The Impact of the United Nations Human Rights Treaties on the Domestic Level: Twenty Years On

The Impact of the United Nations Human Rights Treaties on the Domestic Level: Twenty Years On

Second Revised Edition

Edited by

Christof Heyns†, Frans Viljoen and Rachel Murray

BRILL | NIJHOFF

LEIDEN | BOSTON

This is an open access title distributed under the terms of the CC BY-NC-ND 4.0 license, which permits any non-commercial use, distribution, and reproduction in any medium, provided the original author(s) and source are credited. Further information and the complete license text can be found at https://creativecommons.org/licenses/by-nc/4.0/

The terms of the CC license apply only to the original material. The use of material from other sources (indicated by a reference) such as diagrams, illustrations, photos and text samples may require further permission from the respective copyright holder.

Funder: Millennium Trust; Start Year of Funding: 2021.

Library of Congress Cataloging-in-Publication Data

Names: Heyns, C. H. (Christof H.), editor. | Viljoen, Frans, editor. | Murray, Rachel (Rachel H.), editor.
Title: The impact of the United Nations human rights treaties on the domestic level : twenty years on / edited by Christof Heyns, Frans Jacobus Viljoen, and Rachel Murray.
Description: Second revised edition. | Leiden ; Boston : Brill/Nijhoff, 2024. | Includes index.
Identifiers: LCCN 2023055039 (print) | LCCN 2023055040 (ebook) | ISBN 9789004377646 (hardback) | ISBN 9789004377653 (ebook)
Subjects: LCSH: Human rights. | International and municipal law. | International law and human rights. | Treaties. | United Nations.
Classification: LCC K3240 .I487 2002 (print) | LCC K3240 (ebook) | DDC 341.4/8—dc23/eng/20231201
LC record available at https://lccn.loc.gov/2023055039
LC ebook record available at https://lccn.loc.gov/2023055040

Typeface for the Latin, Greek, and Cyrillic scripts: "Brill". See and download: brill.com/brill-typeface.

ISBN 978-90-04-37764-6 (hardback)
ISBN 978-90-04-37765-3 (e-book)

Copyright 2024 by Christof Heyns†, Frans Viljoen and Rachel Murray. Published by Koninklijke Brill NV, Leiden, The Netherlands.
Koninklijke Brill NV incorporates the imprints Brill, Brill Nijhoff, Brill Schöningh, Brill Fink, Brill mentis, Brill Wageningen Academic, Vandenhoeck & Ruprecht, Böhlau and V&R unipress.
Koninklijke Brill NV reserves the right to protect this publication against unauthorized use.

This book is printed on acid-free paper and produced in a sustainable manner.

Christof Heyns served as United Nations Special Rapporteur on Extrajudicial, Summary or Arbitrary Executions from 2010 to 2016; and was a member of the UN Human Rights Committee from 2017 to 2020. One of his abiding passions was to better track and understand the actual effect of international human rights on the real lives of people. This concern led him to devise this far-reaching study on the effect of the core United Nations human rights treaties. Christof's instinctive warmth and genuine kindness stemmed from an abundant generosity and sense of humanity. His enthusiasm was boundless and infectious, leaving untouched no one whose life intersected with his. We, the editors of and contributors to this book, dedicate this study and publication to his memory.

May this be a part of his enduring legacy.

Frans Viljoen, Rachel Murray, Sarah Joseph, Adam Fletcher, Anna Lochhead, Thiago Amparo, Odara Andrade, Júlia Piazza, Deborah Bittar, Alexander Agnello, Frédéric Mégret, Rodrigo Uprimny, Sergio Ruano, Gabriella Michele García, Jitka Brodská, Harald Christian Scheu, Mustapha Kamel Al-Sayyid, Omar A El-Gammal, Yasmina Khaled Azzazy, Merilin Kiviorg, Merja Pentikäinen, Miloon Kothari, Surabhi Sharma, Malene Alleyne, Tracy Robinson, Hatano Ayako, Yota Negishi, Matsuda Hiromichi, Alejandro Anaya-Muñoz, Lucía Chávez, Rodolfo Franco-Franco, José Antonio Guevara Bermúdez, Ravi Prakash Vyas, Pranjali Kanel, Anusha Kharel, Katarzyna Sękowska-Kozłowska, Grażyna Baranowska, Łukasz Szoszkiewicz, Aslan Abashidze, Aleksandra Koneva, Aleksandr Solntsev, Ibrahima Kane, Foluso Adegalu, Tess Mitchell, Carlos Villán Durán, Javier Leoz Invernón, Carmelo Faleh Pérez, Carmen Rosa Rueda Castañón, Başak Çalı, Betül Durmuş, İlayda Eskitaşçıoğlu and O'Brien Kaaba

Contents

Foreword XI
List of Figures, Graphs and Tables XIII
Abbreviations and Acronyms XV
Notes on Editors and Contributors XXIV

Introduction
What a Difference do 20 Years Make? The Impact of the Core UN Human Rights Treaties on the Domestic Level in Selected States between 1999 and 2019 1
　Frans Viljoen and Rachel Murray

1 The Impact of the United Nations Human Rights Treaties on the Domestic Level in Australia 33
　Sarah Joseph, Adam Fletcher and Anna Lochhead-Sperling

2 The Impact of the United Nations Human Rights Treaties on the Domestic Level in Brazil 94
　Thiago Amparo, Odara Andrade, Júlia Piazza and Deborah Bittar

3 The Impact of the United Nations Human Rights Treaties on the Domestic Level in Canada 156
　Alexander Agnello and Frédéric Mégret

4 The Impact of the United Nations Human Rights Treaties on the Domestic Level in Colombia 227
　Rodrigo Uprimny, Sergio Ruano and Gabriella Michele García

5 The Impact of the United Nations Human Rights Treaties on the Domestic Level in the Czech Republic 288
　Harald Christian Scheu and Jitka Brodská

6 The Impact of the United Nations Human Rights Treaties on the Domestic Level in Egypt 355
　Mustapha Kamel Al-Sayyid

7 The Impact of the United Nations Human Rights Treaties on the Domestic Level in Estonia 422
　Merilin Kiviorg

8   The Impact of the United Nations Human Rights Treaties on the Domestic Level in Finland   482
    Merja Pentikäinen

9   The Impact of the United Nations Human Rights Treaties on the Domestic Level in India   532
    Miloon Kothari and Surabhi Sharma

10 The Impact of the United Nations Human Rights Treaties on the Domestic Level in Jamaica   569
    Malene C. Alleyne and Tracy Robinson

11 The Impact of the United Nations Human Rights Treaties on the Domestic Level in Japan   608
    Ayako Hatano, Hiromichi Matsuda and Yota Negishi

12 The Impact of the United Nations Human Rights Treaties on the Domestic Level in Mexico   699
    Alejandro Anaya-Muñoz, Lucía Guadalupe Chávez-Vargas, Rodolfo Franco-Franco and José Antonio Guevara-Bermúdez

13 The Impact of the United Nations Human Rights Treaties on the Domestic Level in Nepal   749
    Ravi Prakash Vyas, Pranjali Kanel and Anusha Kharel

14 The Impact of the United Nations Human Rights Treaties on the Domestic Level in Poland   823
    Katarzyna Sękowska-Kozłowska, Grażyna Baranowska, Joanna Grygiel-Zasada and Łukasz Szoszkiewicz

15 The Impact of the United Nations Human Rights Treaties on the Domestic Level in the Russian Federation   899
    Aslan Abashidze, Aleksandra Koneva and Alexander Solntsev

16 The Impact of the United Nations Human Rights Treaties on the Domestic Level in Senegal   1003
    Ibrahima Kane

17 The Impact of the United Nations Human Rights Treaties on the Domestic Level in South Africa   1077
    Foluso Adegalu and Tess Mitchell

18 The Impact of the United Nations Human Rights Treaties on the
    Domestic Level in Spain   1147
    Carlos Villán Durán

19 The Impact of the United Nations Human Rights Treaties on the
    Domestic Level in Turkey   1225
    Başak Çalı, Betül Durmuş and İlayda Eskitaşçıoğlu

20 The Impact of the United Nations Human Rights Treaties on the
    Domestic Level in Zambia   1273
    O'Brien Kaaba

Conclusion
Contours of a Conclusion, into the Sixth UN Treaty System Decade   1320
  Frans Viljoen and Rachel Murray

Index   1353

Foreword

During my six-year term as UN High Commissioner for Human Rights, with responsibility for the UN human rights treaty bodies, I spent much time, throughout my mandate, seeking to strengthen them and consolidate the so-called 'human rights treaty body system'. The treaty bodies are a pillar of the international human rights protection system. Their system has grown significantly since the establishment of the first treaty body in 1969, enhancing human rights protection. So why did I have to work on the consolidation of these treaty bodies? Because of the many concerns, complaints and misunderstandings that filtered to me from states, civil society organisations and the expert members of these bodies.

Civil society actors complained of exclusion and little or no consultation as well as the lack of implementation of the recommendations. They underlined that the expert members of the Committees were not sufficiently resourced and asked for wider dissemination of their jurisprudence. States objected to disrespectful questioning by what they perceived as unaccountable Committee members and felt that their reporting obligations were too onerous and, most chilling of all, some argued for the disbanding of the treaty body system, indicating that it could be replaced by the then newly established Universal Periodic Review of the Human Rights Council. This would have replaced independent review by experts with a multilateral forum made of states.

It is in this context that the UN General Assembly in 2014 adopted Resolution 68/268, deciding 'to consider the state of the human rights treaty body system', notably 'to ensure their sustainability'. This included a direction to my Office to provide further assistance to states, where it was needed, to comply with the treaty bodies' findings. Yet, at the time of my departure from office in 2014, I keenly felt that we still did not know enough about how the treaty body system protects and promotes human rights at the domestic level, how it permeates to people through States. We needed better data and a comprehensive study of their impact.

This new publication *The Impact of the United Nations Human Rights Treaties on the Domestic Level: Twenty Years On* meets exactly this need. And it meets it superbly! Professors Christof Heyns, Frans Viljoen and Rachel Murray assembled a monumental work, covering the impact of nine core United Nations human rights treaties, ten UN treaty bodies and three substantive Protocols over a period of twenty years. This new study picks up from an earlier review of the treaty bodies conducted by Professors Heyns and Viljoen, which had covered the period 1969 to 1999. These two publications together provide an important baseline, evidencing how human rights percolate from the United Nations to the rights-holders.

Sadly, my dear friend Christof Heyns passed away on 28 March 2021, as this study was being finalised. His untimely death threw the human rights world into deep mourning for the loss of this giant who had played an incredible, leading role in the advancement of human rights.

I welcome this study with enthusiasm. It is a substantial and comprehensive report based on country-specific research that reinforces and amplifies the findings that the treaty bodies have had an enormous influence and impact at the domestic level. The publication presents the larger picture and tracks changes in attitude, ideas, perception and understanding of norms and standards espoused by the treaty body system. It addresses cultural or ideological changes in the appreciation of human rights advances.

This publication is an invaluable source for all of us: for spreading awareness among civil society actors and encouraging them to engage more vigorously with the treaty bodies and for states to see the positive benefits of their cooperation with the treaty bodies.

Judge Navi Pillay
UN High Commissioner for Human Rights (2008–2014)

Figures, Graphs and Tables

Figures

0.1	Territorial reach: '20 selected countries' (follow-up study shown)	7
0.2	Average delay (in months) in submission of state reports (from ratification date to 1999; from 2000 to 30 June 2019)	18
0.3	Total number of individual communications registered, 2012 to (Oct) 2019	22
11.1	Reference to COs by Diet	644

Graphs

4.1	Total references to decisions of Constitutional Court compared with TBS	244
4.2	Mentions of selected soft law by the Constitutional Court	247
12.1	Number of decisions by Mexico's federal judiciary that mention UN human rights treaties (2000 to 2019)	711

Tables

0.1	Core UN human rights treaties and substantive protocols	12
0.2	UN treaty bodies	16
0.3	State acceptance of optional complaints procedures and SPT mandate	17
0.4	Number of final decisions on communications adopted per treaty body, 2015 to (31 October) 2019	21
0.5	Number of communications in which TBs found violations against WEO states	22
0.6	Number of communications in which TBs found violations against East European states	23
0.7	Number of communications in which TBs found violations against 'Asian' states	23
0.8	Number of communications in which TBs found violations against African states	24
0.9	Number of communications in which TBs found violations against GRULAC states	24
0.10	Number of communications in which TBs found violations against all 20 states	24

4.1	Decisions of the Constitutional Court in which a UN treaty was mentioned	244
4.2	Mentions by the Constitutional Court of different UN treaties and committees	245
6.1	Citations of UN core human rights treaties in a sample of Egyptian newspapers 2014–2019	366
6.2	Egyptian government's reporting to the UN human rights treaty bodies until June 2019	369
11.1	Membership of treaty bodies (as of 2021)	637
11.2	Number of independent/parallel (CSOs) reports under ratified treaties on the occasion of state reporting (cycle, year)	641
12.1	Decisions by Mexico's Federal judiciary that mention human rights treaties and treaty bodies (2000 to 2019)	712
21.1	Legislation implementing CRPD in 20 study countries	1334

Abbreviations and Acronyms

2SLGBTQQIA	two-spirit, lesbian, gay, bisexual, transgender, queer, questioning, intersex and asexual
AAT	Administrative Appeals Tribunal (Australia)
ACF	Active Citizens Fund (Estonia)
ACHR	American Convention on Human Rights
African Charter	African Charter on Human and Peoples' Rights
African Children's Charter	African Charter on the Rights and Welfare of the Child
African Commission	African Commission on Human and Peoples' Rights
African Court	African Court on Human and Peoples' Rights
African Women's Protocol	Protocol to the African Charter on Human and Peoples' Rights on the Rights of Women in Africa
AGD	Attorney-General's Department (Australia)
AHRC	Australian Human Rights Commission (Australia)
AHRC	Arab Human Rights Charter
AI	Amnesty International
AJS	Senegalese Female Lawyers' Association
ALP	Australian Labour Party
ALRC	Australian Law Reform Commission
ANSD	National Statistics and Demography Agency (Senegal)
ASEAN	Association of Southeast Asian Nations
BAOJS	Reception and Referral Offices (Senegal)
BIJS	Citizen Advice Bureaux (Senegal)
BOE	*Boletín Oficial del Estado* (Spain)
CAPE	Child Protection Support Unit (Senegal)
CAT	Convention against Torture and Other Cruel, Inhuman and Degrading Treatment or Punishment
CC	Constitutional Court (Spain; Czech Republic)
CChR	Commissioner for Children's Rights (Poland)
CCL	Centre for Child Law (South Africa)
CCNDHDIH	National Advisory Council on Human Rights and International Humanitarian Law (Senegal)
CCOHR	Secretariat for the Continuing Committee of Officials on Human Rights (Canada)
CCPR	International Covenant on Civil and Political Rights
CCRC	Canadian Coalition for the Rights of Children
CED	International Convention for the Protection of all Persons from Enforced Disappearance
CED Cttee	Committee on Enforced Disappearance

CEDAW	Convention on the Elimination of All Forms of Discrimination Against Women
CEDAW Cttee	Committee on the Elimination of Discrimination against Women
CEDCAS	State Councils for the Rights of the Child (Brazil)
CENA	Independent National Electoral Commission (Senegal)
CERD Cttee	Committee on the Elimination of Racial Discrimination
CERD	International Convention on the Elimination of All Forms of Racial Discrimination
CERMI	Spanish Committee of Representatives of Persons with Disabilities
CESCR	International Covenant on Economic, Social and Cultural Rights
CESCR Cttee	Committee on Economic, Social and Cultural Rights
CESE	Economic, Social and Environmental Council (Senegal)
CGE	Commission for Gender Equality (South Africa)
CHIN	Children in Need Network
CHR	Council for Human Rights
CHRC	Canadian Human Rights Commission
CHRM	Commission on Human Rights and Minorities (Brazil)
CHRT	Canadian Human Rights Tribunal
CIDE	Interschool Centre for Children's Rights
CIEDP	Commission of Enforced Disappeared Person (Nepal)
CINPE	National Intersectoral Committee for the Protection of Children (Senegal)
CINPE	National Intersectoral Child Protection Committee (Senegal)
CJEU	Court of Justice of the European Union
CMDCAS	Municipal Councils for the Rights of the Child (Brazil)
CMU	Universal Health Coverage Programme (Senegal)
CMW	International Convention on the Rights of All Migrant Workers and Members of their Families
CNDH	National Human Rights Commission (Mexico)
CNLCTE	National Intersectoral Committee against Child Labour (Senegal)
CNLTP	National Human Trafficking Unit (Senegal)
CNRA	National Broadcasting Regulatory Council (Senegal)
CNV	National Truth Commission (Brazil)
CoE	Council of Europe
CONAPRED	National Council for the Prevention of Discrimination (Mexico)
COS	Concluding Observations
CPT	European Committee for the Prevention of Torture and Other Inhuman or Degrading Treatment or Punishment
CRC	Convention on the Rights of the Child
CRC Cttee	Committee on the Rights of the Child

ABBREVIATIONS AND ACRONYMS

CREI	Court for the Suppression of Unlawful Enrichment (Senegal)
CRIA	Child Rights Impact Assessment (Canada)
CRPD	Convention on the Rights of Persons with Disabilities
CSDH	Senegalese Human Rights Committee
CSFR	Czech and Slovak Federative Republic
CSM	Higher Council of the Judiciary (Senegal)
CSOS	civil society organisations
DANIDA	Danish International Development Assistance
DCI Spain	Defence of Children International
DFAT	Department of Foreign Affairs and Trade (Australia)
DFID	Department for International Development
DIP	Special Police and the Image and Advertising Department (Brazil)
DPJ	Democratic Party of Japan
DPO	Organisation of Persons with Disabilities (Finland)
DPRK	Democratic People's Republic of Korea
DPSP	Directive Principles of State Policy
EÇHA	Network for the Rights of Children with Disabilities (Turkey)
ECHR	European Convention of Human Rights
ECOSOCC	Economic, Social and Cultural Council (African Union)
ECOWAS	Economic Community of West African States
ECPT	European Convention on the Prevention of Torture and Inhuman or Degrading Treatment or Punishment
ECRI	European Commission against Racism and Intolerance
ECtHR	European Court of Human Rights
EDJA	African Legal Publishers
EHRO	Egyptian Human Rights Organisation
EIDHR	European Instrument for the Development of Human Rights
EIHR	Estonian Institute of Human Rights
EOUS	Equal Opportunity Units (Egypt)
ESCR	economic, social and cultural rights
ESPEN	National School of Criminal Services (Brazil)
EU	European Union
EWUA	early warning urgency actions
FAFIA/AFAI	Canadian Feminist Alliance for International Action Canada
FAO	Food and Agriculture Organisation
FC	Brazilian Federal Constitution
FCA	Federal Court of Appeal (Canada)
FCC	Federal Court of Canada
FGM	female genital mutilation
FGTS	Employee's Severance Guarantee (Brazil)

FIC	Financial Intelligence Centre (Zambia)
FMHR	Forum of Ministers on Human Rights (Canada)
FNHRI	Finnish National Human Rights Institution
F-P-T	Federal-Provincial-Territorial (Canada)
FUNAI	National Indian Foundation (Brazil)
GANHRI	Global Alliance of National Human Rights Institutions
GCHR	Government Commissioner for Human Rights (Czech Republic)
GEED	Gender Equity and Equality Directorate (Senegal)
GESI	gender equality and social inclusion (Nepal)
GIZ	Germany Development Cooperation
GNI	gross national income
GONGOS	government organised non-governmental organisations
GRECO	Group of States against Corruption
GSIA	Sociology Group of Childhood and Adolescence (Spain)
HAC	Highest Administrative Court (Czech)
HCA	High Court of Australia
HCCL	Higher Local Authorities Council (Senegal)
HIV/AIDS	human immunodeficiency virus/acquired immunodeficiency syndrome
HRC	Human Rights Council
HRCA	Human Rights Council of Australia
HRCttee	UN Human Rights Committee
HRD	Human Rights Department (Czech)
HRHAD	Human Rights and Humanitarian Affairs Division (Japan)
HRLC	Human Rights Law Centre (Australia)
HRLRC	Human Rights Law Resources Centre (Australia)
HRW	Human Rights Watch
IACtHR	Inter-American Court of Human Rights
IACHR	Inter-American Commission of Human Rights
ICC	International Criminal Court
ICTR	International Criminal Tribunal for Rwanda
IDC	Interdepartmental Committee on International Treaty Obligations (South Africa)
IDHP	Human Rights and Peace Institute (Senegal)
IHRL	international human rights law
IHRLA	International Human Rights Law Association
ILO	International Labour Organisation
IMCHR	Inter-Ministerial Committee on Human Rights (Jamaica)
IMF	International Monetary Fund
IMM	Independent Monitoring Mechanism (South Africa)
INAI	National Institute on Access to Information (Mexico)

ABBREVIATIONS AND ACRONYMS

INDECOM	Independent Commission of Investigations (Jamaica)
INEGI	National Institute of Statistics and Geography (Mexico)
INESC	Institute of Socio-Economic Studies (Brazil)
INSLM	Independent National Security Legislation Monitor (Australia)
IOM	International Organisation for Migration
IPEA	Institute of Applied Economic Research (Brazil)
IPPDH	Institute of Public Policies on Human Rights (Brazil)
IRB	Immigration and Refugee Board of Canada
Istanbul Convention	Council of Europe Convention on Preventing and Combating Violence Against Women and Domestic Violence
JCPC	Judicial Committee of the Privy Council
JCTR	Jesuit Centre for Theological Reflection
JDF	Japan Disability Forum
JFBA	Japan Federation of Bar Associations
JICS	Judicial Inspectorate for Correctional Services (South Africa)
JSC	Judicial Service Commission (South Africa)
JURICAF	Jurisprudence of Francophone Supreme Courts
LCI	Law Commission of India
LDP	Liberal Democratic Party (Japan)
LEAF	West Coast Legal Education and Action Fund (Canada)
LGBT	lesbian, gay, bisexual and transgender
LHR	Lawyers for Human Rights (South Africa)
LICHR	Legal Information Centre for Human Rights (Estonia)
LOIPR	List of Issues Prior to Reporting
MDGS	Millennium Development Goals
MERCOSUR	Argentina, Brazil, Paraguay, Uruguay, Venezuela, Bolivia, Chile, Colombia, Ecuador, Guyana, Peru, Surinam
MFDC	*Mouvement des Forces Démocratiques de Casamance* (Senegal)
MISA	Media Institute of Southern Africa Zambia Chapter (Zambia)
MMD	Movement for Multiparty Democracy (Zambia)
MMIWG	murdered missing indigenous women and girls (Canada)
MNPCT	National Mechanism for the Prevention and Combat of Torture (Brazil)
MOFA	Ministry of Foreign Affairs Japan
MPS	Members of Parliament
NATO	North Atlantic Treaty Organisation
NC	National Congress (Brazil)
NCC	National Children's Commissioner (Australia)
NCCM	National Council for Childhood and Motherhood (Egypt)

NCCPIMTIP	National Coordinating Committee for Preventing and Combating Illegal Migration and Human Trafficking (Egypt)
NCHR	National Council of Human Rights (Egypt; Brazil)
NCPCR	National Commission for the Protection of Child Rights (India)
NCRB	National Crime Records Bureau (India)
NCRC	National Children's Rights Committee (South Africa)
NCW	National Council for Women (Egypt)
NDIS	National Disability Insurance Scheme (Australia)
NDS	National Disability Strategy (Australia)
NED	National Endowment for Democracy (Zambia)
NEGES	National Gender Equity and Equality Strategy (Senegal)
NEPAD	New Partnership for Africa's Development
NFDN	National Federation of Disabled Population, Nepal
NGOCC	Non-Governmental Gender Coordinating Council
NGO	non-governmental organisation
NHRAP	National Human Rights Action Plan (Nepal)
NHRC	National Human Rights Commission (India)
NHRI	national human rights institution
NHRI	Defensor del Pueblo (Spain)
NHRI	Human Rights and Equality Institution (Turkey)
NJA	National Judicial Academy (Nepal)
MMIWG	missing and murdered indigenous women and girls (Canada)
NMRF	National Mechanism for Reporting and Follow-Up (South Africa)
NPAC	National Programme of Action for Children (South Africa)
NPM	National Preventive Mechanism (under OP-CAT)
NPM	National Preventive Mechanism (Finland)
NRC	National Register for Citizens (India)
NSCJ	National Supreme Court of Justice (Mexico)
NSNP	National Schools Nutrition Programme (South Africa)
NWAC	Native Women's Association of Canada
NWAC	National Women's Association of Canada
OAS	Organisation of American States
OAU	Organisation of African Unity
OCA	Office of the Children's Advocate (Jamaica)
OCASI	Ontario Council of Agencies Serving Immigrants
ODIHR	Office for Democratic Institutions and Human Rights
OECD	Organisation for Economic Co-operation and Development
OHADA	Organisation for the Harmonisation of Business Law (Senegal)
OHCHR	UN Office of the High Commissioner for Human Rights
OICS	Office of the Inspector of Custodial Services (Australia)

ABBREVIATIONS AND ACRONYMS

OMCT	World Organisation Against Torture
OMHR	Office of the Minister of Human Rights (Czech Republic)
ONLPL	National Detention Centre Observatory (Senegal)
OP1-CCPR	(first) Optional Protocol to the International Covenant on Civil and Political Rights
OP2-CCPR	Second Optional Protocol to the International Covenant on Civil and Political Rights aimed at the abolition of the death penalty
OP-CAT	Optional Protocol to the Convention against Torture and Other Cruel, Inhuman or Degrading Treatment or Punishment
OP-CEDAW	Optional Protocol to the Convention on the Elimination of All Forms of Discrimination against Women
OP-CESCR	Optional Protocol to the International Covenant on Economic, Social and Cultural Rights
OP-CRPD	Optional Protocol to the Convention on the Rights of Persons with Disabilities
OP-CRC-AC	Optional Protocol to the Convention on the Rights of the Child on the Involvement of Children in Armed Conflict
OP-CRC-CP	Optional Protocol to the Convention on the Rights of the Child on a Communications Procedure
OP-CRC-SC	Optional Protocol to the Convention on the Rights of the Child on the Sale of Children, Child Prostitution and Child Pornography
OPD	Office of the Public Defender
OPDR	Office of the Public Defender of Rights (Czech Republic)
OPS	Optional Protocols
OSCE	Organisation for Security and Co-operation in Europe
OTIT	Organisation for Technical Intern Training (Japan)
PD	Public Defender (Czech)
PF	Patriotic Front (Zambia)
PJCHR	Parliamentary Joint Committee on Human Rights (Australia)
PKK	Kurdistan Workers' Party (Turkey)
PMTCT	prevention of mother-to-child transmission (of HIV)
PNDS	National Health Development Plan (Senegal)
PRI	Institutionalised Revolutionary Party (Mexico)
PSCHR	Permanent Supreme Committee of Human Rights (Egypt)
PSE	Emerging Senegal Plan
PSSD	Strategic Plan for Digital Health (Senegal)
RC	Royal Commissions (Australia)
RDC	Race Discrimination Commissioner (Australia)
RDP	Reconstruction and Development Programme (South Africa)

RICA	Regulation of Interception of Communications and Provision of Communication Related Information Act (South Africa)
SAARC	South Asian Association of Regional Cooperation
SAC	Supreme Administrative Court (Czech Republic)
SAC	Supreme Administrative Court (Finland)
SACCORD	Southern African Centre for Constructive Resolution of Disputes
SAHRC	South African Human Rights Commission
SALRC	South African Law Reform Commission
SANDF	South African National Defence Force
SC	Supreme Court (Finland)
SCC	Supreme Constitutional Court (Egypt)
SCC	Supreme Court of Canada
SCCR	Supreme Court of the Czech Republic
SCE	Supreme Court of Estonia
SCI	Supreme Court of India
SCIELO	Scientific Electronic Library Online
SCN	Supreme Court of Nepal
SDA	Sex Discrimination Act 1984 (Cth) (Australia)
SDG	Sustainable Development Goals
SDS	Statistics Master Plan (Senegal)
SEDH	Special Secretariat for Human Rights (Brazil)
SEPPIR	Special Secretariat for Policies for the Promotion of Racial Equality (Brazil)
SIPIA	System on Information about Childhood (Brazil)
SNDES	National Economic and Social Development Strategy (Senegal)
SNEEG	National Strategy for Gender Equity and Equality (Senegal)
SNHIS	National Housing of Social Interest System (Brazil)
SNPE	National Child Protection Strategy (Senegal)
SNPS	National Social Protection Strategy (Senegal)
SOCHR	Senior Officials Committee on Human Rights (Canada)
SOGI	sexual orientation and gender identity
ŞÖNİM	Centres for Preventing and Monitoring Violence
SPM	Special Secretariat of Policies for Women (Brazil)
SPSP	National Human Rights Commission Strategic Plan Support Project (Nepal)
SPT	Sub-Committee on Prevention of Torture and Other Cruel, Inhuman or Degrading Treatment or Punishment
SSDP	School Sector Development Plan (Nepal)
SSHRCC	Social Sciences and Humanities Research Council of Canada
SSRP	School Sector Reform Programme (Nepal)

ABBREVIATIONS AND ACRONYMS

STF	Federal Supreme Court (Brazil)
STJ	Superior Court of Justice (Brazil)
TB	treaty body
TBS	treaty body system
TOHAD	Social Rights and Research Society (Turkey)
TRC	Truth and Reconciliation Commission (Nepal)
TRC	Truth and Reconciliation Commission (Canada)
UDHR	Universal Declaration of Human Rights
UMS	Judges' Union of Senegal
UN	United Nations
UNDP	United Nations Development Programme
UNDRIP	UN Declaration on the Rights of Indigenous Peoples
UNESCO	United Nations Educational, Scientific and Cultural Organisation
UNFPA	United Nations Population Fund
UNHCHR	United Nations High Commissioner for Human Rights
UNHCR	United Nations High Commission for Refugees
UNICEF	United Nations Children's Fund
UNMIN	United Nations Mission in Nepal
UNODC	United Nations Office on Drugs and Crime
UNSC	United Nations Security Council
UNSDGS	United Nations Sustainable Development Goals
UNSP	United Nations Special Procedures
UNTBS	United Nations treaty bodies
UPND	United Party for National Development (Zambia)
UPR	Universal Periodic Review
VANE	Rights of Persons with Disabilities (Finland)
WACSI	West African Civil Society Institute
WEFE	Women Empowerment and Gender Equality Bill (South Africa)
WGAD	Working Group on Arbitrary Detention
WiLDAF	Women in Law and Development in Africa
WTO	World Trade Organisation
ZLDC	Zambia Law Development Commission

Notes on Editors and Contributors

Aslan Abashidze
is the head of the Department of International Law at Peoples' Friendship University of Russia (RUDN University) in Moscow, professor of International Law and Honoured Lawyer of the Russian Federation. He is a member, Vice-Chair and Rapporteur of the Committee on Economic, Social and Cultural Rights (since 2010) and a former member of the UN Working Group on Arbitrary Detention (2008 to 2009). He is also a professor at the Moscow State Institute of International Relations and emeritus professor at the Russian-Tajic Slavonic University (Tajikistan) and at the LN Gumilyov Eurasian National University (Kazakhstan). He has established the joint LLM Programme 'International Protection of Human Rights' (in Russian and in English) as the first Master's programme in human rights in Russia, supported by the Office of the UN High Commissioner for Human Rights. Within this programme he has developed various human rights courses and learning materials, including the course and the textbook *Human Rights Treaty Bodies*, which is the first and only discipline and textbook of this kind in Russia. He has published more than 1 000 research works, including monographs, textbooks and teaching guides.

Foluso Adegalu
is a doctoral researcher, Centre for Human Rights, University of Pretoria, and a co-manager of its Litigation and Implementation Unit. He holds an LLM degree from the University of Ibadan.

Alexander Agnello
is a researcher and Master of Laws (LLM) candidate at McGill University, where he also obtained Juris Doctor (JD) and Bachelor of Civil Law (BCL) degrees. He has worked for the OECD, the Asian Development Bank, and the Ombudsperson of British Columbia.

Malene Alleyne
is a human rights lawyer and founder of Freedom Imaginaries. She holds a Master of Laws from Harvard Law School and a Master of Advanced Studies from the Graduate Institute of International Studies, Geneva.

Mustapha Kamel Al-Sayyid
is Professor of Political Science, Faculty of Economics and Political Science, Cairo University. He has also taught at American University in Cairo; Law

School, Harvard; and Colgate University. He was a visiting scholar at the University of California, Los Angeles (UCLA), and a Research Associate at Carnegie Endowment for International Peace. He has published in English, French and Arabic on issues related to civil society, human rights and the politics of development in Arab countries.

Thiago Amparo
is a law professor at São Paulo Law School of Fundação Getulio Vargas (FGV), Brazil, teaching human rights, international law and constitutional law. Amparo holds doctorate and master's degrees from Central European University (Budapest, Hungary) and was a visiting scholar at Columbia Law School.

Alejandro Anaya-Muñoz
is a research professor at the Department of Social, Political and Legal Studies at ITESO, Jesuit University in Guadalajara, Mexico. He holds a PhD degree in government, from the University of Essex. He has been Fulbright Scholar at the Human Rights Programme of the University of Minnesota and Mexico Public Policy Scholar at the Woodrow Wilson International Centre for Scholars, in Washington DC. His most recent book is *Mexico's Human Rights Crisis*, co-edited with Barbara Frey (University of Pennsylvania Press 2018).

Odara Andrade
is a Master's student at the Law Faculty of São Paulo-USP; Researcher Assistant at São Paulo Law School of Fundação Getulio Vargas (FGV).

Hatano Ayako
is a research fellow at the Centre of Human Rights Education and Training (Japan) and a DPhil (PhD) candidate at University of Oxford (Law Faculty). She has experience in research and practice in the fields of international human rights law, gender and development with international organisations, governments and civil society organisations. She holds a JD and a MA from the University of Tokyo and an LLM from New York University School of Law (Fulbright Scholar).

Yasmina Khaled Azzazy
holds an MA from the American University in Cairo, for a thesis 'Backsliding to autocracy: The case of Turkey under Erdogan', May 2021.

Grażyna Baranowska
PhD in law, is an assistant professor at the Institute of Law Studies of the Polish Academy of Sciences and a Marie Skłodowska-Curie Post-Doctoral Research at the Hertie School in Berlin. Previously she worked as a researcher and policy advisor to a member of the UN Committee for Enforced Disappearances. Her book *Rights of Families of Disappeared Persons. How International Bodies Address the Needs of Families of Disappeared Persons in Europe* was published with Intersentia in 2021.

Deborah Bittar
is an undergraduate student at the Faculty of Law of the University of São Paulo (USP); intern and research assistant at São Paulo Law School of Fundação Getulio Vargas (FGV).

Jitka Brodská
is a diplomat, currently working as the Deputy Permanent Representative of the Czech Republic to the United Nations in Geneva. During her diplomatic career, she was posted at the Embassy of the Czech Republic to the Kingdom of The Netherlands (covering legal and multilateral issues) and the Permanent Mission of the Czech Republic to the United Nations Office and Other International Organizations in Geneva, Switzerland (human rights and humanitarian affairs). She also worked as the Deputy Director of the Human Rights and Transition Policy Department at the Ministry of Foreign Affairs of the Czech Republic in Prague. Jitka Brodská has a degree in law from the Faculty of Law of the Charles University in Prague, Czech Republic, and in international trade from the Faculty of International Relations of the University of Economics in Prague, Czech Republic. She further studied at the Diplomatic Academy of the Ministry of Foreign Affairs of the Czech Republic and at the Clingendael Institute of International Relations in The Hague, The Netherlands.

Başak Çalı
is co-director of the Centre for Fundamental Rights and professor of international law at the Hertie School, Berlin. She is also a faculty member at Koç University Law School, Istanbul and the Chairperson of the European Implementation Network, Strasbourg.

Lucía Guadalupe Chávez-Vargas
has a law degree from the Universidad Nacional Autónoma de México and a Master's Degree in Human Rights, Rule of Law and Democracy in Iberoamerica

from the Universidad de Alcalá de Henares, Spain. Since 2008 she has worked in the field of human rights with civil society organisations, and from 2011 to 2014 in the Mexico City ombudsman office. She has participated as coordinator and author in books and articles for national and international academic journals; likewise, in conferences, congresses, training courses, diplomas, and as a tutor in various courses related to human rights and transitional justice. Currently, she is a professor at the Universidad Tecnológica Latinoamericana and deputy-director of Analysis and Strategy of the Mexican Commission for the Defence and Promotion of Human Rights.

Carlos Villán Durán
is a professor of international human rights law and co-director of the Master on International Protection of Human Rights at the University of Alcalá (Madrid). He is the author and co-editor of 19 books and some 165 articles and chapters on international human rights law. He is a member of the editorial boards of four Latin American periodicals, president of the Spanish Society for IHRL and former staff member of OHCHR (1982 to 2005).

Betül Durmuş
is a research assistant in public international law and a PhD candidate in public law at Koç University. She is also a Human Rights Law Reporter for Oxford Reports on International Law. She holds an LLM degree in public law from Koç University.

Omar A El-Gammal
has an MPhil in Development Studies from the University of Cambridge. He previously graduated from the American University in Cairo with a BA (Hons) in economics and political science. He also obtained a Bachelor of Laws from Ain Shams University.

İlayda Eskitaşçıoğlu
is a PhD candidate in public law at Koç University, a fellow at the UNESCO Chair for Sustainable Development and Gender Equality and a researcher at Koç University Gender Studies Centre. She holds an LLM degree in European and International Human Rights Law from Leiden University.

Adam Fletcher
is a lecturer at RMIT University, having previously worked at Monash University, as well as in the government and NGO sectors. He holds a PhD from

Monash University on the subject of human rights scrutiny in the Australian Parliament.

Rodolfo Franco-Franco
is deputy-director of programmes at the Mexican Commission for the Defence and Promotion of Human Rights. He has extensive experience in human rights advocacy projects. He has collaborated with national and international organisations on migration issues, reproductive rights and the rule of law. He co-led the project 'Citizen-led Forensics' in 2014, which created the first independent DNA database for the identification of disappeared persons in Mexico. He holds an MA in Political Science from the University of British Columbia (2006) and a BA in International Relations from Tec de Monterrey (2004).

Gabriella Michele García
is a Political Science major at Stanford University (Class of 2024). Her research about human rights violations during the construction of the World Cup infrastructure was published through Centro para la Apertura y el Desarrollo de América Latina (CADAL), which led to a campaign to heighten awareness around the issue. Additionally, she has had research published at LawFare through the Stanford-MIT Healthy Elections Project regarding the United States 2020 general election. Her main interests lie between the intersection of design thinking, government, campaigns, and human rights.

Joanna Grygiel-Zasada
is a research assistant and PhD candidate at the Poznań Human Rights Centre of the Institute of Law Studies, Polish Academy of Sciences. She conducts research on the compliance of national standards of human rights protection with international standards, in particular in the field of fundamental rights and freedoms, criminal proceedings and protection from torture. Since 2020 she has been a trainee attorney-at-law at the District Bar Association in Poznan. She is also human rights activist in a local group of Amnesty International Poland.

José Antonio Guevara Bermúdez
holds a law degree from the Universidad Iberoamericana, Mexico City and a PhD in Human Rights from the Carlos III University of Madrid, Spain. Since 2015 he is a professor of international human rights and international criminal law at the Faculty of Law and Criminology of the Autonomous University of Tlaxcala, Mexico. He was one of the five members of the Working Group

on Arbitrary Detention of the Human Rights Council of the United Nations Organisation (2014 to 2020).

Christof Heyns

held the degrees LLB and MA (Pretoria), LLM (Yale) and PhD (Witwatesrand). He was Professor of Human Rights Law, Director of the Centre for Human Rights, Dean of the Faculty of Law, and Director of the Institute for International and Comparative Law in Africa at the University of Pretoria. He was the United Nations Special Rapporteur on Extrajudicial, Summary or Arbitrary Executions from 2010 to 2016; and a member of the UN Human Rights Committee from 2017 to 2020. He was, with Frans Viljoen, the co-study leader and co-editor of *The Impact of the United Nations Human Rights Treaties on the Domestic Level* (2002). Christof authored numerous publications, with a focus on human rights in Africa and the right to life. He passed away on 28 March 2021.

Matsuda Hiromichi

is an associate professor at International Christian University, where he teaches constitutional law, international law and human rights law. He obtained his Doctor of Laws at the University of Tokyo in Japan and LLM at Columbia Law School in the United States of America.

Javier Leoz Invernón

holds a PhD from the University of Zaragoza and is a staff member of OHCHR.

Sarah Joseph

is a Professor of Human Rights Law at Griffith University in Brisbane. Prior to her appointment in 2020, she was the Director of the Castan Centre for Human Rights Law at Monash University for 15 years. Her expertise ranges across civil, political, economic, social and cultural rights, as well as international human rights law and human rights in Australia.

O'Brien Kaaba

(LLB (London), LLM (Zambia), LLD (UNISA)) is a lecturer in the Department of Public Law, Assistant Dean Research in the School of Law, University of Zambia and a senior research fellow at the Southern African Institute for Policy and Research (SAIPAR). O'Brien also holds a diploma in philosophy from St Augustine's Catholic Philosophical College. He is an associate editor of the *SAIPAR Case Review Journal*. Prior to joining academia, O'Brien worked in development cooperation. His teaching subjects currently are constitutional law, jurisprudence, international humanitarian law, and legal process.

Ibrahima Kane

is a Senegalese human rights lawyer and activist. Founding member of RADDHO, a Senegalese human rights organisation, he worked at Interights for 10 years as a senior lawyer in charge of the Africa programme of the organisation. Kane has collaborated closely with and litigated before the African Commission on Human and Peoples' Rights, the African Union Commission, the African Committee of Experts on the Rights and Welfare of the Child, the Court of Justice of the Economic Community of West African States (ECOWAS) and the Court of Justice of the East African Community (EAC). Since 2007 he heads Open Society's Africa Union Advocacy Programme. He is an author of a number of reports and articles on the African Union, the African Commission on Human and Peoples' Rights, and the protection of human rights by regional economic community bodies. He has also been an associate lecturer at the law faculty of the University of Essex in the United Kingdom.

Pranjali Kanel

is the programme assistant and a BA LLB candidate at Kathmandu School of Law.

Anusha Kharel

is a teaching assistant at Kathmandu School of Law. She is a BA LLB graduate from Kathmandu School of Law.

Merilin Kiviorg

(DPhil Oxford, mag iur Tartu) is an associate professor in international law at the University of Tartu School of Law. She obtained her doctorate as well as taught international law at the University of Oxford. She was a Max Weber Fellow at the European University Institute in Florence. She has advised governmental bodies in Estonia. She is a member of the Advisory Panel of Experts on Freedom of Religion or Belief of the Organisation of Security and Cooperation in Europe/ODIHR and a member of the Chancellor of Justice's Human Rights Advisory Board in Estonia. She is a principal investigator in the Project 'Russia and Consolidation of Regional International Law in Eurasia'. She is the author of multiple articles and books in the field of human rights, constitutional rights, and public international law.

Aleksandra Koneva

is a senior lecturer at the Department of International Law, RUDN University. She holds a PhD in Law from RUDN University on the subject of strengthening the human rights treaty body system. She has been awarded the Grant of the President of Russia for state support of young scientists on the topic 'Human Rights Treaty Body System: Yesterday, Today and Tomorrow' (2018 to 2019). She published the textbook *Human Rights Treaty Bodies* (2nd edn, 2015) in co-authorship with Aslan Abashidze.

Miloon Kothari

is an expert on human rights and social policy, located in New Delhi and Geneva. He served from 2000 to 2008 as the UN Special Rapporteur on the Right to Adequate Housing and took the lead in preparing the UN Basic Principles and Guidelines on Development-Based Evictions and Displacement. Between 2015 and 2022, he was the president of UPR-Info, an independent organisation that promotes the UPR process. Mr Kothari has published widely and has lectured and taught at leading academic institutions around the world. He has extensive experience in fact finding, research and training on UN human rights as a consultant with governments, UN agencies, local governments, national human rights institutions, judicial bodies, academic institutions and civil society organisations. In 2021 he was appointed by the UN Human Rights Council as Commissioner, UN Independent Commission of Inquiry on the Occupied Palestinian Territory, including East Jerusalem, and Israel.

Anna Lochhead

is a lawyer currently working at the Royal Commission into Violence, Abuse, Neglect and Exploitation of People with Disability. She has principally worked in the area of indigenous rights, including at the Office of the High Commissioner for Human Rights and the Australian Human Rights Commission.

Frédéric Mégret

is full professor and William Dawson Scholar at the Faculty of Law, and the co-director of the Centre for Human Rights and Legal Pluralism, Faculty of Law, McGill University. From 2006 to 2016 he held the Canada Research Chair on the Law of Human Rights and Legal Pluralism. Before coming to McGill, he was an assistant professor at the University of Toronto, a research associate at the European University Institute, and an attaché at the International Committee of the Red Cross. He is the editor, with Philip Alston, of the forthcoming second edition of *The United Nations and Human Rights: A Critical Appraisal* and the co-editor of the *Oxford Handbook of International Criminal Law*. His research interests in general are international law, the laws of war, human rights and international criminal justice. We would like to thank Emily Williams for her careful review of the chapter and valuable comments. Emily Williams is a Master of Laws (LLM) candidate at the National University of Ireland, Galway. She has worked with Canada's intergovernmental committee responsible for international human rights.

Tess Mitchell

works in social development, with a focus on gender and youth. She has been based in West Africa for three years (currently for the UNRCO in Sierra Leone, and previously for WHO in Guinea-Bissau). She has a Masters of International Humanitarian Law and Human Rights (Geneva Academy, Switzerland). The opinions expressed in the chapter she co-authored are her own and do not reflect the views of the UN or WHO.

Rachel Murray

holds the degrees LLB (Leic), LLM (Bristol), PhD (W England). She is Professor of International Human Rights and Director, Human Rights Implementation Centre, School of Law, University of Bristol. Rachel has experience in advising governments, NGOs, NHRIs and regional and international organisations on human rights issues. She has a particular interest in the African human rights system, the Optional Protocol to the UN Convention Against Torture, and National Human Rights Institutions. She is the author of *Implementation of the Findings of the African Commission on Human and Peoples' Rights* and editor of *Reflections on the Implementation of Human Rights Law: Research Handbook on Implementation of Human Rights Law* (with Debra Long).

Yota Negishi

is an LLM and PhD holder at Waseda University in Tokyo. He engaged in research projects of comparative public law and international law as doctoral and post-doctoral research fellow of the Japan Society for the Promotion of Science (2013 to 2017). Dr Negishi stayed as a visiting scholar at Max Planck Institute for Comparative Public Law and International Law in Heidelberg (2014 to 2017).

Merja Pentikäinen

is a lawyer and Doctor of Laws (University of Lapland, Finland) with specialisation in international law and human rights in particular. She has a DES from the Graduate Institute of International Studies (Geneva). She worked for over 20 years in academia as a researcher and teacher of international law, also as an acting professor of international law (University of Turku, Finland). She is the author of a number of monographs, academic articles and popular writings on human rights. Since 2015 she has worked as an independent expert and entrepreneur with the focus on human rights, corporate responsibility and sustainable development.

Carmelo Faleh Pérez

holds a PhD and is a professor in public international law and human rights at the University of Las Palmas de Gran Canaria and legal adviser to the Spanish Society for International Human Rights Law. He is the author of numerous publications on international human rights law.

Júlia Piazza

is an undergraduate student at São Paulo Law School of Fundação Getulio Vargas (FGV), and lead researcher for the Inter-American human rights moot court team at FGV.

Tracy Robinson

is a senior lecturer in the Faculty of Law, University of the West Indies (UWI), Mona and a co-founder and co-coordinator of the Faculty of Law UWI Rights Advocacy Project (U-RAP). She was a member of the Inter-American Commission on Human Rights (2012 to 2015) and served as its president between 2014 and 2015.

Sergio Ruano

is a lawyer and LLM from the Universidad Nacional de Colombia and is a student at the Geneva Academy of International Humanitarian Law and Human Rights. He has been a professor of International Law at the Universidad Católica de Colombia and Lecturer at Universidad Nacional. Sergio has principally worked in Human Rights and the transitional justice field.

Carmen Rosa Rueda Castañón

is former secretary of the Human Rights Committee's working group on communications and member of the Spanish Society for International Human Rights Law.

Harald Christian Scheu

was educated at the University of Salzburg (Dr Iur, 1995, Mag Phil, 1996) and the University of Prague (PhD, 1997, Doc, 2006). He teaches and conducts research in the fields of international and European law and international human rights law; since 2013 member of the Council of the Government of the Czech Republic for Human Rights; since 2014 member of the Czech Government's Legislative Council' from 2015 to 2020 member of the Management Board of the European Union Agency for Fundamental Rights; since 2020 member of the Advisory Committee on the Framework Convention for the Protection of National Minorities.

Katarzyna Sękowska-Kozłowska
PhD in law, is an assistant professor and the head of Poznań Human Rights Centre of the Institute of Law Studies, Polish Academy of Sciences. She is lecturer in anti-discrimination law at SWPS University; member of the Scientific Board of the Interdisciplinary Centre for Cultural Gender and Identity Studies of Adam Mickiewicz University; expert of the European Commission and Council of Europe. Her field of research is international human rights law with a focus on gender issues.

Surabhi Sharma
holds the degree LLM in International Humanitarian Law and Human Rights. She worked as a Lecturer at Jindal Global Law School and subsequently worked with vulnerable communities, particularly in providing legal representation to asylum seekers.

Aleksandr Solntsev
is an associate professor and deputy head of the Department of International Law, RUDN University. He studied at RUDN University and University of Amsterdam, holds PhD in Law from RUDN University. He is the author of more than 700 publications. He developed the innovative course 'Human Rights and Environment' and published a handbook *Human Rights and Environment* (in 3 editions, 2021).

Łukasz Szoszkiewicz
PhD in law, is an assistant professor at the Faculty of Law and Administration of Adam Mickiewicz University. His research is focused on the areas of artificial intelligence and human rights as well as children's rights. Since 2018 he has been actively engaged in the preparation of the UN Global Study on Children Deprived of Liberty and currently leads one of its follow-up projects on immigration detention of children.

Rodrigo Uprimny

is a Colombian Lawyer with PhDin economics (University of Amiens). He is Professor of Constitutional Law at the National University of Colombia. Member, senior researcher at the Center of Studies "Dejusticia" and member of the International Commission of Jurists. He was a member of the UN Committee on Economic, Social and Cultural Rights 2015–2022, executive director of Dejusticia 2005–2015, and deputy justice at the Constitutional Court 1994–2005. He has written extensively on transitional justice, human rights, judicial system and drug policy.

Frans Viljoen

holds the degrees LLB, MA and LLD (Pretoria) and LLM (Cambridge). He is Professor of International Human Rights Law and Director of the Centre for Human Rights, Faculty of Law, University of Pretoria. He is the author of *International human rights law in Africa*. He was, with Christof Heyns, the co-study leader and co-editor of *The Impact of the United Nations Human Rights Treaties on the Domestic Level* (2002).

Ravi Prakash Vyas

is an assistant professor of International Law and Human Rights at Kathmandu School of Law (KSL). He holds a Master's in Human Rights and Democratisation from the University of Sydney and an undergraduate degree in law from India. He is member of the Global Campus Council and programme coordinator of the Asia Pacific Master's in Human Rights and Democratisation at KSL. He has previously worked as a consultant (proceedings) at India's National Human Rights Commission. He is also managing editor of the Kathmandu School of Law Review.

Negishi Yota

is associate professor (Public International Law), Seinan Gakuin University, Fukuoka, Japan (2017–present).

Introduction

What a Difference do 20 Years Make? The Impact of the Core UN Human Rights Treaties on the Domestic Level in Selected States between 1999 and 2019

Frans Viljoen and Rachel Murray

1   Introduction

1.1   *Background to this Study*

This introductory chapter provides a background to a collection of chapters discussing the impact of the core United Nations (UN) human rights treaties at the domestic level during the 20 years between 1 July 1999 and 30 June 2019. This is a follow-up to the study by Christof Heyns and Frans Viljoen, conducted with the assistance of country-based researchers, and published as *The Impact of the United Nations Human Rights Treaties on the Domestic Level*.[1] In that study, Heyns and Viljoen aimed to track and understand the impact of the core UN human rights treaties during the 30 years between the entry into force in 1969 of the first of these treaties (the 1965 Convention on the Elimination of All Forms of Racial Discrimination (CERD)) and 30 June 1999.

Although the chapters in the present book can stand separately, in their own right, in many ways they serve as an updated complement to the initial study. For the follow-up study, Heyns and Viljoen were joined by Professor Rachel Murray, Director of the Human Rights Implementation Centre, University of Bristol, as co-study leader. The country studies were close to completion when co-editor, friend and colleague Christof Heyns so unexpectedly, untimely and sadly passed away on 28 March 2021.[2] Together with many who knew him and had the privilege of working with him, we miss Christof immensely. He pioneered the initial study and energised its follow-up. In fact, at the time of his passing, Christof was on a sabbatical, busy working on this study. The two remaining co-editors have subsequently brought the work to finality.

---

[1] Kluwer Law International 2002 (*Impact* 2002). The editors gladly acknowledge the contributions of Professor William Gravett, who coordinated the logistics of the study for much of its duration.

[2] On Christof's contributions, more generally, see F Viljoen and others (eds), *A Life Interrupted: Essays in Honour of the Lives and Legacies of Christof Heyns* (Pretoria University Law Press 2022); and Daniel Bradlow and Frans Viljoen 'Christof Heyns (1959–2021): Human Rights Lawyer, Legal Educator and Activist' (2021) 117(7–8) South African Journal of Science 1–2.

The initial study covered 20 selected countries, four from each of the five UN regions. With three exceptions, the follow-up study countries are the same as in the initial study.

The treaty system has played a pivotal role in developing the substantive norms of the global human rights project over the last five decades. On the one hand, the future of the treaty system depends on whether it will continue to lead the way in substantively advancing the scope and content of the body of human rights. On the other hand, to enhance its visibility and broaden its ownership by a global audience, treaty norms will have to increasingly find their way into domestic law and practices. This study aims to better understand and assist in bridging the gap between expanding standard-setting and challenging implementation.[3]

This introductory chapter deals with the main changes pertinent to the impact of the 'core UN human rights treaties' in the 20 years between 1999 and 2019, related to the UN treaty body system, the UN Charter-based system, regional human rights systems, and at the national level.

The study presents a portrait of a particular moment in time, namely, the end of the fifth decade in the relatively brief life of the UN human rights treaty system. Tracking and assessing impact will always be 'work-in-progress', in need of continuous updating. While a strict cut-off date (30 June 2019) applies to the treaty body directives (eg recommendations and views) that are covered in the study, the discussion of the domestic impact of these directives is based on an extended time frame, sometimes up to 2022. Because there is a time lag between the study's cut-off date and its publication, some chapters occasionally refer to pertinent subsequent developments.

Many changes that are relevant to the effectiveness of the 'core UN human rights treaties' have occurred during these 20 years. Against the background of and accounting for these changes, the introduction aims to track and better understand aspects of the impact of these treaties at the domestic level. These changes are embedded in the broader socio-political and geopolitical context, including factors such as the increasing securitisation after the events of 11 September 2011; the rise of populism and authoritarianism across the world; shrinking space for civil society engagement in many states; an increased wavering of belief in science-based rationality; and the effects of growing

---

3 See C Heyns and F Viljoen, 'What Difference Does the UN Human Rights Treaty System Make, and Why? A New, Global Academic Study to Answer this Question is Launched in Collaboration with the UN High Commissioner for Human Rights' <https://www.openglobalrights.org/what-difference-does-un-human-rights-treaty-system-make/> accessed 30 September 2021.

global inequalities.[4] The scope of our study does, however, not allow the spotlight to fall on any of these important contextual factors.

1.2 Defining 'Impact'

In the initial study, 'impact' was understood as referring to 'any influence that these treaties may have had in ensuring the realisation of the norms they espouse in individual countries' through constitutional or legislative adoption/incorporation/transformation, policy changes, judicial decisions, the implementation of Concluding Observations (COs), and through the work of civil society, the media, and the academia.[5] For the purpose of the follow-up study, the 'impact' of the UN human rights treaty system is more closely defined as the 'overall domestic effect, influence or repercussions' of the nine core UN human rights treaties, the three substantive Protocols thereto, and the findings and recommendations and normative guidance emanating from the nine UN human rights treaty bodies (UNTBs) established under the nine core treaties, as well as the Sub-Committee on the Prevention of Torture (SPT), established under an optional protocol to one of the treaties.[6] Direct impact we define as 'observable change in the conduct of those' a treaty '*directly targets*'.[7] Indirect impact affects a much broader range of stakeholders. For example, the indirect 'impact' of a remedial order or recommendation would be on persons who are not parties to the case or directly involved in the litigation.[8]

We distinguish between the material and symbolic impact of the UN treaty system.[9] Material impact entails tangible effects that in some way are attributable to the UN treaty system (treaties and treaty bodies), such as the adoption of laws and the use of treaty provisions to influence the outcome of judicial decisions. Symbolic impact is much more intangible and relates to an effect on ideas, understandings and narrative framing. The aim of our study in the first instance is to chart legal, policy and institutional (*de jure*) changes rather than

---

4   The Senegalese chapter, for example, emphasises that the eradication of poverty in the country is the primary purpose of government, and that human rights will be meaningless in a country where the majority of the population is extremely poor.
5   *Impact* 2002 (n 1) 1.
6   The Sub-Committee on Prevention of Torture and other Cruel, Inhuman or Degrading Treatment or Punishment is established under the Optional Protocol to CAT (OP-CAT).
7   César Rodríguez-Garavito, 'Beyond Enforcement: Assessing and Enhancing Judicial Impact' in Malcolm Langford, César Rodríguez-Garavito and Julieta Rossi (eds), *Social Rights Judgments and the Politics of Compliance: Making it Stick* (Cambridge University Press 2017) 84 (emphasis added).
8   ibid.
9   ibid 75.

to provide data on improvements in the actual enjoyment or *de facto* realisation of rights.

From the perspective of a state party to a treaty, 'compliance' with a treaty is the condition of having fufilled its treaty obligations. 'Compliance' is a term best used in relation to the duty bearer under a treaty. To Von Staden, the concept refers to 'conformity of an actor's observed behaviour with the behaviourial requirements of a normative pre-or proscription applicable to that actor'.[10] Giving effect to treaty provisions by setting up a national mechanism, as required by the treaty, or by giving effect to a treaty body's remedial recommendation, are examples of direct material impact. Indirect and symbolic impact includes the raising of public awareness, the reframing of an issue in the press, a change in public perception, increasing the negotiating power of non-governmental organisations (NGOs), and opening up possibilities for public participation on policy making.[11] 'Impact' is therefore broader than but includes 'compliance'. Given its most expansive meaning, impact refers to the contributions to the actual fulfilment of the rights in question.[12]

Under 'implementation' we understand the process of taking measures at the domestic level in response to obligations arising from UN human rights treaties or directives of treaty bodies.[13] In this sense, implementation often is a feature of (or means to achieve) compliance and direct material impact. Often, indirect material impact, as well as symbolic impact, occurs outside the process of implementation. So, for example, greater awareness and public debate may result from exactly the opposite of implementation (that is, from a failure or refusal to implement).

1.3 Scope of the Initial (1999) and Follow-Up (2019) Study

We now examine the study's substantive scope ('core UN human right treaties') and its territorial reach ('20 selected countries').

---

[10] Andreas von Staden, *Strategies of Compliance with the European Court of Human Rights: Rational Choice within Normative Constraints* (University of Pennsylvania Press 2018) 30.

[11] Rodríguez-Garavito (n 7) 83–93.

[12] ibid 78.

[13] Rachel Murray and Debra Long, *The Implementation of the Findings of the African Commission on Human and Peoples' Rights* (Oxford 2015) 27; Kal Raustiala, 'Compliance and Effectiveness in International Regulatory Cooperation' (2000) 32 Case Western Reserve Journal of International Law 387, 392.

1.3.1 Core Human Rights Treaties

The 'core' UN human rights treaties are those UN human rights treaties that provide for self-standing, separate supervisory bodies composed of independent experts. The study can be understood as being premised on the notion that treaties *with treaty bodies* stand a better chance – all things being equal – to be better implemented and thus, be more effective than treaties without such treaty bodies. The premise is that the existence of a treaty body (in a generic sense, or UNTB, specifically), with the concomitant process of generating compliance with normative standards, does 'make a difference'. Six treaties were included in the scope of the initial study: CERD; the 1966 International Covenant on Civil and Political Rights (CCPR), which entered into force in 1976; the 1966 International Covenant on Economic, Social and Cultural Rights (CESCR), which also entered into force in 1976; the 1979 Convention on the Elimination of All Forms of Discrimination against Women (CEDAW), which entered into force in 1981; the 1984 Convention against Torture and Other Cruel, Inhuman or Degrading Treatment (CAT), which entered into force in 1987; and the 1989 Convention on the Rights of the Child (CRC), which entered into force in 1990.

Certainly, there are many more UN treaties of relevance to human rights, broadly understood. However, these treaties do not have independent expert treaty bodies.[14] An example of a 'human rights-related' treaty without a treaty body is the 1951 UN Convention Relating to the Status of Refugees (UN Refugee Convention), which for its implementation depends on the UN High Commissioner for Refugees, a more diplomatic, political and bureaucracy-driven mechanism. Although the impact of the UN Refugee Convention is undeniable,[15] it lacks a system of independent oversight and quasi-judicial accountability. What distinguishes treaty bodies from other forms of oversight in the UN is their rule-based and quasi-judicial role, which removes them and sets them apart from the realm of pragmatic politics.

---

14 Other relevant treaties without treaty bodies include the 1948 Convention on the Prevention and Punishment of the Crime of Genocide, and the 1973 International Convention on the Suppression and Punishment of the Crime of Apartheid. The interpretation, application and implementation of these treaties is adjudicated by the International Court of Justice (ICJ); see eg its 1996 judgment in *Application of the Convention on the Prevention and Punishment of the Crime of Genocide (Bosnia and Herzegovina v Serbia and Montenegro)*.

15 Nergis Canefe, 'The Fragmented Nature of the International Refugee Regime and its Consequences: A Comparative Analysis of the Applications of the 1951 Convention' in James C Simeon (ed), *Critical Issues in International Refugee Law* (CUP 2010) 206.

1.3.2 Twenty Selected Countries

Four countries from each of the five UN regions were covered in the initial study. These are, in the African region: Egypt, Senegal, South Africa and Zambia; in the Asia-Pacific region: India, Iran, Japan and the Philippines; in the Eastern European region: the Czech Republic, Estonia, Romania and the Russian Federation; in the Group of Latin America and Caribbean countries (GRULAC): Brazil, Colombia, Jamaica, and Mexico; and in the West European and Other (WEO) region: Australia, Canada, Finland and Spain. The selection of counties was aimed at identifying a 'fairly representative mix of countries in which the treaty system has had an opportunity to effect a change'.[16] Factors informing the specific choices were the level of the country's wealth, development and political stability; national-level diversity; and ensuring a mixture of states with long-standing engagement (having ratified the relevant treaties for some time) and states with a more recent engagement with the UN human rights treaty system.

The territorial scope of the follow-up study is 20 UN member states. Ideally, this list of countries would have been exactly the same as that of the previous research study. However, due to the unavailability of researchers or other institutional and logistical difficulties, two countries in the Asia-Pacific region included in the original study (Iran and the Philippines) have been replaced (by Turkey and Nepal), and one in the East Europe region, with Poland replacing Romania.

With a civil war largely resolved and in the context of the demise of the monarchy, the inclusion of Nepal instantiates a least-developed country poised for the first time in its history to come to terms with the impact of international human rights law. Turkey's position within the UN spatial geometry reflects its location on the cusp between East and West. While it participates fully in both the WEO and Asia-Pacific group, for electoral purposes it is considered a member of the WEO group only. However, for the purposes of this study we categorise Turkey as part of the Asia-Pacific group. Clearly, the lack of a perfect symmetry complicates comparisons between the two studies at a level beyond the individual country.

The choice means that some of the most politically and economically influential states in our world were not included. Of the five UN Security Council members, only the Russian Federation is included; and of the world's five largest economies (USA, China, Germany, Japan and India) only two (Japan and India) are included. In our view, the inclusion of all the regional hegemons

---

16   *Impact* (2002) (n 1) 2.

INTRODUCTION   7

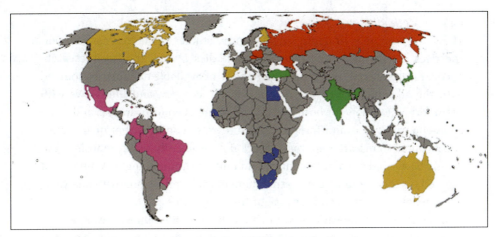

FIGURE 0.1   Territorial reach: '20 selected countries' (follow-up study shown)

would have risked skewing the study. However, the omission of these countries does not imply that they are not important in painting a holistic picture of the impact of UN treaties globally. In this regard, we note published contributions that deal with this topic in, for example, China,[17] the USA,[18] and the United Kingdom (UK),[19] which should be viewed as complementing our study.

With only 20 (out of 193) UN member states covered, the number of countries is rather limited. It provides a limited snapshot at a particular moment in those countries that may quickly be overtaken by events. It was not our aim to draw generalisable conclusions for all UN member states, based on an accurately-designed representative sample. Although the study countries shed light on the larger population of states, the sample size is too limited to allow conclusive claims relating to general patterns and trends.

---

17 See eg Sonya Sceats and Shaun Breslin, 'China and the International Human Rights System' October 2012 The Royal Institute of International Affairs, 2012 <http://dspace.jgu.edu.in:8080/jspui/bitstream/10739/173/1/NPHR8%20China%20%26%20Int%20HR.pdf>; Sanzhuan Guo, 'Implementation of Human Rights Treaties by Chinese Courts: Problems and Prospects' (2009) 8 Chinese Journal of International Law 161–179; Björn Ahl, 'Exploring Ways Of Implementing International Human Rights Treaties in China' (2010) 28 Netherlands Quarterly of Human Rights 361–403; Sophia Woodman, 'Human Rights as Foreign Affairs: China's Reporting under Human Rights Treaties' (2005) Hong Kong Law Journal 179; and Ann Kent, *China, the United Nations, and Human Rights: The Limits of Compliance* (University of Pennsylvania Press 2013).

18 See eg Kenneth Roth, 'The Charade of US Ratification of International Human Rights Treaties' (2000) 1 Chinese Journal of International Law 347.

19 See eg Brice Dickson, *International Human Rights Monitoring Mechanisms: A Study of Their Impact in the UK* (Edward Elgar 2022).

1.4 Methodology

The study combines in-depth single-country studies with cross-country perspectives. Twenty in-depth single country studies, by country-based researchers or research teams, based on desk reviews of available documents, sourced with the advantage of close proximity to the country, and interviews with key informants, allow for both careful and rigorous country studies and some cross-country trends and insights. The study also confirms that quantitative and qualitative research approaches are not necessarily polar opposites, but should be viewed as complementary and mutually reinforcing.[20] A number of researchers incorporate quantitative elements, in combination with analysing documents and drawing on the insights of interviewees.

Interviewees in the various countries include a wide range of respondents, such as high-ranking government officials who are directly responsible for or involved in the preparation of reports; activists advocating the implementation of UN human rights treaties; legal practitioners who have relied on treaty body decisions and recommendations in their cases in court; and members of treaty bodies from the country. A general University of Pretoria certification of 'ethical approval' was secured for the interviews conducted as part of the project as a whole.

Two expert meetings, at which the country researchers presented work-in-progress, were organised in Geneva, Switzerland. The first expert meeting was hosted by the Office of the High Commissioner for Human Rights, in Geneva, in March 2019. The second expert meeting was hosted by the Geneva Academy of International Humanitarian Law and Human Rights, in September 2019. The two expert meetings were attended by UN treaty body members, renowned experts on domestic influence of human rights treaties, practitioners and researchers of international human rights law worldwide. In 2020 a number of virtual meetings were also held, during which work-in-progress were presented, and researchers commented on one another's work.

As part of this study, primary documents from the domestic system (such as policy papers, laws and judgments) referenced in the chapter are collated in electronic form. Following wide consultation, a process of setting up an online database, where information on the impact of the system in all UN member

---

20   See eg B Simmons, *Mobilizing for Human Rights: International Law in Domestic Politics* (Cambridge University Press 2009); and Malcolm Langford, 'Interdisciplinarity and Multimethod Research' in BA Andreassen, HO Sano and S McIernet-Lankford, *Human Rights Research Methods* (Edward Elgar 2017), available as University of Oslo Faculty of Law Research Paper No 2016–30 <https://papers.ssrn.com/sol3/papers.cfm?abstract_id=2854037> accessed 14 November 2022.

states will be posted, is underway. The 20 country studies mentioned above, as well as the supporting documentation, will for a start be posted on the website. In the meantime, clinical groups are being formed at universities around the world, where international students are gathering the relevant information on their home countries, to be posted on the website.[21]

To the extent possible, the study aims to identify *correlation* between a treaty provision or treaty body recommendation and a domestic measure. Impact does not necessarily show or depend on causality (showing, for example, that the treaty system is an *indispensable condition* for the observed change). *Correlation* is the relationship or connection between two or more things. The relationship can be one of influence or contribution. *Influence* is the capacity to have an effect on someone or something. *Contribution* is the role played by a person or thing in bringing about a result. The impact of UN treaties or treaty body recommendations at the domestic level can therefore be described as their *discernible influence on or contribution to* changes at the domestic level.

The most obvious form of discernible correlation is *exact similarity or conformity (for example, between a UNTB recommendation and a domestic measure taken)*. When there is no clear-cut conformity, correlation can be *deduced from*, for example, the following:

- *explicit recognition in documentary form:* The influencing role on the treaty or treaty body recommendations is explicitly 'acknowledged' by relevant domestic actors, as reflected in textual evidence (for example, in the Preamble to a statute).
- *explicit recognition acknowledged and recorded during interviews:* The influencing role on the treaty or treaty body recommendations is explicitly 'acknowledged' by relevant domestic actors, during interviews.
- *chronological sequence:* The material effect (domestic measure) came about *consequent to* (in temporal sequence) to the treaty ratification, or the adoption by the treaty body of a recommendation.

The normative and institutional expansion of human rights have two major implications for the 2019 study:

> First, the expansion of the landscape to treaties and mechanisms that were not in place in 1999 limits the 'conversation' between the two studies, in that comparative data or discussions about the treaties and mechanisms that came into force subsequently do not exist. Therefore, it is not

---

21 See 'Impact database 2020+' <http://www.icla.up.ac.za/countries-researchers-database-2020> accessed 14 November 2022.

possible to make a complete or all-encompassing comparison between the two periods (the 30 years before and the 20 after 1999).

In the second place, it brings into stark relief the imperfect nature of a study that aims to dissect and view the impact of one part of the UN human rights architecture – the treaty body system – in isolation from the UN Charter-based and relevant regional human rights system. From a domestic perspective, the Universal Periodic Review (UPR) and the activities of a plethora of special procedures have a significant impact on human rights that may often be difficult to isolate or separate from the impact of the UN treaty system. There is increasing evidence that the UN treaty-based and Charter-based systems overlap and act in mutually-reinforcing ways, to produce a cumulative effect.[22] While this study focuses on the treaty system, study researchers point to the most salient instances of influence or impact of the UPR, UN special procedures, and regional human rights systems.

After deliberation, we decided to keep the focus on the core treaties and treaty bodies, mainly for the sake of continuity and potential comparison. Retaining the focus of this study on the treaty body system allowed for a contribution to ongoing debates and discussions on the UN treaty body system within the framework of the ongoing Human Rights Treaty Bodies Review 2020 process.[23] The study departs from the premise that the reality of the actual implementation of these treaties should be an important factor in the streamlining and strengthening of the UN treaty system.[24] Even if there are overlaps between the UN treaty bodies, special procedures and the UPR, as quasi-judicial bodies, treaty bodies play a particular role in norm-elaboration through their close and detailed analysis of treaty provisions.

---

[22] Olivier de Frouville, 'Building a Universal System for the Protection of Human Rights: The Way Forward' in M Cherif Bassiouni and William A Schabas (eds), *New Challenges for the UN Human Rights Machinery. What Future for the UN Treaty Body System and the Human Rights Council Procedures?* (Intersentia 2011) 251; F Cowell, 'Reservations to Human Rights Treaties in Recommendations from the Universal Periodic Review: An Emerging Practice?' (2021) 25 International Journal of Human Rights 274.

[23] Jasper Krommendijk, 'Less is More: Proposals for How UN Human Rights Treaty Bodies Can Be More Selective' (2020) 38 Netherlands Quarterly of Human Rights 5–11; Jeremy Sarkin, 'The 2020 United Nations Human Rights Treaty Body Review Process: Prioritising Resources, Independence and the Domestic State Reporting Process Over Rationalising and Streamlining Treaty Bodies' (2020) 25 International Journal of Human Rights 1.

[24] On reform, see generally Sarkin (n 23).

INTRODUCTION

1.5 Format of Chapters

The chapters follow the same structure, with each containing six parts. The first two parts are introductory, and provide an introduction to human rights in the country, and to the relationship of the country with the international human rights system in general. The third part is a schematic table of formal engagement of the country with the UN human rights treaty system. Part 4 provides an overview of the role and overall impact of the UN human rights treaties in the country. Here, the aim is to discern the big picture, not the detail. On the one hand, this part paints an overall picture of the role of the UN human rights treaties in the country, and deals with cross-cutting issues related to the treaties that a particular country has ratified. On the other hand, it provides a succinct summary of the main trends emerging from the detailed discussion in part 5. Part 5 provides a detailed impact of the different UN human rights treaties on the domestic level. The last part is a conclusion.

The length of the chapters varies, depending on factors such as the extent and duration of a particular state's engagement with the UN human rights system. An initial intention to have more succinct chapters was met with the reality of the abundance of state and other practice.

2 Changed Human Rights Landscape: UN Treaty Body System

2.1 Core Treaties – from Six to Nine 'Core' Treaties in Force

The effectiveness of the UN treaty system is premised on the acceptance by states of formal obligations under UN human rights treaties, which is a prerequisite for empowering 'individuals, groups, or parts of the state with different rights preferences that were not empowered to the same extent in the absence of the treaties'.[25] The very concept 'core UN human rights treaties' has seen a clear evolution. Over the last 20 years, three further treaties entered into force: the Convention on the Protection of the Rights of All Migrant Workers and Members of Their Families (CMW, adopted as far back as 1990) in 2003; the 2006 Convention on the Rights of Persons with Disabilities (CRPD) in 2008; and the 2006 Convention for the Protection of All Persons from Enforced Disappearance (CED) in 2010. These additions increased the number of 'core' treaties under the study's purview to nine, three up from the six at the time of the initial study.

---

25 Simmons (n 20) 25.

TABLE 0.1   Core UN human rights treaties and substantive protocols

TREATY, adoption	Entry into force
CERD, 1965	1969
CCPR, 1966	1976
CESCR, 1966	1976
CEDAW, 1979	1981
CAT, 1984	1987
CRC, 1989	1990
CMW, 1990	2003
CED, 2006	2010
CRPD, 2006	2008
OP2-CCPR, 1989	1991
OP-CRC-AC, 2000	2002
OP-CRC-SC, 2000	2002

To these should be added optional protocols elaborating on the *substance* of the core treaties.[26] Two substantive optional protocols entered into force in the last 20 years: the 2000 Optional Protocol to CRC on the Sale of Children, Child Prostitution and Child Pornography (OP-CRC-SC); and the 2000 Optional Protocol to CRC on the Involvement of Children in Armed Conflict (OP-CRC-AC) (which both entered into force in 2002). The Council of Europe (CoE) Lanzarote Convention is addressing the same issues as OP-CRC-SC, allowing for two divergent arguments by CoE member states, namely, either that ratification of both treaties therefore is not required; or that ratification of the other treaty does not create obstacles.

By 1999 only four study states had not accepted all six core treaties: Jamaica was not a state party to CAT; South Africa was not a party to CESCR; India not to CAT and Iran not to CAT and CEDAW. By 2020 South Africa and India had ratified CESCR and CAT, respectively. (Iran still is not a party to CAT and CEDAW.) The new study countries, Nepal, Poland and Turkey, are party to all six of these treaties. In other words, of the 2019 study countries, only one state covered in the follow-up study has not accepted all of the initial six treaties – Jamaica, which has not yet become a party to CAT.

---

26   One such protocol, the 1989 Second Optional Protocol to CCPR, aimed at the abolition of the death penalty (OP2-CCPR), having entered into force in 1991, was already in force.

In respect of the three treaties that entered into force after 2000, the position is as follows:
- CRPD – all 20 2019 study countries ratified or acceded to (in line with global trend, with a total of 184 state parties);
- CED – half (10, or 50 per cent) of the 2019 study countries ratified or acceded to (in line with but higher than the global trend, with a total of 64 state parties (or 33 per cent of UN membership) becoming party to CED);
- CMW – only 7 (or 35 per cent) of the new states ratified or acceded to (in line with global trend, with a total of 56 state parties (29 per cent of UN membership));
- OP-CRC-AC and OP-CRC-SC are ratified by all study countries except Zambia (but it is not clear why).

A variety of reasons explain ratification. The study confirms that political leadership and political context are important factors favouring ratification. Under the rule of Egyptian President Mubarak (1981 to 2011) who adopted a softer style of authoritarianism, CCPR, CESCR, CRC, CAT, CRPD, CMW, CRC-OP-AC and CRC-OP-SC were all ratified. Mexico, the only country among the 20 to have become party to all nine core treaties, as well as OP-CAT, OP2-CCPR, OP-CRC-AC and OP-CRC-SC, has under President Vicente Fox (2000 to 2006) seen a paradigmatic shift in Mexico's human rights foreign policy, with a permanent representative of the Office of the High Commissioner for Human Rights (OHCHR) being established in Mexico City. The surge in ratifications in the 2000s and the late ratification of the twin Covenants in 2003 correspond with Turkey's Europeanisation process, with increased commitment to UN treaties and legal reform driven by its access negotiations with the European Union (EU). Canadian officials cited the federal government's strategy to unify Canada as a catalyst for ratification.

Only two treaties, CMW and CED, enjoy a rate of ratification of 50 per cent or lower. The study countries provide some insight into the reasons for the formal acceptance of these treaties.

The most frequently invoked reasons for non-adherence to CED include that existing obligations under international law and under domestic criminal law make ratification unnecessary or redundant (Australia, Czech Republic); avoidance of responsibility for involvement in forced disappearance in Afghanistan (Canada); and pervasive problems of disappearances (Brazil). As the only treaty Egypt has not ratified, unresolved reported claims of disappearances by the National Council of Human Rights suggest an unwillingness on the part of the government to be held accountable for such practices (Egypt). In other countries, the resistance is less principled. In Estonia, ratification is under consideration; in Nepal, ongoing national processes may have suspended ratification;[27] and in South Africa, bureaucratic hurdles rather than principled opposition have delayed ratification.

Most 'developed countries' that are destinations for international migratory flows are not state parties or even signatories to CMW (Australia, Canada, Japan, Russain Federation). Canada cites a policy of preference for highly-educated and skilled workers as the basis of non-adherence to CMW. It also indicated that migrant management was an area that should remain entirely within its domestic purview. Japan noted that CMW contravened domestic laws and its Constitution, thus invoking national law as a basis for not aligning national law with international standards. The Russian Federation's ratification is impeded by economic reasons (the lack of resources for ensuring the implementation of the Convention's requirements); legal reasons (difficulties in reforming national legislation); and institutional reasons (the absence of necessary institutes for a qualitative implementation of the Convention's norms). No EU member state has accepted CMW. This factor accounts for CMW not being formally accepted by the Czech Republic, Estonia, Finland, Poland and Spain. These states take the view that the EU position was not adequately considered when the UN General Assembly drafted and adopted the Convention; that the CMW is not in line with EU policies and regulations; that it does not distinguish between those migrants lawfully and unlawfully in the country;[28] and they argue that the shared competences on asylum and migration of the EU and its member states are an obstacle to ratify CMW.[29]

Seven states covered in our study have not formally adhered to OP2-CCPR. These states maintain the death penalty under domestic law, even if only *de jure*.

2.2 Treaty Bodies – from Six to Ten Treaty Bodies, and the Addition of Oversight of Detention

CMW, CRPD and CED each established a new treaty body. In addition, a mechanism for allowing visits to places of detention, the Sub-Committee on Prevention of Torture and Other Cruel, Inhuman or Degrading Treatment or Punishment (SPT), was established under the Optional Protocol to the

---

27 At the domestic level in Nepal, the Commission of Enforced Disappeared Persons and Truth and Reconciliation Commission was established in 2015 in accordance with the Enforced Disappearances Inquiry, Truth and Reconciliation Commission Act, 2014.
28 A/HRC/WG.6/8/ESP/1, 19 February 2010 para 20; and A/HRC/29/8, 13 April 2015 para 131.
29 E MacDonald and R Cholewinski, *The Migrant Workers Convention in Europe. Obstacles to the Ratification of the International Convention on the Protection of the Rights of All Migrant Workers and Members of their Families: EU/EEA Perspectives* (UNESCO 2007) 69.

Convention against Torture (OP-CAT), which was adopted in 2002 and entered into force in 2006. The great innovation that OP-CAT brings is that state parties allow on-site visits without the need for state authorisation. Of the 20 2019 study countries, only 11 have accepted OP-CAT. It has not been accepted by Canada, Colombia, Egypt, India, Jamaica, Japan, Nepal, Russian Federation and Zambia. Russian Federation contends that ratification of OP-CAT is not necessary because it already accepts the mandate of the European Committee for the Prevention of Torture, and that accepting the SPT can potentially lead to duplication and overlap.

2.3 Increase in State Reporting

While reporting was required under a possible six treaties, this has increased to a possible nine. For three states in the study cohort (Brazil, Mexico, Senegal) reporting now is required under nine treaties. For all states in the study cohort, reporting under at least one treaty (CRPD) has been added. In addition, the intervening years saw 20 years of reporting cycles continuing. Many more reports have been considered, and Concluding Observations received. However, the period of delay in submission has also increased. For example, Zambia is a total of 19 years overdue with four reports (under CERD, CAT, CESCR, CED) at an average of almost five years per report. With reference to the 17 countries for which we have comparative data: The number of states with an average delay of more than three years per due report has doubled, from four at the end of 1999 (Brazil, Estonia, Jamaica, Zambia), to eight by mid 2019 (Brazil, Egypt, India, Jamaica, Senegal, South Africa, Zambia). Only four study countries (Australia, Colombia, Czech Republic, Estonia) have managed to reduce the period of delay in submission.

The introduction of the 'simplified reporting procedure' is a feature that has become available in the context of increasing reporting obligations. Instead of waiting for states to submit reports, and on the basis of these reports submitting a list of questions/issues to states, the simplified procedure allows treaty bodies to send to state parties a 'list of issues prior to reporting'. The state's responses to the list or issues then effectively becomes the report, replacing the lengthy report. The CAT Cttee was the first treaty body in 2007 to offer states this option.[30] Subsequently, all the other treaty bodies with regular reporting procedures have adopted the simplified procedure (with some variations) as an option. Some of these have been introduced relatively recently, and fall outside the study period.[31]

---

30   A/62/44, paras 23–24.
31   CRC Cttee made this an option for state reports due after 1 September 2019, <https://www.ohchr.org/en/treaty-bodies/crc/reporting-guidelines> accessed 31 March 2023.

TABLE 0.2   UN treaty bodies

1969 – 6/1999	7/1999 – 6/2019
30 years	20 years
6 core treaties	9 core treaties
CERD CESCR CCPR	CERD CESCR CCPR CEDAW CAT CRC
CEDAW CAT CRC	CMW CED CRPD
1 substantive Protocol	3 substantive Protocols
OP2-CCPR	OP2-CCPR OP-CRC-AC OP-CRC-SC
	OP-CAT
3 complaints procedures	9 complaints procedures
76-OP1-CCPR 82-a14-CERD 87-a22-CAT	76-OP1-CCPR 82-art 14-CERD 87-art 22-CAT
	00-OP-CEDAW 08-OP-CRPD
	10-art 31-CED 13-OP-CESCR
	14-OP-CRC-CP

Whether the regular or simplified reporting processes are followed, they culminate in Concluding Observations, to be implemented by states. The HRCttee initiated a process of follow-up to Concluding Observations in 2001. In 2003 the inter-committee meeting of the human rights treaty bodies recommended that all treaty bodies should examine the possibility of setting up a procedure of follow-up to Concluding Observations, and they obliged: the CESCR Cttee in 1999; the CAT Cttee in 2003; the CERD Cttee in 2004; the CEDAW Cttee in 2008; the CRPD Cttee in 2012; and the CED Cttee started in 2014. This follow-up procedure has become an important means of assessing the degree to which compliance with the recommendations of UN treaty bodies has had an impact.

The process broadly entails the following (with variations). The treaty body identifies issues (around one to four) from among the most recently-issued issued Concluding Observations to prioritise. It then requests additional information from state parties, with a view to assessing whether the recommendations have been implemented. The treaty body sets a period (of around one to two years) within which the state is required to provide the relevant information. The treaty body appoints one of its members as rapporteur or 'coordinator' to lead the process. Follow-up is considered on the basis of the state response and replies for NGOs and other actors. The treaty body then assesses

INTRODUCTION

TABLE 0.3 State acceptance of optional complaints procedures and SPT mandate

	OP-CCPR	CERD art 14	CAT art 22	OP-CEDAW	OP-CRPD	CED art 31	OP-CESCR	OP-CRC-CP	CMW art 77	OP-CAT (SPT)	Total per state
Australia	✓	✓	✓	✓	✓	N/A	X	X	N/A	✓	6
Brazil	✓	✓	✓	✓	✓	X	X	✓	N/A	✓	7
Canada	✓	X	✓	✓	✓	N/A	X	X	N/A	X	4
Colombia	✓	X	X	✓	X	X	XX	X	X	X	2
Czech Republic	✓	✓	✓	✓	✓	✓	X	✓	N/A	✓	8
Egypt	X	X	X	X	X	N/A	X	X	X	X	0
Estonia	✓	✓	X	✓	✓	N/A	X	X	N/A	✓	4
Finland	✓	✓	✓	✓	✓	X	✓	✓	N/A	✓	8
India	X	X	X	X	X	X	X	X	X	X	0
Jamaica	X	X	X	X	X	N/A	X	X	X	X	0
Japan	X	X	X	X	X	X	X	X	N/A	X	0
Mexico	✓	✓	✓	✓	✓	✓	X	X	✓	✓	8
Nepal	✓	X	X	✓	X	N/A	X	X	N/A	X	3
Poland	✓	✓	✓	X	X	N/A	X	X	N/A	✓	5
Russian Federation	✓	✓	✓	✓	X	N/A	X	X	N/A	X	4
Senegal	✓	✓	✓	✓	X	X	X	X	X	✓	5
South Africa	✓	✓	✓	✓	✓	N/A	X	X	N/A	✓	6
Spain	✓	✓	✓	✓	✓	✓	✓	✓	N/A	✓	9
Turkey	✓	X	X	✓	✓	N/A	X	X	X	✓	5
Zambia	✓	X	X	X	X	X	X	X	N/A	X	1
Number	16	11	12	14	11	3	2	4	1	11	85/20= 4,25 average

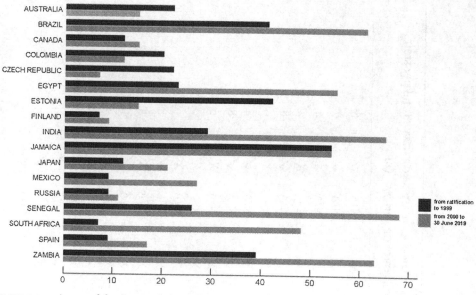

FIGURE 0.2 Average delay (in months) in submission of state reports (from ratification date to 1999; from 2000 to 30 June 2019)

the available information and may take a decision, for example by awarding a grade from A to E.[32]

2.4 Individual Complaints – from Three to Eight (Optional) Individual Complaints Mechanisms in Force

No less than five optional individual complaints mechanisms have come into force since 1999: the Optional Protocol to CEDAW (OP-CEDAW) that was adopted in 1999 and entered into force in 2000; the Optional Protocol to CRPD (OP-CRPD) that was adopted in 2006 and entered into force in 2008;

---

32 See eg Human Rights Committee, Note by the Human Rights Committee on the procedure for follow-up to concluding observations, CCPR/C/108/2 (21 October 2013): (A) Reply/action largely satisfactory: The state party has provided evidence of significant action taken towards the implementation of the recommendation made by the Committee; (B) Reply/action partially satisfactory: The state party has taken steps towards the implementation of the recommendation, but additional information or action remains necessary; (C) Reply/action not satisfactory: A response has been received, but action taken or information provided by the state party is not relevant or does not implement the recommendation; (D) No cooperation with the Committee: No follow-up report has been received after the reminder(s); (E) The information or measures taken are contrary to or reflect rejection of the recommendation.

the Optional Protocol to CESCR (OP-CESCR) that was adopted in 2008 and entered into force in 2013; the Optional Protocol to CRC on a Communications Procedure (OP-CRC-CP) that was adopted in 2011 and entered in force in 2014; and the required number of declarations pursuant to article 31 of CED to ensure that the competence of the CED Cttee to receive and consider individual complaints has been met, thereby securing its entry into force in 2010. A sixth complaints mechanism, provided for under article 77 CMW, was not yet in force by 30 June 2019, since the target of acceptance by 10 state parties required to allow it to enter into force had not been reached. Only one of the countries in the study (Mexico) was among five states globally that had made this declaration.

In the early 2000s Mexico experienced an important political transition from a one-party regime to a more competitive multi-party political system. The government of President Vicente Fox (2000 to 2006) brought about a paradigmatic shift in Mexico's human rights foreign policy. By 1999 it had accepted no optional complaints mechanism. Over the next 20 years, Mexico accepted seven of the nine complaints mechanisms (including under CMW, which is not yet in force).

Four states (Egypt, India, Jamaica, Japan) have not accepted any of the optional complaints mechanisms. This uniform reluctance to open up domestic judicial decisions to international scrutiny suggests principled opposition. This proposition is confirmed by Egypt's justification that the sufficiency of its domestic laws makes international recourse superfluous, and Japan's longstanding argument that accepting the submission of individual communications to UN treaty bodies would undermine judicial independence. Although these positions appear to be rather entrenched, at least in Japan some suggestions regarding the review of this position have been made. Although the experience of Jamaica has been coloured by its denunciation of OP1-CCPR, this withdrawal occurred in a very specific context framed by the death penalty. There seems to be some latitude for future acceptance of the complaints mechanisms under OP-CRPD and OP-CEDAW. Justifications from Indian officials include a fear of exposure of its human rights violations, a fear of overworking of its administrative machinery, a lack of resources to administer the remedies (compensation, and so forth), and unwavering faith in government institutions as the best avenue to secure human rights for individuals.

OP-CESCR is one of the least ratified complaints mechanisms. The main reasons for states' lack of enthusiasm are their misgivings about the justiciability of economic, social and cultural rights (Australia, Poland, Turkey); the resistance against perceived 'control' by (quasi)-judicial bodies over social policies or resource allocation (Australia, Poland); and the argument that accepting

OP-CESCR is unnecessary, since national legislation is sufficient to protect economic, social and cultural rights (Russian Federation).

OP-CRC-CP has a much lower level of acceptance than CRC. In Poland, reluctance to accept this complaint mechanism stems from a fear that it would lead to a questioning of restrictive domestic laws on, for example, abortion and contraception. South Africa advanced the sufficiency of its domestic legal system to justify not becoming a party.

Complaints under these procedures add an important dimension to the 2019 study. By 1999, not only were complaints mechanisms possible under only three treaties (CCPR, through OP1-CCPR, CERD and CAT) but the volume of complaints was also quite limited. Since then, individual complaints have become much more frequent. The number of complaints under the pre-existing three procedures also grew over the years. In many instances, the frequency of these complaints increased, signalling the evolving maturity of these complaints mechanisms. Complaints under the five new procedures also gradually started taking off.

In his 2020 'Status of the human rights treaty body system' report,[33] the UN Secretary-General provided the following pictures of an expanding communications procedure:

What matters most in a discussion on effectiveness are the complaints in which the state has been found in violation, and in which a remedial action is called for. The last 20 years have witnessed an increase in the number of communications in which treaty bodies found violations by state parties that have accepted optional complaints mechanisms. Tables 0.5 to 0.9 below show the increase in violations found, in respect of states from the five UN regions, and in total (Table 0.10) comparing the first and the present periods:

The relevant part of these findings is the remedial recommendation, usually dealing with redress to the author or complainant, and then with measures of a general or systemic nature, aimed at preventing a recurrence of the violation. It is not an easy task to ascertain the implementation status of these findings. There is no central database that shows whether states replied to the treaty body's request to provide information about measures taken, within a stipulated period, or what these measures are. As the number of violation findings grew, and the need for information and data increased, the treaty bodies devised a system of engaging with states in a follow-up process on individual communications.

---

33 Report of the Secretary-General, A/74/643, 10 January 2020 <https://undocs.org/A/74/643>; Annex VI: Individual communications registered as at 31 October 2019.

TABLE 0.4 Number of final decisions on communications adopted per treaty body, 2015 to (31 October) 2019

Treaty body	No. of final decisions on communications adopted in 2015	No. of final decisions on communications adopted in 2016	No. of final decisions on communications adopted in 2017	No. of final decisions on communications adopted in 2018	No. of final decisions on communications adopted as at 31 October 2019
CERD Cttee	3	2	1	2	4
HRCttee	101	109	131	101	134
CESCR Cttee	1	5	2	4	21
CEDAW Cttee	9	12	13	18	19
CAT Cttee	65	53	65	68	39
CRC Cttee	1	1	2	9	17
CRPD Cttee	3	3	8	6	9
CED Cttee	0	1	0	1	0
TOTAL DECISIONS	183	186	222	209	243

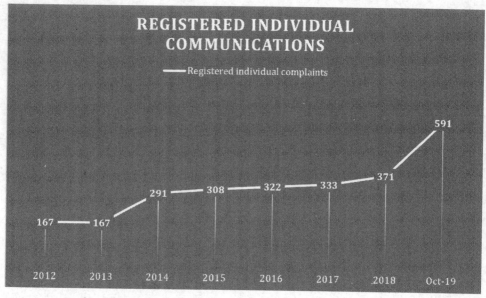

FIGURE 0.3   Total number of individual communications registered, 2012 to (Oct) 2019
SOURCE: A/77/279 ANNEX VIII

TABLE 0.5   Number of communications in which TBs found violations against WEO states

	CERD		CCPR		CAT	
	up to 06/1999	07/1999 – 06/2019	up to 06/1999	07/1999 – 06/2019	up to 06/1999	07/1999 – 06/2019
Australia	0	1	2	33	1	5
Canada	n/a	n/a	8	20	1	8
Finland	0	0	4	1	0	2
Spain	0	0	2	26	1	8
Total	0	1	16	80	3	23

INTRODUCTION

TABLE 0.6 Number of communications in which TBs found violations against East European states

	CERD		CCPR		CAT	
	up to 06/1999	07/1999 – 06/2019	up to 06/1999	07/1999 – 06/2019	up to 06/1999	07/1999 – 06/2019
Czech Republic	n/a	0	2	29	0	0
Estonia	n/a	0	0	1	n/a	n/a
Poland	0	0	0	1	0	0
Russia	0	0	0	39	0	3
Total	0	0	2	70	0	3

TABLE 0.7 Number of communications in which TBs found violations against 'Asian' states

	CERD		CCPR		CAT	
	up to 06/1999	07/1999 – 06/2019	up to 06/1999	07/1999 – 06/2019	up to 06/1999	07/1999 – 06/2019
India	n/a	n/a	n/a	n/a	n/a	n/a
Japan	n/a	n/a	n/a	n/a	n/a	n/a
Nepal	n/a	n/a	0	23	n/a	n/a
Turkey	n/a	n/a	n/a	3	0	0
Total	0	0	0	26	0	0

Thus, another important development over the last two decades has been the inclusion of a follow-up procedure on views, by all treaty bodies (except the CED Cttee). While there are differences between treaty bodies, in the main the process is triggered by and dependent on states (and authors) providing information. A relatively small number of views are considered at any particular opportunity, leading to a small number of cases being closed, and a steady increase in the overall number of cases under the follow-up procedure.

TABLE 0.8 Number of communications in which TBs found violations against African states

	CERD		CCPR		CAT	
	up to 06/1999	07/1999 – 06/2019	up to 06/1999	07/1999 – 06/2019	up to 06/1999	07/1999 – 06/2019
Egypt	n/a	n/a	n/a	n/a	n/a	n/a
Senegal	0	0	1	0	0	1
South Africa	0	0	n/a	1	0	0
Zambia	n/a	0	3	7	n/a	0
Total	0	0	4	8	0	1

TABLE 0.9 Number of communications in which TBs found violations against GRULAC states

	CERD		CCPR		CAT	
	up to 06/1999	07/1999 – 06/2019	up to 06/1999	07/1999 – 06/2019	up to 06/1999	07/1999 – 06/2019
Brazil	n/a	0	n/a	0	n/a	0
Colombia	n/a	0	9	13	n/a	0
Jamaica	n/a	n/a	77	7	n/a	n/a
Mexico	n/a	1	n/a	1	n/a	0
Total	0	1	86	21	0	0

TABLE 0.10 Number of communications in which TBs found violations against all 20 states

	CERD		CCPR		CAT	
	up to 06/1999	07/1999 – 06/2019	up to 06/1999	07/1999 – 06/2019	up to 06/1999	07/1999 – 06/2019
Total	0	2	108	285	3	27

2.5 Inquiry Procedures

At the time of the initial study, only one inquiry procedure, that under article 20 of CAT, was in place. By the end of the second decade of the new century, five further inquiry procedures – those under OP-CEDAW, CED, OP-CRPD, OP-CESCR and OP-CRC-CP – have been put in place and are being used. These inquiry processes are all triggered by the receipt of 'reliable information' indicating that the state party is committing 'grave or systematic violations'. While the possibility of a treaty body initiating an inquiry flows automatically from state adherence to CAT, OP-CEDAW, CED, OP-CRPD and OP-CRC-CP, with an option available under all but CED to explicitly opt out,[34] under OP-CESR an explicit opt-in is required for states to accept this procedure.[35] This distinction makes a considerable difference. As states have shown a reluctance to explicitly opt out,[36] the fallback position is that most of them have acquiesced to the inquiry procedures under CAT, OP-CEDAW, OP-CRPD and OP-CRC-CP. States have equally been slow to make opt-in declarations, resulting in only five state parties to OP-CESR having made opt-in declarations accepting the inquiry procedure. OP-CRC-CP went one step further by establishing a formal 'follow-up to the inquiry procedure', allowing the CRC Cttee to 'invite' the relevant state supply information on the measures it has taken to implement the recommendations resulting from the inquiry.[37]

Because the inquiry procedure allows for the submission of information to UN treaty bodies without requiring the exhaustion of local remedies, it was expected that this avenue would become an important tool to better protect treaty guarantees. However, using OP-CEDAW as measure, by mid-2019 a disappointingly small number had been undertaken.[38] Of the four inquiries concluded under OP-CEDAW, two were to study countries (Canada and Mexico).

By 30 June 1999 only four article 20-inquiries had been undertaken, two of these to study countries (Brazil and Turkey). Article 20 inquiries have subsequently taken off, with eight inquiries undertaken, four of which in respect of study countries: in respect of Mexico (2003), Colombia (2006), Nepal (2006)

---

34 However, states may make an explicit declaration to opt out under CAT (art 28(1)); OP-CEDAW (art 10(1)); OP-CRPD (art 8); and OP-CRC-CP (art 13(7)).
35 Art 11 OP-CESCR.
36 Very few states have made use of the opt-out option. Under OP-CRPD, eg, only two states (Guinea Bissau and Syria) opted out, and in respect of OP-CEDAW, only six states opted out (including one study country, Colombia).
37 OP-CRC-CP, art 14.
38 Catherine O'Rourke, 'Bridging the Enforcement Gap – Evaluating the Inquiry Procedure of the CEDAW Optional Protocol' (2018) 27 American University Journal of Gender, Social Policy and the Law 1.

and Brazil (2008).[39] With the first visit by the SPT taking place in 2007, these visits are of more recent origin. It would appear that since then, the SPT visits are largely eclipsing article 20-visits. In the period between 2008 and 2019, the SPT conducted more than 70 visits. Seven of the study countries received a visit, with two visits to Mexico (2008, 2016), Brazil (2011, 2015) and Senegal (2012, 2019), and one each to Estonia (2009), Turkey (2015), Spain (2017) and Poland (2018).

3   Changed Human Rights Landscape: Beyond UN Treaty Body System

3.1   *UN Charter-Based System*

Within the broader UN human rights framework, a number of far-reaching changes had also taken place. The Human Rights Council (HRC) replaced the Commission on Human Rights, and met for the first time on 19 June 2006. One of the main achievements of the HRC is the UPR. Two UPR cycles have taken place during the 20-year period, a first from 2008 to 2011, and a second from 2012 to 2016. A third cycle, scheduled to run from 2017 to 2022, was underway for part of the study period. In the period between 1 July 1999 and 30 June 2019, each of the states in this study has undergone at least two rounds of review under the UPR, resulting in hundreds of recommendations addressed to each of them.

There has also been an enormous expansion in the special human rights procedures established under the HRC. Many of their thematic mandates to some extent overlap or reinforce aspects of the treaty bodies' work. Some of the newly-established rapporteurs are the Special Rapporteur on the Right of Everyone to the Enjoyment of the Highest Attainable Standard of Physical and Mental Health (established in 2002); the Special Rapporteur in the Field of Cultural Rights (2009); the Special Rapporteur on the Rights to Freedom of Peaceful Assembly and of Association (2010); the Independent Expert on the Enjoyment of All Human Rights by Older Persons (2013); the Special Rapporteur on the Rights of Persons with Disabilities (2014); the Independent Expert on the Enjoyment of Human Rights by Persons with Albinism (2015); and the Independent Expert on Protection Against Violence and Discrimination Based on Sexual Orientation and Gender Identity (2016). It should be noted that, at

---

39   <https://tbinternet.ohchr.org/_layouts/15/TreatyBodyExternal/TBSearch.aspx> accessed 5 November 2022.

the level of the OHCHR, attention has also increasingly been directed to the domestic impact of visits undertaken and appeals made by these procedures.[40]

3.2   Burgeoning Growth in Regional Human Rights Systems

Regional human rights systems also matured, and extended the scope of their work and influence. The 20 years since 1999 have witnessed significant growth in the outputs and domestic resonance of the three major regional human rights systems. In all three of the well-established regional human rights systems, the possibility of a binding judgment by an international court exists. This growth further problematizes efforts to discern the precise contribution of the UN treaty body system to reform at the domestic level.

In Europe, within the CoE, Protocol 11 to the European Convention of Human Rights entered into force in 1998. It made the European Court of Human Rights a full-time institution and abolished the European Commission of Human Rights, which used to decide on the admissibility of applications. The right to individual petition became automatic. The newly-overhauled Court attracted a large number of applications.

While the European Convention for the Prevention of Torture (ECPT) was adopted already in 1987 and entered into force in 1989, the European Committee for the Prevention of Torture (CPT) in the last two decades solidified its role of undertaking missions to state parties to conduct unannounced visits to places of detention. Building on the 1961 European Social Charter, its updated and adjusted reincarnation, the 1996 revised European Social Charter, and its 1995 Additional Protocol to the European Social Charter Providing for a System of Collective Complaints, entered into force in 1999 and 1998, respectively. The European Committee of Social Rights decided its first complaint on 9 September 1999,[41] finding a violation of the Social Charter. To this list can be added the 2007 CoE Convention on the Protection of Children against Sexual Exploitation and Sexual Abuse (Lanzarote Convention), which entered into force on 1 July 2010;[42] and the 2011 CoE Convention on Preventing and Combating Violence against Women and Domestic Violence (Istanbul Convention), which entered into force in 2014.[43] The Charter of Fundamental Rights of the European Union, which entered into force in 2009,

---

40   See 'How do Special Procedure Mandate-Holders Make a Difference?' <https://www.ohchr.org/EN/HRBodies/SP/Pages/Welcomepage.aspx> accessed 5 November 2022.
41   No 01/1998 *International Commission of Jurists (ICJ) v Portugal.*
42   All CoE member states have ratified both OP-CRC-SC and the Lanzarote Conventions.
43   Turkey's withdrew from the Istanbul Convention, which withdrawal took effect on 1 July 2021.

also adds another dimension of rights protection for EU member states. The EU established its Fundamental Rights Agency in 2007, and the EU Charter of Fundamental Rights came fully into effect in 2009.

In the Inter-American human rights system, established under the Organization of American States, a number of treaties are similar in substantive scope to UN treaties. The American Convention is a parallel to CCPR; the 1988 Protocol additional thereto in the Area of Economic, Social, and Cultural Rights, which entered into force in 1999, has many similarities to CESCR. Other self-standing OAS human rights treaties include the 1994 Inter-American Convention on the Forced Disappearance of Persons; the 1994 Inter-American Convention to Prevent, Punish and Eradicate Violence against Women; the 1999 Inter-American Convention on the Elimination of All Forms of Discrimination against Persons with Disabilities (entered into force 2001); the 2013 Inter-American Convention against Racism, Racial Discrimination, and Related Intolerance (in force since 2017); and the 2013 Inter-American Convention Against All Forms of Discrimination and Intolerance (entered into force in 2020 when Mexico became the second state to become party to this treaty). Many of these predate equivalent UN treaties.

At the turn of the millennium, the intergovernmental organisation within which the African regional system is located, transformed itself from the Organisation of African Unity (OAU) into the African Union (AU). Compared to its predecessor (the 1963 OAU Charter) the AU Constitutive Act places human rights much closer to its core. At a normative level, the 1981 African Charter on Human and Peoples' Rights (Africa Charter) is largely inspired by CCPR and CESCR. Importantly, it provides for an automatic right of individual access to the quasi-judicial supervisory body, the African Commission on Human and Peoples' Rights (African Commision). Two AU human rights treaties that are regional parallels to UN treaties entered into force around 2000: the 1990 African Charter on the Rights and Welfare of the Child (African Children's Charter) in 1999, and the 2003 Protocol to the African Charter on Human and Peoples' Rights on the Rights of Women in Africa (Maputo Protocol) in 2005. With the advent of the African Court on Human and Peoples' Rights (African Court) in 2006, after the 1998 Court Protocol on the Establishment of an African Court entered into force in 2004, the possibility of a binding judgment also exists in the African system. It should be noted that the substantive jurisdiction of the African Court extends to UN human rights treaties ratified by respondent states.[44] In Africa, human rights protection at the sub-regional

---

44 African Court Protocol, art 3(1).

level, in particular within the Economic Community of West African States (ECOWAS), also rose in prominence over the last two decades.

3.3 Human Rights at the National Level

As much as significant growth and expansion occurred at the international level, the domestic level also experienced pertinent changes. The earlier study had made proposals for the establishment of inter-departmental fora to deal with reporting and implementation, along the lines of the 'National Mechanisms for Reporting and Follow-up' (NMRF). The OHCHR has put its full weight behind the NMRF process,[45] while further national implementing mechanisms evolved over this period.[46] The role of national human rights institutions has also since 1999 become more pronounced, as more national human rights institutions became established in various regions of the world.[47]

It should be noted that there has also been an evolution towards making the newly-established treaties better attuned to effective and meaningful implementation by requiring the creation of national implementing institutions. If the tendency since the early 1990s has been to increase the role of national human rights institutions in treaty monitoring and implementation, two UN human rights instruments drafted since the turn of the century take a significant step further. Both OP-CAT and CRPD formally require national institutions to play a role in monitoring or implementing states' treaty obligations. State parties to these two instruments are required to give the relevant national institutions the necessary powers to carry out various functions specified in the treaty itself. This is a radical new method of implementing treaties.

---

45 See *National Mechanisms for Reporting and Follow-Up: A Practical Guide to Effective State Engagement with International Human Rights Mechanisms* (UN OHCHR 2016); on the critical elements that states need to consider when establishing or strengthening their national mechanism for reporting and follow-up, see <https://www.ohchr.org/Documents/Publications/HR_PUB_16_1_NMRF_PracticalGuide.pdf> accessed 5 November 2022.

46 Rachel Murray and Christian de Vos, 'Behind the State: Domestic Mechanisms and Procedures for the Implementation of Human Rights Judgments and Decisions' (2020) 12 Journal of Human Rights Practice 22; Lingliang Zeng, 'Implementation Mechanism of the UN Core Human Rights Treaties: Current Situation, Issues and Enhancement' in Lingliang Zeng, *Contemporary International Law and China's Peaceful Development* (Springer 2021) 213.

47 See eg Richard Carver, 'A New Answer to an Old Question: National Human Rights Institutions and the Domestication of International Law' (2010) 10 Human Rights Law Review 1; and T Kayaoglu, 'National Human Rights Institutions: A Reason for Hope in the Middle East and North Africa?' Brookings Doha Centre Analysis Paper (2021) (noting the rise of NHRIs in the MENA region, and their role in more domestic implementation of UN treaties).

OP-CAT's aim is the prevention of torture, primarily by establishing mechanisms for visiting places of detention. The Sub-Committee on Prevention of Torture (SPT) occupies a position analogous to a national mechanism. In parallel with the SPT, OP-CAT also requires state parties to establish a national preventive mechanism within a year of ratification.[48] CRPD explicitly calls for the creation of national 'focal points' and the designation of national human rights institutions to promote, protect and monitor implementation of the Convention.[49] Article 33(2) simply requires state parties to 'designate or establish' independent mechanisms.

An emerging and ongoing challenge is the implementation of UN human rights treaty standards – and research – at the sub-national, encompassing both the federal ('state'/'provincial') level and the district/local authority level.[50] The Inter-American Court of Human Rights has already stated that a state cannot invoke its federal structure to justify its failure to comply with an international obligation.[51]

4   Contribution to Academic Debate

Interest in and scholarship on the 'impact', 'implementation' or 'compliance' by states with international human rights law, generally, and the UN treaty body system, specifically, have blossomed over the last 20 years. In fact, it was in the very year in which the initial study was published, 2002, that Hathaway's seminal article ('Do human rights treaties make a difference?') saw the light.[52] Its comprehensive scope, provocative title, its bleak conclusion, and its methodology are factors that explain the wide citation this article enjoys, and the range of the responses to it.[53]

'Implementation/impact' research on the UN human rights treaty system has since then evolved into many directions. In terms of focus, UN human

---

[48] OP-CAT, art 17.
[49] CRPD, art 33(1).
[50] Barbara Oomen and Baumgärtel Moritz, 'Frontier Cities: The Rise of Local Authorities as an Opportunity for International Human Rights Law' (2018) 29 European Journal of International Law 607.
[51] Corte IDH *Caso Escher y otros v Brasil*, sentença de 06.07.2009, Série C, n. 200, 65–66; Corte IDH, *Caso Garibaldi v Brasil*, sentença de 23.09.2009, Série C n. 203.
[52] Oona A Hathaway, 'Do Human Rights Treaties Make a Difference?' (2002) 111 Yale Law Journal 1935.
[53] See eg Ryan Goodman and Derek Jinks, 'Measuring the Effects of Human Rights Treaties' (2003) 14 European Journal of International Law 171.

rights treaty-impact research may be categorised as country-specific,[54] treaty-specific,[55] or procedure-specific (by, for example, focusing on state reporting),[56] or a combination of any of these.[57] In other contributions, attention is directed to the various pathways of domestic implementation and impact (for example, through the judiciary,[58] or through domestic bills of rights).[59] The reasons or motivation of ratifying states also interrogated,[60] while the effect of international human rights law in particular political contexts is also being

---

[54] See eg Carole J Petersen, 'Sexual Orientation and Gender Identity in Hong Kong: A Case for the Strategic Use of Human Rights Treaties and the International Reporting Process' (2012) 14 Asian-Pacific Law and Policy Journal 28; Marc Gambaraza 'La Mise en Oeuvre de la Convention relative aux Droits de l'enfant en France: Les Enjeux relatifs à la Protection de l'enfance dans une Perspective Internationale' (2021) 19 Droits Fondamentaux; Benoît Eyraud, 'Adopter une approche du handicap par les droits humains? La domestication en spirale de la Convention internationale sur les droits des personnes handicapées en France' (2023) 113(1) Droit et société 55-71..

[55] Linda Camp Keith, 'The United Nations International Covenant on Civil and Political Rights: Does it Make a Difference in Human Rights Behaviour?' (1999) 36 Journal of Peace Research 95; Neil A Englehart and Melissa K Miller, 'The CEDAW Effect: International Law's Impact on Women's Rights' (2014) 13 Journal of Human Rights 22; Susanne Zwingel, 'From Intergovernmental Negotiations to (Sub)-National Change: A Transnational Perspective on the Impact of CEDAW' (2005) 7 International Feminist Journal of Politics 400; Wayne Sandholtz, 'Domestic Law and Human Rights Treaty Commitments: The Convention against Torture' (2017) 16 Journal of Human Rights 25; Frances Raday, 'Gender and Democratic Citizenship: The Impact of CEDAW' (2012) 10 International Journal of Constitutional Law 512 <https://doi.org/10.1093/icon/mor068>; Christopher McCrudden, 'Why Do National Court Judges Refer to Human Rights Treaties? A Comparative International Law Analysis of CEDAW' (2015) 109 AJIL 534.

[56] Cosette D Creamer and Daniel W Simmons, 'The Proof is in the Process: Self-Reporting Under International Human Rights Treaties' (2020) Faculty Scholarship at Penn Carey Law 2145 <https://scholarship.law.upenn.edu/faculty_scholarship/2145> accessed 5 November 2022.

[57] Ursula Kilkelly, Laura Lundy and Bronagh Byrne (eds), *Incorporating the UN Convention on the Rights of the Child into National Law* (Intersentia 2021). At the same time treaty-specific (CRC) and country-specific, in the various chapters, covering mostly states in the WEO UN region (Australia, New Zealand, Iceland, Ireland, Norway, Scotland, Sweden, United States of America, Wales) as well as China, Mexico and South Africa. Three countries are included in this publication as well as in the 1999 and 2019 studies.

[58] McCrudden (n 55) 534; Machiko Kanetake, 'UN Human Rights Treaty Monitoring Bodies Before Domestic Courts' (2018) 67 International and Comparative Law Quarterly 201.

[59] James Raymond Vreeland, 'Political Institutions and Human Rights: Why Dictatorships Enter into the United Nations Convention Against Torture' (2008) International Organization 65.

[60] Oona A Hathaway, 'Why Do Countries Commit to Human Rights Treaties?' (2007) 51 Journal of Conflict Resolution 588; Eric Neumayer, 'Do International Human Rights Treaties Improve Respect for Human Rights?' (2005) 49 Journal of Conflict Resolution 925.

investigated.[61] Various disciplinary perspectives – in particular, law, political science,[62] international relations and sociology – have been brought to bear on the topic, marking the field as particularly multidisciplinary in nature.

This study, 20 years on from the previous, builds upon this broad research providing an insight, through the lens of particular states, into the domestic reach of these international obligations and mechanisms.

---

61 Emilie Hafner-Burton and Kiyoteru Tsutsui, 'Justice Lost! The Failure of International Human Rights Law to Matter Where Needed Most' (2007) 44 Journal of Peace Research 407; Claudio Grossman, 'Implementing Human Rights in Closed Environments through the United Nations Convention against Torture' (2014) 31 Law Context: A Socio-Legal Journal 125.

62 Eg, Daniel W Hill, 'Estimating the Effects of Human Rights Treaties on State Behaviour' (2010) 72 Journal of Politics 1161.

CHAPTER 1

The Impact of the United Nations Human Rights Treaties on the Domestic Level in Australia

Sarah Joseph, Adam Fletcher and Anna Lochhead-Sperling

1   Introduction to Human Rights in Australia

The six British colonies of Australia united to form a federation in 1901, with those colonies becoming six autonomous state governments alongside a new Commonwealth federal government. There are also two self-governing territories.

Australia is a stable liberal democracy, with a long-standing commitment to democratic values, the rule of law and the separation of powers. Political violence is essentially absent. While Australia is a comparatively wealthy, a developed country with numerous social security entitlements for those in need, there is growing income inequality.[1]

Australia's Constitution is contained in section 9 of an Act of the Imperial British Parliament (Commonwealth of Australia Constitution Act 1901 (Imp)). Australia now is fully independent,[2] although it remains a constitutional monarchy.

Australia's Constitution does not contain a Bill of Rights. There are limited guarantees with respect to freedom of religion, trial by jury, and compensation if one's property is compulsorily acquired.[3] There is also an implied constitutional freedom of political communication and an implied constitutional right to vote.[4] However, Australia has an entrenched traditional attachment to parliamentary sovereignty; constitutionally-protected rights undermine parliamentary sovereignty as they significantly constrain the powers of Parliament, the democratically-elected arm of government, and enhance those of the

---

1 See ACOSS and UNSW Sydney, 'Inequality in Australia 2018' <https://www.acoss.org.au/wp-content/uploads/2018/07/Inequality-in-Australia-2018_Factsheet.pdf> accessed 18 March 2022.
2 See Sarah Joseph and Melissa Castan, *Federal Constitutional Law: A Contemporary View* (5th edn, Thompson Reuters 2019) paras 1.155–1.170.
3 ibid, ch 12.
4 ibid, ch 13. An 'implied' right is one which is not explicit in the words of the Constitution.

© SARAH JOSEPH ET AL., 2024 | DOI:10.1163/9789004377653_003
This is an open access chapter distributed under the terms of the CC BY-NC-ND 4.0 license.

unelected judiciary. Even human rights statutes are suspect: As noted by a senior government official who works on human rights implementation during the interview, 'there's a question around the role of judges ... are [they] the right people to be making such determinations?'[5]

There is no comprehensive national human rights statute, a fact that has often been criticised by the UN treaty bodies.[6] However, comprehensive rights-protective statutes have been adopted in three jurisdictions – the Australian Capital Territory (ACT), Victoria and Queensland.[7]

Australia's apex court, the High Court of Australia, has played an important role in protecting the human rights of various parties, including criminal appellants, asylum seekers and those seeking to vindicate implied constitutional rights.[8] However, the constitutional limitations of its role preclude the Court from being a consistent protector of rights.[9]

The principal domestic institution responsible for the protection and promotion of human rights is the Australian Human Rights Commission (AHRC), Australia's national human rights institution. The AHRC is an independent statutory authority with many functions including the conciliation of complaints under federal anti-discrimination law; inquiries into human rights issues; an educational role; and the promotion of human rights generally.[10] Its human rights remit is based on Australia's international treaty obligations. It has 'A status' under the Principles Relating to the Status of National Institutions.[11] Relations between the AHRC and the federal government soured considerably from 2013 to 2017, prompted by the then new government's displeasure over the timing of an AHRC inquiry into immigration detention.[12] Relations

---

5   Senior government official who works on human rights implementation, interview, telephone, 20 August 2019. All interviews are on file with the authors. Interviewees are only named where they agreed to such.

6   See, eg, HRCttee, COs on Australia, UN Doc CCPR/C/AUS/CO/6, paras 5 and 6 (1 December 2017).

7   Human Rights Act 2004 (Act); Charter of Human Rights and Responsibilities Act 2006 (Vic); Human Rights Act 2019 (Qld).

8   See eg *Bugmy v R* [2013] HCA 37; *Plaintiff M70/2011 v Minister for Immigration and Citizenship* (2011) 244 CLR 144; *Brown v Tasmania* (2017) 261 CLR 328; and *Roach v Electoral Commissioner* (2007) 233 CLR 162.

9   See eg *Al-Kateb v Godwin* (2004) 219 CLR 562; *Behrooz v Secretary, Department of Immigration and Multicultural and Indigenous Affairs* (2004) 219 CLR 486; *Magaming v R* [2013] HCA 40; *Thomas v Mowbray* (2007) 233 CLR 307.

10   See Australian Human Rights Commission Act 1986 (Cth).

11   These are known as the Paris Principles; see General Assembly Resolution 48/134 (20 December 1993).

12   Shalailah Medhora and Ben Doherty, 'Tony Abbott Calls Report on Children in Detention a "Transparent Stitch-Up"' *The Guardian* (12 February 2015)

improved after the end of the term of the AHRC president, Professor Gillian Triggs, in 2017, the apparent scapegoat for the government's grievances.[13]

The AHRC has counterparts in the eight state and territory jurisdictions. Other executive institutions such as Ombudsman Offices in each jurisdiction play an occasional rights-protective role, as do parliamentary inquiries and Royal Commissions of Inquiry.

Australia currently faces numerous human rights challenges, including the situations of detainees, those with disabilities and/or mental illness and the homeless.[14] Indigenous people continue to experience lower socio-economic conditions (for instance, regarding health, housing and education), discriminatory attitudes, as well as a much larger rate of incarceration.[15]

The most prominent human rights issue has concerned asylum seekers arriving by boat. Since the 1970s thousands of refugees have sought asylum in Australia via unauthorised boat arrivals.[16] In 1992 new federal laws mandated the detention of such boat arrivals until their claims were processed, or until they left the country. These laws breached international human rights law.[17] Nevertheless, since 2013 Australia's laws have become harsher, with boat arrivals now sent to Nauru as well as, previously, to Papua New Guinea (PNG), where their claims are processed. The government is adamant that these people will

---

    <https://www.theguardian.com/australia-news/2015/feb/12/tony-abbott-rejects-report-children-detention-blatantly-political> accessed 27 March 2019.

[13] It is arguable that the AHRC faced government hostility simply for doing its work: Sarah Joseph, 'Australia's Exceptionalism: Antipathy Towards Human Rights' in Paula Gerber and Melissa Castan (eds), *Critical Perspectives on Human Rights in Australia: Volume 2* (Thomson Reuters, 2022).

[14] AHRC, Information Concerning Australia's Compliance with the International Covenant on Civil and Political Rights, UN Doc INT/CCPR/NHS/AUS/28980/E, 18 September 2017; Disability Rights Now, 2019 Australian Civil Society Shadow Report to the United Nations Committee on the Rights of Persons with Disabilities: UN CRPD Review 2019, UN Doc INT/CRPD/CSS/AUS/35639/E; and Australia's 3rd Universal Periodic Review: Joint NGO Submission on Behalf of the Australian NGO Coalition (April 2020) <https://www.hrlc.org.au/universal-periodic-review> accessed 18 March 2022.

[15] Australian Law Reform Commission, 'Pathways to Justice: Inquiry into the Incarceration Rate of Aboriginal and Torres Strait Islander Peoples' (March 2018), available via <https://www.alrc.gov.au/publication/pathways-to-justice-inquiry-into-the-incarceration-rate-of-aboriginal-and-torres-strait-islander-peoples-alrc-report-133/> accessed 22 March 2022.

[16] See Janet Phillips and Harriet Spinks, 'Boat Arrivals in Australia Since 1976' Parliament of Australia, 23 July 2013 < https://www.aph.gov.au/about_parliament/parliamentary_departments/parliamentary_library/pubs/rp/rp1314/boatarrivals > accessed 18 March 2022.

[17] The first of many such decisions was *A v Australia* UN Doc CCPR/C/59/D/560/1993 (3 April 1997).

never settle in Australia, regardless of any confirmation of refugee status.[18] While some have been able to settle in third countries such as the United States, hundreds of asylum seekers have for years languished on Nauru and in PNG, where there are limited facilities for refugees and underdeveloped immigration, integration and employment programmes, leading to well-documented serious health issues among the asylum seekers.[19] Australia justifies its policies on the basis that it needs to maintain control of its borders, and that the policy stops unsafe boat journeys that have resulted in mass drownings.[20]

In 2009 a National Human Rights Consultation was conducted, resulting in a recommendation for the adoption of a federal human rights charter similar to those then in place in the ACT and Victoria.[21] However, the Australian government baulked at that recommendation and instead adopted a 'Human Rights Framework'.[22] The most important parts of the Framework boosted parliamentary and bureaucratic mechanisms to address human rights. An in-depth study of the first four years of the Framework, however, indicates that it has had little impact on the actual protection of human rights,[23] probably because the Framework lacks judicial teeth. The exclusion of the judiciary from the Framework reflects Australia's traditional adherence to notions of parliamentary sovereignty.[24]

Australia has a 'diverse, pluralistic and sophisticated' civil society,[25] with numerous human rights non-governmental organisations (NGOs) with both

18   AHRC, 'Lives on Hold: Refugees and Asylum Seekers in the "Legacy Caseload"' (2019), Appendix 1: Timeline of Legal and Policy Developments Affecting People in the Legacy Caseload <https://www.humanrights.gov.au/our-work/asylum-seekers-and-refugees/publications/lives-hold-refugees-and-asylum-seekers-legacy> accessed 18 March 2022.
19   See HRCttee, COs on Australia, UN Doc CCPR/C/AUS/CO/6 (9 November 2017) para 35(a).
20   The first argument exaggerates the numbers that arrived in Australia, while the second argument uses the asylum seekers and refugees on Nauru and PNG as a means to an end: Their despair is being used to deter others: Sarah Joseph, 'Operation Sovereign Borders, Offshore Detention and the "Drownings Argument"' *The Conversation* (24 July 2015).
21   National Human Rights Consultation, Report (September 2009), Recommendation 18 <https://alhr.org.au/wp/wp-content/uploads/2018/02/National-Human-Rights-Consultation-Report-2009-copy.pdf> accessed 27 March 2019.
22   Human Rights Law Resources Centre, Australia's Human Rights Framework (22 April 2010) <https://www.hrlc.org.au/news/australias-human-rights-framework-2> accessed 18 March 2022.
23   Adam Fletcher, *Australia's Human Rights Scrutiny Regime* (MUP, 2018). It is unlikely that the effectiveness of the system has improved significantly since those first four years.
24   ibid 87–95.
25   Phil Lynch, Director of International Service for Human Rights and former Director, Human Rights Law Centre, interview, Geneva, 8 May 2019.

general and specific focuses. While most do not use the language of international human rights, their focuses cross the spectrum of human rights within the core treaties. However, there are concerns over laws that have targeted certain protest activity, as well as cuts and threats of more cuts to the funding of such groups (for example, by the removal of the tax-exempt status) which have curtailed activities and narrowed civil space.[26]

2   Relationship of Australia with the International Human Rights System in General

Australia is party to seven of the nine core UN human rights treaties, six Optional Protocols (OPs), and has accepted five of the seven treaty body complaints mechanisms available to it. Australia is also party to a number of other treaties of relevance to human rights, such as treaties relating to refugees and slavery. Australia issued a standing invitation to the Special Procedures of the UN Human Rights Council in 2008, which remains open. It was also a member of the UN Human Rights Council for a term from 2018 to 2020, and has been an engaged participant in the system of Universal Periodic Review (UPR). Since there is no regional human rights mechanism to which Australia can become a party, UN obligations and engagements represent the main international component of human rights in the country.

Australia has a dualist system of law. Thus, international legal obligations must be incorporated into domestic law before they become enforceable in Australian courts. The federal Parliament has the constitutional power to enact statutes to implement human rights treaty obligations, even if the treaties concern subject matters that are within the traditional constitutional realm of the Australian states.[27] The states and territories retain residual powers to enact relevant legislation for their respective jurisdictions. Despite its extensive constitutional power to do so, the federal government seems reluctant to incorporate human rights treaties. Professor Simon Rice of the University of Sydney suggested a reason for such reluctance during an interview: 'States' rights remains a thing ... by and large one respected by [the federal] government.'[28]

Over the past two decades relations between Australia and the UN human rights mechanisms have waxed and waned. Dealings between the government

---

26   See Australian NGO Coalition Submission to the HRCttee, Australia's Compliance with the ICCPR UN Doc INT/CCPR/NGO/AUS/28925/E (September 2017) Part 16.
27   Joseph and Castan (n 2) paras 4.20–4.55.
28   Simon Rice, Professor of Law, University of Sydney, interview, telephone, 15 July 2019.

and the treaty bodies, and the International Convention on the Elimination of All Forms of Racial Discrimination (CERD) Committee in particular, deteriorated around the turn of the century in light of the latter's sharp criticism of Australia's treatment of indigenous Australians.[29]

Relations improved after the election of a new left-wing government in 2007.[30] In late 2013 the conservative coalition returned to power. In May 2015 Prime Minister Abbott responded to a damning report by the Special Rapporteur on Torture on the nation's migration policies by stating that Australians were 'sick of being lectured to by the United Nations'.[31] Nevertheless, albeit under a different Prime Minister, the Coalition government ran a successful campaign to join the United Nations Human Rights Council from 2018 to 2020, and ratified the Optional Protocol to the Convention against Torture and other Cruel, Inhuman and Degrading Treatment or Punishment (OP-CAT) in 2017.[32]

Australia seems generally content to implement the treaties, and recommendations by treaty bodies, Special Rapporteurs and via the UPR to the extent that those recommendations reflect existing laws, policies, practices and aspirations. While Australia's alignment with human rights values is comparatively high compared to many other countries, largely due to Australia's traditions as a liberal welfare state,[33] that circumstance does not seem to have been driven to a significant extent by Australia's United Nations (UN) obligations and engagements.[34] Hence, the impact of the core human rights treaties on Australian law and policy is overall disappointing.

---

[29] See Sarah Joseph, 'The Howard Government's Record of Engagement with the International Human Rights System' (2008) 27 Australian Year Book of International Law 45, 54–58. See further Spencer Zifcak, *Mr Ruddock Goes to Geneva* (UNSW Press 2003).

[30] For a further overview of Australia's engagement with the UN from 2007–2013, see Australia and the UN: Report Card 2013, UN Association of Australia, 2013 <https://www.unaa.org.au/wp-content/uploads/2015/07/Australia-and-the-UN-Report-Card-2013.pdf> accessed 18 March 2022.

[31] See 'Abbott says Australians "Sick of Being Lectured to by UN" After Scathing Report on Asylum Policies' *ABC News Online* (9 March 2015) <https://www.abc.net.au/news/2015-03-09/tony-abbott-hits-out-united-nations-asylum-report/6289892> accessed 18 March 2022.

[32] Phil Lynch stated at the interview (n 25) that the engagement under the coalition since 2013 was similar to that under the preceding ALP government, aside from the fractious issue of refugees.

[33] A Shadow Minister stated at the interview (video, 18 July 2019) that Australia's human rights record was the least one could expect of a 'developed, advanced representative democracy like Australia … we could be doing things so much better'.

[34] This point, regarding Australia's overall compliance but lack of specific responsiveness to international human rights obligations, was also made by Phil Lynch at the interview (n 25).

3 At a Glance: Formal Engagement of Australia with the UN Human Rights Treaty System

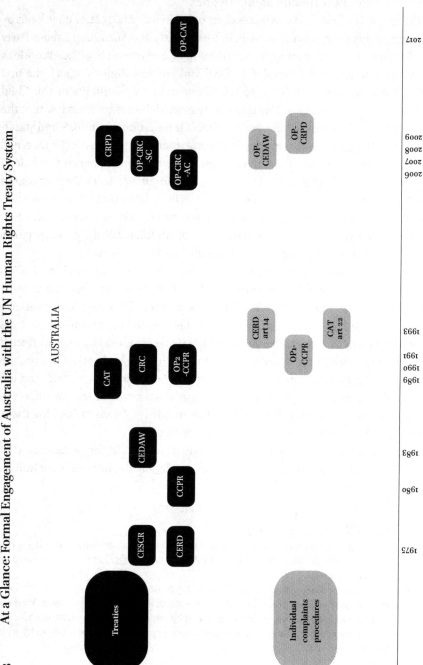

4   Role and Overall Impact of UN Human Rights Treaties in Australian

4.1   *Role of UN Human Rights Treaties*

The majority of ratifications/accessions of human rights treaties have been by governments from Australia's main left-wing party, the Australian Labour Party (ALP), which served from 1972–1975, 1983–1996, and 2007–2013. The exceptions are the International Covenant on Civil and Political Rights (CCPR), the first two Optional Protocols (OPs) to the Convention on the Rights of the Child (CRC), and OP-CAT. A shadow minister suggested during an interview that the ALP historically focuses more on Australia's international relations and standing than the conservative parties.[35] The ALP is also historically less concerned with the implications of treaty ratification for relations between the federal government and the states.[36] In contrast, a senior officer at the Department of Foreign Affairs and Trade ("senior DFAT officer") stated that conservative federal governments, which have ratified fewer human rights treaties than their ALP counterparts, were 'more suspicious of multilateralism', perhaps partly due to its perceived intrusions on domestic 'parliamentary sovereignty'.[37]

Australia has not ratified the International Convention on the Rights of All Migrant Workers and Members of their Families (CMW) nor the International Convention for the Protection of all Persons from Enforced Disappearance (CED). Successive Australian governments believe that migrant workers' rights are protected in other treaties, and that the rights are already largely protected in domestic legislation.[38] The government also feels that the MWC was incompatible with domestic migration policies and Australia's visa regime, and did not adequately distinguish between those migrants working lawfully and those working unlawfully.[39] Finally, no like-minded state has ratified the CMW, reducing international pressure on Australia to do so.

Regarding the CED, the government has rejected calls for ratification during Australia's UPR, and stated that 'Australia already has international human

---

35   Shadow Minister, interview (n 33).
36   Indeed, the ALP for many decades pledged to abolish federalism: See Brian Galligan and David Mardiste, 'Labour's Reconciliation with Federalism' (1992) 27 Australian Journal of Political Science 71.
37   Senior DFAT officer, interview, telephone, 6 May 2019.
38   Human Rights Council of Australia (HCA), 'Australian Ratification of the Migrant Workers' Conventions – Responses to Concerns Raised by the Australian Government, 2012'. The reasons are gleaned from a communication between the then Attorney-General, Nicola Roxon, and the HCA.
39   ibid 7.

rights obligations prohibiting conduct covering enforced disappearances and provides protection against enforced disappearances in its criminal law'.[40]

4.2 *Impact of UN Human Rights Treaties*

4.2.1 Incorporation and Reliance by Organs of State

As explained below, CERD, the Convention Against Torture and Other Cruel, Inhuman or Degrading Treatment or Punishment (CAT) and the Convention on the Elimination of All Forms of Discrimination Against Women (CEDAW) are largely incorporated into Australian law, while the Convention on the Rights of Persons with Disabilities (CRPD) and the CRC are partially incorporated. CCPR and the International Covenant on Economic, Social and Cultural Rights (CESCR) are not incorporated into Australian law. CCPR, however, is relevant to a number of federal statutes, and is the foundation of the three human rights charters in the ACT, Victoria and Queensland. It is also listed in the Act governing the AHRC, so the latter body may receive complaints relating to CCPR (as well as CRC and CRPD).

Importantly, numerous laws protect human rights values enshrined in the treaties, particularly CCPR, in ordinary laws that do not use human rights language, such as laws governing police powers, the admissibility of evidence, and privacy. Nevertheless, Australian law lags in some respects and outright breaches international human rights law in some areas.

All of the core UN human rights treaties to which Australia is a party are instruments to which the Human Rights (Parliamentary Scrutiny) Act 2011 (Cth) applies. A statement of compatibility with regard to Australia's obligations under each of those treaties must be appended to each Bill introduced into the federal Parliament.[41] Furthermore, each of those treaties is within the mandate of the Parliamentary Joint Committee on Human Rights (PJCHR), which issues a report on the human rights compatibility of each Bill. There are significant doubts over the effectiveness of this framework.[42] Simon Rice explained that the system focuses only on legislation, and does not 'speak at all to government action' and day-to-day service delivery.[43] An in-depth academic study indicates that it has had minimal impact on the actual protection of

---

40   'Universal Periodic Review monitoring: Recommendation 50' Australian Government Attorney-General's Department (Web page, 2012) <https://www.ag.gov.au/recommendations/recommendation-50> accessed 4 September 2023.
41   Human Rights (Parliamentary Scrutiny) Act 2011 (Cth), ss 8 and 9.
42   See, eg, HRCttee, COs on Australia, UN Doc CCPR/C/AUS/CO/6 (1 December 2017) paras 11–12.
43   Simon Rice, interview (n 28).

human rights, or even on the attention paid to human rights within the federal Parliament and executive government.[44]

Australia rarely refers to international human rights treaties in announcing policies, including budget measures, of relevance to human rights. It should be noted that the 2014 and subsequent budgets significantly cut funding for the AHRC, leading its president to state that the funding was insufficient to allow it to meet its statutory obligations.[45]

4.2.2 Level of Awareness

Awareness of the human rights treaties is patchy within the public service, although there are high levels of knowledge in certain areas that commonly work with them, such as the Office of International Law within the Attorney-General's Department ('AGD') and certain legal and human rights policy areas of DFAT. Knowledge within other departments is low according to interviewees,[46] although staff in certain parts of government might have specific knowledge of a relevant human right.[47] The greatest familiarity seems to be with certain rights in CCPR, such as freedom of speech and freedom of religion, as well as non-discrimination (perhaps due to the plethora of anti-discrimination laws in Australia).[48]

Members of Parliament generally have low levels of awareness of the treaties, given the dearth of parliamentary discussion about them.[49] A former senior AGD officer, as well as the Shadow ALP Minister, thought that the

---

44 Fletcher (n 23). It is unlikely that the effectiveness of the system has improved significantly since those first four years. Civil society interviewees, such as Phil Lynch (n 25), as well as Ron McCallum, former Chairperson of the CRPD Committee (interview, telephone, 15 May 2019), felt that the framework was ineffective. Cf Zoe Hutchison and Kate Mitchell, 'Australia's Human Rights Scrutiny Regime' (2019) 25(2) Australian Journal of Human Rights 346 (a review of Fletcher's book by members of the PJCHR's secretariat, arguing that the scrutiny regime has been relatively successful given general constraints on parliamentary committee influence).

45 See Stephen Easton, '"Top-Heavy" Human Rights Commission Straining Under Cuts' The Mandarin (9 May 2016) <https://www.themandarin.com.au/64608-top-heavy-human-rights-commission-starting-to-wobble-under-budget-cuts> accessed 18 March 2022.

46 See, eg, Sarah McCosker, formerly of AGD, interview, telephone, 16 May 2019; senior government official who works on human rights implementation, interview (n 5); senior DFAT officer, interview (n 37), Ron McCallum, interview (n 44).

47 The example given by a former senior AGD officer, interview, via telephone, 21 May 2019; was that of arbitrary detention and the Immigration Department.

48 Former senior AGD officer, interview (n 47). senior government official who works on human rights implementation, interview (n 5). However, a Shadow Minister felt that there was 'a great ahistoricity' about debates about freedom of religion in Australia, interview (n 33).

49 Fletcher (n 23).

parliamentary scrutiny regime may nevertheless have increased human rights knowledge within Parliament.[50] Certainly, members and past members of the PJCHR must know more about the treaties given the nature of their committee work.

There is little knowledge in or attention paid to human rights within the mainstream media,[51] with the online *Guardian Australia* probably providing the most consistent coverage of Australia's treaty body engagements.[52] Nick Poynder, a barrister involved in individual communications, remarked at an interview that 'the way that [individual communications] came to the attention of journalists is almost completely arbitrary', with journalists needing an 'angle' beyond the fact of an adverse international decision itself.[53] Olivia Ball of the NGO Remedy Australia felt the media 'often get it wrong'.[54] Furthermore, Australian print media is unhealthily dominated by News Limited papers,[55] which are often hostile to international human rights law.[56] Overall, little pressure is applied to the government by the media to prompt compliance with the UN treaties.

International human rights treaties and associated jurisprudence are rarely raised in Australian courts, except where a treaty is cited as a legitimate source of interpretation for a particular statute. Hence, knowledge of the details of international human rights treaties and associated treaty body jurisprudence

---

50   Former AGD officer, interview (n 47); Shadow Minister, interview (n 33).
51   This conclusion is reached after searches for the treaty acronyms via the Factiva database. See also Fletcher (n 23) 242–249.
52   See, eg, Ben Doherty, 'Report on Australia's Human Rights Record to be Scrutinised by UN committee' *The Guardian* (16 October 2017) https://www.theguardian.com/australia-news/2017/oct/16/report-on-australias-human-rights-record-to-be-scrutinised-by-un-committee accessed 19 March 2022. See also Sarah Joseph, 'Global Media Coverage of the Universal Periodic Review' in Hilary Charlesworth and Emma Larking (eds), *Human Rights and the Universal Periodic Review* (CUP 2014) 147, 149.
53   Nick Poynder, barrister involved in individual communications, interview, telephone, 13 May 2019. See also Olivia Ball, 'Because Every Human Rights Violation Should Be Remedied' in Corinne Lennox, *Contemporary Challenges in Securing Human Rights* (Institute of Commonwealth Studies 2015) 105, 108.
54   Olivia Ball, Remedy Australia, interview, Melbourne, 19 July 2019.
55   See R Finkelstein, 'Report of the Independent Inquiry into the Media and Media Regulation' (28 February 2012), Table 3.1 60, a graph from the International Media Concentration Project <https://catalogue.nla.gov.au/catalog/5971715> accessed 4 September 2023.
56   See, eg, Father Frank Brennan SJ AO, 'The Practical Outcomes of the National Human Rights Consultation' Address to Judicial College of Australia Colloquium (12 October 2013) <http://jca.asn.au/wp-content/uploads/2013/11/P01_13_02_28-Brennan-paper.docx.pdf> accessed 13 September 2019.

is unlikely to be high within the judiciary, given the dearth of relevant arguments before them. Such knowledge is likely increasing among the senior judges in the ACT and Victoria as a response to local human rights statutes with regard to CCPR.[57] Poynder stated, correctly, that most treaty citations are from a select few 'judges with a human rights reputation', such as (formerly) Kirby J of the High Court.[58]

Knowledge of the human rights treaties is very high within, and are a prominent feature of, the work of the AHRC.[59] The treaties, even those such as CESCR and CAT which are not explicitly referenced in its governing statute, are frequently cited in reports and inquiries. It also has the power to make non-binding decisions on breaches of CCPR, CRPD and CRC, which are tabled in Parliament.[60]

Continuing Legal Education for practitioners is mandatory for Australian lawyers in various areas but not in international human rights law. There is occasional human rights training for lawyers on an *ad hoc* basis.[61] Nick Poynder suggested that knowledge amongst immigration lawyers, who are more likely to engage with international law than most other lawyers, of international human rights law was 'moderate' and not detailed.[62] Simon Rice suggested that detailed knowledge was lacking in community legal centres.[63]

Some Australian NGOs, such as the Human Rights Law Centre, are very alert to the core treaties and associated jurisprudence. It also seems that more

---

[57] It is likely that the same will occur in Queensland, now that its Human Rights Act has come into force as from 2020. See, eg, Victorian Equal Opportunity and Human Rights Commission, 2018 Report on the Operation of the Charter of Human Rights and Responsibilities, ch 4 <https://www.humanrights.vic.gov.au/resources/2018-report-on-the-operation-of-the-charter-of-human-rights-and-responsibilities/#:~:text=The%2018%20report%20on%20the,the%20public%20sector%20in%20Victoria> accessed 18 March 2022.

[58] Nick Poynder, interview (n 53).

[59] See, eg, AHRC, Children's Rights Report 2019 – In Their Own Right <https://www.humanrights.gov.au/our-work/childrens-rights/publications/childrens-rights-report-2019>; and AHRC, *Mr Nauroze Anees v Commonwealth of Australia (Department of Home Affairs)* [2019] AusHRC 133 <https://www.humanrights.gov.au/sites/default/files/document/publication/2019_aushrc_133_redacted.pdf>, both accessed 18 March 2022.

[60] See the AusHRC series available via austlii.edu.au.

[61] See, eg, Law CPD, Gillian Triggs, 'Human Rights in Australia: A Charter of Rights and Responsibilities?', online CPD course, accessed 18 March 2022. There are also human rights committees in the legal professional organisations NSW and Victoria that organise occasional professional development events.

[62] Nick Poynder, interview (n 53).

[63] Simon Rice, interview (n 28).

NGOs are engaging with the treaty bodies, particularly the reporting process.[64] Knowledge seems higher in some sectors, such as disability (according to Simon Rice) than others.[65] However, according to Ben Schokman, a human rights consultant formerly with the Human Rights Law Centre, most NGOs have a 'low level of literacy in terms of human rights understanding'.[66] Furthermore, many NGOs consciously avoid human rights language in their advocacy campaigns in favour of the language of social justice, perhaps because explicit human rights arguments are not perceived as likely to be effective.[67]

The Australian public generally lacks specific knowledge of the treaties, and most people have a very limited understanding of how rights are protected.[68] There were differences of opinion among interviewees with regard to public attitudes to human rights. Sarah McCosker, formerly of the AGD, felt Australians were generally liberal and open-minded regarding human rights. Nevertheless, a 'body of conservative opinion' was ill-informed on the matter, and there was definite 'ongoing divisiveness on certain issues, particularly relating to border protection and asylum-seeker policy'.[69] A senior DFAT officer believes that human rights align with Australian values, such as democracy, the rule of law, and common law values.[70] An ALP shadow Minister also felt that the public has a strong attachment to 'underlying principles' such as fairness, openness, integrity, transparency, though there was little knowledge of the specifics of human rights and human rights language.[71]

---

64 See, eg, Disabled People's Organisations Australia, 'People with Disability to Take Concerns to the United Nations' (21 August 2019) <https://dpoa.org.au/people-with-disability-to-take-concerns-to-the-united-nations/> accessed 18 March 2022. Eighty-four organisations also endorsed, in whole or in part, the Australian civil society shadow report to the CRPD in 2019.

65 Simon Rice, interview (n 28).

66 Ben Schokman, human rights consultant, interview, Melbourne, 9 May 2019. See also Rachel Ball, Head of Policy and Advocacy Oxfam Australia, interview Melbourne, 14 May 2019; Olivia Ball, interview (n 54).

67 Simon Rice, interview (n 28); Olivia Ball, interview (n 54).

68 See National Human Rights Consultation, Appendix B Colmar Brunton Community Research Report: Summary <https://alhr.org.au/wp/wp-content/uploads/2018/02/National-Human-Rights-Consultation-Report-2009-copy.pdf> accessed 4 September 2023.

69 McCosker, interview (n 46). The shadow Minister also noted a disturbing trend that for over 30 years Australians 'have come to accept that lesser rights can be afforded to people who are not Australian citizens'; interview (n 33).

70 DFAT officer, interview (n 37).

71 Shadow Minister, interview (n 33).

In contrast, Nick Poynder believes that the Australian public 'has been conditioned by governments to be suspicious of human rights, and to see [them] as a negative'.[72] Rachel Ball, at Oxfam at the time of the interview, believes that the public thinks of human rights as a 'left wing',[73] which generates doubts over their legitimacy. Olivia Ball of Remedy Australia felt that Australians were complacent regarding protection of their rights, and thus did not appreciate the importance of international human rights law.[74] In contrast, she felt that 'oppressed minorities' were more aware of human rights violations.[75] A senior government official who works on human rights implementation felt that 'most people ... probably never really think about human rights', and that human rights language did not resonate.[76] A former senior AGD officer added that the public was not likely to accept the authority of the UN in Geneva: In an echo of former Prime Minister Abbott, they 'don't like being told what to do'.[77]

Overall, little popular pressure is brought to bear on the government to pay greater attention to its international human rights obligations. Such pressure seems unlikely to arise unless an issue becomes one of concern to the majority.

Law faculties within Australian universities commonly have international human rights law units at undergraduate and postgraduate levels.[78] Human rights law is not compulsory for law students, and international human rights law generally is absent from core subjects.[79] There is a growing number of specialist human rights academics and human rights doctorates: Some Australian human rights academics are world renowned.[80] While academic activities are dominated by the discipline of law,[81] there are increasing numbers of non-law

---

72 Nick Poynder, interview (n 53).
73 Rachel Ball, interview (n 66); Nick Poynder agreed, interviews (n 53).
74 Olivia Ball, interview (n 54). Ben Schokman, essentially agreed, interview (n 66). Ron McCallum felt that 'people only get concerned about human rights when they affect them'; interview (n 44).
75 Olivia Ball, interview (n 54).
76 Senior government official who works on human rights implementation, interview (n 5).
77 Former AGD officer, interview (n 47). Senator Nick McKim of the Australian Greens party, (interview, telephone, 29 August 2019) agreed.
78 However, Olivia Ball stated at the interview (n 54) that she felt she had to go overseas to do a Masters in human rights law in the early 2000s.
79 Simon Rice, interview (n 28). Ron McCallum agrees, interview (n 44).
80 Interviewees generally agreed with this statement.
81 Olivia Ball, interview (n 54): 'Human rights is perceived as something that lawyers do'.

human rights academics. Academic outputs from Australia regarding the core UN human rights treaties are too numerous to list.[82]

Some interviewees felt that overall awareness of the international human rights system would be assisted by the adoption of national human rights legislation: Simon Rice felt that such legislation would 'fill a gap in people's minds'.[83] Indeed, knowledge within government and civil society in those jurisdictions with human rights statutes is felt to be much better than in other jurisdictions.[84]

4.2.3 State Reporting

Australia has submitted its periodic reports to the treaty bodies, although its submissions are always delayed. Reporting is a complex process, involving consultation across various government departments as well as six states and two territories.[85] Many of the most important issues are largely matters governed by the states, such as prisons, hospitals and housing. While a senior government official who works on human rights implementation agreed that coordination was difficult, he added that 'states and territories engaged with reporting processes in good faith and did what they could to support federal government'.[86] Delays also arise on the part of the treaty bodies, with regard to the scheduling of the dialogues pursuant to state reports.[87]

Delays in the submission of Australia's reports have shortened in recent years. In this regard, treaty body reforms in the form of word limits and lists of issues have undoubtedly helped. So too, according to a senior DFAT officer, have ongoing civil society consultations that help to focus the reports on matters of the deepest concern.[88]

---

[82] See, eg, Sarah Joseph and Melissa Castan, *The International Covenant on Civil and Political Rights: Cases Materials and Commentary* (3rd edn, OUP 2013); Ben Saul, David Kinley and Jacqueline Mowbray, *The International Covenant on Economic, Social and Cultural Rights: Commentary, Cases and Materials* (OUP 2014); John Tobin, *The UN Convention on the Rights of the Child: A Commentary* (OUP 2019).

[83] Phil Lynch, interview (n 25), former AGD law officer, interview (n 47), Ben Schokman, interview (n 66), Ron McCallum, interview (n 44) agreed.

[84] Rachel Ball, interview (n 66), Ron McCallum, interview (n 44), Simon Rice, interview (n 28), Ben Schokman, interview (n 66).

[85] See Sarah McCosker, interview (n 46), senior government official who works on human rights implementation, interview (n 5).

[86] Senior government official who works on human rights implementation, interview (n 5).

[87] Some delays have been as long as two or three years.

[88] Senior DFAT officer, interview (n 37); Rachel Ball, interview (n 66), however, was sceptical about the utility of that consultation for NGOs. She did not feel such consultation was reflected in the final reports.

Typically, the reporting process involves consultations with relevant Commonwealth government departments and agencies, as well as each state and territory government. There now is a standing mechanism for regular meetings among relevant department officials, along with the AHRC, which has improved coordination across departments' inputting into reports.[89]

The lead agency for all reports, apart from CEDAW, is either the AGD (CCPR, CAT, CRC, CRPD) or DFAT (CERD, CESCR). In 2006/2007, the substantive content of Australia's periodic reports under the two covenants were incorporated into a single 'Common Core Document',[90] necessitating cooperation in drafting between AGD and DFAT.

Australia's periodic reports vary in their thoroughness. The most recent reports, which are more timely, are less comprehensive, possibly due to word limits and the permissibility of focusing on lists of issues from the treaty bodies. Phil Lynch, Director of the International Service for Human Rights and former director of the Australian NGO, the Human Rights Law Centre, stated at interview that there was 'a level of ritualism about' Australia's reports, listing programmes and budgets rather than focusing on 'the extent of implementation' and 'violations'.[91] The reports tend to avoid politically embarrassing statements,[92] although shortfalls are sometimes conceded. Simon Rice agreed, but doubted that Australia's reports were 'any different from most Western states'.[93]

Shadow reports are regularly submitted. The AHRC has generally prepared independent reports since the 2000s, as have NGOs.[94] A feature of shadow reporting for over ten years is the production of an 'NGO coalition report' coordinated by a lead NGO with contributions from dozens of other NGOs,

---

[89] This information emanates from Darren Dick of the AHRC (email on file with authors).

[90] Australian Government, Common Core Document Forming Part of the Reports of States Parties – Australia – Incorporating the Fifth Report under the International Covenant on Civil and Political Rights and the Fourth Report under the International Covenant on Economic, Social and Cultural Rights (June 2006) available via <https://catalogue.nla.gov.au/catalog/4222818> accessed 4 September 2023.

[91] Phil Lynch, interview (n 25). Rachel Ball, interview (n 66) and Ben Schokman, interview (n 66) agreed.

[92] As stated by Simon Rice, interview (n 28): 'Nothing is ever volunteered that is adverse'.

[93] Simon Rice, interview (n 28).

[94] See, eg, AHRC, 'Information Concerning Australia's Compliance with the Convention on the Rights of Persons with Disabilities' UN Doc INT/CRPD/NHS/AUS/35594/E (25 July 2019); and AHRC, 'Information Concerning Australia's Compliance with the CERD' UN Doc INT/CERD/IFN/AUS/29335/E (30 October 2017).

and endorsements from dozens more, which cover the breadth of the treaty or at least the lists of issues.[95] The coalition reports generally are more thorough and engaging than the official state report. Individual NGOs also submit reports on bespoke issues.

Delegations for dialogues with treaty bodies normally include senior public servants from the lead reporting department, staff from other relevant departments such as Immigration or Indigenous Affairs, and senior staff from Australia's Permanent Mission to the UN in Geneva. Sometimes a relevant commissioner from the AHRC will be part of the delegation, such as the Race Discrimination Commissioner for CERD. Ministers and other politicians have not attended since the fractious CERD dialogue in 2000.

Civil society interviewees had a mixed view on Australian delegations. Rachel Ball states that delegation members were occasionally unable to answer pertinent questions,[96] while Ben Schokman felt that sometimes answers were 'factually incorrect' or 'misleading at best'. He also stated that one could almost see the mood change in the room when the issue of refugees arose. Nevertheless, he felt that Australian delegations were willing 'to engage in a constructive way'.[97]

Concluding Observations (COs) for all treaties are published on the website of the AGD.[98] Only the most recent COs are available, and no further dissemination efforts are apparent. A senior government official who works on human rights implementation stated that there has been 'a huge amount of progress in a short amount of time' regarding dissemination, including greater cooperation and information sharing with NGOs and the AHRC.[99]

Implementation and follow-up to COs by Australia is underwhelming. While Australia has cooperated procedurally by responding to the follow-up processes, it often fails to implement recommendations unless a recommendation aligns with domestic political aspirations. A senior DFAT officer felt that they could 'feed into the conversation about policy change' but did not

---

95 See, eg, Australian NGO Coalition Submission to the HRCttee, Australia's Compliance with the ICCPR UN Doc INT/CCPR/NGO/AUS/28925/E (September 2017); and Australian NGO Coalition, CEDAW Shadow Report 2018, UN Doc INT/CEDAW/NGO/AUS/31435/E.
96 Rachel Ball, interview (n 66).
97 Ben Schokman, interview (n 66). See also Simon Rice, interview (n 28).
98 See Treaty Body Reporting, Attorney-General's Department <https://www.ag.gov.au/rights-and-protections/human-rights-and-anti-discrimination/united-nations-human-rights-reporting/treaty-body-reporting> accessed 4 September 2023.
99 Senior government official working on human rights implementation, interview (n 5).

have an 'immediate impact'.[100] Simon Rice did not believe that COs were very useful.[101]

Sarah McCosker stated during her interview that dialogues on reports, from the government's point of view, were overly short and somewhat unreal: 'It was the performance of a dialogue rather than a real dialogue.' She also felt that the format had contributed to the adoption in some dialogues of a defensive attitude by Australia: Perhaps a more regular dialogue might reduce that 'sense of anxiety'.[102] In contrast, a senior DFAT officer stated that members of delegations were now trained so as to engage positively rather than defensively.[103]

A former senior AGD officer felt that treaty body members were unfamiliar with the Australian context, and that some of their conclusions were based on incorrect premises. He added that the reviews were quite 'superficial', especially in contrast to the effort put into the reports. However, he added that specific recommendations can have an impact within government if they are 'practical and direct', rather than vague or 'scattergun'.[104] Phil Lynch agrees that 'the more precise the recommendations are, the more useful they tend to be for domestic advocacy purposes'.[105]

4.2.4 Individual Communications

Australia has dealt with individual communications under CERD, the OPI-CCPR, CAT and the OP-CRPD, as explained below. Selected views from all treaty bodies and government responses are published on the AGD's website.[106] The site refers users to the Treaty Body Jurisprudence Database for other Views.

Australia engages procedurally in individual communications processes by submitting arguments while the case is proceeding. Australia also tends to respond in some way regarding follow-up, though the response may be cursory. Ben Schokman recommended a more formal follow-up process, such as tabled reports in Parliament from the PJCHR. Otherwise he felt follow-up '[fell] into an abyss'.[107]

---

100 Senior DFAT officer, interview (n 37).
101 Simon Rice, interview (n 28).
102 Sarah McCosker, interview (n 46).
103 Senior DFAT officer, interview (n 37).
104 Former senior AGD officer, interview (n 47).
105 Phil Lynch, interview (n 25).
106 Human Rights Communications, Attorney-General's Department <https://www.ag.gov.au/rights-and-protections/human-rights-and-anti-discrimination/human-rights-communications> accessed 4 September 2023.
107 Ben Schokman, interview (n 66).

Nick Poynder stated that interim measures are very 'useful to prevent immediate deportation', and had probably saved lives.[108] A senior DFAT officer agreed that interim orders had an impact, as they triggered a final review of a relevant decision (most often a prospective deportation), even if they are not always complied with.[109]

The views in individual communications have had little impact in Australia.[110] The government's position is that they are 'not legally enforceable' so it will not implement them where it disagrees with the relevant treaty body's interpretation and finding of violation.[111] Government officers generally agreed in their interviews that Australia has often disagreed with the conclusions reached by the treaty bodies on domestic and international law.[112] A senior DFAT officer conceded that implementation therefore is 'rare'.[113] Communications have concerned a wide range of matters, especially those submitted under the OPI-CCPR. Phil Lynch believes that the government has breached its obligation to at least engage with the views 'in good faith'.[114]

While there have been many individual communications against Australia, there are glaring absences in the jurisprudence. Certain matters that seem ripe for submission have not arisen, such as offshore processing of asylum seekers and, largely, indigenous issues. A lack of faith in the likelihood of implementation of views by the Australian government might explain these absences. Furthermore, NGOs might be wary of the possibility that an impugned policy might be exonerated by a treaty body, thus hampering local campaigns against the policy.[115]

Olivia Ball interviewed many authors of individual communications against Australia for her PhD research. She ultimately concluded that there was utility

---

108 See also Olivia Ball interview (n 54) 106; Rachel Ball agreed, interview (n 66).
109 Senior DFAT officer, interview (n 37).
110 Phil Lynch stated at the interview that Australia's record of implementation was 'very very poor', interview (n 25). See, eg, the HRCttee's concern over Australia's failure to implement its views and the fact that victims have not received reparation: HRCttee, COs on Australia UN Doc A/55/40, 2000 paras 520–521; and HRCttee, COs on Australia UN Doc CCPR/C/AUS/CO/5 (7 May 2009) para 10.
111 See, eg, Australian Government, Response of the Australian Government to the Views of the HRCttee in Communication No 2005/2010 Hicks v Australia; and Noble v Australia, Communication 7/2012, UN Doc CRPD/C/16/D/7/2012, views of 2 September 2016.
112 For example, senior DFAT officer, interview (n 37), former AGD officer, interview (n 47).
113 Senior DFAT officer, interview (n 37).
114 Phil Lynch, interview (n 25).
115 Such concerns arose in conversations that Sarah Joseph, one of the authors of this chapter, had over the viability of a complaint regarding marriage equality.

in the complaints process for victims, despite the low level of implementation. In particular, there was value in the 'vindication' received at the international level, especially for those who had lost multiple times while exhausting domestic remedies at home: 'The UN said I was right.'[116] Other benefits (for some) included 'respect among their peers', 'a positive public profile', and 'a sense of achievement and [greater] self-confidence'.[117] Phil Lynch agreed that views could provide 'a victim with a platform and the sense of legitimation and vindication which can be gained from reporting your story on an international stage'.[118]

More negatively, Olivia Ball found that the process was slow,[119] difficult to understand, and that contact with the treaty bodies was difficult for some complainants.[120]

A former senior AGD officer felt that the views were helpful in facilitating policy arguments within government, but only where 'well-reasoned'. He used that word deliberately, as he felt that some views seemed to be based on 'making a call, according to personal politics'.[121] A senior government official who works on human rights implementation stated that they are 'a mechanism for drawing something to a government's attention'.[122]

Rachel Ball felt that individual communications take up 'a lot of resources' without resulting in 'meaningful change'. Their greatest utility, in her view, was if they contributed to a 'broader [civil society] campaign'.[123] Ultimately, Ben Schokman felt that individual communications were 'an instrumental process not an end in themselves'.[124] Less hopefully, Ron McCallum, former Chair of the CRPD Cttee, felt that individual communications did not generally 'help Australians'.[125]

People and organisations are not subjected to reprisals from the government for engagements with the treaty bodies which criticise or make allegations of human rights breaches against Australia.[126]

---

[116] Olivia Ball, interview (n 54); see also Ball (n 53) 108.
[117] ibid 107.
[118] Phil Lynch, interview (n 25); see also Ben Schokman, interview (n 66).
[119] Nick Poynder, interview (n 53) and Ron McCallum, interview (n 44) agreed.
[120] Ball, interview (n 54); see also Ball (n 53) 106.
[121] Former AGD officer, interview (n 47).
[122] Senior government official working on human rights implementation, interview (n5). The senior DFAT officer agreed, interview (n 37).
[123] Rachel Ball, interview (n 66). Phil Lynch, interview (n 25) and Simon Rice, interview (n 28) agreed.
[124] Ben Schokman, interview (n 66).
[125] Ron McCallum, interview (n 44).
[126] Ball (n 53) 106: 'No one felt any pressure to withdraw their UN complaint'.

4.2.5 Other Measures

Beyond reporting and individual communications, Australia's other main engagement with the treaty bodies has been with regard to the urgent action procedure under CERD, discussed in part 5.1.

4.2.6 Treaty Body Membership

There is no officially-documented process for the selection of treaty body members/nominees in Australia. Australia has had six overall (including two positions for the same person, Elizabeth Evatt, on two different treaty bodies). In the last ten years, Australia has successfully nominated two candidates for one committee, the CRPD.[127]

Many interviewees expressed a preference for Australia to push for more nominees on the treaty bodies. One former senior member of the AGD felt that 'vote trading' for UN positions (within and beyond the human rights field) meant that Australia was less inclined to nominate people for treaty bodies, and instead focused on other priorities, such as its successful campaign for the Human Rights Council.[128] Ben Schokman and Rachel Ball felt that Australia might be comparatively good at promoting candidates for UN treaty bodies, when a decision is made to do so.[129]

4.2.7 Conclusion

Given Australia's status as a rich, liberal, democratic state, its engagements with the treaty bodies may be viewed as disappointing. Treaties and treaty body jurisprudence have a soft impact in the form of the creation of advocacy tools for civil society and within government, and to provide vindication for victims. Nevertheless, they rarely lead to actual policy and legislative changes.

While the nadir in relations (1999–2007) has long passed, Australian governments are commonly unimpressed with treaty body processes and outputs. Those processes are beset by under-resourcing,[130] duplication, divergence, inconsistency of quality and efficiency, and discrepancies in procedures.

A senior DFAT officer felt that there was 'a lack of nuance' in some jurisprudence, where the treaty bodies failed to grapple with 'larger public policy

---

[127] In late 2020, outside the reporting period for this chapter, an Australian, Ms Natasha Stott-Despoja, was elected to the CEDAW Committee.
[128] Former senior member of the AGD, interview (n 47). See also Simon Rice, interview (n 28).
[129] Ben Schokman, interview (n 66) and Rachel Ball, interview (n 66).
[130] Sarah McCosker, interview (n 46), Simon Rice, interview (n 28) and Ben Schokman, interview (n 66).

issues'.[131] This comment seems to refer to the fact that the government's priorities are far broader than those of the treaty bodies, and that the treaty bodies are perhaps naïve in their continuing failure to acknowledge those other priorities.

A senior government official who works on human rights implementation believes that the treaty bodies have engaged in problematic 'mission creep', which undermined their effectiveness.[132] The same official also felt that the treaty bodies were dominated by a 'civil law approach'.[133] While Simon Rice felt that some treaty body members lacked experience, he added that 'at their best, you've got really smart people making really thoughtful decisions'.[134]

The senior government official who works on human rights implementation wished for more people on the treaty bodies who 'understood how governments work', especially in democratic countries, and tailored their comments in a more practical manner.[135] Ron McCallum stated that Australia, as a 'wealthy' state, can be an 'easy target', especially for treaty body members from poorer states.[136] This insight may help to explain a sense within the government that it is treated overly harshly. These negative opinions of the quality of treaty body processes and outputs also help to explain Australia's reluctance to consistently implement their recommendations and views.

Rachel Ball stated that civil society increasingly perceived the treaty body processes to be too distant and 'top-down' to solve human rights problems in Australia.[137] On a more positive note, Phil Lynch felt that treaty body jurisprudence, even in the problematic area of refugees, may have helped to prevent 'further regress', and at least helped to put 'violations on the record in relation to future accountability' and 'for learning lessons'.[138]

---

131   Senior DFAT official, interview (n 37). He was focusing on immigration cases, but the comment also seemed to apply beyond that context.
132   Senior government official who works on human rights implementation, interview (n 5). This sentiment was shared by a senior DFAT officer, interview (n 37).
133   Senior government official who works on human rights implementation, interview (n 5). A former senior AGD officer added that Australian representatives would add 'a common law perspective', interview (n 47).
134   Simon Rice, interview (n 28). This point was also made in interviews with the senior government official who works on human rights implementation, interview (n 5) and Ron McCallum, interview (n 44).
135   Senior government official who works on human rights implementation, interview (n 5).
136   Ron McCallum, interview (n 44).
137   Rachel Ball, interview (n 66).
138   Phil Lynch, interview (n 25).

5 The Impact of the Different UN Human Rights Treaties on the Domestic Level

5.1 *International Convention of the Elimination of All Forms of Racial Discrimination*

5.1.1 Ratification, Incorporation, and Main Institutions

Australia signed CERD in 1966 and ratified it on 30 September 1975. Australia deposited the instrument of acceptance of individual communications under CERD on 28 January 1993. Australia did not opt out of the CERD Cttee's Early-Warning Measures and Urgent Procedures.

Australia made a declaration regarding article 4(a) upon ratification that offences regarding racial hatred and incitement to discrimination were not then on the statute books, but that the government intended to legislate 'at the first suitable moment'. Civil offences regarding racist speech were introduced in 1995.[139] The declaration remains, as no criminal law has been enacted at the federal level nor in most states. Maintenance of the declaration also reflects ongoing concerns within government over the free speech implications of hate laws.[140]

The Racial Discrimination Act 1975 (Cth) (RDA) incorporates CERD into Australian law. It applies to all state and territory jurisdictions, as well as the Commonwealth, and is supplemented by legislative prohibitions on race discrimination in the states. The main office charged with promoting the RDA, and indirectly CERD, is the Race Discrimination Commissioner, a post within the AHRC. Within the AHRC there is also the Aboriginal and Torres Strait Islander Social Justice Commissioner, who promotes and investigates human rights matters related to Australia's indigenous peoples.

5.1.2 Policies and Initiatives of Relevance to CERD[141]

Here, we concentrate on those policies most likely to have been driven in some way by the treaties themselves, rather than on every policy of potential relevance to a treaty. In April 2009 the government declared its support for the UN Declaration on the Rights of Indigenous Peoples, which had been withheld

---

139 Racial Hatred Bill 1994. See also Australian Human Rights Commission, 'Race Hate and the RDA' <https://www.humanrights.gov.au/our-work/race-discrimination/projects/race-hate-and-rda> accessed 18 March 2022.
140 The ruling coalition from 2013–2022 professed a desire to roll back the civil offences in s 18C of the Racial Discrimination Act 1975 (Cth), but it lacked the numbers in the upper house of Parliament to do so.
141 See CERD, COs on Australia, UN Doc CERD/C/AUS/CO/18–20 para 3.

by the previous government.¹⁴² A prominent policy development was the federal government's suspension of the RDA in the context of what is known as the Northern Territory Emergency Response ('NTER'). The NTER (colloquially known as The Intervention) was a series of coercive administrative measures initiated by the government in 2007 to address reports of widespread child abuse and related social dysfunction in Indigenous communities in Australia's Northern Territory. The measures, which included the compulsory acquisition of land, the cancellation of a major indigenous employment scheme, compulsorily managed welfare payments and mandatory health checks, were controversially deemed 'special measures' by the government for the purposes of anti-discrimination law. The RDA protections were restored in 2010, but the Emergency Response itself has been extended to 2022.¹⁴³

5.1.3 Use by Courts

The High Court of Australia has, since 1999, drawn on CERD and related jurisprudence in a handful of cases. For example, in *Commonwealth v Yarmirr*,¹⁴⁴ the Court endorsed the use of international law, particularly CERD, in determining common law native title, as had arisen almost a decade earlier in the *Mabo* case (discussed below). However, in *Maloney v The Queen* the High Court unanimously rejected arguments that the RDA ought to be construed in light of CERD Cttee jurisprudence.¹⁴⁵ For example, Kiefel J wrote:

> The views of the committees travel beyond the international obligations that Australia has agreed to and the terms of the Convention they recommend, in effect, are implications. This Court cannot apply views which would have the effect of altering the text of the Convention to

---

142 See Australia's support of the UNDRIP, Australian Human Rights Commission, 2008 <https://www.humanrights.gov.au/publications/australias-support-declaration-rights-indigenous-peoples> accessed 18 March 2022.

143 The complexities and background to the intervention are explained in AHRC, 'The Suspension and Reinstatement of the RDA and Special Measures in the NTER' (2011) <https://www.humanrights.gov.au/publications/suspension-and-reinstatement-rda-and-special-measures-nter> accessed 18 March 2022.

144 *Commonwealth v Yarmirr* [2001] HCA 56 para 294, Gleeson CJ, Gaudron, Gummow and Hayne JJ.

145 For a full analysis, see eg Patrick Wall, 'The High Court of Australia's Approach to the Interpretation of International Law and its Use of International Legal Materials in *Maloney v The Queen*' (2014) 15(1) Melbourne Journal of International Law 211.

which Australia has agreed and which has formed the basis for the relevant measures provided by the RDA, which the Court is required to construe.[146]

Maloney is typical of the High Court's cautious approach to treaty body jurisprudence, if not international legal materials generally.[147]

5.1.4   State Reporting and Its Impact

Since 1999, Australia has submitted reports in 1999, 2003, 2010, and 2016. There has been an average delay of just under 18 months. Australia appeared before the CERD Cttee in 2000, 2005, 2010 and 2017.

In 2000 the government accused the Committee of a 'blatantly political and partisan' approach, particularly in light of its criticism of Australian native title laws, and began to push strongly for 'reform' of the treaty body system.[148] Australia's appearance in 2005 was also fractious.[149] Relations have improved since that very low point.

The CERD Cttee's COs on Australia focus on topics such as the ongoing discrepancies in almost all life outcomes (including life expectancy, education, health and incarceration rates) between indigenous and non-indigenous Australians, Islamophobia, racism against international students, the failure to withdraw Australia's declaration, and the mandatory immigration detention regime.[150]

Australia has responded to the CERD Cttee's requests for follow-up information, but generally in a defensive rather than a compliant manner.[151] The Joint NGO submission to the CERD Committee's 2017 review of Australia stated:

---

146   *Maloney v The Queen* [2013] HCA 28 paras 175–176.
147   See Patrick Wall, 'A Marked Improvement: The High Court of Australia's Approach to Treaty Interpretation in *Macoun v Commissioner of Taxation* [2015] HCA 44' (2016) 17(1) Melbourne Journal of International Law 170. See eg *Western Australia v Ward* [2002] HCA 28 para 658 (fn 769).
148   See Joseph (n 29) 54–58; Zifcak (n 29).
149   See David Cooper, 'Australia Before the UN CERD Committee' ABC Radio National – Perspective (18 March 2005) <https://www.abc.net.au/radionational/programs/archived/perspective/david-cooper/3446652> accessed 18 March 2022.
150   See eg CERD Committee, List of Themes in Relation to the Combined Eighteenth to Twentieth Periodic Reports of Australia UN Doc CERC/C/AUS/Q/18-20 (19 September 2017).
151   CERD Committee, 'Information Received from Australia on Follow-Up to the COs' UN Doc CERD/C/AUS/CO/18-20/Add.1 (27 December 2018); CERD Committee, 'Information Received from the Government of Australia on the Implementation of the COs' UN Doc CERD/C/Aus/CO/15-17/Add.1 (4 October 2011) and 'Comments by the Government of

Overall, Australia has not made significant progress towards addressing the concerns raised in the Concluding Observations of the CERD Committee on 27 August 2010 following Australia's last periodic review. Alarmingly, in some areas, Australia has regressed.[152]

More positively, in 2018 it was announced that the AHRC would begin working with police forces in Australia and New Zealand to follow up on the CERD Cttee's 2017 recommendations regarding anti-racism training for the police,[153] which is one of the few measures objectively attributable to a treaty body recommendation.

5.1.5   Individual Communications

The CERD Cttee has published views in six individual communications against Australia. Only one, *Hagan v Australia* in 2003, resulted in a finding of a violation.[154] *Hagan* concerned the failure by Queensland authorities to remove the sign on a stand at a sports stadium in Queensland named after one ES Brown; the sign bore his offensive nickname of 'Nigger Brown'. The CERD Cttee agreed that the display of the sign breached the treaty and recommended its removal. In 2008 the relevant local authority demolished the stand as it had structural defects.[155] Hence, the views were implemented but due to reasons unrelated to them.

5.1.6   Early Warning Measures and Urgent Procedures

Australia's extreme displeasure with the CERD Cttee at the turn of the century stemmed from the latter's urgent action decision on 14 August 1998, calling on Australia to provide more information on its dilution of statutory native title rights for indigenous peoples. Australia was the first Western democracy to

---

Australia on the COs of the Committee on the Elimination of Racial Discrimination' UN Doc CERD/C/AUS/CO/14/Add.1 (16 May 2006).

152 Australia's Compliance with the International Convention on the Elimination of All Forms of Racial Discrimination – Australian NGO Coalition Submission to the UN Committee on the Elimination of Racial Discrimination, October 2017 (UN Doc INT/CERD/NGO/AUS/29334/E) 4.

153 See AHRC, 'Anti-Racism in 2018 and Beyond' (2015–2018): <https://humanrights.gov.au/sites/default/files/document/publication/NARPS_2018_FINAL-WEB-VERSION.PDF>, 13, accessed 4 September 2023.

154 *Hagan v Australia* UN Doc CERD/C/62/D/26/200214 (20 March 2003).

155 See Remedy Australia, *Hagan v Australia* <https://remedy.org.au/cases/15> accessed 24 March 2022.

be subjected to such a decision.[156] Australia did not resile from its rollback of native title rights despite the CERD Cttee's concerns.

Since then, the CERD Cttee has written to the Australian government on four occasions under its Early Warning and Urgent Action Procedure: in 2009 (twice), 2010 and 2018. The first two concerned the NTER, the third was with respect to the ongoing lack of funding for Aboriginal legal aid,[157] and the most recent one concerned the proposed Carmichael Coal Mine and Rail Project in Queensland and its impact on local indigenous peoples.[158]

In response to the 2009 letters, the government initiated public consultations on future directions for the NTER. As noted above, the suspension of the RDA was reversed in 2010.[159] Australia's response to the 2010 letter has been mixed, with funding increased but subsequently reduced. It has been declining in real terms since 2013, despite an increase in demand.[160]

The Australian government did not respond to the CERD Cttee's 2018 letter in the reporting period for this chapter. It may be noted that the relevant state (Queensland) and Commonwealth governments have both granted the necessary approvals for the impugned mine to proceed.

5.1.7 Treaty Body Membership

No Australian expert has served on the CERD Cttee.

---

[156] See Sarah Prichard, 'Stirrings: Early Warning/Urgent Action Decision Concerning Australia and the UN Committee on the Elimination of Racial Discrimination' (1998) 4(15) Indigenous Law Bulletin 17.

[157] See further Jane Robbins, 'Aboriginal Legal Aid Funding: Discriminatory Policy or a Failure of Federalism?' (2009) 7(10) Indigenous Law Bulletin 15.

[158] See further Wangan and Jagalingou Family Council, 'Australia's Ongoing Violation of its Obligations Under the International Convention on the Elimination of All Forms of Racial Discrimination and its Failure to Protect the Indigenous Wangan and Jagalingou People from Human Rights Violations Arising from the Development of the Carmichael Coal Mine on Our Ancestral Homelands' UN Doc INT/CERD/NGO/AUS/29370/E (31 October 2017).

[159] See John Gardiner-Garden, 'Overview of Indigenous Affairs: Part 2: 1992–2010' Australian Parliamentary Library (10 May 2011) <https://www.aph.gov.au/About_Parliament/Parliamentary_Departments/Parliamentary_Library/pubs/BN/1011/IndigenousAffairs2> accessed 18 March 2022.

[160] See Australia's Compliance with the ICERD Australian NGO Coalition Submission to the UN CERD Committee (October 2017) 41–42 <https://tbinternet.ohchr.org/Treaties/CERD/Shared%20Documents/AUS/INT_CERD_NGO_AUS_29334_E.pdf> accessed 18 March 2022.

5.1.8 Brief Conclusion

CERD's impact in Australia is apparent in its adoption within the RDA, and the work of the Race Discrimination Commissioner and other parts of the AHRC. No impact is evident from the small number of CERD communications, nor does it seem that the COs have compelled policy changes, apart from the commitment to anti-racism training for the police. Urgent actions have borne some fruit in terms of amendments to the NTER, but have otherwise had little noticeable policy impact. Certainly, Australia's relationship with the CERD Cttee has improved from a nadir at the turn of the century.

5.2 *International Covenant on Civil and Political Rights*

5.2.1 Ratification, Incorporation, and Main Institutions

Australia signed CCPR on 18 December 1972 and ratified it on 13 August 1980. The delay was caused by strong opposition by some state governments who believed that ratification would centralise power in the Commonwealth at the expense of the states.[161]

Australia maintains three reservations and one declaration, having withdrawn the majority of its original reservations and declarations in 1984.[162] Regarding article 10(2)(b) (which mandates the separation of juvenile and adult offenders in detention), Australia believes that it is not always desirable to separate offenders, such as where segregation might entail solitary confinement or living conditions less amenable than those of the general prison population.[163] It is also difficult to meet the requirements in remote areas.[164] Regarding the right to compensation for miscarriages of justice under article 14(6), Australia maintains that the right may be provided by administrative procedures rather than legislation. Finally, regarding the prohibition on war propaganda and hate speech in article 20, Australia states that it 'interprets the rights provided for by articles 19, 21 and 22 as consistent with article 20', and as such reserves the right not to introduce further legislation on these matters. The latter reservation is consistent with Australia's declaration under

---

[161] David Kinley, Jennifer Beard and Peter Thomson, 'Australia' in Christof Heyns and Frans Viljoen (eds), *The Impact of the UN Human Rights Treaties on the Domestic Level* (Kluwer Law International 2002) 51.

[162] International Covenant on Civil and Political Rights: Reservations, 1197 UNTS 411. See also Australian Government, Third Periodic Report to the HRCttee: Addendum UN Doc CCPR/C/AUS/98/3 (22 July 1999) para 625; and Australian Government, Sixth Periodic Report to the HRCttee UN Doc CCPR/C/AUS/6 (2 June 2016) paras 47–48.

[163] Australian Government, Third Periodic Report to the HRCttee: Addendum UN Doc CCPR/C/AUS/98/3 (22 July 1999) para 625.

[164] ibid.

CERD. Australia has also made a declaration that it is a federal constitutional system and, as such, 'the implementation of the ICCPR will be effected by the Commonwealth, State and Territory authorities having regard to their respective constitutional powers and arrangements concerning their exercise'. This reflects the federal government's ongoing political commitment to the federal split in powers, mentioned above.

Australia acceded to the OPI-CCPR on 25 September 1991. It ratified OPII-CCPR even earlier, on 2 October 1990, before it came into force.

CCPR has not been incorporated into domestic law and Australia has not adopted a comprehensive legal framework for the protection of CCPR rights at the federal level.[165] However, some statutes incorporate CCPR in part, and rely on Australia's ratification of CCPR for their constitutional basis, such as the Age Discrimination Act 2004 (Cth), the Human Rights (Sexual Conduct) Act 1994 (Cth), and the extension of the Sex Discrimination Act 2004 (Cth) so as to cover men and sexual minorities (discussed below). The Crimes (Torture Prohibition and Death Penalty Abolition) Act 2010 (Cth) implements the Second Optional Protocol. *Non-refoulement* obligations embedded in articles 6 and 7 of CCPR are protected under the Migration Act after the passage of the Migration Amendment (Complementary Protection) Act 2011 (Cth).[166]

CCPR is included in the Schedule to the Australian Human Rights Commission Act 1986 (Cth) so it falls within the AHRC's mandate for receiving complaints. The Human Rights Commissioner within the AHRC largely deals with CCPR rights. The Age Discrimination Commissioner also serves within the AHRC, and has primary responsibility for monitoring and facilitating implementation of the Age Discrimination Act 2004 (Cth).

CCPR sometimes is included in legislation as an object to the Act. For example, section 3 of the National Disability Insurance Scheme Act 2013 (Cth) states that one of the objects of the Act is to give effect to CCPR.[167]

At the sub-federal level, the human rights charters in the ACT, Victoria and Queensland bind public authorities within those jurisdictions to comply with almost all of the rights in CCPR, absent contrary primary legislation. Some CCPR rights are excluded from that legislation, such as the right to self-determination in all three charters.[168] Various reasons have been given for its

---

165 HRCttee, COs on the Sixth Periodic Report of Australia UN Doc CCPR/C/AUS/CO/6 (9 November 2017) paras 5–6; and HRCttee, COs on the Fifth Periodic Report of Australia, UN Doc CCPR/C/AUS/CO/5 (7 May 2009) para 8.
166 See Migration Amendment (Complementary Protection) Bill 2011 (Cth), Explanatory Memorandum.
167 National Disability Insurance Scheme Act 2013 (Cth) s 3(1)(i).
168 The right is mentioned in the Preamble to the Queensland Act.

exclusion, such as its nature as a collective rather than an individual right, as well as controversy over its scope.[169]

Australia asserted in its 2016 report to the Human Rights Committee (HRCttee) that its existing institutions and domestic laws, including common law and statute law, adequately implemented CCPR at the domestic level.[170] Certainly, numerous laws protect civil and political rights, including laws regarding the franchise, privacy and police powers. A senior government official who works on human rights implementation stated that most CCPR rights have found 'their way into Australia's legal system in all sorts of different ways'.[171] However, no compatibility study has been officially undertaken, nor has a programme of domestic legal reform been embarked upon, to give specific effect to the treaty.[172]

5.2.2 Policies and Initiatives of Relevance to CCPR[173]

On 21 April 2011 the Australian government appointed the inaugural Independent National Security Legislation Monitor (INSLM) under the Independent National Security Legislation Monitor Act 2010 (Cth), which has a mandate to review and report on Australia's counter-terrorism and national security legislation.[174] In performing functions under the Act, the INSLM must have regard to Australia's human rights obligations. Accordingly, INSLM reviews have often focused on Australia's obligations under CCPR.[175]

---

169 See, eg, Scrutiny of Acts and Regulations Committee, Review of the Charter of the Victorian Charter of Rights and Responsibilities 2006 <https://www.parliament.vic.gov.au/images/stories/committees/sarc/charter_review/report_response/20110914_sarc.charterreviewreport.pdf> accessed 4 September 2023. ch 3, Recommendation 3.
170 Australian Government, Sixth Periodic Report to the HRCttee UN Doc CCPR/C/AUS/6 (2 June 2016) paras 28–46.
171 Senior government official who works on human rights implementation, interview (n 5).
172 See Australian Law Reform Commission, Traditional Rights and Freedoms – Encroachments by Commonwealth Laws, ALRC Report 129 (December 2015), which assessed federal laws that interfered with 'traditional rights and freedoms' (which cover a few select ICCPR rights), but which did not come to conclusions as to whether those interferences constituted breaches of international human rights law.
173 See Australian Government, Sixth Periodic Report to the HRCttee UN Doc CCPR/C/AUS/6 (2 June 2016).
174 Independent National Security Legislation Monitor Act 2010 (Cth), arts 3 and 8.
175 See eg Independent National Security Legislation Monitor, Report to the Prime Minister: The Prosecution and Sentencing of Children for Terrorism, Dr James Renwick SC, 3rd INSLM 2018 5th Report, via <https://www.inslm.gov.au/reviews-reports/prosecution-and-sentencing-children-terrorism> accessed 18 March 2022.

As discussed below in part 5.5, Australia ratified OP-CAT on 21 December 2017. Its implementation of that treaty will assist in monitoring the implementation of articles 7, 9, 10 and 14 of CCPR.[176]

5.2.3 Use by Courts

The high point of judicial use of CCPR remains *Mabo v Queensland (No 2)*[177] of 1992, the ground-breaking case where the High Court decided that indigenous native title rights were cognisable under the common law. In joining the majority, Brennan J stated at 42:

> The opening up of international remedies to individuals pursuant to Australia's accession to the Optional Protocol to the International Covenant on Civil and Political Rights brings to bear on the common law the powerful influence of the Covenant and the international standards it imports. The common law does not necessarily conform with international law, but international law is a legitimate and important influence on the development of the common law, especially when international law declares the existence of universal human rights. A common law doctrine founded on unjust discrimination in the enjoyment of civil and political rights demands reconsideration.

Since that zenith, the HRCttee has expressed its regret that Australian judicial decisions make little reference to CCPR.[178] It is cited most often in cases where legislation is based on CCPR. For example, CCPR is cited extensively by the High Court in *SZTAL v Minister for Immigration*, which concerned the complementary protection provisions of the *Migration Act*.[179]

The High Court has rejected the use of CCPR to override the clear meaning of legislation.[180] Furthermore, in *Coleman v Power*, Gummow J stated that a particular provision of a statute should not be construed in light of CCPR, as it was enacted before Australia ratified CCPR. However, Kirby J in the same case stated that 'where words of a statute are susceptible to an interpretation that

---

176 Australian NGO Coalition Submission to the HRCttee, Australia's Compliance with the ICCPR UN Doc INT/CCPR/NGO/AUS/28925/E (September 2017) 12.
177 (1992) 1 CLR 175.
178 HRCttee, COs on Australia UN Doc CCPR/C/AUS/CO/5 (7 May 2009) para 8.
179 [2017] HCA 34.
180 See also *Re Woolley* [2004] HCA 49 paras 108–116; *Minister for Immigration and Multicultural and Indigenous Affairs v B* [2004] HCA 20 para 171.

is consistent with international law, that construction should prevail over one that is not'.[181]

The decision of the Supreme Court of Victoria in *Castles v Secretary to the Department of Justice*[182] is an example of citations of CCPR in a case based on a state charter. Articles 10 and 23 of CCPR aided the Court in finding that, under the Victorian Charter, a prisoner had a right to access in vitro fertilisation (IVF) treatment while in prison.

5.2.4 State Reporting and Its Impact

Australia submitted its fifth report in 2007 and its sixth report in 2016. On average, Australia has been late by 26 months with its reports. Australia appeared before the HRCttee in 2000, 2009 and 2017.

The HRCttee's COs on Australia focus on Australia's repeated failure to implement the Committee's views under the Optional Protocol; the policy of mandatory immigration detention and offshore immigration processing centres; counter-terrorism laws, policies and practices; violence against women; lack of respect for the principle of *non-refoulement*; excessive use of force by law enforcement officials; and the rights of indigenous peoples.

Australia first submitted information on follow-up to the HRCttee's 2009 COs on 17 December 2010, which amounted to a delay of nine months.[183] Australia's response to the follow-up question on immigration detention policy received an 'A' evaluation mark, which equates to 'response largely satisfactory'. It may be noted, however, that since that time the policy has regressed significantly. With regard to the remaining three recommendations, Australia's response was not sufficient, earning a 'B2' evaluation from the Committee ('initial action taken, but additional information required').[184] The Committee sent a follow-up letter to Australia requesting it provide further information on these three recommendations. Australia provided a response on 3 February 2012, which included some additional information. However, it disagreed with the Committee's interpretation of some issues, for example, that the definition of a terrorist act in the 2005 counter-terror legislation was vague.[185] The

---

181 *Coleman v Power* [2004] HCA 39 para 240. See also *Attorney-General (WA) v Marquet* [2003] HCA 67 paras 172–186; and *Behrooz v Secretary, Department of Immigration and Multicultural and Indigenous Affairs* [2004] HCA 36 paras 125–129.
182 [2010] VSC 310.
183 HRCttee, Report of the Special Rapporteur for Follow-Up on COs of the HRCttee UN Doc CCPR/C/104/2 (27 April 2012) 14–16.
184 ibid.
185 Australian Government, Information Provided by Australia on the Follow-Up to the COs of the Committee UN Doc INT/CCPR/FCO/AUS/11695/E (3 February 2012) 2.

Committee therefore ranked Australia's response on counter-terrorism legislation and practices as C1 ('not implemented'); its response on indigenous peoples as B1 ('substantive action taken, but additional information required'); and its response on violence against women as B1. The Committee requested that Australia provide information on action taken to address these three issues in its response to the List of Issues for Australia's 2017 review.[186]

The NGO coalition report to that 2017 review listed a large number of areas where Australia had failed to implement the COs, and indeed where it had gone backwards. Those lists dwarfed the list of areas where Australia had made progress in respect of recommendations in the 2009 COs.[187]

The HRCttee requested in its 2017 COs that Australia provide follow-up information on three issues by 10 November 2019.[188] No responses were received in this chapter's reporting period.

5.2.5 Individual Communications

The first individual communication against Australia was *Toonen v Australia*,[189] where Tasmanian laws which banned sex between men were found to breach the right to privacy in article 17. The case led directly to a remedy in the form of the passage of the Human Rights (Sexual Conduct) Act 1994 (Cth), which overrode the impugned Tasmanian laws. No case has since been as successful or impactful.[190]

The HRCttee has since 1999 published views in 67 individual communications against Australia. Of those, 27 were found to be inadmissible.

In 33 communications, 31 of which were finalized since June 1999, the HRCttee found Australia in violation of the CCPR. The communications concerning violations have covered a wide range of issues such as arbitrary detention;[191] life imprisonment without parole for a person who was a child at the

---

186   See, eg, HRCttee, List of Issues Prior to the Submission of the Sixth Periodic Report of Australia, adopted by the Committee at its 106th session, UN Doc CCPR/C/AUS/Q/6 (9 November 2012) para 7.
187   Australian NGO Coalition Submission to the HRCttee, Australia's Compliance with the ICCPR UN Doc INT/CCPR/NGO/AUS/28925/E (September 2017) 9.
188   HRCttee, COs on Australia UN Doc CCPR/C/AUS/CO/6 (1 December 2017) para 56.
189   *Toonen v Australia* UN Doc CCPR/C/50/D/488/1992 (31 March 1994).
190   See also Malcolm Langford and Cosette D. Creamer, 'The Toonen decision: domestic and international impact', SSRN, 3 November 2017, <https://papers.ssrn.com/sol3/papers.cfm?abstract_id=3063850> accessed 14 April 2022.
191   These cases covered the following issues: *Shafiq v Australia* UN Doc CCPR/C/88/D/1324/2004 (31 October 2006) is one of many cases concerning detention pursuant to the mandatory immigration detention regime; *FKAG v Australia* UN Doc CCPR/C/108/D/2094/

time of the relevant crime;[192] the prohibition of torture and cruel, inhuman or degrading treatment or punishment;[193] discrimination on the basis of sexuality;[194] the deportation of long-term resident aliens;[195] the best interests of the child;[196] and denial of the right to family life.[197]

Australia generally responds by disputing the HRCttee's interpretation of CCPR and refusing to implement the views.[198] In 2018 the then Vice-Chairperson of the HRCttee, Professor Yuval Shany, described Australia's record as one of 'chronic non-compliance',[199] with the government routinely rejecting the HRCttee's views.

Some cases are remedied. *Horvath v Australia* concerned the lack of compensation for a woman assaulted by a Victorian police officer.[200] At the time, only the police officer was liable for damages and not the state of Victoria. Victorian law has since been amended so that the state provides for damages if the police officer is unable to pay damages. The relevant police officer also

---

2011 (20 August 2013) concerned the indefinite detention of refugees on security grounds; *Fardon v Australia* UN Doc CCPR/C/98/D/1629/2007 (10 May 2010) concerned preventive detention orders extending beyond the expiry of a sentence; *Hicks v Australia* UN Doc CPR/C/115/D/2005/2010 (5 November 2015) concerned the detention by Australia of David Hicks after he had been released from Guantanamo Bay pursuant to an arrangement with the United States.

192 *Blessington and Elliot v Australia* UN Doc CCPR/C/112/D/1968/2010 (3 November 2014).
193 *FJ & Others v Australia* UN Doc CCPR/C/116/D/2233/2013 (22 March 2016) concerned psychological harm caused by immigration detention.
194 *Young v Australia* UN Doc CCPR/C/78/D/941/2000 (6 August 2003).
195 *Nystrom v Australia* UN Doc CCPR/C/102/D/1557/2007 (18 July 2011).
196 *Z v Australia* UN Doc CCPR/C/115/D/2279/2013 (5 November 2015).
197 *Winata v Australia* UN Doc CCPR/C/72/D/930/2000 (26 July 2001).
198 See, eg, responses to HRC decisions available via <https://www.ag.gov.au/rights-and-protections/human-rights-and-anti-discrimination/human-rights-communications> accessed 4 September 2023. As one specific examples, see Australian Government, Response of the Australian Government to the Views of the HRCttee in Communication No 2005/2010 (*Hicks v Australia*) <https://www.ag.gov.au/rights-and-protections/publications/hicks-v-australia-20052010-australian-government-response>, accessed 18 March 2022 paras 18 and 32. See also the Australian government's response to follow-up by the HRC, for example, on the *Hicks* decision: HRCttee, 'Follow-up progress report on individual communications', UN Doc CCPR/C/119/3, 30 May 2017, pp 6–8.
199 See Ben Doherty, '"Unacceptable: UN Committee Damns Australia's Record on Human Rights' *The Guardian* (19 October 2017) <https://www.theguardian.com/australia-news/2017/oct/19/unacceptable-un-committee-damns-australias-record-on-human-rights> accessed 18 March 2022. See also HRCttee, COs on Australia UN Doc A/55/40 (2000) paras 498–528 3; HRCttee, COs on Australia UN Doc CCPR/C/AUS/CO/5 (7 May 2009) para 10.
200 *Horvath v Australia*, UN Doc CCPR/C/110/D/1885/2009 (27 March 2014).

faced trial.[201] A senior DFAT officer noted the merit in this case highlighting 'a flaw in the system' which was accordingly remedied.[202]

The NGO Remedy Australia tracks Australia's implementation of individual communications across the UN system.[203] It lists only six fully 'remedied' cases, five of which are CCPR cases.[204] Aside from *Toonen*, the other cases seem to have been 'accidentally remedied' by circumstances which were not influenced by the decision. For example, one 'remedied' case is *Hagan*, discussed above, where the 'remedy' was not driven by CERD views.

Remedy Australia's criteria for assessing remedial status are quite stringent. For example, it lists *Kwok v Australia*[205] as only 'partially remedied'. The HRCttee found that Kwok's deportation would breach CCPR and Australia did not in fact deport her. However, it did not pay her compensation for her prior years of detention as recommended.

Remedy Australia's list only goes up to 2017. Two more cases can now be classified as essentially remedied. The violations in *Campbell v Australia*[206] and *G v Australia*,[207] concerning the refusal by Australia to, respectively, recognise same-sex divorce and a married transgender person's right to change her birth certificate, were both driven by Australia's failure to recognise same-sex marriage. This situation changed in late 2017, when Australia amended its marriage legislation to recognise marriage equality. That change, which indirectly remedies the two cases, was not driven by those HRCttee decisions. Rather, it was driven by vigorous local debate and a survey of public opinion which confirmed overwhelming support for marriage equality.

5.2.6 Interim Measures

The HRCttee has requested interim measures from Australia in 13 communications and Australia has complied every time. Most requests have been to

---

201 See, eg, Australian Government, Response of the Australian Government to the Views of the Committee in Communication No 1885/2009, *Horvath v Australia*, via <https://www.ag.gov.au/rights-and-protections/publications/horvath-v-australia-18852009-australian-government-response> accessed 18 March 2022.
202 Senior DFAT officer, interview (n 37).
203 See, eg, remedy.org.au.
204 See, generally, Remedy Australia, Follow-up Report on Violations by Australia of ICERD, ICCPR & CAT in Individual Communications (1994–2014) (11 April 2014) <https://www.remedy.org.au/reports/2014_Follow-Up_Report_to_treaty_bodies.pdf> accessed 15 April 2020.
205 *Kwok v Australia* UN Doc CCPR/C/97/D/1442/2005 (23 October 2009).
206 *Campbell v Australia* UN Doc CCPR/C/119/D/2216/2012 (1 November 2017).
207 *G v Australia* UN Doc CCPR/C/119/D/2172/2012 (17 March 2017).

the effect that Australia refrain from deporting a person prior to finalisation of their communication. Some have concerned a request to provide medical treatment.[208] Australia has on occasion requested that the measures be lifted, successfully[209] and unsuccessfully.[210]

5.2.7 Treaty Body Membership

Elizabeth Evatt AC served as a member of the HRCttee from 1993 to 2000. Professor Ivan Shearer AM served as a member of the HRCttee from 2001–2008, and as Vice-Chairperson from 2007 to 2008.

5.2.8 Brief Conclusion

CCPR probably is the most well-known of the core human rights treaties within Australia among government, civil society and the public. It forms the basis of the three human rights statutes in the ACT, Victoria and Queensland. Otherwise, its incorporation into Australian law has arisen in a piecemeal fashion, such as in the realms of age discrimination and *non-refoulement*. Having said that, its rights and values are reflected in numerous laws that protect civil rights in accordance with Australia's liberal democratic and common law traditions. The Human Rights Commissioner within the AHRC plays a role in conducting inquiries and promoting CCPR, and the AHRC may make non-binding decisions regarding breaches of the treaty. Australia has also incorporated the Second Optional Protocol into domestic law.

There have been many OP decisions against Australia, the vast majority of which have not been implemented, or which have been 'implemented' due to reasons unrelated to the relevant views. Similarly, the COs have not had a significant impact on Australian law or policy. However, interim measures issues by the HRCttee have uniformly been complied with, which will have provided short-term relief to the relevant author of a communication under OP1-CCPR.

5.3 *International Covenant on Economic, Social and Cultural Rights*

5.3.1 Ratification, Incorporation, and Main Institutions

Australia signed CESCR in 1972 and ratified it on 10 December 1975. The treaty was not well understood in Australia at the time, so opposition to ratification was minimal, on the understanding that it would make 'little or no difference

---

208 See *FKAG v Australia* UN Doc CCPR/C/108/D/2094/2011 (28 October 2013).
209 *Leghaei v Australia* UN Doc CCPR/C/113/D/1937/2010 (15 May 2015).
210 *ARJ v Australia* UN Doc CCPR/C/60/D/692/1996 (11 August 1997).

to domestic laws and policies'.[211] Australia lodged no reservations or declarations to CESCR.

Australia is not a party to OP-CESCR. The Human Rights Law Resources Centre (as it was then known) has cogently suggested that the government has misgivings about group complaints, justiciability of economic, social and cultural rights, and the appropriateness of judicial or quasi-judicial bodies determining how a state's resources should be allocated.[212]

Australia has not directly incorporated CESCR into its domestic law. Provisions of legislation pertaining to, for example, public housing, social security and conditions of work all protect Australians' economic social and cultural rights, but make no reference to CESCR. Indeed, minimal attention has been paid to CESCR since its ratification. A senior government official who works on human rights implementation stated that it was harder to demonstrate the way in which social rights are protected in law as effective realisation of social rights did not always lend itself to legal responses: He added that demonstrating 'progressive realisation is really hard ... there will always be competing resource [considerations]'.[213]

No national mechanism, other than the bodies involved in the implementation of the Human Rights (Parliamentary Scrutiny) Act 2011 (Cth), specifically addresses CESCR. However, there are many governmental mechanisms that do work relating to economic, social and cultural rights, including the Fair Work apparatus and the Australia Council for the Arts.

At the sub-federal level, the Human Rights Act 2004 (ACT) and Human Rights Act 2019 (Qld) protect certain economic, social and cultural rights. The Australian Capital Territory statute recognises the right to education in section 27A, while the Queensland Act recognises rights of access to education and health services in sections 36 and 37. These provisions, allowing for justiciable social rights based on CESCR, are ground-breaking in Australian law.[214]

5.3.2 Policies and Initiatives of Relevance to CESCR[215]

Between 1999 and 2007 Australia's national budget remained relatively steady in terms of proportions spent on areas directly affecting economic, social and

---

211 Kinley, Beard and Thomson (n 161) 51.
212 HRLRC, Australia's Ratification of the Optional Protocol to the International Covenant on Economic, Social and Cultural Rights (July 2009) 12–20.
213 Senior government official who works on human rights implementation, interview (n 5).
214 Their inclusion in Queensland is explained by 'stakeholder support'. See Explanatory Note, Human Rights Bill 2018 (Qld) 11.
215 See Australian Government, Australia's Fifth Report under the International Covenant on Economic, Social and Cultural Rights UN Doc E/C.12/AUS/5 (1 February 2016) para 74.

cultural rights, including education, health care, social security and welfare, housing, recreation and culture. From 2008, when the government announced stimulus spending in response to the Global Financial Crisis, the government spent more overall than in the previous decade, and devoted a larger proportion of the budget each year to those areas, until 2013.[216]

From the conservative government's first budget in 2014, attempts have been made to reduce spending in areas such as social security as part of a broader push to reduce spending and bring the budget back into surplus. However, many relevant budget measures have been blocked in Parliament. While the blocking of measures was never based explicitly on CESCR, prominent arguments around 'unfairness' arguably reflected notions of proportionality and non-retrogression in economic and social rights jurisprudence.

5.3.3 Use by Courts

CESCR and the jurisprudence of the CESCR Cttee have featured only sparsely in Australian jurisprudence since (and before) 1999. In *Purvis v NSW*, an anti-discrimination case from 2003 about a student with disability being excluded from his school, Callinan J of the High Court referred to CESCR, but only to note that students with disabilities might 'cause disruption to the education of others', and that this 'rights conflict' had not been adequately addressed by the student's legal representatives.[217]

As a better example, in 2012 Bell J of the Victorian Court of Appeal discussed the right to work in article 6 of CESCR, including the CESCR Cttee's General Recommendation 18. Bell J observed that the Victorian Charter only protected related rights, rather than the right to work as such, but that the common law protected the right to work in certain circumstances.[218] Similarly, in 2018 Bell J discussed General Comment 14 (on the right to health), but went on to note that the right to health was not reflected in Victorian domestic law.[219]

---

[216] See Alan Duncan and Rebecca Cassells, 'Government Spending Explained in 10 charts; From Howard to Turnbull' *The Conversation* (9 May 2017) <https://theconversation.com/government-spending-explained-in-10-charts-from-howard-to-turnbull-77158> accessed 18 March 2022.

[217] *Purvis v NSW* (2003) 217 CLR 92 164 (fn 148).

[218] *WBM v Chief Commissioner of Police* (2012) 43 VR 446, 483; also *ZZ v Secretary, Dept of Justice* [2013] VSC 267 paras 80–82 (Bell J).

[219] *PBU & NJE v Mental Health Tribunal* [2018] VSC 564 para 97–99.

5.3.4 State Reporting and Its Impact

Australia submitted reports to the CESCR Cttee in 2007 and 2016. The average delay for the last 20 years has been approximately two years. Australia appeared before the CESCR Cttee in 2000, 2009 and 2017. The CESCR Cttee's COs on Australia focus on topics such as lack of domestic legal implementation, the treatment of indigenous Australians and asylum seekers, healthcare services, labour relations and trade union rights, as well as the lack of an official poverty line.[220] To these have lately been added lack of action on climate change, business and human rights, the adequacy of social security benefits, gender equality and domestic violence, migrant workers' rights and mental health services.[221]

Australia first submitted information on follow-up to the CESCR Cttee's 2017 COs in December 2018.[222] The government committed to revising the Closing the Gap strategy, which is aimed at improving socio-economic conditions for indigenous Australians, and to re-evaluating the discriminatory indigenous income management measures which have applied in the Northern Territory since before the CESCR Cttee issued its 2009 COs.[223] Finally, the document defends Australia's border protection measures and regional cooperation on irregular migration.[224] Such follow-up documents do not suggest that major shifts in policy have been implemented as a result of COs.

5.3.5 Treaty Body Membership

Professor Phillip Alston served on the CESCR Cttee from 1986 to 1998, and as Chairperson from 1991 to 1998.

5.3.6 Brief Conclusion

Despite being the second human rights treaty ratified by Australia, CESCR has probably had the least impact on Australian law and government policy. Australia's welfare laws are driven by local political and economic considerations rather than by CESCR or the jurisprudence of the CESCR Cttee. Australia

---

220 CESCR Cttee, COs on Australia UN Doc E/C.12/1/Add.50 (11 September 2000) paras 14–23.
221 CESCR Cttee, COs on the Fifth Periodic Report of Australia UN Doc E/C.12/AUS/CO/5 (11 July 2017) paras 11, 13, 21, 27, 29, 31.
222 CESCR Cttee, COs on the Fifth Periodic Report of Australia – Addendum: Information Received from Australia on Follow-Up to the COs UN Doc E/C.12/AUS/CO/5/Add.1 (8 January 2019) (received 21 December 2018).
223 CESCR Cttee, COs on the Fifth Periodic Report of Australia – Addendum: Information Received from Australia on Follow-Up to the COs UN Doc E/C.12/AUS/CO/5/Add.1 paras 7–15.
224 ibid paras 4–6.

also seems wedded to outmoded doubts over the justiciability of economic, social and cultural rights, which is delaying serious consideration of ratification of OP-CESCR. On a more positive note, CESCR jurisprudence can be expected to be utilised in making decisions under the economic and social rights provisions of the ACT and Queensland human rights charters.

5.4 Convention on the Elimination of All Forms of Discrimination against Women

5.4.1 Ratification, Incorporation, and Main Institutions

Australia signed CEDAW in 1980 and ratified it on 28 July 1983. The ratification was directed by a new ALP government towards the end of the UN Decade for Women (1976–1985). Ratification gave Australia the 'constitutional foundation' to enact the Sex Discrimination Act 1984 (Cth) (SDA).[225]

Australia lodged a reservation to article 11(2) of CEDAW with respect to paid maternity leave, stating that for the time being it was reserved for government employees.[226] It also entered a reservation which stated that the Australian Defence Force policy of excluding women from combat and combat-related duties would not be altered (although the definitions of such duties would be reviewed).[227] This latter reservation was revised in 2000 to include only combat, and in 2018 it was withdrawn altogether.[228] The maternity leave reservation remains in effect, due to budgetary considerations.

Australia acceded to OP-CEDAW in 2008. It did not opt out of the CEDAW Cttee's inquiry procedure under article 10 of the Optional Protocol.

The SDA directly incorporates CEDAW into Australian federal law. There is also a range of state and territory laws that prohibit discrimination on the basis of sex. The SDA was amended in 2011 to protect men from sex discrimination; to prohibit workplace discrimination on the basis of family responsibilities; to strengthen prohibitions on sexual harassment; and to establish breastfeeding as a separate ground of discrimination.[229] In 2013 amendments relating to

---

225 See Kinley, Beard and Thomson (n 161) 52. The seminal *Tasmanian Dams* case (*Commonwealth v Tasmania* (1983) 158 CLR 1), which finally confirmed the profound impact of treaty ratification on the constitutional scope of federal legislative authority, was decided on 1 July 1983.
226 See Convention on the Elimination of All Forms of Discrimination against Women: Reservations 1325 UNTS 378.
227 ibid.
228 See depositary notification C.N.592.2018.TREATIES-IV.8 of 14 December 2018.
229 See Australian Government, Eighth Periodic Report on the Implementation of the CEDAW UN Doc CEDAW/C/AUS/8 (8 December 2016) para 2.5.

discrimination on the basis of sexual orientation, gender identity and intersex status were incorporated.[230]

The SDA in 1984 brought with it the office of Sex Discrimination Commissioner in what was then called the Human Rights and Equal Opportunity Commission (later renamed the AHRC). In addition, there is an Office for Women (formerly known as the Office for the Status of Women), which currently is located in the Department of Prime Minister and Cabinet.[231]

5.4.2 Policies and Initiatives of Relevance to CEDAW

Numerous policies are of relevance to CEDAW, even if CEDAW is not expressly cited, such as a number of initiatives aimed at eradicating family violence and violence against women,[232] and the introduction of government-funded paid parental leave in the private sector.[233]

5.4.3 Use by Courts

CEDAW and the CEDAW Cttee jurisprudence arise occasionally in cases under the SDA. For example, in 2007 the Federal Court held that a Victorian law that prohibited the alteration of a married person's sex on their birth certificate was not contrary to the SDA: The majority justified its reasoning by reference to their interpretation of the requirements of CEDAW.[234] CEDAW and related jurisprudence are also raised by female asylum applicants, with varying degrees of success, before Australian tribunals (in relation to their countries of origin failing to respect CEDAW).[235]

5.4.4 State Reporting and Its Impact

The Australian government reported to the CEDAW Cttee in 2004, 2009 and 2016. The average delay was one year and eight months. Australia appeared before the CEDAW Cttee in 2006, 2010 and 2018.

---

230 Sex Discrimination Amendment (Sexual Orientation, Gender Identity and Intersex Status) Act 2013 (Cth).
231 Department of Prime Minister and Cabinet, Office for Women <https://www.pmc.gov.au/office-women> accessed 18 March 2022.
232 See, eg, the National Plan to Reduce Violence against Women and their Children 2010–2022; the National Framework for Protecting Australia's Children 2009–2020.
233 See Paid Parental Leave Act 2010 (Cth).
234 See *AB v Registrar of Births, Deaths and Marriages* [2007] FCAFC 140 (29 August 2007).
235 See eg 1008090 [2010] RRTA 1064 (25 November 2010) in relation to Mongolia; 1205511 [2013] RRTA 4 (9 January 2013) in relation to Bosnia; 1005606 [2010] RRTA 801 (17 September 2010) in relation to Malawi or 0904059 [2009] RRTA 998 (30 October 2009) in relation to Mauritius.

The Office for (the Status of) Women, variously located in different departments over the years, is responsible for reporting under CEDAW. Professor Simon Rice has suggested that CEDAW 'goes missing', as its reports are prepared by an office which shuffles across departments, rather than by a central government department.[236] However, it is arguable that CEDAW reports have in some respects been superior to other reports. The 2004 and 2009 CEDAW reports seem more comprehensive and frank than reports prepared by DFAT or AGD. For example, the 2004 report transparently acknowledged 'areas where progress has been slower and new challenges have emerged'.[237] In contrast, the 2016 report is terse and factual.

The CEDAW Cttee's COs on Australia focus on topics such as the inconsistent implementation of the treaty; a lack of engagement by Parliament; the maintenance of the paid maternity leave reservation; the lack of judicial use of CEDAW; the rejection of quotas for female representation; the prevalence of violence against women; the persistence of people trafficking; and the prevalence of sexual harassment and continuing poor outcomes for vulnerable women (for instance, indigenous women, women in detention and women seeking asylum).[238]

The government's follow-up report of 2012[239] is more detailed than equivalent follow-up reports to other treaty bodies. The report goes into depth on government initiatives to combat violence against women and to support victims, as well as measures to improve the lives of indigenous women.[240] However, there is no indication that anything reported in the follow-up document was being done specifically to implement the CEDAW Cttee's recommendations.

The AHRC prepared an Independent Interim Report in 2012 to evaluate follow-up on the 2010 COs.[241] According to that Interim Report, significant progress had been made from 2010 to 2012 on recommendations relating to family violence and harassment, although in other areas, such as indigenous women's rights, progress was less observable.[242]

---

236 Simon Rice, interview (n 28).
237 See Commonwealth Office of the Status of Women, Australia's Combined Fourth and Fifth Reports to the UN on the CEDAW, UN Doc CEDAW/C/AUL/4–5 (June 2003) paras 14–15.
238 CEDAW Cttee, COs on Australia UN Doc CEDAW/C/AUL/CO/7 (30 July 2010) paras 14–45; also COs on Australia, UN Doc CEDAW/C/AUS/CO/8 (20 July 2018) paras 8–58.
239 Australian Government, Information Provided by Australia on the Follow-Up to the COs of the Committee UN Doc CEDAW/C/AUL/CO/7/Add.1 (17 December 2012) paras 7–121.
240 ibid paras 122–196.
241 AHRC, Independent Interim Report on CEDAW (31 August 2012) <https://www.humanrights.gov.au/independent-interim-report-cedaw> accessed 18 March 2022.
242 ibid.

5.4.5 Individual Communications

Australia has been party to OP-CEDAW since 2008, but to date no relevant communications have been submitted regarding Australia. The absence of cases could reflect a general scepticism over the likelihood of such complaints leading to genuine remedies in Australia.

5.4.6 Treaty Body Membership

Elizabeth Evatt served on the CEDAW Cttee from 1985 to 1992, including as Chairperson from 1989 to 1990.

5.4.7 Brief Conclusion

CEDAW provides the constitutional foundation for the SDA. It has also benefited, at least in the 2000s, from a rigorous reporting process coordinated by the Office for Women, compared to other core human rights treaties, though that Office may suffer from a low profile within government. Some progress is evident in relation to the COs, but it seems likely that such progress is driven by local political and social impetuses towards greater protection of women's rights rather than CEDAW *per se*. The communications procedure has not to date been utilised with regard to Australia.

5.5 *Convention against Torture and Other Cruel, Inhuman or Degrading Treatment or Punishment*

5.5.1 Ratification, Incorporation, and Main Institutions

Australia signed CAT in December 1985 and ratified it on 8 August 1989. Ratification had broad support 'given Australia's prominent part in the work of the UN to find practical ways of combating torture'.[243] Australia did not enter any reservations or declarations upon ratification. Australia accepted the individual and interstate complaints mechanisms under articles 20 and 22 of CAT by means of a declaration on 28 January 1993.

CAT was originally incorporated into Australian law by the Crimes (Torture) Act 1988 (Cth). A decision was made in 2008 to update the 1988 legislation after a recommendation by the CAT Cttee in its 2008 COs. Accordingly, Parliament passed the Crimes Legislation Amendment (Torture Prohibition and Death Penalty Abolition) Act 2010 (Cth). This Act inserted a specific division prohibiting torture as defined in CAT, which is directly cited, in Division 274 of the Commonwealth Criminal Code 1995. This Division also implements the obligation to prosecute or extradite all torturers, although ministerial

---

243 Kinley, Beard and Thomson (n 161) 52.

approval is required to prosecute perpetrators for offences that occur outside Australia.[244]

The Migration Amendment (Complementary Protection) Act 2011 (Cth) amended the Migration Act 1958 (Cth) to enshrine Australia's *non-refoulement* obligations under article 3 of CAT in legislation, rather than leaving them to be exercised via ministerial discretion, as had previously been the practice.[245]

Other provisions of Commonwealth legislation also prohibit conduct which might be characterised as torture or ill-treatment under CAT, particularly in the context of armed conflict and terrorism.[246]

Australia signed OP-CAT in May 2009 and ratified it on 21 December 2017. Ratification was delayed because implementation of this treaty was seen as especially difficult in a federal state requiring cooperation between jurisdictions.[247] However, in the wake of revelations about mistreatment in various detention environments (for instance, youth detention in the Northern Territory),[248] and in the context of a successful campaign for a seat on the Human Rights Council, Australia finally ratified OP-CAT in late 2017.

In announcing ratification, the Commonwealth government indicated that no new legislation was planned at the federal level to establish the National Preventive Mechanism (NPM),[249] but legislation to permit visits by the Sub-Committee on the Prevention of Torture is planned (and in fact is already in place in the two territories).[250] Public consultation on the form and mandate

---

244 See Criminal Code Act 1995 (Cth) s 274.3.
245 See Migration Amendment (Complementary Protection) Bill 2011 (Cth), Explanatory Memorandum.
246 See Attorney-General's Department, Prohibition on Torture and Cruel, Inhuman or Degrading Treatment or Punishment <https://www.ag.gov.au/rights-and-protections/human-rights-and-anti-discrimination/human-rights-scrutiny/public-sector-guidance-sheets/prohibition-torture-and-cruel-inhuman-or-degrading-treatment-or-punishment> accessed 4 September 2023.
247 See further APT, Implementation of the OPCAT in Federal and Decentralised States (March 2011) <https://www.apt.ch/en/resources/publications/implementing-opcat-federal-and-other-decentralised-states-briefing-paper> accessed 18 March 2022.
248 See Royal Commission into the Detention and Protection of Children in the NT <https://www.royalcommission.gov.au/royal-commission-detention-and-protection-children-northern-territory> accessed 18 March 2022 (final report issued 17 November 2017).
249 See Cth Ombudsman, Implementation of the OPCAT: Baseline Assessment of Australia's OPCAT Readiness, September 2019: <https://www.ombudsman.gov.au/__data/assets/pdf_file/0025/106657/Ombudsman-Report-Implementation-of-OPCAT.pdf> accessed 4 September 2023, 10.
250 See Monitoring of Places of Detention (Optional Protocol to the Convention Against Torture) Act 2018 (NT); Monitoring of Places of Detention (Optional Protocol to the Convention Against Torture) Act 2018 (ACT).

of the NPM has been undertaken by the AHRC since 2017, with a final report due in 2019.[251] Accordingly, Australia declared, in accordance with article 24 of OP-CAT, that it would postpone its obligation to establish the NPM for three years.

5.5.2   Policies and Initiatives of Relevance to CAT

The NPM will be the major national mechanism for implementing OP-CAT and, by extension, CAT. It will be coordinated by the Commonwealth Ombudsman and involve agencies conducting visits to places of detention from each state and territory.[252] States and territories are expected to fund NPM member bodies responsible for visiting places of detention within their jurisdictions. The Commonwealth Ombudsman will receive funding of $1,2 million over four years to coordinate the national NPM network.[253]

Western Australia has had an Office of the Inspector of Custodial Services (OICS) since 2003,[254] and similar inspectorates are coming online in other jurisdictions, either in response to the ratification of OP-CAT or due to pre-existing concerns about detention conditions.[255]

5.5.3   Use by Courts

The CAT prohibition on *refoulement* is sometimes discussed in Australian court decisions concerning planned deportations and removals. For example, in 2013 the Full Court of the Federal Court ruled that a departmental assessment that the applicant's removal would not breach CAT (or CCPR) was unlawful because the assessor did not apply the correct standard of proof in assessing his risk of being subjected to torture.[256] Less positively, in 2015 the High Court held that an attempt by the Australian government to intercept a boat carrying

---

251 See AHRC, OPCAT (19 June 2018) <https://www.humanrights.gov.au/our-work/rights-and-freedoms/projects/opcat-optional-protocol-convention-against-torture> accessed 18 March 2022.
252 See Ombudsman media release (n 249).
253 See Minister for Foreign Affairs, 'Improving Oversight and Conditions in Detention' Media Release (9 February 2017) <https://www.dfat.gov.au/news/news/Pages/improving-oversight-and-conditions-in-detention> accessed 18 March 2022.
254 See WA OICS <https://www.oics.wa.gov.au> accessed 18 March 2022.
255 See eg NSW Inspector of Custodial Services <http://www.custodialinspector.justice.nsw.gov.au>; Office of the Custodial Inspector Tasmania <https://www.custodialinspector.tas.gov.au>, both accessed 18 March 2022. Other agencies such as the Victorian Ombudsman also perform inspections of places of detention.
256 *Minister for Immigration and Citizenship v SZQRB* [2013] FCAFC 33 paras 246–248, 297.

153 asylum seekers and to return them to Sri Lankan authorities was lawful under Australian law, *refoulement* concerns notwithstanding.[257]

In 2017 the High Court upheld a finding by the Refugee Review Tribunal that subjection to unsatisfactory prison conditions on return to Sri Lanka was not likely to constitute a breach of CAT, as the Sri Lankan authorities did not 'intend' to subject detainees to such conditions (rather they were due to a lack of resources for the prison system).[258] The Court found that international authorities did not shed any useful light on this question of intention,[259] but did not consider CAT Cttee jurisprudence.

CAT Cttee jurisprudence has also been considered in Tribunal decisions regarding asylum claims.[260] For example, the Refugee Review Tribunal may refer to the CAT Cttee's COs when considering whether an applicant is a person to whom Australia has protection obligations under the Refugee Convention.[261]

5.5.4 State Reporting and Its Impact

Australia reported to the CAT Cttee in 2005, 2013 and 2019. There was an average five months' delay in the delivery of these reports. In our reporting period, a session to discuss the latest report had not yet been scheduled. Australia appeared before the CAT Cttee in 2000, 2008 and 2014.

The CAT Cttee's COs on Australia focus on topics such as violence against women; people trafficking; indigenous Australians in the criminal justice system; TASERs; counter-terrorism legislation; *refoulement*; mandatory immigration detention and offshore processing; child sexual abuse and involuntary treatment of persons with disabilities.[262]

Two of the key recommendations of the CAT Cttee in 2008 were that Australia specifically criminalise, and adequately define, torture in domestic law; as well as prohibit *refoulement* through a legislative regime. As explained above, these reforms were adopted in 2010 and 2011 respectively.[263] These responses might be considered the high water mark in Australian legislative implementation of treaty body COs.

---

257 See *CPCF v Minister for Immigration and Border Protection* (2015) 25 CLR 514.
258 *SZTAL v Minister for Immigration and Border Protection; SZTGM v Minister for Immigration and Border Protection* [2017] HCA 34.
259 ibid paras 84–91.
260 See eg 0807987 [2009] RRTA 591; N99/27139 [1999] RRTA 676; 1008846 [2011] RRTA 14, and 1301683 [2013] RRTA 765.
261 1301683 [2013] RRTA 765.
262 See CAT Cttee, COs on Australia UN Doc CAT/C/AUS/CO/4–5 (23 December 2014) paras 9–20.
263 See, eg, CAT Cttee, COs on Australia, UN Doc CAT/C/AUS/CO/3 (22 May 2008) paras 8 and 15.

Australia produced its first follow-up report for the CAT Cttee in 2009,[264] and another in 2015.[265] Both were relatively detailed, although it does not seem that many policies, apart from those discussed directly above, have changed in light of the latter follow-up.

5.5.5 Individual Communications

Over the last 20 years the CAT Committee has issued views in 27 communications against Australia. Without exception, these concern complaints about prospective removal from Australia to face an alleged risk of a breach of article 3 of CAT in the state to which they are being returned (that is, *refoulement* claims). Australia has prevailed in the majority of these cases, with the proposed deportation being found to breach article 3 (if executed) in only five cases.

The Australian government has published views of the CAT Cttee from 2012, but to date has published only two responses.[266] In these responses Australia refused to accept that it should refrain (or should have refrained) from removing the complainants.[267] We are unaware of any deportation decision that has been stopped due to an adverse CAT decision although, as explained below, deportations have been stayed due to requests for interim measures.

The CAT Cttee's follow-up reports to the Complaints Procedure, issued since 2014, do not contain a report on any of the communications against Australia.

5.5.6 Interim Measures

The CAT Cttee has requested interim measures against Australia on 36 occasions, all of which requested the government to refrain from deporting a person while an article 3 complaint was being considered. Australia has complied on all but three occasions, although it has sometimes (unsuccessfully) requested that such measures be lifted. In two cases, Australia deported a person on the day the interim measures request was issued, but prior to its receipt.[268] In *Thirugnanasampanthar v Australia* the relevant person was deported despite a request for interim measures, as the request 'could not be brought to the

---

264 Australian Government, Information on Follow-Up to the COs UN Doc CAT/C/AUS/CO/3/Add.1 (29 May 2009).
265 Australian Government, Information on Follow-Up to the COs UN Doc CAT/C/AUS/CO/4–5/Add.1 (26 November 2015).
266 See Attorney-General's Department, 'Human Rights Communications' <https://www.ag.gov.au/rights-and-protections/human-rights-and-anti-discrimination/human-rights-communications> accessed 4 September 2023.
267 ibid para 29. See also Response of the Australian Government to the Views of the CAT Committee in Communication 701/2015 (*HK v Australia*) (17 April 2018) para 20.
268 See *MPS v Australia* UN Doc CAT/C/28/D/138/1999 (30 April 2002) and *ZT v Australia* UN Doc CAT/C/31/D/153/2000 (19 November 2003).

attention of the relevant authorities in sufficient time to prevent the complainant's scheduled departure on 25 June 2014'.[269] The CAT Cttee accordingly found that Australia had breached its obligations under article 22 of CAT, under which it is required to cooperate in good faith with the Committee in relation to individual communications.[270]

5.5.7 Treaty Body Membership

There has never been an Australian expert on the CAT Cttee.

5.5.8 Brief Conclusion

CAT and the CAT Cttee jurisprudence have had some impact on Australian law and policy, for example in the passage of a new statute outlawing torture and in the introduction of complementary protection for refugees under migration law. Both developments were explicitly driven by the 2008 COs from the CAT Cttee. In contrast, the subsequent COs have had little impact, nor have CAT decisions in individual communications apparently provided a remedy to the complainants. As with CCPR, the interim measures requests have been generally effective in providing short term relief to complainants.

5.6 Convention on the Rights of the Child

5.6.1 Ratification, Incorporation and Main Institutions

Australia signed CRC on 22 August 1990 and ratified it on 17 December of the same year. Australia's early ratification reflects its prominent role in the development of the treaty.[271] Australia maintains a reservation to article 37(c) of CRC regarding the obligation to separate children from adults in prison, which reflects a similar reservation discussed above regarding CCPR.

Australia signed the OP to CRC on the involvement of children in armed conflict on 21 October 2002 and ratified it on 26 September 2006. It signed the Optional Protocol to CRC on the sale of children, child prostitution and child pornography (OP-CRC-SC) on 18 December 2001 and ratified it on 8 January 2007. The relevant National Interest Analysis made by the government in 2005 suggests that the delay in ratifying the OP-CRC-SC was due to the need to enact new trafficking in persons offences, and to consult with state and territories.[272]

---

269 *Thirugnanasampanthar v Australia* UN Doc UN Doc CAT/C/61/D/614/2014 (9 August 2017) para 6.2.
270 Ultimately, the CAT Cttee did not find that the removal breached art 3.
271 Kinley, Beard and Thomson (n 161) 52.
272 Australian Government, OP-SC: National Interest Analysis [2005] ATNIA 15 (11 October 2005).

Australia has not ratified the OP to CRC on a communications procedure (OP-CRC-CP), despite the urgings of civil society during a public consultation period in 2012.[273] That consultation took place late in the term of the Rudd-Gillard ALP government (2007–2013). It seems likely that Australia's contemporaneous asylum and border policies, under which many children were being detained onshore and offshore, may have discouraged ratification at that time. As noted, conservative governments, which were in power from 2013 to 2022, have never initiated the authorisation of or consented to any of the communications procedures.

CRC has been partially incorporated into Australian domestic law. Implementation of CRC is mentioned specifically in section 60B(4) of the Family Law Act 1975 (Cth) (Family Law Act) as an 'additional object' of Part VII, relating to parenting orders.[274] Australian legislation relating to children also frequently includes provisions on the best interests of the child. For example, CRC is reflected in Part VII, Division 1, Subdivision BA of the Family Law Act, which provides that the 'best interests of the child' are to be a 'paramount consideration' in making parenting (custody) orders. The best interests of the child is also a key principle in child protection legislation in every jurisdiction in Australia.[275] The application of this principle, however, varies widely depending on the jurisdiction.[276]

Section 60B of the Family Law Act was amended in 1995 to reflect CRC and, since 1999, there has been significant work on trafficking in persons, including children, partly in recognition of the OP-CRC-SC.[277] However, there has never been a national compatibility study or programme of domestic legal reform to give effect to the treaty. Although some national initiatives directly or indirectly rely on CRC, they predominantly focus on either specific groups of children or specific themes, notably child abuse.

---

[273] See, eg, Castan Centre for Human Rights Law, Submission in Favour of Australia Signing and Ratifying the Third Optional Protocol to the Convention on the Rights of the Child (April 2012) <https://www.monash.edu/__data/assets/pdf_file/0004/138451/rights-of-the-child-sub.pdf> accessed 18 March 2022.

[274] See Australian Institute of Family Studies, Australian Child Protection Legislation <https://aifs.gov.au/cfca/publications/australian-child-protection-legislation> accessed 18 March 2022.

[275] ibid.

[276] Australian Human Rights Commission, Submission to the Committee on the Rights of the Child (1 November 2018) para 25.

[277] See Australian Government, OP-SC: National Interest Analysis [2005] ATNIA 15 (11 October 2005).

CRC became a 'declared instrument' under section 47 of the Australian Human Rights Commission Act 1986 (Cth) on 22 October 1992, with the result that the AHRC is able to hear complaints with regard to alleged abuses under the treaty.

On 25 February 2013 the government appointed the first National Children's Commissioner (NCC) at the AHRC. The Commissioner monitors the implementation of CRC and tables an annual report in the Australian Parliament on the enjoyment and exercise of human rights by children in Australia. The Commissioner also consults with children and conducts inquiries and leads projects on children's rights.

Each state or territory has a Children's Commissioner, Guardian or Ombudsman that holds independent monitoring powers for children in that jurisdiction. These powers vary and range from child protection to out-of-home care and complaints. In 2013 Victoria appointed a specific Commissioner for Aboriginal Children and Young People.

5.6.2 Policies and Initiatives of Relevance to CRC

The Australian government established two Royal Commissions between 2013 and 2016 that focused specifically on children: the Royal Commission into Institutional Responses to Child Sex Abuse and the Royal Commission into the Protection and Detention of Children in the Northern Territory.[278] Their terms of reference indirectly relied on CRC by referring to Australia's human rights obligations. Both Royal Commissions explicitly referenced CRC in their final reports, as well as in their recommendations. For example, the Royal Commission into Institutional Responses to Child Sexual Abuse released its final report in December 2017 and made 409 recommendations, including that 'all institutions should act with the best interests of the child as a primary consideration' consistent with article 3 of CRC.[279]

The Royal Commission into the Protection and Detention of Children in the Northern Territory made certain findings that the conduct of youth justice officers was inconsistent with article 37(c) of CRC.[280]

---

[278] See the Royal Commission into Institutional Responses to Child Sex Abuse <https://www.childabuseroyalcommission.gov.au/> accessed 18 March 2022; and the Royal Commission into the Protection and Detention of Children in the Northern Territory <https://www.royalcommission.gov.au/royal-commission-detention-and-protection-children-northern-territory> accessed 18 March 2022.

[279] Royal Commission into Institutional Responses to Child Sex Abuse, Final Report Recommendations, Recommendation 6.4.

[280] The Royal Commission into the Protection and Detention of Children in the Northern Territory, Vol 2A 164–66.

In 2017 the government requested that the NCC lead the development of the National Principles for Child Safe Organisations. These principles are based on the ten child-safe standards that were recommended by the Royal Commission into Institutional Responses to Child Sexual Abuse.[281] CRC underpinned the development of the child-safe standards as the Royal Commission's position was that 'by fulfilling children's rights, we believe institutions will create a positive, child safe environment that better protects children from harm'.[282] The principles are 'grounded in a child rights approach, which recognises children and young people as active participants',[283] and each of the principles includes an explicit reference to the relevant article of CRC. The scope of the National Principles extends beyond sexual abuse to other forms of harm.[284] All members of the Council of Australian governments, which includes the Prime Minister and state and territory First Ministers, have endorsed the National Principles.

5.6.3 Use by Courts

When considering Part VII of the Family Law Act, the Full Court of the Family Court of Australia has frequently considered the operation of CRC. For example, in *Re: Jamie*, the Court considered the operation of section 67ZC of the Family Law Act (orders relating to welfare of children) in the context of determining whether a child was competent to consent to the stage two treatment for gender dysphoria. The Court directly relied on CRC to interpret the provision and determine that the child was competent.[285] The Full Court of the Family Court has noted in other cases that the intent of section 67ZC was to extend protection to children in a manner consistent with CRC, in particular articles 19 and 3(2).[286] The Court has also noted that other sections of the Family Law Act that relate to children, such as section 43, should be interpreted in light of

---

281 Royal Commission into Institutional Responses to Child Sexual Abuse, Final Report: Volume 6, Making Institutions Child Safe 13 and Recommendations 6.5 and 6.6.
282 ibid 35.
283 Australian Human Rights Commission, Media Release 'COAG endorses National Principles for Child Safe Organisations' (19 February 2019) <https://www.humanrights.gov.au/about/news/coag-endorses-national-principles-child-safe-organisations> accessed 18 March 2022.
284 ibid.
285 *Re: Jamie* [2013] FamCAFC 110, paras 120–134.
286 *B & B & Minister for Immigration & Multicultural & Indigenous Affairs* [2003] FamCAFC 451 paras 293–288.

CRC.[287] However, the Court emphasised that it was applying the Family Law Act rather than CRC itself.[288]

The Federal Court of Australia has considered CRC in several cases regarding the interpretation of 'the best interests of the child' in the context of a decision to grant or cancel a visa, as well as in applications for Australian citizenship.[289] In these cases, the Court has tended to find that a decision should have considered the best interests of the child as set out in CRC when the relevant provisions referenced the phrase 'best interests of the child', even when there was no express reference to CRC in the provisions.[290]

5.6.4 State Reporting and Its Impact

Australia has submitted six reports since 1996. The average delay has been 30 months. Since 1999 Australia has appeared before the CRC Cttee in 2005, 2012 and 2019. In 2018 the government provided funding to the National Children and Youth Law Centre to support the preparation of a shadow report by an NGO coalition to the CRC Cttee.[291]

The CRC Cttee's COs on Australia focus on areas such as the reservation to article 37(c) of CRC; data collection; budgetary allocations for the realisation of children's rights, the preservation of identity for indigenous children; corporal punishment; child abuse and violence against children; children with disabilities; children in immigration detention facilities; children placed in out-of-home care; and the administration of juvenile justice, in particular the disproportionately high percentage of indigenous children in the juvenile justice system.[292]

---

287 *Re: B and B: Family Law Reform Act 1995* [1997] FamCAFC 33 paras 10.9–10.21.
288 *Ralton & Ralton* [2017] FamCAFC 182 para 18.
289 *Kaur v Minister for Immigration and Border Protection* [2017] FCAFC 184; *Paerau v Minister for Immigration and Border Protection* [2014] FCAFC 28; *Le v Minister for Immigration and Multicultural and Indigenous Affairs* [2004] FCA 875; and *G v Minister for Immigration and Border Protection* [2018] FCA 1229.
290 *Kaur v Minister for Immigration and Border Protection* [2017] FCAFC 184 paras 11–26; *Le v Minister for Immigration and Multicultural and Indigenous Affairs* [2004] FCA 875 para 59; *Paerau v Minister for Immigration and Border Protection* [2014] FCAFC 28 para 103; and *G v Minister for Immigration and Border Protection* [2018] FCA 1229, paras 217–219, 226–230.
291 See National Children's and Youth Law Centre, 'The End Child Marriage Australia: Research Report on the Forced Marriage of Children in Australia' <https://yla.org.au/wp-content/uploads/2019/01/End-Child-Marriage-NCYLC-Research-Report.pdf> accessed 18 March 2022; and National Children's and Youth Law Centre, 'What's Up Croc?' Australia's implementation of the Convention on the Rights of the Child' <https://yla.org.au/wp-content/uploads/2019/04/Whats-up-croc.pdf> accessed 18 March 2022.
292 CRC Cttee, COs on Australia CRC/C/AUS/CO/5–6 (1 November 2019) paras 47–48. See also CRC Cttee, COs on Australia UN DOC CRC/C/AUS/CO/4 (28 August 2012); and CRC Cttee, UN DOC CRC/C/15/Add.268 (20 October 2005).

In 2014 the NCC, together with UNICEF Australia and Plan International Australia, developed a child-friendly version of the 2012 COs. There are two versions of the publication: one for younger children and one for older children and young people.[293]

The CRC Cttee has no official follow-up procedure. Follow-up and the implementation of COs, therefore, are assessed through the subsequent state party reports. In its 2005 and 2012 COs the Committee noted that Australia had made efforts to implement its previous COs, such as through the passage of the Family Law Legislation Amendment (Family Violence and Other Measures) Act 2011 (Cth).[294] The Committee also welcomed legislation to establish a NCC but noted that Australia should provide the NCC with adequate immunities and resources for it to effectively function.[295] More negatively, the CRC Cttee reflected that some of its concerns and recommendations had not been sufficiently addressed.

5.6.5 Treaty Body Membership

Australia has never had a member of the CRC Cttee.

5.6.6 Brief Conclusion

The most consequential developments regarding the implementation of CRC since 1999 in Australia have been the creation of the office of the NCC within the AHRC, and the convening of two Royal Commissions focused on the protection and rights of children in the contexts of institutional abuse and juvenile detention. CRC also forms the basis of certain statutory concepts, particularly in family law, and thus is utilised in those limited instances by decision makers, including courts.

5.7 *Convention on the Rights of Persons with Disabilities*

Australia signed CRPD on 30 March 2007 and ratified it on 17 July 2008, reflecting a strong rhetorical commitment to improving the rights of people with disabilities in Australia. CRPD entered into force for Australia on 16 August 2008.

---

293 Australian Human Rights Commission, 'Child Friendly Version of the United Nations Committee on the Rights of the Child's COs' <https://www.humanrights.gov.au/our-work/childrens-rights/projects/child-friendly-version-united-nations-committee-rights-childs> accessed 18 March 2022. The youth-friendly version is available at <https://www.humanrights.gov.au/our-work/childrens-rights/publications/making-australia-more-child-friendly> accessed 18 March 2022.
294 CRC Cttee, COs on Australia UN DOC CRC/C/AUS/CO/4 (28 August 2012) para 14.
295 See CRC Cttee, COs on Australia UN DOC CRC/C/15/Add.268 (20 October 2005) paras 15–16; and CRC Cttee, COs on Australia UN DOC CRC/C/AUS/CO/4 (28 August 2012) paras 17–18.

Australia has made three interpretive declarations regarding CRPD.[296] Regarding article 12, it states its understanding that CRPD allows for substituted or supported decision-making arrangements. Regarding article 17, Australia declared its understanding that CRPD allows for compulsory assistance or treatment, as a last resort subject to safeguards. Regarding article 18, Australia states its understanding that CRPD does not grant a right for non-nationals to enter and remain in the country, nor does it impact on Australia's ability to impose 'health requirements' on non-nationals. The CRPD Cttee, along with Australian civil society, has recommended that Australia review these interpretative declarations with a view to withdrawing them.[297]

Australia acceded to OP-CRPD on 21 August 2009, and it entered into force for Australia on 20 September 2009. It has not opted out of the inquiry procedure in article 8 of the OP.

CRPD is partially incorporated into domestic law. The Disability Discrimination Act 1992 (Cth) (DDA) is the principal piece of Commonwealth legislation regarding the rights of persons with disabilities. Amendments made to the DDA in 2009,[298] in part, were a response to Australia's ratification of CRPD.[299] The CRPD Cttee has since suggested that the scope of protected rights and grounds of discrimination in the DDA is narrower than the CRPD.[300] Its former Chairperson, Ron McCallum, believes that 'much more should be done' to align the DDA with CRPD.[301]

On 20 April 2009 the Attorney-General declared CRPD a 'relevant international instrument' for the purposes of the Australian Human Rights

---

296 See Australian Government, Initial Reports Submitted by States Parties Under Article 35 of the CRPD UN Doc CRPD/C/AUS/1 (7 June 2012) paras 9, 10, 55 and 107; and Australian Government, Combined Second and Third Periodic Reports Submitted by Australia Under Article 35 of the CRPD, due in 2018 UN Doc CRPD/C/AUS/2–3 (7 September 2018) para 15.

297 See CRPD Cttee, COs on Australia UN Doc CRPD/C/AUS/CO/1 (21 October 2010) [9]. See AHRC, Information Concerning Australia's Compliance with the Convention on the Rights of Persons with Disabilities UN Doc INT/CRPD/NHS/AUS/35594/E (25 July 2019) para 10; Disability Rights Now, Information from Civil Society Organisations for List of Issues Prior to Reporting UN Doc INT/CRPD/NGO/AUS/15451/E (August 2012).

298 Disability Discrimination and Other Human Rights Legislation Amendment Act 2009 (Cth) <https://www.legislation.gov.au/Details/C2009A00070> accessed 18 March 2022.

299 For example, s 12 of the DDA, which sets out the application of the Act, was amended to include an explicit reference to the CRPD.

300 CRPD Cttee, COs on the Initial Report of Australia UN Doc CRPD/C/AUS/CO/1 (21 October 2013) para 14.

301 Ron McCallum, interview (n 44).

Commission Act 1986 (Cth).[302] Hence, certain functions of the AHRC were extended to include the rights under CRPD. The Disability Discrimination Commissioner (DDC) within the AHRC has a special role in promoting and monitoring the implementation of the DDA and CRPD. The AHRC and the DDC are nominated by Australia as the relevant domestic monitoring process for the purposes of article 33 of CRPD.[303]

CRPD is directly cited in section 3 of the National Disability Insurance Scheme Act 2013 (Cth) (NDIS Act), which states that one of the objects of the Act, in conjunction with other laws, is to give effect to Australia's obligations under CRPD.[304]

5.7.1 Policies and Initiatives of Relevance to CRPD

The National Disability Strategy 2010–2020 (NDS) is the primary framework to give effect to CRPD in Australia. All state and territory governments are signatories to the NDS. The NDS states that it adopts the principles in article 3 of CRPD and that its six policy areas are aligned to articles of CRPD, including priority area 2: 'Rights protection, justice and legislation'.[305] Although the NDS has developed significant reforms, civil society and academic research have raised concerns around the implementation, monitoring and evaluation of the strategy.[306]

In 2013 the federal government established the National Disability Insurance Scheme (NDIS), which provides individuals with a permanent and significant disability with direct funding to access the supports and services they need in order to live independently and participate in the community. When it is fully rolled out by 2019–2020, the NDIS will provide insurance for about 460 000 Australians aged under 65.[307] Civil society, persons with disabilities and their

---

[302] Convention on the Rights of Persons with Disabilities Declaration 2009 <https://www.legislation.gov.au/Details/F2009L02620> accessed 18 March 2022.
[303] Australia's 2nd-3rd reports to CRC, UN Doc CRPD/C/AUS/2-3 (5 February 2019) paras 345–348.
[304] National Disability Insurance Scheme Act 2013 (Cth) s 3(1)(a).
[305] National Disability Strategy 2010–2020: An Initiative of the Council of Australian Governments 17, 22 <https://www.dss.gov.au/sites/default/files/documents/05_2012/national_disability_strategy_2010_2020.pdf> accessed 18 March 2022.
[306] University of New South Wales, Social Policy Research Centre, 'Review of Implementation of the National Disability Strategy 2010–2020: Final Report' (August 2018) <http://doi.org/10.26190/5c7494b61edc4> accessed 18 March 2022. See also AHRC, Information Concerning Australia's Compliance with the Convention on the Rights of Persons with Disabilities UN Doc INT/CRPD/NHS/AUS/35594/E (25 July 2019) paras 24–28.
[307] At the age of 65, people can choose to move into the aged care system, or stay in the NDIS system.

representative organisations have called for stronger engagement with persons with disabilities and their representative organisations in the implementation of the NDIS.[308] Concerns have also been raised that some groups of persons with disabilities, such as indigenous people and people from culturally and linguistically diverse backgrounds, may not have equal access to the NDIS.[309]

On 23 July 2013 the ALRC received terms of reference to undertake an inquiry into laws and legal frameworks within the Commonwealth jurisdiction that deny or diminish the equal recognition of persons with disabilities as persons before the law and their ability to exercise legal capacity. CRPD was explicitly referred to in the inquiry's terms of reference. The final report was tabled in the Australian Parliament on 24 November 2014.[310] There has been no official government response to this report.[311]

On 5 April 2019, the Australian government announced the establishment of the Royal Commission into Violence, Abuse, Neglect and Exploitation of People with Disability. The terms of reference for this Royal Commission contain an explicit reference to CRPD and recognise the human rights of persons with disabilities under CRPD.

5.7.2 Use by Courts

The Administrative Appeals Tribunal (AAT) has directly referred to articles of CRPD to interpret sections of the NDIS Act,[312] as well as to determine the meaning of 'reasonable and necessary supports', which is not defined under the Act. However, in *Pavilupillai and National Disability Insurance Agency* [2018] AATA 4641, the Tribunal declined to read into section 34(1)(b) of the NDIS Act the general principles of article 3 of CRPD, due to its adherence to traditional principles of statutory construction.[313]

---

308   See People with Disability Australia, 'NDIS Campaign' <https://pwd.org.au/our-work/ndis/> accessed 18 March 2022; and AHRC, Information Concerning Australia's Compliance with the Convention on the Rights of Persons with Disabilities UN Doc INT/CRPD/NHS/AUS/35594/E (25 July 2019) paras 11 and 32.
309   AHRC (n 308) paras 24–28.
310   ALRC, 'Equality, Capacity and Disability in Commonwealth Laws' (August 2014) <https://www.alrc.gov.au/wp-content/uploads/2019/08/alrc_124_whole_pdf_file.pdf> accessed 18 March 2022.
311   Disability Rights Now, 2019 Australian Civil Society Shadow Report to the United Nations Committee on the Rights of Persons with Disabilities: UN CRPD Review 2019 UN Doc INT/CRPD/CSS/AUS/35639/E 23.
312   *PNFK and National Disability Insurance Agency* [2018] AATA 692, paras 19–22 and 105.
313   *Pavilupillai and National Disability Insurance Agency* [2018] AATA 4641, paras 68–69.

The Federal Court of Australia has relied on CRPD by virtue of section 3 of the NDIS Act in relation to appeals from the AAT on the NDIS.[314] That Court has also relied on the definition of 'reasonable accommodation' in article 2 of CRPD to determine the meaning of 'reasonable adjustments' in section 5(2)(a) of the DDA, as 'adjustment' is not defined in the Act.[315]

The Supreme Court of Victoria has relied on CRPD when interpreting Victoria's Human Rights Charter. The Court has noted that the Charter and CRPD both reflect the paradigm shift whereby persons with a disability are treated not 'as objects of social protection [but] as subjects with rights'.[316] For example, in *PBU & NJE v Mental Health Tribunal* and *Nicholson v Knaggs*, the Court considered article 12 of CRPD in detail, the General Comment thereon, and the *travaux préparatoires*, to support a wide construction of the concept of 'legal capacity'.[317]

In contrast, as explained below, the High Court failed to even cite CRPD in a case about discrimination against deaf people with regard to service on juries, despite relevant CRPD jurisprudence.[318]

5.7.3 State Reporting and Its Impact

Australia submitted its first report to the CRPD Cttee in December 2010, and its combined second and third report was submitted on 7 September 2018. On average, Australia has been three months late in submitting its reports. Australia appeared before the CRPD Cttee in 2013 and 2019. Ron McCallum believes that the government was disappointed in its first review. It expected more praise for the NDIS, rather than criticism over its shortcomings.[319]

COs on Australia focus on topics such as the need to strengthen anti-discrimination laws to address intersectional discrimination; the continuing regime of substitute decision making; the use of prisons for the management of unconvicted persons with disabilities; the sterilisation of boys and girls with disabilities; violence, exploitation and abuse experienced by women and girls with disabilities; the failure to provide all information in accessible formats; segregated education; significant barriers in the voting process; and the lack

---

314   See, eg, *Mulligan v National Disability Insurance Agency* [2015] FCA 544.
315   See, eg, *Tropoulos v Journey Lawyers Pty Ltd* [2019] FCA 436 paras 147–148; *Watts v Australian Postal Corporation* [2014] FCA 370 paras 18–21 and 54; and *Munday v Commonwealth of Australia (No 2)* [2014] FCA 1123.
316   *Nicholson v Knaggs* [2009] VSC 64 para 13. See also *PJB v Melbourne Health & Another (Patrick* case) [2011] VSC 327 paras 130 and 333.
317   *PBU & NJE v Mental Health Tribunal* [2018] VSC 564; *Nicholson v Knaggs* [2009] VSC 64.
318   *Lyons v Queensland* [2016] HCA 38.
319   Ron McCallum, interview (n 44).

of nationally consistent measures for data collection and public reporting of disaggregated data across the full range of obligations under CRPD.

The CRPD Cttee's COs are published on the AGD website via a link to the OHCHR website.[320] However, that website lacks important accessibility features for persons with a disability.[321]

The CRPD Committee has not requested that Australia provide additional information through a follow-up procedure. The AHRC and the NGO shadow report for the 2019 session acknowledged positive reforms since 2013, in particular aspects of the NDIS and the establishment of the Royal Commission.[322] However, many of the key recommendations from the 2013 COs have not been implemented. For example, there is no uniform national legislation to prohibit the sterilisation of persons with disability in the absence of their free, prior and informed consent.[323]

5.7.4 Individual Communications

Up to 30 June 2019 the CRPD Cttee had finalised ten individual communications since the Optional Protocol entered into force for Australia in 2009. Of those, two were discontinued as subsequent developments rendered the complaints moot, one was inadmissible, and seven resulted in a finding of a violation. Three of the latter communications concerned the refusal to accommodate the author's disability so that they could perform jury duty.[324] Three more concerned the indefinite detention of cognitively-impaired men who

---

[320] Australian Government Attorney-General's Department, 'Treaty Body Reporting' <https://www.ag.gov.au/rights-and-protections/human-rights-and-anti-discrimination/united-nations-human-rights-reporting/treaty-body-reporting> accessed 4 September 2023.

[321] Ron McCallum felt that they should be distributed in, for example, braille; interview (n 44).

[322] Disability Rights Now, 2019 Australian Civil Society Shadow Report to the United Nations Committee on the Rights of Persons with Disabilities: UN CRPD Review 2019 UN Doc INT/CRPD/CSS/AUS/35639/E 10; and AHRC, Information Concerning Australia's Compliance with the Convention on the Rights of Persons with Disabilities UN Doc INT/CRPD/NHS/AUS/35594/E (25 July 2019) paras 25 and 28.

[323] CRPD Cttee, COs on the Initial Report of Australia UN Doc CRPD/C/AUS/CO/1 (21 October 2013) paras 39–40; Disability Rights Now, 2019 Australian Civil Society Shadow Report to the United Nations Committee on the Rights of Persons with Disabilities: UN CRPD Review 2019 UN Doc INT/CRPD/CSS/AUS/35639/E 10; and AHRC, Information Concerning Australia's Compliance with the Convention on the Rights of Persons with Disabilities UN Doc INT/CRPD/NHS/AUS/35594/E (25 July 2019) para 6 and s 4.12.

[324] See, eg, *Lockrey v Australia* UN Doc CRPD/C/15/D/13/2013 (30 May 2016).

were found unfit to plead to criminal charges.[325] The final case concerned the right to vote by secret ballot.[326]

In all of its responses to CRPD on findings of violations, the government has disagreed with the findings. In some instances, the government nonetheless expressed an intention to provide some support to the complainant, and noted that it would be grateful for the Committee's guidance on necessary and effective support measures.[327]

In *Lyons v Queensland* the High Court of Australia dismissed a complaint of discrimination under Queensland law by a deaf woman who had been excluded from a potential jury pool.[328] In dismissing her claim, the High Court failed to acknowledge the CRPD decisions against Australia on that exact issue.

The CRPD Cttee's follow-up reports to the complaints procedure, issued since 2013, do not contain a report on any of the communications against Australia.

5.7.5   Treaty Body Membership

Professor Ron McCallum AO was elected as an Australian member of the CRPD Cttee from 2008 to 2014 and held the position of Chairperson of the Committee from 2010 to 2012, and Vice-Chairperson from 2013 to 2014. In 2011 and 2012 he chaired the meetings of all of the treaty body chairs. Rosemary Kayess was elected as a member of the CRPD Cttee in 2018. She was swiftly appointed to Vice-Chairperson in 2019, before being elevated to Chairperson in 2021.

5.7.6   Brief Conclusion

CRPD has been impactful in Australia with regard to amendments to the preexisting DDA, as well as the development and implementation of the National Disability Strategy, including the NDIS. The government's response to CRPD's assessments of the NDIS will be instructive of its overall approach to treaty body engagement. So far, the communications procedure has had a minimal impact, despite there being a reasonably large number of communications in

---

325   *Noble v Australia* UN Doc CRPD/C/16/D/7/2012 (2 September 2016); *Doolan v Australia* UN Doc CRPD/C/22/D/18/2013 (17 October 2019); *Leo v Australia* UN Doc CRPD/C/22/D/17/2013 (18 October 2019).
326   *Given v Australia* UN Doc CRPD/C/19/D/19/2014 (16 February 2018).
327   See, eg, Response of the Australian Government to the Views of the Committee on the Rights of Persons with Disabilities in Communication 7/2012 (*Noble v Australia*) paras 59–64.
328   *Lyons v Queensland* [2016] HCA 38.

a short period of time. The number of cases probably reflects a reasonably high awareness of CRPD among NGOs focused on disability rights.

6 Conclusion

Since 1999 Australia has become a party to CRPD, and Optional Protocols to CRC, CEDAW and CAT. The UN core treaties to which Australia is a party have influenced Australian law. CERD, CEDAW and, since 1999, the OP2-CCPR and CAT have been largely incorporated into Australian law. In descending order, partial incorporation has taken place regarding CRPD, CRC and CCPR, with CESCR lacking translation into domestic laws. An exception arises regarding CCPR in Victoria, Queensland and the ACT and, to a much lesser extent, CESCR in the latter two jurisdictions. All of the sub-national human rights statutes have been adopted since 1999. Important policies adopted since 1999, particularly in the areas of disability rights, children's rights and, possibly, violence against women,[329] have been influenced by Australia's treaty obligations.

Furthermore, the adoption of the Human Rights (Parliamentary Scrutiny) Act 2011 (Cth) ensures that human rights are considered in the policy-making process and by the members of a joint parliamentary committee. However, it has not noticeably led to greater human rights compliance in legislation.

While the treaties themselves have had an influence, Australia's interactions with the UN treaty bodies on the whole are disappointing. While it complies procedurally by submitting reports, and submitting information on communications and urgent actions, its implementation of COs and Committee views is minimal, with some standout exceptions such as the 2008 COs from the CAT Cttee. Australia is developing a reputation as a 'recalcitrant state', according to Senator Nick McKim of the Australian Greens party.[330]

Australia's relationship with the treaty bodies has deteriorated since the first volume of this book. The nadir in the relationship between Australia and the treaty bodies, which roughly lasted from 1999 to 2007, has passed. However, it is perhaps true that Australia's commitment to the treaty body processes has never fully recovered.[331]

Interactions and impact might improve with reforms to the treaty body processes. As noted above, Australian governments, including its public service,

---

329 The extent to which these policies have been influenced by CEDAW and the other treaties is uncertain.
330 Nick McKim, interview (n 77).
331 Simon Rice believed so at the interview (n 28).

have been unimpressed on occasion by the limitations in the treaty body processes. Australia has also participated in and supported UN initiatives aimed at strengthening the UN treaty body system. As commented by Sarah McCosker, such initiatives reflect a widespread recognition among both the UN treaty bodies themselves, and many UN member states, including Australia, that 'if [the treaty body processes] could be more effective, then they'd have greater impact'.[332]

While the former AGD officer felt that Australian governments see value in being a 'good international citizen, domestic political considerations will "always win the day"'.[333] Currently, Australia's human rights obligations do not figure within those considerations for many reasons, including apathy and even scepticism from the public and the media. As explained by the ALP Shadow Minister, polling has indicated that Australians generally care less about 'international perceptions and international affairs when they are asked than was the case 20 or 30 years ago'.[334] In that case, governments too are going to take less account of the statements of international bodies.[335]

The most likely catalyst for an improvement in Australia's record of treaty implementation is a significant intensification of domestic political pressure, including from the media. Such an increase in pressure seems unlikely at present, especially in an international environment of rising nationalism where skepticism over multilateral initiatives is growing rather than receding.[336]

---

[332] Sarah McCosker, interview (n 46).
[333] Former AGD officer, interview (n 47).
[334] Shadow Minister, interview (n 33).
[335] The Shadow Minister added, however, that they cannot take 'no account', interview (n 33).
[336] Also see Nick McKim, interview (n 77), Ben Schokman, interview (n 66).

CHAPTER 2

The Impact of the United Nations Human Rights Treaties on the Domestic Level in Brazil

Thiago Amparo, Odara Andrade, Júlia Piazza and Deborah Bittar

1   Introduction to Human Rights in Brazil

Brazil is a federal democratic republic. It has been independent of Portugal since 1822, although it became a republic only in 1889. The nineteenth century was marked by a constant power struggle and the search for a Brazilian identity. During this period, the 1824 Constitution protected some political and civil rights, although power was concentrated in the hands of the Emperor. In the 1891 Constitution, non-universal suffrage was granted, along with the inclusion of the principles of liberty, equality and justice.

The 1934 Constitution continued to protect some individual rights, but when the Getúlio Vargas government took over, many obstacles to the advancement of human rights appeared, along with the 1937 Constitution, influenced by fascist ideals. On the one hand, populism offered workers many advantages and, on the other, the Special Police and the Image and Advertising Department were part of a structure designed to remove fundamental guarantees. This context was changed in 1946, when the *Estado Novo* period came to an end and the new Constitution restored and expanded individual rights. This scenario of improvement ended soon thereafter, in 1964, when the military dictatorship began, marked by a 21-year period of torture, kidnapping, murders and forced disappearances.

In 1988 the Brazilian Federal Constitution ('citizen Constitution') (FC) entered into force, guaranteeing a wide range of civil, political, economic, social and cultural rights. In 2005 Constitutional Amendment 45 was passed, giving international human rights treaties that have been approved in two rounds by three-fifths of the members of each House of Congress the status of constitutional amendments. In its election for the UN Human Rights Council (HRC) in 2016, the Permanent Representative of Brazil to the United Nations (UN) presented a series of pledges for improving human rights.[1]

---

[1] Letter dated 22 March 2016 from the Permanent Representative of Brazil to the United Nations addressed to the President of the General Assembly <https://digitallibrary.un.org/record/826631> accessed 8 September 2023.

Despite the comprehensive legal framework for the protection of human rights in the country, serious political instability and, more recently, serious setbacks in human rights are being faced. Brazil has a long history of rights violations in a wide range of areas, such as socio-economic inequalities; prison conditions and police violence; discrimination against women; migrants; violations of the rights of persons with disabilities and lesbian, gay, bisexual and transgender (LGBT) persons; a lack of protection of human rights defenders and journalists; and growing concerns over environmental issues and the rights of indigenous peoples.[2]

According to the Brazilian Public Security Forum in 2022, 6,429 people died due to police interventions;[3] 3.2 out of 100 violent deaths are caused by the police, totalling a number of 17 deaths per day.[4] The majority of victims are young black men. The latest statistics also revealed a large amount of sexual abuse: 5.5 girls (aged 13 years or younger) are raped every hour. In 2022, Brazil recorded the highest number of cases of sexual violence in history. There are 109 rape cases per day and incidents of domestic violence are registered every hour. The aggressors are mostly family members and the majority of sexual violence incidents occur in the victim's house.[5] On account of these statistics, Global Witness reports as follows: 'We recorded 24 murders of land and environment defenders in Brazil in 2019, the third-highest number in the world. Almost 90% of these deaths were in the Amazon.'[6] This shows how dangerous it is to live in Brazil if you are not a white man.

Brazil is a federation composed of 26 federal states and the Federal District, which is the seat of the federal government. Each state has its own

---

[2] United Nations, Letter dated 22 March 2016 from the Permanent Representative of Brazil to the United Nations addressed to the President of the General Assembly <https://digitallibrary.un.org/record/826631> accessed 8 September 2023.

[3] FBSP – FÓRUM BRASILEIRO DE SEGURANÇA PÚBLICA. Anuário Brasileiro de Segurança Pública 2023, São Paulo: FBSP, 2023. <https://forumseguranca.org.br/wp-content/uploads/2023/07/anuario-2023.pdf> accessed 8 September 2023.

[4] FBSP – FÓRUM BRASILEIRO DE SEGURANÇA PÚBLICA. Anuário Brasileiro de Segurança Pública 2023. São Paulo: FBSP, 2023. <https://forumseguranca.org.br/wp-content/uploads/2023/07/anuario-2023.pdf> accessed 8 September 2023.

[5] FBSP - FORUM BRASILEIRO DE SEGURANÇA PÚBLICA. Anuário Brasileiro de Segurança Pública, 2023. São Paulo: FBSP, 2023. <https://forumseguranca.org.br/wp-content/uploads/2023/07/anuario-2023.pdf> accessed 8 September 2023.

[6] Global witness Annual Report 2018: Delivering Global Change <https://www.globalwitness.org/en/about-us/annual-report-2018-delivering-global-change/#chapter-0/section-0> accessed 18 April 2022.

constitution, congress, judiciary and executive powers. The Brazilian administration operates on three levels: federal, state and municipal. The municipality is a third-level state entity in the federative order, included by the 1988 Constitution, with its own powers and autonomous government, linked to the member state by indestructible constitutional ties.[7] There is no hierarchy between the levels. The FC clearly stipulates the boundaries of the federal, state and municipal levels. The three levels can legislate and tax what is within their competence established by the FC. With regard to human rights, the federal government is responsible for the national plan for social development (article 21 of FC). All levels are responsible for providing access to culture, education, science, technology, innovation and research, and have the responsibility to protect the environment and to fight against poverty (article 23 of FC).

The budgets for managing social programmes are determined by executive and legislative powers and approved by the judiciary, but this is now linked to the *Teto de Gastos* (spending margin). This notion establishes that by 2036 the budget for each year will be equivalent to the previous year's expenditure with corrections for inflation. The consequence is a battle between the judiciary, legislative and executive powers for budget distribution.

In Brazil the decentralisation of institutionalisation is the key for the maintenance of a minimum standard of human rights. In that way, municipal health agents are essential for the maintenance of Brazilian National Health System (*Sistema Único de Saúde* – SUS) health programmes, such as the dengue prevention policy. Municipal social workers are responsible for the guarantee and protection of children, adolescents and vulnerable groups in the state and the city; the Specialised Reference Centres of Social Assistance are public units of municipal or regional scope whose role it is to constitute a locus of reference, in the territories, of the offer of specialised social work to families and individuals in situations of personal or social risk, for violations of rights.

The actions of civil society are also examples of the strengths of articulation for human rights in Brazil, as they are present in the national territory, also in a decentralised manner and dealing with multiple themes. According to a survey by the Institute of Applied Economic Research (IPEA), there are 820 186 civil society organisations in Brazil, and the south-east region is home to 40 per cent of those organisations, followed by the north-east (25 per cent), the south

---

7 Municipalities have (a) power of self-organisation; (b) power of self-government (election of the mayor, vice-mayor and councillors); (c) own normative power or self-legislation; (d) power of self-administration (providing services of local interest, as well as legislating on taxes and their income).

(19 per cent), the mid-west (8 per cent) and the north (8 per cent).[8] In 2016 there were four organisations per 1 000 inhabitants in Brazil. Another interesting fact revealed by IPEA is that the per capita presence of human rights organisations aimed at defending rights is higher in regions with a lower human development index. The presence of religious civil society organisations is also high in the south-east (Rio de Janeiro being the state where they are mostly concentrated.)

2 Relationship of Brazil with the International Human Rights System in General

Brazil is party to the major UN and regional human rights treaties. However, the country only started to become party to important human rights treaties after the end of the military regime in 1985, despite the ratification of the International Convention on the Elimination of All Forms of Racial Discrimination (CERD) in 1968 and the Convention on the Elimination of All Forms of Discrimination Against Women (CEDAW) in 1984. According to Vilhena,[9] 'the whole movement to pressure the Brazilian government to adhere to these treaties and the contact with international human rights organisations that started to be active in the country at the end of the military period, inspired new organisations with a clearer human rights vision', such as *Comissão Teotônio Vilela* and *Justiça Global*.

Brazil is also a full member of the Inter-American system of human rights, having been found in violation of human rights by the Inter-American Court of Human Rights in twelve cases. Furthermore, Brazil has maintained a working relationship with the UN and the Inter-American systems. Since 2012 the UN maintains a 'UN House' in Brasília, gathering in one place official representations from several UN programmes. Additionally, since 2001 Brazil has offered a standing invitation to all UN thematic special procedures. Yet, key setbacks have been evident. In 2011 former President Dilma Rousseff criticised the Inter-American Commission on Human Rights after an unfavourable resolution protecting indigenous peoples against the construction of the Belo Monte Dam, threatening to cut Brazil's funds for the regional system. In August 2018 the then candidate and now former Brazilian President, Jair Bolsonaro, stated that he intended to withdraw Brazil from the HRC, of which Brazil was a member

---

8   Felix Garcia Lopes, 'Perfil das organizações da sociedade civil no Brasil' Brasília: IPEA, 2018 <https://repositorio.ipea.gov.br/bitstream/11058/8396/1/Perfil%20das%20organizações%20 da%20sociedade%20civil%20no%20Brasil.pdf> accessed 13 November 2023.
9   Oscar Vilhena Vieira, 'Public Interest Law: A Brazilian Perspective' (2008) UCLA Journal of International Law and Foreign Affairs 219.

three times, from 2006 to 2011, 2012 to 2015, and 2015 to 2019, on the grounds that the institution is 'of no use'. However, Brazil secured its seat at the HRC in 2019, for a fourth term, with 153 votes.[10]

The FC contains 14 articles concerning international relations and human rights.[11] The articles relating to international human right treaties bodies are the following: Brazil in its international relations follows human rights principles (article 4); the treaties and international conventions approved in each congress house, in two turns, by three-fifths of the members, have constitutional status equal in status to amendments to the Constitution (article 5, third paragraph); Brazil will advocate the formation of an international human rights court (article 7 of Transition Acts). Apart from the Rome Statute of the International Criminal Court (ICC) and the Convention on the Rights of Persons with Disabilities (CRPD), all other major human rights treaties were ratified before 2005 by ordinary procedure, which means that they have legal status below constitutional norms, but above ordinary legislation. It is what Brazil's Federal Supreme Court calls 'supra-legal status': 'International human rights treaties and conventions, once ratified and internalised, while directly establishing individual rights, hinders the legal effects of other infra-constitutional state acts which prevents their full implementation.'[12]

In the federal government, the main institutions in charge of maintaining a dialogue with the international human rights system are the Ministry of Foreign Affairs and the Ministry of Women, Family and Human Rights (before 2019, and again in 2023, this Ministry was named simply the Ministry of Human Rights).[13] In addition, Brazil has a National Council of Human Rights, with the participation of civil society organisations and state institutions. The National Council of Human Rights is the closest there is in Brazil to a national human rights institution. Yet, it lacks administrative and budgetary independence to be fully considered as such in light of the Paris Principles. In 2019 the National Council issued an open letter criticising the Ministry of Women, Family and Human Rights for firing the coordinator of the Council.[14]

---

10   Conectas, 'Brazil Wins Seat on UN Human Rights Council: Brazil's Election Does Not Give the Government Carte Blanche to Act However It Wishes on the Council' <https://www.conectas.org/en/noticias/brazil-wins-seat-on-un-human-rights-council/> accessed 18 April 2022.

11   See arts 4, 5, 21, 49, 59, 84, 102, 105, 109, 215, 226, 227, 230, 7 of Transition Acts of Brazilian Constitution. Version in English: <https://www2.senado.leg.br/bdsf/item/id/243334> accessed 18 April 2022.

12   Brazil's Federal Supreme Court Case ADI 5.240, 2016.

13   Brazil, Law 13.844/2019, arts 43, 44 and 57-III <http://www.planalto.gov.br/ccivil_03/_ato2019-2022/2019/lei/L13844compilado.htm> accessed 18 April 2022.

14   Conselho Nacional Dos Direitos Humanos, Nota pública em repúdio ao desrespeito à autonomia e independência do cndh, 2019 <https://www.gov.br/mdh/pt-br/acesso-a-informacao/participacao-social/conselho-nacional-de-direitos-humanos-cndh/2019.08.16NotaPblicaemRepdioaoDecreton9.9262019.pdf> accessed 18 April 2022.

IMPACT OF UNHR TREATIES ON DOMESTIC LEVEL IN BRAZIL

3 At a Glance: Formal Engagement of Brazil with UN Human Rights Treaty System

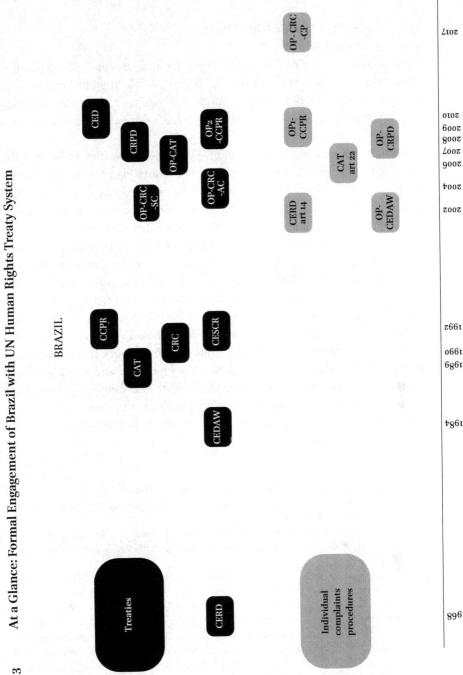

4 Role and Overall Impact of the UN Human Rights Treaties in Brazil

4.1 *Role of UN Human Rights Treaties*
4.1.1 Formal Acceptance

Brazil is party to all core UN human rights treaties, except the International Convention on the Protection of the Rights of All Migrant Workers and Members of Their Families (CMW). All ratifications were made after the military dictatorship (1964–1985), except CERD, ratified in 1968, and CEDAW, ratified in 1984.

Brazil is the only MERCOSUR country that has not ratified CMW. In 1996, Brazil acknowledged in its National Human Rights Plan the need for ratification, but this has not yet materialised.[15] Brazilian scholarship on the topic points to the difficulty of ratification because the treaty has not been harmonised with the outdated 1980 Foreigner's Law.[16] Yet, this Law was replaced in 2017 by the Immigrant Law, thus improving the prospect for ratification, despite resistance by former President Bolsonaro with regard to the rights of migrants. After years of processing, ILO Convention 143 and CMW have not yet been ratified as their provisions do not comply with the 1980 Foreigner's Law. It is expected that with the approval of the Migration Law this reality will be changed. The Migration Law was developed based on a more humanistic view of non-nationals, containing a principled framework that is consistent with the human rights treaties already ratified by Brazil and which expressly contemplates the guarantee of individual rights and freedoms to migrants, not only to regulars, but also to those in an irregular situation in the country, which, as has been seen, may contribute decisively to the ratification of the two analysed conventions.[17]

---

15 Brazil, Programa Nacional de Direitos Humanos – PNDH, 1996 <http://www.biblioteca.presidencia.gov.br/publicacoes-oficiais/catalogo/fhc/programa-nacional-de-direitos-humanos-1996.pdf> accessed 18 April 2022.

16 This Law was replaced in 2017 by the Immigrant Law (Law No. 13,445, of may 24, 2017 <http://www.planalto.gov.br/ccivil_03/_ato2015-2018/2017/lei/l13445.htm> accessed 18 April 2022).

17 Own translation from original text in Portuguese. Alverne; Oliveira; Matos, 'Trabalhador Migrante E A Dificuldade De Incorporação Da Convenção Da OIT E Da Convenção Da ONU Pelo Brasil: Possíveis Contribuições Da Lei De Migrações' (Migrant Worker and the Difficulty of Incorporation of the ILO Convention and the UN Convention for Brazil: Possible Contributions of the Migration Law) (2018) 4 Revista Jurídica Unicuritiba, n. 53, Curitiba, 2018 611-632 DOI: 10.6084/m9.figshare.7701596. <http://www.mpsp.mp.br/portal/page/portal/documentacao_e_divulgacao/doc_biblioteca/bibli_servicos_produtos/bibli_informativo/bibli_inf_2006/Rev-Juridica-UNICURITIBA_n.53.25.pdf> accessed 20 June 2020.

With the 1988 Constitution, human rights language was incorporated into the Brazilian legal system. Most of the treaties were ratified after the promulgation of the Constitution that re-established democracy in the country. Under Amendment 45, treaties adopted since 2005 potentially have constitutional status. Apart from the CRPD, Brazil ratified the other human rights treaties before 2005 by ordinary procedure, which means that they have, in the language of Brazil's Federal Supreme Court, a supra-legal status, that is, a status below the Constitution but above ordinary legislation.

Brazil entered reservations to articles 15(4), and articles 16(1)(a), (c), (g) and (h), and article 29 of CEDAW. The reservations to articles 15 and 16, withdrawn in 1994, were made due to the incompatibility between Brazilian legislation, which was then ruled by the asymmetry between the rights of men and women. The reservation to article 29, which does not refer to substantive rights, is related to disputes between state parties regarding the interpretation of the treaty and remains in force.[18]

4.1.2   Level of Awareness and Impact

The level of support for and commitment to human rights treaties by Brazilian civil society is high. An example of this is CMW, which since 2005 has been a recurring object of campaigns for ratification. A document entitled Charter of Immigrants on World Day Immigrant: Universal Citizenship and Human Rights was sent to the then and current President Luiz Inácio (Lula), and launched in 16 Brazilian cities on 17 December 2005.[19] Such engagement by civil society in 2017 culminated in the approval and enactment of the new immigration law that aims to protect immigrants in the Brazilian territory. Civil society engaged in international campaigns to account for crimes committed by the military regime, to advocate for the investigation into the disappearance of people, to defend the rights of persons with disabilities, and against practices of torture and police violence. There are countless civil associations and movements for the protection of human rights. Such associations also led to mobilisations for adherence to treaties at municipal and state levels, exemplified by the regional

---

18   Brazil, Observatory of Gender Impact. CEDAW, 2013 <https://www.gov.br/mdh/pt-br/navegue-por-temas/politicas-para-mulheres/arquivo/assuntos/acoes-internacionais/Articulacao/articulacao-internacional/onu-1/o%20que%20e%20CEDAW.pdf> accessed 8 September 2023.

19   Reporter Brasil, 'Brasil é único do Mercosul a não assinar convenção da ONU' Repórter Brasil, 2006 <https://reporterbrasil.org.br/2006/12/brasil-e-unico-do-mercosul-a-nao-assinar-convencao-da-onu/> accessed 13 July 2020.

committees created to promote adherence to CEDAW in municipalities and states.

Currently, civil society has articulated mobilisations against austerity policies and dismantling of socio-economic rights, such as the national campaigns against austerity measure 95 adopted in 2016, which froze social spending for 20 years (*Teto de gastos*).[20] Additionally, there are campaigns against declarations of former President Bolsonaro's intention no longer to accept the recommendations by the HRCttee after it ruled in favour of President Lula's petition, requesting Brazil to 'take all necessary measures to ensure that Lula can enjoy and exercise his political rights while in prison, as candidate in the 2018 presidential elections'.[21] Those mobilisations have so far been unsuccessful.

The impacts on judicial decisions are meaningful. Various treaties have different impacts on the Brazilian judiciary. While some have greater adherence (as in the case of CRPD), others are virtually forgotten (such as CAT, in relation to which society often resorts to the Inter-American Commission on Human Rights for protection). However, in 2019, when the federal judiciary reversed the government's decision to dismiss experts of the national mechanism against torture, the direct impact of CAT and OP-CAT was at full display.[22] Although the Brazilian judiciary often uses human rights language, it does not often directly cite human rights treaties.

Legislative power, in turn, in view of public pressure, is responsible for the creation of federal and state regulations that promote the implementation of UN human rights treaties in Brazil. Since 2005, Brazil has seen an increase in laws dealing with human rights. However, after 2016, some austerity measures have been preventing the realisation of socio-economic rights, due to the spending ceiling imposed by the Proposed Amendment to Constitution 95.

At the federal level, Brazil has adopted Law 7437 of 1985 which included as penal contraventions the practice of race, colour, sex and civil state discrimination; Law 7716 of 1989 which defined racial and discriminations crimes, which was amended by Law 12.288 of 2010[23] which established the Racial Equality

---

20 'Brazil's Austerity Package Decried by UN as Attack on Poor People' The Guardian, 2016 <https://www.theguardian.com/world/2016/dec/09/brazil-austerity-cuts-un-official> accessed 15 April 2020.
21 UN, Information Note on Human Rights Committee <https://www.ohchr.org/en/NewsEvents/Pages/DisplayNews.aspx?NewsID=23464> accessed 1 August 2020.
22 Agencia brasil, 'Justiça mantém peritos no combate à tortura' Agencia Brasil, 2019 <https://agenciabrasil.ebc.com.br/justica/noticia/2019-08/justica-mantem-peritos-no-combate-tortura> accessed 20 April 2020.
23 Brazil Law 12.288 of June 2010 <https://www.planalto.gov.br/ccivil_03/_ato2011-2014/2013/lei/l12830.htm> accessed 13 March 2020.

Statute; Law 9140 of 1995[24] which recognised the death of the people forcibly disappeared for political reasons during the dictatorship; Law 9474 of 1997[25] which defined mechanisms for the implementation of the refugee law; Law 9455 of 1997[26] which defined torture crimes; Law 12.847 of 2013[27] which instituted the National System for Preventing and Combating Torture and created the National Committee for the Prevention and Combating of Torture and the National Mechanism for the Prevention and Combat of Torture in line with the UN treaties. Additionally, several federal decrees deal with human rights standards, such as Decree 6044 of 2007 which approves the National Plan for the Protection of Human Rights Defenders; Decree 7037 of 2009,[28] which approves the National Plan for Human Rights; Decree 6872 of 2009,[29] which approved the National Plan for Racial Equality and created a Committee for monitoring the implementation of the Plan. This Committee was replaced in 2019 by Decree 10087[30] under President Bolsonaro's administration.

Another important point to note is that the Brazilian state has been creating special bodies to deal with human rights issues, such as national secretariats for the protection of women and the national secretariat for the protection of human rights of the Presidency of the Republic, and the creation of National Plans on Human Rights from 1996 to 2010. Three national human rights plans were carried out to incorporate UN resolutions for the protection of human rights in Brazil. The last plan assigned the Secretariat of State for Human Rights the responsibility for coordinating the implementation, monitoring and updating of the National Human Rights Programme.[31]

24   Brazil Law 9.140 of 1995 <https://www2.camara.leg.br/legin/fed/lei/1995/lei-9140-4-dezembro-1995-348760-normaatualizada-pl.html> accessed 13 March 2020.
25   Brazil Law 9.474 of 1997 <http://www.planalto.gov.br/ccivil_03/leis/L9474.htm> accessed 13 March 2020.
26   Brazil Law 9.455 of 1997 <http://www.planalto.gov.br/ccivil_03/leis/L9455.htm> accessed 13 March 2020.
27   Brazil Law 12.847 of 2013 <http://www.planalto.gov.br/ccivil_03/_Ato2011-2014/2013/Lei/L12847.htm> accessed 13 March 2020.
28   Brazil Decree 7.037 of 2009 <http://www.planalto.gov.br/ccivil_03/_ato2007-2010/2009/decreto/d7037.htm> accessed 13 March 2020.
29   Brazil Decree 6.872 of 2010 <http://www.planalto.gov.br/ccivil_03/_Ato2007-2010/2009/Decreto/D6872.htm> accessed 13 March 2020.
30   Brazil Decree 10.087 of 2019 <http://www.planalto.gov.br/ccivil_03/_Ato2019-2022/2019/Decreto/D10087.htm#art1> accessed 13 March 2020.
31   Brasil, Secretaria de Direitos Humanos da Presidência da República. B823 Programa Nacional de Direitos Humanos (PNDH-3) / Secretaria de Direitos Humanos da Presidência da República – rev. e atual. – Brasília: SDH/PR, 2010 <https://www.ohchr.org/Documents/Issues/NHRA/ProgrammaNacionalDireitosHumanos2010.pdf> accessed 20 June 2020.

However, during Jair Bolsonaro's government, some changes have been made in Brazilian government ministries. Law 13. 844/2019 transformed the Ministry of Human Rights into the Ministry of Women, Family and Human Rights (MMFDH), and attributed the administrative duties of the Amnesty Law to it.[32] The MMFHD is structured in eight final units: the National Secretariat for Global Protection (SNPG); the National Secretariat for the Rights of Persons with Disabilities (SNDPD); the National Secretariat for Policies for the Promotion of Racial Equality (SEPPIR); the National Secretariat for the Promotion and Defence of the Rights of the Elderly (SNDPI); the Secretariat National Child and Adolescent Rights (SNDCA); the National Secretariat for Policies for Women (SNPM); the National Youth Secretariat (SNJ); and the National Family Secretariat (SNF). One of the main changes is the withdrawal of the LGBT community from the Charter of Human Rights guidelines and the extinction of the secretariat for the community. As for the indigenous population, the Ministry of Agriculture is now responsible for the demarcation of land and no longer by the National Foundation of India (FUNAI). It is also important to highlight the extinction of the Ministry of Culture.

The budget of R $ 398 267 203 approved in the Annual Budget Law for 2019 – about R $ 21 million less than that committed in 2018 – is not sufficient for the protection of human rights in the territory, in view of the budgetary decrease.

As far as the level of awareness among civil society organisations is concerned, Brazil counts with strong non-governmental organisations (NGOs) constantly monitoring what is happening in Geneva at the UN, including Conectas Human Rights, Justiça Global, Plaforma DhESCA Brasil, and Sexuality Policy Watch. Yet, Conectas Human Rights, in an interview for this research, highlighted some challenges in working with the UN treaty bodies, such as a lack of predictability in the calendar of state reporting, unclear procedures regarding the submission of shadow reports (with the UN Special Procedures the communication is more fluid considering urgent appeals, for instance), language barriers for most of Brazilian NGOs, and the existence of the Inter-American system which is perceived as closer to NGOs in Brazil. Yet, Brazilian NGOs have been actively involved in the strengthening process of the UN treaty body mechanisms as well as voiced against budget cuts for those bodies. A handful of Brazilian journalists cover the UN treaty bodies constantly, in particular Jamil Chade, who lives in Geneva and reports to the main news portal in Brazil.[33]

---

32   Brazil, Law *13.844, 18 June 2019* <http://www.planalto.gov.br/ccivil_03/_Ato2019-2022/2019/Lei/L13844.htm> accessed 20 June 2020.

33   See for more <https://noticias.uol.com.br/colunas/jamil-chade/> accessed 20 June 2020.

4.1.3 State Reporting

Brazil lags behind in almost all state reporting. The longest delay was about 12 years, in respect of OP-CRC-SC. In an email interview with the Ministry of Foreign Affairs, Brazilian diplomats highlighted that on 25 February 2019, on the occasion of the High-Level Segment of the 40th session of the HRC, the Minister of Women, Family and Human Rights 'expressed her public commitment in submitting all Brazil's reports pending in treaty bodies during her administration'. In fact, a series of reports were subsequently submitted. Researchers have asked the Ministry how the reports due to the UN treaty bodies are prepared. According to the Ministry of Foreign Affairs, 'the preparation of reports submitted by the Brazilian state to treaty bodies of the international human rights system would be the responsibility of the Ministry of Women, Family and Human Rights', while it is up to the Division of Human Rights (DDH) of the Ministry of Foreign Affairs 'to accompany, coordinate and guide the preparation of Brazil's reports on compliance with the human rights treaties to which it is a party, as well as its respective oral defence', in accordance with the Ministry's Internal Regulations of the Secretariat of State for Foreign Relations (RISE).[34] As far as publication is concerned, Brazil publishes on the website of the Ministry of Human Rights and Citizenship the reports it has submitted to the UN treaty bodies in Portuguese.[35] The website of the Ministry often publishes drafts of human rights reports for consultation, in particular in relation to the Universal Periodic Review (UPR) mechanism. Finally, some NGOs have produced alternative reports for treaty bodies, such as the alternative report regarding social, economic and cultural rights prepared by a group of NGOs in 2007.[36]

---

[34] See for more <https://www.in.gov.br/en/web/dou/-/portaria-n-430-de-22-de-dezembro-de-2022-454144985> accessed 13 November 2023.

[35] Brasil, Ministério dos Direitos Humanos e da Cidadania. Relatórios Internacionais <https://www.gov.br/mdh/pt-br/navegue-por-temas/cooperacao-internacional/relatorios-internacionais-1> accessed 8 September 2023.

[36] Brasil, Contra informe da sociedade civil brasileira sobre o cumprimento do pacto internacional dos direitos econômicos, sociais e culturais pelo Estado brasileiro. / Projeto coordenado pela Articulação dos Parceiros de Misereor no Brasil, Movimento Nacional de Direitos Humanos, Plataforma Brasileira de Direitos Humanos Econômicos, Sociais, Culturais e Ambientais, Processo de Articulação e Diálogo entre Agências Ecumênicas Européias e suas Contrapartes Brasileiras. Brasília / Passo Fundo: MISEREOR; MNDH; DhESC BRASIL; PAD; IFIBE, 2007 <http://www.mpsp.mp.br/portal/page/portal/cao_civel/dh_relevancia_publica/relevancia_diversos/Contra%20Informe%202007%20-%20PIDESC.pdf> accessed 13 November 2023.

4.1.4 Domestic Implementation Mechanisms

In 2014 Brazil developed an online platform called Observatory of International Recommendations on Human Rights,[37] aimed at compiling recommendations 'issued by the UN and OAS with a view to progressively integrating them into national rights action plans, policies and work programmes', as reported by Brazilian diplomats in an interview for this research. Yet, this platform was discontinued by the Brazilian government and is no longer available. At the Inter-American level, there is a similar initiative within the Institute of Public Policies on Human Rights (IPPDH), regarding the Recommendation Monitoring System (SIMORE).[38] SIMORE is still functioning to monitor recommendations from the Inter-American system. In contrast with the lack of uniform procedure for monitoring of UN treaty bodies recommendations, Brazil has been more transparent regarding the UPR procedure.

4.1.5 Treaty Body Membership

A national process for nomination of treaty body members is currently an issue in Brazil. In 2014 a group of NGOs called the Brazilian Committee on Human Rights and Foreign Policy presented a document outlining criteria and procedures for the nomination of treaty body members that is transparent and open to different stakeholders. Although Brazil has not formally endorsed the document, it is a clear impact of the UN treaty bodies in fostering advocacy around issues of their members' nominations.

The criteria outlined in the document include (i) qualification and knowledge of international instruments, standards and principles of human rights or humanitarian law, and fluency in at least one of the official languages of the UN or OAS; (ii) knowledge and experience in the mandate field; (iii) independence and impartiality (anyone occupying a government position, in instances closely linked to state functions or in organisations and private companies that may produce potential conflicts of interest in relation to the inherent responsibilities to the mandate, should be excluded from the selection process); (iv) personal integrity and moral integrity (the nominee cannot have contributed to authoritarian or governments, and have expressed public positions contrary

---

37   Ministério Da Família, Da Mulher E Dos Direitos Humanos. Sociedade Civil pode contribuir com Observatório de Recomendações Internacionais sobre Direitos Humanos até o fim do mês. MFMDH, 2015 <https://www.gov.br/mdh/pt-br/sdh/noticias/2015/janeiro/sociedade-civil-pode-contribuir-com-observatorio-de-recomendacoes-internacionais-sobre-direitos-humanos-ate-o-fim-do-mes> accessed 16 August 2020.

38   OEA, Simore Interamericano <https://www.oas.org/ext/pt/direitos-humanos/simore> accessed 20 July 2020.

to human rights or have had any involvement with public or private organisations known to have violated human rights); (v) availability and flexibility; (vi) gender, race, ethnicity and other expressions of plurality (it is essential that clear parameters for the promotion of equality and equity between genders and with respect to race and ethnicity and other variables are established as criteria for selecting and nominating candidates for vacancies in human rights systems). The process of selection and nomination must also consider other dimensions of socio-cultural plurality, especially in the case of historically discriminated groups. Efforts must also be made to ensure regional diversity.

4.1.6   Overview of Impact

Human rights treaties were incorporated as civil society claims became more prominent. The first decade of 2000 saw the highest volume of public policies in accordance with international recommendations. It was during this period that the National Human Rights Plans were made.

The Brazilian judiciary has to a large extent applied human rights treaties in its decisions. Most treaties are used as a source of interpretation and resource, especially when the parties to the lawsuit invoke the text for the protection of the law in dispute.

The most extensive impacts of human rights treaties were found in decentralised public policies that do not focus on a specific organ or power and are supported by social movements and civil society. An example are the Special Secretariats, such as the Special Secretariat for Women, which was responsible for the implementation of public policies that meet the commitments of CEDAW. Also, the role of civil society in the impact of the treaties is remarkable: civil society organizations and NGOs mobilize to demand the implementation and enforcement of the treaties. In some cases – as in CEDAW and the CRPD – this role is even more outstanding. While there is a large social movement (in particular, anti-carceral movements) supporting it, the implementation of the Convention Against Torture (CAT) has been less pronounced, especially in companies.

Brazil had an individual communication decided by the CEDAW Committee regarding the *Maria de Lourdes Pimentel* case, in which Brazil was accused of violating the right to health and maternity protection. Brazil, through the Special Secretariat for Women, publicly acknowledged its accountability and paid compensation to the victim, showing the relevance of the decentralised action indicated in the previous paragraphs.

The Subcommittee on Prevention of Torture (SPT) conducted visits to Brazil in 2009 and 2015. The SPT's reports pointed out the precarious position of Brazilian prisoners. In its report published in 2016, based on its 2015 visit, the SPT issued warnings that could have prevented prison riots. Brazil has recurrently omitted to pay attention to the needs of public security and to reduce the number of prisoners in the country, being the country with the third major highest number in arrests in the world, with 64 per cent of 727 000 prisoners black. The prison system is an urgent problem that is not yet the object of institutional attention, even though there is a great deal of work by NGOs to do so.

The Universal Declaration of Human Rights, the American Convention on Human Rights and UN human rights treaties had a direct impact on the drafting of the FC. Article 4 of the Brazilian FC states that Brazil governs its international relations with reference to human rights. Article 5 refers to gender equality and the inviolability of the right to life, liberty, equality to security and property. There is also an express mention of the prohibition of torture and cruel punishment; the prohibition of arbitrary imprisonment and the presumption of innocence.

Another important point is that the FC in article 6 declares that education, health, food, work, housing, transportation, leisure, security, social security, maternity and child protection, assistance to the helpless are social rights and also has a chapter on Social Security. The Constitution also expressly provides for workers' rights, including vacation and rest (in article 7). Other impacts can be mentioned, as Piovesan (2012) pointed out, namely, (a) the right of every person to an adequate standard of living; (b) the prohibition of any propaganda in favour of war and prohibition of any apology for national, racial or religious hatred; (c) the right of ethnic, religious or linguistic minorities to have their own cultural lives, to profess and practise their own religion and to use their own language; (d) prohibition on the re-establishment of the death penalty in states that have abolished it, in accordance with article 4(3) of the American Convention; (e) the possibility for states to adopt measures in the social, economic and cultural spheres that ensure the protection of certain racial groups; (f) the possibility for states to adopt temporary and special measures aimed at accelerating *de facto* equality between men and women; (g) prohibition on the use of means to hinder communication and the circulation of ideas and opinions; (h) the right to a double degree of jurisdiction as a minimum judicial guarantee; (i) the right of the accused to be heard; (j) the right of every detained person to be tried within a reasonable time or to be released, without prejudice to the continuation of the process; and (k) the prohibition on extradition or expulsion of a person to another state when there are well-founded reasons that can be subjected to torture or other cruel, inhuman or degrading treatment. 'It should be noted that this list is not exhaustive, but aimed to exemplify rights that are enshrined in the international agreements ratified by Brazil and incorporated into the Brazilian domestic legal order.'[39]

In case of conflict between international law and domestic law, the STF has held that the human dignity principle had primacy. Since 2004, human rights norms with constitutional status, as provided for in article 5 of FC and mentioned above, have a prevalence of human rights over domestic law as a constitutional norm. If the human rights treaty did not meet that threshold, it still has prevalence over domestic law but not from constitution norms.

5 Impact of the Different UN Human Rights Treaties on the Domestic Level in Brazil

5.1 *International Convention on the Elimination of All Forms of Racial Discrimination*

5.1.1 Incorporation and Reliance by Legislature and Executive

Brazil ratified CERD on 27 March 1968 and it was incorporated into domestic law by Decree 65,810 of 8 December 1969, which in its headnote explicitly refers to the promulgation of CERD. In 2002 Brazil accepted CERD's individual complaints procedure under article 14 of CERD.

There has been significant growth in national legal rules involving the fight against racial discrimination. The first law that sought to combat racial discrimination was Law 1.390 of 1951 known as the Afonso Arinos Act, which typified as racism discrimination by public or private entities against people on grounds of colour or race. However, such behaviour was classified only as a 'minor offensive potential offence'. Subsequently, in 1989, Law 7716 was promulgated, characterising as a criminal offence the kind of conduct that blocks access to services, positions and jobs on grounds of race or colour prejudice. In 1997 Law 7716/89 was partially modified by Law 9459/97, which includes new categories of criminal offences. The most expressive rule against any kind of discrimination and, consequently, against racial discrimination, in Brazil is the 1988 FC. In article 5, items XLI and XLII, the FC establishes that 'the law shall punish any discriminatory discrimination against the rights and fundamental freedoms', and that 'the practice of racism constitutes an unreliable and imprescriptible crime, subject to the penalty of imprisonment under the law'.

---

[39] Flávia Piovesan, *Temas de Direitos Humanos* (São Paulo: Saraiva, 2012), p. 40.

Thus, racism had its status as a mere 'criminal misdemeanour' turned into a serious crime.

The Brazilian legislature has directly relied on CERD in numerous legislative proposals. A search of the database of Brazil's House of Representatives shows at least 50 explicit mentions of CERD in legislative proposals.[40] The vast majority of these mentions are from the 2000s onwards despite the fact that Brazil ratified CERD during the military dictatorship in 1969, showing that the impact of UN human rights treaties has occurred primarily after the democratisation from the mid-1980s in Brazil. In order to illustrate this impact, it is possible to cite two concrete examples: (i) in 2003 CERD was cited in a parliamentary inquiry proposing to the executive to establish race-based affirmative action programmes for public service;[41] (ii) in 2004, citing Brazil's obligations under CERD, the executive branch presented a legislative Bill for racial quotas in federal universities.[42]

Brazil has several public policies seeking to tackle racial discrimination, such as (i) the enactment of Law 12.711/2012, known as the Quota Law, in an attempt to repair history and to respond to the provisions of article 2(2) of CERD, which established affirmative action programmes at federal universities based on race and ethnicity;[43] (ii) the enactment of the Statute of Racial Equality (Law 12.288/2010) which details the rights of black people in Brazil and explicitly mentions CERD in its article 38, as follows: 'The implementation of policies aimed at the inclusion of the black population in the labour market will be the responsibility of the public power, observing ... the commitments assumed by Brazil when ratifying the 1965 International Convention on the Elimination of All Forms of Racial Discrimination.' At the executive level, Brazil counted with a Special Secretariat for Policies Promoting Racial Equality between 2003 and 2015 at the President's Office.[44]

---

40 A search was conducted on the website of the Brazil's House of Representatives (Câmara dos Deputados) <https://www.camara.leg.br/busca-portal?contextoBusca=BuscaProposicoes&pagina=1&order=relevancia&abaEspecifica=true&q=%22Convenção%20Internacional%20sobre%20a%20Eliminação%20de%20todas%20as%20Formas%20de%20Discriminação%20Racial%22> accessed 20 June 2020.

41 Brazil's House of Representatives, INC 721/2003 <https://www.camara.leg.br/proposicoesWeb/fichadetramitacao?idProposicao=124916> accessed 20 June 2020.

42 Brazil's House of Representatives, PL 3627/2004 <https://www.camara.leg.br/proposicoesWeb/fichadetramitacao?idProposicao=254614> accessed 20 June 2020.

43 Brazil, Law 12.711, 29 August 2012 <http://www.planalto.gov.br/ccivil_03/_ato2011-2014/2012/lei/l12711.htm> accessed 20 June 2020.

44 Brazil, Law 10.678, 23 May 2003 <http://www.planalto.gov.br/ccivil_03/LEIS/2003/L10.678.htm> accessed 20 June 2020.

5.1.2   Reliance by Judiciary

The most relevant impact of CERD in the Brazilian legal system has been in the paradigmatic case from 2012,[45] in which Brazil's Federal Supreme Court (STF) confirmed that affirmative actions involving racial quotas in universities are constitutional. The reference to CERD by the STF was replayed later in another case,[46] which confirmed the validity of the public university quota system mentioned above. The concept of discrimination outlined in CERD was key to the findings of the Court in favour of affirmative action programmes, and it was cited extensively.

CERD has been very present in Brazilian jurisprudence, especially in the judgments of the Superior Court of Justice (STJ), another higher court in Brazil responsible for the interpretation of federal law (including international treaties). Looking at the jurisprudence of the STJ, the Convention was mentioned in 115 individual decisions,[47] and in eight judgments as a legislative reference.[48] In these, treaties are always mentioned along with the existing Brazilian legislation on the subject, to emphasise how the domestic norms are in conformity with the international treaties. The substantive issues in respect of which the treaties are mentioned are diverse, ranging from cases of racial injury committed on the internet to cases that question whether the federal court is competent to prosecute racist crimes provided for under CERD.[49]

5.1.3   Impact on and through Independent State Institutions

Regarding the impact of CERD on independent state institutions, the promotion of accessibility policies can be mentioned, such as that carried out by the Secretariat of Higher Education, in 2005, which deals with

---

45   STF, ADPF 186 – Presiding Judge: Ricardo Lewandowski – 04/28/2012 <https://redir.stf.jus.br/paginadorpub/paginador.jsp?docTP=TP&docID=6984693> accessed 13 November 2023.

46   STF – RE 597285 – Presiding Judge: Edson Fachin: 05/09/2012 <http://portal.stf.jus.br/processos/downloadPeca.asp?id=207767406&ext=.pdf> accessed 20 June 2020.

47   An individual decision consists of a decision rendered by a single magistrate, from any instance or court.

48   Research conducted in July 2020.

49   STJ – 3ª seção – *CC 146983 / RJ* – Rel. Min. Feliz Fischer – Publicação: 29/06/2017. [Superior Court of Justice. Conflict of Competence 14683/ Rio de Janeiro. Presiding Judge: Feliz Fischer. Published: 29/06/2017].

opening up possibilities for quota holders in the Afro-Attitude Programme.[50] The programme aims to offer opportunities for black students to participate in research, community initiatives and monitoring projects developed by professors and students from participating universities. In 2014 the Public Defenders' Office of the State of São Paulo created quotas for black people in the public selection for Defender of the State (public lawyer).[51] In this context, in 2015, quotas for the magistracy vacancies had been created, based on a dossier on the racial inequality in the judiciary power made by the National Council of Justice (CNJ).[52]

5.1.4 Impact on and through Non-state Actors

The impact through non-state actors is focused on projects to fight against racial inequalities. The Black Women Health Project launched a manual about the Convention,[53] which underscores the importance of CERD in the action against racism, as well as the rights contained in the text and the duties of the state parties. Specifically, the manual, which was drafted in partnership between Conectas Human Rights and the Geledes Black Women Institute, looks closely at the issue of black women's health rights in light of the Convention. NGOs also conducted campaigns to publicise the Convention.[54] These campaigns were essential for the promotion of public policies by state institutions.[55] One of the greatest responses to the adherence by Brazil to CERD has taken the form of dissemination and the promotion of meetings allowing for debates on the themes.

---

50 Brasil, Ministério da Educação Programa Afro-atitude abre oportunidades para cotistas, 2005 <http://portal.mec.gov.br/ultimas-noticias/213-1762821894/2383-sp-392224435> accessed 9 September 2023.

51 Geledes, 'Ações afirmativas deixarão Defensoria Pública mais democrática' Geledes, 2014 <https://www.geledes.org.br/acoes-afirmativas-deixarao-defensoria-publica-mais-democratica/> accessed 20 July 2020.

52 Conectas. Dossiê: Desigualdade no sistema de justiça. Conectas, 2015 <https://www.conectas.org/noticias/dossie-desigualdade-no-sistema-de-justica> accessed 20 July 2020.

53 Geledes, Projeto Saúde da Mulher Negra Lança Manual sobre Projeto de Convenção Contra o Racismo. Geledes, 2009 <https://www.geledes.org.br/projeto-saude-da-mulher-negra-lanca-manual-sobre-projeto-de-convencao-contra-o-racismo/> accessed 20 June 2020.

54 UNIC Rio De Janeiro, Políticas públicas afirmativas são fundamentais para a redução da desigualdade racial, diz Sistema ONU. UNIC, 2012 <https://unicrio.org.br/politicas-publicas-afirmativas-sao-fundamentais-para-a-reducao-da-desigualdade-racial-diz-sistema-onu/> accessed 17 June 2020.

55 Geledés, Geledés no Monitoramento e Incidência em Políticas Públicas Geledes, 2009 <https://www.geledes.org.br/geledes-no-monitoramento-de-politicas-publicas/> accessed 20 June 2020.

5.1.5 Impact of State Reporting

Brazil has also reacted, directly and indirectly, to COs of the CERD Cttee as shown by a handful of concrete examples. In 2004 the CERD Cttee considered Brazil's 14th to 17th report. It welcomed the adoption, in 2002, of the National Affirmative Action Programme as an important mechanism to implement the Durban Declaration and Programme of Action, as well as the second National Human Rights Programme and New Civil Code.[56] It also identified as a positive aspect Brazil's ratification of ILO Convention 169 and reaffirmed its concern about the persistence of deep structural inequalities affecting black and mestizo communities, as well as indigenous peoples.[57] Besides that, the Committee demonstrated uneasiness about the increase in the number of racist organisations, such as neo-Nazi groups, and the spread of racist propaganda on the internet. In its COs in 2004 the Committee also recommended that Brazil 'clarify further the content and application of the relevant provisions of domestic law that address the existence and activity of racist organisations, as well as those that prohibit racist propaganda on the Internet'.[58] Citing CERD directly, a parliamentary hearing was held in 2018 to tackle the issue,[59] and ongoing discussions are underway in Brazil's National Congress regarding hate speech and racism. Also, in 2004 the CERD Cttee requested Brazil to 'provide statistical information on prosecutions launched, and penalties imposed, in cases of offences which relate to racist crimes, and where the relevant provisions of the existing domestic legislation have been applied'. Brazil provided at least part of the required data to the Committee (as stated in its latest report received by the Committee on 14 July 2020). The Brazilian Congress has amended anti-racism criminal legislation citing CERD as a reference. The last change in 2009 has empowered the prosecutor's office to initiate criminal proceedings on the crime of racial slur, provided the victim allows it.[60]

5.1.6 Impact of Individual Communications

No cases have been submitted to the CERD Cttee against Brazil.

---

56 CERD/C/64/CO/2 2.
57 ibid.
58 CERD/C/64/CO/2, 28 April 2004, para 19.
59 Brazil's House of Representatives, REQ 20/2018 <https://www.camara.leg.br/proposicoesWeb/fichadetramitacao?idProposicao=2172136V> accessed 20 June 2020.
60 Brazil, Law 12.033, 29 September 2009 <http://www.planalto.gov.br/ccivil_03/_Ato2007-2010/2009/Lei/L12033.htm> accessed 20 June 2020.

5.1.7 Impact of CERD Urgent Procedures

An important impact of the Committee is in the situation of the indigenous peoples of Raposa Serra do Sul in the state of Roraima, which was the object of all but one early warning communications concerning Brazil and the CERD Cttee between 2006 and 2011. During this time, civil society activists managed to obtain responses from the Brazilian government, through its Permanent Mission in Geneva, regarding the demarcation of this specific indigenous land. In parallel, Brazil's Federal Supreme Court finally decided a case in 2009 formally guaranteeing the right to land to indigenous peoples, mentioning several times in particular the UN Declaration on the Rights of Indigenous Peoples. Although the final court decision did not expressly mention the Committee, the repeated access to the early warning mechanism while the case was pending has shown coordinated tactics by civil society organisations and indigenous defenders.

This case involved the demarcation of a territory that lasted 30 years. It started in 1993, when the National Indian Foundation (FUNAI) proposed to the Ministry of Justice the recognition of the extension of 1,67 million hectares of the Raposa Serra do Sol Indigenous Territory. The violence was present throughout the process of demarcation. The year 2006 was destined for the departure of non-indigenous people from the territory, as part of the integration process. April 2006 was the deadline for non-Indians leaving from the Raposa Serra do Sol Reserve. On 25 April 2006 the Federal Police began to enter rice farmers' farms located in the so-called 'rice belt'.

Thus, in the same year, 2006, the Indigenous People Council, Indigenous Peoples Law and Policy Programme of the University of Arizona, the Rainforest Foundation and the Forest People Programme asking urgent actions from the Committee regarding the violence against peoples of Raposa do Sol (Ingaricó, Macuxi, Patamona, Taurenge and Wapichana). The Committee requested more information from Brazil about the allegations.[61] In June, Judge Helder Girão Barreto ordered the suspension of any actions promoted by Funai and others aimed at removing rice producers from the areas they occupy in Raposa. It is in this conflicting and institutionally nebulous scenario that the Committee issued an 'early warning' to Brazil asking for clarification on the racial attacks and violence experienced by the communities in this process.

In 2009 the Federal Supreme Court finally decreed the demarcation of the land.[62] In the meantime, CERD issued six early

---

61 United nations, Early Warming Brazil Letter, 18 August 2006 <https://www.ohchr.org/Documents/HRBodies/CERD/EarlyWarning/Brazil_letter.pdf> accessed 20 June 2020.

62 Federal Supreme Court (STF), Petition 3388 <https://portal.stf.jus.br/processos/detalhe.asp?incidente=2288693> accessed 9 September 2023.

warnings.[63] An early warning was issued in 2010,[64] alerting to the concern with the land of Raposa Serra do Sol, even after the demarcation, requesting up-to-date information and urging action to stop and prevent violence against indigenous people in the territory. Thus, only in 2011[65] did the Committee issue its last early warming on the Raposa Serra do Sol case, warning Brazil of its withdrawal from the urgent procedures in the Committee.

The only early warning communication that does not deal with Raposa do Sol is the latest one, from May 2019, which is related to the 'building of highways and railroads in the State of Mato Grosso, in Brazil, and its impact on Xavante and other indigenous peoples' rights'.[66] In particular, the Committee requested the suspension of the building of highway BR-080. Although the early warning communication is mentioned in Parliament through a request by opposition politicians to the government,[67] the building of the highway is underway.[68]

5.1.8 Brief Conclusion

The influence of CERD in Brazil can be traced along the axes of the country's political history. Ratified in 1969, during the military dictatorship, its effect on

---

63 Brazil Early Warming, 18 August 2006 <https://www.ohchr.org/Documents/HRBodies/CERD/EarlyWarning/Brazil_letter.pdf> accessed 20 June 2020; Brazil Early Warming, 14 March 2007. <https://www.ohchr.org/Documents/HRBodies/CERD/EarlyWarning/70_Letter_Brazil.pdf> accessed 20 June 2020; Brazil Early Warming, 18 August 2006 <https://www.ohchr.org/Documents/HRBodies/CERD/EarlyWarning/letterbrazil24aug07.pdf> accessed 20 June 2020; Brazil Early Warming, 7 March 2008 <https://www.ohchr.org/Documents/HRBodies/CERD/EarlyWarning/Brazil070308.pdf> accessed 20 June 2020; Brazil Early Warming, 15 August 2008 <https://www.ohchr.org/Documents/HRBodies/CERD/EarlyWarning/Brazil070308.pdfhttps://www.ohchr.org/Documents/HRBodies/CERD/EarlyWarning/Brazil_letter150808.pdf> accessed 20 June 2020; Brazil Early Warming, 28 September 2009 <https://www.ohchr.org/Documents/HRBodies/CERD/EarlyWarning/Brazil28092009.pdf> accessed 20 June 2020.
64 Brazil Early Warming, 30 may 2010 <https://www.ohchr.org/Documents/HRBodies/CERD/EarlyWarning/Brazil31052010.pdf> accessed 20 June 2020.
65 Brazil Early Warming, 11 March 2011 <https://www.ohchr.org/Documents/HRBodies/CERD/EarlyWarning/Brazil_11March2011.pdf> accessed 20 June 2020.
66 CERD/EWUAP/ 98th session/Brazil/JP/ks, 10 May 2019 <https://tbinternet.ohchr.org/Treaties/CERD/Shared%20Documents/BRA/INT_CERD_ALE_BRA_8925_E.pdf> accessed 20 June 2020.
67 Brazil's Congress House, RIC 686/2019 <https://www.camara.leg.br/proposicoesWeb/fichadetramitacao?idProposicao=2206526> accessed 14 September 2020.
68 Agência Brasil, Ministerio-da-infraestrutura-e-df-avancam-na-reforma-da-rodovia-br-080. Agencia Brasil, 2020 <https://agenciabrasil.ebc.com.br/geral/noticia/2020-06/ministerio-da-infraestrutura-e-df-avancam-na-reforma-da-rodovia-br-080> accessed 20 August 2020.

Brazilian legislation became noticeable only after the promulgation of the 1988 Constitution and the return to democracy. Nevertheless, it is important to point out that the legislation on the subject is punitive and also focused on public policies. Public policies regarding the guarantee of rights have become more common since the 2000s, in particular for affirmative action. The role of civil society and organisations in the dissemination of CERD remains of paramount importance in the Brazilian context. Adherence in civil society was and is very important, acting in protection against racial violence in cases such as that of Raposa Serra do Sol land.

5.2   *International Covenant on Civil and Political Rights*

5.2.1   Incorporation and Reliance by Legislature and Executive

The Brazilian Congress approved CCPR by Legislative Decree 226 of 12 December 1991, in which it also approved the CESCR. On 6 July 1992, by Decree 592, it published an annex to the decree promulgating CCPR in the country, establishing its execution and fulfillment entirely as contained therein. In 2009, through Decree 311,[69] Brazil approved OP1-CCPR and OP2-CCPR, while expressing a reservation to article 2 of the latter. Even though it was approved it has not yet been promulgated.[70] In 1996 the National Human Rights Programme was launched by Decree 1904. Decree 4229/2012 brought into being National Human Rights Programme II. These initiatives enabled Brazilian regional governments to develop human rights plans. Many other public policies were created in Brazil, indirectly mentioning CCPR.

The Brazilian legislature has directly relied extensively on CCPR in legislative proposals. A search conduced in September of 2023 in the database of Brazil's House of Representatives showed at least 169 explicit references[71] to CCPR in legislative proposals, the vast majority of them from the 2000s onwards. Brazil ratified CCPR in 1992, shortly after the promulgation of the FC in 1988, illustrating that the impact of UN human rights treaties has occurred

---

69   Brazil's House of Representatives, Decreto Legislativo 311 <https://www2.camara.leg.br/legin/fed/decleg/2009/decretolegislativo-311-16-junho-2009-588912-publicacaooriginal-113605-pl.html> accessed 20 June 2020.

70   In Brazilian law, for a treaty to be "legal" it must be promulgated in addition to ratification. Enactment is an act done by the president of the republic and stands for the approval of its incorporation into the internal regulations, in this way, the treaty can only be "enforceable" if it is promulgated and published.

71   Search was conducted on the website of the Brazil's House of Representatives (Câmara dos Deputados) <https://www.camara.leg.br/busca-portal?contextoBusca=BuscaProposicoes&pagina=1&order=data&abaEspecifica=true&q=%22Pacto%20Internacional%20sobre%20Direitos%20Civis%20e%20Pol%C3%ADticos%22> accessed 9 September 2023.

primarily after the democratisation from the mid-1980s onwards. In order to illustrate this impact, two examples are cited: (i) In 2015, CCPR was cited in a legislative Bill to guarantee fundamental rights in the context of sexual health and reproductive rights;[72] and (ii) in 2015, citing directly Brazil's obligations under CCPR, the legislative branch presented a Bill to establish the duty to a custody hearing within 24 hours after arrest,[73] which was in line with recommendations by the UN Special Rapporteur against Torture.[74]

There were often setbacks or negative impacts, at least indirectly, from the UN Human Rights Committee (HRCttee) COs. In 2015 the HRCttee[75] concluded that the 'state party should ensure that the military police are subject to the institutions and procedures of judicial and civilian accountability. The ordinary courts should have criminal jurisdiction over all serious human rights violations committed by the military police, including excessive use of force and manslaughter, as well as intentional murder.' Previously, in 1996, Law 9299/96 transferred judicial authority over intentional crimes against human life committed by military police officers from military justice to common justice, thereby eliminating the privileged forum that previously shielded military police officers responsible for civilian deaths. In 1997, Law 9455, which defines the crimes of torture, in accordance with CCPR in article 7, was adopted. Yet, in 2017 Brazil enacted Law 13.491/2017 stipulating as follows: 'The crimes, when committed with intention against life and by military personnel in the Armed Forces against civilians, will be the responsibility of the Military Justice.'[76] The problem is that in Brazil part of the police belongs to the armed forces, thus there are cases of police misconduct tried by military courts.

5.2.2 Reliance by Judiciary

The STF on 9 September 2015[77] granted a precautionary measure to determine that judges and courts allow, within 90 days, the holding of custody hearings throughout the country, allowing prisoners to be presented to the judicial

---

[72] Brazil's House of Representatives, PL 882/2015 <https://www.camara.leg.br/proposicoesWeb/fichadetramitacao?idProposicao=1050889> accessed 20 June 2020.

[73] Brazil's House of Representatives, PL 470/2015 <https://www.camara.leg.br/proposicoesWeb/fichadetramitacao?idProposicao=949101> accessed 20 June 2020.

[74] For more, see <https://www.cnj.jus.br/onu-audiencias-de-custodia-sao-importantes-contra-prisao-arbitraria/> accessed 20 June 2020.

[75] For more, see <https://www.cnj.jus.br/onu-audiencias-de-custodia-sao-importantes-contra-prisao-arbitraria/> accessed 9 September 2023.

[76] For more, see <http://www.planalto.gov.br/ccivil_03/_Ato2015-2018/2017/Lei/L13491.htm> accessed 20 June 2020.

[77] In the records of ADPF# (Arrangement for Breach of Non-Compliance) No 347.

authority within 24 hours: 'Judges and courts, subject to articles 9(3) of CCPR and 7(5) of the American Convention on Human Rights, are required to hold custody hearings within ninety days, enabling the prisoner to appear before the judicial authority within maximum of 24 hours from the time of arrest.' When it decided that the accused has the right to attend, to assist and to witness, under penalty of absolute nullity, the procedural acts, notably those that take place during the investigation phase of the criminal procedure, in 2012, the STF mentioned article 14(3)(d) of CCPR.[78]

In 2014 the STF awarded compensations for moral damage as a result of torture during the military regime and highlighted that Brazil is a state party to CCPR, 'incorporated into the legal system by Legislative Decree 226/1991, promulgated by Decree 592/1992, which guarantees that no one will be subjected to torture or cruel, inhuman or degrading treatment or punishment, and provides for judicial protection in cases of human rights violations'. A decision then was issued in accordance with the Covenant.[79] As a last example, the Federal Supreme Court decided, in 2005, that an accused has the right to be present in criminal hearings concerning his case, based on article 14(3)(d) of CCPR.[80]

5.2.3 Impact on and through Independent State Institutions

A key impact of CCPR in Brazil is the establishment of a Police Ombudsman's Office in several states in Brazil to act independently and receive complaints involving crimes and misconduct of police officers. In its COs in 2005, the HRCttee recognised the efforts of Brazil in this regard.[81] For instance, the state of Rio de Janeiro, the Police Ombudsman's Office was established in 1999,[82] and in Bahia state, the Civil Police Ombudsman's Office was created in 2018.[83]

---

78 Federal Supreme Court Habeas Corpus 98.676 judgment 7 February 2012 art 14(3)(d).
79 Federal Supreme Court Resource: RE-AgR-715.268. For more access <https://redir.stf.jus.br/paginadorpub/paginador.jsp?docTP=TP&docID=5930743> accessed 9 September 2023.
80 Federal Supreme Court Habeas Corpus 73.510. To know more, <https://portal.stf.jus.br/processos/detalhe.asp?incidente=1631838> accessed 9 September 2023.
81 UN Human Rights Committee, COs of the Human Rights Committee, CCPR/C/BRA/CO/2 1 December 2005, para. 4.
82 Brazil Law 3.168/1999 <http://alerjln1.alerj.rj.gov.br/contlei.nsf/c8aa0900025feef-6032564ec0060dfff/4504b22c29a5778e032566f900790c88?OpenDocument> accessed 9 September 2023.
83 Governo Do Estado Da Bahia. Polícia Civil. Ouvidoria da Polícia civil <http://www.policiacivil.ba.gov.br/modules/conteudo/conteudo.php?conteudo=41> accessed 9 September 2023.

5.2.4 Impact on and through Non-state Actors

As for the adherence by organisations and non-state actors, there is mainly the complaint of non-compliance with the rules stipulated in the Convention: for example, Human Rights Watch in the article 'Brazil: Mothers arrested despite legal ban' about the imprisonment of mothers.[84] In the same way, specialists from the UN and the Inter-American Commission on Human Rights demanded that the São Paulo government review its newly-created legislation that hardens the rules for protests in the state.[85] Other mentions can be found in legal articles that aim, for the most part, to highlight the context of CCPR and its implications for lawyers' day-to-day functioning. An interesting analysis is the one presented by Criminal Justice Network,[86] which launched a note and criticised the processing of a Bill that defines terrorism. There are also guides to practical actions towards the Convention: Guide to Training in Special Testimony of Children and Adolescents;[87] Guide to Evaluation Impact on Human Rights what Companies should do to Respect the Rights of Children and Adolescents. It is also possible to observe an adherence of the Convention in academic studies.[88] A search at CAPES Periodic (Coordination for the

---

[84] Human's Right Watch, 'Brasil: Mães presas apesar de proibição legal' (Brazil: Mothers Arrested Despite Legal Ban) <https://www.hrw.org/pt/news/2019/05/10/brazil-mothers-risk-illegal-detention> accessed 9 September 2023. Abstract: The law now requires house arrest rather than pre-trial detention for pregnant women, mothers of people with disabilities and mothers of children under 12, except when charged with crimes committed by violence or serious threat, or crimes against their dependents. However, data from 2018 shows that thousands of women who apparently were entitled to these protections remained behind bars under remand. Express mention – art 9(3) of CCPR.

[85] Conectas, 'ONU E OEA PEDEM QUE DÓRIA REVEJA LEI QUE LIMITA PROTESTOS EM SP – Manifestação ocorre após organizações da sociedade civil denunciarem decreto promulgado em janeiro' ('UN and OAS Ask for Dória to Review Law That Limits Protests in SP – Demonstration occurs after civil society organisations denounce decree promulgated in January') <https://www.conectas.org/noticias/onu-e-oea-pedem-que-doria-reveja-lei-que-limita-protestos-em-sp> accessed 20 June 2020.

[86] To know more <http://www.global.org.br/blog/rede-justica-criminal-lanca-nota-e-critica-a-tramitacao-de-projeto-de-lei-que-tipifica-terrorismo/> accessed 20 June 2020.

[87] Childhood Brasil Guia para Capacitação em Depoimento Especial de Crianças e Adolescentes 23/10/2015 – *See for more* <http://www.crianca.mppr.mp.br/2015/10/12202,37/> accessed 20 June 2020. Abstract: Guidebook for the Training of the Various Professionals Involved in Listening to Children and Teenagers Victims of Sexual Violence – *Pact Reference:* 'They are also universally protected by their civil, political, economic, social and cultural rights in international covenants on civil and political rights – the right to protective measures on the grounds that they are minors, registered at birth, of having a name, and a nationality'.

[88] Search was conduced at the CAPES Periodic website: <http://www.periodicos.capes.gov.br/index.php?option=com_pmetabusca&mn=88&smn=88&type=m&metalib=aHR0cHM6Ly9ybnAtcHJpbW8uaG9zdGVkLmV4bGlicmlzZ3JvdXAuY29tL3ByaW1vX2xpYnJhcnkvbGlid2ViL2FjdGlvbi9zZWFyY2guZG8/dmlkPUNBUEVWTX1Yx&Itemid=124> accessed 9 September 2023.

Improvement of Higher Education Personnel) in September 2023 by subject search 'Pacto Internacional de Direitos Civis e Políticos' (CCPR) found 326 papers. CCPR also had relevance in the complaint[89] against the prohibition of the candidacy to the presidency of former President Lula, with, for example, reference to article 25 of the Convention. Although the HRCttee has requested Brazil to 'take all necessary measures to ensure that Lula can enjoy and exercise his political rights while in prison, as candidate in the 2018 presidential elections',[90] this did not materialise until after the election of former President Jair Bolsonaro.

5.2.5 Impact of State Reporting

In 2005 the HRCttee examined the second report submitted by Brazil.[91] The Committee noted as positive aspects the campaign for civil registration of births, needed to facilitate and ensure full access to social services. It recommended that Brazil take stringent measures to eradicate extra-judicial killing, torture, and other forms of ill-treatment and abuse committed by law enforcement officials and conduct impartial investigation of human rights violations.

In its COs in 2005 the HRCttee requested the state party to 'ensure that the constitutional safeguard of federalisation of human rights crimes becomes an efficient and practical mechanism in order to ensure prompt, thorough, independent and impartial investigations and prosecution of serious human rights violations'.[92] The legal instrument of federalisation of severe cases of human rights violations was established in 2004 through Constitutional Amendment 45. Three cases were federalised so far by decisions of the Superior Court of Justice. The first of these, granted in 2010, refers to the killing of the human rights defender Manoel Mattos in 2009, who fought against death squads in the North-East.[93]

---

89   PARTIDO DOS TRABALHADORES, Defesa alerta ONU sobre restrições à campanha de Lula, 2018 <https://pt.org.br/defesa-alerta-onu-sobre-restricoes-a-campanha-de-lula/> accessed 20 June 2020.
90   Reuters. Brazil's Lula should have political rights: UN Human Rights Committee <https://www.reuters.com/article/us-brazil-election-lula-idUSKBN1L21L1> accessed 13 November 2023.
91   CCPR/C/BRA/CO/2.
92   UN HRCttee, COs of the Human Rights Committee, CCPR/C/BRA/CO/2 1 December 2005, para. 13.
93   CONSULTOR JURÍDICO. Caso Manoel Mattos será julgado pela Justiça Federal. Conjur, 28 de outubro de 2010 <https://www.conjur.com.br/2010-out-28/manuel-mattos-federalizado-grave-violacao-direitos-humanos> accessed 20 June 2020.

Brazil has participated in the Follow-Up Procedure of the UN Human Rights Committee. On 18 April 2008 Brazil presented a follow-up report on the 2005 COs of the HRCttee.[94] Brazil listed developments on demarcation of indigenous lands, on police violence, on the rights of people deprived of liberty and, finally, on the accountability for the crimes committed under the military dictatorship. One example of impact cited by Brazil in the follow-up report mentions increasing the number of vacancies in the prison system and improving state penal establishment facilities as a way to meet the Concluding Observation related to the improvement of prison conditions. Yet, this might be highly problematic to be counted as a human rights development considering the country's mass incarceration levels. The Committee requested the state party to provide information on the other recommendations made and on the Covenant as a whole in its next report, which was due by 31 October 2009. However, Brazil only submitted its report on 3 June 2020.

5.2.6   Impact of Individual Communications

No complaints under OP1-CCPR have been submitted against Brazil.

5.2.7   Brief Conclusion

CCPR is perhaps one of the treaties with the most diffuse implications in the country. It has an important role in promoting various civil rights and on various topics, in particular taking into consideration the massive challenges in Brazil regarding issues such as the demarcation of indigenous lands, access to justice, mass incarceration and police violence. The impact of CCPR in the country is considerable, in particular in terms of legislative and judicial impact. Also, the executive engages with the HRCttee, despite the delays in state reporting.

5.3   *International Covenant on Economic, Social and Cultural Rights*

5.3.1   Incorporation and Reliance by Legislature and Executive

Brazil ratified CESCR on 24 January 1992 by means of an accession letter. Its text was approved by the National Congress through Legislative Decree 226 of 12 December 1991. The Covenant entered into force on 24 April 1992. On 6 July 1992 the President, through Decree 591,[95] published an annex to the Decree promulgating the Covenant in the country. Regarding OP-CESCR, which came

---

94   CCPR/C/BRA/CO/2/Add.1.
95   Decree 591/1992. To know more <http://www.planalto.gov.br/ccivil_03/decreto/1990-1994/d0591.htm> accessed 20 June 2020.

into effect on 5 May 2013, internal procedures are ongoing, the reason why it has neither been signed nor ratified.

In assessing the legislative impact of CESCR in Brazil, the Brazilian legislature has directly relied on CESCR in various legislative proposals. A search conduced in September of 2023 on the database of Brazil's House of Representatives reveals at least 110 instances in which CESCR is explicitly mentioned in legislative proposals,[96] the vast majority of these from the 2010s onwards. The following two concrete examples are provided: (i) in 2019 CESCR was cited in a constitutional amendment proposal suggesting that access to drinking water should be included as a social right;[97] (ii) in 2014, citing directly Brazil's obligations under CESCR, the executive branch presented a legislative Bill for free transport to students.[98]

CESCR establishes, in articles 6 and 7, the right for just and favourable work. In this sense, regarding the issue of employment, it is important to point out that since 1943 Brazil has had specific legislation in place to protect workers, the CLT (Consolidation of Labour Laws). However, in recent years the Brazilian Congress House increased flexibility of labour laws through pension reform and labour law reform.[99] Shortly after the promulgation of CESCR in Brazil, Law 8.900/94 was adopted to ensure the guarantee for unemployment benefits. However, this Law was revoked in 2015 by Law 13.134. The rights of domestic employees were regulated by Law 5.859/1972. In 2001, after CESCR, Law 10.208 provided access to the Employee's Severance Guarantee (FGTS) and unemployment insurance. It took until 2015 with Complementary Law 150,[100] known as Domestic Employees Law, to ensure new rights for workers in this category, such as mandatory FGTS, night allowance, unemployment insurance and family allowance.

The first decade of 2000 was a decade in which the idea was to foster demand for consumption for the large portions of the population, which until then were excluded from the consumption of goods and services due to insufficient income. A series of legislative and executive initiatives were enacted over

---

96   Search was conducted on the website of the Brazil's House of Representatives (Câmara dos Deputados) <https://www.camara.leg.br/busca-portal?contextoBusca=BuscaProp osicoes&pagina=1&order=data&abaEspecifica=true&q=%22Pacto%20Internacional %20sobre%20Direitos%20Econ%C3%B4micos,%20Sociais%20e%20Culturais%22> accessed 9 September 2023.
97   Brazil's House of Representatives, PEC 232/2019 <https://www.camara.leg.br/proposicoes Web/fichadetramitacao?idProposicao=2234674> accessed 20 June 2020.
98   Brazil's House of Representatives, PL 7952/2014 <https://www.camara.leg.br/proposicoes Web/fichadetramitacao?idProposicao=622275> accessed 20 June 2020.
99   Law 13467 of 2017 and Law 13.954 of 2019.
100 Brazil, Law No 150, 1 July 2015 <https://www.planalto.gov.br/ccivil_03/leis/lcp/lcp150.htm> accessed 20 June 2020.

the last 20 years in Brazil to foster economic and social rights, such as the Fome Zero (Zero Hunger) Programme, created in 2003, to fight against famine; the Luz para Todos (Light for Everyone) Programme created in November 2003, to bring electricity to 10 million Brazilians living in rural areas by 2008; and Law 10,836, of 2004, which created the famous Bolsa Família (Family Allowance) programme, a cash transfer programme for poor families.[101]

For education (article 13 of the Convention), it is possible to mention the Brasil Alfabetizado (Literate Brazil) Programme, created in 2003, aimed at the literacy of young people, adults and older persons. The Universidade Para Todos (University for Everyone Programme), created in 2004, aimed at providing low-income youth with access to higher education, through the granting of full or partial scholarships. Finally, Decree 6,096, 2007 institutes the programme to Support Federal University Restructuring and Expansion Plans for Expansion of Federal Universities in the country and the Student Financing Fund Programme, which is a programme of the Ministry of Education aimed at financing undergraduate education for students enrolled in non-free higher education courses at the form of Law 10.260/2001.

Soon after that, from 2015, a series of discussions on the social crisis began, which led to the impeachment of former President Dilma Rousseff. In this scenario labour rights were affected, with an austerity measure for spending ceiling in 2016, by Constitutional Amendment 95.[102] This ceiling limits spending by the federal government on social issues for 20 years, impacting on socio-economic rights. In 2018 a group of UN experts warned that Brazil's austerity policies are harming social rights as child mortality increased.[103] Such policies remain in place, although, with the new government, they are linked to the country's revenue growth - that is, it have been made more flexible through Complementary Law 200/2023.[104]

---

[101] CAMPOS, André Gambier. BREVE HISTÓRICO DAS MUDANÇAS NA REGULAÇÃO DO TRABALHO NO BRASIL. Texto para discussão / Instituto de Pesquisa Econômica Aplicada.- Brasília: Rio de Janeiro: Ipea, 2015 <http://repositorio.ipea.gov.br/bitstream/11058/3513/1/td_2024.pdf> accessed 20 June 2020.

[102] 'Brazil Passes the Mother of All Austerity Plans' *The Washington Post* (2016) <https://www.washingtonpost.com/news/worldviews/wp/2016/12/16/brazil-passes-the-mother-of-all-austerity-plans> accessed 20 June 2020.

[103] United Nations, Human Rights Office of the High Commission, 'Brazil Must Put Human Rights Before Austerity, Warn UN Experts as Child Mortality Rises' <https://www.ohchr.org/en/NewsEvents/Pages/DisplayNews.aspx?NewsID=23426&LangID=E> accessed 20 June 2020.

[104] National Congress. "Novo Arcabouço Fiscal entra em vigência no Brasil". <https://www12.senado.leg.br/noticias/materias/2023/08/31/novo-arcabouco-fiscal-entra-em-vigencia-no-brasil> accessed 9 September 2023.

5.3.2 Reliance by Judiciary

The Brazilian Superior Court of Justice referenced CESCR in four judgments.[105] To cite an example of positive impact: in a class action,[106] the Public Defender mentioned article 13 of CESCR to guarantee the right of a student to university transfer. At the Public Civil Action 1.573.573[107] the plaintiff aimed to oblige the educational institution to allow candidates who did not fulfill the requirements of the quota system to still be part of the selection for general vacancies. The Court maintained the sentence that admitted the claim in order to recognise the right to education by expressly mentioning article 13 of the Covenant.

The STF directly mentioned CESCR in Injunction 20–4/1994,[108] guaranteeing the right of public servants to strike. Here, the STF referred to articles 8(c) and (d) of CESCR – concerning the right of trade unions and the right to strike – in order to rule that, although striking is a right, exemptions can apply when it comes to public servants such as limitations 'prescribed by law and which are necessary in a democratic society in the interests of national security or public order or for the protection of the rights and freedoms of others' (CESCR, article 8(c), cited in the case).

5.3.3 Impact on and through Independent State Institutions

The creation of the Special Secretariat for Policies for the Promotion of Racial Equality, in March 2003, was decisive to speed up the regularisation of *quilombola* lands, as the issue received specific appropriations in the 2004–2007 Multiannual Plan and became the subject of wide debate with civil society. Also, the three Special Secretariats under the President's Office, endowed with ministerial status, were created in 2003: the Special Secretariat for Human Rights (SEDH); the Special Secretariat of Policies for Women (SPM); and the Special Secretariat for Policies for the Promotion of Racial Equality (SEPPIR). The institutionalisation of such official bodies came to the attention of the CESCR Cttee several times, in particular in the state reporting process, during which Brazil argued that the institutionalisation of such bodies, which no longer enjoy ministerial status, counted as implementation of the right to equality.[109] These secretariats have the responsibility to coordinate executive

---

105   Superior Court of Justice – STJ: AgRg-REsp-1.243.163, 8 October 2011; AgInt no REsp-1.573.481, 16 April 2016; STJ APn-369, 15 August 2007; AgRg-AR-5.194, 16 September 2011.
106   Superior Court of Justice – STJ: REsp-1.264.116 – 18 October 2011.
107   Superior Court of Justice – STJ: AgInt no REsp-1.573.481-PE.
108   Federal Supreme Court – STF: Injunction No 20-4/1994. To know more <http://redir.stf.jus.br/paginadorpub/paginador.jsp?docTP=AC&docID=81733> accessed 20 June 2020.
109   Economic and Social Council, Third Periodic Report Submitted by Brazil Under Articles 16 And 17 of the Covenant, due in 2014, submitted on 4 June 2020, E/C.12/BRA/3.

and legislative branches in federal, state and municipal levels in matters of gender, race and human rights.

5.3.4 Impact on and through Non-state Actors

The major impact of CESCR on and through non-state actors was its use as a pressure mechanism on Brazilian politics. In 2017 civil society organisations pressured the Minister of Human Rights, Luislinda Valois, in order for Brazil to sign and ratify OP-CESCR.[110] Brazil has so far not ratified the individual complaints procedures of OP-CESCR.

In 2016 United Nations Special Rapporteur on extreme poverty and human rights stated that, if approved, Constitutional Amendment Bill 55, an austerity law that freezes social and economic resources, 'clearly violates Brazil's obligations under CESCR, which it ratified in 1992, not to take "deliberately retrogressive measures" unless there are no alternative options and full consideration has been given to ensure that the measures are necessary and proportionate'.[111] Unfortunately, while the impact of CESCR as a pressure mechanism can be observed in the legislative discussion of the Constitutional Amendment Bill 55, given the UN Special Rapporteur's statement, Brazil's National Congress nevertheless adopted the measure.

One of the main NGOs dealing with social rights, the Institute of Socio-Economic Studies (INESC), continues to use CESCR as the basis for its advocacy for the reversal of the austerity measure. In 2017 INESC released a report stating:

> The signatory states of the International Covenant on Economic, Social and Cultural Rights undertake to adopt measures, mainly at the economic and technical levels, using the maximum of their available resources, which aim to ensure, progressively, by all appropriate means, the full exercise of the rights recognised in the Pact, including, in particular, the adoption of legislative measures. Brazil also fails this test, because Constitutional Amendment 95 adopts an opposite principle: the 'minimum use of available resources', since it puts a ceiling on social spending, but leaves financial expenses completely free. The consequence of

---

110 Conectas, Slow Procedure Conectas, 07/21/ 2017 <https://www.conectas.org/en/noticias/slow-procedure/> accessed 9 September 2023.
111 United Nations, Human Rights Office of the High Commissioner, 'Brazil 20-year Public Expenditure Cap Will Breach Human Rights, UN Expert Warns' OHCHR, 9 December 2016 <https://www.ohchr.org/en/press-releases/2016/12/brazil-20-year-public-expenditure-cap-will-breach-human-rights-un-expert> accessed 9 September 2023.

this is that the country has experienced an expressive transfer of public resources from relevant social programmes to public debt services – which means an inverse and unprecedented redistribution of public resources destined for vulnerable populations to the wealthiest.[112]

As mentioned above, it was only in August of 2023 that the austerity mesure was made more flexible, although is still in place.

5.3.5 Impact of State Reporting

The reporting process to the CESCR Cttee is important for civil society organisations in Brazil. In 2000 civil society organisations prepared a comprehensive report on the compliance by Brazil of its obligations under CESCR.[113] The document received inputs from over 2 000 entities all over Brazil and was coordinated by the National Human Rights Movement, and the Human Rights Commission of the House of Representatives, among others. The main reason for the shadow report by civil society organisations was the fact that in 2000 Brazil had not submitted an official report to the CESCR Cttee, although it was due by 1994. The government submitted its report in August 2001. The last report submitted by Brazil to the CESCR Cttee was due in 2014, but was only submitted in June 2020.[114]

In its COs in respect of Brazil in 2009, the CESCR Cttee focused on challenges related to inequalities in the territory, such as imbalances in the distribution of resources and income and access to basic services in Brazil.[115] Specifically, in its COs in 2009, the Committee requested Brazil to 'take all necessary measures to combat the culture of violence and impunity prevalent in the state party and to ensure the protection of human rights defenders against any violence, threats, retaliation, pressure or any arbitrary action as a consequence of their activities'.[116] As an example of impact, in 2016 former President Dilma Rousseff enacted Decree 8.724 establishing a national programme for the protection of

---

112 David Grazielle, 'Por que revogar a Emenda Constitucional 95' in Outras Palavras, 13 de dezembro de 2018 <https://outraspalavras.net/crise-brasileira/por-que-revogar-a-emenda-constitucional-95/> accessed 20 June 2020.
113 BRASIL. RELATÓRIO – O BRASIL E O PACTO INTERNACIONAL DE DIREITOS ECONÔMICOS, SOCIAIS E CULTURAIS <https://www.camara.leg.br/Internet/comissao/index/perm/cdh/Pidesc%20-%20Relatório%20Final.html> accessed 20 June 2020.
114 E/C.12/BRA/3.
115 E/C.12/1/Add.87 3.
116 E/C.12/BRA/CO/2 12 June 2009, para 8.

human rights defenders,[117] a programme that continues until today despite concerns about its efficacy and independence.

Also, in its COs from 2009, the CESCR Cttee recommended that Brazil take effective measures to end all forms of exploitative labour.[118] Two important developments happened after these COs: (i) In 2014, Constitutional Amendment 81 was adopted establishing the expropriation of properties with a situation of slave labour, including in the Constitution the following provision: 'Art 243. Rural and urban properties in any region of the country where illegal crops of psychotropic plants are located or the exploitation of slave labour in accordance with the law will be expropriated and destined to agrarian reform and popular housing programs, without any compensation to the owner and without prejudice to other sanctions provided for by law';[119] (ii) Brazil created a National Pact for the Eradication of Slavery in 2017, coordinating judiciary, state level governments and the federal government.[120] However, Brazil still faces several challenges regarding slave labour.

The CESCR Cttee urged Brazil to take all effective measures to prohibit discrimination on the basis of race, colour, ethnic origin or sex in all fields of economic, social and cultural life. In its second set of COs,[121] the Committee recommended that Brazil amend article 215 of the Penal Code, dealing with the concept of 'honest woman', previously applied in certain cases of sexual violence against women. The Committee stated, in line with what civil society movements were already saying, that the concept was discriminatory and asked Brazil to create coordinated public employment policies for disadvantaged groups, including indigenous peoples, Afro-Brazilians and women. All those suggestions were implemented. In addition, the CESCR Cttee requested Brazil to adopt the necessary legislative or other measures to enable the Council on the Defence of the Rights of the Human Person to fully conform to the Paris Principles.[122] The CESCR Cttee recommended that Brazil intensifies its efforts to reduce the persisting inequalities and social injustice between different regions, communities and individuals, and its efforts to advance the

---

117   BRAZIL. Decree 8724 of 2016 <http://www.planalto.gov.br/ccivil_03/_Ato2015-2018/2016/Decreto/D8724.htm> accessed 20 June 2020.
118   E/C.12/BRA/CO/2 12 June 2009, para 15.
119   BRAZIL. EC 81/2014 <https://legis.senado.leg.br/norma/540684/publicacao/15642540> accessed 20 June 2020.
120   MINISTÉRIO DA JUSTIÇA E SEGURANÇA PÚBLICA, 'Pacto pelo fim do trabalho escravo é assinado em solenidade no CNJ' <https://www.justica.gov.br/news/pacto-pelo-fim-do-trabalho-escravo-e-assinado-em-solenidade-no-cnj> accessed 20 June 2020.
121   E/C.12/BRA/CO/2 12 June 2009.
122   E/C.12/BRA/CO/2 3.

rights of children (combat children labour, and ensure that street children have access to education, shelter and health care).

5.3.6 Impact of Individual Communications

Brazil has not accepted OP-CESCR. Civil society organisations, including Conectas, Articulation for Monitoring Human Rights in Brazil, National Human Rights Movement (MNDH), Brazilian Human Rights and Foreign Policy Committee (CBDHPE), Institute for Development and Human Rights (IDDH) and FIAN Brasil, on 18 July 2017 sent a letter sent to the Minister of Human Rights, Luislinda Valois, calling on Brazil to sign and ratify OP-CESCR.[123]

5.3.7 Brief Conclusion

The impact of CESCR in Brazil has been substantial. This impact has been circumscribed in legal and institutional reforms. Brazil, by COs Committee, promoted some politics to extinguish inequalities in territory on the last years, namely, the Brazil Free of Homophobia Programme; the National Qualification Plan to coordinate public policies on employment for disadvantaged groups, including indigenous peoples, Afro-Brazilians and women; the National School Food Programme; compulsory licensing of HIV/AIDS anti-retroviral drugs in order to make these affordable and enable the extension of treatment to all patients; and the National Housing of Social Interest System (SNHIS).

5.4 *Convention on the Elimination of All Forms of Discrimination against Women*

5.4.1 Incorporation and Reliance by Legislature and Executive

Brazil ratified CEDAW on 1 February 1984, with reservations to article 15(4), articles 16(1)(a), (c), (g), and (h), and article 29. It was incorporated into domestic law by Decree 89,460 of 20 March 1984, which explicitly refers to the promulgation of CEDAW. This Decree was subsequently repealed and replaced by Decree 4,377 of 13 September 2002.

The FC, which was promulgated in 1988, some four year after the ratification of CEDAW, represents a national historical landmark regarding the protection of women's human rights and the recognition of their citizenship in Brazil. The FC emerged after a long process of deliberations in plenary. Demands of social movements made it possible to include the notion of equal rights from an ethnic, racial and gender perspective. Women's rights in the Constitution was the

---

123 Conectas, 'Slow Procedure' Conectas (21 July 2017) <https://www.conectas.org/en/noticias/slow-procedure/> accessed 9 September 2023.

result of a mobilisation created by the National Women Council campaign, with the Council asking Brazilian women to send articles for the Constitution Assembly. With these proposals, the Letter of Women for the Constitution[124] was created, and suggestions for the text of the Constitution were collected. Suggestions included equality between men and women (article 5), maternity leave (articles 7(18) and (19)); encouraging the work of women, through protective rules (article 7(20)).

In recent years, Brazilian legislation has undergone some important changes, notably in the new content of the Civil Code of 2002, the changes in the Penal Code of 2005, as well as the advent of Law 11,340 in 2006 (Maria da Penha Law), which deals with domestic and family violence against women.

Brazil ratified two treaties that specifically address the eradication of gender inequalities: CEDAW and the Inter-American Convention to Prevent, Punish and Eradicate Violence against Women (Belém de Pará Convention).[125] Brazil ratified OP-CEDAW on 28 June 2002, through Decree 4,316, and without reservation.

In assessing the legislative impact of CEDAW in Brazil, the Brazilian legislature has directly relied extensively on CEDAW in legislative proposals. A search conduced in September 2023 in the database of Brazil's House of Representatives shows at least 286 explicit mentions of the CEDAW in legislative proposals,[126] the vast majority of them from the 2010s onwards. In order to illustrate this impact, two concrete examples are provided: (i) in 2015 CEDAW was cited in a proposed Bill suggesting the ineligibility to any political position of those convicted civilly or criminally in situations of domestic and family violence against women;[127] (ii) in 2018, citing Brazil's obligations under CEDAW, the legislative branch presented a Bill to make political violence against women an electoral crime.[128]

---

124 CONSTITUINTE 1987. CARTA DAS MULHERES AOS CONSTITUINTES <https://www2.camara.leg.br/atividade-legislativa/legislacao/Constituicoes_Brasileiras/constituicao-cidada/a-constituinte-e-as-mulheres/arquivos/Constituinte%201987-1988-Carta%20das%20Mulheres%20aos%20Constituintes.pdf> accessed 20 June 2020.
125 Belém do Pará Convention.
126 Search was conducted on the website of the Brazil's House of Representatives (Câmara dos Deputados) <https://www.camara.leg.br/busca-portal?contextoBusca=BuscaProposicoes&pagina=1&order=data&abaEspecifica=true&q=%22Convem%C3%A7%C3%A3o%20sobre%20a%20Elimina%C3%A7%C3%A3o%20de%20Todas%20as%20Formas%20de%20Discrimina%C3%A7%C3%A3o%20contra%20a%20Mulher%22> accessed 20 June 2020.
127 Brazil's House of Representatives, PLP 195/2015 <https://www.camara.leg.br/proposicoesWeb/fichadetramitacao?idProposicao=2055597> accessed 20 June 2020.
128 Brazil's House of Representatives, PL 9699/2018 <https://www.camara.leg.br/proposicoesWeb/fichadetramitacao?idProposicao=2168798> accessed 20 June 2020.

5.4.2 Reliance by Judiciary

The STF made two direct references to CEDAW. The first is found in an inquiry against former President Bolsonaro, who was accused of the crimes of incitement to rape and injury.[129] The case against Bolsonaro was subsequently opened formally. The second is found in the collective *habeas corpus* that stipulated the replacement of pre-trial detention by domicile of female prisoners who are pregnant or mothers of children up to 12 years of age, and persons with disabilities.[130] CEDAW was mentioned along with other mechanisms of the legislative network for the protection of women in order to build the argument about the situation of female vulnerability in certain situations. Moreover, in analysing the jurisprudence of the STF, four other references to the Convention were found in judgments, all as a legislative reference.[131]

5.4.3 Impact on and through Independent State Institutions

Stimulated by CEDAW and as an answer for civil society's claim, the State of São Paulo created a secretariat for the women of São Paulo. This secretariat stimulated the creation in 1985 of the National Centre for Women. After the re-democratisation, Lula's government in 2003 created the National Secretariat for Women Politics. The Secretariat is the most relevant space to observe the impact of CEDAW in independent state institutions. Between 2003 and 2015, the Secretariat had ministry status, and for this period produced recommendations to promote politics for eradicating discrimination against women and National Plans for Women whose goals was the development policies to revert racism and women discrimination in observance with international conventions and CEDAW recommendations.[132] CEDAW was mentioned among all objectives. In 2015 the Secretariat lost ministry status and was engulfed by the Human Rights, Racial Equally and Women Ministry.[133] In 2016, then President Michel Temer extinguished this ministry and the National

---

129 STF, INQUÉRITO 3.932 21/06/2016 <https://portal.stf.jus.br/processos/detalhe.asp?incidente=4689051> accessed 13 November 2023.

130 STF, HABEAS CORPUS 143.641 SÃO PAULO <https://portal.stf.jus.br/processos/detalhe.asp?incidente=5183497> accessed 13 November 2023.

131 By direct references we mean that CEDAW was used as the main legal basis. In the other decisions, this Conference does not occupy the place of the main legal basis, but is cited, throughout the arguments of the decision, by the Federal Supreme Court.

132 See II PLANO NACIONAL PARA MULHERES [Second National Plan to Women – Portuguese version] <http://portal.mec.gov.br/dmdocuments/planonacional_politicamulheres.pdf> accessed 9 September 2023.

133 The justification was the need for administrative reform to overcome the economic crisis. See <https://g1.globo.com/politica/noticia/2015/10/dilma-anuncia-reducao-de-39-para-31-pastas-na-reforma-ministerial.html> accessed 9 September 2023.

Secretary for Women went to the Justice Ministry. After Bolsonaro's election, the Secretariat went to the Human Rights, Family and Women Ministry and CEDAW was not directly mentioned. In 2023, the Ministry of Women returned was revived as an independent body, with Decree No. 11,351/2023 providing for its organizational structure, which has a National Secretariat for Institutional Articulation, Thematic Actions and Political Participation.[134]

5.4.4 Impact on and through Non-state Actors

The impact of CEDAW on and through non-state bodies in Brazil is significant, especially in the case of feminist NGOs and non-state actors. The work of NGOs related to the implementation of CEDAW has been to elaborate alternative reports on the status of effective implementation of the Convention in Brazil, which are also sent to the CEDAW Cttee. As many as 51 non-state feminist actors participated in the ten alternative reports on the CEDAW website, indicating the extent of social mobilisation around CEDAW in Brazil.

Regarding the impact of CEDAW on the academy, when analysing publications in mechanisms such as SciELO and Google Scholar, several mentions to CEDAW were found and in formats mainly of academic articles or coursework. The analysis, for the most part, is limited to the impact of CEDAW in Brazil from observing the various scopes of women's lives that should be impacted by the Convention (such as the labour market and access to education).

5.4.5 Impact of State Reporting

Brazil's first report submission was only in 2002. The CEDAW Cttee COs, covering reporting cycle I-V, recommended an upgrade in the database of women violence. As a response, Brazil presented the description and data of race, age and ethnicity data programmes.[135] The second report was in 2007,[136] covering reporting cycle VI.[137] In addition to the fight against gender violence, this report showed its enforcement in legislative procedure 'a landmark achievement since publication of Brazil's sixth report had been the passage of the 'Maria da Penha Law on domestic and family violence, which had created special courts to hear domestic violence cases, stiffened the penalties for perpetrators and established protective measures for victims'. The report also

---

134 Ministry of Women website <https://www.gov.br/mulheres/pt-br> accessed 9 September 2023.
135 CEDAW/C/BRA/1-5.
136 Committee on the Elimination of Discrimination against Women 39th session Summary Record of the 795th meeting (Chamber B) held at Headquarters, New York, on 25 July 2007, 2.
137 ibid.

highlighted programmes against gender discrimination and the realisation of the first National Conference for Women Policies. In response to the CEDAW Cttee's preoccupation with the divergence between judicial procedures and treaties, the Brazilian delegation highlighted the importance of Constitutional Amendment 45, which grants functional and administrative autonomy to the State Public Defenders' Offices.

Brazil took numerous institutional and policy measures regarding the issues raised by the CEDAW Cttee, in particular by establishing a National Plan for Women and Secretariat for Women Policy, which has been the most significant influence of CEDAW in Brazil. In the last report, covering reporting cycle VII, the main goal of the country was the consolidation of the national policy for women. This policy included

> [o]n one hand, the construction of the Multi-Annual Plan 2012–2015, a government planning tool that sets guidelines, goals and objectives in order to facilitate the implementation and management of public policies, guide the setting of priorities and assist in promoting sustainable development. On the other, the organization of the 3rd National Conference for Women Policies, which evaluated and redefined the priorities of the second National Plan for Women for the next period.[138]

Also, the Multi-Annual Plan 2012–2015 has had directive guidelines for 'human rights guarantee with the reduction of gender, ethno-racial, regional and social inequalities'. It is important to highlight that the second National Plan for Women Policies was used as a basis document by the Ministry of Planning, which led to the process of drafting the Multi Annual Plan.[139]

Following this, an alternative report to the Brazilian report 2006–2009 was produced, 'a contribution of the feminist and women's movement to support the CEDAW Cttee in its analysis and comments on the official report sent by the Brazilian State in 2010, and ensure appropriate and effective accomplishment of the Convention on the Elimination of All Forms of Discrimination against Women (CEDAW)'.[140] This alternative report focuses on articles 1 and

---

138   51st session of the Committee on the Elimination of Discrimination against Women Geneva, 13 February to 2 March 2012. VII PRESENTATION OF BRAZILIAN NATIONAL REPORT TO THE CONVENTION ON THE ELIMINATION OF ALL FORMS OF DISCRIMINATION AGAINST WOMEN 4.
139   ibid.
140   Alternative Report Seventh Periodic Report of Brazil (CEDAW/C/BRA/7), Committee on the Elimination of All Forms of Discrimination Against Women, CEDAW, 51st session 2.

The National Housing Strategy itself refers to a 'human rights-based approach to housing' and the UN Sustainable Development Goals.[231]

5.3.2 Reliance on the Treaty by Domestic Courts

The Supreme Court of Canada in *Health Services and Support v British Columbia* relied on CESCR for guidance in interpreting the scope of collective bargaining rights under section 2(d) of the Canadian Charter of Rights and Freedoms.[232] In *Saskatchewan Federation of Labour v Saskatchewan*, the Court held that CESCR is relevant to interpreting the Charter with respect to the right to strike. The majority opinion emphasized that Canada's obligations under article 8(1) of CESCR, 'clearly argue for the recognition of the right to strike within s. 2(d) [of the Charter]' (freedom of association).[233] The dissenting opinion emphasized that article 8(2) of CESCR did not prevent a state from imposing lawful restrictions on the right to strike, and that there is 'no clear consensus under international law that the right to strike is an essential element of freedom of association'.[234] Although they provide interpretative guidance, rights protected under CESCR have not formed the basis of successful Charter challenges as the Charter does not explicitly protect economic, social, and cultural rights. Advocates have used the section 7 right to life, liberty and security of the person to 'read in' economic, social, and cultural rights. The most recent case to invoke section 7 on the basis of a violation of social, economic and cultural rights was the Ontario Court of Appeal ruling in *Tanudaja v Canada (Attorney-General)*.[235] The applicants sought a declaration 'that the failure of Canada and Ontario to have implemented effective national and provincial strategies to reduce and eliminate homelessness and inadequate housing violates the applicants' and others' rights to life, liberty and security of the person contrary to s.7 of the *Charter*'.[236] The Ontario Court of Appeal deemed the issue non-justiciable.[237]

---

231 Government of Canada, 'What is the National Housing Strategy?' (nd) <https://www.placetocallhome.ca/what-is-the-strategy> accessed 27 October 2020.
232 *Health Services and Support – Facilities Subsector Bargaining Assn v British Columbia* [2007] 2 SCR 391 paras 72–77.
233 *Saskatchewan Federation of Labour v Saskatchewan* [2015] 1 SCR 245 paras 62–70.
234 ibid paras 155–156.
235 2014 ONCA 852.
236 ibid para 15.
237 Ibid paras 16 and 19.

5.3.3 Impact on and through Non-state Actors

NGOs and civil society: We have not come across examples of NGOs using CESCR in advocacy campaigns or other awareness-raising projects. However, NGOs such as Canada Without Poverty periodically update stakeholders on their engagement with the CESCR Cttee.[238] The most common use of the treaty by NGOs has been in the context of submitting alternative reports to the Committee for the periodic review of Canada.[239]

Academics: To our knowledge, only three academic articles by local researchers deal exclusively with CESCR and Canada.[240] There have been recent articles that focus in part on the Covenant and Canada: a 2015 article on the right to housing;[241] another on monitoring women's socio-economic equality under CESCR;[242] and a third on the justiciability of social and economic rights in Canada.[243]

---

[238] Canada Without Poverty, 'CWP and the CESCR' <http://www.cwp-csp.ca/action/cwp-at-the-un/cwp-and-the-committee-on-economic-social-and-cultural-rights/> accessed 26 June 2019.

[239] OHCHR, 'UN Treaty Body Database' (search results) <https://tbinternet.ohchr.org/_layouts/TreatyBodyExternal/TBSearch.aspx?Lang=en&CountryID=31&TreatyID=9&DocTypeID=14&DocTypeID=12>. The following NGOs and civil society groups have submitted reports: Food Secure Canada; CCPI-SRAC; Income Security Advocacy Centre; the Canadian Human Rights Commission; Canadian Civil Liberties Association; Council of Canadians With Disabilities; Centre for Equality Rights in Accommodation; Pivot Legal Society; FAFIA; Canadian Council for Refugees; First Nations Child and Family Caring Society of Canada; Canada Without Poverty; Amnesty International; Maytree; Indigenous Bar Association in Canada; Income Security Advocacy Centre; Sierra Club British Columbia; David Suzuki Foundation; Human Rights Watch; African Canadian Legal Clinic; Front d'action populaire en réaménagement urbain (FRAPRU); Mining Watch; Ligue des Droits et Libertés; Human Rights and Tobacco Control Network; and the Asubpeeschoseewagong/Grassy Narrows First Nation.

[240] El-Obaid Admed and Kwadwo Appaigyei-Atua 'Human Rights in Africa: A New Perspective on Linking the Past to the Present' (1996) 41 McGill Law Journal 819; Nihal Jayawickrama, 'The Right of Self-Determination: A Time for Reinvention and Renewal' (1993) 57 Saskatchewan Law Review (1993) 1; Robert E Robertson, 'The Rights to Food – Canada's Broken Covenant' (1989–90) 6 Canadian Human Rights Yearbook 185.

[241] Darcel Bullen, 'A Road to Home: The Right to Housing in Canada and Around the World' (2015) 24 Journal of Law and Social Policy 1–9.

[242] Meghan Campbell, 'Monitoring Women's Socio-Economic Equality under the ICESCR' (2018) 30 Canadian Journal of Women and the Law 82.

[243] Martha Jackman and Bruce Porter, 'Justiciability of Social and Economic Rights in Canada' in M Langford (ed), *Socio-Economic Rights Jurisprudence: Emerging Trends in Comparative International Law* (Cambridge University Press 2013).

2 (discrimination); 5 (violence, trafficking and sexual exploitation)' 7 and 10 (education); and 12 (sexual and reproductive health, abortion and HIV/AIDS).

Additionally, Brazil participated in the follow-up procedure of the CEDAW Cttee in February 2014,[141] presenting a lengthy report on the impact of COs. It is important to highlight that NGOs also presented alternative reports for the follow-up procedure, namely, CEDAW Watch Brazil and the Centre for Reproductive Rights, which shows the importance of the procedure for Brazilian civil society. In its reply to Brazil, the Rapporteur for Follow-up on COs of the CEDAW Cttee, the Committee concluded that Brazil had implemented most of the recommendations, either partially or fully. Two examples of full implementation is the establishment in 2013 of a national mechanism against human trafficking and the regional monitoring of data on collection and analysis of data on trafficking and on the exploitation of women in prostitution.

5.4.6 Impact of Individual Communications

In 2008 Maria de Lourdes da Silva Pimentel submitted a communication concerning Alyne da Silva Pimentel, her daughter, who was alleged to have been a victim of a violation by Brazil of her right to life and health under articles 2 and 12 of CEDAW.[142] The CEDAW Cttee found a violation of article 12 (in relation to access to health), article 2(c) (in relation to access to justice) and article 2(e) (in relation Brazil's due diligence obligation to regulate the activities of private health service providers).[143] The CEDAW Cttee issued one recommendation specifically to Ms Da Silva Pimentel Teixeira and six general recommendations.

For the author and the family of Ms Da Silva Pimentel Teixeira, the Cttee recommended that Brazil 'provide appropriate reparation, including adequate financial compensation, to the author and to the daughter of Ms da Silva Pimentel Teixeira commensurate with the gravity of the violations against her'. Brazil paid financial reparation to Ms Da Silva Pimentel Teixeira in March 2014,[144] and symbolically recognised the Brazilian government's responsibilities for Alyne's death. The government, represented by its Women Secretariat, paid compensation of US $55 000 and also, in the solemn ceremony, handed

---

[141] CEDAW/C/BRA/CO/7/Add.1.
[142] The Convention and the Optional Protocol entered into force for the state party on 2 March 1984 and 28 September 2002, respectively.
[143] CEDAW/C/49/D/17/2008 21.
[144] SDH, Mãe de Alyne Pimentel recebe reparação do Estado brasileiro pela morte da filha. SDH, 23 de março de 2014 <https://www.gov.br/mdh/pt-br/sdh/noticias/2014/marco/mae-de-alyne-pimentel-recebe-reparacao-do-estado-brasileiro-pela-morte-da-filha> accessed 20 June 2020.

a certificate to Alyne's mother acknowledging responsibility for the death and committed to undertake public policies for women's health and maternity.[145]

As far as general recommendations are concerned, the CEDAW Cttee issued six recommendations,[146] specifically focused on policies for training health professionals and ensuring adequate sanctions for health professionals who violate women's reproductive health rights. Hereafter, some federal states in Brazil incorporated legislative laws (in state and municipal levels) to protect maternity and reproductive rights, such as São Paulo through Municipal Law 15894/2013 and State Law 15759/2015. The decision also spurred an institutional response: Brazil has 'established an inter-ministerial group to oversee the implementation of the Committee's recommendations'.[147] Yet, the causal link between the CEDAW recommendations and those measures is not clear.

5.4.7 Brief Conclusion

CEDAW and the CEDAW Cttee are very well known at the domestic level. In recent years, CEDAW was an important instrument to guide Brazilian politics for women's protection. This impact is mostly at the institutional level. The Women Secretariat, for example, was the body that represented the Brazilian government on the reparations to the *Alyne Pimentel* case. The decentralised

---

[145] AGÊNCIA BRASIL, Governo indeniza família de grávida morta após atendimento na rede pública. Agencia Brasil, 24 de março de 2014 <https://agenciabrasil.ebc.com.br/direitos-humanos/noticia/2014-03/governo-brasileiro-indeniza-familia-de-jovem-morta-em-2002> accessed 20 June 2020.

[146] CEDAW Cttee, Communication No 17/2008. The six recommendations were the following: '(a) ensure women's right to safe motherhood and affordable access for all women to adequate emergency obstetric care, in line with General Recommendation No 24 (1999) on women and health; (b) provide adequate professional training for health workers, especially on women's reproductive health rights, including quality medical treatment during pregnancy and delivery, as well as timely emergency obstetric care; (c) ensure access to effective remedies in cases where women's reproductive health rights have been violated and provide training for the judiciary and for law enforcement personnel; (d) ensure that private healthcare facilities comply with relevant national and international standards on reproductive health care; (e) ensure that adequate sanctions are imposed on health professionals who violate women's reproductive health rights; (f) reduce preventable maternal deaths through the implementation of the National Pact for the Reduction of Maternal Mortality at state and municipal levels, including by establishing maternal mortality committees where they still do not exist, in line with the recommendations in its COs for Brazil, adopted on 15 August 2007 (CEDAW/C/BRA/CO/6)'.

[147] Plataforma Brasileira de Direitos Humanos Econômicos, Sociais, Culturais e Ambientais, 'A Victory in Alyne's Case' (Media Release, 5 September 2012) as cited in Simone Cusack and Lisa Pusey, 'CEDAW and the Rights to Equality and Non-discrimination' (2013) 14 *Melbourne Journal of International Law* 54, 112.

bodies created for monitoring and guiding the gender questions in Brazil have had the most relevant impact, but this impact is largely limited to the municipal and state level.

5.5 Convention against Torture and Other Cruel, Inhuman or Degrading Treatment or Punishment

5.5.1 Incorporation and Reliance by Legislature and Executive

CAT was incorporated into domestic law by Decree 40 of 15 February 1991. One of the main efforts by the executive branch in Brazil to investigate torture was the establishment of the National Truth Commission (CNV). The CNV was established by the Brazilian government to investigate the serious human rights violations that occurred between 18 September 1946 and 5 October 1988, the period of the military dictatorship. These violations took place in Brazil and abroad, committed by Brazilian public agents, persons in their service, with the support or in the interest of the state. The Committee was made up of seven members appointed by former President Dilma Rousseff, who were assisted by advisors, consultants and researchers. Law 12,528/2011, which instituted it, was passed in 2011, and the Commission was officially installed in 2012. The CNV concentrated its efforts on examining and clarifying human rights violations committed during the latter dictatorship, especially as regards torture.

In 2006 the National Congress approved the ratification of the Optional Protocol to the UN Convention against Torture and other Cruel, Inhuman and Degrading Treatment or Punishment (OP-CAT). On 26 June 2006 – International Day against the Torture – President Luiz Inácio Lula Da Silva established the National Committee for the Prevention and Control of the Torture in Brazil.[148] Among its duties, the Committee is takes to propose actions and programmes to combat torture. It consists of 23 members, 11 of

---

[148] The National Committee for the Prevention and Combat of Torture (SNPCT) is one of the bodies that make up the National System for the Prevention and Combat of Torture (SNPCT). The collegiate is composed of 23 members, 11 of which are representatives of federal agencies and 12 of civil society. The initiative aims to contribute to the fight against this violation in institutions of deprivation of liberty, such as police stations, penitentiaries, places of permanence for the elderly and psychiatric hospitals. This committee was approved before the creation of the National System for the Prevention of Torture, since the National System for the Prevention and Combat of Torture (SNPCT) was established by Law No. United Nations (UN), through the ratification, in 2007, of the Optional Protocol to the Convention against Torture and Other Cruel, Inhuman or Degrading Treatment or Punishment. After creating the National System for the Prevention of Torture, it is linked to the National Committee on Prevention.

whom are representatives of federal executive branch bodies and 12 of professional class councils and civil society organisations.

In 2006,[149] the Commission on Human Rights and Minorities produced a report on the prison situation throughout the country, in which torture is one of the main problems identified. This Commission established an Integrated Action Plan for the Prevention and Combat of Torture that influenced state legislation such as State Management Committee for Monitoring the Implementation of the Plan of Integrated Actions for the Prevention and Combating Torture. Another important point to highlight is the omission of the Brazilian state regarding the applicability of public policies to combat torture. One of the most emblematic actions involving the National Mechanism for Prevention and Combating Torture took place in 2015, when experts delivered to the government a report denouncing the precarious conditions and the climate of tension in Compaj (Anísio Jobim Penitentiary Complex), in Manaus. In this document the experts found that the complex housed 697 prisoners more than the capacity and highlighted the fact that Compaj had agents from a private company, Umanizzare, to make the site safe. In the analysis of the agency, this resulted in deficient training, precarious work, high turnover and insufficient number of security employees – only 153 worked on the day of the visit, compared to 250 under contract. The document was ignored and in 2019 one of the worst massacres in Brazilian prisons, the rebellion of the Penitentiary Anísio Jobim in Manaus, took place.[150]

---

149   COMISSÃO DE DIREITOS HUMANOS E MINORIAS. SITUAÇÃO DO SISTEMA PRISIONAL BRASILEIRO. Brasília 2016 <https://www2.camara.leg.br/atividade-legislativa/comissoes/comissoes-permanentes/cdhm/documentos/relatorios/SitSisPrisBras.pdf> accessed 20 June 2020.

150   According to the report, the torture has continued in democratic periods, because of '(i) institutional resistance within the organs of the Executive Branch both in admitting torture common practice as well as investigating or reporting colleagues in the police career or penitentiary; (ii) lack of material and human resources for distinct independent research that made by the police force, the result of resistance to the establishment of full power of investigation outside the police force. This defence of the police investigative monopoly (even in cases of torture) was evident in the episode of the rejection of the Proposed Amendment Constitutional Law No 37, which expressly granted the monopoly of investigative power to the political, but was overthrown after having been widely criticised in the street demonstrations of June 2013; (iii) impunity for public officials involved in torture cases (police, prison officers), due to the lack of a successful investigation (see item 'i' and 'ii' above), generating the vicious circle of stimulating the practice; (iv) underreporting of cases, generated by the fear of victims or family members of reporting torture, which is reinforced by the confidence in the quick punishment or removal of those involved; (v) persistent speech in certain political sectors and the electorate in which the practice of torture is an effective police investigation (to obtain a 'confession')

IMPACT OF UNHR TREATIES ON DOMESTIC LEVEL IN BRAZIL   137

In assessing the legislative impact of CAT in Brazil, it is key to observe that the Brazilian legislature has quite often placed direct reliance on CAT in legislative proposals. A search conduced in September 2023 in the database of Brazil's House of Representatives has shown at least 49 explicit mentions[151] to CAT in legislative proposals, the vast majority of them from 2005 onwards. Considering the fact that Brazil ratified CAT in 1989, shortly after the promulgation of the Federal Constitution in 1988, it shows that in Brazil the impact of UN human rights treaties has occurred primarily after democratisation. In order to illustrate this impact, two concrete examples are cited: (i) in 2007 CAT was cited in a proposed Bill suggesting that torture should also be an act of administrative 'improbity';[152] and (ii) in 2005, the legislative branch requested an international seminar about OP-CAT.[153]

5.5.2 Reliance by Judiciary

CAT is directly mentioned in several cases on the STF.[154] Reference to CAT is often related to the unconstitutionality of the violations of rights in the prison system, and shows the necessity of the minimum guarantee of personal, and the physical and mental security of detainees as a state duty. One of the key cases in this regard concerns the unconstitutional state of affairs in the prison system in Brazil, in which the STF determined a series of measures to be taken by lower judges, in particular to avoid whenever legally possible ordering prison sentences.[155] In a report, NGOs and the public defender's office analysed

---

or proportional response to practices criminal prisoners (punishment); (vi) lack of break with the dictatorial past, in the face of the absence of the removal of torture agents from the military regime, keeping the tradition of violence against the detainee'. See <https://www.defensoria.sp.def.br/dpesp/repositorio/31/Comenta%CC%81rio%20Geral%20texto%20final%2026.06.pdf> accessed 20 June 2020.

151 Search was conducted on the website of the Brazil's House of Representatives (Câmara dos Deputados) <https://www.camara.leg.br/busca-portal?contextoBusca=BuscaProposicoes&pagina=1&order=data&abaEspecifica=true&q=%22Conven%C3%A7%C3%A3o%20Contra%20a%20Tortura%20e%20Outros%20Tratamentos%20ou%20Penas%20Cru%C3%A9is,%20Desumanos%20ou%20Degradantes%22> accessed 9 September 2023.

152 Brazil's House of Representatives, PL 417/2007 <https://www.camara.leg.br/proposicoesWeb/fichadetramitacao?idProposicao=344662> accessed 20 June 2020.

153 Brazil's House of Representatives, REQ 75/2005 CDHM <https://www.camara.leg.br/proposicoesWeb/fichadetramitacao?idProposicao=294543> accessed 20 June 2020.

154 Resource: RE 580252; Resource: RE 715268 AgR; Arrangement for Breach of Non-Compliance ADPF 153, Ext 112; Habeas Corpus, HC 70389; Arrangement for Breach of Non-Compliance ADPF 54.

155 See <https://www.stf.jus.br/arquivo/informativo/documento/informativo798.htm> accessed 9 September 2023.

the prohibition of torture in the Brazil's judiciary between 2005 and 2010:[156] (1) it has been common to find cases in which the Public Ministry absolves the accused; (2) the production of evidence in cases where the authors are public officials is more deficient than when private agents are involved or if, in fact, there is a different view from the operators of the right in relation to cases, depending on who the perpetrator of the crime is; (3) finally, most of the judgments dealt with the criminal 'torture-punishment' or 'proof-torture', none of them dealt with the crime of 'torture-discrimination', very few dealt with torture in its omissive modality and psychological torture. The understanding of torture is often restricted to physical torture. There is a definite need for Brazil to improve its performance in terms of torture.

5.5.3 Impact on and through Independent State Institutions

There are two important forms of impact of CAT in independent state institutions. First, there is the proliferation of anti-torture mechanisms at the state level, which follows the guidelines of article 17 of OP-CAT. At the state level in Brazil,

> [a]ccording to data from the federal government, until July 2019, Brazil had 22 state committees created, with the exception of the states of Roraima, Mato Grosso, Tocantins, São Paulo and the Federal District. In relation to state mechanisms, the progress was more timid, being verified in only 10 states, namely, Amapá, Maranhão, Espírito Santo, Alagoas, Sergipe, Mato Grosso do Sul, Paraíba, Pernambuco, Rio de Janeiro and Rondônia. It happens that only the mechanisms of the last 4 are in effective operation.[157]

In São Paulo, the state with the largest number of people arrested in the country, a law was passed in December 2018 by São Paulo's Legislative Assembly (ALESP) providing for the creation of an anti-torture mechanism, but it was vetoed in its entirely by Governor João Dória Jr (PSDB). The National System for the Prevention and Combat of Torture is an advisory board also

---

[156] Maria Gorete Marques de Jesus, CALDERONI, Vivian (Coordenadoras). Julgando a tortura:ANÁLISE DE JURISPRUDÊNCIA NOS TRIBUNAIS DE JUSTIÇA DO BRASIL (2005-2010) <https://carceraria.org.br/wp-content/uploads/2018/01/documento_julgando-a-tortura.pdf> accessed 20 June 2020.

[157] Hugo Matias, O compromisso da Defensoria com os mecanismos de combate à tortura no Brasil *Conjur* 14 January 2020 <https://www.conjur.com.br/2020-jan-14/tribuna-defensoria-compromisso-defensoria-combate-tortura-brasil#_ftn5> accessed 20 June 2020.

composed by other entities rather than itself, such as the DEPEN (National Penitentiary Department), organisations of the justice system and community committees.[158]

Second, in 2013, after international pressure, Law 12,847/13 was promulgated, to institute the National Mechanism for the Prevention and Combat of Torture (MNPCT). Yet, in June 2019, former President Bolsonaro signed Presidential Decree 9,831. According to a report by the SPT, this Decree introduced 'a new model', the main differentiating feature of which is that the members/experts of the MNPCT would cease to be remunerated and would exercise their functions on a voluntary basis (article 4 of Decree 9,831 that modifies article 10 of Decree 8,154). The June 2019 Decree also removes the requirement for its membership to be diverse in terms of gender, race and regional representation and, in ways that remain somewhat unclear, dismantles the NPM's administrative support structure.[159] Brazil's President has not revoked the Decree, despite the request by the SPT to do so, but in August 2019 the judiciary maintained the remuneration for the 11 experts of the National Mechanism,[160] citing OP-CAT in support.[161]

5.5.4 Impact on and through Non-state Actors

CAT is usually mentioned in campaigns for the protection of human rights. National human rights NGOs make intensive use of CAT and the CAT Cttee's COs. In 2019 NGOs (*Justiça Global, Terra de Direitos e Instituto de Defensores de Direitos Humanos*) denounced former President Bolsonaro to the UN after he had issued Decree 9,831/2019,[162] which discharged experts from the national

---

158   CONECTAS. THE IMPORTANCE OF THE MECHANISM FOR THE COMBAT OF TORTURE. CONECTAS, 14 August 2019 <https://www.conectas.org/en/noticias/the-importance-of-the-mechanism-for-the-combat-of-torture/> accessed 9 September 2023.

159   See Subcommittee on Prevention of Torture and Other Cruel, Inhuman or Degrading Treatment or Punishment Views of the Subcommittee on Prevention of Torture on the compatibility, with the Optional Protocol to the Convention against Torture, of Presidential Decree No 9.831/2019, relating to the national preventive mechanism of Brazil <https://www.ohchr.org/sites/default/files/Documents/HRBodies/OPCAT/NPM/Views_NPM_Brazil.pdf> accessed 9 September 2023.

160   AGÊNCIA BRASI, Justiça mantém peritos no combate à tortura. Agência Brasil, agosto de 2019 <https://agenciabrasil.ebc.com.br/justica/noticia/2019-08/justica-mantem-peritos-no-combate-tortura> accessed 20 June 2020.

161   JUSTIÇA FEDERAL, AÇÃO CIVIL PÚBLICA N° 5039174-92.2019.4.02.5101/RJ <https://www.conjur.com.br/dl/justica-rio-revoga-exoneracao.pdf> accessed 20 June 2020.

162   A PÚBLICA, Jair Bolsonaro exonera todos os peritos do Mecanismo de Combate à Tortura. A PÚBLICA, 11 junho de 2019 <https://apublica.org/2019/06/jair-bolsonaro-exonera-todos-os-peritos-do-mecanismo-de-combate-a-tortura/> accessed 20 June 2020.

mechanism to combat torture. The CAT Cttee called Bolsonaro to explain the situation. As mentioned above, after this, the controversy went to judiciary power and Federal Justice, which determined the suspension of the exoneration. One of the key NGOs working with the fight against torture in Brazil is *Pastoral Carceraria*, which has developed a series of manuals containing guidelines for monitoring prisons and other places of detention.[163] Those practical guidelines are based on CAT and its Optional Protocol, demonstrating a direct impact of the treaty.

5.5.5 Impact of State Reporting

Brazil has extensively engaged with the CAT Cttee's reporting procedure, with substantial delays in submitting the periodic reports (10 years in the first reporting cycle and 18 years' delay in the second reporting cycle). In 2001 the CAT Cttee requested the state 'to guarantee to any person deprived of his or her liberty the right of defence and, consequently, the right to be assisted by a lawyer, if necessary at the state's expense'.[164] Since then, the number of free legal aid has increased in Brazil with the spread of public defenders' offices across the country, although there is still a need for more public defenders in most of the states.[165] In its 2009 COs,[166] the CAT Cttee recommended that the state party should protect human rights in judicial procedures; carry out awareness-raising campaigns in order to sensitise all sectors of society about the issue of torture and ill-treatment and on the existing conditions of detention centres; and ensure optimal conditions of detention in adult and juvenile detention centres. In this regard, the federal government manages the National School of Criminal Services (ESPEN) which deals with education for public officials, including prison personnel and police, on human rights. One of the key influences of CAT in Brazil is the establishment of custody hearings in 2015, which seek to check, within 24 hours after arrest, the legality

---

163   BRAZIL, Monitoramento de locais de detenção: um guia prático (2ª edição) / Associação para Prevenção da Tortura; Tradução: Fabiana Gorenstein e Liana Rodrigues; Revisão e correção da versão: Mary Murphy; Releitura: Karolina Alves de Castro, Naum Pereira de Sousa e Antonia Portoalegre. – Brasília: Secretaria de Direitos Humanos, 2015.
164   COs of the Committee against Torture on Brazil, A/56/44, A/56/44, para 120.
165   IV Diagnóstico da Defensoria Pública no Brasil (Forth Diagnosis of the Public Defender's Office in Brazil) https://www.anadep.org.br/wtksite/downloads/iv-diagnostico-da-defensoria-publica-no-brasil.pdf accessed 9 September 2023.
166   CAT/C/39/2.

of the arrest, including whether the detainee was subjected to torture or ill-treatment in custody.[167]

5.5.6   Impact of Individual Communications
No communication has been submitted to the CAT Cttee against Brazil.

5.5.7   Impact of Other Measures: SPT Visits and Article 20 Inquiry Procedure

In line with articles 1 and 11 of OP-CAT, the SPT conducted visits to Brazil in 2009 and 2015.[168] The SPT in its first visit highlighted that it had received allegations of beatings and ill-treatment as a form of punishment. In its 2017 report, following its 2015 visit, the SPT recommended that the 'Federal Government, through the federal Human Rights Secretariat, take a more proactive approach as part of an established national public programme, in coordination with state-level authorities, to foster the creation of local mechanisms'.[169] This may include meetings with high-level state authorities, regular advocacy visits to the states, technical support for the drafting of legislation and economic incentives through allocation of funds. This recommendation was implemented. According to Brazil's 2020 report, the Federal Pact for Preventing and Combating Torture was published in the Federal Official Gazette through MMFDH Ordinance 346 of 19 September 2017. In July 2018, MMFDH organised the Third National Meeting of National Committees and Mechanisms for Preventing and Combating Torture. The Third Meeting resulted in the publication of the Brasilia Letter, which gathers a set of proposals resulting from the analysis of the needs in order to strengthen SNPCT. The letter specifically suggests the adoption of a set of actions aiming at encouraging and implementing State Committees and Mechanisms.[170] Yet, there were recent setbacks in the national mechanism against torture in 2019, as mentioned above.

In its report published in 2016,[171] the SPT alerted the Brazilian authorities to the problems of the prisons that ended up leading to the Manaus massacre

---

167   CNJ, Audiencia de custódia <https://www.cnj.jus.br/sistema-carcerario/audiencia-de-custodia/> accessed 9 September 2023.
168   CAT/OP/BRA/1, CAT/OP/BRA/R.2, CAT/OP/BRA/3.
169   CAT/OP/BRA/3, para 97 https://undocs.org/en/CAT/OP/BRA/3 accessed 20 June 2020.
170   CAT/C/BRA/2, para 219.
171   'In accordance with article 16(1) of the Optional Protocol, the present report was transmitted confidentially to the state party on 24 November 2016. On 10 January 2017 the state party made public the present report at https://www.gov.br/mdh/pt-br/sdh/noticias/2017/janeiro/sedh-publica-relatorio-de-subcomite-da-onu-sobre-prevencao-e-combate-a-tortura-e-maus-tratos-no-sistema-carcerario; consequently, in accordance with article

soon thereafter – in 2017.[172] Here, it is important to highlight the failure of the Brazilian authorities to take action on the issue of prisons, with the country being tainted by rebellions in prisons. Yet, some measures taken by the government regarding this issue can still be mentioned. For example, every four years the National Council for Criminal and Penitentiary Policy develops the National Criminal Policy Plan, which sets the guidelines for this policy, in compliance with what is contained in article 64, items I and II of Law 7,210 of 11 July 1994 (Penal Execution Law). The last of these Plans was developed in 2019.

Finally, Brazil has engaged extensively with the inquiry procedure under article 20 of CAT. In 2006 the CAT Cttee presented conclusions regarding an investigation into the Brazilian situation.[173] Later on, the Brazilian government replied to the Committee's concerns. One of the recommendations from the CAT Cttee was that 'the problem of overcrowding in detention centres must be solved by adopting measures urgently, such as awareness-raising of the judiciary of the possibility of applying alternative sentences'.[174] Several measures for inducing the application of alternative sentences have been implemented by the Brazilian judiciary, although the level of mass incarceration in Brazil places the country in the third position in the world. In its comments replying to the inquiry procedure, Brazil recalled the creation of the General Coordination of Alternative Sentencing, and the creation of Special Federal Criminal Courts applying a wider range of crimes to alternative sentences.[175]

5.5.8   Brief Conclusion

CAT has had an important impact in Brazil to protect citizens from torture, mainly after the country's democratisation process, through legislative reforms and judicial decisions. However, despite having guided legal changes at various levels, these changes were not accompanied by consistent public policy projects. There has been a constant neglect in dealing with the subject and increasingly the dismantling of oversight mechanisms, both at the state and

---

16(2) of the Optional Protocol, the present report is published by the Subcommittee'. See <https://digitallibrary.un.org/record/831519> accessed 9 September 2023.

172   The rapporteurs cited frequent occurrences of torture and ill-treatment in prisons, overcrowding and control of penitentiary units by criminal factions with the tacit permission of the state.

173   CAT/C/36/R.1/Add.1.

174   CAT/C/39/2, para 196, See <https://www2.ohchr.org/english/bodies/cat/docs/AdvanceVersions/cat.c.39.2.doc> accessed 20 June 2020.

175   CAT/C/39/2, paras 270–275 <https://www2.ohchr.org/english/bodies/cat/docs/AdvanceVersions/cat.c.39.2.doc> accessed 20 June 2020.

federal levels, indicating that the Brazilian state neglects its international obligations. The need for change remains urgent.

5.6   Convention on the Rights of the Child

5.6.1   Incorporation and Reliance by Legislature and Executive

Brazil ratified the CRC on 24 September 1990, not long after the promulgation of the Federal Constitution in 1988. It was incorporated into domestic law by Decree 99,710 of 21 November 1990. The most important Brazilian law on the subject is the Statute of the Child and Adolescent, which provides for integral child and adolescent protection (Law 8.069 of 13 July 1990). It changed the legal framework for children's rights in Brazil. The Federal Constitution in article 227 also guarantees the fundamental rights of children and adolescents, and safeguards them from all forms of neglect, discrimination, exploitation, violence, cruelty and oppression.

In addition, on 27 January 2004 Brazil ratified the Optional Protocol to the Convention on the Rights of the Child on the Sale of Children, Child Prostitution and Child Pornography (OP-CRC-SC), and the Optional Protocol to the Convention on the Rights of the Child on the Involvement of Children in Armed Conflict (OP-CRC-AC). In 2009, with Constitutional Amendment 59,[176] Brazil made schooling obligatory for students from 4 to 17 years old. In 2016 the legal marker for the start of childhood was institutionalised by Law 13.257.[177] Brazil ratified the Optional Protocol to the Convention on the Rights of the Child on a Communications Procedure (OP-CRC-CP) on 29 September 2017.

The Brazilian legislature has directly relied on CRC extensively in legislative proposals. Two examples are provided: (i) In 2017 CRC was cited in a proposed Bill suggesting that imprisoned women with underaged children should serve their sentences in the form of house arrest;[178] and (ii) in 2019 another proposed Bill aimed at typifying paedophilia as a heinous crime cited CRC.[179] A search conduced in September 2023 on the database of Brazil's House of

---

[176] Brazil EC 59/2009 <http://www.planalto.gov.br/ccivil_03/constituicao/emendas/emc/emc59.htm> accessed 20 June 2020.

[177] Brazil L Law 13.257/2016 <http://www.planalto.gov.br/ccivil_03/_ato2015-2018/2016/lei/l13257.htm> accessed 20 June 2020.

[178] Brazil's House of Representatives, PL 7338/2017 <https://www.camara.leg.br/proposicoesWeb/fichadetramitacao?idProposicao=2128785> accessed 20 June 2020.

[179] Brazil's House of Representatives, PL 2007/2019 <https://www.camara.leg.br/proposicoesWeb/fichadetramitacao?idProposicao=2196711> accessed 20 June 2020.

Representatives revealed at least 237 explicit mentions of CRC in legislative proposals,[180] the vast majority of them from the 2000s onwards.

5.6.2 Reliance by Judiciary

The STJ mentioned CRC directly five times as a mechanism of child protection. Those mentions were announced by three of its *Informativos de Jurisprudência*,[181] documents periodically released with notes on relevant theses defended in STJ judgments, chosen for their legal repercussion and novelty. A *habeas corpus* of 2009 citing CRC was found in 'decisions of the presidency' of the STF. In case law reports, two documents were found that directly cite the Convention. One extraordinary appeal was found, in which CRC is cited. However, the appeal was denied.[182]

5.6.3 Impact on and through Independent State Institutions

CSOs produced alternative reporting to describe the situation of children and CRC.[183] In 2006 all but 8 per cent of Brazilian municipalities had in place Municipal Councils for the Rights of the Child (CMDCAs). Nevertheless, when analysing regional data, striking differences are noted, and 'there is still a precarious balance between forces of government and civil society, what create problems of independence, since 60% of counsellors reported being public servants, coming from the executive, legislative and judicial powers'.[184] State Councils for the Rights of the Child (CEDCAs) were created in all states, but half of them did not structure procedures for monitoring and evaluating policies for children. Brazil has a database for children's rights, *Sistema de Informações para a Infância e Adolescência* (SIPIA), which serves as an important tool to generate data on childhood.[185]

---

180 Search was conducted on the website of the Brazil's House of Representatives (Câmara dos Deputados) <https://www.camara.leg.br/busca-portal?contextoBusca=BuscaProposicoes&pagina=1&order=data&abaEspecifica=true&q=%22Conven%C3%A7%C3%A3o%20sobre%20os%20Direitos%20da%20Crian%C3%A7a%22> accessed 20 June 2020.
181 Informative No 0661 <https://processo.stj.jus.br/jurisprudencia/externo/informativo/>, Informative No 0565 <https://processo.stj.jus.br/jurisprudencia/externo/informativo/>, Informative No 507 <https://processo.stj.jus.br/jurisprudencia/externo/informativo/> accessed 20 June 2020.
182 HC 101985, Rapporteur: MARCO AURÉLIO, judged on 7 February 2013, ELECTRONIC JUDGMENT DJe-036 DISCLOSED 2014-02-20 PUBLIC 2014-02-21.
183 II Alternative Report on the Situation of the Rights of the Child in Brazil to the International Convention on the Rights of the Child (CRC), 2014.
184 ibid 7.
185 ibid 8.

5.6.4 Impact on and through Non-state Actors

The United Nations Children's Fund (UNICEF) joined its voice with Brazilian NGOs for the drafting and approval of article 227 of the Federal Constitution and the Statute of the Child and Adolescent. In addition, UNICEF was in solidarity with the Brazilian Parliament, the government and society in approving Law 9,534/97, which made civil birth registration free for all Brazilians. UNICEF has also taken action for the approval of Constitutional Amendment 59, which made teaching from 4 to 17 years compulsory and also secured more resources for education. These were important victories for education in the country, which UNICEF supported from the outset. Since 1966 in Brazil, Child Fund Brazil is a social development organisation that through solid experience in designing and monitoring social programmes and projects mobilises people for life transformation. Children, adolescents, young people, families and communities at risk are supported so that they can fully exercise the right to citizenship.

In order to promote lasting results, social projects are developed with the involvement of families, communities and society in the creation of protective and caring environments for children, adolescents and young people. Through social projects, Child Fund Brazil benefits more than 140 000 people, of which over 42 000 are children, adolescents and young people. For this, Child Fund Brazil has the partnership of 45 social organisations, which operate in more than 40 municipalities.

The SciELO website revealed direct mention of the Convention in two papers,[186] and the Google Scholar platform showed one direct mention of the Convention.[187]

---

[186] A CONVENÇÃO INTERNACIONAL SOBRE OS DIREITOS DA CRIANÇA: DEBATES E TENSÕES: Identifies and revisits the literature on the socio-political context and the text of the International Convention on the Rights of the Child, as well as some of its repercussions in Brazil.; FÚLVIA ROSEMBERG and CARMEM LÚCIA SUSSEL MARIANO <http://www.SciELO.br/pdf/cp/v40n141/v40n141a03.pdf> published in 2010. Direitos da criança e do adolescente: um debate necessário; "a Convenção deve ser problematizada, levando-se em conta os dez anos em que o pré-texto foi debatido, a complexidade de suas afirmações e as dificuldades existentes para sua efetivação." Esther Maria de Magalhães Arantes published in 2012.

[187] Anderson Pereira de Andrade, A CONVENÇÃO SOBRE OS DIREITOS DA CRIANÇA EM SEU DÉCIMO ANIVERSÁRIO: AVANÇOS, EFETIVIDADE E DESAFIOS Promotor de Justiça Ministério Público do Distrito Federal e Territórios <http://www.escolamp.org.br/ARQUIVOS/15_01.pdf> accessed 20 June 2020.

5.6.5 Impact of State Reporting

In its COs to Brazil, issued in 2004, the CRC Cttee welcomed the Constitution and other law reforms, but noted with extreme concern 'the dramatic inequalities based on race, social class, gender and geographic location which significantly hamper progress towards the full realisation of the children's rights enshrined in the Convention'.[188] In 2015 the CRC Cttee focused its recommendations on violence against children and the end of inequalities. As mentioned in a Master's thesis about the impact of the CRC Cttee in Brazil from 2018,[189] one such inequality is the issue of healthy nutrition and obesity. In this regard, Brazil adopted Resolution 163/2014 of the National Council on the Rights of Children specifically about advertisement for children, including the concern about promotion of healthy nutrition. Additionally, the CRC Cttee also requested Brazil to take all necessary measures to address the issue of children incarcerated with their mothers (paragraph 50). In this regard, Brazil's Federal Supreme Court in 2018 issued a collective *habeas corpus* in favour of mothers incarcerated with their children or pregnant women, ordering their release from prison.[190] However, lower courts remain reluctant to do so.

5.6.6 Impact of Individual Communications

No communications have been submitted to the CRC Cttee against Brazil.

5.6.7 Brief Conclusion

CRC was important for adherence at the municipal, state and national levels of child protection. Here, we can include initiatives taken to create councils and secretariats. Legislative changes were also relevant to the incorporation of the Convention. Still in this context, the need for the country to adopt policies that manage to encompass its different contexts is expressed. There still is a need for an effort to protect children and adolescents more and more.

---

188 CRC/C/15/Add.241 2.
189 Renata Sefarim, As Recomendações Do Comitê Para Os Direitos Da Criança, Da Convenção Das Nações Unidas Sobre Os Direitos Da Criança (1989): Uma Análise Da Sua Aplicação Nas Políticas Públicas Brasileiras. UNIVERSIDADE DO EXTREMO SUL CATARINENSE – UNESC PROGRAMA DE PÓS-GRADUAÇÃO EM DIREITO: Dissertação de mestrado. Orientador Prof Dr Ismael Francisco de Souza. Criciúma, 2019 <http://repositorio.unesc.net/bitstream/1/6760/1/Renata%20Nápoli%20Vieira%20Sera fim.pdf> accessed 20 June 2020.
190 STF Notícias STF: Ministro Lewandowski concede HC para presas com filhos que ainda não foram colocadas em prisão domiciliar. STF, 25 de outubro de 2018 <https://portal.stf.jus.br/noticias/verNoticiaDetalhe.asp?idConteudo=393814> accessed 10 September 2023.

5.7 International Convention for the Protection of All Persons from Enforced Disappearance

5.7.1 Incorporation and Reliance by Legislature and Executive

CED, which Brazil ratified on 29 November 2010, was incorporated into domestic law by Decree 8,767 of 11 May 2016.[191] The Decree explicitly refers to the promulgation of CED. Even before the Convention's incorporation into domestic law, there was a legal reform proposal (PLS 236/2012) that rendered the forced disappearance of people into crimes against humanity and provided for the imposition of a penalty of up to six years on perpetrators.[192] There was also an attempt to insert the crime of enforced disappearance into the current Penal Code (article 149-A), through PL 6.240/2013, with a penalty of up to 12 years' imprisonment. This project is still ongoing in the House of Congress. In assessing the legislative impact of CED in Brazil, it is key to observe that the Brazilian legislature has directly relied extensively on CED in legislative proposals. A search conducted in September 2023 on the database of Brazil's House of Representatives has shown at least 11 explicit mentions to CED in legislative proposals,[193] the vast majority of them dating from 2009 and 2013.

5.7.2 Reliance by Judiciary

The SPT has made no direct or indirect references to CED, although six judgments refer to the Inter-American Convention on Forced Disappearance of Persons.[194] However, it should be noted that the use of the 'forced disappearance' search engine resulted in a total of six judgments, which in turn refer to the Inter-American Convention on Disappearance. In the STJ, as well as the Courts of Justice and other lower courts of the country, no rulings are found that directly mention CED but, again, some reliance was placed on the Inter-American Convention on Forced Disappearance.

---

[191] BRAZI Decree 8767/2016 <http://www.planalto.gov.br/ccivil_03/_ato2015-2018/2016/decreto/D8767.htm> accessed 20 June 2020.

[192] Art 466 of the mentioned project.

[193] Search was conducted on the website of the Brazil's House of Representatives (Câmara dos Deputados) <https://www.camara.leg.br/busca-portal?contextoBusca=BuscaProposicoes&pagina=1&order=data&abaEspecifica=true&q=%22Conven%C3%A7%C3%A3o%20Internacional%20para%20a%20Prote%C3%A7%C3%A3o%20de%20Todas%20as%20Pessoas%20contra%20o%20Desaparecimento%20For%C3%A7ado%22> accessed 20 June 2020.

[194] The majority of the cases concerned the extradition process and the CPED was not the main object. We mention here to highlight that this was remembered by the Brazilian courts. Only one case was after the promulgation of the Convention.

5.7.3 Impact on and through Non-state Actors

In March 2012 Human Rights Watch Brazil praised federal prosecutors for offering criminal charges in relation to abuses during the military regime,[195] which was soon thereafter rejected by the judiciary on the basis of the amnesty law.[196] The denunciation dealt with the charge against Colonel Curió Rodrigues de Moura for forced disappearances in 1974, in Pará. That was the first criminal case in respect of crimes committed during the military regime. CED was mentioned as an obligation of the country to provide reparation to the victims. In April of the same year, the organisation once again denounced Brazil for crimes committed during the dictatorship. In 2011 CED appeared in a request of Conectas and Corporación Humanas to investigate the circumstances surrounding the death of Muammar al-Gaddafi.[197]

While no mention has been made of CED in Brazilian academic articles or research, some references to the Inter-American Convention against Forced Disappearance have been noted.[198]

5.7.4 Impact of State Reporting

Brazil submitted its first report in 2019. The country highlighted that 'there is no law on enforced disappearances in Brazil; however, the country may face forced disappearances perpetrated by persons or groups of persons acting without authorisation, notably related to land conflicts in remote rural areas, drug trafficking/anti-drug actions, and internationally'.[199] The report mentioned the creation in 2017 of the National System for Locating and Identifying Missing Persons of the Prosecutor's Office.

---

195 See <https://www.hrw.org/news/2012/03/13/brazil-human-rights-prosecution-landmark-step> accessed 10 September 2023.
196 See <http://g1.globo.com/politica/noticia/2012/03/justica-rejeita-denuncia-contra-militar-que-combateu-guerrilha-do-araguaia.html> accessed 20 June 2020.
197 <https://www.conectas.org/en/noticias/public-statement-4-2011-prevalence-of-human-rights-in-libya-2/> accessed 11 April 2022.
198 Being (i) by José Carlos Portella Jr; (ii) by Carina Gouvêa, Professor and Lawyer Specialist in Military Law; (iii) Luiz Flávio Gomes; and (iv) Horrancele Barros. Articles have been attached to folder '(c)'. The search was done broadly on the 'SciELO' and 'Google Scholar' platforms. It is important to note that the same phenomenon encountered in jurisprudential research is reiterated here: several references to the Inter-American Convention against Forced Disappearance, few or – as in this case – none in relation to the present research object. In a search in 'jusbrasil', from the 'Articles' filter, four direct mentions were found to the Convention for the Protection of All Persons against Forced Disappearance.
199 CED/C/BRA/1 5.

5.7.5 Brief Conclusion

The ratification of CED was motivated by the country's efforts to overcome a legacy of human rights atrocities, including enforced disappearances, and to progress towards greater democratisation. Brazil's implementation of CED has not been satisfactory. Its first report was submitted only in 2019. While the ratification dates from 2010, the Legal Decree to promulgate it was signed by the President only in 2016.

5.8 Convention on the Rights of Persons with Disabilities

5.8.1 Incorporation and Reliance by Legislature and Executive

Brazil ratified CRPD on 30 March 2007, together with its Optional Protocol, with the result that CRPD and OP-CRPD entered into force in Brazil on 1 September 2008.[200] The National Congress through Legislative Decree 186 of 9 July 2000 approved CRPD and incorporated it into domestic law, with constitutional amendment status, by Decree 6949 of 25 August 2009. Its headnote explicitly refers to the promulgation of CRPD and OP-CRPD.

Other incorporations can be cited, first its 2022 Brazil Plan which establishes goals that the Social Administration and Brazilian society must have achieved in 2022, in the bicentenary of independence. Its Goal 6 states as follows: 'Ensure accessibility for all persons with disabilities; oversee and promote the application of art 9 CRPD'. The 2011 National Plan for Persons with Disabilities provides as follows:

> Art 1 The National Plan of the Rights of Persons with Disabilities – Living Without Limit Plan is hereby established, with the purpose of promoting, through the integration and articulation of policies, programs and actions, the full and equitable exercise of the rights of persons with disabilities according to the International Convention on the Rights of Persons with Disabilities and its Optional Protocol, adopted by Legislative Decree No 186 of 9 July 2008, with constitutional amendment status, and promulgated by Decree No 6,949 of 25 August of 2009.[201]

Other measures include Law 12319/2010 (regulating the profession of translator and interpreter of Brazilian Sign Language (LIBRAS)); *Cidade acessível é Direitos Humanos* (encouraging society to make a commitment to full participation of people with disabilities and demonstrate the importance of

---

200   CRPD/C/12/D/10/2013.
201   BRAZIL Decree 7612/2011 <http://www.planalto.gov.br/ccivil_03/_ato2011-2014/2011/decreto/d7612.htm> accessed 20 June 2020.

providing equal opportunities in cities); Law 12033/2009 (modifying article 145 of the Criminal Code to make possible public prosecution of defamation cases including those referring to persons with disabilities).

The Brazilian legislature has directly relied extensively on CRPD in legislative proposals. A search conduced in September 2023 on the database of Brazil's House of Representatives has shown at least 306 explicit mentions of CRPD in legislative proposals,[202] the vast majority of them from 2015 onwards – when the Brazilian Law for Inclusion was passed.[203] In order to illustrate this impact, it is possible to cite two concrete examples: (i) In 2019 CRPD was cited in a constitutional amendment proposal suggesting the use of 'persons with disabilities' in the Constitution rather than 'disabled people';[204] and (ii) in 2019 another proposed Bill, aimed at eliminating additional fees to students with disabilities in private educational institutions, cited CRPD.[205]

5.8.2 Reliance by Judiciary

CRPD appears in 16 judgments of the STF, of which nine cites CRPD directly. The *Habeas Corpus* case is prominent among those.[206] In this matter, the STF had to determine alternatives to preventive custody of imprisoned women who are guardians or mothers of children of up to 12 years, or persons with deficiencies, while taking into account the alternative measures in article 319 of the Code of Penal Process (CPP). The STF's decision in favour of those suffering consequences of severe burns is another illustration of the strong inclusion of CRPD in Brazil. Other citations include the direct relationship between the Convention and the Constitution of the Republic. In the Superior Court of Justice, there are 29 mentions of CRPD, 20 of them in relation to the Federal Supreme Court's *Habeas Corpus* 143641 judgment.

---

202 Search was conducted on the website of the Brazil's House of Representatives (Câmara dos Deputados) <https://www.camara.leg.br/busca-portal?contextoBusca=BuscaProposicoes&pagina=1&order=relevancia&abaEspecifica=true&q=%22Conven%C3%A7%C3%A3o%20Internacional%20sobre%20os%20Direitos%20das%20Pessoas%20com%20Defici%C3%AAncia%22> accessed 20 June 2020.
203 'Lei Brasileira de Inclusão da Pessoa com Deficiência (Estatuto da Pessoa com Deficiência)' (Brazilian Law of Persons with Disabilities) <http://www.planalto.gov.br/ccivil_03/_ato2015-2018/2015/lei/l13146.htm> accessed 20 June 2020.
204 Brazil's House of Representatives, PEC 57/2019 <https://www.camara.leg.br/proposicoesWeb/fichadetramitacao?idProposicao=2198865> accessed 20 June 2020.
205 Brazil's House of Representatives, PL 3092/2019 <https://www.camara.leg.br/proposicoesWeb/fichadetramitacao?idProposicao=2204477> accessed 20 June 2020.
206 STF, *Habeas Corpus* 143641.

5.8.3 Impact on and through Non-state Actors

NGOs such as Human Rights Watch have highlighted non-compliance with the Convention, for example in its report *'THEY STAY UNTIL DYING: A life of isolation and neglect in institutions for people with disabilities'*.[207] NGOs have organised various seminars on the Convention.[208] A search on the Abraça portal for the term 'Convention on the Rights of Persons with Disabilities'[209] resulted in 51 mentions, among them six manifestos from NGOs.[210] A search in FBASD,[211] for the term 'Convention on the Rights of Person with Disabilities', revealed 33 mentions, among them the organisational statutes of a number of NGOs. At Inclusive portal,[212] a search for the term 'Convention on the Rights of Person with Disabilities' led to 2 700 results. On the Baresi Institute portal, a search for the term 'Convention on the Rights of Person with Disabilities' showed 5 news items that mentioned CRPD. A search of the Down Movement portal for the term 'Convention on the Rights of Person with Disabilities' showed ten news items mentioning CRPD. Using the search term 'Convention on the Rights of Persons with Disabilities' on Google Scholar showed two results. When the same search engine was used on the SciELO portal, specifically selecting Brazilian articles, as it is an international portal and some general results related to Portuguese works, two results were found.[213] All the searches mentioned above were conduced in June 2020.

---

207   Human Rights Watch, 'Eles ficam até morrer' HRW Rio de janeiro, 2016 <https://www.hrw.org/pt/report/2018/05/23/318010> accessed 10 September 2023.

208   See eg Conectas Direitos Humanos – ESPIONAGEM É 1 ENTRE 11 TEMAS ESPINHOSOS PARA BRASIL E EUA EM DIREITOS HUMANOS; CONECTAS DISCUTE EM SP DIREITO DAS PESSOAS COM DEFICIÊNCIA; SEMINÁRIO: CONVENÇÃO DA ONU – DIREITOS DAS PESSOAS COM DEFICIÊNCIA: AVANÇOS, DESAFIOS E PARTICIPAÇÃO DA SOCIEDADE.

209   See ABRAÇA's website <https://abraca.net.br> accessed 10 September 2023.

210   Manifesto Abraça A Favor Da Aprovação Do Pl 1712/2019 Sem Emendas No Senado; (2) Manifesto: Autistar É Resistir! Identidade, Cidadania E Participação Política; (3) Manifesto – Sou Autista E Viver Em Comunidade É Direito Meu!; (4) Manifesto Da Abraça Sobre A Lei Nº 12.438/2017; (5) Manifesto Público Da Abraça Sobre As Medidas Do Governo Interino Michel Temer Com Relação Aos Direitos Humanos Das Pessoas Com Deficiência; (6) Manifesto Público Decreto De Regulamentação Da Lei Dos Autistas.

211   See Federação Down's website <http://federacaodown.org.br/> accessed 20 June 2020.

212   See Inclusive's website <http://www.inclusive.org.br/> accessed 20 June 2020.

213   The Inclusion Pact is an example of the use by business: 'Considering the principles, laws, and norms of respect for the rights of persons with disabilities, in particular the Universal Declaration of Human Rights, the UN Convention on the Rights of Persons with Disabilities, the Brazilian Inclusion Law and the Letter of Commitment from the ILO Global Business and Disability Network (ILO Global Business and Disability Network)'. The Companies that joined the Pact: Grupo Pão de Açúcar, IBM, Accenture, TozziniFreire Advogados, Serasa Experian, JLL, Natura, EY, Dow, Trench Rossi Watanabe, Abril, Ernst

5.8.4 Impact of State Reporting

In 2012 Brazil submitted its first report.[214] In 2015 the Committee sent a list of questions for the country to answer.[215] In 2015, CSOs also submitted information to the Committee.[216] In September of the same year, the Committee issued its COs.[217] These COs acknowledged CRPD as a constitutional landmark. The COs recommended the adoption of policies to address discrimination against disability in all areas, including incarceration policies. In 2015 a permanent commission on the rights of persons with disabilities in the Chamber of Deputies of the National Congress was created, and a national plan for the rights of persons with disabilities entitled 'Living without limits' was approved. In 2016 the Statute for Persons with Disabilities, a national anti-discrimination law on people with disabilities, entered into force. One of the advances brought about by this statute was the prohibition on charging additional fees for enrolments and fees for private educational institutions; legislation requires that 10 per cent of hotel and hostel dormitories be accessible and that at least one accessible unit be guaranteed; and that workers with disabilities must have recourse to the Guarantee Fund for Length of Service when receiving a prescription for orthosis or prosthesis to promote its accessibility.

5.8.5 Impact of Individual Communications

Two communications were submitted against Brazil, and declared inadmissible by the CRPD Cttee.[218]

5.8.6 Brief Conclusion

CRPD is one of the treaties that has had the greatest impact in Brazil. It has influenced a significant number of legislative changes and has inspired important court judgments. Civil society and NGOs showed a strong commitment. Two communications were submitted to the CRPD Cttee, but were declared inadmissible.

    & Young Terco, Gtcon, Magazine Luiza, Oi, Raia Drogasil, Via Varejo, UnitedHealth Group, etc.

214 CRPD/C/BRA/1.
215 CRPD/C/BRA/Q/1.
216 1st Joint Submission to the Committee on the Convention on the Rights of Persons with Disabilities: An overview from the Brazilian Civil Society, July 2015.
217 CRPD/C/BRA/CO/1.
218 Communication 10/2013, CRPD/C/12/D/10/2013 (2 October 2014). The second communication, submitted in 2016, was declared admissible in 2020.

6   Conclusion

Much has changed in Brazil since June 1999 as far as the impact of UN treaty bodies is concerned. By that time, the major impact had been the ratifications of such treaties, as an important initial step towards a more democratic country after the end of the military dictatorship in 1985. As this chapter shows, while the UN treaties still lack extensive implementation in Brazil, civil society organisations and the judiciary have started using UN treaty bodies more often than they did in 1999, either participating in their reporting or complaint proceedings or making use of their recommendations. While preference is still given to the Inter-American system, as was identified in the 1999 study, this chapter shows that UN treaty bodies system influenced policy making in Brazil, in particular in areas such as the prevention of torture and access to justice, women's rights, racial equality and the rights of persons with disabilities.

Brazil currently is party to the major international human rights treaties, whether in the UN or OAS spheres. Brazil started to become a party to important human rights treaties only after the end of the military regime in 1985, illustrating that the history of human rights in the country is the product of its own democratisation movement. The presidency of Bolsonaro underlines that the country's commitment to human rights is as fragile as the process of democratisation itself. Brazil has since 2016 been undergoing a period of political instability, which has influenced the international human rights mechanisms in the country. The sentiment expressed by former President Bolsonaro that Brazil's membership of the HRC is 'of no use' underlines the fragility of the role of human rights and the re-democratisation process more broadly, and the ongoing need to implement UN human rights treaties at the domestic level.

Adherence to international human rights mechanisms has a twofold role in the country. On the one hand, it shows the commitment that different groups and organisations have to the re-democratisation process. On the other hand, taking into account the fragility of the re-democratisation process itself, adherence to international human rights mechanisms (which has been constantly threatened, especially since 2016 when political conflicts intensified in the country) is the means by which different groups under conditions of social vulnerability are granted domestic protection.

There have been advances, but much remains to be accomplished to advance the human rights agenda in Brazil. One of the major advances has been the Constitutional Amendment 45 of 2004, which gives constitutional status to human rights treaties ratified in the country. Numerous treaty body recommendations underline that the Brazilian government needs to do more to make the protection of a minimum of rights viable, based on the institutional mechanisms inherent to a democratic state.

Taking into account the historical-political context of the country and of the region in which it is located, domestic reform cannot detach itself from a reform at the UN level. It is necessary that UN human rights policies are capable of dealing with different regional realities, including authoritarian domestic conditions.

Brazil has entered reservations only in respect of OP2-CCPR and CEDAW (in terms of articles 2 and 29(1), respectively). Three communications were submitted against Brazil, one under CEDAW and two under CRPD. The CRPD Cttee declared the case inadmissible. CEDAW has had significant influence in Brazil. The CEDAW and CRPD Cttees are very well known domestically, mostly on an institutional level. As in the case of CEDAW, CRPD has influenced a significant number of legislative changes and adherence to it by the judiciary is of particular note, since in several cases and respects judicial decisions have gone beyond the main objects of the treaty.

Brazilian commitment to CERD and CED has been unsatisfactory, due mainly to the dictatorial period and of the ongoing instability in democratisation processes. In both cases, there is a need for discussion about promoting these treaties not only in Brazil but in the entire Latin America region. Adherence to CERD in 1969 took place in a particular historical context, dating back to the period of military dictatorship. Its effective implementation only started after the promulgation of the 1985 Constitution and the return to the democratic state. Nevertheless, legislation on the subject is more punitive in nature than focused on public policies. The Brazilian Penal Code is still the same law as the one adopted in the 1940s. Public policies regarding the guarantee of rights have become more common since the 2000s. The role of civil society and organisations in the dissemination of CERD remains of paramount importance in the Brazilian context. The influence of CED is constrained by its relatively recent ratification, the pervasive influence of dictatorship represented by some congressmen and national institutions. Its value is largely symbolic, serving as a signal to enforce the re-democratisation of the country. However, it remains imperative that mechanisms for promoting CED are established at the domestic level.

In terms of municipal, state and national levels of adherence, CRC is the most relevant, as reflected in initiatives taken to create institutions such as councils and secretariats and legislative changes. CAT also inspired legislative reforms. Although CAT has an important treaty body to protect citizens from torture, Brazil had not complied with all recommendations by the SPT. Urgent domestic reform is necessary particularly to address the government's neglect of the prison system. The impact of CESCR has been circumscribed in legal and institutional reforms, although Brazil, by implementing some COs of the CESCR Cttee, promoted some policies to extinguish inequalities in territory in the last years.

Finally, in terms of more diffuse implications in the country, CCPR perhaps is one of the treaties with the most impact. It plays an important role in promoting various civil and political rights.

CHAPTER 3

The Impact of the United Nations Human Rights Treaties on the Domestic Level in Canada

Alexander Agnello and Frédéric Mégret

1   Introduction to Human Rights in Canada

The Dominion of Canada was formed through the British North America Act, 1867 and was recognized as a fully sovereign state in 1931 with the enactment of the Statute of Westminster by the UK Parliament.[1] Roughly half a century later the Constitution Act, 1982 'patriated and Canadianized' the British North America Act.[2] The most recognised part of the Constitution Act is the Charter of Rights and Freedoms (Charter) which, for the first time, provided for a 'constitutional bill of rights' for Canada.[3] Since its adoption the Charter has become recognised around the world, particularly in the common law, as a model document for the protection of rights and freedoms.[4] The Charter has led to considerable litigation, with virtually no area of Canadian law left untouched by this scrutiny.

A number of institutions are responsible for the monitoring and implementation of human rights in Canada. The Department of Justice is responsible for ensuring that federal Bills are consistent with Canada's human rights

---

1 Government of Canada, 'Anniversary of the Statute of Westminster' (19 October 2017) <https://www.canada.ca/en/canadian-heritage/services/important-commemorative-days/anniversary-statute-westminster.html> accessed 18 February 2019.
2 Michael D Behiels, 'The making of a deal: Trudeau, patriation and the Charter' *Policy Options* (1 December 2011) <https://policyoptions.irpp.org/fr/magazines/the-year-in-review/the-making-of-a-deal-trudeau-patriation-and-the-charter/> accessed 18 February 2019.
3 Richard Foot, 'Canadian Charter of Rights and Freedoms' *Canadian Encyclopedia* (28 February 2018) <https://www.thecanadianencyclopedia.ca/en/article/canadian-charter-of-rights-and-freedoms> accessed 3 March 2019; Charles R Epp 'Do Bills of Rights Matter? The Canadian Charter of Rights and Freedoms' (1996) 90 American Political Science Review 765.
4 Mark Tushnet, 'The Charter's Influence Around the World' (2013) 50 (3) Osgoode Hall Law Journal 527–546; John Ibbitson, 'The Charter Proves to be Canada's Gift to the World' *The Globe and Mail* (15 April 2012) <https://www.theglobeandmail.com/news/politics/the-charter-proves-to-be-canadas-gift-to-world/article4100561/> accessed 18 February 2019.

obligations.[5] It also conducts a review of existing laws when Canada considers becoming a party to a human rights treaty, advises on the domestic implementation of human rights treaties, and represents Canada in the litigation of international human rights cases.[6] Global Affairs Canada oversees foreign policy on international human rights and negotiates new international human rights instruments.[7] Canadian Heritage is primarily responsible for international human rights education.[8] It is also home to the Secretariat for the Continuing Committee of Officials on Human Rights (CCOHR)[9] which, *inter alia*, collects input from provincial and territorial (P-T) governments to inform Canada's reports to the human rights treaty bodies and coordinates consultations with P-T governments in cases where the federal government is considering becoming a party to a human rights treaty that engages provincial or territorial laws and powers.[10]

Legislative Acts of Parliament and various parliamentary committees, such as the Standing Senate Committee on Human Rights, also play an important role in the domestic implementation of human rights treaties.[11] In accordance with custom and policy, the federal executive branch will seek the support of provinces and territories before becoming a party to treaties that contemplate

---

5   The Minister of Justice is required by statute to ensure that federal legislation is in conformity with the Bill of Rights and the Charter of Rights and Freedoms. Canadian Bill of Rights SC 1960, ch 44 s. 3; Department of Justice Act RSC 1985, ch J-2, s 4.1; and Statutory Instruments Act RSC 1985, ch S-22, s 3.
6   United Nations, 'Core Document Forming Part of the Reports of States Parties' Canada (12 January 1998) (HRI/CORE/1/Add.91); Department of Justice, 'International Human Rights Law – Roles and Responsibilities' *Government of Canada* (5 August 2021) <https://www.justice.gc.ca/eng/abt-apd/icg-gci/ihrl-didp/index.html> accessed 3 September 2021.
7   ibid.
8   ibid.
9   Canadian Heritage, 'About human rights' *Government of Canada* (23 December 2020) <https://www.canada.ca/en/canadian-heritage/services/about-human-rights.html#a4> accessed 5 August 2021.
10 United Nations, 'Core Document Forming Part of the Reports of States Parties' Canada (12 January 1998) (HRI/CORE/1/Add.91); Department of Justice, 'International Human Rights Law – Roles and Responsibilities' *Government of Canada* (5 August 2021) <https://www.justice.gc.ca/eng/abt-apd/icg-gci/ihrl-didp/index.html> accessed 3 September 2021.
11 Examples of free-standing legislation intended to implement a treaty include the Crimes Against Humanity and War Crimes Act SC 2000, ch 24 implementing the Rome Statute of the International Criminal Court; the Geneva Conventions Act, implementing the Geneva Conventions for the Protection of War Victims; the North American Free Trade Agreement Implementation Act, implementing the North American Free Trade Agreement (NAFTA); and the Canada-European Union Comprehensive Economic and Trade Agreement Implementation Act SC 2017, ch 6 implementing the agreement of the same name.

provincial or territorial laws and powers.[12] However, Canada's general position is that human rights treaties do not require specific implementing legislation in cases where Canada's laws already fulfil Canada's international obligations.[13]

Regarding the enforcement of human rights, most courts at the provincial and federal level have jurisdiction to hear human rights issues, including trial courts, provincial appellate courts, the Federal Court of Appeal, and the Supreme Court of Canada.[14] Courts can not only examine the behaviour of state agents but also engage in the judicial review of laws and strike down those that are found to be in violation of the Charter.[15] They have done this quite often with sometimes momentous consequences for the Canadian legal system.

In addition, an entire *sui generis* system of human rights enforcement exists in Canada. Federal, provincial, and territorial human rights commissions have a unique role in investigating and mediating human rights complaints dealing with discrimination and supporting human rights education.[16] Moreover, human rights commissions may provide some advantages to courts: they are comprised of persons with specialised expertise in human rights; may pursue public reporting or a review of legislation, policy or practice on their own initiative; and may promote a more accessible form of justice insofar as commissions

---

12   See Laura Barnett, 'Canada' Approach to the Treaty-Making Process: 3.3.2 Implementation', Library of Parliament (November 2008) <https://lop.parl.ca/sites/PublicWebsite/default/en_CA/ResearchPublications/200845E#a8> accessed 18 February 2019.

13   Standing Senate Committee on Human Rights, 'Children: The Silenced Citizens – Effective Implementation of Canada's International Obligations with Respect to the Rights of Children' (April 2007) 9-15 <https://sencanada.ca/content/sen/Committee/391/huma/rep/rep10apr07-e.pdf> accessed 18 February 2019.

14   Anne Bayefsky and Gillian Collins, 'Canada' in Christof Heyns and Frans Viljoen (eds) 'The Impact of the United Nations Human Rights Treaties on the Domestic Level' (Kluwer Law International 2002) 115.

15   Charles R Epp 'Do Bills of Rights Matter? The Canadian Charter of Rights and Freedoms' (1996) 90 American Political Science Review 765.

16   The findings of these commissions are enforced only by means of rights and procedures laid out in legislation, as opposed to ordinary recourse through the court system. Moreover, these statutory rights found in legislation applicable to human rights commissions overlap with, but do not mirror, the rights protected constitutionally. See Nancy Holmes, 'Human Rights and the Courts in Canada' Law and Government Division, Government of Canada (2001) <http://publications.gc.ca/Collection-R/LoPBdP/BP/bp279-e.htm> accessed 13 February 2019; Nancy Holmes, 'Human Rights Legislation and the Charter: A Comparative Guide' Law and Government Division, Government of Canada (1997) <https://publications.gc.ca/Collection-R/LoPBdP/MR/mr102-e.htm> accessed 3 September 2021.

involve fewer formal procedures than courts and may represent complainants before a court or tribunal.[17] The Canadian Human Rights Commission (CHRC) – the country's national human rights institution (NHRI) – is empowered by the Canadian Human Rights Act to settle complaints of discrimination in employment matters and in the provision of services within federal jurisdiction.[18] It is also empowered to enforce the Employment Equity Act to help ensure that federally regulated entities provide employment equity for four designated groups: women, persons with disabilities, indigenous people, and visible minorities.[19] Additionally, the CHRC is the body responsible for monitoring the federal government's implementation of CRPD.[20]

Human rights commissions may refer cases to the relevant human rights tribunal. These tribunals are specialised bodies, independent from human rights commissions, with the jurisdiction to hear cases based on statutory rights found in the relevant federal, provincial, or territorial legislation.[21] The Canadian Human Rights Tribunal, for example, is established through the Canadian Human Rights Act and has cases referred to it by the CHRC for adjudication under that Act.[22] Tribunal decisions are reviewable by the Federal Court of Canada.[23] Federal Court decisions can be appealed to the Federal Court of Appeal and then the Supreme Court of Canada.[24]

The Charter has brought about momentous changes to Canadian society.[25] Major human rights milestones were achieved in the areas of women's reproductive rights; two-spirit, lesbian, gay, bisexual, transgender, queer, questioning, intersex, and asexual (2SLGBTQQIA) rights; aboriginal rights; and

---

17 Standing Senate Committee on Human Rights, 'Promises to Keep: Implementing Canada's Human Rights Obligations' (December 2001) s I(B) <https://sencanada.ca/content/sen/committee/371/huma/rep/rep02dec01-e.htm#B.%20%20%20%20%20Domestic%20Human%20Rights%20Mechanisms%20in%20Canada> accessed 23 November 2020.
18 Canadian Human Rights Act RSC 1985, ch H-6, ss 26–38.3.
19 Employment Equity Act SC 1995, ch 44, s 22.
20 Canadian Human Rights Act, s 28.1.
21 Nancy Holmes, 'Human Rights Legislation and the Charter: A Comparative Guide' Law and Government Division, Government of Canada (1997) <https://publications.gc.ca/Collection-R/LoPBdP/MR/mr102-e.htm> accessed 3 September 2021.
22 ibid ss 48.1–48.4.
23 Canadian Human Rights Tribunal, 'Instructions' <https://www.chrt-tcdp.gc.ca/decisions/instructions-en.html > accessed 10 February 2019.
24 ibid.
25 Foot (n 3); Daniel Schwartz, '6 Big Changes the Charter of Rights has Brought' CBC (17 April 2012) <https://www.cbc.ca/news/canada/6-big-changes-the-charter-of-rights-has-brought-1.1244758> accessed 16 February 2019.

minority language education rights.[26] A Charter challenge under the section 7 guarantee of life, liberty and security of the person led the Supreme Court in *R v Morgentaler* to strike down the Criminal Code provision prohibiting abortion, granting women greater control over their reproductive lives and health.[27] The Supreme Court's 1998 *Vriend v Alberta* decision engaged the Charter's section 15 clause on anti-discrimination and recognised sexual orientation as a prohibited ground of discrimination.[28] This decision laid the foundations for the legalisation of same-sex marriage in 2005.[29] While aboriginal and treaty rights do not fall under the Charter, the interpretation and expansion of these rights was greatly influenced by the Charter.[30] The Supreme Court 1990 *Sparrow* decision transformed the negotiating power of indigenous communities by putting forward a duty to consult these communities when government resource development projects affect them.[31] While aboriginal rights fall outside the scope of the Charter, section 25 of the Charter guarantees that the Charter is not interpreted in a way that diminishes the rights of indigenous peoples in Canada.

Despite these major milestones, Canadian society still faces serious human rights challenges. The government struggles to address the severe discrepancy in living standards between indigenous communities and the rest of Canada.[32] Moreover, indigenous women and girls are disproportionately affected by violence. In 2017 indigenous women comprised 4,3 per cent of the female population, yet accounted for 16 per cent of female homicides and 11,3 per cent of missing females in Canada.[33] Black Canadians also remain

---

26 Foot (n 3).
27 *R v Morgentaler* [1988] 1 SCR 30.
28 *Vriend v Alberta* [1998] 1 SCR 493.
29 Civil Marriage Act SC 2005, ch 33.
30 Thomas Isaac, 'Balancing Rights: The Supreme Court of Canada, *R v Sparrow*, and the Future of Aboriginal Rights' (1993) 13(2) The Canadian Journal of Native Studies 210: Isaac argues that the aboriginal and treaty rights contemplated in *R v Sparrow* were subject to a 'justificatory analysis' that is similar to the reasonable limits tests found in s 1 of the Charter of Rights and Freedoms, as interpreted by *R v Oakes*.
31 *R v Sparrow* [1990] 1 SCR 1075; Schwartz (n 23).
32 'Canada: Events of 2018' *Human Rights Watch* (2018) <https://www.hrw.org/world-report/2019/country-chapters/canada> accessed 2 October 2023.
33 'Canada: Events of 2017' *Human Rights Watch* (2017) <https://www.hrw.org/world-report/2018/country-chapters/canada> accessed 2 October 2023.

the target of systemic discrimination, notably by the police.[34] Other issues include growing tension between national security and human rights, particularly in detention powers or surveillance and the risk of torture for deported individuals.[35] This has led to the expansion of the state's surveillance powers. The imposition of limits to religious freedoms, including a proposed law banning religious symbols for persons administering or receiving public services, is also a concern.[36]

2 Relationship of Canada with the International Human Rights System in General

Canada is a founding member of the UN. Canada participates in the UN Human Rights Council's Universal Periodic Review (UPR) and has undergone three periodic reviews (2009, 2013, and 2018).[37] After France and Spain, Canada has provided the most recommendations during the UPR.[38] Since April 1999, Canada has extended a standing invitation to all UN Special

---

[34] Desmond Cole, *The Skin We're In: A Year of Black Resistance and Power* (Doubleday Canada 2020).

[35] Audrey Macklin, 'From Cooperation, to Complicity, to Compensation: The War on Terror, Extraordinary Rendition, and the Cost of Torture' (2008) 10 European Journal of Migration and Law 11.

[36] An Act to foster adherence to State religious neutrality and, in particular, to provide a framework for requests for accommodations on religious grounds in certain bodies, R-26.2.01 (2017); Jacques Boissinot, 'How Will Quebec's Bill 62 Work? What We Know (and Don't) So Far' *The Globe and Mail* (24 October 2017) <https://www.theglobeandmail.com/news/national/quebec-bill-62-explainer/article36700916/> accessed 23 February 2019; Ingrid Peritz, 'Quebec Judge Stays Controversial Face-Cover Law Bill 62' *The Globe and Mail* (1 December 2017) <https://www.theglobeandmail.com/news/politics/quebec-judge-stays-controversial-face-cover-law-bill-62/article37169426/> accessed 23 February 2019; L'Assemblée nationale de Québec, 'Loi 21' <http://www.assnat.qc.ca/fr/travaux-parlementaires/projets-loi/projet-loi-21-42-1.html> accessed 22 November 2020; Benjamin Shingler, 'CAQ Government Wants to Know How Many Teachers Wear Religious Symbols' CBC (28 January 2019) <https://www.cbc.ca/news/canada/montreal/quebec-religious-symbols-1.4995774> accessed 23 February 2019.

[37] Government of Canada, 'Universal Periodic Review' (03 July 2019) <https://www.canada.ca/en/canadian-heritage/services/canada-united-nations-system/universal-periodic-review.html> accessed 10 October 2020.

[38] UPR Info, 'Recommendations' (UPR Info nd) <https://upr-info-database.uwazi.io/en/library> accessed 10 October 2020.

Procedures.[39] Visits of Special Procedures have increased since the election of Mr Justin Trudeau as Prime Minister in October 2015, with six visits during his first term (November 2015–2019), compared to four visits during Mr Stephen Harper's near decade in office (February 2006 – November 2015).[40]

Canada was a member of the UN Human Rights Council (UNHRC) from 2006 to 2009 and a member of the UN Security Council for 12 years in all, spanning six terms (1948–49, 1958–59, 1967–68, 1977–78, 1989–90, and 1999–2000). The country is generally regarded as an engaged member of the UN system and a strong proponent for the promotion and protection of human rights abroad.

Canada joined the Organization of American States (OAS) in January 1990 but has not ratified the principal treaty on the protection of human rights in the Americas, the American Convention on Human Rights,[41] and is not a member of the Inter-American Court of Human Rights.[42] The Convention was negotiated without Canada and certain provisions of the Convention on the right to life, freedom of expression, property rights, and equality rights are arguably not compatible with current Canadian law.[43] Ratifying the Convention with reservations on all these issues would contradict Canada's stated opposition to making numerous reservations to human rights treaties.[44] For these reasons, Canada is a full member of the OAS but does not fully participate in the inter-American human rights system. However, as a member of OAS, Canada acknowledges its international obligations based on the American Charter and, specifically, the 1948 American Declaration of the Rights and Duties of Man. Accordingly, Canada recognises the functions of the Inter-American

---

[39] United Nations Human Rights Office of the High Commissioner, 'Standing Invitations' United Nations Human Rights Office of the High Commissioner (nd) <https://spinternet.ohchr.org/StandingInvitations.aspx?lang=en> accessed 5 May 2019.

[40] United Nations Human Rights Office of the High Commissioner, 'View Country Visits of Special Procedures of the Human Rights Council Since 1998' United Nations Human Rights Office of the High Commissioner (nd) <https://spinternet.ohchr.org/ViewCountryVisits.aspx?visitType=completed&lang=en> accessed 4 November 2020.

[41] The American Convention on Human Rights OAS Treaty Series No 36; 1144 UNTS 123; 9 ILM 99 (1969).

[42] Senatorial Committee on the Rights of the Person (Canada), Report, 'Enhancing Canada's Role in the OAS: Canadian Adherence to the American Convention on Human Rights: Government Concerns' Parliament of Canada (May 2003) s IV <https://sencanada.ca/content/sen/committee/372/huma/rep/rep04may03part1-e.htm#C.%20Discussion%20of%20Interpretive> accessed 4 February 2019.

[43] ibid.

[44] ibid; Committee Evidence, 18 March 2002 8:11 (John Holmes).

Commission on Human Rights, including the Commission's authority to process individual complaints against member states and to put forward recommendations based on these.[45]

Canada played a vital role in establishing the International Criminal Court (ICC), was one of the first countries to ratify the Rome Statute establishing the Court, and became the first country to adopt legislation to directly implement the Rome Statute in domestic law.[46] In September 2018, Canada joined Argentina, Chile, Colombia, Paraguay, and Peru in signing a formal request for the ICC to investigate Venezuela based on a report detailing torture, forced disappearances, and extrajudicial killings under the Nicolás Maduro government.[47] This was the first time that Canada referred a member state to the ICC.[48]

While Canada was proactive in implementing the Rome Statute into its internal law system, this example is an exception to the country's general approach to the domestic implementation of international law. Canada has a dualist legal order, meaning that treaties ratified by the executive branch are required to be implemented by the legislature before they can be considered to be part of domestic law and applied by national courts as such.[49]

---

45 In 2014 the Inter-American Commission on Human Rights released a report expressing the need for a national inquiry into the issue of missing and murdered indigenous women and girls in Canada. See Inter-American Commission on Human Rights (IACHR), 'Missing and Murdered Indigenous Women in British Columbia, Canada', OEA/Ser.L/v/II Doc 30/14 (21 December 2014) <https://www.oas.org/en/iachr/reports/pdfs/indigenous-women-bc-canada-en.pdf> accessed 2 October 2023.

46 Government of Canada, 'Canada and the International Criminal Court' (26 February 2019) <https://www.international.gc.ca/world-monde/international_relations-relations_internationales/icc-cpi/index.aspx?lang=eng> accessed 6 October 2020; Crimes Against Humanity and War Crimes Act SC 2000, ch 24.

47 Organization of American States, 'Report of the General Secretariat of the Organization of American States and the Panel of Independent International Experts on the Possible Commission of Crimes Against Humanity in Venezuela' (29 May 2018) <https://www.oas.org/documents/eng/press/Informe-Panel-Independiente-Venezuela-EN.pdf> accessed 19 February 2019; Global Affairs Canada, 'Canada Joins Hemispheric Partners in Referring Venezuela to ICC' Government of Canada (26 September 2018) <https://www.canada.ca/en/global-affairs/news/2018/09/canada-calls-on-venezuela-to-cooperate-with-international-criminal-court.html> accessed 19 February 2019.

48 CBC News, 'Canada joins multilateral move to take Venezuelan government to International Criminal Court' (25 September 2018) <https://www.cbc.ca/news/politics/canada-joins-effort-sanction-venezuela-1.4838359> accessed 19 February 2019.

49 Kindred, Hugh M, Phillip M. Saunders, and Robert J. Currie, International Law, Chiefly as Interpreted and Applied in Canada: Eighth Edition (2014) at 150.

None of the seven core human rights treaties have been directly implemented into Canadian law and, therefore, cannot be directly applicable in Canada's courts. This is a considerable limitation on the impact of the human rights treaties judicially, although, as discussed above, significant efforts go into ensuring *ex ante* that the ratification of new treaties will not conflict with Canadian law.

Moreover, Canadian courts, led by the Supreme Court, have shown signs of openness to interpreting Canadian law in ways that conform to international human rights norms.[50] They have done so less because these obligations are directly applicable in domestic law than because they involve sister courts (such as the US Supreme Court or the European Court of Human Rights) dealing with similar issues. Furthermore, unimplemented treaties may be used by courts as an interpretative guide to domestic law based on the presumption that Canada would not have wanted to violate its international obligations. As far as possible, harmonious interpretation seeks to reconcile the meaning of Canadian law with that of Canada's international human rights obligations. This means in practice that international human rights law is often relied on to reinforce a certain domestic understanding of the law rather than to depart from it.

Overall, the reception of international human rights treaties in domestic law remains constrained by Canada's dualism and the reluctance of Canadian judges to directly apply international human rights law. This may evolve in the future, while pressure to implement Canada's international human rights obligations remains strong. By contrast, if a norm of customary international law is not displaced by statute, it may be relied on in a Canadian court 'as if it were a common law rule.'[51] Still, the use of customary international law as it pertains to human rights remains limited before Canadian courts.

---

50   *Baker v Canada (Minister of Citizenship and Immigration)* [1999] 2 SCR 817 is a leading example.
51   Gib van Ert, 'Dubious Dualism: The Reception of International Law in Canada' (2010) 44 Val U L Rev 930; Stéphane Beaulac, 'Customary International Law in Domestic Courts: Imbroglio, Lord Denning, *Stare Decisis*' in CPM Waters (ed), *British and Canadian Perspectives on International Law* (Martinus Nijhoff 2006) 379.

IMPACT OF UNHR TREATIES ON DOMESTIC LEVEL IN CANADA 165

3   At a Glance: Formal Engagement of Canada with the UN Human Rights Treaty System

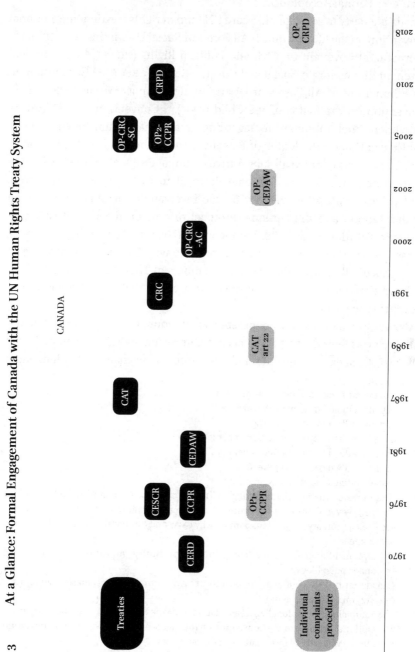

4   Role and Overall Impact of UN Human Rights Treaties in Canada

4.1   *Role of UN Human Rights Treaties*

4.1.1   Formal Acceptance

Canada is a party to seven of nine core UN human rights treaties: International Convention on the Elimination of All Forms of Racial Discrimination (CERD),[52] International Covenant on Civil and Political Rights (CCPR),[53] International Covenant on Economic, Social and Cultural Rights (CESCR),[54] Convention on the Elimination of All Forms of Discrimination against Women (CEDAW),[55] Convention on the Rights of the Child (CRC),[56] Convention against Torture and Other Cruel, Inhuman or Degrading Treatment or Punishment (CAT)[57] and Convention on the Rights of Persons with Disabilities (CRPD).[58] In addition, Canada has adopted all substantive Optional Protocols of the UN human rights system: the Second Optional Protocol to CCPR (OP2-CCPR) (2005), the Optional Protocol to the CRC on the Involvement of Children in armed conflict (2000), and the Optional Protocol to CRC on the Sale of Children, Child Prostitution and Child Pornography (OP-CRC-SC) (2005). However, Canada is not a party to the International Convention on the Protection of the Rights of all Migrant Workers and Members of Their Families (CMW), nor to the Intentional Convention for the Protection of All Persons from Enforced Disappearance (CED).[59]

Canada recognises the competence of four treaty bodies (CCPR,[60] CEDAW,[61] CAT[62] and CRPD)[63] to accept and review individual complaints.[64] However, Canada has not adopted the optional mechanism for individual

---

[52]   Canada ratified CERD on 14 October 1970.
[53]   Canada ratified CCPR on 19 May 1976.
[54]   Canada ratified CESCR on 19 May 1976.
[55]   Canada ratified CEDAW on 10 December 1981.
[56]   Canada ratified CRC on 13 December 1991.
[57]   Canada ratified CAT on 24 June 1987.
[58]   Canada ratified CRPD on 11 March 2010.
[59]   'The Core International Human Rights Treaties and Their Monitoring Bodies' OHCHR <https://www.ohchr.org/EN/ProfessionalInterest/Pages/CoreInstruments.aspx> accessed 3 February 2019. Discussions on why CMW and CPED were not ratified are found in ss 4 and 5.
[60]   The Optional Protocol to CCPR (complaint mechanism) (1976) (OP1-CCPR) was ratified by Canada on 19 May 1976.
[61]   Canada ratified the Optional Protocol to CEDAW (complaint mechanism) (2002) (OP-CEDAW) on 18 October 2002.
[62]   The complaint process for alleging a violation of CAT is found in art 22 of the treaty itself.
[63]   The Optional Protocol to the Convention on the Rights of Persons with Disabilities (2018) (OP-CRPD) was ratified by Canada on 3 December 2018.
[64]   'International Complaints: Complaints Under the International Human Rights Treaties' Government of Canada (25 January 2019) <https://www.canada.ca/en/canadian-heritage/services/human-rights-complaints/international.html#1a> accessed 3 February 2019:

communications under CESCR (OP-CESCR) or the CRC (OP-CRC).[65] In Canada's 6th report for the UPR (2010), the federal government stated that it would need to ensure that F-P-T laws, policies and programmes meet the obligations of OP-CAT before deciding on whether to join the treaty.[66]

Decisions regarding the formal acceptance of the core human rights treaties are an executive prerogative and much of the deliberation has taken place at the CCOHR behind closed doors.[67] For this reason, the motivations behind Canada's decisions to ratify the core treaties are not well-documented. Dominique Clément has argued that Canada's participation in treaty negotiation and ratification was part of the federal government's strategy to strengthen the Canadian confederation.[68] The federal government developed the CCOHR to consult provinces and territories on the implementation of international human rights obligations that would affect provincial and territorial laws and powers.[69]

Non-ratification of CMW and CED: Canada is not a party to the International Convention on the Protection of the Rights of all Migrant Workers and Members of Their Families (CMW) or the Intentional Convention of the Protection of All Persons from Enforced Disappearance (CED).[70]

A 2006 report commissioned by the United Nations Educational, Scientific and Cultural Organisation (UNESCO) identified possible reasons for Canada's objection to CMW.[71] At the time, the Canadian government's general stance

---

The complaint process of CCPR, CEDAW and CRPD are found in optional protocols to the treaties, namely, the Optional Protocol to the International Covenant on Civil and Political Rights, the Optional Protocol to the Convention on the Elimination of All Forms of Discrimination against Women and the Optional Protocol to the Convention on the Rights of Persons with Disabilities.

65 ibid.
66 Government of Canada, 'Convention against Torture and Other Cruel, Inhuman or Degrading Treatment or Punishment, Sixth Report of Canada' (4 October 2010); United Nations, Committee against Torture, 'Consideration of Reports Submitted by States Parties under Article 19 of the Convention, COs of the Committee against Torture' (25 June 2012) (CAT/C/CAN/CO/6).
67 Standing Senate Committee on Human Rights (n 17) s (I)(C)(2)(b)(iii), citing Gérald-A Beaudoin, with the collaboration of Pierre Thibeault, *Le fédéralisme au Canada* (Wilson & Lafleur 2000) 882; Noël Kinsella, 'Some Historical Notes on the Establishment of the Continuing Committee of Officials Responsible for Human Rights' (nd).
68 Dominique Clément, 'Human Rights in Canadian Domestic and Foreign Politics: From "Niggardly Acceptance" to Enthusiastic Embrace' (2012) 34 Human Rights Quarterly 751–778.
69 ibid.
70 'The Core International Human Rights Treaties and Their Monitoring Bodies' OHCHR <https://www.ohchr.org/EN/ProfessionalInterest/Pages/CoreInstruments.aspx> accessed 3 February 2019.
71 CMW, 'Human Rights Commitments' (2015) <http://humanrightscommitments.ca/wp-content/uploads/2015/11/Convention-on-Migrant-Workers-FW-rev-clean-copy-2.pdf>

was that migrant management was an area that should remain entirely within the purview of states. In Canada's view the rationale behind CMW, which seeks to harmonise the 'attitudes of states through the acceptance of basic principles concerning the treatment of migrant workers', were inconsistent with its immigration policies, which favour priority access to migrants who are highly educated and skilled in areas of demand.[72] There does not seem to be any clear change to Canada's migration policy and treatment of migrants as a result of the existence and development of this treaty. While temporary labour migrants make important contributions to Canadian society and pay taxes, governments in Canada do not fund many basic services for these workers.[73] As a result, many temporary workers lack basic access to health and other social services to which they would have been entitled under the treaty.

Canada officially stated during the 2009 UPR that it would not become a party to CED.[74] Canadian law professor Amir Attaran argued that Canada's reported involvement in cases of enforced disappearance in Afghanistan may be a possible reason for its refusal to join CED.[75] The disappearance of indigenous women and girls is of ongoing concern in Canada.[76] Despite not ratifying CED, Canada has supported Asia's first anti-disappearance law.[77] Moreover,

---

accessed 3 February 2019; Victor Piché, Eugénie Pelletier and Dina Epale, 'Identification of the Obstacles to the Ratification of the United Nations International Convention on the Protection of the Rights of All Migrant Workers and Members of their Families: The Canadian Case' UNESCO Series of Country Reports on the Ratification of the UN Convention on Migrants (SHS/2006/MC/9).

[72] Preamble, International Convention on the Protection of the Rights of All Migrant Workers and Members of Their Families, adopted by General Assembly Resolution 45/158 of 18 December 1990 <https://www.ohchr.org/en/professionalinterest/pages/cmw.aspx> accessed 3 February 2019.

[73] Canada Council for Refugees, 'Migrant Workers – The Issues' <https://ccrweb.ca/en/migrant-workers-issues> accessed 3 February 2019.

[74] Universal Periodic Review, 'Report of the Working Group on the Universal Periodic Review: Canada' A/HRC/11/17/Add.1 8 (June 2009) <https://www.icaed.org/fileadmin/user_upload/Canada__A_HRC_11_17_Add1_CAN_E.pdf> accessed 4 February 2019.

[75] Amir Attaran, 'The Ugly Canadian: Forget Middle Power. Forget Model Citizen. We're Becoming One of the Bad Kids on the Block' (2009) Literary Review of Canada <http://reviewcanada.ca/magazine/2009/06/the-ugly-canadian/> accessed 16 March 2019; ICED, *Human Rights Commitments* (2015) <http://humanrightscommitments.ca/wp-content/uploads/2015/11/Convention-on-Protection-from-Enforced-Disappearances.pdf> accessed 8 February 2019; *Amnesty International Canada v Canadian Forces* 2008 FC 162.

[76] Chris Arsenault, 'Native Women "Disappear" in Canada' *Al Jazeera* (19 September 2010) <https://www.aljazeera.com/quoteofday/2010/08/201083018253280225.html> accessed 10 March 2019.

[77] The Philippines passed the landmark Anti-Enforced or Involuntary Disappearance Act in December 2012, making it the first country in Asia to criminalise the practice of enforced

the Chair-Rapporteur of the Working Group on Enforced or Involuntary Disappearance, Mr Bernard Duhaime, is a Canadian national.[78]

4.1.2 Reservations Entered

Canada has entered three reservations with respect to provisions of CRC and CRPD. Canada maintains the right to not apply the provisions of article 21 of CRC regarding permission to adopt a child 'to the extent that they may be inconsistent with customary forms of care among aboriginal peoples in Canada'.[79] Canada also accepts the general principles of article 37(c) of CRC regarding the dignified treatment of children, particularly in cases of detention, but 'reserves the right not to detain children separately from adults where this is not appropriate or feasible'.[80] Moreover, Canada's reservation with respect to article 12 of CRPD preserves the right to use decision making that is not subject to regular review by an independent authority where such decision making would otherwise be subject to review.[81] In the first and latest COs (2017) for CRPD, the Committee expressed concern that Canada's reservation to article 12 of CRPD may contradict the object and purpose of the Convention.[82]

4.1.3 General Attitude of State towards UN Treaty System

Canada regards the UN treaty bodies as legitimate authorities on human rights issues and is responsive to communications, recommendations and inquiries they release, as these processes are covered by mainstream media and affect the domestic and international perception of the country and the government of the day.

---

and involuntary disappearance; see Embassy of Canada in the Philippines, 'Canada Supports Asia's First Anti-Disappearance Law' <https://www.canadainternational.gc.ca/philippines/eyes_abroad-coupdoeil/ADL-LDF.aspx?lang=en> accessed 24 February 2019; OHCHR, 'Philippines Passes Landmark Law Criminalising Enforced Disappearances' <https://www.ohchr.org/en/newsevents/pages/philippinespassescriminalizingenforceddisappearances.aspx> accessed 24 February 2019.

78 OHCHR, 'Working Group on Enforced or Involuntary Disappearances' <https://www.ohchr.org/EN/Issues/Disappearances/Pages/DisappearancesIndex.aspx> accessed 22 February 2019.

79 UN Treaty Collection (UNTC), CRC, Reservations made by Canada <https://treaties.un.org/pages/ViewDetails.aspx?src=IND&mtdsg_no=IV-11&chapter=4&clang=_en#EndDec> accessed 14 March 2019.

80 ibid.

81 UN Treaty Collection (UNTC), CRPD, Reservations Made by Canada <https://treaties.un.org/pages/ViewDetails.aspx?src=TREATY&mtdsg_no=IV-15&chapter=4#EndDec> 16 March 2019.

82 Committee on the Rights of Persons with Disabilities, 'COs on the Initial Report of Canada' (CRPD/C/CAN/CO/1; 8 May 2017) paras 7–8.

4.1.4 Level of Awareness

The level of awareness of the UN treaty system varies across the different actors in Canadian society. Knowledge of the treaties and the work of the treaty bodies among public servants will depend on whether their work requires experience in, or exposure to, international human rights law. Members of standing committees on human rights (for instance, the Standing Senate Committee on Human Rights) will generally have a very strong command of international human rights law.[83] There is little mention of the core UN human rights treaties in many of the current government's priority policies and programmes. For example the Trudeau administration (2015-) has made numerous public statements regarding his government's commitment to women's rights and is behind initiatives such as establishing gender parity in the executive branch of government.[84] His government also launched Canada's first national action plan on gender violence and announced an investment of approximately 3,8 billion by the G7 to support education for women and girls in conflict areas at the 2017 G7 Summit in Canada.[85] However there is no mention of CEDAW in such announcements, in the Parliamentary record, or in media interviews with the Prime Minister and other senior federal officials. In fact, the CEDAW COs regarding Canada's 8th and 9th periodic review (2016) identified the Convention's lack of visibility in Canada as a major issue.[86] Public bodies may not see their work as involving the implementation of Canada's international human rights obligations, especially when the rights in question are thought to enjoy full protection under the Charter.

NGOs and civil society: Awareness and the use of the treaties among NGOs and civil society largely depend on the scope of their mandate and their target stakeholders. Examples of NGOs interacting directly with the treaties include the Canadian Coalition for the Rights of Children (CCRC), which has established a monitoring mechanism for Canada's compliance with the CRC and endeavours to be an active participant in the upcoming 5th and 6th periodic review of Canada.[87] Generally, the treaties have been used by NGOs in

---

83   Standing Senate Committee on Human Rights (n 16).
84   Jennifer Ditchburn, '"Because it's 2015": Trudeau forms Canada's 1st gender-balanced cabinet' (6 November 2015) <https://www.cbc.ca/news/politics/canada-trudeau-liberal-government-cabinet-1.3304590> accessed 1 April 2019.
85   Justin Trudeau, Speech: 'Advancing gender equality and women's empowerment' (10 June 2018) <https://pm.gc.ca/eng/news/2018/06/10/advancing-gender-equality-and-womens-empowerment> accessed 1 April 2019.
86   CEDAW/C/CAN/CO/8-9 (18 November 2016) paras 7–9.
87   Link to previous Canadian Coalition for the Rights of Children (CCRC) reports <http://rightsofchildren.ca/resources/childrens-rights-monitoring/> accessed 16 April 2019.

parliamentary hearings, including before the Standing Committee on Human Rights, as well as in letters, briefs, and petitions to federal cabinet ministers and parliamentarians. Some treaties feature prominently in the advocacy and outreach efforts of some NGOs. This is particularly the case for the relatively recent CRPD. For example, the Council of Canadians with Disabilities has produced a range of thorough and accessible articles, guidebooks, and other materials on the substantive aspects of CRPD.[88] These materials discuss Canada's accession to CRPD[89] and OP-CRPD,[90] provide guidance on how Canada can implement CRPD by involving the disability community at various steps in the process,[91] and report quick facts on the CRPD for the general public.[92] The treaty has also been used in numerous NGO campaigns for Persons with Disabilities Day on 3 December.[93] NGOs have also used the treaty in litigation before tribunals and courts. However, given the limited likelihood of making a successful legal argument on the basis of the core human rights treaties, they are more likely to be invoked for advocacy and legal reform purposes than as part of litigation strategies.

Legal community: Awareness and the use of the core treaties and protocols appear to be localised among lawyers with expertise in international human rights law. International human rights law is taught at all 24 law faculties in Canada but is currently a required course only at one law faculty (the University of Moncton). Dedicated undergraduate programmes in human rights are offered at St Thomas University in New Brunswick and at the University of Winnipeg in Manitoba.[94]

---

88 Council of Canadians with Disabilities, 'Canada and the CRPD Archives' <http://www.ccdonline.ca/en/international/un/canada/archives> accessed 26 May 2019.

89 Council of Canadians with Disabilities, 'Open Letter: Recognising Two Important Rights Milestones of 2018' (21 December 2018) <http://www.ccdonline.ca/en/international/un/canada/CRPD-OP-21December2018> accessed 26 May 2019.

90 Council of Canadians with Disabilities, 'Review of Canada's Accession to the UN OP-CRPD' (16 March 2017) <http://www.ccdonline.ca/en/international/un/canada/CRPD-OP-16March2017> accessed 26 May 2019.

91 Council of Canadians with Disabilities, 'Canada and the CRPD Archives' <http://www.ccdonline.ca/en/international/un/canada/archives> accessed 26 May 2019.

92 Council of Canadians with Disabilities, 'CRPD – 10 Facts Canadians Should Know' <http://www.ccdonline.ca/en/international/un/canada/10-facts> accessed 26 May 2019.

93 National Union of Public and General employees, 'Dec. 3: International Day of Persons with Disabilities' <https://nupge.ca/content/dec-3-international-day-persons-disabilities> accessed 26 May 2019.

94 St Thomas University, 'Programme Structure' <https://www.stu.ca/humanrights/program-structure/>; University of Winnipeg, 'Bachelor of Arts in Human Rights' <https://www.uwinnipeg.ca/global-college/undergradute-programs/index.html> accessed 7 November 2020.

Media: Coverage of the UN treaty system is typically ramped up during a review of Canada and is featured on major Canadian media outlets such as CBC/Radio-Canada, *Le Devoir*, *The Globe and Mail*, and Torstar. These media reports will often highlight areas where Canada needs to improve based on recommendations, inquiries, or communications issued by the treaty body, particularly when they relate to known and ongoing issues in Canadian society. For example, domestic and foreign media have widely reported on the CEDAW Cttee's 2015 report for Canada, which calls for a national inquiry into the issue of missing and murdered indigenous women and girls in Canada.[95] This report and the Committee's work more generally have been mentioned by the media in its coverage of the tragic cases of Tina Fontaine[96] and Cindy Gladue,[97] among others. The media also provides focused analysis and critical commentary on specific law and policy issues related to Canada's treaty performance. For example, media-driven discussions on racism in Canada occasionally mention CERD and provide readers with statistical data for context, such as detailed statistics on hate crime, while identifying solutions for different levels of government to take to meet the demands of the treaty.[98] The media will also occasionally feature stories on civil society organisations and community leaders that are invited to attend treaty body sessions for Canada's periodic review. However, reporters occasionally make errors in covering UN review mechanisms. For example, they might confuse the HRCttee with the Human Rights Council, particularly its special procedures, or reveal gaps in the understanding of the difference between the High Commissioner's technical assistance, political, and expert bodies.

General public: The general public is aware of the existence of some of the core treaties but there is low awareness of the specialised mandate of the treaty bodies and conflicting views about whether ratified treaties legally bind Canada. Popular media certainly helps in engaging the public's interest

---

95   'Canada Commits "Grave Violation" of Rights of Aboriginal Women: UN Report' *CBC* (10 March 2015) <https://www.cbc.ca/news/indigenous/canada-commits-grave-violation-of-rights-of-aboriginal-women-un-report-1.2989320> accessed 5 April 2019.

96   Mali Ilse Paquin, 'Unsolved Murders of Indigenous Women Reflect Canada's History of Silence' *The Guardian* (25 June 2015) <https://www.theguardian.com/global-development/2015/jun/25/indigenous-women-murders-violence-canada> accessed 5 April 2019.

97   Tom McCarthy, 'Canada Has Failed to Protect Indigenous Women From Violence, Says UN Official' *The Guardian* (12 May 2015) <https://www.theguardian.com/world/2015/may/12/canada-violence-indigenous-first-nations-women> accessed 5 April 2019.

98   Amira Elghawaby, 'Canada's Hate Crime Statistics Only Tell Part of the Story' *Ottawa Citizen* (7 December 2018) <https://ottawacitizen.com/opinion/columnists/elghawaby-canadas-hate-crime-statistics-only-tell-part-of-the-story> accessed 11 April 2019.

in the UN human rights system, which may enhance the indirect or symbolic impact of the treaties on Canadian society. However, media reports regarding Canada's review before a treaty body seldom provide background information that would help the public contextualise the treaty body's work within the framework of the UN human rights system. For example, a 2015 CBC report[99] covered a HRCttee hearing regarding CCPR and alleged human rights violations by Canada-based resource companies without drawing the link between CCPR and the HRCttee to point out the Committee's specialised mandate in monitoring the treaty. Nevertheless, there are particular thematic initiatives by the government to increase awareness and knowledge of Canada's human rights treaty obligations and the work of the treaty bodies. The federal government has funded Cape Breton University to implement a high school level children's curriculum focused on teaching children's rights and CRC through art.[100] The New Brunswick Child and Youth Advocate's work offer an annual summer course on CRC in conjunction with the University of Moncton.[101] Moreover, the opening of the Canadian Museum for Human Rights in 2014 may indirectly spur greater public awareness of the UN treaty system.

Local researchers citing the treaties in their work: Mentions of the core treaties by local researchers vary considerably by treaty. CCPR appears to be cited more than any other treaty.[102] By contrast, to our knowledge, there are three works by local researchers dealing exclusively with CESCR,[103] three others that focus in part on CESCR,[104] and one that deals exclusively with

---

[99] 'UN Human Rights Committee Grills Canada Over Mining, Aboriginal Treatment' *CBC News* (8 July 2015) <https://www.cbc.ca/news/politics/un-human-rights-committee-grills-canada-over-mining-aboriginal-treatment-1.3142635> accessed 3 May 2019.

[100] Cape Breton University, 'Children's Rights Centre' <https://archive.crin.org/en/library/organisations/childrens-rights-centre-cape-breton-university.html> accessed 4 November 2020.

[101] New Brunswick Child and Youth Advocate, 'International Summer Course on the Rights of the Child' New Brunswick Child and Youth Advocate (nd) <https://www.umoncton.ca/droitsdelenfant/en> accessed 4 November 2020.

[102] Bayefsky and Collins (n 13) 129–131.

[103] Admed El-Obaid and Kwadwo Appaigyei-Atua, 'Human Rights in Africa: A New Perspective on Linking The Past to the Present' (1996) 41 McGill Law Journal 819; Nihal Jayawickrama, 'The Right of Self-Determination: A Time for Reinvention and Renewal' (1993) 57 Saskatchewan Law Review 1–19; Robert E Robertson, 'The Rights to Food – Canada's Broken Covenant' (1989–90) 6 Canadian Human Rights Yearbook 185.

[104] Darcel Bullen, 'A Road to Home: The Right to Housing In Canada and Around the World' (2015) 24 Journal of Law and Social Policy 1–9; Meghan Campbell, 'Monitoring Women's Socio-Economic Equality under the ICESCR' (2018) 30(1) Canadian Journal of Women and the Law 82; Martha Jackman and Bruce Porter, 'Justiciability of Social and Economic

CERD.[105] Media reports occasionally cite local researchers who are able to provide views on Canada and the human rights treaties and, in some cases, researchers write media features to update the public on the outcome of the communications and actions by treaty bodies.

4.1.5 State Reporting

Reporting obligations: As of 30 June 2019, Canada has submitted 51 reports for periodic review before the treaty bodies, including reports for the optional protocols OP-CRC-AC and OP-CRC-SC. Canada has only submitted two periodic review reports on time, both for CERD. Canada is, on average, one year and five months late in submitting its reports for review. Canada's tardiest submission was their tenth report to CERD, which was submitted five years and three months late. While Canada currently has four reports overdue, it has never failed to submit a report to a treaty body for periodic review.[106]

The situation regarding tardy submissions has improved in the case of CERD: Canada's most recent report (13th report) was only four months late, compared to its 12th (one year and one month late) and 10th report (five years and three months late). The situation regarding submissions for CEDAW has become progressively worse: Canada's 1st report was five months late and its 3rd, 4th, 5th, and 6th reports were late by seven months, eight months, two years and two months, and three years and six months, respectively. The reporting statistics for other treaties have either been too inconsistent to outline a clear trend or, in the case of CRPD, OP-CRC-AC and OP-CRC-SC, there is too little data available with only one report submitted for each treaty.

Preparation of reports to UN treaty bodies: Canada's reports to the UN treaty bodies are prepared by Canadian Heritage in collaboration with the provinces and territories.[107] Canadian Heritage receives technical assistance from the Department of Justice, Global Affairs Canada, Employment and Social Development Canada, and Statistics Canada.[108] This is a somewhat unusual setup internationally, given the primacy of the role of justice or foreign ministries in this process.

Rights in Canada' in M Langford (ed), *Socio-Economic Rights Jurisprudence: Emerging Trends in Comparative International Law* (Cambridge University Press 2013).

105 Ryszard Cholewinski, 'The Racial Discrimination Convention and the Protection of Cultural and Linguistic Ethnic Minorities' (1991) 69(3) Rev D Inter 157.
106 https://tbinternet.ohchr.org/_layouts/15/TreatyBodyExternal/LateReporting.aspx.
107 HRI/CORE/1/Add.91 paras 164–168.
108 ibid.

Dissemination of reports: Global Affairs Canada is primarily responsible for presenting Canada's reports for periodic review to the UN.[109]

NHRI *reports under treaties:* The Canadian Human Rights Commission (CHRC) is invited by the Canadian government to provide input on reports and in fact contributed to Canada's reports for periodic review under CERD, CCPR, CESCR, CAT and CRPD.[110]

Alternative reports by NGOs and CSOs: NGOs and civil society organisations may be invited by the federal government to take part in the preparation of Canada's reports.[111] However, these organisations typically prefer to submit independent alternative reports.

Alternative reports for CERD addressed the issues of systemic discrimination against minorities and indigenous peoples; racial profiling by police and other figures of authority; immigration policies and practices that are contrary to the treaty; and the overrepresentation of certain minorities and indigenous people and in prisons.

Key themes and topics covered in alternative reports to the HRCttee include the incomplete implementation of the treaty at the domestic level; violence and discrimination against (indigenous) women and children; torture in the process of intelligence gathering; the use of solitary confinement; refugee and migrant rights; 2SLGBTQQIA rights; deportation to torture; indefinite detention and detention of children; corporate accountability for human rights violations; and a shrinking space for civil society advocacy and dissent.

Alternative reports to CESCR cover issues regarding the full domestic legal implementation of CESCR; the defunding of programmes promoting economic, social, and cultural rights; restrictions on the political activities of charities through the Income Tax Act; the participation of poor people in social and political life; violence against women and indigenous peoples; the lack of a living minimum wage, decent and stable employment and pay equity; measures to deny refugees access to social supports; health care for undocumented migrants; the right to housing; the right to food; and the right to health.

Core issues discussed in alternative reports to the CEDAW Cttee include violence against (indigenous) women and girls; the disproportionate number of (indigenous) women in maximum security prisons; the rights of sex workers; the gender wage gap; the economic empowerment of women; and discrimination at the intersection of race, economic, and legal status.

---

109 ibid para 166.
110 ibid para 165.
111 ibid para 168.

Key themes and topics covered in alternative reports to the CAT Cttee include the lack of media coverage on the use of solitary confinement and national security measures; the greater risk of indigenous people being subjected to deathly violence by the state; and the non-ratification of OP-CAT.

Alternative reports to the CRPD Cttee feature several joint submission and frame core issues in relation to provisions of CRPD, the Canadian Charter of Rights and Freedoms, and other relevant domestic and international instruments. The alternative reports touch on several key issues, including the lack of incorporation of CRPD into domestic law; intersectional discrimination (article 5 of CRPD); involuntary detentions in psychiatric institutions; sexual assault of PWDs; unemployment or precarious employment and its disproportionate effect on PWDs; and issues at the intersection of disability and medical assistance in dying (MAiD).

There are no submissions to the CRC Cttee available in the UN treaty body database for the time period of this study.

4.1.6 Domestic Implementation Process

Jurisdiction over matters covered by the core treaties and the responsibility for implementing COs and treaty body recommendations is divided between the federal, provincial, and territorial governments.[112] Canadian Heritage coordinates implementation efforts between these different levels of government. The federal government will consult and cooperate with other levels of government in cases where the implementation of COs and treaty body recommendations falls within provincial or territorial jurisdiction. However, there is no formal mechanism to monitor human rights implementation across levels of government or force compliance.

4.1.7 Treaty Body Membership

Candidates are nominated for treaty body membership through Global Affairs Canada. The nomination of a candidate is a ministerial decision.

Canada has nominated one member to CERD, Mr Ronald St John MacDonald, who was elected to sit on the Committee from 19 January 1972 to 19 January 1976.[113] No other Canadian has been elected since.[114] Given Canada's minimal

---

112   Bayefsky and Collins (n 13) 116.
113   Bayefsky and Collins (n 13) 132; Committee on the Elimination of Racial Discrimination, 'Membership' OHCHR <https://www.ohchr.org/EN/HRBodies/CERD/Pages/Membership.aspx> accessed 21 February 2019.
114   Committee on the Elimination of Racial Discrimination, 'Elections' OHCHR <https://www.ohchr.org/EN/HRBodies/CERD/Pages/Elections.aspx> accessed 21 February 2019.

National human rights institutions: The CHRC submits its own report to treaty monitoring bodies and for the UPR. According to the UN treaty body database, the CHRC made two submissions to the Committee (February 2016 regarding Canada's 6th periodic report[244] and February 2015, also regarding Canada's 6th periodic report).[245]

5.3.4　State Reporting and Its Impact

The key issues detailed in the 6th and latest COs include the consistent lack of full domestic implementation and application of CESCR in domestic law; the low levels of development assistance (0,24 per cent of Canada's gross national income (GNI) which is less than half of the internationally-recognised target of 0,7 per cent); the lack of meaningful consultations with indigenous peoples regarding government resource development; ongoing socio-economic disparities between indigenous and non-indigenous peoples; and the overrepresentation of women and minorities in part-time and low-wage labour.[246]

Canada's engagement with COs: There are no follow-up procedures for COs on record, which makes it very difficult to assess whether COs have been implemented by Canada.

5.3.5　Brief Conclusion

The absence of follow-up procedures for COs on record makes it difficult to accurately assess Canada's implementation of CESCR Cttee recommendations. At the same time, key issues detailed in the 6th and latest COs are still negatively impacting CESCR adherence. Canada's official development assistance still makes up less than half of the internationally recognised target of 0,7 per cent.[247] There still exists a wide wage gap and other socio-economic disparities between indigenous and non-indigenous peoples. A 2017 study by the Conference Board of Canada revealed that indigenous people with a high school diploma earned 15 to 19 per cent less than non-indigenous people

---

244　Canadian Human Rights Commission, 'Submission to the Committee on Economic, Social and Cultural Rights on the Occasion of its Review of Canada's 6th Periodic Report' (February 2016) <https://tbinternet.ohchr.org/_layouts/treatybodyexternal/Download.aspx?symbolno=INT%2fCESCR%2fNHS%2fCAN%2f23019&Lang=en>.
245　Canadian Human Rights Commission, 'Submission to the Committee on Economic, Social and Cultural Rights in Advance of its Review of Canada's 6th Periodic Report' (February 2015) <https://tbinternet.ohchr.org/_layouts/treatybodyexternal/Download.aspx?symbolno=INT%2fCESCR%2fIFL%2fCAN%2f19481&Lang=en>.
246　E/C.12/CAN/CO/6 (23 March 2016).
247　Donor tracker: 'Canada's Total ODA' <https://donortracker.org/country/canada> accessed 12 August 2019.

with the same level of education.[248] Available statistics for Canada also illustrate serious disparities between men and women in the job market. Statistics Canada reports that Canadian women earn on average 4,13 CAD less per hour than men.[249] The gap is attributed to women being more statistically likely to work part-time, sacrifice paid hours to attend to family obligations, work lower-wage jobs, among other factors.[250]

On a more positive note, Canada has committed to implementing a national housing strategy, a recommendation made by the CESCR Cttee in COs to the 6th report. However, Canada's lack of follow-up procedures to the COs make it difficult to attribute the national housing strategy to the Committee's recommendation.

5.4 Convention on the Elimination of All Forms of Discrimination against Women

5.4.1 Incorporation and Reliance by Organs of State

Dubravka Šimonović, UN Special Rapporteur on violence against women, its causes and consequences, made the following remarks following her official visit to Canada in 2018:

> [W]omen's human rights in Canada are protected in an incomplete and patchwork way at the federal, provincial and territorial level that are in different level of harmonisation with CEDAW, and thus result in different levels of protection for women's right to life free from violence.[251]

The CEDAW Cttee has expressed similar concerns related to the treaty not being justiciable in Canada because it has not been incorporated into domestic law.[252]

---

248 Conference Board of Canada, 'How Canada Performs: Social Outcomes in the Territories' (July 2017) <https://www.conferenceboard.ca/hcp/territories-aspx> accessed 2 October 2023.
249 Statistics Canada, 'The gender wage gap in Canada: 1998 to 2018' <https://www150.stat can.gc.ca/n1/pub/75-004-m/75-004-m2019004-eng.htm> accessed 13 August 2019.
250 ibid.
251 End of mission statement by Dubravka Šimonović, United Nations Special Rapporteur on Violence against Women, Its Causes and Consequences, Official visit to Canada (23 April 2018) <www.ohchr.org/EN/NewsEvents/Pages/DisplayNews.aspx?NewsID=22981&LangID=E> accessed 17 May 2019.
252 CEDAW/C/CAN/CO/8-9 paras 7-13. Additionally, Dubravka Šimonović, United Nations Special Rapporteur on Violence against Women, its Causes and Consequences, requested that Canada take the necessary steps to implement recommendations from the latest

presence on the Committee throughout its history, it is unlikely that membership has had a notable impact on the role of the treaty at the domestic level.

Four individuals have been elected for membership on the HRCttee. Mr Walter Tarnopolsky was elected to serve on the HRCttee from 1976 to 1983. Ms Gisèle Côté-Harper was elected to serve on the HRCttee from 1983 to 1984.[115] She was re-nominated but not re-elected for membership. Mr Maxwell Yalden was elected to serve on the HRCttee in 1996 and remained a member until 2006.[116] In March 2016 Ms Marcia VJ Kran was elected to serve on the HRCttee.[117] Ms Kran is the first Canadian member of the HRCttee in 10 years. She was re-elected to serve on the HRCttee in 2020.[118] Canada's participation in the treaty body has had a notable impact on the role of the treaty at the domestic level. For example, the CCPR may have influenced Mr Tarnopolsky contributions to the drafting of the Canadian Charter.[119]

One Canadian, Ms Marie Caron, served as a member of the CEDAW Cttee from 1982 to 1988 but was not re-nominated. An alternative report submitted to the Committee in 1997 raised concerns about the fact that Canada had not nominated a woman to any treaty body for several years.[120] From 2008 to present, Canada has not nominated anyone to the CEDAW Cttee.[121] The general lack of initiative to nominate a candidate for CEDAW Cttee membership undermines the Trudeau government's (2015-) official position that women's human rights are a special focus for his administration.

Professor Peter Thomas Burns was elected to serve as a member of the CAT Cttee in 1987, was made Chairperson in 1998, and held that position until 1999.[122] To date, no Canadian has been elected as a member on CESCR or the

---

[115] Bayefsky and Collins (n 13) 132.
[116] ibid.
[117] 'Membership of the Human Rights Committee 1977 to 2014' OHCHR <https://www.ohchr.org/Documents/HRBodies/CCPR/Membership/Membership1977_2014.pdf> accessed 21 February 2019; Matt Meuse, 'West Vancouver Lawyer Elected to UN Human Rights Committee' CBC News (26 July 2016) <https://www.cbc.ca/news/canada/british-columbia/west-vancouver-un-human-rights-1.3695868> accessed 21 February 2019.
[118] 'UM Law alumna Marcia V.J. Kran re-elected to UN Human Rights Committee' UM Alumni <https://news.umanitoba.ca/um-law-alum-marcia-v-j-kran-re-elected-to-un-human-rights-committee> accessed 06 November 2020.
[119] Bayefsky and Collins (n 13) 132.
[120] ibid; Canada – Alternative Report to CEDAW, submitted by Canadian Women's NGOs as represented by the National Action Committee on the Status of Women, January 1997.
[121] Committee on the Elimination of Discrimination Against Women, 'CEDAW Elections' <https://www.ohchr.org/EN/HRBodies/CEDAW/Pages/Elections.aspx>.
[122] Bayefsky and Collins (n 13) 132; 'Peter Burns' Peter A Allard School of Law, UBC <https://allard.ubc.ca/about-us/our-people/peter-burns > accessed 09 May 2019.

CRC Cttee,[123] and no Canadian has been elected or nominated to the CRPD Cttee.[124] A Canadian national, Mr Bernard Duhaime, is the current Chair-Rapporteur (2014-) of the CED Cttee.

4.2   Overview of Impact

4.2.1   Incorporation and Reliance by Legislature and Executive

The executive branch of government possesses the legal authority to negotiate, sign, and ratify treaties. Given that Canada has a dualist legal order, treaties ratified by the executive require implementing legislation before they can be considered to be part of domestic law and applied by national courts as such. Canada has not directly incorporated into its domestic law any of the core UN human rights treaties that it has joined. Moreover, 'there is no formal or public process in Canada that is dedicated to following up on the observations, findings, and recommendations of these bodies with respect to Canada's human rights performance'.[125] Canada's general position is that its domestic laws already provide effect to the obligations of the treaty and thus do not require dedicated legislation for their implementation.[126] In reality, what results is a reliance on an arguably incomplete patchwork of domestic legislation giving partial effect to Canada's human rights treaty obligations.

4.2.2   Reliance by Judiciary

Given that human rights treaties are not directly incorporated into Canadian law, the treaties generally have no direct application or legal effect before a Canadian court. However, the Supreme Court of Canada has held and reaffirmed that the Canadian Charter of Rights and Freedoms 'should generally be presumed to provide protection at least as great as that afforded by similar provisions in international human rights documents which Canada has ratified'.[127]

---

123   'Past Membership of the Committee on the Rights of the Child (1991–2003)' OHCHR <https://www.ohchr.org/Documents/HRBodies/CRC/PastMembers1991-2013.pdf> accessed 4 May 2019.

124   Committee on the Rights of Persons with Disabilities, 'Elected Members of the Committee on the Rights of Persons with Disabilities' OHCHR <https://www.ohchr.org/en/hrbodies/crpd/pages/membership.aspx> accessed 4 May 2019.

125   Standing Senate Committee on Human Rights (n 17) ss I(C)(2)(a) and III-E.

126   ibid s I(C)(2)(b).

127   *Reference Re Public Service Employee Relations Act (Alta)* [1987] 1 SCR 313 para 59; *Health Services and Support – Facilities Subsector Bargaining Assn v British Columbia* [2007] 2 SCR 391 para 70; *Quebec (Attorney General) v 9147–0732 Québec Inc* 2020 SCC 32 para 31.

4.2.3 Impact on and through Non-state Actors

Legal community: A probable reason why we see relatively little explicit treatment of the core human rights treaties in Canadian decisions is because they cannot give rise to a cause of action *per se* in Canada. Therefore, law practitioners are more likely to rely on the Charter and other relevant domestic human rights instruments to make a legal claim in court.

NGOs and civil society: Well-established human rights NGOs have a high awareness of the core treaties and the capacity to undertake information-sharing sessions with other organisations in their collaborations with treaty bodies. The core treaties (most often CCPR) have been used by NGOs in parliamentary hearings, as well as in letters, briefs, and petitions to federal cabinet ministers and other parliamentarians. NGOs have used the treaties in litigation before tribunals and courts but the most consistent use of the core treaties is through alternative reporting to the UN treaty bodies in preparation for Canada's periodic review or through knowledge sharing and other collaborations with other civil society actors. Alternative reports sometimes include the authoring organisation's dialogue with federal, provincial or territorial governments regarding issues raised, and some reports will also recommend questions for the treaty body to pose to the Canadian delegation.

4.2.4 Impact of State Reporting

Generally, it is difficult to assess whether Canada has effectively implemented the COs because of serious, cross-cutting issues tied to knowledge management and a lack of self-critical assessment in Canada's reports. Canada's reports tend to identify initiatives that purport to fulfil Canada's treaty obligations, often without indicating how these initiatives will be implemented or whether past initiatives have been implemented and adequately monitored. The result is a series of reports that detail government initiatives without conducting a retrospective analysis of whether the overall situation is ameliorating, has stayed the same, or is becoming worse.

Treaty bodies have also noted persistent and serious issues with Canada's implementation of recommendations made in the COs. One recommendation that is consistently disregarded is the need for Canada to legislatively implement its human rights obligations under the treaties. There are also great difficulties with monitoring implementation of COs because there are relatively few state follow-ups to COs. Given that there is no streamlined and dedicated mechanism for monitoring the implementation of recommendations contained in COs, one of the few ways to monitor Canada by way of COs is by looking for recurring or repeat issues, which could signal that those have not been (fully) addressed.

4.2.5 Impact of Individual Communications

Canada has accepted the complaints procedures of CCPR, CAT and CEDAW. The relevant UNTBs made a total of 38 findings of violation against Canada, 28 of CCPR, 9 of CAT and one of CEDAW. All but nine of these findings (8 of CCPR and one of CAT) were adopted after 30 June 1999. There is very little information available that would allow us to assess how Canada generally responds to the views of treaty bodies in communications, given that there are only two follow-ups to communications recorded and they are under CCPR.

Canada's legal system does not give legal effect to the treaty bodies' communications because none of the core treaties have been directly incorporated into domestic law. Moreover, the social and political effect of the treaty bodies' communications is weakened by the lack of a 'formal and public process' at the domestic level for follow-up on communications, as well as COs, early warning measures and urgent procedures, inquiries, and other findings and recommendations of the treaty bodies.[128] Nevertheless, Canada's policy is to respect decisions arising from communications, as they go hand-in-hand with Canada's treaty obligations.[129]

Moreover, while the federal government represents Canada on the international stage, under the constitution of Canada, it is the responsibility of provincial governments to implement treaty obligations that fall under the exclusive powers of provincial legislatures.[130] Problems arise when provincial laws, policies, programs or actions put Canada in a situation of non-compliance because there is no clear mechanism to compel a province to honour Canada's human rights treaty commitments.[131]

4.2.6 Impact of CERD Early Warning Measures

Past CERD early warning measures have alerted Canada to the need to engage in meaningful consultation with indigenous peoples where resource development projects affect aboriginal and indigenous treaty rights.[132]

---

128 Standing Senate Committee on Human Rights (n 16) ss s I(C)(2)(a).
129 ibid ss I(C)(1) and III(E).
130 Constitution Act 1867, s 92.
131 Standing Senate Committee on Human Rights, Committee Evidence, 4 June 2001 (Anne Bayefsky). Bayefsky noted: 'If the provinces are able to say that they have no obligation to adhere to those international obligations, and the federal government is able to say that it has no obligation to do more than encourage them, what does our ratification mean?'.
132 See part 5.1 below.

4.2.7 Impact of Inquiries

Canada allows the CEDAW Cttee to undertake inquiries pursuant to articles 8 and 9(2) of OP-CEDAW. The Committee launched an inquiry into the issue of missing and murdered indigenous women and girls (MMIWG) in Canada in 2012.[133] While Canada's initiative to establish a national inquiry on this issue was viewed by the CEDAW Cttee as a positive step, the CEDAW Cttee noted with concern that Canada had not put forward a formal plan to implement 37 other recommendations stemming from the Committee's inquiry.[134]

5 The Impact of the Different UN Human Rights Treaties on the Domestic Level in Canada

5.1 *International Convention of the Elimination of All Forms of Racial Discrimination*

5.1.1 Incorporation and Reliance by Organs of State

Treaty incorporation into domestic law and policy: Canada's reports to the CERD Cttee cover laws and programmes intended to address racial discrimination, advance substantive equality, improve the conditions of marginalised individuals and groups, and give legal effect to the treaty. The Canadian Multiculturalism Act directly references CERD in the Preamble.[135] The Act recognises multiculturalism as a fundamental tenet of Canadian society.[136] Article 4 CERD is reflected in amendments to the Criminal Code that address hate propaganda offences and aim to combat racial violence.[137] The Canadian Human Rights Act (1977) prohibits racial discrimination at any stage of the employment cycle or in the provision of government or private goods and services under federal jurisdiction.[138] Additionally, the Employment Equity Act requires federally regulated entities to advance employment policies and practices that increase the representation of four designated groups: women, persons with disabilities, indigenous peoples, and visible minorities.[139] The Federal Contractors Programme is intended to provide equal employment

---

133   Lara Koerner Yeo, 'A Comment: the UN CEDAW Committee's Concluding Observations of Canada' (2018) 14 Journal of Law & Equality 199, citing CEDAW/C/OP.8/CAN/1 paras 15–17.
134   Yeo (n 133), citing CEDAW/C/CAN/CO/8-9 para 26.
135   Canadian Multiculturalism Act (RSC 1985, ch 24 (4th Supp)).
136   ibid; CERD/C/CAN/21-23 para 10.
137   CERD/C/CAN/19-20 paras 79–82.
138   Canadian Human Rights Act R.S.C., 1985, c. H-6.
139   Employment Equity Act SC 1995, ch 44.

opportunities to the four designated groups and applies to employers with 100 employees or more that have been granted a federal contract of $1 million or more and are provincially regulated.[140] The Legislated Employment Equity Programme requires federally regulated entities to report annually on the number of individuals from the four designated groups in their workplace and the steps they have taken to achieve more equitable representation.[141] Notably, CERD was not referenced in Canada's or Nova Scotia's current anti-racism strategies or Ontario's Anti-Racism Act.[142]

Allocation of budget in light of the treaty requirements: Canada's 21st and 22nd reports to CERD cover investments into programmes at the federal and provincial levels targeting discrimination and diversity as well as reparations for injustices linked to systemic racism.[143] In 2015 Ontario invested $752 800 over three years in an initiative to reduce the dropout rate of Somali youth in Toronto high schools.[144] In 2012 British Columbia introduced the Aboriginal Post-Secondary Education and Training Policy Framework and Action Plan to increase the number of degrees or certificates awarded to indigenous learners by 75 per cent by 2020–2021.[145] The plan includes $25,1 million in funding from 2012 for supporting education and career advancement initiatives between indigenous communities and public post-secondary institutions; $4 million in annual funding to eleven public post-secondary institutions to put in place an Aboriginal Services Plans for Indigenous learners; and a $4,3 million contribution starting in 2012 to support indigenous students experiencing an immediate financial need.

---

140 Government of Canada, 'Federal Contractors Programme' (21 February 2018) <https://www.canada.ca/en/employment-social-development/programs/employment-equity/federal-contractor-program.html> accessed 16 April 2019.

141 Government of Canada 'Legislated Employment Equity Programme' (4 May 2017) <https://www.canada.ca/en/employment-social-development/programs/employment-equity/leep.html> accessed 16 April 2019; Government of Canada, 'Rights in the Workplace' (1 June 2018) <https://www.canada.ca/en/canadian-heritage/services/rights-workplace.html#a2> accessed 16 April 2019.

142 Government of Canada, 'Canada's Anti-Racism Strategy' Government of Canada (nd) <https://www.canada.ca/en/canadian-heritage/campaigns/anti-racism-engagement.html> accessed 4 April 2019; Government of Nova Scotia, 'Count Us In: Nova Scotia's Action Plan In Response to the International Decade for People of African Descent' 2015–2024 (2018) <https://novascotia.ca/international-decade-for-people-of-african-descent/Action-Plan-international-decade-for-people-of-african-descent.pdf> accessed 4 April 2019; Anti-Racism Act, 2017, SO 2017, ch 15.

143 CERD/C/CAN/21–23 (8 June 2016).

144 ibid (8 June 2016) para 28.

145 ibid para 107.

Québec has also implemented measures to close the gap in levels of education between indigenous and non-indigenous students.[146] From 2012–2016, $125 000 per year was allocated to indigenous friendship centres to assist Quebec students who are indigenous and living off-reserve.

The federal government is working to make reparations for past injustices surrounding the legacy of the Indian residential school system through the Indian Residential Schools Settlement Agreement (2006).[147] As of December 2015, Canada has paid over $1,62 billion in reparations (Common Experience Payments) to 79 302 recipients.

Canada's 2018 endorsement of the UN International Decade for People of African Descent (2015–2024) was backed by a CAD 214 million investment in the 2018 federal budget for 'initiatives designed to remove racial barriers, promote gender equality, combat homo-and trans-phobia and enhance the quality of life of black Canadians'.[148]

5.1.2 Reliance on Treaty by Domestic Courts

CERD has received explicit treatment in three milestone Supreme Court of Canada cases: *R v Keegstra*,[149] *Canada (Human Rights Commission) v Taylor*[150] and *R v Zundel*.[151] In *R v Keegstra* the Supreme Court considered the provisions of CERD in interpreting the scope of section 2(b) (freedom of expression) of the Charter. The Court found that the protection provided to freedom of expression by CERD article 5(viii), interpreted in conjunction with article 2, does not cover expression advocating racial or religious hatred.[152] In *Canada v Taylor* CERD is mentioned as evidence that the international community's commitment to eliminating discrimination 'extends to the prohibition of the dissemination of ideas based on religious or racial superiority'.[153] In *R v Zundel*, the Court found that article 4 of CERD emphasized the goal of 'preventing the harm caused by calculated falsehoods which are likely to injure the public

---

146 ibid para 108.
147 ibid at para 150.
148 'One country's example of promoting inclusion, justice, and respect for diversity' (22 March 2018) OHCHR <https://www.ohchr.org/EN/NewsEvents/Pages/AfroDescendantsInCanada.aspx> accessed 4 April 2019.
149 *R v Keegstra* [1990] 3 SCR 697.
150 *Canada (Human Rights Commission) v Taylor* [1990] 3 SCR 892.
151 *R v Zundel* [1992] 2 SCR 731.
152 *R v Keegstra* [1990] 3 SCR 697 752.
153 *Canada (Human Rights Commission) v Taylor* [1990] 3 SCR 892 919–920.

interest in racial and social tolerance', covered by the now-repealed section 181 of the Criminal Code.[154]

5.1.3 Impact on and through Non-state Actors and Independent State Institutions

NGOs and civil society: NGOs and civil society in Canada have used CERD in innovative and informative ways that take advantage of the reach of social media. Organisations that work on equality, diversity, and inclusion issues, such as the National Women's Association of Canada (NWAC) and the Ontario Council of Agencies Serving Immigrants (OCASI), share the treaty body's findings and reports with the public across social media platforms. Organisations also often solicit support from other civil society groups to conduct knowledge sharing for the periodic review process. These organisations also use CERD treaty body reports and COs as a benchmark to assess Canada's performance under the treaty, make direct demands, and, where appropriate, bring shame on different levels of government for their lack of progress.[155] Overall, Canadian civil society is generally well organised and systematic in applying pressure at the international and domestic levels on issues related to racial discrimination in Canada.[156]

Academics: To our knowledge, only one article by a local researcher dealt exclusively with the treaty.[157]

---

[154] *R v Zundel* [1992] 2 SCR 731.

[155] Shree Paradkar, 'NGOs Tell UN Panel Canada is Failing on Ending Racism: Paradkar' *The Star* (14 August 2017) <https://www.thestar.com/news/gta/2017/08/14/ngos-tell-un-panel-canada-is-failing-on-racism-paradkar.html> accessed 18 March 2019.

[156] The following NGOs, indigenous groups, and other civil society actors have submitted alternative reports to the treaty Committee: NWAC; OCASI; South Asian Legal Clinic; Chinese and South East Asian Legal Clinic; African Canadian Legal Clinic; Canadian Race Relations Foundation; CRRAR; KAIROS; Oxfam Canada; Amnesty International; the Canadian Council of Muslim Women; the Canadian Aboriginal AIDS Network (CAAN); the National Aboriginal Circle Against Family Violence; Alliance4Democracy; the Coalition for the Human Rights of Indigenous Peoples; the Canadian HIV/AIDS Legal Network; the National Council of Canadian Muslims; Mining Watch Canada; Interior Alliance of Indigenous Nations; Union of BC Indian Chiefs; Assembly of First Nations (Quebec & Labrador, BC); Mothers and Grandmothers of Maliseet Nations; Skeena Indigenous Groups; Algonquin Nation Secretariat; The Chiefs of Ontario; Union of BC Indian Chiefs; Onion Lake Cree Nation; Lubicon Lake Indian Nation; Mohawks of the Bay of Quinte; Roma Community Centre; The Haudenosaunee of Kanehsatàke; Six Nations of the Grand River; Nishnawbe Aski Nation (NAN); and Tsilhqot'in Nation.

[157] Cholewinski (n 104).

National human rights institutions: The Canadian Human Rights Commission (CHRC) has made two submissions to CERD.[158]

5.1.4 State Reporting and Its Impact

Pertinent issues in COs: The COs for the combined 21st to 23rd periodic reports of Canada pointed to unresolved issues from previous state reports and addressed growing concerns regarding Canada's overall performance in meeting the obligations of CERD.[159] The CERD Cttee reiterated its concern from the 12th report regarding the lack of comprehensive data on the ethnic composition of Canada's population and the representation of minority groups in political life in Canada.[160] This has prevented the Committee from properly evaluating the attainment of civil, political, social, and cultural rights in Canada by minority groups.

The CERD Cttee also recalled its General Recommendation (No 23 (1997)) on the rights of indigenous peoples and restated its previous recommendation that Canada suspend all permits for the Site C dam in British Columbia.[161] It also urged Canada to undertake a full review of the project in cooperation with indigenous peoples to ensure that developers seek free, prior and informed consent from indigenous peoples affected, respect indigenous treaty obligations in the course of development, and identify alternatives to the destruction of indigenous land that may result from the project.[162]

Regarding developing issues, the CERD Cttee also pointed to a lack of a renewed national plan against racism since the previous plan ended in 2010, and a lack of an anti-racism legal framework to meet the requirements of article 4 of CERD.[163] Lastly, the Committee also called on Canada to address racial

---

158 Canadian Human Rights Commission, 'Submission by the Canadian Human Rights Commission to the United Nations Committee on the Elimination of Racial Discrimination on the Seventeenth and Eighteenth Periodic Reports of Canada under the International Convention on the Elimination of All Forms of Racial Discrimination' (January 2007) <https://tbinternet.ohchr.org/_layouts/15/treatybodyexternal/Download.aspx?symbolno=INT%2fCERD%2fNGO%2fCAN%2f70%2f8262&Lang=en>; Canadian Human Rights Commission, 'Submission to the United Nations Committee on the Elimination of Racial Discrimination' (January 2012) <https://tbinternet.ohchr.org/_layouts/15/treatybodyexternal/Download.aspx?symbolno=INT%2fCERD%2fNGO%2fCAN%2f80%2f8284&Lang=en> accessed 5 June 2022.
159 CERD/C/CAN/CO/21–23 (13 September 2017).
160 CERD/C/2007/1 paras 10–12.
161 CERD/C/CAN/CO/19–20 para 20; CERD/C/CAN/CO/21–23 (13 September 2017) para 20.
162 CERD/C/CAN/CO/21–23 (13 September 2017) paras 19–20.
163 ibid paras 9–10.

profiling by police and security agents, specifically through amendments to the Anti-Terrorism Act and other relevant laws.[164]

Canada's engagement with COs: Regarding the possibility of racial profiling in immigration detention, Canada states that its policy is to use detention 'only as a measure of last resort, in limited prescribed circumstances and only after alternatives to detention have been considered'.[165] The government also stated that access to periodic review of detention and other safeguards protected detainees from arbitrary detention through the periodic review of their detention.[166] Canada deferred responding to the Committee's recommendations for follow-up on the Site C dam project, explaining that it would instead address this concern in its response to a CERD Early Warning Urgent Action request.[167]

5.1.5 Individual Communications and Their Impact

There are no individual communications and no inquiries lodged under CERD. While Canada does not recognise the competence of CERD treaty body to accept and review individual complaints, there have been several CERD early warning urgency actions (EWUA) that would be ripe for submission as individual communications were Canada to recognise the CERD complaint mechanism. CERD EWUA reports cover development projects that are being carried out without meaningful consultation with the indigenous peoples affected. This activity could potentially undermine pre-existing aboriginal and treaty rights.

5.1.6 Impact of Other Measures

The CERD early warning measures have been used a total of seven times (15 August 2008; 13 March 2009; 27 May 2016; 3 October 2016; 13 December 2016; 17 May 2017; 13 December 2019). CERD early warning measures were exercised by the Committee to alert Canada to the following:

– the continuance of the Site C dam project and the approval of the Trans Mountain Pipeline Extension project and the Coastal Gas Link pipeline

---

164   ibid at paras 15–16.
165   CERD/C/CAN/CO/21–23/ADD.1 (4 March 2019): COs on the twenty-first to twenty-third periodic reports of Canada, Addendum, Information received from Canada on follow-up to the COs Recommendations 34(a), (b) and (d) para 12.
166   ibid para 13.
167   ibid para 3.

without free, prior and informed consent by indigenous peoples affected (2019);[168]
- alleged violations of the rights of indigenous women in the village of Lote Ocho in Guatemala by employees of a Canada-based resource company (2016);[169]
- the undermining of the indigenous land rights of the Secwepemc Nation and the St'át'imc Nation in British Columbia (2016, 2017);[170]
- absence of certainty regarding the land rights over Lubikon Lake Nation territory and the North Central Corridor Pipeline extending through the territory (2016, 2008);[171]
- the expansion of development projects in indigenous territories without informed consent and the extinguishing of traditional land rights in favour of private interests (2009).[172]

5.1.7   Brief Conclusion

Canada's reports and follow-up submissions to the COs continue to avoid addressing ongoing issues that impede the Committee's work across reporting cycles, such as the lack of comprehensive statistics on the country's ethnic composition. Moreover, despite Canada endorsing the UN Declaration on the Rights of Indigenous Peoples (UNDRIP), the free, informed, and prior consent of indigenous peoples remains an unresolved and contentious issue in the country. At the time of writing, only British Columbia has passed legislation to implement the Declaration.[173]

---

168   'Reference: CERD/100th/EWU/CAN/9026 OHCHR' (25 November-13 December 2019) <https://tbinternet.ohchr.org/Treaties/CERD/Shared%20Documents/CAN/INT_CERD_EWU_CAN_9026_E.pdf>.
169   'Reference: CERD/89th/EWUAP/GH/MJA/ks' (27 May 2019) <https://tbinternet.ohchr.org/Treaties/CERD/Shared%20Documents/CAN/INT_CERD_ALE_CAN_8030_E.pdf>.
170   'Reference: CERD/90th/EWUAP/GH/MJA/ks' OHCHR (3 October 2016) <https://tbinternet.ohchr.org/Treaties/CERD/Shared%20Documents/CAN/INT_CERD_ALE_CAN_8092_E.pdf> accessed 5 June 2022; 'Reference: CERD/92nd/EWUAP/GH/SK/ks' (17 May 2017) <https://tbinternet.ohchr.org/Treaties/CERD/Shared%20Documents/CAN/INT_CERD_ALE_CAN_8206_E.pdf> accessed 5 June 2022.
171   'Reference: CERD/91st/EWUAP/SW/ks' OHCHR (13 December 2016) <https://tbinternet.ohchr.org/Treaties/CERD/Shared%20Documents/CAN/INT_CERD_ALE_CAN_8131_E.pdf> accessed 5 June 2022; 'Reference: TS/JDV/JF (15 August 2008) <https://www.ohchr.org/sites/default/files/Documents/HRBodies/CERD/EarlyWarning/Canada_letter150808.pdf> accessed 5 June 2022.
172   'Reference: TS/JF' OHCHR (13 March 2009) <http://www.ohchr.org/Documents/HRBodies/CERD/EarlyWarning/Canada130309.pdf> accessed 5 June 2022.
173   Declaration on the Rights of Indigenous Peoples Act [SBC 2019] ch 44.

5.2 *International Covenant on Civil and Political Rights*

5.2.1   Incorporation and Reliance by Organs of State

Incorporation of treaty into domestic law: In April 2001 the federal government established the Standing Senate Committee on Human Rights to identify measures needed to fully implement its obligations under CCPR after the HRCttee expressed concern that there may be gaps between the protection of civil and political rights under the Charter and relevant federal, provincial, and territorial (F-P-T) laws.[174] Following the Senate Committee's first report (13 December 2001), a federal Deputy Ministers Committee (October 2002) was established for Canadian governments to more effectively coordinate and share in the responsibility for implementing Canada's international human rights obligations.[175] Since then, a Senior Officials Committee on Human Rights (SOCHR) and the Forum of Ministers on Human Rights (FMHR) have also been established as part of this effort (see part 1).[176] Despite its incomplete incorporation into domestic law, CCPR was considered in the drafting of the Charter.[177] CCPR has also had a stated influence on the Canadian Multiculturalism Act; the Preamble to the Act references Canada's international obligations under CCPR.

Policies related to the treaty: Policies related to the treaty were mandated by the federal government as a response to the HRCttee's recommendations following the country's 5th[178] and 6th[179] (latest) periodic reports to the Committee. The HRCttee paid particular attention to article 2 of CCPR (equal rights and effective remedies) and recommended that human rights legislation be amended to guarantee access to an effective remedy in all discrimination cases.[180] In response the Canadian Human Rights Commission (CHRC) introduced process reforms in May 2003 aimed at reducing its chronic backlog

---

[174]   Standing Senate Committee on Human Rights (n 16); Human Rights Committee, 65th Session, CCPR/C/79/Add.105, 7 April 1999 para 10.

[175]   CCPR/C/CAN/2004/5 (18 November 2004) para 15; Government of Canada, 'Deputy Minister Committees: Committee and Task Force Mandates and Membership' (18 October 2019) <https://www.canada.ca/en/privy-council/programs/appointments/senior-public-service/deputy-minister-committees.html> accessed 27 October 2020.

[176]   Canadian Heritage, 'About human rights' *Government of Canada* (23 December 2020) <https://www.canada.ca/en/canadian-heritage/services/about-human-rights.html#a4> accessed 5 August 2021.

[177]   Bayefsky and Collins (n 13) 132; Walter Tarnopolosky, 'A Comparison Between the Canadian Charter of Rights and Freedoms and the International Covenant on Civil and Political Rights' (1982) 8 Queens LJ 211.

[178]   CCPR/C/CAN/2004/5 (18 November 2004).

[179]   CCPR/C/CAN/6 (28 October 2013).

[180]   CCPR/C/CAN/2004/5 (18 November 2004) paras 10–16; CCPR/C/CAN/6 (28 October 2013) paras 7–14.

of cases.[181] These reforms include using alternative dispute resolution in all stages of the complaints process and referring select cases to the Canadian Human Rights Tribunal.[182]

5.2.2 Reliance on the Treaty by Domestic Courts

In *Canadian Foundation for Children, Youth and the Law v Canada* the Supreme Court of Canada engaged with the Preamble and article 7 of CCPR, and the views expressed by the HRCttee, to find that the CCPR does not require state parties to categorically ban corporal punishment of children, since it permits 'corrective force that is reasonable'.[183]

The extradition case, *USA v Burns*, references CCPR but ultimately finds that the Charter requires Canada to seek assurances that the death penalty will not be imposed by the country requesting extradition 'in all but exceptional cases'.[184] Similarly, the Court in *Suresh v Canada* found that deportation to torture is prohibited – barring exceptional cases – by article 7 of CCPR (prohibition on torture), but ultimately relied on section 7 of the Charter (life, liberty and security of the person) in arriving at the decision.[185] Also in this case, the HRCttee's General Comment 20 was used to inform the Court's interpretation of the principles of fundamental justice in section 7 of the Charter.[186]

5.2.3 Impact on and through Non-state Actors

NGOs and civil society: NGOs generally cite CCPR in their alternative reports to the HRCttee for their periodic review of Canada.[187]

Academics: CCPR appears to be cited more than any other major human rights treaty in Canadian textbooks and journal articles.[188] This may be due

---

181 CCPR/C/CAN/2004/5 (18 November 2004) paras 12–13.
182 CCPR/C/CAN/6 (28 October 2013) paras 10–12.
183 *Canadian Foundation for Children, Youth and the Law v Canada (Attorney-General)* 2004 SCC 4 paras 32–49.
184 *United States v Burns* 2001 SCC 7 paras 8, 87 and 93.
185 *Suresh v Canada (Minister of Citizenship and Immigration)* 2002 SCC 1 paras 66–67 and 78.
186 ibid para 66–75.
187 The following NGOs and civil society organisations have submitted alternative reports: Human Rights Watch; Canadian Human Rights Commission; Canadian Civil Liberties Association; FAFIA-AFAI; Native Women's Association of Canada (NWAC); Franciscans International; Canada Without Poverty; Privacy International; Mercy International Association; ILGA North America; Aboriginal Title Alliances; Amnesty International; International Fellowship of Reconciliation; Quebec Human Rights Commissions; Canadian Federation of University Women; KAIROS; FIACAT; and a statement by Lil'wat.
188 Bayefsky and Collins (n 13) 129 (fn 74).

to the particular emphasis on civil and political rights in Canada, and the fact that the individual complaints mechanism under the Optional Protocol (OP1-CCPR) has been well utilised with respect to Canada.

5.2.4 State Reporting and Its Impact

Pertinent issues in Concluding Observation recommendations: The COs to Canada's 6th report expressed concern in several areas. The HRCttee recommended that Canada consult indigenous people to seek their free, prior and informed consent whenever government resource projects may affect aboriginal and indigenous treaty rights.[189] The HRCttee also expressed concern regarding the alleged human rights abuses committed by Canada-based resource companies operating abroad and recommended the establishment of an independent mechanism with the capacity to undertake complaints about such abuses.[190] The HRCttee also expressed concern about the gender pay gap in Canada, which disproportionately affects low-income women; the differing or non-existent pay equity legislation at the F-P-T levels; the underrepresentation of women in leadership positions in the public and private sectors; and the failure to guarantee equal employment and advancements opportunities within the private sector.[191] The HRCttee noted with concern the conditions in Canada's correctional facilities and, in particular, the high level of overcrowding; the use of segregation for extended periods; reports of suicides in corrections facilities and insufficient support for inmates with mental-health issues.[192] Lastly, the Committee expressed grave concern about the continued high incidences of domestic violence in Canada, specifically against indigenous women and girls and women of colour.[193]

Implementing recommendations in COs: A general comment regarding the implementation of Concluding Observation recommendations to the 6th periodic report is that only a select few recommendations are given attention in the follow-up procedure.[194] Those that are addressed receive only partial implementation. Canada recognised its ongoing duty to consult and accommodate indigenous communities where the government contemplates action that might adversely affect aboriginal treaty rights.[195] An important tool to this

---

189 CCPR/C/CAN/CO/6 (13 August 2015) s C: Indigenous lands and titles.
190 CCPR/C/CAN/CO/6 (13 August 2015) s C: Business and human rights.
191 CCPR/C/CAN/CO/6 (13 August 2015) s C: Gender equality.
192 CCPR/C/CAN/CO/6 (13 August 2015) s C: Prison conditions.
193 CCPR/C/CAN/CO/6 (13 August 2015) s C: Violence against women.
194 CCPR/C/CAN/FCO/25188/E (16 September 2016).
195 CCPR/C/CAN/FCO/25188/E (16 September 2016) s 4.4; *Haida Nation v British Columbia (Minister of Forests)* [2004] 3 SCR 511; *Taku River Tlingit First Nation v British Columbia*

end is the Updated Guidelines for Federal Officials to Fulfil the Duty to Consult (March 2011).[196] Provincial governments have also established similar policies and guidelines for their officials to fulfil the duty to consult.[197] Regarding the resolution of land and resource disputes with indigenous peoples, Canada has implemented a specific claims policy meant to encourage reconciliation through negotiated settlements rather than litigation.[198] Canada committed to developing a new federal reconciliation framework informed by the recommendations ('calls to actions') of the Truth and Reconciliation Commission of Canada for addressing the legacy and impact of Canada's Indian Residential Schools system as well as the principles of UNDRIP.[199] However, the national reconciliation framework remains a work in progress and Canada has yet to legally adopt the UNDRIP at the federal level.[200] In January 2018 the Minister of International Trade announced the establishment of a Canadian Ombudsperson for Responsible Enterprise.[201] However, this measure may not

---

(*Project Assessment Director*) [2004] 3 SCR 550; *Mikisew Cree First Nation v Canada* (*Minister of Canadian Heritage*) [2005] 3 SCR 388.

[196] Indigenous and Northern Affairs Canada, 'Aboriginal Consultation and Accommodation – Updated Guidelines for Federal Officials to Fulfil the Duty to Consult – March 2011' <https://www.rcaanc-cirnac.gc.ca/eng/1100100014664/1609421824729> accessed 2 October 2023.

[197] As examples, see British Columbia <https://www2.gov.bc.ca/gov/content/environment/natural-resource-stewardship/consulting-with-first-nations> accessed 18 April 2019; see also Ontario draft guidelines <https://www.ontario.ca/page/draft-guidelines-ministries-consultation-aboriginal-peoples-related-aboriginal-rights-and-treaty> accessed 18 April 2019; finally, see Government of New Brunswick, 'Duty to Consult Policy' (2011) <https://www2.gnb.ca/content/dam/gnb/Departments/aas-saa/pdf/en/DutytoConsultPolicy.pdf> accessed 18 April 2019.

[198] CCPR/C/CAN/FCO/25188/E (16 September 2016) s 4.3; Government of Canada, 'Ongoing Negotiations' <https://www.rcaanc-cirnac.gc.ca/eng/1100100030285/1529354158736> accessed 21 May 2019.

[199] Truth and Reconciliation Commission of Canada, Final Report (2015) <http://www.trc.ca/websites/trcinstitution/index.php?p=890> accessed 28 May 2019. On 10 May 2016 the Minister of Indigenous and Northern Affairs announced at the 15th Meeting of the United Nations Permanent Forum on Indigenous Issues that Canada is now a 'full supporter of the UNDRIP without qualifications' and that Canada 'will adopt and implement the declaration in accordance with the Canadian Constitution'. See Government of Canada, 'Speech delivered at the United Nations Permanent Forum on Indigenous Issues, New York, May 10' (10 May 2016) <https://www.canada.ca/en/indigenous-northern-affairs/news/2016/05/speech-delivered-at-the-united-nations-permanent-forum-on-indigenous-issues-new-york-may-10-.html> accessed 21 May 2019.

[200] Government of Canada, 'Overview of a Recognition and Implementation of Indigenous Rights Framework' (10 Sept 2018) <https://www.rcaanc-cirnac.gc.ca/eng/1536350959665/1539959903708> accessed 21 May 2019.

[201] Order in Council PC 2019–299 (8 April 2019) <https://orders-in-council.canada.ca/attachment.php?attach=38652&lang=en> accessed 28 May 2019.

fully address the HRCttee's call for an independent mechanism with investigatory power. Local human rights groups have expressed concern that the Ombudsperson lacks independence and the power to obligate companies to comply with Ombudsperson investigations and recommendations.[202, 203] Regarding the level of engagement of Canada with the outcome of follow-up procedures, only one follow-up to COs is found in the UN treaty body database.[204] This demonstrates a low level of engagement with the outcomes of the periodic reporting for CCPR.

5.2.5 Individual Communications and Their Impact

There have been 138 individual communications and no inquiries lodged under CCPR.[205] The HRCttee found violations in respect of 28 communications concerning Canada, 8 covered in the previous study, and 20 adopted since 30 June 1999.[206] Some individual communications brought before the HRCttee have received media attention and have led to law and policy change. For example,

---

[202] Business and Human Rights Resource Centre, 'Canada Creates Independent Ombudsperson and Multi-Stakeholder Advisory Body to Strengthen Responsible Business Conduct Abroad' <https://www.business-humanrights.org/en/latest-news/canada-creates-ombudsperson-multi-stakeholder-advisory-body-to-strengthen-responsible-business-conduct-abroad/> accessed 3 June 2019.

[203] Business and Human Rights Resource Centre (n 202).

[204] CCPR/C/CAN/FCO/25188/E (16 September 2016) (Interim measures following the sixth periodic report of Canada – International Covenant on Civil and Political Rights).

[205] The number of individual communications include communications that were deemed inadmissible.

[206] *Waldman v Canada* CCPR/C/67/D/694/1996 (3 November 1999); *Judge v Canada* CCPR/C/78/D/829/1998 (5 August 2002) (deportation); *Ahani v Canada* CCPR/C/80/D/195/2002 (29 March 2004); *JT v Canada* CCPR/C/89/D/1052/2002 (24 March 2007); *Dauphin v Canada* A/64/40 vol II (2009) (28 July 2009) (deportation); *Dumont v Canada* CCPR/C/98/D/1467/2006 (16 March 2010) (effective remedy); *Hamida v Canada* CCPR/C/98/D/1544/2007 (18 March 2010) (deportation); *Kaba v Canada* CCPR/C/98/D/1465/2006 (25 March 2010) (deportation); *Pillai v Canada* CCPR/C/101/D/1763/2008 (25 March 2011); *Warsame v Canada* CCPR/C/102/D/1959/2010 (21 July 2011); *Thuraisamy v Canada* CCPR/C/106/D/1912/2009 (31 October 2012) (deportation); *Shakeel v Canada* CCPR/C/108/D/1881/2009 (24 July 2013) (deportation); *Choudhary v Canada* CCPR/C/109/D/1898/2009 (28 October 2013) (deportation); *AHG v Canada* CCPR/C/113/D/2091/2011 (25 March 2015) (deportation); *DT & AA v Canada* CCPR/C/117/D/2081/2011 (15 July 2016) (deportation); *Saxena v Canada* CCPR/C/118/D/2118/2011 (3 November 2016) (deportation); *Contreras v Canada* CCPR/C/119/D/2613/2015 (27 March 2017) (deportation); *Budlakoti v Canada* CCPR/C/122/D/2264/2013 (6 April 2018) (deportation); *Toussaint v Canada* CCPR/C/123/D/2348/2014 (24 July 2018); *McIvor and Grismer v Canada* CCPR/C/124/D/2020/2010 (1 November 2018).

the case of Sandra Lovelace led to changes to the Indian Act 'that seek to restore the legal rights of many status Indian women'.[207] Lovelace lost her legal Indian status under the Indian Act because she married a 'non-Indian' and was prevented by the government of Canada from returning to her home reserve. The HRCttee concluded that Canada had violated her cultural minority rights, under article 27 of CCPR.[208]

In the more recent case of *Toussaint v Canada*, the HRCttee concluded that irregular migrants' right to life and equality under CCPR covers access to essential health care services.[209] Nell Toussaint entered Canada in 1999 and developed a serious health condition in 2008 before she could complete the process to regularise her immigration status. Due to her irregular status Toussaint was denied access to essential healthcare services available through Canada's Interim Federal Health Programme. The HRCttee concluded that the right to life may impose positive obligations on governments, in addition to the negative obligation to not discriminate based on regular and irregular migration status. The HRCttee requested that Canada review its legislation to make sure that irregular migrants have access to essential health care in such circumstances.[210] Canada disagreed with the views of the Committee and expressed that it would 'not be taking any further measures to give effect to those views'.[211]

5.2.6   Follow-Up to Individual Communications

There has been very low engagement on the part of Canada with the procedures for follow-up before the HRCttee. Canada has submitted one follow-up progress report on individual communications (CCPR/C/101/3) containing information received since October 2010. The two cases recorded in this single follow-up are *Dumont* and *Hamida*.[212]

---

[207] Heather Conn, 'Sandra Lovelace Nicholas' *Canadian Encyclopedia* (10 January 2018) <https://www.thecanadianencyclopedia.ca/en/article/sandra-lovelace-nicholas> accessed 17 May 2019.

[208] *Sandra Lovelace v Canada*, Communication No 24/1977 Canada 30/07/81, UN Doc CCPR/C/13/D/24/1977.

[209] *Toussaint v Canada*, CCPR/C/123/D/2348/2014, 2018.

[210] ibid ss 10 and 11.

[211] Permanent Mission of Canada to the UN, 'HRCttee 2348/2014 – Response to the Committee's Views' (GENEV-5356) (see <https://www.socialrights.ca/2019/CanadaToussaintResponseonImpl.pdf> accessed 15 April 2022); on the general measures recommended, the government responded: 'Canada reiterates its position that the provision of life-saving emergency medical services to irregular migrants at Canadian hospitals is sufficient to meet Canada's obligations under the Covenant'.

[212] CCPR/C/101/3 (25 May 2011).

Dumont dealt with a violation of articles 2 and 14 of CCPR. In 1991 the Court of Québec found Mr Dumont guilty of sexual assault and sentenced him to 52 months in prison. Mr. Dumont appealed the decision, which was upheld. Prior to Mr. Dumont's appeal, his alleged victim formally attested that she was mistaken about the assailant's identity, yet this was not raised at appeal. Mr Dumont spent 34 months in prison before his conviction was reversed, and was not compensated in accordance with the Québec Guidelines on Compensation for Wrongfully Convicted and Imprisoned Persons.[213] In 2011 the HRCttee concluded that Canada should provide Mr Dumont with an effective remedy, including financial compensation, and take the appropriate steps to avoid similar violations in the future. Mr Dumont maintains that the out-of-court financial settlement he received does not constitute an effective remedy. This follow-up dialogue is considered ongoing by the treaty body.

Hamida dealt with an expulsion order requiring Mr Hamida to return to Tunisia. Mr Hamida argued that the order violated article 7 (prohibition against torture), in addition to article 2 of CCPR. The HRCttee's follow-up recommended a reconsideration of the order with a view to obligation under CCPR to avoid exposing individuals to the risk of torture and other cruel and inhumane treatment. This follow-up dialogue is considered ongoing by the treaty body.

5.2.7   Brief Conclusion

Canada's periodic and follow-up reports tend to cherry-pick recommendations to address; and of those, most receive only partial implementation. Nevertheless, there are moments demonstrating that Canada generally recognises the legitimacy and authority of the HRCttee. In August 2019 Canada delayed the deportation of Mr Abdilahi Elmi, a former Somali refugee and foster child, at the United Nations' request so that the HRCttee could review his case. In response, a spokesperson for the Minister of Public Safety stated that '[i]nterim measures requests from the HRCttee are always considered by Canada'.[214]

---

[213] Quebec Minister of Justice, 'Quebec Guidelines on Compensation for Wrongfully Convicted and Imprisoned Persons' <https://www.justice.gouv.qc.ca/fileadmin/user_upload/contenu/documents/En__Anglais_/centredoc/publications/programmes-services/ej_lignes_directrices-a.pdf> accessed 9 June 2019.

[214] CBC News, 'Former Refugee Abdilahi Elmi Won't Be Deported to Somalia Monday as Scheduled' (23 August 2019) <https://www.cbc.ca/news/canada/edmonton/abdilahi-elmi-deportation-somalia-edmonton-1.5258193> accessed 23 October 2020.

5.3　*International Covenant on Economic, Social and Cultural Rights*

5.3.1　Incorporation and Reliance by Organs of State

In the COs to Canada's 6th periodic report, the CESCR Cttee has expressed concern that the lack of available legal mechanisms in Canada for upholding economic, social, and cultural rights might disproportionately affect disadvantaged and marginalised individuals and groups, including indigenous peoples, the homeless, and persons with disabilities.[215] The Covenant, unlike the Canadian Charter of Rights and Freedoms, explicitly guarantees the right to work and safe and fair working conditions;[216] the right to strike and belong to a trade union;[217] the right to an adequate standard of living;[218] the right to paid maternity leave and social security;[219] and the right to benefit from cultural and scientific developments.[220] To close the rights gap between the Charter and CESCR, the Committee has requested that Canada actively engage with indigenous peoples and other relevant stakeholders to broaden the scope of the Charter to explicitly include economic, social, and cultural rights.[221]

Laws and policies related to the treaty: While not in direct response to the treaty, reforms to the Criminal Code aim to better protect target groups – particularly women and children – from domestic violence (article 10 of CESCR).[222] An Act to amend the Canadian Human Rights Act,[223] extends protection under the Act to first nations registered under the Indian Act by admitting complaints made under the Indian Act that were previously inadmissible.[224] The federal Employment Equity Act seeks to achieve equitable representation in federal workplaces for four designated groups: women, aboriginal persons, persons with disabilities, and members of visible minorities.[225] This helps to promote the progressive realisation of the right of all to gain a living by work under article 6 of CESCR.[226] Government statistics on the representation of designation groups in the federal government and the private sectors show

---

215　E/C.12/CAN/CO/6 (23 March 2016) paras 5–6.
216　CESCR, art 7.
217　CESCR, art 8.
218　CESCR, art 11.
219　CESCR arts 9–10.
220　CESCR, art 15.
221　E/C.12/CAN/CO/6 (23 March 2016) para 6.
222　E/C.12/CAN/6 (23 April 2013) paras 43–46.
223　An Act to Amend the Canadian Human Rights Act SC 2008, ch 30.
224　E/C.12/CAN/6 (23 April 2013) paras 62–63.
225　Employment Equity Act SC 1995, ch 44.
226　E/C.12/CAN/6 (23 April 2013) para 74.

a gradual improvement in the employment situation of the four designated groups since the Act took force in 1986.[227]

Resource allocation in light of treaty requirements: The treaty body and the UN Special Rapporteur on Adequate Housing have both labelled the housing situation in Canada a 'national emergency'.[228] Canada has committed to implementing a national housing strategy. The strategy includes an investment of over $72 billion CAD over 10 years with the aim of cutting homelessness in half, in part by renovating and modernising 300 000 homes, and building up to 160 000 new homes.[229] The National Housing Strategy Act is a rare example of a Canadian law directly referencing a provision of a human rights treaty:

> 4 It is declared to be the housing policy of the Government of Canada to –
> (a) recognise that the right to adequate housing is a fundamental human right affirmed in international law;
> (b) recognise that housing is essential to the inherent dignity and well-being of the person and to building sustainable and inclusive communities;
> (c) support improved housing outcomes for the people of Canada; and
> (d) *further the progressive realisation of the right to adequate housing as recognised in the International Covenant on Economic, Social and Cultural Rights* [emphasis added].

Civil society played a major role in successfully petitioning the federal government to include this provision in the National Housing Strategy Act. After the release of the National Housing Strategy, which signalled the federal government's intention to make housing a right under Canadian law, 1 100 signatories penned a letter to Prime Minister Trudeau urging the government to do so.[230]

---

227 ibid paras 75–78.
228 Miloon Kothari, United National Special Rapporteur on Adequate Housing, 'Preliminary Observations at the End of his Mission to Canada 9–22 October 2007' A/HRC/7/16/Add.4 (Preliminary Observations).
229 Canadian Mortgage and Housing Corporation, 'National Housing Strategy: What Is the Strategy?' <https://www.cmhc-schl.gc.ca/en/nhs/guidepage-strategy> accessed 27 October 2020.
230 Social Rights Advocacy Centre, 'Historic Recognition of the Right to Housing in the National Housing Strategy Act' Social Rights Advocacy Centre (nd) <http://www.socialrights.ca/NHS.html> accessed 29 October 2020.

Nevertheless, certain guarantees in CEDAW have been reflected in constitutional and statutory protections and policies. The Canadian Charter of Rights and Freedoms includes an explicit prohibition on discrimination based on sex.[253] Moreover, under the Canadian Human Rights Act, the Canadian Human Rights Commission may investigate claims of discrimination in federally regulated spheres and refer cases for adjudication to the Canadian Human Rights Tribunal. Moreover, each province and territory has its own anti-discrimination legislation that applies to non-federal spheres and prohibits discrimination in employment and the government provision of goods and services.

Other relevant legislation and programmes identified by Canada in its combined 8th and 9th periodic reports include the Zero Tolerance for Barbaric Cultural Practices Act (2015), to protect girls and women from forced marriage and bans a foreign national or permanent resident from Canada for practising polygamy;[254] the Protecting Canadians from Online Crime Act (2014);[255] the Family Homes on Reserves and Matrimonial Interests or Rights Act (2013; amended in 2014);[256] the Protection of Communities and Exploited Persons Act (2014) to outlaw profiting from prostitution;[257] the Gender Equity in Indian Registration Act (2011);[258] the Action Plan to Address Family Violence and Violent Crimes against Aboriginal Women and Girls (2014);[259] the National Action Plan to Combat Human Trafficking (2012);[260] and the Federal Framework for Aboriginal Economic Development (2009).[261]

COBs by using CEDAW General Recommendation 35 on gender-based violence against women as a unifying benchmark for harmonisation <https://www.ohchr.org/en/NewsEvents/Pages/DisplayNews.aspx?NewsID=22981&LangID=E> accessed 17 May 2019.
[253] Canadian Charter of Rights and Freedoms, Constitution Act 1982 Part 1, s 15.
[254] Zero Tolerance for Barbaric Cultural Practices Act SC 2015, ch 29.
[255] Protecting Canadians from Online Crime Act SC 2014, ch 31.
[256] Family Homes on Reserves and Matrimonial Interests or Rights Act SC 2013, ch 20.
[257] Protection of Communities and Exploited Persons Act SC 2014, ch 25.
[258] Gender Equity in Indian Registration Act SC 2010, ch 18.
[259] Status of Women Canada, 'Action Plan to Address Family Violence and Violent Crimes against Aboriginal Women and Girls' (2014) <https://cfc-swc.gc.ca/fun-fin/ap-pa/index-en.html> accessed 4 October 2020.
[260] Public Safety Canada, 'National Action Plan to Combat Human Trafficking' (2012) <https://www.publicsafety.gc.ca/cnt/rsrcs/pblctns/ntnl-ctn-pln-cmbt/index-en.aspx> accessed 4 October 2020.
[261] Indigenous and Northern Affairs Canada, 'Federal Framework for Aboriginal Economic Development' (2009) <https://www.aadnc-aandc.gc.ca/eng/1100100033498/1100100033499> accessed 4 October 2020.

5.4.2 Policies

As with legislation, Canada's policies may contemplate core treaties such as CEDAW but it is generally difficult to establish this link in a cause-and-effect way, even based on Canada's written submissions to the CEDAW Cttee. The Canadian Feminist Alliance for International Action Canada (FAFIA/AFAI Canada) has been persistent in pressuring the federal government to implement a national gender equality plan.[262] In June 2017, Canada launched 'It's Time: Canada's Strategy to Prevent and Address Gender-Based Violence', a national plan to tackle gender-based violence.[263]

5.4.3 Resource Allocation

Canada's combined 8th and 9th periodic reports also outline budgetary allocations in light of the treaty's obligations. The 2018 federal budget included $100,9 million over five years, and $20,7 million per year ongoing, to implement the national gender equality plan.[264] This included the establishment of the Gender-Based Violence Knowledge Centre within Status of Women Canada (now Women and Gender Equality Canada), which aims to better distribute resources across different levels of government and promote more coordinated action on gender-based violence.

5.4.4 Reliance by Domestic Courts

There is no significant reliance on CEDAW by the Supreme Court or by lower courts and tribunals. The vast majority of cases mentioning CEDAW have come before the Immigration and Refugee Board of Canada (IRB) and the federal courts and involved women who have been denied asylum in Canada or are seeking a stay of deportation in order to avoid the threat of violence by a partner in their country of origin. In these cases, CEDAW is mentioned merely to establish whether the treaty has been ratified by the country of origin so as to

---

262 FAFIA-AFAI Canada, 'Reply to Issues 3, 4, 7, 8, 11, 12 & 13: Report to the Committee on the Elimination of Discrimination against Women on the Occasion of the Committee's Eighth and Ninth Periodic Review of Canada' (October 2016) <http://fafia-afai.org/wp-content/uploads/2016/10/FAFIA-Coalition-report.pdf> 11 July 2019.

263 Government of Canada, 'Strategy to Prevent and Address Gender-Based Violence' <https://cfc-swc.gc.ca/violence/strategy-strategie/index-en.html> accessed 4 October 2020.

264 Government of Canada, 'Gender Equality: A Foundation for Peace: Canada's National Action Plan 2017–2022 – For the Implementation of the UN Security Council Resolutions on Women, Peace and Security' <https://publications.gc.ca/site/eng/9.846056/publication.html> accessed 22 July 2019.

determine whether the country of origin offers protection to women against domestic violence.

5.4.5   Impact on and through Non-state Actors and Independent State Institutions

NGOs and civil society: NGOs generally cite CEDAW in alternative reports to the CEDAW Cttee for the periodic review of Canada. CEDAW is also consistently cited by Human Rights Watch and Amnesty International in their reports on Canada.[265] In 2011 the Native Women's Association of Canada (NWAC) and FAFIA Canada requested that the CEDAW Cttee conduct an inquiry into the murders and disappearances of indigenous women and girls in Canada, given that the federal government in power at the time did not seem inclined to undertake such an inquiry.[266] NWAC, FAFIA and other public interest groups were instrumental in coordinating with the Committee to successfully pressure Canada to launch the National Inquiry into Missing and Murdered Indigenous Women and Girls (MMIWG) in 2015. In addition, NGOs that work on issues related to women's rights in Canada consistently make submissions to the Committee for the periodic review of Canada.[267]

---

265   As examples, see Human Rights Watch, 'Those Who Take Us Away' (February 2013) <https://www.hrw.org/report/2013/02/13/those-who-take-us-away/abusive-policing-and-failures-protection-indigenous-women> accessed 13 May 2019; Amnesty International 'Violence Against Indigenous Women and Girls in Canada: A Summary of Amnesty International's Concerns and Call to Action' (February 2014) <https://www.hrw.org/report/2013/02/13/those-who-take-us-away/abusive-policing-and-failures-protection-indigenous-women> accessed 2 October 2023.

266   Jennifer Ashawasegai Windspeaker, 'UN to Do the Job that Canada Will Not' (2012) <https://ammsa.com/publications/windspeaker/un-do-job-canada-will-not> accessed 13 May 2019.

267   NGOs and civil society organisations have submitted 43 reports to the Committee. The following are NGOs and civil society groups who have submitted reports: Feminist Alliance for International Action (FAIA); Canadian Voice of Women for Peace; FOR Women's Autonomy, Rights and Dignity (FORWARD); Fédération des femmes du Québec; Justice for Girls International; Amnesty International; Six Nations Traditional Women's Council Fire and Haudenosaunee (The People); Human Rights Watch; Chinese & Southeast Asian Legal Clinic; Native Women's Association of Canada; Voice of Women for Peace; African Canadian Legal Clinic; Canadian Human Rights Commission; Poverty and Human Rights Centre in Action; Global Initiative to End all Corporeal Punishment for Children; Action Canada for Sexual Health and Rights; Canadian HIV/AIDS Legal Network; Egale Canada Guman Rights Trust; Canada Without Poverty; Canadian Alliance for Sex Work Law Reform; Pivot Legal Society; DisAbled Women's Network (DAWN) Canada; EarthRights International; Indigenous Women Against the Sex Industry

National human rights institution: The Canadian Human Rights Commission has submitted one independent report (September 2016) to the Committee with regard to Canada's 8th and 9th periodic reports.[268]

5.4.6 State Reporting and Its Impact

Pertinent issues in COs recommendations: The COs regarding Canada's 8th and 9th periodic reports considered unaddressed issues from previous COs such as the particularly low public awareness of CEDAW in the country and the dearth of government initiatives to improve awareness;[269] insufficient steps to render CEDAW justiciable;[270] and the crisis of access to justice in Canada and its distinct effect on women.[271] It also urged Canada to consider, going forward, a whole-of-government national strategy to address gender-based violence against women;[272] the persisting discrepancy in pay between men and women, in part linked to the lack of accessible child-care and other social supports;[273] the conduct of Canada-based resource extraction companies operating abroad and its particular impact on women and girls;[274] and provisions of the Indian Act which continue to unduly discriminate against indigenous women, as reflected in decisions rendered by the HRCttee.[275]

Implementation of COs: In the COs for Canada's 6th and 7th period report,[276] the CEDAW Cttee urged Canada to examine the reasons for failing to investigate cases of missing and murdered indigenous women and girls (MMIWG)

(IWASI); the Feminist Alliance for International Action (FAFIA/AFAI Canada); and the Ma Mawi Wi Chi Itata Centre.

268   Canadian Human Rights Commission, 'Submission to the Committee on the Elimination of Discrimination Against Women in Advance of its Consideration of Canada's 8th and 9th Periodic Reports' (September 2016) <https://tbinternet.ohchr.org/_layouts/15/treatybodyexternal/Download.aspx?symbolno=INT%2fCEDAW%2fIFN%2fCAN%2f25373&Lang=en>.
269   CEDAW/C/CAN/CO/8-9, paras 7-9.
270   ibid paras 10-11.
271   ibid paras 14-15.
272   ibid paras 24-25.
273   ibid paras 38-39.
274   ibid paras 18-19.
275   ibid paras 12-13; CCPR/C/124/D/2020/2010 (*Sharon McIvor and Jacob Grismer v Canada*); Sandra Lovelace v. Canada, Communication No. R.6/24, U.N. Doc. Supp. No. 40 (A/36/40) at 166 (1981); Jessica Deer, 'Indian Act Still Discriminates Against First Nations Women, Says UN Human Rights Committee' *CBC News* (17 January 2019) <https://www.cbc.ca/news/indigenous/indian-act-sex-discrimination-un-committee-1.4982330> accessed 29 April 2019.
276   CEDAW/C/CAN/CO/6-7.

as part of a formal national inquiry and to determine whether this issue is symptomatic of systemic discrimination based on gender and race.[277] In response in its follow-up to COs, Canada explained it was providing funding to the NWAC Sisters in Spirit initiative ($5 million over five years (2005–10)) to conduct research and education pertaining to the underlying factors contributing to gendered racism and violence against indigenous women and girls.[278] The NWAC and the Royal Canadian Mounted Police have established an information-sharing arrangement regarding MMIWG. The NWAC has also established a collaboration with the Department of Justice to develop a protocol for service providers (e.g., police, social workers) who work with indigenous women and girls affected by crime.[279] Canada's follow-up to the COs regarding the 6th and 7th periodic reports did not provide, as requested by the CEDAW Cttee, a firm commitment toward establishing a national inquiry into the issue of MMIWG. In response, the CEDAW Committee launched its own inquiry into the matter.

5.4.7   Individual Communications and Their Impact

The CEDAW Cttee found Canada in violation in one communication, *Cecilia Kell v Canada*,[280] and declared a further three complaints inadmissible.[281] In *Kell*, the Cttee found a violation of articles 1, 2 and 16 of CEDAW. The matter concerned Kell, an indigenous woman, who had been evicted from her home by her abusive partner.[282] Kell filed an individual complaint, claiming that Canada 'failed to ensure that its agents refrain from engaging in any act or practice of discrimination against women, when they removed [Kell's] name from the lease without her consent', and therefore violated article 16 of CEDAW. The Committee recommended that Canada provide Kell housing and financial compensation and take proactive steps to ensure that indigenous women who face domestic violence have adequate and effective access to justice. There are no follow-up reports to communications for CEDAW found in the UN treaty database.

---

277   ibid para 32.
278   CEDAW/C/CAN/CO/7/Add.1 para 41.
279   ibid para 43.
280   CEDAW/C/51/D/19/2008 (28 February 2012) (Communication No 19/2008).
281   *SO v Canada* (CEDAW/C/59/D/49/2013) *MPM v Canada* (CEDAW/C/51/D/25/2010) and *Rivera v Canada* (CEDAW/C/51/D/25/2010).
282   OHCHR, 'Women's Rights Body Rules on *Kell v Canada* Complaint' (16 July 2012) <https://www.ohchr.org/en/stories/2012/07/womens-rights-body-rules-kell-v-canada-complaint> accessed 14 June 2019.

5.4.8 Impact of Inquiries

Canada allows the CEDAW Cttee to undertake inquiries pursuant to articles 8 and 9(2) of OP-CEDAW. The Committee launched an inquiry into the issue of missing and murdered indigenous women and girls in Canada in 2012 followed by an official state visit in 2013.[283] The CEDAW Cttee's 2015 inquiry report[284] concluded that Canada violated several rights under CEDAW and was required to 'take appropriate measures to modify or abolish not only existing laws and regulations, but also customs, practices and stereotypes that constitute discrimination against women',[285] to exercise due diligence and 'strengthen its institutional response' to prevent, address, and provide reparations for violence against indigenous women (articles 2(c), 2(e) and 15(1));[286] and 'ensure that aboriginal women are protected against discrimination committed by public institutions' (articles 2(c), 2(d), 2(e) and 15).[287]

In response to these findings of grave violations of CEDAW, the Committee issued 38 recommendations to 'be considered and implemented as a whole'.[288] The Trudeau administration (2015-) committed $54 million over more than a three-year period to the National Inquiry on Missing and Murdered Indigenous Women and Girls (MMIWG).[289] The inquiry called on over 2 000 witnesses across the country to give testimony and concluded with a report on the findings. The inquiry and its associated report call on F-P-T and indigenous governments to implement 231 'imperative' changes that need to be undertaken by society as a whole to address violence against indigenous women and girls and 2SLGBTQQIA persons.[290]

While Canada's initiative to establish a national inquiry on this issue was regarded by the CEDAW Cttee as a step forward that satisfied one of the 38

---

283 Yeo (n 133, citing CEDAW/C/OP.8/CAN/1 paras 15–17).
284 CEDAW/C/OP.8/CAN/1.
285 ibid para 205.
286 ibid para 207–209.
287 ibid para 210.
288 ibid para 216.
289 National Inquiry into Missing and Murdered Indigenous Women and Girls (MMIWG Report) <http://www.mmiwg-ffada.ca/>; 'MMIWG Inquiry Asks Federal Government for 2-year Extension' *CBC News* (6 March 2018) <https://www.cbc.ca/news/canada/north/mmiwg-inquiry-extension-1.4564254> accessed 5 February 2019; John Paul Tasker, 'Inquiry Into Missing and Murdered Indigenous Women Issues Final Report With Sweeping Calls for Change' (3 June 2019) <https://www.cbc.ca/news/politics/mmiwg-inquiry-deliver-final-report-justice-reforms-1.5158223> accessed 4 June 2019.
290 CBC News '231 "imperative" Changes: The MMIWG Inquiry's Calls for Justice' (2 June 2019) <https://www.cbc.ca/news/indigenous/mmiwg-inquiry-report-1.5158385> accessed 4 June 2019.

recommendations stemming from the Committee's inquiry, the CEDAW Cttee noted with concern that Canada had not provided a concrete plan to carry out the Cttee's other recommendations.[291] The UN High Commissioner for Human Rights has also put pressure on Canada to develop a national MMIWG action plan to fully implement the recommendations of the National Inquiry.[292]

5.4.9 Brief Conclusion

Canada's follow-up to the COs regarding the 6th and 7th periodic reports did not provide, as requested by the CEDAW Cttee, any firm commitment toward establishing a national inquiry into the issue of MMIWG. After the CEDAW Committee launched its own inquiry into the matter in 2012,[293] the Trudeau administration (2015-) later committed $54 million over more than a three-year period to the National Inquiry on MMIWG.[294] While this was regarded by the CEDAW Cttee as a step forward, the Committee remained concerned that Canada had not provided a concrete plan to action 37 outstanding recommendations stemming from its 2012 inquiry.[295]

5.5 *Convention against Torture and Other Cruel, Inhuman or Degrading Treatment or Punishment*

5.5.1 Incorporation and Reliance by Organs of State

Treaty incorporation into domestic law: Canada relies on an incomplete patchwork of constitutional and statutory protections, policies, and programmes to implement CAT, including the Canadian Charter of Rights and Freedoms, the Criminal Code, the Immigration and Refugee Protection Act, the Extradition Act, and the Corrections and the Conditional Release Act.[296] However, some provisions of CAT have been specifically incorporated in Canadian law. The Convention's definition of torture is directly referenced in the Immigration and Refugee Protection Act's definition of a 'person in need of protection' as it applies to the principle of *non-refoulement*.[297] The criminal offence of

---

291 Yeo (n 133) citing CEDAW/C/CAN/CO/8–9 para 26.
292 Olivia Stefanovich, '"It's Time for Implementation": UN High Commissioner Urges Ottawa to Development National MMIWG Action Plan' (17 June 2019) <https://www.cbc.ca/news/politics/stefanovich-un-high-commissioner-visit-mmiwg-plan-1.5179005> accessed 5 July 2019.
293 CEDAW/C/OP.8/CAN/1 paras 15–17.
294 MMIWG Report (n 289); Tasker (n 289).
295 Yeo (n 133), citing CEDAW/C/CAN/CO/8–9 para 26.
296 CAT/C/CAN/7 para 4.
297 ibid para 14.

torture, established in section 269.1 of the Criminal Code, aims to replicate the definition of torture in article 1 of CAT. Moreover, section 269.1(4) of the Criminal Code excluding evidence obtained by torture except as evidence that it was obtained through torture mirrors the 'exclusionary rule' in article 15 of CAT.[298]

Policies based on/related to CAT: There have also been several policy developments through court rulings and acts of legislature which indirectly rely on the provisions or general principles of CAT. In 2014, the Supreme Court of Canada in *Kazemi Estate v Iran* recognised the prohibition of torture as a peremptory norm of international law.[299] Following a 2015 Federal Court of Canada decision,[300] unsuccessful refugee claimants originating from designated countries now have the right to appeal initial determinations made against them by the Refugee Appeal Division of the Immigration and Refugee Board.[301]

5.5.2 Use of the Treaty by Domestic Courts

In *Kazemi Estate v Iran*, the Supreme Court of Canada held that while any acts of torture committed by Canada 'would breach international laws and principles that are binding on Canada', these acts would ultimately be deemed illegal under the Criminal Code and contrary to the Charter section 12 prohibition of cruel and unusual treatment or punishment.[302] The *Kazemi* decision demonstrates the extent to which provisions of CAT are relied on as a guide for the interpretation of Canadian law rather than as a source of legal remedy *per se*. In *France (Republic) v Diab* the Ontario Court of Appeal interpreted article 15 of CAT in finding that extradition should not be authorised where there is a significant risk that the requesting state will use torture to obtain evidence from the extradited person.[303] The Alberta Court of Appeal's decision in *United States v 'Isa*, also interpreted article 15 of CAT to highlight the inadmissibility of evidence obtained by torture.[304]

---

298   ibid.
299   ibid para 6.
300   YZ v Canada (Citizenship and Immigration) 2015 FC 892.
301   CAT/C/CAN/7 para 6; Immigration and Refugee Board of Canada, 'Federal Court Decision Impacting the Right to Appeal to the Refugee Appeal Division' <https://irb-cisr.gc.ca/en/news/2015/Pages/craupd.aspx> accessed 18 May 2019.
302   CAT/C/CAN/7 para 16; *Kazemi Estate v Islamic Republic of Iran* 2014 SCC 62 para 52.
303   CAT/C/CAN/7 para 17; *France (Republic) v Diab* 2014 ONCA 374.
304   CAT/C/CAN/7 para 16; *United States v 'Isa* 2014 ABCA 256.

5.5.3 Impact on and through Non-state Actors and Independent State Institutions

Legal community: CAT has received treatment in reports or findings by ombudsman and human rights institutions, civil liberties associations, and civil society organizations. The subjects of these reports range from the treatment of inmates in corrections facilities and the failure to conduct legally mandated inspections of these facilities under the norms set out by CAT; to coordinated efforts between civil society and the CAT Cttee to stop the forced sterilisation of (indigenous) women; and Canada's reluctance to adopt OP-CAT, despite stating that it would do so.[305]

NGOs and civil society: The CAT mechanisms and processes have also been appealed to by concerned citizens turned advocates. Nurses Linda MacDonald and Jeanne Sarson appeared before the CAT Cttee in 2012 to seek its assistance in convincing the Canadian government to define non-state torture as a distinct crime.[306] As health practitioners, they had seen first-hand the effects of electric shocking, water torture, confinement in basements, mutilation and maiming, among other inhumane and cruel acts. While these acts are already considered crimes, they argued that protracted abuse linked to torture is not captured by currently labelled crimes such as aggravated assault. Accordingly, the CAT Cttee recommended that Canada amend the Criminal Code to include non-state torture as a distinct crime. The pair returned to the Committee in 2018 to increase pressure following Canada's failure to implement the Committee's recommendation.[307]

---

305 See as examples, The Office of the Ombudsperson of British Columbia, 'Under Inspection: The Hiatus in BC Correctional Centre Inspections' (2016) <https://bcombudsperson.ca/investigative_report/under-inspection-the-hiatus-in-b-c-correctional-centre-inspections/> accessed 10 April 2019; International Justice Resource Center, 'Forced Sterilization of Indigenous Women in Canada' (nd) accessed 10 April 2019; Global Detention Project, 'Canada' (nd) <https://www.globaldetentionproject.org/countries/americas/canada> accessed 10 April 2019; Canadian Civil Liberties Association, 'Canada to Join Critical Anti-Torture Protocol' (3 May 2016) <https://ccla.org/criminal-justice/prisons-jails-community-supervision/canada-to-join-critical-anti-torture-protocol/> accessed 10 April 2019.

306 Janice Dickson, 'Nova Scotia Advocates to Tell UN Committee of Women's "Non-State Torture" in Canada' *The Star* (19 November 2018) <https://www.thestar.com/news/canada/2018/11/19/nova-scotia-advocates-to-tell-un-committee-of-womens-non-state-torture-in-canada.html> accessed 1 April 2019.

307 Persons Against Non-State Torture <https://tbinternet.ohchr.org/Treaties/CAT/Shared%20Documents/CAN/INT_CAT_CSS_CAN_32806_E.pdf>.

Academics: While CAT has been mentioned in several Canadian textbooks and academic journal articles in the field of international human rights, we did not find works by local researchers that are devoted to CAT.

National human rights institutions: The Canadian Human Rights Commission (CHRC) has made two submissions under CAT.[308] This does not represent frequent and consistent use of the treaty, but the CHRC have made submissions for the last two periodic reviews and hopefully this is a continuing trend.

5.5.4 State Reporting and Its Impact

Pertinent issues in COs recommendations: The CAT Cttee begins the 7th and latest COs to Canada's periodic report for review[309] by addressing pending follow-up issues from the previous reporting cycle.[310] These include ensuring that the legal mechanism for detention and deportation under the Immigration and Refugee Protection Act – the security certificate process – is consistent with relevant safeguards in international law.[311] The Committee also found that while section 10 of the Charter provides *de jure* procedural safeguards, such as the right to be promptly informed of the reasons for detention and the right to 'retain and instruct counsel without delay', little information was provided on institutional procedures available to ensure the application of these safeguards.[312] Other issues raised included the misuse of solitary confinement; the lack of statistics regarding complaints of torture received through prison complaint mechanisms; deaths in custody; and the need for adequate redress for torture and other inhumane treatment of Canadians detained abroad.[313]

Implementation of recommendations in COs: In line with the Committee's recommendation, the Canada Border Services Agency introduced alternatives to detention in July 2018, including electronic monitoring and community supervision.[314] However, contrary to the Committee's recommendations, Canada has left open the possibility of indefinite immigration detention.[315] Canada justifies this policy by appealing to the 2007 Supreme Court of Canada

---

308 Submission to CAT on the occasion of its consideration of Canada's 7th period report (October 2018); Submission to CAT (April 2012).
309 CAT/C/CAT/CAN/CO/7.
310 CAT/C/CAT/CAN/CO/7 para 9 ff; CAT/C/CAN/CO/6 para 29.
311 CAT/C/CAN/CO/6 paras 12–13, 17; E/CN.4/2006/7/Add.2 para 92.
312 CAT/C/CAT/CAN/CO/7 paras 10–13.
313 ibid paras 13–25.
314 Canada Border Services Agency (CBSA), 'Alternatives to Detention Programme' <https://www.cbsa-asfc.gc.ca/agency-agence/reports-rapports/pia-efvp/atip-aiprp/atd-srd-eng.html> accessed 8 April 2019.
315 CAT/C/CAN/7 para 38.

decision, *Charkaoui v Canada*, in which the Court implicitly rejected the necessity of imposing strict timelines for immigration detention and instead emphasised the need for a 'meaningful process of ongoing review' to accord the detainee 'meaningful opportunities to challenge their continued detention or the conditions of their release'.[316] Canada's statutory scheme for detention was later re-evaluated by the Supreme Court of Canada in the 2019 *Canada v Chhina* decision, where it was held that Canada's statutory scheme is not necessarily as robust as section 10(c) of the Charter (*habeas corpus*).[317]

Regarding the torture of Canadians detained abroad, and in light of the findings of the Iacobucci Inquiry,[318] the CAT Cttee welcomed government compensation and a formal apology to three Canadians tortured by Canadian officials but regretted 'the absence of prosecutions related to Canadian involvement in these alleged offences'.[319]

5.5.5   Impact of Individual Communications and Their Impact

Around 70 individual communications have been submitted to the CAT Cttee against Canada. The CAT Cttee found violations in nine of these communications, one instance predating the current study period, and eight adopted after 30 June 1999.[320] Most of the communications dealt with the obligation not to return non-nationals to places where they face a serious risk of being tortured or experiencing ill-treatment upon their return. The majority of complaints were found inadmissible or discontinued. In one high-profile case, *Boily v Canada*, the Committee determined that Canada violated CAT when it extradited Boily to Mexico where he faced torture. The Committee ordered Canada to review its system of diplomatic assurances. There is no follow-up to the jurisprudence report on record under CAT, so it is difficult to provide full information on the impact of this communication. According to media

---

316   *Charkaoui v Canada* [2007] 1 SCR 350 at 107.
317   *Canada (Public Safety and Emergency Preparedness) v Chhina* 2019 SCC 29.
318   Also known as the 'Internal Inquiry into the Actions of Canadian Officials in Relation to Abdullah Almalki, Ahmad Abou-Elmaati and Muayyed Nureddin' <http://epe.lac-bac.gc.ca/100/206/301/pco-bcp/commissions/internal_inquiry/2010-03-09/www.iacobucciinquiry.ca/en/documents/final-report.htm> accessed 9 April 2019.
319   CAT/C/CAT/CAN/CO/7 paras 38–39.
320   *Enrique Falcon Ríos v Canada* CAT/C/33/D/133/1999 (17 December 2004); *Mostafa Dadar v Canada* CAT/C/35/D/258/2004 (5 December 2005); *Bachan Singh Sogi v Canada* CAT/C/39/D/1297/2006 (16 November 2007); *Régent Boily v Canada* CAT/C/47/D/327/2007 (14 November 2011); *Singh v Canada* CAT/C/46/D/319/2007 (30 May 2011); *Kalonzo v Canada* CAT/C/48/D/343/2008 (18 May 2012); *PSB & TK v Canada* CAT/C/55/D/505/2012 (13 August 2015); *JK v Canada* CAT/C/56/D/562/2015 (23 November 2015).

reports, Canada has not acted on the Committee's order to provide an effective remedy to Boily.[321]

Domestic issues ripe for submission to treaty body that have not been submitted: One domestic issue that might be ripe for submission is the involuntary sterilisation of indigenous women and women with disabilities. Sterilisation without informed consent has been allegedly performed in Canada as recently as 2018.[322]

A House of Common Committee is currently examining this issue as is a F-P-T task force established by Health Canada.[323] These developments came after the COs to Canada's 7th periodic report, which call on Canada to investigate all allegations of involuntary sterilization.[324] The COs also recommended criminalizing coerced sterilization.

5.5.6 Brief Conclusion

It is difficult to provide a comprehensive analysis on the tangible impact of the treaty body's jurisprudence as Canada did not submit any follow-up reports to the CAT Cttee's views. Moreover, Canada has a mixed record of implementing COs made by the CAT Cttee. While Canada has adopted less severe alternatives to detention where appropriate, it has also decided to leave open the possibility of indefinite immigration detention despite the CAT Cttee's concerns.

5.6 *Convention on the Rights of the Child*

5.6.1 Incorporation and Reliance by Organs of State

The COs of the CRC Cttee for the 3rd and 4th periodic reports of Canada expressed concern 'at the absence of legislation that comprehensively covers the full scope of the Convention in national law'.[325] While this broad issue

---

321 Brigitte Bureau, 'UN Pushing Canada to Compensate Quebec Man Tortured in Mexico' *CBC* (06 September 2018) <https://www.cbc.ca/news/canada/ottawa/un-committee-demands-canada-pay-quebec-man-tortured-mexico-1.4809978> accessed 10 April 2019.

322 Penny Smoke, 'UN Committee Recommends Canada Criminalise Involuntary Sterilisation' *CBC News* (7 December 2018) <https://www.cbc.ca/news/indigenous/un-committee-involuntary-sterilization-1.4936879> accessed 22 April 2019; Avery Zingel, 'Indigenous Women Come Forward With Accounts of Forced Sterilisation, Says Lawyer' *CBC News* (18 April 2019)<https://www.cbc.ca/news/canada/north/forced-sterilization-lawsuit-could-expand-1.5102981> accessed 22 April 2019.

323 Jorge Barrera, 'MP Asks RCMP for Criminal Probe of Coerced Sterilisation of Indigenous Women' (21 February 2019) <https://www.cbc.ca/news/indigenous/ndp-rcmp-indigenous-women-coerced-sterilization-1.5028101> accessed 22 April 2019.

324 CAT/C/CAT/CAN/CO/7 para 50.

325 CRC/C/CAN/CO/3–4 paras 10–11.

persists, Canada's 3rd and 4th reports outline sporadic, piecemeal legislative measures aimed at meeting some of Canada's obligations under CRC.[326] The 2009 amendments to the Citizenship Act allow a child adopted by a Canadian citizen to obtain Canadian citizenship without first becoming a permanent resident to reduce the distinction in eligibility for Canadian citizenship that existed between foreign-born adopted children and children born abroad to Canadian parents'.[327] Moreover, 2015 amendments to the Criminal Code establish offences to specifically address human trafficking – a crime that acutely affects children.[328]

5.6.2 Policies and Programmes

Canada's 3rd and 4th reports for periodic review also outline specific policy initiatives undertaken by Canada in consultation with various stakeholders to promote observance of the treaty requirements. In 2004, Canada launched its National Action Plan for Children, A Canada Fit for Children, as a response to commitments it made at the 2002 UN Special Session on Children.[329] Also in 2004, Canada implemented the National Strategy to Protect Children from Sexual Exploitation on the Internet.[330] In June 2012, Canada launched a four-year National Action Plan to Combat Human Trafficking.[331] In addition to these initiatives, the federal government provides funding support to non-profit organisations to promote the principles of CRC. Canada has funded a child-friendly version of OP-CRC-AC and conferences which provide training for first nation youth facilitators, adults, and community workers on the CRC.[332]

At the provincial level, Ontario enacted the Child, Youth and Family Services Act in April 2018 with the explicit aim 'to be consistent with and build upon the principles expressed in the United Nations Convention on the Rights of the

---

[326] CRC/C/CAN/3-4.
[327] CRC/C/CAN/3-4 paras 45–46.
[328] An Act to Amend the Criminal Code (Exploitation and Trafficking in Persons) (SC 2015, ch 16).
[329] CRC/C/CAN/3-4 para 35; Government of Canada, 'A Canada Fit for Children: Canada's Follow-Up to the United Nations General Assembly Special Session on Children' (April 2004) <https://canadiancrc.com/PDFs/Canadas_Plan_Action_April2004-EN.pdf> accessed 12 April 2019.
[330] Public Safety Canada, '2013–2014 Evaluation of the National Strategy for the Protection of Children from Sexual Exploitation on the Internet' <https://www.publicsafety.gc.ca/cnt/rsrcs/pblctns/vltn-prtctn-chldrn-2013-14/index-en.aspx> accessed 12 April 2019.
[331] Public Safety Canada, 'National Action Plan to Combat Human Trafficking' (2012) <https://www.publicsafety.gc.ca/cnt/rsrcs/pblctns/ntnl-ctn-pln-cmbt/index-en.aspx> accessed 5 June 2022.
[332] CRC/C/CAN/3-4 para 36.

Child'.³³³ In New Brunswick, every policy proposal that goes before Cabinet that impacts or may impact children must be accompanied by a Child Rights Impact Assessment (CRIA), which is based on CRC.³³⁴

It is difficult to assess budgetary commitments in light of the treaty because, as the CRC Cttee notes, Canada does not use a 'child-specific approach for budget planning and allocation' at the F-P-T levels.³³⁵ Moreover, Canada's 3rd and 4th reports fail to provide any specific, concrete details on expenditure in relation to child-or youth-related programmes that different levels of government are undertaking.³³⁶ This makes it a serious challenge to assess the impact of financial or other material investments in CRC and in children.

5.6.3 Use by Domestic Courts

In *Baker v Canada*, the majority of the Supreme Court of Canada held that CRC is not directly implemented in Canadian law and therefore could not form the basis of a legal claim before a Canadian court.³³⁷ The majority of the Supreme Court found that while 'the legislature is presumed to respect the values and principles enshrined in international law, both customary and conventional',³³⁸ the provisions of CRC 'have no direct application within Canadian law', although the provisions could still serve as a source for finding the values and principles behind Canadian law.³³⁹ Accordingly, the majority held that the treaty's guiding principle of the 'best interests of the child' should have been a prime factor informing government decision making concerning children in this case, despite CRC not being incorporated into domestic law.³⁴⁰ Following *Baker*, CRC has received explicit treatment as an interpretative guide on questions pertaining to child pornography,³⁴¹ youth protection services,³⁴² corporal punishment,³⁴³ privacy, and the protection of children from cyberbullying.³⁴⁴

---

333 Preamble, Child, Youth and Family Services Act, 2017, S.O. 2017, c. 14, Sched. 1.
334 New Brunswick Child and Youth Advocate, 'Child Rights Impact Assessment: A Primer for New Brunswick' (nd) <https://cwrp.ca/publications/childrens-rights-impact-assessments-primer-new-brunswick> accessed 25 October 2020.
335 CRC/C/CAN/CO/3-4 paras 16–17.
336 CRC/C/CAN/3-4 paras 25–26.
337 *Baker v Canada (Minister of Citizenship and Immigration)* [1999] 2 SCR 817.
338 ibid para 70, citing Ruth Sullivan, *Driedger on the Construction of Statutes* (3rd edn, LexisNexis 1994) 330.
339 ibid para 69–71.
340 ibid paras 69–75.
341 *R v Sharpe* [2001] 1 SCR 45.
342 *Winnipeg Child and Family Services v KLW* [2000] 2 SCR 519.
343 *Canadian Foundation for Children, Youth and the Law v Canada (Attorney General)* [2004] 1 SCR 76.
344 *AB v Bragg Communications Inc* [2012] 2 SCR 567.

5.6.4 Impact on and through Non-state Actors

CRC is sometimes relied on as part of the toolkit in NGO advocacy to put pressure on Canada when the government acts in a manner inconsistent with the treaty. The most common use of CRC by NGOs in this respect is in alternative reports to the CRC Cttee. UNICEF Canada and the Canadian Coalition on the Rights of the Child (CCRC) in particular have also taken initiatives to translate CRC, Canada's reports and correspondences with the UN, and other supporting documents in child-friendly language.[345]

The input of over 100 NGOs was sought for Canada's 3rd and 4th periodic reports.[346] Throughout these consultations, NGO participants noted the lack of opportunities for meaningful participation in the periodic review process by Canadian youth and children in attendance. They also noted that Canada's 3rd and 4th reports to the Committee lacked a focused and coherent strategy for giving effect to the obligations of the treaty.[347]

5.6.5 State Reporting and Its Impact

Pertinent issues in recommendations in COs: Some of the main concerns expressed in the COs to the 3rd and 4th report were carried over from Canada's initial periodic report under the treaty. They include incomplete domestic implementation of the CRC and its Optional Protocols and Canada's failure to follow the CRC Cttee's recommendation to withdraw its reservation to article 37(c) (deprivation of a child's liberty).[348] Emerging issues raised in the COs to the 3rd and 4th periodic reports include the National Plan of Action for Children's lack of a 'clear division of responsibilities, clear priorities, targets

---

[345] UNICEF Canada, 'The Convention on the Rights of the Child in Child-Friendly Language' (nd) <http://www.unicef.ca/sites/default/files/imce_uploads/UTILITY%20NAV/TEACHERS/DOCS/GC/CRCPosterEN_FA.pdf> accessed 26 April 2019; Canadian Coalition on the Rights of the Child (CCRC), 'Children's Rights Monitoring' (nd) <http://rightsofchildren.ca/resources/childrens-rights-monitoring/> accessed 26 April 2019.

[346] The following organisations responded to the invitation: the Canadian Coalition for the Rights of Children (CCRC); UNICEF Canada; Institute of Marriage and Family Canada; BC Aboriginal Child Care Society; Attawapiskat First Nations Education Authority; First Call: BC Child and Youth Advocacy Coalition; Society for Children and Youth of BC; Canadian Parks and Recreation Association; Adoption Council of Canada; BC Government and Service Employees' Union; Child Care Advocacy Association of Canada; Elizabeth Fry Society of Canada; First Nations Summit; First Nations Education Steering Committee; Pivot Legal Society; National Alliance for Children and Youth; and Health Council of Canadians.

[347] CRC/C/CAN/CO/3-4 paras 7 and 9.

[348] CRC/C/CAN/CO/3-4 paras 7 and 9.

and timetables, resource allocation and systematic monitoring';[349] the need for a national ombudsman for children at the federal level given that the Canadian Human Rights Commission can only address discrimination-based complaints;[350] an overrepresentation of indigenous and black children in the criminal justice system or under the care of the state;[351] the rising level of obesity among youth;[352] and the absence of mediums to facilitate meaningful participation of youth in laws and policies that particularly affect them.[353]

Implementation of recommendations of COs: Canada's level of engagement with COs and its commitment to implementing the recommendations therein are difficult to gauge because there are no official follow-up reports to COs on record in the UN treaty body database. The Committee notes in the COs to the 3rd and 4th periodic reports that a number of recommendations from the initial and 2nd country reports were not fully addressed or sufficiently implemented by the federal government. These include inadequate data collection and a lack of mechanisms for independent monitoring and reporting of the situation of children in Canada; and issues of particular concern to children, including: adoption; corporal punishment; economic exploitation; and juvenile justice.[354]

5.6.6 Brief Conclusion

Canada's lack of engagement in the CRC Cttee's monitoring processes makes it difficult to gauge the impact of the treaty at the domestic level. At the time of writing Canada has not issued a follow-up to the Committee's COs to indicate why many of the recommendations from the initial and 2nd reports still have not been implemented. The Supreme Court of Canada's treatment of CRC in a landmark case, *Baker v Canada*, has helped define the place of human rights treaties in Canadian law. Following *Baker*, CRC has received explicit treatment as an interpretative guide in cases regarding child pornography, youth protection services, corporal punishment and the protection of children from cyberbullying.

---

349 CRC/C/CAN/CO/3-4 paras 12-13.
350 CRC/C/CAN/CO/3-4 paras 22-23.
351 CRC/C/CAN/CO/3-4 paras 32-33.
352 CRC/C/CAN/CO/3-4 paras 63-64.
353 CRC/C/CAN/CO/3-4 paras 36-37.
354 CRC/C/CAN/CO/3-4 paras 7-8.

5.7 Convention on the Rights of Persons with Disabilities

5.7.1 Incorporation and Reliance by Organs of State

CRPD is partially implemented by a patchwork of constitutional, statutory, and administrative protections. These include the explicit guarantee of equal treatment for persons with disabilities (PWDs) under section 15 of the Canadian Charter of Rights and Freedoms, which is similar to article 5 of CRPD;[355] the Canadian Human Rights Act, which protects PWDs from discrimination when they are employed by, or receive services from, the federal government or entities regulated by the federal government;[356] and other F-P-T laws, policies, and programmes covering issues that particularly affect PWDs, such as minimum standards for the accessibility of built environments, disability insurance and other social supports.[357]

The obligations of CRPD may also be implemented through the Accessible Canada Act.[358] The Act explicitly references the treaty and sets the goal of making Canada barrier-free by 2040.[359] Generally, the Act has been welcomed by disability groups and stakeholders, given that only three provinces (Manitoba, Nova Scotia and Ontario) have passed accessibility legislation to set a minimum standards on the accessibility of built environments.[360]

The definitions of 'barrier' and 'disability' and the principles (section 6) of the Accessible Canada Act may have been influenced by the language used in the Preamble and articles 1–4 of CRPD. Moreover, Canada's interpretative declaration regarding article 33(2) of CRPD clarifies that the country will establish monitoring mechanisms at multiple levels of government through (quasi-)judicial and administrative bodies.[361] So far, the Canadian Human Rights Commission is one body made responsible for monitoring the federal government's implementation of CRPD.[362]

---

355 The Canadian Charter of Rights and Freedoms, s 15(1).
356 Canadian Human Rights Act RSC 1985, ch H-6.
357 For examples of provincial accessibility legislation, see Accessibility for Ontarians with Disabilities Act, 2005, S.O. 2005, c. 11; The Accessibility for Manitobans Act, CCSM c A1.7; An Act Respecting Accessibility in Nova Scotia, 2017, c. 2, s. 1.
358 Accessible Canada Act (SC 2019, ch 10).
359 ibid preamble and art 5.
360 Rick Hansen, 'Passing Bill C-81 is Critical to Making Canada Accessible for all Canadians' (22 April 2019) <https://www.theglobeandmail.com/opinion/article-passing-bill-c-81-is-critical-to-making-canada-accessible-for-all/> accessed 25 October 2020.
361 United Nations Treaty Collection, 'Chapter IV Human Rights 15. Convention on the Rights of Persons with Disabilities' (New York, 13 December 2006) <https://treaties.un.org/pages/ViewDetails.aspx?src=TREATY&mtdsg_no=IV-15&chapter=4>.
362 Canadian Human Rights Act R.S.C., 1985, c. H-6, s 28.1.

5.7.2 Institutional Reform

The Accessible Canada Act establishes an accessibility commissioner and chief accessibility officer, both of whom are responsible for monitoring compliance with the Act.[363]

5.7.3 Collaborative Approach to Policy Making

Canada included PWDs as members of the Canadian delegation in the negotiation and ratification of the CRPD.[364] Canada has also welcomed and supported NGOs to participate in all conferences of state parties to CRPD and hosted consultations on issues related to persons with intellectual disabilities; the Registered Disability Savings Plan; and the Canada Pension Plan disability benefit.[365]

5.7.4 Budget Allocations

Employment and Social Development Canada has allocated $11 million in annual funding for initiatives addressed barriers to social inclusion experienced by PWDs.[366] In 2013, up to $9 million was earmarked to support projects promoting the accessibility of physical environments.[367] The Social Sciences and Humanities Research Council of Canada was allocated $7 million per year in the 2013 federal budget to conduct research on the labour market participation of PWDs.[368]

5.7.5 Reliance by Domestic Courts

Canadian courts do not adjudicate CRPD or directly apply its articles in their decisions due to a lack of implementation of the treaty into domestic law.

In *Cole v Cole,* the Ontario Superior Court considered whether an 18-year-old person with a disability was a 'child of the marriage' under the federal Divorce Act,[369] or whether they were an adult who should be provided with the support to exercise their own legal capacity and decision-making powers.[370] Under the Divorce Act, 'a child of the marriage' may be a person who 'is the age of majority or over and under their charge but unable, by reason of illness, disability

---

363 Accessible Canada Act SC 2019, ch 10 s 37ff.
364 CRPD/C/CAN/1 para 19.
365 CRPD/C/CAN/1 para 20.
366 CRPD/C/CAN/1 para 21.
367 ibid.
368 ibid, para 17.
369 Divorce Act RSC 1985, ch 3 (2nd Supp.), s 2(1)(b).
370 *Cole v Cole* 2011 ONSC 4090.

or other cause, to withdraw from their charge'. The litigation guardian of the respondent requested that the Court apply the CRPD which requires Canada to recognise and take appropriate measures to ensure that PWDs can exercise legal and decision-making capacity on an equal basis with others.[371] While the Court found the respondent's argument 'most interesting, and worthy of consideration', the 18-year-old remained subject to the child custody order. This case illustrates one of the ways in which Canada's failure to incorporate CRPD into domestic law can act as a barrier to the legal application of CRPD rights. Similarly, the CESCR Cttee has highlighted in its COs to Canada's 6th periodic report that the fact the treaty 'remain[s] non-justiciable in domestic courts … may disproportionately impact disadvantaged and marginalised groups and individuals, including homeless persons, indigenous peoples and persons with disabilities'.[372]

5.7.6 Impact on and through Non-state Actors and Independent State Institutions

NGOs and civil society organisations: Given that CRPD offers rights to persons with disabilities that are more expansive than Canadian law, public interest litigation, as demonstrated by *Cole v Cole*, is making use of the CRPD provisions in the hope of broadening the scope of domestic laws that touch on disability rights. CRPD may also be used in NGO advocacy strategies to pressure the government to do more for PWDs by enacting legislation to fully implement CRPD. The most common use of the treaty is in the submission of alternative reports by NGOs and civil society organisations. Some NGOs have engaged in knowledge sharing practices and have submitted a joint submission.[373]

---

371 See CRPD art 12 (Equal recognition before the law) in particular.
372 E/C.12/CAN/CO/6 para 5.
373 For example, the submission from the Canadian Civil Society Parallel Report Group includes contributions from the ARCH Disability Law Centre; Alzheimer's Society of Canada; Canada Without Poverty; Canadian Association for Community Living; Canadian Association of the Deaf; Canadian Council on Rehabilitation and Work; Canadian Centre on Disability Studies; Canadian National Institute for the Blind; Canadian Labour Congress; Council of Canadians with Disabilities; Disability Rights Promotion International; York University; DisAbled Women's Network of Canada; Independent Living Canada; MAD Canada; Ontario Network of Injured Workers; Income Security Advocacy Centre; Autistic Minority International-Canada; Participation & Knowledge Translation in Childhood Disability Lab; McGill University; and People First Canada (Canadian Civil Society Parallel Report Group, 'Parallel Report for Canada' (CRPD Committee 16th Session – 20 March-7 April 7 2017) <https://archdisabilitylaw.ca/wp-content/uploads/2017/02/CSPRG_Parallel_Report_for_Canada_Feb-2017-A.pdf> accessed 18 March 2019).

National human rights institutions: The Canadian Human Rights Commission and 700 civil society organisations were consulted in the drafting of the report.[374]

5.7.7 State Reporting and Its Impact

The Committee's COs to the initial report made recommendations on several fronts, including to implement CRPD across all levels of government and withdraw the declaration and reservation to article 12 which purportedly preserves substitute decision making counter to the human rights model of disability.[375] Additionally, the lack of quantitative and qualitative data on these issues make it difficult for the Committee to assess the gaps in exercise and enjoyment of rights of PWDs compared to those who do not live with disabilities.

5.7.8 Individual Communications and Their Impact

Canada ratified OP-CRPD only in 2018, and as yet there are no individual communications or inquiries on record in the UN treaty body database.

5.7.9 Brief Conclusion

There is no official follow-up from Canada to the latest COs. The upcoming report for periodic review will give Canada a chance to explain measures it has taken to improve its efforts to implement CRPD.

6 Conclusion

General trends and lessons learned: In December 2001 the Standing Senate Committee on Human Rights released its first report dealing exclusively with Canada's performance on implementing its international human rights obligations.[376] The report noted that the biggest issue across the previous two decades was 'the gap ... between our willingness to participate in human rights instruments at the international level and our commitment to ensuring that the obligations contained in these instruments are fully effective within

---

374 CRPD/C/CAN/1 para 5.
375 CRPD/C/CAN/CO/1 paras 7–10.
376 Standing Senate Committee on Human Rights (n 16). The Standing Committee continues to monitor implementation of and adherence to human rights treaties in Canada, and occasionally holds hearings regarding the work of the treaty bodies (Report of the Standing Senate Committee on Human Rights, 'Thirteenth Report' (25 June 2013) <https://sencanada.ca/Content/SEN/Committee/411/ridr/rep/rep13jun13-e.htm>).

this country'.³⁷⁷ Nearly two decades after the Standing Senate Committee's report, this gap remains apparent. The human rights treaties that Canada has ratified have not received direct implementation and rely for potential domestic effect on an incomplete patchwork of constitutional and statutory protections. Moreover, there still is no formal, coordinated mechanism across governments to monitor and facilitate their full implementation. This in particular has made it challenging to pinpoint and assess Canada's efforts to implement the treaties, as these efforts have often been carried out in indirect and uncoordinated ways. Despite these issues, the human rights treaty system has had notable and important impacts on Canadian society over the last two decades.

The impact of state reporting, inquiries and other interim measures: Treaty body recommendations stemming from the COs appear to have spurred important nation-wide initiatives to address some of Canada's long standing human rights issues.

The federal government's commitment to national action plan for MMIWG and a national reconciliation framework: Following the CEDAW Committee's inquiry into the issue of MMIWG in 2012,³⁷⁸ the Trudeau administration (2015-) committed $54 million over more than a three-year period to the National Inquiry on MMIWG.³⁷⁹ The National Inquiry report calls on F-P-T and indigenous governments to implement 231 'imperative' changes to address violence against indigenous women and girls and 2SLGBTQQIA persons.³⁸⁰ While Canada's initiative to establish a national inquiry on this issue was regarded by the CEDAW Cttee as a step forward, the CEDAW Cttee noted that Canada had not provided a formal plan to implement 37 outstanding recommendations.³⁸¹ The UN High Commissioner for Human Rights has also put pressure on Canada to develop a national MMIWG action plan to fully implement the recommendations of the National Inquiry.³⁸² In 2018 Canada also committed to adopting a national reconciliation framework informed by the recommendations ('calls to actions') of the Truth and Reconciliation of Canada for addressing the legacy and impact

---

377   ibid.
378   CEDAW/C/OP.8/CAN/1 paras 15–17.
379   MMIWG Report (n 289); Tasker (n 289).
380   Tasker (n 289); CBC News, '231 "imperative" Changes: The MMIWG Inquiry's Calls for Justice' (2 June 2019) <https://www.cbc.ca/news/indigenous/mmiwg-inquiry-report-1.5158385> accessed 4 June 2019.
381   Yeo (n 133), citing CEDAW/C/CAN/CO/8–9 para 26.
382   Stefanovich (n 292).

of Canada's Indian Residential Schools system[383] and Canada's obligations under UNDRIP.[384] Canada has committed to implementing the calls to action following pressure by the CEDAW Cttee and domestic civil society, but national reconciliation framework remains a work in progress.[385]

National housing strategy: The CESCR Cttee and the UN Special Rapporteur on Adequate Housing have labelled the housing situation in Canada a 'national emergency'.[386] Canada has responded with a national housing strategy. The strategy includes an investment of over $72 billion CAD over 10 years with the aim of cutting homelessness in half, in part by renovating and modernising 300 000 homes, and building up to 160 000 new homes.[387] Civil society organisations played a significant role in successfully petitioning the federal government to include the human right to housing – recognised in CESCR – in the National Housing Strategy Act.[388]

Establishing an Ombudsperson for responsible business conduct abroad: In response to Canada's 6th report under CCPR, the HRCttee recommended that Canada establish an independent mechanism with the power to investigate complaints of human rights abuses committed by Canada-based resource companies operating abroad.[389] In January 2018 the Minister of International Trade announced the establishment of a Canadian Ombudsperson for Responsible Enterprise.[390] While this measure follows the HRCttee's recommendation, we

---

383 Truth and Reconciliation Commission of Canada, *Final Report* (2015) <http://www.trc.ca/websites/trcinstitution/index.php?p=890> accessed 5 June 2022.

384 CCPR/C/CAN/FCO/25188/E (16 September 2016) s 4.3. On 10 May 2016, the Minister of Indigenous and Northern Affairs announced at the 15th Meeting of the United Nations Permanent Forum on Indigenous Issues that Canada is now a full supporter of the UNDRIP, without qualifications, and that Canada will adopt and implement the UNDRIP in accordance with the Canadian Constitution.

385 Government of Canada, 'Overview of a Recognition and Implementation of Indigenous Rights Framework' (10 September 2018) <https://www.rcaanc-cirnac.gc.ca/eng/1536350959665/1539959903708> accessed 16 June 2019.

386 Miloon Kothari, United National Special Rapporteur on Adequate Housing, 'Preliminary Observations at the End of his Mission to Canada 9–22 October 2007' A/HRC/7/16/Add.4 (Preliminary Observations).

387 Canadian Mortgage and Housing Corporation, 'National Housing Strategy: What Is the Strategy?' <https://www.cmhc-schl.gc.ca/en/nhs/guidepage-strategy> accessed 27 October 2020.

388 Social Rights Advocacy Centre, 'Historic Recognition of the Right to Housing in the National Housing Strategy Act' Social Rights Advocacy Centre (nd) <http://www.socialrights.ca/NHS.html> accessed 29 October 2020.

389 CCPR/C/CAN/CO/6 (13 August 2015) s C: Business and human rights.

390 Order in Council PC 2019-299 (8 April 2019) <https://orders-in-council.canada.ca/attachment.php?attach=38652&lang=en> accessed 17 June 2019.

lack the evidence to draw a clear connection between these events. Moreover, this measure may not fully address the HRCttee's call for an independent mechanism with investigatory power. Local human rights groups have expressed concern that the Ombudsperson lacks independence and the power to obligate companies to comply with Ombudsperson investigations and recommendations.[391] This case in particular demonstrates the monitoring and evaluation issues that arise due to the absence of a formal, direct mechanism for implementing the obligations of the treaties and the recommendations of the treaty bodies.

Direct impact on domestic law and policy: Despite the lack of direct and full incorporation of the core human rights treaties into Canadian law, parts of some human rights treaties have been given legal effect through acts of the legislature. Ontario's Child, Youth and Family Services Act was enacted with the explicit aim 'to be consistent with and build upon the principles expressed in the UN Convention on the Rights of the Child'.[392] Moreover, there are encouraging signs that a significant part of CRPD will be implemented in law by way of Canada's Accessible Canada Act.[393] The Act explicitly references the treaty and sets the goal of making Canada barrier-free by 2040.[394]

Difficulty monitoring the implementation of treaty body recommendations in cos: Examples detailing the implementation of Concluding Observation recommendations are few and far between. Generally, it is difficult to assess whether Canada has effectively implemented the cos because of serious, cross-cutting issues tied to knowledge management and a lack of self-critical assessment in Canada's reports. Canada's reports tend to identify initiatives that purport to fulfil Canada's treaty obligations, often without indicating how these initiatives will be implemented or whether past initiatives have been implemented and adequately monitored. The result is a series of reports that detail government initiatives without conducting a retrospective analysis of whether the overall situation is ameliorating, has stayed the same, or is becoming worse. There are also great difficulties with monitoring and assessing Canada's progress towards implementation of cos because there are relatively few follow-ups by the state. Given that there is no streamlined and dedicated mechanism for monitoring the implementation of Concluding Observation recommendations, the only way to monitor Canada through cos is to look for recurring issues, which could signal that those have not been fully addressed.

---

391 Business and Human Rights Resource Centre (n 202).
392 Preamble, Child, Youth and Family Services Act, 2017, S.O. 2017, c. 14, Sched. 1.
393 Accessible Canada Act SC 2019, ch 10.
394 ibid preamble and art 5.

While Canada reports on legislation, programmes, policies and other measures that purport to implement the core treaties, it is almost always unclear whether the measure was established with the relevant treaty in mind, or whether the connection to the treaty is an *ex post* rationalisation. One way in which Canada could clarify this is by explaining how measures are meant to promote specific provisions of the treaty.

Difficulty giving legal effect to treaty provisions and individual communications: The promotion of treaty rights by way of judicial action constitutes indirect impact, because the treaties cannot give rise to a legal cause of action or remedy *per se*. This was well demonstrated by an Ontario Superior Court decision, *Cole v Cole*, which considered whether an 18-year-old person with a disability was a 'child of the marriage' under the federal Divorce Act,[395] or whether they were an adult who should be provided with the support to exercise their own legal capacity and decision-making powers.[396] The litigation guardian of the respondent requested that the Court apply the CRPD which requires Canada to recognise and take appropriate measures to ensure that PWDs can exercise legal and decision-making capacity on an equal basis with others.[397] While the Court found the respondent's argument 'most interesting, and worthy of consideration', the 18-year-old remained subject to the child custody order. This case illustrates how the reluctance to incorporate international human rights law into Canadian law can leave gaps in legal protection that disproportionately impact individuals and groups that are underserved by Canada's legal system.

Treaties inform NGOs advocacy: Some treaties feature prominently in the advocacy and outreach efforts of some NGOs. For example, the Council of Canadians with Disabilities produces a range of very thorough and accessible articles, guidebooks, and other materials on the substantive aspects of CRPD. These materials discuss Canada's accession to CRPD[398] and OP-CRPD,[399] provide guidance on how Canada can implement CRPD by involving the disability

---

395 Divorce Act RSC 1985, ch 3 (2nd Supp.), s 2(1)(b).
396 *Cole v Cole* 2011 ONSC 4090.
397 See CRPD art 12 (Equal recognition before the law) in particular.
398 Council of Canadians with Disabilities, 'Open Letter: Recognising Two Important Rights Milestones of 2018' (21 December 2018) <http://www.ccdonline.ca/en/international/un/canada/CRPD-OP-21December2018> accessed 26 May 2019.
399 Council of Canadians with Disabilities, 'Review of Canada's Accession to the UN OP-CRPD' (16 March 2017) <http://www.ccdonline.ca/en/international/un/canada/CRPD-OP-16March2017> accessed 26 May 2019.

community at various steps in the process,[400] and report quick facts on the CRPD for the general public.[401]

Treaties act as a benchmark upon which to evaluate Canada's human rights performance and make demands on the state: Civil society actors have used the CERD Cttee reports as a benchmark to assess Canada's performance under the treaty, make direct demands, and, where appropriate, bring shame on different levels of government for their lack of progress. In 2011 the Native Women's Association of Canada (NWAC) and Feminist Alliance For International Action (FAFIA) Canada requested that CEDAW Cttee conduct an inquiry into the murders and disappearances of indigenous women and girls in Canada, given that the federal government in power at the time were not inclined to undertake such an inquiry.[402] NWAC and FAFIA were instrumental in coordinating with the Committee to successfully pressure Canada to launch a national inquiry into MMIWG in 2015.

NGOs act as additional mechanisms for monitoring Canada's compliance with treaty obligations: The Canadian Coalition for the Rights of Children (CCRC) has established a mechanism to monitor Canada's compliance with CRC and aims to be an active participant in the upcoming 5th and 6th periodic review of Canada.[403]

Treaty body committee sessions as a space for civil society advocacy on legal reform: The CAT mechanisms and processes have also been appealed to by concerned citizens turned advocates. Nurses Linda MacDonald and Jeanne Sarson appeared before the CAT Cttee in 2012 to seek its assistance in convincing the Canadian government to define non-state torture as a distinct crime.[404] As health practitioners, they had seen first-hand the effects of electric shocking, water torture, confinement in basements, mutilation and maiming, among other inhumane and cruel acts. While these acts are already considered crimes,

---

[400] Council of Canadians with Disabilities, 'Canada and the CRPD Archives' <http://www.ccdonline.ca/en/international/un/canada/archives> accessed 26 May 2019.

[401] Council of Canadians with Disabilities, 'CRPD – 10 Facts Canadians Should Know' <http://www.ccdonline.ca/en/international/un/canada/10-facts> accessed 26 May 2019.

[402] Jennifer Ashawasegai Windspeaker, 'UN to Do the Job that Canada Will Not' (2012) <https://ammsa.com/publications/windspeaker/un-do-job-canada-will-not> accessed 5 June 2022.

[403] Link to previous Canadian Coalition for the Rights of Children (CCRC) reports: <http://rightsofchildren.ca/resources/childrens-rights-monitoring/> accessed 5 June 2022.

[404] Janice Dickson, 'Nova Scotia Advocates to Tell UN Committee of Women's "Non-State Torture" in Canada' *The Star* (19 November 2018) <https://www.thestar.com/news/canada/2018/11/19/nova-scotia-advocates-to-tell-un-committee-of-womens-non-state-torture-in-canada.html> accessed 5 June 2022.

they argued that protracted abuse linked to torture is not captured by currently labelled crimes such as aggravated assault. Accordingly, the CAT Cttee recommended that Canada amend the Criminal Code to include non-state torture as a distinct crime. The pair returned to the Committee in 2018 to increase pressure following Canada's failure to implement the recommendation.[405]

---

405 Persons Against Non-State Torture <https://tbinternet.ohchr.org/Treaties/CAT/Shared%20Documents/CAN/INT_CAT_CSS_CAN_32806_E.pdf> accessed 5 June 2022.

CHAPTER 4

The Impact of the United Nations Human Rights Treaties on the Domestic Level in Colombia

Rodrigo Uprimny, Sergio Ruano and Gabriella Michele García

1 Introduction to Human Rights in Colombia[1]

The situation of democracy and human rights in Colombia is complex because it is paradoxical not only from a long-term perspective but also in its evolution in more recent times.[2]

On the one hand, and seen from a long-term perspective, Colombia appears to be a well-established and advanced democracy. In the more than two centuries since its independence from Spain in 1819, the country has experienced almost no *coups d'état* or periods of military rule, contrary to the experience of some other countries in Latin America. In addition, Colombia has had a sophisticated legal system and a long tradition of respect for the independence of the judiciary, and review by the courts of laws and actions of the government.[3] Colombian Constitutions, in general, have since the nineteenth century enshrined most fundamental civil liberties. Colombia is an early ratifier of most core human rights treaties. It also has developed a vibrant civil society committed to human rights, with a high number of well-respected non-governmental oganisations (NGOs), such as the Colombian Commission of Jurists (CCJ), the Colectivo de Abogados José Alvear Restrepo (CAJAR),

---

1   See R Uprimny, *Countries at the Crossroads 2011 – Colombia* (Freedom House 2011) <https://freedomhouse.org/sites/default/files/inline_images/COLOMBIAFINAL.pdf> accessed 30 June 2022. See also R Uprimny 'Por una paz incluyente y fundacional' in M García Villegas (ed), *¿Cómo mejorar a Colombia? 25 ideas para reparar el futuro* (Instituto de Estudios Políticos y Relaciones Internacionales – IEPRI Universidad Nacional de Colombia, Editorial Planeta 2018).
2   These paradoxes of Colombian democracy have been stressed by many other authors. See, eg, F Gutiérrez, *El Orangután con sacoleva Cien años de democracia y represión en Colombia (1910–2010)* (Penguin Random House Group Editorial SAS 2014).
3   For a general overview of judicial review in Colombia in the twentieth century, see MJ Cepeda, 'La Defensa Judicial de la Constitución' in Fernando Cepeda (ed), *Las fortalezas de Colombia* (Ariel, BID 2004) 145–87.

CODHES and SISMA Mujer.[4] Compared to other countries in Latin America, Colombia has had a long history of economic stability, at least since the crisis of 1929.

On the other hand, in other areas this rosy picture of Colombia as a strong and stable democracy has to be put in question, as the country faces severe shortcomings that seriously undermine democratic rule and the enjoyment of human rights by the population. Throughout its history, the Colombian state has lacked complete control over the entire territory, with private armed actors filling the void. Furthermore, for over half a century, there has been a complex armed conflict involving different leftist guerrilla groups (FARC, ELN, EPL and M-19); different right-wing paramilitary groups, which have acted in collusion with the Colombian army; the Colombian state armed forces; and drug gangs and other criminal organisations. All these actors, including the official Colombian armed forces, have over the last decades committed heinous crimes.

This armed conflict has been both a symptom and a cause of Colombia's situation, which includes inequality and poverty, in spite of Colombia being an upper middle-income economy that is part of the Organisation for Economic Cooperation and Development (OECD). According to the DANE (the Colombian official statistics institution) in 2021, 39 per cent of the population lived in poverty and 12 per cent in extreme poverty, with one of the highest Gini coefficients at 0,52.[5]

The combination of the protracted armed conflict, the presence of powerful criminal organisations, the persistent inequality and the atrocities committed by all armed actors has resulted in Colombia living, at least since the 1980s, in a continual and severe humanitarian crisis, which has been documented by several reports of well-respected international and local human rights NGOs and international monitoring bodies.[6]

---

4   NGOs have played a significant role in addressing issues such as human rights, poverty and the environment. Many NGOs in Colombia work to promote social and economic development, protect human rights, and provide assistance to marginalised and vulnerable communities. At least 293 NGOs work in the country in these fields. See <https://ngoexplorer.org/country/col> accessed 30 September 2022. For a general overview on the origins and development of the human rights movement in Colombia, see A Vargas Coronel, *Acción para la conciencia colectiva: La defensa de los derechos humanos y las luchas por la configuración de la justicia en Colombia, 1970–1991* (Ediciones Universidad del Rosario 2021).
5   See DANE Pobreza monetaria y grupos de ingreso en Colombia (2022) <https://www.dane.gov.co/files/investigaciones/condiciones_vida/pobreza/2021/Presentacion-pobreza-monetaria_2021.pdf> accessed 31 August 2022.
6   For a general overview of the human rights situation in Colombia in the past few decades, see the different reports of Human Rights Watch, Amnesty International, the Inter-American

This severe and protracted humanitarian crisis has resulted in millions of internally-displaced persons, hundreds of thousands of persons killed or forcefully disappeared or kidnapped, and widespread torture and sexual violence, just to mention some of the atrocities committed in the country in the last decades in relation to the armed conflict.[7]

These long-term paradoxical features of Colombia have persisted over the last 30 years, in spite of very important efforts made to deepen Colombian democracy and achieve peace and security. Two important democratising processes, in particular, have to be highlighted.

First, in 1991 a new Constitution was promulgated which increased judicial protection, ensured equality and non-discrimination, and enhanced systems for citizen participation. At that time, two of the largest four guerrilla groups (M-19 and EPL) demobilised but the other two (ELN and FARC) remained in war. Besides, this new Constitution created the *Defensoria del Pueblo*, a national human rights institution with important roles in the promotion and protection of human rights, and the Constitutional Court, which has developed one of the most progressive and robust jurisprudences on fundamental rights in the world.[8]

Commission on Human Rights, the UN Office of High Commissioner of Human Rights in Colombia (OHCHR), and the Colombian Commission of Jurists. See, eg, a somewhat old report, Comisión Colombiana de Juristas *Situación de derechos humanos y derecho internacional humanitario* (CCJ 2009) <http://es.calameo.com/read/000360549c74ef241ed4b> accessed 31 January 2022. See also Human Rights Watch, Herederos de los Paramilitares La Nueva Cara de la Violencia en Colombia Washington (HRW 2010) <https://www.hrw.org/es/report/2010/02/03/herederos-de-los-paramilitares/la-nueva-cara-de-la-violencia-en-colombia> accessed 30 September 2022. For recent reports, see any of the last reports of OHCHR, eg OHCHR Situación de los derechos humanos en Colombia – Informe de la Alta Comisionada de las Naciones Unidas para los Derechos Humanos (2022) A/HRC/49/19 <https://www.ohchr.org/es/documents/country-reports/ahrc4919-situation-human-rights-colombia-report-united-nations-high> accessed 30 June 2022.

7 According to a report presented in June 2022 by the truth commission established as a consequence of the peace accord of 2016 between the government of Santos and the FARC, some of the numbers of the victims associated with the armed conflict are as follows: Between 1995 and 2004, 450 000 persons were murdered and approximately 121 000 persons were forcibly disappeared. About 80% of the victims were civilians and not combatants. Between 1990 and 2018, some 50 000 persons were kidnapped, principally by the guerrillas, and about 8 million persons were internally displaced between 1985 and 2019. See Comisión para el Esclarecimiento de la Violencia CEV (2022) Informe Final. Hay futuro si hay verdad Book I: Hallazgos y recomendaciones 122–52 <https://www.comisiondelaverdad.co/hallazgos-y-recomendaciones-1> accessed 1 September 2022.

8 On the work of the Colombian Constitutional Court, see MJ Cepeda and David Landau, *Colombian Constitutional Law: Leading Cases* (Oxford University Press 2017).

Second, in 2016, after lengthy negotiations, a peace settlement was reached between the FARC and the government of Juan Manuel Santos, putting an end to the armed uprising by this guerrilla group for about five decades and which, at points, especially at the end of the 1990s, posed an existential threat to the Colombian state.[9] This peace process with the FARC came after another controversial peace process led by previous president, Alvaro Uribe, with the AUC (Autodefensas Unidas de Colombia), a coalition of the most important right-wing paramilitary groups. Both peace processes have triggered a very difficult human rights discussion relating to how to harmonise the pursuit of a negotiated peace settlement with respect for the rights of victims to justice.

In spite of these important efforts for achieving peace and deepening democracy, which have had significant effects in institutional and cultural terms, as will be seen below, the situation of human rights in Colombia unfortunately has remained critical. As the ELN did not demobilise and new armed actors replaced some of the demobilised paramilitary groups, the armed conflict has persisted, even if less intense, thanks in part to the peace processes. Thus, Colombia continues to combine high levels of violence, a protracted armed conflict and gross human rights violations with a stable civilian rule and an important respect for the separation of powers and the independence of the judiciary. Colombia cannot be said to be a democracy, but neither is it a dictatorship.

This paradox has led some scholars to state that Colombia is not a single country but that in reality it is a territory where several and different Colombias coexist; at least two: a more 'civilised' country, with a very sophisticated legal regime, that operates especially in consolidated urban areas, and a more 'uncivilised' one, in some rural areas, in which the armed actors and the illegal economies tend to dominate.[10] This thesis of the different Colombias captures some of the realities of the country, but we should not assume that these two Colombias are separated. That is not the case. What happens in the 'civilised' Colombia has a deep effect in the 'uncivilised', and the other way around. For instance, when the paramilitary groups were controlling some parts of the land and territory, through massacres and displacements of peasants, they were at

---

9 For a general overview of this peace agreement, see Jorge Lui Fabra-Zamora, Andrés Molina-Ochoa and Nancy C Doubleday, *The Colombian Peace Agreement: A Multidisciplinary Assessment* (Routledge 2021).

10 On these different Colombias and their interactions, see JE Revelo, JR Espinosa and M García-Villegas, Los Estados del país. Instituciones municipales y realidades locales (Dejusticia 2011) <https://www.dejusticia.org/publication/los-estados-del-pais-instituciones-municipales-y-realidades-locales/> accessed 31 January 2020.

the same time supporting some candidates for the Congress in order to have legislation approved in favour of their economic interests.[11]

2 Relationship of Colombia with the International Human Rights System in General

In the 1970s Colombia took pride in being one of the few remaining democracies in Latin America, presenting itself as a country with strong adherence to international law. It was thus natural that Colombia began to ratify all human rights treaties, not only in the universal system but also in the regional system of the Americas. With the exception of the Convention on the Elimination of All Forms of Racial Discrimination (CERD), most of the treaties in the universal system were ratified soon after their adoption, at an average of three years after the treaty was adopted.

At the end of the 1980s Colombia had already ratified most of the existing treaties that protect human dignity – not only the human rights treaties *stricto sensu* (such as the American Convention on Human Rights (ACHR) in the Inter-American system; or CERD; the International Covenant on Civil and Political Rights (CCPR); the International Covenant on Economic, Social and Cultural Rights (CESCR); the Convention on the Elimination of All Forms of Discrimination Against Women (CEDAW); and the Convention against Torture and Other Cruel, Inhuman or Degrading Treatment or Punishment (CAT) in the universal system). Importantly, the International Labour Organisation (ILO) conventions and the main treaties relating to international humanitarian law (such as the four Geneva Conventions of 1949) or to international criminal law (such as the Convention on the Prevention and Punishment of the Crime of Genocide and the Convention on the Suppression and Punishment of the Crime of Apartheid) were also ratified.

This trend continued in the ensuing decades until the present time. Thus, besides the ratification of the nine core United Nations (UN) human rights treaties, Colombia has also ratified the Rome Statute of the International Criminal Court (ICC), the two protocols to the four Geneva Conventions of humanitarian law and the other main treaties within the Inter-American system.[12]

---

[11] On that infiltration of the paramilitary of the political system, which was labelled the 'parapolitica', see Mauricio Romero (ed), *Parapolítica; La ruta de la expansión paramilitar y los acuerdos políticos* (Corporación Nuevo Arco Iris, Asdi 2007).

[12] Eg the Inter-American Convention to prevent and punish torture; the Belem do Para Convention on the Prevention, Punishment, and Eradication of Violence against Women;

These ratifications revealed Colombia as a country that, in principle, upholds and supports international human rights, as it appears to be an enthusiastic participant not only in the universal system but also in the Inter-American system. However, two caveats must be introduced: (i) the international monitoring of the Colombian situation of human rights; and (ii) the domestic legal status of these treaties and their enforceability.

First, Colombian governments, in spite of continuing to ratify human rights treaties, have tended to reject most of the conclusions of international monitoring bodies concerning violations of human rights in the country, either in reports made by international NGOs (such as Human Rights Watch or Amnesty International) or those made by official international bodies (such as the Inter-American Commission on Human Rights (IACHR) and the Office of the High Commissioner for Human Rights (OHCHR)). Various governments of Colombia have, with some notable differences among them, used different arguments to generally reject these reports. However, there has been an overriding starting point that has consistently unified their approach, namely, that all these monitoring bodies were biased and did not properly understand the complexity of Colombia, which was not an authoritarian state that violates human rights, but rather a democracy under siege by criminal organisations and terrorist guerrillas.[13] In a sense, this meant that Colombia ratified almost all human rights treaties but was reluctant to accept stringent international monitoring.

Second, as explained by Carrillo in the previous study,[14] until the 1991 Constitution, Colombia operated in a dualist manner in relation to human rights treaties, in spite of being formally a monist country, as is usual in a civil law system such as that of Colombia. Before the 1991 Constitution, human rights treaties were not considered real and hard law by judges, only as reflecting an ideological discourse. Most judges were not even aware of the existence

---

the Inter-American Convention on Forced Disappearances of Persons; and the San Salvador Protocol in the Area of Economic, Social and Cultural Rights.

13 On these attitudes, see Gustavo Gallón, 'Diplomacia y derechos humanos en Colombia: Más de una década de ambigüedad' in M Ardila and others (eds), *Prioridades y desafíos de la política exterior colombiana* (Fescol, Hanns Seidel Stiftung 2002). See also S Borda, 'La administración de Alvaro Uribe y su política exterior en materia de derechos humanos: de la negación a la contención estratégica' (2012) 25 Análisis Político 111–137 <http://www.scielo.org.co/scielo.php?script=sci_arttext&pid=S0121-47052012000200006&lng=en&tlng=es> accessed 30 September 2020.

14 See A Carrillo, 'Colombia' in Christof Heyns and Frans Viljoen (eds), *The Impact of the United Nations Human Rights Treaties on the Domestic Level* (Kluwer Law International 2002) 166.

of these treaties, in spite of the fact that Colombia had already ratified at least 15 of the treaties at that time – if the ILO Conventions are included.[15] For its part, the Supreme Court refused systematically to apply those treaties, even in those cases in which the litigants had asked the tribunal to take them into account in a specific decision.[16]

This Colombian tendency of ratifying human rights treaties, while at the same time severely criticising their monitoring and abstaining from implementing those treaties in the domestic legal system, has led some critics to conclude that this ratification might be purely a 'strategic' one or one intended only to have a 'symbolic effect'.[17] Those ratifications would be oriented to obtain the political benefits of appearing as a country supposedly in favour of human rights, as opposed to a serious commitment to guarantee those rights. The treaties, in fact, were devoid of any legal effect in the domestic order. A legal technique of normative degradation[18] was developed in those years by the Colombian legal system as the country ratified human rights treaties but those rights were not considered self-executing and usually no law developed them. If any legal regulation was approved, it was a restrictive one. Thus, those rights could be infringed with impunity in administrative or judicial procedures.

However, this situation has changed drastically with the promulgation of the 1991 Constitution, which not only incorporated in its articles a long and robust list of civil, political, economic, social and cultural rights, much in line with international law, but also gave to human rights treaties a 'specific and

---

15   See R Uprimny, 'La fuerza vinculante de las decisiones de los organismos internacionales de derechos humanos en Colombia: un examen de la evolución de la jurisprudencia constitucional' in Viviana Krsticevic and Liliana Tojo (eds), *Implementación de las decisiones del Sistema Interamericano de Derechos Humanos: Jurisprudencia, normativa y experiencias nacionales* (Centre for Justice and International Law – CEJIL 2007) <https://www.corteidh.or.cr/tablas/23679.pdf> accessed 30 June 2022.

16   For a critique of the legal doctrine of the Supreme Court under the previous Constitution, See R Uprimny *'Estado de sitio y tratados internacionales: una crítica a la jurisprudencia constitucional de la Corte'* in G Gallón (ed), *Guerra y Constituyente* (Bogotá Comisión Andina de Juristas Seccional Colombiana 1991).

17   On the distinction between symbolic and instrumental effects of promulgating a law or ratifying a treaty, see M García, *La eficacia simbólica del derecho* (Uniandes 1993). On the notion of a purely 'strategic ratification', see S Borda, 'La administración de Alvaro Uribe y su política exterior en materia de derechos humanos: de la negación a la contención estratégica' (2012) 25 Análisis Político 111-137 <http://www.scielo.org.co/scielo.php?script=sci_arttext&pid=S0121-47052012000200006&lng=en&tlng=es> accessed 30 September 2022.

18   See G Gallón and R Uprimny, 'Derecho internacional de los derechos humanos y derecho interno en Colombia' in G Gallón (ed), *Guerra y Constituyente* (Comisión Andina de Juristas Seccional Colombiana 1991).

privileged status':[19] those treaties did not follow the general regulation of other treaties in the Constitution; they have a 'specific' regulation in particular norms of the Constitution, especially in article 93, that establishes that, in general, those treaties have legal pre-eminence in the domestic order and that also constitutional rights have to be interpreted in conformity with the human right treaties ratified by Colombia. Those treaties thus have a 'privileged' status.

This new constitutional framework facilitated a progressive jurisprudence by the recently-created Constitutional Court, which not only has applied human rights treaties in many of its decisions since its inception, but also has recognised that those treaties, in principle, are self-executing and have a constitutional hierarchy. To arrive at that conclusion, the Court has incorporated the French concept of 'constitutional bloc' (*bloc de constitutionnalité*) but in a somewhat different sense. According to the Court, the constitutional bloc in Colombia makes reference to all those rules, principles and rights that do not appear literally in any of the articles of the Constitution but have to be considered as part of the Constitution as the Constitution itself ordered their incorporation. Such was the case, according to the Court, at least since the ruling C-225/25,[20] for the human rights treaties as article 93 provides them with a constitutional and self-executing status.[21]

---

[19] On that situation and the subsequent evolution of the constitutional status of human rights treaties on Colombia, see R Uprimny, 'La fuerza vinculante de las decisiones de los organismos internacionales de derechos humanos en Colombia: un examen de la evolución de la jurisprudencia constitucional' in Viviana Krsticevic and Liliana Tojo (eds), *Implementación de las decisiones del Sistema Interamericano de Derechos Humanos: Jurisprudencia, normativa y experiencias nacionales* (Centre for Justice and International Law – CEJIL 2007) <https://www.corteidh.or.cr/tablas/23679.pdf> accessed 30 June 2022.

[20] There are three types of decisions of the Constitutional Court: (i) constitutionality decisions that are the abstract revision of the conformity with the Constitution of a law, or of some governmental decrees or of some treaties that are decided by the plenary chamber of all nine members of the Court; (ii) ordinary tutela rulings decided by chambers of three justices; and (iii) some *tutelas* of special relevance that are decided also by the plenary chamber of all nine justices. The first rulings are identified with a letter 'C'; the second rulings by a 'T' and the third rulings by 'SU'. After these letters the number of the ruling and its year of emission follow. So, the sentence C-225/95 is the ruling 225 of 1995 and is a constitutionality ruling. The sentences we cite in this chapter will be so identified.

[21] In fact, the doctrine of the constitutional bloc is more complex and controversial in Colombia because of some ambiguities of the text of the Colombian Constitution and of the jurisprudence of the Constitutional Court, which have triggered some complex legal discussions. However, for the purpose of this chapter, it is not necessary to enter into these nuances. For the notion of constitutional bloc and its evolution in Colombia,

Additionally, the 1991 Constitution also incorporated powerful judicial protection for constitutional rights, especially the 'tutela', which is a legal action that allows individuals to request immediate protection of their constitutional rights before any judge, when those rights have been violated, or are at risk of being violated, by the state or by private actors. Any person can present a *tutela*, without the need of a lawyer. The procedure is very informal, and within days the judge has to render a writ of protection. The *tutela* has thus become a very popular, quick and effective means for judicial protection of constitutional rights, which includes international human rights because of the concept of constitutional bloc.[22] All *tutela* decisions go before the Constitutional Court which selects, via a kind of writ of *certiorari*, those cases that allow the Court to establish precedents on the interpretation of constitutional rights.

Thanks to the new constitutional framework and the progressive interpretation by the Constitutional Court, a type of 'rights revolution' has occurred in Colombia since the 1991 Constitution, at least in the judiciary. Not only has the Constitutional Court begun to apply human rights treaties and other human rights standards, but so have other national tribunals.[23]

This rights revolution has favoured the role of human rights NGOs in Colombia, as they can now invoke international human rights standards as binding law not only in their litigation but also in their discussions with the government concerning specific decisions or policies. However, it is important to emphasise that this rights revolution was also, to a certain degree, a product of the activism of those same NGOs, at least for the following two reasons. First, some of those NGOs, in some cases with the support of progressive judges, presented in 1991 to the constitutional assembly some proposals oriented to establish this 'specific and privileged status' of human rights treaties, in order to overcome the previous situation in which Colombia ratified those treaties

---

see R Uprimny, *Bloque de constitucionalidad, derechos humanos y proceso penal* (Escuela Judicial Rodrigo Lara Bonilla 2008).

[22] Between 1992 and 2022 around 9 million *tutelas* were presented asking for protection of fundamental rights. See the statistics at <https://www.corteconstitucional.gov.co/lacorte/estadisticas.php> accessed 30 June 2020.

[23] On the notion of rights revolution, see Ch Epp, *The Rights Revolution: Lawyers, Activists, and Supreme Courts in Comparative Perspective* (Chicago University Press 1998). On this perspective in Colombia and thanks to the Colombian Constitutional Court, see J Jaramillo, 'La Constitución de 1991 en Colombia: la revolución de los derechos' in *Constitución, democracia y derechos* (Dejusticia 2016) <https://www.dejusticia.org/wp-content/uploads/2017/02/fi_name_recurso_828.pdf> accessed 31 May 2020.

but which had no real legal effect on the domestic order.[24] Second, once the Constitution was promulgated, human rights NGOs and other social actors, such as indigenous peoples and many women and lesbian, gay, bisexual and transgender (LGBT) organisations, began to invoke human rights standards in their litigation to defend their interests, facilitating in that manner the role of judges, and especially that of the Constitutional Court, in enforcing human rights standards with a progressive interpretation. A sort of tactical alliance has grown between the Constitutional Court and certain marginalised actors in the development of this rights revolution.[25]

Finally, this rights revolution has been accompanied by an increased focus on human rights in law programmes at universities, as international human rights law has become hard law within the Colombian legal domestic regime. It has thus become relevant, even for ordinary lawyers. For instance, nowadays there are more than 80 postgraduate programmes related to human rights in Colombia.

3 At a Glance: Formal Engagement of Colombia with the UN Human Rights Treaty System

Refer to the chart on the next page.

4 Role and Overall Impact of the UN Human Rights Treaties in Colombia

4.1 *A General Overview*

As we have already seen, Colombia has ratified all nine UN core human rights treaties, and almost without any reservation. Colombia has also adopted all the protocols that establish substantive norms or new rights, such as the second protocol to CCPR abolishing the death penalty, or the two protocols to

---

24 On these proposals by NGOs and groups of judges, see Grupo de Estudio Carlos Valencia García, 'Propuesta a la Asamblea Constituyente' in *Concordancias y discordancias. Derecho Internacional, Derecho Colombiano y Derechos Humanos* (Comisión Andina de Juristas Seccional Colombiana 1991).

25 See MJ Cepeda, 'Democracy, State and Society in the 1991 Constitution: The Role of the Constitutional Court' in E Posada-Carbó (ed), *Colombia: The Politics of Reforming the State* (Macmillan Press 1998) 76.

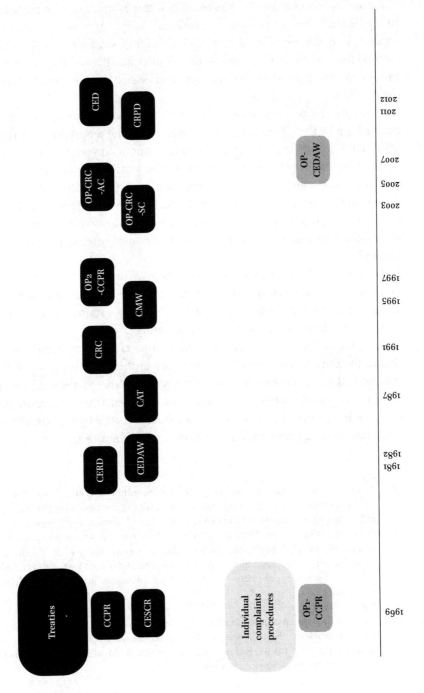

the Convention on the Rights of the Child (CRC) concerning armed conflict or the sale of children, prostitution and pornography.

Colombia has also usually presented in a timely manner all reports to the treaty bodies, with some minor, occasional delays. According to our interviews – and the revision of the minutes of the sessions and Concluding Observations – the reports are usually of good quality and the country has, in general, sent high-level and well-prepared delegations for constructive dialogue with the treaty bodies.[26]

However, the process of reporting still presents two defects, which were pointed out by Carrillo in the previous study:[27] (i) the reports are constructed essentially within the executive branch, without any significant involvement of civil society organisations or even the legislature and the courts; (ii) the conclusions and recommendations made by the treaty bodies are not disseminated by the government to the legislature or to society. This situation has persisted in spite of the creation by the Ministry of Foreign Affairs of a follow-up mechanism for all the recommendations made by treaty bodies.[28]

The process of reporting has in general been assumed by the different governments as a bureaucratic activity to formally comply with an international obligation, but it has not been seen by the Colombian state as an opportunity to improve the policies concerning human rights.

Fortunately, these shortcomings have to a certain extent been overcome thanks to active involvement by some NGOs in the reporting process. Some leading NGOs, on some occasions acting in a coordinated manner, have presented high-quality alternative reports that have enriched the constructive dialogue in Geneva with most UN treaty bodies (UNTBs). Besides, the most important findings and recommendations made by the UNTBs have been

---

26   In addition to interviews referred to specifically, the authors also interviewed the following: In addition to interviews referred to specifically, the authors also interviewed the following persons: Olga Isabel Isaza UNICEF Argentina (February 2021); Paulo Ilich Bacca Dejusticia (March 2021); Monica Cortes-PAIIS (programa de acción por la igualdad y la inclusión social) (March 2021); Roberto Molina. Deputy Justice at the Conseil d'Etat (March 2021); and Lucía Ramírez, expert in migration issues from Dejusticia (May 2020). All notes of interviews are on file with the authors. All notes of interviews are on file with the authors.

27   See Carrillo (n 14) 176, 183.

28   It is the SISREDH (for its initials in Spanish) that is the 'follow-up system for human rights recommendations' <https://www.cancilleria.gov.co/sisredh> accessed 31 October 2022. However, the SISREDH has had no significant impact on the dissemination or the fulfilment of the recommendations by the government.

published by some of these civil society organisations (CSOs), which have also used them as an important tool in their activism.

Colombia has also been one of the first countries to voluntarily access the Universal Periodic Review (UPR) in December 2008. It has undergone three reporting cycles: in 2008, 2013 and 2018. NGOs and other CSOs have also been very active in the UPR, presenting alternative reports. For instance, about 500 organisations presented a detailed report for the third cycle in May 2018. In this cycle, Colombia received 211 recommendations and accepted 183 of these at the adoption of its UPR outcome at the Human Rights Council 39, in September 2018 (an increase of 45 per cent compared to the second cycle). In the last report, there were at least three areas of concern: peace, in which the main recommendation was to implement the final peace agreement with the FARC; discrimination, aimed at primarily eliminating racial discrimination and discrimination against women; and inequality and economic development.

The areas of concern of the states in the UPR are very similar to the recommendations formulated in the Concluding Observations by the different UNTBS with, of course, the thematic specificities of each committee. The Colombian position concerning complaint mechanisms has been markedly different to the ratification of treaties. Initially, Colombia ratified the Optional Protocol to CCPR (OP-CCPR) almost immediately. The Protocol was approved in 1968 by the same law that approved both covenants (CCPR and CESCR) without any special justification to explain the acceptance of this complaint mechanism.[29] Some years later, in 1985, Colombia was also among the first states to accept the competence of the Inter-American Court of Human Rights (IACtHR) to hear individual cases. However, Colombia ratified subsequent human rights treaties without accepting individual complaints.

We did not find a document justifying this reluctance. The most reasonable explanation, according to our interviews, is the one presented by Carrillo in his previous study,[30] namely, the high number of cases already in the Inter-American system. Until 2020, of the 358 cases before the Inter-American Court, 27 cases were against Colombia.[31] Regarding the number of complaints, of the 21 771 submitted to the regional system from 2006 to 2017, 4 073 were filed by Colombians, approximately 20 per cent, and in a single year, such as 2021, the Comisión Interamericana de Derechos Humanos (CIDH) received

---

29   See Law 74/1968 and Carrillo (n 14) 168.
30   See Carrillo (n 14) 169.
31   See CIDH <http://www.oas.org/es/cidh/multimedia/estadisticas/estadisticas.html#por-pais> accessed 30 June 2022.

568 petitions from Colombia.[32] This significant presentation of cases before the Inter-American system since the 1980s might have troubled Colombian authorities in that something similar would happen if they accepted the competence of other treaty bodies. Thus, the different governments decided to move away from the ratification of the competence of the committees to advance individual complaints.

One exception to this reluctance was the ratification of the Optional Protocol to CEDAW (OP-CEDAW) in 2007, which gave competence to the CEDAW Cttee to receive communications. We inquired, through interviews and the revision of the formal procedure of approval of the Protocol by the Law 984/05, whether there was a particular reason for accepting this specific complaint mechanism, especially during the presidency of Alvaro Uribe, perhaps a President who was more reluctant to accept any international monitoring in human rights.[33] We found no convincing explanation for that particular step. There were of course justifications given during the discussion of the approval of that Protocol in Congress, but all the arguments presented, such as the importance to protect women's rights, would apply to the acceptance of other complaint mechanisms.[34] We only found that one internal document of the Ministry of Foreign Affairs recognised that there was high domestic and international pressure on Colombia to accept the competence of the CEDAW Cttee for petitions.[35]

On the contrary, the government of Petro, in office since August 2022, is changing this Colombian attitude. When drafting this chapter, this government had already accepted the competence of the CERD Cttee and intends to accept other complaint mechanisms for other UNTBs.[36] This change of attitude might be partly ascribed to the fact that the current President, Gustavo Petro, received protection of his political rights through a regional complaint mechanism some years ago. In 2020, the IACtHR decided that Petro's political

---

32   See CIDH <http://www.oas.org/es/cidh/multimedia/estadisticas/estadisticas.html#por-pais> accessed 30 June 2022.
33   On several occasions, the government of Uribe criticised statements or reports made by treaty bodies or special procedures or OACNUDH. See S Borda, 'La administración de Alvaro Uribe y su política exterior en materia de derechos humanos: de la negación a la contención estratégica' (2012) 25 111–137 <http://www.scielo.org.co/scielo.php?script=sci_arttext&pid=S0121-47052012000200006&lng=en&tlng=es> accessed 1 September 2022.
34   See the arguments in Gaceta del Congreso No 105, 29 March 2004 and No 226, 27 May 2004.
35   See Memorando 42880/0440/06 of 25 August 2006 from 'Dirección de Derechos Humanos' to Hector Sintura Jefe Oficina Asesora Jurídica 4.
36   According to a personal interview with the Deputy Minister of Foreign Affairs, Laura Gil (November 2022).

rights were violated by Colombia because he was removed from his post as the elected mayor of Bogotá in 2013 by a non-judicial body (the Procuraduría), while the ACHR requires that those decisions have to be taken only by judges.[37]

In any case, the apprehension by previous governments of a possible overflow of petitions before the UNTBs seems to be unjustified, as most NGOs have preferred to use the Inter-American system. Thus, at the time of writing, there were no complaints before the CEDAW Cttee and the petitions before the HRCttee were very few and have even diminished in the last decades, when compared with the increased petitions presented before the IAHRC.

After having conducted interviews with representatives of different organisations,[38] we arrived at the conclusion, similar to that of Carrillo in the previous study,[39] that this preference of the IACHR by Colombian NGOs is due, essentially, to four reasons. First, the possibility exists that, after being examined by the Commission, cases can be reviewed by a court, which ruling is binding on Colombia. This is a substantial difference when compared to the views that UNTBs may deliver. Second, even though this has changed in the last few years due to the significant number of cases being presented to the regional system, reaching a decision before the Inter-American system is considered to be faster than in the UN. Third, the IACHR can pressure the government on cases, by means of on-site visits or the annual report made by the Commission on the situation of all countries in the Americas. Lastly, the Inter-American system appears simpler and more accessible to most Colombians, as it operates in the Americas, is in Spanish and is composed of only two bodies (the Commission and the Court) compared to the UN system, which operates in Geneva with many TBs and special procedures.

As mentioned in the previous study,[40] Colombia adopted Law 288 in 1996 to facilitate the internal implementation of the decisions taken by the treaty bodies through any complaint mechanism, especially in relation to monetary compensations for the violations. A special Committee of four Ministers (Foreign Affairs, Interior, Justice and Defense) studies the international

---

37 See Corte Interamericana de Derechos Humanos. Caso *Gustavo Petro Urrego v Colombia*, Sentencia de 8 de julio de 2020, accessed in January 2023 at <https://www.corteidh.or.cr/docs/casos/articulos/seriec_406_esp.pdf> accessed 31 March 2023.

38 Interviews with Gustavo Gallón from CCJ (June 2022) and Alirio Uribe from CAJAR (June 2022), two of the most important and active NGOs before UNTBs.

39 See Carrillo (n 14) 189, 190.

40 See Carrillo (n 14) 188.

decision and gives an opinion if compensation should be granted. In 2015, in order to strengthen the impact of this mechanism, Resolution 5674/15 of the Ministry of Foreign Affairs created a special group to undertake follow-up for the implementation of all the decisions of treaty bodies. The mechanism established by Law 288 promised to be an interesting option for implementing decisions taken by treaty bodies. Results in relation to the decisions taken by the Inter-American system have been significant, especially because it has allowed the compensation of many cases in which a friendly settlement was reached.[41] However, the mechanism has intrinsic limitations as it is only established for monetary compensations and not for fulfilling other recommendations. Besides, the results in relation to the UN system have been very poor, including with respect to CCPR, which is the only treaty in respect of which a UNTB has adopted views.[42]

Because of the protracted human rights crisis in Colombia and international and national pressure by NGOs and some states, since 1997 Colombia has accepted a large permanent presence of the Office of the United Nations High Commissioner for Human Rights (OHCHR). Its main functions are to observe, systematically and analytically, the situation of human rights and international humanitarian law throughout the country; to advise on and provide technical cooperation; and to inform, disseminate and promote human rights. Furthermore, the OHCHR produces an annual report on the human rights situation in the country. Throughout the prior 24 reports, the main problems on which the Office has focused are violations of the right to life by the state or armed actors in the conflict; attacks on and murders of human right defenders; forced displacement; discrimination against women and ethnic groups; and, since the peace negotiations with the paramilitary groups in 2005, with issues concerning transitional justice. The work of the Office has achieved great relevance and influence in Colombia. On several occasions, some Presidents, especially Uribe and Duque, have tried to limit the role of the OHCHR to merely an advisory body, without the possibility to monitor the situation in the country.

---

41   See below, 5.2. The better impact of the system in the Inter American system vis-a-vis the UN system might be related to the possibility that the case goes before the Inter-American Court if the recommendations of the CIDH are not fulfilled.

42   See 5.2 below; and Alvarez Rosero. LC (2020) Estudio de la aplicación y eficacia de la Ley 288 de 1996 como instrumento de reparaciones en Colombia por recomendaciones de la Comisión Interamericana de Derechos Humanos en vulneración del Derecho a la vida. Dissertação de Mestrado Acadêmico, Universidade Uberlandia <https://repositorio.ufu.br/handle/123456789/29582> accessed 31 March 2023.

However, the persistence of the human rights crisis, and pressure from NGOS, prevented this from happening.

Additionally, in the last two decades, the presence in Colombia of other UN specialised agencies has also increased significantly. As at the time of writing, we have the presence of the following UN agencies: the UN Development Programme (UNDP); the UN Environment Programme (UNEP); the UN Population Fund (UNFPA); UN-Habitat; the UN Children's Fund (UNICEF); the UN Refugee Agency (UNHCR); the UN High Commissioner for Human Rights (UNHCHR); the UN Drug Control Programme (UNDCP); CINU; the UN Department of Safety and Security (UNDSS); the UN Centre for Regional Development (UNCRD); the UN Mine Action Service (UNMAS); UN Women; and, for the Final Peace Agreement, a UN Verification Mission.

Finally, the presence of the ICC in Colombia has become crucial in the last two decades. This is so especially in relation to the issue of justice and impunity in the peace processes with the paramilitary groups and with the FARC, as both negotiations were made after Colombia had ratified the Rome Statute.[43] Thus, in both cases, it was necessary to harmonise the search for a negotiated settlement with the obligations under the ICC Statute to prevent the impunity of international crimes. Under the umbrella of a possible ICC intervention, which took steps to initiate a preliminary investigation into Colombia, an intense discussion on transitional justice blossomed during those years.

4.2 Quantitative Impact of the UN Treaties in the Colombian Constitutional Court

International human rights law has become increasingly important in Colombian law, at least in the judicial decisions. A proxy quantitative indicator of this impact is the mention of UN treaties by courts and judges, especially by the Constitutional Court, which has been the most active tribunal in this respect. To quantify this impact, we consulted the web page of the Court and built a database and counted the decisions in which a UN treaty was cited in relation to the total of decisions that year. Graph 4.1 presents the results: In the upper line we have the total decisions taken by the Court and in the bottom line those which any UN treaty was mentioned.

---

[43] In relation to the ICC in Colombia, see J Easterday, 'Beyond the "shadow" of the ICC: Struggles over control of the conflict narrative in Colombia' in C de Vos, S Kendall and C Stahn (eds), *Contested Justice: The Politics and Practice of International Criminal Court Interventions* (Cambridge University Press 2015).

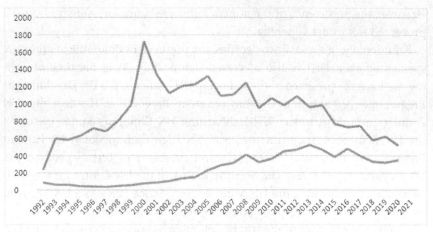

GRAPH 4.1   Total references to decisions of Constitutional Court compared with TBs
SOURCE: DATABASE BUILT BY THE AUTHORS THROUGH CONSULTATION OF THE 'RELATORÍA' IN WEB PAGE OF THE COLOMBIAN CONSTITUTIONAL COURT

As is evident, the tendency of the Court has been to cite UN treaties in more and more decisions, especially since 2002, not only in absolute terms but also as a percentage of the total of decisions taken. In some years, such as the year 2020, the percentage was higher than 65 per cent, as can be seen in Table 4.1, in which we have incorporated only some years and not all, for the sake of clarity.

In total, from 1992 to 2020, the Court adopted 26 640 decisions and in 6 711 of these a UN treaty was mentioned, that is, about 25 per cent, which is a significant percentage of the total number of decisions. Additionally, since 2002, there is a tendency of this percentage to rise.

TABLE 4.1   Decisions of the Constitutional Court in which a UN treaty was mentioned

Years	1993	1995	2000	2005	2010	2015	2020
Decisions mentioning a UN treaty	88	63	78	229	360	383	346
Total decisions	234	598	1725	1322	1065	766	516
Percentage	37.6	10.5	4.5	17.3	33.8	50.0	67.1

SOURCE: DATABASE BUILT BY THE AUTHORS THROUGH CONSULTATION OF THE 'RELATORÍA' IN WEB PAGE OF THE COLOMBIAN CONSTITUTIONAL COURT

TABLE 4.2 Mentions by the Constitutional Court of different UN treaties and committees

Treaty	# Mentions	Committee	# Mentions
CAT	168	CAT	19
CCPR	2282	HRCttee	411
CED	33	CED	0
CEDAW	538	CEDAW	77
CERD	216	CERD	26
CESCR	2137	CESCR	1435
CMW	51		
CRC	1025	CRC	136
CRPD	321	CRPD	26

SOURCE: DATABASE BUILT BY THE AUTHORS THROUGH CONSULTATION OF THE 'RELATORÍA' IN WEB PAGE OF THE COLOMBIAN CONSTITUTIONAL COURT

The Constitutional Court thus is a tribunal that is open to international law and which in a significant number of cases makes reference to UN treaties. However, the use of UN treaties and the reference to UNTBs by this Court has been very different, as seen in Table 4.2.

The two treaties and UNTBs most cited by the Court are CCPR (and HRCttee) and CESCR (and CESCR Cttee), which seems logical as those were the first UN treaties to be ratified by Colombia. Besides, both treaties incorporate all human rights for the entire population. It is natural that these treaties are the most well-known and the most used by the Court. Despite being the oldest UN treaty and the third being ratified by Colombia, CERD has been used infrequently. We offer an explanation for this in the specific analysis of that treaty.[44] By contrast, CRC has been used relatively extensively, compared to other treaties ratified by Colombia before CRC, such as CAT, or almost at the same time, such as CEDAW. A possible explanation is the specificity of CRC, which develops very concrete human rights standards concerning children that were not so clearly established in the Constitution. This specificity has given to CRC and the CRC Cttee a particular interpretative value that could explain its more

---

44   See 5.1. below.

frequent use by the Constitutional Court. Similarly, the high level of reliance on the Convention on the Rights of Persons with Disabilities (CRPD), despite being one of the most recently-ratified treaties, may be ascribed to the standards established by CRPD as being much more concrete and specific than the very general norms in the 1991 Colombian Constitution.[45]

The UNTB most cited is the CESCR Cttee. The question arises as to why, if CCPR and CESCR have a very comparable number of mentions, the mentions of the CESCR Cttee are about 3,5 times higher than those of CCPR, despite the fact that CCPR is an older and, in some academic fields, regarded as a more prestigious treaty body than CESCR, and Colombia has ratified OP-CESCR. A possible answer is that as far as civil and political rights are concerned, the Constitutional Court has also used other international jurisprudence, such as that of the European Court or, especially, that of the IACtHR, which are tribunals that do not deal expressly with economic, social and cultural rights, at least not until quite recently.[46] Thus, the CESCR Cttee has acquired a particular importance in Colombia and has become perhaps the most influential UNTB in the Constitutional Court, as it has been the only international body to produce, especially through its General Comments, a legal doctrine concerning economic, social and cultural rights.

There is increased application by the Constitutional Court of some UN human rights soft law instruments. These soft law documents, in a sense, are an indirect impact of the UN treaties not only because they are adopted in the context of the UN but also because those treaties are an important normative basis for the elaboration of these soft law documents. However, it is difficult to evaluate the impact of all these soft law documents, as they are numerous and diverse. Thus, we decided to evaluate only the use of three of these documents that have been very important in some legal discussions in Colombia, especially concerning internal displacement and transitional justice: the 'Joinet principles' on impunity, the 'Deng principles' on internal displacement,[47] and

---

[45] Eg, in 2019 the Court mentioned CRPD in 33 cases, compared to three references to CAT, one to CED, eight to CERD, three to CMW and 22 to CEDAW. Only CCPR, CECSR and CRC had more mentions that year than CRPD (data taken from the web page of the Constitutional Court and incorporated in our database built for this quantitative analysis).

[46] Some years ago, the IACtHR decided that it could also deal with petitions concerning economic, social and cultural rights. This fact could diminish the importance of CESCR in Colombia and in Latin America, which until recently perhaps was the most influential of the UN treaty bodies in the region.

[47] On the relevance of Joinet principles on discussion on transitional justice in Colombia, see R Uprimny, LM Sánchez and Sánchez Camilo, Justicia para la paz. Crímenes atroces,

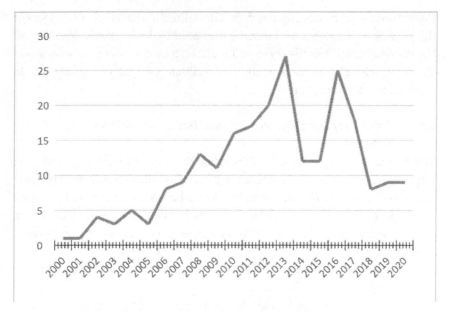

GRAPH 4.2 Mentions of selected soft law by the Constitutional Court
SOURCE: DATABASE BUILT BY THE AUTHORS THROUGH CONSULTATION OF THE 'RELATORÍA' IN WEB PAGE OF THE COLOMBIAN CONSTITUTIONAL COURT

the 'Pinheiro' principles on restitution of property. Thus, we counted the decisions since 2000 in which the Court has cited one of these three documents. The results are summarised in Graph 4.2.

It appears that there is a tendency towards an increased use of these soft law documents, in spite of the complex discussion concerning their legal status in international and constitutional law. Two possible explanations are the following: These documents fill some normative gaps in the UN treaties and the

---

derecho a la justicia y paz negociada. Bogotá. Dejusticia (2014) <https://www.dejusticia.org/wp-content/uploads/2017/04/fi_name_recurso_363.pdf> accessed 1 February 2022. On the relevance of the so-called Deng principles for the discussion on internal displacement in Colombia, see R Goldman, 'Internal Displacement, the Guiding Principles on Internal Displacement, the Principles Normative Status, and the Need for their Effective Domestic Implementation in Colombia' (2009) 2 Anuario Colombiano de Derecho Iinternacional <https://www.corteidh.or.cr/tablas/r25153.pdf> accessed 30 June 2022. On the relevance of the Pinherio Principles, see DL Attanasio and NC Sánchez, 'Return Within the Bounds of the Pinheiro Principles: The Colombian Land Restitution Experience' (2012) 11 Wash U Global Stud L Rev 1 <https://openscholarship.wustl.edu/law_globalstudies/vol11/iss1/2> accessed 30 June 2022.

Constitution which, for instance, do not deal directly and clearly with rights of the victims or the rights of internally displaced persons (IDPs). Because soft law documents such as the three under consideration are written in language akin to articles of a law or a treaty, they facilitate easy judicial application in the form in which they are.

4.3   *Final Considerations on the Global Impact of UN Treaties in Colombia*

The previous paragraphs have illustrated the very important quantitative impact of UN treaties in the decisions of the Constitutional Court. However, two questions need to be answered in order to have a general view of the effective impact of UN treaties in Colombia. First, besides being cited by the Court, do the treaties have had a concrete impact on the decisions or not? Second, what about the impact of the UN treaties on other institutions, such as the executive or the legislature, or on society in general? We proceed to answer these two questions.

The impact of UN treaties and the legal doctrine of the UNTBs in the decisions and jurisprudence of the Constitutional Court have not only been formal but, in fact, very substantive. The Court has not used the treaties only as a formal reference to embellish a decision that would have been taken in any case; in several cases, these standards have deeply modified the orientation of the decisions and even the interpretation of the Constitution.[48] We have attempted to make a similar quantitative analysis in respect of other courts, such as the Supreme Court or the Conseil d'État, or with judges deciding ordinary cases, but it was impossible due to limited time and resources. For similar reasons, we also were not able to develop a quantitative analysis of the use of UN treaties in the discussions in the Congress or in the media or on social networks. Instead, we have undertaken a qualitative study in these areas.

The analysis of some judicial decisions and the interviews of former justices of these courts allow us to conclude that the other courts and judges did not cite UN treaties or UNTBs jurisprudence as frequently as the Constitutional Court. Nevertheless, these other courts or even individual judges have also quite often used these UN standards in very important decisions, with an increase in the last years.[49]

In spite of the fact that the subject of human rights has been present in public debates in the last decades, due to the protracted humanitarian crisis in

---

48   See part 5 below.
49   Interview with Danilo Rojas, former chief justice of the Conseil d'état (September 2022).

Colombia, the references to the UN treaty system in Congress, in the press or on social networks, have been much less frequent than within the judiciary,[50] and have been dependent on the activity of other actors, especially NGOs and the courts, in particular the Constitutional Court. This means that, when a particular UN treaty or a legal doctrine is mentioned in the debates in the Congress, or in the press, it is usually as a consequence of a specific judicial decision that has stated that this treaty is crucial in relation to a particular subject, or because some influential NGOs have stressed the relevance of that treaty in that particular matter.[51] For instance, the Constitutional Court has incorporated a frequent reference to General Comment 14 on health of CESCR in order to analyse the content of or right to health, almost as soon as it was adopted by CESCR.[52] As a result, this General Comment has been very influential in legislative and public discussions on Colombia on health.

5 The Impact of the Different UN Human Rights Treaties on the Domestic Level

5.1 *International Convention of the Elimination of All Forms of Racial Discrimination*

5.1.1 Incorporation and Reliance by Organs of State

Colombia ratified CERD in 1981, some 16 years subsequent to its adoption, representing the longest delay for a ratification of a UN treaty by the state. This delay may be explained because of the myth, at that time, that there was not widespread racism in the country because Colombia was supposed to be essentially a country of *mestizos*, in which the majority of the population was from a mixed racial or ethnic origin. However, racial discrimination has been a significant and persistent problem in Colombia.[53] Thus, the identity of

---

50　Eg, if one uses the search engine of any important media in Colombia and one enters a concrete human rights violation, such as torture, one would obtain thousands of references in one year. However, if one enters a reference to CAT, the references would be very few or none. Eg, we conducted that exercise in *El Tiempo*, the newspaper with the largest audience in Colombia. For 2021, the search engine gave us 3 300 articles in which the word 'torture' appeared in that year, whereas CAT Cttee appeared only in 259 articles and CAT treaty in 211, less than 1% of the cases.

51　This is elaborated upon in part 5 below.

52　This GC was adopted by CESCR in August 2000. Three years later, many rulings of the Constitutional Court made reference to this GC. See, eg, decision T-844/03.

53　C Mosquera and R León, *Acciones afirmativas y ciudadanía diferenciada étnico-racial negra, Afro-Colombiana, palenquera y raizal: entre Bicentenarios de las Independencias y Constitución de 1991* (Universidad Nacional 2009).

Colombia as a *mestizo* country, which has been used to build some national identity, has had some positive aspects, as racial equality was established in law since the early twentieth century and since that time, the Colombian legal system has not contained any open racially discriminatory norms. However, this same idea has also had a negative impact: It made invisible the persistence of a pervasive de facto racial discrimination in the country and thus made it more difficult to eradicate.

This changed with the promulgation of the Colombian Constitution which, in line with CERD, recognises and protects ethnic diversity (article 7) and incorporates most of the rights established in the treaty, especially in article 13, which not only forbids racial discrimination but also envisages affirmative action in favour of groups marginalised or discriminated against, such as ethnic and racial groups. Additionally, other articles of the Constitution establish robust protection for Afro-Colombians or indigenous peoples, such as special forms of representation in Congress, the right to have education according to their language and culture, and recognition of their ancestral lands.[54]

In several decisions, the Constitutional Court has mentioned CERD.[55] However, perhaps due to this strong protection against racial discrimination enshrined in the Constitution, these have in general been supplementary arguments to reinforce the duty of the state to combat discrimination, but they usually have not had a determinant impact on the decision. This robust constitutional protection against discrimination might also explain that, in spite of the persistence of racial discrimination in the country, the use by the Court of this treaty has not been as frequent as its use of other UN treaties. Additionally, Colombia in 1991 ratified ILO Convention 169, which provides strong protection for indigenous peoples in aspects that were not clearly established in the Constitution and are not part of CERD, especially in recognising the right to be informed and previous consultation with indigenous peoples in relation to legislative or administrative measures that may affect them directly. The Court, in a progressive interpretation, gave constitutional status to this ILO Convention and understood that it also protected Afro-Colombian communities.[56] Thus, in relation to previous consultations, which has perhaps been the most controversial discussion in relation to the rights of ethnic groups in Colombia in

---

54 See arts 68, 171, 176, 330 and 55T.
55 See, eg, rulings T-586/07, C-671/14 and T-572/17.
56 For a summary of the abundant jurisprudence of the Constitutional Court on this issue, see Ruling SU-111/20.

the last decades,[57] the constant reference made to international human rights law has been to ILO 169.

However, in some cases, CERD has had an important and direct impact. In particular, the ruling T-1090/05 of the Constitutional Court analysed the case of two Afro-Colombian young women who were not allowed to enter a bar in Cartagena, the most touristic city of the country, while their white and *mestizo* friends were able to enter the location. In spite of the fact that it was a relationship between private actors and that in principle bars and restaurants have the prerogative of denying entrance to a particular customer, the Court found that this bar had discriminated against these two Afro-women. To arrive at this conclusion the Court relied directly on article 5(f) of CERD, which obliges states to eliminate any restriction based on race on the right of persons 'of access to any place or service intended for use by the general public, such as transport hotels, restaurants, cafes, theatres and parks'. Besides, the Court in this decision noted that this was not an isolated case because racial discrimination was pervasive in the country. The Court also noted that the law had no criminal sanction against acts of racial discrimination, which was contrary to article 4 of CERD. Consequently, the Court urged Congress to adopt a law to impose sanctions for racial discrimination in accordance with CERD and recommendations made previously by the CERD Committee.[58]

Some years later Congress, invoking this decision of the Court and the provisions of CERD, adopted Law 1482 of 2011, which criminalises acts of racism and other forms of discrimination based on race, nationality, sex and sexual orientation. In spite of the fact that the CERD Cttee, in 2016, in its Concluding Observations to Colombia, considered that the offence of racism or discrimination established in this law 1482 was 'not in line with the parameters defined in article 1 of the Convention',[59] it was nevertheless a positive development to combat discrimination directly linked to CERD.

During the last 20 years, the distribution of the budget for discrimination policy has changed multiple times. At the central level, there are two departments in charge of racial discrimination issues, namely, the Directorate for Black Community Affairs and the Directorate for Indigenous, Roma persons and Minorities, both in the Ministry of the Interior. In 2009 there was

---

57   Mosquera and León (n 48).
58   See the justification for this Bill, in 'Exposición de motivos del Proyecto de Ley 08 de 2010 Senado' in Gaceta del Congreso No 459 de 2010.
59   See CERD/C/COL/CO/15-16 paras 9 and 10.

a legislative proposal to develop an anti-discrimination statute, which would allow the budget to be centralised and autonomous and to contribute to fighting against discrimination beyond criminal punishment. However, this initiative failed to progress.[60]

5.1.2 Level of Awareness

CERD is not a treaty widely known by the general population or even by its potential beneficiaries. Until now, CERD has not been translated into indigenous languages, which might result in discrimination and contribute to the lack of awareness of this treaty. CERD has hardly been covered by the media, even though many cases of discrimination persist and appear quite frequently in the news. Platforms such as 'El Tiempo', 'Semana' or 'El Espectador' have hundreds of entries for discrimination news each year; however, they cite CERD or the CERD Cttee only in very few cases. Since 2014, the Ministry of Culture has offered a virtual course titled 'Learning about the diversity of Colombia', which promotes knowledge of Colombian languages and recognises the linguistic diversity of Colombia. In terms of public policy, this initiative is very appropriate for promoting cultural diversity. This type of assistance is imperative in light of the fact that discrimination is a form of non-recognition of diversity. These issues, including native tongues and recognition of the cultural diversity of indigenous and Afro-Colombian audiences, are addressed by this initiative.

5.1.3 Use by Non-Governmental Actors

The use of CERD by civil society organisations has increased significantly. For instance, NGOs and grassroots organisations[61] have been actively involved in the latest reporting process.[62] Some of these organisations have also invoked

---

60 Proyecto de Ley número 150 de 2009. Gaceta del congreso: 847. 03/09/2009.
61 For example, such as ONIC; el Proceso de Comunidades Negras; Afrodes; the Program of Global Justice and Human Rights from University of Los Andes Law School; the Comisión Colombiana de Juristas; Dejusticia; the Centro Internacional para el Monitoreo del Desplazamiento; and Global Rights; most of these organisations have participated, at the invitation of the committee, in the follow-up and monitoring mechanism for the periodic reports. Eg, in 2019, the last report was the Parallel report on Colombia for the Committee on the Elimination of Racial Discrimination CERD <https://tbinter net.ohchr.org/_layouts/15/treatybodyexternal/Download.aspx?symbolno=INT%2FC ERD%2FNGO%2FCOL%2F39714&Lang=es>.
62 Some of these organisations have worked with the committee in the presentation of alternative reports and comments to the state's reports; see <https://tbinternet.ohchr.org /_layouts/15/TreatyBodyExternal/Treaty.aspx?CountryID=37&Lang=EN> accessed 30 June 2022.

CERD in their litigation and advocacy strategies. However, most of these organisations prefer to prioritise the Inter-American system for their advocacy, not only because of the general considerations we presented earlier, but also because Colombia has not yet accepted the competence of the CERD Cttee to examine petitions. Besides, on the more controversial issue of the right to previous consultation, these organisations have made more use of ILO Convention 169 and the UN Declaration of the Rights of Indigenous Peoples than the CERD.

5.1.4 State Reporting and Its Impact

Colombia has in general a low average reporting delay. However, it took more than eight years[63] (from 1996 to 2008) for the 10th to 14th periodic reports to be submitted. The Colombian state argued that this delay was because the due date for sending the report had been modified. Several factors contributed to the quality of the reports presented. First, the reporting process led to a dialogue between the government and some NGOs. However, the report has a narrow scope because it is limited to the impact of public policy during the period. The most common objections that NGOs have made when evaluating state reports before the Committee are that the national government does not recognise the problems of registration and identification of Afro-Colombian and indigenous communities; structural discrimination resulting in high poverty levels; and the lack of commitment of the Colombian state to ensure recognition of these historically excluded populations. The reports have been criticised for the lack of frankness of the Colombian government; most of the reports highlight the importance of the normative advance in anti-discrimination matters and the public policies implemented. Nevertheless, the reports omit pointing out the lack of effectiveness in their implementation.[64]

5.1.5 Brief Conclusion

In general, CERD has played a role in addressing issues of racial discrimination and promoting racial equality in Colombia. The Colombian government has taken steps to implement the provisions of the treaty, including the adoption of laws and policies to combat racial discrimination and to promote equality.[65]

---

63 CERD/C/COL/14.
64 Global Justice and Human Rights programme. Alternate Report to the Fourteenth Report presented by the Colombian State to CERD, 2009.
65 UN Committee on the Elimination of Racial Discrimination (CERD Cttee), Concluding Observations on the combined 17th to 19th periodic reports of Colombia, 20 January 2020, CERD/C/COL/CO/17–19.

However, racial discrimination persists and the armed conflict has had a disproportionate impact on ethnic groups.[66] In that context, the use and impact of the treaty has not been as important as might be expected in a country with pervasive racial discrimination and many active civil society organisations combating discrimination. This situation might be explained by the robust direct protection against racial discrimination provided by the Constitution and by the role of ILO 169 in relation to those rights not so clearly stipulated in the Constitution, especially the right to previous and informed consultation for ethnic groups.

5.2 International Covenant on Civil and Political Rights

5.2.1 Incorporation and Reliance by Organs of State

Colombia ratified CCPR approximately two years after its adoption. Colombia simultaneously ratified OP1-CCPR and in 1997 the Second Protocol on the abolition of the death penalty (OP2-CCPR).

Most of the rights and principles of CCPR are incorporated into the Colombian legal system, especially the Constitution.[67] In fact, during the 1991 constitutional drafting process in Colombia, CCPR, along with CESCR, the American Convention on Human Rights and the Universal Declaration of Human Rights, were taken into account when drafting Chapter 2 of the Constitution on fundamental rights.[68]

After ratification, several legislative and administrative mechanisms have emerged to develop and implement some of the rights enshrined in CCPR. For instance, the principles of the Code of Criminal Procedure (Law 906 of 2004) are directly inspired by the content of the right to a fair trial of CCPR and of the American Convention on Human Rights;[69] also the adoption of Law 1448, known as the 'Victims and Land Restitution Act', which establishes mechanisms for providing reparation to victims of the armed conflict and for restoring land and property, was justified invoking UN documents based on CCPR, such as the so-called Joinet UN principles against impunity. However,

---

66   See Special Rapporteur on the situation of human rights and fundamental freedoms of indigenous people para 8.
67   Eg the right to life, liberty, and security of the person; the right to a fair trial; the freedom of thought, conscience, and religion; and the freedom of expression.
68   See eg the report on that chapter in Gaceta Constitucional, No 82 13. On the influence of those documents, especially the Universal Declaration of Human Rights in the constituent process, see JC Upegui, 'Cuatro indicios de la influencia de la Declaración Universal de los Derechos Humanos de 1948 en el constitucionalismo colombiano' (2009) 23 Revista Derecho del Estado.
69   See arts 1–9 of Law 906 and especially art 3.

as with most UN human rights treaties, it is by the judiciary, and especially by the Constitutional Court, that CCPR and the HRCttee have been more clearly invoked and used. In fact, as we have already shown, CCPR is the UN treaty most frequently mentioned by the Court, and the HRCttee is the second most frequently-cited treaty body by this tribunal.

The references to CCPR began around the beginning of the work of the Constitutional Court in 1992,[70] and have continued until today. However, as the protection of civil and political rights is very strong in the Constitution itself, in general they have been supportive and reinforcing certain duties of the state or rights of the individuals, but that usually have not had a determinant impact on the decision. Besides, as Colombia is part of the Inter-American system, the Constitutional Court and the claimants have preferred to invoke the jurisprudence on civil and political rights of the IACtHR rather than the case-law of the HRCttee, when the Court had already developed a particular point.

In spite of this, CCPR and the HRCttee have had a direct and very important influence on the Court and the Colombian legal system in those issues in which the Constitution was ambiguous and the Inter-American system did not provide a clear answer. In those cases, provisions of the CCPR and findings to the HRCttee were not only used to support an argument, but to decide cases. The direct impact of CCPR and the HRCttee case law on the decisions and the jurisprudence of the Constitutional Court is illustrated by the following four examples.

First, in some cases the Court has used legal developments made by the HRCttee to clarify and strengthen a jurisprudence that the Court has already developed on an important matter. That was the case in relation to the duty of the state to protect persons who were at high risk because of threats against their lives. In Ruling T-694/12 the Court invoked the decision of the HRCttee in the case *Jayawardena v Sri Lanka*[71] to reinforce its jurisprudence that in those situations the state has a duty to offer effective protection to those persons.

Second, CCPR has been invoked to fill normative gaps. In particular, the Colombian Constitution is silent on the role of custodial sentences. Thus, article 10 of CCPR, which states that the essential aim of treatment of prisoners 'shall be their reformation and social rehabilitation', has been invoked in many decisions by the Constitutional Court to order measures to ameliorate the penitentiary system, not only to protect the human dignity of prisoners, but also because of the social rehabilitation role that a custodial sentence must have.[72]

---

70 See, eg, Ruling T-011/92.
71 See *Jayalath Jayawardena v Sri Lanka* CCPR/C/75/D/916/2000.
72 See, eg, ruling T.1096/04.

Third, in some cases the impact of those references has been more intense as it has a significant role in the change of the constitutional jurisprudence in a specific matter. That was the case in relation to conscientious objection to military service. The Constitution recognises freedom of conscience but does not specify a right to conscientious objection to military service. In 1994, in a controversial and divided decision,[73] the Court rejected the existence of this right. Citizens could not invoke conscientious objection to avoid military service. However, in 2009[74] the Court changed its criteria and concluded that freedom of conscience included the right to object to military service. One of the main arguments used by the Court for this change was the reference to the doctrine of the HRCttee. In particular, the Court mentioned General Comment 22 on Freedom of Thought, Conscience and Religion,[75] which states that even if '[t]he Covenant does not explicitly refer to a right of conscientious objection', the Committee 'believes that such a right can be derived from article 18, inasmuch as the obligation to use lethal force may seriously conflict with the freedom of conscience and the right to manifest one's religion or belief'. The Court also mentioned the HRCttee decision in the case of *Yeo-Bum Yoon and Myung-Jin Choi v Korea* as relevant.[76] Besides, the Court also took into account the last Concluding Observations to Colombia at that time,[77] in which the HRCttee had recommended that the country recognise conscientious objection to military service. Thus, the Court decided to protect this right and asked the legislature to regulate it, which occurred some years later, with the adoption of Law 1861/07.

Fourth, and perhaps the most intense impact, have been instances when references to CCPR and the HRCttee have led to a reform of the Constitution. This concerned the right of a person to appeal a conviction, established in article 14(5) of CCPR. Even if that right is recognised in article 29 of the Constitution, this guarantee did not apply to high public servants, such as members of Congress who, according to the Constitution, were judged directly by the Supreme Court. These persons could not appeal their conviction, as there was no higher criminal court than the Supreme Court. However, the Constitutional Court, over many years, considered that this fact was not a violation of the right to appeal as those persons have the special guarantee of being judged by the highest criminal court in the country.[78] In recent times, the Constitutional

---

73   See Ruling C-511/94.
74   See Ruling C-728/09.
75   See CCPR/C/21/Rev.1/Add.4 27 September 1993; particularly para 11.
76   CCPR/C/88/D/1321-1322/2004.
77   26/05/2004; CCPR/CO/80/COL.
78   See Rulings C-142/93 and C-411/97.

Court took into account some decisions of the IACtHR and also General Comment 32 of the HRCttee on article 14 of CCPR,[79] especially paragraph 47 which states that even a person tried by the supreme tribunal of the state must have the possibility of having his or her conviction reviewed. With those international standards, the Constitutional Court changed its jurisprudence and in Ruling C-792/14 established that those public servants who were convicted in a single instance by the Supreme Court must have the possibility to appeal their conviction. Thus, some years later, a constitutional reform was approved to provide those public servants with a right to appeal their convictions.[80]

5.2.2 Level of Awareness

CCPR is one of the UN treaties most well-known by legal scholars, lawyers and judges and it is used relatively often in litigation and judicial decisions. However, as explained earlier, in matters of civil and political rights, the impact of the Inter-American system is clearly dominant, which explains that mentions in the media specifically to CCPR or to the HRCttee are not a common occurrence.

5.2.3 Use by Non-Governmental Actors

The most active NGOs frequently use CCPR and the legal doctrine of the HRCttee. Some of these NGOs intervene in the dialogues in Geneva and use and disseminate Concluding Observations. Some of these NGOs have litigated individual cases before the HRCttee.[81] However, as explained before, most of these NGOs prefer to prioritise the Inter-American system for their advocacy and litigation.

5.2.4 State Reporting and Its Impact

Colombia has a low average delay (13 months) concerning its obligation to report. There are at least three main concerns in these reports: the prevention of massive violations relative to armed conflict; reparation of victims; and protection and care for the most vulnerable persons and communities.

Some common issues that the HRCttee highlighted were arbitrary deprivation of life; enforced disappearances; the use and recruitment of children by illegal armed groups; reparation of victims; restitution of land for

---

79 See CCPR/C/GC/32 (2007).
80 See Acto Legislativo 01 of 2018.
81 NGOs such as CAJAR and COLJURISTAS have represented some cases before the HRCttee.

internally-displaced persons; and the protection of human rights defenders.[82] In that context, one of the most critical aspects of monitoring has been the duty to prosecute atrocities because of the massive human rights violations in the internal armed conflict committed by guerrillas, paramilitaries and public servants. Those crimes must be investigated promptly, thoroughly and impartially through transitional or ordinary mechanisms[83] to avoid impunity.[84] For those reasons, during this time the HRCttee has been monitoring the compatibility with international law of some of the mechanisms of transitional justice established during the peace process with the paramilitary groups in 2005 and in the peace accord with the FARC in 2016.

5.2.5 Impact of Individual Communications

The individual communications presented to the HRCttee are related, mainly, to the guarantee of due process into sanctions to public servants;[85] murder and persecution of leaders;[86] arbitrarily deprivation of life;[87] arbitrary interference in the home;[88] and due process in criminal proceedings.[89]

Regarding the effectiveness in the implementation, until 2016 only four decisions have been fully implemented following Act 288 of 1996 to grant compensation in favour of victims of violations of CCPR. Despite the adoption of Decree No 507 of 2017 and the Resolution 9709 of 2017, which aimed to facilitate the compensation, most of the views in which the HRCttee has found a violation of the Covenant have not been fully implemented.[90] Because of that, some victims have used the *tutela* as a mechanism to reach the effective application of the compensations established in the views. The Constitutional Court has validated this possibility.[91]

Most leading NGOs have for a long time prioritised the Inter-American system for submitting individual communications, which explains why in the last

---

82 A/HRC/43/51/Add.1 Report of the Special Rapporteur on the Situation of Human Rights Defenders.
83 CCPR/C/COL/CO/7 paras 11, 13 & 15.
84 For information about cases where there has been a procedural impulse, see CCPR/C/COL/CO/7/Add.1 paras 13, 14, 15, 16.
85 *Becerra Barney v Colombia*, Comm 1298/2004, CCPR/C/129/D/2931/2017, CCPR/C/129/D/2930/2017, CCPR/C/55/D/563/1993.
86 CCPR/C/129/D/2931/2017.
87 CCPR/C/76/D/778/1997, CCPR/C/60/D/612/1995.
88 CCPR/C/71/D/687/1996.
89 CCPR/C/75/D/848/1999.
90 CCPR/C/COL/CO/7 para 7.
91 See Ruling SU-738/14.

15 years the communications presented to the HRCttee have been presented by individuals but not as part of strategic litigation. Consequently, the impact of the views adopted has not been as important as they were 20 years ago.

5.2.6 Brief Conclusion

The awareness and use by different actors of CCPR and the HRCttee have been significant. Its impact in some concrete fields has also been important as it has contributed to crucial jurisprudential developments by the Constitutional Court and even to constitutional reform. However, the humanitarian crisis in Colombia persists with gross violations of civil and political rights. Besides, in that field, the impact of the Inter-American system has to a certain extent limited the direct impact of CCPR and the legal doctrine of the HRCttee, as NGOs and judges have given priority to the jurisprudence of the Inter-American Court of Human Rights.

5.3 *International Covenant on Economic, Social and Cultural Rights*

5.3.1 Incorporation and Reliance by Organs of State

CESCR was adopted in 1966 and ratified by Colombia in 1969, some two years later. Along with CCPR, this Covenant was one of the fastest to be ratified. However, unlike CCPR, Colombia has not ratified the protocol to accept the individual complaints system.

As with CCPR, most of the rights of CESCR are incorporated in the Colombian legal system, especially in the Constitution. For example, the Constitution guarantees individual and collective labour rights and the rights to social security, housing, health, education, and so forth. In fact, as with CCPR, during the 1991 constituent process in Colombia, CESCR was taken into account to draft Chapter 3 of the Constitution on economic, social and cultural rights.[92]

CESCR and the CESCR Cttee have been very influential in the Colombian legal system, especially because the Constitutional Court has invoked and used them widely. In fact, as we have seen, the CESCR Cttee clearly is the treaty body most frequently cited by this tribunal. According to the website of the Court, in recent years the Court cited the CESCR Cttee in an average of 10 per cent of cases.[93]

---

92 See eg the report on that chapter in Gaceta Constitucional, No 82 13.
93 We selected three years to make this consultation: in 2010 the Court took 1 065 decisions and in 111 CESCR was cited, about 8%; in 2015 the Court adopted 866 decisions and in 105 CESCR was cited, about 12%; and in 2020 the Court took 523 decisions and in 57 CESCR was cited, about 11%.

This extensive use of CESCR and of the CESCR Cttee by the Court has triggered other actors, especially the legislature and some governmental agencies, to also take them into account.

In most cases, as with other UN treaties, this judicial reference to CESCR and to the CESCR Cttee was essentially to support or strengthen some constitutional arguments but without a decisive and direct impact on the decision. However, on many occasions those references have had a real substantive impact, as illustrated by the following five examples.

First, some General Comments by the CESCR Cttee have been crucial for the interpretation by the Court and other institutions of the content of constitutional social rights, such as education and health, as the Court has closely followed their doctrine that those rights have to be available, accessible and acceptable and that states not only have an obligation to respect, but also to protect and fulfil those rights.[94] These constant references of the Constitutional Court to the General Comments elaborated by the CESCR Cttee have led other institutions to incorporate these concepts and to take them into account in their decisions. Of particular importance was the adoption of the 'statutory' Law 1751[95] on the right to health that incorporated important parts of General Comment 14 of the CESCR Cttee. Equally important, for some years, the Colombian Ombudsman (La Defensoría del Pueblo) operated a follow-up mechanism to evaluate the policies related to social rights; the indicators of this mechanism were largely based on General Comments of the CESCR Cttee.[96]

Second, the Court has also made constant reference to some General Comments of the CESCR Cttee to determine that social rights, such as education and health, were justiciable in a manner similar to the case of civil and political rights[97] and, thus, that the very powerful 'tutela' could be used to protect those rights. The impact has been vast: Every year, up to half of all tutelas

---

[94] On the right to education, see, eg, ruling T-308/11, which used General Comment 13 on education and on the right to health; ruling T-884/03 and C-313/14, which used General Comment 14 on health.

[95] In Colombia a statutory law (*ley estatutaria*) has higher force than an ordinary law and its approval in Congress requires a stringent majority.

[96] It was called el PROSEDHER, because of its Spanish acronym. An example of this follow-up in relation to education was the book Defensoría del Pueblo, *Sistema de seguimiento y evaluación de la política pública educativa a la luz del derecho a la educación* (Serie DESC 2004) <https://www.corteidh.or.cr/tablas/r26113.pdf> accessed 20 September 2022.

[97] For a defence of the justiciability of the right to health, based largely on General Comment 14, see Ruling T-760/04. For a defence of the justiciability of the right to education, based largely on General Comment 13, see Ruling T-428/12.

presented are related to social rights. For instance, in 2018, close to half of the tutelas presented were related to a possible violation of the right to health.[98]

Third, the Court has also incorporated, with some adjustments, some important legal doctrines of the CESCR Cttee, especially the thesis, stated since General Comment 3, that regressive measures in the protection of social rights imply a violation of those rights, unless the authorities are able to show that the adoption of those measures were necessary and proportionate.[99] The adoption of this doctrine has had practical consequences as some legislative or administrative measures were found regressive without any justification by the Court and thus declared unconstitutional.[100]

Fourth, the references to the CESCR Cttee have also led to the recognition of new rights as fundamental rights in Colombia. In particular, the Constitutional Court has used General Comment 15 to recognise the existence of the right to water in Colombia as a fundamental right,[101] even if the Constitution does not mention this right. This recognition has had very important consequences. For instance, the Court ordered the municipality of Yarumal to take all the necessary emergency measures to guarantee, for a maximum period of one month, access to potable water to the inhabitants in situations of vulnerability, and to develop, within one year, a permanent solution to ensure access to water for human needs.[102] Additionally, as a consequence of this recognition by the Court of water as a fundamental right, some of the largest cities in Colombia, such as Bogotá or Medellin, have adopted municipal regulations and policies to guarantee access to water to their inhabitants.

Fifth, a rather dramatic impact of CESCR and the CESCR Cttee has been the fact that it led to an interpretation of the content of the right to education

---

98   See Defensoría del Pueblo, *La tutela y los derechos a la salud y a la seguridad social* (2019) 65.
99   On this doctrine in Colombia, see R Uprimny and D Guarnizo, '¿Es posible una dogmática adecuada sobre la prohibición de regresividad? Un enfoque desde la jurisprudencia constitucional colombiana' in E Ferrer Mac-Gregor and A Zaldívar Lelo de Larrea (eds), *La ciencia del derecho procesal constitucional. Estudios en homenaje a Héctor Fix-Zamudio en sus cincuenta años como investigador del derecho, T. IV Derechos Fundamentales y tutela constitucional* (UNAM, Instituto de Investigaciones Jurídicas 2008).
100 See, for instance, among many others, Ruling C-1165/00, which declared unconstitutional a law that reduced the financial support for the public health system, and C-931/04, which declared unconstitutional a law that reduced the percentage allocated to public universities in the budget.
101 Eg, see rulings T-279/11, T-946/13, T-418/10, T-028/14, T-790/14 and T-118/18, among many others.
102 See RulingT-129/17.

contrary to the letter itself of the Constitution. Until 2010, in most public schools, parents had to pay for the primary education of their children, which was contrary to article 13 of CESCR, which provides that 'primary education shall be compulsory and available free to all'. However, the governments argued that these fees were legitimate because article 67 of the Constitution clearly authorises their imposition, even for primary education in public schools, at least for those families with the capacity to pay the fees. Some human rights NGOs challenged this possibility before the Constitutional Court, arguing that even if the letter of article 67 of the Constitution allowed these fees, that was contrary to CESCR. The Court, in the Ruling C-376/10, accepted this argument. The Court took into account article 13 of CESCR, General Comments 11 and 13 of the CESCR Cttee on education, and the last Concluding Observations on Colombia by the CESCR Cttee,[103] which recommended that Colombia guarantee primary education free of charge. The Court argued that as a consequence of the *pro personae* principle and the constitutional status of human rights treaties in Colombia, CESCR should prevail over the letter of the Constitution as it provided a more generous protection to the right of education. Thus, the Court concluded that, contrary to the letter of article 67 of the Constitution, primary education in public schools has to be free of charge.

5.3.2 Level of Awareness

The previous analysis illustrates that even if CESCR and the CESCR Cttee are not extensively mentioned by the media, they are widely used by different social actors and institutions and thus have had a considerable impact on everyday life. Even though policy makers have taken steps to protect economic rights, the implementation of that public policy has not reached the majority of the population. This limitation implies the frequent use of judicial actions to protect those rights, spreading the use and knowledge of CESCR. In public demonstrations, it is more common to see claims of social rights. The 2011 students' strike,[104] the 2013 agricultural strike[105] and the 2019 protests against tax reform are some of the instances where the vindication of social rights has been critical. Moreover, in this way, the population recognises the need for reforms to guarantee these rights.

---

103   E/C.12/1/Add.74 para 48.
104   https://www.bbc.com/mundo/noticias/2011/10/111012_colombia_protestas_estudiantiles_aw.
105   https://www.semana.com/nacion/articulo/se-levanta-el-paro-agrario/357014-3/.

5.3.3 Use by Non-Governmental Actors

NGOs regularly make use of CESCR and the CESCR Cttee in their litigation and advocacy strategies, both internationally and internally.[106] Besides, the participation of many NGOs in the dialogues with the CESCR Cttee has been important and robust as most of these are part of a mechanism of coordination, the Colombian Platform on Human Rights, Democracy and Development, which has presented alternative high-quality reports.[107] However, for international individual cases, the litigation strategies of most organisations have focused on the regional system because of the reasons already provided, and the fact that Colombia has not yet accepted the system of individual complaints before the CESCR Cttee.

5.3.4 State Reporting and Its Impact

Colombia has a delay of one year on average in its obligation to report. From 1977 to 2019 there have been six periodic reports. The CESCR Cttee has underlined some issues related to the guarantee of social rights as problems related to labour rights, the right to social security and the right to an adequate standard of living, and has highlighted problems associated with inequality, regressive taxation and the differential economic impact of the armed conflict in rural areas.[108]

Colombia has a regressive taxation system. This is one of the primary sources of inequality, in addition to the gap between rural and urban areas, and the structural deficiencies left by the armed conflict. Despite multiple attempts, it has been very difficult to reform the tax system. Due to corruption, achieving the maximum amount of resources has been difficult, leading to low funding for the realisation of economic, social, and cultural rights. Even though various legislative proposals have been made to combat corruption, according to the recommendations of the Committee, these efforts have been unsuccessful.

---

106 Afro-Colombian National Movement CIMARRON, Comisión Colombiana de Juristas, Comité Ambiental en Defensa de la Vida, Dejusticia – Centro de Estudios de Derecho, Justicia y Sociedad, Corporación Colectivo de Abogados José Alvear Restrepo (CCAJAR), Instituto Latinoamericano de Servicios Legales Alternativos (ILSA) are all part of the so-called 'escr-network', which coordinates international advocacy and litigation in this field. See https://www.escr-net.org/es/miembros.

107 See, eg, the high-quality report for 2010. Plataforma de Derechos Humanos, Democracia y Desarrollo (2010) *Informe Alterno al Quinto Reporte del Estado Colombiano*. Bogotá, author <https://colombiadiversa.org/colombiadiversa/documentos/DIVULGACION/INFORME_COMITE_DESC_1.pdf> accessed 30 June 2022.

108 E/C.12/COL/CO/6.

Rural workers and the structural inequality gap between the cities and the rural areas have also been of critical concern in the dialogues with the CESCR Cttee. The Final Peace Agreement with the FARC, mentioned earlier, aims, through different reforms, to improve the livelihood of peasants, indigenous peoples and Afro-Colombians, in particular through access to land and natural resources.[109] Despite this, there has not been political will to implement these measures effectively. In 2020 only 4 per cent of the provisions agreed on rural reform were fully implemented and 33 per cent have not even started to be executed.[110]

5.3.5 Brief Conclusion

CESCR has been one of the most widely-used UN treaties in Colombia, and clearly the CESCR Cttee has been the most influential treaty body in the country. Their impact in law and jurisprudence has been significant with important practical effects on daily life. However, the enjoyment of economic, social and cultural rights remains precarious, mainly because legislative and executive policy makers' efforts have been inadequate to overcome inequality. This then transfers the burden of protection to the judiciary, and explains the considerable use of the *tutela* to protect social rights such as health. Only limited progress has been made in implementing the recommendations of the CESCR Cttee. Legislative initiatives lack political support, and corruption and inequality remain widespread.

5.4 *Convention on the Elimination of All Forms of Discrimination against Women*

5.4.1 Incorporation and Reliance by Organs of State

CEDAW was ratified in 1982. OP-CEDAW was ratified in 2007, one of three UN complaint mechanisms accepted by Colombia.

During the 1991 constitutional assembly, CEDAW was not widely cited in the debates in spite of the fact that the treaty had already been ratified for more than two decades. However, the Constitution incorporates many articles that not only forbid discrimination against women but that also impose obligations on authorities to develop special measures to achieve equality between men and women, including through the strengthening of the participation of women in the highest decision-making offices in the government.[111]

---

109 E/C.12/COL/CO/5 para 22.
110 Instituto Kroc de Estudios Internacionales de Paz. 'Tres años después de la firma del Acuerdo Final de Colombia: hacia la transformación territorial' 2020.
111 See arts 13, 40 and 44 of the Constitution.

In the last 20 years, many laws have been adopted concerning discrimination against women, such as Law 581 of 2000, which establishes a minimum quota of 30 per cent of women in the highest offices in the executive branch; Law 731 of 2002 in favour of rural women; Law 823 of 2003 on equal opportunities for women; Law 1009 of 2006 which creates an observatory on gender issues in the presidency; Law 1257 of 2008 to combat gender violence; Law 1434 of 2011 which creates a legal commission on equality for women in the Congress; Law 1719 of 2014 which aims to guarantee the right of access to justice for victims of sexual violence, especially sexual violence associated with armed conflict; Law 1761 of 2015, which creates femicide as an autonomous crime; Law 1822 of 2017, which extends maternity leave to 18 weeks and paid paternity leave to 8 working days; and Law 902 of 2017, which provides for the recognition of the care economy and prioritises rural women as beneficiaries of programmes for access to land.

The Colombian government has also implemented programmes in order to fight gender inequality. These include the National Gender Equality Plan,[112] which aims at fostering equality between women. It also includes the National Comprehensive Policy on Gender Equity and Equality, which was approved in 2011 and seeks to ensure the rights of Colombian women.

All these laws and programmes implement the provisions of CEDAW as they are instruments to eradicate discrimination against women. However, it is not easy to evaluate the real impact of CEDAW in their adoption. CEDAW in fact was repeatedly mentioned in some of the debates in Congress or in articles in the media when these laws or programmes were discussed, which illustrates that the treaty has had a certain impact on their approval. For instance, Law 2117 of 2021 was adopted to reform and strengthen the previous 2002 Law 823 on equal opportunities for women. One of the justifications invoked for this law clearly was CEDAW.[113] However, participants in the debates on this law and in other discussions concerning other laws and governmental programmes have also made reference directly to the constitutional provisions on discrimination against women and to other treaties, especially to so-called Belen do Para Convention, an important treaty in the Inter-American system adopted to eradicate violence against women and which was ratified by Colombia in 1996 and has had a clear influence in the country.

In the same vein, it is not easy to evaluate the impact of CEDAW on the judiciary. Compared to CCPR and CESCR, CEDAW is less frequently cited by the

---

112   CEDAW/C/COL/9.
113   See 'Exposición de Motivos' for the Bill 158 of 2019 Cámara in Gaceta del Congreso No 758 of 16 August 2019.

Constitutional Court, despite the fact that all three treaties were already ratified by Colombia when this tribunal began to operate. This can be explained because the Court might have preferred, instead of invoking CEDAW, to directly use the robust constitutional provisions forbidding discrimination against women and ordaining authorities to adopt measures to ensure equality between men and women. Thus, in general, as with other UN treaties, CEDAW has been used by the Court more as a supplementary argument to reinforce a decision that would have been taken in any case, by directly invoking constitutional provisions, than as an autonomous normative basis to reach a conclusion and provide a remedy.

An example of this use is the following: Sometimes affirmative action measures adopted to achieve gender equality have been challenged by arguing that these implied sexual discrimination against men. In general, the Court has upheld these measures, and in many cases it has invoked article 4 of CEDAW which allows temporary special measures aimed at accelerating de facto equality between men and women. However, in all those rulings the Court has also directly used article 13 of the Constitution, which clearly establishes the possibility of these affirmative action measures.[114]

However, in some cases the impact of CEDAW has been more significant and direct, especially where the Constitution was not clear on the issue, as shown by the following two examples.

First, in relation to some cases of domestic violence against women,[115] in most of these cases the Court has directly relied on statutes already adopted by Congress, such as Law 1257 of 2008, to combat gender violence. The Court has also invoked the Inter-American Belem do Para Convention. However, as the Constitution does not contain a strong provision on domestic violence against women, in these cases the Court has extensively used CEDAW and especially several documents adopted by the CEDAW Cttee. In particular, the Court cited General Recommendation 19 which emphasises that domestic violence against women is one of the worst forms of discrimination against women and has to be eradicated. The Court also took into account the 2007 Concluding Observations of the CEDAW Cttee in relation to Colombia regarding the flaws in access to justice of women victims of domestic violence. Additionally, the Court also invoked some cases on domestic violence decided by the CEDAW

---

114   See, eg, Ruling C-677/06 regarding the constitutionality of a law that ordered special measures in favour of women. The Court upheld the law and invoked art 4 of CEDAW but the main normative base of the decision was art 13 of the Constitution.
115   See in particular rulings T-967/14 and T-388/19.

Cttee against other countries, such as the cases of *AT v Hungary* and *Sahide Goekce v Austria*. With all these references, the Court concluded that the prevalence of discriminatory stereotypes on gender roles and the lack of a gender perspective of judges were a clear obstacle for the access to justice of women victims of domestic violence. Thus, the Court ordered the Superior Council of Justice, which is in charge of the judicial training of judges, to provide to all judges dealing with this type of case a special course on gender to reduce and overcome these stereotypes.

A second and even more dramatic example is abortion. The Constitution is silent on this matter, and until 2006 Colombia criminalised all forms of abortion, even in cases of rape. In a controversial and divided decision in 1994, the Constitutional Court upheld this very punitive criminalisation. However, in the 2006 ruling C-355/06 the Court decriminalised abortion in three cases, namely, (i) rape; (ii) when the health and life of the woman was in danger; and (iii) when the fetus was inviable. One of the main arguments of the Court for this dramatic change in jurisprudence was CEDAW, and especially the CEDAW Cttee's doctrine. For this historic decision the Court relied strongly on the CEDAW General Recommendation 24 and on the previous Concluding Observations of the CEDAW Cttee vis-à-vis Colombia in 1999.

5.4.2 Level of Awareness

Issues of violence and discrimination against women have in the last two decades been at the core of many social and political discussions. These are important topics in most media and social networks almost daily. This is due to the discrepancy between the increased strength and presence of feminist movements of a very different nature and the persistence of a pervasive violence and discrimination against women. In a sense, most of the values and rights defended by CEDAW are increasingly accepted in the political and social Colombian culture, except perhaps in relation to abortion, an issue on which there are deep social divisions. However, CEDAW and the CEDAW Cttee are not widely mentioned in the media and on social networks.

5.4.3 Use by Non-Governmental Actors

The most important NGOs working on women's rights have widely used CEDAW and CEDAW Cttee general recommendations in their litigation. For instance, these references have been explicit in some important cases before the Constitutional Court.[116] These NGOs have also extensively used CEDAW in

---

116 See, eg, Ruling C-754/15 concerning health attention to victims of sexual violence. The plaintiffs, members of important NGOs, extensively invoked CEDAW and its General

their advocacy strategy. For instance, these references have been important to defend the notion that the peace accord with the FARC in 2016 had to have a gender perspective and had to deal clearly with issues such as sexual violence, issues that were neglected in previous negotiations with armed groups, such as those made in 2005 with paramilitary groups.[117] This strategy was successful: The 2106 peace accord has a clear gender perspective and forbids amnesty for cases of sexual violence committed during the armed conflict.

5.4.4 State Reporting and Its Impact

In general, Colombia has presented its reports timeously and has participated in the dialogues with a high-level delegation. For instance, the last dialogue in 2019 was led by the Deputy Foreign Affairs Minister and included representatives of the Ministry of the Interior, the Attorney-General's Office, the Constitutional Court, the Congress, the National Gender Commission of the Judiciary, the Office of the Presidential Council for Women's Equity, the Ministry of Foreign Affairs and the Permanent Mission in Geneva.[118] Colombia's ninth periodic report, which covers the period from 2014 to 2018, provides information on the progress made in implementing CEDAW in the country, including on the legal and institutional frameworks for the protection of women's rights and on the situation of women in various areas. It also includes the measures by the government to combat violence against women, including femicides and forced displacement of women.

As with other treaty bodies, the report in this case and the previous reports before the CEDAW Cttee in general were of good quality in relation to the description of the legislative and other measures taken to ensure equality and non-discrimination of women. However, the reflections of the state report on the impact of these measures have been rather poor.

Recommendations and the Court accepted the relevance of those references, especially General Recommendations 19 on women and violence, 24 on women and health and 30 on women and armed conflict.

117 Interview Linda Cabrera, March and October 2022, Director of 'Sisma Mujer'. She stressed the importance in their advocacy of General Recommendations of CEDAW Cttee 9, 23, 25, 28, 30 and 33. See also A Benjumea, C Mejía and L Cabrera, *La inviolabilidad del cuerpo de las mujeres hace la paz sostenible. Claves para un tratamiento diferenciado de la violencia sexual en el mecanismo tripartito de monitoreo y verificación del cese al fuego y de hostilidades y dejación de arma* (Sisma Mujer and Humanas 2016) <https://www.sismamujer.org/wp-content/uploads/2021/08/2016-Claves-para-un-trato-diferenciado-de-la-violencia-sexual-en-mecanismo-tripartito-de-monitoreo-y-verificacion.pdf> accessed 31 October 2022.

118 See CEDAW/C/COL/CO/9.

A coalition of the most important NGOs working on women' rights, such as CCJ, Sisma Mujer, Humanas, Casa de la Mujer and others, has participated in the latest reviews of Colombia and has presented high-quality alternative reports. In general, the reports recognised the legal and jurisprudential advancements made by the state in the last decades, but stressed that discrimination and violence against women remained widespread. The 2013 shadow report concentrated on the lack of real impact of the laws adopted to overcome violence and discrimination against women, as illustrated by the extended violence against women, especially sexual violence associated with the armed conflict.[119] The 2019 report stressed the opportunities opened up by the peace accord reached in 2016 to overcome, or at least diminish, these forms of violence.[120]

In general, the CEDAW Cttee has recognised that the normative advancements made by the state are significant, but has also stressed that the measures adopted have not always been effective to overcome discrimination and violence against women. For instance, the Committee has recognised the importance of Law 1257 adopted to combat violence against women, but expressed its concern about the limited implementation of this law and, thus, has recommended that Colombia 'ensure adequate and sustainable allocation of resources' for the implementation of Act 1257/2008 concerning integrated and accessible services for victims in rural areas, in particular health services, and the provision of shelters for victims in rural areas.[121]

5.4.5 Impact of Individual Communications

No case has as yet been presented to or decided by the CEDAW Cttee in respect of Colombia.

---

[119] See the 2013 report endorsed by about 25 very important NGOs. See Alianza Iniciativa de Mujeres Colombianas por la Paz – IMP and 25 other NGO's, *Una mirada a los derechos de las mujeres en Colombia informe alternativo presentado al Comité CEDAW de Naciones Unidas* (Bogotá 2013) <https://www.dejusticia.org/wp-content/uploads/2017/04/fi_name_recurso_331.pdf> accessed 30 September 2022.

[120] See the 2019 report endorsed by about 20 very important NGOs. See Católicas por el Derecho a Decidir (CDD) and 20 other NGOs, *Mujeres y paz, en búsqueda de plenos derechos informe sombra del grupo de monitoreo para la implementación de la CEDAW en Colombia* (Bogotá 2019) <https://despenalizaciondelaborto.org.co/wp-content/uploads/2019/04/Informe_sombra_MUJERES-Y-PAZ-EN-COLOMBIA-EN-BU%C3%ACSQUEDA-DE-PLENOS-DERECHOS.pdf> accessed 30 September 2022.

[121] See Concluding Observations to the 9th report of Colombia, 2019, CEDAW/C/COL/CO/9 para 26.

5.4.6 Brief Conclusion

In the last decades there has been a clear improvement in the adoption of legislation and public policies aimed at combating gender discrimination and responding to the particular needs and rights of women. CEDAW has had some impact in these legal and political advancements. However, challenges and gaps in the implementation of CEDAW remain. Several factors could explain the situation, including the armed conflict.[122] There also is the persistence of social and economic inequalities and unequal access to justice persists.

5.5 Convention against Torture and Other Cruel, Inhuman or Degrading Treatment or Punishment

5.5.1 Incorporation and Reliance by Organs of State

Colombia ratified CAT in 1985 but has accepted neither the individual complaints mechanism of article 22 of CAT, nor the Optional Protocol that allows regular visits to places of deprivation in the country by the Subcommittee on Prevention of Torture and by national bodies (OP-CAT).

The Constitution establishes in article 12 that nobody may be subjected to torture or cruel or inhumane treatment, and since the ratification of CAT Colombia has criminalised torture in the Criminal Code, with significant penalties.[123] These developments can be considered a form of implementation of CAT.

As we have seen, CAT is one of the UN treaties least cited by the Constitutional Court in spite of the fact that it was ratified before the promulgation of the 1991 Constitution. References to the CAT Cttee are even more scarce. We were also not able to find any direct reliance on CAT in the legislative debates in Congress.

However, there are two important issues in which CAT has had some influence: The first is more indirect, and relates to the overcrowding of prisons in Colombia, which led the Constitutional Court, on several occasions,[124] to declare massive violations of fundamental rights in the penitentiary system, and to order the government to take urgent and structural measures to overcome this situation. In these decisions the Court considered that the conditions in prisons were so dire that they implied torture and inhuman treatment,

---

[122] CIDH, Violence and Discrimination against Women in the Armed Conflict in Colombia (2006) <http://www.cidh.org/countryrep/ColombiaMujeres06eng/TOC.htm>. IDCM Informe Mundial sobre Desplazamiento Interno de 2022 <https://www.internal-displacement.org/global-report/grid2022/spanish/> accessed 30 September 2022.
[123] See art 178 of the current Criminal Code, Law 599 of 2000.
[124] See, eg, Rulings T-388/13 and SU-122/22.

citing the CAT Cttee. However, the Court placed weak reliance on the CAT Cttee as it did not use a direct quotation of the CAT Cttee but made a reference to a report of the CIDH, which in turn cited the CAT Cttee.[125] In a sense this was surprising, because in the previous Concluding Observations on Colombia, the CAT Cttee stressed the appalling conditions in prisons and formulated direct recommendations to Colombia, which the Constitutional Court could have taken into account.[126]

A more direct normative impact is linked to the issue of due obedience within the military forces. Article 91 of the Constitution establishes that even in case of an overtly unconstitutional order, the responsibility lies with the commander who gave the order and not with the officer who executed it. However, this provision contradicts article 2 of CAT, which establishes that 'an order from a superior officer or a public authority may not be invoked as a justification of torture', even in the military forces. Taking CAT into account, the Court in several decisions has established that in spite of the strong rule of due obedience in the military in article 91 of the Constitution, a *pro persona* interpretation of the Constitution must give preference to CAT. Thus, a military officer charged with torture cannot invoke a superior order to justify his conduct and it is his duty to refuse to abide by this order.[127]

5.5.2 Level of Awareness

Even if issues of torture or inhumane treatment by authorities are widely discussed in Colombia, CAT is not well known, even in academic circles, neither is it frequently cited in public or in media debates.

5.5.3 Use by Non-Governmental Actors

Some very important NGOs that work on a wide range of human rights issues, such as CCJ, CAJAR and the Committee for Solidarity with Political Prisoners (CSPP), in alliance with the World Organisation Against Torture, in 2003 created the 'Colombian coalition against torture', in order to do more coordinated work in this area, not only internally in Colombia but also in their international advocacy strategies.

5.5.4 State Reporting and Its Impact

Colombia has fulfilled its reporting obligations, but on two occasions with substantial delays: The third report was presented four years late and the

---

125 See para 121 of Ruling SU-122/22.
126 See paras 17 and 18 of the Concluding Observations of 2015, CAT/C/COL/CO/5.
127 See Rulings C-225/95, C-578/95 and C-570/19.

fourth seven years late. As with other treaty bodies, Colombia has focused its reports on the normative and policy measures taken to prevent and prosecute instances of torture and to provide reparations to victims.

In these dialogues, civil society has participated mainly through the Colombian Coalition against Torture, which has presented very good and systematic shadow reports to the Committee,[128] which in general have stressed that, in spite of legal advancements, torture and inhuman treatment remain widespread in Colombia, especially in prisons. The alternative reports have also underlined the high levels of impunity of these crimes and the cruel treatment of persons captured during protests.

In their Concluding Observations[129] the CAT Cttee has recognised some legal and normative advancements if the country, but has stressed the pervasiveness of torture, the high levels of impunity and the need of urgent measures in relation to the overcrowding and dire conditions of the penitentiary system. The CAT Cttee also emphasised the need to use force by authorities during protests according to international law, in particular taking into account the Basic Principles on the Use of Force and Firearms. However, these recommendations have had minor practical impact as shown by the persistence of the overcrowding and humanitarian crisis in Colombian prisons[130] and the excessive use of force during the protests in 2019 and 2021.[131]

5.5.5 Brief Conclusion

Compared to other UN human rights treaties, the impact of CAT in Colombia has been rather limited. CAT has not had significant influence in legal developments, except on the issue of due obedience in the military. Besides, the evidence is that torture remains pervasive in the country. The lack of acceptance of individual complaints and of the regular visits to places of deprivation of liberty in the country established in the Optional Protocol are crucial factors

---

128 See the reports for the last two revisions of Colombia in 2009 and 2015. See Coalición colombiana contra la tortura *Informe alternativo al 4° informe periódico del Estado colombiano al Comité contra la Tortura* (2009) <https://www.cjlibertad.org/files/Informe_alternativo_al_4_informe_peridico_del_Estado_Colombiano_al_Comit_contra_la_Tortura.pdf> accessed 30 September 2022; Coalición colombiana contra la tortura *Tortura y tratos o penas crueles, inhumanos o degradantes en Colombia. Informe alterno al al Comité contra la Tortura*. Bogotá, OMCT (2015), <https://www.coljuristas.org/documentos/libros_e_informes/informe_sobre_tortura_24-04-15.pdf> accessed 30 September 2022.
129 Concluding Observations of 2015, CAT/C/COL/CO/.
130 On the persistence of the humanitarian crisis in the penitentiary system, see the Ruling SU-122/22 of the Constitutional Court.
131 On the repression of these protests, see R Uprimny, 'El «estallido social» colombiano. Reflexiones sobre protesta y derechos humanos en democracias débiles' (2022) 10 Deusto Journal of Human Rights 133–159, <https://djhr.revistas.deusto.es/article/view/2625/3215> accessed 31 December 2022.

that explain this limited impact,[132] as the problem of torture is more practical than normative and Colombia is refusing the more important practical mechanisms developed in the UN to eradicate torture.

5.6 Convention on the Rights of the Child

5.6.1 Incorporation and Reliance by Organs of State

Colombia ratified CRC in 1991, coinciding with the adoption of the new Constitution in the same year. Colombia also in 2003 ratified the Optional Protocol to the CRC on the Sale of Children, Child Prostitution and Child Pornography (OP-CRC-SC) and the Optional Protocol to the CRC on the Involvement of Children in Armed Conflict (OP-CRC-AC).[133] However, Colombia has not yet ratified the Optional Protocol to the CRC on a Communications Procedure (OP-CRC-CP).

Article 44 of the Constitution in a sense is the Bill of Rights for children as it includes basic rights of life, physical integrity, health and social security, a balanced diet, a name and citizenship, the right to have a family and not to be separated from it, care and love, instruction and culture, recreation, and the free expression of their opinions. Children are protected against all forms of abandonment, physical or moral violence, sequestration, sale, sexual abuse, work or economic exploitation, and dangerous work. The state also upholds that children can exercise their rights guaranteed in laws and international treaties ratified by Colombia. The rights of children take precedence over the rights of others.

In addition, Colombia has passed several Acts that protect children from several harmful practices such as child labour and illegal adoption. For example, in terms of child labour, Colombia has ratified International Labour Organisation (ILO) Conventions 138 and 182, which were adopted under Law No 515 of 1999 and Law No 704 of 2001. Following the promulgation of Law No 985 of 2005, Colombia has adopted measures to curb human trafficking and has taken steps to provide support and protection for trafficking victims. Also, two important laws that equip the state with judicial tools to combat commercial sexual exploitation of children and young persons have been adopted: Law No 679 of 2001 and Law No 1236 of 2009. Law No 1257 of 2008 contains provisions on raising awareness of, preventing and punishing violence and discrimination against women, and Law No 1329 of 2009 is aimed at combating commercial sexual exploitation of children and young persons.

---

132 According to a former member of CAT, Diego Rodriguez Pinzón (interview September 2022).
133 See Law 765 of 2002 and Law 833 of 2003.

All these legal advancements can be seen as forms of implementation of CRC. Additionally, it is possible to establish a direct normative impact of CRC in important legislative and jurisprudential developments.

In 2006 Colombia promulgated the Code of Childhood and Adolescence (Law 1098) which is a very important piece of legislation that in more than 200 articles clarifies the rights of the child, the mechanisms of protection of those rights, the role of different institutions in this area and a juvenile criminal justice system. In addition, the state established units that specialised in the protection of the child through branches of the government required under the terms of this Code. Institutions established are the Counsel-General's Office, through the Office of the Specialised Counsel for Child, Youth and Family Rights, which undertake high-level oversight, prevention, management supervision and intervention functions with respect to the administrative and judicial authorities.

The purpose of this Code, the adoption of which was advocated by an important network of civil society organisations (the Alliance for the Colombian Childhood),[134] was clearly to harmonise legal regulations to CRC, as it is explicitly explained in the presentation of the Bill in Congress, which not only directly mentions CRC but also the work of the CRC Cttee and recognises that the ratification of this treaty implied a deep change of perspective in dealing with children's issues.[135] The purpose of adapting internal regulations to CRC is so clear that article 6 of Law 1098 admonishes that the interpretation and enforcement of this Code must be guided by CRC.

Additionally, as already mentioned, CRC and the CRC Cttee are treaties and treaty bodies widely mentioned by the Constitutional Court. In general, as we have already explained in relation to other treaties, those references in general do not have a specific impact on the decisions as they appear more as a supporting argument. However, CRC, its protocols and the legal developments of the CRC Cttee have had a direct impact on important jurisprudential developments, as shown by these three examples.

First, the legal developments made by the CRC Cttee have informed the doctrine of the Court in this field. On several occasions, the Court has made reference to General Comments of the CRC Cttee. For instance, Ruling C-569/16 emphasised the relevance for the interpretation of the fundamental rights of the child of General Comment 5 on the general measures of implementation of

---

134 The 'Alianza por la niñez colombiana' is a different type of network to those mentioned in this article. It is not composed of classic human rights NGOs but by international organisations, such as Save the Children or Plan International, in coordination with philanthropic business foundations, such as Foundation Barco and Foundation Saldarriaga. See its web page at <https://alianzaporlaninez.org.co/> accessed 30 September 2022.
135 See Exposición de Motivos al Proyecto de Ley 085/2005 Cámara in Gaceta del Congreso No 551 de 2005 25, Exposición de Motivos al Proyecto de Ley 085/ 2005 Cámara de Representantes República de Colombia in Gaceta del Congreso No 551 de 2005 25.

the convention.[136] In Ruling SU-180/22, which deals with the measures of protection that should be adopted for a child of Venezuelan nationality who was abandoned by the parents, the Court relied extensively on General Comment 6 of the CRC Cttee on the 'treatment of unaccompanied and separated children outside their country of origin'.

Second, CRC has had an important impact when the treaty establishes some principles or rules that do not appear directly in the Constitution. That is the case of articles 5 and 12 of CRC, which establish the right of a child who is capable of forming their own views to express those views freely in all matters affecting them, the views of the child being given due weight in accordance with their age and maturity. This right is not part of any article of the Constitution, even if the Court has recognised its existence for children based on a progressive interpretation of certain principles of the Constitution, such as the general protection of autonomy and liberty for all persons, including children. However, the Court has also increasingly relied, and more directly, for defending this right of children in articles 5 and 12 of CRC and in General Comment 12 of the CRC Cttee, on the right of the child to be heard. This jurisprudence has been crucial in many fields, for instance to affirm the right of children to autonomously take medical decisions according to their age and maturity.[137]

Finally, OP-CRC-AC has also had a direct impact in the jurisprudence of the Court on a very sensitive point, namely, the content of the war crime of recruitment of minors. According to this Protocol, a person under the age of 18 years (and not 15 as previously stated in CRC) cannot be recruited in the armed forces and cannot participate in hostilities. This strong rule of the Protocol led the Court to conclude that in relation to Colombia, the recruitment of persons under the age of 18 years by armed groups was a war crime that cannot not be amnestied, in spite of the fact that the definition of this crime in the ICC Statute refers to the recruitment of children under the age of 15 years.[138]

5.6.2 Level of Awareness

As is the case in many other countries, the protection of the rights of children has become crucial in political and social debates. For that reason, CRC is relatively well known for people working in this field. The situation is different for the general public as references to CRC or to the work of the CRC Cttee are not frequent in the media or on social media.

---

136 In the same vein, see Ruling T-200/14.
137 See, eg, ruling C-246/17.
138 See Ruling C-007/18.

5.6.3 Use by Non-Governmental Actors

Several CSOs of a very different nature focus their work on the rights of children, the CRC and the CRC Cttee. Some are more humanitarian groups, while others provide social services for children in vulnerable situations, and others are more classic human rights NGOs. Some of these organisations have regrouped in networks, such as the Alliance for the Colombian Childhood, which was instrumental in the adoption of the Code of Childhood and Adolescence, and Coalico (*Coalición contra la vinculación de niños, niñas y jóvenes al conflicto armado*) which is a coalition of several humanitarian organisations focused on the issue of the recruitment of children in armed conflict.[139] Both networks have submitted reports for dialogues with the Cttee, with different emphases: While Coalico focuses on the impact of armed conflict on children, the Alliance for the Colombian Childhood attempts to present a broader view.[140]

5.6.4 State Reporting and Its Impact

Colombia has in general submitted its reports on time and has participated in the dialogue with qualified delegations. However, as with other treaties, the reports focused on the measures taken by the state and less on impact. Besides, the Concluding Observations formulated by the CRC Cttee are not usually disseminated by the government in the country, which diminishes their possible impact.

5.6.5 Brief Conclusion

CRC and the CRC Cttee have had a significant impact on the legal and cultural understanding of the rights of children in Colombia, as they have stimulated a change of paradigm in this field: Children are now accepted as right holders, with an evolving and progressive autonomy that has to be respected, and not only as objects of protection. This transformation has been possible, as with other treaties, due to the progressive incorporation of this vision by the Constitutional Court, but also through the adoption of the Code of Childhood and Adolescence that follows this new paradigm. However, the practical impact of this change remains limited as children, in particular children of marginalised populations, continue to suffer high levels of violence, especially in territories in which armed actors are still operating. Additionally, due to the persistence of inequality, the enjoyment of social rights of children in

---

[139] See the presentation of Coalico on its web page <https://coalico.org/nosotros/> accessed 30 September 2022.

[140] See, eg, the alternative report of Coalico for the last review: Coalico and CCJ *Informe alterno al informe del Estado colombiano sobre el cumplimiento del Protocolo Facultativo Relativo a la Participación de Niños en los Conflictos Armados* (2009), <https://coalico.org/wp-content/uploads/2020/05/IA10_EspIng.pdf> accessed 30 November 2022.

discriminated groups is still precarious, in spite of improvements in the last decades.

5.7 Convention on the Rights of Persons with Disabilities

5.7.1 Incorporation and Reliance by Organs of State

Colombia ratified CRPD in 2011, making it one of the most recently-ratified UN treaties. However, its influence and impact have been clear and significant.

The Constitution contains some provisions that order authorities to combat discrimination against persons with disabilities and to adopt special measures in their favour, especially in the areas of health, the labour market and education.[141] These norms indicate that the 1991 Constitutional Assembly was sensitive to the discrimination suffered by persons with disabilities and attempted to address it. This was important as it opened the door for some laws and jurisprudential developments in that direction. However, as stressed by some analysts,[142] the language and content of these provisions were anchored in the old medical and rehabilitation paradigm that, in a sense, was superseded and replaced by the social and human rights paradigm enshrined in CRPD. Thus, the ratification of CRPD led to the adoption of laws, policies and new jurisprudential developments, the explicit objective of which was to implement CRPD and to adapt the domestic order to the new paradigm of the CRPD, as illustrated by the following four examples.

First, a statutory law, Law 1618, which is a law of special hierarchy, was adopted in 2013, after the Constitutional Court had revised its compatibility with the Constitution.[143] The purpose of this important law clearly was to implement CRPD[144] and, with that finality, it clarifies the obligations of different national and regional institutions to guarantee full respect for the rights of persons with disabilities. Additionally, this law reiterates important concepts articulated with the new social paradigm on disability, such as 'reasonable accommodation', 'universal design', and so forth, and reiterates the duty of authorities to remove barriers to inclusion and to apply the differential approach for persons with disabilities.

Second, in 2019, after wide consultation with civil society and scholars working on disability, the Congress adopted Law 1996, which is also a very important development for the implementation of CRPD as it not only protects the autonomy and legal capacity of persons with disabilities, a crucial principle of article 12 of CRPD, but expressly established in article 2 that the law must

---

141   See arts 47, 54 and 68 of the Constitution.
142   See MY Díaz Aya, 'Impacto de la CPCD en la reformulación de la política pública: caso Colombia' (2018) 2 Revista Latinoamericana en Discapacidad, Sociedad y Derechos Humanos 1.
143   See Ruling C-765/12.
144   See the justification of this law in *Gaceta del Congreso* No 678 of 2011.

be construed and applied in conformity with CRPD. In addition, according to experts on this matter, this law is one of the most advanced in the Americas on the subject and to a large extent was based in the legal doctrine of the CRPD Cttee, especially on General Comment 1 of 2014 on article 12 of the Covenant on 'equal recognition before the law'.[145]

Third, after the ratification of CRPD, different governments have also adopted policies to implement CRPD with this new perspective. For example, the Colombian armed forces have built a comprehensive rehabilitation centre for children and a functional rehabilitation centre for adults. The National Institute for the Deaf has pushed for reasonable accommodation in state educational institutions and the use of assistive technologies and devices for deaf persons. The National Reading and Writing Plan aims to increase the supply of and access to books in non-conventional settings close to young children and in order to strengthen public libraries. There are various trainings for officials, and with guidance from the National Institute for Blind Persons, the Special Administrative Unit for Support Organisations has developed Braille-format tools and audio material, for the purpose of publicising its institutional services and ensuring effective interaction with persons with sensory disabilities. This extends to the educational sector to provide commodities. In particular, the Government of Juan Manuel Santos adopted the National Public Policy on Disability and Social Inclusion (the so-called CONPES No 163 of 2013) which includes administrative and budgetary measures to advance the implementation of CRPD.

Fourth, CRPD has acquired significant importance in the jurisprudential evolution of all high courts, especially that of the Constitutional Court. As was shown previously, CRPD currently is a treaty very frequently cited by the Constitutional Court, which also is making increasing reference to the legal doctrines developed by the CRPD Cttee. These references have not been purely rhetorical but have had substantial impacts.

In many decisions, the Court has incorporated and given pre-eminence to the language and the perspective of the social paradigm enshrined in CRPD, encouraging all institutional and social actors to embrace this vision.[146] The Court emphasised that this change was substantial as it implied a positive appreciation of diversity and the establishment of specific obligations on the state to remove discrimination and create a favourable environment for the full enjoyment of their rights by persons with disabilities.[147] Additionally, the endorsement of this perspective by the Court has had concrete impacts

---

145 Interview in September 2022 with Juliana Bustamante, director of PAIIS, an expert legal clinic specialising in the rights of persons with disabilities.
146 C-066/13, C-458/15 nd T-468/18.
147 See Ruling T-468/18, para 5.1.5.3.

in the regulation of disability in several fields, such as in the area of language, as the Court has modified certain previous legal expressions as they were discriminatory;[148] in the protection of mothers with disabilities by not being separated from their children only because of their disability, by ordering that the woman must receive all possible social service support for allowing her to keep her child;[149] the need of schools to realise reasonable accommodation to ensure inclusive education for children with disabilities;[150] and the protection of sexual and reproductive rights of persons with disabilities.[151]

5.7.2   Level of Awareness

Awareness among Colombian society concerning rights of persons with disabilities and of the new social paradigm concerning disability has grown enormously in the last decade.[152] Colombia is undergoing a sort of cultural transformation in this field, as a growing number of Colombians now regard persons with disabilities as rights holders. Even if CRPD and the legal doctrine of the CRPD Cttee are not widely cited by the media or the social media, this cultural transformation can be reasonably attributed to the ratification of CRPD, as it is a consequence of the adoption of the new laws adopted to implement CRPD, of the judicial rulings by high courts, and especially the Constitutional Court based on CRPD. Additionally, this cultural change has been linked to the advocacy and pedagogic activities made by groups of scholars and legal clinics, such as PAIIS from the University of Andes, and other civil society organisations working in association with groups of persons with disabilities, forming a large and important coalition called the Colombian Coalition for the Implementation of CRPD.[153] Its role has been important as civil society is necessary to promote awareness and the need to step up efforts to publicise policies, plans and programmes for persons with disabilities, including those with psychosocial disabilities, and to overcome negative stereotypes around persons with disabilities.

5.7.3   Use by Non-Governmental Actors

Non-governmental actors play a significant role in aiding the expansion of services and protections to persons with disabilities. In that respect, as has been

---

148 See Ruling C-458/15.
149 See Ruling T-468/18.
150 Ruling T-231/19.
151 Ruling T-227/20.
152 Interview with Natalia Angel, former director of PAIIS and currently justice of the Constitutional Court Febrero (2021).
153 See the presentation of the coalition, <https://sites.google.com/site/coalicionconvencion/> accessed 30 June 2022.

mentioned, the Colombian Coalition for the Implementation of CRPD has been crucial, as it has been instrumental in the approval of Law 1996 and has also participated actively in the dialogue with the CRPD Cttee.

5.7.4 State Reporting and Its Impact

Colombia timeously presented the first report, and civil society, through the 'Colombian Coalition for the Implementation of CRPD', presented a robust and detailed alternative report.[154] In the dialogue and the Concluding Observations of 2016,[155] the CRPD Cttee, having recognised important legal advancements, stressed several issues, especially the lack of disaggregated data, the absence of strong policies to ensure accessibility and reasonable accommodation for persons with disabilities, and the persistence of negative stereotypes in relation to these persons.

Two intertwined points raised by the Committee deserve particular attention as they have an important impact. First, the Committee expressed concern because of the restrictions in law and judicial decisions concerning legal capacity of persons with disabilities, and recommended that Colombia should bring its legislation into conformity with article 12 of CRPD, taking into account General Comment 1 of the Committee.[156] This Concluding Observation was an important argument used by the Colombian Coalition for the Implementation of CRPD for proposing a Bill on that matter,[157] which resulted in the adoption, some years later, of the very important Law 1996.

Second, the Committee criticised the Colombian law for allowing forced sterilisation of persons with disabilities and the fact that this practice was admitted by some rulings of the Constitutional Court. Thus, it recommended the modification of the law and the adjustment of the criteria of the Court to the protection of the right of sexual and reproductive health of persons with disabilities, as established in article 17 of CRPD.[158] Even if the understanding of the Committee was not totally accurate, as the Court allowed this practice only in very restricted circumstances,[159] the fact remains that this recommendation has had an influence in the Court that developed a more stringent approach.

---

[154] See the alternative report, <https://www.ecoi.net/en/document/1290370.html> accessed 30 June 2022.
[155] See CRPD/C/COL/CO/1.
[156] See CRPD/C/COL/CO/1, paras 30 and 31.
[157] Interview with Juliana Bustamante, director of PAIIS, an expert legal clinic specialised on rights of persons with disabilities (September 2022).
[158] See CRPD/C/COL/CO/1, paras 46 and 47.
[159] See Ruling C-182/16. The Court only allowed this sterilisation without consent when a pregnancy could endanger the life of the person and the person would never be able, according to a scientific evaluation, to give her consent.

Some months later, in Ruling T-573/16, the Court took into account this recommendation and General Comment 1 of the CRPD Cttee and concluded that no sterilisation could be practised on a person with disabilities without their consent, and that authorities should make provision to allow these persons to take this decision. The Court also ordered the Ministry of Health to implement a regulation to guarantee this right, and the Ministry adopted Resolution 1904/17 in that direction. In subsequent decisions, such as Ruling T-410/21, the Court reiterated this prohibition.

5.7.5 Brief Conclusion

As we have seen, the impact of CRPD since its recent ratification has been significant in Colombia. It has influenced legislation, policies and judicial decisions and thus has been the source of important legal and cultural improvements on the situation of persons with disabilities. This impact may be explained because CRPD has brought to the Colombian legal regime a new understanding of disability that had no equivalent in either the Constitution or in the Inter-American system.[160] It transformed the approach of the Colombian legal system to disability in a significant way and, by doing so, it is contributing to a type of cultural transformation in this respect. However, the picture is not only rosy. The situation of persons with disabilities remains problematic. Disability rights remain marginalised in political conversations and more resources need to be allocated, especially at the local level. Discrimination and violence against persons with disabilities persist and the state needs to make an effort to optimise outcomes in cases of violence against persons with disabilities as they are entitled to increased protection under the Constitution.

5.8 International Convention for the Protection of All Persons from Enforced Disappearance

5.8.1 Incorporation and Reliance by Organs of State

Colombia became a party to the International Convention for the Protection of All Persons from Enforced Disappearance (CED) in 2012. This is the last UN treaty ratified by the country.

The problem of enforced disappearances has become serious since the mid-1980s when the number of cases increased so intensively that, two decades later, it surpassed the total number of enforced disappearances by all the

---

[160] Colombia has also ratified the Inter-American Convention on the Elimination of All Discrimination Against Persons with Disabilities even before CRPD. However, this regional treaty has not played an important role in Colombia in that field, perhaps because it is less specific than CRPD, and especially because it does not embrace the new social paradigm vis-à-vis disability as clearly as CRPD.

military regimes in South America.[161] Thus, since the 1980s, several important and courageous civil organisations of members of relatives of disappeared persons, such as *La Asociación de Familiares de Detenidos Desaparecidos* (ASFADDES)[162] and the Nydia Erika Foundation,[163] were created to denounce this outrageous crime, committed not only by government officials but also by paramilitary groups and guerrillas. The advocacy by these organisations, together with the work of important human rights NGOs such as CAJAR, CSPP or CCJ, has not only increased the awareness of the general public about the cruelty and pervasiveness of this crime, but has also led, since the 1990s, to the adoption of important regulations to prevent, combat and prosecute disappearances, many years before Colombia ratified CED. These regulatory frameworks are the Constitution, which in article 12 prohibits enforced disappearances; the Criminal Code (Law 599 of 1999) which in articles 165 to 167 criminalises enforced disappearances as a specific crime different to kidnapping; Law 971 of 2005, which regulates a mechanism of urgent search in cases of possible disappearances; and Law 1408 of 2010, which honours victims of enforced disappearances and strengthens the state's duty to identify and localise victims of this crime.

Additionally, in 2005 Colombia ratified the Inter-American Convention on Enforced Disappearances, which contains norms similar to CED in some of the most important subjects related to enforced disappearances, such as the elements of the crime, the strict limits for establishing a statute of limitations, and the impossibility of invoking superior orders to justify enforced disappearances.

For all these reasons, the impact of CED has been mostly to strengthen normative and policy evolutions that were already taking place in the country, which might explain why CED is the treaty least cited by the Constitutional Court and does not seem to have had a direct and substantive influence on the jurisprudence of high courts or in legislative or political discussions.

However, as stressed by some experts,[164] there is at least one very important point in which the ratification of CED and the work of the CED Cttee has had a direct influence: the duty of states to search and locate disappeared persons, as a humanitarian obligation of states, which is distinct to those to prevent and prosecute enforced disappearances. This obligation has not

---

161 For a general overview of the crime of enforced disappearances in Colombia, see CNMH Centro Nacional de Memoria Histórica *Hasta encontrarlos. El drama de la desaparición forzada en Colombia* CNMH, Bogotá.
162 On ASFADDES, see <https://asfaddes.org/> accessed 31 October 2022.
163 On Nydia Erika Bautista Foundation, see <http://web.nydia-erika-bautista.org/> accessed 31 October 2022.
164 Interview with María Clara Galvis, former member of CED Cttee (March 2022).

previously been given the importance it deserved. Thus, the CED Cttee not only has stressed the centrality of this autonomous obligation in its dialogues with states, but also developed and adopted in its session of April 2019, after a large consultative process, the Guiding Principles for the Search for the Disappeared Persons.

This emphasis of the CED Cttee on the importance and autonomy of the duty to search and locate disappeared persons has had a direct influence on the so-called 'integral system for protection of the rights of victims' created by the Peace Accord with FARC, in particular, in relation to the 'Unit for searching disappeared persons' (UBPD) The UBPD is a humanitarian and non-judicial institution established precisely to fulfil this specific obligation of the state. In fact, the UBPD is not mandated to investigate the crime of enforced disappearance or to establish criminal responsibility. Its role is, according to the Constitutional Court, to 'contribute to the implementation of humanitarian actions to search for and locate living persons reported missing in the context of and due to the armed conflict. In the event that an individual has died, its role is, where possible, to recover, identify and hand over the remains in a dignified manner'.[165] In this regard, the Constitutional Court has specified that 'there is no room for misunderstanding about the Unit's humanitarian mandate of searching for all persons reported missing in the context of and due to the armed conflict, whether they are alive or dead, regardless of the type of crime or conduct that led to the disappearance, the status of the victim or the identification of the alleged perpetrator'.[166] Besides, the UBPD has explicitly incorporated the guiding principles of the CED Cttee as an essential component of its normative framework.[167]

5.8.2 Level of Awareness

The intense activity denunciation made in these decades by human rights NGOs and organisations of relatives of victims, combined with reports made by the Centro Nacional de Memoria Histórica and the Truth Commission (CEV), have made it impossible for Colombians to ignore the tragedy of enforced disappearances in the country. Although the level of awareness of the phenomena is high, neither CEV nor the CEV Cttee has been widely cited by the media or social media.

---

[165] See Ruling C-067/18, in which the Court analyses the legal and constitutional framework of the UBPD and stresses the importance and autonomy of the duty to search for and locate disappeared persons.
[166] Ruling C-067/18.
[167] MC Galvis and R Hule, 'The Impact of the Guiding Principles for the Search for Disappeared Persons Adopted by the Committee on Forced Disappearances' in Grazyna Baranoswka and Milica Kolaković Bojović (eds), *Collection of Papers on the Next Ten Years of the Convention* (to be published in 2023).

5.8.3 Use by Non-Governmental Actors

As mentioned before, since the mid-1980s several CSOs, including some comprising relatives of disappeared persons, have been working intensively and with great courage to prevent and promote the prosecution of enforced disappearances and to attempt to locate disappeared persons. In their work they have relied on international standards. However, for their advocacy and litigation, most CSOs have preferred to invoke the very rich jurisprudence developed by the Inter-American system in relation to enforced disappearances, instead of relying more directly on CED.

5.8.4 State Reporting and Its Impact

Colombia timely presented its first report, which had the usual characteristics of other reports to UN treaty bodies, namely, a report of good quality and a dialogue that was attended by a high-ranking and competent delegation. However, the report centres more on a description of policies and laws rather than on the real impacts of the measures taken. Besides, the process of reporting has not involved civil society or even a strong consultation with other state institutions, and the Concluding Observations have not been widely disseminated.

Civil society organisations, in particular associations of victims or human rights NGOs, have participated in the dialogues through the presentation of good alternative reports.[168] The Committee has recognised important legal advancements in the country in relation to enforced disappearances.[169] However, it has expressed its concerns over the persistence of the practice in the country, the high levels of impunity and the lack of accurate information collected by the authorities on the phenomenon. The Committee has also criticised the fact that the definition of the crime in Colombia includes the possibility of enforced disappearances committed by non-state actors, such as guerrillas or criminal organisations, as the Committee considered that this definition could dilute the responsibility of the state.[170] It has also stressed the importance for Colombia to develop more robust strategies for searching for and locating disappeared persons or, at least, their remains, which is a recommendation that has had an important impact, as we have already seen.

---

168 See, eg, the alternative report presented by a coalition of NGOs <https://coeur opa.org.co/wp-content/uploads/2020/07/Informe-ante-el-Comit%C3%A9-de-Desapar iciones-Forzadas-de-Naciones-Unidas-REVISADO.pdf> accessed 31 October 2022.
169 See CED/C/COL/OAI/1.
170 We do not agree with this recommendation as it is clear that armed actors, such as guerrillas, can commit enforced disappearances. It is not at all clear why a state should abstain from criminalising this conduct by such actors. If the Criminal Code envisages, as Colombia does, an increased penalty when it is committed by a state official, it is difficult to understand that it implies a dilution of the responsibility of the state.

5.8.5 Impact of Individual Communications

Colombia only in 2022 accepted the complaints mechanism established under articles 31 and 32 of CED. As of 31 March 2023, no communications have been decided by the Committee.

5.8.6 Brief Conclusion

The direct impact of CED has not been very strong because the most important and policy legal developments in relation to enforced disappearances were already adopted in Colombia when the treaty was ratified. Besides, the Inter-American system and, particularly, the IACtHR, have developed a very strong jurisprudence in that field, which has been the main source for international human rights standards taken into account by courts and NGOs. In spite of this, CED and the legal doctrine of the CED Cttee have been important to consolidate these previous advances and, especially, to strengthen the notion that the state has an autonomous and specific obligation to search for and locate disappeared persons or their remains.

6 Conclusion

In the last decades, the system of UN human rights treaties has had a significant impact not only on the Colombian legal system but also, to a certain extent, on the Colombian society as a whole. It has contributed to a legal and cultural 'revolution of rights', in the sense that human rights have been recognised as judicially enforceable entitlements that have to be respected by authorities and that began to be at the centre of many key political and social debates. However, the impact of UN treaties has not been uniform, as some treaties and some UNTBs have clearly had a more profound influence than others. In that context, this brief conclusion systematises the responses to two issues already dealt with partially in the text: What explains the significance in the impact of the UN system? Why have some treaties been more influential than others?

The UN system was not the only factor behind this revolution of rights, as other elements, such as the Inter American human rights system, also played a very important role. In particular, a crucial source of this rights revolution that also partly explains the impact of the UN human rights system is the adoption of the very progressive 1991 Constitution. The introduction of the Constitution has three elements that have facilitated such an evolution. First, it led to the constitutionalisation of most human right treaties ratified by Colombia, through the special and privileged constitutional status of human rights treaties and the use of the concept of the 'block of constitutionality' by the Constitutional Court. Second, it created very effective and informal judicial procedural instruments, in particular the *tutela*, that have allowed citizens to directly invoke the protection of judges if one of their fundamental rights were violated or threatened. Third, it created the Constitutional Court as a powerful tribunal to provide a unified and generally accepted binding interpretation of the content of the constitutional rights.

The combined effect of these three features of the 1991 Constitution has been that almost all human rights incorporated into UN treaties ratified by Colombia automatically became self-executing and enforceable rights through the judiciary, and especially through the Constitutional Court. UN human rights treaties could therefore be invoked directly before courts, in particular the Constitutional Court, who began to apply them more and more intensively. This Constitutional Court has since the beginning of its work taken very seriously the legal doctrines developed by treaty bodies as relevant criteria for interpreting the content of constitutional rights. Thus, the normative developments by the treaty bodies, such as their General Comments, began to be used more and more systematically by the Constitutional Court and other tribunals.

This situation explains that the impact of UN treaties has taken a particular form in Colombia: a sort of radiating impact in different steps, like the ripples when a stone is thrown into a pond. First moment: the treaties and the legal doctrine of the UNTBs were used initially mainly by the Constitutional Court, thanks to the special and privileged status of human rights treaties in the Constitution. Then, a second step followed: because of the power of this Court, other institutions had to take into account the content of those treaties and the legal doctrines of the UNTBs as the Constitutional Court had incorporated them as hard law into the domestic legal order. Third, as judges and other institutions began to rely on those treaties for their arguments and decisions, human rights entered more and more into social, cultural and political debates. Finally, a fourth ripple ended the circle and began a new one, with civil society organisations, in particular human rights NGOs, increasingly using those treaties for their advocacy and litigation and induced the Constitutional Court and other institutions to take into account new developments within the UN human rights system.

These factors not only provide a reasonable interpretation of the impact of the UN human rights system in Colombia but also show that providing a particular and privileged constitutional status to human rights treaties and creating judicial procedures to make them enforceable are powerful legal techniques to increase the national impact of those treaties. However, these factors do not explain why some treaties and committees have been more influential than others.

The specific impact in Colombia of the different UN treaties depends on various factors. First, as not only judges but also NGOs have preferred to rely more in the Inter-American system than in the UN system, for the reasons explained in part 4 of the chapter, the influence of a particular UN treaty or a UNTB has been more pronounced when it deals with issues in which the Inter American system is relatively silent. This explains the much stronger influence in Colombia of the CESCR and the CESCR Cttee compared to the CCPR and the HRCttee. The IACtHR has not until very recently had a well-developed jurisprudence on socio-economic rights, but had developed a very strong jurisprudence in relation to civil and political rights issues. Second, UN treaties have had a stronger influence when they deal with issues that were not dealt with in detail or systematically by the Colombian Constitution or specific laws. This explains why important treaties that deal with very relevant issues for Colombia, such as CERD, CAT or CED, have had a relatively minor influence, as the Colombia legal order had already developed important standards and regulations in those fields. By contrast, CRC or CRPD have had a very strong influence, as their thematic focus has not previously been consistently and systematically addressed by the Colombian domestic legal order. Third, and strongly linked with the previous factor but with some independent effect, some UN treaties, such as the CRC or CRPD, or some General Comments of the CESCR, have had also a very strong influence as they have implied a sort of new paradigm to address issues that were already dealt by the Colombian legal order but in a different manner: a strong defense of the justiciability of ESCR, a conception of the child as rights holder and not only as objects of protection, and the replacement of the medical approach to disability by a social and human rights one.

In summary, in these decades, the UN human rights treaties have assisted Colombia in developing a more rights-based legal system and have strengthened the country's democratic culture. However, the Colombian paradox persists, with this cultural and legal rights revolution happening against the backdrop of Colombians living through a deep humanitarian crisis due to the massive and gross human rights violations associated with the protracted armed conflict. The challenge of effectively materialising human rights in Colombia remains, in spite of the significant contributions achieved in respect of the UN human rights system.

CHAPTER 5

The Impact of the United Nations Human Rights Treaties on the Domestic Level in the Czech Republic

Harald Christian Scheu and Jitka Brodská

1 Introduction to Human Rights in the Czech Republic*

On 1 January 1993 the Czech Republic was established as an independent unitary state. This event marked the end of turbulent constitutional development.[1] At the end of World War I, the First Czechoslovak Republic had been established on the ruins of the Austrian-Hungarian Empire, and between 1918 and 1938 it had built a functioning parliamentary democracy surrounded by countries that gradually shifted towards authoritarianism. After a period of occupation by Nazi Germany, Czechoslovakia was restored and became one of the founding members of the United Nations (UN). However, after a *coup d'état* of 1948 the Communist party led Czechoslovakia into an undemocratic rule lasting until 1989.[2] The Communist regime, totalitarian in some respects, was characterised by systematic and massive human rights violations. Communist ideology was dominating the society. Opponents of the regime were persecuted.

In 1989 a non-violent change of government took place in the Czechoslovak Socialist Republic, the 'Velvet Revolution'. The new constitutional order was built on democratic principles, including a pluralist system of political parties and the protection of human rights and freedoms of individuals. A constitutional Act of 1991 stipulated that international treaties on human rights and basic freedoms duly ratified and legally binding to Czechoslovakia should be directly applicable and take precedence over municipal law. Thus, international human rights protection became a crucial point of reference with regard to issues of constitutionality.[3]

---

* Jitka Brodská works at the Ministry of Foreign Affairs of the Czech Republic. The opinions expressed in this chapter are the author's own and do not reflect the views of the Ministry of Foreign Affairs.

1 For an overview of the history of the Czech Republic, see Karolina Adamová, Antonín Lojdek and Karel Schelle (eds), *Velké dějiny Zemí Koruny české* (Praha; Litomyšl 2015).

2 L Šlehofer, 'Ústavní vývoj v letech 1849–1989' in P Mlsna (ed), *Cesty české ústavnosti* (Praha 2010) 70.

3 P Mlsna, 'Ústavní a ústavněprávní vývoj po roce 1989' in P Mlsna (ed), *Cesty české ústavnosti* (Praha 2010) 86.

In 1992 the political representations of the Czech Republic and the Slovak Republic agreed to peacefully dissolve the common state. In principle, Czechoslovakia was the only former Communist country that dissolved without any acts of violence. Since the dissolution, the Czech Republic and Slovakia have maintained excellent mutual relations.[4]

The protection of human rights plays a pivotal role in Czech constitution law. According to article 112 of the Constitution of the Czech Republic, the Charter of Fundamental Rights and Basic Freedoms of 1991 forms an integral part of the Czech constitutional order. Those rights and freedoms are defined as 'inherent, inalienable, non-prescriptible, and irrepealable'. The Charter is divided into different chapters covering fundamental civil rights; political rights; rights of national and ethnic minorities; economic, social and cultural rights; and the right to judicial and other legal protection. In principle, economic, social and cultural rights may be claimed only within the confines of the laws implementing the relevant Charter provisions.[5]

According to article 4 of the Constitution, fundamental rights and basic freedoms enjoy the protection of judicial bodies. According to article 83 of the Constitution, the Constitutional Court, which is composed of 15 judges appointed by the President of the Republic for a period of ten years, is responsible for the protection of constitutionality. For this purpose, it evaluates whether statutes are in compliance with the constitutional order of the Czech Republic. In this context, some international human rights treaties are an important point of reference. The Constitutional Court further decides on constitutional complaints by the self-governing regions against unlawful encroachment by the state and on constitutional complaints against final decisions or other encroachments by public authorities infringing constitutionally-guaranteed fundamental rights and basic freedoms.[6] With a view to the jurisprudence of the European Court of Human Rights (ECtHR), article 87 of the Constitution provides that the Constitutional Court decides on measures necessary to implement a decision of an international tribunal which is binding on the Czech Republic, in the event that it cannot be otherwise implemented.

---

4 For the constitutional development of the Czech Republic, see eg A Gerloch and J Kysela (eds), *20 let Ústavy České republiky. Ohlédnutí zpět a pohled vpřed* (Plzeň, Čeněk 2013).
5 See art 41 of the Charter of Fundamental Rights and Freedoms: 'The rights listed in Article 26, Article 27 para 4, Articles 28 to 31, Article 32 paras 1 and 3, Article 33, and Article 35 of this Charter may be claimed only within the confines of the laws implementing these provisions'.
6 For more details on the competencies of the Czech Constitutional Court, see Wagnerová a kol. Zákon o Ústavním soudu s komentářem (Praha, ASPI 2007); V Sládeček, *Ústavní soudnictví* (2nd edn, Praha 2003).

In 1999 a law on the establishment of the Office of the Public Defender of Rights[7] (Ombudsperson) was adopted. The Public Defender is elected by the Chamber of Deputies of the Czech Parliament for a period of six years.[8] The Public Defender is accountable and submits its regular reports to the Chamber of Deputies. It acts independently from any other authority or body. With a view to the protection of human rights, the Public Defender may recommend amendments to legislation, government policies or administrative procedures and submit such recommendations to the Czech government or the Chamber of Deputies. The Public Defender of Rights provides protection to individuals in cases where public administrative authorities act in violation of the law or of the principles of democratic rule of law or good governance. However, the Public Defender does not have the power to cancel or change decisions. When dealing with individual cases, he may carry out independent inquiries and inform the authorities, including the government and its ministers, about his findings and recommendations.

After the Czech Republic in 2006 had ratified the Optional Protocol to the Convention against Torture and Other Cruel, Inhuman or Degrading Treatment or Punishment (OP-CAT), the functions of the national preventive mechanism in terms of the Optional Protocol are performed by the Public Defender of Rights. The Public Defender of Rights, who previously has been reviewing complaints from individuals harmed by the actions of public authorities, is authorised to undertake systematic preventive visits to places where people are or may be deprived of their liberty.[9] Since 2009, based upon a new Anti-Discrimination Act,[10] the Public Defender has been acting as a national equality body providing assistance to victims of discrimination.[11] In 2017 the Public Defender was given the mandate to monitor the implementation of the Convention on the Rights of People with Disabilities (CRPD).[12]

The Public Defender of Rights already complies with many principles of a national human rights institution according to the Paris Principles. However, accrediting the Public Defender with the Global Alliance of National Human Rights Institution Sub-Committee on Accreditation is still under consideration.[13] In the government, it was the Minister for Human Rights and Equal

---

7   Law No 349/1999. on the Public Defender of Rights.
8   § 2 of Act 349/1999.
9   § 1 para 3 of Act 349/1999. The amendment was introduced by Act 381/2005 Sb.
10 Act 198/2009 Sb.
11 § 21b of Act 349/1999.
12 § 21c of Act 349/1999.
13 The Government has not recently taken concrete steps; there were initiatives within the Senate of the Czech Republic (a seminar organised by a group of senators in October 2019).

Opportunities who was charged with the coordination of the human rights agenda in the Czech Republic (the Minister was appointed for the years 2002–2004; 2007–2010; 2014–2017). Currently, the Government Commissioner for Human Rights coordinates the agenda. The situation in specific areas is monitored by human rights government advisory bodies which are the platform for discussions between the government and civil society. It is primarily the Government Council for Human Rights and committees attached to this Council: the Committee for the Rights of the Child; the Committee for the Rights of Foreigners; the Committee against Torture and Other Cruel, Inhuman and Degrading Treatment; the Committee for Sexual Minorities; the Government Council for National Minorities; the Government Council for Roma Minority Affairs; the Government Council for Gender Equality; the Government Council for Anti-corruption Coordination; and the Interdepartmental Coordination Group for Combating Human Trafficking.

A major task for the Czech Republic is the integration of the Roma minority, combating racism and extremism.

2 Relationship of the Czech Republic with the International Human Rights System in General

From the perspective of the Czech legal system, four different levels of human rights protection are relevant: the universal level, the regional level, the level of European Union (EU) law and the constitutional level.

As for the relationship of the Czech Republic with universal mechanisms, the UN plays the major role. The Czech Republic was elected member of the UN Human Rights Council three times: for the 2006–2007 term, for the years 2011–2014 and 2019–2021. Recently, the Czech Republic presented its candidature for the period 2025–2027. The Czech Republic also actively participates in the Universal Periodic Review (UPR). Its UPR was held in April 2008, October 2012 and November 2017. In addition to its regular national reports, the Czech government submitted a mid-term report in 2015.

On 30 June 1993 the Czech Republic became a member of the Council of Europe. Besides the European Convention on Human Rights (ECHR) the country has ratified a number of crucial human rights documents[14] and accepts regular monitoring exercised by conventional supervisory mechanisms, such

---

14   The list of treaties of the Council of Europe ratified by the Czech Republic is available on the webpage of the Council of Europe, Treaty Office <https://www.coe.int/en/web/conventions/search-on-states> accessed 30 September 2021.

as the European Committee for the Prevention of Torture and the European Committee against Racism and Intolerance.[15] In the late 1990s Europeanisation of the legal order became a major topic for the Czech Republic, as the country was preparing for EU accession. In line with the so-called Copenhagen Criteria adopted by the European Council in 1993, the Czech Republic as a candidate country had to prove compliance with democratic and human rights standards. The European Commission in its regular progress reports examined the human rights situation in the Czech Republic.[16]

In 2015, after intense discussions involving political actors and civil society representatives, the Czech government adopted a new Concept of the Czech Republic's Foreign Policy which defines human dignity, including human rights as one of three global goals.[17] The Concept was, in relation to human rights, further developed by the Human Rights and Transition Promotion Policy Concept, which was adopted also in 2015. According to the Concept Czech foreign policy is based on the assumption that achieving human dignity, while a value of and in itself, also contributes to international security. Therefore, a policy of promoting human rights and democracy is fundamental to the safeguarding of human dignity. Czech foreign policy makes explicit reference to the principles of universality and the indivisibility of human rights. The Concept states that the promotion of human rights includes sharing the Czech experience of the transition to democracy and sustainable social market economy with transition countries and societies interested in this experience. Indeed, the promotion of democracy, human rights and transition represents one of the Czech Republic's foreign policy priorities. Development cooperation shall contribute to the pursuit of the objective of human dignity in part by incorporating cross-cutting principles into its activities, such as good governance, environmental and climate friendliness, and respect for human rights.

The Concept further deals with multilateral activity in the field of human rights protection, within the frame of the UNHRC and other UN bodies, the CoE, the Organisation for Security and Co-operation in Europe (OSCE) and the International Labour Organisation (ILO). Also, the promotion of human rights within the EU shall play an important role. Among the thematic priorities of

---

15 More information is available on the web page of the Council of Europe <https://www.coe.int/en/web/portal/czech-republic> accessed 30 September 2021.

16 See eg Regular Report from the Commission on Czech Republic's progress towards accession 2002, SEC (2002) 1402 final, 9 October 2002.

17 The document is accessible at the website of the Czech Ministry of Foreign Affairs <https://www.mzv.cz/jnp/en/foreign_relations/policy_planning/concept_of_the_czech_republic_s_foreign.html> accessed 30 September 2021.

the Concept one finds the protection of vulnerable and marginalised groups and religious minorities. The Czech Republic should further raise the issue of strengthening women's place in society and within the UN. Support to civil society, participation in political and public affairs, access to information and free media are also listed among the thematic priorities.

Article 10 of the Constitution provides for the incorporation of international treaties into the legal order of the Czech Republic, including international human rights treaties. In a judgment of 2002, the Czech Constitutional Court clarified that some international human rights treaties have the rank of constitutional law, and that the constitutional status of those human rights treaties cannot be changed by any constitutional amendment.[18] The Constitutional Court is using international human rights treaties as a reference criterion for judgments on the constitutionality of laws and legal provisions.[19]

3 At a Glance: Formal Engagement of the Czech Republic with the UN Human Rights Treaty System

Refer to the chart on the next page.

4 Role and Overall Impact of Human Rights Treaties in the Czech Republic

4.1 *Role of UN Treaties*
4.1.1 Formal Acceptance

The Czech Republic has ratified eight of the nine core UN human rights treaties.[20] Six of these – the International Covenant on Civil and Political Rights (CCPR); the International Covenant on Economic, Social and Cultural Rights (CESCR); the International Convention on the Elimination of All Forms of Racial Discrimination (CERD); the Convention on the Elimination of All

---

18 Ruling of the Constitutional Court No 403/2002.
19 For more details, see P Mlsna 'Příprava, vznik a problémy spojené s euronovelou Ústavy ČR'(2013) 59(4) AUC IURIDICA 33.
20 On the motivation for ratifying the first six treaties, see Alena Kroupova and Pavel Bilek, 'Czech Republic' in Christof Heyns and Frans Viljoen (eds), *The Impact of the UN Human Rights Treaties on the Domestic Level* (Kluwer Law International 2002) 201–202.

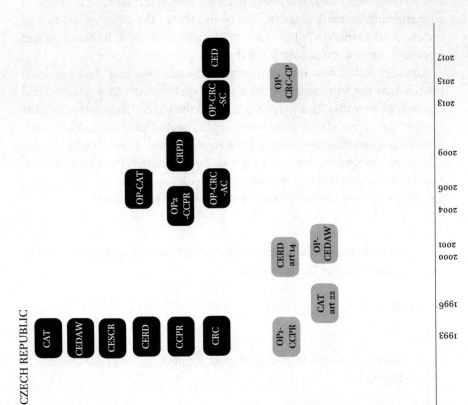

Forms of Discrimination against Women (CEDAW); the Convention against Torture and Other Cruel, Inhuman or Degrading Treatment or Punishment (CAT); the Convention on the Rights of the Child (CRC) – were already ratified during the existence of the former Czechoslovak Socialist Republic. In line with Constitutional Law No 4/1993 Coll on measures associated with the dissolution of the Czech and Slovak Federative Republic (CSFR), the Czech Republic, as of 1 January 1993, assumed all the obligations arising from international law in respect to the former CSFR, except for obligations in respect of the territory of the Slovak Republic. The Czech Republic thus succeeded to the obligations arising from the respective UN human rights treaties – a notification addressed to the UN Secretary-General, the depositary of the Conventions, was submitted in February 1993.

CERD entered into force in respect of the then Czechoslovak Socialist Republic on 4 January 1969. The ratification had been subject to a reservation in respect of article 22 CERD. The Federal Assembly of the CSFR on 16 November 1990 approved the withdrawal of this reservation.

CESCR was signed in the name of the Czechoslovak Socialist Republic on 7 October 1968. After Federal Assembly approval, the President ratified the Covenant with a comment on article 26(1). The Czech Republic has not accepted the individual complaints procedure (OP-CESCR), nor the inquiry procedure under the Optional Protocol (OP-CESCR article 11). There is an ongoing discussion on the possibility of ratification of OP-CESCR, and government officials are working on an analysis which should provide the government with various options for further steps towards ratification.

CCPR took effect in the former Czechoslovak Socialist Republic in 1976; the Czech Republic succeeded, as of 1 January 1993, into the obligations arising from the Covenant including the declaration pertaining to article 48(1) of the Covenant. The declaration pertaining to article 41 was repealed in 1991. At the same time, the Czech Republic accepted the individual complaints procedure. The First Optional Protocol (OP1-CCPR) took effect in 1991. The Czech Republic also succeeded, as of 1 January 1993, into the obligations arising for the former Czech and Slovak Federative Republic from OP1-CCPR. The Czech Republic ratified OP2-CCPR in 2004.

CEDAW was ratified in 1980 and came into force in 1982. The Czech Republic succeeded to the obligations arising from the Covenant for the former CSFR as of 1 January 1993. The Czech Republic ratified the Optional Protocol to the Convention on the Elimination of All Forms of Discrimination against Women (OP-CEDAW) in 2001 and accepted the inquiry procedure (articles 8–9 OP-CEDAW).

The former Czechoslovak Socialist Republic ratified CAT in 1988. The Czech Republic succeeded to the obligations arising from the Covenant for the former CSFR as of 1 January 1993. In 1996, it accepted the individual communications procedure under article 22.

CRC came into effect for the CSFR in 1991. With regard to the Optional Protocol to the Convention on the Rights of the Child on the Involvement of Children in Armed Conflict (OP-CRC-AC), the instrument of ratification was deposited in 2001. In 2013 the Czech Republic ratified the Optional Protocol to the Convention on the Sale of Children, Child Prostitution and Child Pornography (OP-CRC-SC) and in 2015 the Optional Protocol to the Convention on a communications procedure.

The International Convention for the Protection of All Persons from Enforced Disappearance (CED) was ratified by the Czech Republic in 2017. The individual complaints procedure (article 31) and the inquiry procedure (article 33) under the Convention have been accepted.

The instrument of ratification of the Czech Republic for CRPD was deposited in 2009. The Czech Republic has not yet ratified OP-CRPD; there is an ongoing process towards ratification.

The Czech government is not planning to ratify the International Convention on the Protection of the Rights of All Migrant Workers and Members of Their Families (CMW) as it believes that these rights are ensured by existing legislation and measures.[21]

4.1.2 General Attitude of State towards UN Treaty System

The obligations which the Czech Republic accepted under the UN treaty system are reflected at different levels. As for the level of government, advisory bodies regularly review compliance of Czech legislation and legal practice with the recommendations of the UN treaty bodies. Based on suggestions made by UN human rights bodies, the Council for Human Rights of the Czech government quite frequently proposes changes in law and concrete measures to be implemented by various bodies of the executive branch. At present, Czech authorities are preparing for an upgrade of the Office of the Defender of Rights to a national human rights institution (NHRI) as requested by various UN human rights bodies.[22]

---

21 A/HRC/WG.6/28/CZE/1 – National report submitted in accordance with para 5 of the annex to HRC Resolution 16/21 3.
22 'UN Committee Against Torture Calling on the Czech Republic to Establish the National Human Rights Institution by Increasing Powers of the Ombudsman'

At the level of legislation, when proposing new legislation the government has to evaluate compliance of all drafts with different levels of international human rights protection. The Legislative Council of the Czech government is an advisory body for the legislative work of the government. It has been established under 28a of Act of the Czech National Council No 2/1969 Sb on the establishment of ministries and other central governmental authorities of the Czech Republic, of 8 January 1969, as amended. Although human rights obligations under the European Convention and other Council of Europe conventions are more important for the practice of the Legislative Council, reference is also made to obligations under the UN treaty system.

As the UN human rights treaties that have been ratified by the Czech Republic are part of the internal legal order, Czech courts are obliged to use these as a source of law which, in cases of conflicts of law, takes precedence over national law (except the Constitution).

4.1.3 Level of Awareness

In the current system of legal education at the university level, human rights education plays an important role, a part of mandatory courses focusing on both constitutional and international legal aspects. Besides this, courses on international and European human rights protection are also taught as optional courses. This means that state officials who have graduated from law schools, in general, have quite a good understanding of the UN treaty system.

In the Czech Republic, the Judicial Academy as a central state institution is offering training for judges and prosecutors in different fields of law, including international human rights law. The major focus of the training programmes is on the ECHR and the case law of the ECtHR. The training carried out by the Justice Academy guarantees a high level of awareness among judges and state prosecutors. As for practising lawyers, the Czech Bar Association offers training and publications dealing especially with the implementation of the ECHR in the Czech Republic.

<https://www.ochrance.cz/en/news/press-releases-2019/un-committee-against-torture-calling-on-the-czech-republic-to-establish-the-national-human-rights-in/> accessed 30 September 2021: 'The State party should, as soon as possible, complete the process of consolidating the mandate of the Office of the Public Defender of Rights to enable it to act as the national human rights institution with a mandate to protect the full range of human rights and in full compliance with the Paris Principles.' – CCPR/C/CZE/CO/4 2.

The web pages of the government's Council for Human Rights offer a Czech version of the major UN human rights treaties and also of many state reports and COs that have been part of the monitoring procedure.[23]

Awareness about international human rights law is quite high among non-governmental organisations (NGOs) in the Czech Republic as representatives of those organisations are involved into the national monitoring process at the level of advisory bodies of the government as half of the government's Human Rights Council is composed of representatives of civil society. Moreover, the role of the Ombudsperson in the field of promoting human rights must not be underestimated. The publications and reports of the Ombudsperson contribute to the high level of awareness as they regularly take into account the implementation of international human rights obligations.

4.1.4 State Reporting

The Czech Republic generally meets its reporting obligations. In total, 31 reports were submitted (CERD – seven reports were submitted; CCPR – four reports; CESCR – three reports; CEDAW – six reports; CAT – five reports; CRC – four reports; CRPD – one report; and CED – one report). Some of the reports were delayed; the delays are being shortened.[24]

Given general shortcomings and deficiencies in the preparation of reports on the fulfilment of commitments and obligations arising from international treaties on human rights, the government has established the Council for Human Rights[25] to act as an advisory and coordinating body responsible for monitoring domestic compliance with international commitments in the field of human rights.[26]

The Council is currently chaired by the Prime Minister. In the past it was the Government Commissioner for Human Rights who chaired the meetings; the Government Commissioner acts as the vice-president of the Council. The post of the Commissioner for Human Rights[27] was established in 1998. The

---

23 <https://www.vlada.cz/cz/ppov/rlp/rlp-uvod-17537> accessed 30 September 2021.
24 For example, the first report to CERD was submitted with a delay of more than two years, the last one with a four-month delay; the first report to CCPR was submitted with a delay of more than six years, the third one with a one-month delay.
25 Resolution of the Government 809 of 9 December 1998.
26 The information on the Council and the Statute of the Council is available at <https://www.vlada.cz/en/ppov/rlp/government-council-for-human-rights-50632/> accessed 30 September 2021.
27 The position of the Commissioner for Human Rights was established by Resolution of the Government 579/1998 dated 9 September 1998.

Commissioner's mission is to act as an initiative and coordinating body of the government responsible for monitoring and assessing the situation and level of human rights in the Czech Republic. The government has empowered the Council to ensure the fulfilment of its commitments arising from international instruments, and to prepare and submit, in cooperation with the Ministry of Foreign Affairs, reports required by control mechanisms incorporated into such international instruments to relevant international organisations (UN, Council of Europe) unless such tasks have been entrusted to other state administration authorities.[28] In the years 2002–2004, 2007–2010 and 2014–2017 the Council was chaired by the Minister for Human Rights and Equal Opportunities who, at the same time, was a member of the government. Besides representatives of line ministries, representatives of NGOs and academia participate in the Council.

The reports to various committees are usually descriptive and detailed, follow the structure of the Conventions and are compiled by the Section for Human Rights of the Office of the Government based on documentation from central state administration bodies (such as the Ministries of Culture, Defence, Local Development, Labour and Social Affairs, Justice, Education, Youth and Sports, Interior, Foreign Affairs, Health, Agriculture, Environment, the Czech Statistical Office, the Council for Radio and Television Broadcasting). Additional documentation is usually provided by the Ombudsperson, Supreme Courts, members of the government advisory bodies (such as the Government Board for People with Disabilities, the Council for National Minorities), academic institutions and other NGOs cooperating with the Government Commissioner for Human Rights.

The delegation of the Czech Republic presenting the reports in Geneva is mostly headed by a representative at the level of Director and includes representatives of government Ministries (Education; Interior; Labour and Social Affairs, Health, Justice, and so forth). All periodic reports, follow-up and other information for the Committees, their COs and related information are published on the web page of the government in the section of the Government Council for Human Rights (www.vlada.cz). All the documents are available in Czech. Numerous, usually thematic, reports are submitted by civil society.

---

28   Initial Report of the Czech Republic on the Implementation of CCPR for the Period 1993–1999, CCPR/CZE/2000/1.

There were no reports of reprisals against human rights defenders engaging in the reporting process.

4.1.5 Domestic Implementation Mechanism

As stated above, the government has empowered the Council for Human Rights to ensure the fulfilment of its commitments arising from international instruments, unless such tasks have been entrusted to other state administration authorities. The domestic mechanism for implementation of COs is the same as for the preparation of reports. The Secretariat of the Council for Human Rights coordinates the process. The respective ministries (such as the Ministry of Education; Interior; Labour and Social Affairs) are involved, depending on the subject matter of the COs.

4.1.6 Treaty Body Membership

So far, the Czech Republic has had only one member on a treaty body. This was Ms Margerita Vysokajová (from the Charles University in Prague; an expert in labour and social security law) who was a member of the CESCR Cttee and whose term expired in 1996. There is no open national process for nomination of members to the treaty bodies. The impact on the role of the treaty on the domestic level in connection with the treaty body membership has not been registered. The transfer of knowledge and experience was ensured.

4.2 *Overview of Impact*

4.2.1 Involuntary Sterilisations

Several Committees[29] made the recommendation to consider extending or abolishing the statute of limitation with regard to past cases of involuntary (or 'forced') sterilisations and to establish an effective out-of-court compensation mechanism for victims of involuntary sterilisation. In 2016 the Czech Republic also received a communication[30] in the case of *Dzurková & Others v the Czech Republic* (No 102/2016) which related to the issue of involuntary sterilisation.

The main measure taken to prevent involuntary sterilisations for the future was the adoption of an Act on specific healthcare services, which came into

---

[29] CAT (CAT/C/CZE/CO/6 paras 28–29), CERD (CERD/C/CZE/CO/12–13 paras 19–20), CCPR (CCPR/C/CZE/CO/4 paras 22–23).

[30] In a decision adopted by the Committee in July 2019, it was considered that the authors had not exhausted the available domestic remedies and that the communication is inadmissible under art 4(1) of OP1-CCPR.

effect in 2012 and which reinforced the rights of the patient. At the beginning of 2012 the Government Council for Human Rights adopted a proposal which recommended to the government to compensate women who had been sterilised in violation of the law.[31] The Minister for Human Rights prepared a draft compensation mechanism. However, in 2015 the Government decided not to establish an *ex gratia* compensation mechanism. The government is engaged in other methods to redress the harm caused by unlawful sterilisation than pecuniary compensation.

4.2.2 Restitutions

Case law regarding the problem of restitution in the Czech Republic has shown that in cases of conflicts between UN treaty bodies and national authorities the interpretation provided by the Czech Constitutional Court will prevail.[32] The restitution of property to its original owners was conceived as a project of compensating property confiscations and nationalisation programmes carried out by the Communist Czechoslovak government. Therefore, in principle restitution may be understood as compensation for former human rights violations. The major Restitution Law, namely, the Law on Extrajudicial Rehabilitation, which became effective in April 1991, provided that compensable acts of injustice occurred between February 1948 and January 1990. Thus, the Law does not apply, for instance, to property of Sudeten Germans and ethnic Hungarians that was nationalised between 1945 and 1948 due to their former collaboration with the Nazis. The Restitution Law further stipulated that the claimant needed to be a physical person having his citizenship and place of permanent residence in the Czech and Slovak Federal Republic. Thus, the Law precluded foreign nationals or citizens permanently residing abroad from submitting restitution claims. A number of those whose restitution claims had been rejected by the Czech authorities alleged that they had been discriminated against in violation of article 26 CCPR. The Human Rights Committee (HRCttee) found that whereas communications questioning the temporal scope of restitution (post-February 1948) were manifestly ill-founded, that the citizenship requirement was discriminatory and the Committee called upon the Czech Republic to change the Restitution Law.[33]

---

31 CCPR/C/CZE/Q/3/Add.1 11.
32 Ruling of the Constitutional Court sp. zn. Pl.ÚS 33/96 ze dne 4. 6. 1997.
33 Communication 516/1992 (Šimůnek), Communication 586/1994 (Adam).

However, the Czech Constitutional Court in 1997 did not adopt the Committee's interpretation of article 26 CCPR and decided that the citizenship requirement was in line with the international obligations of the Czech Republic as according to the Czech constitutional protection of fundamental rights, some specific rights may be reserved for citizens.[34]

4.2.3 Impact on and through Independent State Institutions

The main independent institution for the protection and promotion of human rights is the Ombudsperson/Public Defender of Rights, who fulfils the majority of the Paris Principles within his or her work. The authority of the Ombudsperson is regulated by a special law.[35] His or her main goal is to check that the public administration works in accordance with the principles of good governance. The Ombudsperson cannot directly interfere with the actions of the administrative bodies or annul or change their decisions and does not have a quasi-judicial authority. However, he or she can perform independent investigations and give recommendations to rectify the mistakes and shortcomings. The authorities have an obligation to cooperate with the Ombudsperson, to fulfil his or her recommendations and to inform them about their correcting measures.

In the activities within his or her legal authority the Ombudsperson also focuses on economic, social and cultural rights. Within the supervision of the state administration he or she primarily focuses on administrative proceedings related to access to economic, social and cultural rights, namely, policies of employment; inspection of working conditions; social security and welfare; social and legal protection of children; investigation of complaints within health care; provision of education; and so forth, where he or she oversees that these proceedings are carried out in compliance with the law and the principles of good governance and that they contribute as much as possible to the fulfilment of the rights of the affected persons.[36] Since 1 December 2009 the Ombudsperson performs the role of the so-called equality body as defined by the Anti-Discrimination Act. In January 2018 the Ombudsperson became the independent monitoring body under CRPD that systematically monitors the rights of persons with disabilities.

---

34 Ruling of the Constitutional Court sp. zn. Pl.ÚS 33/96 ze dne 4. 6. 1997.
35 Act 349/1999 Coll. of 8 December 1999 on the Public Defender of Rights.
36 E/C.12/CZE/Q/2/Add.1 4.

5   The Impact of the Different UN Human Rights Treaties on the
       Domestic Level in the Czech Republic

5.1   *International Convention on the Elimination of All Forms of Racial
       Discrimination*

5.1.1   Incorporation and Reliance by Legislature and Executive

In line with Constitutional Law No 4/1993 Coll on measures associated with the dissolution of the CSFR, the Czech Republic, as of 1 January 1993, assumed all the obligations arising from international law in respect to the former CSFR, except for obligations in respect of the territory of the Slovak Republic. Since ratification had been subjected to a reservation in respect of article 22 CERD, the Federal Assembly of the CSFR on 16 November 1990 approved the withdrawal of this reservation. After the Czech Republic had informed the UN Secretary-General that, as a successor state to CSFR, it intended to remain bound among others by CERD, the Secretary-General notified the succession of the Czech Republic to CERD with effect from 1 January 1993.

The treaty was incorporated into domestic law by virtue of article 10 of the Czech Constitution which stipulated that 'ratified and promulgated conventions concerning human rights and fundamental freedoms which are binding on the Czech Republic are directly applicable and superior to law'. Thus, if a provision of Czech legislation was in conflict with the Convention, the latter took precedence.

The situation of the Czech Republic is specific insofar as the country was ethnically and culturally more homogenous than its neighbours in the eastern European region. State policy towards ethnic minorities is based upon a basic distinction between two groups of minorities. Whereas the situation of traditional national minorities, such as the Polish, Slovak and German minorities, from the beginning was considered rather satisfactory, the situation of the Roma minority was viewed as problematic from the perspective of social integration as most members of the Roma minority lacked education and vocational skills. Basically, the Czech Republic intended to avoid the paternalistic approach towards the Roma minority which had been typical for the Communist regime in Czechoslovakia.[37]

A number of political programmes and an institutional framework for the integration of Roma were created in the 1990s. For example, the Ministry of the Interior in 1997 instructed every town and district authority to create a post of

---

37   On the history of Roma integration in Czechoslovakia, see L Fonádová, *Nenechali se vyloučit: sociální vzestupy Romů v české společnosti (kvalitativní studie)* (Brno: Masarykova univerzita 2014) 22–25.

a 'Roma assistant and adviser' to monitor the situation of the Roma minority and to mediate between the municipalities and the Roma community with a special view to Roma interests.[38] The Ministry of Labour and Social Affairs introduced job promotion measures for Roma and the Ministry of Trade and Industry initiated a programme of financial subsidies for employers hiring Roma. Governmental authorities widened the network of preschool classes for Roma children to overcome their language and socio-cultural handicap and to offer them better employment opportunities in the future. Also in 1997, the Czech government created an inter-ministerial Commission for Roma Community Affairs as a consultative and coordinating body that involves Roma in decision making.[39] The inter-ministerial commission was later renamed the Government Council for Roma Community Affairs. Issues of ethnic discrimination are also dealt with by the Government Council for National Minorities which was established in accordance with article 6(3) of Act 273/2001 Coll, on the Rights of the Members of the National Minorities.

In the 1990s the Czech Criminal Code was amended in order to introduce subsections into a number of provisions on homicide, bodily harm and extortion that make racial motivation for such acts an aggravating circumstance.[40] Moreover, the penalties for racially-motivated crimes were increased. Public prosecutors and investigators were instructed to ensure prompt judicial action in cases of racially-motivated offences.

With regard to political documents that deal with the issue of Roma integration, it has to be noted that there is little reference to international treaties in general and the specifically CERD. The current governmental strategy for Roma integration until 2020, which was adopted in 2015, contains only two short footnotes pointing at CERD: first in the context of equal access to employment and, second, with regard to the prohibition of racial discrimination.

Roma inclusion is being supported by both national and EU funds. Therefore, the European Commission regularly monitors progress in Roma inclusion. According to the European Commission, the Czech Republic should allocate at least 20 per cent of its total European social fund to fighting social exclusion and poverty.[41] Following the judgment of the ECtHR in the case of *DH & Others*

---

38   CERD – Czech Republic – CERD/C/SR.1254 (1998) paras 12 and 13.
39   The Commission was established through the Resolution of the Government of the Czech Republic of 17 September 1997 No 581.
40   Eg § 219 para 2, § 221 para 2 and § 222 para 2 of the Penal Code (Law No 140/1961). Law No 140/1996 was replaced by a new Penal Code in 2009 (Law No 40/2009) which contains similar provisions (eg § 140 para 2).
41   European Commission, The European Union and Roma – Factsheet Czech Republic (2014) <https://commission.europa.eu/strategy-and-policy/policies/justice-and-fundamental-rights/combatting-discrimination/roma-eu/roma-equality-inclusion-and-participation-eu-country/czech-republic_en> accessed 8 September 2023.

v the Czech Republic,[42] the European Commission has called for further legislative efforts in the field of special needs education programmes. The judgment defines standards for equal access of socially-disadvantaged children to Czech education facilities.

5.1.2   Reliance by Judiciary

Czech courts very rarely rely on CERD. In a constitutional complaint of 2013, the complainant argued that his placement in a so-called special school, which at the time was established for children with intellectual disabilities under the legislation, was unconstitutional. The placement took place in 1985. The complainant claimed that he had been placed in a special school because of his Roma origin and that the authorities had discriminated against him on grounds of ethnic origin. According to the complainant, the education deficit was limiting him in the labour market. He therefore demanded apologies by the Czech state and compensation for non-material damage of CZK 500 000. In this case, the Constitutional Court admitted that, for the period since 1985, the applicant in principle could base his claim on CERD. However, the Constitutional Court concluded that as the provisions relating to the right to education were not self-executing, their direct application was precluded.[43]

In 2012 the same case was dealt with by the Highest Court which also addressed the issue of the self-executing nature of CERD provisions.[44] The Highest Court found that articles 5 and 7 CERD cannot be understood as self-executing, since the Convention itself does not qualify as self-executing, and it could be inferred from the circumstances that the CSFR intended to establish such national applicability at the time of accession to this Convention. According to the Highest Court, these standards were not sufficiently specific and unambiguous to directly create rights and obligations for individuals, since they did not impose obligations on the judiciary but only legislative powers to translate the individual articles into national law. The Highest Court concluded that although CERD was binding on the Czech Republic, due to the non-self-executing nature of its provisions on the right to education, individuals cannot claim their rights by simply referring to this Convention.

---

[42]   The case deals with the discrimination of Roma children in the education system of the Czech Republic. Whereas the Chamber of the European Court did not find a violation in the case, the Grand Chamber found that because of their ethnic origin Roma children did not have equal access to education.
[43]   III.ÚS 1136/13 ze dne 12. 8. 2015.
[44]   30 Cdo 4277/2010.

5.1.3 Impact on and through Non-state Actors

In the period from 2015 to 2019 we do not find references to CERD in the professional journals of the Czech Notarial Chamber, the Czech Executive Chamber and the Czech Bar Association. More often CERD is referred to in the statements and publications of NGOs which focus on issues of non-discrimination.[45] Special focus is put, for instance, on the education of Roma children, the collection of ethnic data and hate crimes. In those publications the issue of racial discrimination is quite often linked to the problem of gender discrimination.[46] As an academic teacher, I may confirm that racial discrimination is a relatively popular subject among students preparing a diploma thesis or doctoral thesis at Czech universities.

5.1.4 Impact of State Reporting

Since the 1990s the Committee in its COs has focused on issues related to the situation of the Roma minority in the Czech Republic. Already in its COs of 1998 the Committee found that there was discrimination against Roma in areas such as housing, transport and employment.[47] The 1998 COs also mentioned 'the marginalization of the Roma community in the field of education'. A disproportionately large number of Roma children were placed in special schools, leading to '*de facto* racial segregation'.[48] So, quite logically, the Committee in 1998 recommended the adoption of legal provisions aimed at safeguarding the enjoyment on a non-discriminatory basis of the economic, of social and cultural rights listed in CERD, notably, the rights to work, housing, education, and access to services and places open to the general public. Among other issues, the Committee noted that the Czech Republic should consider the possibility of a declaration under article 14 CERD.

In its COs of 2001 the Committee pointed at progress concerning the establishment of new advisory bodies on matters relevant to combating racism and intolerance, in particular the government's Commissioner for Human Rights and the Council for Human Rights.[49] However, the Committee also expressed its concern about situations of *de facto* segregation in the areas of housing and education of the Roma population and about the continuing lack of effective

---

45 See eg the regular reports of the non-governmental organisations Liga lidských práv. In iustitia and Sdružení pro migraci a integraci.
46 Jachanová Doležalová, Alexandra and others, *Prosazování genderové rovnosti: vybraná témata* (Praha: Česká ženská lobby 2009) 4–9.
47 CERD/C/304/Add.4 para 12.
48 ibid para 13.
49 CERD/C/304/Add.109 para 4.

anti-discrimination legislation. Therefore, the Committee again recommended the adoption of legislative reform.

In 2000 the Czech Republic submitted a declaration under article 14 CERD recognising the competence of the Committee to receive and consider individual communications under CERD. The Czech Republic also accepted the amendment of article 8(6) of CERD concerning the responsibility for expenses of members of the Committee during the performance of their duties. Despite certain positive steps adopted with a view to improving the situation of the Roma and other marginalised groups, including refugees, the Committee, in its COs of 2004, still noted many shortcomings in the fields of racially-motivated violence and discrimination.[50] The Committee found that negative attitudes towards minorities and refugees persisted among public officials, in the media and among the general public and that the judiciary, unlike the police, was not the object of sensitisation and educational activities.

In its COs of 2007, the Committee noted some positive legislative changes related to the new Employment Act of 2004, which prohibits direct and indirect discrimination in the enjoyment of the right to work, in particular on the grounds of race or ethnic origin, nationality, citizenship, descent, language and religion or belief, and to the new Education Act of 2004, which stipulates that basic education will be provided to all regardless of citizenship and legality of residence.[51] However, the problem of Roma discrimination remained urgent. In this respect the Committee for the first time pointed to the issue of coerced sterilisation to which a large proportion of Roma women were subjected before and after 1991. The inquiries undertaken by the Public Defender of Rights on this matter were found insufficient and not sufficiently prompt.[52]

A number of legislative measures were adopted by the Czech Republic in 2008 and 2009, in particular Act 198/2009 on equal treatment and on legal means of protection against discrimination (Anti-Discrimination Act), the 2009 amendment of section 133a of the Rules of Civil Procedure reversing the burden of proof in cases of racial discrimination and the 2008 amendment of the Penal Code, establishing racial motive as an aggravating circumstance in a number of crimes. The enactment of these legislative measures was in line with former recommendations of the Committee. However, it seems that the major reason for the adoption of the new Anti-Discrimination Act, which was

---

50 CERD/C/63/CO/4 paras 9 and 15.
51 CERD/C/CZE/CO/7 para 5.
52 ibid para 14.

disputed in Czech society, was compliance with EU norms and the threat of EU sanctions against the Czech Republic in case of non-compliance.[53]

With regard to the follow-up to the COs of 2011 two major issues have been identified. First, the issue of Roma discrimination in the field of education was again raised, with a special view to a judgment of the ECtHR of 2007, which found a violation of European non-discrimination standards within the Czech system of primary education. The Committee recommended that the state party take concrete steps to ensure effective desegregation of Romani children. In this respect, the Czech Republic stated that by means of a new national action plan and legislative changes this problem would be tackled.[54] Second, the Committee remained concerned about the issue of sterilisation of Romani women without their free and informed consent. Although Czech authorities in 2009 had expressed their regret and a decision of the Supreme Court of June 2011 had waived the statute of limitations, many obstacles remained in place obstructing full reparation and compensation of victims. In this respect, the Czech Republic promised to reconsider the issue of the three-year statutory limitation period and *ex gratia* compensation which would apply to women whose sterilisation prior to 1991 had been motivated by the social care, and also to women for whom the sterilisation was the responsibility of the medical facility where the procedure was performed, and who had no possibility of demanding compensation via legal proceedings, due to the lapse of the statutory limitation period.[55]

Both issues remained on the list for the 2017 follow-up. Following up on the Committee's recommendation concerning the introduction of inclusive education, the Czech Republic provided extensive information about a new system of educating pupils with special educational needs which took effect in 2016.[56] The new system is based on the principle of including these pupils in the mainstream education system. The Act removed the categorisation of children, pupils and students according to their health or social status. As for the issue of compensation damages to illegally-sterilised persons, the Czech government had discussed possible legislative measures. However, the government in 2015 decided not to adopt any such measures after having carefully considered the arguments ensuing from the Czech legal order, the jurisprudence of the Czech courts, including the Constitutional Court, the viewpoints

---

53 In 2008 the European Commission issued a reasoned opinion arguing that the Czech Republic was not acting in compliance with its obligations under EU law.
54 CERD/C/CZE/CO/8–9 para 12.
55 ibid 19.
56 CERD/C/CZE/CO/10–11/Add.1 paras 3–11.

of the Public Defender of Rights, the recommendations of international bodies protecting human rights, and the jurisprudence of the ECtHR. Due to the difficulty of evaluating the individual cases, which often took place a long time ago and the problems of possibly missing medical documentation or other supporting materials, the illegally-sterilised persons could face long and complicated procedures, which might not result in compensation being granted.[57]

5.1.5   Impact of Individual Communications

Although the Czech Republic already in 2000 recognised the competence of the Committee to receive and consider individual communications, so far no individual complaints have been submitted.

5.1.6   Impact of Other Measures

In 1998 the Committee issued Decision 2(52)[58] in which, in line with article 9(1) of CERD, it requested the government of the Czech Republic to provide it with information on the situation in certain municipalities in which measures were allegedly contemplated for the physical segregation of some residential units housing Roma families. The Czech Republic in 1999 provided information on the situation in Maticni Street, Nestemice, where the local authorities intended to prevent the tenants of two residential blocks from direct access to Maticni Street. As the government viewed this intention as a possible interference in human rights, namely, human dignity, equality before the law without distinction as to social and ethnic origin or property, it promised to prevent the erection of a wall separating the tenants of the residential units (90 per cent of whom were Roma).

The President of the Republic and the Government Representative for Human Rights visited the municipality in order to hold talks with members of the local self-government and the Romas. Civic associations established a dialogue with the city hall and removed the garbage which was one of the causes that made the non-Roma residents in Maticni Street call for the erection of a wall. In October 1999 the government expressed its concern over the construction of the fence and also the Chamber of Deputies discussed the case at its proximate session following the parliamentary holiday.

Nevertheless, the Neštěmice municipality, based on a decision of September 1999, had the fence erected in October 1999. On the same day the Chamber of Deputies decided, by 100 votes to 58 (with 28 absentees and 14 abstentions)

---

57   ibid 12–13.
58   CERD Decision 2 (53) on the Czech Republic (11 August 1998).

to repeal the decision on the fence construction. The government, thereupon, authorised its Deputy Interior Minister to start negotiations with the local authorities on the removal of the fence in Matiční Street which had become a symbol of a division in society. The Minister of Finance provided the municipality with 10 million crowns. Approximately one-third of the government subsidy was used in order to buy three single-family homes located in the immediate vicinity of the residential units. So, the home owners moved away. The municipal police established a local station in one of the former single-family homes. However, officers were not permanently present there. An NGO (People in Need) opened a community centre in another of the former single-family homes and started to provide programmes for local Romani children. The rest of the subsidy was spent on the reconstruction of the residential units and for various other social welfare projects. On 24 November 1999 the fence was removed.[59]

Although gaps persisted also after the removal of the fence, the action taken by the Committee, supported by other international human rights actors, has had a clear impact on the solution of the case.

5.1.7 Brief Conclusion

The issue of racial discrimination is very topical in the Czech Republic with regard to the unsatisfactory situation of the Roma minority. Thus far the Committee has been focusing almost exclusively on this minority. The status of other national and social minorities seems to be less problematic in light of CERD. Although in its regular reports the Czech Republic has shown a significant degree of self-criticism and openness to dialogue with the Committee and international organisations, the protracted problem of racial discrimination has many complex causes.

A number of concrete legislative and institutional measures that have been adopted by the Czech Republic as a consequence of its obligations under CERD and EU anti-discrimination law. Concrete legal acts concern a new body of anti-discrimination law and amendments concerning the laws on education and employment and the Criminal Code. The government has installed a set of

---

[59] For more details on the case of Matiční street, see the 1999 Report of the State of Human Rights in the Czech Republic which the Government Commissioner for Human Rights and Chairman of the Council for Human Rights of the government of the Czech Republic submitted to the government under Government Resolution 278 of 7 April 1999. The document is available at the website of the Czech government <https://www.vlada.cz/assets/ppov/rlp/dokumenty/zpravy-lidska-prava-cr/zprava1999_en.pdf> accessed 23 April 2022.

advisory bodies monitoring compliance with international treaties including CERD. The role of the Public Defender of Rights is also very important.

From a pragmatic perspective it seems that the obligations under CERD and the recommendations issued by the Committee are more effectively implemented when they are supported by political pressure from EU institutions, especially the European Commission. Although the Czech Anti-Discrimination Act indeed is reflecting crucial provisions of CERD, its adoption, in the first place, was motivated by the Czech Republic's obligation to implement EU directives into national law. As far as racial discrimination in the field of education is concerned, a prominent judgment of the ECtHR, which is legally binding on the Czech Republic, has more concretely influenced both political debate and the procedure of legislation.

5.2 International Covenant on Civil and Political Rights

CCPR took effect in the former Czechoslovak Socialist Republic on 23 March 1976. As of 1 January 1993, the Czech Republic succeeded to the obligations arising from the Covenant for the former Czech and Slovak Federative Republic, including the declaration pertaining to article 48(1) of the Covenant. The declaration pertaining to article 41 was repealed as of 12 March 1991. Also in 1993, the Czech Republic accepted the individual complaints procedure. A Czech translation of the Covenant exists.[60]

5.2.1 Incorporation and Reliance by Legislature and Executive

Like any other international treaty, the Covenant forms part of the Czech legal order, while also taking precedence over legislative acts.[61] Most of the civil and political freedoms listed in the Covenant are also reflected in the Charter of Fundamental Rights and Basic Freedoms of 1991 which forms an integral part of the Czech constitutional order (there is no direct citation of the Covenant). The Charter also introduces into the law the rights laid down in the CESCR. Commitments and obligations arising from the Covenant are binding upon the Czech Republic even above the framework of what the Charter contains. The fundamental rights and liberties laid down in the Charter require a multitude of legal provisions to be implemented.

Some rights protected in the Covenant were affected by the Czech Republic's accession to the EU on 1 May 2004. This concerns mainly rights of which the holders under the Covenant can only be nationals of the treaty state. Member

---

[60] The Covenant was promulgated in a communication of the Ministry of Foreign Affairs under No 120/1976 of Coll.
[61] Art 10 of the Constitution.

states of the EU, or community law, also acknowledge these rights for the nationals of other member states. They concern, for example, the right to vote and to be elected to the European Parliament, the right to vote and to be elected to representative bodies at the local level and the right of access to a public function.[62]

More than two decades after the 1989 revolution, the complex transformation in the fields of criminal and private law was completed by the adoption of new criminal and civil codes. In 2010 the new Criminal Code[63] entered into force, which focuses primarily on the protection of individual human rights such as the right to life, health, liberty and dignity. Criminal prosecution is regarded as the *ultima ratio*. Another fundamental change was the recodification of the rules of private law in the new Civil Code,[64] as well as the Act on Business Corporations[65] and the Act on Private International Law.[66] The main objectives of the recodification were to develop codices based on respect for European legal thought and to break with the ideology embodied in pre-1989 Communist law.[67] An issue of great importance for the protection of human rights was the adoption of the Anti-Discrimination Act in 2009,[68] designed to strengthen the protection against discrimination in all major areas of social life.

The responsibility for the implementation of the views of the Human Rights Committee in 2003 was assumed by the Ministry of Justice. The procedure was set by a resolution of the government.[69] The Ministry requests the relevant authorities to submit information about measures they had taken (or intend to take) or had suggested (or intend to suggest) in order to implement the views of the Committee with regard to non-compliance with the Covenant by the Czech Republic. The Minister of Justice, in cooperation with relevant authorities, recommends measures to be adopted by the government in order to implement the conclusions contained in the views of the Committee. The government may submit a draft law to the Chamber of Deputies in order to remedy the incompatibility of the legislation with the Covenant.[70] Government

---

62   Second periodic reports of state parties, CCPR/C/CZE/2.
63   Act 40/2009 Coll Criminal Code.
64   Act 89/2012 Coll Civil Code.
65   Act 90/2012 Coll, the Act on Business Corporations.
66   Act 91/2012 Coll, the Act on Private International Law.
67   Such as Constitutional Law No 100/1960 Coll – the Constitution of the Czechoslovak Socialist Republic.
68   Act 198/2009 Coll, on equal treatment and on legal means of protection against discrimination and amending certain laws.
69   Resolution of the Government of the Czech Republic 527 dated 22 May 2002.
70   Comments by the government of the Czech Republic, Follow-up state party report, CPR/CO/72/CZE/Add.1, 27 February 2003.

officials of respective ministries are directly involved in the process of implementation. Moreover, the Ministry of Justice presents its regular reports (in Czech) to the government, and other ministers of the government are thus informed. The information is made public[71] and therefore is easily accessible to those interested in the topic.

The government has adopted comprehensive strategies on the promotion of human rights of various vulnerable groups, such as on the Right to Childhood; the National Action Plan Promoting Positive Ageing; the National Action Plan for the Prevention of Domestic Violence; the National Action Plan for Equal Opportunities for Persons with Disabilities; the Strategy of Roma Integration; and the Strategy for Combating Social Exclusion.[72] These strategies relate directly to the rights contained in the Covenant. However, explicit references to concrete provisions of the Covenant are very rarely found (for instance, in the Strategy of Roma Integration until 2020). The comprehensive strategies contain provisions on resource allocation, both from national resources as well as EU funds.

The protection of human rights and the fulfilment of commitments and obligations arising from the Covenant also fall into the purview of committees of both chambers of Parliament of the Czech Republic, namely, the Petition Committee of the House of Deputies of Parliament, which comprises two sub-committees, one for the application of the Charter of Fundamental Rights and Liberties, the other dealing with nationalities; and the Human Rights, Science, Education and Culture Committee of the Senate of Parliament. Members of Parliament may present interpellations[73] to the government ministers to obtain information about issues relating to human rights treaties.

---

[71] Reports are available in Czech on the web page of the Ministry of Justice and are regularly submitted to the government of the Czech Republic <https://www.justice.cz/web/msp/zpravy-o-cinnosti> accessed 30 September 2021.

[72] Opening Statement by the Head of the Delegation of the Czech Republic, Ms Andrea Baršová, Head of the Human Rights Department-Office of the Government of the Czech Republic, Presentation of the third periodic report of the Czech Republic, Human Rights Committee, 108th Session (16 and 17 July 2013).

[73] See eg the interpellation by Member of Parliament of the Czech Republic Ms Olga Richterová dated 1 August 2019, relating to the policy of the government towards China (Interpelace poslankyně Olgy Richterové na předsedu vlády Andreje Babiše ve věci vládní politiky vůči Číně v souvislosti se zprávami o soustavném porušování lidských práv včetně obchodu s nezákonně odebíranými lidskými orgány).

5.2.2 Reliance by Judiciary

According to article 4 of the Constitution, fundamental rights and freedoms are protected by the judicial power. A particularly important role in the protection of human rights belongs to the Constitutional Court. Courts are responsible for offering protection in the manner stipulated by law. In decision making, judges are bound both by legislative acts and by international treaties.[74] References to the provisions of the Covenant can be found in the decisions of the Supreme Court of the Czech Republic (no reference to treaty body interpretations was found) and administrative courts. The Constitutional Court often refers[75] to the provisions of the Covenant and also uses references to the General Comments to the Covenant (for instance, in the findings Pl.ÚS 8/16 from 19 December 2017 and IV.ÚS 3526/16 from 21 March 2017 where the General Comment was followed) and to the jurisprudence of the Committee (for instance Pl. ÚS 83/06 from 12 March 2008 and finding PL.ÚS 17/10 from 28 June 2011 where the argumentation was followed; in its resolution III.ÚS 93/11 from 11 September 2012 in the case on discrimination on the

---

74 Art 95 para 1 of the Constitution of the Czech Republic.
75 In our research, we studied 226 decisions of the Constitutional Court. In 32 cases, the Court used references to the Covenant in its argumentation to annul either a decision of a court (19 cases) or of a public prosecutor's office or police (9 cases – Finding II. ÚS 860/10 dated 2 September 2010, violation of art 17 of CCPR: questioned inspection of premises; Finding II.ÚS 1414/07 dated 15 July 2010 – house inspection, violation of art 17; Finding II.ÚS 79/07 dated 19 June 2007, violation of art 14 of CCPR, violation of prohibition of forced self-accusation, Finding I. ÚS 636/05 dated 21 August 2006, violation of art 14 of CCPR, forced self-accusation, Finding II. ÚS 642/04 dated 8 March 2006, forced self-accusation, violation of art 14 of CCPR, Finding I.ÚS 671/05 dated 22 February 2006, violation of art 14 of CCPR, forced self-accusation; Finding II.ÚS 89/04 dated 2 February 2006, imposition of an order fine, Finding II.ÚS 552/05 dated 12 January 2006, violation of art 14 of CCPR, forced self-accusation; Finding III.ÚS 561/04 dated 10 March 2005, violation of art 14 of CCPR, forced self-accusation). In six cases (Finding PL.ÚS 18/15 dated 28 June 2016 – a provision of the law on income tax annulled, violation of art 26 of CCPR (cited together with the Charter of Fundamental Rights and Freedoms of the Czech Republic), equality and non-discrimination; Finding PL. ÚS 1/12 dated 27 November 2012, compliance with the prohibition of forced labour, art 8 of CCPR; Finding Pl. ÚS 47/04 dated 8 March 2005, violation of art 26 of CCPR, prohibition of non-discrimination, law on public auctions; Finding Pl. ÚS 28/98 dated 23 November 1999, violation of art 14 of CCPR; Finding Pl. ÚS 2/97 dated 2 July 1997, violation of art 9 of CCPR, law on the police of the Czech Republic; Finding Pl. ÚS 30/95 dated 10 January 1996, violation of art 14 of CCPR, Civil Procedure Code); references were made in the findings of the Constitutional Court which annulled a provision of a law (law on income tax, on public auction, on the police, Civil Procedure Code). The Constitutional Court often refers to the art 14 of the Covenant (fair trial); art 26 (equality before the law and non-discrimination); art 25 (public participation); and art 9 (right to liberty and security of person).

basis of citizenship with respect to restitution of property, the Constitutional Court rejected the argumentation (extensive interpretation of article 26 of the Covenant)).

5.2.3 Impact on and through Non-state Actors

The Covenant forms part of legal education at a general level at law faculties, as well as at the level of specialised training for judges, public prosecutors and other civil servants. The rights guaranteed by the Covenant are taught along with the rights guaranteed by the Charter of Fundamental Rights and Freedoms and public international law courses at all law faculties in the Czech Republic. Additional information on this topic is also provided in the Czech Judicial Academy's training programme for judicial trainees awaiting appointment as judges, as well as for public prosecutors.[76] All civil servants are required to abide by the constitutional order, which includes the Charter of Fundamental Rights and Freedoms, as well as legislative acts and international treaties that form part of the legislation including the Covenant.[77]

Legal professionals use references to the provisions of the Covenant especially in their complaints presented to the Constitutional Court.

NGOs use references to the Covenant in their advocacy campaigns. For example, In Iustitia refers to the Covenant in its campaign on hate crime which refers also to the OSCE documents and the European Convention;[78] the Organisation for Aid to Refugees in its campaign against the V4 (Visegrad Group countries – Czech Republic, Slovakia, Poland and Hungary) policy on migration;[79] *Sdružení pro integraci a migraci* (in English, Association for Integration and Migration) in its advocacy work to support migrant women;[80] and Slovo 21 in its campaign on Roma identity/education,[81] all relied on the Covenant.

---

[76] The list of seminars organised by the Czech Judicial Academy in the area of constitutional and human rights law is available on the web page of the Judicial Academy.
[77] Third periodic reports of state parties, CCPR/C/CZE/3.
[78] Information is available at <https://in-ius.cz/wp-content/uploads/2021/04/zapomen-ute-obeti-final.pdf> accessed 15 September 2023.
[79] Information is available at <https://www.opu.cz/cs/2015/09/k-pristupu-visegradske-ctyrky/> accessed 15 September 2023.
[80] Information is available at <https://www.migrace.com/docs/140925_vysledky-vyzkumu-najemne-prace-v-domacnosti-v-cr.pdf> accessed 30 September 2021.
[81] Information is available at <http://www.slovo21.cz/images/dokumenty/publikace/KHAMORO_Kvalitni_vzdelani_pro_kazdeho_5.pdf.pdf> accessed 30 September 2021.

5.2.4 Impact of State Reporting

The reporting of the Czech Republic is thorough and descriptive.[82] It follows the structure of the Covenant article by article. Reports contain factual information and make reference to previous COs. In 2001 the Committee stated that it missed the information on the implementation of the Covenant rights in practice. When preparing the reports not only government bodies, but also the Ombudsperson, Supreme Courts, members of government advisory bodies and other NGOs cooperating with the Government Commissioner for Human Rights are consulted and are invited to submit their views and opinions, which have been used for the composition of the report. There were no reports of reprisals against human rights defenders engaging in the reporting process. Civil society submits thematic reports.[83]

The Committee had a dialogue with the delegation in July 2001, July 2007, July 2013 and October 2019. The most pertinent issues covered by the COs were the following: in 2001 – restitution of property; the lack of independent mechanisms for monitoring the practical implementation of rights; discrimination against minorities, particularly Roma; discrimination in employment; racial discrimination; representation of women in political life; trafficking of women; domestic violence; and police harassment; in 2007 – restitution of property; police misconduct particularly against Roma; involuntary/forced sterilisation; participation of women in political life; the use of enclosed restraint beds; and discrimination; in 2013 – the mandate of the Ombudsperson/Public Defender of Rights; representation of women in decision-making positions; intolerance against Roma; involuntary/forced sterilisations; and discrimination against persons with mental disabilities.

---

[82] So far, the Czech Republic presented four reports to the Committee. The initial report for the years 1993–1999 was submitted in 2000. According to the provisions of art 40 para 1 of the Covenant, the Czech Republic should have submitted the initial report by 31 December 1993 (a delay of six years and two months). The second periodic report was due in 2005. However, it was submitted in May 2006 (a delay of eight months). The third report was submitted in 2011 (a delay of one month). The fourth periodic report was due to be submitted on 26 July 2018 and was received in August 2018.

[83] Eighteen thematic reports by civil society were the subject to our study. To give a few examples and provide an idea of topics covered by the reports: two briefings of the Global Initiative to End All Corporal Punishment of Children from July 2017 and March 2013 which cover the legality of corporal punishment of children in the Czech Republic. There was one report submitted by the Conscience and Peace Tax International on the topic of conscientious objection to military service in March 2017. The Amnesty International Report from 2006 touches upon three topics: forced sterilisation of women; discrimination against Roma; and racially-motivated attacks on Roma.

All periodic reports, follow-up and other information for the Committee, its COs and related information are published on the web page of the government in the section of the Government Council for Human Rights (www.vlada.cz). All the documents are available in Czech. From the information on follow-up to the COs and replies to the list of issues it can be derived that the Czech Republic is making efforts to implement the key recommendations. It does so often through soft tools such as strategies and action plans (for instance the Roma Integration Strategy, National Action Plan for the Prevention of Domestic Violence). However, measures are mostly of a long-term character.

One of the key issues repeatedly mentioned in the COs are involuntary sterilisations. The main measure taken to prevent it in the future was the adoption of the new rules on sterilisation in the Act on specific healthcare services, which came into effect in 2012 and which reinforced the rights of the patient. Sterilisation for health reasons may only be performed on patients over the age of 18, provided they give their written consent. Sterilisation for other reasons may only be performed on patients over the age of 21 on the basis of their written request, provided there are no serious health counter-indications. At the beginning of 2012 the Government Council for Human Rights adopted a proposal which recommended to the government to compensate women who had been sterilised in violation of the law.[84] The Minister for Human Rights prepared a draft compensation mechanism which was later rejected by the government. The government is further engaged in other methods than pecuniary compensation to redress the harm caused by unlawful sterilisation. In March 2016 the Government Council for Roma Minority Affairs set up the Working Party on Unlawful Sterilisations to identify other ways of public support for unlawfully-sterilised persons than financial compensation. For example, in cooperation with the Czech Psychotherapy Society, experts have provided free psychological assistance to unlawfully-sterilised women.[85] In five cases of unlawful sterilisation the Czech courts have had to deal with pleas of statutory limitation.[86] In two cases, the Supreme Court found the plea *contra bonos mores* and in at least one case the victim received compensation.[87] In the other three cases the Czech courts upheld the statutory limitation. In two cases submitted to the ECtHR, an amicable settlement was reached, with the

---

[84] CCPR/C/CZE/Q/3/Add.1 11.
[85] CCPR/C/CZE/4 12.
[86] CCPR/C/CZE/CO/3/Add.3 para 10.
[87] This case *Červeňáková v Czech Republic* was also heard by the European Court of Human Rights (Application 26852/09). However, as the applicant failed to inform the court of the compensation awarded at national level, her application was found to be inadmissible.

state paying compensation.[88] In one case, the ECtHR has yet to decide.[89] The government is not currently preparing any other out-of-court compensation mechanisms,[90] However, an initiative in this regard was presented by a group of Czech parliamentarians in the Chamber of Deputies of the Parliament of the Czech Republic.[91]

5.2.5 Impact of Individual Communications

The Czech Republic succeeded, as of 1 January 1993, into the obligations arising for the former Czech and Slovak Federative Republic from OP1-CCPR. Fifty-six individual complaints have been lodged with the Human Rights Committee. The HRCtee found the Czech Republic in violation in 29 communications. The predominant topic of individual complaints lodged with the Committee is discrimination on the basis of citizenship with respect to restitution of property. In most of the cases of non-restitution to non-citizens of the Czech Republic the Committee declared violations of article 26 of the Covenant and that the state party is under an obligation to provide the authors with an effective remedy, including compensation, if the properties cannot be returned.[92]

---

88 *RK v Czech Republic* (Application 7883/08) and *Ferenčíková v Czech Republic* (Application 21826/10).
89 *Maděrová v Czech Republic* (Application 32812/13).
90 CCPR/C/CZE/4 11.
91 Initiative of 27 September 2019 by a group of members of parliament of the Czech Republic: H Válková, J Pastuchová, L Dražilová, P Golasowská, M Pekarová Adamová, K Schwarzenberg, M Novák, A Gajdůšková, E Matyášová.
92 *Miroslav Klain and Eva Klain v the Czech Republic* (Communication 1847/2008, views adopted on 1 November 2011); *Oldřiška (Olga) Junglingova v the Czech Republic* (Communication 1563/2007, view adopted on 24 October 2011); *Adolf Lange v the Czech Republic* (Communication 1586/2007, views adopted on 13 July 2011); *Victor Drda v the Czech Republic* (Communication 1581/2007, views adopted on 27 October 2010); *Bohuslav Zavřel v the Czech Republic* (Communication 1615/2007, views adopted on 27 October 2010); *Nancy Gschwind v the Czech Republic* (Communication 1742/2007, views adopted on 27 October 2010); *Nikolaus First Blucher von Wahlstatt v the Czech Republic* (Communication 1491/2007, views adopted on 27 October 2010); *Jaroslav and Alena Slezák v the Czech Republic* (Communication 1574/2007, views adopted on 20 July 2009); *Olga Amundson v the Czech Republic* (Communication 1508/2006, views adopted on 17 March 2009); *Jaroslav Persan v the Czech Republic* (Communication 1479/2006, views adopted on 24 March 2009); *Richard Preiss v the Czech Republic* (Communication 1497/2006, views adopted on 17 July 2008); *Ivanka Kohoutek v the Czech Republic* (Communication 1448/2006, views adopted on 17 July 2008); *Zdenek Vlček v the Czech Republic* (Communication 1485/2006, views adopted on 10 July 2008); *Josef Lněnička v the Czech Republic* (Communication 1484/2006, views adopted on 25 March 2008); *Miroslav Susser v the Czech Republic* (Communication 1488/2006, views adopted on 25 March 2008); *Zdenek and Milada Ondracka v the Czech Republic* (Communication 1533/2006, views adopted on 31 October 2007); *Peter and Eva*

The Committee reiterated that the state party should review its legislation to ensure that all persons enjoy both equality before the law and equal protection of the law. Violations of article 14(6) (miscarriage of justice) of the Covenant were examined in connection with the non-restitution to non-citizens.

The Czech Republic does not share the legal opinion of the Committee regarding the discriminatory nature of the restitution condition of citizenship and therefore it relies on the case law of the Constitutional Court, in which the Court has also referred to the relevant provisions of the Covenant. The opinions of the Committee have been, and will continue to be, implemented through hearings of individual cases by the courts as bodies empowered to protect human rights and fundamental freedoms, and the Constitutional Court as a body established to protect constitutionality.[93]

In the case *Rudolf Czernin v Czech Republic*,[94] which covered the substantive issue of retention of citizenship, the Committee declared a violation of article 14 of the Covenant (views adopted on 29 March 2005). In the case of *Mr LP v Czech Republic*,[95] covering the issue of contact with minor children, the Committee declared a violation of article 17 of the Covenant (views adopted on 25 July 2002).

The implementation of the Committee's observations is governed by the 2011 Act on the Cooperation in the Proceedings before International Courts and Other International Supervisory Bodies requiring the competent bodies to immediately take all necessary individual and general measures intended to halt and prevent any violation of the Covenant or any other international convention. The Ministry of Justice (namely, the government agent) has been

---

Gratzinger v the Czech Republic (Communication 1463/2006, views adopted on 25 October 2007); *Libuse Polackova and Joseph Polacek v the Czech Republic* (Communication 1445/2006, views adopted on 24 July 2007); *Zdeněk Kříž v the Czech Republic* (Communication 1054/2002, views adopted on 1 November 2005); *Bohumír Mařík v the Czech Republic* (Communication 945/2000, views adopted on 26 July 2005); *Alžběta Pezoldová v the Czech Republic* (Communication 757/1997, views adopted on 25 October 2002); *Eliška Fábryová v the Czech Republic* (Communication 765/1997, views adopted on 20 October 2001); *Robert Brok* (Communication 774/1997, views adopted 31 October 2001); *Karel Des Fours Walderode v the Czech Republic* (Communication 747/1997, views adopted 30 October 2001); *Miroslav Blažek, George A Hartman and George Krizek v the Czech Republic* (Communication 857/1999, views adopted on 12 July 2001); *Josef Frank Adam v the Czech Republic* (Communication 586/1994, views adopted on 23 July 1996); *Alina Simunek, Dagmar Hastings Tuzilova and Josef Prochazka v the Czech Republic* (Communication 516/1992, views adopted on 19 July 1995).

93 CCPR/C/CZE/4 2.
94 Communication 823/1998.
95 Communication 765/2000.

delegated to represent the Czech Republic in the proceedings on communications under the Optional Protocol to the Covenant and the implementation of the Committee's views, and is kept informed of implementation measures. The Committee of Experts for the Enforcement of Judgments of the ECtHR – and the opinions of other international bodies – also contribute to their implementation by discussing individual cases and recommending the adoption of implementation measures.

The government agent charged with representation of the Czech Republic in the proceedings on communications under the Optional Protocol publishes regular reports on the state of complaints against the Czech Republic before the international bodies for the protection of human rights. These are available in Czech on the webpage www.justice.cz and contain summary information on the individual complaints (including a short annotation of individual cases).[96]

5.2.6 Brief Conclusion

The Covenant forms part of the Czech legal order. In general, the Czech Republic makes efforts to cooperate with the Committee, submits its reports and provides timely responses within the follow-up procedure. The Czech courts (the Constitutional Court, the Supreme Court and administrative courts) refer to the Covenant in their decisions and NGOs in their advocacy campaigns. Almost half of the individual complaints lodged with the treaty body focus on one topic: non-restitution to non-citizens. The view of the government reflects difficult circumstances occasioned by the transition from a Communist to a democratic state. Property restitution in the Czech Republic was a complex and sensitive issue. It was undeniable that property-restitution had been very generous, the sole restriction being legal residence or citizenship. The Constitutional Court had found the citizenship requirement to be lawful. There was no legal obligation on the state to restore property. Although some might consider the restrictions discriminatory, in terms of legal residence and citizenship, they had not been introduced by the government, but by Parliament, and thus represented the popular will.[97]

5.3 *International Covenant on Economic, Social and Cultural Rights*

By notice of 22 February 1993 the Czech Republic succeeded to the obligations arising from the Covenant for the former CSFR as of 1 January 1993. The Czech Republic has accepted neither the individual complaints procedure

---

96 Reports are available at <https://www.justice.cz/web/msp/zpravy-o-cinnosti> accessed 23 April 2022.
97 CCPR/C/SR.2465 4.

(OP-CESCR) nor the inquiry procedure under OP-CESCR (article 11). The Czech government continues to examine the possibility of ratifying the Optional Protocol and analyses its national implementation.[98]

5.3.1 Incorporation and Reliance by Legislature and Executive

The Covenant forms part of the Czech legal order, while also taking precedence over legislative acts. The Charter of Fundamental Rights and Basic Freedoms of 1991 implements into the legal order the major part of rights set forth in CESCR (there is no direct citation of the Covenant). Steps taken by the Czech Republic to achieve full implementation in the economy of the rights recognised by the Covenant were directly connected to the transformation of the economy which started in 1990 and its transition to a market economy. An issue of great importance was the adoption of the Anti-Discrimination Act in 2009, designed to strengthen the protection against discrimination in all major areas of social life, such as employment, social protection, health care, housing and education.

In the field of economic and social rights, the government's main goal is the social inclusion of every person. The Social Inclusion Strategy for 2014–2020 is the general policy document for the fight against poverty and social exclusion with specific goals to reduce poverty with the help of EU structural funds. The Czech Republic supports equal opportunities for women and men by annually adopting the government's priorities and actions. The Government Council for Equal Opportunities for Women and Men, which includes representatives from the general public and academia, is closely involved in designing and monitoring these measures. The focus mainly is on the reconciliation of the working, private and family life of women and men as well as an increase in the proportion of women in decision-making positions and the elimination of the gender pay gap and domestic violence.

The basic document for the development of the education system in the Czech Republic has become, after 2001, the National Programme of Education Development in the Czech Republic, the so-called White Paper.[99] It formulates the basis and prerequisites of the development of the education system, principles of the education policy, and management and funding principles, and has also set the main strategic lines of the development of education.[100] The

---

98 E/C.12/CZE/3 4.
99 Resolution of the Czech Republic Government 113 of 7 February 2001.
100 Special emphasis is put on the development of human individuality; the strengthening of social cohesion; promotion of democracy and civic society; education towards partnership; cooperation and solidarity; increasing competitiveness of the economy; and social prosperity.

basic principles of education formulated in the National Programme are also reflected in the new Education Act.

In 2003 the government founded the Government Council for Sustainable Development as a permanent advisory, initiating and coordinating body in the area of sustainable development and strategic management.[101] The Government Council for Seniors and Population Ageing was founded in 2006.[102] The Council strives to create conditions for healthy, active and decent ageing and for equal treatment of seniors in all fields of life, for the protection of their human rights and for the development of intergenerational relations in families and in society.

5.3.2 Reliance by Judiciary

Independent courts are protecting the human rights and freedoms of individuals, including economic, social and cultural rights. The judicial body for the protection of constitutionality and domestic law is the Constitutional Court. In a conflict between international and domestic law, the Constitutional Court applies international and regional (European) treaties on human rights, including CESCR.

References to the Covenant were found in 61 decisions of the Constitutional Court. Most often, the Constitutional Court referred to article 11 of the Covenant (the right of everyone to an adequate standard of living for themselves and their family, including adequate food, clothing and housing); article 7 (the right of everyone to the enjoyment of just and favourable conditions of work); and article 12 (the right of everyone to the enjoyment of the highest attainable standard of physical and mental health).[103]

---

[101] The Government Council for Sustainable Development of the Czech Republic.
[102] Statute of the Government Council for Older Persons and Population Ageing.
[103] In one finding of the Court (Pl. 2/15), referring to art 12, a reference to the criticism of CESCR was found (issue of access of foreigners to the public health insurance). The same finding relied on three CESCR General Comments – General Comment 3 on the Nature of States Parties' Obligations; 14 on the Right to the Highest Attainable Standard of Health; and 20 on Non-Discrimination in Economic, Social and Cultural Rights. The Constitutional Court used references to the Covenant in two decisions which annulled the decision of a court (2613/17 and 615/17). The Constitutional Court annuls legal regulations or their parts that are in conflict with the constitutional order of the Czech Republic or with an international treaty. The Constitutional Court made reference to CESCR in seven decisions which annulled an act or its part (Pl. 1/12 – the Court annulled several provisions of the Act on Medical Services, Pl. 83/06 – several provisions of the Labour Code, Pl. 51/06 – several provisions of the Law on Public Non-profit Medical Institutional Facilities, Pl. 40/02 – Act on collective bargaining, Pl. 2/03 – Government regulation on rent of flats).

The Supreme Court made references to the Covenant in 30 decisions. The Supreme Court most frequently referred in general terms to the principles of democratic society respecting human rights enshrined *inter alia* in CESCR (the Charter is always quoted as well) without referring to concrete provisions of the Pact.[104] In five cases the Supreme Court relied on the Covenant when arguing that there is no right to refuse duties towards the state, including military service.[105] In four decisions the Supreme Court referred to concrete articles of the Covenant (articles 6, 7 and 8(1)(d)).[106]

The Supreme Administrative Court also cited the right to an adequate standard of living and adequate housing (article 11(1)) when assessing the legality of tax concessions for some flat transfers or the general principles of solidarity and development and upholding of the right of a human to be free from fear and want pursuant to the Covenant's Preamble.[107] The Supreme Court also focused on the right to an adequate standard of living or adequate housing (article 11(1)) when assessing the regulation of rents of flats and the right to education as well as the issue of discrimination in access to education. The decisions of lesser courts are not centrally monitored; nevertheless, they are also bound by the Covenant and the Charter and other international treaties and must respect them in their decision making. The Covenant and the Charter are also often used for argumentation by parties in court proceedings.[108]

5.3.3 Impact on and through Independent State Institutions

The mandate of the Ombudsperson has been gradually extended to encompass new human rights portfolios as the national equality and anti-discrimination body and the protection of the rights of foreigners during detention and expulsion procedures. In this manner the Ombudsperson exercises many of the functions of a national human rights institution according to the Paris Principles, although not registered as such.

In the activities within their legal authority the Ombudsperson also focuses on economic, social and cultural rights. Within the supervision of the state

---

[104] Case 15 Tz 47/2002, 28 Cdo 2331/2013, 28 Cdo 2680/2009 or 21Cdo 3160/2009.
[105] Cases 15 Tz 47/2002, 5 Tz 40/2003, 5 Tz 8/2001, 15 Tz 67/2003, 5 Tz 26/2001.
[106] Cases 21 Cdo 2489/2000 and 21 Cdo 2104/2001 – reference to art 8/d (right to strike), 21 Cdo 1486/2005 – reference to art 7 (right to the enjoyment of just and favourable conditions of work), 21 Cdo 1803/2003 – reference to art 6 (right to work).
[107] Legal framework and policies of the government of the Czech Republic in the field of housing <https://www.ohchr.org/_layouts/15/WopiFrame.aspx?sourcedoc=/Documents/Issues/Housing/Financialization/CzechRepublic1.docx&action=default&DefaultItemOpen=1> accessed 30 September 2021.
[108] E/C.12/CZE/Q/2/Add1 3.

administration they primarily focus on administrative proceedings related to access to economic, social and cultural rights, that is, for example, policies of employment; inspection of working conditions; social security and welfare; social and legal protection of children; investigation of complaints around health care; the provision of education, and so forth, where they oversee that these proceedings are carried out in compliance with the law and the principles of good governance and that they contribute as much as possible to the fulfilment of the rights of affected persons.[109]

The Ombudsperson cooperates with the government and Parliament, and presents them with recommendations on how to deal with human rights problems. The Ombudsperson also makes comments on most of the government's draft regulations and policies from the perspective of human rights protection. The Ombudsperson works intensively with expert practitioners and with civil society representatives and utilises their experience in their own work.[110]

5.3.4 Impact on and through Non-state Actors

Education in the area of human rights in general has been included in all current documents used in education towards citizenship.[111] The process and results of activities of individual schools in regions are continuously monitored and assessed by the Czech School Inspection. The Covenant forms part of legal education at a general level at law faculties, as well as at the level of specialised training for judges, public prosecutors and other civil servants.

NGOs use references to the Covenant in their advocacy campaigns. To give some examples: Liga lidských práv referred to the Covenant and its particular provisions and cited concrete obligations of the state in its advocacy work on the topic of employment of persons with disabilities;[112] involuntary sterilisation and education of Roma children;[113] Otevřená společnost in its work on social discrimination;[114] Organisation for Aid to Refugees in its campaign on

---

109   E/C.12/CZE/Q/2/Add.1 4.
110   E/C.12/CZE/3, 4, 6.
111   The most often used name of this subject, which is the basic one in providing education to citizenship in the vocational education system, is civics. The issue of the position of men, women and minorities in society is also represented in topics of subjects such as civics and history, but also in vocational subjects (dealing with issues of psychology, law and economy related to the relevant specialisations).
112   Report available at <https://llp.cz/wp-content/uploads/LLP_Analyza_Zamestnavani-lidi-s-postizenim_final.pdf> accessed 30 September 2021.
113   Report available at <https://llp.cz/wp-content/uploads/02_zakladni_vzdelavani_romskych_deti.pdf> accessed 30 September 2021.
114   Report available at <https://www.otevrenaspolecnost.cz/knihovna/1274-socialni-diskriminace-pod-lupou-2006> accessed 30 September 2021.

status of migrant women;[115] and La Strada in its campaigns on human trafficking and forced labour.[116] Civil society organisations further submit their thematic reports.[117]

5.3.5 Impact of State Reporting

The reports to the Committee were prepared by the Human Rights Department of the office of the government of the Czech Republic based on documentation from central state administration bodies.[118] Additional documentation was provided by NGOs and academic institutions.

The reporting of the Czech Republic is rather descriptive, contains detailed statistical data, respects articles 16 and 17 of the Covenant and is based on the Committee's revised general guidelines on the form and content of reports on the fulfilment of obligations arising from the Covenant and relevant facts and new measures adopted by the Czech Republic to fulfil obligations arising from the Covenant in the report period. The Committee itself welcomed the initial report of the state party, which it found to be comprehensive and generally in conformity with its guidelines for the preparation of reports.

---

[115] Report available at <https://www.opu.cz/wp-content/uploads/2016/06/Analýza-k-problematice-migrantek-a-migrantů-v-České-republice.pdf> accessed 30 September 2021.

[116] Report available at <https://documentation.lastradainternational.org/lsidocs/manual.pdf> accessed 15 September 2023.

[117] Several thematic reports by civil society were the subject of our study. In 2013 the League of Human Rights provided a submission concerning the right of everyone to the enjoyment of just and favourable conditions of work and the right of everyone to the enjoyment of the highest attainable standard of physical and mental health. In the same year the Mental Disability Advocacy Centre, the European Disability Forum, and the League of Human Rights submitted a joint report on the rights of children with disabilities to education and their right to be free from discrimination. The League of Human Rights also provided two written submissions to the Committee for consideration when compiling the List of Issues on the Second Periodic Report – one concerned the special protection of young children suspected of having committed an unlawful act and the implementation of the right to the highest attainable standard of health; the second the right to the highest attainable standard of health with respect to children who are subject to compulsory immunisation, the special protection of mothers in relation to childbirth and the right to just and favorable conditions of work in public hospitals taken together with the right to the highest attainable standard of health of doctors and patients.

[118] So far, the Czech Republic has presented three reports to the Committee. The initial report for the years 1993–1999 was submitted in August 2000. The Czech Republic should have submitted the initial report by 30 June 1995 (a delay of five years and one month). The second periodic report was due in 2007. It was submitted in December 2010 (a delay of three years and five months). The third report was submitted in September 2019 and covers the period from 1 January 2013 to 31 December 2018.

The delegation of the Czech Republic that presented the report in Geneva was mostly headed by a representative at the level of director and included representatives of government ministries (Education; Interior; Labour and Social Affairs; Health; Justice; Regional Development). In 2002 the Committee appreciated the candid and open nature of the constructive dialogue with the delegation.

There were no reports of reprisals against human rights defenders engaging in the reporting process.

The Committee had a dialogue with the delegation in April/May 2002 and in May 2014.

In its COs of 2014 the Committee recommended to incorporate all economic, social and cultural rights into the Charter; to revise the mandate and powers of the Ombudsperson with a view to bring them in line with the Paris Principles; to amend the Anti-Discrimination Act; to adopt a human rights-based approach in addressing discrimination against the Roma; to address discrimination against migrants; the gender pay gap; social housing; and inclusive education.[119] In 2002 the Committee recommended to give full effect to the Covenant in its legal system; to repeal the lustration law; to eliminate discrimination against groups of minorities, in particular Roma; to address domestic violence; housing; and to adopt effective measures to reduce tobacco smoking, drug abuse and alcohol consumption, especially among children.[120] The two periodic reports and other information for the Committee and its COs are published on the web page of the government in the section of the Government Council for Human Rights. All the documents are available in Czech. There is no targeted media strategy.

From the periodic reports and replies to the list of issues, it can be derived that the Czech Republic makes efforts[121] to implement the key recommendations, relating to discrimination (in major areas of social life such as employment, social protection, health care, housing and education), combating racism and extremism, and social inclusion. It does so often through soft tools such as strategies and action plans – Roma Integration Strategy; National Action Plan for the Prevention of Domestic Violence; Social Inclusion Strategy for 2014–2020; National Action Plan Promoting Positive Ageing for 2013–2017; Concept of Prevention and Solution of Homelessness until 2020. However, measures are mostly of a long-term character. Problems such as Roma discrimination[122]

---

119   E/C.12/CZE/CO/2.
120   E/C.12/1/Add.76.
121   See the list of strategies and action plans adopted in part (b) Incorporation and reliance by legislature and executive.
122   Discrimination of Roma in the field of education – see the chapter on CERD.

and social housing have not yet been fully addressed. Even though the issue of social housing is covered by the Concept of Social Housing for the years 2015–2025, the relevant legislation has not yet been adopted.[123]

5.3.6 Brief Conclusion

The Czech courts (the Constitutional Court, the Supreme Courts and administrative courts) refer to the Covenant in their decisions and NGOs use it in their advocacy campaigns. Since most of the rights contained in the Covenant are equally protected by the Charter of Fundamental Rights and Freedoms, judges prefer to refer to the corresponding provisions of the Charter. This does not undermine the judicial protection of rights guaranteed by the Covenant, as the content of the rights in the Charter almost fully corresponds to the rights contained in the Covenant. Progress made in the realisation of economic, social and cultural rights is dependent on the economic situation and often also on the political will (which determined, for example, the approach of the government to the issue of compensation mechanism for non-consensual sterilisations[124] of Romani women). The progress made was also influenced by the specific circumstances of the transition from a Communist to a democratic state which included privatisation and a subsequent change of ownership structures with an impact on certain areas of social life such as the provision of social housing. The Czech government continues to examine the possibility of ratifying the Optional Protocol and analyses its national implementation.

5.4 Convention on the Elimination of All Forms of Discrimination against Women

The Czech Republic succeeded to the obligations arising from the Covenant for the former CSFR as of 1 January 1993. The Czech Republic ratified OP-CEDAW on 26 February 2001 and accepted the inquiry procedure (OP-CEDAW articles 8 and 9). A Czech translation of the Covenant exists.[125]

5.4.1 Incorporation and Reliance by Legislature and Executive

The Convention forms part of the Czech legal order, while also taking precedence over legislative acts. In addition to the key regulation of discrimination in the Penal and Civil Codes, specific legislation – the Anti-Discrimination

---

123 See the information on the webpage of the Ministry of Labour and Social Affairs <http://www.socialnibydleni.mpsv.cz/cs/co-je-socialni-bydleni/zakladni-informace-o-sb/zakon-o-sb> accessed 23 April 2022.
124 See also chapters on CERD, CCPR and CEDAW.
125 CEDAW was published in the Collection of Laws under No 62/1987 Coll.

Act – came into force on 1 September 2009.[126] The Anti-Discrimination Act further specifies the general prohibition of discrimination set out in the Charter of Fundamental Rights and Freedoms. The Anti-Discrimination Act is a comprehensive regulation of the right to equal treatment. Since 1 December 2009 the role of the so-called equality body has been performed by the Ombudsperson. The labour inspection authorities (that is, the State Labour Inspection Office and the regional labour inspectorates), based on Act 251/2005 Coll on labour inspection, are authorised to check employers' compliance with labour laws.

In 2001 the advisory body of the government– the Government Council for Equal Opportunities for Women and Men – was established.[127] Its members are representatives of the individual ministries, social partners, the academic sector and civil society and expert public.

On the basis of the 4th World Conference on Women held in Beijing in 1995, the Czech Republic adopted in 1998 a national action plan named Priorities and Procedures of the Government in the Promotion of Equality between Men and Women, a fundamental strategic document in the field of gender equality at the government level.[128] Since 1998 the national action plan for gender equality is adopted annually. Government Resolution 262 of 13 April 2011 approved the National Action Plan for the Prevention of Domestic Violence for the years 2011–2014. Later on, the Strategy of Gender Equality for the period 2014–2020 provided a broader framework and complemented other strategic and conceptual documents of the government associated with the gender agenda.

In terms of visibility of the Convention, the Gender Equality Unit in the Office of the Government discloses general recommendations of the Committee on the website of the Secretariat of the Government Council for Equal Opportunities for Women and Men. Thanks to a project named 'Domestic Violence and Gender-Based Violence/Mainstreaming of Equal Opportunities for Women and Men and Promoting the Reconciliation of Work and Private Life', the implementation of which started in March 2014, a publication informing about the Convention, the Committee's activities and also

---

[126] Act 198/2009 Coll, on Equal Treatment and Legal Protections against Discrimination and amending certain laws.

[127] Government Council for Gender Equality <https://www.vlada.cz/cz/pracovni-a-porad ni-organy-vlady/rada-pro-rovne-prilezitosti/the-government-council-for-equal-opport unities-for-women-and-men-29830> accessed 23 April 2022.

[128] <http://docstore.ohchr.org/SelfServices/FilesHandler.ashx?enc=6QkG1d%2 FPPRiCAqhKb7yhsoVqDbaslinb8oXgzpEhivh71vRngm5VRKNNlaQuonDa3jH4qSDG4iK 75w%2Fu%2Fj%2BtDdOOt4VnGSCZahEy8dJCZosBNpFLMk9YHplNiOTVB5O%2B> accessed 23 April 2022.

about institutional framework for gender equality in the country has been released.[129]

5.4.2 Reliance by Judiciary

In relation to the use of the Convention in the judicature of Czech courts it is possible to refer, for instance, to judgment of the Supreme Court No 30 Cdo 4277/2010 of 13 December 2012, which stated that at the international level, protection against discrimination is regulated by the conventions, by which the Czech Republic is bound, including CEDAW. The judgment concerned racial discrimination. References to the Convention were found in three decisions of administrative courts (reference to article 16) and in three decisions of the Constitutional Court. In a finding of 2017 (PL.ÚS 2/15 #1) a reference to article 12 of the Convention and to the recommendation of CEDAW relating to the health insurance and care to foreign women and children (CEDAW/C/CZE/CO/5, paras 32–33) were found.

5.4.3 Impact on and through Independent State Institutions

The mandate of the Ombudsperson has been gradually extended to encompass new human rights portfolios as the national equality and anti-discrimination body.

5.4.4 Impact on and through Non-state Actors

The Covenant forms part of the Czech legal order. Therefore, the level of awareness among the legal practitioners should be rather high. However, the Committee, in its COs to the sixth periodic report, reiterated its concern that the provisions of the Convention continue to be rarely invoked in proceedings in the Constitutional Court and the ordinary courts, indicating that there is inadequate knowledge among the general public and women themselves, as well as within the judiciary, about the rights of women under the Convention and the procedures available to them under the Optional Protocol; the concept of substantive equality of women and men; and the Committee's general recommendations. These observations correlate with the experience of the Ombudsperson which shows that the problematic aspect of adopting measures to eliminate discrimination against women is the prevailing low percentage

---

[129] Government Strategy for Equality of Women and Men in the Czech Republic for 2014–2020 <https://www.vlada.cz/assets/ppov/rovne-prilezitosti-zen-a-muzu/dokumenty/Government_Strategy_for-Gender_Equality_2014_2020.pdf> accessed 15 September 2023.

of reported and investigated cases (underreporting).[130] In their practice, the Ombudsperson faces the reluctance of victims of discrimination to take their claims to court.[131] This is mainly related to the low awareness of the possibility of such a procedure, a general distrust of citizens in the fairness of the Czech justice system and the unwillingness or inability to bear the related costs.[132]

The rights guaranteed by the Convention are taught along with the rights enshrined in the Charter of Fundamental Rights and Freedoms and public international law courses at all law faculties in the Czech Republic. Additional information is also provided through the Czech Judicial Academy's training programme.[133] However, in general, more attention is paid to the European regional system of protection of human rights (for instance, Training on EU Gender Equality Law for judges and public prosecutors is organised in cooperation with the Academy of European Law). In its COs to the sixth periodic report, the Committee reiterated its previous recommendation that the state party should ensure that the Convention and the Optional Protocol are made an integral part of the legal education and training of judges, lawyers and prosecutors, with a view to enabling them to directly apply the provisions of the Convention and interpret national legal provisions in the light of the Convention.

NGOs use references to the Covenant in their advocacy campaigns. To give some examples of NGOs that focus on discrimination of women: Česká ženská lobby; Forum 50% (focusing on the topics of equal opportunities for men and women in municipalities, Lobbying Kit, Women in Politics);[134] *Otevřená společnost*;[135] (topics: gender discrimination, gender audit, gender at school); *In Iustitia* (sexual violence); *Český svaz žen* (topics: equality at labour market, women in the countryside). Some of the NGOs also submitted shadow reports to CEDAW.

---

130 Office of the Public Defender of Rights, Discrimination in the Czech Republic, Victims of Discrimination and Obstacles Hindering Their Access to Justice, 2015. Final Report on the Research of the Public Defender of Rights.
131 ibid 12.
132 CEDAW/C/CZE/6 12.
133 The list of seminars organised by the Judicial Academy is available at <https://www.jacz.cz/vzdelavani/seznam-seminaru> accessed 30 September 2021.
134 Available at <https://padesatprocent.cz/docs/lobbying-kit.pdf> accessed 30 September 2021.
135 Policy papers are available at <https://www.otevrenaspolecnost.cz/> accessed 30 September 2021.

5.4.5 Impact of State Reporting[136]

The reports submitted so far were elaborated by the Office of the Minister of Human Rights or the Government Commissioner for Human Rights on the basis of information provided by central state administration authorities, higher territorial self-government units, non-governmental non-profit organisations, the academic sector and social partners.

Civil society presented its shadow reports to the CEDAW Cttee. The reports covered the following topics: coercive sterilisation of Romani women (two reports, in relation to articles 10, 12 and 16 of the Convention); trafficking in human beings and Romani women (both by the European Roma rights centre; article 6); obstacles to the free choice of place to give birth, domestic violence, rape and right to education (article 10); right to health (article 12); right to marriage and family life (article 16) (two reports by the League of Human Rights); women with disabilities (International Disability Alliance; Mental Disability Advocacy Centre and Forum for Human Rights); violence against women, trafficking and exploitation of prostitution; participation in political and public life; education; employment; health (joint report of the Czech Women's Lobby, La Strada and Persefona); migrant women (Organisation for Aid to Refugees and Forum for Human Rights). There were no reports of reprisals against human rights defenders engaging in the reporting process.

The delegations of the Czech Republic presenting the reports in Geneva were mostly headed by a representative at the level of director and included representatives of government ministries (Education; Interior; Labour and Social Affairs; Health; Justice; Foreign Affairs).

The Committee reviewed the reports of the Czech Republic in 1998, 2002, 2006, 2010 and 2016.

General recommendations of the Committee are made public on the website of the Secretariat of the Government Council for Equal Opportunities for Women and Men (published in Czech and in English, www.vlada.cz). COs of

---

[136] In 1995 the Czech Republic submitted to the CEDAW Cttee an initial report on the Convention for the years 1993–1994 (a delay of one year and six months). The Committee reviewed the report on 26 and 27 January 1998. At its meeting of 8 August 2002, the Committee reviewed the second periodic report of the Czech Republic for the period from 1 January 1995 to 30 June 1999, which was submitted in March 2000. The third periodic report of the Czech Republic for the period from 1 July 1999 to 31 December 2003 was reviewed by the Committee on 17 August 2006 (submitted in August 2004, a delay of two years and five months). The joint fourth and fifth periodic report of the Czech Republic for the period from 1 January 2004 to 31 July 2008 was reviewed by the Committee in October 2010 (submitted in April 2009). The sixth report was submitted in November 2014 and considered in February 2016. The seventh report is due in March 2020.

the Committee include a recommendation to expeditiously establish a comprehensive system of free legal aid for women without sufficient means to pay for legal assistance in anti-discrimination proceedings; to undertake legislative reforms to allow for the *actio popularis*, including in cases of gender discrimination; to strengthen the efforts to address persistent and deep-rooted gender stereotypes that perpetuate discrimination against women; to take measures to accelerate the process of ratification of the Istanbul Convention; to combat trafficking in women and girls, including at the regional level and in cooperation with neighbouring countries; to amend its electoral law to implement the 'zipper' system for election candidates; to strengthen its measures to ensure substantive equality of women and men in the labour market; to continue to reduce the gender pay gap; to reinforce its social housing policy; and to respect the fundamental rights of migrants, asylum seekers and refugees.

The key recommendations of the COs are taken into account by the government. So far, no significant progress has been registered, for instance, on the issue of ratification of the Istanbul Convention (the ratification process has not yet started) or the amendment to the electoral law to introduce the 'zipper' system (the draft amendment was not approved by the government). The Government Strategy for Equality of Women and Men covers horizontal areas such as gender stereotypes, legislation, data collection, men and gender equality. It includes specific indicators in order to monitor and evaluate progress achieved. The government claims that it has been paying increased attention to gender equality in the labour market. In order to help reconcile work and private life, the Act on Children Groups was adopted and came into force in November 2014. The Act provides the legal framework for providing childcare services on a non-commercial basis, which should be an alternative to educational care provided to children within the pre-school education system.

The Czech Republic provided information on the follow-up to the COs in 2012 (on domestic and sexual violence and on unlawful sterilisations)[137] and in 2018 (on greater representation of women in politics and on coercive and non-consensual sterilisations).[138]

Coercive and non-consensual sterilisations represent a very specific issue for the Czech Republic. The government decided in 2015 not to establish an *ex gratia* compensation mechanism. The Constitutional Court in its ruling ordered courts not to disregard the statute of limitations where this would

---

137   CEDAW/C/CZE/CO/5/Add.1.
138   CEDAW/C/CZE/CO/6/Add.1.

be *contra bonos mores*.[139] In the context of sterilisations, the principal means of remedy for victims of coercive or non-consensual sterilisation remains an application to a court seeking pecuniary or non-pecuniary compensation for non-material harm suffered by an infringement of personal rights.

5.4.6 Impact of Individual Communications

The Ministry of Justice (namely, the government agent) has been delegated to represent the Czech Republic in the proceedings on communications under OP-CEDAW.[140] Based on the available reports of the government agent,[141] the Czech Republic has received two communications. One was declared inadmissible.[142]

5.4.7 Brief Conclusion

The Committee, in its follow-up communications, considers the information provided by the Czech Republic to be thorough and extensive, and the quality of information qualifies as satisfactory. The main factors that influence the impact of the Convention are the inadequate knowledge of legal regulations among the general public and women themselves,[143] the low percentage of reported[144] and investigated cases[145] and, in relation to certain specific issues such as non-consensual sterilisation, the lack of political will.[146] The Ombudsperson,[147] including with his or her role of equality

---

139 Written information on steps taken to implement the recommendations of the CEDAW Cttee on support for increased representation of women in politics <https://www.vlada.cz/assets/ppov/rovne-prilezitosti-zen-a-muzu/dokumenty/Written-Information-on-steps-taken-to-implement-the-recommendations-of-the-UN-Committee-on-the-Elimination-of-Discrimination.pdf> accessed 30 September 2021.

140 Resolution of the Government 155 of 27 February 2017.

141 Zpráva za rok 2017 o stavu vyřizování stížností podaných proti ČR k mezinárodním orgánům ochrany lidských práv, str. 26.

142 CEDAW/C/73/D/102/2016 (19 July 2019), decided just after the cut off date for this study. The case relates to the issue of illegal sterilisation of six women who were not provided an effective remedy. In a decision adopted by the Committee in July 2019, it was considered that the authors had not exhausted the available domestic remedies and that the communication was inadmissible under article 4(1) of OP-CEDAW.

143 The Government Strategy for Equality of Women and Men in the Czech Republic for 2014–2020, Office of the Government, 2014 26.

144 ibid 12.

145 CEDAW/C/CZE/6 12.

146 See the chapter on CCPR.

147 An example of the contribution of the Public Defender of Rights to the discussion on the sterilisations of Romani women: Final Statement of the Public Defender of Rights in the Matter of Sterilisations Performed in Contravention of the Law and Proposed Remedial Measures, Brno, 2005; a leaflet on the issue of discrimination on the basis of sex

body,[148] contributes to the improvement of the situation. In terms of policy making, the role of the Government Council for Equal Opportunities for Women and Men is not negligible.[149] No Czech national has ever been a member of CEDAW Cttee.

The Czech Republic has not yet ratified the Istanbul Convention. The ratification process should start in the near future. The Convention currently receives an unprecedented level of attention from the general public (comments by the Catholic Church,[150] newspaper articles,[151] seminars in Parliament).[152]

5.5 Convention against Torture and Other Cruel, Inhuman or Degrading Treatment or Punishment

5.5.1 Incorporation and Reliance by Legislature and Executive

The Czech Republic, as of 1 January 1993, assumed all the obligations arising from international law in respect to the former CSFR, except for obligations in respect of the territory of the Slovak Republic.

Under the Communist regime, before the Velvet Revolution of 1989, thousands of citizens had been arrested on political grounds and had suffered torture or inhuman or degrading treatment. After the fall of the regime a number of relevant legislative changes were introduced by the Czechoslovak Parliament, for instance, amendments concerning the Criminal Code, the Code of Criminal Procedure, the Code of Civil Procedure, Act 59/1965 on the

---

<https://www.ochrance.cz/fileadmin/user_upload/Letaky/Diskriminace-z-duvodu-pohlavi.pdf> accessed 30 April 2022.

148 Information on the Public Defender of Rights support to the victims of discrimination is available at <https://www.ochrance.cz/diskriminace/pomoc-obetem-diskriminace/> accessed 30 April 2022.

149 See the chapter (b) Incorporation and reliance by legislature and executive; information on the activities of the Government Council for Equal Opportunities, including minutes from the meetings is available at <https://www.vlada.cz/scripts/detail.php?pgid=1074> accessed 30 April 2022.

150 Article in electronic media <https://www.irozhlas.cz/zpravy-domov/knez-pitha-istanbulska-umluva-kazani-trestny-cin-ceska-zenska-lonny_1901141626_lac> accessed 30 April 2022.

151 Examples of articles in electronic media <https://www.novinky.cz/domaci/clanek/valkova-chce-parlamentem-protlacit-istanbulskou-umluvu-podle-kritiku-je-dokument-zbytecny-40299007> accessed 30 April 2022; <https://www.ceska-justice.cz/2019/07/valkova-pomoc-obetem-nasili-praxi-selhava-pomoci-ma-istanbulska-umluva/> accessed 30 April 2022.

152 Invitation to a seminar <https://www.psp.cz/sqw/cms.sqw?z=11866> accessed 30 April 2022; information on a seminar <https://www.vlada.cz/cz/ppov/rovne-prilezitosti-zen-a-muzu/aktuality/odbor-zorganizoval-seminar-pro-poslance-a-poslankyne-na-tema-_istanbulska-umluva_-myty-a-fakta–168836/> accessed 30 April 2022.

enforcement of prison sentences. In 1992 Act 555/1992 on the prison service and court guards of the Czech Republic was adopted. Basic legal protection against acts of torture and inhuman treatment was guaranteed by the Constitution, including the Charter of Fundamental Rights and Freedoms which was promulgated by a constitutional Act on 9 January 1991 and which after 1 January 1993 remained part of the constitutional order of the Czech Republic.

In line with a recommendation issued by the CAT Cttee to the former Czech and Slovak Federative Republic, following the Czechoslovakian initial report on the implementation of CAT, an amendment to the Criminal Code was adopted in 1993 (Act 290/1993) which introduced a new definition of the criminal act of 'torture and other inhuman and cruel treatment' as section 259a of the then Criminal Code.

On 8 January 2008 the Czech Republic adopted a new Penal Code, which entered into force on 1 January 2010. The new Penal Code, as in the case of the former Criminal Code, contains a definition of the crime of torture and other inhuman and cruel treatment but not of torture and inhuman treatment itself. The relevant provision (section 149) reads as follows:

> Whosoever causes physical or mental suffering to another by means of torture or other inhuman and cruel treatment in connection with the exercise of the powers of central government authorities, local authorities, courts or other public authorities shall be punished by imprisonment of between six months and five years.

Two-year and eight-year prison sentences shall be imposed on an offender who commits this offence as an official against a witness, expert or interpreter in connection with the performance of their duties, against another person on the grounds of his actual or perceived race, ethnic group, nationality, political beliefs, religion, or in the actual or perceived absence of beliefs, if such an act is committed by at least two persons or repeatedly. Imprisonment of five to 12 years shall be imposed on an offender who commits the offence on a pregnant woman, on a child under the age of 15 years, in a particularly savage or harrowing manner, or if he causes severe injury as a result of such act. An offender who causes death as a result of committing the offence shall be imprisoned for between eight and 18 years.

It is acknowledged by Czech legal doctrine and legal practice that basic elements of the definition of torture are acts, intent, the effect of severe pain or physical or mental suffering, an objective and the existence of a state element. These factors are included in the constituent elements of the crime of torture and other inhuman and cruel treatment. Intention is a necessary element for all criminal offences, unless the law expressly states that culpability through negligence is admissible. Therefore, intent is envisaged as an element of the crime of torture and other inhuman and cruel treatment.

The Czech Republic has ratified OP-CAT. The Protocol came into force for the Czech Republic on 9 August 2006. The Ombudsman was appointed the national preventive mechanism in the Czech Republic under articles 17 to 23 of the Protocol.[153] Under an amendment to Act 349/1999 on the Ombudsman, the Ombudsman's competences were extended to include the new task of systematically visiting all places (facilities) where detained persons are or may be held (section 1 and 21(a)). It does not matter whether these persons are detained on the basis of a decision or order of a public authority or as a result of the factual situation in which they find themselves.

The Czech Republic is bound by CCPR, the European Convention Rights and the European Convention on the Prevention of Torture and Inhuman or Degrading Treatment or Punishment. In February 1997, the European Committee for the Prevention of Torture and Inhuman or Degrading Treatment or Punishment made its first regular visit to the Czech Republic. Czech courts frequently make reference to the case law of the ECtHR concerning the interpretation and application of article 3 ECHR.

5.5.2 Reliance by Judiciary

As for CAT, we find relatively many references in the jurisprudence of Czech courts. In the decisions of administrative courts we found 140 concrete references to CAT. The vast majority of cases in which the administrative courts, including the Highest Administrative Court, used reference to CAT concerns the issue of extradition, mostly to countries such as Georgia, Russia, Belarus and Moldova. The courts examined whether the decision to extradite a complainant infringed his right under article 3 CAT.[154] As a rule, a violation of article 3 CAT was examined together with article 7 of the constitutional Charter, articles 3 and 6 ECHR and article 7 CCPR. Whereas court decisions in *non-refoulement* cases regularly point at article 3 CAT on a general level, they do not contain a thorough analysis of the provision.[155]

---

153 Czech Republic National Preventive Mechanisms (arts 17–23 of OP-CAT) <https://www.ohchr.org/Documents/HRBodies/OPCAT/NPM/CzechRepublic.pdf> accessed 30 April 2022.
154 Judgment of the Highest Administrative Court in Case 4 Tz 89/2008.
155 So, eg, in its judgment of 25 September 2013 in Case 30 Cdo 4198/2010, the Highest Administrative Court only recalled that under art 4 of CAT it is the duty of the state to assess cases of inhuman treatment as a criminal offence under the Criminal Code.

References to article 3 CAT also appear in a decision of the Constitutional Court concerning the enforcement of a foreign criminal judgment (from Thailand). In the same case the Constitutional Court also refers to the conclusions of the CAT Cttee on conditions in Czech prisons.[156] In another case the Constitutional Court, dealing with an asylum case, stated that CAT contains no provision on the right to asylum.[157]

There is only one judgment in which the Constitutional Court makes reference to articles other than article 3 CAT, namely, articles 12–14 CAT. In this judgment the Constitutional Court deals with the rights of victims in proceedings on a petition to authorise the reopening of proceedings to the detriment of the perpetrator, namely, in connection with the state's obligation to protect the right to life through criminal law. In the same case the Constitutional Court also used article 8 of the Universal Declaration of Human Rights, article 2 CCPR, articles 2, 3, 4 and 30 CRC and article 6 CERD.[158] However, in this case the Constitutional Court interpreted none of the above-mentioned international human rights provisions but without any deeper analysis assumed that those norms, including articles 12–14 CAT, have the same meaning as the relevant constitutional provisions.

5.5.3 Impact on and through Non-state Actors

In the period from 2015 to 2019 we do not find references to CAT in the professional journals of the Czech Notarial Chamber, the Czech Executive Chamber and the Czech Bar Association. In the statements and publications of NGOs we very rarely find references to CAT. Also in academe, CAT and its application is not very popular among students preparing a diploma or doctoral thesis at Czech universities.

5.5.4 Impact of State Reporting

When considering the initial report of the Czech Republic, the Committee in its COs of 1995[159] noted that there were no serious matters of concern regarding implementation by the Czech Republic of CAT. Following up on the only recommendation formulated by the Committee the Czech Republic withdrew its reservation to article 20 of the Convention and made a declaration recognising the Committee's competence to receive and consider communications under articles 21 and 22 of the Convention. The document on the withdrawal

---

156 Case N 34/44 SbNU 417.
157 Case N 17/44 SbNU 217.
158 Case N 151/82 SbNU 385.
159 CAT/C/21/Add.2.

of the reservation, together with the declaration, was deposited with the UN Secretary-General on 3 September 1996.

In its COs of 2001 the Committee welcomed the adoption of the new Aliens Law and the new Asylum Law, both effective from 1 January 2000, the amendment to the Citizenship Law adopted in September 1999, which resolved most problems of statelessness that had disproportionately affected the Roma population, and the introduction of a special detention facility for foreigners, which resolved the problems arising from the detention of foreigners prior to expulsion.[160]

However, it has to be noted that there was no direct link between these legislative measures and obligations under CAT. The Committee expressed concern with regard to instances of racism and xenophobia in society and continuing incidents of discrimination against Roma, including by local officials. It is not clear why the Committee raised such issues that had already been intensively dealt with under the CERD mechanism. The Committee further noted allegations of the excessive use of force by law enforcement officials during and after demonstrations, particularly alleged instances of cruel, inhuman and degrading treatment of persons arrested and detained as a result of the demonstrations during the International Monetary Fund (IMF)/World Bank meeting in Prague in September 2000. There had also been cases of interprisoner violence and bullying in various institutions, including prisons, the military and educational institutions. The Committee called upon the Czech Republic to ensure the independence of investigations of offences committed by law enforcement officials by introducing a mechanism of external control.

In its COs of 2012, the Committee was concerned that the new Czech Penal Code did not define torture and recommended to the Czech Republic to amend its Penal Code in order to include a definition of torture that covers all the elements contained in article 1 CAT. The Committee further expressed concerns related to the acceptance of diplomatic assurances in relation to extraditions of persons to states where those persons would be in danger of being subjected to torture. The Czech Republic did not provide information concerning the type of diplomatic assurances received or requested.

In its most recent COs of 2018, the Committee recalled its previous recommendation to adopt a definition of torture that covers all the elements contained in article 1 CAT and takes into account the Committee's General Comment 2 of 2007 on the implementation of article 2. Although the procedural guarantees are enshrined in Czech domestic legislation, the Committee

---

160   A/56/44 para 108.

found that the right of access to a lawyer was provided only at the concerned person's own expense, and that free legal aid was not available from the very outset of deprivation of liberty. In practice, police officers allegedly did not always respect the right of detained persons to be informed of their rights and to notify a relative of their detention. In this respect state action is needed.

According to the Committee further legislative, administrative and other measures should be adopted in order to ensure that, for instance, all detained persons have the right to request and receive a medical examination by an independent medical doctor, including a doctor of their own choosing, from the outset of the deprivation of liberty, and that medical examinations are conducted out of hearing and out of sight of police officers and prison staff, unless the doctor concerned explicitly requests otherwise. The Health Care Services Act 372/2011 should be amended in order to explicitly provide for the obligation of healthcare professionals to report suspected cases of torture and ill-treatment to the relevant authorities. Reform was needed to strengthen the independence of the General Inspection of Security Forces so that all allegations of torture or ill-treatment made by persons deprived of their liberty will be promptly, impartially and effectively investigated and suspected perpetrators will be duly tried. The conditions of detention remained problematic in some respects. Also, the practice of detaining individuals seeking international protection, including those in particularly vulnerable situations, and the fact that the lack of alternative accommodation for families was subject to the Committee's concern, especially with regard to the fact that asylum-seeking children and their families continued to be detained at the respective facility, often for periods of more than two months.

In our opinion, beyond the scope of CAT, the Committee in its COs of 2018 again mentioned aspects related to the discrimination of the Roma minority in the field of education. This issue indeed was subject to discussion between the Czech delegation and Committee members in May 2019. Committee members argued that the ECtHR had not excluded the fact that the discriminatory treatment of a minority by the majority fell under article 3 of the European Convention. When the representatives of the Czech Republic pointed to the practices of other UN treaty bodies, Committee members recalled that each convention had its own set of specific obligations and legal distinctions. According to the Committee, the placement of children from minority groups in schools not suitable for their intellectual capacity constituted humiliating and degrading treatment as set forth in article 1 CAT.

5.5.5 Impact of Individual Communications

Although the Czech Republic has recognised the competence of the Committee to receive and consider communications under article 22 CAT, so far, no individual complaints have been submitted. Victims of torture or ill-treatment are more likely to file a complaint with the ECtHR rather than using the tool of individual communication under CAT. So far, in 22 complaints against the Czech Republic complainants before the ECtHR alleged a violation of article 3 ECHR. Most complaints were found inadmissible.[161]

5.5.6 Impact of Other Measures

The Public Defender of Rights was established as an independent institution for the protection and promotion of human rights. In many ways the institution fulfils the requirements of the Paris Principles. The scope of operation and the powers of the Public Defender of Rights are regulated by a special law on the Public Defender of Rights. Since 2006 the Public Defender of Rights as the National Preventive Mechanism also deals with the supervision of the places where persons are restricted in personal liberty pursuant to OP-CAT.

In order to strengthen protection from torture and other forms of ill-treatment, the Public Defender of Rights is performing systematic visits to relevant facilities.[162] The visits are carried out at places where freedom is restricted *ex officio* (prisons, police cells) and also in facilities providing care on which the recipients are dependent (retirement homes, treatment facilities for long-term patients). The Public Defender of Rights and his employees are authorised to enter all places in the facility, to inspect all records including medical records and to speak with all persons (employees, patients, prisoners, and so forth) without the presence of third persons. Systematic visits are performed without previous notification and may take place at any time of the day (including

---

161 In the case of *Bureš v the Czech Republic*, the Court in 2012 dealt with the circumstances in a Czech 'sobering-up centre'. The disorientated complainant was strapped to a bed, even though he presented no danger to himself or others. The straps caused injuries to his wrists with the result that his ability to play the cello was impaired. Following his release, Mr Bureš brought a criminal complaint against the hospital and its staff. In this case the European Court found the Czech government responsible for the unjustified use of restraints. The Court criticised the use of restraints as a violation of the right to freedom from torture and inhuman or degrading treatment under article 3 ECHR. The complainant received compensation for this human rights violation.

162 Protection of Persons Restricted in their Freedom <https://www.ochrance.cz/en/letaky/en-protection-of-persons-restricted-in-their-freedom/EN-Protection-of-persons-restricted-in-their-freedom.pdf> accessed 15 September 2023.

non-working days). External experts such as physicians, psychiatrists, nurses, and so forth are involved in the preparation of the systematic visits.

In the past years, the Public Defender of Rights has issued proposals for the improvement of the situation found during the individual visits to the facilities and has also submitted generalised findings and systemic recommendations to the responsible governmental authorities. The Public Defender of Rights has detected a number of systematic problems related, for instance, to the care of the elderly, the unification of care for vulnerable children and the relocation of prisoners (as a means of preserving the family).

Summary reports are accessible to the public.[163] Such reports deal, for instance, with the situation in facilities for institutional and protective education (2006); prisons (2006 and 2016); institutions of social care for adults with disabilities (2006); police facilities (2006 and 2017); facilities for long-term patients (2006 and 2017); facilities for the detention of foreigners (2006); facilities for institutional and protective education (2007); social service facilities for the elderly (2007); psychiatric treatment facilities (2008); homes for persons with disabilities (2009); remand prisons (2010); psychiatric treatment facilities (2010 and 2013); school facilities for institutional and protective education (2012); infant care centres (2013); preventive educational care centres (2013); diagnostic institutions (2013); and 'sobering-up stations' (2014).

At present, the team responsible for carrying out the duties of the National Preventive Mechanism is constituted by eight full-time lawyers and cooperates with 12 external experts during the systematic visits.

5.5.7 Brief Conclusion

The Czech Republic takes its obligations under CAT very seriously. The experience of torture and ill-treatment used by the former Communist regime, particularly in relation to political prisoners, serves as a strong warning for the democratic country. The Czech Republic has been active in supporting the adoption of the OP-CAT providing for the establishment of a National Preventive Mechanism and was among the first countries to ratify OP-CAT. The protection against torture and ill-treatment is part of the constitutional order and stipulated in international human rights treaties to which the Czech Republic is a state party.

In Czech legal doctrine and judicial practice the most prominent place belongs to article 3 ECHR which is frequently referred to by Czech courts. Czech

---

163 Reports for the Chamber of Deputies of Parliament <https://www.ochrance.cz/en/vystupy/annual-report/> accessed 15 September 2023.

jurisprudence also takes into account the relevant case law of the ECtHR. On the European level, the recommendations of the European Committee for the Prevention of Torture and Other Inhuman and Degrading Treatment or Punishment (ECtteePT) also play an important role and are implemented in Czech legal practice.

It has to be noted that by introducing issues going beyond the scope of CAT, such as the problem of discrimination in the field of education, the CAT Committee might be weakening its credibility. In a situation in which the Committees under CERD and CCPR would be more competent to deal with such issues, the activist approach of the CAT Committee might also endanger the consistency of the system of UN human rights treaty bodies.

5.6 Convention on the Rights of the Child
5.6.1 Incorporation and Reliance by Legislature and Executive

The Czech Republic is bound by the Convention as of 1 January 1993. CRC as an international convention under article 10 of the Constitution of the Czech Republic is directly binding, and takes precedence over domestic law. Some rights under CRC have been included in the Charter of Fundamental Rights and Freedoms, which is part of the constitutional order of the Czech Republic. Given the complexity of children's rights that are contained in CRC, it needs a number of legal Acts to properly implement the provisions of the Convention.[164]

On the political level, a National Strategy to Protect Children's Rights was adopted by the government in 2012 covering the period from 2012 to 2018. The creation of this Strategy was prompted by the Committee's COs from 2011 and other international organisations' recommendations.[165] The Strategy aims to create a system to consistently protect all rights of any child and to meet the child's needs, a system to promote the improvement of the lives of children and families, eliminate discrimination and unequal approach to children, and promote the overall development of the child in the natural family or alternative family environments, as appropriate, with the child's participation in

---

164 Such as Act 94/1963 Coll on the family; 140/1961 Coll the Criminal Code; 141/1961 Coll the Criminal Procedure Code; 40/1964 Coll The Civil Code; 99/1963 Coll the Civil Procedure Code; 65/1965 Coll the Labour Code; 50/1973 Coll on foster care; 100/1988 Coll on social security; 114/1988 Coll on the responsibilities of the Czech social security authorities; 29/1984 Coll on elementary and secondary schools (Schools Act); 97/1963 Coll on private international law and rules of procedure; 498/1990 Coll on refugees; and Act 117/95 Coll on state social support, all as subsequently amended.

165 Government Resolution No. 4 of 4 January 2012 on the National Strategy for the Protection of Children's Rights.

relevant decision-making processes. The document establishes fundamental principles, priorities and targets in the protection of the children's rights in the Czech Republic, based on relevant articles of the Convention, the Committee's recommendations and General Comments, and other international conventions or case law. The objectives of the National Strategy are being pursued under national action plans.

5.6.2 Reliance by Judiciary

The vast majority of decisions of the Constitutional Court that make reference to CRC concern the rejection of constitutional complaints against decisions of general courts in family law matters. Such decisions most often deal with the situation of children after divorce, that is, decisions on the custody of a child, on the contact of a parent with the child who is under the custody of the other parent, and on alternate custody. There have been numerous complaints concerning maintenance obligations and the amount of maintenance. In these cases, the Constitutional Court usually confines itself to finding that the best interests of the child pursuant to article 3 CRC have been observed in proceedings before the general courts.[166] Exceptionally, the Constitutional Courts uses references to CRC when it appeals to the parents (the complainants) to act in the best interests of the child.[167]

Article 3 CRC is often used in combination with articles 9, 12 and 18 CRC. Article 9 appears in particular in cases in which the Constitutional Court decides on the right of a child to maintain contact with parents who are dependent on alcohol or other drugs, or in cases concerning the extradition of the parents. Article 12 is used mainly in divorce cases when the courts need to ascertain the child's opinion on intercourse with parents and the selection of an appropriate school. The Constitutional Court relies on article 18 mainly with regard to alternative care and the responsibility of parents for raising a child or their rights to raise a child.[168]

Apart from divorce proceedings, article 3 rarely appears in resolutions, for example in connection with home birth[169] or the execution of imprisonment of one of the parents (especially the mother).[170] Furthermore, article 7 appears

---

[166] Eg ECLI:CZ:US:2018:4.US.2458.18.1; ECLI:CZ:US:2018:3.US.1064.17.2; ECLI:CZ:US:2018:3.US.346.18.1.
[167] Eg ECLI:CZ:US:2018:3.US.346.18.1; ECLI:CZ:US:2018:2.US.2507.18.1.
[168] Eg ECLI:CZ:US:2018:1.US.714.18.1.
[169] Eg ECLI:CZ:US:2012:Pl.US.26.11.1.
[170] Eg ECLI:CZ:US:2017:1.US.3296.17.1. For a more detailed analysis, see HAUPTFLEISCHOVÁ, I. Právo na styk dítěte s vězněným rodičem. Jurisprudence, 2/2018, 14–25.

quite often (either in combination with article 3 or separately) in cases involving the determination of paternity. Articles 27 and 29 CRC appear in relation to maintenance. In one decision of the Constitutional Court, the OP-CRC-SC has been mentioned in connection with combating child pornography.

In the proceedings before the Constitutional Court, the complainants invoke specific provisions not only of CRC but also of the ECHR (most often article 8) and the Charter of Fundamental Rights and Freedoms (in particular articles 32 and 36).

When the Constitutional Court found an infringement of one of the articles of CRC, this was never the only ground for annulment of the contested decision of the general courts. The CRC provisions are always used together with the relevant provisions of the Charter of Fundamental Rights and Freedoms and sometimes with the ECHR. Of the articles of CRC, article 12 (together with articles 36 or 38 of the Charter) appears most often as one of the violated provisions in the operative part of the judgments of the Constitutional Court. In those cases the Constitutional Court concluded that there had been a violation of the participation rights of the child in proceedings concerning, for instance, disputes between parents about the vaccination of a child or the choice of a primary school. There have been some cases of travelling on public transport without paying where the Constitutional Court annulled the decisions of the general courts, because the child who committed the misconduct, in violation of article 12, was not allowed to participate in the proceedings.

5.6.3 Impact on and through Non-state Actors

CRC certainly is the most popular universal human rights convention, as far as media coverage is concerned. Looking at academic journals and textbooks, we find that there is a relatively high level of awareness about the Convention among the broad public. There are a number of national NGOs dealing with different aspects of children's rights. The protection of children's rights is a very popular subject among students preparing a diploma or doctoral thesis.

5.6.4 Impact of State Reporting

The reporting history under CRC shows that it is difficult to overcome certain structural problems related to children's rights. In its CO of 2003, the CRC Cttee reiterated that the Czech Republic continued to deal with socio-economic problems related to the transition to a market economy such as the deterioration of living standards and unemployment. According to the Committee, persisting traditional societal attitudes further hampered the enactment of new legislation and affected implementation of the CRC. Above all, the Cttee found that some of its recommendations contained in the previous CO of 1997 had not been sufficiently addressed, in particular recommendations concerning the development of a comprehensive policy on children, the reduction of discriminatory practices against the Roma population and a comprehensive reform of the system of juvenile justice. Therefore, the Committee reiterated its recommendations on those issues.

The establishment of the institution of a Public Defender of Rights in the Czech Republic was seen by the CRC Cttee as a positive step. However, as the mandate of the Public Defender was limited to action or inaction of the public sector, not all implementation aspects of the Convention were fully covered. According to the Committee, the Czech Republic should establish an independent body competent to deal with the investigation of individual complaints by children in a child-sensitive manner. Therefore, the mandate of the Public Defender should be broadened and supported with the necessary human and other resources. The establishing a separate independent children's commissioner or ombudsperson was seen by the Committee as an adequate alternative.

Also in its CO of 2011 the CRC Cttee found that many of its concerns and recommendations have been addressed insufficiently or only partly and urged the Czech Republic to sufficiently implement the recommendations, particularly those related to the establishment of an independent body to oversee the implementation of the Convention, the collection of relevant data and the full integration of the right to non-discrimination. The Committee criticised the sectoral approach to the Convention, which had led to fragmentation of its implementation. In 2019, the Czech Government Council for Human Rights has identified the issue of guardianship as one of its major priorities. In the past, many promised steps were not fulfilled. Cooperation between Czech human rights institutions and the Ministry of Justice, for a long period, have been unsuccessful.

5.6.5   Impact of Individual Communications

Although the Czech Republic in 2015 accepted the instrument of an individual complaints procedure under the OP-CRC-CP, so far no individual communications have been submitted. This might be due to the fact that in the past, complaints concerning children's rights have been submitted to the ECtHR and the HRCttee. In one of the most famous cases, *DH & Others v the Czech Republic*, the ECtHR decided that the applicants, 18 children of Roma origin, had been discriminated against by the Czech system of school education.

5.6.6 Brief Conclusion

In principle, the Convention has been properly implemented in the Czech legal order. However, some pieces of legislation have not always translated into reality. So far, there is no institution of a children's ombudsman in the Czech Republic, although the Committee has repeatedly called upon the Czech Republic to consider the establishment of an independent body monitoring the implementation of the Convention and leading sensitive investigation of individual children's complaints. When national remedies for violations of the rights guaranteed by the Convention are exhausted, a complaint can be lodged not only with the competent UN Committees but also with the ECtHR. His decisions are binding on the contracting states and, if the Court finds that there has been a breach of the Convention, it may at the same time grant the complainant fair compensation (financial compensation for material or non-material damage). However, the European Convention does not cover all rights under CRC.

5.7 International Convention for the Protection of All Persons from Enforced Disappearance

The Convention was ratified by the Czech Republic in 2017. The individual complaints procedure (article 31) and the inquiry procedure (article 33) under the Convention have been accepted. A Czech translation of the Covenant exists.[171]

5.7.1 Incorporation and Reliance by Legislature and Executive

Based on article 10 of the Czech Constitution,[172] CED forms part of national law. Where the provisions of the treaty are at variance with those of a national legislative act, the international treaty prevails. The ban on enforced disappearance is constitutionally derived from article 8 of the Charter of Fundamental Rights and Freedoms, which guarantees every individual's personal liberty and provides that no one may be prosecuted or deprived of liberty other than on grounds and in the manner laid down by law. The Criminal Code[173] covers enforced disappearance as a criminal act; however, it does not define enforced disappearance, nor does it establish the specific constituent elements of a criminal offence labelled as enforced disappearance. Nevertheless, conduct constituting enforced disappearance, as defined in the Convention, may be

---

171 CED was published in the Collection of Laws under No 13/2017 Coll.
172 Act 1/1993, the Constitution of the Czech Republic.
173 Act 40/2009, the Criminal Code, as amended.

prosecuted – depending on the specific form it takes – as one of several criminal offences built primarily around the personal liberty of the individual: the deprivation of personal liberty (section 170 of the Criminal Code); the restriction of personal liberty (section 171); the transfer of a person against their will (section 172); and, where appropriate, blackmail (section 175) or infringement of another person's rights (section 181).

5.7.2   Reliance by Judiciary

No reference in the decisions of the Constitutional Court or the Supreme Court has been found. A reference to the Convention (article 16) was made in a decision of the Administrative Court (Regional Court in České Budějovice, ref 56 Az 1/2017–73), which cancelled a decision of the Ministry of Interior on the issue of international protection.

5.7.3   Impact on and through Non-state Actors

Given the recent ratification of the Convention, the level of awareness is rather low. Nevertheless, only a few months after ratification the first communication was submitted to the Committee. At the training facilities of the Police Education and Service Training Department, the topic of the protection of persons from the illegal restriction of personal liberty is mainly covered in the qualification courses Basic Training 2018, Public Order Police Qualification Courses, and Criminal Police and Investigation Service Qualification Courses. The above courses encompass the teaching of criminal and constitutional law, including analyses of the constituent elements of the relevant criminal acts. Training is also provided in relation to acts of detention and the possibility of the restriction or deprivation of personal liberty in accordance with the Act on the Police of the Czech Republic and the Code of Criminal Procedure. No reference to the Convention was found in the work of NGOs (in their advocacy campaigns) or in academic research.

5.7.4   Impact of State Reporting

The initial report of the Czech Republic was submitted in May 2019.[174] The report is descriptive and detailed, and follows the structure of the Convention. The Ministries of Justice, Interior, Labour and Social Affairs and Foreign Affairs are involved in the process of implementation of the Convention.

---

[174] CED/C/CZE/1.

5.7.5 Impact of Individual Communications

So far, one communication has been submitted to the Committee, but was discontinued after the matter had been resolved.[175]

5.7.6 Brief Conclusion

It is premature to assess the impact of the Convention as it was ratified only recently. The government submitted its initial report only in May 2019. So far, there is no feedback from the Committee. The first communication within the respective procedure was submitted very shortly after ratification. The Czech Republic has never had a member on the CED Cttee.

5.8 *Convention on the Rights of Persons with Disabilities*

The Czech Republic ratified CRPD in 2009, but has not ratified OP-CRPD.

5.8.1 Incorporation and Reliance by Legislature and Executive

In line with article 10 of the Constitution, the Convention was incorporated in the legal system of the Czech Republic and takes precedence over national law. From the perspective of implementation, the Czech legal system does not contain a unified definition of the terms 'disability' and 'person with disability'. Thus, section 5(6) of the Anti-Discrimination Act states that

> [d]isability is understood as physical, sensory, mental, intellectual or other disability which hinders or may hinder the persons in their right to equal treatment in areas defined by this law; whereas such disability must be of a long term character which has lasted or is supposed to have lasted at least one year according to the findings of the medical science.

---

[175] *Iureva v Czech Republic* (Communication 2/2017 of June 2017) related to the extent of the state party's obligation to provide information as to the whereabouts of a person. The author of the communication (a national of the Russian Federation) submitted that her daughter had disappeared with her husband in October 2015, and had last been seen in the Czech Republic in December 2015. The state party confirmed that the alleged victim and her husband were in the Czech Republic and that they were well but did not wish their location to be revealed. In April 2018, the author advised that her daughter had been located. As the allegations raised by the author were directly linked to the individual situation of her daughter, which had been resolved, the Committee considered that the subject matter of the submitted complaint was moot and decided to discontinue the consideration of communication. The state cooperated during the procedure. Information on the communication was published in the report of the government agent for the year 2017. The Ministry of Justice and the Police of the Czech Republic were involved.

Section 67 of the Act on Employment provides that persons with disabilities are individuals who qualify for disability of the first, second or third degree according to a social security agency or qualify as disadvantaged in terms of health as decided by the Czech Labour Office. A person disadvantaged in terms of health means an individual whose ability to carry out a job or other gainful activity continuously has been preserved. However, it also means that his or her ability to be or remain involved in their work, to perform their previous job or to use their present qualification or to gain new qualification has been substantially limited on the grounds of their long-term unfavourable state of health (that is, a state which is supposed to last for more than one year according to the findings of the medical science, restricts their psychical, physical or sensory abilities substantially and thus their chances of finding employment). For the purpose of the School Act, disability means mental, physical, visual or hearing disability.

The Anti-Discrimination Act provides for protection against direct and indirect discrimination based on disability in fields such as employment, entrepreneurship and other self-employed activities; membership of and activities in trade unions; membership and activities of professional associations; social security and social benefits; health care; education and training; and services that are offered to the public.

As for political programmes, the government has approved and given effect to a number of national plans which formulate the state policy concerning citizens with disabilities.[176] Each ministry has to assess priorities in line with the national plans. The government annually reviews the accomplishment of the national plans. In its initial state report[177] the Czech Republic maintained that the fulfilment of the national plans had probably improved the attitude of the state to persons with disabilities and promoted their social inclusion. The elemental form of the National Plan, both in content and structure, corresponds to the general principles on which the Convention is based. With reference to the individual articles of the Convention, the National Plan is divided into separate chapters. Besides a quotation of the relevant article of the Convention, each chapter also contains a concise description of the existing situation and goals to be achieved by the measures, and a group of fixed terms and continuous measures including an indication of the department in charge of their implementation.

---

[176] Information on the Government Board for People with Disabilities <https://icv.vlada.cz/en/media-centrum/tema/information-on-the-government-board-for-people-with-disabilities-70404/tmplid-676/> accessed 30 September 2021.

[177] CRPD/C/CZE/1.

As becomes clear from their alternative report, NGOs identified some major problems related to the implementation of CRPD, such as the lack of a definition of reasonable accommodation which would reflect the wide understanding of the core disability rights principle of CRPD and the need for a reform of the guardianship system which would introduce a system of supported decision making.

The Czech Republic already in 1991 established the Government Board for People with Disabilities as its coordinating and advisory body for the problems surrounding disability.[178] The Board, which consists of representatives of the government and ministries and representatives of associations of persons with disabilities and their employers, cooperates with the public administration authorities as well as with NGOs. The Board is involved in the preparation of the national plans of action.

5.8.2 Reliance by Judiciary

As for the case law of the Constitutional Court, the CRPD for the first time appeared in a finding concerning the requirements for detention review in a psychiatric hospital.[179] The Constitutional Court found a violation of articles 8, 36 and 38 of the Constitutional Charter and article 5(4) of the ECHR. Articles 13(1) and 14(2) CRPD are mentioned in relation to the obligation to adapt the procedure to persons with disabilities. In a second case the Constitutional Court dealt in more detail with the content and interpretation of CRPD.[180] In this case the Constitutional Court found that it was the duty of the regional authorities to ensure the availability of a suitable social care service to persons with disabilities. A violation of article 19 CRPD was found in conjunction with articles 31 and 36 of the Constitutional Charter and article 11 CESCR. The complainant himself, in addition to other human rights documents, explicitly relied on several articles of CRPD, namely, articles 4(1) and (2), 5, 19 and 26(1)(a). Some of these are also dealt with in the recitals in the reasoning of the Constitutional Court.

The Highest Administrative Court has referred to CRPD in several cases concerning issues of social security. In a judgment of 2017,[181] the Court found that CRPD was an international treaty, which due to its universality is not a law applicable directly within the meaning of article 10 of the Constitution of the

---

178 Government Board for Persons with Disabilities <https://www.vlada.cz/en/ppov/vvzpo/uvod-vvzpo-en-312/> accessed 30 September 2021.
179 ECLI:CZ:US:2015:1.US.1974.14.3.
180 ECLI:CZ:US:2018:2.US.3169.16.1.
181 3 Ads 151/2016–59.

Czech Republic. According to the Court, the provisions of CRPD need to be specified in a broad context by national legislation, depending on local social and economic conditions. Thus, CRPD does not imply any rights with regard to specific welfare services. The provision of section 38 of the Act on Social Services generally defines the purpose of providing social care services and, in particular, it states that social welfare services help persons to ensure their physical and mental self-sufficiency in order to enable them to participate as much as possible in the everyday life of society. The Court concluded that personal claims arising from the Social Services Act must be sought only in individual provisions of the Act and not in CRPD.

In a judgment of 2016,[182] the Highest Administrative Court rejected an argument of the complainant based on article 28 CRPD and decided that the Convention does not contain a provision under which the complainant could claim a special-purpose scholarship. In a case concerning the issue of invalidity pensions,[183] the Highest Administrative Court recalled that CRPD has been acceded to by both the Czech Republic and the EU and that the Convention thus became part of EU law. According to the Court, CRPD does not imply that the Czech Republic undertakes to waive the legal regulation of invalidity pension from the principle of merit, or that it undertakes to equalise the amount of the invalidity pension with the minimum wage. The Court found that under article 4(2) of the Convention, states committed to undertake measures to the maximum extent of their resources. That does not necessarily mean that states are obliged to spend all income on invalidity pensions as the state is obliged to perform a large number of public tasks, which entail a considerable amount of expenditure, and their distribution largely is the result of political consensus. Therefore, according to the Court, the Czech Republic as a state party to CRPD is not obliged to maintain the level of the invalidity pension benefits in a specific proportion to other expenses such as, for example, the level of the minimum wage as suggested by the complainant.

5.8.3 Impact on and through Non-state Actors

For the period from 2015 to 2019, we did not find references to CRPD in the professional journals of the Czech Notarial Chamber, the Czech Executive Chamber and the Czech Bar Association. A number of publications of NGOs use references to CAT in articles concerning the protection of the rights of persons deprived of or limited in legal capacity, involuntary hospitalisation of

---

182   5 As 40/2016 – 59.
183   4 Ads 283/2015–53.

psychiatric patients, the institution of professional guardianship and support, cage beds and the use of restraints in psychiatric facilities and the employment of people with disabilities. In the academia, CRPD is not very popular among students preparing a diploma or doctoral thesis at Czech universities.

5.8.4 Impact of State Reporting

In its COs on the initial report the Czech Republic,[184] adopted in 2015, the CRPD Cttee welcomed the National Plan, the Anti-Discrimination Act, the amendment of the Building Act aiming at the creation of a barrier-free environment and concrete provisions in the Czech Civil Code for supported decision making. The Committee also appreciated the provision of assistance in proceedings under the Code of Civil Procedure. However, a number of issues were the subject of concern. Under the Anti-Discrimination Act, as the duty to provide reasonable accommodation is limited to employment and related labour relations, the Committee suggested that the Czech Republic should extend the prohibition of denial of reasonable accommodation to other areas besides employment and labour relations. In line with Czech public policy, children with disabilities often end up in care institutions and support services for boys and girls with disabilities and their families in local communities are insufficiently developed. Therefore, the Committee called upon the Czech Republic to abandon the concept of residential institutional care for boys and girls with disabilities and to step up its efforts to develop support services for boys and girls with disabilities and their families in local communities.

As the Czech Civil Code provides for the possibility of limiting a person's legal capacity and placing a person with a disability under partial guardianship, the CRPD Cttee found that Czech legislation was not in full compliance with article 12 of the Convention and the Committee's General Comment 1 on equal recognition before the law. It has to be noted that under the election legislation, persons with disabilities with restricted legal capacity may be denied the right to vote or to stand for election. Election materials reportedly are rarely accessible to blind persons or to persons with intellectual disabilities and polling stations often are not physically accessible.

It was not before 1 January 2018 (almost nine years after ratification of CRPD) that the Public Defender of Rights became the independent monitoring body under the Convention that systematically watches over the rights of persons with disabilities. The Public Defender seeks to change systemic shortcomings that prevent persons with disabilities from fulfilling their rights and, to this end,

---

184 CRPD/C/CZE/CO/1.

she is involved in commenting on draft legislation. In 2018 the Public Defender suggested to the authors of an amendment to Decree 98/2012 Coll, on medical documentation, that they had failed to incorporate one of the measures imposed on it by the National Plan for the Promotion of Equal Opportunities for Persons with Disabilities 2015–2020 which concerned mandatory information on the necessary compensatory aids used by a patient.[185] The Public Defender also commented on the proposal to amend Decree 27/2016 Coll, on the education of pupils with special educational needs and gifted pupils.[186] In particular, she pointed out the inconsistency of the proposed amendment with article 24 of CRPD. She found that the envisaged amendments to the decree, such as the limitation of the number of teachers working in parallel in the mainstream classroom or the deletion of the provision whereby pupils with disabilities are preferentially educated in mainstream schools, did not comply with the Convention's concept of inclusive education

5.8.5 Brief Conclusion

According to the National Plan for the Promotion of Equal Opportunities for Persons with Disabilities 2015–2020, which was approved by Resolution of the Government of the Czech Republic 385 of 25 May 2015, the position of persons with disabilities in the Czech Republic may be characterised as stabilised, supported by the existence of a solid legal framework, leaning mostly on positive attitudes of the majority. Indeed, important legislation has been adopted with respect to the social inclusion of persons with disabilities in the Czech Republic. The competent Czech courts are aware of the crucial provisions of CRPD and frequently make reference to the Convention. However, as pointed out by the Public Defender of Rights, society's attitudes to persons with disabilities must change to eliminate certain stereotypes and prejudices. The Public Defender, as the national independent monitoring body, has identified a number of structural weaknesses concerning the effective implementation of rights of persons with disabilities. In response to the initial report of the Czech Republic, the CRPD Cttee has formulated a number of substantial concerns and recommendations.

---

185 Doc. No. MZDR 28667/2017–4/OZS.
186 Opinion of the Public Defender of Rights on the Communication from the Czech authorities concerning enforcement of the judgement of the European Court of Human Rights in the Case of *DH & Others v the Czech Republic* <https://ochrance.cz/fileadmin/user_upload/ESO/49-2019-DIS-VB_Opinion_discrimination_under___21b.pdf> accessed 30 September 2021.

6   Conclusion

With a view to its experience with undemocratic and totalitarian regimes violating basic human rights, today's Czech Republic, as a liberal democracy fully integrated into the process of European integration, places considerable emphasis on the constitutional protection of human rights and on the implementation of both universal and regional human rights obligations into the national legal order. Human rights are also emphasised in the Czech foreign policy.

Whereas state authorities are fully aware of human rights norms adopted within the framework of UN treaty-based protection, in legal practice, that is, in legislation and adjudication, the role of European human rights treaties and especially the ECHR is more prominent. Legal practitioners, in principle, are aware that legally-binding judgments of the ECtHR have a stronger position in the legal discourse than soft law documents issued by the UN treaty bodies. Nevertheless, they also acknowledge the added value of UN documents which go beyond the narrower frame of the ECHR, for instance, in the fields of children's rights, racial discrimination and social rights.

This chapter documents a rather low direct impact of the UN human rights treaties and TB recommendations on two illustrative examples: the issue of involuntary sterilisations and the restitution of property. As for the recommendations relating to national institutions, the Czech Republic still lacks a national human rights institution and a children's ombudsperson.

Compared to the domestic impact as at 1999, this study presents information about the complex transformation in the fields of criminal and private law. The main objectives of the recodification, which was completed more than 20 years after the non-violent change of government in 1989, was to develop codes based on respect for European legal thought and to break with the ideology embodied in pre-1989 Communist law. Another very important piece of legislation adopted in the period covered by the study was the Anti-Discrimination Act of 2009, designed to strengthen the protection against discrimination in all major areas of social life.

CHAPTER 6

The Impact of the United Nations Human Rights Treaties on the Domestic Level in Egypt

Mustapha Kamel Al-Sayyid

1   Introduction to Human Rights in Egypt

The recent history of the Arab Republic of Egypt (ARE) has been marked by the succession of two regimes: a semi-liberal monarchy (1923–1952) and an authoritarian republic (since 18 June 1953). The republican regime hovered between a radical statist model of development and single mass organization (1952–1973), and a model allowing a larger role for the private sector and foreign investments and tolerating a restricted form of party pluralism.[1]

Efforts at economic development undertaken by successive regimes managed to move the country from an agrarian economy during the first half of the twentieth century to a more diversified economy relying on revenues from migrant workers, exports of petroleum and natural gas, tolls of ships going through the Suez Canal, and tourism. Industrialization did not succeed in placing Egypt among newly-industrialized countries. The socio-economic conditions of the majority of people have definitely improved as a result of these efforts. In 2017 the United Nations Development Programme reported that the average life expectancy in the country was 71,7 years, with the mean years of schooling standing at 7,2 years. In terms of the Human Development Index, the country ranked 115 out of 189 countries in 2018. Official statistics suggested that in 2017 more than 32,5 per cent of the population was living below the poverty line.[2]

The human rights situation in Egypt mirrored both the succession of different regimes and models of development and the difficulty of facing the challenge of a large population that reached 99 million in 2019, making Egypt the

---

[1] Afaf Lutfi al-Sayyid Marsot, A History of Egypt (Cambridge University Press 2007).
[2] UNDP, Human Development Indices and Indicators: 2018 Statistical Update. Brief Note for Countries in the 2018 Statistical Update <www.hdr.updateorg/sites/allthemes/hdr/theme/country-notes/EGY.pdf> accessed 27 November 2019; CAPMAS, Income, Expenditure and Consumption Survey 1 October 2017–30 September 2018, CAPMAS, Cairo (2018) 78 (in Arabic).

© MUSTAPHA KAMEL AL-SAYYID, 2024 | DOI:10.1163/9789004377653_008
This is an open access chapter distributed under the terms of the CC BY-NC-ND 4.0 license.

most populous country in the Middle East. Realizing socio-economic rights was a constant challenge to all these regimes but the situation of civil and political rights varied considerably from one regime to the other.

Under the semi-liberal regime of the monarchy, the fortunes of civil and political rights were relatively better than under the republican regime, notwithstanding varying degrees of tolerance for these rights from one administration to the other. The monarchy did not exhibit much concern for socio-economic rights. This category of rights was a major priority for the republican regime, particularly under Gamal Abdel Nasser (1954–1970). The shift to an open market policy, which started under President Sadat, marked the beginning of the deterioration in the exercise of these rights, reaching unprecedented levels from 1991 with the adoption of neo-liberal economic policies. The shift to a hybrid form of multi party system since 1977 did not radically improve the exercise of civil and political rights.

The January 2011 Revolution ushered in a brief period of two years characterized by political instability, on the one hand, and the removal of many restrictions on civil and political rights, on the other. This exceptional period ended with removal by the armed forces of the elected Muslim Brothers' President Mohammed Morsi on 30 June 2013. This move was supported by large sections of the people but opposed by others. It paved the way for a 'restoration' of an authoritarian regime, marked even more than the pre-revolution order by military domination of the country's politics. Under this new regime, the relative liberty that civil society organizations enjoyed during the pre-revolution period shrank enormously.[3]

Human rights were recognized for the first time in independent Egypt in chapter 2 of the 1923 Constitution, and this continued in all successive Constitutions, the most important of which were those of 1956, 1971, 2012 and 2014. Civil and political rights were recognised in all these Constitutions, with the exception of the establishment of political parties, which was prohibited in the Constitutions of 1956 and 1971, but were allowed, under certain conditions, through an amendment to the 1971 Constitution in 1980. All these Constitutions required the exercise of these rights to be in accordance with the law. A wide range of socio-economic rights, including the rights to education, health, work, social protection and the formation of trade unions, were

---

3 On the evolution of Egypt's political system, see Afaf Lutfi Al-Sayyid Marsot, Egypt's Liberal Experiment: 1922–1936 (University of California Press 1977); John Waterbody, The Egypt of Nasser and Sadat. The Political Economy of Two Regimes (Princeton University Press 1983); Bruce Rutherford and Jeannie Sowers, Modern Egypt: What Everyone Needs to Know (Oxford University Press 2018).

included in the 1956 Constitution and such provisions were replicated in all successive constitutions.

The current Constitution is the 2014 Constitution, as amended in 2019. It maintained in its article 93 the reference to human rights treaties ratified by Egypt as part of domestic law, once they are published in the Official Gazette (Al Jarida Al Rasmiyyah).[4]

Human rights are mentioned in school textbooks and should be taught in all universities. A number of civil society organizations and state bodies are engaged in promoting different categories of human rights. The Egyptian Human Rights Organization was founded in 1985, followed by over 200 human rights organizations. The National Council of Human Rights (NCHR) was established in 2006. Three other government-established bodies take care of the rights of children and mothers (1988), women (2000) and persons with disabilities (2004). As for the enforcement of these rights, the Supreme Constitutional Court (SCC) in particular is endowed with the power of judicial review of the constitutionality of laws including disputes involving violations of human rights. The Court has recently been empowered to look into the constitutionality of Bills before they are enacted as laws. However, there are very few cases in which Egyptian courts accepted statements of claims based on Egypt's commitments under United Nations (UN) human rights treaties. Such cases are quite rare as judges argue that such claims are not justiciable unless a law has been adopted giving effect to the rights in a specific human rights treaty. The SCC, the Court of Cassation and the Council of State did issue rulings that reversed decrees of the executive authority. The SCC in 2000 declared the electoral law of 1990 as well as the Law of Associations of 2002 to be unconstitutional. The Council of State ordered the dissolution of the first Constituent Assembly formed under Muslim Brothers' rule in 2012.[5]

While the Egyptian legal system gave effect to many human rights, relevant laws in some cases introduced restrictions on the exercise of the rights rather than enabling and facilitating their exercise.[6] Other laws, such as those on associations or the right to peaceful assembly, in fact deprive categories

---

4   See the text of the Constitution of 2014 in English <www.sis.gov.eg> 15 September 2023. See also Nathan Brown, 'Correcting the Corrective Revolution' Carnegie Middle East Centre, Beirut (27 February 2019).

5   On rulings by the SCC, see <www.hlibrary.umn.edu/arabic/Egypt-SCC-SC/Egypt-SCC-11-Y13.htm> accessed 8 July 2000; <www. hlibrary.umn.edu/arabic/Egypt-SCC-SC/Egypt-SCC-153-Y21.htm>, ruling on 3 June 2000; on rulings by the Council of State <www.manshurat.org/node/1003> (10 April 2012) accessed 29 May 2020 (in Arabic).

6   See, for example, text of Law 8 of 2015 known as the Law of Terrorist Entities in AL-Jarida Al-Rasmia, <www.alamiria.com> 15 September 2023.

of citizens from the possibility of enjoying the most basic of these rights. The country has since 1981 been living almost uninterruptedly under a state of emergency. Under the single mass organization or dominant party system that has been ruling the country since 1953, the head of state was also the virtual power behind the legislative assemblies, as he was the leader of both or the power behind the dominant party. Constitutional amendments of 2019 ended the limited independence of the judiciary by endowing the President with the power to appoint heads of the major judicial bodies in the country, thereby removing all semblance of separation of powers under the Egyptian political system.[7] In addition, the security forces often deride constitutional provisions on the rights to personal freedom, expression and association.[8] While economic resources of the country do not allow for an end to poverty and unemployment, government misallocation of resources and adoption of neo-liberal policies recently contributed to the aggravation of the problem of poverty and the unfair distribution of national income and wealth. Finally, elevating principles of Islamic Shari'a to be the major source of legislation led the government to express reservations on provisions of several UN human rights treaties, arguing that they are incompatible with its teachings. Such a position explains why some of their provisions on the rights of women and children could not be echoed in the country's laws or family practices.

2 Relationship of Egypt with the International Human Rights System in General

As a founding member of the UN, being guided by a legal tradition going back to the semi-liberal period under the monarchy, Egypt has adhered to almost all relevant UN human rights treaties. With the exception of the International Convention for the Protection of All Persons from Enforced Disappearance (CED), Egypt has ratified all nine core UN treaties covered in this chapter. Egypt has even adhered to some human rights treaties already before the establishment of the UN in 1945, such as the Slavery Convention (ratified in 1928).[9] At the regional level, the country ratified the 1981 African Charter on Human and Peoples' Rights (African Charter) in 1984 and ratified the 2004 Arab Human

---

7 For details, see Brown (n 4).
8 For details, see report of the Working Group on the Universal Periodic Report of Egypt in the document UN General Assembly A/HRC/WG.6/34/EGY/2 (2 September 2019).
9 Abdel Monsef Alaa, 'Egypt's Position on Human Rights Conventions' Egyptian Institute for Studies <https//en.eipss-eg.org> accessed 15 September 2023.

Rights Charter in 2019. It has participated fully in UN debates and activities on human rights. However, Egypt has not adhered to some international human rights treaties, claiming that they are not compatible with the country's sovereignty. The most important of these treaties are the Convention on the Status of Stateless Persons; Nationality of Married Women; Consent to Marriage; Reduction of Statelessness; Non-Applicability of Statutory Limitations to War Crimes; and the Rome Statute of the International Criminal Court.[10]

Egyptian diplomats have been active in human rights fora. Egypt's representatives participated energetically in meetings of the UN Commission of Human Rights and of its successor, the UN Human Rights Council (HRC), as well as those of other UN human rights bodies. Egypt was elected to serve on the HRC for the period 2017–2019, and had submitted three Universal Periodic Review (UPR) reports, in 2010, 2014 and 2019.

Moreover, through its representatives, Egyptian diplomacy has always been careful to express respect for all categories of human rights out of concern for the country's good reputation in the international community and its domestic legitimacy.[11] Quite recently, however, President Abdel Fattah El Sisi had several times adopted a cultural relativist-like position on human rights, arguing that Egypt should not be judged by criteria of human rights prevalent in Western countries such as France and the United States (US), but should be judged according to its own specific conditions, particularly its engagement in the fight against terrorism and the mobilization of resources to provide health, education and housing to the Egyptian people. President Sisi stressed that human rights are not limited to civil and political rights, but include economic and social rights such as the right to housing, medical care, education and employment.[12] Such statements emanating from the President were however not followed by any declaration by the Egyptian government that it would withdraw from any of the human rights treaties that had already been ratified.

The OHCHR had on occasions issued statements commenting on government practices that it considered not in line with the country's commitments under core human rights treaties.[13] Spokespersons of the Ministry of Foreign

---

10   Ibid.
11   See the statement issued by the Ministry of Foreign Affairs on the occasion of the 2020 anniversary of the Universal Declaration of Human Rights (10 December 2020) in Facebook.com/AFAEgypt accessed 15 December 2020.
12   See these statements on YouTube in a joint press conference with the French President Emanuel Macron (28 January 2019) <www.youtube.com/watch?v=EWalfi5osYQ&t=16s> accessed 30 January 2019 (in Arabic).
13   Al Ahram (n 12) 13.

Affairs and prominent members of the House of Representatives rejected such positions. Both local and international human rights organisations, namely, Amnesty International and Human Rights Watch, reiterated such negative comments on government practices.[14]

Despite such critical statements, the government never expressed any intention to withdraw from any UN human rights treaty or organ or to cease cooperation with UN officials. Egypt received four visits of special mechanisms, namely, those concerned with trafficking in persons (in 2010); human rights under the state of fighting terrorism (in 2011); and the Independent Expert on the issue of human rights obligations related to access to safe and drinking water and sanitation (in June 2009),[15] and the Special Rapporteur on the right to housing (who condemned forced evictions, housing demolitions, arbitrary arrest, intimidation and reprisals) (2018). The 2018 report of the Special Rapporteur on adequate housing, which stated that some of the people she had interviewed during her visit were subjected to intimidation by the government,[16] led to harsh criticism by the government All the other visits were conducted before the overthrow of former President Hosny Mubarak on 2 February 2011 and the subsequent changes in the Egyptian political system.

In terms of cooperation with regional human rights mechanisms, Egypt is a state party to the African Charter but has not become a party to the Protocol to the African Charter Establishing the African Court on Human and Peoples' Rights. It has cooperated with the African Peer Review Mechanism of the African Union's NEPAD process to which it submitted its first national report published in February 2020.[17]

At the domestic level, human rights treaties have been given a special status in the Constitution of 2014. In terms of article 93 they should have the force of the law, once they have been ratified by the President, following approval by the legislative authority, and published according to prescribed procedures. This is also the general rule of all treaties as provided for in article 151 of the 2014 Constitution.[18]

---

14 See 'Egypt 2019' <www.amnesty.org/en/latest/press-release/2019/10/egypt> accessed 15 September 2023. 'Egypt' <www.hrw.org/middle-east/n.africa/egyypt> accessed 14 June 2020.
15 A/HCR/15/31/Add.3.
16 OHCHR, Special Procedure 'Egypt: UN expert alarmed by treatment of human rights defenders after visit. Egypt: Reprisals.' 4 December 2018 < https://www.ohchr.org/en/press-releases/2018/12/egypt-un-experts-alarmed-treatment-human-rights-defenders-after-visit> accessed 16 April 2022.
17 See the APRMTOOLKIT <http://aprmtoolkit.saiia.org.za/country-reports-and-experiences/egypt> accessed 9 October 2020.
18 ARE Constitution of 2014 26,40.

IMPACT OF UNHR TREATIES ON DOMESTIC LEVEL IN EGYPT 361

3 At a Glance: Formal Engagement of Egypt with the UN Human Rights Treaty System

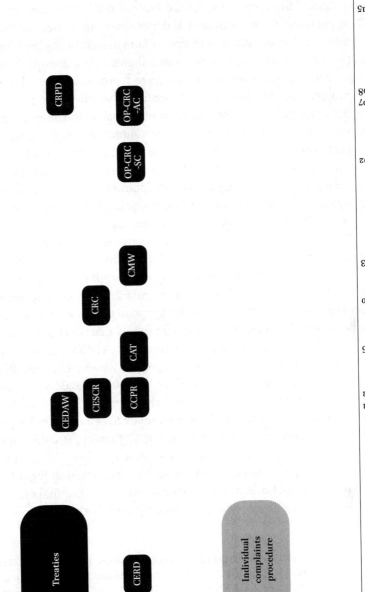

4   Role and Overall Impact of UN Human Rights Treaties in Egypt

4.1   Role of UN Human Rights Treaties

4.1.1   Formal Acceptance

Egypt has become a state party to all core UN human rights treaties, with the exception of the Convention for the Protection of all Persons from Enforced Disappearance (CED), which it did not even sign. The Assistant Foreign Minister of Foreign Affairs in charge of human rights explained this position, stating that many countries have not adhered to this treaty.[19] Human rights organizations, including the NCHR, have reported cases of disappearances of people, some of whom would be declared later by authorities to be under police custody.[20] Of all the claims of disappearances communicated by the NCHR to the Ministry of Interior, the Council received clarifications with respect to only half.[21] One may therefore assume that the unwillingness on the part of the government to be held accountable for such practices, which have definitely increased during periods of confrontation with armed opposition groups between 1981 and 1997, and again since 2011, probably was an important reason for its failure to accede to this Convention.

Four of these treaties were signed between 1967 and 1980, while the International Convention on the Elimination of All Forms of Racial Discrimination (CERD) was signed in 1966 and ratified in 1967. An explanation of the enthusiasm to ratify CERD seven months after its adoption by the UN General Assembly is the fact that the Egyptian government was not expecting to be targeted by this treaty, as it was presumed that the country did not have a history of practicing racial discrimination. Egypt's adherence to CERD could be seen as a sign of solidarity with African peoples who were historically victims of such discrimination by colonial powers. Under the presidency of Gamal Abdel Nasser, in the 1960s Egypt was a leading power in Africa in the fight against colonialism and apartheid. The second treaty to be ratified during this period was the Convention on the Elimination of All Forms of Discrimination against Women (CEDAW), signed in 1980 and ratified in 1981. The third and fourth treaties, the International Covenant on Civil and Political Right (CCPR) and the International Covenant on Economic, Social and Cultural Rights (CESCR), were both signed in 1967 but ratified only 15 years later, in 1982.

---

19   Interview with Mr Ahmed Ihab Gamal El Deen, Assistant Foreign Minister, Human Rights, International Humanitarian and Social Affairs, Ministry of Foreign Affairs, Cairo (5 May 2020). According to the United Nations, 98 countries had signed this Convention with 62 countries ratifying it until May 2020 <https://treaties.un.org> accessed 15 September 2023.
20   Al-majlis al-qawmi lihoqouq al-insaan. Al-taqrir al-sanawi al-rabe' áshr lilmajlis al-qawmi lihoqouq al-insaan 2018–2019 National Council for Human Rights, Fourteenth Annual Report of the National Council for Human Rights, Cairo (2020) (in Arabic). List of claimed disappearances 221–279.
21   ibid 282.

It would be easy also to argue that the country was in a state of war in the period 1967 to 1982, and that it prioritized its attention to these issues at the expense of focusing on international commitments. Egypt was attempting to recover parts of its territory occupied by Israel during the June 1967 war, and was preoccupied with the liberation of occupied territory, a process nearly completed in April 1982. The political regime that ruled Egypt under both Presidents Nasser and Sadat did not welcome the notion of human rights, which was seen as a Western tool to exert pressures on anti-colonial governments or a convenient discourse used by domestic opposition. Ratifying CEDAW, however, was quite compatible with the proclaimed image of the regime that ruled the country since July 1952 as indeed committed to improving the status of women.

As for the other four treaties, namely, the Convention on the Rights of the Child (CRC), the Convention against Torture and Other Cruel, Inhuman or Degrading Treatment or Punishment (CAT), the Convention on the Rights of Persons with Disabilities (CRPD) and the International Convention on the Protection of the Rights of All Migrant Workers and Members of Their Families (CMW), these were all ratified under the rule of President Mubarak (1981–2011). Mubarak in fact had adopted a softer style of authoritarianism by introducing a dose of political liberalization in the country. After Egypt had regained all its occupied territory in the Sinai by 1982, the Egyptian government wanted to be seen as abiding by what it called international legality, a sign that it was adhering to international human rights treaties.

The Egyptian government attached reservations to its ratification to most of these treaties. Several of these reservations relate to provisions seen by the Egyptian government to be incompatible with Islamic Shari'a, such as reservations to the Optional Protocols to CCPR and CESCR, articles 2 and 16 of CEDAW, articles 20 and 21 of CRC, and article 4 of CMW. The object of a second set of reservations was articles seen as infringing on the country's sovereignty by holding it accountable before an international tribunal (the International Court of Justice or international arbitration tribunal). This statist position explains reservations to articles 22 of CERD and article 29 of CEDAW, as well as a reluctance to join the Optional Protocols to most of these treaties calling for acceptance of individual complaints or enquiry procedures. The third category of reservations relates to what was perceived as a matter of national security. This was probably the undeclared rationale of the reservation to article 9(2) of CEDAW calling on governments to grant women equal rights with men with respect to the nationality of their children. This reservation, however, was withdrawn in January 2008.[22] The state party report to the CEDAW Cttee stated

---

22 United Nations Treaty Collection. Chapter IV. Human Rights. 8. Convention on the Elimination of All Forms of Discrimination Against Women. <https://treaties.un.org/pages/ViewDetails.aspx?src=IND&mtdsg_no=IV-8&chapter=4&clang=_en> accessed 9 April 2022.

that the reservation was withdrawn following the adoption of Law 54 of 2004, which granted women such equality.[23]

In other instances, reservations were withdrawn under domestic pressure exerted by some civil society groups. This was indeed the case when the government withdrew reservations to articles 20 and 21 of CRC relating to what should happen when children were separated from one or both of their parents. In his presentation of the third and fourth periodic report to the CEDAW Cttee in December 2008, the representative of Egypt stated the following:[24]

> In response to paragraph 204 of the in document (CRC/C/65/Add.9), Egypt has withdrawn its reservations to article 20 and 21 of the Convention by presidential Decree No 145 of 2003. The National Council of Childhood and Motherhood (the Council) has taken the initiative to call for the withdrawal of reservations and has led a campaign to raise awareness to that end. These efforts were crowned by the said decision of the President of the Republic.

4.1.2 General Attitude of the Egyptian Government towards the UN Treaty System

A major feature of Egyptian foreign policy since the country acquired a semi-independent status in 1922 was respect for 'international legality' including observation of commitments under the founding document of first the League of Nations and later the UN, of which it was a founding member. Egypt tended, in general, to cooperate with the UN and to uphold its Charter. This was also the case with the UN human rights system. While avoiding those human rights treaties that would subject the government to forms of international accountability, Egypt strove to demonstrate that it was not in violation of any of these treaties. This was particularly the case with those treaties that do not give rise to political controversies such as those dealing with women, children, migrant workers, persons with disabilities, or even CESCR. The government had acceded to the two Optional Protocols substantively complementing CRC (the Protocol banning the sale of children, child prostitution and child pornography, in 2002; and the Protocol prohibiting the involvement of children in armed conflicts, in 2007). However, Egypt did not accept any of the individual

---

23 See state party report to the CEDAW Cttee 11 <www.CEDAW/C/EGY/7> accessed 5 September 2020.
24 Egypt state party third and fourth periodic report, UN CRC/C/EGYPT/ (3–4 December 2008) para 14 9.

complaints mechanisms. The conciliatory attitude towards the UN human rights system started to change from August 2013. Statements by spokespersons for the OHCHR, the Secretary of CAT and the UN High Commissioner for Human Rights commenting negatively on the Egyptian government's restrictions of freedom of association, unfair trial or torture of prisoners were met not only by hostile media campaigns but also by strongly-worded rebuttals by the spokesperson of the Ministry of Foreign Affairs.[25]

4.1.3 Levels of Awareness

It is safe to assume that there is general awareness of the UN human rights system as it has occasionally been widely covered in Egyptian media, but the level of awareness of any particular treaty varies among government officials and non-governmental organizations (NGOs) depending on their particular area of concern. The Ministries of Foreign Affairs, Parliamentary and Legal Affairs, Interior and Justice as well as the Office of the Public Prosecutor and the Council of State are definitely the most knowledgeable about the treaties as they have departments in charge of reporting on or responding to complaints on human rights violations. Other ministries or government bodies are knowledgeable about the treaties closer to their area of competence. Among legislators, there is a Commission for Human Rights within the House of Representatives which comments on reports of UN bodies and international NGOs on the human rights situation in the country. More than 200 human rights organizations in Egypt are committed to upholding and disseminating knowledge of human rights among the Egyptian public. As for members of the judiciary, they rarely refer to human rights treaties but they recognize specific human rights only when they are embodied in domestic laws. Professors of law and political science must be familiar with UN core human rights treaties which they all studied in their undergraduate years while others teach some to their students. Other academics are aware of those treaties that relate to their academic disciplines.[26]

Officials' perceptions of UN human rights organs are mixed. They welcome their positive reporting on Egypt and critical reporting on governments that

---

[25] Press Briefing Notes on Egypt, Spokesperson for the UN High Commissioner for Human Rights, Rupert Collville (22 February 2019).

[26] All Egyptian universities are required to teach a course on human rights to all their students. See Human Rights Council, National Report submitted in accordance with paragraph 5 of the annex to Human Rights Council resolution 16/21.A/HRC/WG.6/34/EG/1.4- 15 November 2019 2019, para 86, p 24.

are unfriendly towards the Egyptian government, and would express their displeasure at their reports disapproving certain practices of the Egyptian government. This was particularly the case with some reports of the High Commissioner for Human Rights, or the Secretariat of CAT disapproving of certain violations of human rights in Egypt, which were denounced in the country's media and rebutted by spokespersons for the government as based on insufficient information about the situation in the country or issued under pressure by governments hostile to Egypt.[27] This was also the major theme of many commentators in government-controlled television stations.[28]

All nine core human rights treaties, with the exception of CED, are accessible in Arabic as they have all been published in the official Gazette, which is a formal requirement for all ratified treaties.

The Egyptian public became aware of human rights through media coverage of the different positions taken by the Egyptian government on such issues. Debates on human rights in the media very often fail to specify the relevant treaty related to the issues being covered. The following Table indicates the number of media messages that specifically named one of the eight treaties.

TABLE 6.1 Citations of UN core human rights treaties in a sample of Egyptian newspapers 2014–2019

Convention	Number of references
CERD	4
CCPR	56
CESCR	22
CEDAW	40
CAT	60
CRC	45
CMW	12
CRPD	43

SOURCE: COVERAGE OF MAJOR EGYPTIAN NEWSPAPERS FOR THE PERIOD UNDER STUDY, CARRIED OUT BY THE AUTHOR'S RESEARCH TEAM

---

27 See <https://mfa.gov.eg> accessed 15 September 2023.
28 See the talk show of Ahmed Moussa 'Masr laysa ladayha matókhfihi fi malaff Hoqouq Al'insaan ('Egypt Has Nothing to Hide in the Human Rights File') (18 November 2019) <www.youtube.com/watch?v=1hBcYWdD-m1> accessed 14 June 2020.

The Table is based on the reading of a sample of news items and articles published in major newspapers in Egypt during the period 2014–2019.

The Table demonstrates that CAT and CCPR were the most cited in Egyptian newspapers during the period under study and that CESCR was not very prominent in debates on human rights in the media. The three treaties on rights of children, women and persons with disabilities were in the middle. How could this be explained? In fact, the treaties that received more coverage were those that were most controversial in these debates. Another explanation for the frequency with which a particular treaty was mentioned is the existence of a public institution in charge of its implementation. CRC, CEDAW and CRPD each has a particular institution in charge of promoting the rights it proclaims. Most of those who referred specifically to human rights treaties were either academics, government officials or human rights activists.

In reporting on the treaties, it is very rare to find a comprehensive account of any treaty or treaty body. The media usually covers the part of the proceedings of treaty body meetings of interest to Egypt or that relates to regional issues. Informing readers about the UN human rights system does not seem to be an attractive topic for newspapers or Egyptian media in general.

Human rights are taught in Egyptian public schools. The author had led a team of academics to examine the teaching of human rights for students of primary and secondary schools. Concepts of human rights are presented to young people in a way that corresponds to their age and their knowledge of human rights expands gradually to match their progress in the educational system.[29]

A decision had been taken by the Supreme Council of Universities to introduce the teaching of human rights to all university students across disciplines. The Faculty of Economics and Political Science of Cairo University, the largest and oldest public university in the country, offered this course as an elective for second-year political science students. Some other faculties heeded the decision of the Supreme Council of Universities by introducing such courses, including the Girls Faculty at Ain Shams University as well as Political Science departments at both the American University in Cairo and the British University in Egypt. In my experience, this does not seem to be a general rule, nor does the course in most of the cases include a systematic study of all core treaties.

Some Egyptian academics and scholars published articles and books on several of these treaties. These treaties were used also in graduate dissertations. These works are available in English and Arabic, as could be seen from the

---

[29] Mustapha Kamel Al-Sayyid (ed), 'Huqouq al insaan fi moqarrarat alta'lim alasasi fi masr' Human Rights in Curricula of Basic Education in Egypt, Centre for the Study of Developing Countries, Cairo University (1998) (in Arabic).

analysis conducted for the author of a sample of these works. A preliminary analysis of a tentative list of academic publications on human rights yields the conclusion that most of the scholars who were interested in issues of human rights were more concerned with human rights in general and particularly the compatibility between human rights and Islamic Shari'a. Few academic studies in Arabic dealt with a specific treaty with the exception of CEDAW on which there are a number of studies and dissertations in English. CMW was also the object of several contributions that were published in English.

A number of human rights organizations, particularly the Egyptian Organization of Human Rights, the Cairo Institute for Human Rights Studies, as well as the government, organized workshops to explain the UN human rights system to different categories of people. Human rights organizations catered mostly for human rights activists and university students. Through cooperation with the United Nations Development Program (UNDP) and under the sponsorship of the Ministry of Foreign Affairs, such workshops targeted media people, public prosecution officials and even police officers. The author participated either as a lecturer or evaluator in some of these workshops. National councils for women and children undertook similar activities for lawyers or groups of children.

Despite all these activities on human rights, it would be difficult to claim that there is sufficient knowledge of the core eight human right treaties ratified by Egypt whether within the government, the judiciary, legal profession, NGOs or the public in general, with the exception of those in the government whose task it is to report to UN treaty bodies about Egypt's observance of her commitment under these treaties. One would assume that officials of the four government-established councils for women, children, human rights and persons with disabilities, together with NGOs that care about one particular treaty, know enough about the relevant treaties in their own domains. The educated public probably is aware of the concern by the UN and international NGOs over human rights in general, particularly as their critique of the government's record on such issues has become a matter of public debate in the country. It is doubtful whether the general public has more than a scant knowledge of any of the UN treaties other than CCPR and CAT.

4.1.4   State Reporting

The Egyptian government's record in submitting reports to the eight treaty bodies of which it is a member is quite inconsistent as could be seen by looking at the dates of state party reports. In some cases, the due reporting dates are observed for a while, then are missed for the same treaty body followed by the submission of combined reports for two or several cycles or even giving up on reporting to a specific treaty body for a period close to two decades. The total number of reports submitted to the eight treaty bodies until early 2020 was 35: eleven to the CERD Cttee, six to the HR Cttee, six to the CEDAW Cttee, four to CAT Cttee, three to the CRC Cttee and two each to the CESCR and CMR Cttees. Since the 2000s, Egypt has submitted 12 reports: Three dealt with women's rights and two were submitted to the CERD Cttee, while all the other committees received only one report, namely, those under CCPR, CESCR, CAT, CMW and CRPD. Three reports to each of the CEDAW, CRC and CPRD Cttees were submitted in February 2020. The last report submitted by Egypt to the HR Cttee was on 13 November 2001, but the situation of civil and political rights in the country was included in three of the reports the government sent to the HRC as part of the UPR. Two reports under CMW and CERD were due in January 2018 and have not reached their committees until early 2020. The last report submitted by Egypt to the CAT Cttee was in February 2001. The CMW has not received periodic reports since 2006. The inescapable conclusion is that the government of Egypt became less concerned to submit reports to the treaty bodies since the beginning of the third millennium, but the rate of submission has accelerated towards 2020.This could be the positive effect of the establishment in February 2018 of the Permanent Supreme Committee for Human Rights supported by a technical secretariat at the Ministry of Foreign Affairs.

TABLE 6.2   Egyptian government's reporting to the UN human rights treaty bodies until June 2019

Treaty	Date of last report until June 2019	Reports submitted since 2000	No of dialogues since 2000
CERD	2014	9	4
CCPR	2001	2	2
CESCR	2010	4	5
CEDAW	2008	5	4
CAT	2001	1	2
CRC	2008	3	4
CMW	2006	1	2
CRPD			none
Total		25	23

SOURCE: <www.ohchr.org/en/countries/egypt> ACCESSED 24 AUGUST 2020.

Since 2000, the total number of 25 reports were submitted by the Egyptian government to the eight human rights treaty bodies and were considered by their committees. The CRPD Cttee did not during this period consider any report from the Egyptian government. Egyptian delegations to these treaty bodies participated in 23 dialogues. The reports were initially prepared by experts of the Ministry of Justice and since 2011 by the Ministry of Parliamentary and Legal affairs.[30] Concerned government bodies and government-organized human rights institutions would be consulted as appropriate. Neither other NGOs, nor Members of Parliament were involved in this process.

A decree by the Prime Minister No 2396 of 2018 on 14 November 2018 established the Permanent Supreme Committee for Human Rights chaired by the Minister of Foreign Affairs and includes representatives of five ministries, three government bodies and three government-established human rights institutions. The ministries are Defense, Interior, Justice, House of Representatives Affairs, and Social Solidarity. Government bodies in the Committee are the General Intelligence Services, the Administrative Control Agency and the State Information Service. The NCW, the National Council of Childhood and Motherhood and the National Council for Persons with Disabilities are also members. The Committee may invite two experts to take part in its meetings, but should have no vote. The Committee is supported by a technical secretariat located at the Foreign Ministry and is headed by the Assistant Minister of Foreign Affairs for Human Rights, International Humanitarian and Social Affairs. In the past the Ministry of Justice or that of Parliamentary and Legal Affairs would since 2007 consult with other concerned ministries and government and human rights national institutions while drafting reports to be submitted to UN human rights bodies. The Prime Minister's decree entrusts the new Committee with managing the human rights 'file' and responding to 'claims' about the human rights situation in the country. The Committee should also prepare the UPR to be sent to the UN Human Rights Council, but the decree does not refer to the human rights treaty bodies' reports.[31] The Assistant Foreign Minister for Human Rights, who is also the Secretary of the Committee, stated that the Committee was in charge of preparing all reports to human rights bodies.[32] This might happen in future but the last four reports submitted by Egypt in 2020 were all prepared by relevant ministries with the

---

30 Interview with Assistant Minister of Foreign Affairs, Cairo (1 June 2020).
31 Decree of the Prime Minister No 2396 of 2018. Al-Jarida Al Rasmiyyah No 45bis B (14 November 2018) (in Arabic).
32 The Assistant Minister of Foreign Affairs, Cairo, in a private communication with the author (1 June 2020).

participation of all four national human rights institutions, and were finally reviewed by the Ministry of Foreign Affairs.[33]

The delegations sent to Geneva to take part in the discussion of periodic reports usually comprise senior officials of the ministries or the government bodies concerned by each treaty body together with members of the country's permanent mission in Geneva. Quite often the delegation would be led by an official of legal background from the Ministry of Justice or of the Ministry of Foreign Affairs. The report submitted to the CEDAW Cttee in 2008 had the President of the NCW, herself a former minister, heading the Egyptian delegation.

The COs are not published in Egypt, whether in Arabic or any other language. The only way that an Egyptian citizen would know about them is to search for them on the website of the OHCHR.[34]

Egyptian human rights organizations were present in the last meetings of the treaty bodies that discussed reports by the Egyptian government, including meetings of committees of CERD (one organization), CEDAW (four organizations) and in large numbers in the meetings of CESCR in 2014 in which they numbered seven, but 24 associations put their names in joint declarations. The individual reports of these organizations were quite comprehensive but the joint declarations were thematic in nature. None of those who took part in meetings of treaty bodies was persecuted by the government, although some of those who took part in the discussion of the country's UPR were all victims of repressive measures.[35]

Finally, there are no indications that the government has accepted to make public reports of the Sub-Committee against Torture. In fact, the Committee was denounced in Egyptian newspapers as being politically-motivated and biased against the country.[36]

---

[33] ibid, communication on 3 June 2020.

[34] Interview with the Assistant Minister of Foreign Affairs (5 May 2020).

[35] Miss Mozn Hassan, founder of Nazra for Feminist Studies was put on trial and banned from foreign travel. M Bahey El-Din Hassan of the Cairo Institute for Human Rights left the country and told the author that he had received death threats and Nasser Amin of the Arab Centre for the Independence of the Judiciary and Legal Profession was investigated by public prosecution. Interviews with all three conducted by the author by telephone from Cairo.

[36] A more restrained view is to be found in Hala Mostafa, 'Ma ba'd human rights –What should follow Human Rights Report' Al-Ahram (23 September 2017) <https//gate.ahram.org.eg/daily/News/614965.aspx> accessed 10 April 2020. A much less restrained view is to be found in articles and talk shows of Ahmed Moussa. See his talk show on 11 November 2019 <http://www.facebook.com/pg/AhmedMoussaEG/posts/> accessed 1 June 2020.

4.1.5 Domestic Implementation Mechanism

There is no one single mechanism or process for the domestic implementation of the treaty body recommendations. Several government departments had directorates in charge of human rights, such as Ministries of Foreign Affairs, Justice, Interior, the Office of Public Prosecutor and the Council of State. Reports to UN bodies were usually the responsibility of the Minister of State for Parliamentary and Legal Affairs. This task is to be entrusted to the Technical Secretariat of the newly-formed Permanent Supreme Committee of Human Rights (PSCHR).[37] It is assumed that the institutional entities in charge of the specific domain of certain treaties, namely, the national councils for childhood and motherhood, women and persons with disabilities will be responsible for coordinating government efforts in view of the implementation of recommendations of concern to their targeted constituencies.

4.1.6 Treaty Body Membership

The nomination of members to treaty bodies is entirely in the hands of the government, and particularly the Ministry of Foreign Affairs. The rules are quite informal. Civil society organisations have no insight into how this process is conducted.

Egyptian nationals had been elected to the CERD, CCPR, CESCR, CEDAW and CRC Cttees. An Egyptian national served continuously on the HRCttee between 2001 and 2019, and – with the exception of the period 2002 to 2004 – on the CESCR Cttee. Egyptian female nationals were particularly active in the CEDAW Cttee. Three Egyptians were elected in different cycles to be members of the CRC Cttee, namely, Moushira Gabr, the late Azza Ashmawy and Gehad Madi. An Egyptian national was also elected Chairperson of the HRCttee and CEDAW Cttee. Despite this level of representation, the country's reporting to the human rights treaty bodies has been quite irregular with delays in some instances extending to more than a decade.[38]

The Egyptian representatives who had served on the CEDAW and CRC Cttees, respectively, had the opportunity to benefit from such experience in running state bodies committed to enforce such treaties, when they were later appointed as heads of relevant national bodies. However, very little is known about subsequent involvement in human rights issues of other Egyptian representatives who had served on UN human rights treaty bodies.

---

37 Art 3–2 Decree of the Prime Minister.
38 For details, see sites of the different committees <www.ohchr.org> accessed 30 May 2020.

4.2 Overall Impact of UN Human Rights Treaties

The detailed study of the eight core human rights treaties ratified by Egypt clarifies the extent to which these treaties had an impact on domestic legislative, judicial and policy developments in the country. It is true that this impact is not always easy to discern and varies from one treaty to another. It will be clear that treaties that meet with general consensus in society, particularly between the government, on the one hand, and political opposition and civil society organisations, on the other, and which are of a more functional nature, such as those related to the rights of women, children and persons with disabilities, are likely to produce more of a direct material impact than those that could give rise to mutual recrimination between the government and those who oppose it. The latter category of treaties is more likely to have more of a symbolic influence, perhaps changing attitudes in the medium and long terms towards enforcing the rights they embody. This would be particularly the case of CCPR and CAT.

4.2.1 Incorporation by the Legislature and the Executive

The first direct material impact of all eight treaties is that they became part of domestic law once they have been approved by the country's legislature and ratified by the President and published in the official Gazette. A second direct material impact is that they inspired the adoption of laws that were closely tailored along the structure of specific treaties, or which borrowed the exact language of some treaty provisions. This is the case of domestic legislation on the rights of the child, combating human trafficking, and the law providing protection for persons with disabilities. This material impact could also be seen in several amendments of existing laws in response to recommendations of various treaty bodies, such as the amendment of nationality laws to allow mothers married to foreign husbands to transmit their nationality to their offspring, and redefining racial crimes to correspond to the definition stipulated in CERD.

The symbolic impact could be seen in changes of attitudes on the part of the state or civil society towards some important matters that were not regarded as worthy of special law provisions. This is the case with some practices of sexual harassment of women. Under the influence of CEDAW, these became criminalized in the Penal Code. The call for empowerment of women and persons with disabilities led both the executive and legislature to propose and enact electoral quotas for them. The electoral quota provided for women increased their presence in the House of Representatives to unprecedented levels in the history of the country.

However, the more easily politicized treaties such as CCPR or CAT did not have a similar impact. In fact, they engendered hostility against that part of the UN human rights system monitoring their observance. Responding to statements by these bodies that government officials acted in violation of some of their provisions, the government rejected such statements as inaccurate while continuing the very same practices. Disapproval of such practices by the OHCHR or the CAT Secretariat resulted in the media and spokespersons of the Ministry of Foreign Affairs accusing them of being politically motivated with the head of state objecting to the universal character of human rights or their indivisibility.[39]

4.2.2 Reliance by the Judiciary

There are very few indications that the treaties were used by the judiciary either as a source of remedy or interpretation., with the exception of the Supreme Constitutional Court and criminal tribunals, mostly as sources of interpretation. Judges who were asked why they were reluctant to use international treaties and particularly human rights treaties in their rulings, given that these constitutionally have the force of the law, they responded that articles 93 and 151 of the Constitution address the legislature and not the judiciary. There are few cases in which judges accepted defendant lawyers' arguments based on provisions of human rights treaties. The most famous of these is the case of Public Prosecution against defendants Salah El Din Mostafa Sharaf and 37 others, which involved striking rail workers who had a team of lawyers for their defense including the late lawyer Nabil el Hilali. El Hilali used CESCR as a remedy to argue that their strike of 1986 was lawful due to the government's ratification of CESCR with its provision of the right to peaceful strike. His argument was accepted by the Supreme Emergency State Security Court.[40] In the case of the president of the council of administration of the Islamic Ahl Al-Khair Society against the Minister of Social Affairs and other government officials, the Supreme Constitutional Court upheld freedom of association using paragraph 2 of article 22 of CCPR as a remedy.[41] Finally, in the Khaled Saéid

---

39 'The Ministry of Foreign Affairs in Response to the UN Human Rights Commissioner: The Right to Peaceful Demonstrations is Guaranteed in Terms of the Constitution and the Law' Al Kharejiyyah raddan ála mofawwadiyyat Huqouq al-insan: al Haq fi al tazhahor al-silmi makfoul wefqan li al-qanoun wa al dostour YOUM7/COM/STORY/2019/9/28I (in Arabic).
40 Ruling by the Supreme State Security Court under the State of Emergency No 4190 of 1986, Azbakiiyya (121 Kolliyah Shamal) (in Arabic; text mimeographed).
41 The Supreme Constitutional Court Case 160, Judicial Constitutional Year 37, Ruling declared on 2 June 2018 (mimeographed).

case, the Court of Cassation accepted the argument of the civil lawyer that what the two policemen did with the late Khaled Said in fact was a practice of torture according to CAT, and not cruel treatment as lawyers of defendants had claimed.[42] In a few cases also lawyers used the treaties as a source of remedy such as CRC in which a plaintiff's lawyer found support for his arguments before a court in Alexandria in the summer of 2019.

4.2.3 Impact on and through Independent State Institutions

The NCHR publishes an annual report on the human rights situation in the country, which offers an objective account of this situation. The report is sent to the President and senior officials of the government but is not easily accessible to the public.[43] The NCHR is committed to the universal bill of human rights and monitors the situation of all these rights in its annual report and also carries out activities aimed at raising awareness of the rights for which they provide.[44] The three functional human rights institutions established by the government, the NCW, the National Council for Childhood and Motherhood, and the National Council for People with Disabilities, had framed or amended their statutes to align with the rights and commitments included in the treaties most relevant to their missions. Moreover, they have formulated national strategies to attain their objectives inspired by these relevant treaties, which they admit in the opening pages of such strategies. The NCW had taken the initiative of establishing an Ombudsman Office, while the NCHR receives and investigates complaints by citizens of violations of their rights.

4.2.4 Impact on and through Non-state Actors

Most non-state actors in Egypt concerned with human rights uphold the universal concept of human rights and take treaties relevant to their work as a

---

42 Interview with (the late) Hafez Abou Se'da, President of the Egyptian Human Rights Organization and a human rights lawyer. Cairo at the office of the Egyptian Human Rights Organization on 1 August 2020 (notes on file with author).

43 See, for example, National Council of Human Rights, Al-taqrir al-sanawi lilmajles al-qawmi lihoqouq al-insan. al-thani áshar 2016–2017. The annual report of the National Council of Human Rights. The twelfth report 2016–2017, printed in cooperation with the UNDP, Cairo (2017) (in Arabic).

44 Cairo Institute for Human Rights Studies, 'The Militarization of the Arab Region and the Political Responsibility of Civil Society' Annual Report on Human Rights in the Arab Region 2017–2018 www.cihrs.org/category/cihrs-publications/annual-report/?/lng=en, accessed on 18 June 2019. Egyptian Human Rights Organization. Halat hoqouq el Insan fi Misr 2013; The State of Human Rights in Egypt (2013); the Website of the Organization had been closed but it communicates its activities through the Face Book page facebook.com/TheEgyptianHumanRightsOrganization/ accessed 10 April 2022.

guide in their activities. Such activities include disseminating the content of these treaties, using them as the framework for monitoring the situation of human rights in the country, engaging at the regional and international level in commenting on government's reports and in some cases tailoring their activities so as to promote the rights provided for therein. In a few cases they would even attempt to propose draft laws to rectify defects of national legislation that could allow human rights violations to escape accountability, as was notably the case with the United Lawyers Group. Several of these organizations engage in disseminating ideas of human rights through workshops that address different groups of people in different parts of the country. The two most comprehensive reports are those of the Egyptian Organization of Human Rights and Cairo Institute of Human Rights.[45]

The training of lawyers in particular is very crucial as most of these organizations rely on lawyers to monitor the human rights situation and to file cases in defense of victims of human rights violations. The focus of training would vary depending on the specific interests of the organizations concerned, but the analysis of human rights conventions would constitute an important component in this training.

Egyptian academics manifested a keen interest in the cause of human rights through teaching, research and publications. A sample of over 100 books published in Egypt on human rights shows that most of these books dealt with human rights in general. The themes that were current in many of these publications were the comparison between the universal concept of human rights and Islamic teachings, human rights in Western countries and of all the core human rights treaties, only CEDAW was a privileged theme in their publications.[46]

4.2.5 Impact of State Reporting

In assessing the overall impact of the eight core human rights treaties, it should be noted that three of the treaty bodies have received no report from the Egyptian government for a period ranging between one and two decades despite the fact that the due dates of these reports have passed years ago: nineteen years in the case of both CAT and CCPR, and ten years for CESCR. The rate of positive response by the Egyptian government to COs varied from one treaty to another. One finds more of the positive response with the so-called functional treaties, which deal with specific categories of people or situations, such

---

45   Cairo Institute for Human Rights Studies (n 44).
46   The sample was prepared under supervision of the author using the catalogue of the library of the American University in Cairo.

as CERD, CRC, CEDAW, CMW and CRPD, compared to CCPR and CAT and even CESCR which provide rights for all people. However, the Egyptian government was careful to reply to all the queries formulated by the relevant committees. Apart from CCPR and CAT, there are several instances of direct and indirect material as well as symbolic impact, manifested in the adoption of new laws or amendment of existing ones in response to observations by treaty bodies.

Examples of positive material impact abound, such as the adoption of a Child Law or Law on Combating Human Trafficking and Illegal Migration, amendments of laws on nationality, increasing the penalty for sexual harassment and criminalizing female genital mutilation (FGM). This positive impact also includes withdrawing the government's reservations on certain articles of treaties such as those related to the separation of a child from his parents under articles 20 and 21 of CRC or the definition of family members of the migrant worker under CMW. The positive material impact includes elaborating national strategies to improve the situation of some underprivileged groups such as women and children or dealing with the crime of human trafficking. It also includes institutions that take care of the promotion of human rights in general or certain categories of human rights. The symbolic impact is manifested in encouraging attitudes to welcome women's political empowerment or associating children with discussion of laws and initiatives of concern to them.

On the other hand, the government has been reluctant to change laws or policies that it perceived to be enhancing national security or inherent in Islamic Shari'a. It therefore continued to renew the state of emergency despite calls by CCPR and CESCR to lift it or to join the Optional Protocols attached to any of the conventions, with the exception of the OPs on banning the recruitment of children in armed conflicts and the sexual and economic exploitation of children. More importantly, it remains reluctant to access CED. It is perhaps the government's perception of what it considers threats to national security which drives its members not to respond positively to the CAT Cttee or to disallow trials of children before criminal and state security tribunals, as was demanded by the CRC Cttee. The government continued to insist on maintaining its reservations on articles 2 and 16 of CEDAW which call for equality between men and women in general, and particularly in family and personal status matters, arguing that such equality is incompatible with Islamic Shari'a.[47]

---

47 See the text of reservations in United Nations Treaty Collection, Chapter IV Convention on the Elimination of All Forms of Discrimination Against Women, New York (18 December1979), Status as at 15-12-2020 accessed 15 December 2020.

The Egyptian government, perhaps under a statist understanding of its sovereignty, has declined to accept individual communications or procedures of inquiry, with the exception of the inquiry procedure under article 20 of CAT, which had proved difficult to put into effect. This procedure was invoked in the context of the examination of the CAT Cttee of an Egyptian government report as well as claims by Amnesty International and a number of NGOs of the practice of torture in Egypt. During the consideration of such claims from November 1991 to November 1994, the Committee proposed that the Egyptian government invite the two experts who had examined its report to visit the country. A letter to that effect was sent to the Egyptian government on 28 January 1994 and brought to the attention of its representative in Geneva on 28 April 1994. The CAT Cttee did not receive a reply to this request. The Committee explained the details of its contacts with the Egyptian government on this matter in its report to the UN General Assembly in 1996. The inquiry procedure included in article 20 of CAT has never been invoked with regard to Egypt since then.[48]

4.2.6   Impact of the UN Human Rights System in General

Egypt's membership of the UN and its adherence to all but one of the core human rights treaties has impacted Egyptian politics and society in many other ways. The celebration of human rights treaties has not been manifested only in their all becoming part of the domestic legal order. The last Constitution adopted in January 2014 and amended in 2019 has given them a special status by devoting an article that stated that such treaties have the force of law once they have been ratified and published in the official Gazette. The successive Constitutions of Egypt since 1971 have kept a prominent place for human rights. The 2014 Constitution as amended has listed all the categories of these rights: in article 5 in general, and in chapter 1 of Part II which includes social and economic rights and Part III which provides for public rights and freedoms.[49] It is true that provisions of the Constitution require the exercise of these rights to be according to the law or regulated by the law. One would find

---

[48] See the Report of the Committee against Torture, United Nations General Assembly, Official Records, 51st session, Supplement No 44 (A/51/44) United Nations, New York (1996) Original (July 1996) paras 174–222 29–36.

[49] The reference to the law as regulating the exercise of rights has been included in most provisions on human rights, the most important of which are arts 54 on provisional detention; 57 on privacy; 58 on privacy of homes; 62 on freedom of movement; 64 on freedom of belief; 68 on freedom of information; 70 on freedom of the press; 73 on freedom of association; and 74 on freedom of political parties. See Constitution of the Arab Republic of Egypt 2014 (English translation).

such phrasing, for example, in article 57 with respect to the right to privacy in the use of public means of communications; in article 65 with regard to the establishment of worship places for followers of Abrahamic religions; in article 67 on freedom of artistic and literary creativity; in article 68 on freedom of information; in article 70 on publishing newspapers, and establishing and owning visual, and radio broadcasts stations and online newspapers; and, finally, in article 77 on the establishment of professional syndicates. Some laws in fact limit the exercise of these rights, as was the case of the Law on Terrorist Entities, the Law of Peaceful Assembly and the Law of Association 70 of 2017, amended later in 2019. However, this is not the case of all laws. Laws on the rights of the child or human trafficking and amendments to laws on nationality or sexual harassment have led to the expansion of rights guaranteed by the law and the broadening of the public's understanding of human rights.

The celebration of the universal concept of human rights has encouraged the government to finally authorize the establishment of NGOs devoted to the defense of human rights, set up within government special bodies to promote and protect the exercise of these rights and to order the teaching of human rights in schools and universities.

An awareness of the importance of human rights has emboldened victims of human rights violations to resort to the courts calling for redress of these violations and compensation for the suffering they caused. On several occasions – not in all cases – judges responded favorably and sentenced the perpetrators of these violations within the limits of the Penal Code.

As a result of these treaties and the activities of their treaty bodies, the Egyptian public has become aware of the fact that human rights are not limited to civil and political rights but that they also include rights to be protected for women, children and persons with disabilities. The Egyptian public also became aware that their government is accountable for its practices, not only in reports of international human rights organizations but more importantly before UN inter-governmental organs.

5   The Impact of the UN Human Rights Treaties on the Domestic Level in Egypt

5.1   *International Convention on the Elimination of All Forms of Racial Discrimination*

Egypt ratified CERD on 1 May 1967, attaching a reservation to article 22. The government had not accepted the individual complaint procedure or the early warning procedure.

5.1.1 Incorporation by the Legislature

The principle of non-discrimination has been embodied in Egypt's Constitutions, including the 2014 Constitution, which states in article 53 that all citizens are equal before the law and that they are equal in freedom, rights and public duties without discrimination. The article enumerates the bases on which discrimination is prohibited such as religion, belief, sex, origin, race, color, language, disability, social class, political and geographic affiliation. It adds that discrimination or incitement of hatred is a crime punished by the law. The principle of equality is also mentioned in other articles of the Constitution such as articles 1, 4, 9, 19 and 74, which either elevate equality to be the foundation of the political system or stress that it must be respected in certain areas such as equal opportunity and education.

The Constitution does not refer specifically to CERD, but states in article 93 that all human rights treaties are binding on the state and have the force of law once they are ratified and published in accordance with the relevant procedures.[50] The 2014 Constitution in article 236 calls on the state to establish a plan aimed at the socio-economic development of citizens in border and underprivileged areas in Upper Egypt, Sinai, Matrouh and Nubia, while respecting their cultural traditions. These areas include several groups that are described in the COs as requiring particular attention by the government, mainly Christians,[51] Nubians and Bedouins. It further responded to demands of Nubians to be resettled in their original areas from which they were relocated as a result of the construction of the Aswan High Dam in the 1960s.[52] The author found no citation of this treaty in the work of the legislature. The government carried out actions dealing with attacks on Christian churches by Muslim fanatics or terrorist groups, but the treaty was not cited on such occasions.[53]

---

50 See these articles <http://www.sis.gov.eg/Newvr/Dustor-en001.pdf> accessed 30 September 2021.

51 Christians live together with Muslims in all parts of the country, but they constitute a larger proportion of the population in certain governorates of Upper Egypt where they were targeted by terrorist groups.

52 See the Constitution of the Arab Republic of Egypt, art 236.

53 Kristen Chick, 'Egypt Christians Feel Safer Under Sisi, but Bias and Injustice Persist' Los Angeles Times (15 March 2016) <http://www.latimes.com/world/middleeast/la-fg-egypt-copts-20160305-story.html> accessed 9 April 2022; Alessia Melcangi. Copts and Politics in Egypt from Nasser to Sisi. <www.oasiscenter.eu/en/copts-in-egypt-from-nasser-to-sisi> accessed 3 June 2018.

5.1.2 Reliance by the Judiciary

CERD has not specifically been mentioned or referred to in any court in Egypt. Egyptian judges recognize only articles of international treaties when they are embodied in the country's laws.

5.1.3 Impact on and through Independent State Institutions

The NCHR had participated in the 88th meeting of the CERD Cttee and presented information commenting on the state party report. Several of its recommendations echoed the Committee's observations, particularly with regard to the adoption of a comprehensive legal definition of racial discrimination and the lifting of restrictions on freedoms of associations and peaceful assembly.[54]

5.1.4 Impact on and through Non-state Actors

There are no indications that the treaty was specifically used by non-state actors such as lawyers, academics or business groups. Even activities by some human rights organizations, such as the Andalus Institute for Tolerance and Anti-Violence Studies, in monitoring cases of violations of minority rights were inspired more by their commitment to provisions of non-discrimination in CCPR.[55] Few academic writings dealt with this Convention. Two books, written in Arabic, published by law professors, dealt with the question of discrimination in general, referring to CERD and the work of the CERD Cttee.[56]

5.1.5 State Reporting

Reports on observance of CERD were submitted during the period 1970–1986 with a delay ranging between two months and two years. However, the delay in submitting reports became longer since 1986, ranging between 2,2 years and 6,8 years. The 13th, 14th, 15th and 16th reports were consolidated in one single document submitted to the CERD Cttee on 9 October 2000. These were the

---

[54] See information presented by the National Council for Human Rights, the Committee on the Elimination of Racial Discrimination Reviewing the Reports submitted by the State Party under Article 9 of the Convention on the Elimination of All Forms of Racial Discrimination (nd) 88th sessions <www.ohchr.org> accessed 9 April 2022.

[55] Al-majlis alqawmi lihoqouq alinasaan. The Annual Report of the National Council of Human Rights; The Twelfth Report 2016–2017; The NCHR, Cairo (nd) 186; The Fourteenth Report 2018–2019 29–47 (in Arabic).

[56] El-Minyawi, Mahmoud.al-tamyeez wal tahrid ála alónf fi al-mawatheeq al-dawliyyah. Discrimination and Incitement to Violence in International Instruments. Cairo: Dar Al-Nahda Al-Arabiyyah 2010, Sabbah, Mohammed Sobhi Saéid Jaraém al-tamyeez wal-hath ála alkarahiyah walónf. Derasah moqaranah. Crimes of discrimination and incitement of hatred and violence. Comparative Study (nd).

reports due in 1994, 1996, 1998, and 2000. The report submitted on 15 April 2014 was also a combined report merging the 17th to 22nd reports.

While accepting the statement in the country's report that Egypt is a very homogeneous country, the Committee formulated a number of observations, some of which relate to the situation of minorities while others relate to human rights covered under other treaties. The CERD Cttee invited the Egyptian government to provide information on social and economic conditions of some numerically small ethnic groups such as the Berber, Nubians and Egyptians of Greek and Armenian origins. It called on the government to introduce in its legislation a comprehensive definition of racial discrimination and recognition that ethnic and racial motives are defined as aggravating circumstances for criminal offences. It also called on the government to involve religious leaders in awareness campaigns aimed at promoting religious diversity in the country. On political participation by minorities, the Committee asked the government to consider minorities in the quota electoral system.[57] It called on the government to train its officials in the field of criminal justice in the spirit of respect for human rights,[58] so that they would not have to resort to forceful methods during the interrogation of citizens under investigation, irrespective of their ethnic or religious identity. Moreover, it asked the government to declare its acceptance of the optional declaration provided for in article 14 of CERD recognizing the competence of the Committee to consider individual communications.

Some progress has been made with respect to some of these observations, particularly with respect to associating religious leaders with awareness-raising campaigns promoting religious diversity, the introduction of a quota system that increased representation of Christians in the country's legislature and setting one electoral constituency for Nubians. The country's Penal Code adopted in 1937 already included chapter 11 on misdemeanors related to religions and combating discrimination but it focused on acts targeting people of certain religious communities.[59] The amendment of the Penal Code introduced in 2015 went some way towards accommodating observations of the CERD Cttee.[60] However, no legislation was adopted to consider ethnic and racial motives as aggravating evidence for criminal offenses. There is no

---

57 See the document CERD/C/EGY/CO/17–22 (6 January 2016) paras 10, 29.
58 ibid.
59 See the text of arts 161bis, 171 and 176 in Law 58 of 1937 as amended <www.manshurat.org/node/14677> (in Arabic) accessed 10 April 2022.
60 The date was suggested by Counsellor Yehia Dakroury, former Vice-President of the Council of State in a personal communication (5 June 2020).

evidence that such progress was due in all cases to the influence of the COs of the CERD Cttee.

On the other hand, the government has not heeded the call to make a declaration in terms of article 14 of the Convention, although the Egyptian delegation at the 88th meeting of the Committee stated that the matter was under consideration at the time.[61] This stand is quite consistent with the statist position taken by the Egyptian government on similar provisions in other UN human rights treaties.

5.1.6 Brief Summary

Amendments of the Penal Code in 2015 specifying grounds of discrimination criminalized in articles 161bis and 176 were introduced perhaps in response to recommendations of the CERD Cttee as the representative of Egypt had promised. In this way, it could be said that this perhaps was the only concrete impact of this Convention in the country.

5.2 *International Covenant on Civil and Political Rights*

5.2.1 Incorporation by the Legislature and the Executive

In terms of the country's 2014 Constitution, human rights, as all other treaties approved by the House of Representatives and ratified by the President, have the force of law once they are published in the official Gazette.[62] Egyptian Constitutions, including the present Constitution adopted in January 2014 and amended in April 2019, provide for almost all the rights included in CCPR. Some of these laws would specify conditions for the exercise of these rights that would make the exercise of these rights quite problematic as was the case with the law of associations adopted in 2017 and amended in 2019.

It would be difficult to point to a specific policy to enforce civil and political rights,[63] with the exception perhaps of including the teaching of human rights in the curricula of pre-university schools and university colleges and the training of several categories of government employees, including judges and police officers, in the spirit of respecting human rights. However, these instances cover all generations of human rights, not specifically civil and political rights.

---

61 See the state party report in the document CERD/C/EGY/17–22 (30 June 2014).
62 Art 151 of the 2014 Constitution of the Arab Republic of Egypt.
63 According to Ambassador Ihabl Gamal El-Din, assistant Minister of Foreign Affairs and Secretary-General of the Supreme Committee of Human Rights, the Committee is preparing a national strategy for human rights. Interview, Cairo (5 May 2020).

The monitoring mechanisms provided for in several human rights treaties, including CCPR, led the government to establish several bodies entrusted with the task of responding to claims of violations of human rights in the country, investigating complaints and helping in reporting to international human rights bodies. These include the Supreme Permanent Human Rights Committee within the Ministry of Foreign Affairs set up by the Prime Minister in 2018 headed by the Minister of Foreign Affairs.[64] The Committee works in coordination with offices or departments of human rights that have been operating within certain ministries and state bodies, such as ministries of Justice, Legal Affairs, Interior, and Social Solidarity and both Council of State and the Public Prosecution. Together with the NCHR, established in 2003, all these bodies, with the exception of the Ministry of Solidarity, have a mandate covering all categories of human rights and not specifically civil and political rights. According to the Assistant Minister of Foreign Affairs, the intention of the Supreme Committee of Human Rights is to establish a unit for human rights in all ministries.[65]

Resources that could be used in the enhancement, promotion and protection of civil and political rights are to be found in the budgets of several ministries, including Justice, Interior, Solidarity and Education. However, it would be difficult to pinpoint which part of these resources is exclusively meant for human rights purposes as these ministries undertake other functions. The Secretary-General of the Supreme Permanent Committee of Human Rights declined to specify a figure for the budget of that Committee. Although the NCHR has a broad mandate covering all categories of human rights, its modest budget is an indication of the limited resources allocated to the promotion of civil and political rights. Its budget for the financial year July 2016 to June 2016 did not exceed 23 882 551 increasing to 33 659 596 Egyptian pounds, equivalent to $1 326 and $1 872 million.[66]

5.2.2 Reliance by the Judiciary

The Supreme Constitutional Court used CCPR as a source of a remedy in several cases, one of which referred to freedom of association which has been mentioned in part 4, and in another case, that of Public Prosecution v Mohammed Saéid Abdel Rahman, it stressed the principle that an accused

---

64 Al-Jarida Al-Rasmiyyah No 45 bis(B) (14 November 2018) (in Arabic).
65 Interview with the Assistant Minister of Foreign Affairs (5 May 2020).
66 Almajlis alqawmi Twelfth Report 213.

person is presumed innocent until proven guilty in a fair and legal trial according to articles 2 and 14 of the Covenant.[67]

5.2.3 Impact on and through Independent State Institutions

Of the four independent state institutions (the NCHR, one for Childhood and Motherhood, one for Women, and one for Persons with Disabilities) only the NCHR is concerned with all categories of human rights including civil and political rights. It monitors the human rights situation in the country, receives complaints and communicates with the government with regard to these complaints and organizes visits to prisons to investigate the conditions of imprisonment. It prepares a report submitted to the President on the situation of human rights in the country.[68] It is committed to all core UN human rights treaties, including CCPR, on which it organized several awareness-raising and training workshops for different categories of people.[69] Its fourteenth report of 2018–2019 pointed out several training workshops that targeted 1 012 trainees of various backgrounds including national service volunteers, government employees in different governorates and students. In all these workshops, explaining basic principles of human rights including civil and political rights was a fundamental part of the training.[70]

5.2.4 Impact on and through Non-state Actors

The country's human rights organizations, which number more than 200, are committed to promoting and defending human rights treaties, including CCPR. Several human rights organizations include CCPR in the training workshops they organize for lawyers working for them which they should use as a framework for monitoring the human rights situation in the country. However, aware that judges in Egypt normally rely on provisions of the Constitution, laws and national jurisprudence in their rulings, Egyptian lawyers are reluctant to refer in their pleadings to human rights treaties, including CCPR, even when they are fully familiar with these.[71] There are no indications that CCPR was ever used by Egyptian business groups.

---

67 Supreme Constitutional Court Case No 202, Judicial year 32, session on 3 November 2018 (mimeographed).
68 The Council has submitted 14 reports since it was established in 2006.
69 For more details, see <www.nchr.eg/en> accessed 10 April 2022.
70 Almajlis alqawmi Fourteenth Report 152–158.
71 Interviews with Hafez Abou e'da, Negad Boraéi and Azza Soliman, leaders of several human rights organizations.

University textbooks on human rights, particularly those taught in faculties of law and political science, refer to UN efforts in the domain of human rights, particularly CCPR and CESCR.[72] Scholars concerned with human rights do not seem to focus specifically on this Covenant. A survey of all books written in Arabic on human rights at the library of the American University in Cairo found 68 books dealing with different human rights issues, but none of which was exclusively devoted to CCPR. A survey of all MA and PhD dissertations on human rights at the Faculty of Economics and Political Science of Cairo University found only one MA dissertation focusing on civil and political rights.

5.2.5 State Reporting

Egypt's 2001 state report, its most recent under CCPR during the period of study,[73] was drafted by the Ministry of Justice in consultation with the Ministry of Foreign Affairs. The NCHR established in 2006 had not come into being at the time of drafting the report. The report was presented to the HRCtee by the then president of the Court of Cassation. The HRCttee's COs on the 2001 state party report identified 23 issues, the most important of which were what the Committee considered to be the semi-permanent character of the state of emergency, discrimination against women, impunity of state employees accused of practising torture, the large number of offences that carry the death penalty and concern about the impact of efforts to combat terrorism on the exercise of human rights.[74] In its reply to the list of questions identified by the HRCttee, the Egyptian delegation referred to the Egyptian Constitution and laws as well as courts' rulings to confirm that the country's legal system offers remedies to all the issues of concern to the Committee in a way compatible with Egypt's commitment under CCPR. The reply of the Egyptian delegation was accompanied by statistics on the number of alleged cases of torture that were brought before Egyptian courts and the penalties imposed on perpetrators

---

72 Rashīdī, Aḥmad. Ḥuqūq Al-insān: Dirāsah muqāranah Fī Al-nazạrīyah Wa-Al-tatḅīq (Human Rights - A Comparative Study of Theory and Practice). Maktabat al-Shurūq al-Dawlīyah, al-Qāhirah. 2003 (in Arabic); Badrān, Shibl. Makānat huqūq Al-insān Fī Al-taʿlīm (Human Rights in Education). Ayn lil-Dirāsāt wa-al-Buḥūth al-Insānīyah wa-al-Ijtimāʿīyah, al-Haram, Giza, 2005 (in Arabic).

73 Another report was submitted eighteen years later in 2019 but the definitive list of issues has not been finalized by the Committee. See the government report in CCPR/C/EGY/5, distributed on 18 November 2020.

74 See COs of the Human Rights Committee in its 76th session CCPR/CO/76/EGY/Add.1 (28 November 2002).

convicted of such crimes.[75] However, reports of the HRC as well as the NCHR continue to point to the persistence of the practices that caused concern to the HRCttee, such as the semi-permanent character of the state of emergency, the unlimited duration of pre-trial detention, the frequent practice of torture, and the large and increasing number of offences that carry the death penalty.[76] The Committee also raised the issue of restrictions on activities of NGOs, particularly their capacity to get foreign funding for their activities.[77]

Some progress has been made with respect to a few of the issues raised by the HRCttee, particularly political participation of women. The law of associations has been the object of several legislative efforts, with a new law adopted in 2002, followed by a law of a much more restrictive character in 2017 (Law 70 of 2017). Following protests by Egyptian NGOs and aid donors, it was replaced by the Law 149 of 2019, which is less restrictive, but still retains many features that seriously inhibit the operation of CSOs in the country.[78]

5.2.6 Impact of Individual Communications

The government has not accepted OP1-CCPR. The Assistant Foreign Minister in charge of Human Rights, International Humanitarian and Social Affairs, explained that this is a matter of general policy on the part of the Egyptian government not to adhere to any optional protocols or inquiry procedures.[79] A possible explanation by the author is that such a stand reflects a statist position on human rights in general, which rejects subjecting Egypt to accountability before any inter-governmental body, considering such accountability to be violation of its own sovereignty.

---

75 See the reply by the government of Egypt on the COs of the Committee of Human Rights in CCPR/CO/76/EGY/Add 1 (4 November 2003).

76 For example, 'UN Rights Office Urges Egypt to Halt Death Row Executions' <https://news.un.org/en/story/2019/02/1033301> accessed 30 August 2017; 'Egypt Extends Its Assault on Freedom of Expression <www.ohchr.org/EN/NewsEvents/Page/Display/News> 30 August 2017; Almajlis alqawmi 14th Report 9–32. See one response of the Ministry of Foreign Affairs condemning a statement by the UN High Commissioner of Human Rights on sentences against people involved in the Rab'a Al-Ādawiyya encampment <www.facebook.com/pg/MFAEgypt/posts/?ref/page_internal> (9 September 2018) accessed 5 June 2020.

77 See para 21 of the Concluding Observations of the Committee in its seventy sixth session in CCPR/CO/76/EGY on 28 November 2002.

78 For the texts of the two laws, see <Al-Jarida Al-Rasmiyyah. No. 20, bis on 24/5/207 and No. 33 bis b on 19 August 2019. For a critique of the Law of 2019, see <https://timep.org/reports-briefings/ngo-law-of-2019/> accessed 14 April 2022.

79 Interview with the Assistant Minister of Foreign Affairs (5 May 2020).

5.2.7 Other Forms of Impact

CCPR had also a symbolic impact with civil and political rights becoming an important public issue. This has been reflected in the establishment of governmental, semi-governmental and non-governmental bodies concerned with the promotion and protection of human rights. These included a Supreme Permanent Committee for Human Rights, including representatives of several ministries, government bodies and government established human rights organizations. A NCHR was established. The Egyptian Organization for Human Rights won judicial recognition and was followed by close to 200 other organizations catering for different categories of human rights. A committee for human rights was also created within the country's House of Representatives elected in 2015.

5.2.8 Brief Conclusion

In a few cases, legislative developments echoed the HRCttee's COs, as in the case of the Law of Associations in 2002 and 2019, but that was also due to pressures from civil society organisations and aid donors. The government had taken measures to remove instances of discrimination against women and to increase their political participation, particularly since June 2015, and to encourage the teaching of human rights in schools, universities and to members of security forces and the judiciary. The Covenant was used by both lawyers and judges in cases brought before the Supreme Constitutional Court. Other more important recommendations were not heeded, particularly those related to the continuation of the state of emergency; the long duration of pre-trial detention; the large number of offences carrying the death penalty; the absence of an independent machinery to investigate claims of the practice of torture; and the failure to declare the acceptance of most optional protocols of human rights conventions as well as ending violations of the rights to liberty, expression and peaceful assembly.[80]

5.3 *International Covenant on Economic, Social and Cultural Rights*

5.3.1 Incorporation and Reliance by Legislature and Executive

Most articles of this Covenant have been incorporated into Egyptian Constitutions. The present Constitution recognizes in article 11 the equality of men and women in all rights including economic, social and cultural rights. The following rights are recognized: work (in articles 12 and 13); strike (article 15); social security (article 17); health care (article 180); education (articles 19,

---

[80] See NCHR, Fourteenth Annual Report of the NCHR 8–33.

20); housing (articles 41, 78); food (article 79); cultural identity, and rights to culture (articles 47, 48). Article 9 recognizes the family as the basis of society and calls on the state to support its stability and cohesion and defend its values. Successive governments, whether before 2011 and since 2013, have adopted several policies to improve the economic and social situation in the country, allocated resources and established institutions but none of them in their documents referred to the Covenant. The CESCR Cttee noted some direct material instances of impact. These included the adoption of a national program to reduce disabilities in 2009; the adoption of Law 71 of 2009 providing for the care of psychiatric patients; and the criminalization of female genital mutilation under Law 1266 of 2008 and article 242 of the Penal Code.

5.3.2   Reliance by the Judiciary

The author found only one case in which the defense lawyer (the late lawyer Ahmed Nabil Al-Hilali) invoked CESCR before a court in Egypt, and his pleading was accepted. Al-Hilali invoked the right to strike provided for in article 8(d) of the Covenant in his pleading in defense of striking train workers before the Emergency Supreme State Security Court in 1986. His argument was accepted by the Court against objections by the Public Prosecutor.[81]

5.3.3   Impact through Independent State Actors

The NCHR carried out a number of activities monitoring the situation of socio-economic rights in the country and provided suggestions on the inclusion of these rights in the then new Constitution drafted in 2014.[82] CESCR exerted an indirect impact in this case as it had set the agenda for the NCHR extending its monitoring activities to include socio-economic rights.

5.3.4   Impact through Non-state Actors

Some human rights organizations, run mostly by lawyers, focus on socio-economic rights, and use the Covenant in their awareness-raising campaigns to inform workers of their rights therein and they file cases in defense of victims

---

81   Case 4190 of 1986 Azbakiyya-121 Kolliya North, quoted in Hosam Shekeeb Cases Code. For the text of the text, see 'Hukm mahkamat amn aldawla al'olya tawar'e bibara'at 'ommal al-sikkah alhadid min tohmat Idrab sanat 1986'. 'The ruling by the High Emergency State Security Tribunal Acquitting Railway Workers of the Charge of the 1986 Strike' (September 2011) (in Arabic) <https://ecesr.org> accessed 17 June 2020.

82   See the NCHR Report, Arab' sanawat men al-ámal maán.Kashf Hisaab 2013–2017. Four Years of Working Together. A Balance Sheet 2013–2017, Cairo National Council of Human Rights (2018) (in Arabic).

of violations of such rights. The most active organizations in this respect are the Hisham Mubarak Centre, the Centre for Economic and Social Rights, and the Egyptian Initiative for Personal Rights.[83]

Human rights courses at Egyptian universities include syllabi explaining the categories of rights enshrined in CESCR. This is the case at Cairo University, and Ain Shams and Alexandria Universities, as well as at the American University in Cairo.

Few books published in Arabic deal with CESCR. Of the 68 books found at the library of the American University in Cairo, only one dealt with the right to education. Few dissertations at the Faculty of Economics and Political Science of Cairo University dealt with economic and social rights, including particularly the right to establish trade unions, taking CESCR as the basis of their analysis of the situation of these rights in the country.[84]

5.3.5 Impact of State Reporting

Upon examining the combined state party report, submitted on 11 May 2010, seven years later than its due date and including the second, third and fourth reports, the CESCR Cttee formulated a number of recommendations. It first noted some positive aspects including accession to CRPD in 2008 and the ratification of two Optional Protocols to CRC as well as the adoption of a number of policy and legislative instruments. It also identified a number of principal subjects of concern and recommendations.[85] While expressing its concurrence in general with the views of the Committee, the Egyptian delegation offered replies to the issues that had been identified in the COs. The replies of the Egyptian delegation were based on constitutional, legal and judicial arguments, supported by relevant statistics and accounts of the actions undertaken by the government in order to comply with its engagements under the Covenant.[86]

Some of these recommendations have been heeded by the government, particularly amending the statute of the NCHR to be compatible with the Paris Principles, adopting legislative measures that provided for a higher quota for

---

83 To get an idea about their activities, visit sites of the Egyptian Centre for Economic and Social Rights <https://ecesr.org> accessed 10 April 2022. and the Egyptian Initiative for Personal Rights <https://eipr.org> accessed 10 April 2022.
84 See sample in n 46.
85 Economic and Social Council, Committee on Economic, Social and Cultural Rights, on the combined second to fourth periodic reports of Egypt E/C.12/EGY/CO/2–4 (13 December 2013).
86 See Replies of Egypt to the List of Issues in the document C.12/EGY/Q/2–4/Add 1.

women in the House of Representatives, and probably allocating more financial resources for social services although their share of total expenditure has diminished. A new law on trade unions was adopted in 2019, allowing in principle the formation of independent trade unions upon meeting certain conditions. Trade union activists complain that none of the independent unions that asked for recognition under the new law were granted the official authorization to start operation although they had submitted all the required documents. No comprehensive law banning discrimination has been adopted. On all these issues, the Committee had joined other international and foreign actors, such as the International Labor Organization (ILO) and Amnesty International and aid donors, who had called on the government to introduce these reforms.

However, the government has not acceded to OP-CESCR. The Committee had also recommended the timely submission of the country's fifth periodic report.[87] The fifth report, due in November 2018, as at June 2020 has not yet been submitted.

5.3.6   Other Forms of Impact

The engagement of the Egyptian government in activities under this Covenant resulted in several forms of material and symbolic impact. Some of the instances of this impact were due exclusively to CESCR, while others were the combined outcome of CESCR and other core human rights treaties, particularly CCPR. The ratification by the Egyptian government of this Covenant inspired some civil society organizations to come into being with the specific goal of promoting socio-economic rights. This was the case of the Hisham Mubarak Law Centre and the Egyptian Centre for Economic and Social Rights, established in 1999 and 2009, respectively.[88] The symbolic impact of CESCR of a negative kind is that it emboldened the Egyptian government to reply to those governments and organizations that criticized its record on civil and political rights by claiming that human rights are not limited to those covered by CCPR, but also include socio-economic rights which it has been promoting in the country.[89]

---

87   Intervention by the Egyptian delegation, included in Committee on Economic, Social and Cultural Rights, Summary Records of the 45th meeting, 51st session (24March 2014) <https://digitallibrary.un.org> accessed 13 September 2023.
88   See n 82.
89   President Abdel Fattah Sisi expressed this position in a meeting with presidents of the African Network of National Human Rights Institutions in Cairo (6 November 2019) <http://www.facebook.com/pg?Egy.Pres.Spokesman/posts/> accessed 6 May 2020.

5.3.7 Brief Conclusion

The overall impact of CESCR has been a mixed bag. It had an indirect material impact in those constitutional articles that mirror most of the rights enshrined in the Covenant as well as in some laws that have been adopted in response to recommendations of the COs, as well as a part of its own agenda. The government of President Sisi has adopted policies and undertaken initiatives in order to facilitate access to education, health care, housing and employment. In very few cases, its provisions were invoked by lawyers as a remedy and their arguments were accepted by judges. Some human rights organizations have come into being with the declared objective of promoting the rights enshrined in this Covenant. On the other hand, several recommendations of the CESCR Cttee have not been followed through, such as adhering to OP-CESCR and CRPD. Despite the call to respect trade union freedoms, activists of independent trade unions were harassed and their unions could not be registered despite the fact that they had submitted all required documents.[90] More importantly, the neo-liberal economic policies carried out by the government led to an increase in the rate of poverty in the country, which reached 32 per cent of the population in 2018, two years after the adoption of an 'economic reform' package supported by the International Monetary Fund.[91]

The Egyptian government finds it relatively easy to give effect to some 'soft law'[92] commitments under this Covenant because such action corresponds to the so-called 'Arab social contract' between Arab governments and their people, by which the government undertakes to provide social services to the people in return for their political acquiescence. For this reason, Egyptian leaders at present claim to be giving priority to socio-economic rights over civil and political rights. This populist social contract for generations has been a fundamental feature of Egyptian politics, and more particularly since the 23 July revolution, which brought army officers to run the country. It would be difficult, therefore, to conclude that the selective approach of giving effect to

---

90   Centre for Trade Union and Workers Services (CTUWS), Trade Union Freedoms between Diminished Rights and Deliberate Restrictions, Cairo, CTUWS (17 May 2018).

91   For details, see Heba El-Laithy. Aham natae'j bahth al-dakhl wa al-infaq wa al-da'm al-ghidhda'ei wa mo'áshsherat wa kharitat al-faqr 2017–2018. Most important findings of the Income,Expenditure, Food Subsidies and the Poverty Indices and Map 2017–2018'. Powerpoint presentation (CAPMAS, 2019, p.35) (in Arabic).

92   'Soft' commitments are those that call on the government to increase quotas for women or to raise expenditure on social services, unlike 'hard commitments' which could lead to the establishment of independent trade unions or accepting individual communications and inquiry procedures.

some provisions of CESCR has varied over time, at least since it was ratified in 1982. Compared to other treaties, particularly CCPR and CAT, the Egyptian government has been more responsive towards the 'softer' obligations under this Covenant.

5.4 International Convention on the Elimination of All forms of Discrimination against Women

Upon ratification of this Convention, the government attached reservations to articles 2, 9(2), 16 and 29, arguing that the text of the first three articles is incompatible with the Islamic Shari'a. It did not accept resort to arbitration called for in article 29 'in order to avoid being bound by the system of arbitration in this field'.[93] On 19 October 2008 Egypt withdrew its reservation to article 9(2) relating to the transmission by an Egyptian mother married to a non-national of her nationality to her offspring.[94]

5.4.1 Incorporation and Reliance by Legislature and Executive

As will be discussed in the following paragraphs, a number of laws have been adopted in compliance with the text of the Constitution echoing several recommendations of the CEDAW Cttee on issues varying from the economic empowerment of poor women, combating sexual harassment, eliminating inequality in terms of granting nationality and increasing women's representation in elected bodies, particularly the House of Representatives. The government has also acted to improve the presence of women in the government at its highest levels with the number of female Ministers soaring to almost 25 per cent of all cabinets since 2016.[95]

Policies: These legislative developments reflected the government's commitment to improve the status of women in the country. The major orientations of these policies are outlined in two documents adopted by the National Council for Women (NCW), a semi-governmental body whose members are appointed by the President of the Republic and includes representatives of relevant ministries. The first document is a National Strategy for Combating Violence against Women 2015–2030, and the second is a National Strategy for

---

93 United Nations CEDAW/SP/2006/2 11–12.
94 Presidential Decree No 249 of 2007 as mentioned in 'Combined Sixth and Seventh Periodic Report of State Parties: Egypt' CEDAW/C/EGY/7 (5 September 2008) 34.
95 There were eight female ministers out of 34 members of the cabinet formed in June 2018 <https://cabinet.gov.eg> accessed 18 June 2020.

the Empowerment of Egyptian Women 2017–2030 which specifically mentioned the Convention.[96]

Institutional reform: Although CEDAW was not specifically mentioned in Presidential Decree 90 of 2000 establishing the Council, nor in its amended version of 2018, the reference in it to international treaties ratified by Egypt is understood to include CEDAW. The amended version of this decree in 2018 entrusted the Council with the task of promoting women's rights according to the Constitution and woman-related international conventions (article 2). The Council is also responsible for expressing views on woman-related regional and international conventions, to follow-up those that had been ratified and to work to ensure that their provisions are incorporated as required in national legislation (article 7(7)). It should also represent Egypt in woman-related international meetings (article 7(9)). Finally, it should participate in the preparation of reports that Egypt should regularly submit to woman-related international treaty bodies (article 7(11)). Although articles 2 and 7 of the amended law of the Council of 2018 did not specifically mention CEDAW, it is certain that it was meant by its recurrent reference to woman-related international treaties, of which it definitely is the most important.[97] Another institutional reform was the establishment of Equal Opportunity Units (EOUs) in all ministries between 2000 and 2004. Their main task is to promote gender equality within each ministry, working under the Minister concerned. The Ministry of Finance established its EOU in 2001. This unit became the link between the Ministry and the NCW.

5.4.2 Reliance by the Judiciary

There are no indications that the judiciary referred to CEDAW, either negatively or positively, in their rulings concerning women's rights disputes. Egyptian judges usually base their rulings on Egyptian laws and rarely refer to international treaties.[98]

---

[96] NCW, National Strategy for Combating Violence against Women (2015–2020) <https://evaw-global-database.unwomen.org/en/countries/africa/egypt/2015/natonal-strategy-for-combating-violence-against-women-2015-2020> accessed 13 September 2023.

[97] See arts 2 and 7 of the text of Law 30 of 2018 on the Organisation of the National Council of Women <https://ncw.gov.eg/ar> accessed 24 June 2020.

[98] This is what the author understood from conversations with human rights activists who are mostly lawyers.

5.4.3 Impact on and through Independent State Institutions

The preceding paragraphs have pointed out how the ratification by Egypt of CEDAW led to the expansion of activities of the NCW. The Council was also guided by CEDAW in drawing up its strategy for the promotion of women's rights in the country. Representatives of the NCW participated in meetings of the CEDAW Cttee. Dr Fatma Khafaguy, who was in charge of the Ombudsman Office at the NCW, stated that the Council had organized an orientation workshop on the Convention to a group of about hundred lawyers and urged them to use it in their statements of claim before Egyptian courts. She also said that the Council, together with women groups, used the Convention in campaigns to reform the nationality law in the 1990s. Such campaigning contributed to the reform of the nationality law by the government and its withdrawal of its reservation to article 9(2).[99]

5.4.4 Impact of Treaty through Non-state Actors

Mrs Azza Soliman, president of the Centre of Egyptian Women's Legal Assistance, pointed to awareness-raising activities focused on CEDAW carried out by the Centre.[100] Seven women groups took part in the 2010 session of the CEDAW Cttee submitting shadow reports on Egypt's compliance with provisions of the Convention.[101]

Whenever it took women's complaints to the courts, the legal profession relied more on relevant national legislation.[102] Both Khafaguy and Soliman held the same view, explaining judges' reluctance either due to their ignorance of the Convention or their conservative beliefs regarding women's issues.[103] However, while admitting that the Convention had little impact on the legal profession, Salem argued that it nevertheless had a moral value as women's groups would use it in defending their claims for legal reform.[104]

---

99 Interview with Dr Fatma Khafagy, Cairo (28 July 2019).
100 Interview with lawyer Azza Soliman, Cairo (27 July 2019).
101 For their interventions, see Critical Issues Identified and Presented by the Egyptian NGO's CEDAW Coalition to the CEDAW Committee Pre-session Scheduled 10–14 November 2008, <tbinternet.ohchr.org/-layouts/5/treatybodyexternal/Download.aspx?symbolno=INT%2fCEDAW%2fNGO%2fEGY%2f45%2f8669&Lang=en> accessed 11 April 2022.
102 Nora Salem, 'The Impact of the Convention on the Elimination of All Forms of Discrimination Against Women on the Domestic Legislation in Egypt' thesis defended at the Friedrich Schiller Universitat, Jena; published as a book in International Studies in Human Rights 124 (Brill 2017).
103 Khafaguy, Soliman interviews.
104 Salem (n 102) 190.

As for academic writings, the author found six out of 68 books on human rights written in Arabic at the library of the American University in Cairo dealing with CEDAW, comparing it often with the status of women in Islamic Shari'a.[105] However, none of the 18 Master's and doctoral dissertations on human rights submitted to the Faculty of Economics and Political Science at Cairo University between 2000 and 2019 dealt with the Convention.[106]

5.4.5 Impact of State Reporting

Commenting on the report submitted by Egypt in 2008, the CEDAW Cttee in its 2010 session formulated 60 recommendations and later identified a number of issues for follow-up. Some of these recommendations were echoed in legislative developments. Amendments to the Penal Code in terms of the Decree Laws 11 of 2011[107] and 50 of 2014[108] increased the penalty for acts of aggression against women, and introduced an article defining sexual harassment. Also, the establishment of the Ombudsman office within the NCW went some way towards responding to recommendations 20 and 24 of the COs. The first urged the government of Egypt to 'strengthen the legal complaint mechanism to ensure that women have effective access to justice' and to 'accelerate the establishment of the general ombudsman's office with a mandate to consider complaints'. The second called on the government to adopt comprehensive measures to address violence against women and girls.[109] The call for the political empowerment of women in recommendation 9 was indirectly heeded by Constitutional[110] and electoral law provisions, as well as presidential decrees,[111] which gave women a larger presence in the House of Representatives and the Council of Ministers.[112] In addition, for the first time in the history of the

---

[105] See n 46.
[106] Survey conducted by the author.
[107] Founding documents of the National Council for Childhood and Motherhood are to be found at <https://hrstudies.sis.gov.eg>bodies>councils>local> accessed 13 September 2023.
[108] Presidential Decision No 50 of 2014.in Al-Jaridah Al-Rasmiyyah. No.23 bis 5 June 2014, p.63–64 (in Arabic).
[109] See COs of the CEDAW Cttee in CEDAW/C/EGY/CO/7 (5 February 2010) 4–5 for the government's follow-up response; see CEDAW/C/EGY/CO/7/Add1. (October 2013) 4.
[110] Art 102 of the Constitution of Egypt as amended in 2019.
[111] See art 5 of Presidential Law Decree No 46 of 2014 on the election of the House of Representatives, published in Al Jarida al rasmiyyah No 33 bis (5 June 2014) <www.elections.eg> (in Arabic).
[112] Composition of Madbouli's government in <www.cabinet.gov.eg> accessed 13 September 2023.

country, a woman was appointed as governor and several were appointed as deputy governors.[113] The government also amended the nationality law to allow Egyptian women married to foreign husbands to transfer their nationality to their offspring with a foreign husband, thus providing for equality between women married to Egyptian men and those married to foreigners. This amendment enabled Egypt to withdraw its reservation on article 9(2).[114]

The government did not respond to recommendations of the CEDAW Cttee on two other matters, namely, achieving equality of men and women in marriage and family matters, and ratifying OP-CEDAW. The government maintained its reservation on article 16 of the Convention as it found the equality called for in this article to be incompatible with certain interpretations of Islamic Shari'a. It continued to claim that the withdrawal of the reservation to article 2 and the accession to OP-CEDAW were under consideration.[115]

Progress in these areas could be attributed to political will on the part of the head of state, particularly former President Hosny Mubarak and President Abdel Fattah El Sisi. Under Mubarak, the NCW was established and was headed by his wife, Mrs Suzan Mubarak, who was interested in promoting women's rights. President El Sisi condemned sexual harassment since his first days in office as President of the country in July 2014 and inspired the drafting of constitutional provisions that provided women with a quota in the House of Representatives, which raised the presence of women in the Egyptian Parliament to unprecedented levels.[116] This perhaps was part of his wish to build political capital with Egyptian women who were believed to have supported the uprising on 30 June 2013 against the Muslim Brothers' rule. Part of this progress is due also to campaigns launched by Egyptian women organizations, through the NCW and women's rights groups.

It is true that the Egyptian government still retains its reservation on articles 2 and 16, which call for complete equality between men and women, including in respect of family matters. The state party report of 2008 acknowledged that these matters, together with ratification of OP-CEDAW, were under consideration in government circles.[117] The government's position on these two articles

---

113 ibid.
114 See Combined Sixth and Seventh Periodic Report of State Parties: Egypt CEDAW/C/EGY/7.
115 State Party Report CEDAW/C/EGY/7 (5 September 2008) 15; Government response to the combined sixth and seventh periodic reports (CEDAW/C/EGY/CO/7/Add.1).
116 The new electoral law adopted by the House of Representatives on 18 June 2020 provided for a quota of 25% and 10% for women in the House of Representatives and a restored Shura Assembly respectively. Al-Ahram, (18 June 2020) 3 (in Arabic).
117 State party report to the CEDAW Committee. Combined sixth and seventh periodic reports of State parties. Egypt. CEDAW/C/EGY/7, 5 September 2008. Remark 356 (part of 'Mandatory Reponses to the Committee's Remarks on Egypt's Previous Report', p.14).

has up to December 2019 not changed. The Egyptian Muslim clergy, judges and the political elite in general are rather divided on the extent to which equality between men and women should go with no prejudice to the interpretation of texts of Islamic Shari'a.[118]

5.4.6 Other Forms of Impact

The symbolic impact of CEDAW is seen in the favorable attitude towards women's issues manifested by the government and civil society alike under both Presidents Hosny Mubarak and Abdel Fattah Sisi, and in the presence of two independent state institutions that strive to promote the rights of mothers and women in general, namely, the National Council for Childhood and Motherhood (NCCM) and later the NCW. The ratification by Egypt of CEDAW encouraged the coming into being of several women's rights groups which made their presence felt at both the domestic and international levels.

5.4.7 Brief Conclusion

Although the progress that has marked the position of women in Egypt in terms of legislative changes, state policy, institutional innovations and growth of Egyptian women in public life cannot be attributed exclusively to the impact of the Convention, it is still safe to say that such developments, referred to in preceding paragraphs, are in line with both the provisions of CEDAW and the CEDAW Cttee's recommendation. Some of these developments followed political pressures by civil society and particularly women's groups in Egypt and in international fora. The government's response to the COs of the CEDAW Cttee had been mostly positive, rarely disagreeing with these recommendations. It is true, however, that the response usually came late and that the failure to submit reports on time continued years after the submission of the combined sixth and seventh reports in 2008.

Most of the legislative developments that paralleled articles of the Convention took place under the administration of President Hosny Mubarak, including the establishment of the NCW and the withdrawal of Egypt's reservation to article 9(2). Political participation of Egyptian women substantially increased under President Sisi, although the House of Representatives, which witnessed this spectacular increase in the number of female members, acts mostly as a rubber stamp to the government. Long delays in the submission of state party reports under this Convention were particularly marked following the fall of Mubarak in February 2011.

---

118 Salem (n 102).

Compared to the three preceding instruments, the provisions of CEDAW strike a positive note within the executive authority in Egypt, get support from semi-governmental and civil society institutions and are echoed in several legislative acts and policies by the Egyptian government.

5.5 Convention against Torture and Other Cruel, Inhuman or Degrading Treatment or Punishment

The Egyptian government acceded to CAT on 25 June 1986. It did not ratify OP-CAT.

5.5.1 Incorporation by the Legislature and the Executive

Several articles of the amended Constitution of 2014 specifically ban torture as in articles 52 and 55. Article 52 states that torture in all forms is a crime that is not subject to prescription.

The Egyptian Penal Code, adopted in 1937, nearly five decades before the conclusion of this Convention, has qualified in the strongest of terms torture as a crime and provided for the punishment of the perpetrators whether they were officials of the government or even people claiming to be working for the government using forged identities. This was spelled out in articles 126, 129 and 282. The three articles came close to defining the crime of torture as an act carried out by a public official to force victims to confess (article 126), employs cruelty, commits a breach of honor, incurs bodily harm to the victims (article 129), threatens to kill the victim or torment him or her with physical torture.[119]

It is difficult to point out a specific policy on the part of the Egyptian government concerning the practice of torture, although the country meets some of the conditions to combat this crime as set by CAT. The absence of a specific policy on torture is quite consistent with the government's claim that there is no systematic practice of torture in Egyptian prisons and that claims of the practice of torture relate only to individual cases in violation of the law. The government would insist that effective measures are taken when such claims are made with their perpetrators being brought to trial and punished according to Egyptian laws when proven guilty. The last state party report submitted to the CAT Cttee on 18 October 2001 detailed actions taken by the government with respect to complaints of violations covered by this Convention. Such actions ranged from administrative sanctions, disciplinary and criminal trials and the number of officers subjected to these measures

---

[119] <https://sherloc.unodc.org/cld/document/egy/1937/criminal_code_of_egypt_arabic.html> accessed 24 August 2019.

throughout the period 1996 to 2000. It included a table of the number of civil compensation awards and those that had been implemented. A total of 17 awards were ordered during this period but only three were finally implemented. However, the amount of compensation varied between 7 000 and 10 000 Egyptian pounds, equivalent at the time to no more than $2 000 to less than $3 000.[120] The report referred to some institutional reforms that related more to ensuring respect for human rights in general and not specifically to combat the practice of torture, such as unannounced visits to prisons by public prosecutors and the establishment of a Human Rights Committee at the Ministry of Interior in 1991.[121]

5.5.2 Reliance by the Judiciary

There are very few instances of judges referring to CAT in their rulings. Dr Hafez Abou Se'da, a lawyer and president of the Egyptian Organization of Human Rights, informed the author that he used CAT in the trial of police officers accused of beating to death a young Egyptian, Khaled Sa'eid, believing that he was about to divulge news about corruption within the security forces in Alexandria.[122] The defendants' lawyer insisted that what happened to Khaled Sa'eid was cruel treatment, an argument that was initially accepted by the Penal Court in Manshiyyah, Alexandria. The Court, therefore, sentenced the two policemen to seven years' imprisonment. Using the Convention, Hafez Se'da argued before the Alexandria Court of Appeal that what Sa'eid was subjected to amounted to torture. He added that the Court had accepted his argument and sentenced the two policemen to ten years in prison. The Court of Cassation later supported this sentence.[123] The definition of the crime of torture remains a controversial matter in Egypt, with judicial authorities reluctant to consider cruel and inhuman treatment as constituting torture.[124]

---

120 Egypt state party report fourth periodic report submitted to CAT (October 2001); see CAT/C/55/Add.6 paras 26–27, 122–129.
121 Ordinance No 6181 of 1999 by the Minister of Interior in Annex 2, CAT/C/55/Add.6 34–35.
122 Human rights organizations disseminated widely on Facebook in the summer months of 2010 photos of his deformed skull as a result of police beating. Knowledge of what happened to Khaled Said inflamed discontent with Mubarak's regime and was one of the incidents that aroused public opinion against atrocities of this regime prior to the outbreak of the January 2011 revolution.
123 Interview with Dr Hafez Abou S'eda, Cairo (1 August 2019).
124 This was the point of view of the head of the Human Rights Section at the Public Prosecutor's Office in a conference attended by the author in the summer of 2019.

5.5.3 Impact on and through Independent State Institutions

The NCHR referred in its 2015–2016 report to complaints of torture which it had communicated to the Egyptian Ministry of Interior but got no positive response from the Ministry.[125] Its President met with the head of state and informed him of such abuses and was promised cooperation on such issues.[126] CAT was specifically mentioned in this report with the knowledge that Egypt had ratified the treaty and therefore was bound by its provisions.

The NCHR, together with the Egyptian Human Rights Organization and the Kemet Boutros Ghali Foundation for Peace and Knowledge, in October 2019 convened an international conference on Legislation and Machinery Necessary for Combating Torture in Arab Countries. The 100 participants in the conference included representatives of governmental bodies concerned with human rights as well as eight Arab national human rights institutions, African NGOs, law scholars and diplomats. The Conference discussed 16 papers, four of which specifically compared national legislation on torture to the CAT provisions. Recommendations of the conference called on Arab countries that had not ratified CAT to do so, and on other Arab countries to respond to their reporting commitments under CAT in due course, to lift their reservations on articles 20, 21, and 22 of the treaty and to adhere without delay to its Optional Protocol.[127]

5.5.4 Impact on and through Non-state Actors

The Egyptian Organization for Human Rights convened seminars to inform lawyers of the content of the Convention urging them to use it in their claims before Egyptian courts.[128] The United Group: Lawyers and Legal Advisers, a human rights organization that filed many suits against torture in Egyptian prisons, notified public prosecution of 465 cases of torture in 18 months from January 2014 to June 2015. These notifications, numbering 163, referred to the Convention. It had, moreover, commissioned two judges of the Council of State, namely, Mr Assem Abdel Gabbar and Hesham Ra'ouf, to propose a draft law to ban torture in Egypt and organised a seminar on 11 March 2015 to discuss

---

125 See the Executive Summary of the National Council of Human Rights Annual Report 2015–2016 <https://nchr.eg> accessed 16 April 2022.
126 ibid.
127 NCHR, Publications, Annual Reports. Executive summary of the Fifteenth Annual Report 2019–2020 <www.nchr.eg/Up;oads/publications/en/FinalNCHRexecutivesummary15163 2659283.pdf> accessed 16 April 2022.
128 Interview with Dr Hafez Abou S'eda, Cairo (1 August 2019).

this draft.[129] This draft referred to CAT and was in fact tailored to translate the Convention into Egyptian law. However, the two judges were charged with violating 'their professional duty not to engage in politics'. Mahfouz Saber, at the time the Minister of Justice, asked the President of the Supreme Council of the Judiciary to appoint a judge to examine the eligibility of the two judges to keep their posts following their involvement in working on this draft. The United Group was later banned by the government.[130] Nineteen human rights organisations published a statement deploring measures taken by the government against the two judges of the Council of State and the United Group.[131] The Eligibility and Disciplinary Body within the Supreme Council of the Judiciary on 29 June 2019 found that the two judges were eligible to keep their posts but warned them against repeating the same action.[132]

The United Group had also published a study on the practice of torture in Egypt in which it analysed the socio-economic background of 79 victims of torture.[133] In the introduction to this study, the Group referred to the Convention as binding on the Egyptian government.[134] The Egyptian Initiative of Personal Rights had also referred to the Convention in one of its reports on torture in the country.

Mr Negad Boraéi, director of the United Group, explained to the author that despite the fact that lawyers of the Group had filed more than 150 cases of torture in Egyptian courts, calling for the conviction of the perpetrators using the Convention to qualify the acts constituting the object of these claims as torture, the judges did not accept reliance on the Convention as a source for defining torture. He added that judges usually argue that the constitutional provision on the legal force of international treaties is addressed to lawmakers and not to judges. They would, therefore, base their judgment on Egyptian laws

---

129 See the text of the proposed draft law, United Group, Mashrou'Quanoun lilwiqayah min alt'dtheeb. Proposed Draft Law to Prevent Torture (March 2015).
130 NCHR Al-Taqreer al-sanawi alrabé ashr 2018–2019.The Fourteenth Annual Report of the National Council of Human Rights. 2018–2019, p 29–30 <https://nchr.eg> accessed 11 April 2022 (in Arabic).
131 See statement of the 19 organizations in <www.cihrs.org/rights-groups-referral-judges-hisham-raouf-assem-abd-gabbar-competency-hearings-political-retaliation/?lang=en> accessed 13 April 2022.
132 <https://www.shorouknews.com/news/view.aspx?cdate=29062019&id=355dbade-d2fd-41b7-afee-50ae08c1d06e> accessed 29 June 2019. Personal communication with Mr Negad Bora'ei, former president of United Lawyers Group, Cairo (8 June 2020).
133 United Group Attorney-at-Law, Legal Advisers and Human Rights Advocates, '70 Years of Serving the Law. Torture in Egypt. The Poor Pay the Price. A Socio-Economic Reading of the Crime of Torture and Ill-Treatment' Cairo (December 2014) 22–45.
134 ibid 4.

rather than the Convention. The acts claimed by lawyers of the Group would be qualified by judges to be cruel treatment rather than torture and the perpetrators would receive light sentences. He added that even when police officers were convicted and condemned to a few years' imprisonment, their actions would not be considered by the Ministry of Interior as dishonoring and they would return to the service at the termination of their imprisonment, keeping all the privileges of their ranks as well as their seniority.[135]

5.5.5 Impact of State Reporting

The first four state party reports were submitted close to their due dates. The delays ranged between one month for the first report submitted in 1988, and eight months for the fourth report submitted in 2001. The fifth report was due on 25 June 2004 and had not been submitted by 30 June 2019.[136] No report was submitted until December 27, 2021.

Commenting on the fourth state party report submitted by the Egyptian government in 2001, the CAT Cttee had listed nine issues of concern in its report of 11–12 November 2002.[137] Judging by reports of human rights organizations and the NHRI itself, these issues have not been resolved. Most of these issues were reiterated in the list of questions addressed by the CAT Cttee in its 44th session in 2010 to be considered by the Egyptian government in its preparation of the fifth periodic report. This report has not been submitted nine years after the communication of these questions to the state party.[138] The Committee addressed 59 questions relating to articles 1 to 16 of the Convention.[139] In fact, most of the issues of concern to the Committee have not been resolved. The state of emergency is continually renewed, and reports of the persistence of torture and ill-treatment are frequently issued by credible local and international human rights organizations. Administrative detention is often used by the government. Several human rights organizations that monitor claims of torture not only face restrictions on their activities but some have even been banned by the government, such as Al Nadim Centre, the United Group and Hesham Mubarak Centre for Human Rights Legal Assistance.

In replying to the list of questions in the last session that examined conclusions of the fourth periodic report of Egypt on 24 March 2002, the head of

---

135 Negad Boraéi, interview, Cairo (3 August 2019).
136 <www.tbinternet.ohchr.org/-layouts/15/TreatyBodyExternal/countries.aspx?CountryCode=EGY&Lang=EN> accessed 12 April 2022.
137 See CAT/C/CR/29/4 (23 December 2002).
138 See CAT/C/EGY/Q/5 (13 July 2010).
139 ibid.

the Egyptian delegation, while noting what he considered as the encouraging attitude of members of the Committee towards him and the third and fourth reports of Egypt, nevertheless found the recommendations that were read not in the same spirit and departed from the general trends that prevailed during the examination of the report.[140] He added that some of the responses given by the Egyptian delegation were not taken into account in the recommendations, and that some of the recommendations had already been applied while others were far from the reality that prevailed in the country or were so unclear and too general to be applied. He described the recommendations to be more of a political judgment and that some of them went beyond the mandate of the Committee. He ended by saying that he had hoped that the recommendations would have been concrete and applicable so that they would contribute to progress along the path of promoting human rights. He promised that his delegation would examine these recommendations attentively and would transmit them to his government, hoping that the session would not be the last phase of dialogue between the Egyptian government and the Committee.[141] No other meeting between the Egyptian delegation and the Committee has taken place since 24 March 2002 up to 30 June 2020.

5.5.6 Other Forms of Impact

The symbolic impact of CAT has been manifested in different ways. The debate about Egypt's report before the CAT Cttee and statements by CAT on torture in Egypt and protests by the Egyptian Foreign Ministry and media raised awareness by the Egyptian public not only of claims of torture in the country but, more importantly, that this practice has become an object of concern in the international community. It also became aware that a specific UN body could hold the Egyptian government accountable for such practices. The Convention has also encouraged a number of civil society organizations in the country to focus much of their activities on monitoring cases of torture and helping their victims in several ways, whether through suggesting a law to combat torture or offering psychological and medical care. This is what the United Group, the Nadim Centre, Hisham Mubarak Centre for Legal Aid as well as the Egyptian Initiative of Personal Rights, and the Egyptian Organization for Human Rights attempted to do. The first three of these organizations have been closed down

---

140 See Summary Records of the 29th session of CAT Committee (24 March 2003) CAT/C/SR.543 6.
141 ibid.

by the government.[142] On the other hand, the government since 2002 tended to ignore its reporting commitments under CAT and pro-government media even denounced the CAT Cttee as politically motivated and biased against Egypt.[143]

5.5.7 Brief Conclusion

The mixed symbolic impact of CAT notwithstanding, its impact is limited by the following considerations: the narrow definition of torture in the Egyptian Penal Code, which ignores cruel and inhuman treatment; the reluctance of judges in general to take CAT into account in their judgments; the priority attached to security considerations by government officials; and restrictions on the activities of human rights organizations attempting to monitor torture practices. The government was more conscious of its responsibility under CAT during the first two decades of the Mubarak presidency. Following the examination of its third and fourth reports in 2002, its relations with the treaty body were strained. Since 30 June 2013, the Egyptian government has become dismissive of such reporting commitments. This sequence of events demonstrates that the willingness to abide by provisions of the treaty corresponds to the perceived value of the treaty by policy makers as well as the state of security in the country.

5.6 Convention on the Rights of the Child

The Egyptian government ratified CRC on 6 July 1990, the Optional Protocol on the Involvement of Children in Armed Conflict (OP-CRC-AC) on 12 July 2002 and the Optional Protocol on the Sale of Children, Child Prostitution and Child Pornography (OP-CRC-SC) on 6 February 2007. It attached two reservations to its ratification of CRC in respect of articles 20 and 21, relating respectively to the provision of special assistance and protection to a child deprived, temporarily or permanently, of the family environment, and rules of the adoption system. However, these reservations were withdrawn in 2003.

5.6.1 Incorporation and Reliance by the Legislative and Executive Authorities

Although not specifically mentioning CRC, the 2014 Constitution includes an article that reflects the spirit of the Convention. Article 70 prohibits child labor

---

[142] OHCHR, 'UN Experts Urge Egypt to End Ongoing Crackdown on Human Rights Defenders and Organisations' <www.ohchr.org> accessed 11 April 2016.
[143] Pro-government media hostile comments on CAT; see Hala Mustafa. 'Mab'd human rights', Al-Ahram (n 36).

during the period of compulsory education in jobs that are not fit for their age or that prevents them from continuing their education.[144]

A law of the child (Qanoon al-tifl) was adopted in 1996 and amended in 2008 taking a rights-based approach to the situation of children mirroring in many respects the provisions of CRC.[145] The law mentioned CRC in article 1. In fact, article 1(2) states that '[t]he state ensures, as a minimum, rights of the child as provided for in the Convention of the Rights of the Child and other relevant international instruments in force in Egypt'.[146] Two years before the ratification of CRC, on 24 January 1988, the government established a National Council for Childhood and Motherhood to take care of the situation of children and mothers.[147] Ten years later policy documents of the Council and many of its activities took CRC as a basic reference.[148]

The most recent and comprehensive policy document of the NCCM adopted in 2018, called the Strategic Framework and the National Plan for Childhood and Motherhood in the Arab Republic of Egypt 2018–2030, prepared with the support of the United Nations Children's Fund (UNICEF), referred to the CRC as a basic reference for all members of the drafting group who were required to reach consensus on the activities related to 'each of the fundamental Rights included in the Convention on the Rights of the Child'.[149] The process of preparing the strategy involved meetings with groups of children to establish their expectations of what the NCCM and the government should do for them.[150]

The semi-governmental body that exclusively takes care of children and mothers is NCCM. Data available about its 2020–2021 budget suggests that it is

---

[144] See The Constitution of the Arab Republic of Egypt <www.sis.gov.eg/newvr/the *constitution.pdf*> accessed 12 April 2022.

[145] For the text of the law in Arabic, see Presidency of the Council of Ministers. The National Council of Childhood and Motherhood Law 12 of 1996 issuing the Law of the Child amended by the Law 126 of 2008 <https://hrightsstudies.sis.gov.eg/bodies/councils/> accessed 13 September 2023.

[146] Translated by the author from Al Jaridah Al-Rasmiyyah, No 24 bis (15 June 2008) (in Arabic).

[147] Committee on the Rights of the Child, Consideration of Reports Submitted by State Parties Under Article 44 of the Convention. Third and Fourth Periodic Reports of States Parties Due in 2007, Egypt (29 December 2008), published 4 September 2010 13, CRC/C/EGY/3-4.

[148] Arts 3–9 of the Presidential Decree Establishing the National Council of Childhood and Motherhood. See <www.nccm-egypt.com> accessed 20 May 2020.

[149] National Council for Childhood and Motherhood, The Strategic Framework and the National Plan of Childhood and Motherhood in the Arab Republic of Egypt 2018–2030.

[150] Interview with Dr Hala Abou Sultan, former Secretary-General of the NCCM (August 2015-August 2016) Cairo (9 August 2019).

not sufficient to carry out its own projects. It has been allocated LE 46.250 million, nearly half of which is allocated towards salaries (LE 19.918 million), leaving LE 19.500 million for investments. With this meager budget, equivalent to than $2.803 million, it is hardly conceivable that it could accomplish much for Egyptian children and mothers. In fact, the NCCM has a budget deficit of LE 3.250 million, or nearly 6% per cent of its annual budget, covered by the government.[151]

5.6.2 Impact on and through Independent State Actors

The strategy declared by the NCCM is a rights-based approach drafted so that the activities it called for would lead to the realization of all the rights included in CRC. This was explicitly recognized by the Council in its Strategic Framework and National Plan for Childhood and Motherhood 2018–2030, as follows:[152]

> The Strategic Framework aims at improving childhood and motherhood conditions within the framework of the goals of the Sustainable Development Strategy and the Convention on the Rights of the Child and the new articles in the Constitution of 2014, so that they would be all be embodied in practical mechanisms to be carried out for the benefit of children and mothers.

Moreover, the NCCM in 2015 organized several workshops for children to inform them about the Convention so that they would be able to play a meaningful part in the discussion of the country's sixth periodic report which was due in 2016 but which was submitted only in February 2020.[153] Besides, the NCHR participated in a workshop convened by the National Committee for Combating and Preventing Illegal Migration in cooperation with the International Organization for Migration on The International Legal Framework of the Migration of Unaccompanied Children on 29 and 30 September 2017. One of the items on the agenda of this workshop was CRC and the challenges faced in its implementation.[154]

---

151 'Wakil tadamon alnowwab yaqtareh damg " alomomoumah waltofoulah fi "alqawmi lilmar' 'Vice-chairman of the Solidarity Commission of the House of Deputies proposes merging NCCM in the NCW' (in Arabic) <https://www.youm7.com/story/2023/5/17/6183489> accessed 13 September 2023

152 National Council for Childhood and Motherhood, The Strategic Framework and the National Plan for Childhood and Motherhood in the Arab Republic of Egypt 2018–2030, Cairo, NCCM (March 2018) 17.

153 See Egypt home page <www.OHCHR.org>, reporting status, accessed 18 June 2020.

154 NCHR, Annual Report 112.

5.6.3 Impact on and through Non-state Actors

On 22 June 2019 a number of local human rights organizations issued a statement condemning the criminal trial of children younger than 18 years which, they argued, constituted a violation of CRC by the Egyptian government.[155] These organizations complained that the relevant CRC provisions had been completely ignored by Egyptian authorities who brought children younger than 18 years and even 15 year-olds to trial before criminal and state security tribunals. Some of these children were even initially sentenced to death, but this sentence was later reduced to a lesser penalty by the Court of Appeal. They asked for the referral of these children to the children's courts. CRC was used in this case as a source of remedy.

The Egyptian Coalition of the Rights of Child, which grouped over 100 NGOs concerned with children, submitted a list of proposals to the Committee of Fifty that drafted the Constitution of 2014 to be included in the then new draft Constitution. According to the statement of the Coalition, these proposals were inspired by the four guiding principles of CRC.[156]

The Al-Ahly Sports Club, the most popular sports club in the country, on 21 July 2019 signed an agreement with UNICEF aimed at providing health and physical care to the most vulnerable children in the country. The agreement calls for raising public awareness about children's rights. The country resident representative of UNICEF declared that the agreement was in line with CRC, which called for mobilizing support in view of enforcing children's rights and reaching solutions to provide equal opportunities for girls and boys in order to realize their potential.[157]

Finally, a lawyer filed a suit at the Administrative Court calling on the Court to commit the government to the enforcement of CRC, particularly its provisions related to the shared custody and hosting of a child by the non-fostering family. The Court postponed the date of its ruling to 31 July 2019. In this particular case the lawyer used CRC as a source of remedy since the Law of the Child in Egypt, unlike the Convention, limits the right of the non-fostering parent to see the child rather than hosting him or her. It is not clear whether this

---

155 Egyptian Front for Human Rights, the Beladi Centre for Rights and Freedoms, Cairo Institute for Human Rights, Nadim Centre, the Liberty Initiative, and the Committee for Justice, the Egyptian Commissariat for Rights and Freedoms, Adala Centre for Rights and Freedoms <www.egyptianfront.org/ar/2019/06/kareem-hemeda> accessed 13 April 2022.
156 <www.arabccd.org/page/1194> accessed 13 April 2022.
157 <https://www.unicef.org/mena/press-releases/al-ahly-sporting-club-and-unicef-join-hands-childrens-rights-egypt> accessed 15 September 2023.

case represented a precedent or that there had been other cases in which both lawyers and judges used the Convention.[158]

5.6.4 Impact of State Reporting

The most recent report examined by the CRC Cttee is the combined third and fourth report, submitted in 2008, and examined in 2011. The combined fifth and sixth report was due in March 2016, but was received on 4 February 2020.[159] In its 2011 COs, the CRC Cttee expressed its appreciation of the government's efforts at implementing past reports and outlined the difficulties that impeded the implementation of the Convention. The Egyptian government responded positively to some of the 85 recommendations, including the withdrawal of the reservations to articles 20 and 21. It has also acted upon other recommendations in several ways. In its recommendation 13, the Committee called on the state party to continue work in order to adopt a strategy inspired by a rights-based framework paralleling the child rights provided for in the Convention and to invite children and civil society organisations to take part in its preparation.[160] The NCCM involved children in discussions of the draft combined fifth and sixth periodic report and conducted a number of workshops to raise their awareness of their rights under the Convention.[161] The statement of seven human rights organizations in 2019 condemning criminal trials of children younger than 18 years demonstrates the delay by the Egyptian government in sufficiently responding to recommendations of CRC in 2011 to reform the administration of juvenile justice.[162] The Committee noted the large number of children aged between 12 and 18 years who were deprived of their liberty during investigation and called on the government to ensure that the deprivation of liberty of children is only a measure of last resort and for the shortest possible period.[163] The statement by these organisations noted that some of the children who had been tried were condemned to the death penalty.

The difficulties that obstruct the full implementation of CRC and the COs are due to the perception by the government of threats to political instability and national security. Budget constraints required by an agreement signed with

---

[158] Al-Watan newspaper (23 June 2019) <www.elwatannews.com/news/details/4225163> accessed 13 April 2022.
[159] See home page <www.OHCHR.org,Egypt> accessed 13 April 2022.
[160] See the recommendation of the CRC Cttee in CRC/CEGY/CO/3-4 4; text of the plan on the home page of NCCM.
[161] Interview with Dr Hala Abou Ali (n 150).
[162] See recommendation 86-b in CRC/C/EGY/CO/3-4 (15 July 2011) 23.
[163] ibid 24.

the IMF in 2016 probably was one of the reasons explaining the insufficient resources allocated to activities that could contribute to the improvement of the situation of children. Those children suffer the full impact of the high rate of poverty in a country where poverty afflicts 32 per cent of the population.

5.6.5 Other Forms of Impact

The NCCM could obtain financial and technical assistance from foreign governments (Italy) and specialized UN agencies (UNICEF) to support implementation of some of its activities, such as increasing awareness of CRC by children and preparing a national strategy to improve the conditions of children and mothers.

5.6.6 Brief Conclusion

Some instances of the direct material impact of this Convention include the withdrawal of Egypt's reservations on articles 20 and 21 of the Convention, and the inclusion of a new definition of the child, consistent with provisions of CRC, in the new draft labour law. The indirect material impact of the Convention is seen in the new framework strategy and national plan for childhood and motherhood, which was specifically inspired by CRC. The symbolic impact of the Convention was manifested in the establishment of numerous children's rights associations, which formed a coalition that sought to secure the inclusion of provisions stressing children's rights as stipulated in CRC in the 2014 Constitution.

The Convention served as a guide for NCCM, the institution that was established to help improve the conditions of children and mothers. It inspired several of its activities and, more notably, was used as a framework in the preparation of its national strategy for childhood and motherhood, deliberately tailored to match the range of children's rights in the Convention.

The impact of the Convention was enhanced during the first two decades of the life of the NCCM by the political support from Mrs Suzan Mubarak, the President's wife, who at the time chaired its Technical Advisory Committee, and the assistance it received from some foreign governments and UNICEF. With political instability in the country and at the top of the NCCM, the government did not heed the recommendation of the COs of 2011 to submit its periodic report on time. The combined fifth and sixth report was due in 2016, but was only submitted in February 2020.

Compared to other human rights instruments, CRC had more of an institutional, legislative, material and symbolic impact perhaps because of its relatively 'soft' character as it targets a group of the population, namely, children, who are not seen as constituting a security threat to the government. However,

IMPACT OF UNHR TREATIES ON DOMESTIC LEVEL IN EGYPT 411

if they were seen in this light, the administration of justice also disregarded children's rights under the CRC.

5.7 International Convention on the Protection of All Migrant Workers and Members of their Families

The Egyptian government acceded to this Convention on 19 February 1993, attaching two reservations to its accession. Egypt has not accepted the individual complaints mechanism under CMW.

5.7.1 Incorporation and Reliance by Legislature and Executive

The 2014 Constitution refers only to the right of Egyptians to migrate to foreign countries as part of their freedom of movement, stating in article 62 that freedom of movement, residence and emigration shall be guaranteed to all Egyptian citizens.[164]

The Convention was not specifically cited in the legislation dealing with the status of foreign migrants in Egypt. The most relevant of these are the Law on Combating Human Trafficking No 64 of 2010 and the Law on Combating Illegal Migration and Smuggling of Migrant Workers No 82 of 2016.[165] Law No 82 of 2016 provided for the establishment of the National Coordinating Committee for Combating and Preventing Illegal Migration and Human Trafficking, operating under the authority of the Prime Minister and located at the Ministry of Foreign Affairs.[166] However, foreign workers would fall under the scope of this law only when they are victims of illegal migration or trafficking in persons. Otherwise, those who enjoy the status of being legally recognized migrant workers would be covered by the Labor Code adopted in 2003, which provides for rights and obligations of workers in general with no distinction based on nationality.[167]

The establishment of a national committee to coordinate government efforts in dealing with human trafficking was an institutional development responding to the call by the Convention and recommendations of the Committee to the state party to undertake efforts to combat human trafficking and to deal with the situation of migrants in irregular situations.[168] This

---

164 ibid 19.
165 Art 18 of Law No 64 of 2010 and art 22 of Law No 82 of 2016.
166 For the texts of these laws, see <www.nccpimandtip.gov.eg> accessed 13 April 2022.
167 Taqa, Sheiban Al-Itar al-quanouni lihoqouq al-ómmal almohajereen fi aldowal al'arabi-yyah. The legal framework of the rights of migrant workers in Arab countries. Analytical Study by the Arab Network of Migrant Rights, Amman (2013) 80–85 (in Arabic).
168 See the List of Issues in the CMW Cttee document CMW/C/EGY/QPR/2 (18 May 2017) para 27.

Committee was preceded in 2007 by the National Coordination Committee to Combat Trafficking in Persons and in 2014 by the National Coordination Committee to Combat Illegal Migration, which were merged on 23 January 2017 under the name of the National Coordinating Committee for Preventing and Combating Illegal Migration and Human Trafficking (NCCPIMTIP). The Committee has undertaken a number of activities in many areas, including raising awareness about the risks and dangers caused by human trafficking and illegal migration; capacity building for Egyptian, Arab and African institutions working in this area; the protection of victims of human trafficking and illegal migration; and cooperation with other regional and international organizations and foreign governments concerned with such issues, particularly the International Organization for Migration, UNICEF, the ILO, the United Nations Office on Drugs and Crime (UNODC), the European Union (EU) and with the governments of Italy and Germany. It also helped in the preparation of the national law on fighting human trafficking and illegal migration as well as in elaborating a national strategy to this effect. The Committee was headed by an Egyptian former ambassador who had served four times on the CEDAW Cttee.[169]

5.7.2 Reliance by the Judiciary

There are no indications that this Convention was used in legal proceedings before Egyptian courts.[170]

5.7.3 Impact on and through Independent State Institutions

The Convention was used by the NCHR in its monitoring of the situation of migrant workers in Egypt as was made clear in a statement by a representative of the Council during the consideration of Egypt's report to the CMW Cttee in 2007.[171]

5.7.4 Impact on and through Non-state Actors

One human rights organization, the Egyptian Initiative of Personal Rights, was guided by the Convention in its reporting on the situation of migrant workers in Egypt.[172] The presence of migrant labor in Egypt has attracted a

---

169 For details, see <www.nccpimandtip.gov.eg> 13 April 2022.
170 <https://www.almasryalyoum.com/news/details/1240177>; see also for another case <https://www.shorouknews.com/news/view.aspx?cdate=26032017&id=b7361f9b-d445-4673-a3ed-cfeb32b97b30> accessed 13 April 2022.
171 CMW/C/SR.49 5–7; during its 49th meeting of the sixth session held on 23 April 2017.
172 ibid 7, 9–10.

number of scholars and research centers. The detention of migrants in Egypt also attracted the attention of the Global Detention Project.[173] This could be regarded as an indirect impact echoing concerns of the Convention. One study focused on irregular workers in Egypt and discusses the government's position on this Convention.[174]

5.7.5 Impact of State Reporting

The Egyptian government submitted only one periodic report to the CMW Cttee in 2007. A second report, due by 1 May 2018, had not been submitted until May 2020. In its COs on the first report, the Committee noted positive steps taken by the state party to carry out commitments under the Convention and asked the government to undertake further action for its compliance with the Convention to become complete. The issues of concern covered 27 paragraphs of its report.[175]

On the one hand, the Egyptian government had already implemented a number of these COs. Some of these recommendations related to the civil rights of migrant workers, such as freedom of association, have been covered also by other treaties. In terms of the Electoral Law in force since 2012, the government extended voting rights to migrant Egyptian workers as well as to all Egyptians of voting age residing abroad.[176] It has incorporated combating illegal migration and human trafficking in one law, Law 82 of 2016 on Combating and Preventing Illegal Migration and Human Trafficking, and established a committee to enforce its provisions.[177] The scope of the Law as well as the jurisdiction of its Committee could relate to CMW only when the status of foreign workers is considered by Egyptian authorities to be illegal or when they become victims of human trafficking.

---

173 The most recent of these studies is Francoise De Bel-Air, Migration Profile: Egypt, published by Robert Schuman Centre in February 2016.The study by Ray Jureidini on Regulation of Migration in Egypt, published by the Middle East Institute in March 2010, used no less than seven studies on the same issue by Egyptian and foreign scholars.
174 Ray Jureidin, 'Irregular Workers in Egypt: Migrant and Refugee' (2009) 11 International Journal of Multicultural Societies 75–90.
175 See the COs of CMW.
176 Art 29 of the Presidential Elections Law No 22 of 2014 <http://constitutionnet.org/sites/default/files/law_22_of_2014-presidential_elections.pdf>; art 30 of the Presidential Elections Law No 174 of 2005 as amended by decreed Law No 12 of 2012 <https://pres2012.elections.eg/images/Laws/preselections2005-174_e2012.pdf> accessed 14 April 2022 (in Arabic).
177 For these developments, see <www.nccpimandtip.gov.eg> accessed 14 April 2022.

On the other hand, the government has not heeded other important recommendations of the CMW Committee. The most pertinent are: the government maintaining its reservations on articles 4 and 8(6) of the Convention; the non-acceptance of communications by individuals; and the non-acceptance of ILO Conventions 97 and 143.

5.7.6 Other Forms of Impact

One manifestation of the symbolic impact of CMW is the fact that the EU, and Germany in particular, encouraged Egypt to take an active part in combating illegal migration and offered assistance to the country to help it meet this challenge. The Egyptian government has done more in recent years to combat illegal migration and human trafficking than it did in order to take care of foreign migrant workers in the country whose numbers have been estimated, according to official statements, to range between 300 000 and five million (but with no distinction drawn in these numbers between refugees and migrant workers).[178]

5.7.7 Brief Conclusion

The government has responded to calls by the CMW Cttee to protect Egyptian workers abroad and to grant them some constitutional rights, such as participation in elections which they did not enjoy in the past. However, the government has maintained its reservations to articles 4 and 18(6) of the Convention. For this reason, it is fair to conclude that unlike the other human rights treaties of a functional character, interest by the Egyptian government in this particular Convention has been more limited, with no discernible difference among successive governments.

5.8 *Convention on the Rights of Persons with Disabilities*

5.8.1 Incorporation in Legislation and the Executive

The rights of persons with disabilities are enshrined in several articles of the 2014 Constitution. Article 53 bans discrimination among citizens on a number of grounds, including disability. Article 81 recognises the economic, social, cultural and political rights as well as educational and sporting rights of persons with disabilities. It commits the state to provide jobs and allocate a certain percentage of job opportunities to these persons. It also calls on the state to adapt public facilities and their surrounding environment to their special needs.[179]

---

[178] EuroMed Rights, 'EU-Egypt Migration Cooperation: At the Expense of Human Rights' Brussels EuroMed Rights (July 2019) 17.

[179] For the relevant articles see: The Constitution of the Arab Republic of Egypt in <www.sis.gov.eg> accessed 13 April 2022.

The Convention was incorporated in three legal documents: Law 10 on Persons with Disability of 2 February 2018; Law 11 of 5 March 2019 establishing the National Council for Persons with Disabilities; and Law 2733 of 2018 which set out the ground for the implementation of Law 10. These three pieces of legislation identify their objective as ensuring the rights of persons with disabilities in light of international treaties ratified by the government, including CRPD. The Law on Persons with Disability is divided into eight parts, closely echoing the structure of the Convention. It recognizes the necessity of adhering to the Convention both in its introduction and in the explanatory note attached to it.[180] The Prime Minister further issued a bylaw (2733 of 24 December 2018) to the Law of the Rights of Persons with Disabilities). Measures in favor of persons with disabilities were detailed in the bylaw of 2018. It called on the government to provide a number of public services and facilities for those persons in areas of health, education, rehabilitation and employment, as well as private facilities used by people with disabilities.[181] However, once they knew of the draft of the bylaw, NGOs concerned with the rights of persons with disabilities complained that the Prime Minister's text restricted the exercise of rights of persons provided for in the relevant law. They added that the text of the bylaw left some important provisions of the law unexplained.[182]

Law No 10 of 2018 in its article 20 stressed the State's obligation to ensure their rights to professional instruction, training and work and to ensure their right to receive equal work opportunities commensurate with their academic qualification and professional training and to provide protection to them in fair labor conditions on equal footing with others. Article 22 of the same law required firms with 20 or more employees to ensure that at least 5 per cent of employees are disabled. However, difficulties were encountered in implementing this requirement. Another policy was to issue a special identity card for persons with disabilities to enable them to have free access to state services

---

180 Al Jaridah Al Rasmiyyah No 10 (2 February 2018).
181 Arab Republic of Egypt, Prime Minister's Office, R'eis Majlis alwozara' usder alla'ehah altanfidthiyyah liqanoun hoqouq al-ashkhas dthawi al'e.qah. The Prime Minister issues the executive bylaw of the Law of Persons with Disabilities No 2733 of 2018 <www.cabinet.gov.eg/Arabic/Mediacenter/CabinetNews/pages>. For the text of the bylaw, see <www.modawanaeg.com> (in Arabic) accessed 13 April 2022.
182 Televised debate <https://www.Youtube.com/watch?v=LMOChpdGL4> (28 June 2018) accessed 15 August 2019.

including a pension from a conditional cash transfers scheme known as Karama and Takaful, carried out by the Ministry of Solidarity.[183]

The country already had one institution caring for the situation of persons with disabilities. A 'National Council for Handicapped Affairs' was established by the Prime Minister in 2012, but was replaced on 13 January 2019 by a 'National Council for Handicapped Persons'. The law of the new council stressed in article 1 that it should aim at protecting the rights and dignity of persons with disabilities provided for in the Constitution and consolidating and promoting such rights in light of international treaties ratified by Egypt. Its functions, according to article 5, include proposing public policies for rehabilitating persons with disabilities, coordinating its work with all state-concerned ministries and entities and sharing its views with other governmental and non-governmental bodies in view of preparation of reports to be periodically submitted by the state in terms of clauses of the international treaties on persons with disabilities.[184]

5.8.2   Reliance by the Judiciary

Few cases were submitted to vindicate the rights of persons with disabilities in Egypt. In one such case, the ruling referred to international treaties, without specifically naming the Convention. The case was filed before the Administrative Court of the Presidency and was concluded on 28 May 2016. The first sentence preceded the adoption of the Convention in 2006, but the second came almost ten years after the adoption of the Convention. The two sentences referred to international instruments providing care for persons with disabilities and cited the UN General Assembly Declaration on Rights of Disabled Persons of 19 December 1975. It could be understood why the Supreme Constitutional Court did not mention a relevant international instrument that did not exist at the moment of its deliberations.[185] The Administrative Court of the Presidency did however not have the same excuse as the Convention had already been concluded and ratified eight years earlier.[186]

---

183 Alternative Policy Solutions. Disability and Employment Policies in Egypt <www.aps.aucegypt.edu/en/articles/49/disability-and-employment-policies-in-egypt> accessed 13 April 2022.
184 Al Jarida Al-Rasmiyyah No 9 bis A (3 March 2019).
185 ibid.
186 Reported in <youm7.com/story/2016/5/28/2737198> accessed 15 August 2019.

5.8.3 Impact on and through Independent State Institutions

A national Council for Disabilities Affairs was established and strove to carry out activities aimed at facilitating life and improving conditions of persons with disabilities. One of its tasks is to try to increase from 5 to 7 per cent the percentage of people with disabilities employed in government.[187] The electoral law provides for a quota of eight people with disabilities in the House of Representatives. The total number of elected members is 540.[188]

5.8.4 Impact on and through Non-state Actors

There are no indications that lawyers used the CRPD in their statements to advocate for the rights of persons with disabilities, nor was there a reference to it in activities of the few NGOs that cater for them. The only exception was Ma't for Peace, Development and Human Rights, a human rights organization which published a study suggesting a new approach to improve conditions of persons with disabilities using the Convention as one element of the legal framework of this new approach.[189]

5.8.5 Impact of State Reporting

The first periodic report was due on 3 June 2010, but was submitted to the Committee only on 4 February 2020, ten years later, and has by 30 June 2020 not yet been examined.[190] A possible cause for this delay is the political instability in the country following the 25 January 2011 revolution, which was accompanied by organisational and leadership changes in the institutions that are in charge of preparing the report. The 'National Council for Handicapped Affairs' was established in 2012 and was replaced in 2019 by the 'National Council for Handicapped Persons'. A law on the rights of persons with disabilities was adopted in 2018, and a bylaw issued to facilitate greater access for persons with disabilities to public services.

5.8.6 Other Forms of Impact

The CRPD alerted the Egyptian government to the gravity of the situation of persons with disabilities. Interest in the issue was manifested by the President who invited young people with disabilities to take part in the youth conferences he has held since 2017. This presence of people with disabilities in media-covered public meetings attended by the President as well as their membership

---

187 See Facebook of the Council: facebook.com/NCPDEGYPT accessed 13 April 2022.
188 Al Jarida Al-Rasmiyyah No 23 (followed) (5 June 2014) art 5 39–40.
189 <www.maatpeace.org/2016/2> accessed 13 April 2022 (in Arabic).
190 See Egypt home page <https://www.ohchr.org> accessed 28 May 2020.

in the House of Representatives in terms of the electoral law should be seen as signs of the symbolic impact of the Convention.[191] Another sign of this symbolic impact is the international support Egypt received particularly from the EU in its efforts to deal with the situation of persons with disabilities.

5.8.7 Brief Conclusion

CPRD stimulated interest by the Egyptian government in the state of persons with disabilities. It encouraged the government to adopt three legal documents, namely, two laws and one executive regulation, a law on promoting their rights and its accompanying regulation and another law establishing the institution that would suggest relevant public policies and coordinate work of the government in this regard. Political interest in the situation of persons with disabilities drove the government to adopt these measures. However, a lack of clarity on how to implement the provisions of the laws in both the government and private sector constituted difficulties which hampered their full implementation. There was not much of a follow-up of the country's commitment under the Convention for almost one decade following it becoming a party to CRPD in 2008, but renewed efforts have been undertaken since early 2018.

6 Conclusion

Egypt is one of the founding members of the UN and since its participation in the San Francisco Conference considered the UN, its Charter and treaties as the standard of international legality and legitimacy. The UN General Assembly sided with Egypt when it was the object of a tripartite war by the UK, France and Israel in October-November 1956. It is not surprising, therefore, that Egypt adhered to eight of the core UN human rights treaties. The only core treaty that it has not accepted is CED. It has also not accepted the Optional Protocol to CAT (OP-CAT), and the Second Optional Protocol to the International Covenant on Civil and Political Rights aiming to the abolition of the death penalty (OP2-CCPR).

In ratifying these treaties, the Egyptian government was careful not to accept any individual complaint or inquiry procedures, with the exception of enquiry procedures under CAT in 1985, which has never been put into effect. The author found no general statement by the Egyptian government

---

[191] Watch a video of their presence in the Youth Conference <www.youtube.com/watch?v+y-4dt0xBqxM> accessed 28 May 2017. The meeting was held on 26 April 2017.

explaining such a stand. However, declining to accept any of these procedures is in line with the statist position taken by the government on human rights issues, in general, claiming that the Egyptian Constitution, laws and judicial institutions offer sufficient guarantees for the full protection of human rights and that resort to regional or international bodies, therefore, is not necessary.

The ratification by the country of these treaties and participation in activities of their treaty bodies have impacted on the country's legal structure and institutions in different ways and to a degree that varied from one treaty to another. The relative weight a particular treaty has at the domestic level is a function of the type of political system in the country at the time, its political culture and its level of socio-economic development. Both CCPR and CESCR were signed in 1967 under the harsh authoritarian regime of Nasser, but were ratified only in 1982, under the soft authoritarian regime of Mubarak. Treaties that were perceived by an authoritarian government to empower the opposition were not likely to be ratified soon after adoption of the treaty or given serious effect in practice. The authoritarian government was concerned that giving effect to these treaties might jeopardize its own stability. Other treaties that were seen as contributing to the government's legitimacy and support by the people had a better chance of finding their provisions incorporated in national legislation and institutions. Hard core authoritarian regimes, such as those of Egypt under Nasser and Sadat, would therefore make symbolic gestures by signing CCPR and CESCR, while the soft authoritarian regime of Mubarak ratified them. Another example of this symbolic function is the recent setting up of the Supreme Committee of Human Rights under President Abdel Fattah Sisi to counter charges of the Egyptian government's denial of human rights to its citizens.

While CCPR and CAT did not have much impact in the country, the influence of CEDAW, CRC, and CMW has been much more pronounced. CCPR and CAT were regarded as the most embarrassing to the Egyptian government. Egypt missed several deadlines for the submission of its periodic reports to the HRCttee and CAT Cttee. It showed more interest in participating actively in meetings of the treaty bodies dealing with socio-economic rights in general or those of women, children, and persons with disabilities or migrant workers. Delays in submitting reports to the treaty bodies under CRC, CEDAW, CMW and CRPD are due more to technical constraints, such as the lack of a bureaucratic apparatus to provide the data necessary for the report or political instability in the country which could engender a high turnover rate among heads of the relevant government agencies. President El Sisi publicly emphasised that human rights are not only civil and political but also include socio-economic rights and claimed that his government is doing much to promote the latter category of rights. Such discourse is rather appealing in a country in which one-third of the people live under the poverty line. Undoubtedly, the failure to fully provide socio-economic rights to the majority of citizens is due not only to government policies but also to a lack of physical, human and financial resources. If these rights are not completely enjoyed by all the people, it would be unfair to attribute this failure exclusively to government policies.

Some provisions of these treaties were rather problematic for successive Egyptian governments that expressed reservations thereto. These provisions were seen as incompatible with certain interpretations of Islamic Shari'a. Whether these governments took this position because they wanted to placate large sections of public opinion or were genuinely opposed to what they considered alien cultural concepts and practices, the outcome was the same, namely, diluting the universal character of these provisions.

In the Egyptian context, human rights treaties served three functions for the Egyptian government: a ceremonial role by showing it to be respectful of standards of legitimacy in the international system; a legitimizing function in the face of its people when it undertakes efforts to promote socio-economic rights; and a warning sign for authoritarian regimes of the consequences for their hold over power if citizens exercise their civil and political rights enshrined in some of these treaties.

The ceremonial functions could be seen in the place of human rights in Egyptian Constitutions since the beginning of the softening of authoritarianism, hesitantly with the Constitution of 1971 and later more firmly in the Constitutions of 2012 and 2014. The last Constitution of Egypt has given human rights treaties a prominent status by devoting a special article to them (article 93) emphasizing that they have the force of law once they have been ratified and published in the official Gazette, over and above what has been recognised for all treaties in general in article 151. This Constitution lists all the categories of rights. It is true that provisions of the Constitution require the adoption of laws to specify conditions for the exercise of these rights. Some laws set enabling rules that facilitate citizens' exercise of these rights, while others set hurdles, such as was the case of the Law on Terrorist Entities, the Law of Peaceful Assembly and Law of Association No 70 of 2017 amended in 2019. Enabling laws include those on the rights of children or human trafficking and amendments to laws on nationality or sexual harassment. These laws have led to the expansion of rights guaranteed by the Constitution and the broadening of the public's understanding of human rights in general. One could see in these constitutional provisions and enabling laws examples of direct and indirect impact of the human rights treaties.

An example of the material impact of some treaties is the adoption of national strategies to promote the rights of certain categories of people such as women, children and persons with disabilities, inspired or even modelled after parts of the relevant core treaties. The material impact of the treaties presented itself in an indirect manner as could be seen in the rise of 200 civil society organizations that adhere to the universal concept of human rights and try to promote and defend the exercise of these rights in the country in a way that would give effect to the provisions of the treaties. Few of these organizations monitor all human rights whereas others are more concerned with specific rights, namely, economic and social, the rights of women, workers, children, and the rights of expression or personal rights. Few of them devoted more efforts to training or research.

The symbolic impact of these treaties could be seen in the institutional developments in Egypt within the government and in 'government organized non-governmental organizations' (GONGOs). The Ministries of Foreign Affairs, Justice, Interior, Solidarity and both the Council of State and the Public Prosecution all have departments, committees or offices concerned with human rights. GONGOs include four national councils for human rights, women, childhood and motherhood and persons with disabilities. The functions entrusted to these bodies vary. The activities of such civil society organizations have emboldened victims of human rights violations to resort to courts or to civil society organizations to help them in filing cases to redress these violations and to provide compensations for the suffering they caused. On several occasions – not in all cases – judges responded favorably and sentenced perpetrators of these violations within the limits of the Penal Code.

As a result of these treaties and the activities of their treaty bodies, certain sections of the Egyptian public have become aware of the fact that human rights are not limited to civil and political rights but also include socio-economic rights. The treaties also provide for the rights of specific groups such as women, children and persons with disabilities. The Egyptian public became aware that their government is accountable for its practices, not only before international human rights NGOs but, more importantly, before UN bodies.

CHAPTER 7

The Impact of the United Nations Human Rights Treaties on the Domestic Level in Estonia

Merilin Kiviorg

1   Introduction to Human Rights in Estonia*

The independent Republic of Estonia was born in the aftermath of World War I (1914–1918) when it broke away from the Russian empire. The Proclamation of Independence was followed by the War of Independence of 1918 to 1920. The date of Estonian independence is 24 February 1918.[1]

The first (1920) Estonian Constitution[2] was influenced by the liberal thinking prevalent in Europe after World War I. The 1920 Constitution emphasised the principle of a state based on the rule of law. One of its essential components was the acknowledgment of the fundamental rights of the person. As a result, it was one of the most democratic constitutions in Europe at the time. The 1930s saw significant political changes in Estonia, characterised by the centralisation of the state administration, the concentration of power, a decline of democracy and the expansion of state control. The second (1937) Estonian Constitution introduced a number of amendments on fundamental rights.[3] It laid down a new philosophy, according to which the legal rights and duties of

---

*   This article is written with support from the Estonian Research Council grant PRG 969 'Russia and Consolidation of Regional International Law in Eurasia'.
1   For a more detailed account on these turbulent times in Estonian history, see, eg, T Raun, *Estonia and Estonians* (2nd edn, Hoover Institution Press 2001); DJ Smith, *Estonian Independence and European Integration* (Routledge 2001); RJ Misiunas and R Taagepera, *The Baltic States: Years of Dependence, 1940–1990* (expanded and updated edn, University of California Press 1993).
2   Estonian Constitution, RT 1920, 113/114, 243. The Constitution entered into force on 21 December 1920. In 1933 the Constitution was substantially changed to the extent that it started to be called the 1933 Constitution. Legally speaking, the 1920 Constitution had just been amended, and the amendments entered into force on 24 January 1934. R Narits and others, 'Sissejuhatus' in Ü Madise jt (toim), *Eesti Vabariigi põhiseadus. Kommenteeritud väljaanne* (Juura 2017); M Luts-Sootak H Siimets-Gross, Eesti õiguse 100 aastat (Post Factum 2019) 19.
3   Estonian Constitution, RT 1937, 71, 590. The Constitution entered into force on 1 January 1938.

© MERILIN KIVIORG, 2024 | DOI:10.1163/9789004377653_009
This is an open access chapter distributed under the terms of the CC BY-NC-ND 4.0 license.

individuals emanated from their status as member of a commonwealth. This reflected the more collectivist (communitarian) orientation of the era.

The outbreak of World War II disturbed the peaceful development of the country, which subsequently was occupied by the Soviet Union (1940–1941, 1944–1991) and Nazi Germany (1941–1944). A resurgence of Estonian national identity began in the late 1980s, leading to the break-up of the Soviet Union and Estonian independence in 1991. Estonia started to rebuild its legal order on the principle of restitution, while at the same time acknowledging the changes over time in the European legal order and thinking.

The present (1992) Constitution in a number of ways is a compilation of aspects of Estonia's previous Constitutions.[4] It has continued the democratic spirit of the 1920 Constitution, with some added mechanisms to maintain the balance of power in the state. In drafting the document, considerable attention was paid to fundamental rights. United Nations (UN) treaties,[5] the European Convention on Human Rights (ECHR or European Convention)[6] and constitutions of other democratic states were used as models. During the deliberations of the Constitutional Assembly it was pointed out that as Estonia would seek to become a member of the Council of Europe (CoE) and a party to the ECHR it would make sense to tailor constitutional provisions similarly to those of the European Convention.[7]

The Constitution defines fundamental rights, liberties and duties in Chapter 2, immediately after the seven general provisions listed in Chapter 1. The fact that the fundamental rights have such a prominent place informs the interpretation of the entire Constitution and testifies that the intention after the collapse of the Soviet occupation was to build a society strongly adhering to human rights protection.[8]

---

4   Estonian Constitution, RT 1992, 26, 349. The Constitution entered into force on 3 July 1992.
5   Riigikogu, Põhiseaduse Assamblee, 'Stenogrammid' <https://www.riigikogu.ee/tutvustus-ja-ajalugu/riigikogu-ajalugu/pohiseaduse-assamblee/pohiseaduse-assamblee-stenogrammid/ > accessed 19 April 2022. The Assembly was called upon to draft the new Constitution. During its 30 sessions almost at every session, membership in the UN and obligations regarding human rights were discussed or at least mentioned. The importance of the UN treaties in the creation of the Constitution has also been mentioned by the Supreme Court. Supreme Court *en banc* Case 3-1-3-10-02 (17 March 2003) para 21.
6   European Convention for the Protection of Human Rights and Fundamental Freedoms 1950 (European Convention) 213 UNTS 221.
7   V Rumessen, *Põhiseadus ja Põhiseaduse Assamblee* (Juura 1997) 172; M Ernits, 'Sissejuhatus, Peatükk II' in Ü Madise jt (toim), *Eesti Vabariigi põhiseadus. Kommenteeritud väljaanne* (Juura 2017).
8   See also Madise (n 7).

The catalogue of fundamental rights and liberties includes both liberal rights and social rights. One of the main principles of the Constitution postulates the equality of Estonian citizens and citizens of foreign states as well as stateless persons (article 9(1)). The Constitution extended fundamental rights to legal persons (eg organisations) in so far as these rights are in accordance with the general aims of legal persons and with the nature of such rights (article 9(2)). The Estonian Constitution also recognises collective rights providing protection, for example, for cultural minorities and for their autonomy (article 50). The rights and freedoms set out in the catalogue of fundamental rights do not preclude other rights and freedoms that arise from the spirit of the Constitution or are in accordance therewith, and conform to the principle of human dignity and of a state based on social justice, democracy, and the rule of law (article 10).

The basic rights of the Estonian Constitution have a subjective character, which means that they grant claims to individuals. Basic rights have full binding force. The fundamental rights apply in the relationship between the individual and the state and also have effect among private persons. The fundamental rights affect all areas of the law. According to article 15 of the Constitution, every person has a right of recourse to courts for protection of their fundamental rights and freedoms.[9] The Supreme Court has emphasised, although with reference to the European Convention, that the right of recourse to the courts must ensure as complete and effective protection of constitutional rights as possible.[10] The Constitution also establishes the duty of the legislature, the executive, the judiciary, and of local authorities, to guarantee the rights and freedoms provided in the Constitution (article 14). All courts are competent to deal with questions of human rights. According to article 152(1) of the Constitution, if any law or other act contradicts the Constitution, it shall not be applied by the courts hearing a case. The Supreme Court, as the court of constitutional review,[11] declares invalid any law or other legislation in conflict with the letter and spirit of the Constitution (article 152(2) of the Constitution).

---

9   '(1) Everyone whose rights and freedoms have been violated has the right of recourse to the courts. Everyone is entitled to petition the court that hears his or her case to declare unconstitutional any law, other legislative instrument, administrative decision or measure which is relevant in the case. (2) The courts observe the Constitution and declare unconstitutional any law, other legislative instrument, administrative decision or measure which violates any rights or freedoms provided in the Constitution or which otherwise contravenes the Constitution'.

10 Supreme Court *en banc* Case no 3-1-3-10-02 (17 March 2003) para 17.

11 See also Constitutional Review Court Procedure Act, RT I 2002, 29, 174, art 1.

In addition, there are two important institutions for human rights protection: Chancellor of Justice and Gender Equality and Equal Treatment Commissioner. The institution of Chancellor of Justice was established by the 1937 Constitution and re-established by the 1992 Constitution on the principle of legal continuity.[12] Since then its obligations have been gradually expanded. Since 1 January 2019, it has acted as a national human rights institution (NHRI). The institution of Gender Equality and Equal Treatment Commissioner was created in 2005. At present, the Commissioner can only give opinions that are not legally binding, but this may change in the future.[13] These institutions will be discussed in greater detail below. To foreshadow, the expansion of the duties of these institutions has been influenced by the comments provided by the UN treaty-monitoring bodies.

The Constitution contains four general limitation clauses: the first sentence of article 3(1),[14] article 11, article 13(2),[15] and article 19(2). However, article 11, is the most important of the limitations clauses: 'Rights and liberties may be restricted only in accordance with the Constitution. Restrictions may be implemented only insofar as they are necessary in a democratic society, and their imposition may not distort the nature of the rights and liberties.' Thus, every case of restriction of rights and liberties has to be justified and pass the test of proportionality. This has also been emphasised by the Supreme Court of Estonia.[16] The Supreme Court has provided three important interpretive principles as to the limitation of fundamental rights and freedoms.[17] First, many restriction clauses in the Fundamental Rights and Freedoms Chapter of the Constitution (for example articles 11 and 47) permit reservations in accordance with law. The term 'law' used in these restriction clauses means an act of Parliament (*Riigikogu*). This means in effect that restrictions must appear in

---

[12] N Parrest and others, 'Õiguskantsler. Peatükk XII' in Ü Madise jt (toim), *Eesti Vabariigi põhiseadus. Kommenteeritud väljaanne* (Juura 2017) para 3.
[13] National Report, CCPR, Estonia, UN Doc CCPR/C/EST/4 (29 August 2018) para 24.
[14] 'State power shall be exercised solely on the basis of the constitution and such laws which are in accordance with the Constitution'.
[15] 'The law shall protect all persons against arbitrary treatment by state authorities'.
[16] Constitutional Review Chamber Case 3-4-1-2-01 (5 March 2001) para 16; Constitutional Review Chamber Case 3-4-1-16-08 (26 March 2009) para 28; Supreme Court *en banc* Case 3-3-1-101-06 (3 January 2008) para 27.
[17] See Decisions of the Constitutional Review Chamber of the Supreme Court Case *3-4-1-18-07* (26 November 2007) para 35; Case 3-4-1-5-05 (13 June 2005) paras 7–9; Supreme Court *en banc* decision Case 3-4-1-7-01 (11 October 2001) para 12.

the Constitution or as set forth in laws enacted by Parliament.[18] Setting limitations to rights and liberties in lower administrative or executive acts would be unconstitutional. Second, relating to the former principle, the Supreme Court has also ruled that Parliament cannot delegate its legislative powers regarding duties specifically vested in it by the Constitution.[19] Third, restrictions to the fundamental freedoms and rights are unconstitutional if they are not clear and detailed enough to enable the putative subjects of law to determine their conduct on the bases of informed choice.[20] The Supreme Court's understanding echoes international understanding of permissible limits to fundamental rights.

However, no country is without problems as far as human rights protection is concerned. Despite the strong position of human rights in the Constitution, there are various areas where Estonia could improve. The main issues will be pointed out under specific treaties later on in connection to the COs of treaty-monitoring bodies.

2   Relationship of Estonia with the International Human Rights System in General

Article 3 of the 1992 Estonian Constitution stipulates that universally-recognised principles and standards of international law shall be an inseparable part of the Estonian legal system. Under article 3 of the Constitution, the universally-recognised principles and standards of international law have been incorporated into the Estonian legal system and do not need further transformation. They are superior in force to national legislation and binding on legislative, administrative and judicial powers. It should be noted that article 3 incorporates both international customary norms and general principles of law into the Estonian legal system. International treaties (ratified by Parliament) are incorporated into the Estonian legal system by article 123(2) of the Constitution. Article 123 states that if Estonian legal acts or other legal instruments contradict foreign treaties ratified by Parliament, the provisions

---

18   Supreme Court, Constitutional Review Chamber of the Case III-4/A-1/94 (12 January 1994) para 2; Supreme Court, Administrative Law Chamber Case 3-3-1-36-05 (18 November 2005) para 12.
19   Constitutional Review Chamber Case no III-4/A-1/94 (12 January 1994) para 4.
20   Supreme Court *en banc* Case 3-4-1-5-02 (28 October 2002) para 31; P Roosma, 'Protection of Fundamental Rights and Freedoms in Estonian Constitutional Jurisprudence' (1999) IV Juridica International 35.

of the foreign treaty shall be applied. This rule of superiority of foreign treaty law over domestic legislation applies also to internal laws enacted after the ratification of the treaty. The Constitution mentions nothing about the legal position in the hierarchy of norms of international treaties concluded by the Estonian government, but not ratified by Parliament. In practice, many such international treaties exist and the majority view among legal scholars is that these treaties have the same position in the norm hierarchy as international treaties ratified by Parliament. This interpretation is also in conformity with the international obligations of Estonia under the 1969 Vienna Convention on the Law of Treaties (VCLT).[21]

Estonia became a member of the UN on 17 September 1991. An indication of the general attitude of the state towards the UN treaty system and human rights, at least to some degree, is evident in Estonia's active participation in the work of the Human Rights Council (HRC) during its membership of 2013 to 2015. This was noted by the Report of the Working Group on the Universal Periodic Review (UPR) in 2016.[22] Estonia was also the chair of the Consultative Committee of the UN Development Fund for Women in 2007–2009. Estonia has contributed to the advancement of the situation of women as a member of the Commission on the Status of Women in 2011–2015, the UN Entity for Gender Equality and the Empowerment of Women as the Executive Board Member in 2011–2012.[23] Likewise, Estonia's standing invitation to special procedure mandate holders of the HRC can be seen as an indication of the accommodating approach taken by the state.[24]

Estonia's first UPR in the UN HRC took place in February 2011. Estonia submitted a mid-term report on the implementation of the accepted recommendations in March 2014. The second UPR took place in 2016. The 2016 national report was prepared by the Ministry of Foreign Affairs. Prior to submission the report was sent for feedback to NGOs dealing with human rights in Estonia

---

21 L Mälksoo and others, 'Välissuhted ja välislepingud' in Ü Madise jt (toim), *Eesti Vabariigi põhiseadus. Kommenteeritud väljaanne* (Juura 2017) paras 5–6; K Merusk and R Narits, *Eesti Konstitutsiooniõigusest* (Juura 1998) 26–32.
22 HRC, Report of the Working Group, Estonia, UPR, UN Doc A/HRC/32/7 (12 April 2016) para 7. The rights of women and children, consideration of the gender perspective in conflict situations, the fight against impunity, protection of the rights of indigenous peoples, freedom of expression, including on the internet, and non-discrimination against lesbian, gay, bisexual, transgender and intersex persons were the focus of the work of Estonia during its membership of the Council.
23 See eg National Report, CEDAW, Estonia, UN Doc CEDAW/C/Est/5-6 (24 March 2015) para 7.
24 See eg Voluntary Pledge, GA, Estonia, UN Doc GA, A/67/121 (2 July 2012).

and was also published on the Governmental Information System for Draft Legislation.[25] This is a platform that facilitates public consultation of draft documents, thus creating access to everybody interested in becoming involved in the reporting process. All documents and results from the 2016 UPR are publicly available on the Ministry of Foreign Affairs website in either English or Estonian (including the 2018 interim report in English).[26] Estonia's third UPR is coming up in 2021.

Estonia became a member of the UN on 17 September 1991. In the same year it joined the Organisation for Security and Cooperation in Europe (OSCE). Since 14 May 1993 Estonia is also a member of the CoE. Estonia joined the European Union (EU) on 1 May 2004,[27] and the North Atlantic Treaty Organization (NATO) in 28 March 2004. In 2010 it joined the Organization for Economic Cooperation and Development (OECD) and in 1999 the World Trade Organisation (WTO).

Estonia has ratified key treaties protecting fundamental freedoms and rights. Among the international human rights instruments, the ECHR[28] is the most influential along with the Charter of Fundamental Rights of the EU.[29] Estonia has been a party to the Rome Statute of the International Criminal Court (ICC) since its entry into force in 2002.[30] Estonian diplomat Tiina Intelmann was the president of the ICC Assembly of States Parties from 2011 to 2014. Since 2011 Estonia has also had a representative in the Assembly of States Parties Committee on Budget and Finance. Estonia has made, and claims to continue to make, donations to the ICC Trust Fund for Victims and to non-governmental organisations (NGOs) fighting for the universality of the principles of the ICC. It also supports capacity building of the state parties' law enforcement authorities (Coalition for the ICC, Parliamentarians for Global Action, and so forth). Estonia has stressed the importance of following the principles of the Responsibility to Protect (R2P).[31]

---

25   Eelnõude infosüsteem (EIS) <http://eelnoud.valitsus.ee> accessed 19 April 2022.
26   UPR, Mid-Term Report of Estonia on the Implementation of the UPR Recommendations (December 2018).
27   Treaty of Accession, RT II 2004, 3, 8.
28   Estonia became a member of the Council of Europe on 14 May 1993, and on the same day signed the treaty of the European Convention of Human Rights. The Estonian Parliament ratified the Convention on 13 March 1996 (RT II 1996, 11/12, 34), the letters of which were deposited on 16 April 1996.
29   However, one could argue that although EU law is part and parcel of life in Estonia today, the Charter remains relatively unknown and unused in practice.
30   Rome Statute of the International Criminal Court 1998, UNTS, Vol 2187, No 38544.
31   Ministry of Foreign Affairs, 'The Fight Against Impunity' <https://vm.ee/en/fight-against-impunity> accessed 19 April 2022.

Estonia represents a more monistic approach to the relationship of international and municipal law.[32] The direct applicability of international norms in Estonia depends on the quality of that norm. First of all, the norm has to be a part of the Estonian legal system. Directly applicable norms have to be in force internationally and binding upon Estonia (in this regard, also, reservations to international treaties have to be taken into account). Second, the norm has to be self-executing.[33]

Although there are no major issues regarding human rights protection in Estonia today, there are tensions that are related to processes in Estonia and beyond. Tensions that may influence the impact of human rights treaties in the future have flared up by factors such as migration,[34] economic concerns and, not least, the rise of far-right movements and populism. Some politicians, especially from the far right, have questioned Estonia's membership in the EU and in the CoE. These ideas gained further momentum after Russia's voting rights were restored in the CoE in June 2019.[35]

Rhetoric similar to that against European institutions seems to be absent regarding UN and UN human rights treaties. Although the effectiveness of the entire UN system has been discussed occasionally,[36] Estonia's election to the non-permanent membership in the UN Security Council on 6 June 2019 for the period 2020 to 2021 was celebrated and covered mainly positively in the media.[37]

---

32   It theoretically is debatable whether Estonia has adopted a moderate dualist approach or a moderate monist approach to international law. See eg M Kiviorg, 'Application of Freedom of Religion Principles of the European Convention on Human Rights in Estonia' in A Emilianides (ed), *The Application of the European Convention on Human Rights in the European Union* (Peeters 2011) 121; see also reflections on this matter in the commentaries to the Estonian Constitution in Mälksoo and others (n 21).

33   Kiviorg (n 32); see also Supreme Court, Administrative Law Chamber Case 3-3-1-58-02 (20 December 2002) para 11.

34   Since the end of the Soviet occupation (1991), Estonia has not been a country of extensive immigration. On the contrary, it has experienced a rather troubling net outward migration. Due to the extensive in-migration administered by the government of the Soviet Union after World War II, Estonia is left with a considerably large Russian-speaking minority. Of the total population, approximately 26% is from an immigrant background. However, the exact numbers are debatable and depend on what is taken as the basis for determining immigrant background. For a more detailed account on the matter, see M Kiviorg, *Law and Religion in Estonia* (3rd edition, Kluwer Law International 2021).

35   The voting rights were removed due to events in Ukraine and specifically in Crimea.

36   See eg an overview of the challenges in the UN in M Kolga, 'Kolmveerand sajandit ÜRO d – mille nimel?' *Diplomaatia* (Tallinn, 15 August 2019).

37   See eg 'Juhtkiri: hääl maailma pealinnas' *Postimees* (Tallinn, 9 June 2019); L-E Lomp, 'Marko Mihkelson: kogu töö alles seisab ees' *Postimees* (Tallinn, 7 June 2019).

However, one may argue that the entire human rights framework has become more fragile than it has been since the end of World War II and after the Soviet occupation. As recently pointed out by Estonia's former President Toomas Hendrik Ilves, for the first time after the collapse of the Soviet regime, Estonia is in a situation where many are worried about continuance of democratic governance.[38] Similar concerns were expressed by President Kersti Kaljulaid in her speech at the celebration of the Day of Restoration of Independence on 20 August 2019.[39] At the end of her speech, she emphasised that one can never talk too much about democracy and freedom, as there is never too much democracy and freedom.[40] The truth probably is that the social and political situation and atmosphere (also globally) is changing very rapidly, and it has become increasingly more complex to scientifically rationalise over the processes that take place and how these processes influence the impact of international treaties. The following will assess the role of UN human rights treaties in Estonia in general and then focus on the impact of specific treaties and point out challenges in their implementation primarily within the time period under consideration in this study.

3   At a Glance: Formal Engagement of Estonia with the UN Human Rights Treaty System

Refer to the chart on the next page.

4   Role and Overall Impact of UN Human Rights Treaties in Estonia

4.1   *Role of UN Treaties*
4.1.1   Formal Acceptance

Out of nine UN human rights treaties under discussion in this study Estonia has ratified seven. Since the 1999 study,[41] it has ratified the Convention on the

---

[38]   TH Ilves, 'Me seisame kahe riigi väraval' *Postimees* (Tallinn, 20 August 2019).

[39]   On 20 August 1991 Estonia declared formal independence during the Soviet military *coup* attempt in Moscow, reconstituting the pre-1940 state. Every year, 20 August is celebrated as the Day of Restoration of Independence.

[40]   K Kaljulaid, 'Kersti Kaljulaid: demokraatiat ja vabadust ei saa olla kunagi liiga palju' *ERR* (20 August 2019) <https://www.err.ee/972153/kersti-kaljulaid-demokraatiat-ja-vabadust-ei-saa-olla-kunagi-liiga-palju> accessed 19 April 2022. Presidential speeches (also in English) are available on the official website of the President. See <https://www.president.ee/en/official-duties/speeches> accessed 19 April 2022.

[41]   M Hion, 'Estonia' in C Heyns and F Viljoen (eds), *The Impact of the United Nations Human Rights Treaties on the Domestic Level* (Kluwer Law International 2002).

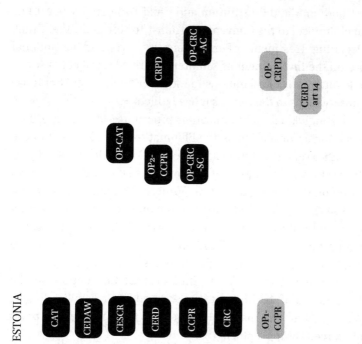

Rights of Persons with Disabilities (CRPD) and its Optional Protocol (OP-CRPD), the Second Optional Protocol to the International Convention on Civil and Political Rights aimed at the abolition of the death penalty (OP2-CCPR), the Optional Protocol to the Convention on the Rights of the Child on the Sale of Children, Child Prostitution and Child Pornography (OP-CRC-SC), the Optional Protocol to the Convention against Torture and Other Cruel, Inhuman or Degrading Treatment or Punishment (OP-CAT), and the Optional Protocol to CRC on the Involvement of Children in Armed Conflict (OP-CRC-AC). It has made interpretive declarations to CRPD, CERD and CRC, but it has not made any reservations to the treaties it has ratified.[42]

It has accepted individual communication procedures under OP1-CCPR, under the International Convention on the Elimination of All Forms of Racial Discrimination (CERD) and the Optional Protocol to Convention on the Rights of Persons with Disabilities (OP-CRPD). It has not ratified the Optional Protocol to the Convention on the Elimination of All Forms of Discrimination against Women (OP-CEDAW), the Optional Protocol to the International Covenant on Economic, Social and Cultural Rights (OP-CESCR) and Optional Protocol to the Convention on the Rights of the Child on a Communications Procedure (OP-CRC-CP). It has accepted the inquiry procedures under CAT and CRPD.

Estonia has chosen not to ratify the International Convention on the Protection of the Rights of All Migrant Workers and Their Families (CMW) and has not yet ratified the International Convention for the Protection of All Persons from Enforced Disappearance (CED).

4.1.2   General Attitude of State towards UN Treaty System

As noted above, after regaining independence as a result of the collapse of the Soviet regime, Estonia sent out a very strong message of taking a democratic path and adhering to international law and human rights. President Lennart Meri (1992–2001) in an interview in 1998 noted that 'the nuclear bomb of small states is international law'.[43] In general terms, this positive attitude towards international law and thus towards the UN treaty system has continued to the present. One can see the trend that state authorities are generally following the Concluding Observations (COs) of treaty-monitoring bodies as to country

---

[42] The analysis of the impact of the treaties in this article will primarily focus on the period between 30 June 1999 and 30 June 2019. However, some exceptions are made. The exceptions are indicated, for example, such as Estonia's latest report on implementation of CERD in July 2019 which was actually due in 2018.

[43] L Mälksoo, 'State Responsibility and the Challenge of the Realist Paradigm' (2003) Baltic Yearbook of International Law 71.

performance quite closely. Sometimes suggested changes do not materialise due to political opposition to implementing certain recommendations or financial constraints. However, sometimes the recommendations themselves are not nuanced enough to facilitate changes. During this study also some inconsistencies between the COs of different committees were identified, as well as occasional inaccuracies. The quality of state reports has also been fluctuating. Some examples of this will be provided under specific treaties.

As noted already in the 1999 study, six treaties under discussion then were ratified in one session, a month after Estonia had regained its independence, without the relevant treaties even having been translated into Estonian.[44] It was, indeed, to make it clear where Estonia wanted to belong after the Soviet occupation by demonstrating, in this way, a clear break with its authoritarian past. It showed 'that it was a full member of the UN intending to cooperate with other members to fulfil the aims of the UN'.[45]

The process of ratification may have slowed down or, perhaps it is more accurate to say, has normalised by now. Estonia is consistently reviewing its international obligations and considering the ratification of human rights treaties to which it is not yet a party. For example, the 2016 UPR indicated the need to ratify several instruments including CED, CMW, OP-CRC-CP and OP-CESCR. Although Estonia expressed its intention to ratify CED and clarified that there are no substantial objections to the ratification, the ratification has not yet materialised during the period under consideration (30 June 1999 to 30 June 2019).[46] Moreover, it has clearly indicated that it is not planning to ratify CMW, because the EU common immigration policy guarantees equal treatment of third country citizens.[47] Estonia is considering the recommendation to ratify OP-CRC-CP and the recommendation to sign and ratify OP-CESCR is under consideration. However, neither of the instruments has been ratified during the period here under review. In its voluntary pledge to the UN General Assembly in 2012 for membership of the HRC, Estonia mentioned that it was considering recognising the competence of the CEDAW Cttee under OP-CEDAW.[48] However, it has not yet ratified this instrument, but has again indicated in its 2018 Mid-Term Report on the Implementation of the UPR

---

44   Heyns and Viljoen (n 41) 9, 251.
45   M Hion, 'Estonia' in Heyns and Viljoen (n 41) 251–252.
46   This data is valid up to 8 October 2020.
47   Views on Conclusions and/or Recommendations, UPR, Estonia, Un Doc A/HRC/32/7/Add.1 (2 June 2016) 4.
48   See eg Voluntary Pledge (n 24).

Recommendations that the relevant authorities are preparing the necessary legislative proposals to sign and ratify the Protocol.[49]

4.1.3 Level of Awareness

As noted by the HRCttee in its COs in 2019, CCPR is rarely invoked by domestic courts.[50] The same cannot be said of the ECHR. Up to the year 2000 the references to the ECHR constituted approximately 60 per cent of the total references to international treaties.[51] It could be argued that this holds true today as well. In addition, since 2004 references to EU law have come to be of considerable importance. References to EU law and cases and to the European Court of Human Rights (ECtHR) cases are commonplace in Estonian legal practice.

CCPR was referenced by the Supreme Court of Estonia in six cases between 30 June 1999 and 30 June 2019.[52] CESCR was referenced in two cases.[53] A reference to CERD came up once, in a case concerning elections of municipal councils.[54] Reference to CRC figured three times.[55] There has been no case in the Supreme Court explicitly mentioning CEDAW. The explicit reference to CAT and its CAT Cttee was made once in a Supreme Court case.[56] There have been quite a few cases related to disability in the Supreme Court. However, during

---

49 UPR, Mid-Term Report of Estonia on the Implementation of the UPR Recommendations (December 2018).
50 HRC, CCPR/C/EST/CO/4, 26 March 2019.
51 See H Vallikivi, 'Euroopa inimõiguste konventsiooni kasutamine Riigikohtu praktikas' (2000) VI Juridica 401.
52 Constitutional Review Chamber Case 3-4-1-7-17 (6 July 2017); Constitutional Review Chamber Case 3-4-1-44-13 (2 October 2013); Constitutional Review Chamber Case 3-3-1-61-09 (9 November 2009); Constitutional Review Chamber Case 3-3-1-101-06 (3 January 2008); Supreme Court, Criminal Law Chamber Case 3-1-1-55-07 (19 October 2007); Supreme Court *en banc* decision, Case 3-1-3-10-02 (17 March 2003). The Court's decisions are available on the Supreme Court website <www.riigikohus.ee> accessed 19 April 2022. Some decisions of the Constitutional Review Chamber and of the *En Banc* of the Supreme Court have been translated into English. All Supreme Court decisions and lower courts decisions from 2006 are also available on the official site of the State Gazette (*Riigi Teataja*) <https://www.riigiteataja.ee/kohtulahendid/koik_menetlused.html> accessed 19 April 2022.
53 Administrative Law Chamber Case 3-3-1-65-03 (10 November 2003); Administrative Law Chamber Case *3-3-1-58-02* (20 December 2002).
54 Constitutional Review Chamber Case 3-4-1-47-13 (15 October 2013).
55 Administrative Law Chamber Case 3-3-1-61-09 (9 November 2009); Supreme Court *en banc* Case 3-2-1-4-13 (17 December 2013); Constitutional Review Chamber Case *3-4-1-16-16* (31 March 2017).
56 Administrative Law Chamber Case 3-3-1-14-10 (21 April 2010) para 11.

the period under study CRPD has been explicitly mentioned only once.[57] The details of the references to international treaties will be discussed under each specific treaty later on.

In addition to international treaties, the human rights documents of international organisations have also been referred to in court cases.[58] Until 1999 the awareness and knowledge about international human rights instruments, including among legal professionals, was not widespread.[59] Although the situation is still not ideal, the quality of reliance on international law has since then improved from year to year. It also appears that overall reasoning regarding interpretation of rights and freedoms is in compliance with their interpretation at the international level even in cases where these international human rights instruments have not been explicitly mentioned. At the same time, in the above-mentioned cases (with a few exceptions) where the treaties were mentioned explicitly there was no extensive argumentation presented that was directly based on the interpretation of these treaties, for example by mentioning monitoring bodies' decisions or General Comments. Although the Estonian legal framework may not be perfect, it provides remedies against violations of the rights and freedoms of individuals. The laws have been consistently and gradually changed to comply with international and also EU law. Thus, for that reason, it seems that the references are first of all made to domestic law. The details will be discussed later on under specific treaties.

While teaching about human rights was just taking off in the 1990s, by now human rights law training is provided by universities as an obligatory or at least as an optional course. Law training is provided by three main universities, namely, the University of Tartu, the University of Tallinn and Tallinn Technical University.[60] Continuing legal training of law professionals is now commonplace. It is organised by several institutions, including professional organisations and governmental institutions. Of course, there is room for improvement. One also needs to notice that there is more emphasis on the

---

57 Constitutional Review Chamber Case 3-4-1-16-16 (31 March 2017). In this particular case several international instruments were mentioned.
58 Eg Constitutional Review Chamber Case 3-4-1-44-13 (2 October 2013).
59 See in this respect also M Hion, 'Estonia' in Heyns and Viljoen (n 41) 253.
60 For example, international human rights law is taught as an obligatory course in the international Master's programme on international law and human rights at the University of Tartu. The University also provides courses on comparative human rights, introduction to international human rights in its obligatory course on public international law. Additionally, there is an optional course on human rights. There is also a course on specific issues of human rights implementation in Russia and a course on law, religion and politics that discusses freedom of religion or belief.

European framework.[61] Regarding human rights in education generally, it is incorporated into school curricula. The Basic Schools and Upper Secondary Schools Act specifically mentions the Universal Declaration of Human Rights (UDHR) and CRC enshrining important fundamental values of general education schools.[62] However, 2017 research shows that there are deficiencies in practice. For example, it was pointed out that it is yet to be fully assessed whether and to what extent these laws apply in practice, 'as the usage and application of human rights in the teaching process is quite often episodic'.[63]

Estonia is a highly-digitised country. Most of the relevant information regarding the impact of human rights treaties is easily accessible on the internet. Unofficial translations into English and Russian of the texts of selected Estonian legal acts can be found at the web page of the State Gazette (*Riigi Teataja*) or via a link provided on the webpage.[64] This is an official webpage of the state *Gazette* where all the laws and other legislative acts and court decisions of Estonia are electronically available. It also publishes translations into Estonian of foreign treaties concluded by Estonia. The site also offers annotations in Estonian of the cases decided in the ECtHR. Unfortunately, similar annotations are not done for the opinions of the UN treaty-monitoring bodies, including the HRCttee. This, as noted before, may be due to the perception that decisions of the ECtHR carry more weight, but there are also financial constraints to producing the annotations.

The reports to treaty-monitoring bodies and COs are available on the Ministry of Foreign Affairs web page in both English and Estonian.[65] However, there seems to be a time delay in publishing the latest reports and COs in some instances. For example, the 2016 COs of the CEDAW Cttee and the state party's report are not available either in English or in Estonian on that specific

---

61 See eg National Report, CCPR, Estonia, UN Doc CCPR/C/EST/4 (29 August 2018) para 26.
62 Basic Schools and Upper Secondary Schools Act, art 3(2), RT I 2010, 41, 240.
63 The deficiencies, for example, were pointed out in the 2017 research ordered by the Ministry of Education and Research. M Käger and others, *Inimõigused ja inimõiguste alusväärtused Eesti koolis ja hariduspoliitikas. Nende avaldumine hariduspoliitilistes dokumentides ja rakendumine koolisüsteemis* (Balti Uuringute Instituut, Eesti Inimõiguste Keskus 2017) 76 <https://www.hm.ee/sites/default/files/uuringud/io_lopparuanne.pdf> accessed 19 April 2022.
64 Riigi Teataja <https://www.riigiteataja.ee/en/> accessed 30 January 2020. The translations have no legal force and cannot be relied on in judicial or any other official proceedings. In Estonia, legislation has legal force only in Estonian.
65 Ministry of Internal Affairs, 'International Organisations', 'Estonia's Reports to International Organisations on the Implementation of Conventions' <https://vm.ee/et/inimoigusalaste-konventsioonide-taitmine-0> accessed 19 April 2022.

webpage. However, the latest reports regarding CCPR and CESCR from 2019 are available.

Similar to the findings in the 1999 study, media interest in the UN treaties, including ratification, reports, findings of treaty bodies (including COs) does not seem to be very high. The majority of articles on human rights deal with human rights situations globally and do not specifically cover UN treaties that Estonia has ratified. For example, in the last 12 months under review here (30 June 2018 to 30 June 2019) human rights-related articles in a major newspaper *Postimees* were primarily related to global issues, Estonia's membership in the UN Security Council, climate change and domestic political debates over hate speech. No media article was found that covered findings in the latest 2019 COs of the CESCR Cttee and HRC ttee.[66] This does not mean that there is no interest in human rights in the media, but merely indicates that these specific instruments were not covered. For example, there was an article on a report produced under the auspices of the United Nations Children's Fund (UNICEF) in 2019.[67]

Two surveys were conducted in 2012 and 2016 under the auspices of the Estonian Institute of Human Rights (EIHR) on human rights knowledge and perceptions of the human rights situation in Estonia among 15 to 74 year-olds. The 2016 survey concluded that although some indicators are better than in 2012, over 50 per cent of the population is not familiar with the topic. Although the survey reveals a lack of knowledge, it also shows that human rights problems are not something that people have had to deal with or think about on a daily basis. According to the survey, this also indicates that human rights problems do not often occur and thus do not trigger interest or become important for people.[68] The survey did not probe into specific knowledge of UN human rights treaties. In 2018 the Institute conducted a comparative study on human

---

66 *Postimees* <https://www.postimees.ee> accessed 19 April 2022.
67 L Saue, 'UNICEFi raport: Eesti perepoliitika on arenenud riikide parimate seas' *Postimees* (Tallinn, 14 June 2019). The article covered results published in the Y Chzhen, A Gromada and G Rees, 'Are the World's Richest Countries Family Friendly? Policy in the OECD and EU' (UNICEF 2019).
68 Estonian Institute of Human Rights, 'Avaliku arvamuse uuring Eestis. Küsitlus 15 – 74 a. elanikkonna seas' (Turu-uuringute AS 2016) 7 <https://www.humanrightsestonia.ee/wp/wp-content/uploads/2016/12/AvalikArv_Kokkuvõte.pdf> accessed 19 April 2022. Mälksoo has pointed out that in his view, people do not know or care too much about the treaties. See interview with Lauri Mälksoo, Professor of International Law at University of Tartu, School of Law, 29 May 2020, Tallinn (notes of interviews on file with author).

rights in the Baltic states.[69] Although the survey revealed that there is still a lack of knowledge about human rights, 73 per cent of Estonians think that there is no problem with human rights protection in their country. No specific data was gathered about the UN human rights treaties.

4.1.4 State Reporting

Estonia's record as to keeping to the submission timeline with the reports seems to have improved since 1999. According to the 1999 report, on average Estonia was three years and six months late with its reports; ranking eighteenth among the 20 countries under study.[70] In the time period under consideration in this chapter, the reporting has been approximately 1,3 years behind schedule.[71] There also does not seem to be any major problem with involvement of different actors in preparation of the reports. The reports seem to be generally open and made available for input and comments. The reports are prepared in various ways, but the most common is to have a relevant ministry dedicated for reporting on a specific treaty to prepare the report in cooperation with various actors. For example, the 2015 state party report on CRPD was drafted by the Ministry of Social Affairs, in cooperation with all other ministries and their relevant agencies, and with input from the civil society. The Estonian Chamber of Disabled People, the Estonian Human Rights Centre, the Estonian Institute of Human Rights (EIHR) and the Estonian Patient Advocacy Association were invited to submit their views on the fulfilment of the Convention.[72] The most recent report submitted in July 2019 on CERD was prepared by the Ministries of Education and Research, Justice, Defence, Culture, Interior and Social Affairs. The report was submitted for information to the Chancellor of Justice and the Gender Equality and Equal Treatment Commissioner. The report was also submitted for comments and opinions to three NGOs: the Estonian Human Rights Centre; the EIHR; and the Legal Information Centre for Human Rights (LICHR). The latter two provided feedback, which is reflected in the report.[73]

One also needs to note that there is an effort made by the government to explain the overall situation in Estonia. For that purpose, a common core

---

69 Estonian Institute of Human Rights, 'Inimõigused Balti Riikides. Eesti, Läti ja Leedu võrdlev uuring 2018' <https://www.humanrightsestonia.ee/wp/wp-content/uploads/2019/02/Inimõigused_est.pdf> accessed 19 April 2022.
70 M Hion, 'Estonia' in Heyns and Viljoen (n 41) 255.
71 See state parity's reporting status at the High Commissioner of Human Rights webpage: 'Human Rights by Country', 'Estonia', 'Reporting Status'.
72 Initial Report, CRPD, Estonia, UN Doc CRPD/C/EST/1 (4 December 2015).
73 National Report, CERD, Estonia, UN Doc CERD/C/EST/12-13 (15 October 2019).

document has been published on the Ministry of Foreign Affairs webpage and submitted to accompany all reports by the government to monitoring bodies.[74] The first such document was published in 2001. It was replaced by a new document in 2015. This document is, however, publicly available only in English.[75] Considering that the document was produced in 2015, it is not an ideal document. The need for updating it to comply with the harmonised guidelines on reporting under the international human rights treaties was also pointed out by the CESCR Cttee in 2019.[76]

4.1.5 Domestic Implementation Mechanism

The 2019 COs of the HRCttee mention a lack of information on a national mechanism to monitor the implementation of its recommendations and the absence of effective mechanisms and legal procedures for authors of individual communications to seek, in law and in practice, the full implementation of views adopted under OP-CCPR.[77] There are mechanisms in place; however, they may not be as clear as they could be for individual applicants and for the implementation of recommendations.

According to the Foreign Relations Act, if a national legal act is contrary to a treaty binding on Estonia, the government of the Republic, the corresponding ministry or the State Chancellery initiates the bringing of such legal act into conformity with the treaty.[78] If a law or other legal act is contrary to a treaty ratified by Parliament, an institution responsible for implementation of the law (judicial or administrative) is entitled and obliged not to apply that law.[79] As noted above, all courts are competent to deal with questions of human rights. According to article 15(1) of the Constitution, everyone whose rights and freedoms have been violated has the right of recourse to the courts. The Constitution also guarantees everyone's right to petition the court that hears the case to declare unconstitutional any law, other legal act or measure which is relevant in the case. This may trigger the constitutional review procedure.[80]

---

74 Ministry of Internal Affairs, 'International Organisations', 'Estonia's Reports to International Organisations on the Implementation of Conventions' <https://vm.ee/et /https://vm.ee/et/inimoigusalaste-konventsioonide-taitmine-0> accessed 19 April 2022.
75 Välisministeerium, Inimõigusalaste konventsioonide täitmine, 'Ülevaatedokument (Common Core Document 2015)' <https://vm.ee/et/inimoigusalaste-konventsioon ide-taitmine-0 > accessed 19 April 2022.
76 CESCR Cttee, COs, Estonia, UN Doc E/C.12/EST/CO/3 (27 March 2019) para 60.
77 HRCttee, COs, Estonia, UN Doc CCPR/C/EST/CO/4 (18 April 2019) 5.
78 Foreign Relations Act, art 24(2), RT I 2006, 32, 248.
79 L Mälksoo and others (n 21) para 9. See also art 123 of the Constitution.
80 See arts 15(2), 146 and 152 of the Constitution and Constitutional Review Court Procedure Act, RT I 2002, 29, 174.

As noted by Uno Lõhmus, fulfilling the obligations stemming from the international treaties that Estonia has adhered to requires interpretation of the domestic law and also the Constitution in compliance with these international treaties and their practice.[81]

In very specific cases, for example, the Code of Administrative Court Procedure foresees the review procedure of the court decisions that have entered into force. One of the grounds of review can be the fact that the ECtHR has established a violation of the ECHR in the making of the court decision, and the violation cannot be reasonably cured or compensated in any other manner than by review.[82] Analogous provisions are included into the Code of Civil Procedure[83] and Code of Criminal Procedure.[84] There is no such explicit mention of the review in these codes on the basis of decisions of the UN treaty bodies. This can be attributed to the quasi-judicial nature of these decisions and to the leeway international law gives for establishing domestic enforcement mechanisms. However, as mentioned before, everybody has a constitutional right to recourse to courts for the protection of their fundamental rights and freedoms[85] and international treaties can be directly applicable.

In addition to the government and courts there are two important institutions in Estonia that internally monitor the implementation of human rights and international human rights instruments: the Chancellor of Justice and the Gender Equality and Equal Treatment Commissioner. Since 2007 the Chancellor of Justice exercises supervision over the compliance of the legislation with international agreements.[86] The Chancellor of Justice's role also includes the verification of compliance of legal instruments with the Constitution and laws (constitutional review competence); supervision over the activities of representatives of public authority; and the protection of people from arbitrary actions of public authority and officials (ombudsman competence). The Chancellor also arranges for conciliation proceedings in discrimination

disputes between persons governed by private law (competence to resolve discrimination disputes) and promotes the principles of equality and equal

---

81   U Lõhmus, *Õigusriik ja inimese õigused* (Ilmamaa 2018) 59. Uno Lõhmus is a former judge of the ECtHR, ECJ and Chief Justice of the Estonian Supreme Court.
82   Halduskohtumenetluse seadustik, art 240(2)(8), RT I, 23.02.2011, 3.
83   Code of Civil Procedure, art 702(2)(8), RT I 2005, 26, 197.
84   Code of Criminal Procedure, art 366(1)(7), RT I 2003, 27, 166.
85   Estonian Constitution, art 15 (n 9).
86   Chancellor of Justice Act, art 1(6), RT I 1999, 29, 406; RT I 2007, 11, 52.

treatment. Each year the Chancellor reports/conveys her concerns to Parliament.

As for the Gender Equality and Equal Treatment Commissioner, the competency of the former Gender Equality Commissioner was broadened with the Equal Treatment Act[87] that entered into force on 1 January 2009. In addition to gender equality, the Commissioner now deals with equal treatment on the basis of ethnic origin, race, skin colour, religion or political views, age, disability and sexual orientation. However, the Commissioner can only give opinions that are not legally binding. The latter has been pointed out as an issue, for example, by the HRCttee,[88] although the 2018 state report to the HRCttee[89] indicated a change in that respect as the amendments of the Equal Treatment Act were under preparation.[90] This change was suspended in February 2019 not least because of the various controversies in the amendments and financial constraints.[91]

Issues of sufficient funding and manning of these institutions have been repeatedly called in question also by treaty-monitoring bodies. Economic factors remain an issue. However, there have been some improvements regarding allocations from the state budget.[92] The Gender Equality and Equal Treatment Commissioner has also obtained funding from the EU and other European funding bodies.[93]

The UN human rights treaties, especially CRC, CAT and CRPD, have had a direct effect on changes of the Chancellor of Justice's mandate domestically. The details will be elaborated later on under specific treaties. The most recent sign that recommendations of monitoring bodies[94] are taken seriously and have an effect at the domestic level is the amendment to the Chancellor of Justice Act[95] on 13 June 2018. This amendment extended the role of the Chancellor of Justice, who currently in Estonia performs the function of a

---

[87] RT I 2008, 56, 315.
[88] National Report, CCPR, Estonia, UN Doc CCPR/C/EST/4 (29 August 2018) para 10.
[89] National Report, CCPR, Estonia, UN Doc CCPR/C/EST/4 (29 August 2018) para 24.
[90] See also HRCttee, COs, Estonia, UN Doc CCPR/C/EST/CO/4 (18 April 2019) para 10.
[91] See for the controversies Justiitsministeerium, 'Vastuskiri võrdse kohtlemise seaduse muutmise seaduse eelnõule' No 8-2/3091 (31 May 2018).
[92] See eg National Report, CCPR, Estonia, UN Doc CCPR/C/EST/4 (29 August 2018) para 21.
[93] National Report, CCPR, Estonia, UN Doc CCPR/C/EST/4 (29 August 2018) para 23.
[94] The establishment of a national human rights institution has been recommended by several human rights monitoring bodies, for example, the CERD Cttee, the HRCttee, the European Union Agency for Fundamental Rights (FRA), the UN Human Rights Council and the UN Committee against Torture. Representatives of Estonian civil society have also drawn attention to this issue.
[95] Chancellor of Justice Act, RT I, 03.07.2018, 14.

national human rights institution (NHRI) as of 1 January 2019 in accordance with UN Resolution 48/134 of 20 December 1993 (Paris Principles).[96] The NHRI was accredited in December 2020.[97] Since February 2019 the Chancellor of Justice is also a member of the European Network of National Human Rights Institutions which has given its support for the accreditation process.[98]

In March 2019 the Chancellor of Justice's Advisory Committee on Human Rights was established. The Advisory Committee's 50 members were selected via an open competition and include people with expertise in various fields of human rights.[99] The establishment of the NHRI has thus been further strengthened. In the capacity of the NHRI the Chancellor of Justice submitted its first report in February 2019 regarding CRPD.[100]

5   Impact of the Different UN Human Rights Treaties on the Domestic Level in Estonia

5.1   *International Convention of the Elimination of All Forms of Racial Discrimination*

5.1.1   Incorporation and Reliance by Legislature and Executive

CERD entered into force with regard to Estonia on 20 November 1991.[101] It was one of the treaties that was ratified 'in bulk' at the beginning of 1990s directly after Soviet occupation, together with CAT, CCPR, CESCR, CRC and CEDAW.

As noted in the introduction, during its deliberations the Constitutional Assembly paid significant attention to UN and European human rights treaties.

---

96   Chancellor of Justice Act, art 1 (10), RT I 1999, 29, 406.
97   The institution was granted A-status (highest status) under the Paris Principles by the Subcommittee on Accreditation of the Global Alliance of National Human Rights Institutions.
98   Chancellor of Justice, 'Chancellor's Year in Review 2018/2019' <https://www.oiguskantsler.ee/annual-report-2019/> accessed 19 April 2022.
99   Chancellor of Justice, 'Chancellor of Justice's Advisory Committee on Human Rights to Convene Today', 26.03.2019 <https://www.oiguskantsler.ee/en/chancellor-justice's-advisory-committee-human-rights-convene-today> accessed 19 April 2022; Chancellor of Justice, 'Chancellor's Year in Review 2018/2019' <https://www.oiguskantsler.ee/annual-report-2019/ > accessed 19 April 2022.
100   Email consultation with Liiri Oja, Andres Aru, Indrek-Ivar Määrits, Office of Chancellor of Justice, 12 June 2020, Tallinn; written contribution of the Chancellor of Justice of the Republic of Estonia on implementation of the UN Convention on the Rights of Persons with Disabilities, 11th pre-session: country briefing of Estonia, February 2019.
101   Eesti Vabariigi ühinemisest rahvusvaheliste lepingutega, mille depositaariks on ÜRO peasekretär, RT 1991, 35, 428.

Almost at every session, membership in the UN and obligations regarding human rights were discussed or at least mentioned. The importance of the UN treaties in the creation of the Constitution has also been mentioned by the Supreme Court.[102]

The wording of the prohibition on discrimination in the Constitution was influenced by international instruments, including the UDHR and European Convention. The principle of equality is explicitly set forth in the first sentence of article 12(1) of the Constitution, which states that all persons shall be equal before the law. The second sentence of article 12 sets out the principle of non-discrimination, prohibiting discrimination on the basis of nationality, race, colour, sex, language, origin, religion, political or other views, property or social status, or on other grounds. The purpose of the second sentence is to protect minorities.[103] Article 12(2) sets forth that 'incitement to ethnic, racial, religious or political hatred, violence or discrimination is prohibited and punishable by law'.[104]

The prohibition on discrimination is also governed by various legislative acts. The Equal Treatment Act,[105] the Gender Equality Act,[106] the Employment Contracts Act,[107] the Penal Code[108] and other legal instruments and policy documents include relevant provisions. The adoption of the first two Acts can primarily be attributed to developments in the EU anti-discrimination legislation.[109] There is no explicit reference in the text of these laws to CERD or any other UN treaty under consideration here. However, the explanatory note to the Equal Treatment Act explicitly mentions CERD and the need to comply with European and international standards of protection against discrimination, including racial discrimination.[110]

As for examples of impact on policies, three national integration strategies have been adopted in Estonia since 1999 for the periods of 2000–2007, 2008–2013 and 2014–2020. These documents specifically mention CERD among

---

102 Supreme Court *en banc* Case 3-1-3-10-02 (17 March 2003) para 21.
103 M Ernits, 'Paragrahv 12' in Ü Madise jt (toim), *Eesti Vabariigi põhiseadus. Kommenteeritud väljaanne* (Juura 2017) para 26.
104 Estonian Constitution, art 12(2), RT 1992, 26, 349.
105 Equal Treatment Act, RT I 2008, 56, 315.
106 Gender Equality Act, RT I 2004, 27, 181.
107 Employment Contracts Act, RT I 2009, 5, 35.
108 Penal Code, RT I 2001, 61, 364.
109 Namely, the Council Directive (EC) 2000/78 on Employment Equality [2000] OJ L195/16 and the Council Directive (EC) 2000/43 on Implementing the Principle of Equal Treatment between Persons Irrespective of Racial or Ethnic Origin [2000] OJ L180/22.
110 Võrdse kohtlemise seaduse seletuskiri (385) 06.11.2008, 3 and 14.

other UN and European human rights instruments that have been taken into account in creating these strategies. In these documents there is no explicit mention of any COs, although they seem to have been taken into account.[111]

5.1.2 Reliance by Judiciary

According to the Supreme Court practice, since 2011 the first and second sentence of article 12 of the Constitution should be treated together.[112] This also means that the list of specific grounds in the second sentence is open-ended and exemplary. The Supreme Court also emphasised that listed grounds have different weights. If the difference in treatment is based on grounds that do not depend on a person's will, for example, race, age, disability, genetic makeup, as well as mother tongue, more substantial justifications would be needed.[113] Thus, the difference in treatment on the grounds covered by CERD requires special attention.

As noted above, there was one Supreme Court case where CERD was explicitly mentioned. This case concerns elections of municipal councils. The electoral committee refused to register a person as a candidate in the local municipality council elections of 2013 as he did not have citizenship.[114] The Municipal Council Election Act in article 5(5) limits candidacy to Estonian citizens and citizens of the EU who have the right to vote, have attained 18 years of age and whose permanent residence is located in the corresponding municipality.[115] In his complaint the applicant referred among other legal texts to article 5 of CERD. Regarding the Convention, the Court explained that according to article 1(2) of CERD the Convention does not apply to distinctions, exclusions, restrictions or preferences made by a state party to this Convention *between citizens and non-citizens*.[116] Thus, the Convention did not support the

---

111   See eg Ministry of Culture, 'The Strategy of Integration and Social Cohesion in Estonia 2020' <https://www.kul.ee/kultuuriline-mitmekesisus-ja-loimumine/strateegilised-dokumendid/loimuv-eesti-2020> accessed 19 April 2022. This type of document was first adopted in 1998 in Parliament ('Eesti riikliku integratsioonipoliitika lähtekohad mitte-eestlaste integreerimiseks Eesti ühiskonda').
112   Supreme Court *en banc* Case 3-1-1-12-10 (7 June 2011), para 31; Constitutional Review Chamber Case 3-4-1-23-11 (27 December 2011) para 41.
113   Supreme Court *en banc* Case 3-1-1-12-10 (7 June 2011) para 32.
114   Constitutional Review Chamber Case 3-4-1-47-13 (15 October 2013).
115   Kohaliku omavalitsuse volikogu valimise seadus, art 5(5), RT I 2002, 36, 220. In contrast to the passive right to vote (the right to stand as a candidate for elections) the law grants the active right to vote in local elections to all permanent residents, regardless of their citizenship.
116   Supreme Court, Constitutional Review Chamber Case 3-4-1-47-13 (15 October 2013) para 20.

complainant's arguments.[117] No further elaboration was made regarding the Convention. It needs to be re-emphasised here that international treaties can be applied directly in Estonian courts.

5.1.3 Impact on and through Independent State Institutions

On 1 January 2004 amendments to the Chancellor of Justice Act came into force granting competence to the Chancellor of Justice for the resolution of disputes related to discrimination in the private sphere (for instance, on the basis of race, ethnicity and skin colour).[118] Although the explanatory note to the amendment mentions EU directives[119] and the European Convention, the creation of this type of institution has been recommended by the CERD Cttee as well.[120] From 1 January 2019, as the NHRI, the Chancellor of Justice's role also includes issues concerning the prohibition on racial discrimination. Between 2014 and 2019 the Chancellor dealt with two cases that involved race as a ground and with eight cases involving nationality and ethnicity.[121] Among other engagements the Chancellor of Justice represents Estonia in the European Commission against Racism and Intolerance (ECRI). Annual reports of the chancellor between 2017 and 2019 did not have a reference to CERD. However, one needs to notice that reports are written in a very accessible way for an audience with no specific legal knowledge.

5.1.4 Impact on and through Non-state Actors

Estonian academic legal literature seems to rely heavily on European human rights instruments and case law.[122] For example, 2017 Commentaries to the Constitution only once explicitly mention CERD in the context of article 12 (equal treatment and non-discrimination) while EU law is mentioned multiple

---

117 Neither did the court find any contradiction in his case with Estonian Constitution or European Union legal acts.
118 Õiguskantsleri seaduse muutmise ja sellega seotud seaduste muutmise seadus, RT I 2003, 23, 142.
119 Council Directive (EC) 2000/78 on Employment Equality [2000] OJ L195/16 and Council Directive (EC) 2000/43 on Implementing the Principle of Equal Treatment between Persons Irrespective of Racial or Ethnic Origin [2000] OJ L180/22.
120 CERD Cttee, COs on the fifth periodic report of Estonia, UN Doc A/57/18 (22 August 2002) para 358.
121 National Report, CERD, Estonia, UN Doc CERD/C/EST/12-13 (15 October 2019) para 89; see also Chancellor's Year in Review 2018/2019 <https://www.oiguskantsler.ee/annual-report-2019/> accessed 19 April 2022.
122 See eg U Lõhmus, *Põhiõigused kriminaalmenetluses* (Juura 2014).

times.[123] No elaboration on the Convention is provided. The Commentaries of the Constitution are a prominent, if not authoritative, source of information for the Estonian legal community and society. It is authored by distinguished legal scholars and practitioners. Somewhat surprisingly, also the latest reports by Estonian Human Rights Centre (an NGO) on the human rights situation in Estonia do not discuss any of the issues in light of CERD. For example, in the context of hate speech only criticism of European institutions (both from the CoE and EU) is pointed out.[124] However, the Centre recently secured funding from the Active Citizens Fund (ACF) for a project to raise awareness and capabilities of civil society organisations engaged in human rights equal treatment advocacy to work with international and European human rights protection mechanisms. One of the main activities during the project is to draft the civil society shadow report for the UPR third cycle review of Estonia due to take place early 2021.[125] The latter, of course, is not only focused on CERD, but on Estonia's overall performance regarding human rights. Regarding the Centre's activities generally, it is also evident that some topics have acquired more attention, for example, under CRPD and CRC. As explained below, this can be attributed to the areas of strong local expertise. In 2016 and 2018 the Centre also sent out letters to political parties to inspire coalition talks and election platforms, respectively. The letters reference several UN treaties and COs of treaty-monitoring bodies.[126]

---

123   M Ernits, 'Paragrahv 12' in Ü Madise jt (toim), *Eesti Vabariigi põhiseadus. Kommenteeritud väljaanne* (Juura 2017). The commentaries are available online in Estonian <https://www.pohiseadus.ee> accessed 19 April 2022.

124   K Käsper (ed), *Inimõigused Eestis, Eesti Inimõiguste Keskuse aastaaruanne 2016-2017* (SA Eesti Inimõiguste Keskus 2017); K Käsper ja E Rünne (eds), *Inimõigused Eestis, Eesti Inimõiguste Keskuse aastaaruanne 2020, Areng aastatel 2018-2019* (SA Eesti Inimõiguste Keskus 2020) eg 47.

125   Human Rights Centre, Projects: VOIVIK: Capable Civil Society Protecting Human Rights <https://humanrights.ee/en/activities/voivik-voimekas-vabakond-inimoiguste-kaitsel/> accessed 19 April 2022.

126   Inimõiguste Keskus, 'Ettepanekud inimõiguste, sallivuse ja võrdõiguslikkuse edendamiseks Eestis' (14 november 2016) <https://humanrights.ee/app/uploads/2016/11/koali tsioonikiri.pdf> accessed 19 April 2022; Inimõiguste Keskus, 'Ettepanekud inimõiguste, sallivuse ja võrdõiguslikkuse edendamiseks Eestis' (15 May 2018) <https://humanrig hts.ee/app/uploads/2018/05/inimoiguste-keskuse-ettepanekud-150518-1.pdf> accessed 19 April 2022.

5.1.5 Impact of State Reporting

By June 2019 Estonia had gone through five full cycles of reporting.[127] The latest state report to the CERD Cttee, which was due in August 2018, was submitted in July 2019 and reflects on issues that were raised in COs and specifically in the COs from September 2014.[128] There have been a few recurring issues that have been reflected in the five COs. Of these, three stand out. The Committee has repeatedly expressed concern about the protection of minorities in Estonia, especially regarding language requirements that mostly affect the Russian-speaking population, the education of Roma children and statelessness. Some of these issues were also pointed out by UN Special Rapporteur Doudou Diène in his 2007 report on contemporary forms of racism, racial discrimination, xenophobia and related intolerance after his visit to Estonia.[129] The issue of awareness about CERD has also been in focus.

As for minority protection, one can at least partially attribute the aforementioned national integration strategies to the implementation of CERD, as it is explicitly mentioned in these documents.[130] As to statelessness, the Citizenship Act was changed in 2015 to allow minors under 15 years of age who were born in Estonia or who immediately after birth took up permanent residence in Estonia, together with their parents, to be granted Estonian citizenship by naturalisation at the moment of their birth. Estonian citizenship by naturalisation is also granted to children of persons with undetermined citizenship who are under 15 years of age.[131] The amendment also simplified the Estonian language examination requirements for citizenship applicants over 65 years of age.[132] However, the explanatory note to the law amendment did not mention CERD, but article 7(1) of CRC was mentioned.[133]

It may be argued that the impact of the COs on Roma issues can be seen in the implementation of the above-mentioned integration strategies. As noted above, CERD is explicitly mentioned in these strategies. The latest strategy for the period 2014–2020 specifically also mentions the importance of

---

127 At the time of the 1999 study there was only one completed cycle considering reports I–IV (combined) which did not meet the submission deadlines.
128 National Report, CERD, Estonia, UN Doc CERD/C/EST/12–13 (15 October 2019).
129 Report of the Special Rapporteur, Mission to Estonia, UN Doc A/HRC/7/19/Add.2 (17 March 2008).
130 'The Strategy of Integration and Social Cohesion in Estonia 2020' (n 111).
131 Citizenship Act, arts 13–14, RT I 1995, 12, 122.
132 Citizenship Act, art 34, RT I 1995, 12, 122.
133 Vabariigi Valitsus, Seletuskiri kodakondsuse seaduse ja riigilõivuseaduse muutmise seaduse eelnõu juurde (737 SE) <https://www.riigikogu.ee/tegevus/eelnoud/eelnou/e0669e30-f9d1-4a51-86d3-77232eba1eb9> accessed 19 April 2022, 12.

the integration of Roma.[134] Thus, it may be argued that although the CERD Cttee COs are not explicitly mentioned, they have been taken into account. In 2016 an Advisory Council for Roma Integration was set up at the Ministry of Culture.[135] This step stemmed from the integration strategies. The 2017 governmental report on implementation of the 2014–2020 strategy in 2016 brings out the establishment of the Council as an achievement in Roma integration.[136]

To diminish discrimination in the labour market, efforts are being made to raise employers' awareness of discrimination and to improve their willingness and ability to act. Collaboration with the Estonian Human Rights Centre, the Ministry of Social Affairs has developed the concept of the Diverse Workplace Label. However, these projects are also influenced by European initiatives.

One of the specific issues CERD had noted in the 2014 COs was the fact that racial motivation did not constitute an aggravating circumstance for crimes and recommended that Estonia include a specific provision to the Penal Code to ensure that the motive of ethnic, racial or religious hatred is taken into account as an aggravating circumstance in criminal proceedings.[137] According to article 58(1) of the current Penal Code, aggravating circumstances are self-interest or other base motives.[138] The Supreme Court has explained that this provision includes an open-ended list that the case law must define.[139] It has also noted that the commission of a criminal offence for a base motive requires deliberate intent pursuant to article 16(2) of the Penal Code.[140] Thus, in principle, racial motives can be taken into account. The above was used in the 2019 report to explain why COs in that respect were disregarded.[141]

---

134 See eg 'The Strategy of Integration and Social Cohesion in Estonia 2020' (n 111).
135 Ministry of Culture <https://www.kul.ee/kultuuriline-mitmekesisus-ja-loimumine/rahvusvahemused-ja-rahvuskaaslased/romade-loimumise-noukoda> accessed 19 April 2022.
136 Aruanne lõimumisvaldkonna arengukava „Lõimuv Eesti 2020" täitmise kohta 2016. aastal (Kultuuriministeerium 2017) 12.
137 CERD Cttee, COs, Estonia, UN Doc CERD/C/EST/CO/10–11 (22 September 2014) para 8. There is a slight discrepancy between the COs made by the CERD Cttee and the HRCttee, namely, the HRCttee is concerned that sexual orientation and gender identity are not aggravating circumstances for all offences. It does not mention racial motivations in that respect as did the CERD Cttee. HRCttee, COs, Estonia, UN Doc CCPR/C/EST/CO/4 (18 April 2019) para 12.
138 RT I 2001, 61, 364.
139 Supreme Court, Criminal Chamber Case 1-15-10119 (9 November 2017) para 34.
140 Supreme Court, Criminal Chamber Case 3-1-1-141-04 (2 March 2005) para 10.2.
141 National Report, CERD, Estonia, UN Doc CERD/C/EST/12-13 (15 October 2019) para 112.

5.1.6 Impact of Individual Communications

Estonia only in 2010 made the declaration pursuant to article 14(1) of CERD recognising the competence of the CERD Cttee to receive communications from individuals or groups.[142] It has recognised the CERD Cttee's competence on condition that it will not consider any communications without ascertaining that the same matter is not being considered or has not already been considered by another international body of investigation or settlement. The explanatory note to the law regarding the declaration specifically mentions both the High Commissioner for Human Rights and the CERD Cttee insisting that Estonia make the declaration under article 14(1) of CERD.[143] It also points out that Estonia had made a promise in its 2009 report regarding the declaration and strongly suggests the adoption of the law on the declaration by Parliament before the CERD Cttee presents its next COs.[144] The explanatory note does not discuss what 'other international bodies of investigation or settlement' were kept in mind. However, it mentions that Estonia has also recognised the individual communication procedure under CCPR.[145]

Up to 30 June 2019, no individual complaints against Estonia have been submitted to the CERD Cttee.

5.1.7 Brief Conclusion

CERD has had an impact on some legislative changes and has contributed to developing policies. It has been referenced by courts. It is a relatively well-known instrument among legal professionals. However, the possibilities it offers to individuals are not widely known which is perhaps also reflected in the lack of individual communications. However, considering that Estonia accepted individual communications only in 2010, this is not surprising. For example, OP1-CCPR was ratified in 1991 and only five cases have made it to

---

142 Rassilise diskrimineerimise kõigi vormide kõrvaldamise rahvusvahelise konventsiooni artikli 14 lõike 1 alusel deklaratsiooni tegemise seadus RT II 2010, 17, 78.

143 See eg CERD Cttee, COs on sixth and seventh periodic reports of Estonia, UN Doc CERD/C/EST/CO/7 (31 July-18 August 2006) para 22.

144 Vabariigi Valitsus, Seletuskiri Rassilise diskrimineerimise kõigi vormide kõrvaldamise rahvusvahelise konventsiooni artikli 14 lõike 1 alusel deklaratsiooni tegemise seaduse (731 SE) juurde s 6 (Seaduse mõjud) <https://www.riigikogu.ee/tegevus/eelnoud/eelnou/3e9fbe2e-97ab-74e9-78a6-0f8f66cf479e/Rassilise%20diskrimineerimise%20kõigi%20vormide%20kõrvaldamise%20rahvusvahelise%20konventsiooni%20artikli%2014%20lõike%201%20alusel%20deklaratsiooni%20tegemise%20seadus/> accessed 19 April 2022.

145 ibid.

the HRCttee by June 2019. The common problem of a lack of awareness of UN human rights treaties generally and the belief in more effective European mechanisms seem to be factors as well.

5.2 International Covenant on Civil and Political Rights

5.2.1 Incorporation and Reliance by Legislature and Executive

It has been argued that CCPR had a significant impact in the dissolution of the USSR. The USSR ratified CCPR in 1973. During the *perestroika* era, the language of human rights enabled dissatisfied societal forces to finally express what to their mind was wrong in the USSR.[146] Mälksoo argues that

> no impact has been more profound than the disappearance of the USSR, one of the two former superpowers, from the world historical stage. Of course, the USSR did not disintegrate exclusively because of the controversy over human rights, but human rights became an idea that came to undermine its ideological self-confidence.[147]

This ideological shift was also important for Estonia in regaining its independence.

CCPR has been in force in re-independent Estonia from 21 January 1992.[148] Estonia has also ratified OP1-CCPR and OP2-CCPR. As noted above, UN treaties including CCPR have had a role in creating the Estonian legal framework. CCPR was mentioned in the debates of the Constitutional Assembly, for example, in connection with the permissible grounds for limiting rights and freedoms.[149] The importance of CCPR in the creation of the Constitution has also been explicitly mentioned by the Supreme Court, for example in the *en banc* decision on constitutionality of the Penal Code: 'The Constitution was worded on the model of article 15(1) of the UN International Covenant on Civil and Political Rights, the wording of which coincides with that of § 23 of the Constitution.'[150] As in the case of CERD, CCPR emerges as one of the

---

[146] L Mälksoo, 'The Controvercy Over Human Rights, UN Covenants, and the Dissolution of the Soviet Union' (2018) 61 Japanese Yearbook of International Law 260, 261.
[147] ibid 261.
[148] RT II 1993/10-11/11.
[149] Riigikogu, Põhiseaduse Assamblee, 'Stenogrammid', '9. istung, 28. oktoober 1991' <https://www.riigikogu.ee/tutvustus-ja-ajalugu/riigikogu-ajalugu/pohiseaduse-assamblee/pohiseaduse-assamblee-stenogrammid/> accessed 19 April 2022.
[150] Supreme Court *en banc* Case 3-1-3-10-02 (17 March 2003) para 21.

main documents that were relied on in creating national integration strategies since 1999.[151]

5.2.2 Reliance by Judiciary

The HRCttee pointed out in its latest observations that CCPR has been rarely relied on by courts and that the country should intensify its efforts to raise awareness about the Covenant and its Optional Protocol, including by widely disseminating the Committee's recommendations and by providing specific training on the Covenant to government officials and legal professionals.[152] As noted above, CCPR is used in Supreme Court cases, but there is some prevalence of the regional human rights instruments and European Convention specifically. Article 25(b) of CCPR and HRC General Comment 25 were discussed in the case concerning the rights of prisoners to be candidates at municipal council elections.[153] The Court did not find the restrictions in the Municipal Council Election Act[154] to be discriminatory or unjustified and in contradiction with CCPR as the author of the application claimed. The Court also noted that General Comments are not legally binding and that General Comment 25 paragraph 14 deals with voting rights and not with the right to be a candidate.[155] As explained in part 5.3 below, despite the fact that General Comments are not legally binding, the Court regards the Comments as important for interpreting rights enshrined in the treaties.

CCPR was mentioned alongside CRC in the case about residence permits. However, it did not play a decisive role in the outcome of the case.[156] Article 26 of CCPR was invoked in the case concerning the refusal of naturalisation/citizenship of a former (technical/secretarial) employee of the KGB.[157] The Court decided to rely mainly on article 12 of the Estonian Constitution (equality and non-discrimination) rather than on CCPR, as this constitutional paragraph, in the words of the Court, echoes the content of article 26 of CCPR and is in conformity with it.[158] CCPR was mentioned in the constitutional

---

151 See part 5.1 of this chapter above. 'The Strategy of Integration and Social Cohesion in Estonia 2020' (n 112).
152 HRCttee, COs, UN Doc CCPR/C/EST/CO/4 (26 March 2019) para C.6.
153 Constitutional Review Chamber Case 3-4-1-44-13 (2 October 2013).
154 Kohaliku omavalitsuse volikogu valimise seadus, *RT I 2002, 36, 220*.
155 Constitutional Review Chamber Case 3-4-1-44-13 (2 October 2013) para 24. See also CCPR General Comment 25, art 25, Participation in Public Affairs and the Right to Vote para 14.
156 Constitutional Review Chamber Case 3-3-1-61-09 (9 November 2009).
157 KGB (Komitet Gosudarstvennoy Bezopasnosti; Committee for State Security), the secret police, the main security agency for the Soviet Union in 1954-1991.
158 Constitutional Review Chamber Case 3-3-1-101-06 (3 January 2008).

review case where the applicant essentially claimed that his right to freedom of association had been violated. The Court made some general remarks on requirements stemming from CCPR and the European Convention stating that international law *per se* does not require criminalisation of acts against freedom of association.[159]

In the case concerning a person convicted for repeated drunken driving the Court explained that his right to be present at his trial was not violated in the appellate court's admissibility decision (resulting in the unanimous dismissal of his appeal). Besides referencing the ECtHR case law,[160] the Court noted that the right was also regulated by article 14(3)(d) of CCPR. The Court explained that this article should be interpreted systematically together with article 14(5) of CCPR which guarantees the right to review of a conviction and sentence by a higher tribunal according to law.[161] It summed up that international law leaves wider room of discretion for states on the basis of the principle of opportunity to regulate the appeal process than first instance proceedings.[162] None of these six decisions were taken to the HRCttee.

5.2.3 Impact on and through Independent State Institutions

The COs of the HRCttee have contributed to the establishment of the Chancellor of Justice as the NHRI. Various chancellors during the time under observation have been actively promoting rights enshrined in CCPR. For example, the Chancellor of Justice pointed out already in 2005 similarly to the 2019 COs of the HRCttee that the blanket ban on prisoners' rights to vote in parliamentary elections is contrary to the Estonian Constitution and international commitments.[163] According to article 4(3) of the Riigikogu Election Act, 'a person who has been convicted of a criminal offence by a court and is imprisoned shall not participate in voting'.[164] This contradiction has been later confirmed also by

---

159   Constitutional Review Chamber Case 3-4-1-7-17 (6 July 2017) para 23. Note that art 155 of the Estonian Penal Code criminalises acts against freedom of association (RT I 2001, 61, 364).
160   *Lundevall v Sweden* App 38629/97 (ECtHR, 12 November 2002) paras 34–37.
161   Supreme Court, Criminal Law Chamber Case 3-1-1-55-07 (19 October 2007) para 10. The Court summed up that international law leaves wider room of discretion for states to take into account the principle of opportunity when regulating the appeal process than when regulating the first instance process.
162   Supreme Court, Criminal Law Chamber Case 3-1-1-55-07 (19 October 2007) para 10.
163   Õiguskantsler, 'Õiguskantsleri 2006. aasta tegevuse ülevaade' (Tallinn 2007) <https://www.oiguskantsler.ee/sites/default/files/6iguskantsleri_2006._aasta_tegevuse_ylevaade.pdf> accessed 19 April 2022; HRCttee, COs, Estonia, UN Doc CCPR/C/EST/CO/4 (18 April 2019) para 33.
164   Riigikogu Election Act, RT I 2002, 57, 355.

the Supreme Court, albeit without reference to CCPR but to the ECHR Protocol 1 article 3 and ECtHR case law.[165] In the opinion provided to the Court in this case, the Chancellor of Justice restated that the blanket ban on prisoners' right to vote was in contradiction with the Constitution and with ECHR Protocol 1 article 3.[166] These and earlier statements reflect the prominence attached to this issue in the ECtHR, especially after the *Hirst v UK* case in 2005.[167] However, the law change has not yet materialised.

5.2.4 Impact on and through Non-state Actors

In comparison with the previous Convention there seem to be more references to CCPR in Estonian academic legal literature. For example, the 2017 Commentaries to the Constitution explicitly mention CCPR several times.[168] CCPR has been mentioned in academic articles.[169] However, the predominance of the European system is clearly visible. The latest report by the Estonian Human Rights Centre on the human rights situation in Estonia does not discuss any of the issues explicitly in light of CCPR.[170]

5.2.5 Impact of State Reporting

By June 2019 Estonia had gone through four full cycles of reporting, three of which took place after June 1999 (that is, after the 1999 study). As CCPR is the most comprehensive of the UN treaties, many of the issues that are pointed out under theme-specific treaties, reoccur in reporting cycles of CCPR. In this respect, separating the impact of individual treaties is nearly impossible. It also raises a question of the effectiveness of the treaties and about the resource waste both domestically and at the UN level, which can be avoided with more consolidated reporting. Below only a selection of issues picked up in the COs and their impact can be addressed.

---

165   Supreme Court *en banc* Case 3-4-1-2-15 (1 July 2015). Several references were made to the European Convention Protocol 1 art 3 and ECtHR case law including *Hirst v UK* (no 2) App 74025/01 (ECtHR, 6 October 2005) para 82; *Frodl v Austria* App 20201/04 (ECtHR, 8 April 2010) para 28; *Söyler v Turkey* App 29411/07 (ECtHR, 17 September 2013) para 42.
166   Supreme Court *en banc* Case 3-4-1-2-15 (1 July 2015) paras 22-25.
167   *Hirst v UK* (No 2) App 74025/01 (ECtHR, 6 October 2005).
168   Ü Madise jt (toim), *Eesti Vabariigi põhiseadus. Kommenteeritud väljaanne* (Juura 2017).
169   See eg K Albi, 'The Right to Use Minority Languages in the Public Sphere: Evaluation of Estonian Legislation in Light of the International Standards' (2003) VIII Juridica International 151, 152.
170   K Käsper ja E Rünne (eds), *Inimõigused Eestis, Eesti Inimõiguste Keskuse aastaaruanne 2020, Areng aastatel 2018–2019* (SA Eesti Inimõiguste Keskus 2020).

As in the case of the CERD Cttee, the HRCttee has pointed out deficiencies in the regulation of hate speech in the Estonian Penal Code. In the HRCttee's view it does not provide comprehensive protection against hate speech and hate crimes due to the light penalties and the high threshold for the offence of incitement to hatred, violence or discrimination under article 151 of the Criminal Code, which requires 'danger to the life, health or property' of the victim.[171] There is no explanation of reasons provided in the state report to the HRCttee of not taking this issue into account. The reasons are provided in the latest and more comprehensive report to the CERD Cttee that was due in 2018 but was submitted only outside the framework of the current study (July 2019). This report emphasises the value of the right to freedom of speech in Estonian society. It explains the preference of settling such disputes through civil law measures (including in the court),[172] as finding an adequate balance between free speech and other rights may be tricky.[173] The report provides a reminder that claims to court can be brought by anyone whose rights have been infringed. This indicates the understanding that the broad definition of hate speech in criminal law may have a chilling effect on freedom of speech. The Penal Code[174] was extensively reviewed and changed in 2015 and many of the recommendations that have been pointed out in COs were taken into account, some of which are reflected later in this chapter under other treaties. Prior to the adoption, there were extensive domestic debates over the scope of article 151 of the Code. There was widespread opposition to the recommended change, including the opposition by the Estonian Council of Churches against broadening the scope of the article.[175]

5.2.6 Impact of Individual Communications

By 30 June 2019, seven communications against Estonia were submitted to the HRCttee. Of the five finalised in this period,[176] only one concluded in a

---

[171] HRCttee, COs, Estonia, UN Doc CCPR/C/EST/CO/4 (18 April 2019) para 12.
[172] Some of these type of cases have also been referred to the ECtHR. See eg *Tammer v Estonia* App 41205/98 (ECtHR, 4 April 2001) and *Delfi v Estonia* App 64569/09 (ECtHR Grand Chamber Decision 16 June 2015).
[173] National Report, CERD, Estonia, UN Doc CERD/C/EST/12–13 (15 October 2019) para 106.
[174] RT I 2001, 61, 364.
[175] Eesti Kirikute Nõukogu, 'EKNi seisukoht Karistuseadustiku, Kriminaalmenetluse seadustiku, Vangistusseaduse ja Väärteomenetluse seadustiku muutmise seaduse eelnõu kohta' 28 November 2012 <http://www.ekn.ee/lakitus.php?id=20> accessed 30 January 2020.
[176] Two communicatiosn were concluded after the cut off mark of 30 June 2019: *PL and ML v Estonia* Comm 2499/2014, CCPR/C/127/D/2499/2014 (HRCttee, 8 November 2019); *PEEP v Estonia* Comm 2682/2015, CCPR/C/128/D/2682/2015 (HRCttee, 13 March 2020).

finding of violation by Estonia. In four remaining cases the HRCttee found no violation.[177]

In *Akhliman Avyaz Ogly Zeynalov v Estonia*,[178] the HRCttee found a violation of article 14(3)(d) of the Covenant. The applicant claimed that his right to be represented by counsel of his choice and his right to have adequate time and facilities for the preparation of his defence were denied by the state. In the domestic processing of these cases no explicit mention of CCPR was made. Thus, the impact of CCPR can be seen in the mere fact of awareness of these individual applicants or their counsel of the possibility to submit the case to the HRCttee.

As for the impact of the *Zeynalov* case, the HRCttee emphasised that Estonia is obliged to provide the applicant with adequate compensation and to take steps to prevent similar violations occurring in the future.[179] The government reported to the HRCttee on the actions taken. As to the compensation, in the state's opinion, Zeynalov had the possibility to use the HRCttee's views as part of evidence in several ongoing and newly-initiated court proceedings, which were related to the proceedings reviewed by the HRCttee. It also noted that the author had initiated a review procedure of his case with the Supreme Court. In these circumstances the state considered the measures outlined to constitute an effective and appropriate remedy.[180] However, the HRCttee assessed

---

[177] *Vjatšeslav Borzov v Estonia* Comm 1136/2002, CCPR/C/81/D/1136/2002 (HRCttee, 25 August 2004); *Gennadi Sipin v Estonia and Russia* Comm 1423/2005, CCPR/C/93/D/1423/2005 (HRCttee, 9 July 2008); *Vjatseslav Tsarjov v Estonia* Comm 1223/2003, CCPR/C/91/D/1223/2003 (HRCttee, 26 October 2007); *Sedljar and Lavrov v Estonia v Estonia* Comm 1532/2006, CCPR/C/101/D/1532/2006 (HRCttee, 29 March 2011). In *Vjatšeslav Borzov v Estonia* the author argued that refusal of his citizenship was insufficiently reasoned and discriminatory. Similarly, in *Gennadi Sipin v Estonia* the author claimed that automatically excluding him from receiving Estonian citizenship on the basis that he is a former member of the armed forces of another country violates art 26 of the Covenant. In the case of *Vjatseslav Tsarjov v Estonia* the author argued that he was discriminated against on the basis of origin, contrary to art 26 of the Covenant, as he was denied a permanent residence permit for being a former employee of the foreign (Soviet) intelligence and security service (KGB). In *Sedljar and Lavrov v Estonia* the authors claimed that their rights under art 14(1) and 14(3)(e) were violated.
[178] *Zeynalov v Estonia* Comm no 2040/2011, CCPR/C/115/D/2040/2011 (HRCttee, 4 November 2015).
[179] ibid para 11.
[180] HRCttee, Follow-up progress report on individual communications, UN Doc CCPR/C/119/3 (30 May 2017) 16.

this response to be non-satisfactory and noted that follow-up proceedings are ongoing.[181] There was no indication of actual compensation being discussed or paid.

Zeynalov brought an application to the Supreme Court to reopen the court proceedings based on the HRCttee's views. This application was rejected.[182] This type of review is done only in exceptional cases. As mentioned earlier, this kind of review exists in the administrative, civil and criminal procedure. One explicit ground for the review is that the ECtHR has found a violation of the ECHR. There is no such explicit mechanism in Estonian law to review the court decisions (which have domestically taken effect) after the HRCttee has found a violation.[183]

Subsequently, the state informed the HRCttee that Zeynalov had been released on parole on 23 January 2018, that is three years, five months and 10 days before the expiry of the term of punishment and a precept to leave was issued by the police and Border Guard Board. He agreed to move to Azerbaijan after release, where he has social connections and relatives (including his mother, wife and daughter).[184]

5.2.7 Brief Conclusion

The treaty is relatively well known. It has been referenced in Estonian courts. The knowledge about the treaty is also reflected in the individual applications made to the HRCttee. Out of three accepted individual communication procedures only the procedure provided by OP1-CCPR has been 'used' during the period under review in this chapter. The impact of the treaty can also be seen in the making of the Constitution, legislation and policies. However, as similar commitments to CCPR are stemming from the European counterpart (especially the European Convention) and there is an overlap between observations made in COs under different UN treaties, an assessment of the individual impact of CCPR is problematic.

---

181 ibid.
182 ibid.
183 See also interview with Uno Lõhmus, judge ret, former judge of the ECtHR, ECJ and Chief Justice of the Estonian Supreme Court, 28 May 2020, Tartu.
184 See interview with Mai Hion, Counsellor, Legal Department, Ministry of Foreign Affairs, 10 June 2020, Tallinn.

5.3   International Covenant on Economic, Social and Cultural Rights

5.3.1   Incorporation and Reliance by Legislature and Executive

Estonia acceded to CESCR on 21 October 1991. Estonia has not ratified OP-CESCR. CESCR is mentioned as one of the international treaties that were at the basis of the creation of the Welfare Development Programme for 2016–2023.[185]

5.3.2   Reliance by Judiciary

As noted above, during the period of study CESCR has been referenced twice in the Supreme Court. One of the most important interpretations of the applicability of UN treaties and specifically CESCR was mentioned in a Supreme Court case already in 2002. The case concerned an applicant who wanted to rely directly on the Covenant explaining that his rights to certain subsidies were better protected by the Covenant than by domestic law.[186] The Court noted that Estonia had ratified CESCR and that it was one of the treaties that can be directly applied. However, for direct applicability the rights have to be self-executing and should not require further elaboration in Estonian law. The Court recognised that treaty provisions can sometimes be more precise than domestic law. Despite the possibility to rely directly on the international treaty, in the view of the Supreme Court, the domestic courts should first look for relevant articles in the Constitution and other legal acts. In this particular case it suggested among other legal acts to analyse articles 27(5), 28(2) and (3) of the Constitution.[187] Before coming to this conclusion, it noted that even if they are not directly applicable, international treaties can also be helpful for interpreting local law. Importantly, the Court also explained that when interpreting CESCR, General Comment 3 (paragraph 5) from 1990 needs to be taken into account especially regarding effective remedies for everybody and recognition of direct justiciability of at least some of the rights in the Covenant.[188]

---

[185]   Sotsiaalministeerium, *Heaolu arengukava 2016–2023*, 45. The programme is available both in Estonian and English <https://www.sm.ee/et/heaolu-arengukava-2016-2023> accessed 19 April 2022.

[186]   Supreme Court of Estonia, Administrative Law Chamber Case 3-3-1-58-02 (20 December 2002).

[187]   However, in this respect one also needs to re-emphasise for clarity that the Estonian Constitution sets forth the rule of superiority of foreign treaty law over domestic legislation. Art 123 states that if Estonian legal acts or other legal instruments contradict foreign treaties ratified by Parliament, the provisions of the foreign treaty shall be applied. See part 2 above.

[188]   Supreme Court of Estonia, Administrative Law Chamber Case 3-3-1-58-02 (20 December 2002) para 11.

Articles 2, 9 and 12 of CESCR were substantially relied upon in the case where the constitutionality of the termination of health insurance to an individual, due to a change of law, was at issue. The Supreme Court pointed out in this case that it did not agree with the explanation provided by governmental authorities regarding the new law, namely, that socio-economic rights are solely objective rights that are non-justiciable in the courts. Article 28(1) of the Estonian Constitution sets forth the subjective right to health and article 15 guarantees its judicial protection.[189] Besides extensively referencing the European Social Charter,[190] the Court also pointed out that the legislature needs to take into account international treaties ratified by Estonia and general principles of international law. The Court explained that according to article 9 of CESCR the state parties recognise the right of everyone to social security, including social insurance. It further explained that article 12(1) of the Covenant recognises the right of everyone to the enjoyment of the highest attainable standard of physical and mental health and that article 12(2)(d) requires taking steps to achieve the full realisation of this right for the creation of conditions which would assure to all medical service and medical attention in the event of sickness. It also pointed out obligations stemming from article 2(1) of CESCR.[191] The Court decided for the applicant on the basis of the relevant provisions in the Constitution, the European Social Charter and CESCR. Drawing simultaneously on these three instruments the Court decided that the state has an obligation to guarantee accessibility and compensation of health care to people who cannot find employment and have no financial means.[192]

Thus, one could argue that the court has given to at least some of the rights in this Covenant a strong position recognising them as justiciable and not merely as programmatic rights. In light of these two cases it is strange that the 2011 COs of the CESCR Cttee express concern that the Estonian judiciary sees the Covenant as containing merely non-self-executing obligations not giving rise to subjective claim rights at the domestic level.[193] Stating that, the relevant information was not provided in the national reports. It also is not adequately provided in the 2015 Common Core Document[194] as claimed in the

---

189   Supreme Court of Estonia, Administrative Law Chamber Case 3-3-1-65-03 (10 November 2003) para 14.
190   Parandatud ja täiendatud Euroopa sotsiaalharta ratifitseerimise seadus, RT II 2000, 15, 93.
191   Supreme Court of Estonia, Administrative Law Chamber Case 3-3-1-65-03 (10 November 2003) para 18.
192   ibid para 19.
193   CESCR Cttee, COs, Estonia, UN Doc E/C.12/EST/2 (12 July 2010) para C.6.
194   Välisministeerium, Inimõigusalaste konventsioonide täitmine, 'Ülevaatedokument (Common Core Document 2015)' <https://vm.ee/et/inimoigusalaste-konventsioonide-taitmine-0> accessed 19 April 2022.

state's 2019 Report.[195] Thus, there are deficiencies in quality of both COs and national reports.

5.3.3 Impact on and through Independent State Institutions

Differently from the HRC ttee, the CESCR Cttee has never been concerned about the fact that the Gender Equality and Equal Treatment Commissioner does not have standing in domestic court proceedings.[196] However, the Commissioner was engaged in strategic litigation within the scope of the project 'Achieving gender equality with gender integration and legal protection' between 2013 and 2016. The strategic litigation entailed the Office of the Commissioner making a selection of cases related to discrimination, providing help to the victims of these cases with their litigation and organising legal assistance for them. The small number of court rulings in cases of discrimination was one of the reasons that triggered the launching of strategic litigation in discrimination disputes.[197]

5.3.4 Impact on and through Non-state Actors

CESCR is mentioned in the 2017 Commentaries to the Constitution in the context of article 37 (right to education).[198] Alongside with the Covenant the Commentaries also refer to General Comment 14 in the context of article 28 (right to protection of health).[199] The last two reports by the Estonian Human Rights Centre do not discuss any of the issues in light of CESCR.[200] The 2014 report mentioned it in connection with the right to education.[201] CESCR has been mentioned in academic literature.[202]

---

[195] National Report, CESCR, Estonia, UN Doc E/C.12/EST/3 (29 September 2019) para 5.
[196] It has only been concerned about insufficient financing of the commissioner. See eg CSECR Cttee, COs, Estonia, UN Doc E/C.12/EST/CO/3 (8 March 2019) para 10.
[197] National Report, CESCR, Estonia, UN Doc E/C.12/EST/3 (29 September 2017) para 42.
[198] N Parrest and T Annus, 'Paragrahv 37' in Ü Madise jt (toim), *Eesti Vabariigi põhiseadus. Kommenteeritud väljaanne* (Juura 2017) para 1.
[199] A Henberg and K Muller, 'Paragrahv 28' in Ü Madise jt (toim), *Eesti Vabariigi põhiseadus. Kommenteeritud väljaanne* (Juura 2017) para 11.
[200] K Käsper (ed), *Inimõigused Eestis, Eesti Inimõiguste Keskuse aastaaruanne 2016-2017* (SA Eesti Inimõiguste Keskus 2017); K Käsper and E Rünne (eds), *Inimõigused Eestis, Eesti Inimõiguste Keskuse aastaaruanne 2020, Areng aastatel 2018-2019* (SA Eesti Inimõiguste Keskus 2020).
[201] A Remmelg, 'Õigus haridusele' in E Rünne and K Käsper (eds), *Inimõigused Eestis 2014–2015* (SA Eesti Inimõiguste Keskus 2015) 84.
[202] A Nõmper and T Annus, 'The Right to Health Protection in the Estonian Constitution' (2002) VII Juridica International 117, 119.

5.3.5 Impact of State Reporting

By 30 June 2019 Estonia had gone through three full cycles of reporting. Many of the issues are again repetitive of the themes brought out by other committees, for example, statelessness, gender equality and the protection of minorities. Further, as multiple issues have been pointed out by the CESCR Cttee during the three reporting cycles only some can be discussed as having an indication of impact. For example, the CESCR Cttee expressed concern in 2011 about the prevalence of domestic violence in the state and the absence of a specific provision of domestic violence as an offence in the Penal Code. It also noted deficiencies in the media campaigns about domestic violence.[203] The Penal Code was changed considerably in 2015, as well as provisions on aggravating circumstances which now include committing an offence against a former or current family member of the offender or committing an offence in the presence of a minor.[204] The elements of physical abuse were specified and stricter punishment (imprisonment of up to five years) was set for abuse in a close relationship or relationship of subordination.[205] There have been improvements in strategies and public awareness. For example, the prevention of violence and other measures were included and carried out according to the Strategy for Prevention of Violence 2015–2020.[206] Public awareness has been raised through various campaigns and information events. These achievements were also mentioned in Estonia's latest report to the CESCR Cttee.[207] However, CESCR or COs were not referred to in the abovementioned Strategy for Prevention of Violence itself. Various CoE and EU instruments and commitments were mentioned under the title 'Following international recommendations'.[208] Thus, the attribution of impact to CESCR can only be partial.

A more direct form of impact of CESCR and the CESCR Cttee COs is visible in an attempt to change the Equal Treatment Act. In its last two COs the CESCR Cttee expressed concern that the Equal Treatment Act only prohibits discrimination on the grounds of religion or views, age, disability and sexual

---

[203] CESCR Cttee, COs, Estonia, UN Doc E/C.12/EST/CO/2 (16 December 2011) para 20.
[204] Penal Code, arts 58(4) and 13, RT I 2001, 61, 364.
[205] Penal Code, art 121 (2.2), RT I 2001, 61, 364.
[206] Ministry of Justice, Strategy for Preventing Violence for 2015–2020 (Tallinn 2015) para 57 <https://www.kriminaalpoliitika.ee/sites/krimipoliitika/files/elfinder/dokumendid/strategy_for_preventing_violence_for_2015-2020.pdf> accessed 19 April 2022.
[207] National Report, CESCR, Estonia, UN Doc E/C.12/EST/3 (29 September 2017) para 123.
[208] Ministry of Justice, Strategy for Preventing Violence for 2015–2020 (n 159) para 57.

orientation in areas relating to working life and the acquisition of professional qualifications. Thus, it does not prohibit discrimination on all grounds stipulated in article 2(2) of CESCR in the enjoyment of all economic, social and cultural rights.[209] The incompatibility of the law with international standards, but also with article 12 of the Constitution was pointed out already in 2009 by the Chancellor of Justice Indrek Teder.[210] As noted before, the law was adopted primarily due to EU directives. An attempt was made in 2016 to change the law. The explanatory note to the law specifically points out both the local criticism from the Chancellor of Justice and criticism from international monitoring bodies. It does not explicitly name the CESCR Cttee (or any other UN treaty body) but seems to be in line with the views expressed by the Committee.[211] The change in law, however, has not yet materialised.

5.3.6 Impact of Individual Communications

Estonia has not recognised the individual communication procedure under OP-CESCR. In its 2019 report the CESCR Cttee has encouraged Estonia to ratify the Optional Protocol to CESCR. It seems that the conclusion in the 1999 study still stands in respect that other instruments, such as CCPR, have been regarded as more important.[212] As noted above, CCPR has been argued to have played a significant role in the process leading to the dissolution of the Soviet Union. However, the ratification of OP-CESCR has not been set aside either. According to the MFA, '[t]he discussions on accepting the individual communications procedures under different instruments are constantly ongoing in the Ministries and possible adherence to these will depend on further developments and analyses'.[213]

5.3.7 Brief Conclusion

The Covenant has been referenced in the court and the Supreme Court has recognised its direct applicability and justiciability, at least partially. CESCR has been at the basis of policy making. Assessment of the impact attributable

---

209 CESCR Cttee, COs on the second periodic report of Estonia, UN Doc E/C.12/EST/CO/2 (14 November-2 December 2011) para 8; CESCR Cttee, COs on the third periodic report of Estonia, UN Doc E/C.12/EST/CO/3 (8 March 2019) paras 10–11.
210 Õiguskantsleri 2008. aasta tegevuse ülevaade (Tallinn 2009) 18 <https://www.oiguskantsler.ee/sites/default/files/6iguskantsleri_2008._aasta_tegevuse_ylevaade.pdf> accessed 19 April 2022.
211 Võrdse kohtlemise seaduse muutmise seaduse seletuskiri 196.
212 M Hion, 'Estonia' in Heyns and Viljoen (n 41) 252.
213 Email consultation with Mai Hion, Ministry of Foreign Affairs (10 June 2020, Tallinn).

solely to this comprehensive treaty on social, economic and cultural rights, however, is complicated as it overlaps with Estonia's European commitments, for example, with the implementation of the European Social Charter.[214] There is also an overlap with COs under other UN treaties, for example, regarding gender equality which is discussed below.

5.4 Convention on the Elimination of All Forms of Discrimination against Women

5.4.1 Incorporation and Reliance by Legislature and Executive

Estonia acceded to the Convention on 26 September 1991. It has not ratified OP-CEDAW or accepted the inquiry procedure under articles 8 and 9 of OP-CEDAW.

CEDAW is mentioned alongside CESCR as one of the international treaties that was at the basis of the creation of the Welfare Development Programme for 2016–2023 by the Ministry of Social Affairs.[215] It is also mentioned alongside CRC and CRPD in the Ministry of Social Affairs Strategy of Children and Families 2012–2020.[216] The CEDAW Cttee pointed out in its latest 2016 COs that Estonia lacks a comprehensive national strategy for gender equality.[217] There is a policy document adopted to tackle this issue, namely, the Gender Equality Programme 2019–2020.[218] However, CEDAW is not explicitly mentioned in this document as are EU commitments.

5.4.2 Reliance by Judiciary

The need to raise awareness about the treaty has been pointed out by the CEDAW Cttee. The lack of awareness, in the eyes of the Committee, is also evident in the lack of court cases referring to CEDAW.[219] Gender discrimination has been discussed on several occasions in the Supreme Court, but with

---

214 Estonia ratified the European Social Charter in 2000. Parandatud ja täiendatud Euroopa sotsiaalharta ratifitseerimise seadus, RT II 2000, 15, 93.
215 Sotsiaalminiateerium, *Heaolu arengukava 2016–2023* 45.
216 Sotsiaalministeerium, *Targad vanemad, toredad lapsed, tugev ühiskond. Laste ja perede arengukava 2012–2020* (Tallinn 2011, toim 2013) 9, 41 (also available in English): Ministry of Social Affairs, *Smart Parents, Great Children, Strong Society. Strategy of Children and Families 2012–2020* (Tallinn 2011) 14, 46, 65 <https://www.sm.ee/sites/default/files/content-editors/Lapsed_ja_pered/lpa_fulltxt_eng_83a4_nobleed.pdf> accessed 19 April 2022.
217 CEDAW Cttee, COs, UN Doc CEDAW/C/EST/CO/5-6 (18 November 2016) para 12.
218 Sotsiaalministeerium, *Soolise võrdõiguslikkuse programm 2019–2022* <https://www.sm.ee/sites/default/files/lisa_4_soolise_vordoiguslikkuse_programm_2019-2022_0.pdf> accessed 19 April 2022.
219 CEDAW Cttee, COs, UN Doc CEDAW/C/EST/CO/5-6 (18 November 2016) para 8.

reference to domestic law or EU law and not directly to CEDAW.[220] Restrictions on women's rights and discrimination on the basis of sex were mentioned, for example, in the context of a case where the Supreme Court decided over not granting international protection to an Uzbekistan citizen accused of being a member of Hisb ut-Tahrir in Uzbekistan.[221] However, the references were not made to CEDAW, but to relevant cases in the ECtHR[222] and the EU Court of Justice.[223] It is true that there could be references to CEDAW, but if the issue is covered by a multitude of international or EU instruments it seems that the Court finds it sufficient to rely mostly on the European instruments.

5.4.3 Impact on and through Independent State Institutions

The CEDAW Cttee in 2016 called on the state to address discriminatory stereotypes regarding the roles and responsibilities of women and men in the family and in society.[224] The Estonian Gender Equality and Equal Treatment Commissioner's Office together with Estonian Public Broadcasting, Tallinn University, SA Innove, Estonian Ministry of Education and Research, Office of the Equal Opportunities Ombudsperson of Lithuania and the Centre for Gender Equality in Iceland, for example, conducted a European Commission-funded project 'BREAK' in 2017 to 2019. Many cross-media activities were carried out to raise awareness of gender stereotypes (primarily in employment). There is no mention of CEDAW in publicly-available project documents. References are made to EU law, and also to the Council of Europe strategies and programmes, for example, to the Council of Europe Gender Strategy 2018–2023.[225]

5.4.4 Impact on and through Non-state Actors

CEDAW is mentioned in the 2017 Commentaries to the Constitution several times, for example, in the context of article 12 (right to equality and non-discrimination).[226] CEDAW and also CEDAW Cttee cases are mentioned in

---

220 For example, Supreme Court, Civil Law Chamber Case 3-2-1-135-11 (4 January 2012); Administrative Law Chamber Case 3-3-1-50-11 (19 December 2011); Supreme Court *en banc* Case 3-3-1-41-09 (20 November 2011); Civil Law Chamber Case 2-16-708 (21 November 2018).
221 Administrative Law Chamber Case 3-17-1026 (1 October 2018).
222 *Hizb Ut-Tahrir & Others v Germany* App 31098/08 (ECtHR 12 June 2012).
223 Joined cases C-57/09 and C-101/09 *Bundesrepublik Deutschland v B and D* (EUCJ, Grand Chamber, 9 November 2010) and Case C-373/13 *H T v Land Baden-Württemberg* (EUCJ, First Chamber, 24 June 2015).
224 CEDAW Cttee, CO s, UN Doc CEDAW/C/EST/CO/5-6 (18 November 2016) para 16.
225 BREAK <https://brea-k.eu/en/b-re-a-k/> accessed 19 April 2022.
226 M Ernits, 'Paragrahv 12' in Ü Madise jt (toim), *Eesti Vabariigi põhiseadus. Kommenteeritud väljaanne* (Juura 2017) para 4.

the context of article 26 (right to privacy and family life). The commentaries explicitly mention *AS v Hungary*[227] on forced sterilisation, *LC v Peru*[228] on abortion and *Alyne da Silva Pimentel Teixeira v Brasil*[229] on maternal deaths. The Commentaries emphasise the importance of the last-mentioned case as a landmark case treating maternal mortality as a violation of international human rights.[230] CEDAW and its commentary 25 is mentioned in the context of article 30 (access to civil service).[231] These are but a few examples. The last three reports by the Estonian Human Rights Centre surprisingly do not explicitly mention CEDAW.[232] However, the need for ratifying OP-CEDAW is mentioned in the Centre's letter to political parties in 2018.[233] One may argue that the impact on and through non-state actors is visible but patchy.

5.4.5   Impact of State Reporting

By June 2019 Estonia had gone through three full cycles of reporting. Gender equality has been one of the issues pointed out in several COs by the HRCttee[234] and also by the CESCR Cttee.[235] Thus, establishing the individual impact of CEDAW is problematic. Estonian commitments in other frameworks, especially European ones, also blur the picture. For example, the Council of Europe Convention on Preventing and Combating Violence against Women and Domestic Violence (Istanbul Convention) was signed by Estonia in 2014

---

227   *AS v Hungary* Comm 4/2004, CEDAW/C/49/D/17/2008 (CEDAW Cttee, 29 August 2006). CEDAW 29.08.2006.

228   *LC v Peru* Comm 22/2009, CEDAW/C/50/D/22/2009 (CEDAW Cttee, 17 October 2011). CEDAW 17.10.2011.

229   *Alyne da Silva Pimentel Teixeira v Brasil* Comm 17/2008, CEDAW/C/49/D/17/2008 (CEDAW Cttee, 27 September 2011) CEDAW 27.09.2011.

230   K Jaanimägi and L Oja, 'Paragrahv 26' in Ü Madise jt (toim), *Eesti Vabariigi põhiseadus. Kommenteeritud väljaanne* (Juura 2017) para 21.

231   O Kask and T Annus, 'Paragrahv 30' in Ü Madise jt (toim), *Eesti Vabariigi põhiseadus. Kommenteeritud väljaanne* (Juura 2017) para 8.

232   K Käsper (ed), *Inimõigused Eestis, Eesti Inimõiguste Keskuse aastaaruanne 2016–2017* (SA Eesti Inimõiguste Keskus 2017); K Käsper and E Rünne (eds), *Inimõigused Eestis, Eesti Inimõiguste Keskuse aastaaruanne 2020, Areng aastatel 2018–2019* (SA Eesti Inimõiguste Keskus 2020); E Rünne and K Käsper (eds), *Inimõigused Eestis 2014–2015* (SA Eesti Inimõiguste Keskus 2015).

233   Inimõiguste Keskus, 'Ettepanekud inimõiguste, sallivuse ja võrdõiguslikkuse edendamiseks Eestis' (15 May 2018) 3 <https://humanrights.ee/app/uploads/2018/05/inimoiguste-keskuse-ettepanekud-150518-1.pdf> accessed 19 April 2022.

234   Eg HRCttee, COs, Estonia, UN Doc CCPR/C/EST/CO/4 (18 April 2019) para 15.

235   Eg CSECR Cttee, COs, Estonia, UN Doc E/C.12/EST/CO/3 (8 March 2019) paras 18–21.

and finally ratified three years later.[236] In these three years many legislative changes took place to comply with the Convention. However, considering that the Istanbul Convention itself refers to UN treaties and specifically to CEDAW and its General Comment 19, there has been a CEDAW impact on the changes, although this impact may be indirect.

As an example of this blurred impact, the 2016 COs of CEDAW Cttee recommended specifically the criminalisation of sexual harassment.[237] Article 153[1] on sexual harassment was added to the Penal Code in 2017.[238] CEDAW is not specifically mentioned in the explanatory note to the amendment, but the Istanbul Convention is.[239] The 2016–2017 report by the Estonian Human Rights Centre also seems to associate changes in law with the Istanbul Convention.[240] The emphasis on certain instruments may also depend on the expertise and preferences of people writing reports.

5.4.6   Brief Conclusion

The Convention is relatively well known among the legal profession and state authorities. However, assessing the separate domestic impact of CEDAW probably is the most difficult as gender equality features prominently in the agenda of European (CoE, EU, OSCE) and other bodies of which Estonia is a member, for example the International Labour Organisation (ILO). Having said that, CEDAW has been at the basis of policy making and some changes in law and policy can at least partially be attributable to this Convention. During the period of study CEDAW has not been referenced in the Supreme Court.

5.5   *Convention against Torture and Other Cruel, Inhuman or Degrading Treatment or Punishment*

5.5.1   Incorporation and Reliance by Legislature and Executive

Estonia has ratified CAT, which entered into force in respect of Estonia on 20 November 1991. No declaration has been made under article 22 to allow

---

236 Naistevastase vägivalla ja perevägivalla ennetamise ja tõkestamise Euroopa Nõukogu konventsiooni ratifitseerimise seadus, RT II, 26.09.2017, 1. The Convention entered into force for Estonia on 1 February 2018.
237 CEDAW Cttee, COs, UN Doc CEDAW/C/EST/CO/5–6 (18 November 2016) para 19.
238 Karistusseadustiku muutmise ja sellega seonduvalt teiste seaduste muutmise seadus, RT I, 26.06.2017, 69.
239 Vabariigi Valitsus, 'Seletuskiri karistusseadustiku ja välismaalaste seaduse muutmise seaduse eelnõu juurde' <https://www.riigikogu.ee/tegevus/eelnoud/eelnou/f9a7291c-8c46-4ad8-a740-4e1c55c83964> accessed 19 April 2022.
240 See eg M Meiorg, 'Sooline võrdõiguslikkus' in K Käsper (ed), *Inimõigused Eestis, Eesti Inimõiguste Keskuse aastaaruanne 2016–2017* (SA Eesti Inimõiguste Keskus 2017) 93.

individual communications. However, inquiry proceedings under article 20 are accepted. Estonia also ratified OP-CAT in 2006.

As noted above, UN treaties, including CAT, were relied on in the creation of the 1992 Constitution.

Explicit references to UN human rights treaties in laws themselves are rare in Estonia. However, OP-CAT is explicitly mentioned in article 1(7) of the Chancellor of Justice Act.[241] Estonia ratified OP-CAT on 18 December 2006.[242] The explanatory note to the ratification law thoroughly describes the obligations stemming from OP-CAT and assures that the obligations are not substantially new being similar to those under the European Convention for the Prevention of Torture and Inhuman or Degrading Treatment or Punishment.[243] The ratification law also names the Chancellor of Justice as the national preventive mechanism. The relevant amendments to the Chancellor of Justice Act entered into force soon after, on 18 February 2007. CAT is also mentioned in the Obligation to Leave and Prohibition on Entry Act article 17. This article, alongside with the 1951 UN Convention Relating to the Status of Refugees and its Protocol, sets forth that an alien may not be expelled to a state to which expulsion may result in consequences specified in article 3 of the European Convention or article 3 of CAT, or in the application of death penalty.[244]

5.5.2 Reliance by Judiciary

Definition of torture has been discussed in the Supreme Court without explicit reference to CAT.[245] The prohibition of torture as something that is incompatible with the values and principles in the Estonian legal system was mentioned in the case that dealt with prisoners' right to vote. No explicit connection was made with CAT.[246] Recommendations of the CoE Committee on Prevention of Torture (CPT) were mentioned in the case concerning the subjection of prisoners to loud music, but not CAT.[247] CPT findings were also mentioned in the

---

241 Chancellor of Justice Act, RT I 1999, 29, 406.
242 RT II 2006, 24, 63.
243 Piinamise ning muu julma, ebainimliku või inimväärikust alandava kohtlemise ja karistamise vastase konventsiooni fakultatiivse protokolli ratifitseerimise seaduse (916 SE) seletuskiri <https://www.riigikogu.ee/tegevus/eelnoud/eelnou/5c0a147c-11b4-3734-ac8c-eb01651c3b83/Piinamise%20ning%20muu%20julma,%20ebainimliku%20või%20inimväärikust%20alandava%20kohtlemise%20ja%20karistamise%20vastase%20konventsiooni%20fakultatiivse%20protokolli%20ratifitseerimise%20seadus> accessed 19 April 2022.
244 Obligation to Leave and Prohibition on Entry Act, RT I 1998, 98, 1575.
245 Criminal Law Chamber Case 3-1-1-54-16 (30 June 2016) para 2.2.
246 Supreme Court *en banc* Case 3-4-1-2-15 (5 July 2015) para 5.
247 Administrative Law Chamber Case 3-3-1-17-14 (21 April 2014) para 12.

case that concerned the use of pepper gas in prison.[248] The ECtHR case of *Julin v Estonia*[249] was relied upon in the Supreme Court case that dealt with a violation of the prohibition of torture on account of the applicant's confinement to a restraint bed.[250] CAT was not mentioned. However, CAT and OP-CAT were explicitly mentioned alongside with European counterparts[251] in the case that dealt with inhumane prison conditions.[252] The Court recalled that under these conventions independent international bodies make regular visits to detention facilities to prevent undermining human dignity and make recommendations for the improvement of prison conditions. It pointed out that under article 3 of OP-CAT each state party has to set up, designate or maintain at the domestic level one or several visiting bodies for the prevention of torture and other cruel, inhuman or degrading treatment or punishment (national preventive mechanism). It also noted that in Estonia, according to the Chancellor of Justice Act article 1(7), this body is the Chancellor of Justice. Most importantly, it went further to explain that if the presenting of evidence on prison conditions cannot be obtained with reasonable efforts or obtaining this information is not possible, a court can rely on findings of the control visits that are done under the above-mentioned treaties.[253]

5.5.3   Impact on and through Independent State Institutions

As noted, amendments to the Chancellor of Justice Act entered into force in 2007.[254] Since then, according to article 7(1) of the law, the Chancellor of Justice is the national preventive mechanism provided for in article 3 of OP-CAT.[255] Article 27 of the Chancellor of Justice Act provides the Chancellor of Justice with relevant tools to act as the national preventive mechanism, facilitating access to relevant institutions and documents. Since the change of law several visits have been made to individuals held in general care homes and places of detention. This in itself is evidence of the impact of the treaty. During these visits several deficiencies and violations of law were discovered.[256] For example,

---

248   Administrative Law Chamber Case 3-3-1-69-14 (14 January 2015) para 7.
249   *Julin v Estonia* App 16563/08, 40841/08, 8192/10 and 18656/10 (ECtHR, 29 May 2012).
250   Administrative Law Chamber Case 3-3-1-47-13 (3 October 2013).
251   European Convention for the Prevention of Torture and Inhuman or Degrading Treatment or Punishment, ETS No 126; Protocol No 1 to the European Convention for the Prevention of Torture and Inhuman or Degrading Treatment or Punishment, ETS No 151.
252   Administrative Law Chamber Case 3-3-1-14-10 (21 April 2010) para 11.
253   ibid para 11.
254   RT I 2007, 11, 52.
255   RT I 1999, 29, 406.
256   See eg Chancellor's Year in Review 2018/2019 <https://www.oiguskantsler.ee/annual-report-2019/> accessed 19 April 2022.

attention was drawn[257] to the fact that care homes were not suitably equipped for people with dementia and that their freedom of movement was often unlawfully restricted (for instance, by locking them into a room or tying them up to a wheelchair). This has led to a policy change and additional financing. For example, in the period 2018–2019 €1,5 million was allocated to improve the conditions of persons with dementia in these facilities.[258] All care-providing institutions could apply for project financing. The office of the Chancellor of Justice was participating in setting the requirements for the application and project.[259] After visits to care homes it has also been repeatedly pointed out that the absence of medical personnel leaves inhabitants without sufficient medical care. Moreover, the need for vaccinations for people in care homes has been emphasised. These observations have led to a law change[260] that now addresses both these issues.[261] There has also been an impact of the control visits on improving conditions in the detention facilities and the protection of the rights of persons detained in these facilities.[262]

5.5.4 Impact on and through Non-state Actors

In comparison with other UN treaties, CAT has been referenced more often in Estonian academic legal literature. For example, 2017 Commentaries to the Constitution explicitly mention CAT and OP-CAT and recommendations of treaty-monitoring bodies. Rait Maruste, a former judge of the ECtHR, commenting on article 18 of the Estonian Constitution, makes several references to these documents. He also points out some of the criticism at international and European level regarding domestic regulations and explains the function and importance of the SPT.[263] Somewhat surprisingly, again, the 2020 report by the Estonian Human Rights Centre does not explicitly mention CAT or related

---

257 Eg Õiguskantsler, Kiri sotsiaalministrile, Vanaduspensioniikka jõudnud dementsetele suunatud hooldusteenuse arendamise vajadus, 19.10.2016 nr 7-7/161162/1604229; Õiguskantsler, Ringkiri üldteenuse osutajetele, 11.07.2017 nr 7-9/170458/1703022.
258 Interview with Liiri Oja, Andres Aru, Indrek-Ivar Määrits, Office of Chancellor of Justice, 12 June, Tallinn.
259 Sotsiaalkaitseministri 13. detsembri 2018. a käskkirjaga nr 99 „Taotlusvoor teenusekohtade kohandamiseks dementsusega inimestele" kinnitatud „Taotlusvooru teenusekohtade kohandamiseks dementsusega inimestele tingimused ja kord" seletuskiri <https://www.sm.ee/sites/default/files/seletuskiri.pdf> accessed 19 April 2022.
260 Eesti Haigekassa tervishoiuteenuste loetelu, RT I, 24.03.2020, 14, arts 7 and 8.
261 Email consultation with Liiri Oja, Andres Aru, Indrek-Ivar Määrits, Office of Chancellor of Justice, 12 June 2020, Tallinn.
262 ibid.
263 R Maruste, 'Paragrahv 18' in Ü Madise jt (toim), *Eesti Vabariigi põhiseadus. Kommenteeritud väljaanne* (Juura 2017) para 10.

instruments, even in the chapter that specifically deals with torture, inhuman and degrading treatment, while making multiple references to ECtHR and Supreme Court practice.[264]

5.5.5 Impact of State Reporting

By 30 June 2019 Estonia had gone through three full cycles of reporting. The latest COs were issued in 2013. The new national report was due in 2017 but has not yet been submitted.

In 2013 the CAT Cttee expressed concern that that the definition of torture in the Penal Code does not reflect all the elements contained in article 1 of the Convention, such as the infliction of mental pain.[265] In 2010 the HRCttee expressed similar concerns that the definition contained in the state party's Penal Code is too narrow and not in conformity with the definition provided in article 1 of CAT and article 7 of CCPR.[266] The Penal Code was substantially changed in 2015, including the definition of torture. In the legislative process CAT and criticism from the CAT Cttee and from European institutions were mentioned as the main reasons for changing the definition of torture in the Penal Code.[267] However, no further elaboration on the incompatibility with CAT was provided.

5.5.6 Brief Conclusion

One could argue that CAT and its Protocol have created the most visible impact especially regarding significant improvements in prison conditions since the collapse of the Soviet Union in 1991. CAT and OP-CAT and recommendations of independent monitoring mechanisms have been mentioned in the courts and in law making. As noted above, OP-CAT is explicitly mentioned in two laws.[268] The work of the office of the Chancellor of Justice as the national preventive mechanism has been important. However, as noted before, the attribution of the sole impact of the treaty can sometimes be difficult as there is an overlap

---

264 E Lumiste and K Paalmäe, 'Piinamise, ebainimlikult või alandavalt kohtlemise ja karistamise keeld' in K Käsper ja E Rünne (toim), *Inimõigused Eestis, Eesti Inimõiguste Keskuse aastaaruanne 2020, Areng aastatel 2018–2019* (SA Eesti Inimõiguste Keskus 2020).
265 CAT Cttee, COs, Estonia, UN Doc CAT/C/EST/CO/5 (17 June 2013) para 7.
266 HRCttee, COs, Estonia, UN Doc CCPR/C/EST/CO/3 (4 August 2010) para 7.
267 Vabariigi Valitsus, 'Karistusseadustiku ja sellega seonduvalt teiste seaduste muutmise seaduse seletuskiri' 75 <https://www.just.ee/sites/www.just.ee/files/elfinder/article_files/karistusseadustiku_ja_sellega_seonduvalt_teiste_seaduste_muutmise_seaduse_eelnou_seletuskiri_3.12.2013.pdf> accessed 19 April 2022.
268 See part 5.5 of this chapter above.

between the UN treaties themselves (especially CCPR) and with European counterparts.

5.6 Convention on the Rights of the Child
5.6.1 Incorporation and Reliance by Legislature and Executive

Estonia acceded to CRC on 26 September 1991. Estonia also ratified OP-CRC-SC and OP-CRC-AC, but it has not accepted individual communications under OP-CRC-CP.

As mentioned above, the Basic Schools and Upper Secondary Schools Act specifically mentions UDHR and CRC as providing important fundamental values for general education schools.[269] CRC is mentioned in the Strategy of Children and Families 2012–2020 alongside CEDAW and CRPD.[270] The Chancellor of Justice Act was amended in 2011. Since 2011, when the amendments came into force, there has been one explicit reference to CRC. According to article 1(8) of the Act the Chancellor of Justice performs the functions of protection of the rights of children and the promotion thereof according to article 4 of CRC.[271] Importantly, CRC is also explicitly mentioned in articles 2 and 5 of the Child Protection Act as a basis of the law.[272] Article 5 of the Act, for example, lists principles embodied in CRC.

CRC and OP-CRC-AC have been mentioned in the legislative process. Both instruments were mentioned in the explanatory note[273] to proposed changes in the Penal Code. The note criticised the then existing regulation for not dealing with the recruitment of children in armed conflict.[274] As mentioned before, the Penal Code was heavily revised in 2015 and relevant changes were introduced.[275] As noted in part 5.1 of this chapter, above, article 7(1) of CRC was

---

269   Basic Schools and Upper Secondary Schools Act, art 3(2), RT I 2010, 41, 240.
270   Sotsiaalministeerium, *Targad vanemad, toredad lapsed, tugev ühiskond. Laste ja perede arengukava 2012–2020* (Tallinn 2011) 9, 41 (also available in English): Ministry of Social Affairs, *Smart Parents, Great Children, Strong Society. Strategy of Children and Families 2012–2020* (Tallinn 2011) 14, 46, 65.
271   RT I 1999, 29, 406; RT I, 09.03.2011, 1.
272   Child Protection Act, RT I, 06.12.2014, 1.
273   According to the Rules for Good Legislative Practice and Legislative Drafting (RT I, 29.12.2011, 228) legislative changes need to be accompanied by a substantial explanation of legislative intent and assessment of impact.
274   Vabariigi Valitsus, 'Karistusseadustiku ja sellega seonduvalt teiste seaduste muutmise seaduse seletuskiri' 47 <https://www.just.ee/sites/www.just.ee/files/elfinder/article_files/karistusseadustiku_ja_sellega_seonduvalt_teiste_seaduste_muutmise_seaduse_eelnou_seletuskiri_3.12.2013.pdf> accessed 19 April 2022.
275   Penal Code, art 102^3, RT I 2001, 61, 364.

mentioned in the process of changing the Citizenship Act. Special guidelines have also been created by the Ministry of Justice for specialists working with children in criminal proceedings.[276] However, CRC is not explicitly mentioned in these guidelines, but European documents are.[277]

5.6.2 Reliance by Judiciary

As mentioned above, there have been three explicit references to CRC in the Supreme Court during the period of study. The first case concerned refusal of residence permits and a review of the deportation order.[278] No substantive discussion emerged on the basis of this Convention. The second case essentially concerned access to education of a disabled child.[279] The Constitutional Review Chamber pointed out that inclusive education is an internationally-recognised principle. In this regard, it made specific reference to article 23 of CRC and article 24 of CRPD alongside the Salamanca Statement and Framework for Action on Special Needs Education.[280] However, the legality of the contested local government Act in this case was decided primarily on the basis of domestic law. The third case concerned access to a child and the consequences of impeding the access. The centrality of the best interests of the child figured in this case. 'The enforcement officer must find a balance of interests and place the child's interests in the foreground.'[281] It was stated further that under article 3 of CRC, article 24 of the Charter of Fundamental Rights of the EU and article 3 of the Estonian Child Protection Act, 'when enforcing a judicial decision concerning a child, the best interests of the child shall be a primary consideration'.[282] However, apart from this single mention of CRC, no further elaboration on the Convention was provided. The technicalities of the case were decided with the references to the domestic law.

---

276 UPR, Mid-Term Report of Estonia on the Implementation of the UPR Recommendations (December 2018) 10.
277 Justiitsministeeriumi kriminaalpoliitika osakond, 'Meelespea' (2018) <https://www.kriminaalpoliitika.ee/sites/krimipoliitika/files/elfinder/dokumendid/lapsesobraliku_menetluse_meelespea.pdf> accessed 19 April 2022. The guidelines are explicitly created on the basis of the material from the European Union Agency for Human Rights 'Child-friendly Justice – Checklist for Professionals' (2017).
278 Administrative Law Chamber Case 3-3-1-61-09 (9 Nov 2009). No extensive elaboration of the link between the case and the Convention was provided by either party.
279 Constitutional Review Chamber Case 3-4-1-16-16 (31 March 2017) para 24.
280 ibid para 24.
281 Supreme Court *en banc* Case 3-2-1-4-13 (17 December 2013) para 9.
282 ibid.

5.6.3 Impact on and through Independent State Institutions

Estonia created the position of Ombudsman for Children on 19 March 2011. As noted, the Chancellor of Justice Act mentions CRC explicitly in that respect.[283] The duties of the Ombudsman are carried out by the Chancellor of Justice. The Children's Rights Department of the Office of the Chancellor of Justice performs the everyday functions of the Ombudsman.[284] Substantial awareness-raising activities have been carried out. For example, events and campaigns have been organised in schools, in media and social media. There is a special telephone line for children where they can raise their concerns and ask for help. In the 2015 report of the Chancellor of Justice to the CRC Cttee the need for the state to adhere to OP-CRC-CP was specifically mentioned.[285] It will also be mentioned in the next UPR report.[286]

5.6.4 Impact on and through Non-state Actors

The 2017 Commentaries to the Constitution explicitly mention CRC and Estonia's obligations, for example, in the context of article 27 (protection of family life);[287] article 37 (right to education);[288] and article 139 (Chancellor of Justice).[289] CRC is mentioned, although without substantive discussion, in a recent article on the role of the Supreme Court in the implementation of international treaties.[290] The article is published in the main law journal in Estonia, *Juridica*. The Estonian Human Rights Centre's 2020 report covering the period 2018–2019 on the human rights situation in Estonia mentions CRC several times explicitly in the chapter on the rights of children.[291] In 2017 there

---

283 RT I 1999, 29, 406; RT I, 09.03.2011, 1.
284 UPR, National Report, Estonia, UN Doc A/HRC/WG.6/24/EST/1 (28 December 2015) 3.
285 Report of the Chancellor of Justice of the Republic of Estonia on Implementation of the UN Convention on the Rights of the Child, about the fourth and fifth regular report of the Republic of Estonia, November 2015.
286 Consultation with Liiri Oja, Andres Aru, Indrek-Ivar Määrits, Office of Chancellor of Justice (12 June, Tallinn).
287 K Jaanimägi and L Oja, 'Paragrahv 27' in Ü Madise jt (toim), *Eesti Vabariigi põhiseadus. Kommenteeritud väljaanne* (Juura 2017) paras 18, 32, 28-41.
288 N Parrest and T Annus, 'Paragrahv 37' in Ü Madise jt (toim), *Eesti Vabariigi põhiseadus. Kommenteeritud väljaanne* (Juura 2017) para 1.
289 N Parrest and others, 'Paragrahv 139' in Ü Madise jt (toim), *Eesti Vabariigi põhiseadus. Kommenteeritud väljaanne* (Juura 2017) paras 14, 40.
290 M Torga, 'Riigikohtu tsiviilkolleegiumi roll Eesti välislepingute kohaldamisel: kas lihtsalt järgija või õiguse edasiarendaja?' (2019) 9 Juridica 687, 688.
291 H Saar, 'Lapse õigused' in K Käsper ja E Rünne (toim), *Inimõigused Eestis, Eesti Inimõiguste Keskuse aastaaruanne 2020, Areng aastatel 2018–2019* (SA Eesti Inimõiguste Keskus 2020).

was a study conducted by the Human Rights Centre and Institute of Baltic Studies on human rights in education. The study noted that although the legal basis for human rights education in schools has been created, it still depends on the competence of teachers to provide it.[292] Substantial academic work has focused on CRC.[293] In 2015 a special issue of *Juridica* on children's rights was published including articles referencing CRC.[294]

5.6.5 Impact of State Reporting

By June 2019 Estonia had gone through two full cycles of reporting under CRC. One cycle of reporting each has been concluded under OP-CRC-AC[295] and OP-CRC-SC.[296]

The first Child Protection Act was adopted in 1993.[297] In 2014 a new law was adopted to replace the 1993 Act.[298] The new Child Protection Act entered into force in 2016. The explanatory note to the law explicitly states that the 1993 law in many ways was a reciting of CRC. It further mentions criticism expressed in the 2003 COs of the CRC Cttee that many of the provisions of the 1993 law have not been fully implemented through detailed regulations.[299] Thus, this criticism was one of the reasons to adopt the new law.

Some specific issues related to implementation of CRC have also been brought out under other treaties. For example, corporal punishment of

---

292 Balti Uuringute Instituut, Inimõiguste Keskus, 'Inimõigused ja inimõiguste alusväärtused Eesti koolis ja hariduspoliitikas' (Tartu 2017) 77 <https://www.hm.ee/sites/default/files/uuringud/io_lopparuanne.pdf> accessed 19 April 2022.
293 K Luhamaa, *Universal Human Rights in National Contexts: Application of International Rights of the Child in Estonia, Finland and Russia* (PhD thesis, University of Tartu, 2015); J Strömpl and A Markina, 'Children's Rights and the Juvenile Justice System in Estonia' (2017) 25 Juridica International 66.
294 A Aru and K Paron, 'Lapse parimad huvid' (2005) 6 Juridica 375; S Hakalehto-Wainio, Lapse õigused koolis (2005) 6 Juridica 387; E Ahas, Kas perest eraldamine on liigne sekkumine perekonnaautonoomiasse või üks lapse huve tagavatest meetmetest? (2005) 6 Juridica 397; K Žurakovskaja-Aru, 'Lapse õigus *vs*. võimalus suhelda vangistuses vanemaga – vanglavälisest suhtlemisest ümberpööratuna' (2005) 6 Juridica 405; K Kask, 'Alaealise kannatanu videosalvestatud ülekuulamise analüüs kriminaalmenetluses' (2005) 6 Juridica 427; K Albi, 'Saatjata sisserändajast alaealise vastuvõtmine' (2005) 6 Juridica 435.
295 CRC Cttee, COs, Estonia, UN Doc CRC/C/OPAC/EST/CO/1 (8 March 2017).
296 CRC Cttee, COs, Estonia, UN Doc CRC/C/OPSC/EST/CO/1 (5 March 2010).
297 Child Protection Act, RT 1992, 28, 370.
298 Child Protection Act, RT I, 06.12.2014, 1.
299 Vabariigi Valitsus, 'Seletuskiri lastekaitseseaduse eelnõu juurde' 2 <https://www.riigikogu.ee/tegevus/eelnoud/eelnou/f3beec87-7eaf-4aad-afa0-aacbdde93a4c> accessed 19 April 2022; CRC Cttee, COs, Estonia, UN Doc CRC/C/15/Add.196 (17 March 2003) para 5.

children was mentioned with concern in the 2013 CAT Cttee.[300] The same concern was expressed in the 2003 COs of the CRC Cttee recommending to the State to 'prohibit corporal punishment and take all measures to prevent all forms of physical and mental violence, including corporal punishment and sexual abuse of children in the family, in schools and in institutions'.[301] The Child Protection Act that entered into force in 2016 explicitly prohibits corporal punishment in article 24.[302] The explanatory note to the Act in parallel to European commitments repeatedly referred to CRC. Moreover, the CRC Cttee concerns in 2003 COs were explicitly mentioned as one of the reasons for creating article 24 in the Child Protection Act.[303] In this respect the explanatory note also refers to paragraph 11 of the CRC Cttee General Comment 8 specifying that according to the Committee corporal or physical punishment is any punishment in which physical force is used and intended to cause some degree of pain or discomfort, however light. It further highlights that, in the view of the Committee, corporal punishment is invariably degrading of the child's dignity.[304]

The CRC Cttee's 2017 COs[305] were discussed at the government-established Children Protection Council meeting in 2018.[306] Some legislative changes have been taking place since the 2017 COs, for example, regarding juvenile offenders.[307] For example, on 1 January 2018 several changes in the system of treating

---

300 CAT Cttee, COs, Estonia, UN Doc CAT/C/EST/CO/5 (17 June 2013) para 21.
301 CRC Cttee, COs, Estonia, UN Doc CRC/C/15/Add.196 (17 March 2003) para 31(b).
302 Child Protection Act, art 24, RT I, 06.12.2014, 1.
303 Vabariigi Valitsus, 'Seletuskiri lastekaitseseaduse eelnõu juurde' 54 <https://www.riigik ogu.ee/tegevus/eelnoud/eelnou/f3beec87-7eaf-4aad-afa0-aacbdde93a4c> accessed 19 April 2022.
304 ibid 55. See also CRC Cttee General Comment 8, arts 19; 28, para. 2; and 37 *inter alia*, The right of the child to protection from corporal punishment and other cruel or degrading forms of punishment, para 11.
305 CRC Cttee, COs, Estonia, UN Doc CRC/C/EST/CO/2-4 (8 March 2017).
306 The Council consists of representatives from the Estonian Union for Child Welfare; the Association of Estonian Cities; the Association of Estonian Rural Municipalities; the Estonian School Student Councils' Union and the Union of Estonian Youth Associations; as well as the Minister of Education and Research; the Minister of Culture; the Minister of Justice; the Minister of Interior Affairs; the Minister of Finance; and directors of the Estonian National Social Insurance Board and the National Institute for Health Development. H Saar, 'Lapse õigused' in K Käsper ja E Rünne (toim), *Inimõigused Eestis, Eesti Inimõiguste Keskuse aastaaruanne 2020, Areng aastatel 2018–2019* (SA Eesti Inimõiguste Keskus 2020) 128.
307 See concerns in the CRC Cttee, COs, Estonia, UN Doc CRC/C/EST/CO/2-4 (8 March 2017) para 48.

offenders who are minors came into force.[308] The explanatory note to the law amendments did not explicitly mention CRC. However, it mentions that recommendations of various European and international organisations have been taken into account.[309]

5.6.6 Brief Conclusion

CRC and its Protocols have been influential. CRC has been referenced in the Supreme Court. It has had a significant impact on legislative changes and policies. It is explicitly mentioned in laws themselves (in the Child Protection Act, Basic Schools and Upper Secondary Schools Act and the Act of Chancellor of Justice). The work of the Chancellor of Justice as Children's Ombudsman has contributed to the impact of CRC and its Protocols. It has also had an impact on the works of NGOs such as the Human Rights Centre. It is possible to argue that the impact of CRC and its Protocols has been significant also due to the rights of children being perhaps least politically sensitive and disputable and thus more readily accepted. It also may be due to significant local expertise and research interests in the area as evidenced in the above-mentioned academic works.

5.7 *Convention on the Rights of Persons with Disabilities*

5.7.1 Incorporation and Reliance by Legislature and Executive

The Estonian Parliament ratified CRPD on 30 May 2012. Prior to ratification of CRPD Estonia reviewed its legislation and determined that it to be in conformity with the requirements of the Convention.[310] It has also ratified OP-CRPD allowing for individual communications. However, Estonia has made the following declaration to CRPD:

---

308   See eg Karistusseadustiku muutmise ja sellega seonduvalt teiste seaduste muutmise seadus (alaealiste õigusrikkujate kohtlemise muutmine), RT I, 05.12.2017, 1.
309   Vabariigi Valitsus, 'Seletuskiri karistusseadustiku muutmise ja sellega seonduvalt teiste seaduste muutmise seaduse (alaealiste õigusrikkujate kohtlemise muutmine) eelnõu juurde' 3 <https://www.riigikogu.ee/tegevus/eelnoud/eelnou/56a447c6-1e2a-4243-a488-4647f80062eb/Karistusseadustiku%20muutmise%20ja%20sellega%20seonduvalt%20teiste%20seaduste%20muutmise%20seadus%20(alaealiste%20õigusrikkujate%20kohtlemise%20muutmine)> accessed 19 April 2022. The explanatory note, eg, explicitly mentions the UN Interagency Panel on Juvenile Justice Compendium of International Instruments Applicable to Juvenile Justice (2014) <https://www.ojp.gov/ncjrs/virtual-library/abstracts/compendium-international-instruments-applicable-juvenile-justice> accessed 27 September 2023.
310   Initial Report, CRPD, Estonia, UN Doc CRPD/C/EST/1 (4 December 2015) para 2.

The Republic of Estonia interprets article 12 of the Convention as it does not forbid to restrict a person's active legal capacity, when such need arises from the person's ability to understand and direct his or her actions. In restricting the rights of the persons with restricted active legal capacity the Republic of Estonia acts according to its domestic laws.[311]

As is apparent from the explanatory note to the law on ratification[312] and in the state's initial report,[313] Estonia continues to adhere to the declaration despite indications from the CRPD Cttee that change may be necessary.[314] The explanatory note points out that one of the reasons for the declaration is that article 12 of CRPD cannot be interpreted as an obligation on the state to remove all the possibilities for restricting active legal capacity. It also notes that legal capacity is sufficiently protected in Estonia by appointed guardianship.[315]

As mentioned, CRPD is referred to in the 2012–2020 Strategy of Children and Families.[316] Obligations stemming from CRPD are also mentioned in the Welfare Development Programme for 2016–2023.[317] CRPD is listed as one of the documents at the basis of the Strategy of Integration and Social Cohesion in Estonia 2020.[318]

The Chancellor of Justice Act was changed in 2018 and the law now makes explicit reference to the Convention in its article 1(11) stating that 'based on Article 33(2) of the Convention on Rights of Persons with Disabilities, the

---

[311] Declaration made by Estonia, UNTC, Depositary, Status as at 28-12-2018.

[312] Seletuskiri „Puuetega inimeste õiguste konventsiooni ratifitseerimine ja konventsiooni fakultatiivprotokolliga ühinemine" seaduse eelnõu kohta Seletuskiri <https://www.riigikogu.ee/tegevus/eelnoud/eelnou/1774015b-86a2-4540-aed8-4ae25d214f16/Puuetega%20inimeste%20õiguste%20konventsiooni%20ratifitseerimise%20seadus> accessed 19 April 2022.

[313] Initial Report, CRPD, Estonia, UN Doc CRPD/C/EST/1 (4 December 2015) para 79.

[314] CRPD Cttee, List of Issues, Estonia, UN Doc CRPD/C/EST/Q/1 (10 May 2019) para 9.

[315] Seletuskiri „Puuetega inimeste õiguste konventsiooni ratifitseerimine ja konventsiooni fakultatiivprotokolliga ühinemine" seaduse eelnõu kohta Seletuskiri 19–20 <https://www.riigikogu.ee/tegevus/eelnoud/eelnou/1774015b-86a2-4540-aed8-4ae25d214f16/Puuetega%20inimeste%20õiguste%20konventsiooni%20ratifitseerimise%20seadus> accessed 19 April 2022.

[316] Ministry of Social Affairs, *Smart Parents, Great Children, Strong Society. Strategy of Children and Families 2012–2020* (Tallinn 2011) 14, 46, 65.

[317] Sotsiaalministeerium, *Heaolu arengukava 2016–2023*, 45. The programme is available both in Estonian and English <https://www.sm.ee/et/heaolu-arengukava-2016-2023> accessed 19 April 2022.

[318] 'The Strategy of Integration and Social Cohesion in Estonia 2020' (n 111).

Chancellor of Justice shall perform the functions of promoting the implementation, protection and monitoring of the Convention'.[319]

5.7.2 Reliance by Judiciary

During the period under study, CRPD has been explicitly mentioned once in the Supreme Court practice.[320] As noted, the case essentially concerned access to education of a disabled child. In this particular case several international instruments were mentioned, including article 24 of CRPD, article 23 of CRC and the Salamanca Statement and Framework for Action on Special Needs Education.[321]

5.7.3 Impact on and through Independent State Institutions

From 1 January 2019, the Chancellor of Justice performs the tasks of an independent mechanism to promote, protect and monitor implementation of CRPD in accordance with article 33(2) of the Convention. The new task also brought some additional funding from the state budget. This facilitated the appointment of a Head of Disability Rights in the Chancellor of Justice's office.[322] In May 2019 the Chancellor convened the Advisory Council for Persons with Disabilities.[323] Members of the Advisory Council are persons with disabilities and representatives of their organisations. The annual report 2018–2019 of the Chancellor of Justice has been included for information among the documents for reviewing Estonia's initial report to the CRPD Cttee. The Chancellor and her advisers actively participate in awareness raising in public and specialist debates, speak at seminars and conferences, and in the media. For example, advisors of the Chancellor have published an article on CRPD.[324] As noted, in the capacity of the NHRI the Chancellor of Justice submitted her first report in February 2019 regarding CRPD.[325]

---

319 Chancellor of Justice Act, RT I, 03.07.2018, 14.
320 Constitutional Review Chamber Case 3-4-1-16-16 (31 March 2017).
321 ibid para 24. See also part 5.6. above.
322 'Protection of the Rights of People with Disabilities', Chancellor's Year in Review 2018/2019 <https://www.oiguskantsler.ee/annual-report-2019/> accessed 30 January 2020.
323 Õiguskantsler, 'Õiguskantsler kutsub kokku puuetega inimeste nõukoja' <https://www.oiguskantsler.ee/et/õiguskantsler-kutsub-kokku-puuetega-inimeste-nõukoja> accessed 30 January 2020.
324 N Parresti and K Mulleri, '*ÜRO puuetega inimeste konventsioon lõhkumas eestkostesüsteemi*' (2015) 1 Sotsiaaltöö 51.
325 Email consultation with Liiri Oja, Andres Aru, Indrek-Ivar Määrits, Office of Chancellor of Justice (12 June, Tallinn).

In 2018 the Chancellor of Justice submitted an application to the Supreme Court to declare unconstitutional several provisions in laws. She also pointed out contradictions with positive obligations stemming from international treaties including CRPD, CRC and the European Social Charter.[326] In its decision of December 2019, which is outside the period under revision in this chapter, the Court found several provisions in the laws to be unconstitutional.

5.7.4 Impact on and through Non-state Actors

CRPD is mentioned several times in the 2018–2019 report of the Estonian Human Rights Centre. The report mentions the 2019 List of Issues of the CRPD Cttee[327] in respect of its concern that Estonia is creating a hierarchy of discrimination grounds in the Equal Treatment Act.[328] The Estonian Chamber of Disabled People has been very proactive in trying to give momentum to the implementation of CRPD. In 2019 the Chamber submitted a shadow report to the CRPD Cttee which was created in consultation with various other organisations in the field.[329] Academic literature seems to be engaging with the theme as well. For example, the 2017 Commentaries to the Constitution also reference CRPD several times.[330]

5.7.5 Impact of State Reporting

By June 2019 Estonia has not yet gone through a full cycle of reporting.

5.7.6 Impact of Individual Communications

Although Estonia has recognised the individual complaints procedure under OP-CRPD, there have been no individual applications submitted to the CRPD Cttee during the period of this study.

---

326 See Constitutional Review Chamber Case 5-18-7 (9 December 2019) para 6.
327 List of Issues, Estonia, UN Doc CRPD/C/EST/Q/1 (10 May 2019).
328 A Habicht, 'Puuetega inimeste olukord' in K Käsper ja E Rünne (toim), *Inimõigused Eestis, Eesti Inimõiguste Keskuse aastaaruanne 2020, Areng aastatel 2018–2019* (SA Eesti Inimõiguste Keskus 2020) 145.
329 A Habicht and H Kask (toim), 'Puuetega inimeste eluolu Eestis: ÜRO puuetega inimeste õiguste konventsiooni täitmise variraport' (Eesti Puuetega Inimeste Koda 2018) <https://www.epikoda.ee/wp-content/uploads/2018/03/EPIK_variraport_webi.pdf> accessed 19 April 2022. For the English version, see UN High Commissioner of Human Rights <https://tbinternet.ohchr.org/_layouts/15/treatybodyexternal/Download.aspx?symbolno=INT%2fCRPD%2fICO%2fEST%2f33965&Lang=en> accessed 19 April 2022.
330 A Henberg, 'Paragrahv 28' in Ü Madise jt (toim), *Eesti Vabariigi põhiseadus. Kommenteeritud väljaanne* (Juura 2017) paras 44–47.

5.7.7 Brief Conclusion

The impact of CRPD and OP-CRPD is visible. It may be indicative of the fact that the impact of a treaty may also depend on the subject matter. Disability touches many people personally either directly or through their family members and it is not a topic that is overly politicised. One also needs to notice the active role of various civic organisations in Estonia in this field that have been promoting rights of persons with disabilities, but also the work of the Chancellor of Justice. There has been a dramatic change in the way in which disability was seen in Soviet times compared to how it is now seen.

6 Conclusion

Has the UN system made a difference at the domestic level? It certainly has. As discussed, '[t]he UN human rights covenants were important in the process of the restoration of independence of the Baltic states because these norms and commitments were also binding for the USSR'.[331] The UN treaties, and CCPR especially, played a significant role when Estonia regained its independence in 1991 and started to rebuild its legal order thereafter. There has been an explicit impact of COs on legislative changes, for example, regarding the establishment of the NHRI, changes in the citizenship laws and treatment of minorities, persons with disabilities and other vulnerable groups, in the treatment of people in detention facilities. There have been references (albeit limited) to the treaties in the courts' practice and most notably in the practice of the Supreme Court of Estonia, which is influencing the way in which legal reasoning is steered in the country. The influence of the UN system in general is reflected in the ratification of most human rights treaties by Estonia and their Protocols as a clear message of how this country wanted to proceed after the collapse of the Soviet Union.

However, regarding the domestic impact, largely, the regional human rights system has received more prominence than the UN in Estonia. This was brought out already in the 1999 study with respect to the ECHR.[332] The conclusion here, in that respect, does not differ. The system under the ECHR is still considered to be more effective and accessible, decisions of the ECtHR (since joining the EU in 2004 also the European Court of Justice) are legally binding, and thus are perceived to carry more weight. This is also reflected in

---

331 See also email consultation with Lauri Mälksoo, Professor of International Law at University of Tartu, School of Law (29 May 2020, Tallinn).
332 M Hion, 'Estonia' in Heyns and Viljoen (n 41) 261.

the number of individual applications made to the ECtHR.[333] Although within the CoE framework the ECHR definitely has the most impact, Estonia is a party to several other European human rights treaties (ECPT, ESC, and so forth). As for the European Union, EU law has regulated a significant part of the Estonian legal order since 2004, and the importance of interpretation of the law in the European Court of Justice has been growing. Thus, at least partly, overlapping commitments of Estonia primarily in the CoE and EU have pushed UN treaties into relative obscurity.

When changes have been made to laws it also sometimes is difficult to assess whether the change was influenced more by the European or UN treaties as similar recommendations or directives have been coming from both systems. The cross-referencing of treaties in UN and European treaty monitoring (the comparative approach) also seems to be on the increase. This is a positive tendency, even if it may blur the picture of separate impact. As a minor issue, one also needs to note that attributing impact, for example, a change in legislation, to a particular UN human rights treaty is also complicated as the same issue is often addressed under different UN human rights treaties.

One significant difference between the extent of domestic impact in 2019, as compared to 1999, is the fact of more awareness of the treaty system, as also reflected in the state's reports and legislative changes. The awareness and use of the UN human rights treaties seems to have increased with Estonia's membership in the UN Security Council, simply also by reason of more publicity in different media publications and also by a professional (heightened) need to better understand the UN system. However, this simply is speculation, and developments will continue to depend on multiple factors including the reforms in the UN itself to make it more attractive, accessible and effective to individuals, but also on efforts (including financial) made to provide UN-supported capacity building locally.[334] The establishment of the NHRI in 2019 certainly will also help.

One also needs to note that only a few full cycles of reporting had been finalised by June 1999 compared to June 2019, which had an impact on the

---

333   The list of cases is available on the web page of the State Gazette (*Riigi Teataja*), Riigi Teataja, Kohtuteave, Euroopa Inimõiguste Kohtu lahendite kokkuvõtted <https://www.riigiteataja.ee/kohtuteave/eik_liigitus.html> accessed 19 April 2022.

334   The 1999 study already reflected on the fact that the Council of Europe supports its human rights system better than the UN in Estonia, by means of seminars, financial assistance and assistance with compatibility studies. The regional system is seen as more efficient, more technical assistance is provided, the case law is more readily available and is also translated into local languages. See Heyns and Viljoen (n 44) 34.

legislative changes and judicial practice. Moreover, in the 1990s Estonia was rapidly rebuilding its domestic legal system after the collapse of the Soviet Union, changing from a totalitarian to a democratic country that complies with international standards. In this state of flux, it often happened that laws contradict one another in terminology and substance and rapid and repeated changes in laws were needed. This somewhat schizophrenic situation was challenging for both lawyers and politicians. The 1999 study also pointed out that due to rapid changes in domestic legislation, reports to and COs from treaty-monitoring bodies soon become obsolete, which also affected reporting generally.[335] One may argue that this frantic learning and rebuilding process is not present in 2019 Estonia, which also is reflected in more up-to-date reporting to treaty-monitoring bodies. There are also different challenges today, for example, dealing with the ever-growing amount of information (specifically case law) that needs to be absorbed or analysed by lawyers to stay on top of human rights protection both in Europe and globally. There are also different political challenges today. However, despite the rise of populism and right-wing movements, one can also say, with relative confidence, that Estonia has not changed its policy to adhere to democratic principles and human rights. At the end of the day, one needs to realise that the impact of the UN treaties needs three main factors: time, willingness and effort.

Acknowledgements

I am very thankful to feedback and email consultations provided by Uno Lõhmus, Lauri Mälksoo, Mai Hiion, Karri Käsper, Liiri Oja, Andres Aru and Indrek-Ivar Määrits. Kari Käsper, Head of the Human Rights Centre from January 2012 to January 2020 (27 May 2020, Tallinn); Lauri Mälksoo, Professor of International Law at University of Tartu, School of Law (29 May 2020, Tallinn); Liiri Oja, Andres Aru, Indrek-Ivar Määrits, Office of Chancellor of Justice (12 June 2020, Tallinn); Mai Hion, Estonian Ministry of Foreign Affairs (10 June 2020, Tallinn); Uno Lõhmus, judge ret., Former judge of the ECtHR, ECJ and Chief Justice of the Estonian Supreme Court (28 May 2020, Tartu).

---

335   M Hion, 'Estonia' in Heyns and Viljoen (n 41) 261.

CHAPTER 8

The Impact of the United Nations Human Rights Treaties on the Domestic Level in Finland

Merja Pentikäinen

1 Introduction to Human Rights in Finland[*]

Finland declared independence in 1917. The parliamentary reform of 1906 had already introduced equal suffrage for women and men.[1] After the civil war that broke out in 1918, a republican form of government and the Constitutional Act of Finland, which included a brief catalogue of fundamental rights, were adopted in 1919. The political and legal reforms, particularly in the 1960s and 1970s, created the basis for the Nordic welfare state model paving the way for the egalitarian society with a high standard of living. Characteristic of the Finnish national political system is its multi-party nature and the formation of coalition governments, which has prevented abrupt changes in political agendas and emphases.

Finland has a decentralised system for securing the implementation of its international human rights obligations at the domestic level. The Ministry for Foreign Affairs represents Finland's human rights policy in international fora. It also coordinates the preparation of the state's periodic human rights reports and acts as government agent in international human rights processes. Various ministries are responsible for the implementation of human rights in their respective fields of responsibility. The Ministry of Justice coordinates the inter-ministerial Government Network of Contact Persons for Fundamental and Human Rights.

---

[*] The study on Finland was commissioned and resourced by the Human Rights Centre (HRC) of the Finnish NHRI.

[1] As a result, Finnish women were the first women in Europe to acquire the right to vote and the first women in the world to be able to stand as candidates for Parliament. In the first parliamentary elections held in 1907, 19 women – the first female parliamentarians in the world – were elected to the unicameral 200-member Parliament. For more, see eg <https://finland.fi/life-society/finlands-parliament-pioneer-of-gender-equality/> accessed 13 April 2022.

The Finnish National Human Rights Institution (NHRI, A-status 2014 and 2019) was established by law in 2012. The NHRI consists of the Human Rights Centre, its pluralistic 20 to 40-member Human Rights Delegation[2] and the Parliamentary Ombudsman (established 1920). The HRC is an autonomous and independent expert institution tasked with promoting and monitoring the implementation of fundamental and human rights in Finland as well as increasing cooperation and exchange of information between various actors in the field. The Human Rights Centre represents the Finnish NHRI in international NHRI cooperation. The NHRI collectively has a special statutory task to promote, protect and monitor the implementation of the United Nations (UN) Convention on the Rights of Persons with Disabilities (CRPD). In addition to its own supervisory duties, the Parliamentary Ombudsman has special tasks with respect to the Convention on the Rights of the Child (CRC), the Convention Against Torture and Other Cruel, Inhuman or Degrading Treatment or Punishment (CAT)[3] and the CRPD.

The Parliamentary Ombudsman, part of the NHRI, oversees that authorities and private entities performing public tasks observe the law. The Parliamentary Ombudsman also places a strong focus on the rights of older persons. The responsibilities of the Chancellor of Justice include supervising the lawfulness of the acts of government, the ministries and the President of the Republic.[4] The Ombudsman for Equality, the Non-Discrimination Ombudsman and the Ombudsman for Children as well as the Data Protection Ombudsman and the new Intelligence Ombudsman exercise ombudsman functions with more specific mandates.[5] They are all members of the Human Rights Delegation.

The Parliament's Constitutional Law Committee has an important role in guaranteeing the implementation of constitutional and human rights. The Committee's main function is to issue statements on the constitutionality and human rights conformity of matters submitted to it, including government Bills. The constitutional reform of 2000 strengthened the role and duties of all

---

2 The Human Rights Delegation functions as a national cooperative body for fundamental and human rights actors. See <https://www.humanrightscentre.fi/about-us/human-rights-delegation/> accessed 13 April 2022.
3 The Ombudsman has since November 2014 functioned as the Finnish National Preventive Mechanism (NPM) under OP-CAT.
4 For the Chancellor of Justice, see <https://www.okv.fi/en/> and the Parliamentary Ombudsman <https://www.oikeusasiamies.fi/en/web/guest> accessed 14 April 2022.
5 See <https://tasa-arvo.fi/en/front-page, https://syrjinta.fi/en/front-page, http://www.lapsiasia.fi/en/> accessed 13 April 2022. There is also the Consumer Ombudsman whose tasks have links to human rights.

public authorities and the courts of law in the area of the protection of constitutional and human rights.

Finland's membership in the Council of Europe (CoE) from 1989 and the ratification of the European Convention on Human Rights (ECHR) in 1990 is a major human rights milestone for Finland. The next significant milestone was the reform of the constitutional rights catalogue in 1995. The aim of the reform was to ensure that the constitutional rights at a minimum were compliant with Finland's international human rights obligations. The provision of the duty of all public authorities to guarantee the observance of human rights was an important addition to the Constitution (section 22). One of the aims of the reform was to strengthen the justiciability of constitutional and human rights. The revised Constitution also introduced an important provision guiding the courts of law to give primacy to the provisions of the Constitution.[6] Finland's membership in the European Union (EU) from 1995 linked Finland to the EU's legal and policy framework, including its human rights components. Regarding structural developments during the past 20 years, the establishment of the Ombudsman for Children (2004) and the Non-Discrimination Ombudsman (2015) as well as that of the HRC and Finland's NHRI in 2012 are also important milestones.

Discrimination against persons belonging to various vulnerable or disadvantaged groups, such as minorities, including the Roma and the Sami,[7] persons with disabilities, sexual minorities (especially transgender persons), persons with immigrant backgrounds and women is a cross-cutting human rights issue. For instance, discrimination in the labour market is commonplace, and certain forms of labour exploitation exist. Discrimination on multiple grounds is also prevalent.

Violence against women, and also against children, in private relationships is among the most serious human rights problems in Finland. The rights and care of older persons, even neglect in care homes, is a burning issue. Hate speech, including in the populist rhetoric of politicians, has gradually increased in the last 15 years and in particular since 2017. Recently violations of privacy due to digitalisation and the limits of freedom of speech have been actively discussed. Racism and intolerance, including anti-semitism and islamophobia, are polarising society. The treatment of asylum seekers and their insufficient legal protection has been vocally criticised.

---

6 According to s 106: 'If, in a matter being tried by a court of law, the application of an Act would be in evident conflict with the Constitution, the court of law shall give primacy to the provision in the Constitution'.

7 The Sami is the only group of indigenous peoples in Finland.

The implementation of socio-economic rights and particularly their justiciability has for years been debated. The economic challenges since the global financial crisis of 2008 have resulted in further challenges to socio-economic rights in the form of cuts to social benefits and lowering the basic subsistence level. Poverty of families with children has increased, and mental health and child protection services are insufficient. Self-determination and the linguistic and cultural rights of the Sami require improvement.

Due to the costs of and financial risks relating to court proceedings and legal assistance as well as insufficient legal aid provided by the state, actual legal protection and access to justice have deteriorated. The general awareness of human rights is at a low level. Regarding structural issues, the self-governance of municipalities and fragmented and partially under-resourced national structures to protect and guarantee human rights cause challenges. The emerging human rights issues relate to the climate crisis and technological development.

Finland has a lively civil society with a high number of non-governmental organisations (NGOs), with whom the Finnish public administration has engaged quite actively in domestic exchanges of views on human rights. Government support for civil society actors through providing funding has been part of this dynamic, also somewhat unique to the Finnish system. However, cuts to government funding have affected the work of civil society actors when resources are forced to be sought from other sources.

2 Relationship of Finland with International Human Rights System in General

Finland became a member of the UN in 1955. During the Cold War era Finland was vocal in adhering to the policy of neutrality in relation to political conflicts. However, Finland ratified the main UN human rights treaties adopted at that time, demonstrating its willingness to be part of the international community. The UN was the main international human rights framework for Finland until the end of the 1980s. The end of the Cold War, which enabled Finland's membership in the CoE in 1989 and the subsequent ratification of the ECHR, opened a new era for human rights in Finland. Human rights emerged in domestic discussions and legal reforms were introduced in the 1990s. The revision of constitutional rights in 1995 stands as a concrete example of the new attention attached to human rights.

During the past three decades (1989 to 2019) Finland has become an active actor in the area of human rights at the international level. Since becoming a member of the EU in 1995, the government's actions in the EU context have come to the fore. Finland ratified the Statute of the International Criminal Court (ICC) in 2000. Finland has vigorously supported the rule-based international order as the guarantor of stability in international relations. This is also reflected in Finland's positive attitude towards both ratifying international treaties and the international inter-state forums of cooperation such as the UN system generally.

Although Finland has been an active participant in the human rights work of the UN, including in various UN human rights procedures such as the Universal Periodic Review (UPR), since the 1990s the main international component of human rights in the country has been provided by the CoE (particularly the ECHR). Since the entry into force of the Lisbon Treaty in 2009, the EU, with its binding Charter of Fundamental Rights and the EU Fundamental Rights Agency, has gained importance.[8]

The high number of asylum seekers to Europe in 2015, particularly due to the war in Syria, made the asylum issue a burning European question. It also resulted in the reception of a record number of asylum seekers in Finland, over 30 000 in 2015 alone, putting pressure on the national systems. The situation triggered statements from politicians (including some right-wing parliamentarians) on the need to revise the international rules on international protection. There were even suggestions that Finland should withdraw from the international treaties regulating the international protection of refugees.

The rejection of most asylum applications by Finland and the decline in the quality of the Finnish asylum procedure (including the deterioration of legal safeguards) after the 2015 influx have led to harsh criticism from civil society actors, official human rights bodies, academics and legal professionals. A number of expulsion cases against Finland have been submitted to the European Court of Human Rights (ECtHR). The low ambition human rights agenda of the coalition government that governed between 2015 and 2019 had a negative impact on human rights in Finland, particularly on socio-economic rights. The government led by social democrat Prime Minister Sanna Marin, however, adopted a much stronger human rights agenda with its government programme for 2019–2023.[9]

---

8   The EU Charter of Fundamental Rights was initially adopted as a legally non-binding instrument in 2000. It became legally binding by its incorporation into the Treaty of Lisbon establishing the constitutional basis of the EU signed in 2007 and entering into force in 2009.
9   Programme of Prime Minister Sanna Marin's Government 2019–2023.

Finland is a so-called dualistic country as regards the relationship between international law and the domestic legal order. When an international treaty falls within the realm of legislation and affects the rights or duties of individuals, its ratification requires consent by Parliament and its incorporation through an Act of Parliament. This takes place through a treaty-specific act or ordinance, depending on the material content of the treaty. Most human rights treaties binding on Finland have been incorporated by way of an Act of Parliament, and this has been the approach followed now in the past decades (see also parts 4 and 5).

Finland has more than 300 municipalities, of which the capital city of Helsinki with its more than 630 000 residents is the largest. The municipalities belong to one of 19 regions, 18 on the mainland and the autonomous province of the Åland Islands. Local authorities with strong self-government based on local democracy and decision making and the right to levy taxes have broad responsibilities for providing basic public services to their residents. Municipalities hold an important role in the national implementation of human rights, since they have responsibility for many services having close links to human rights, including social and health care, and basic education.[10]

The self-governing province of the Åland Islands off the southwest coast of Finland is an autonomous and demilitarised region of Finland with the population of approximately 28 000 inhabitants. The legal status of the Åland Islands is linked to the international law obligations accepted by Finland. Finland is a bilingual country with the official languages of Finnish and Swedish, but according to the Autonomy Act regulating the status of Åland, the only official language in the province is Swedish. The Åland Parliament has a broad competence to pass legislation in areas of relevance to human rights, including education and culture, health and medical care, as well as policing.[11] While the special status of the Åland Islands has come to the fore in the questions and views of international human rights monitoring bodies, the visible domestic discussion on the implementation of human rights, which are binding on Finland, is practically non-existent with respect to the Åland Islands.[12]

---

10   Association of Finnish Municipalities <https://www.localfinland.fi/finnish-municipalities-and-regions> accessed 13 April 2022.

11   Ministry for Foreign Affairs of Finland, The special status of the Åland Islands <https://um.fi/the-special-status-of-the-aland-islands> accessed 13 April 2022.

12   The interviewees in the study at hand as a rule stated that the question did not appear in their work. List of interviews (conducted telephonically unless otherwise indicated; the location (Helsinki) is indicated when the interview was conducted face-to-face): *Fredman, Markku*, Doctor of Laws, Attorney-at-law, 30 September 2019, Helsinki; *Hakalehto, Suvianna*, Professor of Law (child law and education law), University of

3 At a Glance: Formal Engagement of Finland with UN Human Rights Treaty System

Refer to the chart on the next page.

4 Role and Overall Impact of the UN Human Rights Treaties in Finland

4.1 Background and Role of UN Human Rights Treaties in Finland[13]

4.1.1 Formal Acceptance

Finland has ratified seven of the nine UN human rights treaties. Finland has filed reservations only to the International Covenant on Civil and Political

---

Eastern Finland, 29 November 2019; *Heinämäki, Leena*, Doctor of Laws, Docent in indigenous peoples rights, university researcher, University of Lapland, 27 September 2019; *Helander, Petri*, Judge, Supreme Administrative Court, ex-council to the Parliament's Constitutional Law Committee, 26 September 2019; *Hyttinen, Sanna*, lawyer, Finnish Medicines Agency (FIMEA), 12 September 2019; *Joronen, Mikko*, Expert, Finnish Human Rights Centre, 18 November 2019 and 18 May 2020; *Kasa, Tuija*, Master of Social Science, Project Planner (Human Rights, Democracy, Values and Dialogue in Education project 2019–2020), Faculty of Educational Sciences, University of Helsinki, 25 September 2019; *Laajapuro, Niina*, Policy Director, Amnesty International, Finnish section, 30 October 2019; *Laine, Marjaana*, Leading Legal Councel, Finnish Refugee Advise Center, 15 March 2020; *Laukko, Helena*, Executive Director, UN Association of Finland, 12 November 2019; *Lavapuro, Juha*, Professor of Public Law, University of Turku, 23 October 2019; *Leikas, Leena*, Expert, Human Rights Centre, 6 September 2019; *Makkonen, Timo*, Head of Unit of Autonomy and Equality, Ministry of Justice, 14 October 2019, Helsinki; *Marttunen, Matti*, Council to the Parliament's Constitutional Law Committee, 18 September 2019, Helsinki; *Mattila, Kaari*, Secretary General of the Finnish League for Human Rights, 27 September 2019; *Nousiainen, Kevät*, Professor of Comparative Law and Legal Theory (emerita), University of Turku, 2 October 2019; *Oinonen, Krista*, Director, Unit for Human Rights Courts and Conventions, Ministry for Foreign Affairs, 20 September 2019, Helsinki; *Ojala, Johanna*, Attorney-at-law, 26 September 2019 and 16 March 2020; *Pirjatanniemi, Elina*, Professor of International Law, Director of the Institute for Human Rights, Åbo Akademi University, 22 October 2019; *Rautiainen, Pauli*, Associate Professor in Public Law, University of Tampere, interviewed 20 September 2019, Helsinki; *Sakslin, Maija*, Deputy Parliamentary Ombudsman, 22 October 2019; *Scheinin, Martin*, Professor of International Law and Human Rights, European University Institute, 23 October 2019; *Suurpää, Johanna*, Director General, Department for Democracy and Public Law, Ministry of Justice, 3 October 2019; *Tervo, Jaana*, Lawyer, Office of the Ombudsman for Children's Rights, 27 November 2019; *Toivanen, Reetta*, Professor of Sustainability Science, Helsinki Institute of Sustainable Science, University of Helsinki, 24 September 2019. (Notes of interviews on file with author).

13 The questions on attitude, awareness, etc, addressed in this part, were put to the interviewees in the study.

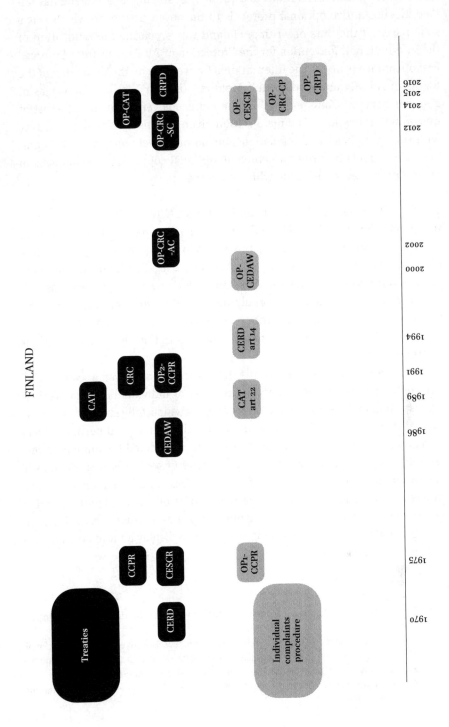

Rights (CCPR), with reservations to three articles still in place. Finland has ratified all substantive optional protocols to the seven treaties to which it is a state party. At the time of writing, Finland was preparing the ratification of the International Convention for the Protection of All Persons from Enforced Disappearance (CED).[14] The International Convention on the Protection of the Rights of All Migrant Workers and Members of their Families (CMW), as of 2011, has been officially removed by the Finnish government from the list of upcoming ratifications. The main reason given for this is its non-conformity with the EU policies and regulations, including aspects relating to EU competencies.[15] Finland further accepted all optional complaints mechanisms in respect of the seven treaties to which it is a state party.

4.1.2   General Attitude of Finland towards UN Treaty System

In general, the attitude in Finland towards the UN treaty system is positive and the government is supporting the efforts to strengthen treaty bodies. It is understood that the UN human rights treaties are legally-binding instruments under international law. However, the emphasis on the CoE and the EU as well as constitutional rights has generally directed the attention away from the UN treaties. The Finnish Constitution is seen to incorporate UN treaty standards, thus diminishing the need to pay attention to the UN treaties and their interpretation.

A certain level of distrust towards the UN treaty body system can also be detected, manifesting particularly in the cases of individual complaints filed against Finland. There are views according to which international monitoring bodies do not sufficiently take the national situation and pertinent facts into account in their deliberations.[16] They are considered recommendations with little legal significance. Also, the expertise of some UN treaty bodies is clearly challenged. Many state officials and judges regard the more court-like processes and judgments of the European Court of Human Rights (ECtHR) and the EU Court of Justice as being binding and more trustworthy. However, younger professionals (such as judges) appear to display a more positive attitude towards the UN treaties.[17]

---

[14]   Finland ratified CED in 2023.
[15]   Other reasons raised concern a broad personal coverage of the rights stipulated in the treaty.
[16]   See also the remarks in J Krommendijk, 'The Domestic Effectiveness of International Human Rights Monitoring in Established Democracies. The Case of the UN Human Rights Treaty Bodies' (2015) 10 Review of International Organisations 489–512.
[17]   The observations put forth in the paragraph were raised in the interviews conducted for the study at hand.

4.1.3 Level of Awareness

The general awareness of the UN treaties in the state administration has increased since 1999. The highest level of awareness is in the Ministry for Foreign Affairs and the Ministry of Justice. The knowledge in other ministries varies significantly, and is often dependent on individuals. Only a handful of parliamentarians are well-informed about human rights, in general, and the UN treaties, specifically. The prevailing view in Parliament is that human rights belong essentially to the Parliament's Constitutional Law Committee. While the Committee attaches some importance to UN treaties, they do not appear visibly in its work. The Committee assesses rights and freedoms primarily through constitutional rights and regional human rights standards.

The awareness of the UN treaties among legal professionals is quite limited, which essentially is the result of the absence of systematic human rights teaching in law schools (see below). As far as the general public is concerned, it is noted that while human rights talk and activism clearly have increased in the past 20 years, the understanding of the content of human rights remains rather limited and often misunderstood.

The perception of treaty-monitoring bodies (among government officials and others) is affected by a certain indifference, sometimes even distrust, as noted above. The work of the treaty bodies is not well known.

Translation of the treaties or any information on the system into local languages: All international treaties ratified by Finland are included in the official national treaty series (*Sopimussarja* (SopS)) and translated into both national languages, Finnish and Swedish. Links to the Finnish translations of the treaties may be found, for instance, on the website of the Ministry for Foreign Affairs. The website of the National Human Rights Institution (NHRI) contains links to the Foreign Ministry's website and provides an overview of the international human rights system with links to the UN pages.[18] In the past years the recommendations of the treaty bodies have been translated at least into Finnish, Swedish and one or more Sami languages.

Media coverage of the treaties:[19] While the media gives hardly any attention to human rights and the UN system more broadly, at times the UN treaties appear in the media. Media coverage has been given clearly to the Convention on the Rights of the Child (CRC) and CRPD as well as CCPR in the Sami issues and regarding hate speech. If the treaty bodies' recommendations to Finland

---

[18] See <http://www.formin.fi and http://www.ihmisoikeuskeskus.fi> accessed 13 April 2022.
[19] The information is based on the perceptions of the interviewees and the author of the study at hand.

contain remarks on burning issues, or individual violations, they may exceed a publishing threshold.

General training and teaching in schools (especially in law schools): The study commissioned by the NHRI and published in 2014 revealed a lack of a coherent and systematic human rights teaching and education in Finland at all levels of education.[20] Recently there have been positive developments, for instance, the introduction of human rights into the general curricula for secondary and high schools. The problem of insufficient human rights teaching for educators persists. The NHRI has co-funded a university project for the development of education for democratic citizenship and human rights education in teacher education for 2018 to 2021.[21] In general, human rights courses in universities are voluntary. With a few exceptions, UN treaties are not visible in compulsory courses in law schools.

The treaties in the work of local researchers and NGOs: According to the study on constitutional and human rights research in Finland commissioned by the NHRI and published in 2017, much research has been done in the area in various disciplines in universities as well as research institutions.[22] The research done in the area of law clearly focuses on constitutional rights and the ECHR. Of the UN treaties CRC has attracted the interest of researchers, particularly in the form of doctoral theses. The problem is that the research results produced in the academic arena mostly do not sufficiently inform political and practical work. The awareness of NGOs about the UN treaties has over the years increased and widened.

4.1.4 Overall Level of Awareness of the Treaties and the Treaty System

CCPR, the International Covenant on Economic, Social and Cultural Rights (CESCR), the Convention on the Elimination of All Forms of Discrimination Against Women (CEDAW) and CRC are the most widely-known UN treaties within the state administration. Generally, the awareness is the most widespread with respect to CRC. CCPR is most visible in the cases relating to the rights of the Sami. As a more recent treaty, CRPD receives visibility that is strengthened by the attention given to it by the active role of the NHRI and

---

20 HRC, *Human rights education in Finland* (Human Rights Centre 2014).
21 See University of Helsinki, 'Human Rights, Democracy, Values and Dialogue in Education' <https://www.helsinki.fi/en/projects/human-rights-democracy-values-and-dialogue-in-education> accessed 13 April 2022.
22 The study is available in Finnish: Ihmisoikeuskeskus (HRC), Assi Harkoma, *Perus-ja ihmisoikeustutkimuksesta Suomessa – asiantuntijoiden näkemyksiä* (2017).

NGOs on disability rights. CEDAW, CRC and CRPD are visible in sectoral politics. CERD is the least known, but it sometimes comes to the fore, for instance in the cases concerning the rights of the Sami, non-nationals and ethnic minorities. With its very specific material scope of application, CAT is not well known by the public. The Parliamentary Ombudsman has used the CAT Cttee's conclusions and recommendations in particular in its monitoring of prisons and closed institutions well before it became the National Preventive Mechanism (NPM). Additionally, lawyers specialised particularly on asylum cases rely on CAT.

4.1.5 State Reporting

As at 30 June 2019 Finland had submitted 23 state reports under CERD, six reports each under CCPR, CESCR and CRC, and seven reports each under CEDAW and CAT. The record of the Finnish government in submitting state reports and the level of engagement of the government with the outcome of the follow-up procedures is relatively good. Some delays, for instance in the submission of the latest reports under CEDAW as well as CRC and its protocols, have occurred. This is mainly due to a lack of resources.

Finland has a standing interministerial mechanism for reporting and follow-up.[23] The Legal Service Department in the Ministry for Foreign Affairs[24] serves as a national competent authority and focal point for preparing the government's periodic reports. It produces the initial draft reports itself. The Unit works closely with the Ministry of Justice, which coordinates the Government Network of Contact Persons for Fundamental and Human Rights with representatives from all ministries. One of its tasks is to monitor the implementation of the national human rights action plan and the implementation of concluding observations within their own ministries.

The preparation process for the reports involves many stakeholders, including ministries, administrative and research institutions and agencies. The various specialised human rights bodies, the NHRI, universities and NGOs are consulted, but usually submit their own statements or reports directly to the treaty bodies. The specific list of invitees for written comments and public hearings depends on the particular treaty.

---

23   See OHCHR, 'National Mechanisms for Reporting and Follow-Up – A Study of State Engagement with International Human Rights Mechanisms' (2016) <https://www.ohchr.org/Documents/Publications/HR_PUB_16_1_NMRF_Study.pdf> accessed 13 April 2022.
24   The task more specifically belongs to the Unit for Human Rights Courts and Conventions of the Legal Service.

The government's reports are loaded with information, often programmatic in nature rather than by providing data. NGOs have criticised their unfocused nature in the past. Limiting the word count of state reports has been welcomed, for instance, by NGOs and researchers as having resulted in a more focused consideration of the issues and better crystallising of the 'big picture'. The government has communicated well with the treaty-monitoring bodies and substantive responses have been provided in the follow-up procedures. The bodies have often commended the Finnish government for its self-critical and honest reports and open and constructive dialogue in the monitoring processes.[25]

The NHRI follows all periodic reporting processes. It has submitted its own statements on implementation directly to the treaty-monitoring bodies since its establishment (in 2012).[26] It also participates in the hearings before the treaty bodies. Other national supervisory institutions also occasionally submit their statements to international bodies (see part 5).

The government delegation in the hearings of treaty bodies consists of the representatives from relevant ministries, in recent years also an independent observer from Parliament's Constitutional Law Committee.

The Ministry for Foreign Affairs circulates the Concluding Observations (COs) of the treaty bodies within the state administration and public actors and posts these on the Ministry's website. There is no media strategy, but the Ministry usually publishes press releases on the process and its outcome. As a rule, the COs have been translated into Finnish and Swedish.

The NHRI website contains links to the relevant pages of the Foreign Ministry's website.[27] Additionally, the NHRI disseminates information on reporting processes as well as on their results widely, encouraging and supporting NGOs to participate with guidance on reporting if needed. All relevant reporting information is available on the NHRI website.

The interest of civil society actors to submit their own alternative reports and statements for the various international treaty-monitoring bodies has clearly increased in past years. NGOs often produce joint reports. Universities, research institutions and individual researchers have also presented views to

---

[25] See eg the CERD Cttee's COs in 2017, CERD/C/FIN/CO/23 (accessed 13 April 2022), para 2. Finland submitted its updated Core Report to the UN in March 2020.

[26] For HRC's statements, see HRC's annual reports <https://www.humanrightscentre.fi/publications/action-plans-and-annual-reports/> accessed 13 April 2022. For HRC's submissions to the UN treaty bodies, see also <https://tbinternet.ohchr.org/_layouts/15/TreatyBodyExternal/Countries.aspx?CountryCode=FIN&Lang=EN> accessed 13 April 2022.

[27] See <https://www.humanrightscentre.fi/monitoring/periodic-reporting-un-coe/> accessed 13 April 2022.

the monitoring bodies.[28] No cases of reprisals against human rights defenders engaging in the reporting process have been reported.

4.1.6   Domestic Implementation Mechanism/Process

The implementation of the COs and recommendations of the UN treaty bodies essentially takes place under the sectoral ministries. The Ministry for Foreign Affairs distributes these to Parliament and ministries as well as to civil society actors. The Government Network of Contact Persons for Fundamental and Human Rights has been set up to streamline the work on constitutional and human rights, ensure the flow of information, reporting and follow-up actions within the state administration and among ministries. While this network has improved the dissemination of information, it is difficult to assess the impact of the UN treaty bodies' COs and recommendations within the various sectors of administration.

4.1.7   Treaty Body Membership

Experts from Finland have served as members of the UN treaty bodies on four occasions: once, each, in the HRCttee (Martin Scheinin) and the CRC Cttee (Elisabeth Tigerstedt-Tähtelä) and twice in the CEDAW Cttee (Pirkko Mäkinen and Niklas Bruun). The membership of the experts from Finland has activated debate on the respective treaties and their implementation at the national level.

4.2   *Overall Impact of UN Human Rights Treaties*[29]

4.2.1   Incorporation and Reliance by Legislature and Executive

All UN human rights treaties ratified by Finland have been incorporated into the domestic legal order, as a rule by Acts of Parliament, with the exception of

---

28   See <https://tbinternet.ohchr.org/_layouts/15/TreatyBodyExternal/Countries.aspx?CountryCode=FIN&Lang=EN> accessed 13 April 2022.

29   Both this part and part 5 include observations by the interviewees in the study. In the preliminary phase of the study on the impact of the UN human rights treaties in Finland since 1999, the author of the study consulted both databases and some Finnish human rights researchers and law professors about the existence of pertinent impact analyses carried out in Finland. While a study by H Niemi (*National Implementation of Findings by United Nations Human Rights Treaty Bodies: A Comparative Study* (Institute for Human Rights, Åbo Akademi University 2003)) was found, no impact analyses covering the past two decades were discovered. In the course of the study the author came across an impact study concerning the implementation of CRC in Finland (see pt 5.6). See also the remarks on the non-existence of relevant studies concerning national case law in fn 46. It is notable that Finland has appeared in some international studies. See eg Krommendijk, *The Domestic Impact and Effectiveness of the Process of State Reporting under UN Human Rights Treaties in The Netherlands, New Zealand and Finland: Paper-Pushing or Policy*

CERD and CESCR.[30] The treaties have been visible in government Bills and parliamentary debates and have affected legislation in different ways. The policy of the Finnish government is to bring the national legislation into line with the human rights treaties prior to their ratification. However, this has often been done with minimum legal modifications. The implementation reviews indicate that there is still much to be done to comply with ratified treaties.

CRC and CRPD have had clear impacts on legislation and structures. The official role assigned to the NHRI, and in the case of CRC also to the Ombudsman for Children, in the promotion and protection of these treaties has increased this impact. Issues covered by CRPD receive back-up through the EU legislation and policies on the basis of the EU's ratification of the treaty and its monitoring mechanism. CCPR has also been relied upon quite visibly by the legislature and executive. With its specific material scope of application, CAT has been paid attention to by both the legislature and executive, and its impact is most visible in the questions supervised by the Parliamentary Ombudsman, not least in its work as the NPM.

Although CERD, CESCR and CEDAW appear in the work of the legislature and executive, their impact appears limited. The impact of CERD and CESCR is affected by the fact that in the past 20 years the main motivations for the specific legislative developments in the areas covered by the treaties have come from the CoE and the EU. While CEDAW had some important impact on legislation at the time of its ratification, including the enactment of the Equality Act and the establishment of the Ombudsman for Equality, in the past 20 years CEDAW has been at the margins and mainly used as an additional argument to the CoE and EU standards. Indicative of this marginalisation is the particular concern raised by both the CEDAW Cttee and the Parliament's Constitutional Law Committee about the invisibility of CEDAW. One of the reasons for CEDAW's marginalisation is the lack of national structures to promote its implementation. This task is not designated fully even to the Ombudsman for Equality.

The domestic implementation of human rights binding on Finland has been nationally assessed in and guided by various *human rights policy documents* prepared by state administration since 1998. The latest Human Rights

---

Prompting? (Intersentia 2014); Krommendijk (n 16) 489–512; J Krommendijk, 'Finnish Exceptionalism at Play? The Effectiveness of the Recommendations of UN Human Rights Treaty Bodies in Finland' (2014) 32 Nordic Journal of Human Rights 18–43; K Luhamaa, *Universal Human Rights in National Contexts: Application of International Rights of the Child in Estonia, Finland and Russia* (University of Tartu Press 2015) (PhD thesis).

30   Both were incorporated by a presidential decree instead of an Act of Parliament.

IMPACT OF UNHR TREATIES ON DOMESTIC LEVEL IN FINLAND 497

Report by the government was submitted to Parliament in 2014. This report contains very general notes on the UN human rights treaties. The objective of the National Action Plan on Fundamental and Human Rights is to promote the obligation of the public authority to guarantee the observance of basic rights and liberties and human rights as stipulated in section 22 of the Constitution.[31] The first Action Plan was adopted for 2012–2013 and the second Action Plan for 2017–2019. The latter notes the recommendations of the international treaty-monitoring bodies to Finland, including those of the UN treaty bodies urging Finland to increase general awareness of human rights treaties, Finland's periodic reports and recommendations concerning Finland among the authorities, NGOs and the general public.[32] The third National Action Plan has been scheduled for 2020–2023. There are also a number of policy documents addressing specific issues.

4.2.2 Reliance by Judiciary

The judgments of the highest courts are important due to their precedent-setting value and reliance on them in domestic legal processes which also renders the visibility of the international human rights treaties therein important. In the past 20 years the number of references to the UN treaties in the highest courts has increased significantly, suggesting that legal counsel particularly is increasingly relying on these treaties and the work of the treaty bodies in court proceedings. Of the UN treaties CCPR was most often cited, while CRC has also received attention. The references to CERD or the CERD Cttee have visibly appeared, particularly in the cases of the Supreme Administrative Court since 2011. Cases including references to CCPR and CERD often concern the rights of the Sami. However, while these treaties and the work of the treaty bodies are noted in the proceedings, the courts have not necessarily followed the views of the bodies.

Previously, CESCR was invisible in the judgments of the highest courts, but in the past 20 years there have been cases including references to it or the work of the CESCR Cttee. CAT or the CAT Cttee has appeared only a few times in the judgments of the Supreme Administrative Court. By contrast, the most recently-ratified treaty, CRPD, has since 2016 been considered already in at least eight cases. It is particularly striking that the only time the highest court

---

31 See <https://www.humanrightscentre.fi/human-rights/fundamental-and-human-rights-in-/national-action-plan-on-fundamental/> accessed 13 April 2022.
32 National Action Plan 35. References are made to the recommendations of the HRCttee, CESCR Cttee, CERD Cttee, CAT Cttee, CEDAW Cttee and CRC Cttee.

has explicitly referred to CEDAW was in a Supreme Administrative Court case in 2005.

4.2.3 Impact on and through Independent State Institutions and Non-state Actors

The UN treaties are visible in the work of the NHRI. The NHRI – mainly the Human Rights Centre – participates in the international treaty-monitoring processes of all treaties and raises problems of non-implementation therein. It organises seminars and events to discuss, inform and educate about the COs of most treaties. It also disseminates information and training materials on its website and in social media. Of the UN treaties CAT, CRC and CRPD have also acquired special attention from the Parliamentary Ombudsman due to the special tasks designated to it with respect to these treaties (OP-CAT and CRC alone and CRPD collectively as the NHRI).

The visibility of the UN human rights treaties in court proceedings to a large extent depends on lawyers' arguments before the courts. Thus, lawyers' level of awareness of the treaties and the work of the treaty bodies is crucial. Generally, the know-how of lawyers about the UN treaties is limited. Lawyers rely more easily on the treaties with case law concerning Finland. Therefore, the lack of Finland-specific case law may explain the low number of references to UN treaties.

Civil society actors, including NGOs, actively use the UN treaties, including the treaty bodies' COs, and increasingly also participate in the treaty-monitoring processes by submitting their own reports. Of the UN treaties CRC has attracted the most attention among researchers and academics. In the rapidly-developing area of corporate responsibility and business and human rights, particularly CCPR, CESCR and CRC, and to some extent also CRPD, have come to the fore.

4.2.4 Impact of State Reporting

The lack of a systematic follow-up mechanism for the UN treaty bodies' COs diminishes their impact in the state administration and beyond, on a local level. The recurrence of the same issues in the COs signals a lack of impact. Often the reasons for the lack of progress are related to the funding of measures but also to the lack of political will. For instance, in the case of CEDAW the problem of violence against women has persistently been on the agenda in the reporting process concerning Finland, but only the entry into force of the CoE Convention on Preventing and Combating Violence against Women and Domestic Violence (Istanbul Convention) and the EU Fundamental Rights Agency's survey results on violence against women triggered the necessary action. While improvements have taken place, the continuous existence of the problem suggests an inadequacy of effective measures. On the positive side is the establishment of the Ombudsman for Children, in line with the CRC Cttee's recommendation in its COs. The COs often impact through the work of the NHRI and the NGOs.

4.2.5 Impact of Individual Communications

The individual communication procedure under CCPR has been used most often. It was relied upon particularly prior to 1999. The ratification of the ECHR with similar substantial coverage and the detailed judgments by the ECtHR caused a shift. However, the long processing times and the more stringent admissibility criteria taken by the ECtHR in the past years have raised some new interest towards CCPR. The cases in the HRCttee against Finland in recent years have concerned particularly the rights of the Sami. CCPR, with its provisions on self-determination (article 1) and minority rights (article 27), has provided a better channel for these concerns than the ECHR.

Since 2002 (and by 30 June 2019) the CAT Cttee has found violations of CAT by Finland in four cases concerning the deportation or expulsion of non-nationals. In 2018 the CEDAW Cttee found violations of the Convention in the first individual communication filed against Finland. No views on the violations of the Convention in individual cases have been given in respect of Finland under CRC or CESCR. There are communications against Finland pending before several UN treaty bodies.

In the event of individual communications against Finland, the relevant ministries have the responsibility to provide information for the submissions of the Finnish government, presented eventually to the treaty bodies by the Ministry for Foreign Affairs. At times there has been some reluctance or delay in implementing the specific recommendations put forth by the UN bodies. This is visible, for instance, in the cases related to the rights of the Sami or the non-implementation of the recommendations of the CEDAW Cttee in the first case concerning Finland. Non-state actors clearly rely on the cases concerning Finland. For instance, the first case considered by the CEDAW Cttee has been used by lawyers before national courts as well as by NGOs in their work.

4.2.6 Additional

Although all recommendations and many of the General Comments issued by the UN treaty bodies have been translated into the national languages, they receive only marginal attention in Finland. They are often viewed as legally irrelevant and being too general, and sometimes their quality has been challenged. However, the NHRI, the ombudsman institutions and NGOs have found these useful in their monitoring activities and promotional work. The first references to the CRC Cttee's General Comment in the highest courts in recent years deserve particular note. The Universal Declaration of Human Rights is occasionally mentioned in law reforms. For instance, when the Non-Discrimination Act was modified in 2014 the government Bill referred to the Declaration and its non-discrimination provision (article 2).[33]

5   Detailed Impact of the Different UN Human Rights Treaties on the Domestic Level in Finland

5.1   *International Convention of the Elimination of All Forms of Racial Discrimination*

5.1.1   Incorporation and Reliance by Legislature and Executive

Finland ratified CERD in 1970. The treaty was incorporated into domestic law with the hierarchical status of a presidential decree, that is, with a decree inferior to the Acts of Parliament and formally of a lower rank in the domestic hierarchy of norms.[34] The ratification of CERD resulted in amendments to the Penal Code in order to criminalise 'incitement to racial hatred' and discrimination in services offered to the public, in organising public meetings and in all activities of public authorities. Although the government saw no obstacles to recognising the competence of the CERD Cttee to consider individual communications, the declaration under article 14 was made only in 1994. Among the reasons given for this is that Finland waited for other states to first make the declaration.[35]

Regarding the visibility of CERD in the work of the legislature and the executive, in the period from 2000 to 30 June 2019 CERD or the CERD Cttee was referred to at least in 28 government Bills considered by Parliament. In that period, references to CERD or the CERD Cttee were inserted at least in 13 documents of the parliamentary committees.[36]

---

33   Government Bill 19/2014, 22. Note also references to the reform of the Act below.
34   As noted above, this nowadays is an exception.
35   S Hyttinen and M Scheinin, 'Finland' in C Heyns and F Viljoen (eds), *The Impact of the United Nations Human Rights Treaties on the Domestic Level* (Martinus Nijhoff Publishers 2002) 276.
36   The information collected by the Information Service of the Library of Parliament for the study at hand. Due to the differences, eg in reference techniques followed over the years, the numbers presented in this study should not be taken as exhaustive and reflecting the exact number of documents but rather indicative of the general situation. While the information on government Bills may be considered pointing more or less towards the right number, the references to other documents only suggest that some hits were found. The Finnish Parliament has 16 permanent special committees and the Grand Committee, which focuses mainly on EU affairs. The special committees prepare government Bills,

CERD's impact on legislation was imminent and discernible at the time of its ratification. Although CERD and the CERD Cttee have been referred to in the context of the later law reforms, it is difficult to distill their impact on laws. While CERD and the CERD Cttee have sometimes been noted, the attention of the legislature and executive on the issues covered by CERD has been geared towards the state obligations deriving from the CoE and the EU. For instance, while CERD was mentioned in the context of the reform of the Penal Code at the turn of the 2010s, it was merely stated that CERD was the basis of the amendments to the Penal Code 1970 and CERD is a treaty that defines racial discrimination.[37] Furthermore, CERD was mentioned when amendments were made to the Non-Discrimination Act in 2014. The Act was initially enacted in 2004 to implement two EC directives,[38] and in the 2014 reform more attention was drawn to various human rights obligations binding on Finland. In the government Bill, CERD is mentioned in passing and the CERD Cttee's COs concerning Finland in 2012 were noted among the reasons to expand the material scope of the Act.[39]

The government's Human Rights Report of 2014 makes only very general references to CERD and the CERD Cttee.[40] The National Action Plan on Fundamental and Human Rights 2017–2019 notes CERD and the CERD Cttee's recommendations in several contexts, including in the remarks on increasing general awareness of human rights treaties, discrimination experienced by various groups, ethnic profiling, promoting equality and tolerance, the rights of the Sami, and hate speech.[41] In the course of the years the Finnish government has also adopted other policy documents addressing more specific issues relating to the questions covered by CERD. These include policy documents on combating hate speech, ethnic discrimination and racism, asylum policy, migration strategy, the Roma, and the integration of immigrants.

---

legislative initiatives, government reports and other matters for handling in Parliament's plenary session. While one committee is responsible for doing this type of preparatory work and to give its report (*valiokuntamietintö*) some other committees may be asked to give their statements (*valiokuntalausunto*) on the issues at hand. See <https://www.eduskunta.fi/EN/valiokunnat/Pages/default.aspx> accessed 13 April 2022.

[37] Government Bill 317/2010, 5, 7 and 35.
[38] EC Directive 2000/43/EC of 29 June 2000 and EC Directive 2000/78/EC of 27 November 2000.
[39] Government Bill 19/2014, 6, 22 and 29.
[40] Government Human Rights Report 2014, 15, 59 and 91.
[41] National Action Plan, 38, 46, 50, 53, 59, 60, 64, 74, 97 and 106.

5.1.2 Reliance by Judiciary

Prior to 1999 the judgments of the highest courts (the Supreme Court and the Supreme Administrative Court) included no references to CERD or the CERD Cttee.[42] From 2000 to 30 June 2019 at least 12 references were found. One of these is the judgment of the Supreme Court in 2012 in which the issues were freedom of expression and incitement to religious hatred. The other cases are from the Supreme Administrative Court, all decided since 2011, concerning discrimination and harassment of the Roma, environmental permits for machine gold prospecting in Lapland (the northernmost area in Finland), and predominantly questions concerning the rights of the Sami.[43]

The CERD Cttee's recommendations have been visibly discussed by the Supreme Administrative Court when it considered the definition of the Sami and made decisions on the eligibility of individuals in the elections of the Sami Parliament. In its COs on Finland's periodic reports, the CERD Cttee considered both the self-identification of individuals and the self-determination of the Sami people as a defining factor. While the CERD Cttee earlier stressed self-identification,[44] later it put more emphasis on self-determination.[45] The Supreme Administrative Court that has the ultimate say in Finland on the access to the electoral lists of the Sami Parliament has made a note of the earlier views of the CERD Cttee but has not followed the newer recommendation stressing self-determination. In these cases the views of the HRCttee under CCPR were also considered (see part 5.2).

5.1.3 Impact on and through Independent State Institutions and Non-state Actors

The NHRI participated in the monitoring process of CERD by submitting its views on the implementation of CERD in Finland in 2014 and 2017. In its latest submission the NHRI, for instance, raised the issues of the need to improve and

---

42 Hyttinen and Scheinin (n 35) 277.
43 The court cases were collected by the Information Service of the Library of Parliament by relying on the databases Edilex and Finlex. Due to the differences, eg in reference techiques followed over the years, the number of cases presented here does not necessarily cover all cases of relevance for the topic at hand. Since the treaties and bodies have not been referred to in a systematic manner in the case law, the lists are not exhaustive but rather indicative. Furthermore, no study of the individual cases has been carried out in order to assess how the treaty or treaty body's comment or recommendation has concretely affected the judgment.
44 CERD Cttee, Concluding Observations on the 17th-19th periodic reports of Finland, paras 13–14.
45 CERD Cttee, Concluding Obervations on the 23rd periodic report of Finland, paras 14–15.

clarify human rights structures in Finland, the prevalence of hate speech, the rights of the Sami (the definition of the Sami, their languages and culture, participation and self-determination), the rights and protection of asylum seekers, and the need for improved human rights education.[46] Many of these issues have been reoccurring in the daily work and events organised by the NHRI.

While some lawyers rely on CERD and the views of the CERD Cttee in their work, the understanding about the treaty is rather narrow among legal professionals. Some NGOs use CERD in their work on related issues and continue to remind the government about its obligations under it. The interest of NGOs is also reflected in their willingness to submit their observations on the implementation of CERD in Finland to the CERD Cttee.[47] CERD and the work of the CERD Cttee neither come to the fore in the work of researchers and academics nor in the activities of business actors.

5.1.4 Impact of State Reporting

Finland has submitted 23 periodic state reports to the CERD Cttee, some considered simultaneously by the Committee. In the period between 2000 and 2019, Finland submitted reports in 2001, 2007, 2011 and 2015. The 24th report was due in 2021. The CERD Cttee gave its COs on the 23rd periodic report in 2017. Its concerns and recommendations relate to many issues that have persisted for a long time. In the past 20 years the CERD Cttee has constantly expressed its concern, for instance, about the situation of the Roma, the Sami (especially the definition of Sami and the land rights) and asylum seekers as well as the existence of racist and xenophobic attitudes and the lack of statistics.[48] It is difficult to crystallise the very impact of CERD or the views of the CERD Cttee on positive developments.[49] At least CERD and the CERD Cttee's views have put some pressure to underline the importance of paying attention to issues such as hate speech and the rights of the Sami.

5.1.5 Impact of Individual Communications

No individual communications concerning Finland have yet been considered by the CERD Cttee.[50]

---

46 HRC/NHRI's submissions to the CERD Cttee in 2017.
47 See State reporting and CERD: <https://tbinternet.ohchr.org/_layouts/15/TreatyBodyExternal/Countries.aspx?CountryCode=FIN&Lang=EN> accessed 13 April 2022.
48 See the CERD Cttee, Concluding Observations on the 15th to 23rd periodic reports of Finland.
49 See eg the positive aspects raised by the CERD Cttee, Concluding Observations on the 23rd periodic report of Finland, paras 3–5.
50 By December 2019, one communication was pending.

5.1.6 Other Forms of Impact of the Treaty and the Treaty Body

CERD and the work of the CERD Cttee receive attention, for instance, in the work of the Parliamentary Ombudsman, the Non-Discrimination Ombudsman and the Ombudsman for Equality.[51] This attention for its part keeps CERD on the domestic human rights agenda.

The National Non-Discrimination and Equality Tribunal,[52] a judicial body deciding cases of discrimination and supervising compliance with the Non-Discrimination Act, closely follows the work of the CERD Cttee and draws on CERD and the CERD Cttee's opinions in its own interpretations when dealing with cases of discrimination.

5.1.7 Brief Conclusion

CERD had the clearest impact on national legislation at the time of its ratification, when some amendments were made to the Penal Code. In the past 20 years the main motivations for the specific legislative amendments concerning the issues covered by CERD have come from the CoE and the EU. CERD and the CERD Cttee have been noted in policy documents. While the visibility of CERD and the CERD Cttee has diminished over the years in the work of the legislature, the CERD Cttee's recommendations have been on the agenda of the highest courts in a few cases, especially in the Supreme Administrative Court since 2011 when it considered the cases concerning the rights of the Sami. However, the Court has not followed the more recent views of the CERD Cttee put forth in its COs.

5.2 *International Covenant on Civil and Political Rights*

5.2.1 Incorporation and Reliance by Legislature and Executive

Finland ratified CCPR in 1975 and the treaty became effective with respect to Finland in 1976. The compatibility assessment carried out at the time resulted in Finland entering seven reservations to CCPR.[53] Subsequently, some of these initial reservations have been lifted after amendments to national laws.[54] The reservations to articles 10(2)(b) and (3), 14(7) and 20(1), however, remain in

---

[51] The references are inserted eg in these actors' annual reports to Parliament. The information collected by the Information Service of the Library of Parliament for the study at hand.
[52] National Non-Discrimination and Equality Tribunal <https://www.yvtltk.fi/en/index.html> accessed 13 April 2022.
[53] Hyttinen and Scheinin (n 35) 272.
[54] The reservations concerned art 9(3), art 13, art 14(1) and (3).

place.[55] Finland ratified OP1-CCPR in 1976 and OP2-CCPR on abolishing the death penalty in 1991. CCPR and its optional protocols were incorporated into domestic law through Acts of Parliament.

The explanatory part of the government Bill to modify the fundamental rights catalogue of the Constitution in the mid 1990s includes a number of references to CCPR.[56] Regarding the visibility of CCPR in the work of the legislature, in the period from 2000 to 30 June 2019, CCPR, its optional protocols and the HRCttee were referred to at least in 108 government Bills considered by Parliament. In that period, the references to them may be found in at least 19 documents of the parliamentary committees.[57] CCPR has also appeared in some written questions by parliamentarians and the pertinent ministers' answers to these questions and legislative motions initiated by parliamentarians, particularly in recent years.[58]

The government's Human Rights Report of 2014 makes only very general references to CCPR.[59] The National Action Plan on Fundamental and Human Rights 2017–2019 notes CCPR or the HRCttee's recommendations in several contexts, including in the text on increasing general awareness of human rights treaties, trafficking in human beings, the rights of the Sami, equality, hate speech, self-determination, violence against women, sexual violence, physical integrity and personal freedom.[60]

5.2.2 Reliance by Judiciary

Prior to 1999 references to CCPR could be found in 32 cases of the highest courts.[61] From 2000 to 30 June 2019 references to CCPR or the HRCttee could be found at least in 95 cases, of which more that a half were decided by the Supreme Court. The cases before the Supreme Court concerned, for instance, the questions of equality and discrimination and freedom of religion and

---

[55] Arts 10(2)(b) and (3) concern absolute separation of juvenile offenders from adult inmates; art 14(7) concerns changing a sentence to the detriment of the convicted person; and art 20(1) concerns the prohibition of propaganda for war.

[56] Government Bill 309/1993.

[57] See the remarks on parliamentary committees and the information collected in n 36 supra.

[58] The information collected by the Information Service of the Library of Parliament for the study at hand. Legislative motions by parliamentarians concern the enactment of new legislation or the amendment or repeal of existing legislation. They are considered by Parliament in the same order as government Bills; <https://www.eduskunta.fi/EN/kansanedustajat/Pages/default.aspx> accessed 13 April 2022.

[59] Government Human Rights Report 2014, 15, 59 and 91.

[60] National Action Plan, 38, 46, 50, 53, 70, 73, 74, 82, 83 and 84.

[61] Hyttinen and Scheinin (n 35) 278.

conscience, discrimination and privacy in the work life, freedom of speech and defamation, incitement to religious hatred, *ne bis in idem*, and the right to family life and restraining orders. The number of judgments referring to CCPR or HRCttee has clearly increased since 2010.[62]

Regarding the cases before the Supreme Administrative Court, the judgments concerning the rights of the Sami clearly stand out. For instance, the issue of the definition of Sami has recurred in matters before the Court. Additionally, the use of land for mining and gold prospecting in Lapland and in the Sami homeland has caused disputes regarding the implementation of the rights of the Sami. Another theme often considered by the Court and in which CCPR or the HRCttee's views are also raised is that concerning asylum seekers and international protection as well as foreigners and residence permits. Other cases include, for instance, portraying the Roma on television and freedom of speech, the teaching of religion and ethics in school, and freedom of assembly.

It often is difficult to distill the very impact of CCPR or the HRCttee on the judgments of the highest courts due to the practice of the courts to refer in the same judgments also to other human rights treaties binding on Finland and constitutional rights. Among the most visible cases in which CCPR and the views of the HRCttee have been discussed in more detail concern the rights of the Sami and the judgments by the Supreme Administrative Court on the definition of the Sami and the elections of the Sami Parliament. In these cases, the Court has also often considered the views of the CERD Cttee.[63] The Supreme Administrative Court has contested the views of the HRCttee on the question of the definition underlining the self-determination of the Sami[64] and followed the earlier CERD Cttee's views on the matter.

In its latest COs (issued in 2013) the HRCttee raised its concerns about the insufficient invocation and use of CCPR in cases before national courts, and recommended that Finland take appropriate measures to raise awareness of CCPR among judges, lawyers and prosecutors in order to ensure that its provisions are taken into account before national courts.[65]

---

[62] The court cases were collected by the Information Service of the Library of Parliament; see also n 43 supra.
[63] The HRCttee has addressed the issue both in its COs on state reports and in the views adopted in the cases concerning Finland.
[64] The most recent judgments were given after the time period covered by this study.
[65] HRCttee, Concluding Observations on the sixth periodic report of Finland, para 5.

5.2.3 Impact on and through Independent State Institutions and Non-state Actors

The NHRI participates in the treaty-monitoring processes of CCPR. In 2018 the NHRI submitted its latest views for the preparation of the List of Issues Prior to Reporting (LOIPR) by Finland before the HRCttee. The NHRI, for instance, raised the issues of the fragmented national human rights structures and the decreasing support for the NGOs due to cuts in government funding, also the insufficient knowledge and implementation of human rights standards, the lack of resources for human rights work and the non-existence of over-arching human rights impact assessment, including the compound effects of legislative changes to access to rights. The substantive issues raised included the polarised and populist climate against human rights; the invisibility and discrimination of minorities; access to justice by persons with disabilities and asylum seekers; the rights of the Sami; the treatment of the elderly in care homes; and participation of all in society.[66] The NHRI has also organised events, training and made statements on many of these themes.

Some lawyers use CCPR and the HRCttee's case law in their legal argumentation, and most references to CCPR or the views of the HRCttee in the judgments are the outcomes of these arguments. The submission of statements and reports by various civil society actors (including NGOs) for the treaty-monitoring processes of CCPR signals these actors' interest towards CCPR.[67] CCPR and the HRCttee also to some extent appear in the work of researchers and academics working, for instance, on issues concerning the Sami. Regarding business actors, the rights stipulated in CCPR have become relevant for corporate responsibility through the 2011 UN Guiding Principles on Business and Human Rights which Finnish companies are increasingly using as a tool to implement the expectation to respect human rights in business activities.

5.2.4 Impact of State Reporting

Finland has submitted six periodic reports to the HRCttee, two of them in the past 20 years (in 2003 and 2011). The LOIPR for the seventh periodic report of Finland was issued in 2019.[68] Many concerns raised by the Committee with respect to Finland's sixth report[69] also appear on the LOIPR. These include

---

66   HRC/NHRI's submissions to the HRCttee in 2018.
67   See <https://tbinternet.ohchr.org/_layouts/15/TreatyBodyExternal/Countries.aspx?CountryCode=FIN&Lang=EN> accessed 13 April 2022.
68   HRCttee, List of issues prior to submission of the seventh periodic report of Finland. The seventh state report was submitted in April 2020.
69   HRCttee, COs on the sixth periodic report of Finland.

non-discrimination; gender equality; violence against women; the treatment of aliens; freedom of conscience and treatment of conscientious objectors; freedom of expression; and rights of indigenous peoples. It is difficult to distill the specific impact of the HRCttee's COs at the domestic level, since similar issues are raised also in other monitoring processes. The very fact that the rights of the Sami have been actively and systematically considered in the reporting processes of CCPR has helped to keep the rights of the Sami on the government's agenda, thus having had some impact on national policies.

5.2.5   Impact of Individual Communications

Prior to 1999 the individual complaints procedure of CCPR was used relatively often. A total of 27 cases were submitted to the HRCttee, and the violations found resulted in some legislative changes.[70] In the past 20 years the procedure has been used much more infrequently. From 2000 to 30 June 2019 the HRCttee gave its views with respect to Finland in only five cases, and found Finland in violation in three cases. These cases concerned the rights of the Sami.[71] In the two most recent cases addressing the eligibility in the elections of the Sami Parliament,[72] the HRCttee found violations of CCPR since the Supreme Administrative Court did not give due weight to the self-determination of the Sami. As a remedy the HRCttee recommended that Finland review its legislation, particularly the Sami Parliament Act. The State party is also under an obligation to take all steps to prevent similar violations in the future. The preparations for the review of the Sami Parliament Act started by the Ministry of Justice at the end of 2019 and the government Bill was expected to be submitted to Parliament in mid-2021. The HRCttee's views on the need to review the Act are given as one of the reasons and basis for the amendments.

5.2.6   Other Forms of Impact of the Treaty and Treaty Bodies

CCPR and the work of the HRCttee have been given attention, for instance, in the work of the Parliamentary Ombudsman, the Chancellor of Justice, the Non-Discrimination Ombudsman and the Ombudsman for Children.[73] This work for its part keeps CCPR on the domestic human rights agenda.

---

70   Hyttinen and Scheinin (n 35) 289.
71   A limited violation of fiar trial rights was found in *Mrs. Anni Äärelä and Mr. Jouni Näkkäläjärvi v Finland* UN Doc CCPR/C/73/D/779/1997 (24 October 2001).
72   *Tiina Sanila-Aikio v Finland*, UN Doc CCPR/C/124/D/2668/2015 (1 November 2018); *Klemetti Käkkäläjärvi et al v Finland* UN Doc CCPR/C/124/D/2950/2017 (2 November 2018).
73   The references are inserted eg in these actors' annual reports to Parliament. The information collected by the Information Service of the Library of Parliament for the study at hand.

5.2.7 Brief Conclusion

There are a number of questions in which the implementation of CCPR falls short in Finland.[74] In the past 20 years the use of CCPR has been visible in the legislature, executive and the courts of law. CCPR and the HRCttee appear also in policy documents. There has been a noticeable decline in the number of individual complaints against Finland under CCPR, undoubtedly as a result of a more active use of the ECHR in similar subject matters. In the past years the complaints procedure of CCPR has been most visibly applied in the cases concerning the rights of the Sami. This is because CCPR, with its provisions on self-determination and minority rights, remains the only international human rights provision binding on Finland that provides added value for the rights of indigenous peoples. This situation will undoubtedly persist as long as Finland has not ratified ILO Convention 169 on Indigenous and Tribal People. The CCPR has acquired some attention among non-state actors, including lawyers, as is reflected in the increase of the visibility of the treaty in domestic court proceedings.

5.3 *International Covenant on Economic, Social and Cultural Rights*

5.3.1 Incorporation and Reliance by Legislature and Executive

The ratification of CESCR took place in Finland at the same time as that of CCPR, in 1975, and also took effect in 1976. A superficial compatibility analysis of CESCR was undertaken at the time of ratification. The government wanted to see CESCR as a 'programmatic' treaty rather than a treaty with effective and justiciable provisions. The 'programmatic' nature of CESCR was the reason for its incorporation into domestic law through a presidential decree inferior to parliamentary laws, unlike CCPR. In 2014 Finland accepted the complaints procedure of CESCR by ratifying OP-CESCR. Finland has also accepted the inquiry procedure under article 11 of OP-CESCR.

Regarding the visibility of CESCR in the work of legislature and executive, in the period from 2000 to 30 June 2019 CESCR or the CESCR Cttee was referred to at least in 50 government Bills considered by Parliament. In that period, the references to these may be found at least in three documents of the parliamentary committees. CESCR has also appeared in some written questions by parliamentarians and the pertinent ministers' answers to these questions and

---

[74] For the NHRI's statements, see the HRC's annual reports <https://www.humanrightscentre.fi/publications/action-plans-and-annual-reports/> accessed 13 April 2022. For the NHRI's submissions to the HRCttee, see <https://tbinternet.ohchr.org/_layouts/15/TreatyBodyExternal/Countries.aspx?CountryCode=FIN&Lang=EN> accessed 13 April 2022.

legislative motions initiated by parliamentarians. For instance, in 2018 CESCR appeared in at least one written question and one legislative motion.[75]

The government's Human Rights Report of 2014 makes general references to CECSR, for instance, by reminding of the legal bindingness of economic, social and cultural rights.[76] The National Action Plan on Fundamental and Human Rights 2017–2019 notes CESCR and the CESCR Cttee's recommendations, for instance, in the texts on increasing general awareness of human rights treaties, the rights of the Sami, equality and self-determination, violence against women and sexual violence.[77]

5.3.2 Reliance by Judiciary

Prior to 1999 no judgments of the highest courts could be found with references to CESCR.[78] From 2000 to 30 June 2019, the highest courts have referred to CESCR or the CESCR Cttee at least in seven cases. Four of these seven cases are judgments of the Supreme Court given since 2013, and they concern work life, including contracts, collective agreements, discrimination, striking and freedom of association. The three judgments decided by the Supreme Administrative Court were handed down between 2003 and 2014, and concern the rights of foreigners, residence permits and family reunification and basic social benefits for a convict.[79]

5.3.3 Impact on and through Independent State Institutions and Non-state Actors

The NHRI participates in the treaty-monitoring processes of CESCR. In 2018 the NHRI submitted its latest views for the preparation of LOIPR by Finland. The HRC raised the same structural issues as in the monitoring of CCPR. Substantive issues raised included discrimination in working life; sports; education and health care; inequalities due to digitalization; problems in the employment of persons with disabilities; the insufficient level of social security and social benefits; violence against women; child poverty; a lack of mental health services; the health care of undocumented migrants; the rights of

---

75 The information collected by the Information Service of the Library of Parliament for the study at hand. See also the remarks on parliamentary committees, parliamentarians' legislative motions and the information collected in notes 36 and 58.
76 Government Human Rights Report 2014, 15, 59, 78–79.
77 National Action Plan, 38, 46, 50, 70, 82 and 83.
78 Hyttinen and Scheinin (n 35) 277.
79 The court cases were collected by the Information Service of the Library of Parliament; see also n 43 supra.

persons caring for family members; sexual education; and the non-visibility of minorities and the Sami in education materials.[80] The NHRI has also organised events and training and made statements on many of these themes.

CESCR is not actively used by lawyers. However, in the past 20 years CESCR has become visible in the work of the highest courts, indicating that it has appeared in legal argumentation before courts. The willingness of a number of civil society actors to submit their views on the implementation of CESCR in Finland to the international supervisory bodies demonstrates their interest towards the treaty.[81] CESCR does not appear very clearly in the work of researchers and academics. Together with CCPR, CESCR has acquired some significance in the area of corporate responsibility through the 2011 UN Guiding Principles on Business and Human Rights on which business actors, including companies, are increasingly relying to demonstrate their respect for human rights.

5.3.4 Impact of State Reporting

Finland has submitted six periodic state reports to the CESCR Cttee, three of them between 1999 and 2011. LOIPR for the seventh periodic report of Finland was issued in April 2019.[82] Many concerns in the COs in 2013[83] also appear on the latest LOIPR. These include the issue of business and human rights; the rights of the Sami; inequalities between men and women in the labour market; and an adequate standard of living (including social benefits).[84] The actual impact of state reporting and recommendations included in the COs of the CESCR Cttee is difficult to assess, since similar issues are raised also in other monitoring processes, including that of the European Social Charter of the CoE.

5.3.5 Impact of Individual Communications

No individual communications concerning Finland have been considered by the CESCR Cttee.

---

80   HRC/NHRI submissions to the CESCR Cttee in 2018.
81   See <https://tbinternet.ohchr.org/_layouts/15/TreatyBodyExternal/Countries.aspx?CountryCode=FIN&Lang=EN> accessed 13 April 2022.
82   The seventh state report was submitted in April 2020.
83   CESCR Cttee, *Concluding Observations on the sixth periodic report of Finland* (accessed 13 April 2022).
84   CESCR Cttee, List of issues (LOIPR) prior to the submission of the seventh periodic report of Finland to the CESCR Cttee.

5.3.6 Other Forms of Impact of the Treaty and Treaty Bodies

CESCR and the work of the CESCR Cttee receive attention, for instance, in the work of the Parliamentary Ombudsman, the Non-Discrimination Ombudsman and the Ombudsman for Equality.[85] This work keeps CESCR on the domestic human rights agenda.

5.3.7 Brief Conclusion

Although CESCR has been noted in the work of the legislature and the executive, including in many government Bills and policy documents, its impact on the national legislation and practices is not easy to be specified. The binding nature of economic, social and cultural rights remains debated. In the area of these rights attention is also usually drawn to the instruments and work of the CoE and the EU rather than to those of the UN. However, the increased visibility of CESCR and the CESCR Cttee in the judgments of the highest courts in the past 20 years deserves to be noted. In addition, CESCR is visible in the work of non-state actors.

5.4 *Convention on the Elimination of All Forms of Discrimination against Women*

5.4.1 Incorporation and Reliance by Legislature and Executive

Finland ratified CEDAW in 1986. The compatibility assessment at the time of the ratification resulted in changes to the Child Custody and Right of Access Act, the Guardianship Act, the Nationality Act and the Surnames Act. The ratification resulted in the adoption of the first separate equality legislation in Finland: The Act on Equality between Women and Men (Equality Act) was enacted in 1986.[86] The Ombudsman for Equality was established to supervise the implementation of the Act. The incorporation of CEDAW with a broad material scope of application nevertheless was done with insufficient legal modifications.[87] Finland ratified OP-CEDAW in 2000.

Regarding the visibility of CEDAW in the work of the legislature and the executive, in the period from 2000 to 30 June 2019 CEDAW, OP-CEDAW or the CEDAW Cttee were referred to at least in 27 government Bills considered by

---

85 The references are inserted eg in these actors' annual reports to Parliament. The information collected by the Information Service of the Library of Parliament for the study at hand.

86 Hyttinen and Scheinin (n 35) 277.

87 K Nousiainen and M Pentikäinen, 'Rise and Fall of the CEDAW in Finland: Time to Reclaim its Impetus' in A Hellum and H Sinding Aasen (eds), *Women's Human Rights. CEDAW in International, Regional and National Law* (Cambridge University Press 2013).

Parliament. In that period, the references to these may be found in some documents of the parliamentary committees, in some written questions by parliamentarians and the pertinent ministers' answers to these questions as well as in legislative motions initiated by parliamentarians. For instance, in 2018 CEDAW clearly appeared at least in four written questions and in two legislative motions.[88] CEDAW and the CEDAW Cttee's views have been noted when the Equality Act has been modified in the course of the years, also in the context of the most recent reform in 2014 (taking effect in 2015).[89]

The government's Human Rights Report of 2014 makes general references to CEDAW, including in the text on hate speech against girls and women belonging to ethnic minorities.[90] The National Action Plan on Fundamental and Human Rights 2017–2019 notes CEDAW and the CEDAW Cttee's recommendations in several contexts, including in the references to the Parliament's Constitutional Law Committee's view on the importance of increasing awareness of CEDAW and of its interpretative practice in Finland. It is noted that according to the Constitutional Law Committee, CEDAW should be better reflected in the definition of future fundamental and human rights policy lines and CEDAW should be implemented more effectively. In addition, the Action Plan notes CEDAW and the CEDAW Cttee in the texts on increasing general awareness of human rights treaties, discrimination against various population groups, the promotion of equality, physical integrity and trafficking in human beings, gender minorities (transsexuals), violence against women, sexual violence and hate speech.[91]

Gender equality has been addressed in separate government Action Plans for Gender Equality, the latest running in 2016 to 2019. There have also been other policy documents focusing on more specific issues such as reducing violence against women (2010 to 2015) and preventing the circumcision of girls and women (2012 to 2016). Gender equality is said to be taken into account as a cross-cutting principle in measures of the selected priority areas.[92]

---

88 The information collected by the Information Service of the Library of Parliament for the study at hand. See also the remarks on parliamentary committees, parliamentarians' legislative motions and the information collected in notes 36 and 58 supra.
89 Government Bill 19/2014, 22 and 29.
90 Government Human Rights Report 2014, 15, 59 and 67.
91 National Action Plan 2017–2019, 22, 38, 53, 59, 60, 73, 74, 82, 83 and 106.
92 ibid, 22.

5.4.2   Reliance by Judiciary

There are no judgments by the highest courts referring to CEDAW prior to 1999.[93] From 2000 to 30 June 2019 there appears to be only one judgment of the Supreme Administrative Court clearly referring to CEDAW. This judgment, handed down in 2005, concerns non-nationals, residence permits and child marriage.[94]

5.4.3   Impact on and through Independent State Institutions and Non-state Actors

The NHRI participates in the treaty-monitoring processes of CEDAW. In 2014 the NHRI submitted its views for the examination of the seventh periodic report by Finland. In its submission the NHRI, among other things, referred to the problem of violence against women and trafficking of women in Finland; the lack of human rights education; discrimination against women in the field of employment; and highly-insufficient resources allocated for the national implementation and supervision of human rights.[95] The NHRI has paid particular attention to the problem of violence against women, taking into account the Istanbul Convention by organising events, training and making statements.

The lack of references to CEDAW in the highest courts suggests that CEDAW has not been actively resorted to by lawyers. Since lawyers tend to rely on international case law concerning Finland, the first case concluded by the CEDAW Cttee in 2018 is of significance. The activities by women's NGOs and an increasing number of submissions by various civil society actors for the treaty-monitoring processes of CEDAW signal an interest towards CEDAW.[96] While CEDAW and the work of the CEDAW Cttee receive some attention in the work of researchers and academics, they are not known among business actors.

5.4.4   Impact of State Reporting

Finland has submitted seven periodic state reports to the CEDAW Cttee, three of them between 1999 and 2011.[97] The eighth

---

93   Hyttinen and Scheinin (n 35) 278.
94   The court cases were collected by the Information Service of the Library of Parliament; see also n 43 supra.
95   HRC/NHRI's submissions to the CEDAW Cttee in 2014.
96   See <https://tbinternet.ohchr.org/_layouts/15/TreatyBodyExternal/Countries.aspx?CountryCode=FIN&Lang=EN> accessed 13 April 2022.
97   ibid.

report, which was due in 2018, was scheduled to be submitted in 2020.[98]

Many concerns raised in the CEDAW Cttee's COs on Finland's seventh report have persisted for a long time. These include the insufficient legal and institutional framework to ensure equality and non-discrimination; violence against women; employment and reconciliation of work and family life (including the pay gap); and the situation of particular groups of women (including immigrant, Roma, Sami and disabled women).[99] The CEDAW Cttee has expressed its particular concern about the invisibility of CEDAW, OP-CEDAW and the CEDAW Cttee's recommendations in the work of public actors, including that of Parliament and courts of law.[100]

The CEDAW Cttee's COs have been mentioned, for instance, when modifications have been introduced to the Equality Act in the course of the years. On the other hand, the fact that certain issues have persisted for a long time on the agenda of the CEDAW Cttee casts doubts over the actual impact of CEDAW regarding those matters.

5.4.5 Impact of Individual Communications

Finland has been found in violation in respect of one communication.[101] The communication was filed in 2016, and the CEDAW Cttee adopted its views on it in March 2018. The case concerns the custody of a child and violence against women. The CEDAW Cttee found violations of several provisions of CEDAW and recommended the reconsideration of the custody case in a court of law, the payment of compensation to the victim in the case, and far-reaching general measures.[102] As of July 2020 Finland has not implemented these recommendations. Some lawyers have relied on the findings of the case in domestic court proceedings concerning child custody and domestic violence. The impact of these references on court decisions, however, is not visible. In its submission to the CAT Cttee in 2019 the NHRI paid attention to the recommendations of the CEDAW Cttee and the first individual communication against Finland.[103] A second

---

98   The information from the Ministry for Foreign Affairs in June 2020.
99   CEDAW Cttee, List of issues and questions with regard to the fifth and sixth periodic reports of Finland.
100 CEDAW Cttee, Concluding Observations on the seventh periodic report of Finland, paras 7–9.
101 *JI v Finland* UN Doc CEDAW/C/69/D/109/2016 (5 March 2018).
102 Ibid, para 10 (eg, to 'conduct an exhaustive and impartial investigation to determine whether there were structural failures in the State party's system and practices that may cause victims of domestic violence to be deprived of protection').
103 HRC/NHRI's submissions to the CAT Cttee in 2019.

individual communication concerning the problem of violence against women was filed in December 2016.[104]

5.4.6 Other Forms of Impact of the Treaty and Treaty Bodies

CEDAW and the work of the CEDAW Cttee are given attention, for instance, in the work of the Parliamentary Ombudsman, the Chancellor of Justice, the Ombudsman on Equality, the Non-Discrimination Ombudsman and the Ombudsman for Children.[105] The Council for Gender Equality (*tasa-arvoasiain neuvottelukunta* (TANE)), a parliamentary council appointed by the government from nominations from the parliamentary parties, often uses CEDAW and CEDAW Cttee in its activities to promote gender equality. This work has a role to keep CEDAW on the domestic human rights agenda.

5.4.7 Brief Conclusion

Although the domestic implementation of CEDAW was effected with insufficient changes in the national legislation, at the time of its ratification CEDAW impacted national laws. The enactment of the Equality Act, which also resulted in the establishment of the Ombudsman for Equality, was the most important outcome. CEDAW and the work of the CEDAW Cttee are noted also in some subsequent legislative reforms as well as in policy documents. The very fact that a number of issues have persisted since the ratification of the treaty and are repeatedly raised in the monitoring process suggest that the impact of CEDAW at the national level leaves much to be desired. It is also notable that both the CEDAW Cttee and the Parliament's Constitutional Law Committee have expressed their particular concern over the invisibility of CEDAW at the national level in Finland. Explicit references to CEDAW in only one case of the Supreme Administrative Court over the course of the years is indicative of this invisibility.

Among the reasons for CEDAW's scant impact at the national level is the lack of national structures for the effective promotion of its implementation. For instance, the tasks of the Ombudsman for Equality do not include the promotion of the implementation of CEDAW comparable to the tasks of the Ombudsman for Children with respect to CRC. Additionally, the questions covered by CEDAW are viewed as belonging to the social rather than the legal

---

104 In March 2020 the CEDAW Cttee declared the communication inadmissible on the basis of non-exhaustion of domestic remedies.

105 The references are inserted eg in these actors' annual reports to Parliament. The information collected by the Information Service of the Library of Parliament for the study at hand.

sphere, which is reflected by the designation of the Ministry for Social Affairs and Health as the ministry with the central responsibilities with respect to the treaty. Generally, the implementation of CEDAW is effected by means of policy documents rather than legal tools.

5.5 Convention against Torture and Other Cruel, Inhuman or Degrading Treatment or Punishment

5.5.1 Incorporation and Reliance by Legislature and Executive

Finland ratified CAT in 1989, at the same time accepting the individual complaints procedure under article 22. The compatibility study carried out during the ratification process led to some changes in the Penal Code. The Aliens Act was found to be incompatible with article 3 of CAT, including the principle of non-refoulement, but the incompatibilities were only later removed. At present the Finnish Constitution Act prohibits the deportation of a non-national to a country where that. person might face the risk of torture.[106] Finland ratified the Optional Protocol to CAT (OP-CAT) in 2014. At the same time the Parliamentary Ombudsman was appointed as the National Preventive Mechanism (NPM), as required by OP-CAT.[107]

Regarding the visibility of CAT and OP-CAT in the work of the legislature and executive, in the period from 2000 to 30 June 2019 these treaties or the CAT Cttee were referred to at least in 21 government Bills considered by Parliament. In that period, some references to them may be found at least in five documents of the parliamentary committees, in one written question by a parliamentarian and the relevant minister's answers to the questions as well as in one legislative motion initiated by a parliamentarian.[108]

The government's Human Rights Report of 2014 makes general references to CAT.[109] The National Action Plan on Fundamental and Human Rights 2017–2019 notes CAT and the CAT Cttee's recommendations, for instance, in the texts on increasing general awareness of human rights treaties, physical integrity, violence against women, sexual violence, personal freedom and mental health patients.[110]

---

[106] Hyttinen and Scheinin (n 35) 271.
[107] See <https://www.oikeusasiamies.fi/en_GB/web/guest/opcat-the-national-preventive-mechanism> accessed 13 April 2022.
[108] The information collected by the Information Service of the Library of Parliament for the study at hand. See also the remarks on parliamentary committees, parliamentarians' legislative motions and the information collected in notes 36 and 58.
[109] Government Human Rights Report 2014, 15, 16 and 63.
[110] National Action Plan, 30, 38, 72, 73, 82, 83 and 84.

5.5.2 Reliance by Judiciary

There are no judgments of the highest courts expressly referring to CAT prior to 1999.[111] From 2000 to 30 June 2019, only three cases including references to CAT or the CAT Cttee were found, all of them judgments of the Supreme Administrative Court. The cases, dating from 2012 to 2017, concern non-nationals, international protection, asylum, non-refoulement and residence permits.[112]

5.5.3 Impact on and through Independent State Institutions and Non-state Actors

The NHRI participates in the treaty-monitoring processes of CAT. In 2019 the NHRI submitted its views for the preparation of the latest LOIPR by Finland. The NHRI reiterated the same structural problems as in its submission to the HRCttee and the CESCR Cttee in 2018 (see above). In addition, it raised the problems of violence against women and domestic violence; 'honour'-based crimes; trafficking in human beings; non-refoulement and access to justice; torture, cruel, inhuman or degrading treatment of various groups of people (including trans-people, older persons and children placed in substitute care homes); liberty; security and treatment of persons deprived of their liberty; the rights of the child; and sexual harassment and violence. As noted above, in its submission to the CAT Cttee the NHRI also raised the recommendations of the CEDAW Cttee and the first individual communication against Finland considered by the CEDAW Cttee.[113]

The Parliamentary Ombudsman has for decades been following CAT at the domestic level and used it, for example, to argue repeatedly for prison reform and improved hygienic conditions in prisons. The so-called 'chamber pots' in cells was a recurring issue for the CAT Cttee, which it followed through systematically with the Finnish government and one which has also been finally resolved. According to the Ombudsman, CAT – in combination with the CoE visits organised pursuant to the CoE Convention for the Prevention of Torture and Inhuman or Degrading Treatment or Punishment (ECPT) – led to many improvements also in detention conditions.[114] The designation of

---

111 The references to the non-refoulement rule of art 3 of CAT nevertheless was noted at least in a case concerning Russian aircraft hijackers in the Supreme Court. Hyttinen and Scheinin (n 35) 278.
112 The court cases were collected by the Information Service of the Library of Parliament; see also n 43 supra.
113 HRC/NHRI's submissions to the CAT Cttee in 2019.
114 The information received from the Parliamentary Ombudsman's Office, its OPCAT coordinator, Iisa Suhonen, by email in June and October 2020.

the Ombudsman as the NPM in 2014 has increased the visibility and impact of CAT through increased attention given to the OP-CAT function and its more frequent inspection visits to the closed institutions. The NPM function that is often carried out in cooperation with persons with special expertise on the issues at hand has developed the supervisory work of the Ombudsman. The Ombudsman's recommendations have had impacts in several areas, for instance in that of child welfare. The recommendations have resulted in legislative amendments to require the child welfare institutions to issue a plan on better treatment of children, including the hearing of children in preparation of these plans. All closed institutions to which the Parliamentary Ombudsman has paid visits have improved the conditions in which individuals are held.[115] The Finnish NPM has also been actively participating in international cooperation of NPMs and in the treaty monitoring by issuing statements to the CAT Sub-Cttee and privately discussing matters with this Committee during the examination of the report.

In general, CAT and the work of the CAT Cttee are not well known among lawyers, with the clearest exception of a few lawyers working with asylum issues and the rights of aliens. For instance, the lawyers of the Finnish Refugee Advice Centre rely on CAT and the findings of the CAT Cttee in their advocacy work and in domestic legal prodeedings concerning the deportation or expulsion of non-nationals. Some cases have been considered in the Supreme Administrative Court. Some civil society actors have submitted their statements to the CAT Cttee in the context of treaty-monitoring processes.[116] CAT and the CAT Cttee do not receive much attention in the work of researchers and academics, and they are not visible in activities of business actors.

5.5.4 Impact of State Reporting

Finland has submitted seven periodic state reports to the CAT Cttee, some of which were considered simultaneously (as combined reports). Three reports were considered between 2000 and 30 June 2019.[117] In its COs on the seventh report the CAT Cttee lists a number of concerns and recommendations.[118] Many of these were also earlier on the list of issues, including the separation

---

[115] See Summary of the Annual Report 2018 of the NPM. Information was also received from the Ombudsman's office in June 2020.
[116] See <https://tbinternet.ohchr.org/_layouts/15/TreatyBodyExternal/Countries.aspx?CountryCode=FIN&Lang=EN> accessed 13 April 2022.
[117] The due date for Finland's eighth report is December 2020.
[118] CAT Cttee, Concluding Observations on the seventh periodic report of Finland.

of juveniles from adults in detention; the situation of remand prisoners; the accelerated asylum procedures; and violence against women.[119]

Regarding the impact of state reporting, it is worth noting that the CAT Cttee's list of positive aspects included in the COs on the seventh report of Finland is rather long. This list includes a number of references, for instance, to legislative amendments and the adoption of national action plans, suggesting that CAT and the CAT Cttee's COs have had some impact on these developments. The CAT Cttee welcomes Finland's initiatives to revise its legislation in areas of relevance to CAT by referring, for instance, to the amendments to the Criminal Investigation Act, the Coercive Measures Act, the Police Act, the Prison Act, the Remand Imprisonment Act and the Aliens Act. Of the action plans the CAT Cttee notes, for instance, the National Action Plan to Reduce Violence against Women for the period 2010–2015 and the Action Plan for the Prevention of Circumcision of Girls and Women 2012–2016.[120]

5.5.5   Impact of Individual Communications

Prior to 1999 no communication concerning Finland was considered by the CAT Cttee.[121] From 2000 to 30 June 2019 the CAT Cttee considered six communications against Finland, all concerning the deportation or expulsion of non-nationals. The CAT Cttee found violations in four of these communications,[122] based on article 3 of CAT, including the principle of non-refoulement in relation to the deportation of a non-national to a country of their origin. Regarding the impact of the CAT Cttee's findings, it is difficult to discern any broader impact on national processes or structures, but impact is limited to the individual cases considered by the CAT Cttee. The Finnish authorities as a rule follow the CAT Cttee's findings in individual cases.

5.5.6   Impact of Other Measures

The Finnish NPM submits its annual report to CAT and the Subcommittee on Prevention of Torture (SPT). The NPM has regular dialogue with the SPT, but there has not yet been a visit to Finland by the SPT.

---

119 See eg the list of issues prior to the submission of the combined fifth and sixth periodic reports of Finland, CAT/C/FIN/Q/5-6.
120 CAT Cttee, Concluding Observations on the seventh periodic report of Finland, paras 3–5.
121 Hyttinen and Scheinin (n 35) 289.
122 *Mr X and Mr Z v Finland* UN Doc CAT/C/2/D/483/2001 & UN Doc CAT/C/52/D/485/2001 (12 May 2014) (Iran); *EKW v Finland* UN Doc CAT/C/54/D/490/2012 (4 May 2015) (DRC); *AP v Finland* UN Doc CAT/C/60/D/465/2100 (10 May 2017) (Russia).

5.5.7 Other Forms of Impact of the Treaty and Treaty Bodies

CAT, OP-CAT and the work of the CAT Cttee are given attention, for instance, in the work of the Parliamentary Ombudsman (within the NPM mandate and in the regular Ombudsman work), the Chancellor of Justice and the Non-Discrimination Ombudsman. OP-CAT has also been raised in the work of the Finnish CoE delegation in the CoE Parliamentary Assembly.[123]

5.5.8 Brief Conclusion

CAT with its specific material scope of application has impacted the situation at the domestic level. It has been given attention in legislative processes as well as in the work of the Parliamentary Ombudsman that functions as the NPM. As mentioned, CAT has been an important factor in improving the prison and detention conditions in Finland over time. The cases concerning the rights of foreigners and the right to asylum brought against Finland in the CAT Cttee suggest that in these matters the impact of CAT at the national level has been weaker, probably due to the strong influence of the EU in these subject matters.

5.6 *Convention on the Rights of the Child*

5.6.1 Incorporation and Reliance by Legislature and Executive

Finland ratified the CRC in 1991. The government Bill concerning ratification concentrates on describing the contents of CRC with minor comparative aspects. The Act on Religious Freedom was identified as being inconsistent with article 14 of the treaty. However, no changes were introduced to the domestic laws at the time of the ratification of CRC.[124] The Ombudsman for Children carried out the first comprehensive compatibility analysis between the Finnish legislation and CRC in 2018.[125] Finland ratified the first Optional Protocol to CRC (OP-CRC-SC) in 2002, the second (OP-CRC-AC) in 2012 and the third on the communications procedure (OP-CRC-CP) in 2016.

Regarding the visibility of CRC in the work of the legislature and executive, in the period from 2000 to 30 June 2019 CRC, its Optional Protocols and the CRC Cttee were referred to at least in 94 government Bills considered by Parliament. In that period, references to them may be found in at least 28 documents of the parliamentary committees, in more than 20 written questions by

---

123 The references are inserted eg in these actors' annual reports to Parliament. The information collected by the Information Service of the Library of Parliament for the study at hand.
124 Hyttinen and Scheinin (n 35) 272.
125 The analysis was carried out by lawyer Merike Helander and was included in the Ombudsman for Children's Report to Parliament 2018, 133–203.

parliamentarians and the ministers' answers to these questions and explicitly in two legislative motions initiated by parliamentarians.[126] While the visibility of CRC in the work of legislature has clearly increased in the past 10 to 20 years and the treaty having concretely impacted on national laws, the compatibility analysis of 2018 noted above points out that a number of implementation deficits remain in the Finnish legislation and practices.

The government's Human Rights Report of 2014 makes general references to CRC.[127] The National Action Plan on Fundamental and Human Rights 2017–2019 notes CRC and the CRC Cttee's recommendations in several contexts, including in the text on increasing general awareness of human rights treaties, discrimination, promoting equality, physical integrity (including violence), personal freedom and violence against women.[128]

5.6.2   Reliance by Judiciary

Prior to 1999 four judgments of the highest courts refer to CRC.[129] From 2000 to 30 June 2019 at least 16 cases make reference to CRC or the CRC Cttee. Of these seven cases were decided by the Supreme Court and nine by the Supreme Administrative Court. The cases in the Supreme Court concern the confirmation of paternity and equality; the use of violence; child custody and the child's right to be heard; the right to family life; and a restraining order. The cases in the Supreme Administrative Court concern non-nationals; international protection; asylum; residence permits; the best interests of the child; child pornography; the internet and freedom of speech; basic education and subsidised school travels; the teaching of religion and ethics in school; family life; and a restraining order. It is notable that the highest courts have recently started to refer to the CRC Cttee's General Comments.[130]

---

126   The information collected by the Information Service of the Library of Parliament for the study at hand. See also the remarks on parliamentary committees, parliamentarians' legislative motions and the information collected in notes 36 and 58 supra.
127   Government Human Rights Report 2014, 15 and 59 (including references to the optional protocols).
128   National Action Plan, 38, 53, 59, 60, 72, 73 and 82.
129   Hyttinen and Scheinin (n 35) 278.
130   See eg the case KHO 2017:81 (in Finnish) of the Supreme Administrative Court. The issue at hand concerned the hearing of a child in an asylum process and the Court referred to arts 3(11) and 12 of the CRC as well as the CRC Cttee's General Comment 14. The court cases were collected by the Information Service of the Library of Parliament; see also n 43 supra.

5.6.3 Impact on and through Independent State Institutions and Non-state Actors

CRC, its protocols and the work of the CRC Cttee are regularly referred to in the work of the Parliamentary Ombudsman (also part of the NHRI). The Parliamentary Ombudsman has special supervisory tasks with regard to the rights of the child.[131] This work has had an important impact on the rights of the child, especially in recent years with regard to children placed in substitute care or other institutions.[132] Additionally, the work of the Ombudsman for Children, established in 2004, has clearly positively impacted the rights of the child in Finland.

Several lawyers rely on CRC and the work of the CRC Cttee in their legal argumentation. This has increased the number of cases in the highest courts referring to the treaty or the CRC Cttee. There is also a very strong body of NGOs promoting and actively using CRC in their work and in the national discussions on children's rights. Attention has been drawn to CRC and the CRC Cttee in the work of researchers and academics. Due to the active work of organisations focusing on children's rights and their increased interest towards issues of corporate responsibility, CRC has acquired attention in the area of corporate responsibility. For instance, in the past years the Finnish Committee for the United Nations Children's Fund (UNICEF) has actively raised children's rights and CRC in its work. It has also sought concrete cooperation with business actors in business and human rights issues.

5.6.4 Impact of State Reporting

Finland has submitted six periodic state reports to the CRC Cttee, two of them between 2000 and 30 June 2019 (in 2003 and 2008). The government of Finland submitted its overdue combined fifth and sixth report in July 2019. Finland submitted its initial report under OP-CRC-SC in 2004 and the CRC Cttee gave its COs on Finland's report in 2005. The initial report under the OP-CRC-AC was due in 2014.[133]

---

[131] See <https://www.oikeusasiamies.fi/en/web/lasten-ja-nuorten-sivut/> accessed 13 April 2022.

[132] The Deputy Parliamentary Ombudsman referred to CRC in its recent decision concerning the organisation of school events (such as those before Christmas breaks) in places of religion (eg in churches). According to the decision, eg on the basis of art 14 of CRC, school events should not be organised in such places. Decision on complaint EOAK/2186/2018 (in Finnish, November 2019).

[133] The report was finally submitted in June 2020.

The CRC Cttee lists a number of concerns and recommendations in its COs on Finland's fourth state report.[134] The CRC Cttee also lists a number of positive developments,[135] suggesting that CRC and the CRC Cttee's recommendations have had an impact, for instance, on domestic legislation. The CRC Cttee has recommended the adoption of a national strategy on children for Finland, to be prepared in 2020–2021.[136]

5.6.5   Impact of Individual Communications
Since the entry into force of the individual communications procedure in 2016, only one case against Finland has been submitted in 2016 and declared inadmissible by the CRC Cttee in 2019.[137]

5.6.6   Other Forms of Impact of the Treaty and Treaty Bodies
While CRC, its Optional Protocols and the work of the CRC Cttee have attracted special attention from the Parliamentary Ombudsman and the Ombudsman for Children, other national actors such as the Chancellor of Justice and the Non-Discrimination Ombudsman have also drawn attention to questions concerning children.[138]

5.6.7   Brief Conclusion
Of all the UN human rights treaties CRC perhaps has attracted the most attention throughout the years at the national level both in the work of public authorities and civil society actors. Particularly the activities of the Parliamentary Ombudsman, the Ombudsman for Children and the large and active body of NGOs have contributed to concrete impacts of CRC at the national level. Despite this the Finnish legislation and practices still contain challenges from the viewpoint of the provisions of CRC. For instance, according to many lawyers

---

134   The Committee eg raised the issues of non-discrimination, the best interests of the child, and respect for the views of the child. CRC Cttee, Concluding Observations on the fourth periodic report of Finland.
135   ibid., paras 3–5.
136   Government of Finland, National Child Strategy – Committee report, Publications of the Finnish Government 2022:16 (published 23 February 2022, English version 5 April 2022) <https://julkaisut.valtioneuvosto.fi/bitstream/handle/10024/163977/VN_2022_16.pdf?sequence=1&isAllowed=y> accessed 20 April 2022.
137   There were six communications pending in the Committee (in December 2019) and two inadmissibility decisions (in July 2020); see <https://juris.ohchr.org/Search/Results> accessed 13 April 2022.
138   The references are inserted eg in these actors' annual reports to Parliament. The information collected by the Information Service of the Library of Parliament for the study at hand.

specialised in CRC, the implementation of the principle of the best interests of the child, the legal personality of the child and the right to self-determination fall short of the requirements stipulated in the treaty.

5.7 Convention on the Rights of Persons with Disabilities

5.7.1   Incorporation and Reliance by Legislature and Executive

The ratification of CRPD and its entry into force in respect of Finland took place in 2016. The lapse of time between the adoption of the treaty in 2006 and its acceptance by Finland was due to the need to amend a number of national laws in order to ensure compatibility with the treaty. Some amendments to the Act of Special Care for Persons with Intellectual Disabilities, the Non-Discrimination Act, and the Municipality of Residence Act and the Social Welfare Act were especially considered necessary prior to ratifying the treaty.[139] The modifications concerned, for instance, the issues of self-determination and participation and the hearings of persons with disabilities. The debate around the need for more legal changes has continued particularly around the issue of self-determination, even in parliamentary plenary sessions.[140] Finland ratified OP-CRPD allowing individual communications simultaneously with the main treaty, and also accepted the inquiry procedure under article 6.

Regarding the visibility of CRPD in the work of the legislature and executive, CRPD and the CRPD Cttee have appeared in government Bills since 2008. In the period from 2008 to 30 June 2019 these were referred to at least in 51 government Bills considered by Parliament. In that period, the references to CRPD or the CRPD Cttee may be found at least in 25 documents of the parliamentary committees. CRPD also appeared in some written questions by Parliamentarians and ministers' answers to these questions concerning the ratification of CRPD. Furthermore, CRPD was mentioned in the parliamentary discussion on EU legislation addressing the same subject matter.[141]

---

139 Initial report, CRPD, Finland, paras 9–11.
140 In February 2020 a plenary discussion was held in the Finnish Parliament initiated by 125 (out of 200) members of Parliament in December 2019. The discussion focused on gaps in the implementation of CRPD in Finland and what could be done to improve the situation. While it is too early to say whether there will be any concrete outcomes, it was encouraging to see such strong support by a large number of parlamentarians across all the parties to CRPD. See <https://www.eduskunta.fi/FI/vaski/KasittelytiedotValtiopaivaasia/Sivut/KA_9+2019.aspx> accessed 13 April 2022.
141 The information collected by the Information Service of the Library of Parliament for the study at hand. See also the remarks on parliamentary committees and the information collected in n 36 supra.

The national focal point under article 33 of CRPD is composed of the Ministry of Social Affairs and Health, the Ministry for Foreign Affairs and a representative of an organisation of persons with disabilities (DPO) appointed by the Advisory Board for the Rights of Persons with Disabilities (VANE). At the Ministry of Social Affairs and Health, the responsibilities of the focal point include the implementation of CRPD, including preparatory work on legislation; various reports; the provision of information relating to the treaty; information gathering; and the collection of statistics. At the Ministry for Foreign Affairs, the responsibility of the focal point is to coordinate the periodic reporting under article 35 of CRPD. In addition to participating in the work of the focal point, VANE is the national coordination mechanism under CRPD and its function is to promote the national implementation of the treaty and to take into account the rights of persons with disabilities in all aspects of government.[142]

At the time of finalisation of the government's Human Rights Report of 2014 Finland had not yet ratified CRPD. However, the report mentions the treaty.[143] The National Action Plan on Fundamental and Human Rights 2017–2019 includes numerous references to persons with disabilities and notes CRPD and the CRPD Cttee's recommendations, for instance, in the texts on human rights education, equality, self-determination, accessibility and older persons.[144]

There have been various reports, programmes and policy papers, including action plans, that focus on persons with disabilities. The Advisory Board for the Rights of Persons with Disabilities appointed for 2019–2023 was tasked to prepare a new action plan for the following years.[145]

5.7.2 Reliance by Judiciary

Since the entry into force of CRPD in respect of Finland in 2016, up to 30 June 2019, there have been at least eight cases making explicit reference to CRPD in the highest courts. One of these judgments is by the Supreme Court, concerning discrimination in employment. Seven judgments of the Supreme Administrative Court concerned disability services (including transportation); the responsibilities of municipalities; subsidised school meals; and personal

---

142 See <https://vane.to/en/frontpage> accessed 13 April 2022.
143 Government Human Rights Report 2014, 15 and 48 (a note on the accession to the treaty by the EU).
144 National Action Plan, 25, 30, 34, 50, 51, 68, 71, 75, 77, 81, 89 and 104.
145 For the National Action Plan, see <https://stm.fi/en/artikkeli/-/asset_publisher/yk-n-vammaissopimuksen-kansallinen-toimintaohjelma-lisasi-tietoisuutta-vammaisten-henkiloiden-oikeuksista> accessed 13 April 2022.

assistance. In some cases the impact of CPRD has been directly discernable. This is evident in the case in the Supreme Administrative Court concerning the right to personal assistance and the covering of the costs of assistance during studies undertaken abroad. The Court referred the case to the Court of Justice of the EU for a preliminary ruling and in its decision the EU Court relied on article 19 of CRPD addressing the questions of living independently and being included in the community.[146]

5.7.3 Impact on and through Independent State Institutions and Non-state Actors

The NHRI has a special statutory task to promote, protect and monitor the implementation of CRPD under article 33 of the treaty. The NHRI participates in the treaty-monitoring process before the CRPD Cttee. The promotional activities of the NHRI include awareness-raising activities such as seminars and training, as well as campaigns. The NHRI (comprising the Parliamentary Ombudsman) handles individual complaints by persons with disabilities and is mandated to carry out inspections, for instance, in the housing units of persons with disabilities.

A few lawyers have specialised using CRPD in their legal argumentation. The number of cases argued before the highest courts within a short period of time bears evidence of this expertise. In addition, there is a wide spectrum of civil society actors, particularly disability organisations, that actively promote and rely on CRPD in their work. CRPD has become a central instrument in the work of many NGOs focusing on disability questions. These NGOs also use their expertise and provide assistance in court proceedings. They promote the social status and well-being of persons with disabilities and collect information on the situation, among others, for the participation in the treaty-monitoring process.[147] CRPD has received some attention also in the work of researchers and academics, but in general research in the area is rather sporadic. In the area of corporate responsibility (business and human rights) persons with disabilities have acquired attention as one of the vulnerable groups. This attention derives from the legislative amendments to the Non-Discrimination Act requiring reasonable adjustments to ensure the equality of persons with disabilities in accordance with CRPD requirements.

---

146   Supreme Administrative Court (KHO) 2018:145 (in Finnish). The court cases were collected by the Information Service of the Library of Parliament; see also n 43 supra.
147   See <https://vammaisfoorumi.fi/en/frontpage/#pll_switcher> accessed 13 April 2022.

5.7.4 Impact of State Reporting

Finland submitted its initial report (due in 2018) to the CRPD Cttee in 2019. At the time of writing, the report had not yet been examined. In addition to the state reporting, data collection and analysis by disability organisations have also been conducted as they prepare for their own reports to the CRPD Cttee.

5.7.5 Impact of Individual Communications

No individual communication has yet been considered by the CRPD Cttee in respect of Finland. One individual communication is pending before the Committee.

5.7.6 Other Forms of Impact of the Treaty and Treaty Bodies

CRPD and the work of the CRPD Cttee are also receiving attention, for instance, by the Chancellor of Justice and the Non-Discrimination Ombudsman, on a general level but also in individual cases.[148]

5.7.7 Brief Conclusion

CRPD has been very visible on the agenda of national actors. This attention has also turned into concrete impact in the areas of legislation and national practices. However, issues such as self-determination and access to rights in general remain, and require further attention. The impact of CRPD is substantially affected by the special tasks of the NHRI with respect to the treaty.

6 Conclusion[149]

The significance and impact of international human rights has over time varied in Finland. The 1990s clearly were the 'golden years' for human rights development at the national level, especially due to Finland becoming a member of both the CoE and the EU as well as the reform of the constitutional rights catalogue. At the time the attention in the human rights work also shifted from the UN to the European contexts. The worldwide war on terror since 2001, the financial crisis of 2008 and the rise of the far right-wing politics in recent years in Europe have brought challenges to human rights also in Finland. Despite this, the human rights culture, or at least the general awareness of human

---

148 The references are inserted eg in these actors' annual reports to Parliament. The information collected by the Information Service of the Library of Parliament for the study at hand.

149 The remarks in this part echo many observations raised by the interviewees of the study.

rights, has taken steps forward in the course of the past 20 years. Human rights talk has become more visible, but there are also stronger domestic voices challenging human rights.

While in international comparison Finland is doing relatively well in adhering to and implementing international human rights, gaps and problems remain. The general knowledge of human rights and particularly that of the UN human rights treaties remain limited – even among legal professionals. The national human rights structures are fragmented and resources channelled for human rights work remain insufficient. With many actors involved, coordination requires efforts and time and energy is lost.

The UN human rights treaties considered in this study have had their clearest direct impact at the time of their ratification. Most of the treaties have resulted in some changes in national legislation. However, the incorporation has often been done with minimal or insufficient legislative modifications. To a large extent the attitude has been that after the ratification process no further attention is necessary to be cast on the UN treaties. The views of the UN treaty bodies appear not to trigger on their own a change in policy or legislation, but they can have a role in intensifying the actions of domestic actors.[150] The outcomes of the international treaty-monitoring processes indicate that there are compliance deficits in Finland's implementation record. The focus on the regional human rights instruments and processes for its part limits the attention paid to the UN treaties.

Of the UN treaties considered in this study, the visibility and impact of two of the more recent UN treaties – CRC and CRPD – have been the clearest at the national level in Finland. The factor contributing hereto is that they both have national structures monitoring and supporting their implementation. The impact of CRC has even increased in the past two decades, resulting particularly from the support from the Parliamentary Ombudsman and the Ombudsman for Children. The impact of the most recently-ratified CRPD can be expected to be visible also in the future due to the institutional back-up for it from the NHRI. Additionally, CRPD's impact is strengthened indirectly through the EU's ratification of the treaty and taking the CRPD's provisions into account in the EU work, including in EU legislation.

---

150   This echoes the conclusions of Krommendijk who studied the effects of the COs of six UN treaty bodies (CERD, CCPR, CESCR, CEDAW, CAT and CRC) eg in Finland. He notes that COs have not on their own been a sufficient cause to instigate a change in policy or legislation, but that they rather had an intensifying or catalyst effect. Krommendijk (n 16) 506 and 508–509.

The impact of CRC and CRPD is also linked to the fact that there are no treaties covering the same subject matters within the CoE. The impact of CCPR and CESCR is affected by the CoE treaties that address the same kinds of rights and freedoms. The attention in Finland clearly is attached to the CoE processes. CEDAW stands out as the UN treaty having received the least serious attention and the weakest institutional back-up at the national level in Finland. The national steps to implement CEDAW have clearly fallen short of the requirements of the treaty obligations.

Finnish civil society has increasingly been participating in the exchanges of views on human rights, including the submission of their views in the context of the monitoring work of the UN treaty bodies.

Generally, the implementation of human rights in Finland is characterised by a certain selectivity. The issues raised in international monitoring processes but which lack national consensus or which are politically controversial at the national level, such as the implementation of the rights or the definition of the Sami or the need of continuous work in the area of gender equality, lack determinant domestic measures and results. The understanding of horizontal effects of human rights and state responsibility to provide protection against human rights threats emanating from non-state actors remains highly underdeveloped in Finland. This is particularly visible in problems such as hate speech, domestic violence and violence against women. It is also easier to resolve, for instance, a problem relating to the length of judicial processes than to address problems that need structural changes. The latter challenges are evident, for instance, in the area of socio-economic rights. Additionally, there often is incoherence between external and internal human rights policies.

The impact of the UN human rights treaties is also influenced by the perception among key national actors that at least some of the treaty monitoring bodies do not understand domestic realities. This results in downplaying the findings of such bodies. This attitude is partly explained by a thin understanding of international law and the significance and the binding nature of international human rights treaties as well as the role of their monitoring mechanisms.

The major factor contributing to the insufficient understanding of human rights is the marginal role of education regarding aspects of international law and human rights at the university level, including in law schools. Also, teachers are not systematically educated to teach human rights. There is also insufficient understanding of human rights at the municipal level that has a central role in the implementation of many fundamental human rights.

Improving the impact of the UN treaties and the implementation of human rights in general at the national level in Finland require the enhancement of the level of understanding and knowledge of international law, including international human rights law. It will further require the development of a coherent national human rights strategy and a well-functioning follow-up mechanism for human rights beyond the central level authorities. Furthermore, national human rights work requires more resources and more comprehensive independent national structures to monitor and promote human rights. The improvement of the UN human rights treaty system itself undoubtedly would also contribute to the better impact of the UN treaties at the national level.

Acknowledgements

The staff of the Centre, particularly LLM expert Leena Leikas, supported the work in a significant way by providing the information, e.g. on the work of the NHRI. She also gave comments on the manuscript. The director of the Centre, Sirpa Rautio, gave her invaluable comments in the text's finalisation phase. The Centre's Mikko Joronen was among the interviewees and gave his insights particularly on the impact of CRPD. Erika Bergström and Sari Koski from the Information Service of the Library of Parliament provided their important assistance to obtain information regarding reliance on the UN treaties and treaty bodies by the legislature, executive and judiciary.

CHAPTER 9

The Impact of the United Nations Human Rights Treaties on the Domestic Level in India

Miloon Kothari and Surabhi Sharma

1   Introduction to Human Rights in India

The Republic of India was established on 15 August 1947 after India had gained independence from the British. With a population of 1,3 billion, India houses nearly one-fifth of the global population. India is a multi-ethnic, multi-linguistic and multi-religious country that follows common law traditions. These traditions are generally adapted to Indian conditions. Ancient Hindu culture and traditions and medieval Islamic culture and traditions can also influence the Indian legal system.

The Constitution of India came into effect on 26 January 1950. A list of 'fundamental rights' is contained in Part III of the Constitution. These rights are justiciable, inviolable (therefore, any law violating a fundamental right is void),[1] and are amendable only to a limited extent.[2] The Directive Principles of State Policy (DPSP)[3] are contained in Part IV. These are not justiciable.[4] Six sets of fundamental rights are enumerated in Part III of the Constitution, which grants the right to a remedy with the help of the writ jurisdiction of the Supreme Court of India in respect of the rights contained in that part (under article 36). Also, the writ jurisdiction of the various High Courts can be invoked to the same effect (under article 226). These are the rights to equality (articles 14–18); the rights to freedom (articles 19–22); the rights against exploitation (articles 23 and 24); the right to freedom of religion (articles 25–28); cultural and educational rights (articles 29 and 30); and the right to constitutional remedies (articles 32–35).

The starting point for the domestic promotion and protection of human rights is the Indian Constitution. Any victim of a violation of the rights recognised in Part III (article 32) of the Constitution may seek a remedy from the

---

1 VN Shukla and MP Singh, *The Constitution of India* (Eastern Book Company 2017) A-42.
2 Fundamental rights are amendable to the extent they do not alter the Basic Structure of the Constitution.
3 Part IV, Constitution of India Act, 1950.
4 Shukla and Singh (n 1) A-44.

© MILOON KOTHARI AND SURABHI SHARMA, 2024 | DOI:10.1163/9789004377653_011
This is an open access chapter distributed under the terms of the CC BY-NC-ND 4.0 license.

Supreme Court and, under article 226, from the High Courts as well. Other persons can do likewise on behalf of victim(s) through public interest litigation.

In addition to the courts, the National Human Rights Commission (NHRC) of India, which was established under the Protection of Human Rights Act, 1993, serves to protect human rights. The NHRC inquires into complaints of violations of human rights or failure to prevent such violations and studies international human rights treaties to make recommendations for their effective implementation by the government.[5] The Protection of Human Rights Act was amended in 2019. The primary changes were related to who can be appointed to the Commission, the length of their terms and other aspects related to membership.[6] The NHRC is an 'A' grade institution in accordance with the Paris Principles. States in India may also establish human rights commissions. Presently there are such commissions in 25 states.

The realisation of economic, social and cultural rights is deeply inadequate. In the period 2011 to 2012, 21,9 per cent of the population of 1,3 billion people lived below the poverty line.[7] This makes the Indian subcontinent one of the poorest countries in the world. Women and children are most affected. India ranks 102 out of 117 in the 2019 Global Hunger Index.[8] Between 2016–2018, 14,5 per cent of the population was undernourished.[9] There are serious problems concerning suicide among farmers; the public distribution of grain is inefficient;[10] and access to the determinants of health, including safe water, is deteriorating.[11] Growing homelessness and forced evictions are commonplace,[12] including through project-induced displacement.[13]

---

5   National Human Rights Commission, 'Vision and Mission' <http://nhrc.nic.in/about-us/vision-and-mission> accessed 14 November 2022.

6   For the text of the amendment, see 'The Protection of Human Rights (Amendment) Act, 2019' <https://nhrc.nic.in/acts-&-rules/protection-human-rights-act-1993-1> accessed 14 November 2022, and a press release on the Act from the Press Information Bureau, 'Parliament Passes the Protection of Human Rights (Amendment) Bill, 2019 unanimously' (22 July 2019) <https://pib.gov.in/newsite/PrintRelease.aspx?relid=192090> accessed 14 November 2022.

7   <https://mospi.gov.in/sites/default/files/publication_reports/India_in_figures-2018_rev.pdf> accessed 15 September 2023.

8   2019 Global Hunger Index <https://www.globalhungerindex.org/india.html> accessed 14 November 2022.

9   Food and Agriculture Organisation, 'The State of Food Security and Nutrition in the World' (2019) <http://www.fao.org/3/ca5162en/ca5162en.pdf> accessed 14 November 2022.

10 WGHR Factsheet UPR 2017 India, Factsheet on Right to Food.

11 WGHR Factsheet UPR 2017 India, Factsheet on Right to Water and Sanitation.

12 See, for example, the annual reports from the Evictions Observatory of the Housing and Land Rights Network (HLRN) <https://www.hlrn.org.in/documents/Forced_Evictions_2018.pdf> accessed 14 November 2022.

13 WGHR Factsheet UPR 2017 India, Factsheet on Right to Adequate Housing.

The violation of civil and political rights is also rife. Allegations of custodial torture, extra-judicial killings and a lack of impartial investigations into mass graves on the part of the government are prevalent. For example, protests related to the Citizen Amendment Act led to the death of numerous people in the State of Uttar Pradesh.[14] Legislation such as the Armed Forces (Special Powers) Act, 1958 confers impunity for the use of force by law enforcement officials which often leads to human rights violations.[15] A total of 12 journalists have been killed in India since 2015 for their work.[16] Capital punishment is still retained in India.[17] Most recently, those convicted in the 2012 Delhi gang rape and murder case were hanged.[18] Legislation such as the Foreign Contributions Regulation Act 2010 threatens the right to freedom of association. Sedition laws and the National Security Act curb freedom of speech.[19] India leads the world in the number of internet shutdowns.[20] Since independence there has been persistent caste-based discrimination due to non-implementation of protective laws. Access to justice issues for Dalit communities persists as does the practice of manual scavenging.[21] In 2019 the Indian government revoked the constitutionally-mandated status of Kashmir.[22] Concern has been expressed that the population of Indian-administered Kashmir continues to be deprived of human rights after the revocation. The

---

14   'Why This Indian State is Witnessing the Country's Most Violent Anti Citizenship-Law Protests' (*Time Magazine* 1 January 2020) <https://time.com/5757332/uttar-pradesh-citizenship-protests/> accessed 14 November 2022; 'As India Violence Gets Worse, Police Are Accused of Abusing Muslims' (*New York Times* 2 January 2020) <https://www.nytimes.com/2020/01/02/world/asia/india-protests-police-muslims.html> accessed 14 November 2022.
15   WGHR Factsheet UPR 2017 India, Factsheet on Militarisation and Armed Conflict.
16   Committee to Protect Journalists <https://bit.ly/2YBC1v3> accessed 14 November 2022.
17   WGHR Factsheet UPR 2017 India, Factsheet on Death Penalty.
18   'Delhi Court: Nirbhaya Case Convicts Hang 6 am on March 3' (*Deccan Chronicle* 19 February 2020) <https://www.deccanchronicle.com/nation/current-affairs/180220/delhi-court-nirbhaya-case-convicts-hang-6am-on-march-3.html> accessed 14 November 2022.
19   Human Rights Watch, 'There is No Democracy Without Dissent' (14 February 2019) <https://www.hrw.org/news/2019/02/14/there-no-democracy-without-dissent> accessed 15 September 2023.
20   Scroll.in, 'In Charts: India Shut the Internet Down More Than 100 times in 2019' <https://scroll.in/article/947880/in-charts-india-shut-down-the-internet-than-100-times-in-2019> accessed 14 November 2022.
21   WGHR Factsheet UPR 2017 India, Factsheet on Discrimination Based on Work and Descent (Rights of Dalits).
22   'Press Briefing on India Administered Kashmir' (29 October 2019) <https://www.ohchr.org/en/NewsEvents/Pages/DisplayNews.aspx?NewsID=25219&LangID=E> accessed 14 November 2022.

central government imposed an internet and telecommunications shutdown in the state.[23]

In the Gender Inequality Index of 2018 of the United Nations Development Programme (UNDP), India ranked 127th in the world.[24] According to the World Bank, less than 30 per cent of working-age women are currently in work compared to nearly 80 per cent of men in India.[25] Data from the National Crime Records Bureau (NCRB) of India shows that there has been no decline in the rate of crimes against women from 2001 to 2016.[26] In the five-year period from 2012 to 2016, 170 000 women in India have reported rape.[27] Cases under the category of 'crimes against women' had reportedly increased by 2,9 per cent from 2015 to 2016.[28] The majority of these cases were categorised as 'cruelty by husband or his relatives' (32,6 per cent); followed by 'assault on women with intent to outrage her modesty' (25 per cent); 'kidnapping and abduction of women' (19 per cent) and 'rape' (11,5 per cent).[29] Marital rape is not criminalised.[30]

Discrimination and violence against persons belonging to the LGBTIQ+ community persists despite the decriminalisation of same-sex relationships.[31] The 'third gender'[32] has been recognised by the Supreme Court, but they still face discrimination in respect of, for example, the right to housing and to work.[33] Furthermore, the Transgender Persons (Protection of Rights) Bill, 2016 does not conform to international human rights standards.[34] The Madras High

---

[23] 'UN Rights Experts Urge India to End Communications Shutdown in Kashmir' <https://www.ohchr.org/en/NewsEvents/Pages/DisplayNews.aspx?NewsID=24909&LangID=E> accessed 14 November 2022.

[24] UNDP, 'Human Development Reports – Statistical Report 2018' Gender Inequality Index 40 <https://bit.ly/2OPJK5i> accessed 14 November 2022.

[25] The World Bank, 'Labour Force Participation Rate, Female (% of Female Population Ages 15+) (modelled ILO estimate) – India' <https://data.worldbank.org/indicator/SL.TLF.CACT.FE.ZS?contextual=default&locations=IN> accessed 14 November 2022.

[26] National Crime Records Bureau, Ministry of Home Affairs, 'Crime in India 2016' <http://ncrb.gov.in/> accessed 14 November 2022.

[27] ibid.

[28] ibid.

[29] ibid.

[30] WGHR Factsheet UPR 2017 India, Factsheet on Women.

[31] International Commission of Jurists, 'Living with Dignity: Sexual Orientation and Gender Identity-Based Human Rights Violations in Housing, Work, and Public Spaces in India' <http://bit.ly/2PgCQGH> accessed 14 November 2022.

[32] *National Legal Services Authority v Union of India* (2014) Writ Petition (C) No 604/2013 (NALSA).

[33] International Commission of Jurists (n 31).

[34] Human Rights Watch, 'India: Transgender Bill Raises Rights Concerns' (23 July 2019) <https://www.hrw.org/news/2019/07/23/india-transgender-bill-raises-rights-concerns#:~:text=%E2%80%9CThe%20Transgender%20Persons%20Bill%20should,director%20at%20Human%20Rights%20Watch> accessed 15 September 2023.

Court has ordered the Tamil Nadu government to prohibit 'normalising' surgeries for intersex children.[35]

India is the country with the world's largest number of children, with 36,68 per cent of its population of an estimated 1,27 billion under the age of 18 years. India continues to have the most widespread incidence of child labour in the world. Gaps in legislative protection has hampered the prohibition of child labour. India has one of the highest sex-selective abortion (foeticide) incidence in the world. In a significant move, the government enacted the Protection of Children from Sexual Offences (POSCO) Act, 2012, to address all forms of sexual offences against children, irrespective of gender, in November 2012. However, this has not reduced the incidence of crimes against children, with a rise of 5,3 per cent in all crimes against children in 2015 as compared to 2014 in India. There has been a 67,5 per cent increase in reported sexual crimes against children.[36]

Persons with disabilities face challenges related to mobility and accessibility, a lack of opportunities for employment and a lack of access to educational facilities.[37] There are also gaps in the implementation of the Rights of Persons with Disabilities Act and the Mental Health Act.[38]

The implementation of refugee and asylum-related laws is ineffective and not in conformity with international standards.[39] India has also deported Rohingyas in violation of the principle of *non-refoulement*.[40] The central government published the updated National Register for Citizens (NRC) (an official record of all Indians who legally qualify as citizens as per the Citizenship Act, 1955) in the state of Assam which resulted in 1,9 million people being termed illegal immigrants.[41] The Home Ministry has stated that the NRC would again

---

35 Human Rights Watch, 'Indian Court Decides in Favour of Informed Consent Rights for Intersex People' (29 April 2019) <https://www.hrw.org/news/2019/04/29/indian-court-decides-favor-informed-consent-rights-intersex-people> accessed 15 September 2023.
36 WGHR Factsheet UPR 2017 India, Factsheet on Rights of the Child.
37 WGHR Factsheet UPR 2017 India, Factsheet on Persons with Disabilities.
38 'Committee on Persons with Disabilities Reviews India's Initial Report, Asks About Violence Against Persons With Disabilities in Institutions' (3 September 2019) <https://www.ohchr.org/EN/NewsEvents/Pages/DisplayNews.aspx?NewsID=24944&LangID=E> accessed 14 November 2022.
39 WGHR Factsheet UPR 2017 India, Factsheet on Refugees and Asylum Seekers.
40 'India: UN Human Rights Experts Condemn Rohingya Deportations' (2 April 2019) <https://www.ohchr.org/en/NewsEvents/Pages/DisplayNews.aspx?NewsID=24437&LangID=E> accessed 14 November 2022.
41 'What is NRC: All You Need to Know About National Register of Citizens' *India Today* (18 December 2019) <https://www.indiatoday.in/india/story/what-is-nrc-all-you-need-to-know-about-national-register-of-citizens-1629195-2019-12-18> accessed 14 November 2022. Also see, Scroll, Explainer: 'What Exactly is the National Register for Citizens'

be conducted in Assam,[42] and those left out of the NRC face the risk of being stateless persons. After the updating of the NRC, the Citizen Amendment Act was passed, stating that persons belonging to the Hindu, Sikh, Buddhist, Jain, Parsi or Christian communities from Afghanistan, Bangladesh or Pakistan and who entered India on or before 31 December 2014 shall not be treated as illegal immigrants.[43] The Act has been criticised as being discriminatory against the Muslim population, and violating India's obligations under the International Covenant on Civil and Political Rights (CCPR) and the International Convention on the Elimination of All Forms of Racial Discrimination (CERD).[44] The implementation of the Act has led to (sometimes violent)[45] protests across the country.[46]

<https://scroll.in/article/930482/explainer-what-exactly-is-the-national-register-of-citizens> accessed 14 November 2022.

42 *India Today* (n 41).

43 Art 2, Citizenship Amendment Act, 2019 reads: '2. In the Citizenship Act, 1955 (hereinafter referred to as the principal Act), in section 2, in sub-section (1), in clause (b), the following proviso shall be inserted, namely: Provided that any person belonging to Hindu, Sikh, Buddhist, Jain, Parsi or Christian community from Afghanistan, Bangladesh or Pakistan, who entered into India on or before the 31st day of December, 2014 and who has been exempted by the Central Government by or under clause (c) of sub-section (2) of section 3 of the Passport (Entry into India) Act, 1920 or from the application of the provisions of the Foreigners Act, 1946 or any rule or order made thereunder, shall not be treated as illegal migrant for the purposes of this Act'.

44 International Commission of Jurists, 'India: Discriminatory Citizenship Law Passed by Parliament Violates International and Constitutional Law' <https://www.icj.org/india-discriminatory-citizenship-law-passed-by-parliament-violates-international-and-constitutional-law/>; OHCHR, 'Press Briefing on India' (13 December 2019) <https://www.ohchr.org/EN/NewsEvents/Pages/DisplayNews.aspx?NewsID=25425&LangID=E> accessed 14 November 2022.

45 NDTV.com, 'On Hate Speeches: Court Gives Centre A Month to Update on Action Taken' (27 February 2020) <https://www.ndtv.com/india-news/delhi-violence-centre-police-ask-high-court-for-more-time-to-file-firs-over-hate-speech-videos-2186602> accessed 14 November 2022.

46 'Shaheen Bagh: A New Kind of "Satyagraha" with a Fresh Grammar of Protest' (*Business Standard* 6 February 2020) <https://www.business-standard.com/article/current-affairs/shaheen-bagh-a-new-kind-of-satyagraha-with-a-fresh-grammar-of-protest-120011601102_1.html> accessed 14 November 2022; *The Indian Express*, 'Why Shaheen Bagh Matters: It Offers Protest Template, Rejects Clergy, Challenges Patriarchy' <https://indianexpress.com/article/opinion/shaheen-bagh-caa-protests-6271972/> accessed 14 November 2022; Observer Research Foundation, 'Taking a Close Look at Shaheen Bagh' (4 February 2020) <https://www.orfonline.org/expert-speak/taking-a-close-look-at-shaheen-bagh-61045/> accessed 14 November 2022.

There is targeted violence against religious minorities particularly with regard to lynching by cattle vigilantes over the storage of beef.[47] The reason for the lynching is that cows are considered sacred in Hinduism. Attacks against Christians due to the presence of anti-conversion laws also exist.[48] Nomadic, semi-nomadic and denotified tribes are not recognised, and face social and economic exclusion and police atrocities.[49] Between 2016 and June 2019, the NHRC registered 2008 cases of harassment against minorities.[50]

The expansive interpretation of article 21 on the right to life by the Supreme Court in 1985 to include a host of socio-economic rights is a significant milestone. The Supreme Court has recognised that article 21 includes the right to water, the right to livelihood,[51] the right to an unpolluted environment,[52] the right to adequate food and nutrition (making article 47 as a directive principle of state policy justiciable)[53] and the right to privacy.[54] The 86th Constitutional Amendment (and insertion of article 21A) enacted in 2002 has made free and compulsory education a fundamental right. The central government has enacted the National Education Policy, 2020,[55] which follows a human rights-based approach. The Rights of Persons with Disabilities Act, 2016 recognises 21 disabilities as opposed to the 1995 Act which recognised seven, and is more inclusive.[56] The Supreme Court of India upheld the constitutional rights of transgender persons;[57] the right to self-determine one's gender identity; and has decriminalised homosexuality;[58] women army officers would be eligible

---

[47] Human Rights Watch, 'India: Vigilante "Cow Protection" Groups Attack Minorities' (18 February 2019) <https://www.hrw.org/news/2019/02/19/india-vigilante-cow-protection-groups-attack-minorities#:~:text=%E2%80%9CCalls%20for%20cow%20protection%20may,director%20at%20Human%20Rights%20Watch> accessed 15 September 2023.

[48] WGHR Factsheet UPR 2017 India, Factsheet on Religious Minorities.

[49] WGHR Factsheet UPR 2017 India, Factsheet on Nomadic, Semi-Nomadic and De-Notified Tribes (NT-DNTs).

[50] 'With 43% Share in Hate Crimes, UP Still Most Unsafe For Minorities, Dalits' (*India Today* 19 July 2019) <https://bit.ly/35dBZfh> accessed 14 November 2022.

[51] *Olga Tellis v Bombay Municipal Corporation* (1985) 3 SCC 545.

[52] *Narmada Bachao Aandolan v Union of India* (2000) 10 SCC 664.

[53] WGHR Factsheet UPR 2017 India, Factsheet on Right to Food.

[54] *Justice Puttaswamy (Retd) & Another v Union of India* Writ Petition (Civil) No 494 of 2012.

[55] 'National Education Policy, 2020', Ministry of Human Resource Development, Government of India <https://www.mhrd.gov.in/sites/upload_files/mhrd/files/NEP_Final_English_0.pdf> accessed 14 November 2022.

[56] WGHR Factsheet UPR 2017 India, Factsheet on Persons with Disabilities.

[57] See Nalsa v Uoi, Writ Petition (Civil) No 400 of 2012; see WGHR Factsheet UPR 2017, Factsheet on Sexual Orientation and Gender Identity.

[58] 'India Ruling to Decriminalise Same-Sex Relations is Victory for Equality, and Other States Should Follow, says UN expert' (7 September 2018) <https://www.ohchr.org/en/NewsEvents/Pages/DisplayNews.aspx?NewsID=23514&LangID=E> accessed 14 November 2022.

for permanent commission;[59] and daughters in coparcenary property would have equal rights.[60]

2 Relationship of India with the International Human Rights System in General

India has played an active role in the development of the international human rights system from the time of the drafting of the Universal Declaration of Human Rights (UDHR). In the drafting process of the UDHR, India was able to convey demands for the emancipation of all oppressed groups.[61] India also actively participated in the drafting of numerous United Nations (UN) human rights treaties, including the International Covenant on Economic, Social and Cultural Rights (CESCR); CCPR; the Convention on the Elimination of All Forms of Discrimination Against Women (CEDAW); and the Convention on the Rights of the Child (CRC). India has been an active supporter of the UN's inter-governmental human rights system, in particular the UN Human Rights Council (HRC). India was a strong supporter of the establishment of the Universal Periodic Review (UPR) and continues to defend this mechanism.[62] India has undergone its third UPR cycle.

The active historical role of India in the development of the international human rights system, however, does not extend to its own record of reporting to the UN treaty bodies, as outlined later in this study. Although India has extended standing invitations to all thematic special procedures, few special procedures have in fact been invited to India since 2014 and some have not been invited despite requests. In the period between 2000 and 2019, at least

---

59 'Women Army Officers Eligible for Permanent Commission, Rules SC' (18 February 2020) <https://www.thehindu.com/news/national/women-officers-can-be-given-permanent-commission-sc/article30840323.ece> accessed 14 November 2022.

60 *Vineeta Sharma v Rakesh Sharma & Others* (11 August 2018) <https://www.livelaw.in/know-the-law/daughters-rights-sc-explains-the-impact-of-hindu-succession-amendment-act-2005-161301> accessed 14 November 2022.

61 Miloon Kothari, 'India's Contribution to the Universal Declaration of Human Rights' (2018) 17 Journal of the Indian National Human Rights Commission. Also see Miloon Kothari, 'Remembering India's Contribution to the Universal Declaration of Human Rights', The Wire <https://thewire.in/rights/indias-important-contributions-to-the-universal-declaration-of-human-rights> accessed 14 November 2022.

62 <https://timesofindia.indiatimes.com/india/india-says-unhrcs-upr-mechanism-a-visible-instrument-for-rights-protection-should-not-be-tinkered/articleshow/76397353.cms> accessed 14 November 2022.

nine Special Rapporteur visits took place to India.[63] India is also not a party to the Rome Statute of the International Criminal Court (ICC).

In order to make international treaties enforceable in India, domestic legislation is required.[64] According to article 51(c) of the Constitution, the state shall endeavour to 'foster respect for international law and treaty obligations in the dealings of organised peoples with one another'. Article 253 of the Constitution gives the power to Parliament to make any law for the implementation of international instruments. In *Apparel Export Promotion Council v AK Chopra* in 1999 the Supreme Court noted that 'the domestic courts are under an obligation to give due regard to international conventions and norms for construing domestic laws when there is no inconsistency between them'.[65] Both the Indian High Courts and the Supreme Court routinely cite international standards in their judgments. The lower courts are however much more reluctant to use international standards.

3 At a Glance: Formal Engagement of India with the UN Human Rights Treaty System

Refer to the chart on the next page.

4 Role and Overall Impact of the UN Human Rights Treaties in India

4.1 Formal Acceptance

India has ratified six of the nine UN human rights treaties: CERD; CESCR; CCPR; CRC; CEDAW; and the Convention on the Rights of Persons with Disabilities (CRPD). It has done the same with respect to the Optional Protocol

---

63 Visits by the Special Rapporteurs on violence against women (2000), freedom of religion (2008), health (2007), toxic waste (2010), human rights defenders (2011), extrajudicial, summary or arbitrary executions (2012), violence against women (2013), housing (2016) and the rights to water and sanitation (2017).
64 *Jolly George Verghese & Another v The Bank of Cochin* 1980 AIR 470.
65 *Apparel Export Promotion Council v AK Chopra* AIR (1999) SC 625.

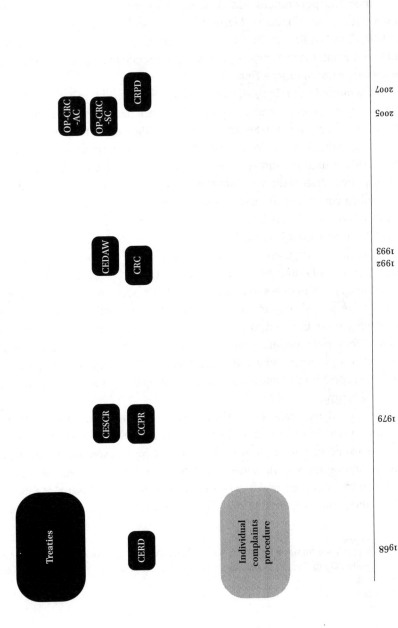

to the Convention on the Rights of the Child on the involvement of children in Armed Conflict (OP-CRC-AC) and the Optional Protocol to the Convention on the Rights of the Child on the Sale of Children, Child Prostitution and Child Pornography (OP-CRC-SC). India has not ratified OP2-CCPR, the Convention against Torture and Other Cruel, Inhuman or Degrading Treatment or Punishment (CAT), the Convention for the Protection of All Persons from Enforced Disappearances (CED), nor the International Convention on the Protection of the Rights of Migrant Workers and Members of their Families (CMW). The Council of Ministers, on the recommendation of the Ministry of External Affairs and nodal ministries, recommends to the President of India whether or not to ratify a treaty.[66]

India ratified CERD in 1968. Mahatma Gandhi, a key figure in the Indian independence movement, had campaigned against racial discrimination against people of Indian origin in South Africa, and India was the first to take the question of apartheid to the UN. It supported the idea of a convention to eliminate racial discrimination and led the Non-Aligned Movement. This participation greatly motivated India to ratify the Convention and through ratification it wanted to covey that the movement against racial discrimination had a vital wider application in the international community.[67] The declaration to article 22 of CERD was made because India wanted to limit the role of the International Court of Justice (ICJ), which had lost the confidence of African and Asian countries after the infamous judgment in the South West Africa cases.[68]

Widespread violations of human rights in the wake of a state of emergency during the period 1975 to 1977 led to a massive reaction resulting in India becoming more inclined towards international human rights and its institutions. When the emergency rule was lifted and the new government came to power in 1977, emergency victims and civil society successfully pleaded for India's succession to CESCR and CCPR. Consequently, these two treaties were ratified in 1979.

One of the main reasons for the acceptance of a declaration/reservation to Common Article 1 of CCPR and CESCR was the government's fear that some groups would use the right of self-determination as a weapon to secede from India. Among these groups are militants in the state of Jammu and Kashmir and insurgents in the north-eastern states, particularly Assam, Manipur and Nagaland. France, Germany and The Netherlands have made objections to

---

[66] Yogesh Tyagi, 'India' in Christof Heyns and Frans Viljoen, *The Impact of the United Nations Human Rights Treaties on the Domestic Level* (Kluwer Law International 2002) 297 at 300.
[67] ibid.
[68] ibid.

this declaration. However, the Indian government does not find these objections tenable and believes that it fought hard for its position on the right to self-determination.

The main reason for the other declarations/reservations is that the constitutional guarantees fall short of the applicable Covenant provisions.[69] With reference to article 9 of CCPR, India declared that the provisions of this article shall be applied in consonance with article 22(3) and (7) of the Constitution of India and that there is no enforceable right to compensation for persons claiming to be victims of unlawful arrest or detention against the state under the Indian legal system. However, even though this declaration/reservation has not been formally withdrawn, it has effectively been overruled by a series of court decisions where the court awarded compensation. For example, in *Rudul Sah v State of Bihar*[70] the petitioner was detained for 15 years in spite of an acquittal. The petitioner sought release on the grounds of unlawful detention and compensation for illegal incarceration. The Supreme Court granted him compensation. The HRCttee has noted the reservations/declarations made by India and invited the state party to review these with a view to withdrawing them.[71]

India ratified CRC in 1992. The main motivation for accession was the desire to ensure development of the country by investing in children. Soon after the adoption of the Convention in 1989, various individuals, non-governmental organisations (NGOs) and other institutions took up the issue of India joining the regime. For example, the National Law School of India University, a leading institution for teaching in law, organised a seminar in Bangalore on the Convention in 1990. These processes gathered momentum after the entry into force of the Convention.

India signed CEDAW in 1980 but only ratified it in 1993. The 13-year gap between signature and ratification represents the dilemma of traditional Indian society. The main motivation to ratify CEDAW was the pressure generated by supporters of the Convention and the government's desire to demonstrate its gender sensitivity and human rights sincerity to the world.[72] Between 1980 and 1990, India implemented a slew of law reforms for women and changes in the international fora with regard to liberalisation and the rising space for women in the public and political arena which led India to ratify CEDAW in 1993.

---

[69] ibid.
[70] *Rudul Sah v State of Bihar* 01.08.1983-SC, AIR 1983 SC 1086.
[71] Heyns and Viljoen (n 66).
[72] ibid.

India has not yet ratified CAT, despite having signed it in 1997. The protection of the right to freedom from torture, cruel, inhuman, and degrading treatment under the Indian Constitution is not as stringent as under the Convention and torture is a widely-accepted phenomenon in the country, which is perceived as being necessary to maintain law and order. In addition, India places significant importance on domestic jurisdiction.[73]

India became a signatory to CED but has not yet ratified it. India participated in the drafting of the Convention and favoured a definition of enforced disappearance that included specific intent as the main element. However, this suggestion was not adopted. India also suggested that the proposed treaty would better function as an optional protocol to CCPR instead of a separate convention with its own monitoring body. However, this suggestion was also not reflected in the final result.[74] A question was posed to the Minister of Home Affairs in 2017 on whether the government was planning to ratify CED, to which the Minister replied that the matter of ratification was under examination.[75] Although CED has not been ratified by India, it has been mentioned in passing in *Zulfikar Nasir*[76] by the Delhi High Court.

In India's first and second UPR, recommendations were made for India to ratify CMW. These recommendations were noted by the government and not accepted. The reason for the reluctance to ratify is not known.

India ratified OP-CRC-AC in 2005 and OP-CRC-SC in 2007. India signed CRPD in 2007 and ratified it in 2007.

India has not accepted any of the individual petition procedures under the treaties it has ratified. It in particular has not acceded to OP1-CCPR for various reasons, including a fear of exposure of its human rights violations, fear of overworking of its administrative machinery and a lack of resources to administer the remedies (compensation, and so forth) to be granted by the HRCttee in cases where violations are found. In India itself, there has been a mixed response to the non-acceptance of the OP1 procedure with some arguing that governments are in the best position to secure human rights for individuals

---

[73] ibid.
[74] 'A Right to Remedy for Enforced Disappearances in India: A Legal Analysis of International and Domestic Law Relating to Victims of Enforced Disappearances' (April 2014) IHRLC Working Paper Series No 1 <https://www.law.berkeley.edu/wp-content/uploads/2015/04/Working-Paper-1-India-Right-to-a-Remedy-151027.pdf> accessed 14 November 2022.
[75] <https://www.mha.gov.in/MHA1/Par2017/pdfs/par2017-pdfs/rs-080217/681.pdf> accessed 14 November 2022.
[76] *Zulfikar Nasir & Others v State of Uttar Pradesh & Others* (31.10.2018 – DELHC) para 109.

and others arguing for India's accession to OP1-CCPR. There is no consensus on whether India should join the OP1 procedure.

4.1.1 General Attitude of State towards UN Treaty System

While India has played an active role in the development of many UN human rights treaties, the improvement of and the engagement with the UN human rights treaty system has never been a priority for the government. The level of importance given to the system, in fact, has declined in recent years. This is reflected in the 'lower' level of delegations that appear before the treaty bodies, in particular, when compared, for example, to the composition of delegations to the UPR. This is also reflected in the fact that there is little change in the 'overdue' status of many reports to the treaty bodies and the continued lack of a broader consultation process in the preparation of treaty body reports by the government.

4.1.2 Level of Awareness

The level of awareness varies across treaties and across stakeholders. For example, CRC is better known among officials in the central government ministries. Generally, the level of awareness is lower when it comes to regional and local level officials and governance systems. As pointed out by the United Nations Children's Fund (UNICEF), even the officials that are aware of the treaties need to be updated on a regular basis about the work and function of the treaty bodies in India.[77] There appears to be limited knowledge of CEDAW among the officials in the government who handle issues related to women and children.[78] In some cases they are not even aware that CEDAW is a binding legal instrument.[79] With regard to CRC, the Optional Protocols do not receive much attention in the government or civil society. Government officials seem to be unaware that they are supposed to be reporting on the Optional Protocols as well.[80] Among those officials who deal with legislative matters, there is a general recognition that India's international obligations are binding, but otherwise there is little awareness.[81] International human rights law is generally taught as a part of public international law during the undergraduate degree. Separate diplomas are offered on international human rights law for which

---

[77] Based on interviews with relevant UN agencies (notes on file with authors).
[78] ibid.
[79] Based on interviews with relevant civil society organisations and UN agencies.
[80] Based on interviews with relevant UN agencies.
[81] Interview, Jayna Kothari, Co-founder, Centre for Law and Policy Research, CLPR office, Bangalore, Karnataka (10 January 2020).

students can opt.[82] With regard to CEDAW, the government has not translated the Conventions into local languages. This work has been carried out by civil society and UN Women.[83] With regard to CRC, the Convention and the COs are in the local language but the translations are generally left to civil society and UNICEF.[84] With regard to CERD, there are also no official government translations of the Convention into local languages. Civil society groups have translated CERD into local languages at the time of advocacy work to include the issue of caste in the UN agenda.[85] It is clear that the inability of the government to translate the instruments and take them to the local levels, communities and local government systems has hampered deeper penetration of the treaties and the work of treaty bodies.

4.1.3 State Reporting

India has stated its commitment to 'cooperate with treaty monitoring bodies and engage constructively with them in the context of fulfilling its human rights obligations'.[86] India has complied with its reporting obligations in the previous reporting cycles under CEDAW, CRC, OP-CRC-AC, OP-CRC-SC and CRPD. However, some of these reports were submitted after a delay of two to five years.[87] India has not submitted a report to CCPR since 2001. Recently, the HRCttee decided to review India *in absentia*.[88] India's report has been outstanding to CERD since 2010,[89] and to CESCR since 2011.[90]

4.1.4 Domestic Implementation Mechanism

The NHRC monitors the implementation of substantive human rights treaty obligations at the domestic level, while the UN Division of the Ministry of External Affairs of the government of India supervises the implementation of procedural treaty obligations at the international level.[91] There is no formal structure to monitor the implementation of the treaty obligations.

---

82 ibid.
83 Based on interviews with relevant UN agencies.
84 ibid.
85 Dalit Groups interview.
86 This was most recently (2018) stated in India's pledge to the UN Human Rights Council at <https://undocs.org/en/A/73/394> accessed 14 November 2022.
87 Office of the High Commissioner for Human Rights, Treaty Bodies, Reporting Status of India <https://tbinternet.ohchr.org/_layouts/15/treatybodyexternal/TBSearch.aspx?Lang=En&CountryID=79> accessed 14 November 2022.
88 ibid.
89 ibid.
90 ibid.
91 Heyns and Viljoen (n 66).

The Ministry of External Affairs coordinates the preparation of reports to the treaty bodies. This Ministry has on occasion outsourced the drafting of the reports. The Indian National Law School University in New Delhi has often been entrusted with the reports both to the treaty bodies and for the UPR.

4.1.5 Treaty Body Membership

India has not taken much interest in nominating members to the treaty bodies. While over the years India has nominated members for CERD, CESCR, CEDAW and the HRCttee (see list below), in spite of the extensive expertise in the country, no one has ever been nominated to CRC. The recent nomination of a former diplomat to the CESCR Cttee also does not inspire much confidence in India's ability to nominate 'independent' experts. The following candidates served as members of UN treaty bodies: CERD Cttee: Ms Shanti Sadiq Ali (1993–2002); Mr Dilip Lahiri (2008–2011); CESCR Cttee: Ms Chokila Iyer (-2006); Ms Arundhati Ghose (-2009); Ms Preeti Saran (2019–2022); Mr Chandrasekhar Dasgupta (2008–2018); HRCtee: Mr Prafullachandra Natwarlal Bhagwati (1995–2009); CEDAW Cttee: Ms Indira Jaising (2009–2012).

4.2 Overview of Impact

4.2.1 Incorporation and Reliance by the Legislature and the Executive

With the exception of CERD, all ratified treaties have been used by legislatures and referred to by courts. Treaties to which India is only a signatory are also used by courts. This is seen especially in the case of the CAT. CCPR and CESCR have been incorporated into domestic law through the Protection of Human Rights Act, 1994. Legislation has also been enacted to give effect to the provisions of specific articles of CEDAW and CRPD, details of which will be provided under part 5.

4.2.2 Reliance by Judiciary

In accordance with article 51(c) of the Constitution, the state has a duty to foster respect for India's treaty obligations, but this does not mean that all India's treaty obligations are automatically binding on India. However, courts have respected international law when it is not in contradiction with domestic law.[92] From the cases examined, it appears that it is largely the Supreme Court

---

[92] In *National Legal Services Authority v Union of India* (2014) 5 SCC 438 the Supreme Court stated: 'Any international convention not inconsistent with the fundamental rights and in harmony with its spirit must be read into those provisions, eg, articles 14, 15, 19 and 21 of

and High Court judgments that rely on treaties for their findings.[93] CCPR is used most frequently. It is difficult to estimate the impact of this on the ground as many judgments in India are not fully implemented.

4.2.3 Impact on and through Non-state Actors

In the High Courts, only a small percentage of lawyers make reference to international treaties for cases they file. The approach of lawyers differs, with reliance on international treaties more pronounced in public interest litigation. Additionally, in some cases lawyers would use treaties before the tribunals and lowers courts, but tribunals and lower courts are not very familiar with international treaties.[94] In the Supreme Court, a growing number of legal practitioners rely on international treaties as part of their arguments.[95] For understandable reasons, courts give more preference to treaty provisions than to General Comments.[96] Courts in some cases rely on UDHR provisions in addition to core UN treaties.

5 Detailed Impact of the Different UN Human Rights Treaties on the Domestic Level

As a general practice in this section, cases where the treaties and treaty body jurisprudence have influenced the findings of courts are discussed in the text. Cases where the treaties and work of the treaty bodies are mentioned merely in passing are enumerated in the footnotes. The selection and analysis of judgments is not exhaustive as there are far too many judgments where the Indian judiciary has referred to UN treaties, and space does not allow for all of these to be presented in this study. The selection of cases, however, attempts to capture the cases that have been most significant in the development of jurisprudence in India.

---

the Constitution to enlarge the meaning and content thereof and to promote the object of constitutional guarantee'.

[93] The term 'courts' in this chapter refers to the High Courts or the Supreme Court unless specifically stated otherwise.

[94] Interview, Jayna Kothari, Co-founder, Centre for Law and Policy Research, CLPR office, Bangalore, Karnataka (10 January 2020).

[95] Interview, Vrinda Grover.

[96] Interview, Jayna Kothari, Co-founder, Centre for Law and Policy Research, CLPR office, Bangalore, Karnataka (10 January 2020).

5.1 International Convention on the Elimination of All Forms of Racial Discrimination

5.1.1 Incorporation and Reliance by Legislature and Executive

The Indian executive has had a difficult relationship with CERD. This fraught relationship is due to India's reluctance to have its human rights record relating to the Dalit community monitored by any international body. India's position is that 'caste' and 'race' are separate categories and that the Dalit community in India is not viewed as a 'minority' community and are thus not covered under international instruments.

5.1.2 Reliance by the Judiciary

In general treaty provisions and treaty body jurisprudence are simply mentioned and not relied upon by courts. We found 13 references to CERD by Indian courts and tribunals. These appear in four judgments of the Supreme Court. The Supreme Court tends to take CERD more seriously and relies on it when coming to its finding but this is not the case with the High Courts. In *Karma Dorjee*, a petition was filed for setting down guidelines to curb discrimination against persons from the north-eastern states in India. The Supreme Court relied on CERD, citing articles 2 and 5 of the Convention[97] and domestic law and directed the central government to set up a monitoring and redressal committee to oversee efforts relating to curbing discrimination against persons from these states.[98] In *PK Koul*[99] the Delhi High Court relied on CERD when affirming that the petitioners have a right to shelter. The petition in this case was filed by a minority from the state of Jammu and Kashmir who could not return to Jammu and Kashmir due to the fear of 'ethnic cleansing'. They relocated to New Delhi and were evicted from the government premises where they were staying. The Delhi High Court held that the petitioners had a right to shelter, stating that

> the Respondents ... must meet the principles laid down in the aforenoted pronouncements of the courts, the international conventions, the standards in the guiding principles for IDPs and ensure the rights of the Petitioners[100] ... the above International instruments and Guidelines for IDPs provide not only for the right to adequate shelter and housing services but also refer to access to land on equitable basis to all.[101]

---

97 *Karma Dorjee & Others v Union of India (UOI) & Others* AIR 2017 SC 113 para 3.
98 ibid para 9.
99 *PK Koul v Estate Officer & Others* (30.11.2010 – DELHC) para 31.
100 ibid para 248.
101 ibid.

CERD has also been mentioned in passing by the Supreme Court[102] and High Courts.[103]

5.1.3 Impact on and through Independent State Institutions

India has a National Commission for Scheduled Castes[104] but it rarely uses CERD. The website of the Commission also does not appear to have any mention of the Convention. The Indian National Commission on Human Rights has more authority to use CERD.[105] The Indian Law Commission has referred to CERD in its report on hate speech.[106]

5.1.4 Impact on and through Non-state Actors

The civil society groups working on discrimination issues in India do not use CERD to a great extent in the courts, but rather rely on the Scheduled Castes and Tribes (Prevention of Atrocities) Act, 1989. The groups, however, extensively use CERD for advocacy with the media and other sectors. They also use CERD in public hearings and fact-finding missions to pressurise the government on discrimination issues.[107] With regard to the impact on academics, there has been no significant academic work that draws on CERD. In the aftermath of the Durban Racism Conference, the Indian Institute of Dalit Studies

---

102   In *Pravasi Bhalai Sangathan v Union of India (UOI) & Others* (12.03.2014 – SC) para 19, CERD is mentioned in passing. In *National Commission on Dalit Human Rights and Others v Union of India* para 6 the Court mentioned CERD and General Recommendation XXIX in passing.
103   In *Prakash v State of Maharashtra & Others* ((04.10.2007 – BOMHC) para 8 counsel for the respondent relied on CERD. The Bombay High Court acknowledged this but did not rely on it for its finding. CERD was mentioned in passing in *Metro Waste Handling v Delhi Jal Board* ((29.05.2018 – DELHC) para 23; *Union of India & Others v Vijay Mam* ((01.06.2012 – DELHC) para 25 by the Delhi High Court. The Delhi High Court also mentioned the Convention in passing in *Mohd Ahmed v Union of India and Others* ((17.04.2014 – DELHC) para 53 in addition to several regional human rights instruments. CERD was mentioned in passing in *Union of India and Others v Fancy Babu* ((03.10.2016 – KERHC) para 29 by the Kerala High Court in addition to similar law other jurisdictions and other human rights instruments such as UDHR. The Convention was also mentioned in passing in *Ramdas Janardan Koli & Others v Secretary, Ministry of Environment and Forests & Others* (27.02.2015 – NGT) para 60, by the National Green Tribunal and in *Vijay Verma v Union of India & Others* ((01.06.2018 – UCHC) para 42 by the Uttarakhand High Court.
104   NCSC website <https://ncsc.nic.in/> accessed 15 September 2023.
105   Dalit groups interview.
106   Law Commission of India, Report No 267, 'Hate Speech' (March 2017) <https://cdnbbsr.s3waas.gov.in/s3caodaec69b5adc880fb464895726dbdf/uploads/2022/08/2022081654-1.pdf> accessed 15 September 2023.
107   Dalit groups interview.

issued a publication.[108] Aside from this publication, there appears to be very little academic work in India related to CERD and its impact.[109]

5.1.5 Impact of State Reporting

State reporting to CERD is overdue but there is no explanation forthcoming from the government as to the reason for the delay. Based on a series of interviews and reviews of government positions over time, it seems that there is resistance to the work of CERD, especially related to issues of caste.[110]

5.2 *International Covenant on Civil and Political Rights*

5.2.1 Incorporation and Reliance by Legislature and Executive

CCPR is incorporated into Indian law by the Protection of Human Rights Act, 1994.[111]

5.2.2 Reliance by Judiciary

CCPR has been referred to close to 390 times by Indian courts. It appears approximately 70 times in judgments of the Supreme Court. In most of the High Court cases examined, the various High Courts refer to the Covenant in the context of relying on earlier Supreme Court judgments.

In *Kirloskar Brothers*[112] and *The People's Union for Civil Liberties v Union of India*,[113] the Supreme Court referenced CCPR to grant justice to victims.[114] The Supreme Court relied upon CCPR in its finding in *Re Inhuman Condition in 1382 Prisons*.[115] In this case the applicants prayed that prisoners sentenced to death should be treated at par with other prisoners and should be provided with all similar facilities that are provided to other prisoners.[116] The Court relied on CCPR and the UDHR in addition to the relevant constitutional provisions when holding that death row prisoners are entitled to meet mental health professionals for a reasonable period of time and with reasonable frequency.[117] The Court in this case went on to state as follows:[118]

---

108 Sukhadeo Thorat and Umakant, *Caste, Race and Discrimination: Discourses in International Context* (Indian Institute of Dalit Studies and Rawat Publications 2004).
109 Dalit groups interview.
110 ibid.
111 The Protection of Human Rights Act, ss 2(d) and 2(f).
112 *Kirloskar Brothers Ltd v Employees State Insurance Corp* 24.01.1196, 1996 (2) SCC 682.
113 *People's Union for Civil Liberties v Union of India (UOI) & Others* (05.02.1997 – SC).
114 Heyns and Viljoen (n 66).
115 *Re Inhuman Condition in 1382 Prisons* 13.12.2018 para 10.
116 ibid para 1.
117 ibid para 10.
118 ibid para 11.

We make it clear that we have only reiterated the law laid down by this Court over several decades and which is based not only on the provisions of our Constitution but is also in conformity with international instruments. Accordingly, the State Governments and Union Territory Administrations must modify the prison manuals, Regulations and Rules accordingly.

In the case of *Justice KS Puttaswamy & Others v Union of India (UOI) & Others*,[119] the petitioners challenged the constitutional validity of the Aadhar Act, 2016,[120] primarily on the ground that it violates the right to privacy which falls within the ambit of the fundamental right to life and personal liberty as under article 21 of the Constitution. In coming to its judgment on the constitutional validity of the Act, the Court had to determine whether there was a right to privacy recognised under the Constitution. Relying on CCPR, CESCR, other international instruments and domestic law, the Court held that there is a fundamental right to privacy.

The Court also relied on CCPR when coming to its judgment in the case of *Navtej Singh Johar*.[121] In this case writ petitions were filed for declaring section 377 of the Indian Penal Code, 1860[122] to be unconstitutional.[123] The Court relied on CCPR, General Comment 16 of the Human Rights Committee[124] in addition to article 2 of CESCR,[125] other international instruments, cases from foreign jurisdictions and domestic law and cases when it read down the section to the extent of decriminalising consensual sexual acts of adults in private. The Court stated:[126]

---

119 26.09.2018 – SC paras 619–621.
120 Under the Aadhar Act, 2016, a Unique Identification Authority of India (UIDAI) was established. The body was given the task of developing a system for issuing Aadhar numbers to individuals and also perform authentication of the numbers. All residents in India were eligible to obtain an Aadhar number. To enable a resident to obtain an Aadhar number, demographic as well as biometric information in addition to name, date of birth and address was to be provided by the individual.
121 *Navtej Singh Johar & Others v Union of India & Others* AIR 2018 SC 4321 paras 523.1, 450–454; see also paras 5 and 151.
122 S 377: 'Unnatural offences: Whoever voluntarily has carnal intercourse against the order of nature with any man, woman or animal, shall be punished with imprisonment for life, or with imprisonment of either description for a term which may extend to ten years, and shall also be liable to fine. Explanation: penetration is sufficient to constitute the carnal intercourse necessary to the offence described in this section'.
123 *Navtej Singh Johar* (n 121) para 10.
124 ibid para 454.
125 ibid paras 452, 453.
126 ibid para 456.

In adjudicating the validity of this provision, the Indian Penal Code must be brought into conformity with both the Indian Constitution and the Rules of principles in international law that India has recognized. Both make a crucial contribution towards recognizing the human rights of sexual and gender minorities.

In *Shatrughan Chauhan*[127] petitions were filed for the commutation of the death sentence to life imprisonment. Relying on provisions of the CCPR, including the right to privacy, other international instruments and domestic law, the Supreme Court commuted the death sentence of one convict on the ground that mental illness is a supervening circumstance.

CCPR is also mentioned in passing by the Supreme Court and the High Courts.[128]

---

127   *Shatrughan Chauhan & Others v Union of India (UOI) & Others* (21.01.2014 – SC) para 73.
128   In GRSE *Ltd Workmen's Union & Others v State of West Bengal & Others* (02.12.2016 – CALHC) para 15, the Calcutta High Court mentioned CCPR in passing in the context of referring to precedent. In *All Manipur Students' Union (AMSU) & Others v Adradeep Kumar Singh & Others* (10.04.2002 – GUHC) para 2 the petitioners contended that there had been an infringement of art 19 of CCPR. However, the Guwahati High Court did not take this into consideration when passing judgment. In *Abhay Shrenikbhai Gandhi v State of Gujarat* (24.01.2017 – GUJHC) para 16 the Gujarat High Court mentions CCPR in passing. In *Manjula Devi & Others v The State of Bihar* (02.03.2017 – PATNAHC) para 7 the Patna High Court had made reference to CCPR in passing only; the Patna High Court cited *Sher Singh alias Partapa v State of Haryana* 2015 CRILJ 1118 para 15 which made reference to art 14(3)(g) of the Covenant. However, the Court did not take the provisions of the Covenant into account when coming to its finding. In *Kavitha G Pillai v The Joint Director, Director of Enforcement, Government of India* (26.07.2017 – KERHC) para 100 the Kerala High Court makes passing reference to art 14(3)(g) of CCPR in addition to a similar provision in the UDHR. The Kerala High Court does not seem to place very much reliance on the Covenant in this case. In *Aaqil Jamil & Others v State of UP & Others* (19.04.2017 – ALLHC) para 22 the Allahabad High Court referred to CCPR but only in passing as it was referred to in the context of relying on *Charu Khurana & Others v Union of India & Others*. Other cases have only had a passing mention of the Covenant; as in *Federation of Obstetrics and Gynecological Society (FOGSI) v Union of India & Others* 03.05.2019 para 7, the petitioner placed reliance on the presumption of innocence enshrined in art 14(2) of CCPR; *Ashwini Kumar v Union of India* 05.09.2019 para 4, the applicant placed reliance on art 7 of CCPR and art 5 of the UDHR; *Subhash Kashinath Mahajan v The State of Maharashtra & Others* 20.03.2018 – paras 43 and 45. The Supreme Court reiterated the law on compensation for unnatural deaths and in this regard referred to its earlier judgments in *Nilabati Behera v State of Orissa* 1993 2 SCC 746 and *DK Basu v State of West Bengal*, both of which mention CCPR; *Lourembam Deben Singh & Others v Union of India (UOI) & Others* (12.11.2018 – SC) para 65, the UDHR and ECHR have also been mentioned. In *Common Cause (A Regd Society) v Union of India (UOI) & Others* (09.03.2018 – SC), which dealt with voluntary

5.2.3 Impact on and through Independent State Institutions

The Indian Law Commission has in numerous reports referred to CCPR. In its report on the death penalty,[129] the Commission made reference not only to CCPR but also its OP2-CCPR. In its report on hate speech the Commission also referred to CCPR.[130] In its Report No 277 on Wrongful Prosecution (Miscarriage of Justice), in the section on legal remedies, the Commission referred to CCPR and the Human Rights Committee's General Comment 32.[131]

5.3 International Covenant on Economic, Social and Cultural Rights

5.3.1 Incorporation and Reliance by the Legislature and Executive

CESCR is incorporated into Indian law by the Protection of Human Rights Act, 1994.[132] The Statement of Objects and Reasons in the National Food Security Act, 2013 states that it is enacted in pursuance of India's international obligations under CESCR.[133]

5.3.2 Reliance by Judiciary

We found 188 cases where CESCR has been cited by the Supreme Court and various High Courts. The Supreme Court of India has referenced CESCR approximately 32 times. The High Courts often refer to settled law by the Supreme Court in relation to international treaties when arriving at their judgments.

In *Navtej Singh Johar*, the Supreme Court placed reliance on the right to health as enshrined in article 12 of the Covenant and General Comment 14 of the CESCR Cttee[134] when reading down section 377 of the Indian Penal Code, 1860, to decriminalise consensual sexual acts of same-sex adults in private. In *Lillu*,[135] an appeal was filed in the Supreme Court against the conviction and sentence for rape by trial in a lower court and affirmed by the High Court. The Court found that the circumstances did not warrant any interference and maintained the conviction and sentence. The Supreme Court relied on CESCR in addition to other international instruments and domestic law when coming

---

euthanasia, the Court mentioned CCPR in passing acknowledging that there are certain relevant obligations enshrined in the Covenant, paras 111–113.
[129] Indian Law Commission, Report No 262 on 'Death Penalty'.
[130] Indian Law Commission, Report No 267 on 'Hate Speech'.
[131] Indian Law Commission, Report No 277 on 'Wrongful Prosecution (Miscarriage of Justice)'.
[132] The Protection of Human Rights Act, ss 2(d) and 2(f).
[133] See iv <https://rajyasabha.nic.in/rsnew/publication_electronic/National_Food_security_Act2013.pdf> accessed 14 November 2022.
[134] *Navtej Singh Johar & Others v Union of India (UOI) & Others* (2018) 10 SCC 1 para 421.
[135] *Lillu & Others v State of Haryana* (09.04.2013 – SC) paras 12, 114.

to its finding that 'rape survivors are entitled to legal recourse that does not retraumatise them or violate their physical or mental integrity and dignity'.[136] It also held that the two-finger test 'violates the right of rape survivors to privacy, physical and mental integrity and dignity'.[137] In *Apparel Export Promotion Council v AK Chopra*,[138] the Court relied on CESCR and CEDAW when coming to its finding. The case required the Court to determine whether an order of dismissal of a senior officer because he sexually harassed a female employee was valid. The Court relied on CESCR, in particular article 7 of the Convention, other international instruments and domestic law when upholding the dismissal. It stated:[139]

> This Court has in numerous cases emphasized that while discussing constitutional requirements, court and counsel must never forget the core principle embodied in the International Conventions and Instruments and as far as possible give effect to the principles contained in those international instruments. The Courts are under an obligation to give due regard to International Conventions and Norms for construing domestic laws more so when there is no inconsistency between them and there is a void in domestic law ... In cases involving violation of human rights, the Courts must forever remain alive to the international instruments and conventions and apply the same to a given case when there is no inconsistency between the international norms and the domestic law occupying the field.

In the case of *Rajive Raturi*[140] the Court placed reliance on India's international obligations to come to its finding.[141] The petition in this case was filed on behalf of visually-impaired persons for proper and adequate access to public places. The Court made reference to General Comment 5 of the CESCR Cttee and relied on domestic law when directing the state to do the required. In the *PG Gupta* case, concerning the allotment of government accommodation and the right to housing, the Supreme Court took cognisance of article 11(1) of

---

136   ibid para 12.
137   ibid para 13.
138   *Apparel Export Promotion Council v AK Chopra* (20.01.1999 – SC).
139   ibid para 28.
140   *Rajive Raturi v Union of India (UOI) & Others* (15.12.2017 – SC) paras 7, 14. 'The very Preamble to the Disabilities Act discloses that this Act was enacted by the legislature to fulfil its international obligation to enact a disability specific law nationally'.
141   ibid.

CESCR, which recognises the right to an adequate standard of living, including adequate food, clothing and housing.[142] CESCR has also been mentioned in passing by the Supreme Court[143] and High Courts.[144]

5.3.3 Impact on and through Independent State Institutions

The Law Commission of India in its 205th report on proposals to amend the Prohibition of Child Marriage Act, 2006, referred to CESCR.[145]

5.4 *Convention on the Elimination of All Forms of Discrimination against Women*

5.4.1 Incorporation and Reliance by Legislature and Executive

In terms of national norms that have a bearing on women's rights, the Sexual Harassment of Women at Workplace (Prevention, Prohibition and Redressal) Act, 2013 explicitly aligns with CEDAW commitments. The Preamble to the Act states that it has been enacted to give effect to CEDAW for the protection of women against sexual harassment at the workplace. A number of provisions similar to those of CEDAW are to be found in legislation such as the Equal Remuneration Act, 1976 and the Maternity Benefit Act, 1961.[146]

CEDAW General Recommendations have often been used by state governments. General Recommendation 26, for example, was used by the government of Andhra Pradesh and Telangana to support the passing a state order regarding the migration of women domestic workers.[147]

There are not many indications that the government takes CEDAW very seriously. Some of the government officials directly dealing with CEDAW state that they would like to make more progress within the government hierarchy, but

---

142 Heyns and Viljoen (n 66).
143 Reliance was placed by the petitioner on art 11(1) of CESCR in connection with the right to shelter by the petitioner in the case of *Ashwani Kumar v Union of India (UOI) & Others* (13.12.2018 – SC) paras 24–25, but the Supreme Court did not rely on it when coming to its final judgment, stating: 'We are in full agreement with the view expressed by the Petitioner but we must be aware of the caution given by this Court to the effect that the right to shelter is subject to "economic budgeting" by the State'. CESCR was mentioned in passing in the case of *Dilip K Basu v State of West Bengal & Others* (24.07.2015 – SC) para 8.
144 *Vijay Laxmanrao Dak & Others v The Union of India & Others* (09.03.2018 – BOMHC) para 34; *Sarfaraz Khan v State of UP & Others. Maharajdeen v State of UP* (06.10.2017 – ALLHC) para 57.
145 Law Commission of India, 'Proposal to Amend the Prohibition of Child Marriage Act, 2006, and other allied laws'. Report No 205 <https://cdnbbsr.s3waas.gov.in/s3ca0daec69b5ad-c880fb464895726dbdf/uploads/2022/08/2022081072-1.pdf> accessed 15 September 2023.
146 Heyns and Viljoen (n 66).
147 CEDAW interview.

the Ministry of Women and Children is a 'weak' ministry and needs approval from other more powerful ministries. This is the reason why UN Women and many civil society groups have been advocating a separate Ministry for Women.[148]

5.4.2 Reliance by Judiciary

We have located 138 cases where CEDAW has been cited by the courts. It has been referenced approximately 19 times by the Supreme Court. High Courts refer largely to Supreme Court judgments where the apex court relied on CEDAW. In most cases CEDAW is mentioned as it appears in the case that is being referred to by the Court and therefore it is mentioned only in passing. As stated in an exhaustive report on the impact of CEDAW in India, '[t]he predominant use of CEDAW in judicial pronouncement has been interpretive, helping to engender constitutional rights to minimise explicit discrimination in the law'.[149]

The fact that the judiciary has played a leadership role in domesticating CEDAW is demonstrated through the setting of guidelines for law making as seen in the 1997 case of *Vishaka v State of Rajasthan*.[150] In the *Vishaka* case the Court drew upon the principle of 'legitimate expectation' (that is, citizens may legitimately expect that rights enshrined in a treaty ratified by the state will be protected) which emanated from the ratification of the treaty and General Recommendation 19 setting out guidelines that should be enacted as law, thereby plugging the legislative vacuum on sexual harassment in the workplace.[151]

The Supreme Court relied on the Convention, particularly articles 11 and 12, in addition to domestic law when arriving at its 2017 finding in *Z v The State of Bihar & Others*.[152] In this case an appeal was filed before the Supreme Court against an order of the High Court which dismissed the application of the appellant for medical termination of pregnancy. The Court did not allow medical termination of pregnancy as the time period for safe termination had

---

148 ibid.
149 Madhu Mehra, 'India's CEDAW Story' <https://pldindia.org/advocacy/submissions-to-domestic-and-international-bodies/womens-human-rights-cedaw-in-international-regional-and-national-law-indias-cedaw-story-studies-on-human-rights-conventions-2013/> accessed 15 September 2023.
150 *Vishaka & Others v State of Rajasthan* (13.08.1997 – SC) paras 7, 12, 13–16.
151 ibid.
152 *Z v The State of Bihar & Others* (2018)11SCC572 (17.08.2017 – SC) para 57.

lapsed, but instead provided the appellant with compensation of Rs 10 00 000. Relying on articles 11 and 12 of CEDAW, the Supreme Court stated (in para 57):

> Before parting with the case, we must note that India has ratified the Convention on the Elimination of All Forms of Discrimination Against Women (CEDAW) in 1993 and is under an international obligation to ensure that the right of a woman in her reproductive choices is protected.

In *Githa Hariharan*,[153] the petitioners challenged the constitutional validity of section 6(A) of the Hindu Minority and Guardianship Act, 1956. The section stated that the mother is the guardian of the Hindu minor child 'after' the father and that the father is the natural guardian. The Supreme Court placed reliance on CEDAW and domestic law when upholding the constitutionality of the section, but interpreted it widely so that it would mean that both father and mother are natural guardians.

In *Independent Thought*,[154] the Supreme Court in 2017 relied on CEDAW, other international instruments and domestic law when arriving at its final decision. In this case the Supreme Court had to determine whether sexual intercourse between a man and his wife, a girl between 15 and 18 years of age, is rape. The Court held that sexual intercourse with a girl below 18 years of age is rape, regardless of her marital status. It further stated that the distinction created between a married girl child and an unmarried one under Exception 2 to section 375 of the Indian Penal Code, 1860 is untenable[155] and read down the exception to mean that the same will not apply to minors.

---

153 *Githa Hariharan & Others v Reserve Bank of India & Others* (1999) 2 SCC 228. (This case extended guardianship of the ward to mothers while the father was living, or in cases where the father was physically absent, was unfit or had delegated his duty.) (17.02.1999 – SC) para 14.

154 *Independent Thought v Union of India (UOI) & Others* (2017) 10 SCC 800 (11.10.2017 – SC) paras 1, 33, 40.

155 S 375 of the Indian Penal Code 1860 reads as follows: 'Rape – A man is said to commit "rape" if he – () penetrates his penis, to any extent, into the vagina, mouth, urethra or anus of a woman or makes her to do so with him or any other person; or (b) inserts, to any extent, any object or a part of the body, not being the penis, into the vagina, the urethra or anus of a woman or makes her to do so with him or any other person; or (c) manipulates any part of the body of a woman so as to cause penetration into the vagina, urethra, anus or any part of body of such woman or makes her to do so with him or any other person; or (d) applies his mouth to the vagina, anus, urethra of a woman or makes her to do so with him or any other person, under the circumstances falling under any of ... seven descriptions'.

In *Seema v Ashwani Kumar*,[156] the Supreme Court directed the states and central government to notify rules to make registration of marriages compulsory notwithstanding India's reservation to CEDAW with regard to making reservation of marriages compulsory.

In *Santi Ruidas v Coal India Ltd*,[157] the Calcutta High Court relied on CEDAW when coming to its judgment. In this case an appeal was filed against the order of a High Court which dismissed the petition of the appellant regarding 'compassionate appointment' because she was a female. The Court relied on CEDAW and domestic law and held:[158]

> Writ Petitioner who had completed 15 years of age but not 18 years of age on the death of her mother who was an employee of the Appellant-authority, was entitled to have her name kept on the live Register for employment upon completion of 18 years of age.

CEDAW has also been mentioned in passing by the Supreme Court[159] and High Courts.[160]

5.4.3 Impact on and through Independent State Institutions

There appears to be no mention of the Convention on the website the National Commission for Women.[161] The State Women's Human Rights Commissions,

---

156 *Seema v Ashwani Kumar* (14.02.2006 – SC).
157 *Santi Ruidas v Coal India Ltd* (25.02.2010 – CALHC).
158 ibid paras 12 and 13.
159 In *State of Maharashtra & Others v Indian Hotel and Restaurants Assn & Others* reliance was placed by the appellant on the Convention. However, the Court's finding was not in favour of the appellant and it did not place reliance on the Convention when coming to its finding. In *Sakshi & Others v Union of India (UOI) & Others* counsel for the petitioner placed reliance on arts 17(e) and 19 of CEDAW. However, the Court did not place reliance on this when coming to its finding. In *Supreme Court Women Lawyers Association (SCWLA) v Union of India (UOI) & Others* the Court mentions CEDAW but does not place reliance on it. In *Santhini v Vijaya Venketesh* the Court mentions CEDAW in passing but does not place reliance on it.
160 In *Debjani Sengupta v The Institute of Cost Accountants of India & Others* (03.05.2019 – CALHC) para 12 the Calcutta High Court mentions CEDAW but does not rely on it when coming to its finding. In *K Hema Latha v State of Tamil Nadu & Others* (08.03.2018 – MADHC) para 25 the Madras High Court referred to the relevant portions of *Vishaka & Others v State of Rajasthan & Others* which referred to CEDAW. However, this was not a contributing factor when the High Court came to its decision. In *Tripti Manish Sahni & Others v Manish Gobindram Sahni & Others* (20.03.2013 – BOMHC) para 75 mentions the mandate of CEDAW to bring about gender equality but only in passing.
161 NCW website <http://ncw.nic.in/> accessed 14 November 2022.

for example, the Commission's in Maharashtra, Assam and Rajasthan, are more effective than the national women's commission.[162]

5.4.4 Impact on and through Non-state Actors

There is a great level of NGO work on CEDAW, including through the preparation of parallel reports. There is very little coverage in the media on CEDAW and the work of the CEDAW Cttee. Trainings with journalists have taken place, including by UN Women, but not many examples of media coverage could be found.

5.5 Convention against Torture and Other Cruel, Inhuman or Degrading Treatment or Punishment

CAT has not been ratified by India. However, the call for the ratification of CAT and robust domestic anti-torture legislation has been reiterated by the National Human Rights Commission, the Law Commission of India, the Supreme Court, UN bodies, national and international civil society organisations, and independent experts. We found 10 references to CAT in judgments of Indian courts. The Supreme Court referred to it three times. In a civil writ petition filed before the Supreme Court of India by Dr Ashwini Kumar,[163] the petitioner sought directions to the central government to enact a suitable stand-alone, effective and purposeful legislative framework/law based upon CAT. The Supreme Court issued notice to the central government regarding creating such a framework. In 2017 the Law Commission of India released its 273rd report on the implementation of CAT.[164]

The judiciary has considered a number of cases alleging torture by some law enforcement officials. It has granted relief in some of these cases on the basis of the right to freedom from torture in the Constitution. For example, in *Francis Coralie Mullin v Adman, Union Territory of Delhi and Others* the Supreme Court observed as follows: '[T]here is implicit in Article 21 the right to protection against torture or cruel, inhuman or degrading treatment.'[165] In other cases, the courts issued guidelines regarding solitary confinement and the use of handcuffs, and non-compliance with these guidelines has been interpreted as a violation of the article 21 constitutional right to human dignity

---

162 Based on interviews with relevant UN agencies.
163 Writ Petition (Civil) No 738 of 2016.
164 Law Commission of India, Report No 273, Implementation of the United National Convention against Torture, Cruel, Inhuman and Degrading Treatment' <https://cdnbbsr.s3waas.gov.in/s3caodaec69b5adc880fb464895726dbdf/uploads/2022/08/2022081620.pdf> accessed 15 September 2023.
165 Heyns and Viljoen (n 66).

and freedom from torture.[166] The Supreme Court relied on the Convention in the case of *Abu Salem Abdul Qayoom Ansari*,[167] stating:

> Furthermore obligations entered by many countries of the world, including India, in the form of Covenant on Civil and Political Rights, and The Convention Against Torture and Other Cruel, Inhuman or Degrading Treatment or Punishment (to which India is a Signatory), would preclude a total and unconditional observance of the principle of non-inquiry. Even though, non-inquiry is not an absolute doctrine, but in facts of the present case, it operates.

In the 2010 case of *State v Chandra Kumar & Others* the Court of the Metropolitan Magistrate relied on CAT, CEDAW, CCPR, other international conventions and domestic law when quashing an order of deportation of a refugee back to his country of origin. In this case, a First Information Report was filed against the accused (who was convicted) under the Foreigner's Act, 1946 for cheating, impersonation and forgery. The prosecutor prayed that deportation should form part of the order on sentence. The judge relied on CAT and other international instruments when recognising the *jus cogens* nature of *non-refoulement* and noting that India is bound by customary international law. The judge relied on CAT, despite India not having ratified it for the reason that '[a] state that signs a treaty is obliged in good faith, from acts that would defeat the object and purpose of the treaty'[168] when quashing the order of deportation. The Court has also in some cases mentioned CAT in passing.[169]

---

166 Heyns and Viljoen (n 66).
167 *Abu Salem Abdul Qayoom Ansari v State of Maharashtra & Others* (10.09.2010 – SC) para 51.
168 *State v Chandra Kumar & Others*, Court of Metropolitan Magistrate, New Delhi, 20.09.2010 para 73.
169 *National Legal Services Authority v Union of India (UOI) & Others* (15.04.2014 – SC) paras 24 and 47. In the case of *Selvi & Others v State of Karnataka* (05.05.2010 – SC) paras 196 and 199 the appellants relied on CAT in their submission. However, the Court stated that they are not bound by CAT even though India is a signatory because it has not been ratified by Parliament in the manner provided under art 253 of the Constitution and neither is there any national legislation that has provisions similar to CAT. Therefore, in the opinion of the Court, CAT does not hold significant persuasive values; *Sakshi Sharma & Others v The State of Himachal Pradesh & Others* (18.06.2012 – HPHC) paras 31, 32 and 76, the Himachal Pradesh High Court mentions CAT but does not rely on it for its final finding; *Shreemad Jagadguru Shankaracharya Shree Shree Raghaveshwara Bharati Swamiji v State of Karnataka* (03.12.2014 – KARHC) para 8, by the Karnataka High Court. CAT was mentioned in passing in the case of *Union of India & Others v Fancy Babu* (03.10.2016 – KERHC) para 29, by the Kerala High Court but was not relied upon for its finding; *Essar Telecom Infrastructure (P) Ltd v State of Kerala* (11.03.2011 – KERHC) para 66, but not relied

5.6 Convention on the Rights of the Child

5.6.1 Incorporation and Reliance by Legislature and Executive

CRC is one of the instruments with which government officials in India are most familiar. Many Indian laws dealing with children recognise the provisions of CRC. The Preamble to the Commission for Protection of Child Rights Act, 2005 states that it is enacted to give effect to the provisions of CRC. The Preamble to the Juvenile Justice (Care and Protection of Children) Act, 2015 states that the Act is enacted to 'make comprehensive provisions for children alleged and found to be in conflict with law and children in need of care and protection, taking into consideration the standards prescribed in the Convention on the Rights of the Child'. The Preamble to the Prevention of Children from Sexual Offences Act, 2017 states that it is enacted to carry out the provisions of CRC.

However, there is a lack of knowledge of CRC at the more junior levels of government where the officers are not concerned about normative standards but rather policy directives. With regard to the perception of CRC Cttee among government officials, the Optional Protocols do not receive much prominence in the government or civil society. Government officials seem largely unaware that they are supposed to be also reporting on the Optional Protocols.

The general attitude of the government towards CRC and the CRC Cttee is favourable. However, there is resistance to some children's rights, especially child participation and protection.

In terms of the legitimacy and authority of the Committee, the government respects the process. The government, however, is not self-critical and seems to want to engage with CRC to demonstrate all the steps they are taking to promote children's rights in the country.

The COs of CRC are practical. That is why these are a good tool for advocacy. National policy for children was a success because it relied on the COs.

---

upon by the Kerala High Court because 'while it may have persuasive effect unless and until it is implemented by making a law as contemplated under the Constitution, it may not be legally binding as such'.

A Rahul v The State of Tamil Nadu & Others (11.03.2011 – KERHC) para. 66, the Madras High Court mentioned CAT in passing but acknowledged it. CAT was mentioned in passing by the Patna High Court in *Chief Commissioner of Income Tax (CCA), Patna & Others v The State of Bihar & Others* (02.02.2012 – PATNAHC) para 19, referring to the definition of torture as stated in the Convention.

5.6.2 Reliance by Judiciary

CRC has been referred to by the courts, as far as we could establish, around 206 times. The Supreme Court referenced CRC approximately 27 times. In some cases the Court has extensively discussed India's international obligations and it is evident that CRC was a major contributing factor when arriving to its judgments. In *Salil Bali,*[170] petitions were filed seeking a declaration that Juvenile Justice Act, 2000[171] was unconstitutional, in particular praying for reconsideration of sections 2(k),[172] 2(l)[173] and 15[174] of the Act in light of the rise in criminal cases by persons within the range of 16 to 18 years. The Supreme Court upheld the constitutionality of the Act stating that it was in line with the Constitution and CRC.[175] In *Jitendra Singh,*[176] an appeal was filed against an order and judgment of the Allahabad High Court which upheld the conviction and sentence of the appellant for dowry death.[177] The punishment awarded by the High Court was Rs 100. The appellant was a juvenile[178] as at the date of the offence. The Supreme Court upheld the conviction but set aside the punishment deeming it grossly inadequate. The issue of quantum of punishment was remitted to the jurisdictional juvenile justice board. Relying on CRC and domestic law, the Court stated:[179]

---

170   *Salil Bali v Union of India (UOI) & Others* (17.07.2013 – SC).
171   This Act has been repealed. The Juvenile Justice Act, 2015 is the Act in force.
172   S 2(k), Juvenile Justice Act, 2000: '"Juvenile" or "child" means a person who has not completed eighteenth year of age'.
173   S 2(l), Juvenile Justice Act, 2000: '"Juvenile in conflict with law" means a juvenile who is alleged to have committed an offence and has not completed eighteenth year of age as on the date of commission of such offence'.
174   S 15, Juvenile Justice Act, 2000: Orders that may be passed regarding a juvenile.
175   *Salil Bali v Union of India (UOI) & Others* (17.07.2013 – SC) para 44.
176   *Jitendra Singh & Others v State of UP* (10.07.2013 – SC) paras 58, 62, 69.
177   S 304B, Indian Penal Code, 1860: '(1) Where the death of a woman is caused by any burns or bodily injury or occurs otherwise than under normal circumstances within seven years of her marriage and it is shown that soon before her death she was subjected to cruelty or harassment by her husband or any relative of her husband for, or in connection with, any demand for dowry, such death shall be called "dowry death", and such husband or relative shall be deemed to have caused her death. Explanation. For the purpose of this subsection, "dowry" shall have the same meaning as in section 2 of the Dowry Prohibition Act, 1961 (28 of 1961). (2) Whoever commits dowry death shall be punished with imprisonment for a term which shall not be less than seven years but which may extend to imprisonment for life'.
178   As under art 2(k) of the Juvenile Justice Act, 2000.
179   *Jitendra Singh & Others v State of UP* (10.07.2013 – SC) para 69.

Keeping in mind our domestic law and our international obligations, it is directed that the provisions of the Code of Criminal Procedure relating to arrest and the provisions of the Juvenile Justice (Care and Protection of Children) Act, 2000 being the law of the land, should be scrupulously followed by the concerned authorities in respect of juveniles in conflict with law.

There are cases where CRC has only been mentioned by the Supreme Court[180] and High Courts.[181]

5.6.3 Impact on and through Independent State Institutions

The mandate of the National Commission for the Protection of Child Rights (NCPCR) is to 'ensure that all Laws, Policies, Programmes, and Administrative Mechanisms are in consonance with the Child Rights perspective as enshrined in the Constitution of India and also the UN Convention on the Rights of the Child'.[182] The Commission has played an important role in advocacy around

---

180 Counsel for the petitioner relied on CRC in its submission in the case of *Mazdoor Kisan Shakti Sangathan v The Union of India (UOI) & Others* (23.07.2018 – SC) para. 20, but the Court did not attach much importance on this when arriving at its judgment. The Supreme Court mentioned CRC in passing in the case of *Kanika Goel v State of Delhi & Others* (20.07.2018 – SC) para 18. However, it did not place much reliance on it when coming to its judgment. In *Alakh Alok Srivastava v Union of India (UOI) & Others* AIR2018SC2440 (01.05.2018 – SC) para 11 the Court again simply mentions CRC.

181 In *ABC v The Bombay Municipal Corporation of Greater Mumbai* (13.03.2018 – BOMHC) para 17 the Bombay High Court refers to CRC when citing a case decided by the apex court but CRC is mentioned only in passing; *Varsha Sanjay Shinde & Others v The Society of Friends of the Sassoon Hospitals & Others* (18.10.2013 – BOMHC) para 13, CRC is mentioned in passing by the Bombay High Court. The Bombay High Court also refers to the Hague Convention on Protection of Children and Cooperation in Respect of Inter-Country Adoption, 1993 on which it places a higher degree of reliance when coming to its judgment. In *Tajel Sk & Others v The State of West Bengal* (02.03.2016 – CALHC) paras 32, 35, the Calcutta High Court mentions CRC in passing and also refers to the Juvenile Justice Act, which in its statement of object and purpose gives importance to the implementation of CRC at the domestic level. In *Rohit Sitapatikumar Verma v State of Gujarat & Others* (08.11.2012 – GUJHC) para 7, the Gujarat High Court mentions CRC but only in the context of referring to the Juvenile Justice (Care and Protection of Children) Act, 2000. Mentioned in passing in the case of *Ruhe v State of Gujarat* (23.07.2010 – GUJHC) para 22 by the Gujarat High Court in the context of referring to the case of *Amarsinh @ Dipsinh Sursinh v State of Gujarat* 2007 [2] GLH 1. CRC is mentioned in passing in the case of *Prajwala v Union of India & Others* (20.11.2018 – HYHC) para 6, by the Hyderabad High Court. In *Reni Krishnan v State of Kerala* (05.02.2018 – KERHC) para 7, the Kerala High Court mentions CRC but only in the context of referring to the Juvenile Justice Act.

182 NCPCR website <https://www.ncpcr.gov.in/> accessed 14 November 2022.

the Convention and COs. However, it is largely caught up in a case management role and monitoring the implementation of COs is not a priority.[183]

5.6.4 Impact on and through Non-state Actors

CRC is taught in the general law school curriculum, and as part of public international law but only as an elective, not as a foundational course. There are, however, child rights centres in a number of law schools. These centres rely extensively on CRC and also carry out research on international law.[184]

5.6.5 Impact of State Reporting

With regard to CRC, the government prepares the report (upon reminders by UNICEF which has provided advice regarding the steps to be taken and the need to include civil society organizations in the process). On occasion, critical comments were included in the initial stages of drafting but removed in subsequent draft. The presentation of reports in Geneva is usually done by the joint secretary and on one occasion by the Secretary.

5.7 *Convention on the Rights of Persons with Disabilities*

5.7.1 Incorporation by Legislature and Executive

The Preamble to the Rights of Persons with Disabilities Act, 2016 states that it is enacted to give effect to CRPD. The Preamble to the Mental Healthcare Act, 2016 states that it is enacted to 'align and harmonise the existing laws with CRPD'.

5.7.2 Reliance by Judiciary

CRPD has been referred to by the courts of India close to 50 times. CRPD has been referred to by the Supreme Court seven times. In *Jeeja Ghosh*,[185] the petitioner was compelled to deboard an aircraft operated by a private company due to her disability. The Court relied on CRPD[186] and domestic law when stating that the deboarding was illegal and awarding her a compensation of Rs 10 00 000.[187] It further stated that fulfilment of the rights under the instruments guaranteeing rights to persons with disabilities is not limited to the state but also private entities.[188] In the 2009 case of *Suchita Srivastava*

---

183   UNICEF interview.
184   ibid.
185   *Jeeja Ghosh & Others v Union of India (UOI) & Others* (12.05.2016 – SC).
186   ibid paras 11, 42.
187   ibid para 34.
188   ibid para 18.

& Others v Chandigarh Administration an appeal was filed against orders of the High Court which ruled that it was in the best interests of the appellant to undergo medical termination of pregnancy due to her mental disability. The Supreme Court stayed the High Court order stating that consent is necessary for termination of the pregnancy. The Supreme Court relied on CRPD and domestic law stating that '[w]e must also bear in mind that India has ratified the Convention on the Rights of Persons with Disabilities (CRPD) on October 1, 2007 and the contents of the same are binding on our legal system'.[189] CRPD has also been mentioned in passing by the Supreme Court[190] and High Courts.[191]

5.7.3 Impact on and through Independent State Institutions

The Law Commission of India has in some of its reports explicitly referred to CRPD and urged the government to repeal or amend legislation that runs counter to the provisions of CRPD.[192]

6 Conclusion

It is difficult to generalise regarding the impact of the treaty system in India. Some of the treaties, for example CRC and CEDAW, have received more attention than others.

---

[189] *Suchita Srivastava & Others v Chandigarh Administration* (28.08.2009 – SC) para 26.

[190] In *Purswani Ashutosh v Union of India (UOI) & Others* (24.08.2018 – SC) paras 1 and 2, the Court mentioned CRPD in the context of stating that the Persons with Disabilities Act, 2016 was enacted to give effect to CRPD. The Court then relied on CRPD for its finding. It was referred to in the same context in *Justice Sunanda Bhandare Foundation v Union of India (UOI) & Others* (25.04.2017 – SC) para 8. The Convention was relied on by counsel for the petitioner in the context of the 2016 Act in *Pranay Kumar Podder v State of Tripura & Others* (23.03.2017 – SC) para 23 but was not relied upon by the Court when rendering its judgment. CRPD was mentioned in passing in *Z v State of Bihar & Others* 17.08.2017 – SC para 35.

[191] *Jadhav Vishwas Haridas v Union Public Service Commission & Others* (27.10.2016 – DELHC) para 25, when stating that it was relied upon by counsel for the appellants. It was also mentioned in passing in *Yusufbhai Hatimbhai Kachwala v. Municipal Commissioner* (24.01.2014 – GUJHC) para 8; *Susanta Kumar Sahoo v Union of India* (04.12.2014 – ORIHC) para 13; *Arora v Lt Governor of Delhi & Others* (03.04.2014 – DELHC) para 7; *DS Chauhan v Railway Board, Ministry of Railways* (15.10.2012 – DELHC) para 2.

[192] See, for example, the report 'Eliminating Discrimination Against Persons Affected by Leprosy' (2015), Law Commission of India, Report No 256 <https://cdnbbsr.s3waas.gov.in/s3caoodaec69b5adc880fb464895726dbdf/uploads/2022/08/2022081662.pdf> accessed 15 September 2023.

While the use of treaties and treaty body work is quite extensive in the Indian judicial system, it is difficult to make an estimate of the impact of this on the ground. It is clear, however, that the use of treaty bodies and their work has increased substantially over the past 20 years, especially in the legislative and civil society arenas. Moreover, the treaty system plays an extensive role as an advocacy tool and a mobilising tool for civil society in India. There is also little doubt that since the advent of the UPR, knowledge of the treaty system has increased. Given the cross sectoral nature of civil society coalitions working on the UPR, and the UPR's comprehensive review of human rights, work of the treaty bodies has received a new profile.

At the same time, the importance of the treaty system for the Indian government may have declined in recent years. This is reflected in the 'lower' level of delegations that appear before the treaty bodies (as opposed to the UPR or global conferences). This is also reflected in the fact that there is little change in the 'overdue' status of many reports to the treaty bodies and the continued lack of a broader consultation process in the preparation of reports by the government. This is also evident in the fact that India is not active in nominating members to the treaty bodies. In spite of the extensive expertise in the country, India has, for example, never nominated a member to CRC. The recent nomination of a former diplomat to the CESCR Cttee also does not inspire much confidence in India's ability to nominate 'independent' experts. The inability of the government to translate the instruments and take them to the local levels, communities and local government systems has hampered deeper penetration of the treaties and the work of the treaty bodies.

The impact of COs is also patchy. The CRC COs have been useful as they contributed to the national plan of action on the rights of the child. The COs of other treaty bodies seem to have had no discernible impact either at the policy level or on the ground.

Civil society and some of the UN agencies are the principal users of the work of treaty bodies. Civil society uses the treaty body work extensively as an advocacy tool, along with the government, media and national human rights institutions, but also has a strong engagement with the treaty bodies through the preparation of parallel reports, participation at their meetings in Geneva, and so forth.

For the treaties and the work of treaty bodies to have greater impact, the government would need to take their reporting obligations more seriously as well as devote more time and resources to publicising the work of treaty bodies, including the COs. The government also needs to initiate a broad consultative process during the preparation of its reports, nominate senior level officials to be part of their delegations for the treaty body reviews, ensure an active role in nominating 'independent' members to serve on the treaty bodies and coordinate follow-up work on the COs.

CHAPTER 10

The Impact of the United Nations Human Rights Treaties on the Domestic Level in Jamaica

Malene C. Alleyne and Tracy Robinson

1   Introduction to Human Rights in Jamaica

Jamaica is a small-island developing state with a population of nearly 3 million.[1] Jamaica has a Human Development Index value of 0,726 (2019), which means that it is in the high human development category.[2] Significant inequality exists in Jamaica and the number of Jamaicans living in poverty increased to approximately 19 per cent in 2017.[3]

Jamaica's colonial history is mired with grave human rights abuses, including the decimation of the indigenous population and African slavery. In 1962 Jamaica became an independent nation and a member of the British Commonwealth. Human rights were guaranteed in Chapter 3 of the independence Constitution of 1962, which covered largely civil and political rights and established a parliamentary democratic system, which is also a constitutional monarchy. There are a number of civil society organisations (CSOs) in Jamaica, some of which promote human rights. However, their efficacy is undermined by a lack of resources.

Jamaica reached a major milestone in 2011 when it replaced Chapter 3 of the independence Constitution with a Charter of Fundamental Rights and Freedoms, broadening the scope of human rights, including some social and economic rights.[4] However, the 2011 Charter contains provisions that significantly limit judicial review of laws in place before 2011 dealing with sexual offences, obscene publications, offences related to the life of the unborn, and

---

1 World Bank, 'Country Profile: Jamaica' <https://data.worldbank.org/country/jamaica> accessed 12 April 2022.
2 United Nations Development Programme, 'Human Development Indicators, Jamaica' <http://hdr.undp.org/en/countries/profiles/JAM> accessed 12 April 2022.
3 The World Bank, 'The World Bank in Jamaica' <https://www.worldbank.org/en/country/jamaica/overview> accessed 12 April 2022.
4 Jamaica Charter of Fundamental Rights and Freedoms (Constitutional Amendment) Act 2011.

© MALENE C. ALLEYNE AND TRACY ROBINSON, 2024 | DOI:10.1163/9789004377653_012
This is an open access chapter distributed under the terms of the CC BY-NC-ND 4.0 license.

marriage.[5] Charter provisions also seek to reverse progressive human rights rulings of the Judicial Committee of the Privy Council (JCPC) in relation to Jamaica dealing with undue delays in carrying out the death sentence and inhumane conditions of detention.[6] The JCPC, based in London, serves as Jamaica's final court of appeal.

The courts are the main avenue for addressing human rights violations. The Supreme Court has original jurisdiction to hear complaints about breaches of the human rights provisions in the Jamaican Constitution.[7] There are also Commissions of Parliament with specific human rights mandates. The Office of the Public Defender (OPD) has jurisdiction to investigate human rights complaints brought against the state and seek redress in the courts. The Office of the Children's Advocate (OCA) provides legal representation to children, investigates complaints made by and on behalf of children against government entities and reviews the adequacy of services for children. The Independent Commission of Investigations (INDECOM) undertakes investigations concerning actions by members of the security forces that result in death or injury to persons or the abuse of the rights of persons.

The most intractable human rights issues in Jamaica relate to citizen security. Economic and social inequalities continue to drive high rates of violent crime, resulting in a precarious human rights situation, particularly for the poorest and most marginalised, including women and children. The state's generally repressive approach to security has generated extrajudicial killings and torture, the incarceration of children in need of protection, arbitrary detentions, inhumane conditions of detention, abuse during detention, and the extensive use of states of emergency, accompanied by preventive detention. For example, in May 2010 Jamaica declared a state of emergency, which culminated in mass detentions and a joint military/police operation in which more than 70 persons were killed.[8] The Law Reform (Zones of Special Operations) (Special Security and Community Development Measures) Act was enacted in 2017 to tackle the security situation in communities with high criminality rates. During 2018 and 2019 Jamaica also declared several states of emergency,[9]

---

5   Jamaica Constitution, ss 13(12), 18.
6   ibid ss 13(8)(a), (b). See *Pratt v Attorney-General* (1993) 43 WIR 340 (JCPC Jam).
7   Jamaica Constitution, s 19.
8   Jamaica, *Western Kingston Commission of Enquiry Report* (15 June 2016) para 2.4.
9   'Prime Minister declares State of Emergency in St James' Gleaner (Kingston 18 January 2018) <https://jamaica-gleaner.com/article/lead-stories/20180118/prime-minister-declares-state-emergency-st-james> accessed 12 April 2022; 'Prime Minister declares state of public emergency in St. Catherine North' Gleaner (Kingston 18 March 2018) <https://jamaica-gleaner.com/article/lead-stories/20180318/prime-minister-declares-state-public-emergency-st-catherine-north> accessed 12 April 2022; 'Sections of Corporate

raising serious concerns about arbitrary detention and the privacy rights of those detained.[10]

Jamaica faces serious challenges with respect to the administration of justice, as evidenced by significant case backlogs and inadequate legal aid services. Discrimination against vulnerable groups, including persons with disabilities and lesbian, gay, bisexual, transgender and queer or questioning (LGBTQ) persons, and disparities in access to social services, housing and social security severely undermine the enjoyment of human rights. Environmental justice is also a salient issue as environmental pollution and climate change disproportionately impact socio-economically disadvantaged communities, including the indigenous communities of Maroons. CSOs and local communities have consistently raised concerns about the human rights and environmental impact of extractive activities, particularly in the context of bauxite mining in ecologically-sensitive areas.[11]

The issue of the death penalty remains a concern in Jamaica. A *de facto* moratorium on executions has been in place since 1988. There has been a significant reduction in death sentences, in part because the mandatory death penalty was judicially abolished in 2004.[12] In addition, the JCPC has ruled that the discretionary sentence of death must be reserved for the 'worst of the worst' cases.[13] At the end of 2018 there was no one known to be under the sentence of death in Jamaica.[14]

Area now under state of emergency' Gleaner (Kingston 23 September 2018) <https://jamaica-gleaner.com/article/news/20180923/sections-corporate-area-now-under-state-emergency> accessed 12 April 2022; 'States of Public Emergency Declared in St James, Westmoreland and Hanover' Jamaica Information Service (Kingston 30 April 2019) <https://jis.gov.jm/states-of-public-emergency-declared-in-st-james-westmoreland-and-hanover/> accessed 12 April 2022; 'PM Announces State of Emergency for South St Andrew' Jamaica Information Service (Kingston 7 July 2019) <https://jis.gov.jm/pm-announces-state-of-emergency-south-st-andrew-police-division/> accessed 12 April 2022; 'PM Holness Announces SOE for Clarendon and St Catherine' The Office of the Prime Minister (Kingston 5 September 2019) <https://opm.gov.jm/news/pm-holness-announces-soe-for-clarendon-and-st-catherine/> accessed 12 April 2022.

10   Interview with Arlene Harrison Henry, Public Defender (Kingston, Jamaica, 11 September 2019) (notes of all interviews on file with authors).
11   The increase in oil exploration activities offshore Jamaica suggests that the issue of extractive industries will become even more salient for human rights and environmental advocates.
12   *Watson v R* [2004] UKPC 34, (2004) 64 WIR 241 (JCPC Jam).
13   *Trimmingham v R* [2009] UKPC 25 (JCPC St Vincent & Gren).
14   Amnesty International, *Amnesty International Global Report: Death Sentences and Executions 2019* (Amnesty International 2020).

The efficacy of human rights protection is diminished by the absence of a human rights institution compliant with the Principles Relating to the Status of National Institutions for the Promotion and Protection of Human Rights (Paris Principles).

2   Relationship of Jamaica with the International Human Rights System in General

Jamaica joined the United Nations (UN) in September 1962, a month after it had become independent. Jamaica's relationship with the UN treaty system is strengthened by the presence of UN agencies and programmes. Jamaica has undergone two cycles of the Universal Periodic Review (UPR) process in 2010 and 2015. Jamaica supported the recommendation made in the UPR that it should prepare and regularly submit periodic reports to the relevant treaty bodies. Jamaica also supported recommendations that it should establish a national human rights institution in line with the Paris Principles.[15] Jamaica has not extended a standing invitation to special procedures to visit. The country accepted a visit from the Special Rapporteur on extrajudicial, summary or arbitrary executions in 2003 and the Special Rapporteur on torture and other cruel, inhuman or degrading treatment or punishment in 2010. Since 2010 Jamaica has accepted no other requests for visits from special procedures.[16] In 2015 a joint study visit to the Caribbean, including Jamaica, was conducted by the UN Special Rapporteur on violence against women and the Rapporteur on the rights of women of the Inter-American Commission on Human Rights (IACHR).

The Inter-American human rights system has assumed greater significance in the monitoring of the protection of human rights in Jamaica since the denunciation of OP1-CCPR. Jamaica has since 1969 been a member of the Organisation of American States. Jamaica ratified the American Convention on Human Rights (ACHR) in 1978, but has not accepted the jurisdiction of the Inter-American Court of Human Rights (IACtHR). The Inter-American

---

15   UN Human Rights Council, Universal Periodic Review of Jamaica – Second Cycle, Thematic List of Recommendations <https://www.ohchr.org/EN/HRBodies/UPR/Pages/JMindex.aspx> accessed 12 April 2022.

16   Interview with Birgit Gerstenberg, Senior Human Rights Advisor to UN in Jamaica, 2014–2018 (Kingston, 13 July 2018).

Commission has used various modalities to monitor the human rights situation in Jamaica: a country visit in 2008 and country report in 2012;[17] the above-mentioned joint study visit in 2015; its annual reports, public hearings, precautionary measures, and individual petitions. A Jamaican human rights defender identified these modalities, including web-cast public hearings 'in our time zone', as mutually reinforcing tools for holding the state accountable in the inter-American system, for which there was 'no close comparison' in the UN human rights system.[18]

Historically Jamaica is part of the dualist tradition in which treaty ratification is a matter for the executive and international human rights treaties do not form part of domestic law until they have been incorporated into domestic legislation. Notwithstanding this classification, the trend of the highest courts in the Anglophone Caribbean, including the JCPC, is to directly and indirectly give effect to unincorporated treaties in statutory and constitutional interpretation.[19] As a general rule of interpretation, the Constitution of Jamaica, ordinary legislation and the common law should, as far as possible, be construed so as to avoid creating a breach of the state's international obligations.[20] In decisions that bind Jamaica the JCPC has held that, where there is ambiguity in the domestic law, the meaning consistent with the treaty should be chosen by the courts.[21] On the other hand, if the domestic law is clear, and is in conflict with the unincorporated treaty, the court must follow the domestic law. Beyond this, it is open to the Jamaican courts to use international human rights treaties and treaty bodies' jurisprudence as highly persuasive precedents. However, the use of international human rights law is uncommon in Jamaican courts.

---

17   IACHR, 'Report on the Situation of Human Rights in Jamaica' (OEA/Ser.L/V/II.144 Doc. 12, 2012).
18   Interview with Rodjé Malcolm, Executive Director of Jamaicans for Justice (Kingston, 1 October 2018 and 1 February 2019).
19   Melissa Waters, 'Creeping Monism: The Judicial Trend toward Interpretive Incorporation of Human Rights Treaties' (2007) 107 Columbia L Rev 628.
20   *Watson v R* [2004] UKPC 34, (2004) 64 WIR 241 (JCPC Jamaica); *Boyce v R* [2004] UKPC 32, 64 WIR 37 (JCPC Barbados). But see also the less expansive approach in *Morrison v R* [2023] UKPC 14 (JCPC Jamaica).
21   *Boyce* (n 20).

3   At a Glance: Formal Engagement of Jamaica with UN Human Rights Treaty System

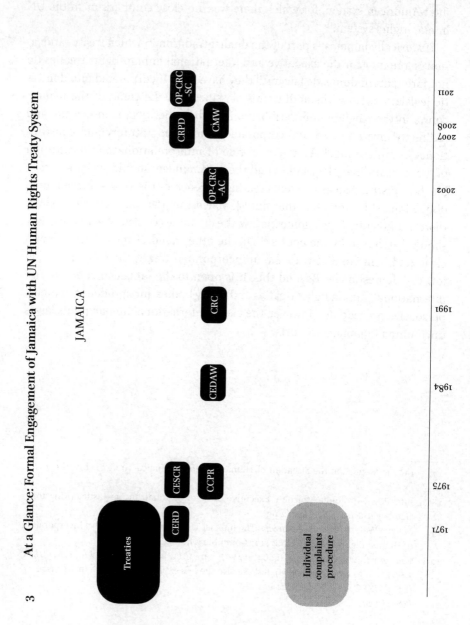

4 Role and Overall Impact of the UN Human Rights Treaties[22]

4.1 Formal Acceptance

Jamaica is party to seven of the nine core international human rights treaties. In 1966, four years after gaining political independence, Jamaica signed the International Convention on the Elimination of All Forms of Racial Discrimination (CERD); the International Covenant on Civil and Political Rights (CCPR); and the International Covenant on Economic, Social and Cultural Rights (CESCR). Jamaica ratified CERD in 1971 and CCPR and CESCR in 1975. In 1984 Jamaica ratified the Convention on the Elimination of All Forms of Discrimination Against Women (CEDAW) and in 1991 the Convention on the Rights of the Child (CRC).[23] Jamaica signed and ratified the Convention on the Rights of Persons with Disabilities (CRPD) in 2007. In 2008 Jamaica signed and ratified the International Convention on the Protection of the Rights of All Migrant Workers and Members of Their Families (CMW). Jamaica has signed, but not ratified, the Convention Against Torture and Other Cruel, Inhuman or Degrading Treatment or Punishment (CAT) and the International Convention for the Protection of All Persons from Enforced Disappearance (CED).

Jamaica maintains reservations to article 4(a) of CERD on the basis that the provisions in this article could infringe the constitutional guarantee of freedom of expression.[24] Jamaica also maintains reservations to article 29(1) of CEDAW, consistent with its 'longstanding understanding about not accepting the jurisdiction of the ICJ'.[25] In 1995 Jamaica withdrew its reservation to article 9(2) of CEDAW.

Jamaica has ratified the Optional Protocol to CRC on the Involvement of Children in Armed Conflict (OP-CRC-AC) and the Optional Protocol to the CRC on the Sale of Children, Child Prostitution and Child Pornography (OP-CRC-SC), but not OP2-CCPR.

Jamaica does not participate in any of the individual complaint mechanisms established under these treaties, having withdrawn from the Optional Protocol

---

[22] The assessment of impact below and throughout this chapter is based on desk research and interviews with 15 sources conducted in Jamaica between February 2018 and August 2020. The information obtained from interviews is not used here to make conclusive or broad generalisations about impact, but rather to provide specific examples of how UN treaties have impacted the attitudes, perceptions and understandings of key stakeholders about norms embodied in UN treaties.

[23] On the motivation for ratifying these traceries, see Lloyd Barnett, 'Jamaica' in Christof Heyns and Frans Viljoen (eds), *The Impact of the UN Human Rights Treaties on the Domestic Level* (Kluwer Law International 2002) 353–354.

[24] State Report, CERD, Jamaica, UN Doc CERD/C/JAM/21-24 (3 April 2019) para 26.

[25] Interview, Ministry of Foreign Affairs and Foreign Trade: Tyesha Turner, Acting Assistant Director, International Organisation Department, and Michelle Walker, Head of the Legal Unit (Kingston, 8 April 2019).

to the International Covenant on Civil and Political Rights (OP1-CCPR) and not having accepted any of the other optional complaint procedures. Jamaica became the first country to denounce OP1-CCPR in 1997, withdrawing the right of individual petition to the HRCttee. This decision may be understood in the context of a 'human rights backlash' in the Caribbean against decisions of the JCPC and international human rights bodies in respect of the death penalty.[26] There is no intention to re-accede to OP1-CCPR at this time.[27] Jamaica has signed, but not ratified, the Optional Protocol to CRPD (OP-CRPD). There is an expectation that, once Jamaica establishes a Disability Rights Tribunal, it will ratify OP-CRPD.[28] Jamaica has also expressed a commitment to acceding to the Optional Protocol to CEDAW (OP-CEDAW).[29]

Jamaica's early engagement with UN treaties in the 1960s may be understood in the context of its post-independence diplomacy, which focused on pushing the UN to intensify its efforts regarding human rights.[30] More generally, government officials have emphasised the fact that Jamaica's decision to ratify treaties has been driven by a 'commitment to the promotion and protection of basic human rights and fundamental freedoms for all human beings'.[31] However, the timing of ratification 'is predicated on the legislative/constitutional space for Jamaica to fulfill the mandates of such treaties/optional protocols'.[32]

4.1.1 General Attitude of the State towards the UN Treaty System

Interviews with relevant actors suggest that state officials generally are unfamiliar with, or may not have received specific training on, UN treaties, treaty body recommendations and General Comments.[33] Some officials question the

---

[26] Laurence Helfer, 'Overlegalising Human Rights: International Relations Theory and The Commonwealth Caribbean Backlash Against Human Rights Regimes' (2002) 102 Colum L Rev 1832, 1860.

[27] Interview, Ministry of Foreign Affairs and Foreign Trade: Tyesha Turner, Acting Assistant Director, International Organisation Department and Michelle Walker, Head of Legal (Kingston, 8 April 2019).

[28] Interview with Birgit Gerstenberg, Senior Human Rights Advisor to UN in Jamaica, 2014–2018 (Kingston, 13 July 2018).

[29] 'Remarks by Sen Hon Sandrea Falconer, Minister Without Portfolio (Information) Office of the Prime Minister to the Opening Ceremony of the Government-NGO Dialogue: Towards Effective Implementation of the Convention on the Elimination of All Forms of Discrimination Against Women (CEDAW)' (Kingston, 17 September 2013) < https://jis.gov.jm/media/Falconer-NGO-Dialogue-on-CEDAW-02.pdf> accessed 12 April 2022.

[30] Steven Jensen, *The Making of International Human Rights: The 1960s, Decolonisation, and the Reconstruction of Global Values* (Cambridge University Press 2016) 71, 101.

[31] Email from Nicola Barker-Murphy, Assistant Director, International Organisations Department, Ministry of Foreign Affairs and Foreign trade (Kingston, 14 August 2020).

[32] ibid.

[33] Interview with Terrence Williams, Commissioner of the Independent Commission of Investigations (Kingston, 16 September 2019); interview with Arlene Harrison Henry,

authoritativeness of UN instruments. One official, for example, questioned the legitimacy of ratified unincorporated treaties as sources of law, noting that, in Jamaica, treaties are ratified by the executive and the obligations they incur do not require parliamentary approval. Therefore, the official considered that the principles of democracy and separation of powers that undergird Westminster-type constitutions preclude the executive changing domestic law through unilateral action at the international level without the participation of parliament. The official also expressed concern about the open-ended nature of the language used in UN treaties. Moreover, the official questioned the legitimacy and authority of treaty bodies to interpret treaty provisions with binding effect, especially since these bodies do not have the character of an independent judiciary.[34] Non-state actors have also noted that the state does not consider General Comments to be binding.[35]

4.1.2 Level of Awareness

Only a few human rights activists, human rights academics and government officials directly involved with UN treaty implementation and reporting demonstrate a high level of awareness of UN treaties. CCPR, CESCR, CEDAW and CERD are the treaties that are most widely referred to in several academic books and articles dealing with the human rights situation in Jamaica or the wider Anglophone Caribbean. Neither CMW nor CED has given rise to any notable academic discussions in relation to Jamaica. The treaties and jurisprudence of treaty bodies appear to receive the most attention in academic literature dealing with polemical human rights issues in Jamaica and the wider Anglophone Caribbean, notably the death penalty,[36] sexual orientation[37] and the corporal punishment of children.[38]

Public Defender (Kingston, 11 September 2019); interview with Judith Grant, Chief Parliamentary Counsel (Kingston, 28 August 2019).

34 Interview with the Chief Justice of Jamaica, Hon Mr Justice Bryan Sykes OJ, CD (Kingston, 28 August 2019).

35 Interview with Birgit Gerstenberg, Senior Human Rights Advisor to UN in Jamaica, 2014–2018 (Kingston, 13 July 2018).

36 For example, Stephen Vasciannie, *International Law and Selected Human Rights in Jamaica* (Council of Legal Education 2002).

37 For example, Conway Blake and Philip Dayle 'Beyond Cross-Cultural Sensitivities: International Human Rights Advocacy and Sexuality in Jamaica' in Corrine Lennox and Matthew Waites (eds), *Human Rights, Sexual Orientation and Gender Identity in the Commonwealth: Struggles for Decriminalisation and Change* (School of Advanced Study, University of London 2013) 455; Delores Smith, 'Homophobic and Transphobic Violence against Youth: The Jamaican context' (2018) 23 Intl J of Adolescence and Youth 250.

38 For example, Corin Bailey, Tracy Robinson and Charlene Coore-Desai, 'Corporal Punishment in the Caribbean: Attitudes and Practices' (2014) 63 Social and Economic

UN treaties and the UN treaty system are covered in the curriculum of legal education institutions in Jamaica[39] and, to some extent, in training programmes targeting professionals involved in the administration of justice, including judges and the police.[40] However, there is a low level of awareness of UN treaties among legal practitioners, except for a small group of advocates who litigate human rights issues.[41]

There is limited, often cursory, coverage of UN treaties by Jamaica's main newspapers. CCPR, CEDAW and CRC are the most extensively-covered treaties by the news media. Experts and academics, including a former member of the CEDAW Cttee, have used newspapers to raise awareness of UN treaty obligations.[42]

4.1.3 State Reporting

Jamaica generally does not meet its reporting obligations on time, having thus far submitted a total of 23 reports with an average delay of three and a half years. There currently are two outstanding state reports, which should have been submitted to the CESCR Cttee and CEDAW Cttee in 2018 and 2016, respectively. Since ratifying CMW in 2008, Jamaica has not submitted a report to the CMW Cttee. Relevant domestic state actors attribute the delay in reporting to a lack of resources.[43] In 2016 there was an improvement in reporting to the HRC ttee, which received Jamaica's most recent report with a four-month delay.

Studies 207; Delores Smith, 'Corporal Punishment of Children in the Jamaican Context' (2016) 7 Intl J of Child, Youth and Family Studies 27.

39 Interview with Nancy Anderson, Associate Tutor, Norman Manley Law School and member, Independent Jamaica Council for Human Rights (Kingston, 6 February 2019); email from Alicia Dixon-Stone, Lecturer, Law Faculty, University of Technology (Kingston, 30 April 2019).

40 Interview with Rodjé Malcolm, Executive Director, Jamaicans for Justice; interview with Birgit Gerstenberg, Senior Human Rights Advisor to UN in Jamaica, 2014–2018 (Kingston, 13 July 2018); interview, Ministry of Foreign Affairs and Foreign Trade: Tyesha Turner, Acting Assistant Director, International Organisation Department and Michelle Walker, Head of Legal (Kingston, 8 April 2019).

41 Interview with Nancy Anderson, Associate Tutor, Norman Manley Law School and member, Independent Jamaica Council for Human Rights (Kingston, 6 February 2019).

42 For example, Glenda Simms, 'Creating a Culture That Says "No" to Violence Against Women' *Gleaner* (Kingston 25 November 2002); Glenda Simms, 'Justice for the Forgotten' *Gleaner* (Kingston 4 September 2011) <http://jamaica-gleaner.com/gleaner/20110904/focus/focus8.html> accessed 12 April 2022.

43 Interview with the Ministry of Foreign Affairs and Foreign Trade; Tyesha Turner, Acting Assistant Director, International Organisation Department and Michelle Walker, Head of Legal (Kingston, 8 April 2019).

The quality of Jamaica's reporting appears to be highest under CRC.[44] Other treaty bodies have expressed concern about the lack of sufficient information in Jamaica's state reports.[45]

Jamaica has engaged in 15 dialogues with treaty bodies since 1990: four with the HRCttee; two with the CESCR Cttee; and three each with the CRC Cttee, the CEDAW Cttee and the CERD Cttee. The absence of any representative of the government of Jamaica at the CESCR Cttee's consideration of Jamaica's second state report triggered concern among committee members.[46] Jamaica consistently sends high-level officials to the CRC Cttee and CEDAW Cttee, but in other cases representatives from the capital are not consistently present. Limited resources may, in part, explain deficiencies in state dialogues.[47]

On 25 June 2018 Cabinet approved the formal establishment and institutionalisation of the Inter-Ministerial Committee on Human Rights (IMCHR) as the official national entity for reporting and follow-up to the UN human rights mechanisms.[48] The IMCHR meets quarterly and comprises a range of ministries, departments and agencies, but noticeably does not include parliamentary commissions. Members of the IMCHR serve as the core points of contact on human rights issues in their respective ministries, departments and agencies. Their functions include preparing Jamaica's national reports to the Human Rights Council and treaty bodies, reviewing recommendations by the treaty bodies, and developing an action plan for implementation.

There is a low level of alternative reporting to UN treaty bodies. A small, but effective, group of local civil society organisations presents alternative reports, often in conjunction with foreign non-governmental organisations (NGOs). However, domestic organisations do not report consistently across all treaty bodies and do not always involve a diversity of groups. The Ministry of Foreign Affairs and Foreign Trade has expressed an intention to strengthen

---

44   The CRC Cttee has commended Jamaica's submission of disaggregated data in its state report. CRC Cttee, COs, Jamaica, UN Doc CRC/C/15/Ad.2104 (30 May 2003) para. 2.
45   CERD Cttee, COs, Jamaica, UN Doc CERD/C/60/CO/6 (4–22 March 2002) para 2; CEDAW Cttee, COs, Jamaica, UN Doc CEDAW/C/JAM/CO/6-7 (9–27 July 2012) para 2; CESCR Cttee, COs, Jamaica, UN Doc E/C.12/1/Add.75 (12–30 November 2001) para. 2, noting Jamaica's failure to submit written replies to the list of issues.
46   CESCR Cttee, COs, Jamaica, UN Doc E/C.12/1/Add.75 (12–30 November 2001) para 2.
47   Interview with Ministry of Foreign Affairs and Foreign Trade: Tyesha Turner, Acting Assistant Director, International Organisation Department and Michelle Walker, Head of Legal (Kingston, 8 April 2019).
48   Jamaica, 'Terms of Reference, Inter-Ministerial Committee on Human Rights' (March 2019).

and institutionalise consultation with civil society actors during the reporting process and consultations are being held and requested prior to reporting.[49]

4.1.4   Domestic Implementation Mechanism

The IMCHR has a mandate to develop action plans to implement the recommendations of international human rights bodies. However, interviews with relevant domestic actors suggest that there still is no systematic work with respect to the implementation of treaty body recommendations.[50]

4.1.5   Treaty Body Membership

Current research was unable to find evidence of a formal national process for nomination of treaty body members. Nonetheless, Jamaica has had, and continues to have, members on UN treaty bodies, including Verene Shepherd, who is a member of the CERD Cttee (term expiring in 2024).[51] Former treaty body members include Barbara Bailey (CEDAW Cttee 2009–2016); Glenda Simms (CEDAW Cttee 2005–2008); Marjorie Taylor (CRC Cttee 2003–2004); Alison Anderson (CRC Cttee 2004–2007); Laurel Francis (HRC ttee 1993–1996); and Kenneth Rattray (CESCR Cttee 1986 to 2004).[52] Outside the period covered by this chapter, on 30 November 2020 Floyd Morris was elected to the CRPD Cttee (2021–2024).[53]

---

[49] Interview with Ministry of Foreign Affairs and Foreign Trade: Tyesha Turner, Acting Assistant Director, International Organisation Department and Michelle Walker, Head of Legal (Kingston, 8 April 2019).

[50] Interview with Birgit Gerstenberg, Senior Human Rights Advisor to UN in Jamaica, 2014–2018 (Kingston, 13 July 2018).

[51] OHCHR, 'Committee on the Elimination of Racial Discrimination' <https://www.ohchr.org/EN/HRBodies/CERD/Pages/Membership.aspx> accessed 12 April 2022.

[52] OHCHR, 'Committee on the Elimination of Discrimination Against Women' <https://www.ohchr.org/EN/HRBodies/CEDAW/Pages/Membership.aspx> accessed 12 April 2022; OHCHR, 'Past Membership of the Committee on the Rights of the Child (1991–2003)' <https://www.ohchr.org/Documents/HRBodies/CRC/PastMembers1991-2013.pdf> accessed 12 April 2022; OHCHR, 'Membership of the Human Rights Committee 1977 to 2014' <https://www.ohchr.org/Documents/HRBodies/CCPR/Membership/Membership1977_2014.pdf> accessed 12 April 2022; OHCHR, 'Committee on Economic, Social and Cultural Rights (CESCR) Membership from 1986–2018' <https://www.ohchr.org/EN/HRBodies/CESCR/Pages/Membership.aspx> accessed 12 April 2022.

[53] OHCHR, 'Committee on the Rights of Persons with Disabilities' https://www.ohchr.org/EN/HRBodies/CRPD/Pages/Elections2020.aspx> accessed 12 April 2022.

4.1.6 Incorporation and Reliance by Legislature and Executive

In the past two decades, Jamaica has embarked upon a process of legal reform that incorporates some of its UN treaty obligations into domestic law. The new Charter of Fundamental Rights and Freedoms expands the scope of civil and political rights and recognises a few social and economic rights. In addition, Parliament has enacted landmark legislation, such as the Child Care and Protection Act 2004, the Sexual Offences Act 2009 and the Disabilities Act 2014, which broaden the scope of human rights protection, although some aspects of these laws are inconsistent with UN treaties.[54]

In 2015 the Minister of Justice emphasised that 'Jamaica is committed to its obligations' under the core international human rights treaties Jamaica has ratified, and that this commitment 'is buttressed by legislation to give effect to those obligations in law'.[55] While human rights laws do not explicitly refer to UN treaties, parliamentary debates suggest that in some instances, UN treaties, particularly CRC, CEDAW and CRPD, have played a role in law and constitutional reforms. Moreover, key policies and action plans also refer to UN treaty norms, particularly those policies related to women,[56] children[57] and development.[58]

Despite Jamaica's progress, Jamaica's compliance with UN treaty obligations is slow and incomplete. Parliament has acknowledged the 'inordinate lapse of time between the ratification of a treaty by Jamaica and its incorporation into domestic law'.[59] Importantly, significant gaps in the law remain and some laws are inconsistent with UN treaty norms, including with respect to cross-cutting principles such as equality and non-discrimination. Jamaica, for example, is yet to enact comprehensive anti-discrimination legislation. Treaty bodies have consistently commented on the narrow scope of prohibited grounds of discrimination in the Charter and, in particular, on the absence of sexual orientation,

---

54   See part 5.
55   For example, Ministry of Justice, 'Ministry of Justice Human Rights Day 2015 Message' *Jamaica Information Service* (Kingston, 10 December 2015) <https://jis.gov.jm/ministry-of-justice-human-rights-day-2015-message/> accessed 12 April 2022.
56   For example, Bureau of Gender Affairs, *National Strategic Action Plan to Eliminate Gender-Based Violence (NSAP-GBV) 2017–2027* (Bureau of Gender Affairs 2017).
57   Office of the Children's Advocate, 'Child Justice Guidelines' (July 2013) <https://www.welcome.oca.gov.jm/resources/> accessed 12 April 2022.
58   Jamaica, Vision 2030 Jamaica National Development Plan: Gender Sector Plan (Final Edition June 2010) 88 <http://lslandr.com/vision2030/wp-content/uploads/sites/4/2020/12/Microsoft-Word-Gender.pdf> accessed 12 April 2022.
59   Jamaica, 'Report of the Joint Select Committee on its Deliberations on the Bill Entitled an Act to Amend the Constitution of Jamaica to Provide for a Charter of Rights and for Connected Matters' (Kingston 2001).

disability, health status, and marital status as prohibited grounds.[60] Instead of prohibiting discrimination on the grounds of sex or gender, the Charter speaks to discrimination on the basis 'of being male or female',[61] an approach designed to ensure that 'sexual orientation' would not be indirectly included.

The Charter also contains savings clauses, which limit judicial review of certain criminal laws, such as those laws dealing with consensual same-sex conduct and abortion.[62] These provisions place an even greater responsibility on the legislature to ensure that Jamaica's laws are in compliance with the Constitution and with UN treaties. Yet, Parliament generally is reluctant to address issues such as the decriminalisation of same-sex conduct, because of what a parliamentary committee describes as the 'sensitive nature' of these provisions and the existence of savings clauses.[63]

Another obstacle is Jamaica's delay in establishing a national human rights institution in accordance with the Paris Principles, despite the Minister of Justice's statements in 2014 welcoming discussion on how Jamaica could establish an effective and sustainable NHRI.[64]

4.1.7 Reliance by Judiciary

Jamaica's judiciary rarely uses UN treaties as a source of law in judicial decision making, even when adjudicating constitutional challenges dealing with human rights. Based on a systematic review of case law, judges only make brief references to UN human rights treaties in a small number of cases.[65] CCPR appears to be the most frequently-cited UN treaty. No references have been found to CERD, CRPD, CEDAW or CMW. Jamaican judges rarely observe the principle of

---

60 HRCttee, COs, Jamaica, UN Doc CCPR/C/JAM/CO/4 (18 and 19 October 2016) para 15; CESCR Cttee, COs, Jamaica, UN Doc E/C.12/JAM/CO/3–4 (29 April–17 May 2013) para 8; CEDAW Cttee, COs, Jamaica, UN Doc CEDAW/C/JAM/CO/6–7 (9–27 July 2012) para 11.
61 See Jamaica Constitution, s 13(3)(i)(i)(ii).
62 See part 1 of this chapter.
63 Jamaica, 'Report of the Joint Select Committee Appointed to Complete the Review of the Sexual Offences Act Along With the Offences Against the Person Act, the Domestic Violence Act and the Child Care and Protection Act' (December 2018) 38 <https://japarliament.gov.jm/attachments/article/2050/JSC%20Sexual%20Offences%20Report.pdf> accessed 12 April 2022.
64 'Jamaica Takes Steps to Establish National Human Rights Institution' *Jamaica Information Service* (Kingston 23 July 2014) <https://jis.gov.jm/jamaica-takes-steps-establish-national-human-rights-institution/> accessed 12 April 2022.
65 The researchers carried out systematic searches in the Caribbean Law Online (CARILAW) database hosted on JustisOne database. CARILAW is the most extensive database of written decisions in the Anglophone Caribbean dating back to 1950.

relying on treaty obligations where there is ambiguity in the domestic law or as persuasive precedent.

4.1.8 Impact on and through Independent State Institutions

The UN treaty system generally does not have a pronounced impact on or through independent state institutions. UN treaties do not influence the work of most parliamentary commissions with human rights mandates. The Public Defender and the Commissioner of INDECOM acknowledged during interviews that they generally do not cite UN treaties or receive copies of COs.[66] In the case of INDECOM, the inter-American system has had a more significant impact on its work due to the Inter-American Commission's individual petition and case system, which has produced jurisprudence that shaped the normative foundation of INDECOM's work. On the other hand, there is evidence that UN treaties have played an influential role in the work of OCA. CRC and its General Comments, for example, inform the formulation of the OCA's recommendations to Parliament[67] and normative standards, such as the Child Justice Guidelines, which were developed by the OCA with the support of UNICEF Jamaica.[68]

4.1.9 Impact on and through Non-state Actors

The UN treaty system has a noticeable impact on the work of non-state actors, mostly human rights experts and academics with an interest in this area. NGO representatives rely on these treaties to strengthen their advocacy and to shape the normative aspects of their work.[69] These NGOs focus mostly on CRC, CEDAW and CCPR. Some NGOs use COs and General Comments to

---

[66] Interview with Terrence Williams, Commissioner of INDECOM (Kingston, 16 September 2019).

[67] Office of the Children's Advocate, 'Focusing on the Uncontrollable Child: Recommendations to the Houses of Parliament' (Kingston 2013) <https://www.welcome.oca.gov.jm/resources/> accessed 12 April 2022.

[68] Office of the Children's Advocate, 'Child Justice Guidelines' (July 2013) <https://www.welcome.oca.gov.jm/resources/> accessed 12 April 2022.

[69] Interview with Linette Vassell, Board Advisor, Women's Resource and Outreach Centre (Kingston, 4 July 2019); interview with Rodjé Malcolm, Executive Director, Jamaicans for Justice (Kingston, 1 October 2018 and 1 February 2019); interview with Glenroy Murray, Associate Director of Programmes and Advocacy, Jamaica Forum for Lesbians, All-Sexuals and Gays (Kingston, 6 September 2018); interview with Christopher Harper, Policy and Advocacy Officer, Jamaica Youth Advocacy Network (Kingston, 26 September 2018).

develop training materials and shape institutional knowledge.[70] The Women's Resource and Outreach Centre, for example, has organised workshops and published a booklet that uses CEDAW and General Comments as tools for educating women's organisations.[71] Academics also cover UN treaties in their academic research and teaching and have sought membership on UN treaty bodies. They have also been involved in training state officials and non-state actors on the treaties.[72] On the other hand, the UN treaty system has not had a significant impact on members of the Jamaican legal profession who generally do not use UN treaties or mechanisms in their legal work or continuing legal education.[73]

Jamaica's withdrawal from or lack of participation in UN individual complaints mechanisms has significantly diminished the impact of UN treaties on the work of non-state actors around redress. The Inter-American human rights system has had a more pronounced impact on their work, due, in part, to the existence of quasi-adjudicatory mechanisms that offer important avenues for redress.

4.1.10   Impact of State Reporting

Jamaica does not generally implement COs. Jamaica, for example, has not fully implemented any of the HRCttee's 2016 recommendations selected for follow up, such as the recommendations to amend abortion legislation; to amend the law in order to remove the possibility of incarcerating a child on the basis of him or her being 'beyond parental control';[74] to amend laws

---

70   Interview with Linette Vassell, Board Advisor, Women's Resource and Outreach Centre (Kingston, 4 July 2019); interview with Rodjé Malcolm, Executive Director, Jamaicans for Justice, (Kingston, 1 October 2018 and 1 February 2019).
71   Women's Resource and Outreach Centre, 'Rights a di plan, wid CEDAW in wi Hand. CEDAW for Jamaicans'; interview with Linette Vassell, Board Advisor, Women's Resource and Outreach Centre (Kingston, 4 July 2019).
72   For example, Ramona Biholar, an international human rights law lecturer at the University of the West Indies, Mona, has been a facilitator in training on treaties and reporting to treaty bodies with OPD (November 2015); government officials (October 2016, March 2018), various civil society organisations (May 2018), the Rastafari community (October 2018); email from Ramona Biholar (8 May 2020).
73   Interview with Nancy Anderson, Associate Tutor, Norman Manley Law School, and member of the Independent Jamaica Council for Human Rights (Kingston, 6 February 2019).
74   Jamaica has committed itself since 2013 to amend the law to remove the possibility of incarcerating a child deemed to be beyond parental control. As of 2020 no reforms have taken place.

to prohibit discrimination on the basis of sex, sexual orientation and gender identity; and to decriminalise same-sex conduct. Parliamentary debates suggest that the existence of savings clauses that limit judicial review of criminal laws dealing with same-sex sex and abortion negatively impact the legislature's responsiveness to treaty body recommendations.[75] The low impact of COs on Jamaica's domestic legal system is acknowledged by relevant actors during interviews, some of whom suggest that any mirroring between domestic reforms and COs is coincidental.[76] COs have the most impact on NGOs, who strategically use UN treaty body recommendations in their advocacy.[77]

4.1.11 Impact of Individual Communications

Individual communications are no longer available. In 1997 Jamaica withdrew from OP1-CCPR. In the most recent cycle of reporting under CCPR, the government indicated that it was 'unable to re-accede' to OP1-CCPR, noting that alternative means of redress exist at the domestic and inter-American level.[78] Since Jamaica's withdrawal from OP1-CCPR, the HRCttee issued 16 decisions in respect of individual complaints that were still pending at the time of Jamaica's withdrawal from OP1-CCPR. Most of these decisions deal with the death penalty and conditions of detention. The resulting jurisprudence has shaped the JCPC's jurisprudence on the mandatory death penalty. Jamaica has signed, but not ratified, OP-CRPD.

---

[75] Jamaica, 'Report of the Joint Select Committee Appointed to Complete the Review of the Sexual Offences Act Along with the Offences Against the Person Act, the Domestic Violence Act and the Child Care and Protection Act' (December 2018) 38 <https://japarliament.gov.jm/attachments/article/2050/JSC%20Sexual%20Offences%20Report.pdf> accessed 12 April 2022.

[76] Interview with Rodjé Malcolm, Executive Director, Jamaicans for Justice (Kingston, Jamaica, 1 October 2018 and 1 February 2019); interview with Birgit Gerstenberg, Senior Human Rights Advisor to UN in Jamaica, 2014–2018 (Kingston, 13 July 2018).

[77] Interview with Linette Vassell, Board Advisor, Women's Resource and Outreach Centre (Kingston, Jamaica, 4 July 2019); interview with Rodjé Malcolm, Executive Director, Jamaicans for Justice (Kingston, Jamaica, 1 October 2018 and 1 February 2019); interview with Glenroy Murray, Associate Director of Programmes and Advocacy, Jamaica Forum for Lesbians, All-Sexuals and Gays (Kingston, 6 September 2018); interview with Christopher Harper, Policy and Advocacy Officer, Jamaica Youth Advocacy Network (Kingston, 26 September 2018).

[78] State Party's Report, CCPR, Jamaica, UN Doc CCPR/C/JAM/4 (18 March 2015) paras 68–69.

5 Detailed Impact of UN Human Rights Treaties on the Domestic Level in Jamaica

5.1 *International Convention on the Elimination of All Forms of Racial Discrimination*

5.1.1 Incorporation and Reliance by Legislature and Executive

CERD has not been fully incorporated into domestic law and it is not a driver of legal reform. The Constitution guarantees the right to equality before the law[79] and the right to freedom from discrimination on the ground of race, which preceded Jamaica's ratification of CERD in 1971.[80] Jamaica, however, still has not adopted comprehensive anti-discrimination legislation containing a clear definition of racial discrimination as required under CERD.[81] Moreover, Jamaica has not adopted specific legislation to give effect to article 4 of CERD prohibiting racist propaganda and racist organisations.

5.1.2 Reliance by Judiciary

There is no significant body of litigation on discrimination generally, including based on race, colour, descent, or national or ethnic origin.[82] A systematic study of domestic case law shows that courts do not refer to or rely on CERD.

5.1.3 Impact on and through Non-state Actors

NGOs and human rights advocates do not use CERD in their campaigns or sensitisation initiatives, although it has been discussed and considered in recent training with some NGOs.[83] Furthermore, NGOs do not engage with the CERD Cttee around its review of Jamaica's implementation of CERD. According to Jamaica's most recent periodic report to the CERD Cttee, NGOs did not respond to the government's calls for public consultation.[84] COs on Jamaica's compliance with CERD are discussed in some analyses of racial discrimination[85] and

---

79 Jamaica Constitution, s 13(3)(g).
80 ibid s 13(3)(i)(i)(ii).
81 Arts 1, 2 and 6.
82 See, eg, CERD Cttee, COs, Jamaica, CERD/C/JAM/CO/16–20 (21 and 22 August 2013) para 9.
83 OHCHR, 'Rastafari Rights Under the Covenant on Economic, Social and Cultural Rights: International Human Rights Reporting Standards and Mechanisms Training Workshop for the Rastafari Community and CSOs' (Kingston, October 2018).
84 State Party's Report, CERD, Jamaica, UN Doc CERD/C/JAM/21–24 (3 April 2019) para 2.
85 For example, Monique Kelly and Stanley Bailey, 'Racial Inequality and the Recognition of Racial Discrimination in Jamaica' (2018) 24 Soc Identities 688; Henrice Altink, *Public Secrets: Race and Colour in Colonial and Independent Jamaica* (Liverpool University Press 2019).

race and language rights in Jamaica.[86] State reports on Jamaica's compliance with CERD are referred to in some non-legal publications simply for data on the racial distribution of Jamaica.[87]

5.1.4 Impact of State Reporting

The CERD Cttee has issued COs on seven occasions in the context of its review of Jamaica's reports. Jamaica has rejected the CERD Cttee's recommendations to enact legislation that prohibits racial discrimination on the basis that there are sufficient measures in place under the Constitution.[88] Similarly, the government has rejected the CERD Cttee's recommendation to withdraw its reservations to article 4(a), which prohibits 'dissemination of ideas based on racial superiority or hatred, incitement to racial discrimination', on the basis that it could infringe the constitutional guarantee of freedom of expression.[89]

5.1.5 Brief Conclusion

CERD has not had an impact on Jamaica's legal system, primarily due to a general lack of awareness of CERD among the population and the attitude of state officials who generally consider CERD to be irrelevant to Jamaica's context.

5.2 *International Covenant on Civil and Political Rights*

5.2.1 Incorporation and Reliance by Legislature and Executive

There is no single piece of legislation incorporating CCPR. Some provisions of CCPR are contained in the Constitution, as amended by the Charter of Fundamental Rights and Freedoms, and various pieces of legislation. The new Charter broadened the protection of civil and political rights, for example, by recognising the right to vote in free and fair elections and the right of every citizen to be granted a passport.[90] The Charter more clearly guaranteed and broadened the right to privacy, which includes 'respect for and protection of private and family life'.[91] The Charter also introduced additional prohibited grounds of discrimination, including 'social class', but failed to add other key

---

86 For example, Danielle Boaz, 'Examining Creole Languages in the Context of International Language Rights' (2008) 2 Hum Rts and Globalisation L Rev 45.

87 For example, Sherrie Russell-Brown, 'Labour Rights as Human Rights: The Situation of Women Workers in Jamaica's Export Free Zones' (2004) 24 Berkeley J Emp & Lab L 179; Rachael Irving and others, 'Demographic Characteristics of World Class Jamaican Sprinters' (2013) Scientific World J 1.

88 State Party's Report, CERD, Jamaica, UN Doc CERD/C/JAM/21–24 (3 April 2019) para 25.

89 ibid para 26.

90 Jamaica Constitution, ss 13(3)(m) & (n).

91 ibid s 13(3)(j)(ii).

grounds. Progress is undermined by the inclusion of 'savings clauses' that are contrary to CCPR in that they shield from constitutional challenge certain laws and punishments, even if they violate the Constitution and UN treaties.[92]

The HRCttee has taken note of legislative reforms in Jamaica that address some of their consistent concerns, such as the enactment of the Sexual Offences Act 2009 and the Law Reform (Flogging and Whipping) (Abolition) Act 2013. A notable achievement is the creation of parliamentary commissions, such as the OPD and INDECOM, with specific mandates to investigate and remedy human rights abuses. However, Jamaica retains legislation that violates key human rights norms recognised in CCPR, such as the continued criminalisation of consensual same-sex conduct, despite the multiple recommendations of the HRCttee to remove these provisions.[93] Parliament is reluctant to review the law because of the 'sensitive nature' of these provisions and the special protection from challenge they enjoy under the savings clause in the Charter.[94]

5.2.2 Reliance by Judiciary

A systematic review of electronic case law databases shows that Jamaican courts referred to CCPR only in a handful of cases and, even then, the references were generally brief.[95] In 1994 in a Jamaican case, the JCPC rejected the HRCttee's decision on the scope of the right to legal representation,[96] stating that '[a]lthough Jamaica is a signatory to the Covenant, it has not been incorporated into Jamaican law'.[97] In Jamaica's common law system, this ruling was binding precedent on the Court of Appeal, which followed it in 2015.[98] Regrettably, the Court of Appeal did not acknowledge that the JCPC's later cases had shown a greater willingness to rely on UN treaties, especially where the Constitution is open to multiple meanings. In 2000, in *Lewis v Attorney-General*, the JCPC enforced the treaty obligation of access to the individual

---

92   Jamaica Constitution ss 13(7), 13(8), 13(12). See also HRCttee, COs, Jamaica, UN Doc CCPR/C/JAM/CO/4 (18 and 19 October 2016) para 15.
93   For example, HRCttee, COs, Jamaica, UN Doc CCPR/C/JAM/CO/4 (18 and 19 October 2016) para 15.
94   Jamaica, 'Report of the Joint Select Committee Appointed to Complete the Review of the Sexual Offences Act Along with the Offences Against the Person Act, the Domestic Violence Act and the Child Care and Protection Act' (December 2018) 38 <https://japarliament.gov.jm/attachments/article/2050/JSC%20Sexual%20Offences%20Report.pdf> accessed 12 April 2022.
95   Information obtained from the Caribbean Law Online (CARILAW) database hosted on JustisOne database.
96   HRCttee, *Robinson v Jamaica*, Communication No 223/1987, 30 March 1989 para 10.3.
97   *Dunkley v R* (1994) 45 WIR 318, 325 (JCPC Jam).
98   *Leslie Moodie v R* [2015] JMCA Crim 16 (Court of Appeal Jam) para 60.

complaints system through the constitutional right to the protection of the law for persons on death row.[99]

In dealing with cases from Jamaica Jamaican courts and the JCPC have shown more willingness to rely on jurisprudence related to the European Convention on Human Rights (ECHR) as a guide to interpretation. In *Grant v R*, for example, the JCPC stated that 'the Board readily accepts the relevance of the Strasbourg jurisprudence' because the ECHR applied to Jamaica before it became independent (because it was binding on the United Kingdom) and because 'the close textual affinity' between the relevant articles in the ECHR and the Constitution 'makes it appropriate to pay heed to authority on the one when considering the meaning and effect of the other'.[100] Ironically and by comparison, Jamaica's binding obligations under CCPR received scant attention.

5.2.3 Impact on and through Independent State Institutions

The researchers were unable to find evidence of the impact of CCPR on commissions of parliament with human rights mandates. The OPD and INDECOM do not rely significantly on UN treaties, including CCPR, in their work.[101]

5.2.4 Impact on and through Non-state Actors

The impact of CCPR on the work of NGOs is severely diminished by Jamaica's withdrawal from the OP1-CCPR individual complaints mechanism, which between ratification and withdrawal received more than 150 communications from Jamaica.[102] For this reason, the Inter-American system of human rights, in particular the work of the Inter-American Commission, is more impactful as an engine of change.[103]

CCPR is the most widely-considered treaty in academic discussions on human rights in Jamaica. Academic and policy publications dealing with Jamaica's human rights situation that refer to multiple treaties almost always reference CCPR.[104] The jurisprudence developed by the HRCttee in the many

---

99 *Lewis v Attorney-General* (2000) 57 WIR 275 (JCPC Jam).
100 *Grant v R* [2006] UKPC 2 (2006) 68 WIR 354 (JCPC Jam).
101 Interview with Arlene Harrison Henry, Public Defender (Kingston, 11 September 2019); interview with Justice Bryan Sykes OJ, CD, Chief Justice of Jamaica (Kingston, 28 August 2019).
102 See part 3.
103 Interview with Rodjé Malcolm, Executive Director, Jamaicans for Justice (Kingston, 1 October 2018 and 1 February 2019); interview with Arlene Harrison Henry, Public Defender (Kingston, 11 September 2019).
104 For example, Danielle Barrett, 'Culture or Rights Violation: An Examination of the Role of Jamaica's Sociopolitical Culture on Women's Rights' (2005) 14 Buff Women's J 11.

death penalty cases from Jamaica and the rest of the Caribbean has given rise to significant academic discussions.[105] Jamaica's withdrawal from OP1-CCPR garnered significant international attention and academic interest.[106]

5.2.5 Impact of State Reporting

The HRCttee has issued COs on four occasions in the context of reviewing Jamaica's periodic reports. As noted by the Special Rapporteur for Follow-Up in 2013, Jamaica generally does not implement the HRCttee's recommendations.[107] In some cases the state has accepted the HRCttee's recommendation, but has been slow to implement the required reforms. In other cases, the state has rejected or has been reluctant to adopt recommendations. Jamaica, for example, has rejected calls to amend its laws to prohibit discrimination on the basis of sex, sexual orientation and gender identity and to decriminalise same-sex conduct. In 2017 the Minister of Justice made it clear that Parliament would not take any decision on the decriminalisation of same-sex conduct without allowing Jamaicans to vote in a referendum.[108] In addition, the HRCttee recommended that states of emergency be brought in line with CCPR, noting in particular the 2010 state of emergency.[109] Since then, especially during 2018

---

105 For example, Saul Lehrfreund, 'International Legal Trends and the "Mandatory" Death Penalty in the Commonwealth Caribbean' (2001) 1 OUCLJ 171; Joanna Harrington, 'The Challenge to the Mandatory Death Penalty in the Commonwealth Caribbean' (2004) 98 AJIL 126; Margaret Burnham, 'Indigenous Constitutionalism and the Death Penalty: The Case of the Commonwealth Caribbean' (2005) 4 ICON 582; Dennis Morrison, 'The Judicial Committee of the Privy Council and the Death Penalty in the Commonwealth Caribbean: Studies in Judicial Activism' (2005) 30 Nova L Rev 403; Stephen Vasciannie, 'The Decision of the Judicial Committee of the Privy Council in the Lambert Watson Case from Jamaica on the Mandatory Death Penalty and the Question of Fragmentation' (2008) 41 NYUJ Int'l L & Pol 837; Lord Anthony Gifford, 'The Death Penalty: Developments in Caribbean Jurisprudence' (2009) 37 IJLD 196.

106 For example, Natalia Schiffrin, 'Jamaica Withdraws the Right of Individual Petition Under the International Covenant on Civil and Political Rights' (1998) 92 AJIL 563; Laurence Helfer, 'Overlegalising Human Rights: International Relations Theory and the Commonwealth Caribbean Backlash against Human Rights Regimes' (2002) 102 Colum L Rev 1832; Ezekiel Rediker, 'Courts of Appeal and Colonialism in the British Caribbean: A Case for the Caribbean Court of Justice' (2013) 35 Mich J Int'l L 213.

107 Follow-up Report of the Special Rapporteur on follow-up on COs, CCPR/C/107/2 (107th session, 11–28 March 2013).

108 'Chuck: Buggery Law Will Only Be Changed by a Referendum' *Jamaica Observer* (Kingston, 16 June 2017), <https://www.jamaicaobserver.com/news/chuck-buggery-law-will-only-be-changed-by-a-referendum/> accessed 10 September 2023.

109 HRCttee, COs, Jamaica: UN Doc CCPR/C/JAM/CO/4 (18 and 19 October 2016) paras 27, 28.

and 2019, multiple states of emergency over large sections of the island, and for extensive periods of time, have been institutionalised.

5.2.6 Impact of Individual Communications

A total of 152 communications were submitted against Jamaica under OP1-CCPR. Most of these complaints relate to death penalty cases and conditions of detention. In 95 of these, the HRCttee found Jamaica in violation of CCPR. The HRCttee issued 82 of these before and 13 of these views after 30 June 1999, the cut-off date for the previous study.[110] Jamaica denounced OP1-CCPR on 23 October 1997. The Government's stated reason for denunciation is that the 5-year timeline between sentencing and execution stipulated by the JCPC in *Pratt v Attorney General* 'was not sufficient to allow persons to exhaust all their domestic appeals and their petitions to international human rights bodies.'[111] Following Jamaica's withdrawal, the HRCttee concluded a significant number of complaints that were still pending at the time of the denunciation. The HRCttee's jurisprudence has shaped the JCPC's jurisprudence on the mandatory death penalty, which was declared unconstitutional in Jamaica in 2004.[112]

5.2.7 Brief Conclusion

CCPR has had limited impact on Jamaica's legal system, although there are signs of symbolic impact on human rights defenders who find empowerment in its normative framework. While some of the CCPR provisions have been domesticated, significant gaps remain, including with respect to cross-cutting principles such as non-discrimination. Furthermore, Jamaica has enacted and retains legislation that violates key CCPR norms, despite the consistent recommendations by the HRCttee to amend these laws. Jamaica's ability to respond to its UN treaty obligations is greatly diminished by savings clauses that not only limit judicial review of certain laws, but also make legislators reluctant to amend 'sensitive' laws that are inconsistent with CCPR. Jamaica's withdrawal from the CCPR's independent complaint mechanism also significantly limits CCPR's potential impact and has undermined the importance that CCPR had assumed and would likely have continued to hold.

---

110   Heyns and Viljoen (n 23) 367–379, updated with reference to <https://tbinternet.ohchr.org/_layouts/15/TreatyBodyExternal/TBSearch.aspx?Lang=en&DocTypeID=17&DocTypeCategoryID=6> accessed 3 April 2022.
111   State Report, CCPR, Jamaica, UN Doc CCPR/C/JAM/4 (18 March 2015) para 68.
112   See *Reyes v R* [2002] UKPC 11, 60 WIR 42 (JCPC Belize) para 41; *Watson* (n 12).

5.3 *International Covenant on Economic, Social and Cultural Rights*

5.3.1 Incorporation and Reliance by Legislature and Executive

CESCR has not been fully incorporated into the domestic legal system, although some progress has been made through processes of domestic legal reform. The 2011 Charter of Fundamental Rights and Freedoms broadened the protection of economic, social and cultural rights in Jamaica, for example, by recognising the right to enjoy a healthy and productive environment free from the threat of injury or damage from environmental abuse and degradation of the ecological heritage.[113]

At the policy level, Jamaica's development plan, Vision 2030, is based on human rights and environmentally sustainable principles. The plan states that the economic and social rights set out in the Universal Declaration of Human Rights and in CESCR 'have served as broad indicators for social and economic policy'.[114] In 2003 Jamaica adopted a National Cultural Policy aimed at promoting and protecting cultural diversity and expression, including that of indigenous communities such as Maroons and Rastafari.

However, major implementation gaps exist. The Charter does not include the right to enjoyment of the highest attainable standard of health. Additionally, the Charter fails to prohibit discrimination on grounds such as health status and disability. Moreover, there still is no comprehensive legislation clearly prohibiting gender discrimination. Jamaica is yet to adopt its Occupational Safety and Health Bill[115] and the work around cultural diversity at the policy level has not translated into legislation that specifically addresses the protection of traditional knowledge of the Maroons and Rastafari. The long-debated Sexual Harassment Act 2021 came into force in 2023.

Furthermore, some of the laws that actually exist do not adequately reflect human rights norms. The Employment (Equal Pay for Men and Women) Act 1975 only guarantees equal pay for 'similar' or 'substantively similar' work, rather than 'equal remuneration for work of equal value'.[116]

---

113 Jamaica Constitution, s 13(3)(l).
114 Jamaica, 'Vision 2030 Jamaica National Development Plan' (2009) 120 <http://www.vision2030.gov.jm/Portals/0/NDP/Vision%202030%20Jamaica%20NDP%20Full%20No%20Cover%20(web).pdf> accessed 10 May 2020.
115 Ainsworth Morris, 'Occupational Safety and Health Bill Passage Expected by Year End, Jamaica Information Service' (Kingston, 23 May 2019) <https://jis.gov.jm/occupational-safety-and-health-bill-passage-expected-by-year-end/> accessed 12 April 2022.
116 Jamaica Employment (Equal Pay for Men and Women) Act 1975, s 2.

5.3.2 Reliance by Judiciary

A systematic review of electronic case law databases[117] shows that Jamaican courts only referred to CESCR on one occasion, namely, in the case of *West v Miller* before Jamaica's Supreme Court.[118] The Supreme Court made a rare acknowledgment of Jamaica's obligations under CESCR, stating that, by ratifying CESCR, state parties commit to act in conformity with their legal obligations under that treaty and must provide judicial remedies for alleged violations of economic, social and cultural rights. In a particularly rare occurrence, the Court relied on the CESCR Cttee's General Comment 4 as an interpretative tool.

5.3.3 Impact on and through Independent State Institutions

The researchers were unable to find evidence of the impact of CESCR on parliamentary commissions with human rights mandates. The OPD and INDECOM do not use CESCR in their work, even in cases where their work centres on the rights recognised in the treaty. For example, one of the priority issues arising out of the work of the OPD relates to the environment and the land rights of Maroon and Rastafari communities. However, the OPD has never used CESCR in submissions to Parliament or in other public reports to frame the nature of state obligations.[119] Moreover, the OPD has never presented reports to the CESCR Committee in the context of the Committee's review of Jamaica's periodic state reports.

5.3.4 Impact on and through Non-state Actors

There is limited evidence of CESCR's impact on the work of non-state actors. Interviews with NGOs and human rights activists show that they rarely, if at all, rely on CESCR in human rights litigation or in the context of campaigns. There is general acknowledgement that CESCR is not a central focus, although economic and social issues are integral to their human rights work.[120]

CESCR is considered in some publications that look at multiple treaties in examining the human rights situation in Jamaica.[121] CESCR has received

---

117 Information obtained from the Caribbean Law Online (CARILAW) database hosted on JustisOne database.
118 *West v Miller* JM 2017 SC 51 (Supreme Court Jam).
119 Interview with Arlene Harrison Henry, Public Defender (Kingston, 11 September 2019).
120 Interview with Rodjé Malcolm, Executive Director, Jamaicans for Justice (Kingston, 1 October 2018 and 1 February 2019).
121 For example, Ramona Biholar, *Nuttin Nuh Gwaan Fi We: Challenges Faced by Adult Ex-Inmates Upon Their Release in Jamaica* (Kingston, Stand Up For Jamaica, 2017).

attention in academic publications looking specifically at economic and social development in Jamaica,[122] as well as a publication considering an emerging human rights issue in Jamaica about protecting the tradition of Rastafari and Maroons.[123]

CESCR is covered in the curricula of legal education institutions in Jamaica in courses on Public International Law and International Human Rights Law.[124] There has been training for government officials and civil society focused on CESCR.[125] In 2018 the Faculty of Law, University of the West Indies, Mona, held a human rights symposium for high-school students focused on the right to education that highlighted the Committee's General Comment 13.[126]

5.3.5 Impact of State Reporting

The CESCR Cttee has issued COs on three occasions in the context of its consideration of Jamaica's periodic reports. Jamaica generally does not implement COs. In the most recent observations, published in 2013, the Committee reiterated many of the cross-cutting issues highlighted by other treaty bodies, such as the absence of a national human rights institution and issues around discrimination against women and sexual minorities.[127]

5.3.6 Brief Conclusion

CESCR has had a discernible, though limited, impact on the domestic legal order. Some of CESCR's provisions are enshrined in the Constitution and other pieces of legislation. While CESCR is not specifically mentioned in these laws, Jamaica's development plan explicitly states that the rights set out in CESCR are broad indicators of economic and social policy. One of the factors limiting

---

[122] For example, Vanus James and Rosalea Hamilton. 'Enhancing Democracy for Development in Jamaica: Key Issues and Strategies' in Kenneth Hall and Myrtle Chuck-A-Sang (eds), *Economic Transformation and Job Creation: The Caribbean Experience* (Trafford Publishing 2013) 55.

[123] Marcus Goffe, 'Protecting the Traditions of the Maroons and Rastafari: An Analysis of the Adequacy of the Intellectual Property Laws of Jamaica and Proposals for Reform' (2009) 5 SCRIPTed 575.

[124] Email from Alicia Dixon-Stone, Lecturer, Law Faculty, University of Technology (30 April 2019).

[125] OHCHR, 'Training Workshop for Government Officials: Reporting to CESCR' (March 2018); OHCHR, 'Rastafari Rights under the Covenant on Economic, Social and Cultural Rights: International Human Rights Reporting Standards and Mechanisms Training Workshop for the Rastafari Community and CSOs' (October 2018).

[126] The University of the West Indies, 'MonaLaw Human Rights Day Symposium' (10 December 2018).

[127] CESCR Cttee, COs, Jamaica, UN Doc E/C.12/JAM/CO/3-4 (29 April-17 May 2013).

the transformative potential of CESCR is the absence of NGO advocacy around its provisions. There is some evidence of impact in academic publications, but this is consistent with the general observation that awareness of UN treaties is limited to human rights experts and academics, and officials charged with the implementation of UN treaties.

5.4 Convention on the Elimination of All Forms of Discrimination against Women

5.4.1 Incorporation and Reliance by Legislature and Executive

CEDAW has had an important impact on Jamaica's legal system, although the legal and policy framework remains deficient. The Charter of Fundamental Rights and Freedoms prohibits discrimination on the ground of 'being male or female', instead of 'sex' or 'gender'.[128] Jamaica has adopted legislative measures aimed at eliminating discrimination against women, including the Sexual Offences Act 2009; the Domestic Violence Act 1995; the Property Rights of Spouses Act 2004; the Maintenance Act 2005; and the Sexual Harassment Act 2021. Additionally, a Joint Select Committee of Parliament recently concluded its review of the Sexual Offences Act and related laws, calling for increased protection for women, children and the elderly.

CEDAW is not explicitly mentioned in the relevant laws, but there is ample evidence that CEDAW played a role in legal reform. The parliamentary debates surrounding the adoption of the Domestic Violence Act show acute awareness of CEDAW, with the Minister of Justice noting that 'Jamaica is a party to this convention, and we are therefore committed to taking this sort of action'.[129] Similarly, debates around the process of constitutional reform suggest that CEDAW has had an impact on the new Charter of Fundamental Rights and Freedoms, which somewhat expands the protection of women's rights to be free from discrimination. In discussing this reform, one senator commented that '[w]e have finally taken the step to comply with Article Two of [CEDAW]. Article Two calls on all parties to embody the principle of equality of men and women in their national constitutions, or other appropriate legislation.'[130]

At the policy level, Vision 2030, Jamaica's national development plan, has a 'Gender Sector Plan' that makes reference to CEDAW and expresses a commitment to 'ensure enactment of new laws and continuing reform of existing laws

---

128 Jamaica Constitution, s 13(3)(i)(i).
129 Jamaica, Parliamentary Proceedings of the House of Representatives (14 March 1995) 287.
130 'Senate to Close Debate on Charter of Rights, Friday' *Jamaica Information Service* (Kingston 1 April 2011) <https://jis.gov.jm/senate-to-close-debate-on-charter-of-rights-friday-2/> accessed 12 April 2022.

in keeping with international conventions that address gender equality'.[131] The National Policy for Gender Equality 2011 similarly expresses a commitment to 'updating existing legislation affecting women to ensure consistency with CEDAW'.[132] The National Strategic Action Plan to Eliminate Gender-Based Violence in Jamaica (2017–2027) is also grounded in CEDAW.

Notwithstanding this impact, important gaps remain. The Constitution still has no definition of discrimination against women. Furthermore, there still is no comprehensive legislation clearly prohibiting gender discrimination in employment. Importantly, Jamaica has not amended its abortion legislation to help women address unplanned pregnancies. In 2018 the Joint Select Committee reviewing the proposal for reform of the Sexual Offences and related acts rejected a proposal to allow for abortion in certain specified cases, noting that the existing law concerning abortion was protected under a savings clause that shields it from constitutional challenge.[133]

5.4.2 Reliance by Judiciary

A systematic search of electronic case law databases shows that CEDAW has not been referred to in any decisions by Jamaican courts.[134] This is remarkable, given that issues related to gender-based violence and discrimination are key human rights challenges in Jamaica.[135] Domestic violence in Jamaica is litigated before parish courts and family courts. No written decisions are issued, except that criminal cases get written decisions on appeal. Therefore, in the area of domestic violence there are many cases, but not many opportunities for written decisions and, thus, public records.

---

[131] Jamaica, *Vision 2030 Jamaica National Development Plan: Gender Sector Plan* (Final Edition June 2010) 88 <http://lslandr.com/vision2030/wp-content/uploads/sites/4/2020/12/Microsoft-Word-Gender.pdf> accessed 12 April 2022.

[132] Jamaica, The National Policy for Gender Equality 2011, 26.

[133] Jamaica, 'Report of the Joint Select Committee Appointed to Complete the Review of the Sexual Offences Act Along with the Offences Against the Person Act, the Domestic Violence Act and the Child Care and Protection Act' (December 2018).

[134] The researchers carried out systematic searches in the Caribbean Law Online (CARILAW) database hosted on JustisOne database. CARILAW is the most extensive database of written decisions in the Anglophone Caribbean dating back to 1950.

[135] Peta-Gay Hodges, 'Nearly 15 Per Cent of Jamaican Women Experience Violence from A Male Partner' *Jamaica Information Service* (Kingston, 23 November 2018) <https://jis.gov.jm/nearly-15-per-cent-of-jamaican-women-experience-violence-from-a-male-partner/> accessed 12 April 2022.

5.4.3 Impact on and through Independent State Institutions

The researchers were unable to find evidence of the impact of CEDAW on parliamentary commissions with human rights mandates. The OPD and INDECOM do not use UN treaties in their work.

5.4.4 Impact on and through Non-state Actors

CEDAW has had a remarkable impact on the work of non-state actors in Jamaica. NGOs focusing on women's rights centre their advocacy and awareness-raising campaigns around CEDAW and the jurisprudence of the CEDAW Cttee. One of the leading women's rights organisations has published a CEDAW booklet, which uses Jamaican language to explain CEDAW's normative framework. The booklet makes extensive reference to the CEDAW Cttee's General Comments and also reproduces the Committee's COs.[136]

CEDAW is cited in a range of publications addressing women's rights in Jamaica.[137] The most extensive analysis of CEDAW is found in a book devoted to the implementation of article 5 of CEDAW in Jamaica.[138]

5.4.5 Impact of State Reporting

The CEDAW Cttee has issued COs on four occasions in the context of reviewing Jamaica's periodic reports.

Relevant domestic actors have expressed a commitment to implementing the CEDAW Cttee's recommendations.[139] In the most recent COs, published in

---

[136] WROC, 'Rights a di plan, wid CEDAW in wi han' (2008) (translation: Rights is the plan with CEDAW in our hand).

[137] Leith Dunn and Alicia Mondesire, *Poverty and Policy Coherence: The Case of Jamaica* (North-South Institute 2002); Danielle Barrett, 'Culture or Rights Violation: An Examination of the Role of Jamaica's Sociopolitical Culture on Women's Rights' (2005) 14 Buff Women's LJ 11; Jimmy Tindigarukayo, 'Perceptions and Reflections on Sexual Harassment in Jamaica' (2006) 7 J Intl Women's Studies 90; J Peters and others, 'Sexual Harassment and Sexual Harassment Policy in Jamaica: The Absence of a National Sexual Harassment Policy, and the Way Forward' (2012) 4 Asian Journal of Business Management 1; Heather Ricketts and David Bernard, 'Unlimited Unskilled Labour and the Sex Segregation of Occupations in Jamaica' (2015) 154 International Labour Rev 475; Carol Watson Williams, *Women's Health Survey 2016: Jamaica* (IADB 2018).

[138] Ramona Biholar, *Transforming Discriminatory Sex Roles and Gender Stereotyping: The Implementation of Article 5(a) CEDAW for the Realisation of Women's Right to be Free from Gender-Based Violence in Jamaica* (Utrecht University 2013); Fred Spiring, *Investigating Gender and Gender-Based Violence in Jamaica* (SAGE Publications 2016).

[139] For example, 'Remarks by Sen Hon Sandrea Falconer, Minister Without Portfolio (Information) Office of the Prime Minister to the Opening Ceremony of the Government-NGO Dialogue: Towards Effective Implementation of the Convention on the Elimination of All Forms of Discrimination Against Women (CEDAW)' (Kingston, 17 September

2012, the Committee focused its attention on a variety of issues, including the failure to criminalise all instances of marital rape and the criminalisation of abortion. However, the most recent assessment of the Rapporteur for Follow-up on COs has found that recommendations selected for follow-up had either not been implemented, been partially implemented, or could not be assessed due to insufficient information.[140]

In 2018 the Joint Select Committee reviewing the proposal for reform of the Sexual Offences and related acts addressed some of the issues raised by the CEDAW Cttee in its COs, but made no reference to the Committee's recommendations and, in some cases, articulated positions that are inconsistent with them. The Joint Select Committee, for example, rejected a proposal to allow for abortion in certain specified cases, noting that the existing law concerning abortion was protected under a savings clause that shields it from constitutional challenge.[141] On the other hand, the Joint Select Committee in 2018 recommended that all marital rape be criminalised, but makes no reference to the CEDAW Cttee's COs recommending the same in 2012.[142]

A high-level delegation consistently appears before the CEDAW Cttee. However, the Committee has noted that the state report does not provide sufficient data. Moreover, the reports are generally submitted with delays.

5.4.6 Brief Conclusion

CEDAW has had a discernible impact on the domestic legal order, not only through the domestication of treaty norms, but also through the work of women's rights groups who centre their advocacy around CEDAW. Jamaica has adopted laws aimed at eliminating discrimination against women. While CEDAW is not explicitly mentioned in these laws, parliamentary debates and policies confirm the awareness of lead government ministers and key policy makers of Jamaica's obligation to update existing legislation to ensure consistency with CEDAW. We also see evidence of Jamaica's commitment to CEDAW in the high-level delegation that appears before the CEDAW Cttee.

2013) <https://jis.gov.jm/media/Falconer-NGO-Dialogue-on-CEDAW-02.pdf> accessed 12 April 2022.

140 Rapporteur on follow-up, Committee on the Elimination of Discrimination against Women, Reference: DB/follow-up/Jamaica/66 (26 April 2017) <https://tbinternet.ohchr.org/Treaties/CEDAW/Shared%20Documents/JAM/INT_CEDAW_FUL_JAM_27292_E.pdf> accessed 12 April 2022.

141 Jamaica, 'Report of the Joint Select Committee Appointed to Complete the Review of the Sexual Offences Act Along with the Offences Against the Person Act, the Domestic Violence Act and the Child Care and Protection Act' (December 2018).

142 ibid.

However, significant gaps remain in existing laws, which still do not adequately protect women against discrimination. Importantly, Jamaica retains laws that are inconsistent with CEDAW, such as the law criminalising abortion. Notwithstanding the public statements from officials expressing a commitment to implementing the Committee's recommendations, the reporting process does not appear to be a significant driver of reform. It is telling that the CEDAW Cttee's 2012 COs were not mentioned by the 2018 Joint Select Committee reviewing the proposal for reform of the Sexual Offences and related Acts that considered the decriminalisation of abortion or a second parliamentary committee that addressed abortion and reported in early 2020.

CEDAW's impact is also limited by the absence of case law that advances the interpretation of CEDAW's provisions and Jamaica's failure to participate in CEDAW's independent complaint mechanism.

5.5   Convention on the Rights of the Child

5.5.1   Incorporation and Reliance by Legislature and Executive

Some provisions of CRC are reflected in the Constitution and other laws. The 2011 Charter of Fundamental Rights and Freedoms broadened the protection of children's rights in the Constitution.[143] For example, the Constitution now recognises the rights of children to measures of protection and publicly funded pre-primary and primary school level education.[144]

CRC was instrumental in the enactment of the Child Care and Protection Act in 2004. While CRC is not mentioned in this Act, in the parliamentary debates preceding the Act one parliamentarian noted that it was 'a giant step in fulfilling [Jamaica's] obligations under the Child Rights Convention'.[145] Jamaica has enacted a variety of other laws in the past two decades that advance children's rights, including the Child Pornography Act, 2009; the Trafficking in Persons Act, 2007; and the Maintenance Act, 2005.

The United Nations Children's Fund (UNICEF) representative to Jamaica has also noted that CRC has led to the establishment of key institutions, such as the Early Childhood Commission in 2003; the OCA in 2004; the Child Development Agency in 2004; and the Office of the Children's Registry in 2007.[146] CRC has also had an important impact on the development of policies

---

143   Jamaica Constitution, s13(3)(k).
144   ibid s 13(3)(k)(i), (ii).
145   Parliamentary Proceedings of the House of Representatives (2 March 2004) Session 2003–2004, 2055.
146   'Children's Advocate Wants Public Support for Rights of the Child Convention' *Jamaica Information Service* (23 November 2009) <https://jis.gov.jm/childrens-advocate-wants-public-support-for-rights-of-the-child-convention/> accessed 12 April 2022.

and best practices, some of which make explicit reference to CRC and the CRC Cttee.[147]

Despite this progress, important gaps remain, particularly in the area of juvenile justice. The Child Care and Protection Act, for example, empowers judges with the authority to imprison a child for life, in violation of article 37 of CRC. Importantly, section 24 of the Child Care and Protection Act permits the incarceration of children considered to be beyond parental control, thus making such conduct a poorly-defined status offence since it is not conduct that would be considered a crime if committed by adults.

Furthermore, while corporal punishment in the juvenile justice system is unlawful, there has been no legislative reform around abolishing corporal punishment in educational institutions and family settings. This much-needed reform remains at the policy level.

5.5.2 Reliance by Judiciary

A systematic search of case law produced one case before the Supreme Court that made very brief reference to CRC.[148] In *Stockhausen v Willis*,[149] the Supreme Court referred to article 9 of CRC, in a child custody case, but the analysis turned on jurisprudence from other common law jurisdictions, rather than jurisprudence from the CRC Cttee.

5.5.3 Impact on and through Independent State Institutions

The OCA extensively relies on CRC in its normative documents. The Child Justice Guidelines, for example, explicitly state that CRC 'informed the formulation of these Guidelines' and they reproduce specific articles of CRC.[150] The OCA has also developed public service announcements[151] that 'highlighted

---

147 See, eg, Jamaica, *Vision 2030 Jamaica National Development Plan: Social Welfare and Vulnerable Groups Sector Plan* (Revised, Kingston June 2009) <http://lslandr.com/vision2030/wp-content/uploads/sites/4/2020/12/Microsoft-Word-SWVG-Plan.pdf> accessed 12 April 2022; Office of the Children's Advocate, 'Child Justice Guidelines' (Kingston, July 2013) <https://www.welcome.oca.gov.jm/media/CHILD-JUSTICE-GUIDELINES.pdf> accessed 12 April 2022; Jamaica Constabulary Force, 'The Jamaica Constabulary Force Child Interaction Policy and Procedure' (November 2015, revised January 2017).

148 Information obtained from the Caribbean Law Online (CARILAW) database hosted on JustisOne database. In *Morrison* (n 20), the JCPC rejected CRC as an interpretive aid to the Jamaica Constitution.

149 *Stockhausen v Willis* (16 July 2008) (Supreme Court Jam).

150 See, eg, Office of the Children's Advocate, 'Child Justice Guidelines' (July 2013).

151 OCA, Annual Report 2012–2013 <https://www.welcome.oca.gov.jm/resources/> accessed 12 April 2022.

different aspects of the [CRC]'. The OPD and INDECOM do not use CRC in their work.[152]

5.5.4 Impact on and through Non-state Actors

CRC is one of the treaties with the most significant impact on the work of non-state actors due, in part, to the presence of UNICEF in Jamaica and the impact of that office in galvanising advocacy around children's rights. CRC is referred to in a range of academic publications addressing the rights of children in Jamaica.[153]

5.5.5 Impact of State Reporting

The CRC Cttee has issued COs on three occasions in the context of reviewing Jamaica's periodic reports. Jamaica is yet to implement the CRC Cttee's recommendations, particularly in the area of the administration of juvenile justice. In the most recent COs, published in 2015, the Committee expressed concern about Jamaica's failure to implement many of the Committee's recommendations from its 2003 COs. The CRC Cttee welcomed information from the state that children deemed 'uncontrollable' would no longer be criminalised. However, as at the end of 2019 no reforms had been implemented.[154] In 2018 the Joint Select Committee reviewing the proposal for reform of a number of

---

[152] Interviews with Arlene Harrison Henry, Public Defender (Kingston, 11 September 2019); Terrence Williams, Commissioner of the Independent Commission of Investigations (Kingston, 16 September 2019).

[153] Angela Steely and Ronald Rohner, 'Relations Among Corporal Punishment, Perceived Parental Acceptance, and Psychological Adjustment in Jamaican Youths' (2006) 40 Cross-Cultural Research 268; Michael Witter, 'Fiscal Expenditure on Services for Children in Jamaica' (GOJ-UNICEF 2006); Kerry-Ann Morris and Michelle Edwards, 'Disaster Risk Reduction and Vulnerable Populations in Jamaica: Protecting Children within the Comprehensive Disaster Management Framework' (2008) 18 Children Youth and Environments 389; C Bakker, M Elings-Pels and M Reis, *The Impact of Migration on Children in the Caribbean* (UNICEF 2009); Janet Brown and Sharon Johnson, 'Childrearing and Child Participation in Jamaican families' (2008) 16 Intl J of Early Years Education 31; Paul Miller, Kemesha Kelly and Nicola Spawls, 'Human Rights as Safeguarding: The Schooling Experiences of HIV+ Children in Jamaica' (2011) 5 Education, Knowledge & Economy 125; Helen Baker-Henningham and others, 'Experiences of Violence and Deficits in Academic Achievement among Urban Primary School Children in Jamaica' (2009) 33 Child Abuse & Neglect 296; Alexay Crawford, 'The Effects of Dancehall Genre on Adolescent Sexual and Violent Behaviour in Jamaica: A Public Health Concern' (2010) 2 North American J of Medical Sciences 143; Paul Miller, 'Children at Risk: A Review of Sexual Abuse Incidents and Child Protection Issues in Jamaica' (2014) 1 Open Rev of Educational Research 171; Delores Smith, 'Corporal Punishment of Children in the Jamaican Context' (2016) 7 Intl J of Child, Youth and Family Studies 27.

[154] Jamaica Child Care and Protection Act, 2004.

laws, including the Child Care and Protection Act, addressed the issue of children deemed 'uncontrollable', but did not refer to the CRC Cttee's recommendations on this issue.[155]

5.5.6 Brief Conclusion

CRC is the treaty that has had the most discernible impact on the domestic legal order, not only through the incorporation of treaty norms, but also through the work of NGOs and state functionaries who rely heavily on the CRC's normative framework. In the past two decades Jamaica has adopted various laws aimed at broadening the protection of children's rights, the most notable being the Child Care and Protection Act 2004. While CRC is not explicitly mentioned in these laws, parliamentary debates and policies confirm the influencing role of CRC in driving reform. We also see evidence of Jamaica's commitment to CRC in the establishment and operation of OCA, an independent institution that explicitly grounds its work in CRC's normative framework.

However, the impact of CRC is diminished by the state's repressive approach to juvenile justice and the existence of legislation that directly contradicts CRC norms, such as section 24 of the Child Care and Protection Act, which permits the incarceration of children considered beyond parental control. Even where the government expresses a commitment to treaty bodies to bring legislation in line with CRC, progress is slow. Another factor that limits the impact of CRC is the near absence of case law that advances interpretation of CRC's provisions. Jamaica's failure to participate in CRC's independent complaint mechanism also limits CRC's potential impact.

5.6 *International Convention on the Protection of the Rights of All Migrant Workers and Members of their Families*

5.6.1 Incorporation and Reliance by Legislature and Executive

CMW has not been incorporated into domestic law. Several laws on migration are obsolete and have not been harmonised with CMW. The Deportation (Commonwealth Citizens) Act 1942, the Aliens Act 1946 and the Immigration Restriction (Commonwealth Citizens) Act 1945 criminalise irregular immigration. There are discriminatory provisions in the Immigration Restriction (Commonwealth Citizens) Act, which lists prohibited immigrants, and in the Aliens Act, which prescribes the eligibility criteria for entry and prohibits

---

[155] Jamaica, 'Report of the Joint Select Committee Appointed to Complete the Review of the Sexual Offences Act Along with the Offences Against the Person Act, the Domestic Violence Act and the Child Care and Protection Act' (December 2018).

entry to persons with disabilities, among others (although Jamaica asserts that such laws are not enforced).[156] Thus, alongside CERD, CMW is one of the least impactful treaties, although there is evidence of a growing impact. Jamaica has adopted the Trafficking in Persons (Prevention, Suppression and Punishment) Act of 2007 (amended in 2013) which contributes to the implementation of CMW. At the institutional level, the appointment of the National Rapporteur on Trafficking in Persons in 2015 is also a notable achievement. The 2017 National Policy on International Migration and Development is replete with references to CMW, and articulates Jamaica's desire to fulfil its obligations under this convention.

5.6.2   Reliance by Judiciary
A systematic search of electronic case law databases shows that CMW has not been referred to by Jamaican courts.[157]

5.6.3   Impact on and through Non-State Actors
The researchers were unable to find evidence of the impact of CMW on commissions of parliament with human rights mandates. The OPD and INDECOM do not use CMW in their work.

5.6.4   Impact on and through Non-State Actors
The researchers were unable to find evidence of the impact of CMW on and through non-state actors.

5.6.5   Impact of State Reporting
State reporting under CMW has had no impact on Jamaica's legal system. Jamaica has never submitted a state report to the CMW Cttee, which issued COs on one occasion in 2017 in the absence of a state report.[158] The Committee expressed concern that the delegation, composed of the representatives of the Permanent Mission of Jamaica to the UN Office and other international organisations in Geneva, was unable to fully provide detailed information. The Committee also expressed specific concerns on a variety of issues, including the absence of implementing legislation; discriminatory provisions in the Immigration Restriction (Commonwealth Citizens) Act; the fact that the detention of irregular migrants under the Aliens Act is not a measure of last

---

156   CMW Cttee COs, Jamaica, UN Doc CMW/C/JAM/CO/1 (4 and 5 April 2017) para 28.
157   Information obtained from the Caribbean Law Online (CARILAW) database hosted on JustisOne database.
158   CMW Cttee, COs, Jamaica, UN Doc CMW/C/JAM/CO/1 (4 and 5 April 2017).

resort; and the provisions of the Immigration Restriction (Commonwealth Citizens) Act, which provide that children under 16 who are dependents of a prohibited immigrant are considered prohibited immigrants.

5.6.6 Brief Conclusion

CMW has had little impact on the domestic legal order. CMW has not been incorporated into domestic law and has not been the subject of civil society advocacy. However, policy statements could be evidence of an emerging trend towards an increasing impact of CMW in the future. The 2017 National Policy on International Migration, for example, articulates Jamaica's desire to comply with CMW.

5.7 *Convention on the Rights of Persons with Disabilities*

5.7.1 Incorporation and Reliance by Legislature and Executive

CRPD has not been fully incorporated into domestic law. The Constitution does not specifically mention persons with disabilities. However, Jamaica values and highlights its leadership on disability rights at the international level.[159] There is an ongoing process of legislative and institutional reform that culminated in the passage of the Disabilities Act in 2014. The Act builds on a National Policy for Persons with Disabilities, approved by Parliament in 2000. CRPD is not explicitly mentioned in the Disabilities Act. Nevertheless, CRPD obligations were present in the minds of some parliamentarians in the debates leading to the new law. One Minister noted that Jamaica was one of the first countries to ratify CRPD and that 'we are in effect reinforcing in our domestic legislation the obligations that we have made at the international level'.[160] The Act, which is yet to enter into force, envisions the creation of a disabilities rights tribunal to settle claims of discrimination. It also established the Jamaica Council for Persons with Disabilities, a department that currently exists within the Ministry of Labour and Social Security, which promotes the protection of the rights of persons with disabilities.

5.7.2 Reliance by Judiciary

A systematic search of electronic case law databases shows that CRPD has not been referred to by Jamaican courts.[161]

---

159 'Legislation Coming to Protect the Disabled' *The Gleaner* (Kingston, 2 October 2006) A3.
160 Parliamentary Proceedings of the House of Representatives, 22 July 2014, 1415.
161 Information obtained from the Caribbean Law Online (CARILAW) database hosted on JustisOne database.

5.7.3 Impact on and through Independent State Institutions

We were unable to find evidence of the impact of CRPD on commissions of Parliament with human rights mandates.

5.7.4 Impact on and through Non-state Actors

We were unable to find extensive evidence of CRPD's impact on non-state actors. CRPD was featured heavily in a special workshop on 'ICT Empowering Persons with Disabilities', which focused on the theme 'ICT Accessibility in the Convention on the Rights of Persons with Disabilities'.[162]

5.7.5 Impact of State Reporting

The state reporting process has had no impact on the domestic legal order. However, in 2018 Jamaica submitted its initial report to the CRPD Cttee, which is pending review.[163] This could point to the future impact of the reporting process.

5.7.6 Brief Conclusion

CRPD has had an evident impact on the domestic legal order. The enactment of the Disabilities Act in 2014 is a notable milestone in advancing CRPD norms in Jamaica. While CRPD is not specifically mentioned in this Act, parliamentary debates confirm that some legislators had a desire to fulfil Jamaica's obligations under CRPD. Nonetheless, the impact of CRPD is diminished by Jamaica's slow progress in bringing the 2014 Act into force and setting up a disability rights tribunal, and its failure to participate in the individual complaints procedure under OP-CRPD. Another factor limiting the impact of CRPD is the absence of case law that makes reference to CRPD. Jamaica's recent submission of its initial state report to the CRPD Cttee could however strengthen engagement with the UN reporting process in the future.

6 Conclusion

None of the seven treaties ratified by Jamaica has been fully incorporated into domestic law. Progress is inconsistent across the various treaties, but generally reporting is marred by delays and the lacklustre implementation of COs.

---

[162] Rodger Hutchinson, 'ICT Conference to Empower Persons with Disabilities' *Jamaica Information Service* (Kingston, 28 November 2013) <https://jis.gov.jm/ict-conference-empower-persons-disabilities/> accessed 12 April 2022.

[163] State Party's Report, CRPD, Jamaica, UN Doc CRPD/C/JAM/1/Rev.1 (25 June 2018).

CEDAW, CRC and CRPD have the most perceptible impact on Jamaica's laws and policies. In the case of each of these three treaties, there are state agencies or functionaries such as the Bureau of Gender Affairs and OCA, human rights defenders, academics, and research institutes that concentrate on issues related to women, children, and persons with disabilities respectively and that call attention to the state's obligations under the treaties in their work. In addition, there are UN agencies in Jamaica and the Caribbean that promote awareness of and compliance with CEDAW and CRC. By contrast, CERD, CESCR and CMW have had little impact, despite the participation of a Jamaican as a member of the CERD Cttee.

On the other hand, CCPR holds a place of historical influence in Jamaica. Jamaica ratified CCPR in 1966, four years after obtaining independence. The HRCttee considered a large number of death penalty cases in respect of Jamaica in the 2000s and their impact on the Caribbean's constitutional jurisprudence. In addition, the rights covered in CCPR, have a strong and long standing comparability with those in Jamaica's Constitution. Finally, monitoring by the HRCttee tackles some of the most endemic human rights problems in Jamaica related to citizen insecurity, actions by the security forces, and discrimination and inequality.

The denunciation of OP1-CCPR, which gave rise to many individual complaints to the HRCttee, set back the impact of treaties in Jamaica in the new millennium. It deprives persons in Jamaica of a valuable avenue to access justice for human rights violations. Moreover, with denunciation, treaty bodies receded entirely into ones that monitored the human rights situation every five to ten years, or, in the case of CMW, not at all. In this context, the inter-American system gained in importance since 2000, given the availability of quasi-adjudicatory mechanisms and the possibility of more frequent and diverse forms of monitoring the human rights situation.

State officials cite CRC, CEDAW and CCPR in the law-making process and acknowledge the state's obligation to comply with these treaties. However, they tend to do so at a general level and without reference to the specific recommendations made to Jamaica in COs or the overall jurisprudence of the treaty bodies that clarify in detail what the treaties mean. In some cases, the very legislation associated with responding to treaty obligations include obvious violations of those treaties. The most flagrant example of this duality is found in the 2011 Charter of Fundamental Rights and Freedoms, which replaces the old Chapter 3 of the Jamaica Constitution. The Charter includes clauses shutting out the judicial protection of human rights in critical areas such as sexual offences, abortion and the death penalty. Parliamentary debates show that these savings clauses cast a thick pall over legislative reform processes and are used to rationalise legislative resistance to comply with human rights norms.

The establishment of a national human rights institution and a more robust operation of the inter-ministerial committee could play a decisive role in transforming UN treaty implementation and protection of human rights generally. Jamaica's experience with the UN treaty system provides important lessons for future treaty body reforms that could have a positive impact on UN treaty implementation. First, treaty bodies must address the limited capacity in small states such as Jamaica to engage with the UN treaty system. Second, the growing importance of the inter-American system with its varied monitoring tools and sessions and in-country visits suggests that more direct engagement of UN treaty bodies on the ground and virtually 'in [Jamaica's] time zone' could yield promising results. It also suggests opportunities for more collaboration between the UN treaty system and the regional Inter-American system. Finally, interviews with stakeholders suggest that the Sustainable Development Goals (SDGs) may be an entry point in Jamaica for advocacy around UN treaty implementation. The challenge, therefore, is to emphasise the human rights foundation of the SDGs and how UN treaties are integral to advancing key targets.

CHAPTER 11

The Impact of the United Nations Human Rights Treaties on the Domestic Level in Japan

Ayako Hatano, Hiromichi Matsuda and Yota Negishi

1 Introduction to Human Rights in Japan

The protection of fundamental human rights with respect to the dignity of an individual is the foundational principle of the Japanese Constitution. Based on the reflection of the devastation of World War II, the post-war Japanese Constitution contains an article on the renunciation of war and contains an elaborate Bill of Rights[1] that lists civil and social rights as justiciable rights.[2]

Japan is a constitutional democracy with a multi-party parliamentary system in which the emperor has strictly ceremonial duties. The National Diet, Japan's bicameral legislature, is the sole law-making organ of the state, composed of a lower house called the House of Representatives and an upper house, the House of Councillors. Both houses are elected directly using a parallel voting system. The Prime Minister is the head of the government and the leader of the national cabinet, where executive power is vested.[3] The Supreme Court and the lower courts conduct judicial reviews independently under the

---

1 Constitution of Japan <https://japan.kantei.go.jp/constitution_and_government_of_japan/constitution_e.html> accessed 29 May 2021, art 9. Some scholars and lower courts argue that the second paragraph of the Preamble and art 9 guaranteed the right to live in peace, eg T Fukase, *Sensō Hōkito Heiwateki Seizonken* (*Renunciation of War and the Right to Live in Peace*) (Iwanami 1987) 225–228; Nagoya High Court, Judgment, 17 April 2008, 1313 *Hanrei Times* 137, 146 (recognising the justiciability of the right to live in peace as a concrete right). However, the Supreme Court has not recognised the justiciability of the right to live in peace. While there have been constant attempts to amend the Constitution by the conservative ruling party, the Constitution of Japan remains in effect without a single amendment as of 2020. S Matsui, 'Fundamental Human Rights and "Traditional Japanese Values": Constitutional Amendment and Vision of the Japanese Society' (2018) 13 Asian Journal of Comparative Law 59.
2 Constitution of Japan, arts 11, 13 and 14.
3 The Prime Minister is appointed by the emperor after being designated by the National Diet and must enjoy the confidence of the House of Representatives to remain in office.

Constitution.[4] The separation of powers is guaranteed under the Constitution of Japan.[5]

During the period covered by this study, from 1999 to 2019, Japan's political landscape was deemed relatively stable, with the conservative Liberal Democratic Party (LDP) continuing in power, except for a brief break from 2009 to 2012 when the Democratic Party of Japan (DPJ) held power. In general, the country's population has enjoyed peace without direct engagement in war and good socio-economic status with a highly developed free-market economy.[6]

However, Japan faces numerous human rights challenges. According to the white paper on human rights in Japan,[7] the Japanese government has identified a list of human rights issues in Japan including those related to women

---

4   The judiciary consists of three main levels: district courts (trial courts), high courts, which are the first level of appeal, and the Supreme Court, the highest and final appeal court. See the Constitution of Japan <https://japan.kantei.go.jp/constitution_and_government_of_japan/constitution_e.html> accessed 29 May 2021, arts 76, 77 and 78. There is no 'constitutional court' in Japan which determines the constitutionality of any laws without being accompanied by legal disputes and issues. All courts (the Supreme Court, High Courts and district courts) can examine compatibility of domestic laws with constitution and treaties. The Supreme Court is composed of the chief justice and 14 justices with a grand bench made up of all 15 justices and three petty benches with five justices each. The cases are first assigned to one of the three petty benches, and these cases that involve constitutional questions are transferred to the grand bench for its inquiry and adjudication. There are also different types of courts, such as family courts and summary courts, which deal with specific types of cases.
5   Prime Minister's Office, 'Constitution of Japan' <https://japan.kantei.go.jp/constitution_and_government_of_japan/constitution_e.html> accessed 29 May 2021. At the end of the 19th century, the Empire of Japan adopted the Meiji Constitution (1889) and pursued a programme of industrialisation and modernisation. Under the Meiji Constitution, the emperor used to be the sovereign, and protection of human rights was limited. The new Constitution of Japan was enacted in 1946 during the occupation after its defeat in World War II, with a declaration of the popular sovereignty principle and of the emperor as the symbol of the state and of the unity of the people.
6   Japan's economy grew to become the world's second largest behind the US from 1968 until 2010, when it was overtaken by China. Japan struggled with economic deficiencies in and after the so-called 'lost decade' of the 1990s with growing economic inequalities. See M Koraha, and F Ohtake, 'Rising Inequality in Japan: A Challenge Caused by Population Ageing and Drastic Changes in Employment' in B Nolan and others (eds), *Changing Inequalities and Societal Impacts in Rich Countries: Thirty Countries' Experiences* (OUP 2014).
7   Ministry of Justice (MOJ), 'The Protection of Human Rights FY2019' (December 2019) <https://www.moj.go.jp/ENGLISH/HB/activities/pdf/booklet2019.pdf> accessed 16 November 2022; MOJ, '*Reiwa 2 Nen ban Jinken Kyōiku Keihatsu Hakusho* (White Paper on Human Rights Education and Awareness-Raising FY2020)' <https://www.moj.go.jp/JINKEN/jinken04_00043.html> accessed 16 November 2022.

(sexual harassment, domestic violence, forced engagement in pornography);[8] children (bullying, corporal punishment, sexual exploitation, and child abuse); elderly people, *Burakumin* (Dowa issues);[9] Ainu people;[10] foreign nationals;[11] HIV and Hansen's disease patients; people released from prison after serving their sentence; crime victims; human rights violations on the internet; victims abducted by North Korean authorities; homeless people; persons with disabilities; people with alternate sexual orientation and gender identity (SOGI);[12] human trafficking; and human rights problems arising after natural disasters. While the Government of Japan emphasises its efforts and the measures taken in the white paper,[13] Japan faces severe criticism from international and domestic human rights organisations in several areas.[14] The treaty bodies have repeatedly expressed their concerns to Japan because it has not established national human rights institutions (NHRIs) in accordance with the Paris Principles, nor has it accepted individual communications mechanisms under any of the human rights treaties and their optional protocols or the enactment of a comprehensive anti-discrimination law.

---

8   The country ranks 116th out of 146 countries in terms of gender equality according to the World Economic Forum. See World Economic Forum, 'Global Gender Gap Report 2022' <http://www3.weforum.org/docs/ WEF_GGGR_2022.pdf> accessed 12 October 2022.

9   The *Burakumin*, or *Buraku* people, is an outcast group in Japan's feudal order and has been discriminated against for a long time, even after the feudal caste system formally ended in the late 19th century. Buraku Liberation League, 'What is Buraku Discrimination' <http://www.bll.gr.jp/en/index.html> accessed 13 December 2020.

10 The Ainu are an indigenous people of the lands surrounding the Sea of Okhotsk, including Hokkaido Island, recognised by the Japanese government. See the Advisory Council for Future Ainu Policy, 'Final Report' <http://www.kantei.go.jp/jp/singi/ainu/dai10/siryou1_en.pdf> accessed 13 December 2020.

11 The ethnic minority groups residing in Japan and often subjected to discriminatory treatment include, but are not limited to, residential Koreans (*Zainichi* Koreans who came to Japan from the Korean peninsula before and during World War II and their descendants, and newcomers) and other residents of foreign origin.

12 Organisation for Economic Co-operation and Development (OECD), 'Society at a Glance 2019: A Spotlight of LGBT People' (27 March 2019) <http://www.oecd.org/japan/sag2019-japan-en.pdf> accessed 9 February 2020.

13 See n 7.

14 Eg, see Human Rights Watch, 'World Report 2019: Japan' <https://www.hrw.org/world-report/2019/country-chapters/japan#> accessed 22 March 2021; Human Rights Watch, 'World Report 2020: Japan' <https://www.hrw.org/world-report/2020/country-chapters/japan> accessed 22 March 2021; Human Rights Watch, 'World Report 2022: Japan' <https://www.hrw.org/world-report/2022/country-chapters/japan> accessed 10 April 2022.

This chapter explores the impact of the United Nations (UN) human rights treaties on Japanese law, policy, judicial decisions, and society during the 20 years after 1999.[15]

2 Relationship of Japan with the International Human Rights System[16]

Japan has developed its relationship with the international human rights system in line with its political priorities as well as with prudent consideration of legal consistency between international and domestic laws. As a matter of general principle, human rights issues were not allowed to interfere with central concerns such as the pursuit of economic self-interest and national security. Thus, it is said that 'Japan's foreign policy towards human rights was almost non-existent until the 1980s'.[17] Such a passive stance in human rights diplomacy often resulted in contradictions with its pro-Western diplomatic allies in multilateral forums. While it has taken human rights into account in its foreign policy since the late 1970s, the Japanese Government's response to human rights violations in the international community has generally been passive.

Japan joined the UN in 1956 and has become one of its most significant financial contributors.[18] Japan is a party to all core human rights treaties, with the exception of the International Convention on the Protection of the Rights of All Migrant Workers and Members of their Families (CMW).[19] Japan acceded to the 1951 Convention Relating to the Status of Refugees in 1981 and the 1967

---

[15] The main period of focus is between 30 June 1999 and 30 June 2019, while some recent important developments after this period may be covered in the chapter. This chapter does not aim to cover all relevant issues but rather to highlight some critical cases and evident narratives during the period.

[16] This section includes Japan's relations with the UN human rights mechanism except for the UN human rights treaty mechanism which will be detailed in the next section.

[17] Y Yokota and C Aoi, 'Japan's foreign policy towards human rights: Uncertain changes' in D P Forsythe (ed), *Human Rights and Comparative Foreign Policy: Foundations of Peace* (United Nations University 2000).

[18] Japan contributed 8,5% of the UN regular budget in 2020, while its voluntary contribution to the UN Office of the High Commissioner for Human Rights (OHCHR) was less than 0,1% of the total amount in 2020. Ministry of Foreign Affairs (MOFA), '2020–2022 Nen Kokuren Tsujō Yosan Buntanritsu Futankin (2020–2022 UN Regular Budget Contributions and Assessment Rates)' <https://www.mofa.go.jp/mofaj/gaiko/jp_un/yosan.html> accessed 10 April 2022; United Nations, 'Human Rights Report 2020' <https://www.ohchr.org/Documents/Publications/OHCHRreport2019.pdf> accessed 13 December 2020.

[19] For details, see part 4 below.

Protocol Relating to the Status of Refugees in 1982[20] and ratified the Rome Statute of the International Criminal Court (ICC) in 2007.[21] However, Japan has not ratified the Convention on the Prevention and Punishment of the Crime of Genocide on the grounds that it may conflict with the Constitution and domestic law.[22] It also has yet to ratify two of the eight core conventions of the International Labour Organization (ILO) on the grounds of possible inconsistencies with the domestic legal framework.[23] While there is no regional international human rights mechanism in East Asia, the Government of Japan conducts regular dialogues with the human rights body of the Association of Southeast Asian Nations (ASEAN)[24] and bilateral 'human rights dialogues' with

20   See UNHCR, 'States Parties to the 1951 Convention Relating to the Status of Refugees and the 1967 Protocol' <https://www.unhcr.org/protection/basic/3b73b0d63/states-parties-1951-convention-its-1967-protocol.html> accessed 13 December 2020.

21   MOFA, '*Kokusai Keiji Saibansho* (International Criminal Court)' <http://www.mofa.go.jp/mofaj/files/000162093.pdf> accessed 26 January 2020. It took a long discussion before Japan ratified the ICC Rome Statute as the 105th signatory state. After its ratification, Japan has been the significant financial contributor to the ICC. For the status of Japanese ratification of the major international treaties regarding human rights, see Hurights Osaka, '*Shuyōna kokusai jinken jōyakuto hijun jōkyōno ichiran* (List of major international human rights treaties and their ratification status)'. <https://www.hurights.or.jp/archives/treaty/un-treaty-list.html> accessed 9 January 2021.

22   '*Kempōto Jōyaku: Ryōritsuwa Eienno Jiremma* (The Constitution and Treaties: Their Compatibility is an Eternal Dilemma)' (Mainichi, 20 May 2002) <https://mainichi.jp/articles/20020520/org/00m/010/999000c> accessed 16 January 2021.

23   ILO, 'Ratification for Japan' <https://www.ilo.org/dyn/normlex/en/f?p=NORMLEXPUB:11200:0::NO::P11200_COUNTRY_ID:102729> accessed 18 March 2021; Japan Trade Union Confederation, '*8tsuno Jūyōna ILO Jōyaku, Nihonga 2tsu Mihijunna Wake: Chūkakuteki Rōdō Kijun 4 Bunya, 8 Jōyaku* (Eight Important ILO Treaties, Why Japan Has Not Ratified Two of Them: Core Labour Standards, Four Areas, Eight Treaties)' <https://www.jtuc-rengo.or.jp/shuppan/teiki/gekkanrengo/backnumber/data/201703why.pdf?91> accessed 18 March 2021; ILO, 'C105 – Abolition of Forced Labour Convention, 1957 (No 105)' <https://www.ilo.org/dyn/normlex/en/f?p=NORMLEXPUB:55:0:::55:P55_TYPE,P55_LANG,P55_DOCUMENT,P55_NODE:CON,en,C105,/Document> accessed 18 March 2021; ILO, 'C111 – Discrimination (Employment and Occupation) Convention, 1958 (No 111)' <https://www.ilo.org/dyn/normlex/en/f?p=NORMLEXPUB:12100:0::NO::P12100_ILO_CODE:C111> accessed 18 March 2021.

24   In 2009 the ASEAN established the ASEAN Intergovernmental Commission on Human Rights (AICHR) to promote human rights in the 10 ASEAN countries. See also ASEAN Commission on the Promotion and Protection of the Rights of Women and Children (ACWC), 'ASEAN Commission on the Promotion and Protection of the Rights of Women and Children (ACWC) Work Plan 2021–2025' <https://asean.org/book/asean-commission-on-the-promotion-and-protection-of-the-rights-of-women-and-children-acwc-work-plan-2021-2025/> accessed 7 September 2023. As a related entity, the ASEAN Committee on Women (ACW) was established as a subsidiary body of the ASEAN Ministerial Meeting on Women. ACW has organised ACW+3 meetings with Japan, China, and Korea since

several countries such as Cambodia, Myanmar, Iran, Sudan and the People's Republic of China.[25]

Japan has undergone the Human Rights Council's Universal Periodic Review (UPR) in the first (2008), second (2012), and third (2017) cycles.[26] The number of recommendations received in each review steadily increased to 26, 174, and 217, respectively.[27] From the first to the third review, the country has continuously received numerous recommendations in the areas of the abolition of the death penalty, the establishment of a domestic human rights institution, the introduction of an individual communications mechanism, discrimination against women, and racial discrimination. This highlights the current gap between international human rights standards and the country's situation.

2009. ASEAN, 'AMMW – Overview' <https://asean.org/asean-socio-cultural/asean-ministerial-meeting-on-women-ammw/overview/#:~:text=(ASCC)%20Pillar.-,ASEAN%20Committee%20on%20Women%20(ACW).,work%20plan%2C%20and%20managing%20partnerships> accessed 15 November 2020; Gender Equality Bureau Cabinet Office, '*Joseini kansuru ASEAN+3 iinkai* (ASEAN+3 Committee on Women ACP+3)'. <https://www.gender.go.jp/international/int_kaigi/int_acw3/index.html> accessed 15 November 2020.

25 For example, MOFA, 'The Seventh Japan-Myanmar Human Rights Dialogue' (21 February 2020) <https://www.mofa.go.jp/press/release/press4e_002579.html> accessed 9 January 2021.

26 OHCHR, 'Universal Periodic Review – Japan' <https://www.ohchr.org/EN/HRBodies/UPR/Pages/JPindex.aspx> accessed 1 November 2020. See also UPR Info, 'Japan' <https://www.upr-info.org/en/review/Japan?device=c&gclid=EAIaIQobChMIlt3yoe-C7QIViuJ3Ch2_MQaQEAAYASAAEgLijvD_BwE> accessed 9 January 2021.

27 Japan has consistently accepted more than 60% of recommendations from the UPR, with a slight decrease in the latest cycle. OHCHR, 'Infographics' <https://lib.ohchr.org/HRBodies/UPR/Documents/Session28/JP/JAPAN_Infographic_28th.pdf> accessed 1 November 2020. In the second cycle of UPR in 2012, Japan accepted 125 recommendations (71,8%) out of 174. It accepted 145 recommendations out of 217 (66,8%) in the third cycle in 2017. As for contents, the 145 recommendations accepted in the third cycle include those concerning national human rights institutions, individual complaints mechanism, human rights education, business and human rights, human trafficking, sexual exploitation, prohibition of corporal punishment, gender equality, persons with disabilities, migrant workers, and the Fukushima nuclear accident. Japan partially accepted to follow up on 10 recommendations, such as those regarding the recognition of same-sex marriage at the national level. However, it did not accept to follow up on 34 recommendations, including those on the death penalty, comfort women, ratification of the Nuclear Weapons Convention, independence of the media, abolition of the substitute prison system, extension of the application of the Atomic Bomb Survivors' Assistance Act to the second generation of atomic bomb survivors, and inclusion of Korean schools in the free high school education scheme in Japan. It 'noted' 28 recommendations, including the enactment of anti-discrimination laws. Human Rights Council, 'Report of the Working Group on the Universal Periodic Review, Japan, Addendum, Views on Conclusions and/or Recommendations, Voluntary Commitments and Replies Presented by the State Under Review' <https://www.mofa.go.jp/mofaj/files/000346500.pdf> accessed 2 March 2021.

This also indicates that there have been no noticeable improvements over the past decade even in those areas where the government agreed to follow up.

Japan has maintained its active membership in the Human Rights Council (HRC). It was a member during the periods of 2006–2008,[28] 2009–2011,[29] 2013–2015,[30] 2017–2019,[31] and, subsequent to the cut-off mark of this study, 2020–2022.[32] With the issue of abductions of Japanese citizens by the Democratic People's Republic of Korea (DPRK), Japan has been submitting a resolution on the situation of human rights in the country to the Human Rights Council almost every year since 2008.[33] Japan maintains a generally positive attitude in supporting human rights resolutions and declarations adopted by the UN, except for resolutions not compatible with its domestic and foreign policies, such as resolutions against the death penalty.[34] Japan received 12 visits

---

[28] OHCHR, 'Membership of the Human Rights Council 19 June 2006 – 18 June 2007 by Regional Groups' <https://www.ohchr.org/EN/HRBodies/HRC/Pages/Group20062007.aspx> accessed 1 November 2020.

[29] ibid.

[30] OHCHR, 'Membership of the Human Rights Council, 1 January – 31 December 2013 by Regional Groups' <https://www.ohchr.org/EN/HRBodies/HRC/Pages/Group2013.aspx> accessed 1 November 2020.

[31] OHCHR, 'Membership of the Human Rights Council, 1 January – 31 December 2017 by Regional Groups' <https://www.ohchr.org/EN/HRBodies/HRC/Pages/Group2017.aspx> accessed 1 November 2020.

[32] OHCHR, 'Current Membership of the Human Rights Council for the 14th Cycle, 1 January – 31 December 2020' <https://www.ohchr.org/EN/HRBodies/HRC/Pages/CurrentMembers.aspx> accessed 1 November 2020.

[33] Japan did not join the submission of the resolution in 2019. United Nations Human Rights Council, 'Documents and Resolutions' <https://www.ohchr.org/en/hrbodies/hrc/pages/documents.aspx> accessed 1 November 2020.

[34] Eg, in 2007 the UN adopted the Declaration on the Rights of Indigenous Peoples (United Nations Declaration on the Rights of Indigenous Peoples (A/RES/61/295, 13 September 2007)). Japan voted in support of this declaration. House of Councillors, '*Ainu Minzokuwo Senjū Minzokuto Surukotoo Motomeru Ketsugi* (Resolution Seeking Government's Recognition of the Ainu as Indigenous People)' (6 June 2008) <http://www.sangiin.go.jp/japanese/gianjoho/ketsugi/169/080606-2.html> accessed 1 February 2020. On the other hand, Japan abstained from voting on the UN General Assembly's resolution of 14 November 2018 strongly condemning rights abuses against Rohingya Muslims and other minority groups in Myanmar. UN General Assembly, 'Promotion and Protection of Human Rights: Human Rights Situations and Reports of Special Rapporteurs and Representatives' <https://undocs.org/A/74/399/Add.3> accessed 13 December 2020. The situation behind Japan's inaction on the Rohingya issues is their intimate relationship with the Myanmar government that is boldly pushing forward economic development of the country. Human Rights Watch, 'Japan's Cold-Blooded Approach to the Rohingya Crisis' <https://www.hrw.org/news/2019/06/20/japans-cold-blooded-approach-rohingya-crisis> accessed 13 December 2020. Following the coup by the military in 2021, which led to deteriorated political and humanitarian situations, Japan and some 60 countries

through the Special Procedures of the HRC between 1999 and 2019.[35] It has also extended a standing invitation to thematic special procedures since 1 March 2011.[36]

There seems to be a significant disparity between international commitment and domestic implementation. For example, in the international fora, Japan has played a pivotal role in advancing rights of lesbian, gay, bisexual, and transgender (LGBT) people, particularly in the UN system. Japan was one of the drafters of the statement presented in the General Assembly that affirmed that international human rights protections include SOGI.[37] It voted for two Human Rights Council (HRC) resolutions to end violence and discrimination

---

submitted the General Assembly Resolution of 18 June 2021 condemning lethal violence by Myanmar's Armed Forces. United Nations, 'General Assembly Reappoints Secretary-General to Second Five-Year Term, Adopting Resolution Condemning Lethal Violence by Myanmar's Armed Forces' <https://www.un.org/press/en/2021/ga12339.doc.htm> accessed 6 July 2021; *'Myanmā "buki ryūnyū soshi" ketsugi saitaku kokuren sōkaide saitaku chūronado kiken* (Myanmar "Weapon Inflow Prevention" Resolution Adopted by UN General Assembly with Abstentions by China and Russia and so on)' (*Mainichi*, 19 June 2021) <https://mainichi.jp/articles/20210619/k00/00m/030/055000c> accessed 6 July 2021.

[35] Special Rapporteur on contemporary forms of racism, racial discrimination, xenophobia, and related intolerance (2005), Special Rapporteur on human trafficking, especially women and children (2009), Special Rapporteur on the human rights of migrants (2010), Independent expert on the issue of human rights obligations related to access to safe drinking water and sanitation (2010), Special Rapporteur on the right of everyone to the enjoyment of the highest attainable standard of physical and mental health (2012), Independent expert on the effects of foreign debt and other related international financial obligations of states on the full enjoyment of all human rights, particularly economic, social, and cultural rights (2013), Special Rapporteur on the situation of human rights in the Democratic People's Republic of Korea (2014), Special Rapporteur on the sale and sexual exploitation of children (2015), Special Rapporteur on the promotion and protection of freedom of opinion and expression (2016), Special Rapporteur on the situation of human rights in the Democratic People's Republic of Korea (2016), Special Rapporteur on adequate housing as a component of the right to an adequate standard of living, and on the right to non-discrimination in this context (2017), Special Rapporteur on the situation of human rights in the Democratic People's Republic of Korea (2017). OHCHR, 'Country Visits of Special Procedures of the Human Rights Council Since 1998, Japan' <https://spinternet.ohchr.org/ViewCountryVisits.aspx?visitType=all&country=JPN&Lang=en> accessed 11 November 2020.

[36] OHCHR, 'Standing Invitations' <https://spinternet.ohchr.org/StandingInvitations.aspx> accessed 1 November 2020.

[37] General Assembly, 'Letter Dated 18 December 2008 from the Permanent Representatives of Argentina, Brazil, Croatia, France, Gabon, Japan, the Netherlands and Norway to the United Nations Addressed to the President of the General Assembly' (A/63/635, 18 December 2008) <https://undocs.org/A/63/635> accessed 2 March 2021.

on the basis of sexual orientation and gender identity in 2011 and 2014.[38] However, it is ranked low at the 25th position among 36 Organisation for Economic Co-operation and Development (OECD) countries for social acceptance of homosexuality at the domestic level[39] and second to last in legal LGBT and intersex inclusivity, which has improved at a more modest pace than in other countries.[40]

Despite its general pledge of commitment and cooperation with the international human rights system,[41] there are some highly contentious issues, such as so-called 'comfort women'. The Special Rapporteur on Violence against Women highlighted the issue of military 'sexual slavery' in wartime in her report in 1996.[42] The Japanese government does not acknowledge that comfort

---

[38] General Assembly, 'Resolution adopted by the Human Rights Council: 17/19 Human rights, sexual orientation and gender identity' (A/HRC/RES/17/19, 14 July 2011); General Assembly, Resolution adopted by the Human Rights Council: 27/32 Human rights, sexual orientation and gender identity' (A/HRC/RES/27/32, 2 October 2014). On the other hand, Japan voted against the UN Human Rights Council resolution to condemn the imposition of a death penalty as a sanction against apathy, disbelief, adultery, consenting to homosexual acts, and so forth, in 2017 (General Assembly, 'Human Rights Council Thirty-sixth Session Agenda Item 3: Promotion and Protection of All Human Rights, Civil, Political, Economic, Social and Cultural Rights, Including the Right to Development, 36/ ... The Question of the Death Penalty' (A/HRC/36/L.6, 22 September 2017)). This is explained as the purpose of this resolution being rather towards the abolition of the death penalty and to seek a moratorium. Japan also became a member of the UN LGBT Core Group, an informal cross-regional LGBT group established in 2008, alongside other states, the European Union, the Office of the United Nations High Commissioner for Human Rights (OHCHR), and two civil society organisations (CSOs). UN LGBTI Core Group, 'Members' <https://unlgbticoregroup.org/members/> accessed 18 November 2022.

[39] OECD, 'Society at a Glance 2019: OECD Social Indicators' <https://www.oecd-ilibrary.org/social-issues-migration-health/society-at-a-glance-2019_soc_glance-2019-en> accessed 2 March 2021.

[40] OECD, 'Over the Rainbow? The Road to LGBTI Inclusion' <https://www.oecd-ilibrary.org/social-issues-migration-health/over-the-rainbow-the-road-to-lgbti-inclusion_8d2fd1a8-en> accessed 2 March 2021.

[41] Eg, see MOFA, 'Japan's Human Rights Commitments and Pledges' (January 2019) <https://www.mofa.go.jp/files/000175306.pdf> accessed 9 January 2021; see also MOFA, 'Commitment and Pledges of Japan as Candidate of Human Rights Council 2020–2022' <https://www.mofa.go.jp/mofaj/files/000175485.pdf> accessed 9 January 2021.

[42] The report recommends that the Japanese government '(a)cknowledge that the system of comfort stations set up by the Japanese Imperial Army during the Second World War was a violation of its obligations under international law and accept legal responsibility for that violation' and '(p)ay compensation to individual victims'. Economic and Social Council, 'Report of the Special Rapporteur on Violence Against Women, its Causes and Consequences, Ms Radhika Coomaraswamy, in Accordance with Commission on Human Rights Resolution 1994/45: Report on the Mission to the Democratic People's Republic of Korea, the Republic of Korea and Japan on the Issue of Military Sexual Slavery in Wartime'

women were forcibly recruited by the Japanese military or authorities.[43] It maintains that the issue has been legally settled by treaties and agreements.[44] The Japanese government repeated this position at the Third Committee of the UN General Assembly, the HRC, and country reviews by treaty bodies.[45] The treaty bodies and international and national human rights groups severely criticise the government from the standpoint of women's rights and transitional justice.[46]

(E/CN.4/1996/53/Add.1, 4 January 1996) <https://documents-dds-ny.un.org/doc/UNDOC/GEN/G96/101/23/PDF/G9610123.pdf?OpenElement> accessed 9 January 2021. This report received significant guidance from humanitarian law but also had a reference to human rights law, such as CCPR, CESCR and CAT. Similar views were expressed in a report on systematic rape, sexual slavery, and slavery-like practices during armed conflict, which was submitted in June 1998 to the UN Economic and Social Council by Special Rapporteur Ms Gay J McDougall. G J McDougall, 'Contemporary forms of Slavery: Systematic rape, Sexual Slavery, and Slavery-Like Practices During Armed Conflict' (22 June 1998) <https://digitallibrary.un.org/record/257682/files/E_CN.4_Sub.2_1998_13-EN.pdf> accessed 9 January 2021. For the most recent response on this issue by the Japanese government, see HRCttee, 'Seventh Periodic Report Submitted by Japan Under Article 40 of the Covenant Pursuant to the Optional Reporting Procedure, due in 2018' (CCPR/C/JPN/7, 28 April 2020); Nippon Television Network, 'Ianfu Mondai Meguri, Nikkanga Kokurende Shuchōno Ōshu (Japan and Korea Argue at the UN over the Issue of Comfort Women)' (16 October 2012) <https://www.news24.jp/articles/2012/10/16/10215887.html> accessed 9 January 2021.

43 MOFA, 'Japan's Efforts on the Issue of Comfort Women' <https://www.mofa.go.jp/policy/postwar/page22e_000883.html> accessed 21 November 2022.

44 See 'Agreement on the Settlement of Problems Concerning Property and Claims and on Economic Co-operation between Japan and the Republic of Korea' (22 June 1965) <https://worldjpn.grips.ac.jp/documents/texts/JPKR/19650622.T9E.html> accessed 2 March 2021; MOFA, 'Japan-ROK agreement' (28 December 2015) <https://www.mofa.go.jp/a_o/rp/page24e_000277.html> accessed 2 March 2021.

45 Eg, state party report under the List of Issues Prior to Reporting for the Human Rights Committee, Seventh periodic report submitted by Japan under article 40 of the Covenant pursuant to the optional reporting procedure, due in 2018 (HRCttee (n 42) paras 148–54); Permanent Mission of Japan to the United Nations, United Nations Committee on Human Rights: Japan Defends Human Rights of Citizens Abducted by DPRK (6 November 2012) <https://www.un.emb-japan.go.jp/pressreleases/110612.html> accessed 13 December 2020; United Nations, 'Japan's Stance on "Comfort Women" Issue Violates Victims' Rights – UN Official' *UN News* (August 2014) <https://news.un.org/en/story/2014/08/474572-japans-stance-comfort-women-issue-violates-victims-rights-un-official> accessed 13 December 2020.

46 For example, see OHCHR, 'Japan / S Korea: "The Long Awaited Apology to 'Comfort Women' Victims is Yet to Come" – UN Rights Experts' (OHCHR, 11 March 2016) <https://www.ohchr.org/EN/NewsEvents/Pages/DisplayNews.aspx?NewsID=17209> accessed 9 January 2021; see also Women's Active Museum on War and Peace (WAM) <https://wam-peace.org/en/> accessed 2 January 2021, and their submission to the treaty bodies (eg, WAM, 'On Japan's Military Sexual Slavery Issue' (24 July 2017) <https://tbinternet.ohchr.org/_layouts/15/treatybodyexternal/Download.aspx?symbolno=INT%2fCCP

Like the Coomaraswamy report mentioned above, observations and reports of the Special Rapporteurs often face harsh criticism from Japan. In May 2017, the Special Rapporteur on the right to privacy issued an open letter to the Prime Minister of Japan. The letter says that a controversial anti-conspiracy bill may breach the rights of privacy under article 17(1) of the International Covenant on Civil and Political Rights (CCPR).[47] The Japanese government strongly opposed the letter, condemning it for its lack of correct understanding of the Bill.[48] Similarly, in May 2017 the Japanese government issued a statement opposing the report of the UN Special Rapporteur on freedom of expression released for the Human Rights Council's 35th session.[49] The Japanese government argued that its recommendations were based on mistaken and misrepresented facts and uncertain information.[50] The cabinet emphasised that 'the views of the Special Rapporteur are expressed in his or her individual capacity and are *not* the views of the United Nations or of the Human Rights Council'.[51] Some Special Rapporteurs, including the UN Special

---

R%2fICS%2fJPN%2f28281&Lang=en> accessed 2 January 2021). Women's International Tribunal on Japanese Military Sexual Slavery in 2000, a people's tribunal organised by Violence Against Women in War-Network Japan (VAWW-NET Japan), attracted international attention to this issue. CM Chinkin, 'Women's International Tribunal on Japanese Military Sexual Slavery' (2001) 95 American Journal of International Law 335–41; Y Matsui, 'Women's International War Crimes Tribunal on Japan's Military Sexual Slavery: Memory, Identity, and Society' (2001) 19 East Asia 119–42.

47 MOFA, '*Kokuren Jinken Rijikaino "Puraibashīno Kenri" Tokubetsu Hōkokushani Yoru Kōkai Shokanni Taisuru Nihon Seifu Kenkai* (Japanese Government's Views on the Open Letter from the UN Special Rapporteur on the right to privacy)' (18 May 2017) <https://www.mofa.go.jp/mofaj/fp/is_sc/page3_002110.html> accessed 25 January 2020.

48 'UN Privacy Expert Shoots Down Japan's Complaints About 'Anti-Conspiracy' Bill Criticism' (Mainichi, 22 May 2017) <https://mainichi.jp/english/articles/20170524/p2a/00m/0na/014000c> accessed 25 January 2020.

49 For the Report of the Special Rapporteur on the Promotion and Protection of the Right to Freedom of Opinion and Expression on his mission to Japan, see Human Rights Council, 'Report of the Special Rapporteur on the Promotion and Protection of the Right to Freedom of Opinion and Expression on His Mission to Japan' (A/HRC/35/22/Add.1, 15 June 2017) <https://documents-dds-ny.un.org/doc/UNDOC/GEN/G17/163/96/PDF/G1716 396.pdf?OpenElement> accessed 7 July 2021.

50 For the Japanese government's comments, see Human Rights Council, 'Report of the Special Rapporteur on the Promotion and Protection of the Right to Freedom of Opinion and Expression on His Mission to Japan: Comments by the State' (A/HRC/35/22/Add.5, 30 May 2017).

51 House of Representatives, '*Shūgiin Giin Ōsaka Seijikun Teishutsu Kokuren Jinken Rijikaino Tokubetsu Hōkokushani Taisuru Seifuno Teigini Kansuru Shitsumonni Taisuru Tōbensho* (Answers to Questions Submitted by Member of the House of Representatives Seiji Osaka Regarding the Definition by the Government of the Special Rapporteur of the United

Rapporteur on hazardous substances and waste, have not been accepted for a visit, despite repeated requests. The press release and report issued in October 2018 by the UN Special Rapporteur on hazardous substances and wastes regarding nuclear accidents in 2011 in Fukushima triggered a strong reaction from the Japanese government condemning the statement as full of erroneous content based on a one-sided claim.[52]

Furthermore, with the background of active advocacy and individual communications by civil society groups in Japan, the Working Group on Arbitrary Detention (WGAD) adopted opinions on the following cases: two Greenpeace Japan employees arrested and detained (2009);[53] a man with schizophrenia forcibly hospitalised after being arrested (2018);[54] a protester against the relocation of a US military base in Okinawa detained for about five months (2018);[55] a woman detained by police officers and compulsorily hospitalised (2018);[56] the lengthy detention of Turkish and Iranian asylum seekers with deportation orders (2020);[57] and Carlos Ghosn, a former head of a global

Nations Human Rights Council)' (30 May 2009) <http://www.shugiin.go.jp/internet/itdb_shitsumon.nsf/html/shitsumon/b193333.htm> accessed 16 January 2021.

[52] OHCHR, 'Japan Must Halt Returns to Fukushima, Radiation Remains a Concern, Says UN Rights Expert' (25 October 2018) <https://www.ohchr.org/EN/NewsEvents/Pages/DisplayNews.aspx?NewsID=23772&LangID=E> accessed 15 November 2020.

[53] Human Rights Council Working Group on Arbitrary Detention, 'Opinions Adopted by the Working Group on Arbitrary Detention' (A/HRC/13/30/Add.1, 4 March 2010) <https://documents-dds-ny.un.org/doc/UNDOC/GEN/G10/116/72/PDF/G1011672.pdf?OpenElement> accessed 15 November 2020.

[54] Human Rights Council Working Group on Arbitrary Detention, 'Opinions Adopted by the Working Group on Arbitrary Detention at its Eighty-First Session, 17–26 April 2018 Opinion No 8/2018 Concerning Mr. N (whose name is known by the Working Group) (Japan)' (A/HRC/WGAD/2018/8, 23 May 2018) <https://www.ohchr.org/Documents/Issues/Detention/Opinions/Session81/A_HRC_WGAD_2018_8.pdf> accessed 15 November 2020.

[55] Human Rights Council Working Group on Arbitrary Detention, 'Opinions Adopted by the Working Group on Arbitrary Detention at its Eighty-Second Session, 20–24 August 2018 Opinion No 55/2018 Concerning Yamashiro Hiroji (Japan)' (A/HRC/WGAD/2018/55, 27 December 2018) <https://www.ohchr.org/Documents/Issues/Detention/Opinions/Session82/A_HRC_WGAD_2018_55.pdf> accessed 15 November 2020.

[56] Human Rights Council Working Group on Arbitrary Detention, 'Opinions Adopted by the Working Group on Arbitrary Detention at its Eighty-Third Session, 19–23 November 2018: Opinion No 70/2018 Concerning Ms H (whose name is known by the Working Group) (Japan)' (A/HRC/WGAD/2018/70, 16 January 2019) <https://www.ohchr.org/Documents/Issues/Detention/Opinions/Session88/A_HRC_WGAD_2020_58_Advance_Edited_Version.pdf> accessed 15 November 2020.

[57] Human Rights Council Working Group on Arbitrary Detention, 'Opinions Adopted by the Working Group on Arbitrary Detention at its Eighty-Eighth Session, 24–28 August 2020, Opinion No 58/2020 Concerning Deniz Yengin and Heydar Safari Diman (Japan)'

automobile company, arrested and detained four times (2020).[58] Some critical recommendations of the WGAD were taken up in questions against the government at the National Diet.[59] However, the government has not provided a substantial response to these questions or requests by the WGAD.

There is an active civil society in Japan, with countless non-profit organisations (NPOs) and civil society groups.[60] Their role in providing public goods has grown due to insufficient government response to emergencies, such as large earthquakes after the economic slowdown in the 1990s.[61] It is

---

(A/HRC/WGAD/2020/58, 25 September 2020) <https://www.ohchr.org/Documents/Issues/Detention/Opinions/Session88/A_HRC_WGAD_2020_58_Advance_Edited_Version.pdf> accessed 15 November 2020.

[58] Opinions Adopted by the Working Group on Arbitrary Detention at its Eighty-Eighth Session, 24–28 August 2020, Opinion No 59/2020 Concerning Carlos Ghosn (Japan) (A/HRC/WGAD/2020/59, 20 November 2020) <https://www.ohchr.org/Documents/Issues/Detention/Opinions/Session88/A_HRC_WGAD_2020_59_Advance_Edited_Version.pdf> accessed 16 January 2021. This case attracted international attention with criticism of the Japanese 'hostage justice' system. R Wingfield-Hayes, 'Carlos Ghosn and Japan's "Hostage Justice" System' (BBC, 31 December 2019) <http://www.bbc.com/news/world-asia-47113189> accessed 25 January 2020.

[59] House of Councillors, 'Dai 197 Kai Kokkai Rinjikai Shitsumon Dai 13 Gō Sochi Nyūinwo Shiiteki Kōkinto Suru Kokuren Shiiteki Kōkintō Sagyō Bukai Kankokuni Kansuru Shitsumon Shuisho (The 197th Diet Extraordinary Session, Question No. 13, Statement of Question on the UN Working Group on Arbitrary Detention's Observation that Compulsory Hospitalisation is Arbitrary Detention)' (24 October 2018) <https://www.sangiin.go.jp/japanese/joho1/kousei/syuisyo/197/syuh/s197013.htm> accessed 15 November 2020. In 2019 Seong-Phil Hong, a member and the ex-Chairperson of the WGAD, visited Japan, upon invitation by a civil society group to attend events hosted by the JFBA and civil society organisations (CSOs). Keiji Bengo Oashisu, "Shimpojiumu "Nipponno Shintai Kōsoku – Sore, Shiiteki Kōkindeha Arimasenka?" (Symposium "Physical Restraint in Japan – That is Arbitrary Detention, Isn't It?")' <https://www.keiben-oasis.com/4193> accessed 8 September 2023.

[60] The number of officially acknowledged NPOs under the 'Law to Promote Specified Non-profit Activities' (NPO Law 1998) is 51,793 (as of 28 February 2022). See Cabinet Office NPO Homepage, 'Ninshō shinsei jurisū / ninshōsū (shokatsuchobetsu) (Numbers of Applications for Certification Received and approved (by Authority))' <https://www.npo-homepage.go.jp/about/toukei-info/ninshou-zyuri> accessed 10 April 2022. There are also many civil society groups that are not accredited under the law. For details of the legal system on charity organisation and its problems, see S Yamasaki, 'Charitable Organisations in Japan: Overview' Thomson Reuters Practical Law <https://uk.practicallaw.thomsonreuters.com/w-019-3735?transitionType=Default&contextData=(sc.Default)&firstPage=true> accessed 12 January 2021.

[61] R Pekkanen, 'Japan's New Politics: The Case of the NPO Law' (2000) 26 Journal of Japanese Studies 111. However, most of those organisations and groups do not enjoy sufficient funds and resources due to legal, political and social constraints. Zhu and Iwatsubo, who study the challenges faced by Japanese NPOs, point out that the amount of contribution

noteworthy that the human rights defenders and CSOs take greater advantage of the special procedures concerning individual cases and communications as there is no individual complaints mechanism under treaty bodies available to them.

3 At a Glance: Formal Engagement of Japan with the UN Human Rights Treaty System

Refer to the chart on the next page.

4 Role and Overall Impact of the UN Human Rights Treaties in Japan

4.1 *Role of the UN Human Rights Treaties*

4.1.1 Formal Acceptance

Japan ratified the CCPR and the International Covenant on Economic, Social and Cultural Rights (CESCR) in 1979, and the Convention on the Elimination of All Forms of Discrimination against Women (CEDAW), the Convention on the Rights of the Child (CRC), the International Convention on the Elimination of All Forms of Racial Discrimination (CERD) and the Convention Against Torture and Other Cruel, Inhuman, or Degrading Treatment or Punishment (CAT) in 1985, 1994, 1995 and 1999, respectively. After the turn of the 21st century, Japan joined two other UN human rights treaties and the two protocols. It ratified the Optional Protocol to the Convention on the Rights of the Child on

---

received by NPOs in Japan is still relatively small when compared to their counterparts in some other countries. While approximately 4.000 NPOs are newly established every year, the total amount of yearly contributions to NPOs is stagnant at around 600 billion yen. This amount corresponds to one-fortieth of 23,7 trillion yen in the United States. H Zhu and K Iwatsubo, 'Financial Constraints on NPO in Japan: The Role of Intermediaries' (2010) 18 Journal of Business Administration and Information 35. The Cabinet Office's Survey on Specified Non-Profit Organisations depict similar situations. Cabinet Office, '*Heisei 25 Nen Tokutei Hieiri Katsudō Hōjinni Kansuru Jittai Chōsa* (Survey on Non-Profit Organisations in 2013)' (24 December 2013) <https://www.npo-homepage.go.jp/toukei/npojittai-chousa/2013npojittai-chousa>; Cabinet Office, '*Heisei 29 Nendo Tokutei Hieiri Katsudō Hōjinni Kansuru Jittai Chōsa* (Survey on Non-Profit Organisations in FY 2017)' (30 March 2018) <https://www.npo-homepage.go.jp/toukei/npojittai-chousa/2017npojittai-chousa> accessed 12 October 2022.

JAPAN

Year	Treaties	Individual complaints procedure
1979	CESCR, CCPR	
1985	CEDAW	
1994	CRC	
1995	CERD	
1999	CAT	
2004	OP-CRC-AC	
2005	OP-CRC-SC	
2009	CED	
2014	CRPD	

the involvement of children in armed conflict (OP-CRC-AC) in 2004 and the Optional Protocol to the Convention on the Rights of the Child on the sale of children, child prostitution, and child pornography (OP-CRC-SC) in 2005.[62] Subsequently, the government ratified the International Convention for the Protection of All Persons from Enforced Disappearance (CED) in 2009, including the acceptance of the interstate communication procedure under the Convention.[63] In 2014, Japan ratified the Convention on the Rights of Persons with Disabilities (CRPD) after a revision of pertinent domestic laws to meet treaty requirements.[64] Japan neither signed nor ratified the International Convention on the Protection of the Rights of All Migrant Workers and Members of Their Families (CMW) as it contravenes domestic laws and the Constitution,[65] and is not a party to the Optional Protocol of the

---

[62] C Heyns and F Viljoen, 'The Impact of the United Nations Human Rights Treaties on the Domestic Level' (2003) 23 Human Rights Quarterly 483; OHCHR, 'Ratification Status for Japan' <https://tbinternet.ohchr.org/_layouts/15/TreatyBodyExternal/Treaty.aspx?Country ID=87&Lang=EN> accessed 11 November 2022.

[63] There was significant concern and interest among the Japanese government and nationals on people abducted by the Democratic People's Republic of Korea (DPRK). This issue was raised by the government representative during the consideration of the first report submitted by Japan. Committee on Enforced Disappearances, 'Consideration of Reports of States Parties to the Convention, Initial Report of Japan (CED/C/SR.257, 23 November 2018)' <https://tbinternet.ohchr.org/_layouts/15/treatybodyexternal/Download.aspx?symbolno=CED%2fC%2fSR.257&Lang=en> accessed 13 December 2020. See also art 32 of CED.

[64] The civil society had a major role in this ratification process of CRPD. See the following section on CRPD.

[65] N Piper, 'Obstacles to, and Opportunities for, Ratification of the ICRMW in Asia' in R Cholewinski, P de Guchteneire and A Pécoud A (eds), *Migration and Human Rights: The United Nations Convention on Migrant Workers' Rights* (Cambridge University Press 2009) 171–92. The reluctance of ratification may be explained by Japan receiving many migrant workers, as other non-party developed countries. S Ago, '*Hitono Kokusai Idōto Rōdō: Kokusai Soshikino Yakuwari* (Migration and Labour: The Role of International Institutions)' (2014) 357/358 Ritsumeikan Law Review 1573, 1582. For general obstacles to ratification of the receiving countries, see A Pecoud, 'United Nations Migrant Workers Convention' <https://link.springer.com/referenceworkentry/10.1007%2F978-981-13-2898-5_142> accessed 8 November 2020. According to the comment of the director of MOFA at the Committee of Legal Affairs at the House of Representatives, '[i]f Japan is to ratify ICMW, we must carefully consider the possible issues in relation to various domestic systems such as Japan's basic labour policy, immigration control, elections, education, criminal procedures, and social security, as well as whether migrant workers will be given preferential treatment over citizens or foreigners other than migrant workers and there will be problems in relation to the principle of equality or not'. National Diet Library, '*Dai 123 Kai Kokkai Shūgiin Hōmu Iinkai Dai 7 Gō* (The 123rd Diet, House of Representatives

Convention against Torture (OP-CAT),[66] and the Second Optional Protocol to the International Covenant on Civil and Political Rights, aiming at the abolition of the death penalty (OP2-CCPR). Japan has also not accepted any of the complaints mechanisms under the Optional Protocol to the International Covenant on Civil and Political Rights (OP1-CCPR), the Optional Protocol to the International Covenant on Economic, Social and Cultural Rights (OP-CESCR), the Optional Protocol to the Convention on the Elimination of All Forms of Discrimination against Women (OP-CEDAW), the Optional Protocol to the Convention on the Rights of the Child on a communications procedure (OP-CRC-CP), the Optional Protocol to the Convention on the Rights of Persons with Disabilities (OP-CRPD), CERD, CAT or CED.[67] In the past, the government reasoned that the acceptance of individual communications would be contrary to judicial independence.[68] However, through internal studies of issues related to a possible organisational framework for implementing the procedure,[69] the government admitted that it is 'not necessarily required to change the judicial system ... in association with individual communication mechanisms'.[70]

Committee on Judicial Affairs, Case no 7)' (14 April 1992) <https://kokkai.ndl.go.jp/simple/detail?minId=112305206X00719920414&spkNum=0#s0> accessed 8 March 2021.

[66] United Nations Treaties Collection, 'Optional Protocol to the Convention against Torture and Other Cruel, Inhuman or Degrading Treatment or Punishment' <https://treaties.un.org/pages/ViewDetails.aspx?src=IND&mtdsg_no=IV-9-b&chapter=4&lang=en> accessed 4 July 2019; OHCHR, 'Optional Protocol to the Convention against Torture and Other Cruel, Inhuman or Degrading Treatment or Punishment' (4 July 2019) <https://www.ohchr.org/Documents/HRBodies/OPCAT/StatRatOPCAT.pdf> accessed 8 November 2020.

[67] OHCHR, 'View the Ratification Status by Country or by Treaty' (*UN Treaty Body Database*) <https://tbinternet.ohchr.org/_layouts/15/TreatyBodyExternal/Treaty.aspx?Treaty=CCPR&Lang=en> accessed 8 November 2020.

[68] National Diet Library, '*Dai 169 Kai Kokkai Sangiin Yosan Iinkai Dai 3 Gō* (The 169th Diet, House of Councillors Committee on Budget, Case no. 3)' (1 February 2008) <https://kokkai.ndl.go.jp/#/detail?minId=116915261X00320080201&current=1> accessed 6 June 2021.

[69] In the course of this process, the Division for Implementation of Human Rights Treaties was set up in the MOFA in April 2010, and the Division has held 20 seminars on the procedure with the relevant ministries and agencies. See International Human Rights Instruments, 'Common Core Document Forming Part of the Reports of States Parties: Japan' (HRI/CORE/JPN/2019, 14 October 2020), for the status as of September 2019.

[70] National Diet Library, '*Dai 201 Kai Kokkai Sangiin Gaikō Bōei Iinkai Dai 6 Gō* (Diet 201st Session, the House of Councillors, Committee on Foreign Affairs and Defence, Case no 6)' (26 March 2020) <https://kokkai.ndl.go.jp/txt/120113950X00620200326/112> accessed 10 July 2021. The government established the Division for Implementation of Human Rights

Japan entered reservations to several articles in multiple treaties, including one on articles 4(a) and (b) of CERD, which calls for the criminalisation of so-called racial hate speech. The government claims that this is because the provision may conflict with the protection of freedom of speech under the Japanese Constitution.[71] Regarding CESCR, Japan entered several reservations and declarations upon ratification. In the application of article 7(d) of the Covenant, Japan reserves the right not to be bound by the 'remuneration for public holidays' referred to in said provisions; it also reserves the right not to be bound by article 8(1)(d) of the Convention on the right to strike, except in relation to the sectors in which the right referred to in said provisions is in accordance with the laws and regulations of Japan at the time of ratification of the Covenant. Further, the government declares that 'members of the police' referred to in article 8(2) as well as in article 22(2) of the Covenant be interpreted to include fire service personnel in Japan. In September 2012, Japan withdrew the reservation made upon article 13(2)(b)(c) of the Covenant regarding free secondary and tertiary education,[72] while it reserves the right not to be bound 'in

---

Treaties in the Ministry of Foreign Affairs in April 2010, aiming for the consideration and preparation to accept individual complaints mechanisms under human rights treaties. Government of Japan, 'Mid-Term Report on the Progress Made in the Implementation of the Recommendations Issued at the Second Cycle of the Universal Periodic Review' <http://www.mofa.go.jp/mofaj/files/000225031.pdf> accessed 10 October 2020.

[71] International Convention of the Elimination of All Forms of Racial Discrimination, Declarations and Reservations-Japan, UNGA Res 2106 (XX) (A/RES/2106(XX), 21 December 1965): 'In applying the provisions of paragraphs (a) and (b) of article 4 of the [said Convention], Japan fulfils the obligations under those provisions to the extent that fulfilment of the obligations is compatible with the guarantee of the rights to freedom of assembly, association, and expression, and other rights under the Constitution of Japan, noting the phrase "with due regard to the principles embodied in the Universal Declaration of Human Rights and the rights expressly set forth in article 5 of this Convention" referred to in article 4.' The government maintains that CERD recommendations are already covered by existing laws or incorporated in several laws targeting specific groups, despite there being no comprehensive law against racial discrimination. These laws principally aim at raising and promoting understanding among the general public through human rights education and awareness-raising activities. CERD, 'Tenth and Eleventh Combined Periodic Report by the Government of Japan under Article 9 of the International Convention on the Elimination of All Forms of Racial Discrimination' (CERD/C/JPN/10–11, 25 September 2017) para 105.

[72] In 2010 the government under DPJ ruling decided to make upper secondary education free. Ministry of Education, Culture, Sports and Science and Technology (MEXT), 'Kōtō Gakkōtō Shūgaku Shienkinno Shikyūni Kansuru Hōritsu (Act on Provision of High School Enrolment Support Fund)' (31 March 2010) <https://www.mext.go.jp/a_menu/shotou/mushouka/detail/__icsFiles/afieldfile/2014/08/06/1346770.pdf> accessed 6 June 2021.

particular by the progressive introduction of free education referred to in the said provisions'.[73]

Japan also entered reservations to the CRC upon ratification. Regarding article 37(c) of the Convention, Japan reserves the right not to be bound by the provision in its second sentence, that is, 'every child deprived of liberty shall be separated from adults unless it is considered in the child's best interest not to do so'. This is based on the government's view that in Japan, as regards persons deprived of liberty, those who are below 20 years of age are generally to be separated from those who are 20 years of age and over under its national law. Japan also declares that article 9(1) of the Convention 'be interpreted not to apply to a case where a child is separated from his or her parents as a result of deportation in accordance with its immigration law'. As for article 10(1), Japan decided that 'the obligation to deal with applications to enter or leave a state party for the purpose of family reunification "in a positive, humane and expeditious manner" be interpreted not to affect the outcome of such applications'.[74]

4.1.2 General Attitude toward the UN Treaty System

Although human rights treaties are ranked higher than statutory law, courts are not very active in the application of human rights treaties. The Constitution, with supremacy in the Japanese legal system, stipulates its relationship with international law as follows: 'The treaties concluded by Japan and established laws of nations shall be faithfully observed' (article 98(2)). It has been construed that treaties and customary international law are treated respectfully, as placed under the Constitution but superior to domestic laws and can be invoked in the same way as laws in domestic courts.[75]

---

[73] United Nations Treaties Collection, 'International Covenant on Economic, Social and Cultural Rights, article 23' <https://treaties.un.org/pages/ViewDetails.aspx?src=IND&mtdsg_no=IV-3&chapter=4&clang=_en#23> accessed 8 November 2020.

[74] United Nations Treaties Collection, 'Convention on the Rights of the Child' <https://treaties.un.org/Pages/ViewDetails.aspx?src=IND&mtdsg_no=IV-11&chapter=4#EndDec> accessed 11 July 2020; Y Saito, 'Convention on the Right of the Child and Problems on Domestic Law System' (2000) 22 Bunkyo University Life Science Studies 59.

[75] Y Iwasawa, *International Law, Human Rights, and Japanese Law: The Impact of International Law on Japanese Law* (OUP 1998) 28–36, 95–103; Y Iwasawa, 'Domestic Application of International Law' (2016) 378 Recueil des Cours 9. See also H-B Shin, 'Japan' in Dinah Shelton (ed), *International Law and Domestic Legal Systems: Incorporation, Transformation, and Persuasion* (OUP 2011) 360, 365–76. The government takes the standpoint that it does not necessarily presuppose the absolute supremacy of the Constitution over treaties but determines the relative primacy in light of their substance. See the Statement of the Director-General of the Cabinet Legislation Bureau Shuzo Hayashi, the 33rd National Diet, the Budget Committee of the House of Councillors (17 November 1959)

However, Japanese courts have been reluctant to apply international law to domestic cases. Former justice of the Japanese Supreme Court, Itsuo Sonobe, frankly commented that '[s]ince our Constitution is well established, in particular with regard to human rights protections, we can solve most disputes without drawing upon support from international human rights law', and 'in practice of examination of cases, domestic laws come first, and the Constitution second, and subsequently depending on the allegation of the parties, if necessary, international human rights and other international law can be referred'.[76] This view that international human rights law is merely a supplementary yardstick to be used when the existing jurisprudence does not help judges to square the statutory circle is widely shared in the Japanese legal hierarchy.[77]

It is worth noting that the Japanese justice system is traditionally considered to have two unique tendencies in this connection. First, the courts have a tendency to ignore claims based on international human rights law. Under Japan's Code of Civil Procedure, appeals on violations of international human rights law are often dismissed without further investigation and consideration of the actual situation on the grounds that such violations are mere violations of the law in general. For instance, the Supreme Court in 1995 rejected the appeal that the fingerprinting of aliens violated CCPR, saying that it was merely an allegation of violation of the law and did not constitute a legitimate ground for appeal.[78]

<https://kokkai.ndl.go.jp/#/detail?minId=103315261X00419591117&current=6>accessed 29 May 2021. See also V Mazzuoli and D Ribeiro, 'The Japanese Legal System and the Pro Homine Principle in Human Rights Treaties' (2015) 15 Anuario Mexicano de Derecho Internacional 239; H Yamamoto and Y Negishi, 'Japan' in F Palombino (ed), *Duelling for Supremacy: International vs National Fundamental Principles* (Cambridge University Press 2019).

[76] I Sonobe and A Kotera, '*Saikō Saibanshoto Kokusaihō* (Supreme Court and International Law)' (2009) 1387 Jurist 16. While Justice Sonobe acknowledges the potential role of international law in cases for which there is no applicable domestic law, he emphasises it would be a last resort for the courts to directly apply international law only after efforts to use the Constitution directly or indirectly had failed. See also I Sonobe, '*Nihonno Saikō Saibanshoni Okeru Kokusaijinkenhōno Saikin no Tekiyō Jyōkyō* (Recent situations of the application of international human rights law in Japan's supreme court)' in K Serita, T Munesue, K Yakushiji and S Sakamoto (eds), *Kokusaijinkenhō to Kempō [International Human Rights Law and Constitution]* (Shinzansha 2006) 17–24.

[77] T Webster, 'International Human Rights Law in Japan: The View at Thirty' (2010) 23 Colombia Journal of International Law 242, 245.

[78] Supreme Court, Judgment, 15 December 1995, 49 Keishū 842, 847.

Second, the courts tend to conduct a detailed examination of the violations of the Constitution and dismiss claims based on international human rights law. Based on the interpretation that international human rights law and the human rights provisions of the Constitution of Japan have the same meaning and scope of application, and therefore international human rights law does not guarantee human rights beyond the Constitution, the Supreme Court appears to only give cursory attention to claims of international human rights law violations, often dismissing them without thorough examination. For instance, the Supreme Court in 1989 held that the right to take notes in court should be respected in the spirit of article 21 of the Constitution and that article 19(2) of CCPR serves the same purpose.[79]

In recent years, certain studies contend that Japanese domestic courts have demonstrated a more active invocation and application of international human rights law. This trend is particularly notable in cases concerning the rights of vulnerable individuals and groups, such as women and persons with disabilities.[80]

The government is also of the view that the Constitution and statutory laws provide the principal legal protection of human rights. Institutionally, the statutory laws are meticulously formulated to align with the obligations stipulated in the international human rights treaties that Japan has ratified. This process involves a thorough examination by the Legislation Bureau of the Cabinet Office.[81] While the government states that it takes its obligation under international law seriously, when it comes to politically sensitive issues, the Japanese government expressed its defensive or even negative attitudes toward its obligation under international human rights law. For example, its cabinet decision in 2013 declared that the recommendation from the UN treaty bodies is not legally binding.[82] Some human rights CSOs and academics severely criticise this attitude toward international human rights and urge the government

---

79 Supreme Court, Judgment, 8 March 1989, 43 Minshū 89, 93.
80 Eg, see K Ishibashi, 'Implementation of International Law in Japanese Courts: From Their Traditional Reluctance in Invoking International Law to Some Innovative Rulings Based upon International Human Rights Law' (2015) 3 Korean Journal of International and Comparative Law 139–70.
81 In Japan, when the Diet introduces a statute, the Legislation Bureau of the Cabinet Office very carefully checks the bill's compatibility and consistency with the Constitution, existing law, and international obligations. On the one hand, this attentive approach leads to implementing human rights obligations in good faith. On the other hand, the cautious Japanese approach tends to hinder immediate and drastic change of domestic law and active judicial review. See H Matsuda, 'International Law in Japanese Courts' in C Bradley (ed), *The Oxford Handbook of Comparative Foreign Relations Law* (OUP 2019) 541.
82 Cabinet, '*Tōbensho Dai 118 Gō* (Counterstatement No 118)' (18 June 2013) <https://www.sangiin.go.jp/japanese/joho1/kousei/syuisyo/183/toup/t183118.pdf> accessed 9 June 2021.

to take proactive, concrete, and fast-paced measures to fill the gap between national and international standards.[83]

There have been constant gaps in communication among the government, treaty bodies, and civil society groups.[84] For instance, while many treaty bodies have expressed their concerns about the 'comfort women' issue, the government repeats its legal point of view that retroactive application of treaties is not allowed, and the issues have already been resolved at the diplomatic level.[85] Another example may be the controversial Japanese criminal justice system. While the Japanese government alleges that it is one of the countries with the most advanced and fair criminal justice system despite some shortcomings,[86] CSOs and UN treaty bodies have criticised the Japanese criminal legal system,

---

[83] Amnesty International, '*Ibento Hōkoku: Kokuren Kankoku "Shitagau Gimu Nashi" ni Igi Ari! Kinkyū Shūkaiwo Kaisai* (Event Report: Disagreement with 'no obligation to follow UN recommendations'! We held an urgent meeting)' <https://www.amnesty.or.jp/hrc/2013/0718_4065.html> accessed 1 November 2020.

[84] Interview with an International Human Rights Law Expert (Geneva, Switzerland, 27 August 2019); Interview with an International Human Rights Law Expert (Geneva, Switzerland, 11 February 2019) (notes of all interviews on file with authors). One of the experts mentioned that even though the Japanese government tries to explain its stance and provide thorough information to help the committee to understand it, this often does not reach the heart of the discussion or address the questions of the committee members.

[85] The government also states that it made an official apology towards the victims and made efforts to remedy the situation through the Asian Women's Fund established by the Japanese government in cooperation with the people of Japan. See CEDAW Cttee, 'Consideration of Reports Submitted by States Parties Under Article 18 of the Convention, Seventh and Eighth Periodic Reports of States Parties Due in 2014: Japan' (CEDAW/C/JPN/7–8, 16 September 2014) paras 97–102; MOFA, 'The Convention on the Elimination of All Forms of Discrimination against Women Statement by the Head of the Delegation of Japan for the Seventh and Eighth Periodic Reports' (16 February 2016) <https://www.mofa.go.jp/mofaj/files/000133481.pdf> accessed 9 June 2021; and Summary of Remarks by Mr Shinsuke Sugiyama, Deputy Minister for Foreign Affairs in the Question and Answer session in the same CEDAW session (16 February 2016, Geneva), Ministry of Foreign Affairs, 'Convention on the Elimination of All Forms of Discrimination against Women Consideration of the Seventh and Eighth Periodic Reports (16 February 2016, Geneva) (Summary of remarks by Mr Shinsuke Sugiyama, Deputy Minister for Foreign Affairs in the Question and Answer session)' <https://www.mofa.go.jp/mofaj/files/000140100.pdf> accessed 8 March 2021. In 2017 the government issued comments regarding the concluding observations (COs) on the third to fifth periodic reports of the Republic of Korea issued on 12 May 2017. Government of Japan, 'Comments by the Government of Japan Regarding the COs on the Third to Fifth Periodic Reports of the Republic of Korea' (12 May 2017) <https://tbinternet.ohchr.org/Treaties/CAT/Shared%20Documents/KOR/INT_CAT_COB_KOR_27508_E.pdf> accessed 22 March 2021.

[86] The Statement of the Human Rights Ambassador of Japan in 2013 in the review of the government report to implement of the CAT. Kyodo, '"Shut up!" UN Rights Envoy Quits Over Tirade in Geneva' *Japan Times* (21 September 2013) <https://www.japantimes.co.jp/news/2013/09/21/national/shut-up-u-n-rights-envoy-quits-over-tirade-in-geneva/> accessed 8 November 2020.

including its practice of not allowing criminal suspects to have defence lawyers with them during interrogation, and the 'substitute prison' system to use police stations as legal substitutes for detention centres or prisons.[87] These different perspectives and approaches have long impeded the progress of a 'constructive dialogue' on specific issues, keeping discussions on parallel tracks.[88]

4.1.3 Level of Awareness

The level of awareness of the human rights treaty system has been increasing over the past 20 years in general, but different actors have varying levels of understanding.

Government officials in the pertinent divisions of ministries, responsible for the human rights treaty system, possess a certain level of familiarity with the system. However, they undergo rotations every few years. Thus, the level of awareness of international human rights law and standards is not high among government officials, especially in the ministries primarily dealing with domestic matters.

Likewise, international human rights mechanisms and treaties are not generally well known or acknowledged by members of parliament (MPs). Some MPs openly show their opposition or voice complaints against international human rights standards or recommendations by human rights treaty bodies.[89] However, several other MPs are active in leveraging the international human rights treaty mechanism for support or pressure from external authorities, aiming to address specific issues on the contentious domestic human rights agenda.[90]

The government introduced basic training for judges and prosecutors for international human rights law. However, as indicated in former Justice Sonobe's comments above,[91] the awareness among judges on international human rights law does not seem high in general as there are not many chances

---

87 CCPR/C/JPN/CO/6, 20 August 2014; CAT/C/JPN/CO/2, 28 June 2013.
88 One of the experts points out that the translation of the dialogue in the review between English and Japanese may make the correct understanding of each side difficult, with some essential points lost in translation (Comment from International Human Rights Law Expert, 5 May 2020).
89 For example, MP Mio Sugita urged the government to withdraw from CEDAW and abolish the Basic Act for Gender Equal Society, stating that gender equality was an anti-moral delusion that could never be achieved. National Diet Library, '*Dai 187 Kai Kokkai Shūgiin Honkaigi Dai 9 Gō* (The 187th Diet session, House of Representatives, Main Conference Case no. 9)' (31 October 2014) <https://kokkai.ndl.go.jp/#/detail?minId=118705254X00920141031 &spkNum=30&single> accessed 15 November 2020.
90 See the CERD part below regarding the development process of anti-hate speech law.
91 See n 76.

for them to use it in actual cases.[92] These attitudes of the courts or judges have discouraged lawyers from invoking international human rights law in their complaints and arguments, as they think it is unlikely for judges to show a positive attitude in the domestic judicial review towards reference to international human rights law or standards. Thus, many practicing lawyers do not believe that international human rights law can make a strong case in most cases.[93]

Meanwhile, there are some prominent lawyers who ardently learn about international human rights mechanisms, and some CSOs proactively use UN mechanisms in human rights advocacy. For example, the Japan Federation of Bar Associations (JFBA), a mandatory association of lawyers in Japan,[94] and also the largest, has worked intensively on the advancement of international human rights through domestic advocacy and lobbying to the committees, and complaints in some recent human rights litigations have seen more allegations with reference to international human rights law.[95]

---

[92] Interviews with International Human Rights Law Experts (Geneva, Switzerland, 11 February 2019; Online, Paris, France, 17 February 2019).

[93] International public law is one of the Japanese Bar Exam's selective subjects in Japan, but only 1,3% of applicants choose this subject, which may relate to the awareness among legal professions of the international human rights law in domestic proceedings. Ministry of Justice, 'Situation of the Bar Exam 2020' <http://www.moj.go.jp/content/001332199.pdf> accessed 13 December 2020. A Japanese attorney of law argues that Japanese lawyers also are neither familiar with international human rights law and standards, nor being used to using it strategically in domestic cases. Interview with a Japanese Lawyer (Online, 22 November 2020).

[94] Founded in 1949, the JFBA self-regulates the legal profession and strives to further the primary role of attorneys in society: the protection of fundamental human rights and the realisation of social justice. JFBA, 'About us' <https://www.nichibenren.or.jp/en/about/us.html> accessed 9 June 2021.

[95] For example, the lawsuits for marriage equality which started in 2019 argues the inability of same-sex couples to marry is a violation of the Constitution and international human rights law and standards. Marriage for All, '*Saiban Jōhō* (Lawsuit Information)' <https://www.marriageforall.jp/plan/lawsuit/> accessed 8 November 2020; interviews with Lawyers for the Plaintiffs (Online, Tokyo, Japan, 10 May 2020 and 14 May 2020). Further, in the litigation seeking redress for victims of the compulsory sterilisation undertaken under the state's eugenics programme and the now-defunct Eugenic Protection Act, after the redress was denied at the trial court as statute-barred, the lawyers for plaintiff brought forward the argument that the forced sterilisation constitutes 'torture' referred to in CAT; hence, 'in light of the spirit of the convention, any time limit that hinders victims from filing a lawsuit must not be in place and applying the statute of limitations to the damage in this case is contrary to the intention of the convention'. JFBA, 'Statement on Redress for Victims of the Now-defunct Eugenic Protection Act in the Wake of the Tokyo District Court's Judgment' <https://www.nichibenren.or.jp/en/document/statements/200715.html> accessed 8 March 2021. According to one of the lawyers, this argument is influenced by the advice that the Special Rapporteur on the elimination of discrimination

While civil society groups and activists have been working hard to raise awareness regarding the human rights treaty mechanism and international human rights standards among the general public, the majority of the general public do not have knowledge of international human rights treaties.[96] Although the importance of human rights is generally accepted, it is more frequently referred to in moral discourse than in legal discourse.

A lack of intensive coverage of human rights law in media and education may be behind this generally low level of awareness among people. The media and newspapers highlight international human rights treaties as far as they relate to controversial or sensational issues in international and domestic politics, such as comfort women, migrants, refugees, or some high-profile cases. However, they do not often refer to treaties regarding the discussions of domestic policies and their implementation. Human rights, including the UN human rights treaty system, are taught in universities as a theory.[97] Still, pedagogy does not lead citizens to reach a level at which they are aware of their ability to use the UN treaty body system to protect their rights.[98]

---

against persons affected by leprosy and their family members made on the litigation when she visited Japan in February 2020. Interview with a Human Rights Lawyer (Online, 22 November 2020).

[96] For example, the level of awareness of the terminology '*joshi sabetsu teppai jōyaku*' ('CEDAW' in Japanese) was 34,7% in 2019, while it was 36,1% in 2016, 34,8% in 2012, 35,1% in 2009, 35,3% in 2007, 32,8% in 2004, and 37,2% in 1999. Gender Equality Bureau Cabinet Office, 'Yoron Chōsa (*Danjo Kyōdō Sankakuni Kansuru Mono*) (Public Opinion Survey (on Gender-Equal Society))' <htttp://www.gender.go.jp/research/yoron/index.html> accessed 25 January 2020. The government was aiming to increase it to more than 50% by 2020. Gender Equality Bureau Cabinet Office, '*Daiyoji Danjo Kyōdō Sankaku Kihon Keikakuni Okeru Seika Shihyōno Dōkō*' (4th Men and Women Joint Participation Basic Plan Result Indicators Status)' <https://www.gender.go.jp/about_danjo/whitepaper/h28/zentai/html/shisaku/ss_shiryo_5.html> accessed 15 September 2023. The official statistics on the level of awareness regarding other treaties are not available, which is a problem to be addressed. Interview with International Human Rights Experts (Geneva, Switzerland, 11 February and 10 April 2019, respectively). A survey conducted by an international CSO shows that in Japan, only 8,9% of children and 2,2% of adults know the content of CRC, and 31,5% of children and 42,9% of adults have never heard about CRC. Save the Children Japan, '*3 Mannin Ankētokara Miru Kodomono Kenrini Kansuru Ishiki* (Attitudes to Children's Rights seen through a Survey of 30 000 People)' (11 November 2020) <https://www.savechildren.or.jp/news/publications/download/kodomonokenri_sassi.pdf> accessed 8 March 2021.

[97] It is pointed out by an international human rights law expert that there is not substantial human rights education in education programmes in primary and secondary school. Interview with an International Human Rights Law Expert (Online, 17 February 2019).

[98] MEXT, '*Jinken Kyoiku* (Human Rights Education)' <https://www.mext.go.jp/a_menu/shotou/jinken/siryo/index.htm> accessed 26 January 2020; MEXT, '*Dai 2 Shō Dai 2 Setsu 1: Jinken Kyōikuno Naiyō Kōsei* (Chapter 2 Section 2–1: Human Rights Education Contents

4.1.4 State Reporting

The Ministry of Foreign Affairs (MOFA), which stands at the forefront of dealing with the international human rights treaty mechanism in the international fora, is primarily responsible for state reporting in collaboration with other ministries, in particular with the Ministry of Justice (MOJ), which is in charge of human rights issues at the domestic level.[99] The Human Rights and Humanitarian Affairs Division (HRHAD) within the MOFA consolidates the contributions of other ministries and submits them to the committees.[100] For CEDAW, the Gender Equality Bureau of the Cabinet Office leads the consolidation of contributions by each ministry to put together the government's report.[101] The MOFA then translates and sends the report to the UN secretary-general, who transmits it to the committee for consideration. The government also holds consultation meetings with CSOs and its citizens for public comments and opinions on the national report.[102] However, it is not mandatory treatment under the law, but rather a voluntary commitment by the government.

The Japanese government generally complies with reporting obligations across ratified treaties. While occasionally its reports have not been submitted within the time limit, there is no specific pattern for the reason for delay. The vertically divided institutional tradition may cause structural problems that prolong the preparation of relevant documents, especially when the human

---

and Structure)' <https://www.mext.go.jp/a_menu/shotou/seitoshidou/jinken/06082102/009.htm> accessed 26 January 2020. A number of universities and law schools in Japan offer international human rights law courses but mostly as electives.

[99] See under the Act for Establishment of the Ministry of Foreign Affairs. According to art 4(5) of the Act, the interpretation and implementation of treaties and other international agreements, as well as established international law, fall under the MOF's purview, explicitly defining its full and unique responsibility in this regard. Government of Japan, 'Gaimushō Setchi Hō (the Act for Establishment of the Ministry of Foreign Affairs)' <https://elaws.e-gov.go.jp/document?lawid=411AC0000000094_20160401_427AC0000000066> accessed 8 September 2023. T Mori, 'The Current Practice of Making and Applying International Agreements in Japan' in Curtis Bradley (ed), *The Oxford Handbook of Comparative Foreign Relations Law* (OUP 2019) 191.

[100] Interview with the Director of the Human Rights and Humanitarian Affairs Division (Tokyo, Japan, 3 December 2018).

[101] Gender Equality Bureau Cabinet Office <htttp://www.gender.go.jp/english_contents/index.html> accessed 25 January 2020.

[102] Gender Equality Bureau Cabinet Office, *'Joshi Sabetsu Teppai Jōyaku Jisshi Jōkyō Dai 7/8 Kai Hōkokushoni Tsuite Kiku Kai* (Meeting to Hear about the Combined Seventh and Eighth Periodic Report of Japan for CEDAW)' <https://www.gender.go.jp/kaigi/renkei/ikenkoukan/60/index.html> accessed 8 March 2021.

rights matters involve multiple ministries and agencies.[103] The degree of complexity among ministries and agencies also varies depending on the kinds of human rights issues in question when preparing the reports.

As individual complaints procedures are not available in Japan, state reporting is the main channel for CSOs to directly engage in dialogue with treaty bodies. Many CSOs actively engage in the state reporting mechanism by lobbying the treaty bodies by submitting parallel reports and using their recommendations for their domestic advocacy to pressure the government.

4.1.5 Domestic Implementation Mechanism

In principle, the MOFA translates the recommendation and relevant documents regarding international human rights treaties into Japanese to upload on its website.[104] Other ministries, in particular the MOJ, are primarily engaged in the implementation of the recommendation by treaty bodies at the domestic level by setting an agenda for drafting domestic laws and policies. The Human Rights Bureau of the MOJ acts as an administrative organ engaging in human rights promotion and protection in coordination with its regional offices and branches, as well as human rights volunteers, who are private citizens appointed by the MOJ.[105] They are collectively referred to as 'the human rights bodies of the MOJ', which cooperatively carry out national, regional, and community-level human rights promotion and protection activities. The human rights volunteers provide human rights counselling for the investigation of alleged human rights violations.[106] They also conduct human rights education and awareness-raising activities to disseminate knowledge of

---

103 Interview with the Director of the Human Rights and Humanitarian Affairs Division (Tokyo, Japan, 3 December 2018).

104 Not all the General Comments or recommendations are translated into Japanese. Regarding CEDAW, the Gender Equality Bureau of the Cabinet Office is in principle in charge of the dissemination of information and awareness-raising activities regarding the Convention. There is a recent practice that each ministry takes responsibility of the translation of relevant documents related to treaty bodies. Comments by a government official on 8 March 2021.

105 *Jinken Yōgo Iin* (human rights volunteers) are private citizens appointed by MOJ to engage in human rights counselling and the dissemination of the concept of human rights based on the Human Rights Volunteers Act. Ministry of Justice, 'Human Rights Volunteers' <http://www.moj.go.jp/ENGLISH/HB/about/volunteers.html> accessed 25 January 2020.

106 An international human rights expert points out the ineffective monitoring system with the human rights volunteers. Interview with an International Human Rights Expert (Online, 17 February 2019).

international human rights for people in Japan.[107] There are several national, public, and state-funded institutes that support these educational activities and campaigns, such as the National Women's Education Centre[108] and the Centre for Human Rights Education and Training.[109]

However, the effectiveness of the system in monitoring and ensuring human rights protection and promotion has been questioned, in particular without independent national human rights institutions (NHRI).[110] As neither the MOFA nor the MOJ is in a position to recommend other ministries to implement the treaty bodies' recommendations in the vertically-segmented administrative system with bureaucratic sectionalism, the system may not be the most effective in realising the recommendations from the treaty bodies, including raising awareness among government officials.[111] As for promoting the implementation of international standards of gender equality, the National Machinery for the Promotion of the Formation of a Gender Equal Society,[112] the Council for Gender Equality and Specialist Committees[113] all exist to promote gender equality at the domestic level while monitoring the implementation of CEDAW recommendations.[114] Nevertheless, the effectiveness of this national machinery in promoting and monitoring the implementation of CEDAW has

---

[107] MOJ, 'Human Rights Bureau' <http://www.moj.go.jp/ENGLISH/HB/hb.html> accessed 25 January 2020.

[108] National Women's Education Centre, 'Top Page' <https://www.nwec.jp/en/index.html> accessed 2 January 2021.

[109] Centre for Human Rights Education and Training, 'Centre for Human Rights Education and Training (English version)' <http://www.jinken.or.jp/en> accessed 2 January 2021.

[110] In particular, the human rights volunteers system has been widely criticised as ineffective, and a reform has been proposed. MOJ, *'Jinken Yōgo Suishin Shingikaino "Jinken Yōgo Iin Seidono Kaikakuni Kansuru Ronten Kōmoku" ni Taisuru Iken Boshūno Kekkani Tsuite* (Results of the Human Rights Promotion Council's Request for Opinions on the Reform of the Commissioner for Human Rights)' <http://101.110.15.201/JINKEN/public_jinken06_result_jinken06.html> accessed 15 November 2020; Y Kure and J Hiramine, 'The Reality and Problems on the System of Civil Liberties Commission' (2009) 16 Constitutional Law Review 89.

[111] An expert mentions that the treaty bodies' review where the Japanese delegation consists of the representative of each ministry may function to disseminate the knowledge and awareness of international human rights standards among government officials. Interview with an International Expert (Geneva, Switzerland, 27 August 2019).

[112] Gender Equality Bureau, Cabinet Office, 'National Machinery for the Promotion of the Formation of a Gender-Equal Society' <http://www.gender.go.jp/english_contents/about_danjo/prom/national_machinery.html> accessed 25 January 2020.

[113] ibid.

[114] The Gender Equality Bureau of the Cabinet Office facilitates the meeting of these machineries.

been questioned. Yoko Hayashi, a former CEDAW member, highlighted that the national machinery for gender equality does not operate as intended. She noted that the Minister of State for Gender Equality and other members of the machinery lack progressiveness in promoting gender equality and instead have a conservative political record. Additionally, she observed that the minister's busy schedule, often holding concurrent ministerial positions, is a common practice, further hindering effective attention to gender equality issues.[115] Regarding the rights of persons with disabilities, the Commission on Policy for Persons with Disabilities placed in the Cabinet Office functions as the monitoring framework specified in article 33 of CRPD.[116] The Commission informs the preparation process of the government's implementation report of CRPD, with the engagement of a range of actors beyond the Commission.[117]

4.1.6 Treaty Body Membership

Japanese experts have consistently been members of various treaty bodiestreaty bodies. (See Table 11.1 below.)

4.2 Overview of Impact

4.2.1 Incorporation and Reliance by Legislature and the Executive

Since the Japanese government generally assumes that the Bill of Rights in the Constitution and existing statutory laws cover a wide range of human rights, it is uncommon to see explicit reference to international human rights treaties in the Japanese legislature and the executive. A significant impact is often seen when the government decides to enter a treaty. Iwasawa observes that the government makes 'scrupulous effort to bring Japanese law into conformity with the treaty' and '[i]f there is any conflict between the treaty

---

115 Y Hayashi, *Jendā Byōdō Shakaieno Tembō* (Prospects for a Gender-Equal Society)' (2020) 280 Monthly Zenroren 16–17. It is also pointed out that the abolition of the specialised committee to monitor the implementation of the Basic Plan for Gender Equality and the recommendation of CEDAW hindered the effective work of the national machinery. A comment from an international human rights law expert on 17 February 2019. Interview with an International Human Rights Expert (Online, 17 February 2019).

116 The commission has duties that include providing study and experts comments for the development of the Basic Programme for Persons with Disabilities; monitoring the implementation status of Basic Programme for Persons with Disabilities (making recommendation to relevant ministers if deemed necessary); and monitoring the implementation status of CRPD in Japan. Cabinet Office, 'Commission on Policy for Persons with Disabilities (Overview)' <https://www8.cao.go.jp/shougai/english/pdf/pc-1.pdf> accessed 8 March 2021.

117 CRPD, 'Initial Report Submitted by Japan Under Article 35 of the Convention, due in 2016' (CRPD/C/JPN/1, 4 October 2017) <https://undocs.org/CRPD/C/JPN/1> accessed 8 March 2021; CRPD, 'List of Issues in Relation to the Initial Report of Japan' (CRPD/C/JPN/1, 29 October 2019) <https://undocs.org/CRPD/C/JPN/Q/1> accessed 15 November 2020.

TABLE 11.1   Membership of treaty bodies (as of 2021)

CRC	Ms Mikiko Otani (2017–present)
CERD	Ms Keiko Ko (2018–2022)
CRPD	Mr Jun Ishikawa (2017–2020)
CEDAW	Ms Ryoko Akamatsu (1987–1994), Ms Ginko Sato (1995–1998), Ms Chikako Taya (1999–2001), Ms Fumiko Saiga (2002–2007), Ms Yoko Hayashi (2008–2018), and Ms Hiroko Akizuki (2019–present)
CCPR	Mr Nisuke Ando (1987–2006), Mr Yuji Iwasawa (2007–2018), and Mr Shuichi Furuya (2019–2022)
CESCR	Ms Chikako Taya (1986–1990, 1992–1996)
CED	Mr Kimio Yakushiji (2011–2017) and Mr Koji Teraya (2017–2019)

SOURCE: <HTTPS://WWW.OHCHR.ORG/EN/TREATY-BODIES> UNDER 'MEMBERSHIP' FOR EACH CTTEE, ACCESSED 9 SEPTEMBER 2023.

and domestic law, the government makes sure that domestic law is amended before it enters into the treaty' with careful and thorough examinations by the relevant bureaus.[118] Such significant reformation of domestic laws and policies in harmony with human rights treaties was explicitly seen at the time of the ratification of CEDAW and CRPD.[119] The impact of human rights treaties after the ratification or accession of treaties may not be as explicit or drastic as it is at the time of entry into force. In most cases, as examined in the following part of this chapter, strong persuasion and pressure from civil society seem to have been significant drivers of the reformation process for legal and policy changes informed by the recommendations of the treaty bodies and treaties. While a few parliamentarians are actively promoting its standards with reference to it in the Diet, some politicians are strongly critical and concerned about the international human rights intervention as its principles and recommendations may alter the traditional values and practices of the country.[120]

---

118   Iwasawa 1998 (n 75) 306.
119   The enactment of the basic law and revisions to related laws were made before and after ratification of those treaties.
120   See National Diet Library (n 89) for MP Mio Sugita's statement urging the Japanese government to withdraw from the CEDAW. See also n 306 for MP Satsuki Katayama's support for a CSO that called for the immediate dismissal of a Japanese member on CEDAW which criticised the Japanese government on the issue of comfort women.

In recent years, local governments have played an important role in the implementation of human rights treaties. More closely connected with local or community-based civil society groups, some local governments are very active in urging the national government to comply with international human rights treaties.[121] Further, there are many initiatives to develop local ordinances in line with international human rights standards.[122]

4.2.2 Reliance by Judiciary

Under the Constitution, the Supreme Court can review the constitutionality of any particular law, order, regulation, or official act in relation to an individual case of a specific dispute as a court of appellate instance.[123] Despite its wide scope of justiciability, since 1946, as of December 2019, the Supreme Court had identified only 10 cases in which statutes were deemed unconstitutional. In some highly political cases, the Supreme Court was restrained from

---

[121] For example, at least 196 local assemblies have adopted statements of position asking for the ratification of the Optional Protocol of CEDAW (as of 15 March 2023). See OP CEDAW ACTION, 'Kakuchino Ikensho Kaketsu Jōkyō (Status of Adoption of Statements of Position in Various Regions)' <https://opcedawjapan.wordpress.com/> accessed 15 September 2023. Regarding hate speech, over 230 municipalities sent comments to the government as of November 2015 seeking to strengthen countermeasures against hate speech, including the legal development, most of which referred to the Kyoto Korean School case and its ruling to demonstrate the seriousness of the issue to justify their allegation. See All-Japan Prefectural and Municipal Workers Union. 'Jichitaikara Hasshinnsuru Jinken Seisaku (Human Rights Policies Initiated by Local Governments)' <https://www.jichiro.gr.jp/jichiken_kako/sagyouiinnkai/36-jinkenseisaku/contents.htm> accessed 15 November 2020.

[122] For example, 97,9% of the prefectures and 100% of the ordinance-designated big cities (*seirei shitei toshi*) enacted local ordinances on gender equality. See Gender Equality Bureau Cabinet Office, 'Danjo Kyōdō Sankakuni Kansuru Jōreino Seitei Jōkyō (Current Situation of the Enactment of Local Ordinances on Gender Equality)' (1 April 2019) <http://www.gender.go.jp/research/kenkyu/suishinjokyo/2019/pdf/rep/02-1.pdf> accessed 15 November 2020. Kawasaki City in Kanagawa Prefecture enacted an ordinance on children's rights and established a children's conference to hear their opinions. Namie City in Hokkaido Prefecture enacted an ordinance on children's rights and started an election among teenagers. See H Otsu, 'Kokusaijinkenhoshōni Okeru Jichitaino Kennōto Gimu (The Functions and Responsibilities of Municipalities in International Human Rights Protection)' in K Serita, K Tonami, T Munesue, K Yakushiji and S Sakamoto (eds), *Kokusaijinkenhōno Kokunaiteki Jisshi* (*The Domestic Implementation of International Human Rights Law*) (Shinzansha 2011) 20.

[123] Art 81 of the Constitution of Japan 1947 ('the Supreme Court is the court of last resort with power to determine the constitutionality of any law, order, regulation or official act'). However, the Court cannot examine constitutional questions without being accompanied by legal disputes and issues.

dealing with constitutional questions.[124] This may arguably indicate that the Supreme Court of Japan has not played a pro-active, formative role in light of constitutional questions.[125] Since judges tend to believe that the Constitution and statutory laws already protect human rights to the level that treaties require and are not familiar with international human rights law,[126] it is rare for Japanese courts to invalidate domestic law based on international human rights law. Human rights advocates have often criticised the courts for not seriously considering arguments based on international human rights laws or recommendations.[127]

In the concluding observations (COs) of the review of the fourth periodic report of Japan in 1998, the Human Rights Committee strongly recommended that training of judges, prosecutors, and administrative officers in human rights under the Covenant be made available, which the JFBA had also strongly advocated.[128] Following this recommendation, some lectures on international

---

[124] See the *Naganuma Nike* case, in which residents of Naganuma, Japan, alleged that the existence of Japan Air Self-Defence Forces (JASDF) violated art 9 of the Japanese Constitution, which prohibits armed forces and the maintenance of 'war potential'. The Supreme Court dismissed the case based on the political question doctrine without making judgments on whether the existence of JASDF was against the Constitution. See WR Slomanson, 'Judicial Review of War Renunciation in the *Naganuma Nike* Case: Juggling the Constitutional Crisis in Japan' (1975) 9 Cornell International Law Journal 24. It seems the highest court's position of self-restraint from taking a clear position leads to the stance to wait for the problem to be decided in a political process rather than by the judiciary.

[125] Some argue that the Constitution has not been regarded as law to be applied by judges, which is the most unfortunate reason for judicial passivism. S Matsui, 'Why is the Japanese Supreme Court So Conservative?' (2011) 88 Washington University Law Review 1375, 1413; DS Law, 'The Anatomy of a Conservative Court: Judicial Review in Japan' (2009) 87 Texas Law Rev 1545. On the other hand, some argue this reflects a very prudent approach of the Japanese judiciary. Through its contribution to bring about stability with pro-government and pro-business judicial decisions, the Supreme Court has indirectly helped achieve economic growth and a relatively egalitarian civil society. H Itoh, *The Supreme Court and Benign Elite Democracy in Japan* (Ashgate 2010).

[126] See also Iwasawa 1998 (n 75) 288; K Teraya, '*Heito Supichi Jiken* (Hate Speech Case)' (2014) 1466 Jurist 292, 292.

[127] Iwasawa 1998 (n 75) 288–306; D Zartner, *Courts, Codes, and Custom: Legal Tradition and State Policy toward International Human Rights and Environmental Law* (OUP 2014) 241–244. See T Ebashi, '*Kenri Hoshō Kihan to shiteno Kempō to Kokusai Jinken Kiyaku* (The Constitution and the International Covenants on Human Rights as Norms to Guarantee Rights)' (1994) 1037 Jurist 109.

[128] See HRCttee, 'Concluding Observations of the Human Rights Committee: Japan' (CCPR/C/79/Add.102, 19 November 1998) <https://undocs.org/CCPR/C/79/Add.102> accessed 8 March 2021; HRCttee (n 42) para 3; JFBA, '*Kaikaku Semarareru Nihonno Jinken Hoshō Shisutemu* (Japan's Human Rights Protection System Under Pressure to Reform)' (1 March 2009) <http://www.moj.go.jp/content/000055359.pdf> accessed 15 November 2020.

human rights law have been incorporated into the curricula of the Legal Research and Training Institute and continuing legal training for legal experts and legal professionals, namely, judges, prosecutors, and lawyers, who must take courses on international human rights treaties during their training period before obtaining judicial qualifications.[129] However, the JFBA argues that the quality and quantity of these lectures are extremely inadequate.[130] Continuing training for prosecutors is also designed to study international human rights treaties at a certain frequency, but their specific contents are not clear, or distributed materials have not been published.[131]

In the Japanese legal system, an alleged violation of international law is not an explicit ground for a final appeal to the Supreme Court, as explained earlier.[132] An international expert pointed out that it leads to human rights lawyers' allegations that the courts do not adequately respect international human rights law.[133] Although Japanese courts are reluctant to use international law to invalidate domestic law, the Supreme Court of Japan in some recent cases began actively referring to international sources and recommendations as persuasive authorities, particularly CCPR, CERD, and CRC.[134]

4.2.3 Impact on and through Non-state Actors

As examined in the following part of this chapter, human rights CSOs and minority organisations have been the main drivers of change in light of the passive or reticent attitude of the government toward the incorporation of international human rights standards into domestic law and policies. CSOs leveraged the state reporting mechanism under the human rights treaties.[135]

---

129 HRCttee (n 42) para 3.
130 JFBA, 'Report of JFBA Regarding the Seventh Periodic Report by the Government of Japan based on Article 40(b) of the International Covenant on Civil and Political Rights' (16 July 2020) <https://www.nichibenren.or.jp/library/pdf/activity/international/library/human_rights/iccpr_7en.pdf> accessed 10 June 2021, para I-1-(2).
131 ibid. The impact of this training, such as how it changes the understanding and attitude of legal professionals towards international human rights treaties in particular in their judicial decision and allegations in courts has still not been examined.
132 Code of Civil Procedure 2011, art 312, and Code of Criminal Procedure 2011, art 405, list a violation of constitutional law as the grounds for final appeal, without mentioning a violation of international treaties.
133 Interview with an International Human Rights Law Expert (Online, 17 February 2019). Some argue that the lack of acceptance of individual communications leads to negligence of the courts of international human rights treaties.
134 See the sections below.
135 Given Japan's lack of acceptance of any individual complaints mechanism under the treaty bodies, civil society groups have urged the government to adopt the individual complaints procedure. For example, the JFBA adopted a resolution in 2019 requesting the government

TABLE 11.2   Number of independent/parallel (CSOs) reports under ratified treaties on the occasion of state reporting (cycle, year)

CERD	NA (1st–2nd in 2001); 6 (3rd–6th in 2010); 10 (7th–9th in 2014); 12 (10th–11th in 2018)
CCPR	45 (5th in 2008); 54 (6th in 2014); 78 (7th in 2022)
CESCR	3 (2nd in 2001); 38 (3rd in 2013)
CEDAW	18 (6th in 2009); 27 (7th–8th in 2016), 17 (9th in 2020)
CAT	5 (1st in 2007); 12 (2nd in 2013)
CRC	45 (4th–5th in 2019)
CED	3 (1st in 2018); 0 (2nd in 2020)

Note: UN Treaty Body Database <https://tbinternet.ohchr.org/_layouts/15/TreatyBodyExternal/Countries.aspx> accessed 29 September 2020. There is yet to be a first state reporting session for CRPD.

They regularly submit independent reports to treaty bodies and make use of their recommendations in their advocacy for the revision of domestic law and policies.[136] In addition, the number of independent reports submitted from CSOs, as well as the number of CSOs involved in providing information to each committee in the state reporting cycle, have increased as follows:

Several CSOs submit joint independent reports to the committees when they review the government's periodic report, coordinating a group of grassroots organisations, and consolidating different claims of multiple groups under specific treaties.[137] Albeit partially, CSOs are involved in consultation with relevant ministries and agencies to exchange views in the process of developing a

---

for implementation of an individual complaints procedure. JFBA, 'Resolution Requesting the Implementation of an Individual Complaints Procedure and the Establishment of a National Human Rights Institution' <www.nichibenren.or.jp/en/document/statements/2019_2.html> accessed 26 January 2020. For the history of how minority groups in Japan expanded their activism since the late 1970s empowered by global human rights ideas and institutions, see K Tsutsui, *Rights Make Might: Global Human Rights and Minority Social Movements in Japan* (Oxford Academic, 2018).

136 See Table 3 below for further details.
137 See eg, International Movement Against All Forms of Discrimination and Racism (IMADR), '*Jinshu Sabetsu Teppai* (Elimination of Racial Discrimination)' <http://imadr.net/activity/erd/> accessed 25 January 2020; Japan NGO Network for CEDAW (JNNC), 'NGO Joint Report (Japan)' (10 January 2016) <https://tbinternet.ohchr.org/Treaties/CEDAW/Shared%20Documents/JPN/INT_CEDAW_NGO_JPN_22777_E.pdf> accessed 25 January 2020.

government report on the implementation of treaties.[138] They also hold campaigns and meetings to pressure the government to implement committee recommendations.[139] An expert in international human rights mentioned that cooperation among civic groups working for international human rights is a key for civil society groups to gain effective access to treaty bodies, and ardent follow-up by civil society groups after treaty bodies' recommendations is important for domestic incorporation of the treaty bodies' recommendations.[140]

Furthermore, it is also noteworthy that the international human rights law and treaty body mechanism, although indirectly, contributed to the development of active research institutes and associations on international human rights. They have provided evidence-based research on the human rights situation to inform the government or the general public and conducted training and campaigns, which also contributed to raising awareness of human rights treaties among public officials and people. For example, the Centre for Human Rights Education and Training was restructured in 1997 as a national centre for human rights education.[141] The Kyoto Human Rights Research Institute also conducts research on human rights issues and promotes academic exchange with domestic and foreign research institutes in the field of human rights, with more than 100 researchers.[142] The International Human Rights Law Association was established in 1988 as a platform for discussions on the examination of domestic implementation of international human rights standards with the participation of researchers of international human rights law, constitutional and other fields of domestic law, and legal practitioners.[143]

Concerning non-state actors' activism, it may be a unique phenomenon in Japan that some organisations and activists who argue against recommendations by human rights treaty bodies or allegations of other human rights CSOs

---

[138] E.g., the meeting for the exchange of views between the government and CSOs upon the Tenth and Eleventh Combined Periodic Report under article 9 of CERD, held on 19 August 2016. The Ministry of Foreign Affairs of Japan, 'Jinshusabetsuteppai Joyaku (CERD)' <https://www.mofa.go.jp/mofaj/gaiko/jinshu/index.html> accessed 15 September 2023.

[139] An expert observes that while civil society so far tends to focus on providing the information to the committee to have recommendations to reflect their arguments, they should work more on the follow-up procedure, with a focus on the domestic process to implement existing recommendations. Interview with an International Human Rights Expert (Geneva, Switzerland, 11 February 2019).

[140] Interview with an International Human Rights Law Expert (Geneva, Switzerland, 11 February 2019).

[141] Centre for Human Rights Education and Training, 'Information' <http://www.jinken.or.jp/information> accessed 22 March 2021.

[142] Kyoto Human Rights Research Institute, 'Top page' <http://khrri.or.jp/> accessed 8 November 2020.

[143] International Human Rights Law Association, 'Top Page' <http://www.ihrla.org> accessed 29 September 2020. It holds annual academic conferences, and many practitioners and

zealously provide information on several controversial issues to the committees as civil society actors. They actively engage in the state reporting process in Geneva, which has been observed since the 2000s. They claim that the committees have often misunderstood the Japanese historical background, culture, and political sensitivity, and in some cases even object to the basic principles or legitimacy of the human rights treaties and treaty bodies' work, which causes controversy in both international and domestic spheres.[144]

4.2.4   Impact of State Reporting

The state reporting system is the main window for the Japanese government as well as civil society groups and victims of human rights violations to engage with treaty bodies. Through the state reporting cycle, the government revisits its activity through the human rights lens and constructive dialogues with the committees, including responses to their questions. This process potentially offers opportunities for governmental officials from domestically-focused ministries to familiarize themselves with international human rights standards through their involvement in the development of periodic reports and committee sessions.[145] A variety of measures have been taken by the state party to promote human rights through the process of state reporting as a positive impact at the domestic level.[146] This observation is substantiated by empirical analysis, which reveals a greater inclusion of references to international human rights treaties and the committees' recommendations in legislative processes. For example, as indicated in the graph below, the number of references to COs by MPs in the discussion at the Diet has increased over the years.

---

scholars participate in the discussion on actual human rights cases. Additionally, some constitutional scholars pay more attention to international human rights law. Eg, see M Sogabe, 'Jinkenhōtoiu Hassō (The Approach of Human Rights Law)' (2020) 482 *Hogaku Kyoshitsu* (Legal Studies Class) 72.

144   For example, they say that the committees misunderstand the 'comfort women' issue by recognizing them as 'sex slaves.' Their arguments include that it is legally justifiable for the government not to subsidize Korean high schools in Japan and withhold local suffrage from foreigners. Furthermore, they assert that Okinawan people are not indigenous, and that Ainu people have not historically faced mistreatment or oppression. eg, Happiness Realization Research Institute, 'Report Submitted to the Committee on the Elimination of Discrimination Against Women' <https://tbinternet.ohchr.org/Treaties/CEDAW/Shared%20Documents/JPN/INT_CEDAW_NGO_JPN_22837_E.docx> accessed 1 February 2020; Japan NGO Coalition against Racial Discrimination (JNCRD), 'NGO Report in Relation to the Tenth to Eleventh Periodic Reports of JAPAN' (14 July 2018) <https://tbinternet.ohchr.org/Treaties/CERD/Shared%20Documents/JPN/INT_CERD_NGO_JPN_31798_E.pdf> accessed 1 February 2020. These groups are not funded by the government, but some conservative members of parliament have explicitly shown support for these allegations.

145   A comment from an international human rights law expert (Geneva, Switzerland, 27 August 2019).

146   For the impact of state reporting of each treaty, see the following sections.

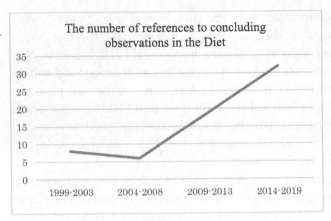

FIGURE 11.1   Reference to COs by Diet
SOURCE: THIS GRAPH IS BASED ON THE NUMBER OF REFERENCES TO COS IN THE DATABASE SYSTEM PROVIDING FULL-TEXT OF MINUTES OF THE DIET'S PARLIAMENTARY PLENARY SITTINGS AND COMMITTEE MEETINGS (SEE: KOKKAI GIJIROKU KENSAKU SYSTEM <HTTPS://KOKKAI.NDL.GO.JP/> ACCESSED 12 NOVEMBER 2020). THE JAPANESE TERM "SOKATSUSHOKEN (CONCLUDING OBSERVATIONS)" WAS USED AS THE KEYWORD TO SEARCH.

5   Detailed Impact of UN Human Rights Treaties on the Domestic Level in Japan

5.1   *International Convention on the Elimination of All Forms of Racial Discrimination*

5.1.1   Incorporation and Reliance by Legislature and Executive Powers

There was no legal reformation or development at the time of the ratification of CERD in 1995. The Bill on the protection of human rights, including the prohibition of racial discrimination, was submitted to the Diet in 2002 and 2005 but was scrapped facing opposition from both conservatives and progressives.[147] However, several changes in legislation and ordinances aimed at eliminating racial discrimination have been observed in recent years. For example, the Act on the Promotion of Efforts to Eliminate Unfair Discriminatory Speech and Behaviour against Persons Originating from Outside Japan (Hate Speech Elimination Act) was enacted in 2016 to encourage national and local governments and the general public to eliminate hate speech, which had been

---

[147]   House of Representatives, '*Jinken Yōgo Hōan* (Human Rights Protection Bill)' <https://www.shugiin.go.jp/Internet/itdb_gian.nsf/html/gian/honbun/houan/g15405056.htm> accessed 18 March 2021.

rampant around 2010.[148] According to the MOJ, this law was developed 'in response' to the recommendations set out in '[the] Concluding Observations on the Sixth Periodic Report of Japan by the UN Human Rights Committee in July 2014 and [the] Concluding Observations on the Combined Seventh to Ninth Periodic Reports of Japan by the UN Committee on the Elimination of Racial Discrimination in August of the same year'.[149] While the law itself does not contain explicit reference to these treaties and does not make hate speech illegal, its development process was informed by the state reporting process and its recommendations, as well as domestic judicial decisions on hateful demonstrations that made significant reference to CERD.[150] It is noteworthy that the supplementary resolutions of both houses of the Diet attached to the law and the background documents on legal development explicitly mention that the law should be interpreted in view of CERD.[151] The development of the Hate Speech Elimination Act contributed to several developments in policies,

---

148 Government of Japan, 'Act on the Promotion of Efforts to Eliminate Unfair Discriminatory Speech and Behavior against Persons with Countries of Origin other than Japan' <https://www.japaneselawtranslation.go.jp/en/laws/view/4081/en> accessed 8 September 2023. The term 'unfair discriminatory speech and behaviour against persons originating from outside Japan' in the Act, despite its problematic scope (addressed later in this chapter), is considered to be equivalent to what is known as 'hate speech' in principle, as indicated on the website of Japan's Ministry of Justice. See MOJ, 'Promotion Activities Focusing on Hate Speech' <http://www.moj.go.jp/ENGLISH/m_jinken04_00001.html> accessed 5 May 2019.

149 ibid.

150 See A Hatano, 'Hate Speech and International Law: The Internalisation of International Human Rights in Japan' in Y Nasu and S Higaki (eds), *Hate Speech in Japan: The Possibility of a Non-Regulatory Approach* (Cambridge University Press 2021). As a consequence of the intense argument over the protection of freedom of speech and the regulation of hate speech, the law does not have provisions on the punishment of a person who displays unfair, discriminatory speech and behaviour and protects only those 'persons originating exclusively from a country or region other than Japan or their descendants and who are lawfully residing in Japan'. Some have criticised the law as toothless and narrow, not fully complying with the recommendations of treaty bodies including CERD. See Hate Speech Elimination Act 2016, art 2; Tomohiro Osaki, 'Diet Debates Hate-Speech Bill that Activists Call Narrow and Toothless' *Japan Times* (19 April 2016) <https://www.japantimes.co.jp/news/2016/04/19/national/politics-diplomacy/diet-debates-hate-speech-bill-activists-call-narrow-toothless/> accessed 28 April 2019.

151 House of Councillors Committee on Judicial Affairs, 'Supplementary Resolution for the Act on the Promotion of Efforts to Eliminate Unfair Discriminatory Speech and Behaviour against Persons Originating from Outside Japan' <https://houseikyoku.sangiin.go.jp/bill/pdf/h28-068ks.pdf> accessed 8 September 2023; House of Representative Committee on Judicial Affairs, 'Supplementary Resolution for the Act on the Promotion of Efforts to Eliminate Unfair Discriminatory Speech and Behaviour against Persons Originating from Outside Japan' <https://www.shugiin.go.jp/internet/itdb_rchome.nsf/html/rchome/Futai/houmu684D38F3EE8DA72649257FBD00182F0C.htm> accessed 8 September 2023.

regulations, and ordinances to curb hate speech and racial discrimination in response to the prior recommendation of CERD.[152] In these processes, there was active engagement of some MPs who strongly pressured the government to take measures against hate speech with reference to international human rights standards.[153]

In addition, the Act on Promoting Measures to Realise a Society in which the Pride of the Ainu People is Respected was promulgated in April 2019. The Act recognises the Ainu as indigenous people in Japan and obligates the government to adopt policies to facilitate people's understanding of the traditions of the Ainu and the importance of the diversity that ethnic groups contribute to society.[154] While there is no reference to CERD in the law, the development

---

152 See Hatano 2021 (n 150) 3, 69–79. For example, on 2 June 2016 the Kawasaki Branch of the Yokohama District Court issued its first ever provisional injunction preventing an anti-Korean activist from holding rallies, again referring to the Hate Speech Elimination Act. Yokohama District Court, Kawasaki Branch, Judgment, 2 June 2016, 2296 Hanji 14. The government conducted a survey of the situation of hate speech in 2016 and another survey of foreign residents in Japan in 2017, both of which were commissioned by the MOJ. An analytical report of the survey was submitted to CERD on the occasion of the review of Japan's tenth and eleventh periodic reports. This responded to the prior CERD request for the Japanese government to collect comprehensive, reliable, and up-to-date data on the ethnic composition of the country's population in the COs on the combined seventh to ninth periodic reports. CERD, 'Tenth and Eleventh Periodic Reports of States Parties due in 2017' <http://docstore.ohchr.org/SelfServices/FilesHandler.ashx?enc=6QkG1d%2fPPRi CAqhKb7yhskWEDuvHColMabuZoOD1HY3EyquAhGLvla1aU%2bU7v%2ffuOPReM5Y jd9g0crsHkePSXOZYbvzKrKbpDj%2bmnQnVkrwcY2byN%2fqnZAgPWpZv6Hon> accessed 16 November 2020. Centre for Human Rights Education and Training, 'Analytical Report of the Foreign Residents Survey – Revised Edition' (June 2017) <https://tbinter net.ohchr.org/Treaties/CERD/Shared%20Documents/JPN/INT_CERD_AIS_JPN_30363 _E.pdf> accessed 15 November 2020; CERD, 'Concluding Observations on the Combined Seventh to Ninth Periodic Reports of Japan' (CERD/C/JPN/CO/7–9, 29 August 2014) <http: //docstore.ohchr.org/SelfServices/FilesHandler.ashx?enc=6QkG1d%2fPPRiCAqhK-b7yhskWEDuvHColMabuZoOD1HYoSfxlfB1VeioXttAzGv30UoRk%2bkdMAGVYyIt-J663GQIU8ZU21%2fekVAPTf2ZAumBFlK3%2fSvEnalM10Sl5jPCCBP> accessed 16 November 2020.

153 Some MPs have joined in the country report reviews in Geneva. For example, MP Yoshifu Arita participated in the review of combined tenth and eleventh periodic reports of Japan for the CERD in 2018 in Geneva. Nishinippon Shimbun, '*Aritashi Heito Taisakude Seifu Hihan Shakumeini "Jidai Okure"* (Arita Criticises Government on Anti-hate Measures, says their Explanation is "Outdated")' (18 August 2018) <https://www.nishinippon.co.jp/item/o /442107/> accessed 15 November 2020.

154 National Printing Bureau, '*Hōritsu* (Law)' (Kampo, 26 April 2019) <https://kanpou.npb .go.jp/old/20190426/20190426g00087/20190426g000870005f.html> accessed 26 January 2020.

of this law followed and resonated with the resolutions adopted in June 2008 at both Houses of the Diet requesting the government to recognise the Ainu as indigenous people, which is informed by the Declaration on the Rights of Indigenous Peoples adopted at the UN General Assembly in 2007 and the recommendations of the CERD Cttee and other treaty bodies.[155]

Regarding the *Buraku* people,[156] Japanese government, has disagreed with the view of the CERD Cttee and human rights CSOs over whether the issues of the *Buraku* people fall within the scope of CERD, more specifically, if *Buraku* people can be seen as a type of 'descent' as defined in article 1(1) of CERD. The Japanese government considers that, historically, the *Buraku* people were a class defined by a very specific occupation and governed by a special status and not regarded as 'descent' in the scope of article 1(1) of CERD.[157] Thus, despite the CERD Cttee's repeated requests to the Japanese government to cover the issue of the *Buraku* in state reporting,[158] the government has never done so throughout their reporting to date.[159] This attitude of the government

---

155 House of Councillors, '*Ainu Minzokuwo Senju Minzokuto Surukotowo Motomeru Ketsugi* (Resolution Seeking Government's Recognition of the Ainu as Indigenous People)' (6 June 2008) <https://www.sangiin.go.jp/japanese/gianjoho/ketsugi/169/080606-2.html> accessed 1 February 2020; House of Representatives, '*Ainu Minzokuwo Senju Minzokuto Surukotowo Motomeru Ketsugi* (Proposal of a Resolution Seeking Government's Recognition of the Ainu as Indigenous People)' (6 June 2008) <https://digitallibrary.un.org/record/438749?ln=en> accessed 15 September 2023.

156 The *Buraku* people *or Burakumin*, although of Japanese ethnic origin, were treated as pariahs and relegated to the most demeaning jobs in the Japanese feudal system. Even after the hierarchical system was over, '*Buraku* Lists' circulated to private companies have denied this group access to contractual employment and exposed them to discrimination in society. CERD Cttee, 'Summary Record of the 1443rd Meeting' (CERD/C/SR.1443, 15 March 2001) <https://digitallibrary.un.org/record/438749?ln=en> accessed 15 September 2023.

157 CERD Cttee, 'Summary Record of the 1444th Meeting' (CERD/C/SR.1444, 11 June 2001) <https://digitallibrary.un.org/record/438765?ln=en> accessed 15 September 2023.

158 CERD Cttee, 'Concluding Observations of the Committee on the Elimination of Racial Discrimination: Japan' (CERD/C/304/Add.114, 27 April 2001) <https://tbinternet.ohchr.org/_layouts/15/TreatyBodyExternal/Download.aspx?symbolno=CERD%2FC%2F304%2FAdd.114&Lang=en> accessed 15 September 2023.

159 There has been no reference to the issue of *Buraku* in Japan's state reports to CERD so far. See OHCHR, 'Reporting Status for Japan' <https://tbinternet.ohchr.org/_layouts/15/TreatyBodyExternal/countries.aspx?Country Code=JPN&Lang=EN> accessed 15 November 2020.

drove Japanese activists for *Burakumin*'s rights to take action for international solidarity. The *Buraku* and Dalit organisations in India worked together and actively lobbied at the Asian Regional Meeting and the Durban Conference in 2001 to have the Durban Declaration and Action Plan clearly state that the reason for racial discrimination is 'caste' and *'Buraku'* discrimination.[160] Although this did not happen in the end after intense arguments, the process drove activists and organisations for *Buraku* rights to actively lobby at the CERD Cttee for the development of General Recommendation 29 on article 1, paragraph 1 of the Convention (Descent) in 2002.[161] In this context, the passage of the Act on the Promotion of the Elimination of *Buraku* Discrimination in December 2016 should not be considered as a direct impact of CERD but rather as a consequence of a mixture of international and national pressures on the legislature. The *Buraku* Act sets out the basic principles and responsibilities of the state and local governments in relation to the elimination of *Buraku* discrimination without establishing penalties in the case of non-compliance.[162] The *Buraku* Act of 2016 does not contain any language of CERD provisions or

---

160   Comments from international human rights CSO staff on 30 May 2020.

161   CERD Cttee, 'Sixty-First Session (2002), General Recommendation XXIX on Article 1, Paragraph 1, of the Convention (Descent)' <https://tbinternet.ohchr.org/_layouts/15/treatybodyexternal/Download.aspx?symbolno=INT%2fCERD%2fGEC%2f7501&Lang=en> accessed 12 January 2021. In the meantime, the Subcommittee on Human Rights started to develop principles and guidelines on the topic of discrimination based on work and descent. IMADR and other CSOs contributed to the research and development of the report of Special Rapporteurs on the topic of discrimination based on work and descent, including Japanese international law expert Yozo Yokota. A draft of the principles and guidelines was submitted to the newly-established Human Rights Council, but it was never submitted to the Human Rights Council as a draft resolution due in large part to the strong opposition of the Indian government. See the final report published for the Human Rights Council session in June 2009 (A/HRC/11/CRP.3, 18 May 2009); Comments from international human rights CSO staff on 30 May 2020.

162   Government of Japan, 'Act on the Promotion of the Elimination of Buraku Discrimination' <https://elaws.e-gov.go.jp/search/elawsSearch/elaws_search/lsg0500/detail?lawId=428AC1000000109> accessed 15 November 2020; IMADR, 'Act on the Promotion of the Elimination of Buraku Discrimination' <https://imadr.net/wordpress/wp-content/uploads/2016/12/Act-on-the-Promotion-of-the-Elimination-of-Buraku-Discrimination-2.pdf> accessed 15 November 2020. It obliges the central and local government to establish consultation systems and undertake surveys into *buraku* discrimination, as well as raise awareness against *buraku* discrimination. Act on the Promotion of the Elimination of Buraku Discrimination <https://imadr.net/wordpress/wp-content/uploads/2016/12/Act-on-the-Promotion-of-the-Elimination-of-Buraku-Discrimination-2.pdf> accessed 1 February 2020. While *buraku* discrimination was also advocated by civil society as a violation of the rights protected under CERD, the government of Japan does not agree to deal with it as racial discrimination.

recommendations, nor any human rights treaties, although it acknowledges that discrimination against *Buraku* communities exists and declares that it is the government's responsibility to root it out based on the principle of fundamental human rights.[163]

5.1.2   Reliance by Judiciary

CERD had a significant impact as interpretative standards on some discrimination cases between private parties. For example, the Shizuoka District Court applied CERD to private relations in 1999.[164] In 2002, the Sapporo District Court further acknowledged that the actions of private persons could constitute racial discrimination under CERD.[165] It used international law as an interpretative standard to recognise the tort of racial discrimination.[166] These lawsuits have helped blur the public-private divide that traditionally insulated people from international law. The application of CERD to the private sphere marked a critical passage in Japan's ongoing integration of international law norms into its domestic law.[167] In part, this development may be because Japan had introduced no new legislation to implement CERD after its accession.[168] In the absence of domestic legislation, judges can step in to fill a legislative void and often rely on international law.[169]

The rulings of the Kyoto Korean School case from 2013 to 2015 follow these precedents within the existing legal framework, but with further references to CERD.[170] The courts condemned hateful demonstrations against Korean residents in Japan as 'racial discrimination' as defined by article 1(1) of CERD and ordered the xenophobic individuals and groups who conducted hostile demonstrations to pay a weighted amount of compensation, being informed

---

163   See Government of Japan, 'Act on the Promotion of the Elimination of Buraku Discrimination' <https://www.japaneselawtranslation.go.jp/en/laws/view/4080/en> accessed 11 September 2023.
164   Shizuoka District Court, Hamamatsu Branch, Judgment, 12 October 1999, 1045 *Hanrei Times* 216, 217.
165   Sapporo District Court, Judgment, 11 November 2002, 1150 *Hanrei Times* 185. In this case a plaintiff sued a bathhouse that refused entry to non-Asian looking foreigners for racial discrimination and the Otaru municipal government for not taking adequate measures to ban racial discrimination.
166   ibid.
167   Webster (n 77) 245.
168   ibid 267.
169   ibid.
170   A Hatano, 'Can Strategic Human Rights Litigation Complement Social Movements? A Case Study of the Movement Against Racism and Hate Speech in Japan' (2019) 14 University of Pennsylvania Asian Law Review 228, 4.

by CERD.[171] Furthermore, the trial court decision by the Kyoto District Court, in this case, made it clear that the national courts have a 'direct obligation' to interpret domestic laws to conform with CERD, referring to articles 2(1) and 6 of the Convention.[172] It is considered that this landmark decision demonstrates a positive attitude among the judiciary towards acknowledging its own role in realising international human rights law in the form of judicial redress for victims.[173] These cases align with the argument that the Japanese court has gradually warmed up to claims brought under international law and have applied CCPR and CERD in domestic litigation to hold acts of racial discrimination illegal, even though no domestic law specifically proscribes such conduct.[174] The rulings took Japan farther along a path reflecting a gradual change in the attitude of the Japanese judiciary towards international law, even if those cases may not have drastically changed the existing framework of jurisprudence.

5.1.3 Impact on and through Non-state Actors

While Japan's decision to accede to the Convention in 1995 occurred nearly 30 years after CERD was adopted, the ascent of the domestic movement for *Buraku* liberation played a pivotal role in driving this accession.[175] The accession of CERD and its state reporting process have encouraged civil society groups to work proactively in advocating the human rights of foreigners and racial

---

[171] The trial court ruled that when a tort is racially discriminatory or racially motivated, the intangible damage the court determines would be 'aggravated based on the direct influence of the ICERD on the interpretation of the Civil Code' and that 'the amount of compensation should be enough to ensure effective protection and remedy against the racial discrimination' under art 6 of CERD, which is specifically addressed to national courts. This is also in line with CERD General Recommendation 26. See A Hatano, 'The Internalization of International Human Rights Law: The Case of Hate Speech in Japan' (2018) 50 New York University Journal of International Law and Politics 637; Kyoto District Court, Judgment, 7 October 2013, 2208 Hanrei Jihō 74; Osaka High Court, Judgment, 8 July 2014, 2232 Hanrei Jihō 34; Supreme Court, Judgment, 9 December 2014, TKC 25505638; Hatano 2019 (n 170).

[172] The trial court also referred not only to treaty provisions but also to the COs in the review of the government reports before CERD. K Teraya, '*Heito Supīchi Jiken* (Hate speech case)' (2014) 1466 Jurist 292, 293.

[173] T Saito, 'The Situation of Domestic and International Laws Over the Measures Against Hate Speech' (2016) 19 Quarterly Jurist 91, 94.

[174] Webster (n 77) 263.

[175] Buraku Liberation and Human Rights Research Institute, 'Success in implementing the Convention on the Elimination of Racial Discrimination in Japan and the World Conference on Anti-Racism and the Elimination of Discrimination!' <https://blhrri.org/old/info/koza/koza_0021.htm> accessed 15 November 2020.

minorities in Japan, including the *Buraku* people, Ainu indigenous people, Ryukyu-Okinawan people,[176] and resident Koreans. The NGO Network for the Elimination of Racial Discrimination Japan (ERD Net), a nationwide network of CSOs and individuals working on issues of racial discrimination, was founded in 2007.[177] In addition, active organisations and groups were developed against racial discrimination with the impact of CERD accession and review process. For example, *Gaikokujin Jinkenhō Renrakukai* (Association for the Protection of the Human Rights of Foreigners) was formed in 2015 by lawyers, activists, and researchers with an aim to realise the basic principle of CERD.[178]

CERD's influence on domestic legislation and policy transformation through non-state actors is exemplified by the development of the aforementioned Hate Speech Elimination Act. Since hate speech emerged as a social issue in Japan around 2009, CSOs and anti-racist activists have actively involved in advocating for treaty compliance. This engagement encompasses the submission of relevant information to committees and active participation in the review processes of government reports.[179] These efforts were reflected in the

---

176   The *Ryukyu-Okinawan* are a group of population with its origin in the Ryukyu Islands located in the southmost of Japan. The islands used to constitute the independent Ryukyu Kingdom before their annexation to Japan in 1872. While some argue that the *Ryukyu-Okinawan* are a group of indigenous peoples, the Japanese government does not recognise them as indigenous nor minority group. Minority Rights Group, 'Ryukyuans (Okinawans)' <https://minorityrights.org/minorities/ryukyuans-okinawans/> accessed 19 November 2022.

177   ERD Net was founded with strong support and commitment of the International Movement Against All Forms of Discrimination and Racism (IMADR), an international non-profit, non-governmental human rights organisation devoted to eliminating discrimination and racism and the Buraku Liberation League, a burakumin's rights group in Japan. As of April 2012, 84 organisations and 29 individuals are members of ERD Net. The International Movement Against All Forms of Discrimination and Racism is a facilitating organisation of the network. ERD Net, *'Jinshu Sabetsu Teppai NGO Nettowāku no Gaiyō* (Overview of General Description on ERD Net)' <https://imadr.net/wordpress/wp-content/themes/imadr2017/pdf/p_erd01.pdf> accessed 26 May 2019. According to the human rights advocate from a CSO, IMADR and the Buraku Liberation League made efforts to develop a network of a variety of minority groups and civic associations, including the resident Koreans, Ainu, and Ryukyu-Okinawan peoples. Comments from international human rights CSO staff on 30 May 2020.

178   There is an observable influence of CERD on the foundational purpose of the organisation, which says 'towards the realisation of a multi-ethnic and multicultural society, we aim for the enactment of the Basic Law for the Human Rights of Foreign and Ethnic Minorities and the Law on the Elimination of Racial Discrimination and the realisation of a National Human Rights Institution'. Association for the Protection of the Human Rights of Foreigners, 'About Us' <https://gjhr.net/about/> accessed 15 November 2020.

179   Y Morooka, *Heitosupīchi Towa Nanika* (What Is Hate Speech) (Iwanami Shoten 2013) 18, 74–78.

recommendations on hate speech in 2010 and 2014 by the CERD Cttee and in 2014 by the HRCttee.[180] Civil society groups have engaged in a wide range of activities, not only requesting relevant ministries to implement the recommendations by treaty bodies but also organising study groups, supporting counter-demonstrations against hateful rallies, establishing links with domestic and foreign groups, supporting legal battles against hate crime and defamation, and disseminating anti-racism advertisements.[181] The JFBA, the largest civic organisation of lawyers in Japan, actively engaged in the movement with a statement that asked the government to implement measures against hate speech based on the principles of CERD.[182] The above-mentioned advocacy effort leveraging the treaty bodies' recommendations and engaging members of parliament reached an agreement through the adoption of the Hate Speech Elimination Act at the National Diet in 2016, in particular its direct reference to CERD in the supplementary resolutions.[183] Moreover, in June 2018 the Tokyo Bar Association requested that local authorities enact an ordinance for the elimination of racial discrimination following international standards and proposed a draft model ordinance of racial discrimination with points of concern based on the recommendations of the human rights treaty body.[184] Kawasaki City, inhabited by many people of foreign heritage including *Zainichi*

---

180 CERD/C/JPN/CO/3–6, 6 April 2010; CERD/C/JPN/CO/7–9, 25 September 2014; CCPR/C/JPN/CO/6, 20 August 2014.

181 Some argue that this advocacy movement can emerge from networks of 'invisible civil society' stemming from the social movement of the new-left in 1960s Japan. See D Shibuichi, 'The Struggle Against Hate Groups in Japan: The Invisible Civil Society, Leftist Elites and Anti-Racism Groups' (2016) 19 Social Science Japan Journal 1, 71, 78; Norikoe Net, <https://norikoenet.jp> accessed 7 March 2019.

182 JFBA, *'Jinshutōwo Riyuto Suru Sabetsuno Teppaini Muketa Sumiyakana Shisakuwo Motomeru Ikensho* (Statement of Opinion for Speedy Measure for the Abolition of Discrimination on the Basis of Race)' (7 May 2015) <http://www.nichibenren.or.jp/activity/document/opinion/year/2015/150507_2.html> accessed 26 May 2019.

183 Interview with Human Rights CSO staff (Tokyo, Japan, 27 July 2016). This law is criticised as it mainly focuses on awareness raising, and CSOs keep calling for a more comprehensive ban on discrimination with a reference to CERD. See JFBA, 'Honpōgai Shusshinsha ni Taisuru Futō na Sabetsuteki Gendō no Kaishō ni Muketa Torikumi no Suishin ni Kansuru Hōritsuan no Ichibu Kaisei o Motomeru Kaichō Seimei (President's Statement Calling for Partial Revision of the Hate Speech Elimination Act)' <https://www.nichibenren.or.jp/activity/document/statement/year/2016/160510.html> accessed 26 May 2019.

184 Tokyo Bar Association, *'Chihō Kōkyō Dantai ni Jinshu Sabetsu Teppai Jōrei no Seitei o Motome Jinshu Sabetsu Teppai Moderu Jōreian o Teiansuru kotoni Kansuru Ikensho* (Statement of Opinion about Asking Local Governments to Establish the Racial Discrimination Abolition Ordinance and Proposing the Racial Discrimination Abolition Model Ordinance Draft)' (8 June 2018) <https://www.toben.or.jp/message/pdf/180608ikensho.pdf> accessed 26 May 2019.

Koreans, enacted in December 2019 Japan's very first ordinance imposing criminal penalties on hate speech, which is informed by international human rights treaties.[185] This shows that local municipalities play important roles as key actors in implementing human rights treaties.

5.1.4 Impact of State Reporting

Japan submitted the first and second combined report in 2000, the third to sixth combined report in 2008, the seventh to ninth combined report in 2013, and the tenth and eleventh combined report in 2017. The CERD Cttee adopted the Concluding Observation for each report in 2001, 2010, 2016, and 2018. The state party's reports on their follow-up to COs were also submitted in 2011, 2016, and 2019.

The process of state reporting has facilitated dialogue between the government and the CERD Cttee. In the case of the technical intern training programme for migrant workers, which has come under scrutiny for alleged labour rights violations, occupational health and safety issues and lax administrative oversight, the Committee recommended in its COs for the seventh to ninth combined report that the state party reinforces its legislation to protect the trainees.[186] Against this background, the government stated in its tenth

---

185 Kawasaki City, '*Kawaski shi Sabetsu no nai Jinken Sonchō no Machzukuri Jōrei* (Kawasaki City Ordinance on Respecting Human Rights without Discrimination)' <https://www.city.kawasaki.jp/shisei/category/60-1-10-0-0-0-0-0-0-0.html> accessed 8 September 2023; S Saito, 'Kawasaki Eyes Criminal Action for Those Who Stir Hate Speech' *Asahi Shimbun* (25 June 2019) <http://www.asahi.com/ajw/articles/AJ201906250041.html> accessed 26 June 2019; 'Kawasaki Enacts Japan's First Bill Punishing Hate Speech' *The Japan Times* (12 December 2020) <http://www.japantimes.co.jp/news/2019/12/12/national/crime-legal/kawasaki-first-japan-bill-punishing-hate-speech/#.XjelPWjolPY> accessed 2 February 2020. As is noted later in the chapter, civil society and human rights advocates played an important part in the development of this anti-hate ordinance in Kawasaki.

186 The technical intern training programme was established in 1993 to promote international development by transferring skills, technologies, and knowledge from Japan to foreign workers from developing countries. However, the government-run program has been criticized as it is used to counteract the lack of low-skilled workers around the business sector and trainees are often subject to abusive labor conditions. In the COs on the Combined Seventh to Ninth Periodic Reports of Japan, the CERD Cttee expressed its concern "about reports that the rights of foreign technical interns are violated through the non-payment of proper wages, subjection to inordinately long working hours, and other forms of exploitation and abuses". See Japan International Trainee & Skilled Worker Cooperation Organization (JITCO), 'What is the Technical Intern Training Program?' <https://www.jitco.or.jp/en/regulation/> accessed 19 November 2022; Global Skills Partnership, 'Technical Intern Training Program (TITP)' <https://gsp.cgdev.org/legalpathway/technical-intern-training-program-titp/> accessed 19 November 2022;

and eleventh combined report that it had taken several steps, including the enactment of the Act on Proper Technical Intern Training and Protection of Technical Intern Trainees in November 2017.[187] In its COs for the latest report, the CERD Cttee evaluated the legislative measure as a positive aspect but, at the same time, requested information on the implementation and impact of the act in the state party's next periodic report.[188] Following this recommendation, the government provided relevant information, including the Organization for Technical Intern Training (OTIT)'s on-site inspections of supervising organisations and implementing organisations, bilateral agreements with countries that intend to send technical intern trainees, and surveys by a project team that studied cases of disappearance and death of technical intern trainees and reviewed the operation status of the current system.[189] While acknowledging the efforts indicated in the follow-up report, the Committee considered that the response to this recommendation was only partially satisfactory and voiced concerns that the licensing system introduced by the Act was not strictly enforced, had insufficient human and financial resources allocated to the OTIT for its on-site inspections, and had poor working conditions for technical intern trainees.[190]

CERD Cttee, COs on the Combined Seventh to Ninth Periodic Reports of Japan (CERD/C/JPN/CO/7–9, 26 September 2014) para 12 <https://tbinternet.ohchr.org/Treaties/CERD/Shared%20Documents/JPN/CERD_C_JPN_CO_7-9_18106_E.pdf> accessed 19 November 2022;U.S. Department of State, 'Trafficking in Persons Report 2016'<https://2009-2017.state.gov/j/tip/rls/tiprpt/2016/index.htm> accessed 19 November 2022. See also Business and Human Rights Resource Center, "Japan: NGO publishes new report on migrant women's pregnancy and maternity, revealing 71% of surveyed technical trainees experience constraints" <https://www.business-humanrights.org/en/latest-news/japan-ngo-publishes-new-report-on-migrant-womens-pregnancy-and-maternity-revealing-71-of-surveyed-technical-trainees-experience-constraints/> accessed 19 November 2022.

187 CERD Cttee, 'Consideration of Reports Submitted by States Parties Under Article 9 of the Convention, Tenth and Eleventh Periodic Reports of States Parties Due in 2017, Japan' (CERD/C/JPN/10-11, 14 January 2017) <https://undocs.org/en/CERD/C/JPN/10-11> accessed 11 July 2021, paras 46–51; MOJ, 'Act on Proper Technical Intern Training and Protection of Technical Intern Trainees' <https://www.moj.go.jp/content/001223425.pdf> accessed 13 October 2022.

188 CERD Cttee, 'Concluding Observations on the Combined Tenth and Eleventh Periodic Reports of Japan' (CERD/C/JPN/CO/10-11, 26 September 2018) <https://undocs.org/en/CERD/C/JPN/CO/10-11> accessed 11 July 2021 paras 31–32.

189 MOFA, 'Comments by the Government of Japan regarding the Concluding Observations of the Committee on the Elimination of Racial Discrimination' (CERD/C/JPN/CO/10-11) <https://www.mofa.go.jp/files/000514197.pdf> accessed 11 July 2021, paras 8–11.

190 OHCHR, 'Letter Dated 24 September 2020' <https://tbinternet.ohchr.org/Treaties/CERD/Shared%20Documents/CHN/INT_CERD_FUL_CHN_43684_E.pdf> (CERD/101 st session/FU/MJA/ks, 24 September 2020) accessed 11 July 2021.

5.1.5 Impact of Other Measures

Early warning measures and urgent procedures under CERD were used by civil society groups, which submitted information to the CERD Cttee in March 2012 concerning the construction of new US military bases in Okinawa.[191] The report claimed that it was racial discrimination against the Ryukyu-Okinawan people to construct new US military bases there, given that the prefecture already hosted most of the existing US military bases in Japan.[192] In response, the CERD Cttee requested the Japanese government to provide information under the early warning procedure on 9 March 2012.[193] The government responded that it does not recognise the Ryukyu-Okinawan people as 'indigenous' under CERD; thus, it is not an issue covered by the treaty.[194] The Committee followed up on 31 August 2012 reiterating the concerns expressed in its COs and those by the Special Rapporteur on Contemporary Forms of Racism regarding the persistent discrimination suffered by the people in Okinawa and asked the government to provide detailed and updated information in its seventh, eighth and ninth periodic reports.[195] However, these periodic reports do not

---

[191] OHCHR, 'Letter Dated 9 March 2012' <https://www.ohchr.org/Documents/HRBodies/CERD/Early Warning/CERD_Japan.pdf> accessed 9 March 2021.

[192] ibid.

[193] OHCHR, 'CERD Early Warning Letter' <https://www.ohchr.org/Documents/HRBodies/CERD/Early Warning/CERD_Japan.pdf> accessed 1 February 2020.

[194] The government stated that '[r]egarding Article 1(1) of the Convention, the Government of Japan understands "racial discrimination" as discrimination against groups of people or individuals belonging to the groups who are generally considered to share biological characteristics, and groups of people or individuals belonging to the groups who are generally considered to share cultural characteristics … the Government of Japan does not consider that there is a prevailing view in Japan that the people living in Okinawa prefecture or born in Okinawa have different biological and cultural characteristics from other Japanese citizens. Therefore, the Government of Japan understands that they could not be covered by "racial discrimination" as provided for in the Convention.' The response letter contains a detailed explanation of the US military base plan in Okinawa. MOFA, 'Jinshu Sabetsu Teppai Jōyaku (Convention on the Elimination of Racial Discrimination)' <https://www.mofa.go.jp/mofaj/gaiko/jinshu/index.html> accessed 16 January 2021; MOFA, 'Response to the Request for Information from the Committee on the Elimination of Racial Discrimination Dated March 9, 2012 Based on Article 9 of the Convention on the Elimination of Racial Discrimination and Article 65 of the Procedure Regulations of the Committee on the Elimination of Racial Discrimination' (31 July 2012) <https://www.mofa.go.jp/policy/human/pdfs/req_info_120731_en.pdf> accessed 16 January 2021.

[195] CERD/C/JPN/CO/3-6; E/CN.4/2006/16/Add.2; OHCHR, 'CERD Early Warning Letter' <http://www.ohchr.org/Documents/HRBodies/CERD/EarlyWarning/Japan31082012.pdf> accessed 1 February 2020. It must be noted that the Japanese government does not recognise the Ryukyu-Okinawan people as indigenous and does not formally accept this being discussed under the framework of CERD, as mentioned above.

contain information on the Okinawan people, and in its tenth and eleventh periodic reports the government repeated its view that it does not recognise the Okinawan people as indigenous, and 'the recommendations by the UN treaty bodies which regard the people of Okinawa as "indigenous people" are regrettable and they should be retracted'.[196] Thus, the measures taken by CERD under the early warning measures and urgent procedures in this case have not been as effective as intended.

5.1.6 Other Forms of Impact

Regarding the *Buraku* issue, the Law for the Promotion of Human Rights Education was enacted in 2000 to eliminate discrimination against the *Buraku* people. This action was taken as the laws providing positive measures against *Buraku* discrimination were set to expire and be abolished.[197] The Law for the Promotion of Human Rights Education is important for the implementation of human rights treaties, but it was allegedly developed not as a direct impact of the recommendations but rather because of the strong demand of the Buraku Liberation League out of concern that the discrimination would not disappear before the expiration of the time-limited laws.[198] The indirect impact of the treaties can be seen as the Buraku Liberation League has been actively engaged in international advocacy through IMADR. However, this example shows that some legal and policy developments that appear to be the direct implementation of the treaty may be a result of domestic circumstances including civic group's advocacy and public opinions rather than a direct effect of the reporting procedure and recommendations. Thus, the indirect impact of treaties on the general public cannot be overlooked. For instance, before the development of the aforementioned Hate Speech Elimination Act, CERD and its recommendations regarding hate speech gained greater recognition among the general populace, serving as a symbol of the anti-racism and anti-hate movement.[199]

---

196   Eg, CERD Cttee (n 71) paras 34–36.
197   MEXT, 'Jinken Kyōiku Oyobi Jinken Keihatsuno Suishinni Kansuru Hōritsu (Heisei 12 Nen 12 Gatsu 6 Ka Hōritsu Dai 147 Gō) (Act on the Promotion of Human Rights Education and Human Rights Awareness-Raising (Act No 147 of December 6, 2000))' <https://www.mext.go.jp/a_menu/shotou/jinken/siryo/1318152.htm> accessed 16 January 2021.
198   Interview with Human Rights CSO staff (Tokyo, Japan, 27 July 2016).
199   When Tokyo Anti-Discrimination March filled downtown streets in Tokyo in September 2013, participants adopted a resolution calling for the Japanese government to act in good faith with CERD. See 'Anti-Hate Speech March Fills Streets Around Shinjuku' *Mainichi* (23 September 2016) <http://mainichi.jp/english/english/newsselect/news/20130923p2a00m0na010000c.html> accessed 28 April 2019.

5.1.7 Brief Conclusion

There is a direct and indirect impact of the recommendations by the CERD Cttee in terms of enhancement of the indigenous Ainu's rights, the development of measures against hate speech and racial discrimination against *Zainichi* Koreans, and legislative measures on the issue of foreign workers, particularly technical intern trainees. However, the state has excluded some issues, such as the *Ryukyu-Okinawan* people and *Buraku* people, from the scope of CERD. Even though some measures have been implemented, they are not regarded as fully aligning with the recommendations of the CERD Committee. This is because they are often soft policy instruments – such as encouraging efforts against racial discrimination, promoting human rights education, and raising awareness – without binding regulations accompanied with punishments for non-compliance. The state does not consider the development of a comprehensive anti-discrimination law. The relatively frequent application of CERD in cases of discrimination against foreigners by the judiciary may be against the background that there is no basic domestic law to define racial discrimination.

In this situation, the impact of CERD recommendations is leveraged more indirectly through civic groups' domestic advocacy efforts, supported and informed by CERD. Some examples shown in this section demonstrate the observed symbolic impact of CERD and other treaties to sensitise and encourage civil society groups and the general public, as well as to push local authorities to develop regulations. However, this symbolic impact or impact at the local municipality and community level is difficult to fully capture in the state reporting system.

5.2 *International Covenant on Civil and Political Rights*

5.2.1 Incorporation and Reliance by Legislature and Executive Powers

The government has maintained a supportive attitude toward CCPR on the ground that the Covenant is very well aligned with the Japanese constitution and the domestic laws. It has explained in its initial report to the HRCttee that 'almost all the rights provided for in the Covenant are guaranteed by the Constitution of Japan', and 'the rights referred to in the Covenant, including rights not specifically mentioned in the Constitution, are guaranteed under domestic legislation'.[200] However, in addition to the legislative revision of family law following the judicial reviews mentioned below, CCPR seems to play a unique role at the domestic level regarding some emerging issues that the government might not have had in mind when it ratified CCPR in 1979, such

---

[200] CCPR/C/10/Add.1, 24 October 1980, para 1.

as the aforementioned case on anti-hate speech legislation and SOGI-based discrimination.[201]

Regarding prisoners' rights, Japanese CSOs and human rights lawyers have long lobbied for the amendment of the Prison Act as a series of mistreatment and extreme correctional treatment of prisoners in Japanese prisons under the outdated law enacted in 1908.[202] They have provided parallel reports to the HRCttee and the CAT Cttee since the 1990s, conducting research and advocacy on prisoners' rights in Japan in light of international human rights treaties. In 1998, the HRCttee in its COs showed its concern about the frequent use of protective measures, such as leather handcuffs, which may constitute cruel and inhuman treatment at the fourth periodic review of the Japanese government's report.[203] In 1999, the MOJ issued a new directive regarding appropriate use of 'protection cells' and leather handcuffs, after which the use of handcuffs decreased sharply.[204] The case where inmates at Nagoya Prison had been injured and died from the use of leather handcuffs in 2002 sparked intense discussion on the revision of the Prison Act, with an eye to aligning the law

---

[201] CCPR Cttee and HRCttee's recommendation in 2014 on hate speech have been referenced in the development of the Hate Speech Elimination Act and its supplementary resolutions with CERD, as mentioned above.

[202] MOJ, 'Penal Institutions (Prisons/Juvenile Prisons/Detention Houses)' <http://www.moj.go.jp/EN/kyousei1/kyousei_kyouse03.html> accessed 9 March 2021.

[203] Centre for Prisoners' Rights Japan, 'Submission to the Human Rights Committee the Task Forces for the Sixth Periodic Report by the Japanese Government 109th session (14 October–1 November 2013)' <http://cpr.jca.apc.org/sites/all/themes/cpr_dummy/Doc/ICCPR_Japan_CPR20130809.pdf> accessed 9 March 2021; Centre for Prisoners' Rights Japan, 'Prison and the Death Penalty in Japan: Stakeholder's Information Report for the 14th Session of the Working Group on the UPR – April 2012' <http://cpr.jca.apc.org/sites/all/themes/cpr_dummy/Doc/FIDH-CPR%20UPR%20submission%20April%202012%20-%20FINAL%202.pdf> accessed 9 March 2021; Centre for Prisoners' Rights Japan, 'The Alternative Report on the Fifth Periodic Reports of the Japanese Government under Article 40 of the International Covenant on Civil and Political Rights' (September 2008) <http://cpr.jca.apc.org/sites/all/themes/cpr_dummy/Doc/reportOct2008.pdf> accessed 9 March 2021; Centre for Prisoners' Rights Japan, 'Human Rights Situation in Japanese Prisons: Alternate Report Submitted to HRC' (September 1998) <http://cpr.jca.apc.org/sites/all/themes/cpr_dummy/Doc/1998SepfourthICCPR_English.pdf> accessed 9 March 2021.

[204] House of Councillors, 'Sangiin Giin Fukushima Mizuhokun Teishutsu Kōkin Shisetsuni Okeru Kawatejō Oyobi Hogobō Shiyouni Kansuru Shitsumonni Taisuru Tōbensho (Written Response to the Questions from Member of House of Councillors Mizuho Fukushima on the Use of Leather Handcuffs and Protection Cells)' (26 May 2000) <https://www.sangiin.go.jp/japanese/joho1/kousei/syuisyo/147/touh/t147021.htm> accessed 9 March 2021. For instance, in the Fuchu Prison in Tokyo, the use of leather handcuffs dropped from 191 in 1995 to three in 1999.

with international standards and the recommendations of the HRCttee.²⁰⁵ This triggered the MOJ to establish the Investigation and Review Committee on Execution Management with the submission of the study report on measures to prevent the recurrence of such cases to the report to the Correctional Administration Reform Council in April 2003.²⁰⁶ The Council's discussion, which was informed by the recommendations of the HRCttee, played a central role in the development of the Act on Penal Detention Facilities and Treatment of Inmates and Detainees enacted in 2005 with the establishment of a third-party monitoring mechanism.²⁰⁷

Concerning asylum seekers and undocumented immigrants, complementary protection based on international human rights law was proposed by the expert committee to the MOJ to clarify the scope of protection, but has not yet been introduced.²⁰⁸ Article 53 of Japan's Immigration Control Act prohibits the extradition against article 33(1) of the 1951 Refugee Convention, article 3(1) of CAT and article 16(1) of CED but not CCPR.²⁰⁹ The HRCttee expressed its concern that the principle of non-refoulement is not implemented effectively in practice with reported cases of ill-treatment during expulsion and detention of

---

205 JFBA, 'Chairman's Statement on Assault and Atrocities in Nagoya Prison' <https://www.nichibenren.or.jp/document/statement/year/2002/2002_16.html> accessed 9 March 2021. In 2010 the Nagoya District Court ruled that the guards of Nagoya Prison should pay damages in connection with the fatal abuse of prisoners. Nagoya District Court, Judgment, 25 May 2010 <https://www.courts.go.jp/app/files/hanrei_jp/529/080529_hanrei.pdf> accessed 11 July 2021.

206 House of Councillors Committee on Judicial Affairs, '*Kangokuhōno Zenmen Kaisei* (The Full Revision of the Prison Act)' <https://www.sangiin.go.jp/japanese/annai/chousa/rippou_chousa/backnumber/2006pdf/20060721l0.pdf> accessed 9 March 2021. MOJ, '*GyōkeiKaikakuKaigi(Dai1Kai)niOkeruHōmuDaijinAisatsu* (Remarks by the Justice Minister at the First Meeting of the Correctional Administration Reform Council)' <http://www.moj.go.jp/shingi1/kanbou_gyokei_kaigi_gaiyou01-01.html> accessed 9 March 2021.

207 Government of Japan, 'Act on Penal Detention Facilities and Treatment of Inmates and Detainees' <http://www.japaneselawtranslation.go.jp/law/detail/?vm=04&re=01&id=142> accessed 9 March 2021. According to the comments on 4 December 2020 by a human rights lawyer working on this prisoners' right, there is a significant impact on the process of revision of the Prison Act.

208 Expert group on refugee recognition system, '*Nanmin Nintei Seidono Minaoshino Hōkōseini Kansuru Kentō Kekka (Hōkoku)* (Results of Examination on the Direction of Review of the Refugee Recognition System (Report))' <https://www.moj.go.jp/isa/content/930003065.pdf> accessed 8 September 2023.

209 Government of Japan, 'Article 53, Paragraph 3, Immigration Control and Refugee Recognition Act, Revised 2009' <http://www.japaneselawtranslation.go.jp/law/detail/?vm=2&re=02&lvm=02&id=173> accessed 22 March 2021.

asylum seekers and undocumented immigrants.[210] While the HRCttee as well as other treaty bodies repeatedly urge the government to ensure that detention is resorted to for the shortest appropriate period and only if the existing alternatives to administrative detention have been duly considered, the Immigration administration practice has been based on the principle that all suspected undocumented foreigners shall be detained in immigration facilities in the system which allows indefinite detention after the issuance of a deportation warrant.[211] It is severely criticised by CSOs for violating international human rights standards, given that there are numerous suspected cases of deaths attributed to the ill-treatment or negligence of immigration officers at the detention facilities.[212]

5.2.2 Reliance by Judiciary

The previous impact study criticised 'the poor record and quality of rulings rendered by the Japanese judiciary with regard to the Covenant'.[213] However, there were two significant Supreme Court cases in 2008 and 2013.

Nationality Act case (2008): Under the *jus sanguinis* principle, the Nationality Act did not allow a child born out of wedlock to a Japanese father and a non-Japanese mother to acquire Japanese nationality without legal marriage of the parents.[214] In the *Nationality Act* case, the Grand Bench of the Supreme

---

[210] CCPR/C/JPN/CO/6, 19 August 2014, para 19; CERD/C/JPN/CO/10-11, 26 September 2018, para 36; CAT/C/JPN/CO/2, 28 June 2013, para 9.

[211] Article 39(1) of the Immigration Control Act stipulates 'An immigration control officer may, if he has reasonable grounds to believe that a suspect falls under any of the items of Article 24, detain the suspect pursuant to a written detention order'. This provision is interpreted in practice as that all suspected cases shall be detained. Government of Japan, 'Immigration Control and Refugee Recognition Act' <https://www.japaneselawtranslation.go.jp/en/laws/view/1934/en> accessed 14 November 2023.

[212] As of May 2021, at least 24 detainees were reported to have died since 1997, including the death of a Nigerian man on hunger strike in a detention centre in June 2019, and the death of a Sri Lankan woman after immigration officers' negligence and ill-treatment of her health in March 2021. These incidents fuelled outrage for critics of Japan's immigration system among human rights defenders as well as publics. 'Japan Is Shaken After a Detainee, Wasting Away, Dies Alone in Her Cell' (*New York Times*, 25 June 2019) <https://www.nytimes.com/2021/05/18/world/asia/japan-refugee-wishma-rathnayake.html> accessed 22 November 2022. See also Human Rights Now, '*Nyūkanshisetsu ni okeru shiiteki shūyō no haishi oyobi hōteki kaizen o motomeru seimei* (Statement calling for the abolition and legal improvement of arbitrary detention in immigration facilities)' (18 October 2019) <http://hrn.or.jp/wpHN/wp-content/uploads/2019/10/c973721f4723730c9804e01b635b5bdb-1.pdf> accessed 22 November 2022.

[213] C Heyns and F Viljoen, *The Impact of the United Nations Human Rights Treaties on the Domestic Level* (Martinus Nijhoff Publishers 2002) 398.

[214] At this time, the Nationality Act provided that '[a] child who has acquired the status of a child born in wedlock as a result of the marriage of the parents and the acknowledgment

Court of Japan invalidated a part of article 3(1) of the Nationality Act as it violated article 14(1) (equality clause) of the Constitution. In this reasoning, the Court referred to CCPR and CRC as persuasive authority, which is considered ground-breaking in light of the conventional practice of the Court, which has been reluctant to adjudicate using international human rights law. The Court held that '[o]ther states are moving toward scrapping the law's discriminatory treatment against children born out of wedlock; in fact, the ICCPR and the CRC, which Japan has ratified, also contain such provisions to the effect that children shall not be subject to discrimination of any kind because of birth.'[215] Justice Izumi further discussed in his concurring opinion:

> The gist of the provision of Article 3, para 1 of the Nationality Act is to grant Japanese nationality to children who were born to Japanese citizens as their fathers or mothers and are ineligible for application of Article 2 of the said Act,[216] and the 'marriage of the parents' is merely one of the requirements to be satisfied to achieve this. Therefore, the gist of the provision should be maintained to the greatest possible extent even if the part requiring the 'marriage of the parents' is unconstitutional, and this is what the lawmakers would have intended. Furthermore, applying Article 3, para 1 of the Nationality Act in this manner conforms to the gist of Article 24, para 3 of the CCPR which provides that 'every child has the right to acquire a nationality' and that of Article 7, para 1 of the CRC.[217]

While conducting interpretation consistent with the existing treaties, Justice Izumi also carefully paid attention to the relationship between the judiciary and the legislature by mentioning that this construction 'may not be permissible when there is a clear probability that the Diet, from the legislative perspective, will not maintain the provision of said paragraph'.[218]

---

by either parent ... may acquire Japanese nationality ... if the father or mother who has acknowledged the child was a Japanese citizen at the time of the child's birth, and such father or mother is currently a Japanese citizen'. See art 3(1) of the Nationality Act (prior to its revision in 2018). Government of Japan, 'Nationality Act' <http://www.japaneselawtranslation.go.jp/law/detail_main?re=02&vm=04&id=185> accessed 1 February 2020.

215   Supreme Court, Judgment, 4 June 2008, 62–6 Minshu 1367, ILDC 1814 (JP 2008) <http://www.courts.go.jp/app/hanrei_en/detail?id=955> accessed 1 February 2020.
216   Art 2(1) of the then Nationality Act provided that a child was a Japanese citizen if the father or mother was a Japanese citizen at the time of birth. Government of Japan (n 214).
217   Supreme Court (n 215).
218   ibid.

Children born outside of wedlock case (2013): Article 900(4) of the Civil Code grants half inheritance to children born out of wedlock, compared to what is inherited by their siblings born in wedlock.[219] The Supreme Court ruled that provision on children born out of wedlock as constitutional in 1995 (Grand Bench decision) and then in 2000, 2003, 2004, and 2009. The 1995 decision of the Supreme Court stated that the provision reconciles respect for legal marriage and the protection of illegitimate children, and it could not be said to be discrimination without reasonable grounds or violate equality under the provision of article 14 of the Constitution. However, on 4 September 2013, the Grand Bench of the Supreme Court overturned its previous rulings in its unanimous decision and invalidated this statutory law by referring to the views and recommendations issued by the HRCttee and the CRC Cttee.[220] In response to this decision, in December 2013 the Civil Code was revised to eliminate these provisions. The case demonstrated that the UN human rights system has made a significant difference in the field of family law through CCPR and CRC.[221]

Prisoners' rights cases: CCPR also had a significant impact on lower court cases concerning prisoners' rights. For example, the Chiba District Court in its judgment of 2000 referred to CCPR articles 7 and 10(1) when declaring excessive usage of leather handcuffs illegal under Japanese prison law.[222]

5.2.3 Impact on and through Non-state Actors

CCPR and the work of the HRCttee have had a significant impact on the work of many non-state actors to advocate a variety of human rights issues to the committee in light of broad issues covered by the Covenant.[223] For example,

---

[219] Japanese Civil Code, art 900 stipulates as follows: 'If there are two or more heirs of the same rank, their shares in inheritance shall be determined by the following items ... (iv) if there are two or more children, lineal ascendants, or siblings, the share in the inheritance of each shall be divided equally; provided that the share in inheritance of a child out of wedlock shall be one half of the share in inheritance of a child in wedlock, and the share in inheritance of a sibling who shares only one parent with the decedent shall be one half of the share in inheritance of a sibling who shares both parents.' Government of Japan, 'Civil Code (Part IV and Part V (tentative translation))' <http://www.japaneselawtranslation.go.jp/law/detail/?id=2252&vm=2&re=02> accessed 9 March 2021.

[220] Supreme Court, Judgment, 4 September 2013, 67–6 Minshu 1320, ILDC 2060 (JP 2013).

[221] For example, a lower court declared a decision of deportation illegal by referring to the spirit of article 23 of CCPR. Tokyo District Court, Judgment, 12 November 1999, TKC 2541005.

[222] Chiba District Court, Judgment, 7 February 2000, TKC 28072863.

[223] In the review of the 6th state reporting in 2014, more than 50 CSOs submitted alternative reports to the committee. See the aforementioned 'Number of information submissions (reporting cycle, year)'.

in the above mentioned case of children born out of wedlock, there were active advocacies of the plaintiff and civic groups who brought the issue into the review of the committee through the state reporting system after they had failed in the domestic justice mechanism. In 1988, some groups of advocates started to seek justice for discrimination against children born out of wedlock and remedy it in domestic administrative and legal procedures.[224] As domestic litigation was not successful, one of the groups, including the plaintiff in the litigation, started lobbying international treaty bodies, namely, the HRCttee, and the CESCR, CRC and CEDAW Cttees. In addition to submitting information to the committees on occasions of review of state reports, these advocates visited Geneva to directly engage with committee members. Their efforts over decades resulted in over a dozen recommendations in the Concluding Observations of those committees.[225] They made significant use of these recommendations in their domestic advocacy and subsequent allegations in litigation. This resulted in tangible outcomes, including the previously mentioned shift in judicial decisions, the submission of petitions by local municipalities to the central government, urging the eradication of discrimination and unjust treatment towards children born out of wedlock, and changes in pertinent laws and policies.[226]

5.2.4 Impact of State Reporting

Japan submitted its first report in 1980, the second report in 1987, the third report in 1991, the fourth report in 1997, the fifth report in 2006, and the sixth report in 2012. The HRCttee adopted the COs for each report in 1982, 1988, 1993, 1998, 2008 and 2014 respectively. In the COs in 2014, the HRCttee positively assessed legislative and institutional steps such as the amendment of the Nationality Act in 2008 and of the Civil Code in 2013 which, with the influence of judicial decisions examined above, removed discriminatory provisions

---

[224] Interview with members of the Society for Abolishing the Family Registration System and Discriminations against Children Born out of Wedlock (AFRDC) (Geneva, Switzerland, 17 January 2019). See *Nakusou Koseki to Kongaishisabetsu Kōryukai* (Group for Abolishing the Discrimination Against Children Born out of Wedlock) <http://www.grn.janis.or.jp/~shogokun/> accessed 22 March 2021.

[225] HRCttee's recommendation in 1993, 1998, and 2008; CRC Cttee's recommendation in 1998, 2004, 2013, and 2019; CESCR Cttee's recommendation in 2001 and 2013; and CEDAW Cttee's recommendation in 2003, 2009, and 2016. Even after the 2013 judicial decision and revision of the Civil Code the government have sought to maintain the distinction between legitimate and illegitimate children in the family register system.

[226] Interview with members of AFRDC (Geneva, Switzerland, 17 January 2019). They mentioned that '[w]e felt confidence about a tangible result from local authorities when we lobbied them with accumulated recommendations by the human rights treaty bodies'.

against children born out of wedlock.[227] However, in the review process, Mr Nigel Rodley, the chairperson of the HRCttee, did not hide his frustration and concern about the persistence of serious human rights issues, stating that 'from one review to the next, the State party did not take account of the Committee's concerns and recommendations', and 'the continued applicability of the system of substitute detention (*Daiyo Kangoku*),[228] despite its flagrant incompatibility with the Covenant and repeated calls by the Committee and the international community for its abolition, was particularly telling in that regard'.[229] COs required the government to provide additional information regarding several key points and assessed the government's actions based on its reply, namely, the issues of the interrogation system, the death penalty, so-called 'comfort women' and 'substitute detention system' and forced confessions, which have not seen any progress since the start of the periodic review of state report in the 1980s.[230]

Furthermore, the HRCttee, along with other committees, has strongly recommended that Japan adopt comprehensive anti-discrimination legislation that prohibits discrimination on all grounds and provides victims of discrimination with effective and appropriate remedies, which has not been met with a concrete response by the state.[231]

Against the recently-developed Conspiracy Law and specifically the Designated Secrets Act, CSOs and journalists have raised more concerns about the threats and attacks on freedom of expression, freedom of the press, freedom of assembly, and right to know and have become active in lobbying the HRCttee.[232]

227　CCPR/C/JPN/CO/6, 20 August 2014, paras 3–4.
228　*Daiyō kangoku* are detention cells found in police stations that are used as legal substitutes for detention centres or prisons. They are seen as problematic in light of separation between the functions of investigation and detention.
229　CCPR/C/JPN/CO/6, 20 August 2014.
230　ibid.
231　ibid para 11.
232　The law constitutes a key element of ex-PM Abe's agenda to strengthen its national security. In essence, it aims to increase the power of authorities over information control for the sake of security and may allow police to seek wiretap warrants to investigate more crimes with supposed links to terrorism. Freedom House, 'Japan' <https://freedomhouse.org/country/japan/freedom-net/2017> accessed 19 November 2022. Japan is ranked 67th (problematic situation) in the 2019 World Press Freedom Index. See Reporters without Borders, 'Japan' <https://rsf.org/en/japan> accessed 27 February 2020; NGO Coalition for Free Expression and Open Information in Japan, 'Joint NGO Report on the International Covenant on Civil & Political Rights (CCPR) Articles 18, 19 & 21: For the 7th Periodic Review of Japan at the UN Human Rights Committee Session' (30 September 2020) <https://sites.google.com/view/ncfoj> accessed 22 March 2021.

The impact of state reporting can also be seen in the area of treatment of asylum seekers. The COs in 2014 expressed concerns on reported cases of ill-treatment during deportations, insufficient implementation the non-refoulement principle, the lack of an independent appeal mechanism with suspensive effect against negative decisions on asylum, as well the prolonged periods of administrative detention without adequate giving of reasons and without independent review of the detention decision.[233] In the subsequent COs in 2022, the Committee welcomed the information on the development of an improvement plan on treatment in detention facilities, and the revision of the deportation procedure establishing the scheduled date of deportation to be at least two months after the delivery of notification on the decision, as well as the State party's willingness to consider measures to avoid long-term detention.[234]

5.2.5   Impact of Other Measures

The impact of the treaty is demonstrated in the civic groups' active use of recommendations of the HRCttee in ongoing litigation on discrimination against LGBT persons. The Committee expressed concerns about discrimination against LGBT people in its COs in 2008.[235] In the following COs in 2014, the Committee showed its disappointment with the non-implementation in the first place and put stronger recommendations to urge the state to take measures to prevent stereotypes, prejudice and harassment, as well as remaining discriminatory practices against LGBT persons in housing services.[236] These recommendations, together with the recommendation by the CESCR Cttee in 2013,[237] have been referred to in the complaints to support the allegation of the plaintiff for the right to same-sex marriage in ongoing strategic litigation for marriage equality in Japan filed across the country in 2019.[238] It is noteworthy

---

233   CCPR/C/JPN/CO/6, para 19.
234   CCPR/C/JPN/CO/6, 3 November 2022, para 32.
235   CCPR/C/JPN/CO/5, 18 December 2008, para 29.
236   CCPR/C/JPN/CO/6, 20 August 2014, para 11.
237   E/C.12/JPN/CO/3, 10 June 2013, para 10.
238   Four suits were filed in Osaka, Nagoya, Sapporo and Tokyo on 14 February 2019. 'Same-sex marriage lawsuits to be filed on Valentine's Day by 13 couples nationwide' *Mainichi* (4 February 2019); 'LGBT couples speak of their suffering in lawsuit seeking marriage for all in Japan' *Japan Times* (15 April 2019) <https://www.japantimes.co.jp/news/2019/04/15/national/lgbt-couples-speak-suffering-lawsuit-seeking-marriage-japan/#.XPMNK9NKjX8> accessed 9 March 2021. On 5 September 2019 another lawsuit was filed in Fukuoka. Call4, 'Marriage for All Litigation (Same-Sex Marriage Litigation)' <https://www.call4.jp/search.php?type=material&run=true&items_id_PAL[]=match+comp&items_id=I0000031> accessed 9 March 2021.

that unlike in previous domestic human rights litigation, the complaints and expert opinions for the strategic litigation for marriage equality contained numerous references to the human rights treaties and other international human rights instruments. The plaintiffs refer to articles 2(1), 17 and 26 of CCPR, COs of the HRCttee and CESCR Cttee, General Comments or recommendations of the HRCttee, the CESCR Cttee and the CEDAW Cttee,[239] and views of the HRCttee related to LGBT rights,[240] to bolster their argument that banning same-sex marriage constitutes unfair treatment.[241]

5.2.6   Other Forms of Impact

The WGAD gave opinions on the issues surrounding penal, preventive and immigration detention in Japan with reference to the relevant provision of CCPR, General Comments, and views of the HRCttee.[242]

5.2.7   Brief Conclusion

The CCPR, considered together with the CRC, has had a significant impact on the Japanese judiciary and legislative change in the field of family law and child rights, such as the revision of the Civil Code provision on children born outside of wedlock and the Nationality Act. Some gradual changes and revisions of the criminal justice system and practice were observed, including the decline in the use of solitary confinement and leather handcuffs in alignment with CCPR and the recommendations by the HRCttee. However, persistent gaps remain between the recommendations of treaty bodies and state practices regarding civil and political rights. Although the HRCttee repeatedly called for the abolition of the death penalty, the government maintains that international law does not prohibit the death penalty and performed consecutive executions of death row inmates, citing that the vast majority of its nationals support the death penalty.[243] As such, there has been no significant

---

239   HRCttee General Comment 28 (CCPR/C/21/Rev.1/Add.10, 29 March 2000); CESCR Cttee General Comment 14 (E/C.12/2000/4, 11 August 2000), 15 (E/C.12/2002/11, 20 January 2003), 18 (E/C.12/GC/18, 6 February 2006), 20 (E/C.12/GC/20, 2 July 2009); CEDAW General Recommendation 29 (CEDAW/C/GC/29, 30 October 2013).
240   CCPR/C/81/D/901/1999, 26 August 2004; CCPR/C/89/D/1361/2005, 14 May 2007; CCPR/C/50/D/488/1992, 31 March 1994; CCPR/C/78/D/941/2000, 18 September 2003.
241   Call 4, 'Written Claim About the Situation, Vol. 2, for the Second Lawsuit in Sapporo' (30 September 2019) <https://www.call4.jp/file/pdf/201910/6923167f6495109abcea96d242124 61b.pdf> accessed 9 March 2021.
242   See the previous section on the WGAD.
243   For example, in 2018 a total of 15 death row inmates were executed, including *Aum Shinrikyo* cult founder Shoko Asahara. As of December 2019, Japan has 110 inmates on death row. These inmates have limited access to legal counsel and are only notified of their execution

progress in the controversial issues with diplomatic, historical or political backgrounds, including comfort women, the substitute detention system and the ill-treatment of asylum seekers and undocumented immigrants in the detention and asylum process, on which the state maintains that they are a matter of government policy discretion.[244]

There was active and persistent advocacy and engagement of civic groups behind the successful incorporation of the HRCttee's recommendations in the *Nationality Act* case and *Children born outside of wedlock* cases, as well as other legal and policy changes. These examples illustrate that it takes a long time with accumulative recommendations and strong civic group advocacy to bring the recommendations into real practice in Japan.

5.3 International Covenant on Economic, Social, and Cultural Rights

5.3.1 Incorporation and Reliance by the Legislature and Executive Powers

Japan ratified CESCR without taking any new legislative development because the government considered economic, social, and cultural rights under the Convention to be already well protected by the Constitution or by existing

---

on the day it takes place. Some were even executed after their lawyers had filed requests for retrials. MOJ, '*Hōmu Daijin Rinji Kisha Kaikenno Gaiyō*' (Justice Minister Press Conference Overview)' <https://www.moj.go.jp/hisho/kouhou/hisho08_01083.html> accessed 26 January 2020; Human Rights Watch, 'Japan Events of 2019' <https://www.hrw.org/world-report/2020/country-chapters/japan> accessed 26 January 2020. The state repeats in its latest report that '[w]hether to retain or abolish the death penalty is basically an issue that should be determined by each country at its discretion with careful examination from various viewpoints, such as the realisation of justice in society, taking public opinion into full account. The majority of citizens in Japan consider that the death penalty is unavoidable for extremely malicious and atrocious crimes. In light of the current situation in Japan, where there is no sign of decline in atrocious crimes such as mass murder and robbery-murder, it is considered unavoidable to impose the death penalty on the offender who has committed an atrocious crime and bears serious criminal responsibility. Therefore, the Government is of the view that it is not appropriate to abolish the death penalty.' CCPR/C/JPN/7, 30 March 2020, para 67. According to the survey of the Cabinet Office, in 2019, over 80% accepted the death penalty in Japan as inevitable. Government of Japan, '*Shikei Seidoni Taisuru Ishiki* (Awareness of the Death Penalty)' <https://survey.gov-online.go.jp/r01/r01-houseido/2-2.html> accessed 22 March 2021.

244 The so-called 'hostage' justice system, in which criminal suspects are held for long periods under harsh conditions to coerce a confession, came under international criticism. The issue received renewed attention after Carlos Ghosn, a former head of Renault and Nissan, was arrested in November 2018 for alleged financial misconduct. Brad Adams, 'Japan's Hostage Justice System' *The Diplomat* (10 January 2019) <https://www.thediplomat.com/2019/01/japans-hostage-justice-system/> accessed 26 January 2020.

legislation.[245] Despite the fact that many of its provisions are reflected in the Constitution, it was a concern of the CESCR Cttee that the state party had not given effect to the provisions of the Covenant in domestic law in a satisfactory manner.[246] The government interprets the obligations under article 2 of the Covenant as not having an immediate effect, which has led to significant cuts to budget allocations for social assistance guaranteed under articles 9 and 11 thereof.[247]

5.3.2   Reliance by Judiciary

Given the negative attitudes of the legislative and executive powers as backdrop, domestic courts in the state party have made decisions that restrict the applicability of the Covenant's provisions.[248] In the *Shiomi* case the Supreme Court stated that '[a]rticle 9 of CESCR ... does not provide for a concrete right to be granted to individuals immediately'.[249] Following this logic, Japanese courts are extremely restrained in exercising judicial power over economic, social, and cultural rights cases.[250] However, the Osaka High Court, in dealing with the case regarding the abolition of the old-age assistance addition system, noted that 'the contents of CESCR should be reflected in the interpretation of constitutional and legislative provisions' in terms of article 98(2) of the Constitution.[251] Furthermore, the Court recognised the prohibition of retrogressive measures by referring to General Comments 3 and 19 of the CESCR Cttee, although the abolishment in question was evaluated as in conformity with the constitutional and legislative standards.[252]

---

245   K Yakushiji, 'Implementation of Human Rights Convention in Japan' (2003) 46 Japanese Annual International Law 1, 2.
246   E/C.12/JPN/CO/3, 17 May 2013, para 7.
247   ibid paras 7, 9.
248   ibid para 7.
249   Supreme Court, Judgment, 2 March 1989, 741 *Hanrei Times* 87, 90.
250   Eg, despite the recommendations of the CESCR Cttee on the discrimination against children born out of wedlock, the aforementioned Supreme Court judgment, which made a reference to CCPR and CRC, made no reference to CESCR.
251   This case concerns the abolition of special additional welfare support reserved for low-income populations aged 70 and above. Osaka High Court, Judgment, 25 December 2015, TKC 25543687.
252   ibid.

5.3.3 Impact on and through Non-state Actors

Although it was once called the 'forgotten human rights treaty', CESCR has received more attention from civil society groups and human rights activists since the 2000s.[253]

In the state reporting process, many civic groups have submitted their reports and information to the Committee on a wide range of issues such as children born out of wedlock; civil servants' rights; homeless people; victims of disasters; domestic violence; comfort women; labour rights, including migrant and foreign workers' labour conditions and ratification of ILO treaties; and discrimination on various grounds, including race, gender, marital status, nationality, and SOGI. In particular, after the Great East Japan earthquake and the Fukushima nuclear accident in 2011, the issue of rights to relief and healthcare has become a major concern among civic groups.[254]

The JFBA is concerned about the lack of follow-up procedure and pointed out that the 2013 recommendations of the CESCR Cttee about 'reported incidents in nuclear power stations and the lack of transparency and disclosure of necessary information regarding the safety of such installations, and also the lack of advance nationwide and community preparation for the prevention and handling of nuclear accidents' were not reflected in legal and policy measures at the time of the 2011 earthquake.[255]

5.3.4 Impact of State Reporting

Japan submitted its first report in 1982, the second in 1998, and the third in 2009. The CESCR Cttee adopted the COs for each report in 1982, 2001, and 2013.

---

[253] In 2001, Japan's government underwent its second review under CESCR, a process that garnered significant attention and active participation from civil society. On the other hand, little is known about the first review, as there were almost no efforts by CSOs. Behind the fact that the Covenant has continued to be a 'forgotten human rights treaty' in Japan is the classical understanding and interpretation of social rights (and the Covenant) based on the dichotomy of human rights and extremely restrictive application in courts, which led to the indifference of CSOs. Hurights Osaka, 'Challenges and Potential of the Covenant on Social Rights' <https://www.hurights.or.jp/archives/newsletter/section2/2001/11/post-62.html> accessed 22 March 2021.

[254] ibid. Many non-state actors addressed these issues in their parallel reports for the third state reporting cycle and the committee's review in 2013 for providing relief and reconstruction efforts for communities affected by the Great East Japan Earthquake and the Fukushima nuclear accident.

[255] JFBA, Shakaikenkiyakuiinkai Sokatsushoken no Ikashikata to Kongo no Kadai ('CESCR: How to Make use of the Concluding Observations and Future Challenges)' <https://www.nichibenren.or.jp/library/ja/kokusai/humanrights_library/treaty/data/society_rep3_pam.pdf> accessed 22 March 2021.

In the COs of the third periodic report, the CESCR Cttee welcomed the state party's ratification of human rights instruments relating to children's rights and enforced disappearance. It also showed its satisfaction with the withdrawal of the state party's reservation to article 13(2)(b) and (c) of CESCR on the progressive introduction of free education.[256] However, the Committee did not hesitate to express its concern regarding significant cuts to budget allocations for social assistance that have negatively impacted the enjoyment of economic and social rights, particularly for disadvantaged and marginalised groups of the population.[257] Notwithstanding this concern, independent experts under the Special Procedures of the Human Rights Council criticised this move as failing the requirements of retrogressive measures under CESCR.[258] As was warned by the Special Rapporteurs and independent experts under the special procedures of the HRC, the retrogressive effect reviewed a series of planned benefit cuts threatening minimum social protection for the poor. In particular, the lack of support for those with disabilities, single parents and their children, and older people was aggravated by the subsequent measures taken in 2018.[259]

There have been repeated recommendations by the CESCR, CERD, and CRC Cttees to call for the state to stop discriminatory treatment of Korean schools, excluding them from the state's tuition fee waiver programme for high school education.[260] However, despite repeated calls from civil society groups working for minorities, this recommendation has been neglected. The government explained that this was due to a lack of agreement among Japanese nationals, as those schools are alleged to have a close relationship with North Korea, which abducted a number of Japanese people.[261]

---

256 E/C.12/JPN/CO/3, 17 May 2013, paras 4–6.
257 ibid para 9.
258 H-B Shin, 'Jinken Jōyaku Tekigōtekina Kokunaihō Kaishaku (Consistent Interpretation of Domestic Law in Conformity with Human Rights Treaties)' in S Taira, T Umeda and T Hamada (eds), Kokusaihōno Furontia (The Frontier of International Law) (Nihon Hyoronsha 2019) 195, 209–214.
259 OHCHR, 'Japan: Benefit Cuts Threaten Social Protection of the Poor, UN Rights Experts Warn' (24 May 2018) <https://www.ohchr.org/en/NewsEvents/Pages/DisplayNews.aspx?NewsID=23124&LangID=E> accessed 9 January 2021.
260 E/C.12/JPN/CO/3, 17 May 2013.
261 Korean high schools lodged lawsuits against the state for stopping the exclusion of the schools from the tuition fee waiver programme, but the Japanese courts were not in favour of the schools and ruled that the treatment was legitimate within the scope of the government discretion. The Osaka District Court decision in favour of schools was nullified by the September 2018 judgment of the Osaka High Court, and in August 2019, the Supreme Court rejected appeals. House of Councillors, 'Questionnaire Regarding the Application of Free High School Tuition to Korean School'

5.3.5 Brief Conclusion

The impact of CESCR on the Japanese legal order has been limited, especially in the public domain. The Supreme Court adopted a narrow interpretation of the right to social security under the Covenant. Political branches are also unwilling to actively pursue the advancement and improvement of social security in line with the recommendations put forth by the CESCR Cttee. Societal challenges, including disparities in minority access to social protection, inequality, and health issues arising from disasters and nuclear incidents, are increasingly apparent in the twenty-first century. CSOs actively participate in a dialogue with the Committee, critiquing the government's economic, social, and cultural policies in light of CESCR standards. However, in some areas, such as the discriminatory treatment of Korean schools, comfort women, and issues regarding nuclear power plants and policies, there has been no progressive implementation of the CESCR Cttee's recommendations. The reluctance to address these matters may stem from their classification as highly diplomatic or political issues intertwined with national interests or national pride.

5.4 Convention on the Elimination of All Forms of Discrimination against Women

5.4.1 Incorporation and Reliance by Legislature and Executive Powers

Upon ratification of CEDAW, the state made significant changes in domestic laws and policies. The Equal Employment Opportunity Law was enacted in 1985; the Nationality Law was also amended in the same year so that people of matrilineal Japanese descent can acquire Japanese nationality; and the curriculum guideline of the Ministry of Education, Culture, Sports, Science and Technology for the subjects of technology and home economics at school was revised in 1989.[262]

<https://www.sangiin.go.jp/japanese/joho1/kousei/syuisyo/176/syuh/s176123.htm> accessed 22 March 2021; Supreme Court, Judgment, 27 August 2019; Hatano 2021 (n 150) 293.

[262] Y Iwasawa, *International Law, Human Rights, and Japanese Law* (Clarendon Press 1999) 211–31; Government of Japan, 'Act on Securing, Etc of Equal Opportunity and Treatment between Men and Women in Employment' <http://www.japaneselawtranslation.go.jp/law/detail/?id=60&vm=04&re=01> accessed 22 March 2021; Government of Japan, 'Nationality Act' <http://www.japaneselawtranslation.go.jp/law/detail/?vm=04&re=01&id=1857> accessed 22 March 2021; Gender Equality Bureau, Cabinet Office, '*Gakushū Shidō Yōryōni okeru Gijutsu Katei Hoken Taiikuno Hensen* (Transition of Technology, Home Economics, and Health and Physical Education in the Courses of Study)' <https://www.gender.go.jp/about_danjo/whitepaper/r01/zentai/html/column/clm_02.html> accessed 20 November 2022.

Subsequently, the Beijing Declaration and Platform for Action adopted on 15 September 1995 complements the implementation of CEDAW with national mechanisms for gender equality established under the framework.[263] The Basic Act for Gender Equal Society was established in 1999 and has been the basis for the Basic Plan for Gender Equality as well as for public policies for women.[264] National machinery for gender equality promotes the advancement of gender equality in law and policy, while also raising awareness of CEDAW in Japanese society.[265]

One of the normative impacts advocated by CEDAW is the internalisation of the concept of 'indirect discrimination'. In 2006, a provision concerning indirect discrimination was inserted into the revised Equal Employment Opportunity Law article 7.[266] Further, there were several legislative developments in line

---

[263] United Nations, 'Beijing Declaration and Platform for Action' <https://www.un.org/en/events/pastevents/pdfs/Beijing_Declaration_and_Platform_for_Action.pdf> accessed 3 February 2020. The Headquarters for the Promotion of Gender Equality, established within the cabinet, has the Prime Minister as president and the cabinet ministers as members. The Council for Gender Equality, an advisory organ to the Prime Minister, is chaired by the Chief Cabinet Secretary/Minister of State for Gender Equality and is composed of ministers designated and intellectuals appointed by the Prime Minister, monitoring the implementation of these policies and surveying the effects of government measures. An expert mentioned that the machineries are not functional. Interview with an International Human Rights Law Expert (Online, Paris, France, 17 February 2019).

[264] The Basic Plan for Gender Equality, initially launched in 2000, lays out the government's political priorities for gender equality. While the Basic Act for Gender Equal Society was groundbreaking, it is also criticised by some civil society groups who question the concept of gender equality in this legislation. They allege that the Japanese term *danjo kyōdō sankaku*, which the government uses to correspond to the term 'gender equality', literally means 'equal participation of men and women' in English. According to the JNNC report submitted to the Committee, 'the expression "equal participation of men and women" signifies in the text of the "Basic Act for Gender Equal Society" equal enjoyment of interests and equal sharing of responsibilities between men and women, ensured primarily by equality in opportunity of participation. While Article 3 of this Act stipulates that the Act is aimed at eliminating discrimination against women, there is no provision directly defining the guarantee of equality or the prohibition of discrimination. Moreover, the definition of discrimination in the Act is narrower than that of the Convention.' JNNC, *List of Issues and Questions from NGOs For the Japan Seventh and Eighth Periodic Reports* (JNNC 2015) <https://tbinternet.ohchr.org/Treaties/CEDAW/Shared%20Documents/JPN/INT_CEDAW_NGO_JPN_20839_E.pdf> accessed 3 August 2020.

[265] Gender Equality Bureau, 'The Organisational Structure of the National Machinery in Japan' <https://www.gender.go.jp/english_contents/about_danjo/lbp/basic/toshin-e/org-e.html> accessed 22 March 2021.

[266] Y Hayashi, '*Josei Sabetsu Teppai Jōyaku: 30nenmeno Seikato Kadai* (Convention on the Elimination of All Forms of Discrimination Against Women – Achievements and Agendas at the 30th year)' (2010) 21 *Kokusai Jinken* (International Human Rights) 100.

with the recommendations of CEDAW, such as the enactment of the Childcare Leave Law (1991) and its revisions (1995, 2001).[267]

The CEDAW recommendations also promoted legislation on violence against women, such as the enactment of the Stalker Regulation Act (2000) and the Domestic Violence Prevention Act (2001). CEDAW paved the way for the significant revision of the provision of the Penal Code on sexual violence in 2017 for the first time since its establishment 110 years ago.[268] Hayashi, a Japanese lawyer and former CEDAW Cttee member, holds that the recommendations of CEDAW helped to internalise the concept of 'violence against women' in Japanese society and led to a series of legal developments on sexual and gender-based violence.[269]

The response to the problem of human trafficking serves as an illustrative example of the combined impact of the CEDAW and other international pressures on legislative and policy development. Early in 2003, CEDAW urged the state to increase its efforts to combat the trafficking of women and girls.[270] When Japan faced further severe criticism in the US Trafficking in Persons Report for its handling of trafficking issues in 2014, the Japanese government heeded the call for action. This response encompassed the commencement of cross-ministerial meetings, the development of comprehensive action plans to combat trafficking, and the incorporation of criminal penalties for human trafficking via the revision of the Penal Code in 2005.[271, 272] From 2006 to 2007 the MOJ

---

[267] Act on Childcare Leave, Caregiver Leave, and Other Measures for the Welfare of Workers Caring for Children or Other Family Members (Act No. 76 of 1991) <https://www.japaneselawtranslation.go.jp/en/laws/view/3543/en#:~:text=Article%2016%2D5(1),caregiver%20leave%22)%20upon%20application%20to> accessed 18 September 2023.

[268] Then committee member Yoko Hayashi and women's rights activist and lawyer Yukiko Tsunoda had played an important role as norm entrepreneurs who internalised CEDAW recommendations and norms into the discussion for revision of legislations on gender-based violence as members of expert committees for the government. See A Hatano, 'A Study on Penal Code Revision and Social Movements on Sexual Violence in Japan: From the Viewpoint of Internalization of International Human Rights Norms' (2020) Asian Gender Culturology Res 73; Y Tsunoda, *Jendāto Hōritsu (Gender and Law)* (Iwanami Shoten 2013); Y Tsunoda, *Jendā Sabetsuto Bōryoku (Gender Discrimination and Violence)* (Yuhikaku 2001).

[269] Y Hayashi, '*Kōenroku 21 Seikini Okeru Kokusaijinkenhōno Yakuwari: Josei Sabetesu Teppai Iinkaino Katsudōo Reito Shite* (Lecture Record: Role of International Human Rights Law in the 21st Century: Taking the Activities of the Committee on the Elimination of Discrimination Against Women as an Example)' (2015) 11 Niben Frontier 2–6.

[270] The CEDAW Cttee already showed its concern about the sexual exploitation of migrant women in Japan early in its review of the second and third state reports. See A/50/38, 31 May 1995, para 635; A/58/38(SUPP), 17 December 2003, paras 363–364.

[271] US Department of State, 'Trafficking in Persons Report 2004' <https://2009-2017.state.gov/documents/organization/34158.pdf> accessed 22 March 2021. Japan was placed in Tier 2 watch list.

[272] Penal Code 2005, arts 226, 227.

revised its requirements for the 'entertainer visa' because of the large number of victims entering Japan on such visas. Ultimately, these actions represent the fulfillment of recommendations from treaty bodies such as the CEDAW Cttee, the HRCttee, and the CAT Cttee. Nevertheless, it is crucial to acknowledge that external influences, including pressures from the United States, and broader factors such as the global initiative against human trafficking exemplified by the adoption of the United Nations Convention against Transnational Organized Crime in 2000, might have played a significant role in shaping these actions. The interplay of these factors likely contributed to propelling these development.

Certain legislative changes were prompted by judicial decisions. Subsequent to a Supreme Court judgment discussed in the following section, the Diet amended article 733 of the Civil Code in 2016. This revision addressed the prohibition that previously prevented women from remarrying within six months after divorce, a practice that the CEDAW Cttee had consistently called upon Japan to abolish.[273] Under the revised provision, women are subject to a shorter remarriage prohibition period of 100 days, which minimises the interval where the father of a child may be redundantly presumed to be either the previous husband or the current husband at the time of the birth of a child.[274]

Japan has also enacted laws to promote the equal participation of women in economic and political fields, namely, the 2015 Act on Promotion of Women's Participation and Advancement in the Workplace and the 2018 Act on Promotion of Gender Equality in the Political Field.[275] The enactment of the former was spurred by the economic recovery policy of the government, rather than the CEDAW recommendation to increase women in leadership positions. On the other hand, the latter was the result of the active advocacy by women's rights groups that have been encouraged by the CEDAW Cttee's call for more women in political leadership and have actively engaged in the law development process with the Non-Partisan League on the Promotion of Gender Equality in the Political Field, which led the drafting process for the 2018 Act.[276] Since both

---

[273] K Ishibashi, 'Further Developments in Fukushima and Other New Movements for Implementing International Human Rights Law in Japan' in S Lee and HE Lee (eds), *Asian Yearbook of International Law, Volume 21* (Brill 2015).

[274] Civil Code 2015, art 733.

[275] Act on Promotion of Women's Participation and Advancement 2015; Act on Promotion of Gender Equality in the Political Field 2018.

[276] The Association Promoting the Quota System, or the Q Association for short, has played an active role in development process of the 2018 Act. The Q Association was established in June 2012 by Ryoko Akamatsu, former Minister for Education and former CEDAW Cttee member who had been actively working to increase the number of female Diet members and for the incorporation of a global gender equality agenda in Japan. In the fall of 2011, she called on major women's groups across the country to work on the quota system. Nine organisations, including the Japan's Association of International Women's Rights, became

5.4.2 Reliance by Judiciary

The impact of CEDAW on domestic judicial examinations and rulings is limited.[277] In 2015 and 2021 the Supreme Court upheld the constitutionality of the law that requires married couples to adopt the same surname.[278] Article 750 in the Civil Code is criticised as discriminatory law by the CEDAW Cttee, which urged the Japanese government to revise the article in order to enable women to retain their maiden surnames in its COs on the combined seventh and eighth periodic reports of Japan. In the 2015 ruling, five justices, including all three female judges, submitted their opinions that the Civil Code provision was incompatible with article 24 of the Japanese Constitution, which stipulates matrimonial equality. One of these opinions made reference to the ratification of CEDAW and its associated recommendations.[279] In the 2021 decision, dissenting opinions referred to CEDAW and pronounced the Civil Code unconstitutional. Although the Court urged the legislature to discuss this issue, discussions among lawmakers have not progressed due to the strong backlash by some conservative groups.[280]

---

the core members of the association at the request of Akamatsu. The association has enthusiastically engaged in lobbying activities while meeting with Diet members.

[277] It is also noteworthy that in the aforementioned *Children Born out of Wedlock* case the Supreme Court did not refer to CEDAW, despite its recommendations on that issue.

[278] Supreme Court, Judgment, 16 December 2015, 69–8 Minshu 2586; Supreme Court, Decision, 23 June 2021, 1488 *Hanrei Times* 94. Article 750 of Japan's Civil Code states that "A husband and wife shall adopt the surname of the husband or wife in accordance with that which is decided at the time of marriage." In reality, approximately 95,5% of the couples choose the husband's surname when getting married. Japanese Law Translation, 'Civil Code (Act No. 89 of 1896; Act No. 94 of 2013)' <https://www.japaneselawtranslation.go.jp/en/laws/view/2252> accessed 21 November 2022; Ministry of Justice, '*Sentakuteki Fūfu Bessei Seidoni Tsuite* (About the Selective Surname System for Married Couples)' <https://www.moj.go.jp/MINJI/minji36.html#Q4> accessed 21 November 2022; CEDAW/C/JPN/CO/7–8, 10 March 2016, para 12–13.

[279] Y Hayashi, '*Josei Sabetsu Teppai Jōyakuto Nihonno Kazokuhō* (CEDAW and Japanese Family Law)' in S Ninomiya and S Watanabe (eds), *Kokusaikato Kazoku* (Internationalisation and Family) (Nippon Hyoronsha 2020) 25; Association Supporting the Separate Surname Litigation, 'Top Page' <http://www.asahi-net.or.jp/~dv3m-ymsk/> accessed 13 June 2021.

[280] Since 2018 several new lawsuits over the same surname were brought before the courts. Association Supporting the Separate Surname Litigation <https://bessei2018.wixsite.com/bessei2018> accessed 22 March 2021.

In 2015, the Supreme Court of Japan ruled that the provision of Civil Code 733(1) was partially unconstitutional as it prohibited women from remarrying for a period longer than 100 days.[281] Although one Supreme Court justice mentioned the recommendations by the CEDAW Cttee and the HRCttee in a separate opinion, the majority opinion did not refer to the CEDAW Cttee,[282] even though UN bodies had adopted repeated recommendations on the issue.[283]

5.4.3   Impact on and through Non-state Actors

Empowered by the global momentum of the women's rights movement, Japanese civil society groups have been actively engaged in the state reporting system for CEDAW. This involvement, facilitated by organizations like the Japan NGO Network for CEDAW (JNNC), has allowed the coordination of diverse groups addressing various women's issues and promoting gender equality.[284] JNNC submits a comprehensive report to both the pre-session working group and the main session, and they appoint a representative to deliver oral presentations, frequently organizing a separate briefing session with committee members.[285]

CSOs not only champion specific issues concerning different groups of women but also emphasize the intersectionality of discrimination, encompassing gender and other factors, as well as the underlying structural causes and discriminatory social norms prevalent in Japan. The groups have leveraged the CEDAW recommendations in their domestic advocacy for legislative and policy changes and monitored the implementation of the recommendations. However, it is also pointed out that more follow-up activities with strategic domestic

---

281   Supreme Court (n 278); see also Waseda University Institute of Comparative Law, 'The Case in Which a Part of Article 733(1) of the Civil Code, Stipulating a Prohibition Period for Remarriage Specific to Women, was Ruled as Unconstitutional' <https://www.waseda.jp/folaw/icl/news/2017/03/29/5721/> accessed 22 March 2021.

282   Supreme Court (n 278).

283   Eg, A/49/38, 12 April 1994, paras 35–6 and CEDAW/C/JPN/CO/6, 7 August 2009, paras 17–8, which is also highlighted in their follow-up procedure. Hayashi (2020) points out that even though the Supreme Court did not make explicit mention of those recommendations, the international trend that the court considered in its judgment includes the existence of those recommendations. Hayashi (n 115) 23.

284   JNNC, a coalition of Japanese CSOs, was established on 23 December 2002, in alignment with the consideration of the 4th and 5th periodic reports of Japan at the 29th session of CEDAW in 2003.

285   Y Yamashita, 'Tokushu – Josei sabetsu teppai jōyaku 30 shūnen NGO no shiten kara: Sōron – Jikkosei Kakuho to NGO no Yakuwari (General Comment – How to Secure Effectiveness of CEDAW and the Role of NGOs – Special Edition: 30 Years Anniversary of CEDAW from the NGO Perspective)' (2015) 29 Kokusai Josei (International Women) 38.

movement, rather than focusing on obtaining recommendations from CEDAW, are necessary for effective implementation of the recommendations.[286]

The international lobbying efforts of civil society groups had a significant impact on empowering plaintiffs in gender discrimination cases.[287] In 1994, two women who had endured workplace discrimination based on their gender received support from a civil society group to attend a session of the state report review. During this session, they presented their case as a stark illustration of gender inequality in the Japanese workplace. This experience and the recommendation of CEDAW declaring this issue as an 'indirect discrimination' encouraged the two women to bring the case to the domestic court.[288] This move, and the public appeal they made for their case in front of the Japanese media, marked a significant step in their subsequent activities to seek gender equality.

There have been continuous legal efforts to address gender-based unfair treatment utilizing CEDAW. In 2000, when asked about the legality of the wage gap between men and women, the Osaka District Court in the first instance turned down the plaintiff's claims based on CEDAW, asserting that the Convention did not have a retroactive effect on cases predating its ratification.[289] However, for the examination of the appealed case in the Osaka High Court, many legal experts, scholars specialising international human rights law, provided their opinions criticising the judgment of the first court. CSOs appealed to the general public in and outside of the country about the gender discriminatory practices of Japanese companies and the gender bias in the Japanese judiciary.[290] The plaintiffs also participated in the CEDA session for Japan's state reporting in July 2003 to lobby the Committee and deliver a discussion on the judicial examination back home.[291] The COs by CEDA Cttee in

---

[286] Interview with an International Human Rights Law Expert (Geneva, Switzerland, 11 February 2019).

[287] The *Sumitomo Electric* case. Osaka High Court, Recommendation of Reconciliation, 24 December 2003; see also Kelly Barret, 'Women in the Workplace: Sexual Discrimination in Japan' (2004) 11 HRB 5.

[288] Y Yamashita, *CEDAW and Japan* (Shogakusha 2010) 316–7.

[289] Osaka District Court, Judgment, 31 July 2000, 1080 Hanrei Times 126. The Equal Employment Opportunity Law and CEDAW do not allow a company or the state party to redress the practice prior to their entry into force.

[290] See the Working Women's Network, 'WWIN News NO.13 Sept. 7. 2003' <http://wwn-net.org/english/2008/10/10> accessed 21 November 2022.

[291] M Miyachi, '*Tokushu 1–Daisankai Nihon Repōto Shingi Forōappu (5) Sumitomo Denkō Danjo Chingin Sabetsu Soshō Shori Wakai de Kaiketsu* (Special Edition 1 Follow-up to the 3rd Review of the State Report of Japan (5): Sumitomo Electric Case on the Discriminatory Wage Gap Between Men and Women)' (2004) 18 Kokusai Josei (International Women) 67.

August 2003 recommended that the Japanese government take action to close the existing wage gap and prevent direct and indirect discrimination against women.[292] The CEDAW Cttee recommendations played a pivotal role in providing a foundation for the plaintiffs to build their cases during court-mediated settlement discussions.[293] Consequently, the settlement record from the Osaka High Court issued on 1 December 2003 emphasized the global consensus that strives for an egalitarian society for both men and women, The record encapsulates the idea of women cultivating their skills and abilities without encountering discrimination, ensuring every woman's right to benefit from reforms aimed at eradicating gender discrimination, including the ratification of CEDAW and the enactment of the Equal Employment Opportunity Law.[294]

5.4.4 Impact of State Reporting

The CEDAW state reporting had a significant impact on cases regarding the dual-track employment system practised by the corporate sector, which indirectly discriminated against women in terms of promotion and wages. Encouraged by the moral support of the Committee during the session for state reporting in 1994, female employees working for *Sumitomo Electric* filed a lawsuit against the company, seeking compensation for indirect discrimination against them in 1995.[295] In the following years, *Sumitomo Chemical* and *Sumitomo Metal* also faced similar lawsuits from female employees.[296] In this case of *Sumitomo Group*, the complainants also sued the Japanese government for failing to implement article 2 of CEDAW. This lawsuit, the first case in which the Japanese court interpreted CEDAW, attracted considerable media attention, which exerted pressure on the Japanese government to take measures against gender discrimination in the workplace.

In its COs adopted in 2003, 2006, 2009, and 2016, the CEDAW Cttee expressed its concern over gender inequality in family law, whose wording has become stronger as time passed. In the follow-up procedure for the COs, the Committee

---

[292] A/58/38(SUPP), 18 Aug 2003.
[293] MOJ (n 107).
[294] Working Women's Network, '*Wakai Kankoku* (Settlement Recommendation)' (1 December 2003) <http://wwn-net.org/wp-content/themes/WWN/pdf/07.pdf> accessed 3 February 2020.
[295] See L Savery, *Engendering the State: The International Diffusion of Women's Human Rights* (Routledge 2007) 147–85.
[296] M Miyachi, 'Sumitomo Mēkā Danjo Chingin Sabetsu Soshō Kara Mita Kaisei Kintōhōno Mondaiten (Problems of the Revised Equal Employment Law as Seen in the Sumitomo Group Gender-based Wage Discrimination Case)' (2006) 20 Kokusai Josei (International Women) 128.

highlighted gender equality upon marriage.[297] The Committee took as a positive change that a Bill was submitted in March 2018 to the National Diet with a proposition to raise the legal age for marriage for women to 18 years, making 18 the marriageable age for both men and women, in alignment with the 2009 CEDAW Cttee recommendation. The Committee also welcomed the adoption of the Act for the Partial Revision of the Civil Code, which shortened the period of prohibition of remarriage from six months to 100 days. However, the CEDAW showed its concerns as Japanese government has taken no legislative steps to allow optional separate surnames for married couples and to abolish the period for prohibition of remarriage for women. This suggests that CEDAW recommendations have initiated incremental changes in family law. However, certain legislative adjustments might necessitate waiting for a shift in social norms, which often requires persistent efforts through multi-layered awareness-raising campaigns and sensitization, coupled with human rights litigation, to reach the tipping point in public opinion.

CEDAW's recommendation in its COs adopted in March 2016 on forced sterilisation under the old Eugenic Protection Act also became a trigger for nationwide discussions and lawsuits.[298] The recommendation, which called for the clarification of facts, the prosecution and punishment of perpetrators, and remedies for victims, gained traction within the Diet. Subsequently, the Ministry of Health, Labour, and Welfare initiated interviews with the alleged victims.[299] This development prompted the victims to file lawsuits seeking redress for illegal forced sterilizations under the now-defunct Eugenic Protection Act. Starting with the pioneering case filed in the Sendai District Court in January 2018, several similar lawsuits have since emerged across the country.[300] The bipartisan parliamentary group and the working group of the

---

[297] CEDAW/C/JPN/CO/7-8/Add.1.
[298] Under the Eugenic Protection Act (effective from 1948–1996) the state sought to prevent births of children with diseases or disabilities and, as a result, subjected persons with disabilities to forced sterilisation. This recommendation of CEDAW made clear the intersectional forms of discrimination of women with disabilities.
[299] IMADR, 'Yūsei Hogohō Mondaiga Nagekakeru Mono (What the Eugenics Protection Act Issue Highlights)' <https://imadr.net/books/199_2/> accessed 22 March 2021.
[300] A total of 20 people have filed lawsuits in seven district courts across Japan demanding compensation for the treatment they suffered under the law. The first ruling of the Sendai court in May 2019 held that the old eugenics law was unconstitutional, but it rejected damages for victims. 'Japan Court Rules Old Eugenics Law Unconstitutional, but Rejects Damages for Victims' *Mainichi* (28 May 2019) <https://mainichi.jp/english/articles/20190528/p2a/00m/0na/013000c> accessed 11 July 2021; S Yoshimoto, 'Forced Sterilisations in Japan: The Push for Justice' (7 August 2018) <https://www.nippon.com/en/currents/d00421/> accessed 13 June 2021.

ruling party to address this issue were quickly established. In April 2018, the 'Law on a Lump Sum Payment to those who underwent eugenic surgery based on the former Eugenic Protection Law' was enacted.[301]

5.4.5 Other Forms of Impact

Alongside the movement for gender mainstreaming, the 2000s was also the period when so-called 'backlash' surged against the gender equal law and policy which had advanced after the ratification of CEDAW.[302] Conservatives became proactive in opposition to feminism, the 1999 Basic Act for Gender Equal Society, and the recommendations by the CEDAW Committee, deeming them excessively radical and potentially undermining traditional values. This anti-feminist movement has grown and intertwined with nationalist agenda, often resulted in statements against the CEDAW and its recommendations, particularly concerning issues related to national history, such as the so-called comfort women.[303] The CEDAW Cttee criticised the 2015 agreement between Japan and the Republic of Korea on the comfort women issue as it considered the agreement to have dismissed the views of the victims.[304] In response, right-wing groups in Japan launched retaliatory actions then-Japanese CEDAW member Yoko Hayashi. In 2016, *Ianfuno Shinjitsu Kokumin Undō* ('Truth of Comfort Women' National Movement) submitted a petition to the MOFA asking for her immediate dismissal from the position under the auspices of a member of the House of Councillors.[305]

5.4.6 Brief Conclusion

CEDAW made a substantial impact on shaping law and policy for gender equality under the national machinery for the promotion of gender equality despite gender backlash from conservative politicians and civil society actors. Even

---

301 This is the law concerning lump sum payment to those who have undergone eugenic surgery based on the former Eugenic Protection Law 2019. This quick measure was appreciated at large, however, the victims lamented that the amount of 3,2 million yen per person is not at all sufficient. IMADR (n 299).
302 Japan Women's Study Association and others, *Q&A Danjo Kyōdō Sankaku Gendā Furī Basshingu (Q&A Gender Equality Gender Free Bashing)* (Akashi Shoten 2006).
303 See n 89. Those official statements against international human rights and gender norms have gained the support of conservative civic groups.
304 CEDAW/C/JPN/CO/7–8, paras 28–29.
305 Sankei Shimbun, '*Kokuren Nihonjin Iinchō Sokuji Kaininseyo Ianfu Mondai Futō Kenkai Kokumin Undōga Gaishō Ateni Shomei Teishutsu* (UN Japanese Chair "Must be Immediately Dismissed" over Unjust Views on Comfort Women Issue: 'National Movement' Submitted Petition to Foreign Minister)' (28 November 2016) <http://www.sankei.com/politics/news/161128/plt1611280006-n1.html> accessed 25 January 2020.

indirectly, it exerted a significant influence on the discourse within the women's movement as a legitimate guideline, empowering women, feminists, and civil society groups to be change agents in advocacy and lobbying for gender equality at both international and domestic levels. Despite certain legislative advancements, the adoption of a gender perspective has not yet become mainstream within Japan's judicial system. Consequently, CEDAW's impact on the judiciary remains limited, with only a few cases directly referencing CEDAW in a favourable manner within their judgments. Despite Japanese women having attained some legal equality in these legislative advancements, deep-rooted cultural and social norms have, in practical terms, have hindered greater progress in gender equality, resulting in the country lagging behind in numerous areas.[306] Article 5 of CEDAW stipulates that to make a legal framework effective to ensure gender equality, there must be a shift in social and cultural patterns of behavior away from entrenched stereotypes and prejudices. As illustrated in this section, further realisation of this goal will require both legal advocacy and social awareness campaigns to internalise the principle of gender equality outlined in CEDAW at the domestic level.

5.5 Convention against Torture and Other Cruel, Inhuman, or Degrading Treatment or Punishment

5.5.1 Incorporation and Reliance by Legislature and Executive Powers

The Constitution of Japan prohibits torture.[307] After the ratification of CAT, article 3(1) (*non-refoulement* principle) was explicitly incorporated into the Immigration Control and Refugee Recognition Act article 53(2) in its revision in 2009.[308] However, as is examined in the part on CCPR, the recommendation regarding criminal justice issues such as the death penalty, the substitute detention system and the improvement of the conditions of detention have not seen a positive response by the government.[309]

---

306 See World Economic Forum (n 8).
307 Constitution of Japan, art 36 ('The infliction of torture by any public officer and cruel punishments are absolutely forbidden').
308 Y Ando, '*Gaikokujinno Taikyo Kyōseini Okeru Gōmontō Kinshi Jōyakuno Nonrufuruman Gensokuno Katsuyō* (How to apply the principle of *non-refoulement* under the Convention against Torture concerning deportation of foreigners)' (2010) 2 Migration Policy Review 90.
309 See the part of general attitude towards the UN treaty system. See also the part of CRC for the revision of law on corporal punishment.

5.5.2 Reliance by Judiciary

CAT article 3 (*non-refoulement*) has a tangible impact on the Japanese judiciary. For example, the Osaka High Court referred to the spirit of CAT article 3 when declaring the deportation of a refugee illegal.[310] In another case, the Osaka High Court referred to the Immigration Control and Refugee Recognition Act article 53(2), which incorporates CAT article 3(1) when declaring that an Iranian national 'cannot be deported' to Iran.[311]

5.5.3 Impact on and through Non-state Actors

Various CSOs submit their reports to CAT for a review of state reports.[312] The information covered various torture-related issues, including asylum-seeking processes, prisoners' rights, criminal investigation methods, domestic violence, violence against children, abortion, detention of people with disabilities, workers' rights, minority rights, and the so-called comfort women issue. In the CSO reporting to CAT, in particular about issues in the criminal justice system, JFBA lawyers played a central role. They incorporated the CAT recommendations into their domestic advocacy, but their efforts and activities have not garnered widespread support from the general public. Consequently, they did not witness significant legal and systemic changes aligned with the CAT recommendations.[313]

5.5.4 Impact of State Reporting

While the government had to submit a report within one year after joining the treaty in 1999, the initial report had been submitted with a delay in 2005. The broad range of recommendations issued in 2007 did not progress further and were repeated in the second COs in 2013.[314] In particular, in the follow-up procedure for COs considering the 2nd report, the Committee highlighted some important issues. A positive advancement regarding inadmissibility in court of confessions obtained under torture and ill-treatment, the Code of Criminal Procedure was revised in 2017 to include an obligation to take audio-video recordings of the entire process of interrogations in line with the CAT Cttee's recommendations. The domestic impact of the COs has been harshly limited because of the conservative position of the government. In relation to the CAT Cttee's recommendations regarding the comfort women issue, the

---

310 Osaka High Court, Judgment, 15 June 2005, TKC 28111464.
311 Osaka High Court, Judgment, 27 November 2015, 2015WLJPCA11276001.
312 OHCHR (n 159).
313 See JFBA, *Gomon Kinshi Jōyaku Houkokusho Shinsa* (Review of CAT State reports, <https://www.nichibenren.or.jp/activity/international/library/human_rights/torture_report.html>
314 COs on the second periodic report of Japan, adopted by the Committee at its 50th session (6–31 May 2013). CAT/C/JPN/CO/2, 28 June 2013.

cabinet expressed its position that those 'recommendations are not legally binding and ... do not impose an obligation on States Parties to the Convention to follow them'.[315]

5.5.5 Brief Conclusion

Some positive impacts of CAT are observed in the legislative and judicial incorporation of *non-refoulement* clauses. Nonetheless, the executive body restricted the normative significance of the CAT Cttee recommendations by rejecting the legal bindingness of the COs.

5.6 *Convention on the Rights of the Child*

5.6.1 Incorporation and Reliance by Legislature and Executive Powers

At the time of the ratification of CRC, there was no development of a new law or revision of the existing law, as the government considered that there was no inconsistency between CRC and domestic laws.[316] After the ratification of CRC, several legislations were enacted, including the Act on Promotion of Development and Support for Children and Young People (2009).[317] The Act was enacted to support the government's efforts to respect the best interests of children and young people with reference to CRC in its very first section.[318] In 2016, the government enacted and implemented the revised Child Welfare Act, of which article 1 clearly states that it embraces the principles of 'the Convention of the Rights of the Child'.[319] The Child Welfare Act attempts to protect children's rights and the rights of persons with disabilities in alignment

---

[315] House of Councillors, '*Tōbensho Dai n8 Gō* (Written Response No 118)' <https://www.sangiin.go.jp/japanese/joho1/kousei/syuisyo/183/toup/t183118.pdf> accessed 9 January 2020.

[316] M Ishikawa and A Morita (eds), *Jidōno Kenri Jōyaku: Sono Naiyō Kadaito Taiō* (Convention of the Rights of the Child: Its Content, Challenges and Response) (Ichiryusha 1995).

[317] Headquarters for Promotion of Development and Support for Children and Young People, 'Vision for Children and Young People' (Cabinet Office, July 2010) <http://www8.cao.go.jp/youth/suisin/pdf/vision_english.pdf> accessed 26 January 2020. An expert commented that the law was enacted when the DPJ was in power and has been weakened since the conservative LDP returned to power. This may explain how political dynamics affect the implementation of the treaty obligations and recommendations. Interview with an International Human Rights Law Expert (Geneva, Switzerland, 17 February 2019).

[318] Cabinet Office, '*Kodomo Wakamono Ikusei Shien Suishinhō* (the Act on Promotion of Development and Support for Children and Young People)' <https://www8.cao.go.jp/youth/whitepaper/h22honpenhtml/html/honpen/sanko_01.html> accessed 26 January 2020.

[319] Government of Japan, '*Jidō Fukushi Hō* (Child Welfare Act)' <https://elaws.e-gov.go.jp/search/elawsSearch/elaws_search/lsg0500/detail?lawId=322AC0000000164_20180402_429AC0000000069&openerCode=1#A> accessed 25 January 2020.

with international human rights law.[320] A number of municipal governments set ordinances on children's rights to implement the principles of CRC in their local context.[321]

5.6.2 Reliance by Judiciary

CRC has had a significant impact on the Japanese judiciary. For example, the Supreme Court referred to CRC together with CCPR for children born out of wedlock and the *Nationality Act* case.[322] It is noteworthy that the Supreme Court also referred to the recommendations of the CRC Cttee. Article 3 of CRC (best interests of children) was refereed by a lower court in a case that nullified the deportation of children of illegal immigrants to Iran.[323]

5.6.3 Impact on and through Non-state Actors

Many CSOs have provided parallel reports to the CRC Cttee at the state report review on various issues regarding children's rights.[324] However, the CSOs are not coordinated in the development and submission of their reports and lobbying the CRC Cttee in the sessions, particularly when compared to such engagement with the CEDAW Cttee.[325]

Some major CSOs actively promote CRC and its Committee's recommendations at the domestic level. For example, as part of the advocacy effort of prohibiting corporal punishment, Save the Children Japan conducted a survey and events and campaigns to raise public awareness.[326] These efforts led to the amendment of the law on corporal punishment in line with the recommendations of the CRC Cttee.[327]

---

[320] The 'family-based care' principle of the 2016 Child Welfare Act guarantees a family setting, such as adoption and foster care, for children unable to live with their birth parents; laws to ban corporal punishment against children by parents and other guardians; revision of the basic law to protect the rights of people with disabilities in 2011. See the revision of the Child Abuse Prevention Act and the Civil Code in line with CRC in the following section.

[321] General Research Institute of the Convention of the Rights of the Child, '*Kodomono Kenri Jōreitōwo Seiteisuru Jichitai Ichiran* (List of Local Governments that Enact Child Rights Ordinances, etc)' <http://npocrc.a.la9.jp/siryou/siryou_jyorei.htm> accessed 22 March 2021.

[322] For the *Nationality Act* case, see the section above on reliance by judiciary under CCPR.

[323] Tokyo District Court, Judgment, 19 September 2003, TKC 28082829.

[324] See OHCHR (n 159).

[325] Interviews with an International Human Rights Law Expert (Geneva, Switzerland, 11 February 2019), and a Child Rights Advocate (Geneva, Switzerland, 17 January 2019).

[326] Save the Children Japan, '*Sankō Shiryō Ichiran* (Reference List)' <https://www.savechildren.or.jp/lp/phpreference/> accessed 22 March 2021.

[327] See the next section on the impact of state reporting.

The UNICEF National Committee and the UNICEF Tokyo Office also engaged in awareness-raising activities of CRC in Japan. In particular, the UNICEF National Committee has published more than 13 reports on child poverty in developed countries, including Japan, and engaged in research and advocacy for issues regarding children's rights.[328] However, while in developing countries, recommendations from the CRC Cttee may be incorporated into programmes of support and cooperation by UNICEF and other UN agencies and international CSOs, such opportunities and processes are very limited in developed countries such as Japan.[329]

5.6.4 Impact of State Reporting

The COs had a great impact on the discussion for the revision of domestic laws by raising questions on various legal provisions that the government did not consider to be a problem in terms of CRC, or which it did not even discuss at the time of ratification. One of the observable impacts of the CRC Cttee recommendations is the ratification of the Hague Convention on the Civil Aspects of International Child Abduction.[330] Against the background of increasing pressure at the international level and the CRC Cttee's COs on the second periodic report of Japan, the government took legislative measures to ratify the Convention in 2013.[331] Otani, a Japanese lawyer, international human rights law expert and CRC Cttee member, points out that the amendment of the Hague Convention Implementation Act in 2019 was also in line with the recommendations of the CRC Cttee on the combined fourth and fifth periodic report.[332]

---

[328] UNICEF National Committee, '*Kodomono Hinkon Mondai* (Issue of Child Poverty)' <https://www.unicef.or.jp/about_unicef/advocacy/about_ad_poverty.html> accessed 2 February 2020.

[329] Interview with an international human rights law expert (Geneva, Switzerland, 11 February 2019).

[330] Hague Conference on Private International Law, '28. Convention on the Civil Aspects of International Child Abduction' (concluded 25 October 1980) <https://assets.hcch.net/docs/e86d9f72-dc8d-46f3-b3bf-e102911c8532.pdf> accessed 21 November 2022.

[331] M Otani, '*Kodomono Kenri Jōyaku*' ('The Convention on the Rights of the Child') in Syuhei Ninomiya (ed), *Gendai Kazokuhō Kōza: Kokusaikato Kazoku (Contemporary Family Law: Internationalisation and Family)* (Nihon Hyoronsya 2021) 29–55.

[332] ibid 45. See also MOFA, 'Outline of Amendment of the Hague Convention Implementation Act' <https://www.mofa.go.jp/mofaj/files/100039100.pdf> accessed 22 March 2021; CRC Cttee, 'Concluding Observations on the Combined Fourth and Fifth Periodic Reports of Japan' (CRC/C/JPN/CO/4–5, 5 March 2019) para 31.

In the COs on the combined fourth and fifth periodic reports of Japan, the CRC Cttee urged the government to prohibit all corporal punishment in law, particularly in the Child Abuse Prevention Act and the Civil Code,[333] referring to their General Comment 8[334] on the right of the child to be protected from corporal punishment and other cruel or degrading forms of punishment and reiterating their previous recommendation to Japan.[335] This was followed by the amendment of the Child Welfare Act and the Child Abuse Prevention Act in 2019 to strengthen measures to prevent child abuse 'in accordance with the international progress in the protection of children's rights'.[336] On 24 May 2019, the House of Representatives approved the revised Act, along with a supplementary resolution, which urges the government to take appropriate measures to 'develop guidelines that provide concrete examples with reference to the CRC at an early stage in promoting parenting that does not involve corporal punishment'.[337] Likewise, the House of Councillors adopted another supplementary resolution, including the same text, along with the revised Act on 19 June 2019.[338] The CRC Cttee's COs on the fourth and fifth periodic reports regarding corporal punishment were also expressly cited in the discussion for reviewing article 822 of the Civil Code on parental discipline.[339]

---

333 CRC Cttee (n 332) para 26.
334 CRC Cttee, 'General Comment No 8 (2006): The Right of the Child to Protection from Corporal Punishment and Other Cruel or Degrading Forms of Punishment' (CRC/C/GC/8, 2 March 2007).
335 CRC Cttee, 'Concluding Observations on the Third Periodic Report of Japan' (CRC/C/JPN/CO/3, 20 June 2010) para 48.
336 House of Representatives, *Jidō Gyakutai Bōshi Taisakuno Kyōkawo Hakarutameno Jidō Fukushi Hōno Ichibuwo Kaiseisuru Hōritsuanni Taisuru Futai Ketsugi* (Supplementary Resolution on the Revision on the Child Welfare Act and the Child Abuse Prevention Act)' <http://www.shugiin.go.jp/internet/itdb_rchome.nsf/html/rchome/Futai/kourouAA374A90540C32634925840400355A30.htm> accessed 9 January 2021; CRC Cttee (n 332) paras 25–6. See art 14 of the revised Act on the Prevention, etc of Child Abuse promulgated on 26 June 2019, and which entered into effect on 1 April 2020. Government of Japan, *Jidō Gyakutaino Bōshitōni Kansuru Hōritsu* (Act on the Prevention, etc of Child Abuse)' (promulgated on 26 June 2019) <https://elaws.e-gov.go.jp/search/elawsSearch/elaws_search/lsg0500/detail?lawId=412AC1000000082> accessed 9 January 2020.
337 House of Representatives, '198th Diet Session, House of Representatives' Committee on Health, Labour and Welfare' (24 May 2019) <https://kokkai.ndl.go.jp/#/detail?minId=119804260X02120190524&spkNum=284&single> accessed 9 January 2020.
338 House of Councillors, '198th Diet Session, House of Councillors, Main Conference, No 27' (19 June 2019) <https://kokkai.ndl.go.jp/#/detailPDF?minId=119815254X02720190619&page=36&spkNum=60&current=3> accessed 9 January 2020.
339 House of Representative, '198th Diet Session, Plenary Session of the House of Representative, No 23' (5 June 2019) <https://kokkai.ndl.go.jp/#/detail?minId=119815254X02320190605&current=1> accessed 12 November 2022; Legislative Council of the Ministry

There have been other revisions of the domestic legislation and policies in line with the provisions of CRC and the recommendations of the CRC Cttee.[340]

5.6.5 Other Forms of Impact

While nearly all junior high and high school textbooks introduce the principles of CRC, this introduction remains limited and falls short of fostering systematic participation of children in safeguarding their own rights through the utilization of human rights treaty mechanisms and principles.[341] The Special Rapporteur on the Sale of Children, Child Prostitution, and Child Pornography visited Japan in 2015 as part of her work to draft a report on the sexual exploitation of children in Japan. In her statement on the 31st session of the Human Rights Council on 8 March 2016, she urged the government to fully ban the so-called JK business, which targeted high school-aged girls, potentially leading to their sexual abuse and exploitation, with reference to OP-CRC-SC.[342] Responding to the surge of criticism of the "JK business", the Tokyo metropolitan government adopted relevant ordinances in 2017 with the police conducting surveys and the investigations into the issue.[343]

---

of Justice, Working Group on Civil Code, 2nd session (10 September 2019) <https://www.moj.go.jp/shingi1/shingi04900402.html > accessed 12 November 2022.

340 For example, the revision of the Civil Code in 2018 that sets the minimum age of marriage at 18 years for both women and men; the amendment to the Penal Code in 2017; the amendment of the Act on Regulation and Punishment of Acts Relating to Child Prostitution and Child Pornography and the Protection of Children, in 2014, which now criminalises the possession of child pornography; the law development in 2016 and revision of the Civil Code in 2019 on child adoption; the revision of the Civil Enforcement Law in 2019 on child support; and the Domestic Relations Case Procedure Act 2011 to ensure the right of children to have their views heard. For the influence on family law, see Otani (n 331) 29–55.

341 S Yamagishi, 'Kodomo (jidou) no kenri joyaku (CRC)' (1996) 2 Journal of Child Study 131.

342 OHCHR, 'Statement by Ms Maud De Boer-Buquicchio, Special Rapporteur on the Sale of Children, Child Prostitution and Child Pornography at the 31st Session of the Human Rights Council' (8 March 2016) <https://www.ohchr.org/EN/NewsEvents/Pages/DisplayNews.aspx?NewsID=19975&LangID=E> accessed 25 January 2020; her statement that 13% of schoolgirls in Japan had experienced Enjo Kosai (compensated dating) was severely criticised as clueless by Japan's MOFA and so was her report. MOFA, 'Reply from the Special Rapporteur on the Sale of Children, Child Prostitution and Child Pornography' (11 November 2015) <http://www.mofa.go.jp/press/release/press4e_000915.html> accessed 25 January 2020. A/HRC/31/58/Add.1, 3 March 2016; A/HRC/31/58/Add.3, 7 March 2016.

343 Tokyo Metropolitan Government Human Rights Division, 'The Issue of Children's Rights' <https://www.fukushi.metro.tokyo.lg.jp/jicen/annai/keriyougo.html>accessed15September 2023; Tokyo Metropolitan Government, 'Tokutei Isei Sekkyaku Eigyōtōno Kiseini Kansuru Jōrei (The Ordinance on Business with Specific Service to the Customer of the Opposite Sex)' <https://www.keishicho.metro.tokyo.jp/about_mpd/keiyaku_horei_kohyo/horei_jorei

5.6.6 Brief Conclusion

The influence of the CRC is evident across various domains, especially through its integration and reliance by the legislature and executive authorities to safeguard the rights of children. This is exemplified by the revisions made to numerous laws and policies pertaining to child rights. Domestic advocacy and awareness-raising campaigns of civil society groups have promoted the government's implementation of CRC and the Committee's recommendations. However, a survey has revealed that only a limited number of individuals are familiar with CRC and its content.[344] This underscores the need for increased efforts to raise awareness about CRC.

5.7 International Convention for the Protection of All Persons from Enforced Disappearance

5.7.1 Incorporation and Reliance by Legislature and Executive Powers

Japan signed CED in 2007 as the first state to do so in the Asia-Pacific region and ratified it based on the unanimous approval of both the House of Representatives and the House of Councillors in 2009. The state has shown great interest in raising international awareness of the issue of enforced disappearances against the background of the abductions of Japanese citizens by North Korea.[345] In 2009, together with CAT and the 1951 Refugee Convention, article 16(1) of CED was incorporated as grounds for non-extradition in the revised Immigration Control and Refugee Recognition Act.[346]

Despite its political appeal at the international level, the Japanese legal system has not been fully consistent with the Convention's standards. Some measures were taken in line with the Convention in the field of trafficking in persons and child prostitution and pornography.[347] However, the Committee, in its COs on the first report submitted by Japan,[348] expressed its concerns

---

/jkbusiness_reg.files/jorei.pdf> accessed 12 July 2021; National Police Agency, *"JK Bijinesu" no Eigyō Jittaitōno Chōsa Kekka* (Results of the Survey on the Situation of "JK Business"') <https://www.npa.go.jp/safetylife/syonen/R1all-JK-chosa.pdf> accessed 12 July 2021.

344 See Save the Children Japan (n 96). The survey indicates only 8,9% of children and 2,2% of adults know the content of CRC, and 31,5% of children and 42,9% of adults have never heard about CRC.

345 CRC, Consideration of reports submitted by state parties under article 29 (1) of the convention, reports of state parties due in 2012 (CED/C/JPN/1, 25 August 2016) paras 2–3.

346 Government of Japan (n 211) art 53, para 3.

347 COs on the report submitted by Japan under art 29(1) of the Convention, CED/C/JPN/CO/1, 19 November 2018. However, as examined in the previous parts, it is not clear whether these developments are an impact of CED and the CED Cttee's recommendations.

348 CED/C/JPN/CO/1, 5 December 2018, paras 11–44.

over a number of issues.[349] In particular, the Committee showed concerns on the lack of an absolute prohibition of enforced disappearance, the offence of enforced disappearance and fundamental legal safeguards in domestic law. The Japanese government was requested to provide information on its implementation of recommendations within one year after the issuance of the COs.[350]

The extensive list of issues highlighted in the COs reveals the ambivalence of the government's attitude in international and domestic arenas. The discord between international and domestic discourses can also be seen at a more fundamental level. For example, international law scholar and former CED member Kimio Yakushiji has drawn attention to the disparity between the CED and the Japanese government regarding the definition and criminalisation of enforced disappearance. Yakushiji emphasizes that the Japanese government asserts that its existing legal framework is comprehensive enough, and additional provisions are unnecessary to define enforced disappearance as a standalone crime. However, this stance is considered insufficient by the CED Committee.[351]

5.7.2 Reliance by Judiciary

The Osaka High Court referred to the Immigration Control and Refugee Recognition Act 53.3, which incorporates CED 16(1) when declaring that an Iranian national 'cannot be deported' to due to the high risk of the complainant being sentenced to death in Iran.[352]

---

349 ibid. The issues highlighted in the COs include: the lack of legislative and executive measures in the prohibition and offence of enforced disappearances; appropriate penalties and mitigating and aggravating circumstances; criminal responsibility of superiors and due obedience; statute of limitations; jurisdiction over offences of enforced disappearances; reporting and investigating cases of enforced disappearances; judicial cooperation in criminal matters; expulsion, return, surrender and extradition mechanisms; fundamental legal safeguards; remedies concerning the lawfulness of a detention; registers of persons deprived of liberty; training on the Convention; the definition of 'victim' and the right to obtain reparation and prompt, fair, and adequate compensation; the legal situation of disappeared persons and their relatives, and legislation concerning the wrongful removal of children.

350 CED/C/JPN/CO/1, 5 December 2018, para 48.

351 K Yakushiji, 'Kyōsei Shissō Jōyakuni Okeru "Kyōsei Shissō" no Teigito Sono Kokunai Hanzaika Gimu (Definition of "Enforced Disappearance" under the Convention on Enforced Disappearances and Obligation of Domestic Criminalisation)' (2019) 24 Kenkyū Kiyō (Research Bulletin) 1 <https://khrri.or.jp/publication/docs/2019070 24001%281.102KB%29.pdf> accessed 22 November 2022.

352 Osaka High Court, Judgment, 27 November 2015, 2015WLJPCA11276001. In the Osaka High Court judgement, the deportation of the Iranian man itself was held to be lawful but the part of the ruling of the first instance that Iran was the destination of repatriation was declared illegal and ordered to be annulled.

5.7.3 Impact on and through Non-state Actors

There were three submissions from CSOs for the first review of the state party report in 2018.[353] In addition to the JFBA, which addressed criminal justice issues as they did with the HRCttee and the CAT Cttee, other CSOs requested the CED Cttee to urge the state to conduct thorough fact-finding research into so-called comfort women issues and to ensure the rights to truth and reparations of the victims/survivors.[354] The CED Cttee urged the Japanese government to take action on this issue.[355]

5.7.4 Impact of State Reporting

Japan submitted its first report in 2016, and the CED Cttee adopted the COs for this report in 2018. Additional follow-up information was provided by the government in 2020.

In responding to the COs, the government representative sent a letter to the chairperson of the Committee to raise opposition to their view pertinent to comfort women.[356] The Japanese government showed a grave concern regarding the recommendation, as it holds that the issue should not be examined by the Committee *ratione temporis* under article 35(1) of the Convention.[357] Further, it maintains that the COs include factual errors on the issue and do not reflect the information provided by the Japanese government to the Committee. The Japanese government holds that it is inappropriate for the CED Cttee to express regret regarding the agreement between Japan and South Korea on the comfort women's issue that the issue was resolved finally and irreversibly.[358]

5.7.5 Brief Conclusion

Despite its generally plausible attitude toward ratification of international treaties in general, Japan has shown its willingness to ratify CED at an early

---

[353] For example, WAM, 'Japan's Military Sexual Slavery Issue' <https://tbinternet.ohchr.org/Treaties/CED/Shared%20Documents/JPN/INT_CED_CSS_JPN_32734_E.pdf> accessed 2 February 2020.

[354] ibid; Korean Council for the Women Drafted for Military Sexual Slavery by Japan, 'Written Submission by The Korean Council for the Women Drafted for Military Sexual Slavery by Japan for the Committee on Enforced Disappearances (CED) 15th Session (05–16 November 2018), Japan' <https://tbinternet.ohchr.org/Treaties/CED/Shared%20Documents/JPN/INT_CED_CSS_JPN_32759_E.pdf> accessed 22 March 2021.

[355] CED/C/JPN/1, 25 August 2016, paras 25–6.

[356] MOFA, 'Letter to the CED Chair' (30 November 2018) <http://www.mofa.go.jp/mofaj/files/000424972.pdf> accessed 2 February 2020.

[357] ibid.

[358] ibid.

instance and has made active efforts to raise international awareness about enforced disappearances by promoting other countries to ratify CED. The Convention has exerted domestic impacts in Japan by transforming some national legal schemes in conformity with its criteria, such as the revision of the Immigration Control Act. The impact on judicial decisions has been observed in the application of the domestic legal provisions incorporating CED. However, when it comes to politically sensitive issues such as comfort women, the government does not hesitate to take an opposing position against the CED Cttee. The number of CSOs to submit information to the Committee in the state periodic report has been smaller than for other treaties, which may be due to the limited scope of the Convention. Given the small number of CSOs engaged, as well as the fact that most of the issues dealt with by CED are highly sensitive, long-standing, unresolved matters also related to other treaty bodies, it remains unclear whether CED would have a unique impact on the progress of those issues at the domestic level.

5.8 Convention on the Rights of Persons with Disabilities

5.8.1 Incorporation and Reliance by Legislature and Executive Powers

Japan signed CRPD in September 2007, one year after its adoption by the UN General Assembly. However, its ratification was delayed until 2014, due to requests from the disability rights movement, urging the government to prioritize substantial legal and policy reforms in alignment with the CRPD before proceeding with ratification.[359] A progressive government came into power in September 2009, which, in its manifesto, committed to earnestly working on harmonising with the CRPD before finalising the ratification. The ministerial board of disability policy reform, headed by the Prime Minister, stood out for its unique composition: the majority of its 24 members represented organisations of persons with disabilities, along with representatives from organisations of family members of persons with disabilities, and almost half of the members themselves were persons with disabilities.[360] In addition, disability rights leaders joined the government as staff members of the Committee secretariat. With this robust engagement of the disability rights movement, various reforms were implemented, such as the revision of the Basic Act for

---

359   Interview with an expert on the rights of the persons with disabilities (Geneva, Switzerland, 10 April 2019); the disability rights movement did not support 'cosmetic' ratification and thus successfully blocked the ratification in March 2009. O Nagase, 'Challenges of the Harmonization and Ratification of Convention on the Rights of Persons With Disabilities by Japan' (2013) 10(2) Journal of Policy and Practice in Intellectual Disabilities 93–5.
360   ibid.

Persons with Disabilities in 2011, the revision of the Services and Supports for Persons with Disabilities Act in 2012, the enactment of the Act for Eliminating Discrimination against Persons with Disabilities, and the revision of the Act for Employment Promotion of Persons with Disabilities in 2013.[361]

The revision of the Basic Act for Persons with Disabilities is noteworthy for expanding the definition of 'persons with disabilities' to incorporate the concept of the so-called social model. This revision marked the inclusion of provisions related to reasonable accommodation, as outlined in article 2 of CRPD, within Japan's domestic laws for the first time.[362] Also, the Commission on Policy for Persons with Disabilities, established as a monitoring mechanism in article 33 of CRPD, oversees the implementation of the Basic Programme for Persons with Disabilities.[363] The adoption of CRPD led to the further development of special needs education in Japan. Schools for children with special needs were urged to take measures for reasonable accommodation in line with the requirements of the Act for Eliminating Discrimination against Persons with Disabilities which was enacted in 2013.[364]

5.8.2   Reliance by Judiciary

The impact of CRPD in Japanese courts is not evident as courts tend to depend on domestic laws for their judgments rather than directly referring to CRPD. For example, in the Osaka District Court, a plaintiff with autism and a mental handicap, who was rejected for re-employment, submitted a CRPD-based claim for the confirmation of status as an employee and compensation. However, the trial court denied the plaintiff's claim, holding that the rejection of re-employment does not conflict with CRPD.[365] However, the settlement has been reached on appeal in this case. The defence lawyers' group believes

---

361 The Revised Basic Act for Persons with Disabilities 2011, the revision of the Services and Supports for Persons with Disabilities Act 2012, the enactment of the Act for Eliminating Discrimination against Persons with Disabilities, and the revision of the Act for Employment Promotion etc of Persons with Disabilities 2013.

362 Government of Japan, 'Act for Eliminating Discrimination Against Persons with Disabilities' <http://www.japaneselawtranslation.go.jp/law/detail/?id=3052&vm=04&re=02> accessed 10 October 2020.

363 See Cabinet Office, 'Policy for Persons with Disabilities' <http://www8.cao.go.jp/shougai/english/index-e.html> accessed 2 February 2020; Cabinet Office, 'Commission on Policy for Persons with Disabilities (Overview)' <http://www8.cao.go.jp/shougai/english/pdf/pc-1.pdf> accessed 2 February 2020.

364 Japanese Law Translation, 'Act for Eliminating Discrimination against Persons with Disabilities' <https://www.japaneselawtranslation.go.jp/en/laws/view/3052/en> accessed 21 November 2022.

365 Osaka District Court, Judgment, 13 February 2019, 2019WLJPCA02136001.

that the court actively promoted the settlement in this case because of the change in environment surrounding the employment of persons with disabilities, including the ratification of the CRPD, the revision of the Basic Law for Persons with Disabilities, the establishment of the obligation to provide reasonable accommodation through the revision of the Act to Facilitate the Employment of Persons with Disabilities, and other advancements in the legal system concerning persons with disabilities.[366]

5.8.3   Impact on and through Non-state Actors

The disability rights movement, represented by the Japan Disability Forum (JDF), which includes 13 organisations of and for persons with disabilities, played a major role in the aforementioned disability policy reform before ratification of the treaty. The JDF has engaged in the negotiation process of the development of CRPD at the UN and collaborated at the domestic level with the bipartisan parliamentary league on the international standards for the rights of persons with disabilities.[367] Under the slogan of 'nothing about us without us', the disability rights movement ardently advocated for legislative and policy reforms, recognising that as it saw that the country was not adequately prepared for an effective implementation of CRPD.[368] They also believed participation of persons with disabilities in the reform process has been critical, ultimately resulting in a paradigm shift in laws and policies pertaining to persons with disabilities.[369]

After ratification, CSOs such as the Japan National Assembly of Disabled Peoples International (DPI-Japan), which is connected to international CSOs,[370] actively use the treaty mechanism for their domestic advocacy by

---

366 Minshu Hōritsu Kyōkai, '*Suitashi Chiteki Shōgaisha Kōmuin Kekkaku Jōkō Yatoidome Jikennno Kōsai Wakaini Tsuite* (About the High Court Settlement of the Case concerning Suita City's Clause on the Termination of Employment of Persons with Mental Disorders as Public Civil Servants)' <https://www.minpokyo.org/incident/2019/11/6675/> accessed 21 November 2022.

367 Disability Information Resources, '"*Shōgaisha Kenri Jōyaku*" *Hijunto Seido Kaikaku* (Ratification of the Convention on the Rights of Persons with Disabilities and Institutional Reform)' <https://www.dinf.ne.jp/doc/japanese/rights/rightafter/131204_JDF/mori.html> accessed 22 March 2021.

368 Interview with the expert on the rights of the persons with disabilities (Geneva, Switzerland, 10 April 2019). See JDF, 'Top Page' <http://www.normanet.ne.jp/~jdf/en/> accessed 2 February 2020.

369 ibid.

370 DPI-Japan was founded in 1986 as a national organisation of Disabled Peoples' International (DPI). Persons with disabilities play a central role in the activities of the organisation with the aim of realisation of an inclusive society. As of February 2021,

facilitating cooperation and policy consolidation of diverse groups working for various needs of persons with disabilities.[371] An expert also reiterates the significance of the convention as a 'weapon' in consultation with domestic authorities to promote the policy for persons with disabilities.[372]

5.8.4   Impact of State Reporting

The initial state report of the Government of Japan was submitted in 2016 for the first reporting cycle under CRPD. Significantly, Japan's inaugural periodic report to the CRPD Committee explicitly underscored its openness to opinions from a diverse spectrum, encompassing persons with disabilities. The report also acknowledged the intersectionality of discrimination, a distinction not commonly observed in other reports.[373] Even in the first round before the issuance of a letter of intent, a number of parallel reports were provided by CSOs, reflecting a heightened level of attention within civil society. In September 2019,[374] around 30 activists from JDF engaged in lobbying efforts with the CRPD Cttee in Geneva, providing inputs for the Committee to develop a list of issues for the Japanese government. The process of consolidating the parallel reports and lobbying endeavours themselves serves to unite the voices of diverse organisations and enhance cooperation for effective advocacy.[375]

5.8.5   Impact of Other Measures

Jun Ishikawa, who served as a CRPD Cttee member from 2017 to 2020, played an important role in connecting international standards to domestic policy.

DPI-Japan is a coalition of 93 organisations nationwide. See DPI-Japan <http://dpi-japan.org/en/about/> accessed 2 February 2021.

371   Comments from staff of a CSO advocating the rights of persons with disabilities on 27 February 2021. However, there are still some challenges in coordinating and collaborating with the organisation for persons with psycho-social disabilities and in addressing the intersectional discrimination.

372   Interview with an International Human Rights Expert (Geneva, Switzerland, 10 April 2019). He mentions that 'CRPD is the strongest weapon when they consult with the domestic authorities, even though it has its limit with indirect application at the domestic level'.

373   See the initial report submitted by Japan under art 35 of the Convention (CRPD/C/JPN/1) para 3. 'Based on the recognition that the implementation of the Convention requires sustained effort, the Japanese government has committed itself to implementing policies *while receiving opinions from persons with disabilities as well as other relevant persons* ... as well as *cross-sectional challenges such as "women with disabilities" and "statistics concerning persons with disabilities"'* (emphasis added).

374   Comments from staff of a CSO advocating the rights of persons with disabilities on 27 February 2021.

375   ibid.

He was also actively involved in domestic policy-making, serving as the chairperson of both the Commission on Policy for Persons with Disabilities and the Commission on Disability Policy at the Cabinet Office.[376]

5.8.6   Brief Conclusion

The ratification process of CRPD had a significant impact on the reform and development of disability laws and policies, as well as their implementation mechanism, with active engagement of the CSOs of and for persons with disabilities and their families. CRPD brought a shift from the old individual and charity models of disability to the social model, empowering persons with disabilities as agents of change. The internalisation of 'reasonable accommodation' is also seen as a significant paradigm change in disability policies. The state reporting mechanism works as a platform for cooperation among CSOs focusing on different kinds of disabilities, fostering opportunities for cross-learning and breaking down informational silos.

6   Conclusion

From 1999 to 2019, Japan ratified three international human rights treaties and two optional protocols. Alongside these ratifications, Japan revised several existing laws and enacted legislation in alignment with international human rights standards. Further, the courts began to actively refer to international human rights laws in some areas, including racial discrimination and children's rights. Civil society's engagement has grown not only in terms of the number of organisations participating in state reporting mechanisms, but also in the scope and impact of their involvement in international human rights legal mechanisms and their domestic application.

However, in contrast to the period from 1979 to 1999, when the surge in ratification of major human rights treaties had a direct and clear impact on Japanese legal and policy framework,[377] the impact of the UN human rights treaties observed during the period from 1999 to 2019 was much more diverse, obscure, and rather moderate. In general, despite some tangible progress seen

---

376   *The Japan Times*, 'Blind Activist Elected to UN Disability Committee' <https://www.japantimes.co.jp/news/2016/06/15/national/blind-activist-elected-u-n-disability-committee/#.XX33cSj7RPY> accessed 2 February 2020. He says that he would like to raise awareness of the challenges people with disabilities face through the implementation of CRPD. Aiming for the Tokyo 2020 Olympic Games, he advocated greater inclusion of persons with disabilities in culture and sports.

377   See the previous study, Heyns and Viljoen (n 62) 395.

in these years regarding the rights of women, children, persons with disabilities, and racial minorities, the change has come at a very gradual pace. Limited progress has been evident in specific domains, particularly those entailing highly politically sensitive issues linked to national security or history, such as the 'comfort women' matter, or in human rights matters lacking substantial public support for change, such as the death penalty. This situation persists despite recurrent recommendations from various treaty bodies, causing significant frustration among committee members. Then-HRCttee member Sir Nigel Rodley, for example, remarked 'from one review to the next, the State party did not take account of the Committee's concerns and recommendations ... Japan was, in many ways, a country that respected human rights ... but it remained concerned by the persistence of serious problems that adversely affected human rights'.[378]

The gradual pace of change can be attributed, in part, to the cautious approach within Japan's bureaucratic apparatus regarding the execution of international obligations. The Cabinet Legislation Bureau in Japan tends to conduct careful and meticulous reviews of its domestic law and policy before formally accepting international legal obligations to maintain legal stability and consistency with existing domestic law. On the one hand, this approach ensures the implementation of human rights obligations in good faith once it is incorporated into the domestic framework. On the other hand, it may also hinder immediate and drastic changes in domestic laws and active judicial review due to the cautious and legally coherent process.

In combination with this careful procedure for legislative change and development, the long-lasting rule of the conservative party, particularly during most of the period under review, may also explain the reluctance of implementation of treaty bodies' recommendations. As observed in this study, human rights issues have not been prioritised in the political sphere or even faced strong opposition or backlash, particularly in cases involving sensitive matters perceived to be linked to national interests or 'traditional Japanese values.' Against this background, even if legislation for human rights protection is agreed and passed in the Diet, it is often a product of compromise such as a mere declaration of principle with non-binding obligations for efforts, without stipulating any punishment for non-compliance. With this 'soft-law approach' often taken to form non-binding flexible guidelines instead of legally binding

---

378 United Nations, 'Comment of the Chairperson of the Human Rights Committee (Sir Nigel Rodley) at the session of the Human Rights Committee' (16 July 2014) <https://documents-dds-ny.un.org/doc/UNDOC/GEN/G14/088/30/PDF/G1408830.pdf?OpenElement> accessed 5 May 2022.

rules, the impact of the international human rights treaties has been observed only obscurely in legislation.

In principle, the judiciary tends to defer to the discretion of the political branch in the implementation of human rights treaties. Thus, the impact of human rights treaties is not conspicuous in judicial decisions. However, certain cases have shown some substantial impact of the UN human rights treaties, utilising them as guiding principles and interpretative tools for domestic law. Especially in the context of CCPR, CERD, and CRC, the Supreme Court has recently adopted a more active approach by referring to international human rights law and recommendations as persuasive authorities when interpreting domestic law.

While Japanese civil society has traditionally been considered relatively weak, during the period covered by this research, it has become increasingly active in the field of human rights. This research found a tangible impact of treaty mechanisms on and through civic groups. Examples include the active participation of civil society in legislative and policy reform before the ratification of CRPD and the persistent efforts of women's and children's rights movement against discriminatory treatments in law and policy. These movements have leveraged treaty provisions and recommendations as legitimate guiding principles for their advocacy. As the individual complaints mechanism with treaty bodies is not available, CSOs and activists take advantage of the state reporting system by submitting parallel reports and directly lobbying treaty body members to draw recommendations. In a sense, the impact of international human rights treaties is not limited to their direct incorporation into policies, legislation, and court judgments. Rather, the state reporting process and the recommendations of treaty bodies have acted as catalysts for policy action and social change by influencing people's behaviour and social norms from a universal perspective of human rights. Despite the gap between active CSOs and the general public in terms of direct knowledge of international human rights treaties, the standards and norms derived from these treaties have spread through social movements and campaigns, facilitated by the Internet. Increasingly, references to international standards and treaties are being made in human rights litigation and movements addressing various human rights issues. In Japan, there is limited political leadership and proactive judicial intervention regarding the use of international human rights treaties. However, democratic government or even courts consider public opinion and sentiments. Given this situation, civil society's intervention and advocacy play a pivotal role in making the human rights treaty system effective on the ground.

Acknowledgements

Appreciation is extended to Ikuru Nogami for providing substantial support throughout the research and writing process. The authors are grateful to everyone who offered valuable comments, shared insightful information, and provided personal experiences relevant to this study. Translations from Japanese to English, unless otherwise noted, are provided by the authors.

CHAPTER 12

The Impact of the United Nations Human Rights Treaties on the Domestic Level in Mexico

Alejandro Anaya-Muñoz, Lucía Guadalupe Chávez-Vargas, Rodolfo Franco-Franco and José Antonio Guevara-Bermúdez

1   Introduction to Human Rights in Mexico

Mexico formally is a democratic state. It acquired its independence from Spain in 1821. *Coups* and abrupt changes in government, constant civil war and several invasions by foreign powers marked the country's history during the nineteenth century. The twentieth century was marked by the legacy of the 1910 Revolution – which was fought in the name of democracy, social rights and land reform – and the hegemonic dominance of the post-revolutionary regime, embodied in the Institutionalised Revolutionary Party (PRI). The 1857 Constitution had included the civil liberties catalogue characteristic of the liberal constitutions of the time. The 1917 Constitution also included these traditional civil liberties and political rights but at the time was praised for its novel inclusion of some social rights.

In 2011 Congress approved a paradigmatic reform to the Constitution, which established that international treaties ratified by the Senate have the same legal standing as the Constitution.[1] Human rights, enshrined in the Constitution and international treaties ratified by the Senate, are justiciable and can be invoked as a source of remedies and to challenge the constitutionality of domestic law. Claims of unconstitutionality are often addressed by federal tribunals, including the National Supreme Court of Justice (Supreme Court).

Despite the rights-based constitutional tradition, human rights have been and continue to be regularly violated in Mexico. In the late 1960s and early 1970s, government and paramilitary forces brutally repressed a students' movement that called for democratisation. Throughout the 1970s, hundreds of peasants allegedly involved in guerrilla activities were forcibly disappeared and/or extra-judicially executed by the armed forces, particularly in the state

---

1   *Diario Oficial de la Federación* (6 November 2011) <http://dof.gob.mx/nota_detalle.php?codigo=5194486&fecha=10/06/2011http://dof.gob.mx/nota_detalle.php?codigo=5194486&fecha=10/06/2011> accessed 1 February 2019.

© ALEJANDRO ANAYA-MUÑOZ ET AL., 2024 | DOI:10.1163/9789004377653_014
This is an open access chapter distributed under the terms of the CC BY-NC-ND 4.0 license.

of Guerrero. During the 1980s the political opposition was harassed, and blatant electoral fraud was recurrent. In the mid-to late-1990s military forces and paramilitary groups perpetrated grave violations of human rights against indigenous communities in the state of Chiapas. In the late 1990s and early 2000s disappearances and killings of hundreds of women in Ciudad Juárez, Chihuahua shocked domestic and international public opinion.

More than 220 000 homicides were perpetrated between 2007 and 2018 and the homicide rate per 100 000 habitants increased from 8,1 in 2007 to 25,7 in 2017, in the midst of a 'war on drugs'.[2] Violence reached yet another high point in 2018, with nearly 37 000 homicides – 29 per 100 000 habitants.[3] Over 98 600 persons were by 2022 disappeared in Mexico, with most of these cases originating from the 2007–2022 period.[4] Torture continues to be a widespread practice, particularly used in the context of criminal investigations. These and other human rights violations take place with almost complete impunity and in a context of a militarised approach to public security.[5]

A parallel and equally long history of poverty and extreme inequality has unfolded, in the midst of the implementation of a neo-liberal model of economic development and high levels of governmental corruption. Mexico's population by 2016 stood at 119 530 753, with more than 55,3 million people living in poverty and 4 749 057 being illiterate.[6] Nearly 10 per cent of the Mexican population is indigenous.[7]

Mexico is a federation composed of 32 states including Mexico City, which is the seat of the federal government. Each state has its own Constitution, congress, judiciary and executive powers, together with its own autonomous human rights institution. The main institution responsible for the promotion

---

2   Laura Y Calderón, Kimberly Heinle, Octavio Rodríguez Ferreira and David A Shirk, 'Organised Crime and Violence in Mexico', Justice in Mexico, Department of Political Science and International Relations, University of San Diego (2019).

3   Anthony Harrup, 'Mexico's Murder Rate Hit Record High in 2018' *The Wall Street Journal* (25 July 2019) <https://www.wsj.com/articles/mexicos-murder-rate-hit-record-high-in-2018-11564079972> accessed 2 February 2020.

4   National Registry of Disappeared and Missing Persons <https://versionpublicarnpdno.segob.gob.mx/Dashboard/Index> accessed 4 April 2022.

5   For the current human rights crisis, see Alejandro Anaya-Muñoz and Barbara Frey (eds), *Mexico's Human Rights Crisis* (University of Pennsylvania Press 2018).

6   See International Human Rights Instruments 'Common Core Documents Forming Part of the Reports of State Parties. Mexico (HRI/CORE/MEX/2017)' (21 December 2016) 3, 10, 11, 12.

7   Human Rights Council 'National Report Submitted in Accordance with Paragraph 15(A) of the Annex to Human Rights Council Resolution 5/1. Mexico' (A/HRC/WG.6/4/MEX/1) (10 November 2008) para 114.

and protection of human rights at the federal level is the National Human Rights Commission (CNDH).[8]

Mexico's human rights non-governmental organisations (NGOs) are numerous and diverse, and their professionalisation has continued to evolve over time.

2 Relationship of Mexico with the International Human Rights System in General

During the 1970s Mexico was cautious in adopting international human rights commitments. The International Convention on the Elimination of All Forms of Racial Discrimination (CERD) was ratified in 1975, and the International Covenant on Civil and Political Rights (CCPR) and the International Covenant on Economic, Social and Cultural Rights (CESCR) only in 1981, alongside the American Convention on Human Rights (ACHR). This was in line with the prevailing model of foreign policy based on the principle of national sovereignty and non-intervention. Since the 1980s Mexico has ratified new UN human rights treaties soon after their adoption. However, until the early 2000s the national sovereignty approach continued to dominate.

This changed radically in the early 2000s, when the country experienced an important political transition from a one-party regime to a more competitive multiparty-political system, both at the federal and local level. The government of Vicente Fox (2000 to 2006) implemented a paradigmatic change in Mexico's human rights foreign policy, opening the country to international scrutiny. A permanent office of representation of the Office of the United Nations High Commissioner for Human Rights (OHCHR) was established in Mexico City. The government issued an 'open and standing' invitation to United Nations (UN) special procedures and accepted the individual communications procedures of the UN treaty bodies,[9] withdrew some reservations, and ratified other relevant treaties, including the Rome Statute of the International Criminal Court.[10]

---

[8] The CNDH addresses cases of violations perpetrated by federal authorities (including when the latter act in concurrence with local authorities).

[9] The jurisdiction of the Inter-American Court of Human Rights (IACtHR) was recognised in 1998.

[10] See Alejandro Anaya Muñoz, 'Transnational and Domestic Processes in the Definition of Human Rights Policies in Mexico' (2009) 31 Human Rights Quarterly 35, 58.

Important innovations in domestic policy followed, including the establishment of a Special Prosecutor's Office for the investigation of human rights violations of 'the past', the abolition of the death penalty and the creation of two human rights under-secretary posts in the Ministries of the Interior and of Foreign Affairs. The government entrusted the OHCHR with the elaboration of a diagnosis of the overall situation of human rights in the country and adopted a National Human Rights Plan of Action. The 2003 Diagnosis of the OHCHR included a recommendation to establish a programme for the withdrawal of reservations and interpretative declarations, as well as to ratify all pending human rights treaties.[11]

This 'U-turn' in human rights policy and discourse has been explained as the result of intense transnational pressure by domestic and external human rights organs and advocates and by the coming to power of a new political elite that tried to 'lock in' its preferences for democracy and human rights.[12]

In this context of openness, numerous UN human rights organs and procedures closely monitored the situation in Mexico. Since 2001, in addition to the scrutiny by treaty bodies, which will be described in detail later in this chapter, around 20 UN Special Rapporteurs and Working Groups of the Human Rights Council (HRC) have conducted fact-finding missions to the country and Mexico has been examined under the Universal Periodic Review (UPR) three times (in 2009, 2013 and 2018).[13] Before 2001 only three fact-finding missions by UN special procedures, and one by the Inter-American Commission on Human Rights (IACHR), had taken place, while in 1998 the UN Sub-Commission on the Protection and Promotion of Human Rights issued a resolution concerning the situation in Mexico.[14] Between 1994 and 2019 UN human rights organs and procedures have made over 3 000 recommendations to the Mexican state.[15]

Before 2011 international human rights treaties ratified by the Senate were part of Mexico's legal framework, in principle below the Constitution but

---

[11] Oficina de la Alta Comisionada de Naciones Unidas para los Derechos Humanos 'Diagnóstico Sobre la Situación de los Derechos Humanos en México' (2003) VII, 2, 3, 77, 87 <https://hchr.org.mx/publicaciones/diagnostico-sobre-la-situacion-de-derechos-humanos-en-mexico-2003/#:~:text=La%20Oficina%20en%20M%C3%A9xico%20del,y%20defini%C3%B3%20recomendaciones%20y%20propuestas> accessed 4 April 2022.

[12] ibid.

[13] A high-ranking Mexican ambassador presided over the first session of the newly-established UN Human Rights Council in 2006.

[14] Christof Heyns and Frans Viljoen, *The Impact of the United Nations Human Rights Treaties on the Domestic Level: Mexico* (Kluwer Law International 2002) 421.

[15] All these recommendations can be consulted at www.recomendacionesdh.mx.

above legislation adopted by federal or local congresses. In practice, however, only human rights NGOs invoked international human rights treaties or jurisprudence from international bodies in their reports and legal work. As already mentioned, a key constitutional reform, adopted in 2011, improved the legal standing of international human rights treaties. According to the reformed article 1 of the Constitution,

> [a]ll persons shall enjoy the human rights recognised in this Constitution and in international treaties of which the Mexican state is a party … Human rights norms will be interpreted in conformity to this Constitution and the international treaties, favouring persons at all times with the broadest protection.

All authorities, in the sphere of their functions, have the obligation to promote, respect, protect and guarantee human rights in conformity with the principles of universality, interdependence, indivisibility and progressivity. Therefore, the state shall prevent, investigate and punish human rights violations, and provide reparations, in the terms established by law.[16]

3 Table of Formal Engagement of Mexico with the UN Human Rights Treaty System

Refer to the chart on the next page.

4 Role and Overall Impact of the UN Human Rights Treaties in Mexico

4.1 *Role of UN Treaties and Treaty Bodies*
Mexico has ratified all core UN human rights treaties, together with those of the Inter-American system. Mexico has recognised most of the optional

---

16 *Diario Oficial de la Federación* (n 1).

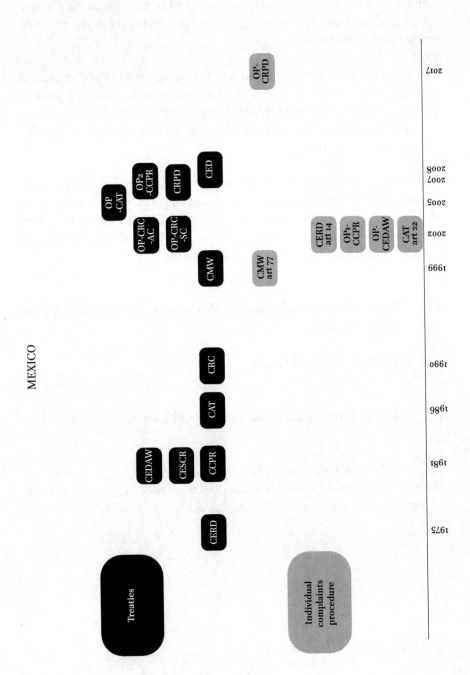

complaints and inquiry procedures, except for the communications procedures under the CESCR and the Convention on the Rights of the Child (CRC). In August 2018 Mexico reported to the UN HRC that it was 'holding inter-institutional consultations to consider ratifying' OP-CESCR and OP-CRC-CP.[17] Despite having actively participated in the elaboration of OP-CESCR, the recommendations by the CESCR Cttee and demands by domestic NGOs for its acceptance of OP-CESCR,[18] Mexico has not recognised the competence of the CESCR Cttee to receive communications. The underlying reasons for this have not been spelled out by the government, which has limited itself to state that 'consultations are being taken'. Mexico is not a party to OP-CRC-CP, despite the CRC Cttee's recommendations to that effect.[19] In early October 2020 Mexico accepted the CED Cttee's communications procedure.[20]

In general, government officials do not openly question the validity of the treaties as such or the legitimacy of treaty bodies or mandate holders to monitor the situation in the country, and to express critical conclusions and to issue recommendations. Furthermore, Mexico has recognised the legally-binding nature of the competence of some treaty bodies.[21] However, some officials argue that Mexico's 'reality' is different from 'the ideal' that treaty body members and mandate holders have in mind, questioning the latter's understanding of the specific situation of the country.[22] During the presidency of Enrique Peña Nieto (2012–2018), the Mexican government became less tolerant of international criticism and adopted a more confrontational approach, particularly towards some treaty bodies (for instance, the International Convention for the Protection of All Persons from Enforced Disappearance (CED) Cttee)

---

[17] Human Rights Council 'National Report Submitted in Accordance with Paragraph 5 of the Annex to Human Rights Council Resolution 16/21 Mexico (A/HRC/WG.6/31/MEX/1)' (23 August 2018) paras 11, 12.

[18] E/C.12/MEX/CO/5-6 para 72. In 2011 a domestic campaign to this effect generated a petition signed by 18 000 persons.

[19] CRC/C/MEX/CO/4-5 para 74.

[20] Mexico's Permanent Mission to the UN, Notification ONU-03759 to the Treaties Section of the UN Office of Legal Studies (2 October 2020).

[21] For example, Mexico's 'Declaration for the Recognition of the Competence of the Committee Against Torture' stated that '[t]he United Mexican States recognize as legally binding the competence of the Committee Against Torture established by article 17 of the Convention'. *Diario Oficial de la Federación* (3 May 2002) 7 <https://aplicaciones.sre.gob.mx/tratados/muestratratado_nva.sre?id_tratado=431> accessed 4 April 2022.

[22] Interview with Alan García, Director of the Juridical and Analysis Unit of the Mexico Office of the UNHCHR, Skype interview by Alejandro Anaya-Muñoz, 7 March 2019; interview with Cristina Hardaga, Adjunct Director of the *EnfoqueDH* project, Skype interview by Alejandro Anaya-Muñoz, 14 June 2019 (notes for all interviews on file with authors); Centro Prodh, 'Revertir la Impunidad. Diagnóstico y Propuestas a Partir del Trabajo del

and mandate holders (for instance, the UN Special Rapporteur on torture and other cruel, inhuman or degrading treatment or punishment), openly questioning their methodology, the validity of their findings and even their motivations.[23] This took place in the context of intense international pressure and criticism in the aftermath of the disappearance of 43 students from the Ayotzinapa rural teachers' college in Guerrero.[24]

Government officials from the federal agencies or specific bureaus that specialise in human rights are more clearly aware of human rights treaties and (to a lesser extent) the treaty bodies than officials from other agencies and, particularly, from sub-national (state and municipal) governments. Overall, however, the level of awareness by government officials regarding the treaties and the treaty bodies is significantly higher than that found in the previous study on the impact of UN human rights treaties on domestic actors and practices, published in 2002 (the previous study on the impact of UN treaties).[25] CCPR, CESCR, the Convention on the Elimination of All Forms of Discrimination Against Women (CEDAW), the Convention Against Torture and Other Cruel, Inhuman or Degrading Treatment or Punishment (CAT), CRC and CED are more widely known than CERD, the International Convention on the Protection of the Rights of All Migrant Workers and Members of their Families (CMW) or the Convention on the Rights of Persons with Disabilities (CRPD). Similarly, as legislative discussions and reforms on human rights have intensified over time, the level of awareness among legislators has increased, particularly those involved in the Senate's or the Chamber of Deputies' human rights

---

Grupo Interdisciplinario de Expertos Independientes (GIEI) y del Centro de Derechos Humanos Miguel Agustín Pro Juárez' (Centro Prodh 2017) 34 <http://centroprodh.org.mx/wp-content/uploads/2018/11/InformeRevertirImpunidad.pdf> accessed 4 April 2022.

23 Alejandro Anaya Muñoz, 'Política Exterior y Derechos Humanos Durante el Sexenio de Enrique Peña Nieto' (2019) 59 Foro Internacional 1049, 1075.

24 CMDPDH, 'Mexico's Human Rights Foreign Policy: From Commitment to Compliance' in Conectas Direitos Humanos, Centre for Human Rights, Law Faculty, University of Pretoria, Commonwealth Human Rights Initiative and CMDPDH in 'A Collection of Thoughts from the Global South on Foreign Policy and Human Rights: Experiences and Strategies from the Field' (2018) 27, 32 <https://conectas.org/wp-content/uploads/2018/06/A-COLLECTION-OF-THOUGHTS-FROM-THE-GLOBAL-SOUTH-ON-FOREIGN-POLICY-AND-HUMAN-RIGHTS.pdf> accessed 4 April 2022; Olga Guzmán, 'México and its Foreign Policy of Denial' (2017) 26 Sur International Journal on Human Rights 3, 95; interview with Juan Carlos Gutiérrez, General Director of the NGO *Idheas Strategic Litigation in Human Rights*, Skype interview by Alejandro Anaya-Muñoz, 14 July 2019; interview with Olga Guzmán, International Advocacy Coordinator of the NGO *Comisión Mexicana de Defensa y Promoción de los Derechos Humanos*, Skype interview by Alejandro Anaya-Muñoz, 3 July 2019.

25 Heyns and Viljoen (n 14) 427–248.

committees. The same is true for the judicial branch, particularly after the 2011 constitutional reform.[26] Awareness clearly is less developed among legislators and judicial operators at the sub-national level.

Highly professionalised human rights NGOs and some specialised organisations focused on the rights of specific groups (such as women, children or persons with disabilities) are acutely aware of the UN treaties and treaty bodies. NGOs extensively use the treaties, COs and, to a lesser extent, the General Comments in their litigation, campaigns and elaboration of reports. Historically, however, Mexican NGOs have turned to the IACHR rather than the UN treaty bodies to litigate petitions on individual cases. Only recently have some organisations started to use the communications procedures of treaty bodies.

In this respect, in addition to the insights gathered through interviews, we reviewed the in-depth reports published by three important NGOs and registered the number of references they made to each UN treaty and treaty body. We found that these NGOs cite UN treaties and treaty bodies very frequently. Some treaties – CCPR, CED and CEDAW – and their treaty bodies are cited much more often than the rest.[27]

The academic human rights literature published in Mexico, mostly law-oriented in thematic scope, sometimes deals with the UN treaties and treaty bodies. However, it gives much more attention to the treaties and organs of the Inter-American system. The number of scholars that produce research and teach courses related to human rights has been growing consistently. A survey undertaken in 2002 found that a good number of universities in different regions of the country included human rights courses in their curricula. Most of these courses included the study of international law, but in general devoted more time to conceptual, historical and theoretical discussions, domestic

---

26   In interviews, however, experts have stressed that knowledge of the specificities of the treaties and the treaty body jurisprudence among judicial operators in lower courts is highly superficial and limited. Interview with María Sirvent, Coordinator of the NGO *Documenta. Analysis and Action Center for Social Justice*, Skype interview by Alejandro Anaya-Muñoz, 1 April 2019; interview with Juan Carlos Gutiérrez; interview with Olga Guzmán.

27   We reviewed 102 in-depth reports produced by the CMDPDH, the 'Miguel Agustín Pro Juárez' Human Rights Centre (Centro Prodh), and the *Grupo de Información sobre Reproducción Elegida* (GIRE). We identified 204 references to the UN treaties and 304 to the treaty bodies. We included in this exercise all the reports available in the organisations' websites. See <http://cmdpdh.org/publicaciones/>; <https://centroprodh.org.mx/category/publicaciones/; and https://gire.org.mx/informes/> accessed 4 April 2019.

legislation and judicial remedies and the faculties of the CNDH. The survey did not find postgraduate degrees specialised in human rights.[28]

For the elaboration of this chapter we reviewed the curricula of the law degrees of 32 leading public universities (one for each federal state and Mexico City). We found that in all but one of these universities, the curricula included general courses on human rights. In addition, over one-third of the universities have incorporated courses exclusively focused on international human rights law and organs. We also identified at least 15 Masters' programmes in human rights offered in the country. This demonstrates that human rights education has advanced considerably in Mexico in the past two decades.[29]

The Mexican press has also made ample use of human rights treaties. We conducted a search in three major national newspapers (*La Jornada*, *Reforma* and *El Universal*) and identified nearly 2 300 news and opinion articles published between 2000 and 2018 that explicitly mention the UN human rights treaties.[30] There is a large variation in the use of treaties. For example, while CRC is mentioned in 673 articles, CESCR is mentioned in 282 and CERD in only 47 articles. The specific content of treaties is not elaborated with detail in the news or opinion articles and knowledge by journalists remains superficial. Only a limited number of highly-specialised reporters have been trained by some NGOs and thus are aware of the specific content of treaties and the functions of treaty bodies.[31]

Mexico has submitted 22 periodic reports to the UN treaty bodies in the period 2000 to 2018. On average, these reports have been 17 months late.[32] Mexico's reports highlight reforms to the legal-institutional framework, formal

---

28   Academy on Human Rights and Humanitarian Law of American University Washington College of Law and Human Rights Programme of Universidad Iberoamericana 'Diagnóstico sobre la Educación Legal en Derechos Humanos en México' (2002) <www.corteidh.or.cr/tablas/28977.pdf> accessed 4 April 2019.
29   The previous study on the impact of UN treaties found that even if a few universities had incorporated human rights issues into the curricula of their law degrees, 'international human rights [did] not form a compulsory part of the curriculum'. Heyns and Viljoen (n 14) 423.
30   The exercise was made using the search engines of the newspapers' websites. In the case of *El Universal*, information is only available for post-2014 editions, so the search was limited to 2014 to 2018. This extensive use of UN human rights treaties by the press in Mexico contrasts sharply with the situation reported in the previous study on the impact of UN treaties, which found a 'very limited interest in the treaties and the monitoring bodies' by these actors. Heyns and Viljoen (n 14) 428.
31   Interview with Juan Carlos Gutiérrez; interview with Olga Guzmán.
32   The previous study on the impact of UN treaties reported that on average Mexico had been nine months late with the submission of reports. Heyns and Viljoen (n 14) 433.

policy programmes and numerous and diverse specific actions taken by a broad array of government agencies. However, reports lack an explicit effort to analyse and evaluate the impact in practice of reforms, programmes and actions. In general, reports lack sufficient data and indicators to allow an analysis of the situation of human rights on the ground and, as also reported in the previous study on the impact of UN treaties in Mexico,[33] they are not self-critical.

The drafting of reports falls under the responsibility of the Ministry of Foreign Affairs, which normally works in close collaboration with other agencies and local governments. Numerous other governmental agencies participate, providing information. Occasionally, the government organises consultations in which some civil society actors participate. However, important NGOs critical of the government distrust these consultations and generally do not attend. Experts argue that the government's consultations are only a simulation that do not result in the incorporation of the organisations' views or concerns,[34] although they stress that, in some periods, government officials have legitimately tried to undertake sincere consultations.[35]

The government has not established a national mechanism for reporting and follow-up. However, during some periods mechanisms have been established for specific treaties, such as CERD and CRPD. During the Fox administration, for example, the Ministry of Foreign Affairs entrusted leading universities to prepare drafts of periodic reports (on torture and civil and political rights), seeking objectivity and a balanced assessment of the human rights situation in the field.

Mexico's human rights NGOs are highly active participants in the reporting procedure. They have submitted over 150 alternate or shadow reports in the period since 1999. In contrast, national human rights institutions (NHRIs) are less active – they have sent only 15 documents or reports.[36]

In collaboration with the UNHCHR and academic institutions, the Ministry of Foreign Affairs created an online database that contains all reports and recommendations to Mexico issued by international human rights organs.[37] COs

---

[33] Heyns and Viljoen (n 14) 441.
[34] Interview with Regina Tamés, President of Mexico's National Commission to Prevent and Eradicate Discrimination, telephone interview by Alejandro Anaya-Muñoz, 15 February 2019; interview with María Sirvent; interview with Cristina Hardaga; interview with Juan Carlos Gutiérrez; interview with Olga Guzmán; interview with Stephanie Brewer.
[35] Interview with Juan Carlos Gutiérrez.
[36] With information from the UN Treaty Data Base <https://tbinternet.ohchr.org/_layouts/15/treatybodyexternal/TBSearch.aspx?Lang=en> accessed 4 April 2022.
[37] See www.recomendacionesdh.mx. This is in sharp contrast to the situation reported in the previous study on the impact of UN treaties, which found that COs by treaty bodies were not made public by the government. Heyns and Viljoen (n 14) 437–438, 442.

and 'views' are not translated into indigenous languages. The government has not established a specific, comprehensive, inter-agency mechanism or procedure to coordinate the implementation of the recommendations included in COs or views.

The government has not established a clear and transparent national procedure for the nomination of candidates to the treaty bodies. Mexican individuals have been members of different treaty bodies, such as the CAT, the Subcommittee on Prevention of Torture and other Other Cruel, Inhuman and Degrading Treatment or Punishment (SPT), CEDAW, CED and CMW Cttees.[38] In a few cases, the government has nominated renowned academics or experts from civil society. On other occasions, however, it has nominated retired or active diplomats, something that has been controversial. A few years ago, the government withdrew the candidacy of a renowned Mexican expert, supported by the NGO community, to the CAT Cttee. Similarly, the Peña Nieto government decided not to nominate for a second term the Mexican national who was serving as president of the CED Cttee, and who had previously served for six years as member of the Working Group on Enforced Disappearances.[39] Recently, the Lopez Obrador government nominated for re-election an 'eminent ambassador' as member of the CAT Cttee.[40]

4.2 Overview of Impact

After the aforementioned 2011 human rights constitutional reform, the political and legal saliency of human rights treaties increased significantly. Graph 12.1 shows the number of times that UN human rights treaties have been explicitly mentioned in the decisions of the federal judiciary (National Supreme Court, Collegiate Circuit Courts and Circuit plenums) from 2000 to 2019.[41] Clearly, the incorporation of treaties into the federal judiciary's decisions

---

[38] Other Mexican nationals have been members of the organs of the Inter-American regime and mandate holders of different UN special procedures.
[39] Anaya-Muñoz (n 23) 1049, 1075.
[40] Eminent ambassador who, in accordance with applicable rules, receives a monthly stipend from the federal budget equivalent to the salary of high-level officials of the federal government.
[41] By 'decisions' of Mexico's federal judiciary we mean (a) the decisions by the National Supreme Court or Collegiate Circuit Courts that establish non-mandatory criteria for the interpretation of legal rules (*tesis aislada* in Spanish); (b) decisions by the National Supreme Court, Collegiate Circuit Courts and Circuit plenums that establish jurisprudence. The rules for the adoption of jurisprudence are established by the Amparo Writ Law (arts 215 to 230).

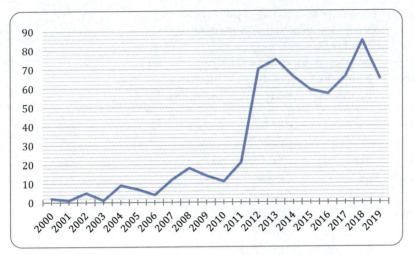

GRAPH 12.1   Number of decisions by Mexico's federal judiciary that mention UN human rights treaties (2000 to 2019)
SOURCE: PREPARED BY THE AUTHORS WITH DATA FROM MEXICO'S NATIONAL SUPREME COURT OF JUSTICE

sharply increased after the 2011 constitutional reform.[42] However, most of these decisions only mention the treaty or the treaty bodies; the actual content of the treaty or the General Comments or COs generally is not discussed or developed in depth. In addition, it is unclear whether this influence has permeated to lower-level courts, particularly at the sub-national level. As one expert interviewed for this research put it, the 'mental frame' and the 'everyday practices' of judges at different levels have not changed significantly.[43] In addition, research has shown that the Supreme Court uses international instruments and jurisprudence more as a source of interpretation than as a source to establish remedies.[44]

---

42 Some experts agree that as a result of the 2011 constitutional reform, the Supreme Court has made important efforts to train federal judges and increase awareness regarding international human rights treaties. Interview with Alexandra Haas, President of Mexico's National Commission to Prevent and Eradicate Discrimination CONAPRED, telephone interview by Alejandro Anaya-Muñoz, 15 February 2019; interview with María Sirvent. In this respect, the previous study on the impact of UN treaties found an 'extremely limited' use of treaties by federal judiciary authorities. Heyns and Viljoen (n 14) 431.
43 Interview with María Sirvent.
44 Karina Ansolabehere, 'Human Rights and Justice in Mexico: An Analysis of Judicial Functions' in Anaya-Muñoz and Frey (n 5) 227, 249.

TABLE 12.1   Decisions by Mexico's Federal judiciary that mention human rights treaties and treaty bodies (2000 to 2019)

Treaty	Number of mentions	Treaty body	Number of mentions
CERD	1	CERD Cttee	1
CCPR	184	HRC Cttee	10
CESCR	92	CESCR Cttee	27
CEDAW	47	CEDAW Cttee	3
CAT	6	CAT Cttee	0
		SPT	0
CRC	250	CRC Cttee	8
CMW	5	CMW Cttee	0
CED	11	CED Cttee	1
CRPD	52	CRPD Cttee	1
ACHR	936	IACHR	22
		IACtHR	252

SOURCE: PREPARED BY AUTHORS WITH DATA FROM MEXICO'S NATIONAL SUPREME COURT (HTTPS://SJF.SCJN.GOB.MX/SJFSIST/PAGINAS/TESIS.ASPX)

As shown in Table 12.1, the number of decisions by the federal judiciary that mention UN human rights treaties and treaty bodies varies significantly. For instance, CRC is mentioned 250 times; CESCR 91 times, CMW only five times, whereas CERD is mentioned only once. It is also worth noting that the federal judiciary mentions the ACHR and the Inter-American organs much more often than the UN treaties and organs.[45]

---

[45] A 2011 Supreme Court ruling determined that federal judges have to interpret the Constitution taking into account the jurisprudence of the IACtHR, under the figure of 'conventionality control'. *Diario Oficial de la Federación* (4 October 2011) <http://dof.gob.mx/nota_detalle.php?codigo=5212527&fecha=04/10/2011> accessed 11 November 2019.

One of the key faculties of the CNDH is the elaboration of 'general recommendations' or general reports in which it addresses human rights violations that have a structural character. The CNDH adopted the first 'general recommendation' in 2001 and had adopted 39 of these by 1 November 2019. To trace the influence of UN treaties and treaty bodies over the CNDH, we have analysed the content of these general reports, finding an extensive use of treaties and General Comments. The CNDH not only mentions the treaties but often analyses specific rights and their interpretation by treaty bodies. However, we found a considerable degree of variation in the use of the different treaties and treaty bodies: Whereas CCPR, CESCR, CEDAW and CRC and their committees are widely used by the CNDH, CED and CRPD and their committees are not used at all.

Since the Vicente Fox administration, every incoming federal government has adopted a National Human Rights Plan of Action, which includes a long list of policy objectives and actions, intended to adopt a human rights approach to public policy. The UN treaties and some treaty bodies were mentioned or quoted in these programmes. The actual implementation and impact of these human rights programmes has not been formally assessed.

Recently, NGOs and other civil society actors that traditionally have not adopted a human rights approach have started to invoke UN treaties and bodies and to participate in the reporting procedure, elaborating alternate or shadow reports and attending interactive dialogues.[46]

Numerous laws related to human rights have been adopted and/or reformed in Mexico. According to one expert, '[m]any new laws in Mexico are very, very much based on international treaties; [and] they are very, very progressive laws'.[47]

Up to 2018, treaty bodies had issued 1 327 recommendations in their COs to Mexico, in which they repeatedly highlight the country's human rights shortcomings. In a parallel process, the Mexican state has reformed its legal and institutional framework, significantly improving the harmonisation of the domestic framework with international norms. However, as the COs themselves have pointed out, important challenges remain in terms of the implementation of reforms and the harmonisation of state and municipal-level laws. This legal and institutional reform agenda is the result of a long process of transnational and domestic pressures, in which the treaty bodies and their

---

46   Interview with Stephanie Brewer; interview with Juan Carlos Gutiérrez; interview with María Sirvent; interview with Olga Guzmán.
47   Interview with María Sirvent.

COs (together with the UN Human Rights Council and its special procedures and the Inter-American organs) have also played a prominent role.[48]

However, the Mexican state has failed to implement many of the important recommendations by the treaty bodies. To provide a notable example, Mexico continues to fail to investigate, prosecute and punish perpetrators of human rights violations, which has been recurrently recommended by all treaty bodies. The near collapse of Mexico's judicial system and the resulting almost absolute impunity is one of Mexico's most daunting human rights challenges. In addition, overall, the Mexican government has failed to fully implement numerous recommendations regarding the adoption of reparations, the generation of statistical information and indicators, the allocation of sufficient financial resources for human rights compliance and the internalisation of norms by government officials and society in general.

As already noted, only recently did a few Mexican NGOs start to submit communications to the UN treaty bodies, after decades of focusing their litigation efforts on the Inter-American organs.[49] As reported with further detail in part 5, until 2018 the HRCttee has adopted views on five cases, and the CAT, CEDAW and CERD Cttees on one case each. All of these decisions were relatively recently taken, and while the government has formally accepted them, victims and NGOs had to exert intense political pressure to achieve improvements in the (partial) implementation of remedies. According to two experts interviewed for this research, the government approaches individual communications following a 'denial litigation' strategy – that is, the automatic denial of the facts presented by victims.[50]

---

[48] See, for example, Alejandro Anaya Muñoz 'El País Bajo Presión. Debatiendo el Papel del Escrutinio Internacional de Derechos Humanos sobre México' (2012) CIDE; Alejandro Anaya-Muñoz 'Bringing Willingness Back in. State Capacities and the Human Rights Compliance Deficit in Mexico' (2019) 41 Human Rights Quarterly 441, 464.

[49] Interview with María Sirvent,; interview with Santiago Aguirre, General Director of the Centro Prodh, personal interview by Alejandro Anaya-Muñoz, Guadalajara, Mexico, 17 June 2019; interview with Juan Carlos Gutiérrez; interview with Olga Guzmán; interview with Stefanie Brewer, International Advocacy Coordinator of the Centro Prodh, Skype interview by Alejandro Anaya-Muñoz, 17 July 2019.

[50] Interviews with Juan Carlos Gutiérrez and Olga Guzmán.

5 The Impact of the UN Human Rights Treaties on the Domestic Level in Mexico

5.1 *International Convention on the Elimination of All Forms of Racial Discrimination*

5.1.1 Incorporation and Reliance by Legislature and Executive

Since the adoption of reform measures concerning indigenous peoples' rights in August 2001, article 1 of the Constitution prohibits discrimination based on ethnic or national origin, among other grounds.[51] Congress has also adopted a number of reforms to the country's legal and institutional framework,[52] including the 2003 Federal Law to Prevent and Eliminate Discrimination, which established the National Council for the Prevention of Discrimination (CONAPRED). In different Bills that preceded the adoption of this law and the creation of CONAPRED, legislators mentioned CERD several times.[53] CERD was also quoted a few times in the many Bills that preceded the 2011 constitutional reform on human rights.[54]

5.1.2 Reliance by the Judiciary

In January 2019 the Supreme Court ruled that the federal executive and congress were in breach of their obligation to take legislative measures to give effect to articles 4(a) and (b) of CERD (regarding the punishment by law of hate speech, the incitement of racial attacks and the participation in organisations that promote racial discrimination). To justify its position, the Supreme Court explicitly relied on the 2012 COs by the CERD Cttee that urged Mexico to 'step up its efforts to … pass a law specifically to define the various manifestations of

---

[51] *Diario Oficial de la Federación* (14 August 2001) <www.dof.gob.mx/index.php?year=2001&month=08&day=14> accessed 1 February 2019.

[52] For details on policy plans and other government actions regarding discrimination, see Committee on the Elimination of Racial Discrimination 'Reports Submitted by States Parties Under Article 9 of the Convention. Fifteenth Periodic Reports of States Parties Due in 2004. Addendum. Mexico (CERD/C/473/Add.1)' (19 May 2005) paras 13, 17.

[53] For example, *Cámara de Diputados*, 'Dictamen de la Comisión de Justicia y Derechos Humanos, con Proyecto de Decreto por el que se Expide la Ley Federal para Prevenir y Eliminar la Discriminación' (9 April 2003) <http://legislacion.scjn.gob.mx/Buscador/Paginas/wfProcesoLegislativoCompleto.aspx?q=1K5PMk8y/k4kiy/XL1ao5JO8Fk7Z3uW6o2VhBnJYo6xstRJ4BKcu4Un1gvWHlTZh4lvmWPTufuHcSEFBgYVchA==> accessed 4 April 2022.

[54] *Cámara de Diputados*, 'Decreto por el que se Modifica la Denominación del Capítulo I del Título Primero y Reforma Diversos Artículos de la Constitución Política de los Estados Unidos Mexicanos (DOF 10-06-2011) Proceso Legislativo' <www.diputados.gob.mx/LeyesBiblio/proceso/lxi/117_DOF_10jun11.pdf> accessed 30 August 2019.

racial discrimination as an offence punishable by law'.[55] From a different perspective, as shown in Table 12.1 in part 4, in its jurisprudence the federal judiciary has cited CERD and the CERD Cttee only once. This stands in clear contrast to other UN treaties and treaty bodies, which have been quoted extensively.

5.1.3   Impact on and through Independent State Institutions

CERD and the CERD Cttee are only mentioned in two 'general recommendations' by the CNDH. For instance, General Recommendation 27, regarding the right of indigenous peoples to free, informed and prior consultation, draws on General Comment 23 by the CERD Cttee to make its argument on the guarantee of indigenous peoples' effective participation in public affairs.[56]

5.1.4   Impact on and through Non-state Actors

CERD is not the most widely used human rights treaty in Mexico. The Convention figures among the least-cited treaties in the review of in-depth reports by domestic NGOs, undertaken for the elaboration of this chapter.[57] Similarly, CERD is the treaty that has received less attention by the press in Mexico.

5.1.5   Impact of State Reporting

In its COs to Mexico, the CERD Cttee focused on challenges related to indigenous peoples' rights, notably the implementation of the right to consultation and 'free, prior and informed consent', and urged Mexico to adopt legislation on this matter.[58] Noting with concern the attacks and killings of defenders of indigenous peoples' rights, the CERD Cttee requested Mexico to legislate and establish a mechanism for the protection of human rights defenders.[59] The CERD Cttee also showed its concern regarding the rights of people of African descent and the lack of data and statistics about them. In this sense, it recommended Mexico to recognise 'people of African descent as an ethnic group'.[60]

---

55 Committee on the Elimination of Racial Discrimination, 'Consideration of Reports Submitted by States Parties Under Article 9 of the Convention: COs of the Committee on the Elimination of Racial Discrimination. Mexico (CERD/C/MEX/CO/16–17)' (4 April 2012) para 11; e-mail communication from Alexandra Haas (27 February 2019).
56 CNDH 'Recomendación General 27' (11 July 2016) 10 <https://www.cndh.org.mx/sites/default/files/doc/Recomendaciones/Generales/RecGral_027.pdcmd> accessed 25 November 2019.
57 n 25.
58 CERD/C/MEX/CO/16–17 para 17.
59 CERD/C/MEX/CO/16–17.
60 CERD/C/MEX/CO/16–17 para 10.

For its latest follow-up procedure, the CERD Cttee included the recommendations on the provision of data and statistical information on people of African descent and the recognition of the latter as an ethnic group, and the implementation of consultations with indigenous peoples in cases of development projects that affect them.[61]

In part, in response to the CERD Cttee's COs, in the 2015 inter-census survey Mexico's National Institute of Statistics and Geography (INEGI) started to gather demographic information on people of African descent. Recently the Mexican Constitution was reformed to recognise Afro-Mexican peoples and communities as part of the pluri-ethnic composition of the country and to grant them the same rights as those of indigenous peoples.[62]

5.1.6 Impact of Individual Communications

CERD has not adopted decisions on communications against Mexico.

5.1.7 Brief Conclusion

Important legislative and institutional reforms have been implemented in relation to the rights included in CERD. CERD has been taken into consideration by legislators in the process leading to these reforms. The clearest instance of CERD's impact in Mexico are specific actions pertaining to the recognition of the rights of people of African descent, notably their inclusion in the country's census data and in the constitutional recognition of their collective rights. However, as noted by the CERD Cttee itself, racial discrimination remains

> deeply rooted in the state party despite the highly developed institutional framework for combating it. The Committee also note[d] with concern the lack of information on the real impact and outcomes of [legal and institutional reforms] and the related programmes, plans and strategies.[63]

Impact, therefore, has been clearly circumscribed to the adoption of legal and institutional reforms, while CERD norms continue to be violated in practice.

---

61 CERD/C/MEX/CO/16–17 para 24.
62 *Diario Oficial de la Federación* (9 August 2019) 2 <https://dof.gob.mx/nota_detalle.php?codigo=5567623&fecha=09/08/2019> accessed 30 August 2019.
63 CERD/C/MEX/CO/16–17 para 9.

5.2 International Covenant on Civil and Political Rights

5.2.1 Incorporation and Reliance by Legislature and Executive

The Constitution enshrines the principles and rights included in CCPR. As noted below, however, an important exception is made by the Constitution itself as to the principle of presumption of innocence, which is violated by the practice of *arraigo* – the pre-charge, prolonged detention, particularly used in cases presumably related to organised crime. The Covenant was explicitly cited numerous times in different draft Bills that were advanced between 2006 and 2011 as part of the legislative process that led to the adoption of the 2011 human rights constitutional reform.[64]

High-profile reforms and initiatives have been adopted, in relation to criminal justice, torture, disappearances, violence against women and femicides, victims' rights and the protection of human rights defenders and journalists.[65] However, CCPR and the HRC Cttee were not explicitly cited in draft Bills on these key reforms, whereas other UN treaties (CED and CAT) and procedures (the Special Rapporteur on the Rights of Human Rights Defenders) and the Inter-American human rights organs were explicitly mentioned.[66]

5.2.2 Reliance by the Judiciary

Table 12.1 in part 4 shows that the federal judiciary has on numerous occasions made explicit reference to CCPR and the HRC Cttee. However, the ACHR and the rulings of the IACtHR are mentioned far more often. Some Supreme Court *amparo* writ rulings use CCPR to establish the procedural means for their effective implementation.[67]

---

64 *Cámara de Diputados* (n 54).
65 The previous study on the impact of UN treaties stressed that the key legislative reforms related to the rights enshrined in CCPR were mostly related to electoral rights (Heyns and Viljoen (n 14) 430).
66 For example, *Cámara de Diputados*, 'DECRETO por el que se Expide la Ley para la Protección de Personas Defensoras de Derechos Humanos y Periodistas. (DOF 25 June 2012) Proceso Legislativo', n/d, <www.diputados.gob.mx/LeyesBiblio/proceso/lxi/257_DOF_25jun12.pdf> accessed 4 April 2022; *Cámara de Diputados*, 'DECRETO por el que se Expide la Ley General de Víctimas (DOF 9-01-2013). Proceso Legislativo', on file with the authors; *Cámara de Senadores*, 'Dictamen de las Comisiones Unidas de Derechos Humanos, Justicia y Gobernación y Estudios Legislativos, de la Minuta con Proyecto de Decreto por el que se Expida la Ley General para Prevenir, Investigar y Sancionar la Tortura y otros Tratos o Penas Crueles, Inhumanos o Degradantes' (25 April 2017) <www.senado.gob.mx/comisiones/justicia/reu/docs/dictamen_250417.pdf> accessed 4 April 2022.
67 See, for example, Primera Sala, 'Recurso de Inconformidad. Su Ratio Constitucional y Convencional' (2017) 42 Gaceta del Semanario Judicial de la Federación 260 <https://www.scjn.gob.mx/sites/default/files/gaceta/documentos/2017-06/libro42.pdf> accessed 4 April 2022.

5.2.3 Impact on and through Independent State Institutions

CCPR and/or the HR Cttee are explicitly used in most 'general recommendations' by the CNDH. The references to both the treaty and the Committee are numerous and substantial, in the sense that they are not only mentioned but used in some detail to interpret the rights in question. For example, General Recommendation 26 makes explicit reference to General Comment 23 of the HR Cttee to make an argument in favour of the rights of indigenous persons and communities.[68]

5.2.4 Impact on and through Non-state Actors

National human rights NGOs regularly make use of CCPR and the HR Cttee's COs. CCPR and the HRC Cttee figure among the most often-cited sources in our review of in-depth reports published by important domestic human rights NGOs.[69] In the same sense, CCPR is one of the treaties most widely cited by the press in Mexico.

5.2.5 Impact of State Reporting

In its COs to México, issued in 2010, the HRCttee urged the Mexican state to reform its Constitution and to harmonise its contents with CCPR. Other recommendations focused on violence against women and femicides. The COs also dealt with the investigation of cases of grave violations of human rights and the prosecution of those responsible; the participation of the military in public security; the elimination of *arraigo*; the elimination of military jurisdiction; and the protection of human rights defenders and journalists.[70] For its follow-up procedure, the Committee focused on its recommendations regarding violence against women, the elimination of *arraigo* and the rights of journalists and human rights defenders.[71]

As already suggested, important legislative reforms and institutional innovations have been adopted, related to the protection of human rights defenders and journalists, victims' rights, the elimination of violence against women and femicide, torture and disappearances. In addition, the Code of Military Justice was partially reformed in 2014.[72] All of these reforms resulted from long

---

[68] CNDH, 'Recomendación General 27' (n 56).
[69] n 27.
[70] Human Rights Committee, 'COs of the Human Rights Committee. Consideration of Reports Submitted by States Parties Under Article 40 of the Covenant. Mexico' (CCPR/C/MEX/CO/5) (17 May 2010).
[71] CCPR/C/MEX/CO/5 paras 8, 9, 15, 20.
[72] For a critique of this reform, see CMDPDH, 'La incompatibilidad del Código de Justicia Militar con el Derecho Internacional de los Derechos Humanos' (2014) CMDPDH.

and intense processes of transnational and domestic pressures, in which the HRCttee's COs played a role, alongside numerous other external and internal actors.[73]

Despite all these reforms, violence against women continues to be 'widespread' and femicide has not abated, while the harmonisation of sub-national legislation with the General Law on Women's Access to a Life Free from Violence remained highly wanting. Attacks against human rights defenders and particularly journalists also persisted and the government did not provide the Mechanism to Protect Human Rights Defenders and Journalists the resources needed to fulfil its challenging mandate. In addition, torture and disappearances are considered to be 'widespread' in the country. The practice of *arraigo* has not been eliminated (from the law or in practice) and a militarised approach to public security was formalised and strengthened by a 2019 constitutional reform that established the National Guard. In sum, numerous problems stressed in the HRCttee's COs have not been adequately addressed.

5.2.6   Impact of Individual Communications

By 30 June 2019, the HR Cttee has adopted views on the merits of two communications lodged against Mexico.[74] In the first communication, the HRCttee did not find a breach of the Covenant.[75] In the second, the HR Cttee found violations, including discrimination, torture and arbitrary detention, and ordered the state to provide the author with an effective remedy.[76] After the adoption of the decision, different government agencies held three follow-up meetings. However, according to Article 19 (who supported the victim in the proceedings), by the end of the administration of President Peña Nieto (1 December 2018) the government had failed to comply with numerous remedies established by the HR Cttee and denounced a clear lack of willingness, urging the new government to comply.[77] In January 2019 the incoming

---

73   Anaya Muñoz, 'El País Bajo Presión' (n 48); interview with Olga Guzmán.
74   Human Rights Committee, 'Views on Communication No 2202/2012 (CCPR/C/108/D/2202/2012)' (29 August 2013); Human Rights Committee, 'Views on Communication No 2767/2016 (CCPR/C/123/D/2767/2016)' (29 August 2018). A number of violations were found subsequent to the cut-off date of 30 June 199: Human Rights Committee, 'Views on Communication No 2750/2016 (CCPR/C/126/D/2750/2016)' (5 August 2019); Human Rights Committee 'Views on Communication No. 2760/2016 (CCPR/C/127/D/2760/2016)' (16 December 2019); Human Rights Committee, 'Views on Communication No 2766/2016 (CCPR/C/127/D/2766/2016)' (24 October 2019).
75   CCPR/C/108/D/2202/2012 para 8.
76   CCPR/C/123/D/2767/2016 (17 July 2018) para 11.
77   Article 19, 'Gobierno de AMLO Debe Cumplir con Resolución de la ONU y Reparar el Daño a Lydia Cacho' (Article 19, 2 December 2018) <https://articulo19.org/gobierno-de-amlo-debe-cumplir-con-resolucion-de-la-onu-por-las-agresiones-contra-lydia-cacho/> accessed 1 February 2019.

López Obrador government complied with one of the reparation measures requested by the HRCttee – holding a public act in which it formally recognised the responsibility of the Mexican state and offered a public apology to the victim.[78]

5.2.7 Brief Conclusion

The levels of awareness regarding CCPR and the HRC Cttee and the use of the treaty and COs by different actors has been high. In this context, many relevant reforms have been adopted. CCPR and particularly the COs and views decisions have been part of broad and complex processes of domestic and transnational pressures and influences that prompted these reforms. However, numerous other COs have not been complied with and the impact of reforms on the levels of respect of human rights in practice has been clearly limited.

5.3 *International Covenant on Economic, Social and Cultural Rights*

5.3.1 Incorporation and Reliance by Legislature and Executive

All the rights included in CESCR are enshrined in the Mexican Constitution and legislation. For example, article 3 of the Constitution includes the right to education; article 4, the rights to health, food and access to culture; while articles 5 and 123 deal with labour rights and the right to social security. In 2011 Congress reformed the Constitution to include the right to 'nutritious, adequate and good-quality food'.[79] As all the other human rights treaties ratified by Mexico, CESCR has mandatory force, at the same hierarchical level as the Constitution.

Different Bill proposals and legislative documents related to the 2011 human rights constitutional reform cite or mention CESCR numerous times.[80] The Covenant has also been cited in other reform Bills pertaining to specific rights. For example, the most recent constitutional reform Bill on education, adopted in early 2019, made specific reference to CESCR, when discussing the right of access to scientific knowledge.[81]

---

[78] Interview with Santiago Aguirre; Antonio Baranda, 'Ofrece Estado Disculpa Pública a Cacho' (Reforma, 10 January 2019) <www.reforma.com/ofrece-estado-disculpa-publica-a-cacho/ar1581258?v=4> accessed 4 April 2022.

[79] *Diario Oficial de la Federación* (13 October 2011) <http://dof.gob.mx/nota_detalle.php?codigo=5213965&fecha=13/10/2011> accessed 4 April 2022.

[80] Cámara de Diputados (n 54).

[81] Grupos Parlamentarios del Partido Acción Nacional, del Partido Revolucionario Institucional, de Movimiento Ciudadano y del Partido de la Revolución Democrática, 'Iniciativa que Reforma los Artículos 30, 31 y 73 de la Constitución Política de los Estados

5.3.2 Reliance by the Judiciary

Table 12.1 in part 4 shows that the federal judiciary has numerous times made explicit reference to CESCR and the CESCR Cttee. The CESCR Cttee in fact is the UN body most frequently cited. Federal tribunals have adopted a number of rulings in which they uphold economic, social and cultural rights, following the CESCR Cttee. For example, in a paradigmatic ruling on the right of access to health of an indigenous community in the state of Guerrero, the judiciary referred to the CESCR Cttee's General Comments to motivate its decision.[82] However, the executive branch has failed to implement such rulings.[83] In this sense, the CESCR Cttee recently expressed concern about the access to effective judicial remedies for victims and 'the lack of effective enforcement of the judgments handed down in *amparo* proceedings in which violations of economic, social and cultural rights have been found'.[84]

5.3.3 Impact on and through Independent State Institutions

CESCR and the CESCR Cttee are also widely used by the CNDH in its 'general recommendations'. In fact, they are the treaty and Committee with the largest number of references. For instance, General Comments 3, 9 and 14 are used to analyse the issue of atmospheric contamination in cities and the resulting damage to the rights to health, an adequate standard of living, a healthy environment and public information.[85]

Unidos Mexicanos' (6 February 2019) <http://sil.gobernacion.gob.mx/Archivos/Documentos/2019/02/asun_3807542_20190206_1549475825.pdf> accessed 4 April 2022.

82 Interview with Juan Carlos Arjona, high ranking official of Mexico City's Human Rights Commission, Skype interview by Alejandro Anaya-Muñoz, 5 March 2019. See Rodrigo Gutiérrez Rivas and Aline Rivera Maldonado, 'El Caso Mininuma: un Litigio Estratégico para la Justiciabilidad de los Derechos Sociales y la No Discriminación en México' (2009) 251 Revista de la Facultad de Derecho de México 89, 122.

83 Centro de Derechos Humanos de la Montaña 'Tlachinollan' and others, 'La Defensa de Casos de Derechos Económicos, Sociales, Culturales y Ambientales y la Respuesta del Estado Mexicano: Retos y Obstáculos en el Cumplimiento de Resoluciones Judiciales' (Fundar, October 2014) <www.fundar.org.mx/mexico/pdf/InformejusticiabilidadDESCA_MEXICO_Casos.pdf> accessed 12 July 2019.

84 Committee on Economic, Social and Cultural Rights, 'COs on the Combined Fifth and Sixth Periodic Reports of Mexico' (E/C.12/MEX/CO/5–6) (17 April 2018) para 5.

85 CNDH 'Recomendación General 32' (24 July 2018) <https://www.cndh.org.mx/documento/recomendacion-general-322018> accessed 27 November 2019.

5.3.4 Impact on and through Non-state Actors

National NGOs regularly make use of CESCR and the CESCR Cttee's COs and General Comments in their litigation and advocacy strategies.[86] In our review of in-depth reports by important human rights NGOs, we found that CESCR and the CESCR Cttee are frequently cited.[87]

5.3.5 Impact of State Reporting

As noted, the CESCR Cttee has expressed concern in its COs regarding the issue of access to effective judicial remedies for victims of the violation of economic, social and cultural rights, and the effective implementation of rulings. The Committee has also stressed issues related to violence against defenders of economic, social and cultural rights, the lack of measures to protect them and the related impunity.[88] As already mentioned in relation to CCPR, a Mechanism to Protect Human Rights Defenders and Journalists has been established. However, in 2018 the Mexican Centre for Environmental Law registered at least 49 attacks and 21 killings of environmental activists. Between 2013 and 2018 (after the establishment of the Protection Mechanism) it documented 440 attacks, including acts of harassment, threats and killings.[89]

In December 2018 Congress adopted a new law for the National Institute for Indigenous Peoples, which is in charge of the implementation of prior, free and informed consultations with indigenous peoples. The CESCR Cttee has expressed in its COs concerns regarding the effective implementation of consultations and fears that this right has not been upheld in practice, particularly in cases of strategic development projects.[90] Similarly, the CESCR Cttee's recommendations regarding violence against women have not been implemented, including those related to obstetric violence in poor areas of the country.[91]

---

[86] In an online survey made for purposes of this research, important NGOs – *Asilegal, Centro Prodh*, GIRE and *Impunidad Cero* – reported that they use CESCR in their litigation strategies.

[87] n 25.

[88] E/C.12/MEX/CO/5–6; Committee on Economic, Social and Cultural Rights, 'Consideration of Reports Submitted by States Parties Under Articles 16 and 17 of the Covenant. COs of the Committee on Economic, Social and Cultural Rights. Mexico (E/C.12/MEX/CO/4)' (9 June 2006).

[89] Alejandra Leyva and others, 'Informe Sobre la Situación de las Personas Defensoras de los Derechos Humanos Ambientales México 2018' (March 2019) 12 <www.cemda.org.mx/wp-content/uploads/2019/03/Informe_defensores.pdf> accessed 4 April 2022.

[90] E/C.12/MEX/CO/5–6 para 12.

[91] E/C.12/MEX/CO/5–6 para 62–64; interview with Regina Tamés.

5.3.6 Brief Conclusion

Congress and judiciary operators have relied on CESCR and the CESCR Cttee. Legal and institutional reforms have been adopted, regarding the rights included in CESCR. However, important recommendations by the CESCR Cttee have not been complied with and, as concluded by the CESCR Cttee itself, groups such as indigenous peoples, human rights defenders, migrants and women remain particularly vulnerable to the violation of their economic, social and cultural rights.

5.4 *Convention on the Elimination of All Forms of Discrimination against Women*

5.4.1 Incorporation and Reliance by Legislature and Executive

Article 1 of the Constitution prohibits discrimination on the basis of gender. CEDAW was cited several times in the numerous draft Bills related to the 2011 constitutional reform.[92] Other high-profile reforms and programmes have been adopted in relation to the elimination and prevention of violence against women and the promotion of equality between women and men.[93] CEDAW and its Committee were cited several times in draft Bills regarding the 2007 General Law on the Access of Women to a Life Free of Violence.[94] The Law explicitly defines the 'rights of women' as those included in CEDAW and the Inter-American Convention on the Prevention, Punishment and Eradication of Violence against Women (Convention 'Belem do Para').[95] CEDAW was also cited in draft Bills regarding the elaboration of the General Law for Equality between Women and Men.[96]

---

92 *Cámara de Diputados* (n 54).
93 In this respect, the previous study on the impact of UN human rights treaties highlighted the enactment of the Law Against Intra-Family Violence. Heyns and Viljoen (n 14) 430.
94 *Cámara de Diputados,* 'DECRETO por el que se Expide la Ley General de Acceso de las Mujeres a una Vida Libre de Violencia. (DOF 01-02-2007). Proceso Legislativo', n/d, on file with authors.
95 *Diario Oficial de la Federación* (1 February 2007) Article 5 (VIII), <https://www.gob.mx/cms/uploads/attachment/file/209278/Ley_General_de_Acceso_de_las_Mujeres_a_una_Vida_Libre_de_Violencia.pdf> accessed 4 April 2022.
96 Lucero Saldaña Pérez and Enrique Jackson Ramirez, 'Proyecto de Decreto que Expide la Ley General para la Igualdad Entre Mujeres y Hombres, y Reforma, Deroga y Adiciona Diversas Disposiciones de la Ley del Instituto Nacional de las Mujeres' (9 November 2004) <http://sil.gobernacion.gob.mx/Archivos/Documentos/2004/11/asun_1499777_2 0041109_1507199.pdf> accessed 4 April 2022. According to the Executive Director of GIRE, legislators sometimes copy the organisation's reports, including the references to CEDAW and other treaties. Interview with Regina Tamés.

5.4.2 Reliance by the Judiciary

Table 12.1 in part 4 shows that CEDAW and its Committee are not among the most often mentioned by the federal judiciary in its thesis and jurisprudence, although CEDAW was cited more often than the Convention 'Belem do Pará'. However, the Supreme Court has relied on CEDAW, for instance, when arguing in favour of the recognition of women's rights to make autonomous decisions regarding their sexuality and reproduction and has made reference to the CEDAW Cttee's General Comment 24 in relation to the decriminalisation of abortion medical procedures.[97]

5.4.3 Impact on and through Independent State Institutions

Although they are not among the most widely quoted, CEDAW and its Committee are used in a number of 'general recommendations' by the CNDH. For example, General Recommendation 31 makes reference to General Comment 24 by the CEDAW Cttee to argue on the importance of the right to health and in particular to the obstetric health of pregnant women.[98]

5.4.4 Impact on and through Non-state Actors

Civil society organisations, journalists and academics in general are highly aware of CEDAW. According to experts interviewed for this chapter, CEDAW is one of the most widely-known human rights treaties in Mexico.[99] According to one of these experts, it is 'the treaty that is totally internalised amongst many sectors'.[100] In its *Cotton Field* ruling, the IACHR included a large number of references to the 2004 special enquiry report by the CEDAW Cttee on the disappearances and killings of women in Ciudad Juárez.[101]

Although the level of expertise among NGOs varies, women's rights organisations make extensive use of CEDAW and the Committee's COs and General Comments, including in their domestic litigation arguments and strategies.[102]

---

[97] Pleno de la SCJN, 'Acción de Inconstitucionalidad 146/2007 y su Acumulada 147/2007' (28 August 2018) <https://www.cndh.org.mx/sites/default/files/doc/Acciones/Acc_Inc_2007_146_Demanda.pdf> accessed 4 April 2022.

[98] CNDH, 'Recomendación General 31' (31 July 2017) 11, 59 <https://www.cndh.org.mx/sites/default/files/documentos/2019-07/RecGral_031.pdf> accessed 4 April 2022.

[99] Interview with Alexandra Haas; interview with Juan Carlos Arjona; interview with Alan García; interview with Regina Tamés; interview with Santiago Aguirre.

[100] Interview with Juan Carlos Arjona.

[101] Inter-American Human Rights Court 'Caso González y otras ('Campo Algodonero') v México' (16 November 2009).

[102] Interview with Alexandra Haas; interview with Juan Carlos Arjona; interview with Regina Tamés.

Our review of in-depth reports published by important Mexican NGOs also shows a frequent use of CEDAW's content and the Committee's arguments.[103]

In interviews, experts stressed that numerous Mexican NGOs travel to Geneva to participate in the interactive dialogues. In the words of one of them, 'everybody goes' to these Committee sessions.[104]

CEDAW is widely cited by the Mexican press. One expert noted, in this respect, that the interactive dialogues that capture most attention from the Mexican press are those of the CEDAW Cttee.[105]

5.4.5 Impact of State Reporting

The CEDAW Cttee issued four COs reports on Mexico from 2000 to 2018[106] and one report under article 8 of the Optional Protocol to the Convention.[107] The COs focused on issues such as the prevention and punishment of violence against women; the elimination of trafficking in persons; the sexual exploitation of women and girls and the effective implementation of the relevant legislation; the killings and disappearances of women in Ciudad Juárez and the inclusion of the crime of femicide in federal and state-level criminal codes; and the effective implementation of the General Law of Women's Access to a Life Free of Violence, the Gender Alert, the Amber Alert and the Alba Protocol (related to the search of disappeared women and girls). The COs also stressed the CEDAW Cttee's concerns regarding the pending challenges on equality between women and men, in particular in relation to labour rights, together

---

103   n 25. For obvious reasons, the CEDAW and CEDAW Cttees are the most often cited sources in GIRE reports, as this organisation focuses on reproductive rights.

104   Interview with Alexandra Haas; interview with Juan Carlos Arjona; interview with Santiago Aguirre.

105   Interview with Juan Carlos Arjona.

106   Committee on the Elimination of Discrimination against Women, 'Report of the Committee on the Elimination of Discrimination Against Women Twenty-Sixth Session (14 January-1 February 2002), Twenty-Seventh Session (3–21 June 2002), Exceptional Session (5–23 August 2002)' (A/57/38)' paras 420, 453; Committee on the Elimination of Discrimination Against Women, 'Concluding Comments of the Committee on the Elimination of Discrimination Against Women: Mexico (CEDAW/C/MEX/CO/6)' (25 August 2006); Committee on the Elimination of Discrimination Against Women, 'COs of the Committee on the Elimination of Discrimination Against Women. Mexico (CEDAW/C/MEX/CO/7–8)' (7 August 2012); Committee on the Elimination of Discrimination Against Women, 'COs on the Ninth Periodic Report of Mexico (CEDAW/C/MEX/CO/9)' (15 July 2018).

107   Committee on the Elimination of Discrimination against Women, 'Report on Mexico Produced by the Committee on the Elimination of Discrimination Against Women Under Article 8 of the Optional Protocol to the Convention, and Reply from the Government of Mexico (CEDAW/C/2005/OP.8/MEXICO)' (25 January 2005).

with reproductive health and the access to safe abortion (under the terms established by Mexican law). The Committee issued recommendations on the effective protection of female journalists and human rights defenders.[108]

For its follow-up procedure, the CEDAW Cttee focused on the enforced disappearance of women and girls, the harmonisation of federal and state legislation on abortion,[109] the penalisation of femicides in all states, and early warning and gender violence alert mechanisms.[110]

As already suggested, Mexico took numerous legislative, institutional and policy measures regarding the issues raised by the CEDAW Cttee's COs, notably the adoption of the General Law for Equality Between Women and Men.[111] In addition, Congress adopted the General Law of Women's Access to a Life Free of Violence. Furthermore, the government established different early warning and gender violence alert mechanisms; created special prosecutors' offices on violence against women, femicides[112] and trafficking in persons; and created institutions such as the National Institute for Women and the National Commission to Prevent and Eradicate Violence Against Women. The CEDAW Cttee has commended Mexico for such an important legislative agenda. However, it has also stressed its concern regarding the insufficient efforts to implement reforms, lack of sufficient budget and insufficient actions to monitor and evaluate the impact of new laws, institutions or programmes. The Committee has also noted with concern the persistence of inequality between women and men; the continuation of violence against women; the increase in domestic violence and femicides; the incomplete harmonisation of state-level legislation; and the ineffective implementation of the gender violence alert mechanisms.[113]

5.4.6 Impact of Individual Communications

In August 2017 the CEDAW Cttee adopted views on a communication filed against Mexico in August 2014. The communication concerned a femicide case. The Committee found that the state had failed 'to act with due diligence

---

108 CEDAW/C/MEX/CO/7-8, CEDAW/C/MEX/CO/9.
109 CEDAW/C/MEX/CO/7-8 paras 19b, 33a, 33b.
110 CEDAW/C/MEX/CO/9 paras 24c, 24d, 24e, 24h.
111 According to the director of CONAPRED, the CEDAW Cttee was highly influential in the adoption of this Law. Interview with Alexandra Haas.
112 According to Amnesty International, Mexico was the country with more femicides in Latin America in 2017, with 3 357 cases. Jessica Xantomila, 'Ocupa México Primer Lugar de América Latina en Feminicidios: AI' (*La Jornada*, 9 April 2019) <www.jornada.com.mx/2019/04/09/politica/010n1pol> accessed 4 April 2022.
113 CEDAW/C/MEX/CO/9.

in order to ensure an investigation and trial, with the result that the offence went unpunished, and that the authors are victims of a denial of justice'.[114] In the case's proceedings, the state informed the CEDAW Cttee that it had recently adopted legislative reforms on women's access to justice, but did not provide any information regarding the implementation of this new legislation or the evaluation of its impact. According to the authors of the communication, the reforms in question 'have not changed the general condition of women's access to justice'.[115] In its 2018 COs on Mexico's ninth periodic report, the CEDAW Cttee lamented the limited progress in the implementation of the reparations included in its views on the case and stressed that Mexico had to accelerate their implementation.[116]

5.4.7 Impact of Other Measures

In 2003–2004 the CEDAW Cttee undertook its first ever special enquiry under article 8 of OP-CEDAW, to investigate the 'abduction, rape and murder' of women in Ciudad Juárez, Chihuahua. The resulting report, found 'grave and systematic violations' of CEDAW's provisions.[117] This report and the preceding fact-finding mission by the CEDAW Cttee were very important components of an unprecedented wave of reports and other documents and actions by all sorts of actors that exerted pressure over the Chihuahua and federal governments, resulting in the adoption of many of the legal and institutional reforms regarding violence against women highlighted here.[118]

5.4.8 Brief Conclusion

CEDAW and the CEDAW Cttee are well known and often used by domestic actors. In this context, Mexico has adopted many legal and institutional reforms pertaining to women's rights, following the agenda set forth by the Committee and other (domestic and international) actors. In this way, the impact on Mexico in the area of women's rights has been particularly salient.

---

114 Committee on the Elimination of Discrimination Against Women, 'Views Adopted by the Committee under Article 7, Paragraph 4, of the Optional Protocol, Concerning Communication No 75/2014' (CEDAW/C/67/D/75/2014) (29 August 2017) para 9.6.

115 Reyna Trujillo Reyes and others, 'Informe Sombra Relativo a la Comunicación 75/2014 Emitida por el Comité CEDAW' (nd) <https://tbinternet.ohchr.org/Treaties/CEDAW/Shared%20Documents/MEX/INT_CEDAW_NGO_MEX_31434_S.pdf> accessed 4 April 2022.

116 CEDAW/C/MEX/CO/9.

117 CEDAW/C/2005/OP.8/MEXICO para 258.

118 Anaya-Muñoz, 'El País Bajo Presión' (n 48); Alejandro Anaya Muñoz, 'Explaining High Levels of Transnational Pressure Over Mexico' (2009) 15 International Journal of Human Rights 339, 358.

However, this impact has been highly circumscribed to the legal and institutional frameworks. New laws have not been effectively implemented and new government agencies have failed to achieve significant improvements on the respect of women's rights in practice.

5.5 Convention against Torture and Other Cruel, Inhuman or Degrading Treatment

5.5.1 Incorporation and Reliance by Legislature and Executive

The Constitution recognises the prohibition of torture and other cruel, inhuman or degrading treatment in various articles. Article 20 section B stipulates that torture, incommunicado detention and intimidation shall be prohibited by law and stipulates that they should be considered crimes under criminal law. The article also stipulates that confessions rendered without the assistance of a defence lawyer shall be deprived of any evidentiary value. Article 22 enshrines that the death penalty is forbidden in Mexico as well as the punishments of mutilation, scourge or torment of any type. Article 29 includes the right not to be tortured as one of the rights that cannot be suspended in times of emergency or armed conflict. CAT was explicitly cited numerous times in the draft Bills[119] regarding the General Law for the Prevention, Investigation and Punishment of Torture or other Cruel, Inhuman or Degrading Treatment or Punishment (General Law on Torture).[120] CAT was also cited in the Bill proposals for the adoption of the 2011 human rights constitutional reform.[121]

Numerous reforms to the legal and institutional framework and policy programmes related to the prevention of torture have been adopted by the government, including the aforementioned 2017 General Law on Torture. In 2015 the National Conference of Prosecutors prepared the Protocol for the Investigation of the Crime of Torture which is to be followed by all the country's prosecutors, forensic experts and police forces.[122] Accordingly, in January 2018 the Prosecutor-General of Mexico announced the creation of a Special Prosecutor for the Investigation of the Crime of Torture.[123]

---

119 See, for example, *Cámara de Senadores* (n 66).
120 *Diario Oficial de la Federación* (26 June 2017) <http://dof.gob.mx/nota_detalle.php?codigo=5488016&fecha=26/06/2017> accessed 4 April 2022.
121 *Cámara de Diputados* (n 54).
122 Procuraduría General de la República, 'Protocolo Homologado para la Investigación del Delito de Tortura' (2 October 2018) <https://www.gob.mx/cms/uploads/attachment/file/342267/Protocolo_Tortura_agosto_2015.pdf> accessed 4 April 2022.
123 *Diario Oficial de la Federación* (26 January 2019) <www.dof.gob.mx/nota_detalle.php?codigo=5511525&fecha=26/01/2018> accessed 4 April 2022.

5.5.2 Reliance by the Judiciary

Table 12.1 in part 4 shows that the federal judiciary has not made much explicit reference to CAT in its decisions, while it has not at all cited the CAT Cttee. However, for example, the Supreme Court relied on CAT's definition of torture to establish in an *amparo* writ the state's human rights obligations and the criminal elements of torture.[124] In addition, in 2014 the Supreme Court issued a protocol to be followed by the members of the judiciary while solving cases that involve torture, which is based in CAT and the Committee's COs and General Comments.[125]

5.5.3 Impact on and through Independent State Institutions

CAT is only used in a few of the CNDH's 'general recommendations'. The CAT Cttee is only quoted in one of these, in which the CNDH recalls the recommendations issued in COs regarding the issue of the protection of human rights defenders in Mexico.[126]

5.5.4 Impact on and through Non-state Actors

National human rights NGOs make intensive use of CAT and its Committee's COs and General Comments.[127] In our review of in-depth reports published by leading Mexican NGOs, we found that CAT and the CAT Cttee have been cited numerous times. The Mexican press has also frequently cited CAT, although it is not the most often-mentioned UN treaty in news reports. Recently, numerous civil society organisations that previously did not engage with the CAT Cttee for the first time attended the interactive dialogue with the Mexican government and participated in the elaboration of alternate reports.[128]

---

[124] Primera Sala, 'Juicio de Amparo Directo Penal 9/2008' (12 August 2009) <https://miguelcarbonell.me/wp-content/uploads/2020/05/EngroseActealPu%CC%81blico.pdf> accessed 4 April 2022.

[125] Suprema Corte de Justicia de la Nación, 'Protocolo de actuación para quienes imparten justicia en asuntos que involucren hechos constitutivos de tortura y malos tratos' (2014) <https://www.scjn.gob.mx/registro/sites/default/files/page/2020-02/protocolo_tortura_malos_tratos.pdf> accessed 4 April 2022.

[126] CNDH, 'Recomendación General 25' (8 February 2016) 44, 46 <https://www.cndh.org.mx/documento/recomendacion-general-252016> accessed 4 April 2022.

[127] Interview with Santiago Aguirre; interview with Stephanie Brewer; interview with María Sirvent.

[128] Although these organisations' overall knowledge of the details of CAT's articles, the Committee's jurisprudence or rules of procedure remains limited. Interview with Olga Guzmán.

5.5.5 Impact of State Reporting

In its 2012 COs the CAT Cttee stressed the issue of legal harmonisation[129] and specifically recommended Mexico to adopt a general law on torture.[130] The COs also included recommendations pertaining to the elimination of *arraigo* and urged Mexico to redouble efforts to prevent torture and to establish a mechanism to protect human rights defenders and journalists. The COs also highlighted the need to ensure that confessions extracted under torture are not used as evidence in criminal proceedings, to ensure the adequate application of the Istanbul Protocol, and to reform the military justice system to preclude the possibility that military courts could have jurisdiction over cases involving human rights abuses.[131] For its follow-up procedure, the CAT Cttee emphasised its recommendations related to the strengthening of legal standards for the protection of persons in custody and the investigation of cases of torture and the adoption of sanctions for perpetrators.[132]

Some of the legislative reforms and institutional innovations already mentioned are relevant to implement the recommendations of the CAT Cttee, particularly the adoption of the General Law on Torture. The mere existence of CAT and the recommendations by the Committee and the SPT are likely to have had an impact on the adoption of this and other torture-related reforms.[133]

5.5.6 Impact of Individual Communications

By 30 June 2019, the CAT Cttee had received three communications. It found Mexico in violation of CAT in one of these communications (*Ramiro Ramírez Martínez v Mexico*);[134] the others were concluded after the cut off mark for this study.[135] In *Martínez*, the CAT Cttee found violations of several CAT articles. In particular, it concluded that the victims had been arbitrarily detained by the armed forces, subjected to incommunicado detention and *arraigo*, brutally tortured, exhibited to the press and forced to confess to crimes that they had not committed. The CAT Cttee urged Mexico to immediately release the victims and grant them full reparations; to investigate, prosecute and punish

---

129 Committee against Torture, 'COs on the Combined Fifth and Sixth Periodic Reports of Mexico as Adopted by the Committee at its Forty-Ninth Session (29 October-23 November 2012) (CAT/C/MEX/CO/5-6)' (11 December 2012) paras 8(a), (b), (c), (d).
130 CAT/C/MEX/CO/5–6 para 12.
131 CAT/C/MEX/CO/5–6 paras 9, 25.
132 CAT/C/MEX/CO/5–6 para 27.
133 Interview with Alan García; interview with María Sirvent; interview with Juan Carlos Arjona; interview with Santiago Aguirre; interview with Olga Guzmán.
134 CAT/C/71/D/759/2016 (23 July 2021) (violation found).
135 CAT/C/72/D/992/2020 (18 November 2021) (violation found).

perpetrators; and to amend the law to eliminate *arraigo* and military criminal jurisdiction.[136] After the adoption of the decision, judicial authorities released the victims and the Ministry of the Interior held meetings with family members and their representatives to explore avenues to further implement the reparations requested in the CAT Cttee's views. However, both the Peña Nieto and López Obrador governments had failed to comply in full. Another communication against Mexico is currently being considered by the CAT Cttee.[137]

5.5.7 Impact of other measures

From 23 August to 12 September 2001, the CAT Cttee undertook its first fact-finding visit to Mexico in accordance with the article 20 confidential inquiry procedure, designed to investigate well-founded indications that torture is being systematically practised in the territory of a state party. The resulting report found that 'the police commonly use torture and resort to it systematically as another method of criminal investigation, readily available whenever required in order to advance the process' and made recommendations to address the issue.[138] In line with its new openness policy, the Vicente Fox government agreed to the publication of the Committee's full report in 2003. More than twenty years after the adoption of this CAT Cttee report, the overall torture situation in Mexico has not improved.

5.5.8 Impact of Visits by SPT

The SPT visited Mexico in 2008 and 2016.[139] The SPT focused on issues also highlighted by the CAT Cttee's COs, such as the need to advance legal harmonisation, the elimination of *arraigo* and the prevalence of impunity. However, the SPT gave specific attention to the situation of persons deprived of their liberty, including the conditions and practices that facilitate the proliferation of

---

136 *Martínez* para 19.
137 Interview with Juan Carlos Gutierrez.
138 Committee Against Torture, 'Report on Mexico Produced by the Committee Under Article 20 of the Convention, and Reply from the Government of Mexico' (CAT/C/75) (26 May 2003) para 218.
139 Sub-Committee on Prevention of Torture, 'Report on the Visit of the Subcommittee on Prevention of Torture and Other Cruel, Inhuman or Degrading Treatment or Punishment to Mexico (CAT/OP/MEX/1)' (31 May 2010); Sub-Committee on Prevention of Torture, 'Advanced Unedited Version. Visita a México del 12 al 21 de Diciembre de 2016 Observaciones y Recomendaciones Dirigidas al Estado Parte. Informe del Subcomité' <https://hchr.org.mx/comite/informe-del-subcomite-para-la-prevencion-de-la-tortura-visita-a-mexico-del-12-al-21-de-diciembre-de-2016-observaciones-y-recomendaciones-dirigidas-al-estado-parte/> (nd) accessed 4 April 2022.

torture in detention centres. The government withheld the publication of the second SPT report for several months, until it was forced to do so by a decision of Mexico's National Institute on Access to Information (INAI) after a request filed by a group of domestic human rights NGOs.[140] The conditions and practices in detention centres that elicit torture, identified by the SPT, have not been eliminated.

5.5.9 Brief Conclusion

CAT and the CAT Cttee are also highly known to and extensively used by domestic advocates. Congress has adopted important reforms, in particular, the General Law on Torture, which addresses a good number of CAT Cttee and SPT recommendations regarding legal harmonisation. However, Mexico has failed to implement other key recommendations, such as the elimination of *arraigo* and those pertaining to the continuation of impunity. Furthermore, once again, legal developments have failed to result in significant changes in practices and patterns of human rights violations. Torture and other cruel and inhuman treatment continue to be 'widespread' in Mexico and impunity remains almost absolute.[141]

5.6 Convention on the Rights of the Child

5.6.1 Incorporation and Reliance by Legislature and Executive

The rights included in CRC are enshrined in the Mexican Constitution and secondary legislation. Article 4 of the Constitution enshrines a list of children's rights related to food, health, education, leisure and 'integral development'.[142] A reform to this article, adopted in October 2011,[143] established the state's obligation to safeguard the principle of the best interests of the child.[144] Article 3 of the Constitution enshrines the right to education. This article was reformed

---

140 CMDPDH and others, 'Subcomité para la Prevención de la Tortura Confirma la Práctica Generalizada de la Tortura en México' (CMDPDH, April 2018) <http://cmdpdh.org/2018/04/subcomite-para-la-prevencion-de-la-tortura-confirma-la-practica-generalizada-de-la-tortura-en-mexico/> accessed 22 April 2022.

141 See, for example, CMDPDH, 'Huellas Imborrables: Desapariciones, Torturas y Asesinatos por Instituciones de Seguridad en México 2006–2017' (CMDPDH, November 2018) <www.cmdpdh.org/publicaciones-pdf/cmdpdh-idoc-analisis-recomendaciones-violaciones-graves-ddhh.pdf> accessed 4 April 2022.

142 Constitución Política de los Estados Unidos Mexicanos, 4<https://www.diputados.gob.mx/LeyesBiblio/pdf/CPEUM.pdf> accessed 7 April 2022.

143 *Diario Oficial de la Federación* (12 October 2011) <www.dof.gob.mx/nota_to_imagen_fs.php?codnota=5213826&fecha=12/10/2011&cod_diario=241442> accessed 4 April 2022.

144 ibid.

in 2019 to establish the best interests of the child in the access, permanence and enjoyment of education services.[145] Article 29 includes children's rights in the list of rights that cannot be suspended in times of emergency or armed conflict. The General Law on Children's and Adolescents' Rights was published in 2014.[146] This new Law recognises children and adolescents as rights holders and enshrines numerous specific rights.[147]

CRC, its two Protocols and the CRC Cttee are cited in numerous occasions in the draft Bills that were advanced for the 2011 human rights constitutional reform.[148] CRC is also cited in other draft Bills, including some related to the General Law on Children's and Adolescents' Rights. The implementation of CRC is one of the 'lines of action' of the 2008–2012 National Human Rights Programme,[149] while CRC is cited as a reference in the elaboration of the 2014–2018 National Human Rights Programme.[150]

5.6.2 Reliance by the Judiciary

Table 12.1 in part 4 shows that CRC is the UN human rights treaty most often cited by the federal judiciary in its jurisprudence. The latter has also referred to the CRC Cttee's General Comments, for example, on decisions pertaining to children's rights to be heard, the right to equality, the best interests of the child and the right to a life free of violence, although the CRC Cttee has not been cited as often as other treaty bodies, such as the CESCR Cttee and the HR Cttee. The CRC has also been used by the Supreme Court to interpret certain rights. For example, in a 2019 unconstitutionality action ruling, the Supreme Court used CRC to develop the concept of the interests of the child[151] and in an

---

145 *Diario Oficial de la Federación* (15 May 2019) <www.diputados.gob.mx/LeyesBiblio/ref/dof/CPEUM_ref_237_15may19.pdf> accessed 4 April 2022.
146 *Diario Oficial de la Federación* (4 December 2014) <www.diputados.gob.mx/LeyesBiblio/ref/lgdnna/LGDNNA_orig_04dic14.pdf> accessed 4 April 2022.
147 ibid.
148 *Cámara de Diputados* (n 54).
149 Poder Ejecutivo, Secretaría de Gobernación 'Programa Nacional de Derechos Humanos 2008–2012' (29 August 2008) <www.cndh.org.mx/sites/all/doc/Programas/VIH/Programa%20Nacional%20de%20derechos%20humanos%202008_2012/PROGRAMA_NACIONAL_DE_DERECHOS_HUMANOS_2008_2012.pdf> accessed 4 April 2022.
150 Gobierno de la República, 'Programa Nacional de Derechos Humanos 2014–2018' (nd) <https://www.gob.mx/publicaciones/articulos/programa-nacional-de-derechos-humanos-2014-2018-105443?idiom=es> accessed 4 April 2022.
151 Pleno de la SCJN, 'Acción de inconstitucionalidad 2/2010' (16 August 2010) <https://www.scjn.gob.mx/sites/default/files/listas/documento_dos/2019-07/A.R.%2057-2019..pdf> accessed 4 April 2022.

amparo writ to allow the use of *cannabidiol* (CBD) for the medical treatment for a child.[152]

5.6.3   Impact on and through Independent State Institutions

CRC is used extensively by the CNDH in its 'general recommendations'. For instance, General Recommendation 39, related to child obesity, quotes CRC 28 times.[153] The CRC Cttee is used in only four 'general recommendations', but in an extensive manner. General Recommendation 39, for example, includes 34 quotations to General Comments (particularly General Comments 7, 14, 15, 19 and 20) and also COs by the CRC Cttee.[154]

5.6.4   Impact on and through Non-state Actors

National NGOs that work on children's rights regularly make use of CRC in their litigation strategies.[155] However, in our review of in-depth reports by important domestic human rights NGOs with a broader human rights agenda, we found that CRC and the CRC Cttee are not cited very frequently. Similarly, domestic human rights NGOs do not usually send numerous alternative or shadow reports to the CRC Cttee. On the other hand, however, CRC is the UN human rights treaty most often cited by leading newspapers in Mexico.

5.6.5   Impact of State Reporting

In its COs on Mexico's periodic reports,[156] the CRC Cttee stressed concerns related to the comprehensive respect and guarantee of the rights included in CRC and urged the state to generate statistics on the impact of legal and institutional reforms and policy programmes.[157] The CRC Cttee also stressed

---

152 Segunda Sala, 'Amparo en revisión 57/2019' (2019) <www.scjn.gob.mx/sites/default/files/listas/documento_dos/2019-07/A.R.%2057-2019..pdf> accessed 4 April 2022.

153 CNDH, 'Recomendación General 39' (15 October 2019) <https://www.cndh.org.mx/sites/default/files/documentos/2019-10/RecGral_39.pdf> accessed 4 April 2022.

154 ibid.

155 In an online survey made for this research, important NGOs – *Asilegal*, Instituto de Justicia Procesal Penal (*IJPP*), *Centro Prodh*, GIRE and *Impunidad* Cero – reported that they use CRC in their national litigation strategies.

156 Committee on the Rights of the Child, 'Consideration of Reports Submitted by States Parties Under Article 44 of the Convention. COs of the Committee on the Rights of the Child, Mexico' (CRC/C/15/Add.112) (10 November 1999); Committee on the Rights of the Child, 'Consideration of Reports Submitted by States Parties Under Article 44 of the Convention. COs: Mexico' (CRC/C/MEX/CO/3) (8 June 2006); Committee on the Rights of the Child, 'COs on the Combined Fourth and Fifth Periodic Reports of Mexico (CRC/C/MEX/CO/4–5)' (3 July 2015).

157 CRC/C/15/Add.112 para 13; CRC/C/MEX/CO/3 paras 13, 14, 43, 46, 47, 52; CRC/C/MEX/CO/4–5 paras 6, 21, 22, 40, 56, 58, 60, 62.

the need to evaluate how the best interests of the child are affected by budget cuts or the lack of public investment.[158] The CRC Cttee has also issued recommendations regarding the adoption of a gender perspective in all government actions that affect girls[159] and requested the generation of data on the number of children detained, wounded or killed in the context of the 'war on drugs'.[160]

Mexico is a party to the Protocols to CRC on children in armed conflict and the sale of children, child prostitution and the use of children in pornography. Therefore, the CRC Cttee has issued two reports, one on each Protocol. In its report on the participation of children in armed conflicts, the CRC Cttee expressed concern over the recruitment of children by non-state armed groups, that is, paramilitaries and organised criminal organisations.[161] In relation to the sale of children, child prostitution and the use of children in pornography, the CRC Cttee stressed the need to harmonise Mexico's legislation with the Protocol and emphasised its concern regarding impunity.[162] The implementation of the Committee's COs has been deficient. Violence against children and adolescents prevails in the country. Official figures indicate that, at the end of 2017, over 5 000 children had disappeared in Mexico, while homicides, femicides, sexual violence, exploitation, the use of children in pornography and the recruitment of children by organised crime continue to severely undermine children's rights.[163]

5.6.6 Brief Conclusion

Mexico's legislation enshrines the rights included in CRC. The Convention and the CRC Cttee have been considered by legislators in important reforms. CRC is very frequently cited in Supreme Court decisions and by the Mexican press. Impact, however, is circumscribed to legal reforms. The implementation of

---

158   CRC/C/MEX/CO/3 para 12; CRC/C/MEX/CO/4–5 para 14.
159   CRC/C/MEX/CO/4–5 para 18.
160   CRC/C/MEX/CO/4–5 para 30.
161   Committee on the Rights of the Child, 'Examen de los Informes Presentados por los Estados Partes en Virtud del Artículo 8 del Protocolo Facultativo de la Convención Sobre los Derechos del Niño Relativo a la Participación de Niños en los Conflictos Armados (CRC/C/OPAC/MEX/CO/1)' (7 April 2011) para 22.
162   Committee on the Rights of the Child, 'Examen de los Informes Presentados por los Estados Partes en Virtud del Párrafo 1 del Artículo 12 del Protocolo Facultativo de la Convención sobre los Derechos del Niño Relativo a la Venta de Niños, la Prostitución Infantil y la Utilización de Niños en la Pornografía (CRC/C/OPSC/MEX/CO/1)' (7 April 2011) para 30.
163   UNICEF, 'Panorama estadístico de la violencia contra niñas, niños y adolescentes en México' (2019) <www.unicef.org/mexico/media/1731/file/UNICEF%20PanoramaEstadistico.pdf> accessed 4 April 2022.

most of the CRC Cttee's COs has been highly limited and the impact of legal reforms and policy programmes on the actual enjoyment of children's rights is not clear, as the severe violation of children's rights continues unabated.

5.7 International Convention on the Protection of the Rights of All Migrant Workers and Members of Their Families

5.7.1 Incorporation and Reliance by Legislature and Executive

As noted in part 2, article 1 of the Mexican Constitution establishes that '*all persons* shall enjoy the human rights recognised in this Constitution and in international treaties of which the Mexican state is a party'.[164] In the same sense, article 11 of the Constitution establishes that '*all persons* have the right to enter' the country and request asylum.[165] Prior to a 2011 reform on migration, article 33 of the Constitution established that the executive power held the 'exclusive faculty' to, without trial, expel foreigners 'whose permanence [in the country] is deemed inconvenient'.[166] The reformed article 33 of the Constitution confirms the executive's faculty to expel foreigners, but in contrast to the previous provisions, expulsions are to be made in accordance with the law and after a hearing. In addition, the reformed article 33 now establishes that foreigners 'shall enjoy the human rights and guarantees' recognised in the Constitution.[167] Mexico's Migration Law was also significantly reformed in 2011. The reformed Law established numerous clauses regarding the human rights of migrants and eliminated the dispositions that explicitly criminalised undocumented migration.[168] CMW was cited in at least one draft Bill on the 2011 Migration Law and in another draft Bill on the 2011 human rights constitutional reform.[169]

---

164 *Diario Oficial de la Federación* (n 1) (emphasis added).
165 Constitución Política de los Estados Unidos Mexicanos, *Diario Oficial de la Federación* (6 July 2019) <https://www.seguridadbc.gob.mx/Planeacion/marcolegalPDF/1.pdf> accessed 4 April 2022 (emphasis added).
166 Cuauhtémoc Manuel de Dienheim Barriguete, 'El Artículo 33 de la Constitución y la Expulsión de Personas Extranjeras' in Eduardo Ferrer Mac-Gregor Poisot, José Luis Caballero Ochoa and Christian Steiner (eds), 'Derechos Humanos en la Constitución: Comentarios de Jurisprudencia Constitucional e Interamericana' vol 2 (Suprema Corte de Justicia de la Nación, Instituto de Investigaciones Jurídicas-UNAM and Fundación Konrad Ahenauer 2013) 1636.
167 ibid 1635, 1659.
168 *Diario Oficial de la Federación* (25 May 2011) <www.diputados.gob.mx/LeyesBiblio/ref/lmigra/LMigra_orig_25may11.pdf> accessed 4 April 2022; see, in particular, arts 6 to 17.
169 Humberto Andrade Quezada and others, 'Iniciativa con Proyecto de Decreto por el que se Expide la Ley de Migración' (9 December 2010) <http://sil.gobernacion.gob.mx/Archivos/Documentos/2010/12/asun_2721389_20101209_1291911767.pdf> accessed 4 April 2022; *Cámara de Diputados* (n 54).

5.7.2 Reliance by the Judiciary

According to the data shown in Table 12.1 in part 4 above, the federal judiciary has mentioned CMW in its jurisprudence a very limited number of times, while it has not mentioned the CMW Cttee at all. In its 2011 COs on Mexico's second periodic report, the CMW Cttee expressed concern regarding information 'that the handling of judicial proceedings by some public prosecutors and the judicial decisions of some judges reflect insufficient knowledge of the provisions of the Convention'.[170]

5.7.3 Impact on and through Independent State Institutions

CMW is not mentioned in the CNDH's 'general recommendations', while the CMW Cttee is only quoted in General Recommendation 36, regarding the rights of agricultural workers. In this 'general recommendation', the CNDH makes reference to the CMW Cttee's COs on Mexico's third periodic report.[171]

5.7.4 Impact on and through Non-state Actors

CMW and the CMW Cttee do not figure among the most widely-known and used human rights treaties and treaty bodies in Mexico. To a good extent, their use is limited to some NGOs and other civil society actors (that is, migrants' shelters) that specialise in the advocacy of the human rights of migrants – CMW is only occasionally cited in NGO reports that address migration issues and the CMW Cttee is not a widely-used source.[172] Domestic NGOs (often in collaboration with international counterparts) produced a number of shadow or alternative reports to the CMW Cttee, for the review process of Mexico's second and third periodic reports. However, this interaction is clearly more moderate than in the case of other treaty bodies. Similarly, CMW is one of the human rights treaties least often cited by the Mexican press.

---

170   Committee on the Protection of the Rights of All Migrant Workers and Members of Their Families, 'COs of the Committee on the Protection of the Rights of All Migrant Workers and Members of Their Families. Mexico' (CMW/C/MEX/CO/2) (3 May 2011) para 22.
171   CNDH, 'Recomendación General 36 (20 May 2019) 22, 23. <https://www.cndh.org.mx/sites/default/files/documentos/2019-05/RecGral_036.pdf> accessed 4 April 2022.
172   See, for example, Fabienne Venet Rebiffé and Irene Palma Calderón, 'Seguridad para el Migrante: una Agenda por Construir' (INEDIM 2011); José Antonio Guevara Bermúdez, 'Marco Institucional y Normativo en Materia de Migración' (INEDIM 2011); INEDIM, 'Diagnóstico de Instituciones del Estado de Coahuila con Enfoque de Derechos Humanos de Personas Migrantes' (INEDIM, Casa del Migrante de Saltillo and Universidad Iberoamericana Puebla 2017).

5.7.5 Impact of State Reporting

The CMW Cttee has issued three sets of COs on Mexico. In its more recent COs, issued in September 2017, the CMW Cttee reiterated its concerns over the lack of harmonisation of the 2011 Migration Law with the contents of CMW. In addition, the CMW Cttee noted the lack of sufficient knowledge of the contents of CMW by government officials, despite training received to that effect; the increase in violent crimes perpetrated against migrants and the threats and attacks suffered by migrant activists; and the persistence of discriminatory attitudes and xenophobia by government officials and society in general. The CMW Cttee also noted the continued impunity regarding massacres of migrants perpetrated in 2010 and 2012; the conditions in administrative detention or 'holding centres', which in some cases amount to cruel, inhuman and degrading treatment; the expulsion of migrants from the country; the detention of children; and the lack of sufficient protections for unaccompanied children.[173] For its follow-up procedure, the CMW Cttee underlined its recommendations regarding legal harmonisation, the impunity on the massacres of migrants, the conditions of detention in 'holding centres' and the protection of migrant children.[174]

Although, as already noted, Mexico's Migration Law was reformed in 2011, as stressed by the CMW Cttee in its 2011 and 2017 COs, tensions remain between Mexico's legal framework and the contents of CMW. Furthermore, the sources of concern identified by the CMW Cttee in 2017 do not differ much from those expressed six years before, suggesting that in this case the impact has been particularly limited.

5.7.6 Impact of Individual Communications

Mexico recognised the competence of the CMW Cttee to receive individual communications in 2006. However, the CMW provisions regarding individual communications have not yet entered into force.

5.7.7 Brief Conclusion

The impact does not seem to be particularly high with respect to CMW and the CMW Cttee. In contrast to other treaties and treaty bodies, the agenda advanced by the CMW Cttee has not made much progress in Mexico, not even

---

[173] Committee on the Protection of the Rights of All Migrant Workers and Members of Their Families, 'COs on the Third Periodic Report of Mexico (CMW/C/MEX/CO/3)' (27 September 2017).

[174] CMW/C/MEX/CO/3 para 63.

in the legislative and institutional spheres. The treaty, furthermore, is among the least used by civil society organisations, the judiciary and the press.

5.8 International Convention for the Protection of All Persons from Enforced Disappearance

5.8.1 Incorporation and Reliance by Legislature and Executive

The crime of enforced disappearances was included in Mexico's Federal Criminal Code in 2001. However, the definition used was criticised for failing to conform to international standards. The General Law on Enforced Disappearance, Disappearance by Non-State Actors and the National Search System (General Law on Disappearances) was adopted in November 2017, almost nine years after Mexico's ratification of CED.[175] CED and the CED Cttee were quoted in different draft Bills on the matter, advanced between 2014 and 2016.[176] Article 29 of the Mexican Constitution includes the right not to be subjected to enforced disappearance as one of the rights that cannot be suspended in times of emergency or armed conflict.

The General Law on Disappearances creates the National Search System, which entails the establishment of a new institutional machinery (including a National Search Commission), the implementation of search protocols and the creation of databases.[177]

The adoption of the General Law and the establishment of the National Search System came about in the midst of the political crises and intense domestic and international pressure produced by the aforementioned disappearance of the 43 Ayotzinapa students and overall the current national crisis of disappearances.

---

175 *Diario Oficial de la Federación* (17 November 2017) <http://www.diputados.gob.mx/LeyesBiblio/pdf/LGMDFP_171117.pdf' \h> accessed 10 June 2019.

176 See, for example, Omar Fayad Meneses, 'Proyecto de Decreto por el que se Expide la Ley General para Prevenir y Sancionar la Desaparición Forzada de Personas' (Gaceta Oficial del Senado, 16 April 2016) <www.senado.gob.mx/64/gaceta_del_senado/documento/54063> accessed 12 November 2019; Angélica de la Peña and others, 'Iniciativa con Proyecto de Decreto por el que se Expide la Ley General para Prevenir, Investigar, Sancionar y Reparar la Desaparición Forzada de Personas y la Desaparición de Personas por Particulares' (Gaceta Oficial del Senado, 17 September 2015) <http://infosen.senado.gob.mx/sgsp/gaceta/63/1/2015-09-17-1/assets/documentos/INIC_PRD__Des_Forzada_Part.pdf> accessed 4 April 2022.

177 *Diario Oficial de la Federación* (n 175) art 44 ff.

5.8.2 Reliance by the Judiciary

Table 12.1 in part 4 shows that CED and the CED Cttee have not been cited often by the federal judiciary. CED entered into force in 2011, when the Supreme Court's use of international human rights standards was on the increase. Many of the decisions adopted by the federal judiciary regarding enforced disappearances do not cite CED or its Committee. Some specialists consider that the effect of CED or the Committee's jurisprudence over the judiciary in Mexico has been limited.[178] However, the Supreme Court has started to use CED in some decisions. For example, the Supreme Court relied on CED in an *amparo* writ related to the Ayotzinapa disappearances case, in which it established the obligation of the authorities to undertake an immediate, exhaustive and impartial investigation.[179]

5.8.3 Impact on and through Non-state Actors

The ratification and entry into force of CED and the monitoring activities by the CED Cttee have lent considerable leverage to civil society.[180] Specialised NGOs and those dealing with gross human rights violations constantly cite CED and the CED Cttee in reports and use them for litigation. Our review of in-depth reports by leading NGOs shows an intense use of both CED and the CED Cttee's COs.[181] Moreover, CED and the reporting process to the CED Cttee have provided a focal point for the articulation of an important network composed of traditional human rights NGOs and victims' collectives, which was highly influential in the legislative process that led to the adoption of the new General Law on Disappearances.[182] In addition, regardless of its recent adoption, CED has been mentioned numerous times in articles by the press.

5.8.4 Impact of State Reporting

By the time the CED Cttee released its COs in 2015, the pressure on the government in relation to the disappearance of the 43 Ayotzinapa students was at its peak. The COs noted that Mexico's legal framework did not conform to CED and expressed concern over the generalised occurrence of enforced disappearances in the country. The Committee recommended, specifically, the adoption

---

178 Interview with Juan Carlos Gutiérrez.
179 Poder Judicial de la Federación 'Amparo en Revisión 203/2017' (31 May 2018) <http://sise.cjf.gob.mx/SVP/word1.aspx?arch=508/05080000211078340011012.doc_1&sec=Jes%C3%BAs_Desiderio_Cavazos_Elizondo&svp=1> accessed 4 April 2022.
180 Interview with Olga Guzmán.
181 See n 21.
182 Interview with Olga Guzmán; interview with Juan Carlos Gutiérrez.

of a general law on the matter and stressed the importance of the development of specific programmes or policies to search and locate victims.[183] Hence, the timing of the COs secured a crucial impact on the legislative process which in due course led to the adoption of the General Law on Disappearances and the creation of the National Search System. The COs offered a clear blueprint for NGOs, legislators and other stakeholders in the process of enacting the General Law in 2017.[184]

5.8.5   Impact of Individual Communications

Despite intense domestic and international pressure to this effect – including through the CED Cttee's COs – the Enrique Peña Nieto government staunchly refused to recognise the CED Cttee's communications procedure. As already mentioned, this reluctance took place in the context of important tensions between the Mexican government and critical international human rights organs, including the CED Cttee. A specialised Mexican NGO lodged three communications regarding cases of enforced disappearances to the HR Cttee, one of which has already resulted in the adoption of views by the HRC Cttee.[185] In early 2019 a Federal Court ordered the recognition of the CED Cttee's communications procedure[186] and on 30 August 2019 (the International Day of the Victims of Enforced Disappearances) President Amlo's government announced that it would recognise the procedure.[187] As already mentioned, this pledge was fulfilled in early October 2020.

5.8.6   Impact of Urgent Actions

Some specialised Mexican NGOs and victims' collectives have been submitting a very large number of urgent actions requests to the CED Cttee. Accordingly, the Committee has requested Mexico to take all the necessary measures to locate disappeared persons in 332 cases – this is 66 per cent of all such requests

---

183   Committee on Enforced Disappearances, 'COs on the Report Submitted by Mexico Under Article 29, Paragraph 1, of the Convention' (CED/C/MEX/CO/1) (25 March 2015).
184   Interview with Olga Guzmán; interview with Stephanie Brewer.
185   Interview with Juan Carlos Gutiérrez.
186   Interview with Stephanie Brewer. Also see Emir Alonso Olivares, 'Instan al Gobierno Federal a Aceptar Competencia del Comité CED' (*La Jornada* 1 February 2019) 11 <www.jornada.com.mx/2019/02/01/politica/011n1pol> accessed 15 July 2019.
187   Amnesty International, "México: Autoridades dan importante paso al anunciar que aceptarán la competencia del Comité de la ONU sobre desapariciones forzadas", Press Release, August 30, 2019, https://www.amnesty.org/es/latest/news/2019/08/autoridades-mexicanas-aceptan-comite-de-onu-sobre-desapariciones-forzadas/ accessed 6 April 2022.

made by the CED Cttee to all states.[188] However, according to a seasoned advocate directly involved in these petitions, the impact of these requests by the CED Cttee has been highly limited, particularly because the government has insisted that they are not legally binding.[189] Nevertheless, for other NGOs the urgent actions of CED have been an important mechanism to force prosecutors to take into account the views of the families and their representatives in the investigation of cases of enforced disappearance and to implement protective measures to family members under threat.[190]

5.8.7   Brief Conclusion

In spite of its short existence, CED and the CED Cttee are well known by domestic human rights advocates, including victim's collectives, who refer to them in their advocacy and litigation actions. The adoption of the General Law on Disappearances, and the resulting creation of the National Search System, are highly relevant reforms, which resulted from an intense process of domestic and external pressures, of which CED and the CED Cttee's COs were a particularly relevant component. However, beyond this legislative impact, disappearances in Mexico remain generalised. At the time of writing, there are more than 70 000 disappeared persons in the country.[191] In addition, according to public information requests by a leading NGO, there are at least 1 606 mass graves, located in 24 federal states, containing 2 320 bodies, 169 skeletons and 548 bone fragments.[192] Impunity, meanwhile, remains almost absolute.

5.9   *Convention on the Rights of Persons with Disabilities*

5.9.1   Incorporation and Reliance by Legislature and Executive

Article 1 of the Constitution was reformed in 2001, to prohibit discrimination on the basis of disability. Some of the draft Bills regarding the 2011 human constitutional reform discussed in some detail the prohibition of discrimination and the rights of persons with disabilities, citing Convention 111 of the International

---

188   Requests made by the Committee between March 2012 and June 2018. Committee on Enforced Disappearances, 'Urgent Actions Registered by the Committee' (nd) <www.ohchr.org/EN/HRBodies/ced/Pages/CEDIndex.aspx> accessed 10 July 2019.
189   Interview with Juan Carlos Gutiérrez; interview with Olga Guzmán.
190   General Assembly, 'Report of the Committee on Enforced Disappearances (A/69/56)' (2014) para 61. Also see <https://cmdpdh.org/no-olvidamos/daniel-ramos/> accessed 4 April 2022.
191   National Registry of Disappeared and Missing Persons (n 4).
192   CMDPDH, 'El Fenómeno de las Fosas Clandestinas en México' (Animal Político, 1 July 2019) <www.animalpolitico.com/verdad-justicia-y-reparacion/el-fenomeno-de-las-fosas-clandestinas-en-mexico/> accessed 4 April 2022.

Labour Organisation (ILO) and the Inter-American Convention for the Elimination of all forms of Discrimination against Persons with Disabilities, but not CRPD.[193] As also mentioned in part 5.1 above, in 2003 Congress adopted the Federal Law to Prevent and Eliminate Discrimination and established the CONAPRED. In 2011, a few years after Mexico's adherence to CRPD, Congress adopted the General Law on the Inclusion of Persons with Disabilities and created the National Council for the Development and Inclusion of Persons with Disabilities.[194] CRPD is mentioned several times in this General Law and was repeatedly cited in draft Bills proposed for its adoption.[195]

5.9.2 Reliance by the Judiciary

Table 12.1 in part 4 shows that the jurisprudence of the federal judiciary has made explicit reference to CRPD on numerous occasions – considerably more than other treaties, such as CAT and CED. For example, in an *amparo* writ, the Supreme Court relied on CRPD to understand disabilities as a social construct.[196] However, the CRPD Cttee has been cited only once by the federal judiciary. In an interview, one practitioner actively involved in the litigation of cases related to the rights of persons with disabilities stated that judges in lower courts often take decisions that are completely contrary to the norms established in CRPD.[197]

5.9.3 Impact on and through Non-state Actors

Specialised national NGOs that work on issues related to the rights of persons with disabilities widely use CRPD in their advocacy and litigation work.[198] Disability-focused organisations have recently started to use CRPD and to engage with the CRPD Cttee, for example participating in interactive dialogues and elaborating shadow reports.[199] CRPD was quoted many times in the

---

193 *Cámara de Diputados* (n 54).
194 *Diario Oficial de la Federación* (30 May 2011) <http://dof.gob.mx/nota_detalle.php?codigo=5191516&fecha=30/05/2011> accessed 4 April 2022.
195 Claudia Edith Anaya Mota, 'Que Expide la Ley General para la Integración Social de las Personas con Discapacidad' (16 February 2010) <http://sil.gobernacion.gob.mx/Archivos/Documentos/2010/02/asun_2632606_20100219_1266602812.pdf> accessed 4 April 2022.
196 Primera Sala, 'Amparo en revisión 410/2012' (21 November 2012) <www2.scjn.gob.mx/ConsultaTematica/PaginasPub/DetallePub.aspx?AsuntoID=140322> accessed 4 April 2022.
197 Interview with María Sirvent.
198 ibid.
199 ibid. In 2014 the Committee published a list of issues related to Mexico's initial report. In response, Mexican civil society organisations submitted seven documents and the Human Rights Commission of the Federal District one document to the Committee.

in-depth reports by leading human rights organisations we reviewed for the elaboration of this chapter.[200] According to our review of three major national newspapers, CRDP was mentioned in hundreds of news or opinion articles – only CRC and CCPR were mentioned more often. This is worth noting, particularly if one considers the fact that the Convention was ratified by Mexico only in late 2007.

5.9.4 Impact of State Reporting

In its 2014 COs on Mexico's initial report and in a 'list of issues in relation to the initial report of Mexico', the CRPD Cttee expressed concern in relation to the harmonisation of national legislation with CRPD, particularly at the sub-national level. The Committee also mentioned the following causes of concern: the insufficient budgetary resources allocated to combat discrimination on the bases of disabilities; the lack of systematic data and statistical information; the lack of access to justice and violations of due process; the lack of administrative and criminal investigations of abuses; violations of the right to education of children with disabilities; the violation of labour rights; and violence against women and girls with disabilities.[201]

Most of these concerns have not been addressed. The harmonisation of state-level legislation remains insufficient; the government's efforts to generate data and statistics are still limited; persons with disabilities continue to face severe problems of discrimination; and access to justice is highly restricted and impunity prevails, including in cases of violence against women with disabilities, to name but a few of the remaining challenges of compliance.[202]

5.9.5 Impact of Individual Communications

The CRPD Cttee has not yet adopted views on communications against Mexico. A domestic NGO that specialises in the access to justice of persons with disabilities recently filed a communication to the CRPD Cttee on a case

---

200 See n 21.
201 Committee on the Rights of Persons with Disabilities, 'COs on the Initial Report of Mexico' (CRPD/C/MEX/CO/1) (27 October 2014); Committee on the Rights of Persons with Disabilities, 'List of Issues in Relation to the Initial Report of Mexico (CRPD/C/MEX/Q/1)' (30 April 2014). At the time of writing, the COs on Mexico's second-third periodic reports had not been released.
202 CNDH, 'Informe Especial de la Comisión Nacional de los Derechos Humanos sobre el estado que guarda los derechos humanos de las personas con discapacidad en las entidades federativas del país' (4 December 2018) <http://informe.cndh.org.mx//images/uploads/nodos/40481/content/files/Estudio-Personas-Discapacidad.pdf> accessed 4 April 2022.

regarding access to justice. According to the director of this organisation, the Committee's mere request for information to the authorities 'opened wide doors', particularly in the judiciary, which was more receptive to issues concerning access to justice for persons with disabilities and started to implement training programmes.[203] At the time of writing, the case continued under the review of the CRPD Cttee.

5.9.6 Brief Conclusion

As in the case of CED and the CED Cttee, CRPD and the CRPD Cttee have become known to domestic advocates and other actors in a relatively short period of time. In addition, important legislative reforms have been adopted and policy programmes were created to advance the rights established in CRPD. The dissemination of CRPD as such and the COs by the CRPD Cttee have been instrumental for advocates and other actors that have influenced the legislative processes that led to such reforms. As in the case of all other treaties and treaty bodies, however, many of the recommendations in the COs have not been complied with, and the adoption of legal reforms and institutional or policy innovations have not in practice resulted in the improvement of the rights of persons with disabilities.

6 Conclusion

The UN human rights system has been a key element of the political and juridical dynamics of change around human rights in Mexico. Treaties and treaty bodies have come a long way in the country – from the early days of cautious and late ratification and the dominance of the doctrine of national sovereignty, to the more recent period of openness to international monitoring and scrutiny. Most UN human rights treaties and treaty bodies are known to political actors, legislators, members of the judiciary, civil society and the media, although the depth of this knowledge and use diminishes significantly at the subnational level. Reliance by the judiciary has expanded, particularly by the Supreme Court after the 2011 human rights constitutional reform. Nevertheless, it seems that the use of international jurisprudence and norms has been more relevant for the interpretation of national norms and not so much for the adoption of remedies.

---

203 Interview with María Sirvent; see communication CRPD/C/22/D/35/2015, the case was finalised on 6 September 2019 (violation found).

UN treaties and treaty bodies, together with the UN Human Rights Council, its special procedures and the Inter-American organs have been part of broader processes of transnational and domestic activism and litigation that have led to important reforms to Mexico's legal and institutional frameworks. The 2011 human rights constitutional reform no doubt is the centrepiece of a long and broad process of legal harmonisation. As shown in this chapter, the constitutional reform was preceded and has been followed by numerous specific reforms and innovations, all of which related to the rights included in UN human rights treaties and monitored by the treaty bodies.[204] Views on individual communications are few and recent, but they have already started to have some impact as well.[205] Much remains to be done, however, at the sub-national level, where diffusion and influence of international norms and treaty bodies has been much more limited and where important harmonisation challenges remain.

The overall impact of the UN human rights system over Mexico in the period covered in this study (1999 to 2020) clearly is broader and deeper than the influence achieved before. The previous study on the impact on Mexico, published in 1999, concluded that 'the treaty system … had a very limited impact' in the country.[206] The subsequent strengthened impact is the result of perseverance; it reflects the accumulation of government responses to domestic and transnational pressures over time, by a broad and diverse network of actors, in a context of governmental openness to international scrutiny and technical assistance and growth and consolidation of a national human rights movement with significant transnational counterparts.

As shown in this chapter, the key development in this process of interaction between the Mexican government and its internal and external critics has been legal and institutional reform. However, as the treaty bodies themselves have repeatedly underlined, huge challenges in implementation and compliance remain. Legal and institutional reforms have not led to clear and significant improvements in the field. 'Rights in theory' have not led to 'rights in practice'.[207] In other words, compliance remains the key challenge for human

---

204 In contrast, the previous study on the impact of UN treaties only found 'limited legislative reforms [adopted] with reference to the treaties' (Heyns and Viljoen (n 14) 430).
205 This also is in sharp contrast to the situation found by the previous study, which stressed that no individual communications procedure had at the time been accepted by Mexico (Heyns and Viljoen (n 14) 443).
206 Heyns and Viljoen (n 14) 444.
207 Joe Foweraker and Todd Landman, *Citizenship Rights and Social Movements: A Comparative Statistical Analysis* (Oxford University Press 1997).

rights organs and advocates, including the UN treaty bodies. Greater emphasis has to be given by treaty bodies to the issue of implementation of reforms and to compliance with COs and remedies or reparations, many of which have been ignored in practice. Stronger and more effective mechanisms of follow-up are needed.

Recent research has stressed the gap between commitment and compliance in the case of Mexico and concluded that despite numerous formal reforms, the Mexican state has been 'unable and unwilling' to comply with international and domestic human rights norms.[208] In this sense, commitments with international norms and organs and formal legal and institutional reforms are best understood as mere 'tactical concessions'.[209] Transforming the entrenched structures of interests, practices and cultural understandings that underlay human rights violations in Mexico requires, in addition to adequate laws, strong state institutions and willing political elites at all levels of government. In this sense, adopting international commitments and reforming formal legal and institutional structures is a necessary but not a sufficient condition for ultimate human rights change in Mexico. Treaty bodies and the other UN actors should be aware of this and step up the momentum of critical scrutiny and pressure and, as already suggested, design stronger and more effective procedures to follow-up on their recommendations and decisions.

---

208 Anaya-Muñoz, 'Bringing Willingness Back In' (n 48).
209 Thomas Risse and Kathryn Sikkink, 'The Socialisation of International Human Rights Norms Into Domestic Practices: Introduction' in Thomas Risse, Stephen C Ropp and Kathryn Sikkink (eds), *The Power of Human Rights. International Norms and Domestic Change* (Cambridge University Press 1999) 1, 38.

CHAPTER 13

The Impact of the United Nations Human Rights Treaties on the Domestic Level in Nepal

Ravi Prakash Vyas, Pranjali Kanel and Anusha Kharel

1   Introduction to Human Rights in Nepal

Nepal is a federal democratic republic with a long and rich history. Its geographical shape changed over time. Nepal was never colonised. People in Nepal have fought for their rights since the very inception of the country. They have always raised their voice for want of human rights and democracy, with the intent to incorporate international human rights mechanisms and have attempted to create a legal system based on the principles of human rights. The popular movement of 1990 against the political turmoil led the path towards restoring a multiparty parliamentary system in Nepal. A decade-long (1996 to 2006) armed conflict between the Maoists and the government impeded this process.

Nepal witnessed gross human rights violations during the decade-long armed conflict that lasted from 1996 to 2006. Thousands of people were killed or forcibly disappeared by the armed forces. Nepal held the distinction for the highest number of disappearances in any country during 2003 and 2004.[1] The Comprehensive Peace Agreement signed in 2006 raised hopes for improvements in the human rights situation after the conflict. The interim Constitution (2007) strengthened the legal framework for guaranteeing human rights in Nepal. It extended due process rights, such as the right to legal assistance upon arrest, the presumption of innocence and the prohibition of untouchability.[2]

After 2006, the promulgation of the interim Constitution saw the human rights of minorities, including women and children, being held to a higher standard.[3] The year 2015 was a turning point in Nepalese political and social

---

[1]   Sonal Singh, Khagendra Dahal & Edward Mills, 'Nepal's War on Human Rights: A Summit Higher Than Everest' (2005) 4 International Journal for Equity in Health 9 <https://equityhealthj.biomedcentral.com/articles/10.1186/1475-9276-4-9> accessed 30 June 2022.

[2]   'Human Rights in Nepal: One Year After the Comprehensive Peace Agreement' UNHCR, December 2007.

[3]   See *Meera Dhungana and Others v Office of the Prime Ministers and Others* (Writ No 131 of the Year 2063) (2007). In this case a petition was filed for revision of the law prohibiting

history. A new Constitution was promulgated. The 2015 Constitution proclaims the essence of democratic norms and values, and human rights.[4] The Constitution contains cross-cutting human rights principles such as accountability, non-discrimination, inclusion and participation. It embeds the fundamental principles of human rights as mentioned in the Universal Declaration of Human Rights and in United Nations (UN) treaties, ranging from the right to life with dignity (article 16); the right to liberty (article 12); the right to equality (article 18); the right to justice (article 20); the rights of victims (article 21); the right against torture (article 22); the right to education (article 31); and the right to privacy (article 28). The Constitution characterises these rights as justiciable and provides for a constitutional remedy (article 46) to enforce these rights. The Constitution bestows the power on the judiciary of Nepal to apply recognised principles of justice along with constitutional and other legal provisions.[5]

The promulgation of the 2015 Constitution also saw the enactment of new laws. The Labour Act, the Children Act and the Social Security Act are examples of legislation that came to be implemented after 2015, in the span of a few years, which was progressive and inclusive of Nepal's international obligations.[6] Despite the progress, the Nepalese government in other respects strayed by not aligning its legislation with human rights instruments. The Citizenship Bill came under scrutiny with its discriminatory provisions towards women despite Nepal's international obligation and opposition by independent organisations and civil society in Nepal. The Information Technology Bill introduced in 2019 has been widely criticised by domestic and international organisations for its provisions that threaten freedom of expression.[7]

---

dowries. The law imposed a much stricter sentence on the bride's family than the groom's, making it inconsistent with the equal rights provisions in art 11 of the Constitution of the Kingdom of Nepal and international human rights standards. The Court's decision to revise the law, which cited earlier rulings based on art 11, shows a continued dedication to transforming the Nepalese Legal Code in the interests of gender rights and equality.

4 Geeta Pathak, 'Paradigm Shifts in Internalisation of International Law: A Case Study of Growing Human Rights Jurisprudence in Nepal' (2008) 6 Kathmandu School of Law Review 12.
5 Constitution of Nepal, 2015 art 126(1).
6 Ravi Prakash Vyas, 'Strategic Roadmap for Nepal: Integrating United Nations Guiding Principles on Business and Human Rights into Domestic Law' (2020) Global Campus of Human Rights <http://doi.org/20.500.11825/1618> accessed 30 June 2022.
7 Bhrikuti Rai, 'Everything You Need to Know About the Nepal Government's New IT Bill' *The Kathmandu Post* (29 February 2019) <https://kathmandupost.com/national/2019/02/22/everything-you-need-to-know-about-the-governments-new-it-bill> accessed 30 June 2022; Amnesty International, 'Nepal: Information Technology Bill Threatens Freedom of

In the early 1990s Nepal became one of the first nations in South Asia to abolish capital punishment. Article 16 of the Constitution provides for the 'right to live with dignity', expressly banning capital punishment.[8] However, several non-governmental organisations (NGOs) and activists have questioned the abolition of capital punishment and have demanded capital punishment in respect of perpetrators of rape and other crimes against women.[9]

The Nepalese Constitution under article 40 provides for the right of Dalits. However, these are of no avail to them, as time and again there have been reports of atrocities against the Dalits.[10] Incidents of targeting a particular caste or echelon of society have persistently been reported. These instances are not only against the fundamental fabric of human rights but are also in violation of the Constitution. Despite the formulation of laws that are justifiable in nature, the question of whether the mere formulation of law is sufficient persists.[11]

Nepal has an independent constitutional body, namely, the National Human Rights Commission (NHRC) established in compliance with the Paris Principles. The NHRC is responsible to respect, protect, promote and ensure the effective enforcement of human rights.[12] It monitors whether the state has fulfilled its primary responsibility and makes it accountable if it has played an unsatisfactory role in the protection and promotion of human rights.[13] The NHRC has played an instrumental role in highlighting the need to put an end to incidents of caste-based discrimination and untouchability. The Commission's monitoring report in 2019[14] stated how such practices went against human

---

Expression', 9 July 2022 <https://www.amnesty.org/en/latest/news/2020/01/nepal-information-technology-bill-threatens-freedom-of-expression/> accessed 9 July 2020.

[8] Constitution of Nepal, 2015 art 16(2).

[9] Bansari Kamdar, 'Rape Cases Surge in Nepal, Activists Question Death Penalty' *The Diplomat* (18 November 2020) <https://thediplomat.com/2020/11/rape-cases-surge-in-nepal-activists-question-death-penalty> accessed 25 June 2020.

[10] Elisha Shrestha and Aditi Aryal, 'Discrimination against Dalits Continues to Stain Nepal's Social Fabric' *The Kathmandu Post* (Kathmandu, 3 June 2020) <https://kathmandupost.com/national/2020/06/03/discrimination-against-dalits-continues-to-stain-nepal-s-social-fabric> accessed 30 June 2020; Human Rights Watch, 'Nepal: Ensure Justice for Caste Based Killings' (New York, 1 June 2020) <https://www.hrw.org/news/2020/06/01/nepal-ensure-justice-caste-based-killings> accessed 30 June 2022.

[11] 'Nepal: Authorities Must Deliver Justice for Dalit Killings' *Amnesty International* (28 May 2020) <https://www.amnesty.org/en/latest/news/2020/05/nepal-authorities-must-deliver-justice-for-dalit-killings/> accessed 30 June 2022.

[12] Constitution of Nepal, 2015 art 249.

[13] Annual Report Synopsis (FY 2017–18), National Human Rights Commission Nepal (NHRC) 2019.

[14] Nepal Human Rights Commission (NHRC), Monitoring Report on 'Status of Rights against Cased-Based Discrimination and Untouchability' 2019.

rights and their adverse effect on life, liberty, equality and dignity. It has assisted in coordinating efforts between all three tiers of government by incorporating mechanisms to include ending discrimination and untouchability in plans, policies, programmes and budgets. The NHRC has also been able to urge political parties to emphasise social offences against such practices and to incorporate such measures in their documents as to raise awareness about such issues by recognising the proportional inclusion for members of the Dalit community.[15]

The Constitution also mandates the establishment of the National Women Commission;[16] the National Dalit Commission;[17] the National Inclusion Commission;[18] the Indigenous Nationality Commission;[19] the Madhesi Commission;[20] the Tharu Commission;[21] and the Muslim Commission.[22] These commissions are responsible for the protection and promotion of the rights and interests of concerned groups. They also implement the policies adopted by the government, suggest the necessary policies and programmes to be pursued for the upliftment of the respective communities and evaluate their representation in organs of state.

Numerous NGOs and civil society organisations (CSOs) in Nepal play an active role in the protection and promotion of human rights. These organisations have a grass-roots presence and continue to function in diverse areas, including raising awareness, providing free legal aid services, assisting governments while formulating legislation and policies, evaluating the human rights situation and reporting to national and international bodies.

2 Relationship of Nepal with International Human Rights System in General

Nepal's meaningful relationship with the international human rights system can be traced to the 1990s. With the promulgation of the 1990 Constitution, the autocratic Panchayat system was overthrown and a multi-party system

---

15   ibid.
16   Constitution of Nepal, 2015 art 252.
17   ibid art 255.
18   ibid art 258.
19   ibid art 261.
20   ibid art 262.
21   ibid art 263.
22   ibid art 264.

restored. The realisation of the consciousness about social and political rights led to the emergence of the Popular Movement (*Jana Andolan*). The 1990 Popular Movement can be credited with propelling the human rights movement in Nepal, which is still considered young. Followed by the promulgation of the Constitution of Kingdom of Nepal in 1990, the Treaty Act of Nepal (1990) was instrumental in providing scope to international human rights instruments. The Constitution provided that Nepal could be a party to any treaty either by simple majority or by a two-thirds majority of the members of both houses of parliament.[23] In a similar manner, the Treaty Act governs the substantive and procedural aspects of the ratification of and accession to treaties.[24] Nepal ratified most of the human rights treaties after 1990.

Apart from its commitment to the UN treaty system, Nepal's engagement with the international human rights system can be viewed through its attitude towards the regional mechanisms, such as the South Asian Association of Regional Cooperation (SAARC), and the UN system in general.

Nepal is part of SAARC, which primarily focuses on the welfare of the South Asian population. While SAARC does not have a specific human rights protection mechanism, the SAARC Social Charter, adopted in 2004 in Islamabad, places particular emphasis on promoting universal respect for and observance and protection of human rights and fundamental freedoms for all. In particular, the Social Charter references the right to development, gender equality, welfare and the interests of children and the youth along with the promotion of social integration and the strengthening of civil society.[25]

Nepal has complied with its commitment[26] to report under the Universal Periodic Review (UPR). Following its reports in 2011 and 2015, Nepal submitted its third national report for review under the UPR in November 2020. In its report[27] to the UPR Working Group, Nepal welcomed the opportunity for review and represented its achievements, opportunities and challenges in the field of human rights. The report also stated that Nepal had implemented almost all accepted recommendations, 152 out of the 195 recommendations provided by the UPR Working Group.[28] Other than the national reports, the

---

23 Constitution of the Kingdom of Nepal, 2047 (1990) art 126.
24 Nepal Treaty Act, 2047 (1990), s 9.
25 SAARC Social Charter, 2004.
26 OHCHR, 'Universal Periodic Review – Nepal' <https://www.ohchr.org/EN/HRBodies/UPR/Pages/NPindex.aspx> accessed 30 June 2022.
27 UNHRC, 'National Report Submitted in Accordance with Paragraph 5 of the Annex to Human Rights Council Resolution 16/21', A/HRC/WG.6/37/NPL/1 <https://digitallibrary.un.org/record/3893975?ln=en> accessed 30 June 2022.
28 ibid.

national human rights institutions (NHRIS) and NGOs in Nepal have been engaged in submitting reports concerning the overall human rights situation for the UPR cycles. A joint submission by the NHRIs in Nepal, which included NHRC, the National Women Commission (NWC) and the National Dalit Commission (NDC), was made in 2020 for the third cycle of the UPR. While the NHRIs in Nepal continue to work according to the constitutional mandate for protecting and promoting human rights, the 2020 joint submission[29] stated that Nepal was on a downward spiral in committing to its voluntary pledge during the Human Rights Council (HRC) election to strengthen the role of the NHRC. The report indicated that the NHRC Amendment Bill tabled in the Nepal Parliament in 2019 contradicted Supreme Court verdicts, the Paris Principles and amendments proposed by NHRC. It also states that the Bill undermined the constitutional provision as well as the independence and autonomy of the NHRC.[30]

Nepal has also been working with the UN human rights mechanism by extending invitations to the mandate holders under special procedures.[31] From 1996 to 2015, ten different special procedures and mandate holders have visited Nepal. The Special Rapporteur on the Human Rights of Migrants and Violence against Women, its Causes and Consequences visited Nepal in 2018. Nepal continues to work closely with UN human rights mechanisms. It has also accepted the request for country visits by the Special Rapporteur on the right to food and the special rapporteur on extreme poverty.[32]

Only a few years after the ratification of prominent human rights treaties, Nepal underwent a decade-long armed conflict lasting from 1996 to 2006. In 2005 the government of Nepal signed an agreement with the Office of the High Commissioner for Human Rights (OHCHR) to establish an office with a far-reaching mandate on human rights.[33] It aimed at monitoring the human rights situation and observing international humanitarian law along with investigating and verifying allegations of human rights abuses. The decade-long conflict brought out human rights concerns for the victims of the conflict along with

---

29   NHRC, NWC and NDC, 'The NHRI Nepal Joint Submission for The Third Cycle Universal Periodic Review of Nepal' <https://www.np.undp.org/content/nepal/en/home/library/democratic_governance/universal-periodic-report-Nepal.html> accessed 30 June 2022.
30   ibid; see also UNHRC, 'Summary of Stakeholders' Submissions on Nepal' A/HRC/WG.6/37/NPL/3 <https://www.ecoi.net/en/document/2042312.html> accessed 30 June 2022.
31   UNHRC (n 30).
32   ibid.
33   'OHCHR in Nepal (2006–2007)' (OHCHR) <https://nepal.ohchr.org/en/index.html> accessed 30 June 2022.

the operation of militant youth wings at the time from the United Nations Mission in Nepal (UNMIN) as well as the OHCHR.[34] The UNMIN report[35] on the 2008 election of Nepal reported violations of human rights in the form of intimidation of voters and clashes between opposition parties, confirmed by UNMIN and OHCHR monitoring and investigation. Although UNMIN and OHCHR ceased their operations in 2011, it is important to note its significant role in monitoring and assisting Nepal with the protection of human rights in a convoluted political and legal situation.

To administer to the victims of human rights violation during the armed conflict, Nepal passed the Act on Commission on Investigation of Disappeared Persons, Truth and Reconciliation, 2071 (2014) to create two commissions, namely, the Truth and Reconciliation Commission and the Commission on Investigation of Disappeared Persons. The Act is considered a significant step taken by Nepal on transitional justice. However, in its technical note,[36] OHCHR stated that the powers granted to the Commission could result in the avoidance or delay of a criminal investigation which would be inconsistent with international law. With concerns relating to the potential violation of international law that would transpire, NHRC,[37] OHRC and Human Rights Watch (HRW)[38] have time and again urged Nepal to ratify the Rome Statute (ICC).

---

[34] Kantipur Fireside, Interview with Ian Martin, Special Representative of the Secretary-General in Nepal <https://reliefweb.int/report/nepal/nepal-transcript-interview-srsg-ian-martin-fireside-chat-kantipur-tv-01-dec-2008> accessed 30 June 2022, UNMIN (1 December 2020) <https://reliefweb.int/sites/reliefweb.int/files/resources/EFFF3733D75AE92AC125751A0034A9F1-Full_Report.pdf> accessed 30 June 2022; 'Note verbale dated 16 August 2017 from the Permanent Mission of Nepal to the United Nations addressed to the President of the General Assembly' (17 August 2017) A/72/347 <https://undocs.org/en/A/72/347> accessed 30 June 2022.

[35] 'UNMIN Election Report No 2', UNMIN, 30 March 2008' <https://nepal.ohchr.org/en/resources/Documents/English/reports/HCR/2008_03_30_UNMIN_ElectionReport2_E.pdf> accessed 30 June 2022.

[36] OHCHR, 'OHCHR Technical Note, The Nepal Act on the Commission on Investigation of Disappeared Persons, Truth and Reconciliation, 2071 (2014) – as Gazetted 21 May 2014' <https://www.ohchr.org/Documents/Countries/NP/OHCHRTechnical_Note_Nepal_CIDP_TRC_Act2014.pdf> accessed 30 June 2022.

[37] Dewan Rai, 'NHR to govt: Ratify Rome Statute' *The Kathmandu Post* (Kathmandu, 19 February 2016) <https://kathmandupost.com/valley/2016/02/19/nhrc-to-govt-ratify-rome-statute> accessed 30 June 2022.

[38] HRW, 'Letter to the Attorney-General of Nepal' <https://www.hrw.org/news/2018/08/29/letter-attorney-general-nepal> accessed 30 June 2022.

The change in governance and political ambiance tends to have affected the commitment of Nepal to the human rights instruments and their domestic application. However, the laws, including the spirit of the Constitution, remain unwavering towards the respect for international human rights laws and its domestication. The Treaty Act is a separate piece of legislation that has been enacted to domesticate the provisions related to international instruments in Nepal. Article 9 of the Treaty Act stipulates that once ratified by Nepal, a treaty is treated as equal to the national law. While the Constitution of Nepal does not expressly provide for the status of international human rights law, it mentions that any treaty relating to peace and friendship, security and strategic alliance, the boundaries of Nepal and natural resources and the distribution of their use requires a two-thirds majority of the total members in both federal houses of the legislature. With contradicting and ambiguous legal provisions, Nepal's international human rights law is subject to equivocal remarks concerning its constitutional status.

The human rights movement in Nepal is relatively young. However, the conduct of the government of Nepal in line with promulgating a new constitution and the enactment of new legislation in addition to the opinions of the relevant stakeholders depict the tight-knit relationship between Nepal and the UN human rights system.

3 At a Glance: Formal Engagement of Nepal with the UN Human Rights Treaty System

Refer to the chart on the next page.

4 Role and Overall Impact of the UN Human Rights Treaties in Nepal

4.1 *Role of UN Treaties*
4.1.1 Formal Acceptance
Nepal had already ratified the International Convention on the Elimination of All Forms of Racial Discrimination (CERD) in 1971. After 1990, following the rise in the realisation of democratic norms and values among Nepali society, the government of Nepal made a very conscious effort to incorporate human rights and promote democratisation by ratifying a further five of the major UN treaties (the International Covenant on Civil and Political Rights (CCPR);

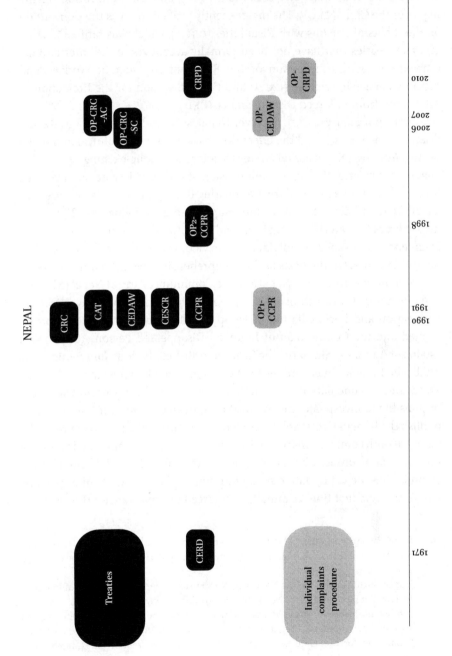

the International Covenant on Economic, Social and Cultural Rights (CESCR); the Convention on the Elimination of All Forms of Discrimination against Women (CEDAW); the Convention Against Torture and Other Cruel, Inhuman, or Degrading Treatment or Punishment (CAT); and the Convention on the Rights of the Child (CRC)). The most recently ratified treaty is the Convention on the Rights of Persons with Disabilities (CRPD), which was ratified in 2010. The two treaties that have not been formally accepted are the International Convention on the Protection of the Rights of All Migrant Workers and Members of Their Families (CMW) and the Convention for the Protection of All Persons from Enforced Disappearance (CED).

Nepal is not a party to CED. However, Nepalese officials are acutely aware that disappearances occur, and the effect they have had on the political and social setting. Although Nepal has taken steps to address the long-existing issue of disappearance by establishing the Commission of Enforced Disappeared Persons (CEDP) and various bilateral treaties relating to migration,[39] it is criticised for its failure to protect the rights of the disappeared by ratifying CED. Nepal witnessed gross human rights violations and atrocities during the 10-year Maoist insurgency. Thousands of individuals were victims of enforced disappearance, rape and torture. On the basis of the Comprehensive Peace Accord concluded between the government of Nepal and the Communist Party of Nepal (Maoist), and the interim Constitution of Nepal, 2007, the Commission for Investigation, Verification and Reconciliation of Disappeared Person Act, 2014 was promulgated and the Commission of Enforced Disappeared Person (CIEDP) was established in 2015. Similarly, the Truth and Reconciliation Commission was established in 2015 in accordance with the Enforced Disappearances Inquiry, Truth and Reconciliation Commission Act, 2014. These Commissions are responsible to investigate the enforced disappeared persons, to establish and publish the human rights violations committed during the armed conflict. The tenure of both commissions was twice extended. However, they failed to resolve the complaints brought by the victims and their families.[40] Additionally, the commissions are yet to publicise their findings. The Penal Code of Nepal 2017 has for the very first time criminalised enforced disappearances. However, the

---

39 Sarah Paoletti and others, 'Migrant Workers' Access to Justice at Home: Nepal' *Open Society Foundations*, 2014 <https://www.refworld.org/pdfid/53aa85ec4.pdf> accessed 30 June 2022.

40 Human Right Watch, 'No Law, No Justice, No State for Victims – The Culture of Impunity in Post-Conflict Nepal' (20 November 2020) <https://www.hrw.org/report/2020/11/20/no-law-no-justice-no-state-victims/culture-impunity-post-conflict-nepal> accessed 30 June 2022; National Human Rights Commission (NHRC), 'The NHRI Nepal Joint Submission for the Third Cycle Universal Periodic Review of Nepal' (March 2020)

rising extra-judicial and enforced disappearance cases, identified by the NHRC, depict a lack of proper security reforms[41] and inadequate application of law by the government. The government of Nepal is continuously urged to ratify CED during UPRs, by the NHRC[42] and the CRC Cttee.[43]

Nepal also is not a party to CMW. Despite this, Nepal recognises that labour migration has become a defining characteristic of its current socio-economic situation and how remittance is one of the primary sources of its economy. It provides for a number of mechanisms to help protect migrant workers' rights through executive action. A wide range of government functionaries, including diplomatic missions, reflect its seriousness towards the issues of migrant workers. Nepal has ratified other international conventions, including 11 International Labour Organisation (ILO) Conventions such as the Forced Labour Convention 1930 and the Abolition of Forced Labour Convention 1957. Moreover, the government regularly reports on many non-ratified conventions and follows up to align relevant laws and policies with those of the conventions and recommendations.[44] The government has been able to establish a well-defined mechanism to address issues concerning migrant labourers. Crucial steps include negotiating minimum wages for migrants; setting up the Foreign Employment Tribunal; skills training; and medical examinations for migrant workers. This helps to ensure the safety and security of the conditions of workers in other countries. The government of Nepal introduced minimum wages for migrant workers in consultation with the diplomatic missions, market trends and other experts. These referral wages are calculated on the basis of prevailing wages, cost of living and other factors. This helps to provide security for Nepali migrants in countries that do not have a system of minimum wages.[45]

    <https://www.nhrcnepal.org/nhrc_new/doc/newsletter/Inner_UPR_Report_Saun_2077_Last_Correction_compress.pdf> accessed 22 December 2020.

41 ibid.
42 NHRC (n 29).
43 Human Rights Council, 'Compilation on Nepal' (29 October 2020) <https://documents-dds-ny.un.org/doc/UNDOC/GEN/G20/274/55/PDF/G2027455.pdf?OpenElement> accessed 30 June 2022.
44 International Labour Organisation, 'Labour Migration for Employment: A Status Report for Nepal 2014/15' (2015).
45 Ministry of Labour, Employment and Social Security, 'National Labour Migration Report 2020' 56 <https://www.developmentaid.org/api/frontend/cms/file/2020/12/Migration-Report-2020-English.pdf> accessed 22 December 2020.

Despite these efforts, a wide range of labour violations has been experienced by Nepali migrant workers both during and after recruitment. The vast majority of migrant workers are unable to access justice in Nepal or abroad.[46] The misrepresentation of the nature and terms of work, overcharging of fees by recruitment agencies, a failure to provide proper documents of employment and recruitment, excessive working hours, wages lower than the stipulated salary, violations of contracts, unsafe working conditions, loss of life, and so forth, are some of the major problems faced by migrant workers. The National Human Rights Institution,[47] the CRC Cttee, UPRs[48] and the Supreme Court of Nepal[49] have all time and again recommended to the government of Nepal to ratify CMW and to adopt national policies to address the interests of migrant workers. Furthermore, the Special Rapporteur on the Human Rights of Migrants on his mission to Nepal also recommended to the government of Nepal to ratify CMW.[50] However, with years of conflict in the past, Nepal is yet to ratify CMW. While the tumultuous political and social setting of Nepal may be identified as a factor for the underlying issue of the government of Nepal not ratifying these treaties, the unwillingness of the government of Nepal is apparent.

Nepal has accepted the individual complaints procedures under CCPR, CEDAW and CRPD.

Nepal has entered no reservations (except in respect of article 22 of CERD) while ratifying, adopting or accessing to the seven treaties. Thus, the provisions of these instruments are applicable in Nepal without any preconditions.

Nepal had promulgated the Constitution of the Kingdom of Nepal after a popular revolt (*Jana Andolan I*).[51] This Constitution restored the multi-party system in Nepal, which had been cast aside. The 1990 Constitution also vested sovereignty in the people of Nepal. The political and social context of the years leading up to 1990 left the people with unfeigned pleasure with their role in fostering a democratic Nepal. With the heightened awareness among the

---

46   Paoletti and others (n 39).
47   NHRC (n 29).
48   Migrant Forum in Asia Network, 'Universal Periodic Review on Nepal' (2015) <https://uprdoc.ohchr.org/uprweb/downloadfile.aspx?filename=2182&file=EnglishTranslation> accessed 30 June 2022.
49   *Prem Chandra Rai and Others v Department of Foreign Employment* Writ No 073-WO-0916.
50   Human Rights Council, 'Report of the Special Rapporteur on the Human Rights of Migrants on His Mission to Nepal' (2018) <https://documents-dds-ny.un.org/doc/UNDOC/GEN/G18/121/49/PDF/G1812149.pdf?OpenElement> accessed 30 June 2022.
51   Gagan B Thapa and Jan Sharma, 'From Insurgency to Democracy: The Challenges of Peace and Democracy-Building in Nepal' (2009) 30 International Political Science Review 205.

Nepalese people following the popular revolt regarding the political and social context along with the rights in a democratic country, the ratification of the core human rights treaties resembles a conscious movement by the government of Nepal to align the interests of the people with the social context along with the political context.

A few years after having ratified some of the significant core human rights treaties, Nepal underwent a tumultuous period of social and political instability, with the Maoist insurgency from 1996 to 2006. The decade-long armed conflict not only saw the disappearance of people but also questioned the approach of recognising and respecting the rights of the minorities in Nepal. The year 2007 saw the promulgation of the interim Constitution of Nepal, which incorporated elements of human rights treaties respecting and protecting the minorities, including women and children.[52] In a similar manner, the 2015 Constitution of Nepal proclaims the essence of democratic norms and values, fundamental rights, civil liberties and human rights.[53] It provides that Nepal can be a party to international treaties either passed by a two-thirds majority or simple majority of the House of Representatives depending on the nature of the treaties.[54] Nepal incorporated these treaties under its 2015 Constitution.

4.1.2   General Attitude of Nepal towards UN Treaty System

The protection and promotion of human rights gained momentum in Nepal since the 1990s. The level of awareness of international human rights instruments certainly has increased in comparison to the initial years of ratification. However, the awareness of treaty bodies is comparatively lower in the provincial and local levels of government than at federal level. The awareness of human rights is intensified among the legislators, which is evident from the internalisation of human rights in the Constitution of Nepal 2015 and the formulation of harmonising domestic laws that has increased the scope of implementation of the human rights treaties to which Nepal is a party. CCPR, CESCR, CEDAW and CRC are more widely cited and better known in Nepal than CAT, CERD and CRDP. The judiciary in Nepal has played an important role in the protection and promotion of human rights by entrenching important principles of internationally-recognised human rights instruments through its judgments.

---

[52] Jill Cottrell and others, 'Interim Constitution of Nepal 2063 (2007) As Amended by the First to Sixth Amendments' (2nd edn, UNDP January 2009).
[53] Constitution of Nepal, 2015, Preamble.
[54] ibid art 279(2).

4.1.3 Level of Awareness

The Constitution of Nepal has mandated the establishment of specialised commissions focused on rights of specific groups (such as women, Dalits, Muslims and Adibasi/Janajati). These commissions are acutely aware of UN treaties and treaty bodies. Furthermore, the NGOs, CSOs and other specialised organisations working towards the protection and promotion of the rights of specialised groups are also aware of UN treaty bodies. The use of treaties, General Comments, Recommendations and COs of CCPR, CESCR, CEDAW and CRC are used extensively in litigation and reports of these organisations. Additionally, different NGOs and CSOs have submitted complementary reports to various human rights treaty bodies,[55] demonstrating that NGOs and CSOs are aware of the treaties and treaty bodies and the level of awareness is constant.

The House of Representatives of the federal parliament in Nepal has constituted a Law, Justice and Human Rights Committee, which is responsible for the status of the implementation of international human rights treaties. The Committee is further responsible to make necessary suggestions to the government of Nepal for the effective implementation of the international human rights treaties to which Nepal is a party. It also studies and monitors the violations of the international treaties and protocols and makes necessary suggestions and instructions to the concerned bodies or officials.[56]

The level of awareness of human rights and its system is also affected by human rights education. Human rights education has been incorporated in the school and university curricula in Nepal.[57] Previously, human rights as a subject were taught only in law studies. However, the human rights themes and content can now be found in other disciplines such as sociology, political science, humanities and arts. While some universities are limited to general or introductory courses in the field of human rights, others offer various specialised courses on particular aspects of human rights.[58] The leading law schools of the country have included human rights courses in their curricula. They also offer LLM programmes and one-year interdisciplinary MA programmes in

---

[55] Sixty complementary reports have been submitted until 2018; <https://tbinternet.ohchr.org/_layouts/15/treatybodyexternal/TBSearch.aspx?Lang=En&CountryID=122> accessed 30 June 2022.

[56] Procedure of the Committee on Law, Justice and Human Rights, 2015, Rule 13.

[57] Human Rights Council, National Report submitted in accordance with paragraph 5 of the annex to Human Rights Council resolution 16/21, Nepal, 2015 9.

[58] Ben Saul, David Kinley and Yubaraj Sangroula, 'Review of Human Rights Education and Training in the Criminal Justice System in Nepal' Sydney Law School Research Paper No 10/114, November 2010 <https://papers.ssrn.com/sol3/papers.cfm?abstract_id=1701476> accessed 30 June 2022.

human rights. In addition to schools and universities, the professionals and law enforcement agencies, such as the National Judicial Academy (NJA), the Nepal Army Staff College, the National Police Academy, the Armed Police Force-Nepal (APF) Training Centre, the Judicial Service Training Centre and the Nepal Administrative Staff College, also organise human rights training courses for judges, prosecutors, legal officers, judicial staff, administrators, lawyers and security personnel.[59]

4.1.4 State Reporting

Nepal's record of state reporting is poor. Nepal has submitted 21 periodic reports to the UN treaty bodies in the period 1993 to 2017. Nepal routinely submits its reports later than on the stipulated time. While the submission of initial reports was delayed only by one or two years, the decade-long armed conflict in the country negatively affected the submission of periodic reports. The government took seven years to submit the second periodic report under CAT and six years to submit the second periodic report under CRC.[60] However, the situation has in recent times improved and Nepal has been more regular in submitting periodic reports. However, the considerations and comments of the relevant treaty bodies are often ignored by the government and the reports are not very self-critical in nature. It does not provide a clear picture of the actual situation of human rights on the ground.

The government of Nepal is responsible for preparing the periodic reports to the treaty bodies. It works in close collaboration with the NHRC, NGOs and CSOs working towards the protection and promotion of human rights and consults with leading experts in the country. The NGOs and CSOs in Nepal are very active in terms of state reporting. They have submitted 60 alternate periodic reports to the treaty bodies on several contextual human rights issues (such as CERD, CEDAW, CRC and CCPR). These reports incorporate the implementation of substantive provisions of the treaties, the actual situation on the ground and the response of the government. They also provide necessary recommendations to the government for effective implementation of treaty bodies.

The treaty bodies have issued 25 COs to Nepal up to 2018. No information about state reporting status can be found in any domestic websites or media sources. Moreover, documentation of the local translations of these COs cannot be traced in Nepal.

---

59 NHRC (n 14).
60 UN Treaty Body Database – Nepal <https://tbinternet.ohchr.org/_layouts/15/treatybodyexternal/TBSearch.aspx?Lang=En&CountryID=122> accessed 30 June 2022.

The NHRIS are less active in terms of submitting shadow or alternative reports to the treaty bodies. Only one report has been submitted by the National Women's Commission of Nepal to supplement the combined fourth and fifth periodic report submitted by the government of Nepal to the CEDAW Cttee.

4.1.5 Domestic Implementation Mechanism

Nepal recognises the legally binding nature of the treaty bodies. The Treaty Act of Nepal, 1990 provides that international treaties ratified by Nepal are enforceable as well as Nepalese laws. Section 9 of the Act further provides that in cases where the provisions of prevailing laws of Nepal are inconsistent with the treaty, the provisions of the treaty prevail.[61] In addition, it is the obligation of the government to initiate and expedite action for the enactment and enforcement of necessary laws.[62]

4.1.6 Treaty Body Membership

While it is difficult to trace a clear and transparent mechanism for the nomination of candidates to the treaty bodies, these are selected on the basis of their expertise and experience in the relevant field. Nepal has only one national on the CEDAW Cttee, Ms Bandana Rana, who was re-elected for a second term in November 2020.

4.2 *Overview of Overall Impact*

4.2.1 Incorporation and Reliance by Legislature and Executive

Nepal has developed a robust legislative framework to comply with international standards set out in human rights treaties. This is the result of intense deliberation and review of previously-existing legislation on the subject of human rights and taking influence from provisions enshrined in the treaties. During these processes, there has been active engagement from all stakeholders so as to ensure compliance at all levels of governance. Civil society groups have successfully moved the government on multiple occasions to adhere to international norms through advocacy campaigns for the ratification of important international treaties. In line with the reflective legislation, directives and policies were initiated to implement and establish mechanisms to achieve objectives laid down and obligations to be complied with by being a party to a particular treaty. Ever since the promulgation of the new Constitution, Nepal has relied greatly on international law to base domestic legislation. The

---

61 Nepal Treaty Act, 1990 s 9(1).
62 ibid s 9(2).

Constitution established several human rights as fundamental rights, thereby guaranteeing their enforceability and legal sanction. These rights include the rights to life and justice, and the right against torture. Subsequently, the existing legislations were amended and the rights were considered while formulating new laws. For example, the Muluki Criminal Code adopted in 2017 criminalised torture and degrading or inhuman treatment and provided a detailed procedure of fair trial to ensure the right to justice. In spite of the commendable speedy drafting process of the legislation, implementation has been an underlying issue for Nepal. With this, Nepal has only begun efforts in working on a particular subject post-ratification which may be concluded as a reason for Nepal's unsatisfactory reporting in the periodical review of the treaty bodies. Foundation lay-out and preparation are important before ratifying an international treaty and its effect on domestic legislation should be gradual. Sudden and frequent changes in legislation and policies have been cited as a hurdle to monitoring the progress of initiatives introduced by the government. In other areas, Nepal has not enacted key legislation to be able to comply with the treaties, such as the lack of a specific law on torture, despite having ratified CAT.[63]

4.2.2 Reliance by Judiciary

The judiciary's role in highlighting the significance of international human rights treaties is noteworthy. Judicial interpretation has evolved to referencing and citing international treaties and Nepal's obligation to comply with international law, even in situations of non-ratification. The Supreme Court of Nepal has on many occasions recognised international law as being superior to domestic law, in cases of inadequacies or inconsistencies in the domestic laws. By way of its directive powers, the courts have instructed the government to take action and legislate on issues that the courts view as essential to be addressed. These have led to the protection of the rights of citizens in many instances. Nepal has marched into an age of judicial activism by way of issuing writs of mandamus, and the Supreme Court has been able to ensure the implementation of rights guaranteed under the Constitution and through legislation promulgated in that regard. In judgments relating to international law and its application, there have been inconsistent pronouncements while deciding on violations of human rights committed by the government, essentially going

---

[63] There is the Compensation Relating to Torture Act 1996, which is a legislation that aims to provide for compensation to the person subjected to torture while in detention. Although there is no specific legislation against torture prevention, torture has been criminalised in the new Country Penal Code (2017), s 167.

against the principles of natural justice that should form the basis for judicial proceedings. The prolongation on deciding on matters relating to human rights has forced the Committees formed under the treaty bodies to by-pass the petitioners' obligations to exhaust local remedies. The government has also been responsible for not adhering to orders passed by the Supreme Court. (The Supreme Court of Nepal is the only court that maintains a record of the cases decided. Thus, the citation of UN treaty bodies by the Trial Courts and the High Courts has not been mentioned in the report.)

4.2.3 Impact of State Reporting

In the past five years Nepal has been regular in submitting its report to the Committees, after a dismal record of not submitting its human rights status submissions. Committees have expressed their concerns over inadequate data regarding the human rights situation in Nepal, which still requires significant improvement. The submissions on the status made through independent reports by human rights commissions mandated by the Constitution and alternative or shadow reports by CSOs help to evaluate disparities in state reporting. Nepal has been able to efficiently respond to concerns and act on recommendations made by the committees. For example, the CERD Cttee recommended the sensitisation of discriminatory traditions and customs[64] by developing concrete legislation and policies to eliminate harmful social practices against the girl child, such as child marriage, *chhaupadi*, dowry and accusations of witchcraft. Accordingly, the National Penal Code not only prohibits marriage under the age of 20 years,[65] but also prohibits the asking for and receiving of dowry from the bridegroom or the bride's side.[66] Further, the Penal Code also criminalises *chhaupadi* during menstruation or the delivery of a child including any similar subjection to inhuman treatment, untouchability and discrimination.[67] The HRCttee recommended that the government of Nepal ensure the effective implementation of the Human Trafficking and Transportation (Control) Act of 2007, while providing victims with adequate protection and assistance.[68] The government has since constituted a national

---

64 CERD, UN Committee on the Elimination of Racial Discrimination: Concluding Observations, Nepal (28 April 2004), CERD/C/64/CO/5 <https://www.refworld.org/docid/411765634.html> accessed 30 June 2022.
65 National Penal Code 2017, s 173.
66 ibid s 174.
67 ibid s 168.
68 UNHRC, 'Concluding Observations on the 2nd Periodic Report of Nepal: Human Rights Committee' (15 April 2014) CCPR/C/NPL/CO/2 para 18 <https://www.refworld.org/docid/539033714.html> accessed 16 December 2020.

committee at the central level for effective implementation of the Act and has ensured reasonable compensation, restitution, rehabilitation, economic support and psychosocial counselling services to the victims of human trafficking under the Act. Similarly, on the recommendation to improve the birth registration process,[69] the Constitution ensures equality between men and women concerning acquiring, retaining and transferring citizenship.

4.2.4 Impact of Individual Communications

As of 30 June 2019, 26 individual communications have been submitted, all of which were under OP1-CCPR. The HRCttee found Nepal in violation of the CCPR in all 23 communications finalised.

Constitutional bodies such as the NHRC, NWC and NDW have continued to play an instrumental role in protecting and promoting the rights of various distinguished groups in society and catering to their specific needs and interests. They also have successfully recommended to the government to implement recommendations made along with strategies. Collaborative efforts between various bodies have also been seen in addressing specific issues, especially notable in their joint submissions on subjects of human rights to various committees. The NHRC, through the Comprehensive Peace Accord, garnered significant legitimacy as an institution that not only monitors human rights violations but also acts as a peace broker between stakeholders.[70] There are two areas that limit their functions. First, the constitutional bodies are yet to obtain financial independence from government influence. Second, the NHRC's influence over thematic constitutional bodies. The NHRC has had greater significance and autonomy compared to the specific commissions. Moreover, the government rarely adheres to recommendations made by the NHRIs or delays decision making. Despite this, the NHRIs have made efforts to make up for lacking execution by the government in launching their own campaigns and initiatives to address human rights issues.

The role of CSOs and NGOs in aiding the process of international law compliance cannot go unnoticed. These organisations have a grass-roots presence and continue to function in varied capacities, including raising awareness; lobbying for legislation; evaluating human rights situations; reporting to international and national committees; and acting as a catalyst for social reform. Their presence in the human rights protection and promotion scene is imperative to ensure some level of success in achieving goals set by the

---

69 ibid para 106.
70 Interview with Prof Kapil Shrestha, Former Commissioner of NHRC. The interview was conducted virtually on 29 January 2021.

government and international organisations. Their collaborative efforts with government institutions and international organisations has contributed immensely in bringing Nepal's international standing to where it is. The government needs to ensure protection of these human rights defenders and prevent the stigmatisation against NGOs while carrying out community-level campaigns.

In examining the impact that individual communications have had, we reached out to the organisations that represented the victims. In doing so, TRIAL International, which represented victims in 13 individual communications, provided the measures taken following individual communications' opinions and recommendations.

The HRCttee in Communication 2556/2015 was of the view to provide an effective remedy, effective reparation, adequate compensation, and appropriate satisfaction measures to the author for the violations suffered. It also noted in paragraph 9 Nepal's obligation to conduct 'a thorough and effective investigation into the facts surrounding the arrest, detention and rape of Ms Nyaya and the treatment she suffered in detention and prosecute, try and punish those responsible for the violations committed'. TRIAL International, who represented the victim in the individual communication, following the Committee's view submitted a report titled 'Guaranteeing the rights of survivors of conflict-related sexual violence in Nepal, with special reference to the Human Rights Committee's decision on the case *Fulmati Nyaya v Nepal*', with the recommendations for the NHRC, the National Women Commission and Indigenous Nationalities Commission and seeking further collaboration to work on the issue. Additionally, TRIAL International also reported on the implementation of the decision of the NHRC to provide a compensation amount referred by the NHRC to Ms Fulmati. TRIAL International reported regular follow-up through email and phone.

TRIAL International also submitted a right to information letter to the office of the Prime Minister and Council of Ministers following the views of the HRCttee in Communication 2000/2010. A reply was provided to RTI by the office of the Prime Minister and Council of Ministers stating that it had forwarded the letters to various ministries. Follow-up since the reply to the RTI has not been documented about the obligations to provide the victim with an effective remedy in paragraph 13 of the communication.

Another organisation that represented the victim facing human rights abuses is Advocacy Forum Nepal. Advocacy Forum Nepal provided the study researchers with information regarding the follow-up measures taken following the HRCttee's view on these individual communications.

In the communication regarding Gyanendra Tripathi, the HRCttee recommended to Nepal to conduct a thorough and effective investigation into the disappearance of the victim, to establish their whereabouts and to prosecute and sanction those responsible. Advocacy Forum Nepal reported that no criminal investigation was carried out; rather, the government reiterated that the case was being considered by the non-judicial transitional justice mechanisms. The victim's remains have not been located, and the person allegedly responsible for the crime has not been prosecuted. While the victim's family received an amount as 'interim relief' as in the case of every victim of enforced disappearance, the HRCttee considered this amount to be insufficient.

As regards recommendations made in relation to the amendment of the domestic legal framework concerning the criminalisation of enforced disappearance in Communications 1863/2009, 1865/2009, 1761/2008, 1469/2006 and 2245/2013 and others; torture has been criminalised in the Penal Code of Nepal. However, there has been little effort in producing legislation, particularly dealing with enforced disappearance as well as torture. In recommendations made by the Committee providing appropriate measures of satisfaction, translation and dissemination of the case, there has been no reply to one or more of the follow-up recommendations.

While organisations representing the victim did follow up with the government agencies regarding the Committee's views, it appears like negligence on the part of the government to ensure transparency regarding the perusal of obligations adhered to by Nepal.

5 Impact of the Different UN Human Rights Treaties on the Domestic Level in Nepal

5.1 *International Convention on the Elimination of All Forms of Racial Discrimination*

Recognising the need for a treaty on the elimination of racial discrimination, Nepal became an early adopter by ratifying CERD as early as January 1971. The caste-based discrimination against the Dalit population, who are subjected to harsh and inhumane treatment by the upper castes of the Hindu caste system, along with their practice of untouchability, gained more attention and initiated dialogue on the issues of oppression against such groups. This was the reason for the momentum for addressing the discrimination based on caste, gender, ethnicity, language, religion, culture, region, age and class during deliberations for the promulgation of the Constitution in 2007 and 2015.

5.1.1 Legislature-Executive Recognition and Implementation

The call for ending all forms of discrimination and oppression in the Preamble to the Constitution is reflective of the Constituent Assembly's intent to develop comprehensive legislation to rid age-old discriminatory practices and further incorporate such ethos into the spirit of the Constitution. Accordingly, the fundamental rights recognised under articles 24 and 40 expressly deal with the rights guaranteed against discrimination and oppression, along with rights of the Dalit population, respectively. However, the intent to incorporate the provisions against all forms of racial discrimination consolidated into legislative form only in 2011 with the Caste-Based Discrimination and Untouchability (Offence and Punishment) Act. The Act provides for an elaborate legal framework to protect the right to equality, freedom and to live with human dignity as enshrined in the Preamble to the Act. Despite the prompt formulation of rules to ensure the effective implementation by creating a mechanism to receive complaints, the Nepalese civil society groups note issues regarding the protection of victims and witnesses, adherence to court decisions and raising awareness about such laws discouraging discrimination and untouchability.[71]

The government of Nepal's Procedure on Elimination of Caste-Based Discrimination along with the Protection and Promotion of Dalit Rights 2016 recognises CERD and the obligations to which Nepal is bound, by being party to the Convention. It details the government's aim to tackle racial and caste-based discrimination by strengthening the already-existing legislation on elimination of caste-based discrimination. It aims to do so by developing a framework with a mechanism intended to target the local level community according to article 2 of CERD. The directive lays out the mechanism at three levels: high level, central and district level mechanisms, with the inclusion of the relevant stakeholders in these levels for inclusive and effective participation to address caste-based discrimination from a grassroots level. In addition, the government has been developing a scheme to track recommendations received through the UPR to track progress on inclusive development in line with CERD. It includes the development of indigenous people, people of ethnic communities, marginalised people, Dalits, backward class/area and Badi community members. The UPR National Action Plan 2016–2011[72] depicts activities

---

[71] Dalit NGO Foundation 'Alternative Report to the UN CERD in Addition to the Govt of Nepal Periodic Reports 17 to 23', CERD 95th Session (2018).

[72] Office of the Prime Minister and Council of Ministers, 'An action Plan for the Implementation of Recommendations Received Through the Universal Periodic Review (UPR)' <https://www.opmcm.gov.np/en/download/an-action-plan-for-the-implementation-of-recommendations-received-through-the-universal-periodic-review-upr/#> accessed 30 June 2022.

planned to be undertaken in response to a recommendation by assigning the appropriate authority along with a supporting source. Further, the Fifth National Human Rights Action Plan 2020–2025 has been adopted with the objectives that the Fourth National Action Plan could not implement. Most importantly, it includes increased funding to the National Dalit Commission which works towards advocating the prohibition of discrimination against Dalits. Through this, the government accords priority to the principle of proportional representation through inclusion and positive discrimination to provide proper representation to the Dalits, Adibasi, Janajatis, Madhesis and Muslims while formulating policies for their social and economic development.

Falling short of Convention commitments, the government failed to adhere to the report submission to the CERD Cttee that parties to the Convention are expected to submit every two years. After the initial 2004 report, the government made its next submission to the Committee only in 2016, after 12 years. Additionally, several provisions of the CBDU Act, 2011 have been identified to create hurdles in implementation. Recommendations have been made to extend the statute of limitations for submitting a complaint, formal recording of complaints through the First Information Registry (FIR), sanction enforcement officials in cases of non-compliance, ensuring implementation and extensively promoting anti-discriminatory laws and complaint mechanisms available.[73]

5.1.2   Reliance by the Judiciary

The Nepalese judiciary has made reflections based on international human rights instruments including CERD. Reflecting on petitioner reliance on CERD, in *Kamanand Ram and Others v HMG and Others*,[74] a judicial pronouncement was made in favour of equality where the petitioners had alleged ill-treatment against higher-caste people who forced them to do the menial service of disposing of dead animals. It also stated that the government was bound by article 14 of the interim Constitution 2007 and were legally obligated to carry out efforts by providing administrative support and initiatives in eliminating untouchability and all forms of discrimination, in conformity with CERD. The Court observed:[75]

---

[73]   CERD Cttee 'Concluding Observations on the Combined Seventeenth to Twenty-Third Periodic Reports of Nepal' UN Doc (C/NPL/17–23).
[74]   'UNDP Nepal Outcome Evaluation of UNDP Nepal Access to Justice and Human Rights 2001–2010' Footnote 21 (UNDP, 2010) <https://erc.undp.org/> accessed 20 April 2022.
[75]   ibid.

In view of the constitutional commitment towards eradication of the malpractice of untouchability and discrimination on the ground of caste, it is not appropriate for Government offices ... to display apathy and negligence in carrying out their legal obligations. Those offices and institutions are duty-bound to work towards the eradication of untouchability and discrimination.

5.1.3 Impact on and through Independent State Actors

The NHRC has been vigilant in taking cognisance concerning crimes committed as an outcome of caste-based discrimination. It has effectively reminded the government of its obligations under CERD ratified by Nepal.[76] Its collaborative efforts and complementing the relationship with civil society organisations continue to play an essential role in upholding the spirit of the Constitution to put an end to all forms of discrimination.[77] The Commission's monitoring report in 2019 stated how such practices went against human rights and its adverse effects on life, liberty, equality and dignity. It has helped to coordinate efforts between all three tiers of government by incorporating mechanisms to include ending discrimination and untouchability in plans, policies, programmes and budgets. The NHRC has also been able to urge political parties to stress social offences against such practices and adopt such measures into their documents to raise awareness about such issues by recognising proportional inclusion for members of the Dalit community.

Article 2 of CERD encourages state parties to encourage organisations to eliminate barriers between races. Despite the presence of constitutionally-mandated bodies such as the NHRC, the NDC, the Tharu Commission and the Madhesi Commission, issues surrounding non-operation or limited operation and insufficient funding restrict these commissions to function according to their objectives. Issues regarding the functionality of these organisations have been raised as a matter of concern.[78]

---

[76] NHRC, Press Release (13 May 2020).

[77] Krishna B Bhattachan, Tej B Sunar &Yasso Kanti Bhattachan, 'Caste-Based Discrimination in Nepal' Working Paper Series on Caste-Based Discrimination, Indian Institute of Dalit Studies, III(8), 2008.

[78] CERD, Concluding Observations on the Combined Seventeenth to Twenty-Third Periodic Reports of Nepal, United Nations, CERD/C/NPL/17–23 <https://www.refworld.org/docid/5a2926844.html> accessed 30 June 2022.

5.1.4   Impact through Non-state Actors

Discrimination has been a cross-cutting issue in Nepal, not only in a social but also in a legal sense.[79] Although domestic legal provisions and international obligations make caste-based discrimination illegal in Nepal, the Dalits continue to face atrocities based on caste.[80] Dalit organisations have played a significant role in working towards ending and advocating against caste-based discrimination. Such organisations have also initiated national consultation programmes in association with government institutions such as the NHRC, NWC, NDC and other civil society organisations working towards the cause while ensuring compliance with the CERD, to highlight issues faced by the vulnerable groups in society and offer recommendations with stakeholders reflecting their needs.[81] There has also been the initiation of a bilateral agency network to work with Dalit NGOs by international donors such as the Danish International Development Assistance (DANIDA).[82]

These organisations had the opportunity to shift their framework from those of social reform to human rights.[83] It has opened the path for a mass mobilisation of Dalit communities by invoking international human rights treaties such as CEDAW and CERD. Through this, they have been able to get for themselves funds allocated for the empowerment of the Dalit community, which has initiated a vital movement to realise land rights to claim land and other resources for their well-being.[84]

However, a hurdle to the recognition of these Dalit NGOs is the fact that international human rights treaties recognise discrimination based on gender,

---

[79]   The socio-legal history of discrimination can be depicted through history by pointing out the provisions of the Muluki Ain 1963. The provisions were discriminatory, where the degree of punishment of the same crime was higher in the case of the 'lower caste' people such as Dalits than the 'upper caste' people.

[80]   'Caste-Based Discrimination Continues Across Nepal: Report' *Himalayan Times* (Kathmandu, 5 March 2020) <https://thehimalayantimes.com/kathmandu/caste-based-discrimination-continues-across-nepal-report/> accessed 30 June 2022.

[81]   Dalit NGO Federation and others, 'Alternative Report to the UN CERD in Addition to the Govt of Nepal Periodic Reports 17 to 23, to be Reviewed at the 95th session' <https://www.ecoi.net/en/file/local/1427938/1930_1522241015_int-cerd-ngo-npl-30737-e.doc> accessed 30 June 2022.

[82]   Indian Institute of Dalit Studies, Working Paper Series on Caste-Based Discrimination, III (8) (2008) 15.

[83]   Luisa Steur, 'Dalit Civil Society Activism' Seminar A Journal of Germanic Studies 633 (2012) <https://www.researchgate.net/publication/281968098_Dalit_Civil_Society_Activism> accessed 5 July 2022.

[84]   Subash Nepali, 'The Role of the Dalit Civil Society in Combating Caste-Based Discrimination' (2019) 5 Georgetown Journal of Asian Affairs 22.

religion, age, ethnicity and race. However, there is no international treaty that expressly acknowledges the need for prohibiting discrimination against the Dalit community. As a result of this, there have been difficulties in identifying and tracking the progress made by Dalit NGOs and reasons for why they have not been able to influence international human rights treaties. Nonetheless, efforts by these groups have shifted towards strengthening organisational structures to monitor and empower the Dalit community socially, economically and politically. Obligations of Nepal as a state party to CERD along with the atrocities faced by the Dalits are largely covered by the media.[85]

5.1.5   Impact of State Reporting

The government of Nepal responded efficiently to the Committee's recommendation to sensitise regarding discriminatory traditions and customs[86] by developing concrete legislation and policies to eliminate harmful social practices against the girl child, such as child marriage, *chhaupadi*, dowry and accusations of witchcraft. Accordingly, the Penal Code not only prohibits marriage under the age of 20 years,[87] but also the concluding of any marriage by asking for any type of property dowry from the bridegroom or the bride's side.[88] Further, the Penal Code criminalises banishing a woman to a shed during menstruation or the delivery of a child, including subjecting her to inhuman treatment, untouchability and discrimination.[89] To raise awareness about these issues, the government proclaimed 8 December as 'Dignified Menstruation Day', to get families to regard menstruation with dignity.[90] The government has also introduced the Acid and Other Harmful Chemical Substance (Regulation) Ordinance 2020 to regulate acid and other harmful substances and create measures to prevent acid attacks. The government had also set an objective of ending child marriage by the year 2020.[91]

---

[85]   Alish Rajopadhyaya, 'History of Dalit Movements in Nepal: Much Has Been Achieved, but Discrimination Still Exists' *OnlineKhabar* (Kathmandu, 1 August 2020) <https://english.onlinekhabar.com/history-of-dalit-movements-in-nepal.html> accessed 5 July 2022.

[86]   UNCERD, UN Committee on the Elimination of Racial Discrimination: Concluding Observations, Nepal (28 April 2004), CERD/C/64/CO/5 <https://www.refworld.org/docid/411765634.html> accessed 5 July 2022.

[87]   National Penal Code 2017, s 173.

[88]   ibid s 174.

[89]   ibid s 168.

[90]   UNHRC, 'National Report Submitted in Accordance with Paragraph 5 of the Annex to Human Rights Council Resolution 16/21' (2020) UN Doc (A/HRC/WG.6/37/NPL/1).

[91]   National Strategy to End Child Marriage 2016.

The Committee had also highlighted the issues on the agricultural bonded labour practice known as *Kamaiya,* despite it being abolished in July 2000.[92] The government response saw the effective implementation of the Kamaiya Prohibition Act 2002, where rehabilitation of the freed *Kamaiyas* was of priority including the allocation of land in city and rural areas, grants for resettlement and skills development training for income generation.[93]

Stressing the need for adequate financial resources and independence for strengthening the NHRIs[94] by the Committee,[95] the government stated that separate financial rules had been approved by the Ministry of Finance to ensure financial autonomy and recognised the importance of supporting the National Dalit Commission and the National Women's Commission by upgrading it as a constitutional body.[96] With this, the NHRC has been able to carry out its mandate as a nation-wide monitoring body.

5.1.6   Impact of Other Measures

The CERD Cttee has highlighted the concerning issues about the indigenous peoples' inadequate representation in the constitution-making process for the drafting of the 2015 Constitution.[97] It did so through its early-warning measures that are aimed at de-escalating tensions and preventing conflicts. The Committee expressed its concern regarding the strict conformity to manifestos of parties to be able to participate in the drafting process[98] and the persecution[99] of the Limbuwan leaders whose territories were militarised

---

[92] CERD (n 78).

[93] Document Name UNHRC submitted by Nepal.

[94] National Human Rights Commission; National Women Commission; National Dalit Commission (NDC); National Inclusion Commission; Indigenous People and Nationalities Commission; Madhesi Commission; Tharu Commission; National Foundation for Development of Indigenous Nationalities (NFDIN); Badi Community Upliftment and Development Committee; Marginalised and Dalit Upliftment and Development Committee; Backward Community Upliftment and Development Committee; and Buddhism Promotion and Monastery Development Committee.

[95] UNCERD, 'Consideration of Reports Submitted by State Parties Under Article 9 of the Convention, Seventeenth to Twenty-Third Periodic Reports of State Parties Due in 2008: Nepal' (20 February 2017) UN Doc CERD/C/NPL/17–23 <https://www.refworld.org/docid/5a2926844.html> accessed 5 July 2022.

[96] ibid.

[97] Cultural Survival, 'CERD Reviews Nepal's Human Rights Record', 2018 <https://www.culturalsurvival.org/news/cerd-reviews-nepals-human-rights-record> accessed 5 July 2022; see also UN Treaty Body Database <https://tbinternet.ohchr.org/_layouts/15/treatybodyexternal/SessionDetails1.aspx?SessionID=1195&Lang=en> accessed 5 July 2022.

[98] Letter from the Office of the High Commissioner for Human Rights, 28 September 2009.

[99] Letter from the Office of the High Commissioner for Human Rights, 13 March 2009.

with clampdowns on raising awareness about the eighteenth century treaties between the Limbuwan inhabitants with the Nepalese Monarchy.[100] Further, the Committee requested information from the government of Nepal on measures adopted to protect the Limbuwan people along with the extent of involvement in the constitution-making process.[101]

CSOs claim that the government did not address the recommendations that were made to resolve the discriminatory treatment of indigenous people, especially by distancing them from the drafting process of the Constitution.[102] The issue was stated to be reflective of the 'deep-rooted' discrimination and systemic exclusion of indigenous people from politics for almost 200 years.[103] News agencies have reported that the critical demands of the marginalised people, such as secularism, proportional representation and identity-based federalism, have not been met, according to representatives of the indigenous people.[104]

5.1.7 Brief Conclusion

CERD realised its impact primarily through the Caste-Based Discrimination Act that helps to protect the lower castes against crimes by other upper-caste Hindus in the caste system, relying on the spirit of the Constitution. The Nepalese legal system has been able to evolve and recognise the importance of international human rights treaties which is visible in claims made by petitioners and instances where the courts of Nepal refer to the Convention in overseeing the claims concerning equal protection of the law. Independent state actors such as the NHRC, NDC and NWC have continued to play an active role relating to cases of caste-based discrimination. However, the impact has been limited due to the lack of complete financial autonomy from the government. The government of Nepal has been able to adequately respond to recommendations of the Committee by incorporating domestic legislation and review mechanisms to track progress, drastically improving the awareness on such issues and the human rights situation of Nepal that was somewhat rocky. However, the top-to-bottom approach with members of the indigenous

---

100 Letter from the Office of the High Commissioner for Human Rights, 31 August 2012.
101 Letter from the Office of the High Commissioner for Human Rights, 30 August 2013.
102 Nepal's Failure to Comply with Recommendations Issued by the UN by the Indigenous Peoples Mega Front & Others on 20 January 2010, paras 8–9.
103 ibid para 9.
104 Shradha Ghale, 'Why Nepal's Janajati's Feel Betrayed by the New Constitution' *The Wire* (27 October 2015) <https://thewire.in/external-affairs/why-nepals-janajatis-feel-betrayed-by-the-new-constitution> accessed 5 July 2022.

communities has been a matter of concern that has garnered international attention during the constitution-making process

5.2 International Covenant on Civil and Political Rights

Nepal ratified CCPR in May 1991, ratified OP1-CCPR on 14 May 1991, and acceded to OP2-CCPR in March 1998.

5.2.1 Legislature-Executive Recognition and Implementation

With the intention of accelerating compliance with CCPR, Nepal has enacted legislation and constitutional measures, including the recognition of fundamental rights under the Constitution of 2015. The National Code of Nepal 1963, Civil Liberties Act 1955, Local Self Governance Act 1999, Human Rights Commission Act 1997, Legal Aid Act 1998, Prison Act 1962 and Prison Rules 1963 are some of the legislation that relate to the rights enunciated in CCPR.[105]

The government has been able to ensure attaining the objectives of CCPR by acting on the recommendations by the HRCttee, which include significant calls for action such as providing equal rights to the lesbian, gay, bisexual, transgender and intersex (LGBTI) community, protecting human rights defenders through the development of guidelines, ensuring implementation of the constitutional right to freedom of expression through online/offline mediums, including efforts to decriminalise defamation.[106] Despite the absence of an explicit guarantee of the right to self-determination, decentralising of dispute settlement to resolve civil legal disputes, it reflects the intention to empower local bodies to manage local affairs.[107] The government has implemented several policies and programmes to implement CCPR. The National Human Rights Action Plan and human rights policies put forward in the Tenth Five-Year Plan are significant steps in this regard.[108]

The blockade of 2015 was a period of significant impact on the civil and political rights of Nepali citizens. It was a year of struggle with regard to the economic-social conditions, as the blockade and strikes nearly halted the rehabilitation and construction work.[109] Despite the situation, Nepal promulgated

---

105 NHRC, The Domestication Status of International Covenant on Civil and Political Rights Nepal, NHRC, May 2007.
106 National Action Plan to Implement Recommendations of UPR, 2016–2011.
107 ibid 10–11.
108 NHRC, The Domestication Status of International Covenant on Civil and Political Rights Nepal, NHRC (May 2007) 9.
109 ibid.

the Constitution of Nepal in 2015 with the progressive realisation of the civil and political rights enshrined in CCPR.

When a preliminary draft of the Constitution was presented for suggestions, the right to peaceful assembly was not being fully observed. There were several incidents where agitators entered prohibited areas. Further, the enforcement of the order of prohibition and curfew began with the vandalising and arson of individual property, government and public offices as well as the offices of political parties. After the murder of the Senior Superintendent of Police using domestic weapons, the government enforced the order of prohibition and implemented a curfew. The rights to freedom and security were additionally impacted as a result of some areas not having the notice of curfew circulated in time.[110]

5.2.2 Reliance by Judiciary

The Nepalese judiciary has recognised the significance of the international human rights treaties by interlinking them with provisions of the Constitution of Nepal. The Constitution identifies civil and political rights and several provisions derive their genesis from CCPR. The Supreme Court in *Advocate Matrika Prasad Niraula v Nepal Government and Office of the Prime Minister*[111] stated that it was the responsibility of Nepal as a state party to CCPR to ensure a conducive environment for the people after the earthquake in order to realise their rights to live with dignity under article 6. The Court made this observation with the post-disaster trauma after the 2015 earthquake. It stated that the government had the duty to provide psychological counselling based on Nepal's state obligation under the UDHR and CCPR.

5.2.3 Impact on and through Independent State Actors

As an institutional framework to protect and promote the right to life, the NHRC has been responsible for conducting routine observations and studies throughout the country along with disseminating information through its publications. The Commission has also been active in training on the implementation of CCPR and periodical reports to harmonise efforts of government action with that of established international standards.[112]

Endowed with the constitutional status provided under the interim Constitution 2007, the NHRC was mandated to monitor the Comprehensive

---

110 ibid.
111 NKP 2072, Decision 9601 <http://nkp.gov.np/full_detail/8644/?keywords=ICCPR#> accessed 5 July 2022.
112 NHRC Annual Report 2004, 14.

Peace Accord[113] that had been endorsed by the government and the CPN-Maoist for monitoring the elections of the Constituent Assembly from a human rights perspective.[114] The role of the NHRC during the constitution-making process was evident where the following actions were taken to de-escalate tensions:

(i) The NHRC monitored the overall human rights situation when the government decided to use the Local Administration Act 2028 to mobilise the Nepal Army in some districts by order of local administrative authorities. Despite this, the protection of the lives of Nepalese citizens and the protection of various aspects of human rights continued to be a challenge.

(ii) Within the context of civic activism during the period of the adoption of the Constitution, there were reports of physical violence perpetrated on 21 journalists. Among these, one was shot and 19 were abused.[115] The NHRC stepped in to implement the Human Rights Protection Guidelines. The National Human Rights Commission also issued the Human Rights Defenders' Guideline in 2011.

5.2.4 Impact through Non-state Actors

NGOs have played an important role in Nepalese society for advocacy regarding civil and political rights. While a number of NGOs have advocated for various rights, organisations such as the Blue Diamond Society have time and again played an instrumental role in emphasising the necessity to recognise persons in the LGBTI community and their participation in the law-making process. The Society also submitted a report on the violation of the rights of LGBTI persons in Nepal by referring to the Supreme Court ruling in *Pant v Nepal,* which acknowledged that LGBTI individuals should benefit from the same legal rights as other citizens of Nepal. It states that despite legal advances in Nepal, the rights of LGBTI persons remain in jeopardy.[116]

In April 2020 it was reported that NHRC in collaboration with NGOs and CSOs would monitor the human rights situation in Nepal. While NGOs continue to work with constitutional bodies, their presence in monitoring human

---

113 Agreement between His Majesty Government of Nepal (HMGN) and the MCP.
114 ibid 18.
115 Federation of Nepal Journalists <http://www.fnjnepal.org/media/?cat=3> accessed 5 July 2022.
116 Blue Diamond Society, 'The Violations of the Rights of Lesbian, Gay, Bisexual, Transgender, and Intersex Persons in Nepal' <https://www.ecoi.net/en/file/local/1036940/1930_138 5650631_int-ccpr-ngo-npl-14738-e.pdf> accessed 5 July 2022.

rights situations and advocating the necessity for adherence to human rights[117] has been reflective since the years of conflict in Nepal. During the armed conflict, some NGOs had to halt their programmes for fear of conflict.[118]

5.2.5 Impact of State Reporting

Nepal has come a long way in empowering vulnerable groups to eliminate their risk of exploitation. This was after recommendations to ensure the effective implementation of the Human Trafficking and Transportation (Control) Act of 2007, while providing victims with adequate protection and assistance.[119] The government has since constituted a National Committee at the central level for effective implementation of the Human Trafficking and Transportation (Control) Act 2007. Accordingly, the victims are entitled to reasonable compensation, restitution, rehabilitation, economic support and psychosocial counselling services under the Act. Further, extracting human organs, unless otherwise specified by law, are considered acts of human trafficking and are criminalised by the Act. In this regard, the Human Trafficking and Transportation (Control) Regulation, 2008 was amended in 2020 for effective implementation of the Act. The government is presently implementing a National Plan of Action against Human Trafficking (2011–2021) which prioritises five specific areas including prevention, protection, prosecution, capacity development and coordination, cooperation and collaboration. Additionally, a separate and specialised Human Trafficking Investigation Bureau has been established under the Nepal police in 2018, which is dedicated to combating human trafficking.[120]

The Committee also recommended ensuring that all Tibetans have proper documentation and ensure that refugees and asylum seekers should not be subjected to arbitrary restrictions of their rights under CCPR, including freedom of expression, assembly and association, while also guaranteeing access to its territory to all Tibetans who may have valid refugee claims and referring them to the UNHCR.[121] Although Nepal is not a party to the 1951 Refugees

---

117   Medani Bhandari, 'Civil Society and Non-Governmental Organisations (NGOs) Movements in Nepal in Terms of Social Transformation' (2014) 15 Pacific Journal of Science and Technology 177.
118   Sonal Singh & others (n 1).
119   UNHRC, 'Concluding Observations on the 2nd Periodic Report of Nepal: Human Rights Committee' para 18 (15 April 2014) CCPR/C/NPL/CO/2 <https://www.refworld.org/docid/539033714.html> accessed 5 July 2022.
120   UNHRC, 'National Report Submitted in Accordance with Paragraph 5 of the Annex to Human Rights Council Resolution 16/21' para 33 (2020) UN Doc (A/HRC/WG.6/37/NPL/1).
121   UNHRC (n 119) para 14.

Convention and its Protocol of 1967, Nepal has provided shelter to thousands of Tibetans and Bhutanese refugees on humanitarian grounds. The Extradition Act 2014 incorporates the principle of *non-refoulement*. It provides that a person should not be extradited to the requesting state if the person would be subjected to torture or other types of harm.[122]

On the recommendation to improve the birth registration process,[123] the Constitution ensures equality between men and women concerning acquiring, retaining and transferring citizenship. This is equally applicable to their children. The Constitution guarantees every child the right to a name and birth registration, along with his or her identity. With the pretext, the Children Act 2018 ensures the right of the child to have a name with their identification and birth registration. The National Identity Card and Registration Act 2020 provides procedural and institutional provision for ensuring this right.[124]

5.2.6 Impact of Individual Communications

A total of 26 individual complaints have been submitted to the HRCttee between 2006 and 30 June 2019. The communications cover subjects relating to torture, enforced disappearance, fair trial, sexual abuse of persons detained by the armed forces, arbitrary arrest and the extraction of confessions using torture. A majority of these communications directly relate to enforced disappearances during the armed conflict of 1996 to 2006.[125] In all 23 communications that had been finalised by 30 June 2019, the Committee found violations of rights under the Covenant and required Nepal to provide impartial investigations and effective remedies. The HRCttee also suggested to Nepal to amend the 35-day statutory limit for claiming compensation for torture, in accordance with international standards. In another communication it directed Nepal to adapt the definition of rape and other forms of sexual violence in accordance with international standards along with abolishing the 35-day statute of limitation for filing complaints of rape. The HRCttee further suggested legislative reforms for the criminal prosecution of those responsible for serious human rights violations such as torture, extrajudicial executions and enforce disappearances. It has also recommended that Nepal provide effective reparation,

---

122   ibid para 106.
123   ibid.
124   ibid para 39.
125   In a communication decided just after the cut-off date for this study, the HRCttee specifically dealt with the matter of child labour and forced labour in line with the prohibition on torture and cruel, inhumane or degrading treatment (CCPR/C/126/D/2773/2016) (15 July 2019).

adequate compensation and appropriate measures of satisfaction to the author for the violations suffered, including arranging an official apology in a private ceremony.

While Nepal participated in the procedure by providing its observations to all the communications that were submitted, there is a discrepancy in terms of affirmative responses to the recommendation provided by the Committee. As for the amendment of the 35-day statutory limitation for the Compensation Relating to Torture Act recommended by the Committee, the provisions continue with the 35-day statutory limitation from the event of torture or the date of release for bringing claims. However, the Country Penal Code, 2017 provides a statutory limitation of six months from the date of commission of the offence or release from arrest under section 170. The definition of rape and the statute of limitation were amended in the Criminal Code in 2017. The statute of limitation for filing complaints of rape is one year from the date of commission of the act. In a recent communication of *Fulmati Nyaya v Nepal,* 2015, the HRCttee held that the new one-year statutory limitation of rape cases is insufficient. Apart from that, torture has been criminalised by the Criminal Code, which was promulgated in 2017.

Dissemination of communications following the adoption of the Committee's views is undertaken, but usually only reaches the legal community. However, given the prominence of enforced disappearance in the country's history, communications dealing with this topic receive much broader attention. Apart from that, there is no clear documentary evidence suggesting Nepal's follow-up procedure with the Committee in communications where it has asked Nepal to submit information on measures taken by Nepal to give effect to the Committee's view within 180 days.

In 2015 the Nepalese government established two commissions to make proposals on how to deal with the perpetrators during the armed conflict of 1996 to 2006, as part of a process of transitional justice aimed at achieving national reconciliation: The Truth and Reconciliation Commission (TRC) and the Commission of Investigation on Enforced Disappeared Persons (CIEDP). The Commissions received 63 000 claims of grave human rights abuses, but only 300 pertained to sexual violence and assaults. Despite the establishment of these Commissions, victims have been concerned about the Commissions' ability to handle their cases confidentially.[126]

---

126 Rukmanee Maharjan, 'Justice for the Victims' (14 July 2020) <https://www.dandc.eu/en/article/nepal-must-urgently-reform-its-sexual-violence-laws> accessed 5 July 2022.

5.2.7 Brief Conclusion

Despite the difficulties it has faced, the government has been able to establish a robust system of laws that align with the ideals of CCPR focused on securing civil and political rights. At the same time, it recovers from authoritarian rule and gives itself the power to govern. The Supreme Court has referred to and relied on provisions from the Covenant to decide cases that are crucial in protecting and promoting civil and political rights. Further, there has been an underlying concern over effective implementation and administration of rules, regulations, guidelines and other laws by officials. Despite the progressive realisation of civil and political rights, the ambitious provisions in the laws of Nepal fail to adequately protect the rights of Nepalese citizens.[127]

The decision that the HRCttee should hear individual complaints, despite non-exhaustion of local remedies on the grounds of prolonged delays in deciding matters by the Courts, reflects diminishing faith in the ability of the legal system to guarantee the rights as prescribed by the Constitution of Nepal and CCPR. A pattern of highly-subjective and inconsistent judicial application and status of international law by the Courts needs to be addressed.

However, the government is yet to enact specific domestic legislation on crimes relating to torture. A considerable effort must be made to engage local government officials to recognise the significance of the Covenant and the need to fulfil duties according to those that have been prescribed by the law to end the long delays and red tape in areas such as reparation for victims of torture.

5.3 *International Covenant on Economic, Social and Cultural Rights*

Nepal acceded to CESCR in 1991, but has not accepted the procedure for individual communication under OP-CESCR.

5.3.1 Legislature-Executive Recognition and Implementation

Part III of the Constitution of Nepal contains numerous economic, social and cultural rights that are enshrined in CESCR. The legal structure comprises the specific Act and regulations to provide for substantive and procedural provisions with particular procedures to offer remedies for human rights violations. These domestic enactments include the Social Welfare Act 1992; the Consumer Protection Act 1998; the Domestic Violence Act 2009; the Compensation Relating to Torture Act 1996; and the Children Act 2018. These laws are made

---

127   Interview with Mr Kapil Shrestha, former Commissioner of NHRC. The interview was conducted virtually on 29 January 2021.

with the intent to protect and promote the rights of various groups and sections of society by ensuring economic, social and cultural rights. In Nepal, there has been discourse over the classifications of rights and the need to harmonise economic, social and cultural rights with development to be able to keep up with the ever-changing needs of society owing to industrial and technological advancement and innovation.[128]

The government of Nepal has developed separate policies to comprehensively approach the situation of human rights in the country by identifying such issues, formulating strategies and monitoring the progress that the constitutional provisions and CESCR aim to guarantee. A notable collaborative venture by the government includes the implementation of the National Human Rights Action Plan (NHRAP) to cater to 12 sectoral areas for policy development including education, health, population, rights of indigenous people, employment, cultural rights, institution and infrastructure.[129] Ensuring access to water, the government implemented a national strategy policy intending to provide safe drinking water and sanitation in rural areas. This involved community-level sanitation programmes that were organised to raise awareness about sanitation. The government has been successful in ensuring safe access to water to 85 per cent of the population,[130] which is disputed by the reports of civil society groups, including the United Nations Children's Fund (UNICEF).[131]

The government has also successfully responded to recommendations to formulate laws surrounding the protection and promotion of rights of indigenous people[132] through the Tribal People's Commission Act 2017 to ensure the

---

128 Geeta Pathak Sangroula, 'Breaking the Generation Theory of Human Rights: Mapping the Scope of Justiciability of Economic, Social and Cultural Rights with Special Reference to the Constitutional Guarantees in Nepal' (2013) 3 Kathmandu School of Law Review 1.

129 CESCR, 'Implementation of International Covenant on Economic, Social and Cultural Rights by Nepal' (12 July 2011) para 17 UN Doc <http://docstore.ohchr.org/SelfServices/FilesHandler.ashx?enc=4slQ6QSmlBEDzFEovLCuWxeiQQmyptl4nBy7D%2bm2Lju SHLp%2fzDMVDtEzoH9s6BIpr1XmYaGS6IgZBCKO136ZAa3miDrYSth1vMXxfiD4dku1 sl2AxxJ69PU8IHn%2f032g> accessed 5 July 2022.

130 CESCR, 'Summary Record of 57th Meeting on Nepal' (20 November 2014) UN Doc <https://tbinternet.ohchr.org/_layouts/15/treatybodyexternal/Download.aspx?symbolno=E%2fC.12%2f2014%2fSR.57&Lang=en> accessed 5 July 2022.

131 UNICEF WASH, Report on Nepal <https://www.unicef.org/nepal/water-and-sanitation-wash#:~:text=%E2%80%9C10.8%20million%20people%20in%20Nepal,access%20to%20basic%20water%20services.%E2%80%9D&text=Only%2025%20per%20cent%20of,per%20cent%20requires%20major%20repairs.> accessed 5 July 2022.

132 OPMCM Nepal, 'UPR Action Plan 2016–2011' (2016) <https://www.opmcm.gov.np/en/wp-content/uploads/2018/03/UPR-Action-Plan-2016-2011_Matrix_Eng.pdf> Recommendations 121.9 and 107.4 accessed 5 July 2022.

representation of indigenous people, Tharu, Madhesi and other disadvantaged groups to be represented in the government.

5.3.2 Reliance by Judiciary

The Supreme Court of Nepal has established for itself a significant role through its positive contributions on the subject, including its frequent references to CESCR and other treaty provisions to help develop judicial guidelines to fill gaps in the law with the objectives of enhancing gender equality in terms of property rights, promoting social security for people with disabilities, enhancing the justiciability of the constitutional rights and other economic, social and cultural guarantees while recognising the interlinkage of the right to live with dignity with the right to equality along with other socio-economic rights.

The Supreme Court has cited international instruments in *Bajuddin Miya and Others v Government of Nepal*,[133] a case involving the right to food, where the petitioners claimed that as a result of there being no barriers in many areas of the wildlife reserves, animals would often escape and destroy the farmers' crops. However, during that time, there were no laws and policies about mitigating damages caused by the escaping animals from the wildlife reserves. The Supreme Court declared that the right to food sovereignty meant the right of every citizen to food security and the right to be free from hunger while citing article 11(2) of CESCR.

Similarly, in *Amrita Thapa Magar and Others v Office of Prime Minister and Council of Ministers*[134] the petitioners had called upon the Court to direct the government to enact laws as envisioned by the Constitution relating to issues of education, health, environment, employment, social security and food. The Court observed that as socio-economic rights were enshrined in the Constitution, it was the responsibility of the government to enact laws for making these rights effective. In this regard, the Court finally issued a directive requiring the government of Nepal to enact the necessary laws for ensuring the rights relating to free education, health, employment, food and social security.

Another example of the Court's focus on the interlinkages of rights was seen in the case *Shanti Balampaki v Government of Nepal*,[135] decided in 2018. The Court in this case related article 10 of CESCR dealing with special protection of and assistance to mothers, family and children to article 38 of the Constitution

---

133 *Bajuddin Minhya and Others v GoN, Prime Minister and the Council of Ministers* Writ No 338, Year 2008.
134 *Amrita Thapa Magar and Others v Office of Prime Minister and Council of Ministers and Others*, 2007, Writ No 0139.
135 *Shanti Balampaki v Government of Nepal* [2015] WN 0484.

on the rights of women and to other state obligations under international treaties such as CEDAW. Such a constitutional culture that is free to cite international law as authority enables the Court to engage with domestic constitutional and international treaty obligations.[136]

5.3.3 Impact on and through Independent State Actors

Nepal became a beacon that highlighted violations of fundamental rights guaranteed by the new Constitution along with the economic, social and cultural rights that were enshrined, drawing inspiration from CESCR. Additionally, Nepal faced an undeclared blockade from India, massively affecting supplies, while having at the time undergone a massive earthquake. With this, the NHRC stepped in to express its concern over the condition of children, the shortages of food supplies, demolished infrastructure due to the earthquake, unemployment and safety.[137]

Ensuring the right to food enshrined in the Convention, the NHRC developed a set of indicators to monitor the compliance and progress relating to the right to food with the support of the Food and Agriculture Organisation (FAO) and the OHCHR. However, the NHRC has received a minimum number of recommendations on subjects relating to economic, social and cultural rights. To a certain degree, this reflects limited awareness on issues relating to education, health, food, housing, and so forth, or the Commission's inability to monitor and investigate such rights. There have been claims by civil society organisations of the NHRC not responding adequately to issues that are raised in the first place.[138] This cyclic process of lack of implementation and lack of response on the part of stakeholders that are involved needs to be addressed.

In line with the government's Gender Inclusion Policy, the NHRC saw the formation of gender equality and social inclusion (GESI) Units in the Commission and the Ministries of Health and Education, Agriculture and Cooperatives that

---

136 Sabrina Singh, 'Realising Economic and Social Rights in Nepal: The Impact of a Progressive Constitution and an Experimental Supreme Court' (2020) Harvard Law Review 33.
137 NHRC, 'Urgent Appeal on Nepal Humanitarian Crisis' (2015) <https://reliefweb.int/sites/reliefweb.int/files/resources/2045759427NHRC_Urgent_Appeal_On_Nepal_Humanitarian_Crisis.pdf> accessed 5 July 2022.
138 FIAN, 'Parallel Information: The Right to Adequate Food in Nepal' (2014) <https://www.fian.org/fileadmin/media/publications_2015/FIAN_Nepal_parellel_information_to_CESCR-final_version10Sep2014_2_.pdf> accessed 5 July 2022.

had gender focal persons that were responsible for monitoring and assessing gender equality and inclusivity of persons in workplaces.[139]

5.3.4 Impact through Non-state Actors

Civil society organisations have had effective collaborations with governmental institutions to work on issues relating to CESCR. While dealing with the issue of justiciable management of squatters, the NHRC relied on the consultations with civil society representatives to put pressure on the government for medical treatment, rehabilitation and the protection of victims that were injured due to clashes during an eviction, while trying to identify squatter settlements.[140]

Further, civil society organisations, both global and regional, have collaborated with the government to protect the rights of Nepali migrant workers that are abroad. Some initiatives include publicising announcements through audio and video clips to raise awareness about safe migration.[141] Such organisations also played a significant role in raising awareness on issues relating to harmful traditions, especially those against women and girls, such as *chhaupadi*, child marriage and dowry demands.[142] In addition, the government has delegated some ground-level work, such as operating helplines for women and children to address their issues.[143] This has helped empower government programmes and initiatives by reaching out at a local level to engage with the community on laws for their protection and other schemes of their government for their overall upliftment.

5.3.5 Impact of State Reporting

Nepal submitted its initial report in 1999, six years later than required under the Convention. In the COs to Nepal's third report, submitted in 2011, the Committee highlighted the need to rehabilitate and integrate bonded labourers,[144] recognising the importance of the issues the government had already started, by providing soft interest loans for buying homes and especially

---

139 Anita Kelles-Viitanen and Ava Shrestha GESI Consultants, *Gender Equality and Social Inclusion: Promoting the Rights of Women and the Excluded or Sustained Peace and Inclusive Development* (2011).
140 NHRC, 'Selected Decisions of the NHRC Nepal' (2017) Vol III.
141 UNHRC, 'National Report Submitted in Accordance with Paragraph 5' (3 November 2020) UN Doc (A/HRC/WG.6/37/NPL/1) para 104.
142 ibid para 110.
143 ibid para 99.
144 CESCR, 'Concluding Observations on the Third Periodic Report of Nepal' (12 December 2014) UN Doc (E/C.12/CO/3) para 18.

helping to provide land and financial assistance to the emancipated bonded labourers for their rehabilitation.[145]

The implementation of the Right to Employment Act 2018 and the Labour Act 2017 addresses issues relating to wages and discrimination by prohibiting all forms of discrimination in respect of wages, to ensure equal pay for equal work and social security on any ground including gender, religion, caste, ethnicity, and so forth. Further, in 2012 the Committee elaborated on the need of ensuring the right to a just and favourable environment by implementing the minimum wage legislation.[146] The government fixed the minimum support price at Rs 13 450 with a daily minimum wage being Rs 517, which has been guaranteed by introducing the Employment Service Centres and the Employment Management Information System at a local level.[147]

Working on the concerns regarding the implementation of measures to prevent the economic exploitation of children,[148] the government introduced the Ten-Year National Master Plan against Child Labour (2018–2028) which aims to eliminate child labour in 2022 and other forms in 2025, in response to concerns over the implementation of the Child Labour (Prohibition) Act 2000.[149] In this regard, Child Helplines were introduced that are run by civil society organisations under the guidance of the Ministry of Women and Children to cooperate with the Child Rights Council to rescue children that may be at risk and provide protection, assistance, counselling and reunion with family.[150]

5.3.6 Brief Conclusion

Nepal has aligned its constitutional provisions with CESCR, as well as with specific legislation that has been incorporated to guarantee economic, social and cultural rights. The unique discourse on CESCR rights in the context of development offers the need to introduce a new perspective towards the applicability of human rights instruments themselves and their influence over domestic legislations. The discourse over the subject seems to have arisen out of a nation-level realisation of the inadequacies of the international treaties in keeping up with time, along with the new Constitution's significant reliance on jurisprudence laid down by international law. The improved legislation

---

145 CESCR, 'Implementation of ICESCR by Nepal Third Periodic Report' (2012) UN Doc (E/C.12/NPL/3) para 278.
146 CESCR (n 145) para 17.
147 UNHRC (n 144) para 52.
148 CESCR (n 145) para 21.
149 UNHRC (n 144) para 98.
150 ibid para 99.

and governmental policies for implementation reflect a new phase for Nepal to review previous legislations and procedures that were ineffective or inadequate in ensuring proper performance. However, there has been an ongoing dispute over the facts that are submitted through government reports to the UN agencies and other civil society organisations. This may create hurdles for international organisations to monitor progress and coordinate efforts with the government to be able to achieve ends if data collections are unclear or inaccurate.

Through collaborative efforts, there has been a rise in civil society organisations specifically coordinating efforts to ensure, evaluate and implement rights under CESCR to help achieve protection and promotion of economic, social and cultural rights. While interacting with NGOs and CSOs, Nepal was able to swiftly respond to recommendations.

5.4 Convention on the Elimination of All Forms of Discrimination against Women

In 1991 Nepal ratified CEDAW; and in 2007 OP-CEDAW, accepting individual complaints.

5.4.1 Legislature-Executive Recognition and Implementation

Through article 38 of the Constitution, the fundamental rights of women have been recognised paving the way for crucial legislation to protect their rights. Ratifying CEDAW and OP-CEDAW in 2007 gave rise to institutional improvements in women's rights through constitutional mechanisms such as the NHRC and NWC.[151] The establishment of the NWC under the National Women Commission Act 2006 was passed with the intention to include women in the mainstream of development and achieve overall development by ensuring gender justice as enshrined in the Preamble to the Act. The establishment of the NWC comes as a positive step by Nepal under its legal obligation under article 2(c) of CEDAW to establish legal protection of women against any acts of discrimination by public institutions.

To ensure the fulfilment of such objectives relating to the protection of rights, there was recognition for the need to press for easy and equal access to education, ultimately leading to the Act Relating to Compulsory and Free Education 2018. Highlighting the importance of health, with abortion being legalised in 2002, women gained increased rights to abortion that were later

---

[151] NAWHRD, 'CEDAW Shadow Report by National Alliance of Women Human Rights Defenders, Nepal' (September 2018).

reinforced in *Lakshmi Dhikta v Nepal* (2009),[152] which ordered the state to ensure that safe and legal abortion was affordably available to women. Further, the Safe Motherhood and Reproductive Health Rights Act 2018 recognises reproductive rights by providing free abortions bringing Nepal closer to the goal of universal access to abortion care and reproductive health services.

The government has identified the need to end gender-based discrimination and for integrating men and women equally into society to ensure equality in all sectors.[153] In this regard, the government has also developed the School Sector Development Plan (SSDP) for the period 2016–2023 to graduate from the status of being the least developed country by the year 2022. This will help instigate growth in the Nepali educational system to create equality in both gender and class divisions. Further, the Second Long-Term Health Plan (1997–2017)[154] sought to address disparities in health care, promote gender sensitivity and ensure access to quality healthcare services. This guiding framework helped build successive health plans to improve the health of the general population, including the establishment of coordinative efforts between public, private and civil society organisations for development. Through the Maternity Incentive Scheme 2005, transportation incentives have been made encouraging delivery in health centres. Nepal aims to ensure that 70 per cent of all deliveries take place by skilled attendants in line with the Sustainable Development Goals (SDG) target in 2030.[155] In its protective efforts against abuse, the government of Nepal has implemented the National Action Plan Against Human Trafficking (2011–2021) in addition to the Guidelines to Control Sexual Exploitation of Workers in Dance and Restaurant Bars, which also aims to prevent sexual abuse. In an attempt to combat the stigma against menstruating women, the government initiated a *Chauppadi* free campaign demolishing the *chhau* sheds in response to recommendations made in 2018.[156] The CEDAW Cttee's[157] recommendation to eliminate harmful practices such as *chhaupadi* resulted in its criminalisation by the Penal

---

152   *Lakshmi Dhikta v Nepal* [2008] WN 757.
153   Gender Equality and Social Integration Policy 2009.
154   The Second-Long Term Health Plan (1997–2017) <http://dohs.gov.np/wp-content/uploads/2014/04/2nd-Long-Term-Health-Plan.docx#:~:text=The%20Ministry%20of%20Health%20of,needs%20are%20not%20often%20met> accessed 5 July 2022.
155   UNHRC (n 141) para 60.
156   Human Rights Watch Submission to the CEDAW Committee on Nepal's Periodic Report for the 71st Session, October 2018.
157   CEDAW, 'Concluding Observations on the Sixth Periodic Report of Nepal' 2018, CEDAW/C/NPL/CO/6 paras 17–18 <https://tbinternet.ohchr.org/_layouts/15/treatybodyexternal/TBSearch.aspx?Lang=En&CountryID=122> accessed 5 July 2022.

Code. In response to the recommendation made by the Committee to ensure equal and full citizenship rights for women, including the right to transfer citizenship to their children and foreign husbands,[158] Nepal stated that it would deliberate the concern as part of the drafting of the new constitution.[159] The promulgation of the new Constitution in 2015 did include aspects of gender in relation to citizenship. However, the constitutional provisions and the submission of the Bill to amend the Citizenship Act were against the principles of equality and non-discrimination. The CEDAW Cttee took note of the discriminatory provision and recommended, in its 2018 Concluding Observations, to Nepal to amend the discriminatory provisions that are contradictory to article 9(2) of CEDAW.[160]

CSOs have expressed concerns regarding the effective implementation of laws relating to violence against women, including the Domestic Violence Act 2010, with calls for impartial and efficient enforcement by competent officials.[161] On the issue of implementation, despite there being several arrangements for seeking remedies, including local governments, the mechanisms are found to be of limited operation as a result of inadequate human and logistic resources and infrastructure.

5.4.2 Reliance by Judiciary

The promulgation of the Constitution of the Kingdom of Nepal 1990 has been recognised as the genesis of the elimination of laws based on gender-based discrimination, property and women's rights.[162] *Meera Dhugana and Meera*

---

158 CEDAW, 'Concluding Observations of the Committee on the Elimination of Discrimination against Women' CEDAW/C/NPL/CO/4–5 para 26(a) <https://tbinternet.ohchr.org/_layouts/15/treatybodyexternal/Download.aspx?symbolno=CEDAW%2fC%2fNPL%2fCO%2f4-5&Lang=en> accessed 5 July 2022.
159 CEDAW, 'Information Provided by Nepal in Follow-Up to the Concluding Observations' CEDAW/C/NPL/CO/4-5/Add.1 para 4–5 <https://tbinternet.ohchr.org/_layouts/15/treatybodyexternal/Download.aspx?symbolno=CEDAW%2fC%2fNPL%2fCO%2f4-5%2fAdd.1&Lang=en> accessed 5 July 2022.
160 CEDAW, 'Concluding Observations on the Sixth Periodic Report of Nepal' CEDAW/C/NPL/CO/6 paras 30–31 <https://tbinternet.ohchr.org/_layouts/15/treatybodyexternal/Download.aspx?symbolno=CEDAW%2fC%2fNPL%2fCO%2f6&Lang=en> accessed 5 July 2022.
161 CEDAW Shadow Report by the National Alliance for Women Human Rights Defenders, Nepal (September 2018) 5.
162 Nutan Chandra Subedi, 'Elimination of Gender Discriminatory Legal Provisions by the Supreme Court of Nepal with Reference to Women's Right to Property' (2009) 24 Tribhuvan University Journal 37 <https://www.nepjol.info/index.php/TUJ/article/download/2615/2312> accessed 5 July 2022.

Khanal v HMG Ministry of Law, Justice and Parliamentary Affairs[163] has been cited as the starting point of legislative reform for women's rights to property. In this case the petitioners claimed violations of constitutional provisions including articles 1, 15 and 16 of the CEDAW. The Court stated:

> The Court observed various issues for the first time and rendered the decision that to make sudden changes in the traditional practices of society and the old social norms, which is adopted since a long time, may create problems in connection to adjustment between male and female in the society. However, this may cause such a situation, which may be beyond the perception. Therefore, before reaching in final conclusion and decision on the issues immediately, it will be better to make some provisions for wide and extensive discussion and deliberation taking into accounts the constitutional provision vis-à-vis equality. As the family law relating to property is to be wholly considered, it is hereby issued this directive order in the name of His Majesty's Government to introduce an appropriate Bill to Parliament within one year from the date of reception of this order, making necessary consultation with recognised women's organisations, sociologists, the concerned social organisation and lawyers as well and by studying and considering the legal provisions in this regard on other countries.

The Supreme Court issued a directive order to the legislature to draft a Bill relating to the matter of partition but did not address the discriminatory provisions enshrined in domestic laws which were in contravention with the international treaties to which Nepal was party. Although the writ petition did not, owing to the traditions and customs, result in a substantive finding on the merits, it opened the doors for other writ petitioners to approach the court relating to violations of rights under CEDAW. After some time, in response to other writ petitions filed pursuant to CEDAW, the apex court established an equal right to property for women and men.[164]

In *Prakashmanai Sharma and Others v HMG/Office of Prime Minister and Council of Ministers*,[165] the petitioners cited inconsistencies with constitutional provisions and articles 1, 2, 3, 4, 5, 6, 15 and 16 of CEDAW and requested

---

[163] *Meera Dhugana and Meera Khanal v HMG Ministry of Law and Justice* Year 2003, Writ No 5.
[164] Susheela Karki, 'A Judicial Response to Gender Justice: A Bird's Eye View' (2012) NJA Law Journal (Special Issue).
[165] *Prakashmanai Sharma and Others v HMG/Office of Prime Minister and Council of Ministers* Year 2008, Writ No 64.

the Court to declare the discriminatory laws on the matter of partition share to be null and void. Accordingly, the Court observed:

> Section 1 of the chapter on partition gives equal right to daughter to get one share, and once she gets the share of property she has full right to enjoy, use, sell or dispose the property, it also compels the daughter to return the remaining property once she gets marriage ... Due to this impugned provision the goal of 11th amendment of National Code to provide equal partition right to daughter has been vitiated and it ultimately results in discrimination as defined in the Article 1 of the CEDAW Convention.

However, despite this recognition, the Court was reluctant to declare the law to be null and void describing it as a subject under the legislative's prerogative and accordingly not under the usurpation of the judicial function. On the same matter under women's exclusive property, *Lily Thapa v Office of Prime Minister and Council of Ministers*[166] held that the provisions under section 2 of the National Code (*Muluki Ain*) 2020 were inconsistent with constitutional provisions including article 26 of CCPR, articles 2 and 3 of CESCR and articles 1, 2, 3 and 15 of CEDAW. The Court stated that the interim Constitution of Nepal and CEDAW, to which Nepal is a party, created a state obligation to provide a strong basis for gender justice. It observed that the government of Nepal should be committed to the 'commitment expressed by the Constitution and the international 7 conventions to which Nepal is a Party and in order to translate those commitments into practice, other laws of the State should also include the provisions expressed in those documents'.[167] The Court stated further:

> The Bench hereby issues a directive order against the Prime Minister and to the Council of Ministers directing the respondents to see that the provisions prescribed under Section 9 and 9(a) on the Chapter of Marriage are consistent with the Interim Constitution, 2063 and with the provisions prescribed in the Convention against Elimination Of All Forms Of Discrimination Against Women (CEDAW) and to amend the law and to make arrangement for appropriate laws.[168]

---

[166] *Lily Thapa v Office of Prime Minister and Council of Ministers* Year 2005, Writ No 47.
[167] 'The Landmark Decisions of the Supreme Court, Nepal on Gender Justice' in Ananda Mohan Bhattarai (ed), (National Judicial Academy & United Nations Fund for Women 2010).
[168] *Lily Thapa* (n 166).

5.4.3   Impact on and through Independent State Actors

The NWC established by the government of Nepal through a separate Act enacted in 2007 is the front-runner in advocating the rights of women in Nepal. It is aimed at monitoring the state's obligations[169] to the provisions of international treaties to which Nepal has been a party and to coordinate[170] with other agencies for mainstreaming gender policy in national development. Since 2009, the NWC began raising issues of women facing problems in being able to acquire and transfer nationality, consistently put forward by women.[171] It also raised awareness about the violence against women and girls in Nepal. In light of the growing incidents of trafficking, rape and domestic violence, child marriage, sex-selective abortions, violence related to dowry and allegations of witchcraft, harmful traditional practices such as *chhaupadi* and *deuki*, the National Women's Commission conducted research in various districts highlighting the rising number of incidents of violence against women, especially against women from marginalised groups such as Dalit women, women with disabilities and Muslim women.[172]

The NWC has resorted to innovative ways to reach out to women. A leading example of this is their promotion of gender-sensitive media by continuously engaging with journalists and inviting them to report and investigate issues concerning the rights of women. The NWC has forged partnerships with different government institutions and civil society organisations, establishing a functional relationship between the Nepal police, different shelter service providers, legal, support and child protection agencies have been established and strengthened.

5.4.4   Impact through Non-state Actors

NGOs have been able to highlight issues that women face by relying on CEDAW and evaluating Nepal's progress in the elimination of all forms of discrimination against women. These specifically include the prevalence of problems with education and health care. Child marriage was cited to be the reason for decreasing enrolments among girls along with a decreasing retention rate and the lack of scholarship opportunities to attract girls, especially those from vulnerable communities, have been catered to through legislation by prohibiting marriage below the age of 20 and by introducing scholarship programmes that

---

169   National Woman Commission Act, 2063 (2006) s 11(h).
170   ibid s 11(a).
171   Nepal's Implementation Status of CEDAW (NWC, 26 June 2011).
172   ibid.

saw an increase in enrolments in schools.[173] This was also reflected in the government's Literate Nepal Mission to eliminate illiteracy by 2015 as was envisioned in the Millennium Development Goals (MDGs). This has been further extended by the United Nations Sustainable Development Goals (SDGs) target in 2030.

Another significant contribution of these NGOs is raising awareness by unifying efforts collaborating with the government to bring about a change in attitude and age-old practices such as child marriage, dowry practice, raising awareness about the harmful *chhaupadi* practices, ending accusations of witchcraft, strengthening healthcare services for women and girls, promoting social security, education and employment. These community-level campaigns help to empower these adolescent girls and develop a dialogue around the issues relating to women and girls.[174]

5.4.5   Impact of State Reporting

Since the Committee's calls for protecting women from violence by strengthening the domestic legislations,[175] the Domestic Violence (Crime and Punishment) Act 2009 was amended in 2015. The amendment has broadened the definition of domestic violence to include physical torture, mental harm, in addition to all forms of sexual violence, including between partners and outside marriage. The Act has also expanded the definition to include torture for dowry-related violence as domestic violence. There have also been measures to protect women in the workplace by enacting the Sexual Harassment at Workplace (Control) Act, 2014 which provides for measures to control and punish sexual harassment at both formal and informal workplaces. Accordingly, the Penal Code criminalises sexual harassment with a punishment of up to three years' imprisonment and a fine 30 000 rupees. The Victims of Crime Protection Act 2018 ensures the protection of the victim of sexual harassment. There is also the Violence against Women Prevention Fund (Operation) 2012, and the Single-Woman Security Fund (Operation) Regulation, 2013 which have established funds providing immediate relief to the victims of violence

---

173   CEDAW Shadow Report Preparation Committee (SRPC), Nepal 2016, 31–32.
174   UNHRC, 'National Report Submitted in Accordance with Paragraph 5 of the Annex to Human Rights Council Resolution 16/21' (2020) UN Doc (A/HRC/WG.6/37/NPL/1) para 110.
175   CEDAW, 'Concluding Observations of the Committee on the Elimination of Discrimination Against Women – Nepal' (11 August 2011) paras 20(a)-(c), CEDAW/C/NPL/CO/4-5, <https://www.refworld.org/docid/4eeb45822.html> accessed 5 July 2022.

against women and provide education, training, relief and treatment of single women.[176] In the area of reproductive health, the Committee had recommended easy access to basic health care and reproductive health services.[177] To achieve this, the government enacted the Safe Motherhood and Reproductive Health Right Act 2018 which explicitly protects the health rights of women, girls, adolescents and new-borns while ensuring easy and affordable access to quality reproductive healthcare services. The Ministry of Health and Population (MoHP) has implemented various programmes related to reproductive health, women and children. In the last five years, the Family Welfare Division trained and listed 1 890 service providers, listed 721 service centres for providing safe abortion services and in the previous five years 440 983 women were served with secure abortion services.[178]

5.4.6 Impact of Individual Communications

Although Nepal has accepted the procedure for individual communication under OP-CEDAW, no communications have been submitted.

5.4.7 Brief Conclusion

The human rights situation of women in the past decades has been significantly improved through elaborate legislations and policies adopted to cater to the needs and rights of women. There have been drastic steps in the development of women through the areas of education, health care, reproductive health, discrimination and protection from exploitation in workplaces. In this connection, NGOs have been instrumental in coordinating efforts along with the government to improve the situation of women by improving the literacy rate to ensure complete literacy of women under the SDGs by the year 2030. CEDAW has acted as a guiding force for the government and the judiciary while taking decisions to protect and promote the rights of women and do away with age-old and orthodox traditions that are inherently discriminatory.[179]

There are still areas where the independent state authorities need to coordinate more efficiently while dealing with matters such as atrocities against Dalit

---

176 UNHRC, 'National Report Submitted in Accordance with Paragraph 5 of the Annex to Human Rights Council Resolution 16/21' (2020) UN Doc (A/HRC/WG.6/37/NPL/1) paras 80–83.
177 CEDAW (n 175) para 32.
178 UN HRC, 'National Report Submitted in Accordance with Paragraph 5 of the Annex to Human Rights Council Resolution 16/21' (2020) UN Doc (A/HRC/WG.6/37/NPL/1) para 57.
179 Interview with Prof Kapil Aryal, Researcher/Consultant. The interview was conducted virtually on 30 January 2021. Mid-term Assessment of Nepal's 2nd Cycle UPR Recommendations, INSEC. April 2018 (the report was submitted to the OHCHR-Geneva).

women, girls and other disadvantaged groups. CSOs have cited issues relating to the implementation of many of these laws relating to access to justice and child marriage. Similarly, despite the emergence of healthcare and reproductive services for women through rules and policies, there are speculations over whether the practical implementation of these schemes actually benefit women. The government will have to encourage the training and development of this sector to create a space that is safe and free from biased attitudes.

5.5 Convention against Torture and Other Cruel, Inhuman or Degrading Treatment or Punishment

Shortly after the restoration of parliamentary democracy, Nepal acceded to CAT in 1991 and accepted the inquiry procedure under article 20 of the Convention. Nepal has not accepted the individual communications procedure under CAT. The 1990 Constitution abolished the authoritarian rule and enshrined the freedom from torture, recognising the fundamental rights of the citizens. Nepal witnessed a significant increase in torture cases through 1996–2006 while both security forces and Maoist rebels used torture to intimidate, suppress and punish victims.[180] With the initiation of institutionalised checks, the reports of such cases have diminished with the restoration of democracy.

5.5.1 Legislature-Executive Recognition and Implementation

The 1990 Constitution recognised the right against torture as a fundamental right, after which the government also ratified CAT in 1991. Five years after the ratification, the Compensation Relating to Torture Act 1996 was enacted as the legislative method of incorporating provisions under CAT into domestic law. The Act encompasses provisions of compensation to any person who is subjected to physical or mental torture during detention in the course of an investigation or inquiry process or any other situation that may arise leading to such cruel and inhuman treatment. However, to be able to achieve this, the provisions against torture should also be applicable outside detention.[181] This provision concerning detention is in line with article 10 of CAT.

The government in association with civil society organisations focused efforts towards imparting training and organising workshops, seminars and other awareness-raising programmes against torture and other cruel, inhuman

---

[180] Advocacy Forum, 'Hope and Frustration: Assessing the Impact of Nepal's Torture Compensation Act 1996' 3 (1st edn 2008).
[181] NHRC, 'Human Rights Situation During and After Promulgation of Constitution Report' (2015) 5, 24–25.

or degrading treatment or punishment.[182] With these efforts, a large number of personnel from the Nepal army, the Nepal police and armed police force have been trained in various issues of human rights, including the subject of torture. Such workshops, training and seminars have been regarded as effective tools not only for changing the behaviour of the targeted officials but also raising general awareness among the mass population against torture. The government of Nepal has also conducted regular monitoring and evaluation of protection and prevention of acts of torture.

Despite this, the most significant hurdles are two-fold: (a) the government has not enacted domestic legislation on torture as prescribed under the Convention; and (b) despite being awarded victim compensation, victims have rarely been able to receive the award from the Chief District Officer (CDO). The former reflects the difficulty in laying down penalties and constitutional provisions against torture in conformity with the international treaty. In the latter, there is a lack of willingness to fulfil duties as prescribed by the law.

5.5.2 Reliance by Judiciary

With the promulgation of the interim Constitution 2007, the Supreme Court reflecting on article 22 issued a directive to criminalise torture and other kinds of ill-treatment. In *Rajendra Ghimire v Office of the Prime Minister*,[183] the Supreme Court recognised Nepal's obligation under CAT to prohibit any kind of inhumane torture to the person in custody or detention. It referred to section 9 of Treaty Act, which provides that the treaties or agreements ratified by Nepal will be applied as Nepal law, and thus there is no ground for the state to get itself absolved from the responsibility determined by these instruments.

The Supreme Court stated that the government must adhere to the obligations of the Convention and enact legislation for criminalising acts of torture:

> It is also the responsibility of the state to create an environment of trust and respect by the victims to the justice system of the state and the feeling among state officials who are guilty that they would not enjoy any immunity from the liability that is created out of their action. This is not a separate and special responsibility of the state rather it is a responsibility

---

182 UNCAT, Comments by the Government of Nepal to the Conclusions and Recommendations of the Committee against Torture (CAT/C/NPL/CO/2) (29 January 2008) UN Doc (CAT/C/NPL/CO/2/Add.1) para 9 <https://www.refworld.org/docid/47aacd6c2.html> accessed 5 July 2022.

183 *Rajendra Ghimire & Others v Office of the Prime Minister* Year 2007, Writ No 3219 <http://www.derechos.org/intlaw/doc/npl5.html> accessed 5 July 2022.

in concord with the commitment of the state towards basic fundamental rights and human rights. This bench has reached the conclusion that in order to fulfil this responsibility the state needs to make such a special law.[184]

This was seen as a significant step in the implementation of domestic law concerning international law and respecting the legal obligations to which Nepal is bound as a party to such treaties. The Supreme Court reiterated this stance in *Advocate Madhav Basnet v Government of Nepal*.[185]

5.5.3   Impact on and through Independent State Actors

The NHRC has been monitoring and giving instructions to the government to ensure peace and to prevent the use of excessive force and torture by advocating dialogue on several occasions.[186] Accordingly, the NHRC has been quick to point out violations of constitutional provisions and international treaties, especially after the promulgation of the 2015 Constitution, highlighting cases of abuse and torture by police officials against human rights activists.[187] During the drafting of the 2015 Constitution, the NHRC recommended the application of provisions against torture for persons outside of detention as well as defined in article 1 of the Convention.[188] The coordination between government and the NHRIS, CSOS for consultations on pending recommendations providing a platform to the NHRC to give feedback on the UPR recommendations, is noteworthy.[189]

The NHRC relies on and takes influence from the treaties to which Nepal is a party in their investigations. The NHRC report relating to the death of Saru Sunar, for example, after having been arrested and in police custody as a result of torture inflicted on him along with its recommendations describing violations of the Universal Declaration of Human Rights, CCPR and CAT is indicative of this.[190]

---

184   ibid.
185   *Advocate Madhav Basnet & Others v Government of Nepal & Others* Year 2014, Writ No 69.
186   Human Rights Situation During and After Promulgation of Constitution Report, NHRC 2015 3.
187   NHRC, 'Human Rights Situation During and After Promulgation of Constitution Report' (2015) 24–25.
188   NHRC Suggestions on Preliminary Draft Constitution of Nepal, 23 July 2015.
189   Suggestions of NHRC Nepal to the Government of Nepal on the Recommendations of UPR Process for 16 March 2016.
190   NHRC, 'Summary Report on the Saru Sunar case' <https://en.setopati.com/political/156318> accessed 5 July 2022.

5.5.4 Impact through Non-state Actors

In Nepal, human rights NGOs have played a significant role in the protection and promotion of human rights since 1990. The NGOs that have been working have played a significant role in monitoring and advocating the right to freedom from torture These NGOs have taken a forefront role in some main areas, which include the following:

(i) monitoring and documenting cases of torture and other human rights violation during the detention of prisoners in custody; NGOs such as Advocacy Forum continues to publish reports and monitoring of detention centres;[191]

(ii) aid in providing legal and other social support for direct communication with the UN Human Rights Committee on behalf of victims to other committees for further investigation and compensation to victims of torture in four individual cases;[192]

(iii) human rights NGOs have been successful in facilitating the Government for policy reform or promulgation of anti-torture law and policies against torture. For instance, many national and international NGOs played an essential role in the process of promulgating the current Compensation Relating to Torture Act (CRTA).[193] After the promulgation of the CRTA in 1996, many NGOs have been working on reviewing the provisions along with the practice of torture and accordingly recommended to the government that it can make new anti-torture laws in Nepal;

(iv) NGOs have been able to effectively communicate with UN human rights mechanisms by submitting reports and the regular issue of findings on cases of torture. Most significantly, the CAT Cttee and

---

[191] Mandira Sharma, 'Ingrid Massage and Kathryn McDonald 'Lawyers' Intervention at Pretrial Stage Helps to Prevent Torture, Illegal Detention and Other Human Rights Violations: Experiences of Advocacy Forum–Nepal' (2012) 4 Journal of Human Rights Practice 253–272.

[192] Human Rights Committee, Views: Communication No 1863/2009, 105th sess, UN Doc CCPR/C/105/D/1863/2009 (2 August 2012) ('*Dev Bahadur Maharjan v Nepal*'); Human Rights Committee, Views: Communication No 1961/2008, 108th sess, UN Doc. CCPR/C/108/D/1761/2008 (27 April 2011) ('*Yubraj Giri v Nepal*'); Human Rights Committee, Views: Communication No 1865/2009, 108th sess, UN Doc CCPR/C/108/D/1865/2009 (28 October 2013) ('*Santa Sedhai v Nepal*'); Human Rights Committee, Views: Communication No 1469/2006 9.

[193] Bhogendra Sharma and Rajendra Ghimire, 'Combating Torture in Nepal Problem and Prospect' Centre for Victims of Torture Nepal' (2006) 30–32.

the Special Rapporteur on Torture have acknowledged the reports and communications made by these human rights NGOs.[194]

Despite the continued efforts by NGOs to raise pertinent issues relating to torture; the government has maintained its distance to prioritise the stance made by the NGOs. The government of Nepal, while replying to a confidential inquiry, stated that 'some reports which were a campaign against Nepal and beyond agenda should not be taken for a credible confidential procedure of the Committee'.[195]

5.5.5 Impact of State Reporting

Nepal has passed no specific legislation dealing with torture as had been recommended by the CAT Cttee.[196] However, the Constitution recognises rights against torture. It prohibits subjecting detained persons to physical or mental torture or cruel, inhuman or degrading treatment as fundamental rights. In this regard, any such act is punishable by law and entails compensation to the victim. The Penal Code has criminalised torture and inhuman treatment. The Penal Code ensures that the plea of superior order does not relieve the accused from any criminal responsibility.[197]

After the CAT Cttee in 2005 had expressed concerns over prolonged detention without trial,[198] the Terrorist and Disruptive Act (Control and Punishment) Ordinance, 2001 was suspended after the enactment of the Terrorist and Disruptive Acts (Prevention and Punishment) Act, 2002. The Act is no longer in existence and to the concerns over prolonged detention, was repealed. The Government clarified that no person had been detained under the Public Security Act. The interim Constitution of Nepal 2007 had included a

---

[194] Report by Special Rapporteur, 'Confidential Inquiry Report 2011', paras 8, 12 UN Doc (A/HRC/C/19/61/Add.3) (1 March 2012) 209–238.

[195] CAT, 'Confidential Inquiry Report' para 113.

[196] CAT Cttee, 'Report of the Committee Against Torture' A/49/44 22–23, para 146 <https://tbinternet.ohchr.org/_layouts/15/treatybodyexternal/TBSearch.aspx?Lang=En&CountryID=122> accessed 5 July 2022; CAT Cttee, 'Consideration of Reports Submitted by States Parties Under Article 19 of the Convention, Conclusions and Recommendations of the Committee against Torture' CAT/C/NPL/CO/2* para 12 <https://tbinternet.ohchr.org/_layouts/15/treatybodyexternal/TBSearch.aspx?Lang=En&CountryID=122> accessed 5 July 2022.

[197] UNHRC, 'National Report Submitted in Accordance with Paragraph 5 of the Annex to Human Rights Council Resolution 16/21' (2020) UN Doc (A/HRC/WG.6/37/NPL/1) para 28.

[198] UNCAT, 'Conclusions and Recommendations of the Committee against Torture: Nepal' (15 December 2005) UN Doc (CAT/C/NPL/CO/2) para 14 <https://www.refworld.org/docid/44n82d90.html> accessed 5 July 2022.

mandatory provision that any person arrested had to be presented to a competent judicial authority within 24 hours of the arrest and no one should be held without an order of court. The government of Nepal expressed its seriousness regarding the implementation of these provisions and added that they were committed to upholding this constitutional imperative.

Both the government and CSOs have been involved in imparting training and organising workshops, seminars and other awareness-raising programmes against torture and other cruel, inhuman or degrading treatment or punishment.[199] With these efforts, a large number of personnel from the Nepal army, the Nepal police and armed police force have been trained in various issues of human rights, including the subject of torture. Consequently, such workshops, training, and seminars have been regarded as effective tools not only for changing the behaviour of the targeted officials but also raising general awareness among the mass population against torture. The government of Nepal[200] has also conducted regular monitoring and evaluation of such training based on the Committee's recommendation.[201] Government agencies such as the Nepal police[202] conduct training regarding rights prohibiting torture and have incorporated it with gender responsiveness in investigative and counselling skills.

A Human Rights Promotion Section has also been established in the Office of the Prime Minister and Council of Ministers. Following this, human rights units have been established in the Ministry of Home Affairs, the Nepal army, the Nepal police and Nepal armed police force. These institutional arrangements have worked towards monitoring human rights protection and helping to bring human rights violators to justice while providing compensation to the victims of such violations.[203]

---

199   UNCAT, 'Comments by the Government of Nepal to the Conclusions and Recommendations of the Committee against Torture' (29 January 2008) UN Doc (CAT/C/NPL/CO/2/Add.1) para 9 https://www.refworld.org/docid/47aacd6c2.html accessed 5 July 2022.

200   UNDP, 'The Strengthening the Rule of Law and Human Rights Protection in Nepal Programme' (2013–2017) <http://webcache.googleusercontent.com/search?q=cache:1mHVcvfR7pYJ:www.undp.org/content/dam/nepal/docs/projects/RoLHR/UNDP_NP_RoLHR_Project-Document.pdf+&cd=9&hl=en&ct=clnk&gl=np> accessed 5 July 2022.

201   UNCAT, 'Conclusions and Recommendations of the Committee against Torture: Nepal' (15 December 2005) UN Doc (CAT/C/NPL/CO/2) para 18 <https://www.refworld.org/docid/441182d90.html> accessed 21 September 2023.

202   Nepal Police, 'Trainer's Manual on Gender-Responsive Investigation and Counselling Skills for Senior Police Officers', Police Headquarters, 2013 <https://nepalindata.com/resource/%22TRAINING-MANUAL-ON-GENDER-RESPONSIVE-INVESTIGATION-AND-COUNSELING-SKILLS%22-FOR-SENIOR-POLICE-OFFICERS--FOR-TRAINERS/> accessed 21 September 2023.

203   UNCAT, 'Comments by the Government of Nepal to the Conclusions and Recommendations of the Committee against Torture' (29 January 2008) UN Doc (CAT/C/NPL/CO/2/Add.1) para 9 <https://www.refworld.org/docid/47aacd6c2.html> accessed 5 July 2022.

5.5.6 Impact of Other Measures[204]

In its COs on the second periodic report of Nepal[205] in November 2005, the CAT Cttee had expressed its concerns about allegations concerning the widespread use of torture, the prevailing climate of impunity for acts of torture and the lack of a legal provision in domestic law to make torture a criminal offence. The Special Rapporteur on torture and other cruel, inhuman or degrading treatment or punishment, after visiting Nepal in September 2005, concluded that

> torture is systematically practiced by the police, armed police and Royal Nepalese Army. Legal safeguards are routinely ignored and effectively meaningless. Impunity for acts of torture is the rule, and consequently victims of torture and their families are left without recourse to adequate justice, compensation and rehabilitation.[206]

In addition to this, in November 2006 the Committee considered information submitted by NGOs on the alleged systematic practice of torture in Nepal. It appeared to the Committee that this information submitted to it under article 19 of CAT was dependable and that it contained indications that torture was systematically practised in the territory of Nepal. In response[207] to the Committee's observation, the government in its comments to the conclusion and recommendation of the CAT Cttee stated that sporadic and isolated incidents must not be generalised into a conclusion that there is systematic practice of torture in Nepal. It reiterated its stand to take legal action against anyone who is found guilty of the use of torture.

5.5.7 Brief Conclusion

The compensation act for victims of torture and efforts made by the government and CSOs to educate security personnel on international human rights and its laws is encouraging. A lack of domestic legislation on torture and concerns regarding implementation have hindered the fulfilment of objectives as prescribed by the Convention. As a result, even though torture became a

---

204 Report on Nepal Adopted by the Committee against Torture under Article 20 of the Convention and Comments and Observations by the State Party, A/67/44, Annex XIII.
205 CAT 'Second Period Report' UN Doc (CAT/C/NPL/CO/2).
206 CAT, E/CN.4/2006/6/Add.5, para 31.
207 CAT, 'Consideration of Reports Submitted by States Parties under Article 19 of the Convention, Comments by the Government of Nepal to the Conclusions and Recommendations of the Committee against Torture' CAT/C/NPL/CO/2/Add.1, 2 para 2 <https://tbinternet.ohchr.org/_layouts/15/treatybodyexternal/TBSearch.aspx?Lang=En&CountryID=122> accessed 5 July 2022.

criminal offence, the law remains silent on many aspects such as reparation. Redress is limited to compensation for cases of physical and not mental torture; the maximum years of imprisonment is five years, which does not match the level of the crimes. Furthermore, the victims' ability to report violations of their rights is limited to six months.

The Supreme Court has expressed its views on the need for specific legislation to rely, legally and otherwise, on such provisions to evaluate the progress of the situation regarding torture. In such cases, government bodies, the judiciary and NGOs, rely on CAT to guide their activities and efforts towards eliminating and protecting people from torture.[208] Torture and enforced disappearances have been criminalised. Moreover, after dissatisfaction with the conditions in the Terrorist and Disruptive Act on prolonged detentions by NGOs, CSOs, along with international bodies, the government repealed the Ordinance.

5.6 Convention on the Rights of the Child

Nepal ratified CRC in 1990; and in 2007 OP-CRC-AC and OP-CRC-SC.

5.6.1 Legislature-Executive Recognition and Implementation

Article 39 of the Constitution recognises the rights of children as fundamental rights with objectives to provide quality education and health care that are essential for a child's development. The Constitution further prescribes punishable offences such as child labour, child marriage, trafficking or being held hostage. The prohibition on recruitment or the use of children in the army, police or any armed group and the protection of children from any physical, mental or sexual abuse provided for in articles 39(6) and (7) of the Constitution complies with the Optional Protocols of CRC. Fulfilling constitutional obligations, the Child Labour (Prohibition and Regulation) Act 2006 prohibits certain forms of child labour, setting boundaries and regulatory mechanisms to protect their rights. The Children Act was enacted in 2018 consolidating the law relating to children in Nepal. The Act aims to maintain the best interests of the child by respecting, protecting, promoting and fulfilling the rights of the child through the establishment of the National Child Council.[209] The Act has been enacted in compliance with CRC and, thus, it has incorporated most of the rights and the provisions of CRC. The rights of child to survival,[210]

---

208 Interview with Prof Dr Yubaraj Sangroula, former Attorney-General of Nepal. The interview was conducted virtually on 26 January 2021.
209 Children Act 2018, s 59.
210 ibid s 3.

development,[211] protection[212] and participation[213] align with the rights enunciated by CRC.

Regarding the situation of children, progress has been made with policies structured to end all forms of violence against children, ending discrimination of any form and strengthening the juvenile justice system.[214] To be able to achieve this, the government has made an effort aimed towards inclusive education by promoting disability rights, including access to education for children.[215] There has also been an emphasis on providing access to education for girls, Dalit children and children belonging to ethnic minorities through strategic incentives such as scholarships and educational support.[216] The School Sector Reform Programme (SSRP) that was implemented in 2010 focused on reducing regional disparities by ensuring compulsory basic education.[217] However, governmental efforts were disrupted due to the 2015 earthquakes in Nepal, putting the teaching of almost a million children in jeopardy.[218] Subsequently, the government responded by increasing budgets and programmes to promote access to education which included an increase in the number of scholarships attracting school enrolments.[219]

In line with the areas of health and safety as provided by CRC in article 3, the Immunisation Act of Nepal, 2016 ensures the right of every child to have access to quality vaccines, striving for 100 per cent immunisation of mothers and children. The government's 'Reach Every Child' initiative has been implemented in this regard. In 2019, 70,2 per cent of children between 12 and 23 months had received all necessary vaccinations.[220] Another initiative based on the Street Children Rescue, Protection and Management Guideline which led to

---

[211] ibid.
[212] ibid s 7.
[213] ibid s 8.
[214] National Action Policy Concerning Children 2012.
[215] Inclusive Education Policy 2016.
[216] National Action Plan to Implement Recommendations of UPR, 2016–2011 2–3.
[217] UN Committee on the Rights of the Child, Third to Fifth Periodic Reports of States Parties Due in 2010: Nepal, para 41, CRC/C/OPSC/NPL/CO/1 (23 December 2013).
[218] UNICEF, 'Nepal Earthquake: Education for Nearly 1 Million Children in Jeopardy' (7 May 2015) <https://www.unicef.org/rosa/press-releases/nepal-earthquake-education-nearly-1-million-children-jeopardy-unicef> accessed 5 July 2022. An estimated 24 000 classrooms were affected by the earthquakes, of which 14 541 of the classrooms were completely destroyed.
[219] National Action Plan to Implement Recommendations of UPR, 2016–2011 2.
[220] UNHRC, 'National Report Submitted in Accordance with Paragraph 5 of the Annex to Human Rights Council Resolution 16/21' (2020) UN Doc (A/HRC/WG.6/37/NPL/1) para 58.

the Street Children Free Kathmandu Valley was implemented, resulting in a Kathmandu free from children on the streets.[221]

5.6.2 Reliance by Judiciary

With the condemnation of corporal punishment of children, the Supreme Court in *Ale (CVICT) and Others v Government of Nepal*[222] declared unconstitutional and 'null and void' section 7 of the Children Act 1992, which provided for 'minor beating' by family members. The Court confirmed the prohibition of torture, cruel and inhuman treatment provision under article 14 of the Constitution of Kingdom of Nepal 1990, and held that it was unlawful and improper to make provisions contrary to obligations laid down in treaties to which Nepal is a party.[223] In September 2018 Nepal enacted the Children Act 2018, which prohibits all corporal punishment of children, and thus became the first South Asian state to achieve such a complete prohibition.

The Supreme Court of Nepal interpreted and elaborated on the freedom of association of children against the backdrop of the Convention in *Tilotam Poudel v Ministry of Home Affairs*.[224] The Court held that not allowing an NGO to be registered just because it was established by children, only, violates their freedom to form associations. The Court applied article 15 of the CRC 'directly and provided/affirmed the supremacy of the Convention, which well reflects the status and significance of the convention in Nepalese legal system'.[225] By reasoning that the provisions of the CRC would be given effect in case of inconsistency between domestic and international law, it subscribed to the superior status of the CRC.

---

[221] UNHRC, 'National Report Submitted in Accordance with Paragraph 5 of the Annex to Human Rights Council Resolution 16/21' (2020) UN Doc (A/HRC/WG.6/37/NPL/1) para 99.
[222] *Ale (CVICT) and Others v Government of Nepal* [2005] WN 57.
[223] In addition to the Constitution, the Court referred to 'treaty related legal obligations created by the commitments made by Nepal at the international sector, universal campaign against physical punishment or torture done to or inflicted on children, and obligation of the State to create environment for the overall development of the child' as the basis of its decision.
[224] *Tilotam Poudel v Ministry of Home Affairs and Others* [2001] NLJ 423.
[225] Prabhat Chettri, 'Rights of the Child to Freedom of Association in the Light of the Leading Case *Tilotam Poudel v Ministry of Home Affairs*' (2016) 1 Journal on Rights of the Child p 145 <https://www.nluo.ac.in/wp-content/uploads/2019/05/Journal-on-the-Rights-of-the-Child.pdf> accessed 30 June 2022.

5.6.3 Impact on and through Independent State Actors

The NHRC's recommendations during the drafting of the 2015 Constitution incorporated several provisions recognising the rights of children in light of CRC. Significant contributions to this effect include providing compensation to each child victim and reparation without discrimination by the state, recognising corporal punishment, making it consistent with article 37 of CRC.[226] The government of Nepal recently acceded the Palermo Protocol in 2020[227] to prevent and punish persons from trafficking women and children based on the NHRC's recommendation, to enhance mutual legal assistance and cooperation with India.[228] The NHRC has supported major seminars on human rights education and worked in coordination with the government to include human rights education in the school curriculum in Nepal.[229]

Collaborative efforts can be seen between the NHRC, the National Women's Commission and the National Dalit Commission to rescue vulnerable children from human right abusers along with civil society organisations working towards protecting the rights of children.[230] The Commission has been monitoring the situation of Nepalese citizens residing on the borders and has provided recommendations to the federal and provincial governments to protect their human rights guaranteed by the Constitution.[231] An elaborate attempt has also been made to effectively train institutions that are involved in community-level efforts to protect children.

5.6.4 Impact through Non-state Actors

The NGOs provide a collaborative platform for civil society action that plays a central role in crucial child rights developments at the international level. These organisations have been able to effectively raise awareness about atrocities committed against children along with media reporting organisations. Through these efforts, NGOs have been able to increase the number of school-going students throughout the country by addressing issues concerning

---

[226] NHRC, 'NHRC suggestions on Preliminary Draft Constitution of Nepal' (23 July 2015).
[227] Palermo Protocol to Prevent, Suppress and Punish Trafficking in Persons, Especially Women and Children 2020.
[228] Suggestions of NHRC Nepal to the Government of Nepal on the Recommendations of UPR Process for 16 March 2016, Recommendation 7.13.
[229] Ravi Prakash Vyas, 'Human Rights Education in Nepal: Integrating Formal and Informal Teaching Strategies' Human Rights Encyclopedia (2020) 10 Human Rights Education in Asia-Pacific 165.
[230] NHRC, 'Implementation Status of UPR on Child Rights' (2013) 9.
[231] Human Rights of Nepalese Living in the Border Area 2020, NHRC.

children, such as healthcare facilities, hygiene and safety.[232] A significant area of contribution involved the sexual exploitation of children by foreigners, where it was found that children were lured by paedophiles who even paid money to unwilling children to engage with them.[233]

International treaties such as CRC help NGOs to coordinate efforts by relying on established international standards for child protection and navigating the process through regular evaluations made in collaboration with government agencies, international organisations and other civil society organisations. The alternative and shadow reports submitted by NGO groups help to identify gaps and falls in governmental policy implementation and their reporting. Additionally, NGOs and CSOs work together with the government during its fact-finding expeditions on the status of children.

5.6.5 Impact of State Reporting

In the COs of 2004, the CRC Cttee raised serious concerns on 'widely prevailing *de facto* discrimination against girls and children belonging to the most vulnerable groups' such as indigenous or ethnic minorities.[234] The Committee also noted the high dropout rate and the significant inequality in access to education, in part due to hidden costs associated with schooling.[235] Several recommendations were made to the government concerning education, including improving the accessibility to education, in particular for girls, and eliminating disparities.[236] The government of Nepal has been emphasising ensuring access to education for girls, Dalit children and children belonging to ethnic minorities through strategic incentives such as scholarships and educational support.[237] The School Sector Reform Programme (SSRP) implemented in 2010 focused on reducing regional disparities by ensuring compulsory basic education.[238] The government has been able to effectively improve the access of education for children with disabilities by developing special and integrated schools that have attracted 46 899 new enrolments in 2019.[239]

---

[232] CWIN, 'State of the Rights of the Child in Nepal 2004/National Report' 31.
[233] ibid 51.
[234] UN Committee on the Rights of the Child, Concluding Observations: NEPAL, CRC/C/15/Add.261 (21 September 2005) para 35.
[235] ibid para 75.
[236] ibid para 76.
[237] National Action Plan to Implement Recommendations of UPR, 2016–2011 2–3.
[238] UN Committee on the Rights of the Child, Third to Fifth Periodic Reports of States Parties due in 2010: Nepal, para 41, CRC/C/OPSC/NPL/CO/1 (23 December 2013).
[239] UN HRC, 'National Report Submitted in Accordance with Paragraph 5 of the Annex to Human Rights Council Resolution 16/21' (2020) UN Doc (A/HRC/WG.6/37/NPL/1) para 66.

Further, the government has made efforts to strengthen its implementation of the existing legislation[240] aimed at the protection and promotion of children's rights through the Act Relating to Children 2018 which ensures all pillars of rights for proper child development such as the right to protection, right to survival, right to development and right to participation. The Act further provides that every child has the right to protection against any physical or mental violence and torture, hatred, inhuman treatment, gender or untouchability-based mistreatment, sexual harassment and exploitation as mandated by the Nepalese Constitution. The Act further provides for the best interests of the child that must be prioritised while establishing the responsibilities of family and guardians, state and media sector towards children. The Act mandates a multi-stakeholder National Child Rights Council chaired by the Minister for Women, Children and Senior Citizens. The Council is represented by various government agencies and civil society organisations working in the field of child rights, child protection, child welfare and juvenile justice. The Council recommends to the government about the policies and programmes to be adopted for achieving these objectives.[241]

The 2004 COs also note the grave concerns of involvement of a significant number of children in child labour, often full-time and in extremely hazardous circumstances.[242] A number of recommendations were made to the government to address child labour, including taking preventative measures, regulating child labour in all areas of work (including the informal sector of the economy) and fully implementing policies, legislation and public awareness campaigns relevant to child labour.[243] The Child Labour (Prohibition and Regulation) Act, 2000 prohibits any form of child labour and restricts the involvement of children in hazardous works. However, child labour remains a widespread problem in Nepal, with more than 2 million children between the ages of 5 and 14 estimated to be engaged in child labour.[244] The most rampant usage of child labour is reported in agriculture, brick factories, the

---

240 UNCRC, 'UN Committee on the Rights of the Child: Concluding Observations, Nepal' (21 September 2005) UN Doc CRC/C/15/Add.261 para 19 <https://www.refworld.org/docid/45377ea30.html> accessed 5 July 2022.
241 UNHRC, 'National Report Submitted in Accordance with Paragraph 5 of the Annex to Human Rights Council Resolution 16/21' (2020) UN Doc (A/HRC/WG.6/37/NPL/1) paras 95–97.
242 UN Committee on the Rights of the Child, Concluding Observations: NEPAL, para 91, CRC/C/15/Add.261 (21 September 2005).
243 ibid para 93.
244 US Department of Labour, 2014 Findings on the Worst Forms of Child Labour 1 (15 October 2015).

stone-breaking industry, and domestic servitude.[245] No clear data of child labour can be found in Nepal since the lockdown induced by the COVID-19 pandemic. The economic impact of the pandemic, along with the disruption of education may lead to an increased risk of child labour in Nepal.

5.6.6 Brief Conclusion

The enactment of the Children Act, 2018 consolidates law specific to the protection, development and participation of children as a significant step towards recognising the rights of children and compliance with the treaty obligations under CRC. The government's policies aimed towards education, health care, removing children from the streets and preventing sexual exploitation are not an end in itself but the initiation of recognition and the improvement of the conditions of many generations to come.[246] The NGOs are the highlight of the implementation processes, where they have set examples for government agencies to follow on many occasions. They can relate better and communicate concerns regarding child rights more effectively to various stakeholders. Nepal currently is in a transitional phase where a systematic attempt is being made by multiple organs of the government to end old practices that were against children, especially the girl child. The judiciary has been able to contribute by setting judicial precedents in line with CRC by abolishing corporal punishment, protecting their freedom of association, and so forth. Moreover, media organisations in coordination with NGOs have been able to highlight issues that children face and demand for calls to action as was seen with an increase in enrolments due to NGOs. It is widely accepted that CRC is relied upon in all spheres to guide and navigate progress, and to sustain efforts in promoting the rights of children.

5.7 *International Convention on the Rights of Persons with Disabilities*

Nepal ratified CRPD and OP-CRPD in 2010.

5.7.1 Legislature and Executive Recognition and Implementation

The Constitution of Nepal comprises provisions specifically protecting the interests of persons with disabilities through the guarantee of the rights to social justice, equality and access to transportation. In 2017 Nepal enacted the Disability Rights Act (DRA) that repealed the previous Disabled Persons

---

245 US Department of State, 2015 Trafficking in Persons Report 287–289 (2015) <http://www.state.gov/documents/organization/226848.pdf> accessed 5 July 2022.
246 Interview with Mr Milan Dharel, Executive Director, National Child Rights Council, Nepal. The interview was conducted virtually on 28 January 2021.

Welfare Act 1982 (DPWA). Although Nepal had legislation to address matters relating to persons with disabilities, the enactment of the 2017 Act serves as adherence to its general obligation under CRPD. The new legislation recognises specific rights accorded by CRPD [247] to persons with disabilities which otherwise was not recognised in 1982. Provisions expressly recognise rights to community life,[248] protection,[249] participation[250] in policy making and cultural life, to form unions,[251] access to services, facilities and justice,[252] social security,[253] movement[254] and information,[255] which denotes progress from provisions relating to 'facilities and privileges'[256] for persons with disabilities previously provided for in the 1982 Act. Moreover, the 2017 Act has made a note to address persons with disabilities and the diversity among them respectfully. Persons with mental, intellectual disabilities or impairments have been defined under 'person with disability',[257] which was otherwise referred to as 'mentally-handicapped' persons[258] in previous legislation.[259]

The government introduced a long-term strategic programme under the School Sector Development Programme 2016–2023 (SSDP), in which the government stressed the need for inclusive education,[260] especially for children with disabilities, by engaging the Department of Education (DoE) to increase enrolments for higher education through several types of scholarships including specific incentives for children from Dalit and other disadvantaged communities.[261] The government also provided support services which included

---

[247] The civil and political rights along with the socio-economic rights enshrined in CRPD along with the general obligation under art 4.
[248] The Act Relating to Rights of Persons with Disabilities, 2074 (2017), s 9 <https://www.lawcommission.gov.np/en/wp-content/uploads/2019/07/The-Act-Relating-to-Rights-of-Persons-with-Disabilities-2074-2017.pdf> accessed 21 January 2021.
[249] ibid s 10.
[250] ibid ss 11, 12, 14.
[251] ibid s 13.
[252] ibid s 15.
[253] ibid s 16.
[254] ibid s 18.
[255] ibid s 17.
[256] Protection and Welfare of the Disabled Persons Act, 2039 (1982), s 2(a) <https://www.lawcommission.gov.np/en/wp-content/uploads/2018/10/protection-and-welfare-of-the-disabled-persons-act-2039-1982.pdf> accessed 21 January 2021.
[257] The Act Relating to Rights of Persons with Disabilities, 2074 (2017) s 2(b).
[258] Protection and Welfare of the Disabled Persons Act, 2039 (1982) s 10.
[259] CRPD, 'Replied of Nepal to the List of Issues' (3 January 2018) UN Doc (CRPD/C/NPL/Q/1/Add.1) para 3.
[260] Inclusive Education Policy 2016.
[261] CRPD (n 259) para 20.

monthly welfare allowances.[262] However, the government discontinued the monthly welfare allowances for women under the age of 60, which has caused discontent among the main stakeholders and the Supreme Court of Nepal.[263] The government further ensured representation of persons with disabilities by providing such persons with a 5 per cent reservation scheme as prescribed under the Civil Services Act 1992. This has also been reduced from 5 per cent to 3 per cent, which may prove disadvantageous for persons with disabilities.[264] Additional efforts have been made to improve the quality of life by introducing vocational training and skills development training to provide persons with disabilities with income-generating capacities. Extending its inclusive measures, the Ministry of Youth and Sports has coordinated with the Paralympic Committee of Nepal to help train and develop the skills of paralympians to prepare them to be able to participate in sport at international level.[265]

With the aim of making places more accessible to persons with disabilities, the Accessible Physical Structure and Communication Service Directive for People with Disabilities 2013 has formulated provisions to ensure more inclusivity and accessibility to safeguard their rights and to provide necessary accommodation in schools, homes and workplaces.[266] However, concerns relating to proper execution and implementation of policies citing inadequate funds have surfaced. It left Nepalese persons with disabilities prone to consequences of insufficiency due to loopholes while making such claims along with a very limited allocation of budgets to address issues.[267]

5.7.2   Reliance on Judiciary

The Constitutional Court has made notable pronouncements on the subject in which the Court has used its judicial activism to issue strict directives for

---

262 ibid para 3. Inclusive Education Policy 2016 para 21.
263 Anup Ojha, 'Single Women and Disabled People Decry Government's Decision to Cut Their Social Security Allowance' *The Kathmandu Post* (26 May 2020) <https://kathmandupost.com/national/2020/05/26/single-women-and-disabled-people-decry-government-s-decision-to-cut-their-social-security-allowance> accessed 5 July 2022.
264 Prithvi Man Shrestha, 'People with Disabilities Protest against Reduction of Quota in Civil Service' *The Kathmandu Post* (4 March 2019).
265 CRPD, 'Replied of Nepal to the List of Issues' (3 January 2018) UN Doc (CRPD/C/NPL/Q/1/Add.1) para 3. Inclusive Education Policy 2016 para 57.
266 S Prasai and A Pant, 'Monitoring Employment Rights of People with Disabilities in Kathmandu, Nepal – Asian Workplace Approach That Respects Equality' (2018) Disability Rights Promotion International (DRPI) & National Federation of Disabled-Nepal.
267 Arne E Eide, 'Living Conditions Among People with Disability in Nepal' (2016) SINTEF Department of Research 46–47.

implementation of the laws and policies enacted by the government in keeping with the international obligations towards respecting, protecting and fulfilling the human rights of persons with disabilities, aligned to the provisions of CRPD.

The first of these cases is *Sudarshan Subedi v Government of Nepal*,[268] where the petitioner had challenged the non-implementation of provisions relating to free education for persons with disabilities under the Disabled (Protection and Welfare) Act in line with CRPD. The Court issued a positive decision stating that no fee should be charged from persons with disabilities during admission at educational institutions, and accordingly issued a directive order for the amendment of the legislation according to CRPD.[269] This is regarded as one the first cases to deal with the protection of the right to education of persons with disabilities. Despite this, it was reported to have taken three years for the Court to decide on the matter, leading to a delay in the implementation of the law. In spite of the favourable judgment, it was for this reason not considered disability-friendly by members of CSOs.[270]

The second instance was *Babu Krishna Maharajan v Government of Nepal* where the non-implementation of the Disabled (Protection and Welfare) Act in its entirety was challenged in line with the state obligation to ensure legislative protection under CRPD.[271] The Supreme Court dealt with the petition with sensitivity and its pronouncement was a favourable interpretation with regard to various rights of persons with disabilities. The Court expressed its concern over the limited implementation of the rights guaranteed under the Act, even after 22 years of enactment. The Court directed the government to provide implementation reports within one year after the judgment was passed. This step is in line with the state obligation under CRPD.

5.7.3 Impact on and through Independent State Actors

State intuitions such as the NHRC have realised their mandate and have collaborated with various relevant government departments and CSOs to develop comprehensive reports on the situation of persons with disabilities in Nepal to present it to the CRPD Cttee.

---

268 Writ No 3586 [2003].
269 *Sudarshan Subedi v Government of Nepal* <http://dhrcnepal.org.np/wp-content/uploads/2016/09/Supreme-Court-Verdict-English.pdf> accessed 5 July 2022.
270 'Fostering Inclusion of Persons with Psychosocial Disabilities in Nepal' (ESCR-Net, 2014).
271 *Petitioner Babu Krishna Maharjan v the Office of Prime Minister and Council of Ministers*, (writ No. 3666 writ petition of the year 2061 B.S.).

Local authorities, including the Nepal police, the National Women Commission and the courts have been implementing the Domestic Violence Act and its Regulation in receiving complaints, investigation, prosecution and ensuring the punishment of perpetrators – especially intervening in such crimes committed against persons with disabilities.

The NHRC has included human rights education programmes, training and 'know-your-rights' activities for persons with disabilities.

Under the National Human Rights Commission Strategic Plan Support Project (SPSP) 2015–2020,[272] the NHRC undertook some important steps in the implementation of CRPD in the context of psychological disability:

(i) There has been a push for greater awareness of human rights issues among persons with disabilities and mental illness through training and workshops and expanded outreach of the NHRC into 48 districts to raise these issues.[273] Awareness of human rights issues was raised through advocacy programmes such as the production of human rights tele-serials and extended human rights film festivals that were organised through coordination and cooperation with civil society organisations and the media groups.

(ii) A baseline survey on the human rights situation of persons with mental disabilities was conducted so that a set baseline could be established for promoting and protecting their right to live a dignified life.

The National Information Commission ensures that every citizen enjoys access to information. The Directives on Communication Service 2012 made provision that the information should be accessible to persons with disabilities, and provision should be made for translators and for news and information to be broadcast in sign language.[274]

---

272 UNDP, 'Annual Progress Report National Human Rights Commission Strategic Plan Support Project (SPSP) 2015–2020' (2020) 6 <https://www.np.undp.org/content/nepal/en/home/projects/spsp.html> accessed 5 July 2022.
273 ibid.
274 NHRC, 'Annual Progress Report on Situation of Human Rights of People with Disabilities (2076–77 BS) 2019–2020' (2020) Doc 22 <https://www.nhrcnepal.org/uploads/publication/Situation_Report_on_PwDs_2076_for_webpage_compressed.pdf> accessed 21 September 2023.

5.7.4 Impact through Non-state Actors

Various stakeholders, including NGOs, CSOs, national institutions and even donor agencies have joined hands to coordinate ways for the effective implementation of CRPD for national legal provisions and policies. CSOs have been actively reviewing all the laws affecting persons with disabilities to establish their compliance with the Convention. In instances where there was a provision stating that a man – not a woman – is entitled to enter into a second marriage if his wife becomes blind, physically or mentally disabled, civil society groups used CEDAW and CRPD, despite non-ratification at the time, to challenge and combat gender and disability-based discrimination.[275]

Some hospitals have begun to be operated by NGOs to provide therapy and rehabilitation services for no or minimal charge to persons with disabilities.[276] Separate admission centres for persons with disabilities and senior citizens have been established in most government hospitals but these are limited, which has been the reason for NGOs to enter into this arena.

Organisations have also engaged at an international level to promote CRPD, for example by highlighting the need for Nepal to ratify the treaty during their participation at various international workshops and conferences. In Nepal, these organisations have also been instrumental in raising wider awareness regarding the importance and relevance of CRPD, while stressing the need for translation of the document into the Nepali language to create accessibility throughout the country.[277] Such efforts ultimately resulted in the agreement to sign and ratify CRPD in 2007. With the focused and persistent advocacy of relevant ministries and government agencies, CSOs have been able to evaluate the progress of the situation of persons with disabilities in the country by publishing reports.[278]

---

275 Rangita de Silwa de Alwis CSW, 'The Intersection of the CEDAW and CRPD: Integrating Women's Rights and Disability Rights into Concrete Action in Four Asian Countries' (4 March 2010).
276 NHRC, 'Report on Situation of Human Rights of People with Disabilities (2076–77 BS) 2019–2020' (2020) Doc <https://www.nhrcnepal.org/uploads/publication/Situation_Report_on_PwDs_2076_for_webpage_compressed.pdf> accessed 21 September 2023.
277 Interview with Prof Geeta Pathak, Professor of International Human Rights Law and Humanitarian Law at Kathmandu School of Law. The interview was conducted virtually on 26 January 2021. She was appointed as *amicus curiae* to the Supreme Court in February 2021.
278 DRPI, 'Monitoring the Employment Rights of People with Disabilities in Kathmandu, Nepal' (June 2018) Doc <http://drpi.research.yorku.ca/wp-content/uploads/2018/08/Nepal-Holistic-Report.pdf> accessed 5 July 2022.

However, there has been a lack in the effective implementation of regular awareness programmes for the population at the local level. A study conducted by the National Federation of Disabled Population, Nepal (NFDN) reflects that community level awareness relating to persons with disabilities is higher in cities than in rural areas.[279] As a result, access to several facilities and services is more prominent and easily available in cities. In addition, there is lack of coordination among the stakeholders on the promotion of rights of persons with disabilities.

5.7.5 Impact of State Reporting

There are three significant areas where recommendations have had an impact on domestic legal and executive actions – gender inclusivity, preventing discrimination and addressing the rights of women with disabilities.

The CRPD Cttee recommended to the government, in line with its General Comment 4, to increase its efforts to achieve inclusive education by adopting inclusive education models and alternative means and modes of communication.[280] In response to the recommendation, the government reiterated that the Constitution guaranteed for every citizen the right of access to basic education, to get compulsory and free education up to the basic level and free education up to the secondary level from the state. The government has been ensuring access to inclusive education for all persons with disabilities at all levels of education. Accordingly, citizens with disabilities, indigent citizens have been guaranteed free higher education and ensuring that persons with visual impairments and those with hearing and speaking impediments have the right to free education by means of using the Braille script and sign language, respectively, including in their mother tongue.[281]

The CRPD Cttee recommended to the Nepalese government to take appropriate measures to protect all persons with disabilities from exploitation,

---

[279] NHRC, 'Report on Situation of Human Rights of People with Disabilities 2019–2020' (2020) 16.

[280] CRPD, 'Concluding Observations of the Initial Report of Nepal' (16 April 2016) UN Doc para 36(b) <http://docstore.ohchr.org/SelfServices/FilesHandler.ashx?enc=6QkG1d%2fPPRiCAqhKb7yhstx8ui%2fT4PIZaaRjmUrkwI7lcboJVv%2fOewLZZ8dySqIb681UnkoYyekvgBTnyNi91bIMeZkhP%2fD9vVkH4tCcr2yfno7bxHAFhIyCwxMjIUUv> accessed 5 July 2022.

[281] UNHRC, 'National Report Submitted in Accordance with Paragraph 5 of the Annex to Human Rights Council Resolution 16/21' (2020) UN Doc (A/HRC/WG.6/37/NPL/1) para 62; s 21, The Act Relating to Rights of Persons with Disabilities, 2074 (2017).

violence and abuse both within and outside the home.[282] This was subsequently ensured by enacting the Act Relating to Rights of Persons with Disabilities 2017, which removed barriers and discriminatory practices towards persons with disabilities. This was followed with the Regulation on the Rights of Persons with Disabilities 2020 to ensure civil, political, economic, social and cultural rights by doing away with discrimination against persons with disabilities and to ensure an environment that enables them to be economically self-reliant by encouraging their participation in the process of policy making and development.

The CRPD Cttee also expressed its concern over the non-inclusion of women with disabilities in decision-making processes and the lack of information on their activities.[283] The government mentioned 'Women and Disability' as one of the priority areas with the aim of creating an equitable society for these women. To attain this, a special programme was launched for women and girls with disabilities so that they can be included in the mainstreaming of gender equity so as to increase the participation of women with disabilities in education, training and livelihood opportunities. Further, the government established a Girls' Education Fund targeting Dalit girl students and girls with disabilities at higher secondary and university levels, where 20 per cent of the total scholarship is reserved for deserving girl students with disabilities.[284]

5.7.6 Impact of Individual Communications

Although Nepal has accepted the procedure for individual communication under OP-CRPD, no communications against the country have been submitted.

5.7.7 Brief Conclusion

With the entry of the new Constitution, Nepal has reviewed its current legislative status regarding provisions for persons with disabilities and re-introduced improved legislation to address and ensure guarantees for persons with disabilities as provided in constitutional and conventional provisions. The judiciary has on multiple occasions stepped in to direct the government to enforce rights. Nepal meets many obligations that the Convention aims to set for state

---

282 CRPD, 'Concluding Observations of the Initial Report of Nepal' (16 April 2018) UN Doc para 28 <http://docstore.ohchr.org/SelfServices/FilesHandler.ashx?enc=6QkG1d%2fPPRiCAqhKb7yhstx8ui%2fT4PIZaaRjmUrkwI7lcboJVv%2fOewLZZ8dySqIb681UnkoYyekvgBTnyNi91bIMeZkhP%2fD9vVkH4tCcr2yfno7bxHAFhIyCwxMjIUUv> accessed 5 July 2022.

283 ibid paras 11–12.

284 CRPD, 'Initial Reports of State Parties Due 2012' (11 November 2015) UN Doc para 62<https://documents-dds-ny.un.org/doc/UNDOC/GEN/G15/272/68/PDF/G1527268.pdf?OpenElement> accessed 5 July 2022.

parties to follow. Moreover, CSOs played a significant role in advocating the ratification of the Convention which was made possible due to their efforts.

Nepal has worked on recommendations made by the Committee by introducing policies, schemes and laws to enable their implementation. The government has also ensured education for all under the Act Relating to Compulsory and Free Education, which is an important pillar in protecting the rights of persons with disabilities. The importance of the Act has also been reiterated by Nepal in its national report submitted to the third cycle of UPR.[285] However, the NHRC notes the lack of implementation and the need to ensure execution after legislation to be able to enhance access to education of persons with disabilities.[286]

This reflects an underlying issue on the implementation of legislation relating to the rights of persons with disabilities by other state actors including the judiciary, NHRIs and other institutions. This is indicative of a lack of preparation and groundwork done prior to the ratification of the Convention. The identified disparity between the effectiveness of implementation between rural and urban areas is also a matter that needs to be addressed. Despite the government's directives regarding architectural restructuring to make buildings more disabled-friendly, reports[287] claim that public buildings themselves do not comply with the directives. A follow-up and specific mechanism to monitor the implementation of laws, directives and court rulings will be essential to bridge paper legislation with actual practical application.

6   Conclusion

The UN human rights treaty system has played a very important part in Nepal and its human rights movement. Nepal signed most of the core human rights

---

[285] UNHRC, 'National Report Submitted in Accordance with Paragraph 5 of the Annex to Human Rights Council Resolution 16/21' A/HRC/WG.6/37/NPL/1 <https://undocs.org/a/hrc/wg.6/37/NPL/1> accessed 5 July 2022.

[286] NHRC, 'The NHRI Nepal Joint Submission for the Third Periodic Review of Nepal' (24 March 2020) Doc <https://media-exp1.licdn.com/dms/document/C561FAQEtDqQj56B7Qw/feedshare-document-pdf-analyzed/0/1607600016113?e=1608699600&v=beta&t=SX-aF1w1Z459H37tE8dqObcPH1kjcwpls41pKFt-A7o> accessed 5 July 2022.

[287] Department of Economic and Social Affairs, 'Disability and Development Report' (United Nations, 2018) <https://www.un.org/development/desa/disabilities/wp-content/uploads/sites/15/2019/07/disability-report-chapter2.pdf> accessed 5 July 2022; 'Nepal: Barriers to Inclusive Education' (HRW, 2018) <https://www.hrw.org/news/2018/09/13/nepal-barriers-inclusive-education> accessed 5 July 2022.

treaties following the years of tumultuous political instability and societal inequality. The core human rights treaties formed a significant part in the years-long democratisation process in Nepal. Although it ratified most of the treaties in 1990, Nepal could not fulfil its obligations as a state party due to the decade-long armed conflict between the Maoists and the government. However, the promulgation of the interim Constitution of Nepal following the year 2007 brought the inclusion of provisions of the Truth and Reconciliation Commission for the people who disappeared in the armed conflict. This was possible mostly due to the conscious realisation of civil and political rights under CCPR and other core treaties.

Nepal's human rights mechanism is largely influenced by the UN human rights treaty system as it is not part of any regional mechanism. The influence of the UN human rights treaty system in the domestic legal system is evident through the use of UN treaties, the treaty bodies and their commentaries in the jurisprudence propounded by the Nepalese judiciary. The recommendations provided by the treaty bodies have influenced and made an impact in Nepal's socio-legal sphere. The recommendation by the HRCttee to include a broad definition of rape and criminalise acts relating to torture, which were amended and added in Criminal Code 2017, is an example of the impact the UN treaties have had on Nepal's human rights situation. The UN treaty body system has especially helped further the protection of human rights that is centred towards women and minorities. The recommendation by the CEDAW[288] and CERD Cttees to eliminate harmful practices such as *chhaupadi* and accusations of witchcraft not only had an impact on the general awareness regarding discrimination, it also propelled the discussion among stakeholders, including the general public, regarding how minorities, such as women, are prone to fall victim to discriminatory traditions and customs.[289] Following the recommendations, Nepal's Penal Code promulgated in 2017 prohibits marriage under the age of 20 and criminalises the *chaaupadi* tradition of banishing a woman to a shed during menstruation or the delivery of a child. Although somewhat late, the government of Nepal, on the recommendation of the CAT Cttee in 1994[290]

---

[288] CEDAW, 'Concluding Observations on the Sixth Periodic Report of Nepal' 2018, CEDAW/C/NPL/CO/6 paras 17–18 <https://tbinternet.ohchr.org/_layouts/15/treatybodyexternal/TBSearch.aspx?Lang=En&CountryID=122> accessed 5 July 2022.

[289] CEDAW, 'Concluding Observations of the Committee on the Elimination of Discrimination against Women' 2011, CEDAW/C/NPL/CO/4–5 <https://tbinternet.ohchr.org/_layouts/15/treatybodyexternal/TBSearch.aspx?Lang=En&CountryID=122> accessed 5 July 2022.

[290] CAT Cttee, 'Report of the Committee Against Torture' A/49/44 22–23, para 146 <https://tbinternet.ohchr.org/_layouts/15/treatybodyexternal/TBSearch.aspx?Lang=En&CountryID=122> accessed 5 July 2022.

and 2007,[291] has criminalised torture in the 2017 Penal Code.[292] However, Nepal is yet to address the concern[293] over the Compensation Relating to Torture Act of 1996 by the CAT Cttee regarding the defective definition of the torture which is not in line to the definition provided in the Convention.

In addition, Nepal has accepted the individual complaints procedures to CCPR, CEDAW and CRPD.[294] Individual complaints have been submitted only to the HRC ttee. The complaints concern cross-cutting issues such as torture and enforced disappearance. The reasons for the submission of most complaints on these issues may be inferred from the lack of proper definition defining the scope of the national legislation on torture despite the CAT Cttee's recommendation and the non-ratification by Nepal of CED. Additionally, the trust in the UN human rights treaty system on the part of the Nepalese legal sphere may be inferred from the 23 individual complaints submitted to the HRC ttee.

Moreover, the suggestions by independent constitutional bodies such as the NHRC, the NWC and the NDC to the government of Nepal to ratify CMW and CED[295] and to implement suggestions by other countries[296] during the UPR to Nepal, depict the importance of the UN human rights treaty system for the human rights movement in Nepal.

In addition to the treaty bodies, the influence of the UPR and special procedures on the Nepalese socio-legal sector cannot be overlooked. The three cycles

---

[291] CAT Cttee, 'Consideration of Reports Submitted by States Parties under Article 19 of the Convention, Conclusions and Recommendations of the Committee against Torture' CAT/C/NPL/CO/2* para 12 <https://tbinternet.ohchr.org/_layouts/15/treatybodyexternal/TBSearch.aspx?Lang=En&CountryID=122> accessed 5 July 2022.

[292] Penal Code 2017, s 167.

[293] CAT Cttee, 'Consideration of Reports Submitted by States Parties under Article 19 of the Convention, Conclusions and Recommendations of the Committee against Torture' CAT/C/NPL/CO/2* para 12 <https://tbinternet.ohchr.org/_layouts/15/treatybodyexternal/TBSearch.aspx?Lang=En&CountryID=122> accessed 5 July 2022.

[294] Ratification Status of Nepal, OHCHR <https://tbinternet.ohchr.org/_layouts/15/TreatyBodyExternal/Treaty.aspx?CountryID=122&Lang=EN> accessed 5 July 2022.

[295] NHRC, 'Suggestion of NHRC Nepal to the Government of Nepal on the Recommendations of UPR Process for 16 March 2016' <http://www.nhrcnepal.org/nhrc_new/doc/newsletter/NHRC_Nepal_UPR_Process_Recommendations_Adoption_Human_Rights_Council_16Mar2015.pdf> accessed 5 July 2022; see also NHRC, 'Eleven Years of the Comprehensive Peace Accord: A Brief Report on the Human Rights Situation' <https://www.nhrcnepal.org/nhrc_new/doc/newsletter/CPA_Report_2074_8_5_Eng.pdf> accessed 5 July 2022.

[296] NHRC, 'Suggestion of NHRC Nepal to the Government of Nepal on the Recommendations of UPR Process for 16 March 2016', para 7.10 2 <http://www.nhrcnepal.org/nhrc_new/doc/newsletter/NHRC_Nepal_UPR_Process_Recommendations_Adoption_Human_Rights_Council_16Mar2015.pdf> accessed 5 July 2022.

of UPR and Nepal's participation with state reporting has made independent bodies such as the NHRC more vigilant towards the government's approach to human rights protection. The concerns raised by the NHRC over the NHRC Amendment Bill tabled in Parliament regarding potential violations of the international commitment is an example of the attentiveness elicited by these procedures.[297] For Nepal, of which a significant part of the economy relies on remittance from Nepalese living abroad, visits by the Special Rapporteur on the human rights of migrants,[298] despite not having ratified CMW, shows the symbolic impact that the UN system has had on the human rights systems in Nepal.

Nepal has strengthened its human rights system with the inclusion of treaty bodies, the UPR, special procedure and assistance of the OHCHR. The history of Nepal dates back to the times of the Rana regime, characterised by inequality and the suppression of democratic norms. The metamorphosis of the human rights situation from the times of the Rana regime to the present has become possible because of the level of awareness of human rights, especially that of civil and political rights among journalists, politicians, lawmakers and bureaucrats. Legislation such as the Labour Act, the Social Security Act and the Children Act are examples of the impact of the UN treaty system on the Nepalese human rights system.

Despite the progress made over time, much still needs to be done. Despite its international legal obligations, the government has strayed into controversies over potential encroachment of human rights through its actions. The tabulation of the IT BiCRCll[299] and the Amendment Bill to the Citizenship Act suggests the divergence of the law-making system from the ethos of the UN treaties respecting the human rights of the people. However, the role of CSOs, academia and the media in the widespread dissent towards these Bills[300]

---

297 NHRC, NWC, NDC, 'The NHRI Nepal Joint Submission for the Third Cycle Universal Periodic Review of Nepal' (National Human Rights Commission, 2020) <https://www.np.undp.org/content/nepal/en/home/library/democratic_governance/universal-periodic-report-Nepal.html> accessed 5 July 2022.

298 UNHRC, 'National Report Submitted in Accordance with Paragraph 5 of the Annex to Human Rights Council Resolution 16/21' A/HRC/WG.6/37/NPL/1 <https://documents-dds-ny.un.org/doc/UNDOC/GEN/G20/278/61/PDF/G2027861.pdf?OpenElement> accessed 5 July 2022.

299 Bhrikuti Rai, 'Everything You Need to Know About the Nepal Government's New IT Bill' *The Kathmandu Post* (22 February 2019) <https://kathmandupost.com/national/2019/02/22/everything-you-need-to-know-about-the-governments-new-it-bill> accessed 5 July 2022.

300 Tika R Pradhan, 'Government Tables Constitution Amendment Bill at House of Representatives'.

reveals the unprecedented role of checks and balances between the government and the general public, which has come about because of the UN system.

There is no definitive research depicting the impact of the UN treaties in Nepal. The ratification and domestication of these treaties can broadly be understood through the lense of events that took place in Nepalese society after 1990. From 1990, there has been a gradual improvement in the realisation of human rights which also aligns with the domestication of UN treaties. The popular movement and the promulgation of the Constitution in 1990, with the restoration of democratic norms and values, heightened the realisation of civil and political rights among the people and the government alike, despite the pretext of discriminatory laws and societal practices. The ratification of core human rights treaties by Nepal in 1991 also suggests the same. Moreover, the realisation and domestication of socio-economic rights can be traced to the Peaceful Settlement of Dispute following the ten-year armed conflict between the Maoists and the government. The interim Constitution of Nepal 2007 followed by the enactment of laws relating to the Truth Reconciliation Commission for the disappeared, and the conscious choice of law makers, media, and the society to collectively promote the legal rights of people of minority groups, including women and children, was the beginning of the realisation of human rights through UN treaties. The enactment of the 2015 Constitution, along with the inclusion of fundamental rights according to the obligations of Nepal under international instruments, demonstrates that although the human rights movement in Nepal might still be young, the extent of domestication of the treaty provisions and their impact is gradually increasing, with greater awareness among the people along with the surge in attention towards the obligations of Nepal as a party to UN treaties.

CHAPTER 14

The Impact of the United Nations Human Rights Treaties on the Domestic Level in Poland

Katarzyna Sękowska-Kozłowska, Grażyna Baranowska, Joanna Grygiel-Zasada and Łukasz Szoszkiewicz

1 Introduction to Human Rights in Poland

The beginnings of the Polish state date back to the tenth century when the country gained its shape and accepted Christianity. In 1791 the first Polish Constitution was adopted – in fact, the first constitution in Europe – which was prepared in the spirit of the Enlightenment and regulated the status of the individual in a modern way, including providing 'townspeople' with a number of rights and freedoms.[1] It is also worth pointing out that Poland has long humanitarian traditions. In the eighteenth century torture was prohibited during criminal trials, and death penalties carried out in a way that caused particular suffering to the convict were banned.[2] Poland remained a state that privileged certain social groups up to the point when its territory was partitioned by the Russian Empire, the Kingdom of Prussia and Habsburg Monarchy at the end of the eighteenth century, when the state lost its independence. In 1918 Poland returned to the map of Europe. The Constitution of 1921 formally guaranteed the protection of life, freedom and property to all people on Poland's territory, regardless of origin, nationality, language, race, religion and equality before the law.[3]

---

1 It is indicated that already in the Middle Ages human rights could be found in Poland, initially in the form of common law. See, for instance, R Kuźniar, 'Prawa człowieka. Prawo, instytucje, stosunki międzynarodowe' (Wydawnictwo Naukowe Scholar 2000) 20–21; G Michałowska, 'Prawa człowieka i ich ochrona' (Wydawnictwa Szkolne i Pedagogiczne Spółka Akcyjna 2000) 7–8; A Łopatka, 'Polskie tradycje w dziedzinie praw człowieka' in A Łopatka (ed), *Prawa człowieka w Polsce* (Wydawnictwo Interpress 1980) 8. Rights and freedoms, such as the right to property and the right to personal inviolability, were initially granted only to elite social groups – knighthood, clergy and nobility. Poland was considered a tolerant country for various religions with people of all origins in its society free from persecution; Kuźniar (above).
2 Łopatka (n 1).
3 Arts 95 and 96 of the Polish Constitution of 17 March 1921, Dz.U. z 1921 r., no 44, item 267. In fact, this regulation was the result of the signature by Poland of the Little Treaty of Versailles

After World War II, Poland came under the influence of the USSR and a socialist government took power. The 1952 Constitutions adopted under the Communist regime did not contain rights and freedoms expressed in the form of fundamental rights.[4] Poland presented an attitude typical for socialist states from the Eastern Bloc, thus social issues (for instance, education, labour rights) were prioritised, while civil rights and freedoms were marginalised and perceived as a potential threat to the regime. The factual disregard for personal and political freedoms, along with a grave economic crisis, was the cause of mass protests in Poland. The gravity of the situation forced the socialist government to initiate talks with the opposition. The first partially free elections took place in 1989 and appeared to be a turning point for the political system in Poland. During the period of Communism the Catholic Church in Poland played an important role, being one of the pillars of the anti-Communist resistance movement. During transition it became an important player in political and social life, with an increasingly influential and institutionalised position, including its official presence in schools, where religious education is conducted. One of the effects of strengthening the role of the Catholic Church have been restrictions in the abortion law, starting from 1993.

The present catalogue of fundamental freedoms and rights was provided in the Polish Constitution adopted in 1997,[5] during the transition, and was a milestone in strengthening the protection of human rights in Poland. The constitutional catalogue of rights and freedoms is similar to the catalogue indicated in international human rights treaties, in particular the International Covenant on Civil and Political Rights (CCPR) and the International Covenant on Economic, Social and Cultural Rights (CESCR).

According to the Constitution, a ratified international agreement shall constitute part of the domestic legal order and shall be applied directly[6] and, furthermore, an international agreement ratified upon prior consent granted by statute shall have precedence over statutes if such an agreement cannot be

---

on minority rights in 1919 (see M Łysko, 'Ochrona praw mniejszości w II Rzeczypospolitej Polskiej w świetle postanowień tzw. Małego traktatu wersalskiego z 1919' MISCELLANEA HISTORICO-IURIDICA 2019 TOM XVIII, Z 1).

4 E Łetowska, 'O znaczeniu praw człowieka dla polskiego systemu prawnego' in T Jasudowicz and C Mik (eds), *O prawach człowieka. W podwójną rocznicę Paktów. Księga Pamiątkowa w hołdzie Profesor Annie Michalskiej* (Dom Organizatora TNOiK 1996) 119.
5 Constitution of the Republic of Poland of 2 April 1997, Dz.U. z 1997 r., no 78, item 483.
6 A ratified international agreement shall be applied directly after its promulgation in the Journal of Laws of the Republic of Poland (*Dziennik Ustaw*) unless its application depends on the enactment of a statute (art 91 para 1 of the Constitution).

reconciled with the provisions of such statutes.[7] This regulation also applies to international human rights treaties. Under the Constitution, one of the roles of the Polish Constitutional Tribunal is to adjudicate the conformity of international agreements with the Constitution[8] and the conformity of domestic law with ratified international agreements.[9] So, the Constitutional Tribunal is entitled to determine whether Polish regulations are in compliance with international standards.

Another constitutional state actor that safeguards human rights in Poland is the Commissioner for Human Rights. Currently, the Commissioner is considered an ombudsman-type National Human Rights Institution (NHRI) with an 'A' accreditation granted by the Global Alliance of National Human Rights Institutions (GANHRI).[10] According to the Constitution, everyone has the right to ask the Commissioner for assistance in protecting freedoms or rights infringed by organs of public authority.[11] The Commissioner also may submit an application to the Constitutional Tribunal to adjudicate the conformity of regulations with the Constitution, ratified international agreements, and with complaints concerning constitutional infringements.[12] Under the Act on the Commissioner for Human Rights, the Commissioner is responsible for safeguarding the liberties and human and citizens' rights as set forth in the Constitution and other normative acts.[13] While performing its tasks, the Commissioner takes into consideration not only domestic standards of human rights protection, but also standards of international law. The Commissioner has also several competences related to the legislature and executive, including presenting opinions and conclusions to the relevant agencies, organisations and institutions, approaching the relevant agencies with legislative initiatives, or issuing or amending other legal acts, approaching participation in the proceedings before the Constitutional Tribunal and taking part in proceedings, requesting the Supreme Court to issue a resolution aimed at explaining legal provisions that raise doubts in practice, or the application of which

---

7   Art 91 of the Constitution. All major UN human rights treaties are classified as the agreements that have precedence over statutes (see art 91 in con with 241 pars 1 of the Constitution).
8   As a side note, the Prime Minister with the application of 30 July 2020 asked the Constitutional Tribunal to adjudicate the conformity of the Istanbul Convention with the Constitution. The case was assigned the reference number K 11/20, but no decision has as yet been issued.
9   Art 188 of the Polish Constitution.
10 See <https://ganhri.org/membership/> accessed 11 April 2022.
11 Art 80 of the Polish Constitution.
12 Art 191 in con with 188 of the Polish Constitution.
13 Art 1 of Law on 15 July 1987, Dz.U. z 2020 r., item 627.

has resulted in conflicting judicial decisions.[14] In the field of children's rights, similar tasks are carried out by the Commissioner for Children's Rights.[15] The Commissioner for Human Rights also remains active on international fora, in particular during the term 2015 to 2019. The NHRI has since 2016 participated (with the right to take the floor) in the UN Open-Ended Working Group on Ageing.[16]

A gradual deterioration in the field of human rights protection in Poland began with the post-2015 constitutional breakdown, when state power was gained by the conservatives from the Law and Justice Party and its supporters.[17] The process of marginalising the rule of law in Poland began with amendments to the law regulating the functioning of Constitutional Tribunal and status of its judges, which resulted in a political takeover of this institution by the ruling party. Since then, constitutionalists have expressed doubts as to whether the rulings of the politicised tribunal have the legal value of judgments.[18]

Subsequently, an attack on judicial independence occurred,[19] as well as the takeover and political instrumentalisation of public media, state-sponsored

---

14 Art 16 of Law on 15 July 1987, Dz.U. z 2020 r., item 627.

15 Art 72(4) of the Polish Constitution. While the official translation of the Constitution translates the name as 'Commissioner for Children's Rights', the Commissioner at times refers to himself also as 'Ombudsman for Children' <https://www.sejm.gov.pl/prawo/konst/angielski/kon1.htm> accessed 11 April 2022.

16 In co-operation with the German NHRI they undertook discussions around the normative content of the UN Convention on the Rights of Older Persons and issued three joint statements in this regard. In 2021 Polish and Georgian NHRIs together spearhead activities in the area of rights of older persons within the European Network of NHRIs. Moreover, the Polish NHRI coordinated preparation of the joint statement of 14 other NHRIs and 37 NGOs calling for launching the process of drafting the Convention. Commissioner for Human Rights, The Joint Statement for the upcoming 11th Session of the UN Open-Ended Working Group of Ageing (OEWGA, 29 March-1 April 2021) <https://www.rpo.gov.pl/en/content/joint-statement-upcoming-11th-session-un-open-ended-working-group-ageing-oewga-29th-march-1st-april#LIST> accessed 11 April 2022; Anna Chabiera, Office of the Polish Commissioner for Human Rights, 31 May 2021, telephone interview (notes of all interviews on file with authors). See recent activities: <https://twitter.com/anna_chabiera> accessed 11 April 2022.

17 The term 'constitutional breakdown' has been borrowed from the monograph W Sadurski, *Poland's Constitutional Breakdown* (Oxford University Press 2019).

18 However, in order to facilitate the reading of this chapter, the authors use the term 'judgment' in relation to the rulings of the Constitutional Tribunal handed down after the constitutional breakdown in 2015.

19 See CJEU judgment of 24 June 2019, C-619/18; CJEU judgment of 19 November 2019, C-585/18, C-624/18, C-625/18; CJEU judgment of 26 March 2020, C-558/18, C-563/18; CJEU judgment of 2 March 2021, C-824/18; Venice Commission, Opinion on the Draft Act amending the Act on the National Council of the Judiciary; on the Draft Act amending the Act on the Supreme Court, proposed by the President of Poland, and on the Act on the Organisation

homophobia and anti-LGBT (lesbian, gay, bisexual and transgender) campaigns[20] further restrictions on abortion laws, and more.[21] Police brutality increased considerably, for example, the mass protests following the 2020 ruling of the Constitutional Tribunal establishing a near-total abortion ban were met with disproportionate use of police force.[22] It should be noted that in recent years Poland has taken significant steps towards denouncing the Istanbul Convention, which may herald a dangerous trend of withdrawal from international obligations in the field of human rights. One of the most recent signs of the crisis of human rights in Poland are steps taken in order to marginalise and politicise the institution of the Commissioner for Human Rights.[23]

2 Relationship of Poland with the International Human Rights System in General

Poland is considered a founding member of the United Nations and since the beginning has actively participated in the activities of the organisation,[24] including the Polish membership in its main organs. For instance, Poland several times was a non-permanent member of the Security Council[25] and

---

of Ordinary Courts on 11 December 2017, Opinion No 904/2017; Venice Commission, joint Urgent Opinion of the Venice Commission and the Directorate General of Human Rights and Rule of Law (DGI) of the Council of Europe on amendments to the Law on the Common courts, the Law on the Supreme court and some other Laws on 22 June 2020, Opinion 977/2020.

20 For detailed information, see Atlas of Hate – a citizen-led project that collects information on discriminatory resolutions adopted by local governments. The initiative has been nominated for the Sakharov Prize 2020. For more, see <https://atlasnienawisci.pl> accessed 11 April 2022.

21 For detailed information, see for example Human Rights Watch, World Report 2021. Events of 2020 547–551.

22 Przemysław Kazimirski, NPM director, 20 May 2021, on-line interview. According to Przemysław Kazimirski, who has worked in the NPM since its creation, there was never such a contemptuous attitude of police authorities toward the NPM recommendation as seen in the last two years, which makes constructive dialogue between the NPM and police authorities nearly impossible.

23 Constitutional Tribunal judgment of 15 April 2021, K 20/20.

24 However, during martial law 1981–1983, Poland formally refused to cooperate with the UN Quasi-Special Procedure due to the distress situation in the state. MA Nowicki, 'Z kart historii: Komitet Helsiński w Polsce w sporze z sekretarzem generalnym ONZ w sprawie oceny sytuacji w PRL w stanie wojennym' (2014) 2 Kwartalnik o Prawach Człowieka 24–31; M Limon and H Power, *History of the United Nations Special Procedures Mechanism. Origins, Evolution and Reform* (Universal Rights Group 2014) 26.

25 During the years 1946–1947, 1960, 1970–1971, 1982–1983, 1996–1997, 2018–2019.

regularly takes part in UN peacekeeping missions. Furthermore, Poland has been elected as a member of the Human Rights Council (HRC) for three terms, the most recent from 2000 to 2022.[26] Poland's membership in the UN has contributed to the domestic institutionalisation of the protection standards for human rights. Poland also ratified the Rome Statue of the International Criminal Court (ICC) in 2001.

Poland has on several occasions been visited by special mechanisms. In March 2001 it extended a standing invitation. Poland was visited by the Special Rapporteur on violence against women in 1996;[27] the Special Rapporteur on freedom of expression in 1997;[28] the Special Rapporteur on health in 2009;[29] the Special Rapporteur on trafficking in 2009;[30] the Special Rapporteur on toxic wastes and human rights in 2011;[31] the Special Rapporteur on food in 2016;[32] the Special Rapporteur on independence of judges in 2017;[33] the Special Rapporteur on cultural rights in 2018;[34] and the Working Group on discrimination against women and girls in 2018.[35] Tin their reports, all these Special Rapporteurs made recommendations to Poland, but these were not always implemented by the government.[36]

---

[26] Poland was a member of the Human Rights Council in 2006–2007, 2011–2013 and was elected for the 2020–2022 term.

[27] Report on the mission of the Special Rapporteur to Poland on the issue of trafficking and forced prostitution of women (24 May to 1 June 1996), E/CN.4/1997/47/Add.1, 10 December 1996.

[28] Report on the mission of the Special Rapporteur to the Republic of Poland, E/CN.4/1998/40/Add.2, 13 January 1998.

[29] Report of the Special Rapporteur on the right of everyone to the enjoyment of the highest attainable standard of physical and mental health, Anand Grover. Addendum. Mission to Poland, A/HRC/14/20/Add.3, 20 May 2010.

[30] Report of the Special Rapporteur on trafficking in persons, especially women and children, Joy Ngozi Ezeilo. Addendum. Mission to Poland, A/HRC/14/32/Add.3, 2 June 2010.

[31] Report of the Special Rapporteur on the adverse effects of the movement and dumping of toxic and dangerous products and wastes on the enjoyment of human rights, Calin Georgescu. Addendum. Mission to Poland (25–31 May 2011), A/HRC/18/31/Add.2, 7 September 2011.

[32] Report of the Special Rapporteur on the right to food on her mission to Poland, A/HRC/34/48/Add.1, 27 December 2016.

[33] Report of the Special Rapporteur on the independence of judges and lawyers on his mission to Poland, A/HRC/38/38/Add.1, 5 April 2018.

[34] Visit to Poland. Report of the Special Rapporteur in the field of cultural rights, A/HRC/43/50/Add.1, 12 May 2020.

[35] Visit to Poland. Report of the Working Group on the issue of discrimination against women in law and in practice, A/HRC/41/33/Add.2, 25 June 2019.

[36] A Hernandez-Połczyńska, Wizyty specjalnych sprawozdawców ONZ w Polsce, Problemy Współczesnego Prawa Międzynarodowego, Europejskiego i Porównawczego, vol. XVI, A.D. MMXVIII 141–142.

By 30 June 2019, Universal Periodic Review (UPR) reports from Poland were reviewed during three cycles, in 2008, 2012 and 2017. In the second cycle Poland accepted 105 of 124 recommendations and in the third cycle 144 of 185.[37] The recommendations in general mainly concerned the ratification of international treaties on equality and non-discrimination, conditions of detention, domestic violence, administration of justice and fair trial, access to sexual and reproductive health and services and the situation of minorities and migrants.[38]

Poland has been a member of the Council of Europe (CoE) since 1991, the Organisation for Security and Co-operation in Europe (OSCE) since its inception and the European Union (EU) since 2004. The main international component of human rights in Poland is provided by the European Convention of Human Rights (ECHR) under the jurisdiction of the European Court of Human Rights (ECtHR). Poland ratified ECHR in 1993 and since then its impact on the domestic law and jurisprudence has been significant. Hundreds of ECtHR's judgments against Poland in which violations were found have caused a significant number of measures to be taken by Poland in recent years.[39] It should be pointed out that also the Istanbul Convention, as ratified by Poland in 2015, has impacted on domestic regulations. However, its implementation is seriously overshadowed by the state-sponsored anti-gender campaign and steps undertaken within the government in order to withdraw.[40] Another leading factor shaping the standards of human rights protection in Poland (for instance, in the area of non-discrimination) is its membership of the EU. The European regional systems have a stronger impact on human rights in Poland than the UN system. For this reason, the impact of the UN human rights framework arguably was more prominent in the 1990s and early 2000s and has gradually been replaced by European regional mechanisms.[41]

---

37   See Infographic <https://www.ohchr.org/sites/default/files/lib-docs/HRBodies/UPR/Documents/Session27/PL/POLAND_Infographic_27th.pdf> accessed 11 September 2023.
38   See Matrix of recommendations to Poland <https://www.ohchr.org/EN/HRBodies/UPR/Pages/PLindex.aspx> accessed 11 April 2022.
39   A Wiśniewski, 'The Impact of the European Convention of Human Rights on the Polish Legal System' (2020) 9 Polish Review of International and European Law 153.
40   See K Sękowska-Kozłowska, 'The Istanbul Convention in Poland: Between the "War on Gender" and Legal Reform' in J Niemi, L Peroni and V Stoyanova (eds), *International Law and Violence Against Women. Europe and the Istanbul Convention* (Routledge 2020) 259–276.
41   Roman Wieruszewski, former HRCttee member, 24 May 2021, on-line interview.

3 **At a Glance: Formal Engagement of Poland with the UN Human Rights Treaty System**

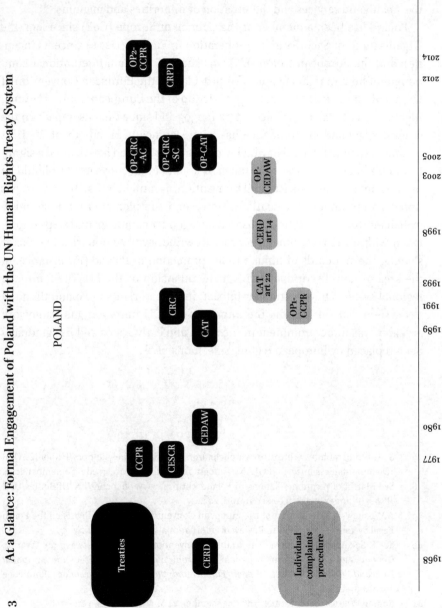

4   Role and Overall Impact of the UN Human Rights Treaties in Poland

4.1   *Role of UN Human Rights Treaties*

4.1.1   Formal Acceptance

The process of Poland's accession to UN human rights treaties can be divided into two periods, split by a significant milestone in Polish history which is the democratic transition in 1989. Although a socialist country until 1989, Poland had by then ratified all core UN human rights treaties: the International Convention on the Elimination of All Forms of Racial Discrimination (CERD) in 1968; CCPR and CESCR in 1977; the Convention on the Elimination of All Forms of Discrimination against Women (CEDAW) in 1980; and the Convention Against Torture and Other Cruel, Inhuman, or Degrading Treatment or Punishment (CAT) in 1989. This step was consistent with its political attitude towards human rights at the time, where commitments were made more for propaganda reasons. Poland accepted international standards in a selective manner, preferring treaties that did not impose any 'troublesome' commitments, or ones of which the subject matter did not directly concern Poland.[42] Consequently, it did not accept the mechanisms of individual complaints under OP1-CCPR, article 14 of CERD and article 22 of CAT. Besides this, it entered a reservation to article 41 of CCPR which provides the mechanism for interstate complaints, and to article 29 of CEDAW allowing for interstate arbitration. This rejection of control mechanisms was typical of the socialist countries.[43]

After 1989 Poland acceded to the Convention on the Rights of the Child (CRC) (in 1991); OP-CAT (in 2005); OP-CRC-AC and OP-CRC-SC (both in 2005). It ratified the Convention on the Rights of Persons with Disabilities (CRPD) in 2012 and OP2-CCPR in 2014. It has not yet acceded to the International Convention on the Protection of the Rights of All Migrant Workers and Members of Their Families (CMW) and the International Convention for the Protection of All Persons from Enforced Disappearance (CED). As for CMW, it has neither been signed nor ratified by Poland, similar to the case in other EU countries.[44] One

---

42   K Drzewicki, 'Zobowiązania międzynarodowe Polski w dziedzinie praw człowieka' (1998) Rocznik Polskiej Polityki Zagranicznej 102–108, cited by A Bieńczyk-Missala, *Human Rights in Polish Foreign Policy After 1989* (PISM 2006) 57.

43   Bieńczyk-Missala (n 42) 57.

44   EU countries have used the indication of shared competences on asylum and migration of the EU and its member states as an essential obstacle to ratify CMW, which may be perceived as a 'convenient alibi' for not undertaking any efforts to ratify this treaty. E MacDonald and R Cholewinski, *The Migrant Workers Convention in Europe. Obstacles to*

of main reasons given for the lack of progress is that CMW requires granting rights to all migrant workers, regardless of their legal status, which is contrary to Polish domestic law.[45] With regard to CED, it was signed in 2013 but has not yet been ratified probably due to the lack of any pressure from politicians or civil society.

Poland has entered substantial reservations and declarations to CRC and CRPD. As for CRC, upon ratification it made reservations to article 7 (on limiting the right of an adopted child to know its natural parents) and to article 38 (on determining the age from which call-up to the military is permissible). Both reservations were withdrawn in 2013. Along with these, Poland entered declarations to CRC related to moral and reproductive issues.[46] Despite CRC Cttee recommendations,[47] Poland has not withdrawn these declarations. Reservations to articles 23(1)(b) and 25(a) of CRPD also concern reproductive rights.[48] Moreover, Poland made a reservation on article 23(1)(a) of CRPD and an interpretative declaration on article 12 of CRPD, both seriously limiting rights in CRPD (see the subsection on CRPD). Although the CRPD Cttee recommended withdrawing these,[49] Poland stated that it had no intention of doing so.[50]

Today Poland is bound by mechanisms allowing for individual complaints under CCPR, CAT, CERD and CEDAW. Poland ratified OP1-CCPR in 1991 and withdrew its reservations to art 41 of CCPR in 1990, to art 22 of CAT in 1993, to art 29 of CEDAW in 1997, and to art 14 of CERD in 1998. It has not ratified OP-CESCR, OP-CRPD and OP-CRC-CP. In all these cases, the reluctance to accept communication procedures is related mostly to controversies over the justiciability of economic, social and cultural rights (see the subsection on CESCR)

---

the Ratification of the International Convention on the Protection of the Rights of All Migrant Workers and Members of their Families: EU/EEA Perspectives (UNESCO 2007) 69.

45   Official response to inquiry 3734 of the Minister of Foreign Affairs, 31 July 2006.

46   'The Republic of Poland considers that a child's rights as defined in the Convention, in particular the rights defined in articles 12 to 16, shall be exercised with respect for parental authority, in accordance with Polish customs and traditions regarding the place of the child within and outside the family; with respect to article 24, paragraph 2(f) of the Convention, the Republic of Poland considers that family planning and education services for parents should be in keeping with the principles of morality'.

47   CRC Cttee, COs on the combined 3rd and 4th periodic reports of Poland, para 7; CRC Cttee, COs on the 2nd second periodic report of Poland, para 10.

48   'The Republic of Poland understands that Article 23.1 (b) and Article 25 (a) shall not be interpreted in a way conferring an individual right to abortion or mandating state party to provide access thereto, unless that right is guaranteed by the national law'.

49   CRPD Cttee, COs on the initial report of Poland, para 6.

50   CRPD Cttee, Summary records, initial report of Poland, paras 41–42.

and the possible economic and legal consequences of decisions against Poland. Moreover, in the case of CRC, ideological issues are also at stake, such as the CRC Cttee's attitude on abortion and contraception (see subsection on CRC).[51]

Since Poland did not ratify OP-CESCR, OP-CRPD and OP-CRC-CP, it also did not accept inquiry procedures under these treaties. It is also not bound by article 20 of CAT empowering the CAT Cttee to carry out a confidential inquiry in case of torture. The only inquiry procedure accepted by Poland is OP-CEDAW (since 2003).

4.1.2   General Attitude of State towards UN Treaty System

In general, Poland seems not to challenge the system of treaty bodies as such. The non-ratification of the individual complaint procedures under CESCR, CRPD and CRC may be perceived as a lack of confidence in the interpretation of some treaty provisions, such as those related to reproductive rights, by the respective treaty bodies. Another problem is the attitude of successive governments towards economic, social and cultural rights. The justiciability of many of these rights is repeatedly undermined by public authorities in state party reports submitted to the CESCR Cttee and to the CRPD Cttee. Polish authorities have on several occasions stated that these treaties contain a large number of provisions that do not establish individual rights which could give rise to judicial remedies,[52] a claim that is related to concerns about financial implications of alleged violations in this field as well as the potential influence of treaty bodies on public policies adopted by the government. This consistent position taken by the government, regardless of the political parties in power, indicates the general reluctance to be subject to control by external actors. Furthermore, referring to the repeated recommendations of treaty bodies, it may be concluded that Poland does not fully implement these, and in the case of access to abortion, legislative changes even go in the opposite direction.[53]

4.1.3   Level of Awareness

References to UN human rights treaties are present in parliamentary debates, inquiries, or motions for amending certain laws. However, this rarely reaches beyond the mere invocation of a provision or a principle (for instance, the best

---

51   Official response to inquiry 8573 to the Ministry of Family, Labour and Social Policy, 11 January 2017.
52   CESCR Cttee, Replies to the List of Issues, Poland, 26 July 2016, para 1; official response to inquiry 323 to the Ministry of Family, Labour and Social Policy, 29 January 2020.
53   Nadaždin Draginja, Director of Amnesty International Poland (term 2007–2021), 29 May 2021, on-line interview.

interests of the child). A particularly popular rhetorical device is invoking the Polish authorship of the CRC. Superficiality promotes the instrumental use of human rights treaties to, for example, justify the absolute nature of the right to life of the child and to restrict access to safe and legal abortion services. Sometimes COs are utilised by the opposition politicians, but this depends on their political agenda.

At the same time, the government perceives the activities of the treaty bodies as a source of uncomfortable criticism and often takes a defensive position. For this reason, press releases typically depict dialogues held in Geneva as 'defence of the submitted report', instead of a 'dialogue', as the treaty bodies refer to the process. Within public authorities, UN human rights standards, along with their reporting procedures, are increasingly raised by the Commissioner for Human Rights and Commissioner for Children's Rights (both institutions are ombudsman-type institutions). Both submit reports to the respective committees, are involved in dialogue with the treaty bodies, and actively disseminate the COs.

Within the judiciary, there is a general awareness of UN human rights treaties, but the jurisprudence remains substantively superficial. The treaties most frequently invoked are CCPR and CRC, which play a major role in judicial review, as well as in the jurisprudence of the lower courts. Nevertheless, some judgments of the Constitutional Tribunal or the Supreme Court have been criticised by academia and non-governmental organisations (NGOs), in particular for their inconsistency with the official position of treaty bodies (the CESCR Cttee, the CRC Cttee, the CRPD Cttee).

With regard to the training of legal professionals, most of the universities in Poland require undertaking at least one human rights course during legal studies. However, a significant number of these relate to either specific human rights issues (for instance, privacy, digital challenges), EU or CoE frameworks.[54] The UN human rights treaty system is but one of several elements typically covered during a general international law or international human rights law course. Further, COs and General Comments are rarely translated into Polish, which influences both legal education as well as jurisprudence (see subsection on state reporting).

As indicated above, legal practitioners acquire a general knowledge about the UN human rights treaties during their studies. However, referring to further education, the national framework for attorneys' training contains

---

54 M Balcerzak, J Kapelańska-Pręgowska and P Sadowski, Dydaktyka w zakresie praw człowieka na polskich uczelniach wyższych. Wyniki Ankiety, conference entitled 'XX lat Katedry Praw Człowieka na UMK w Toruniu', 25 November 2020, Toruń, Poland.

no classes dedicated to human rights issues, without exemption on the UN human rights system.[55] Fragmentary training on this topic may be passed on while discussing other topics, but it is at the discretion of lecturers. In practice, trainee attorneys gain knowledge of the procedural aspects related to the international cooperation (especially in criminal matters) within the EU and representation of clients before regional human rights protection bodies (the ECtHR and the Court of Justice of the European Union (CJEU), while learning about the UN human rights system seems to be impractical. Attorneys in their practice frequently refer to the standards and mechanisms of protection developed by regional systems of human rights protection, in particular to support procedural argumentation.[56] Thus, it can be assumed that lawyers have a general level of awareness about the UN treaty system, but more often and more willingly use the CoE and EU *acquis*.

Media awareness of treaty bodies appears to be scattered. There are several socially and politically sensitive topics that repeatedly appear in the agenda of major media outlets when relevant treaty bodies are mentioned, in particular reproductive rights (for instance, abortion, sex education), discrimination against vulnerable groups and hate speech (for instance, LGBT persons, Roma) and violence against women. For this reason, media coverage remains limited to selected COs from the relevant treaty bodies, and rarely covers the procedure of periodic review comprehensively. In this context, the media have recently extended their interest beyond Poland and reported on the Committees' recommendations and activities around Ireland (HRCttee on abortion law) or Vatican City (CRC Cttee on counteracting paedophilia). One of the topics extensively discussed in the media is the operation of so-called baby boxes (also known as windows of life) that allow parents to abandon a child anonymously. Although criticised by the CRC Cttee as violating the children's right to an identity, baby boxes enjoy significant support from society as well as the Commissioner for Children's Rights and, therefore, remain active.[57] After the post-2015 constitutional breakdown, recommendations by Committees

---

55   As a side note, upon his election as the SPT member in 2020, Jakub Czepek was invited through the Ministry of Justice to come to the central school for prison officers to promote the SPT standards. While the pandemic made such an event impossible, this governmental initiative will lead to a better knowledge of the relevant UN human rights system for professionals, Czepek, Jakub, SPT member, academic, 20 May 2021, on-line interview.

56   Binas Piotr, Attorney and Member of the Training Commission at the Poznań Bar Association, academic, 27 May 2021, on-line interview.

57   TVN24, ONZ wzywa Polskę do likwidacji 'okien życia'. 'Naruszają prawo dzieci do tożsamości', 18 October 2015 <https://tvn24.pl/polska/onz-wzywa-polske-do-likwidacji-okien-zycia-ra587044-3315606> accessed 5 April 2022.

are primarily used to highlight democratic backsliding and governmental attempts to redefine reality. Critical materials therefore appear in major opposition media outlets, reaching approximately half of a highly-polarised society.

There is an increasing awareness of UN core human rights treaties and the findings of the treaty bodies among the general public, in particular after the post-2015 constitutional breakdown, when rights and freedoms are being violated. For example, Amnesty International Poland has since become much more involved in domestic matters.[58] The involvement of civil society in the reporting procedure also plays an important role in terms of awareness raising, in particular within the HRCttee and CRPD Cttee (see the subsection on state reporting). Recommendations are then invoked by NGOs in their human rights advocacy (see the subsections on non-state actors in the sections on the respective treaty bodies).

4.1.4 State Reporting

As of 30 June 2019, Poland had submitted 24 state reports under CERD; seven reports under CCPR; six under CESCR; eight under CEDAW; seven under CAT; one under CRPD; six under CRC; one under CRC-OP-AC; and one under CRC-OP-SC. The state's timeliness towards reporting obligations differs dramatically – from no delays in reporting under CRPD (2014) to over 10 years' delay when reporting under CEDAW (1994–2004). In general, most reports were submitted with delays, which varied depending on the treaty and the time period.[59] The average delay is between one and two years. Delays are now attributable mostly to the overload and overlapping of reporting obligations,[60] as well as organisational reasons related to changes of the governments and ministries in charge of reporting.[61]

The preparation of a state report is coordinated by the ministry responsible for the issues covered by a treaty. This usually is the Ministry of Family and Social Affairs (CESCR, CRC, CRPD); the Ministry of Justice (CCPR, CAT); the Ministry of Interior (CERD); and the Government Plenipotentiary for Equal Treatment (CEDAW). Relevant ministries and public institutions are asked to

---

[58] Nadażdin Draginja, Director of Amnesty International Poland (term 2007–2021), 29 May 2021, on-line interview.

[59] It may be observed that the biggest delays were in the 1990s and early 2000s, which may be attributed to the transition period from socialism to a democratic state, and the reorganisation of the state institutions.

[60] Joanna Maciejewska, Department of International Cooperation, Ministry of Family and Social Affairs, 27 May 2021, on-line interview.

[61] Justyna Chrzanowska, Deputy Director, Department of United Nations and Human Rights, Ministry of Foreign Affairs, 21 May 2021, on-line interview.

provide input, which is then used for drafting the reports. There are no central procedures that regulate reporting – each ministry in charge manages it on its own. Typically, the process is based on gathering data from ministries and public institutions. The final version is accepted by the Council of Ministers.[62] The formalities and logistics (timekeeping, sending reminders to the ministries, corresponding with OHCHR) are coordinated by the Ministry of Foreign Affairs.[63]

In the last two decades, civil society has sometimes been consulted, but it is worth noting that as indicated by some NGOs[64] and ministries,[65] this process has not been effective. This is mostly attributable to different roles of the government and NGOs in the reporting process: the state reports present the government's position on the implementation of the treaty, often highlighting positive aspects, while NGOs express their criticism. Thus, it seems that the consultation process has been frustrating for both civil society, whose comments have not been reflected in the state's reports,[66] and the ministries due to the additional workload and little response from NGOs.[67] In recent years the NHRI has also been asked for input to state reports by some ministries; however, as the Commissioner is an independent body, the current practice of the NHRI is to submit its own alternative reports and not to participate in the creation of state reports. The NHRI reports are drafted after considering the state reports, to include the most current issues and to straighten out or add to information from the report, if necessary.[68]

---

62 Joanna Maciejewska, Department of International Cooperation, Ministry of Family and Social Affairs, 27 May 2021, on-line interview.

63 Justyna Chrzanowska, Deputy Director, Department of United Nations and Human Rights, Ministry of Foreign Affairs, 21 May 2021, on-line interview.

64 K Sękowska-Kozłowska, 'Sprawozdawczość Polski przed organami ochrony praw człowieka ONZ: diagnoza i rekomendacje' (2016), Państwo i Prawo 12 (850).

65 Joanna Maciejewska, Department of International Cooperation, Ministry of Family and Social Affairs, 27 May 2021, on-line interview.

66 K Sękowska-Kozłowska, 'Sprawozdawczość Polski przed organami ochrony praw człowieka ONZ: diagnoza i rekomendacje' (2016), Państwo i Prawo 12 (850).

67 For instance, in the case of CRPD, out of 60 NGOs that received the state's report for consultations, only five submitted their comments. Due to reasons indicated in the text, the Ministry of Family, Labour and Social Affairs decided not to submit a report in 2019 on CRC to consultations (only the Commissioner for Children's Rights was consulted); Joanna Maciejewska, Department of International Cooperation, Ministry of Family and Social Affairs, 27 May 2021, on-line interview.

68 Magdalena Kuruś, Director Department for Equal Treatment in the Office of the Commissioner for Human Rights, 27 May 2021, on-line interview. For example, the Ministry of Home Affairs and Administration is consistently asking for NHRI inputs, while other ministries do not get in touch with the NHRI while preparing reports.

Reports have been presented to the treaty bodies by high-level and multi-sectoral delegations headed by the secretaries or deputy secretaries of state.[69] As of 30 June 2019, representatives of Poland had participated in multiple dialogues before the treaty bodies: fifteen under CERD; seven under CCPR; six under CESCR; five under CEDAW; six under CAT; four under CRC; and one under CRPD.

There are serious shortcomings regarding the publication and dissemination of COs. There is no comprehensive governmental website that publishes the content and documents regarding all treaty bodies and monitoring procedures. This information is split between the websites of the ministries in charge of specific treaties. Moreover, the content is very sparse and fragmented.[70] In particular Polish translations of the recent COs, although prepared by the relevant ministries,[71] are missing. Civil society makes efforts to fill this *lacuna*, and NGOs sometimes prepare and publish their own translations of COs on Poland.[72] The NHRI also regularly reminds the ministries of their obligations to translate COs.[73]

In the last two decades Polish NGOs have become more active in the reporting process, but the level of engagement depends on the treaty under consideration.[74] Most attention is attributed to CCPR and CRPD (ten alternative reports each in the last periodic review) followed by CERD and CAT (six and five reports respectively). NGOs participated in the sessions of the treaty bodies, and delivered additional information such as submissions for sessions and follow-up information. The valuable initiative of preparing comprehensive alternative reports covering the whole scope of the respective treaty by

---

69 The Secretary of State is the highest rank of governmental officials after a minister.
70 Until around 2017 there was much more detailed information and archiving of documents available on the governmental websites. Their content, however, was significantly reduced in order to make them more mobile-friendly.
71 Joanna Maciejewska, Department of International Cooperation, Ministry of Family and Social Affairs, 27 May 2021, on-line interview.
72 Eg translation prepared by Karat: CEDAW Cttee, COs on the 7th and 8th report of Poland <https://www.karat.org/pliki/wp-content/uploads/2014/10/Uwagi-Koncowe-Komitetu-CEDAW%E2%80%8A_PL%E2%80%8A1.pdf> accessed 15 September 2023.
73 Magdalena Kuruś, Director Department for Equal Treatment in the Office of the Commissioner for Human Rights, 27 May 2021, on-line interview.
74 For Amnesty International Poland the key criteria determining the preparation of an alternative report to the treaty body are current critical situations related to the observance of human rights in a specific scope (report to the HRCttee in 2016 and CESCR Cttee in 2009); available resources and the assessment that a report may have a significant impact; Nadażdin Draginja, Director of Amnesty International Poland (term 2007–2021), 29 May 2021, on-line interview.

coalitions of NGOs, as in case of CEDAW and CRPD, is worth noting. It may be observed that, aside from NGOs that specialise in protecting human rights as such,[75] women's rights, LGBT+ and persons with disabilities organisations are the most active before treaty bodies. A growing trend of activity by ultraconservative and church-related movements should be also noted.[76]

The Commissioner for Human Rights (NHRI) has been particularly active in the term 2015–2021, and the first reports prepared by this body have been submitted to the treaty bodies. It delivered information under CCPR (2016), CRPD (2018), CAT (2019) and CERD (2019). In the case of CRC, information was provided by the Commissioner for Children's Rights (2015, 2018).

4.1.5 Domestic Implementation Mechanism/Process

There is no specific process or institutional arrangement in place to implement the COs as a whole or recommendations of the respective treaty bodies. A (partial) exception is CRPD, as article 33(1) requires member states to designate one or more focal points relating to implementation, and this role has been assigned to the Ministry of Family and Social Policy. Until recently, Poland has not adopted a comprehensive strategy for implementing CRPD, a situation which has been criticised by the CRPD Cttee. Similarly, Poland has been criticised by the CEDAW Cttee for not establishing an institutional framework or a comprehensive strategy to implement CEDAW.

4.1.6 Treaty Body Membership

Since 1999 Poland has had four members of treaty bodies: Roman Wieruszewski (HR Cttee 1998–2000 and 2003–2006, vice-chair 2003–2006); Zdzisław Kędzia (CESCR Cttee 2008–2020; 2009–2010 rapporteur, 2011–2012 vice-chair, chair 2013–2014, vice-chair 2017–2018); Zbigniew Lasocik (SPT, 2007–2012); and Jakub Czepek (SPT, 2020–2023). The election process is monitored by the Ministry of Foreign Affairs. A candidate is indicated by a relevant ministry and

---

75   One NGO has remained particularly active in the last 20 years – The Helsinki Foundation for Human Rights managed to submit nine alternative reports: an alternative report to the CAT Cttee in 2007, 2013, 2019; to the HRCttee in 2014, 2016; to the CERD Cttee in 2009, 2014, 2019; and to the CRPD Cttee in 2018. Other NGOs that have made their mark in recent years include, in particular, Amnesty International (CAT Cttee in 2013; HRCttee in 2009, 2016; CESCR Cttee in 2009) and the ultra-conservative *Ordo Iuris* (CAT Cttee 2019; CRC Cttee in 2015, 2018; CRPD Cttee in 2018).

76   *Ordo Iuris* had presented numerous submissions in recent years under CAT, CCPR, CRC and CRPD. See eg *Cultural and Religious Counterrevolution – Is Polish Law under the Threat of Christian Fundamentalists' Ideology?* (The Great Coalition for Equality and Choice 2020).

the election campaign at the UN is run by the Ministry of Foreign Affairs.[77] While there is no transparent process for the nomination of treaty body members,[78] all four members are human rights experts and academics well known in Poland. Roman Wieruszewski and Zdzisław Kędzia, the members of the HRCttee and CESCR Cttee, were both editors of the first Polish commentaries to the two Covenants,[79] thus significantly advancing knowledge about the UN human rights system in Poland. In addition, Roman Wieruszewski, Zdzisław Kędzia and Zbigniew Lasocik have published widely about the UN human rights system, both during their mandates and afterwards.[80] The members of treaty bodies could count on the support offered by the Permanent Mission of the Republic of Poland to the United Nations Office in Geneva for the treaty bodies system while the Ministry of Foreign Affairs and Ministry of Justice were engaged in electoral campaigns in favour of candidates.[81]

4.2 *Overview of Impact*

4.2.1 Incorporation and Reliance by Legislature and Executive

Four of the main treaties (CERD, CCPR, CESCR and CEDAW) were ratified by Poland prior to the democratic transition in 1989 and the adoption of the democratic Constitution in 1997, and thus had had an impact on the constitutionalisation of human rights. In particular CCPR and CESCR have been found to have had a profound impact, as the constitutional catalogue of rights and

---

77 Justyna Chrzanowska, Deputy Director, Department of United Nations and Human Rights, Ministry of Foreign Affairs, 21 May 2021, on-line interview.
78 Treaty body members received proposals to apply from respective ministries, without a formal call and selection; Roman Wieruszewski, former HRCttee member, 24 May 2021, on-line interview; Jakub Czepek, SPT member, academic, 20 May 2021, on-line interview. In the case of CRPD selected candidates were presented to public advisory bodies representing persons with disabilities: Polish Board of Sign Language (in 2018) and National Consultative Council for Disabled Persons (in 2020). The Council adopted the candidature through a vote. Joanna Maciejewska, Department of International Cooperation, Ministry of Family and Social Affairs, 27 May 2021, on-line interview.
79 Z Kędzia and A Hernandez-Połczyńska (eds), *Międzynarodowy Pakt Praw Gospodarczych, Socjalnych i Kulturalnych. Komentarz* (CH Beck 2018); R Wieruszewski (ed), *Międzynarodowy Pakt Praw Obywatelskich (Osobistych) i Politycznych. Komentarz* (Wolters Kluwer 2012).
80 See for example the following books and articles: Kędzia and Hernandez-Połczyńska (n 79); Wieruszewski (n 79); R Wieruszewski (ed), *Mechanizmy ochrony praw człowieka w ramach ONZ. Analiza systemowa* (CH Beck 2017); Z Lasocik and A Męzik, *Krajowy Mechanizm Prewencji Tortur w oczach funkcjonariuszy Służby Więziennej*, Nowa Kodyfikacja Prawa Karnego (54) 2019.
81 Zdzisław Kędzia, former Chair and member of the CESCR Cttee, 25 May 2021, on-line interview; Jakub Czepek, SPT member, academic, 20 May 2021, on-line interview.

freedoms is similar to the catalogue of rights contained in these two treaties.[82] However, the text of the Constitution contains no direct reference to any of the treaties.

The main treaties have been invoked in justification of domestic legislation or policies, as well as during parliamentary debate. For example, CCPR was directly cited in the Preamble to the educational law from 2016 and in some bilateral treaties, and CRC was cited in the law on foreigners. The law on accessibility has explicitly endorsed the CRPD definitions of universal design and reasonable accommodation. Several strategies and policies contain references to treaty bodies, for example concerning combating domestic violence. However, they appear to be merely references, with no impact on the content. No strategies or policies for a more general implementation of each treaty have been adopted.

While direct reference to main treaties occurs, it is not a common phenomenon. For example, Poland ratified CRPD in 2012 and has subsequently introduced legislative changes aimed at better protecting the rights of persons with disabilities, such as amendments to the electoral law and broadcasting law, without referencing CRPD in either the law or the explanatory memorandum. Issues such as labour rights, domestic violence, unequal treatment and discrimination, and sexual and reproductive health, although falling under the scope of CESCR, are instead discussed in Parliament in the context of interpretation developed by other treaty bodies (for instance, the CEDAW and CRC Cttees).

4.2.2 Reliance by Judiciary

The analysis revealed that common and administrative courts, the Supreme Court and Constitutional Tribunal have relied on the main treaties in their jurisprudence. CCPR in particular has had a strong impact, and has been raised in many contexts, such as the right of peaceful assembly, the right to court and the right to liberty and security of the person. Also, the impact of CRC in the case law has been considerable, as it has been raised with regard to many

---

[82] Z Kędzia (ed), *Prawa, wolności i obowiązki człowieka i obywatela w nowej polskiej Konstytucji* (Poznańskie Centrum Praw Człowieka INP PAN 1990); E Łętowska 'O znaczeniu praw człowieka dla polskiego systemu prawa' in T Jasudowicz and C Mik (eds), *O prawach człowieka. W podwójną rocznicę Paktów. Księga Pamiątkowa w hołdzie Profesor Annie Michalskiej* (Dom Organizatora TNOiK 1996) 119. Constitutional Commission of the National Assembly, Bulletin XV, XVI, XVII. As another example, CEDAW was recalled in the drafting process of an article of gender equality, but played a rather peripheral role, see Record of the meeting of the Constitutional Commission of the National Assembly, 25 February 1997; Record of the meeting of the Constitutional Commission of the National Assembly, 28 February 1997.

topics, such as the right to express the child's views freely, and the right of every child to a standard of living adequate for the child's development. CRC is often invoked in order to highlight the priority of the principle of the best interests of the child. The perspective on CESCR differs significantly, as courts have indicated that the provisions of the Covenant cannot be directly applied, and do not expressly provide for individual rights.

Some treaties have been raised by the judiciary with regard to specific topics. For example, CERD has been relied upon by courts in cases concerning racially-motivated violence and hate speech, as well as limits of freedom of assembly. When analysing whether persons who were attempting to stop a protest by far-right groups violated the law, the court invoked the CERD Cttee case law and acquitted them of the alleged offences. CEDAW, on the other hand, has been referred to mostly in the domain of social security, particularly with reference to retirement age, which has for decades been lower for women than for men. CRPD has often been used by claimants in proceedings against public institutions, for example in cases related to entitlement to social benefits or other forms of public support. The majority of cases in which CAT was mentioned in court proceedings concerned compensation cases brought by persons deprived of their liberty.

Throughout the 2000s and 2010s, UN human rights treaties were utilised in the context of judicial review on several occasions. For example, in six cases before the Constitutional Tribunal, article 7 of CESCR (the right to the enjoyment of just and favourable conditions of work) was invoked as the standard for judicial review. Another example is the 2020 ruling of the Constitutional Tribunal establishing a near-total abortion ban, which did not mention CEDAW, while at the same time invoking other treaties and treaty bodies. Overall, while the core treaties have been frequently invoked in domestic courts, this has not led to the comprehensive application of the UN human rights standards.

4.2.3   Impact on and through Independent State Institutions

The Commissioner for Human Rights (NHRI) has been very active in the reporting process for treaty bodies, as well as in the promotion of UN human rights standards, in particular since 2015.[83] It also takes an active part in the

---

[83]   2015 is when Adam Bodnar became the NHRI (term 2015–2021). Before taking this office, he was deputy director of the Helsinki Human Rights Foundation, an NGO involved with treaty bodies, which has a long tradition of submitting alternative reports. For examples of the involvement of NHRI before 2015, see Commissioner for Human Rights, *Informacja Rzecznika Praw Obywatelskich prof Adama Zielińskiego za 1999 rok*, 17–1; Commissioner for Human Rights' address to the Undersecretary of State in the Ministry of Justice,

constructive dialogue in Geneva, including the informal meetings with the treaty bodies' country rapporteurs. The NHRI has submitted observations to treaty bodies' reports, as well as relied on the treaty bodies in domestic proceedings and when making statements, for example on reproductive rights and women on corporate boards. The NHRI has also participated (with the right to take the floor) in the UN Open-Ended Working Group on Ageing since 2016.

Additionally, the NHRI's office has fulfilled the role of the National Preventive Mechanism (NPM) under OP-CAT since 2008. In this role the NHRI has been involved in carrying out numerous visits to places of detention, initiated campaigns, as well as brought cases to courts including the Constitutional Tribunal. Since the ratification of CRPD, the NHRI has also been acting as the independent mechanism under article 33 of CRPD.

Since 2000 Poland has had a Commissioner for Children's Rights, who is responsible for safeguarding the rights of the child as defined in the Constitution, CRC and other legal provisions, respecting the responsibility, rights and obligations of parents. While the Commissioner for Children's Rights is not formally an NHRI, it has also been involved in the reporting procedure with the CRC and in promoting CRC standards, albeit at times only instrumentally.

4.2.4 Impact on and through Non-state Actors

NGOs have been involved in the reporting process and the monitoring of the implementation of recommendations, as well as in promoting the standards of the treaty bodies, for example through preparing guidance manuals, informing about the work of committees when Poland is on the agenda and releasing statements.[84] Coalitions of NGOs to initiate various activities have been formed in particular around CEDAW, CRPD and CRC. The one reporting process that has received significantly less attention from NGOs is CESCR.

RPO-598265-I/08, 15 September 2008. It is also worth paying attention to the exemplary cooperation between Adam Bodnar as the Commissioner (term 2015–2021) and non-governmental organisations, Nadażdin Draginja, Director of Amnesty International Poland (term 2007–2021), 29 May 2021, on-line interview.

84 For instance, Amnesty International Poland, when preparing the statement on the presidential elections in 2020 during the COVID-19 pandemic, recalled the international human rights standards, in particular UN standards, that the state has a duty to ensure that all persons included in the electoral process were able to exercise their rights and freedoms without any obstacles; Nadażdin Draginja, Director of Amnesty International Poland (term 2007–2021), 29 May 2021, on-line interview. The statement is available on the website <https://amnesty.org.pl/wp-content/uploads/2020/04/Stanowisko-AI_-Druk-senacki-nr-99-22042020.pdf> accessed 11 April 2021.

Generally, non-state actors have played a crucial role in strengthening the impact of the treaty bodies. An interesting trend is the recent interest in the UN human rights system by the ultra-conservative organisation *Ordo Iuris*. The organisation has submitted alternative reports to CAT and CRC, stating that the 'system of counteracting domestic violence in Poland is one of the most effective in Europe', and calling for tougher protection of 'unborn children'. In its submissions it included a solid, albeit biased, legal analysis of international human rights law.

4.2.5 Impact of State Reporting

Poland's responses to treaty bodies' COs show that progress has been made. Clearly, over the last three decades Poland's legislative framework has seen significant changes and is more in line with UN human rights standards. At the same time, many changes – including those invoked by state authorities within the reporting procedure – are implemented for other reasons, such as EU law. Authorities have also used treaty bodies in a token way, for example, the right to life in CRC has been invoked in legislation aimed towards restricting abortion law, which remains contrary to the COs and the interpretation of the CRC Cttee. Some cross-cutting topics have been raised by many treaty bodies and have yet to be adopted, such as addressing reproductive rights, gender-based and domestic violence, as well as hate speech. With regard to other subjects, state authorities have also disagreed with the treaty bodies. For example, the CAT Cttee insists on the inclusion of the CAT definition of torture in the Criminal Code, which has been rejected by state authorities, who argue that all the elements specified in the definition of torture in CAT are already encompassed within the Criminal Code. An increase in disagreements between treaty bodies and the government of Poland can be observed since the post-2015 constitutional breakdown. For example, in 2018 the CEDAW Cttee stated that it found Poland's follow-up unsatisfactory, and considered its recommendations not to have been implemented or implemented only partially. Similarly, the HRCttee in 2016 raised concerns about the negative impact of legislative reforms, in particular with regard to the Constitutional Tribunal, which were met with disagreement by state authorities.

4.2.6 Impact of Individual Communications

Overall, 10 communications have been submitted to treaty bodies against Poland, eight to the HRCttee and two to the CEDAW Cttee. Most of those cases were found to be inadmissible and only one resulted in a finding of CCPR being violated.[85] One communication was also brought to the HRCttee by Polish citizens against Russia. It concerned Polish prisoners of war killed during the Katyń massacres in 1940 and was ruled inadmissible.[86] While individual communications can also be brought to the CAT Cttee and CERD Cttee, no cases have yet been submitted. The relatively low use of the communication procedure appears to be due to the high popularity of the ECtHR in Poland, coupled with a low level of recognition of the treaty bodies. Although familiar with this procedure, human rights NGOs rarely use it for strategic litigation. It is employed mostly in cases which, due to some reasons (for instance, temporal issues), do not qualify for the ECtHR. The financial burden related to lodging complaints to the treaty bodies also plays a role.[87]

The individual communication procedure has not yet been accepted for three treaty bodies (CESCR, CRC and CRPD). The reasons raised by the authorities for not accepting these procedures include in particular controversies over the justiciability of claims in the areas of economic, social and cultural rights. The subsequent governments were reluctant to implement the complaint mechanism due to unpredictable financial implications and the alleged influence of treaty bodies on domestic policies.

4.2.7   Impact of Other Measures – Visits by SPT

OP-CAT was ratified in 2006, and the first visit of the Subcommittee on Prevention of Torture and Other Cruel, Inhuman or Degrading Treatment or Punishment (SPT) to Poland was conducted in 2018. While the very short time since the adoption of the recommendation (January 2020) does not allow for analysing the impact of the visit, the SPT pointed out the main challenges, such as the strengthening of anti-torture guarantees, including the definition of torture in the Penal Code and access to lawyers. The SPT report has been mentioned during parliamentary discussion on the use of violence by the police on those taking part in mass protests following the judgment of the Constitutional Tribunal in October 2020 limiting access to abortion.

---

85   HRCttee, *Fijalkowska v Poland* (4 August 2005).
86   HRCttee, *KK and Others v Russia* (16 January 2020).
87   In contrast to applications to the ECHR which can be lodged in Polish, communications to the treaty bodies together with appended documents need to be translated, which incurs significant costs. Marcin Wolny, Lawyer, Helsinki Foundation for Human Rights, 21 May 2021, on-line interview.

5 Detailed Impact of the Different UN Human Rights Treaties on the Domestic Level in Poland

5.1 *International Convention on the Elimination of All Forms of Racial Discrimination*

5.1.1 Incorporation and Reliance by Legislature and Executive

CERD was ratified by Poland in 1968. A number of the CERD Cttee's important recommendations have been realised through changes introduced during the democratic transition that began in 1989, for example through securing minority rights in the 1997 Constitution,[88] and adopting the 2001 law on ethnic and national minorities.[89]

The CERD and the CERD Cttee have been raised a number of times in Parliament, during discussions about political parties or organisations that promote or incite racial discrimination. In 2017 a far-right parliamentarian criticised the fact that the Ministry of Home Affairs was taking action against several far-right organisations and requested action to be taken against the relevant civil servants.[90] When responding to the inquiry, the governmental official mentioned that the initiative that led to those actions was created in order to realise international human rights obligations, including CERD.[91] The 2019 CERD COs (22nd to 24th periodic review of Poland) included 'ensuring effective enforcement of the laws declaring illegal parties or organisations which promote or incite racial discrimination' followed by a list of organisations.[92] The realisation of this recommendation was the subject of an inquiry,[93] to which governmental authorities responded that the CERD Cttee's recommendation was to 'ensure effective enforcement of the laws' and not 'declaring the organisation illegal'.[94] In fact, the listed organisations are still functioning. At

---

[88] Constitution of the Republic of Poland, 2 April 1997, Dz.U. of 1997, No. 78, item 483.

[89] A Gliszczyńska-Grabias, 'Funkcjonowanie procedury sprawozdawczej do Komitetu do Spraw Likwidacji Dyskryminacji Rasowej w odniesieniu do Polski' in R Wieruszewski (ed), *Mechanizmy ochrony praw człowieka w ramach ONZ. Analiza systemowa* (CH Beck 2017) 310–311. On the law on ethnic and national minorities, see also G Baranowska, 'Legal Regulations on National and Ethnic Minorities in Poland' (2014) 2 *Przegląd Zachodni*.

[90] Parliamentary inquiry 9581 to the Minister of Home Affairs and Administration, 25 January 2017.

[91] Official response to inquiry 9581 to the Minister of Home Affairs and Administration, 2 March 2017.

[92] CERD Cttee, COs on the 22nd to 24th periodic review of Poland, para 18(a).

[93] Parliamentary inquiry 157 to the Minister of Home Affairs and Administration, 24 November 2019.

[94] Official response to inquiry 157 to the Minister of Home Affairs and Administration, 11 February 2020.

the same time, the CERD Cttee is not always mentioned when organisations promoting or inciting racial hatred are discussed in Parliament; sometimes only other treaty bodies are mentioned (the CED Cttee, the CAT Cttee).[95]

The CERD and CERD Cttee have also been mentioned in the context of adopting policies for equal treatment,[96] to counteract discrimination[97] and in the context of the situation of the Roma minority in Poland. During a parliamentary discussion in 2020, the Commissioner for Human Rights (NHRI) highlighted that the CERD Cttee paid much attention to the support, everyday functioning and living conditions of the Roma community when reviewing Poland's reports.[98]

5.1.2 Reliance by Judiciary

CERD has been relied upon by domestic courts when adjudicating cases concerning racially-motivated violence and hate speech. Courts have stated that relevant provisions of the Criminal Code should be interpreted taking into account CERD standards.[99] When the Constitutional Tribunal analysed whether the term 'incitement to hatred' (*nawoływanie do nienawiści*) used in the Criminal Code was accurate enough to guarantee freedom of speech and scientific research, it also relied on obligations arising from CERD.[100] Similarly, when examining racial motivation of violence as an aggravating factor, courts have relied on CERD, invoking the obligations arising from article 4.[101]

Another subject matter in which CERD has been invoked by domestic courts concerned the limits of freedom of assembly. In a case brought against a number of demonstrators who were attempting to stop a protest by far-right groups, the District Court invoked the CERD Cttee's decision in *The Jewish Community of Oslo and Others v Norway*,[102] and acquitted them of the alleged offences.[103] In another, very similar, case, the Court went even further and added a two-paragraph analysis of treaty body case law, by invoking the way in which the HRCttee and the CERD Cttee have tackled 'hate speech', in particular in the

---

[95] See for example Official response to inquiry 21624 to the Ministry of Justice, 22 April 2011.
[96] Record of the parliamentary meeting, 14 September 2020.
[97] Parliamentary inquiry 6608 to the Prime Minister, 13 February 2007.
[98] See for example Record of the parliamentary meeting, 25 February 2020.
[99] Appellate Court in Warszawa judgment of 22 September 2017, II AKa 247/17.
[100] Constitutional Tribunal judgment of 24 February 2014, SK 65/12.
[101] Appellate Court in Gdańsk judgment of 19 July 2018, II AKa 192/18; for similar reasoning see also Appellate Court in Warszawa judgment of 23 December 2020, V W 2569/19.
[102] CERD Cttee, *The Jewish Community of Oslo and Others v Norway* (15 August 2004).
[103] District Court in Sieradz judgment of 19 July 2013, I C 114/11; for similar reasoning, see also District Court in Warszawa judgment of 5 March 2019, XI W 717/18.

context of freedom of assembly. The Court stated that, according to the CERD Cttee case law, racist statements violated the rights of all members of the relevant group, even when it is not directly directed at specific persons.[104]

5.1.3 Impact on and through Independent State Institutions

In 2019 the NHRI submitted observations to the report of Poland, which was the first time such comments were submitted to a Polish report to the CERD Cttee. The document contains comments on the implementation of the 2014 CERD Cttee recommendations in four areas: bodies established under international human rights treaties, incitement to hatred and hate crimes, the situation of national and ethnic minorities (in particular Roma and Jewish communities) and discrimination against citizens of other countries.[105] The NHRI has also been involved in the constructive dialogue, including by participating in the informal meetings with the CERD Cttee's rapporteur on the Polish report.[106] Additionally, in March 2021 the NHRI submitted final comments on the implementation of several 2019 CERD Cttee recommendations.[107]

The NHRI has not only been involved in the reporting process, but has also invoked CERD and the CERD Cttee during its work. For example, it cooperates with the Polish Football Association to counteract racism, xenophobia and discrimination in football, *inter alia* in response to the CERD Cttee's recommendations.[108] The NHRI has also invoked CERD in cases brought to the prosecutor's office concerning incitement to racial hatred. In 2018 it did so with regard to an anti-refugee and anti-Muslim election commercial.[109]

---

104   District Court in Warszawa judgment of 4 October 2018, XI W 2059/17.
105   CERD, Observations of the Commissioner for Human Rights of the Republic of Poland concerning measures aimed at the implementation of the provisions of the Convention on the elimination of all forms of racial discrimination in the years 2014–2019.
106   Magdalena Kuruś, Director Department for Equal Treatment in the Office of the Commissioner for Human Rights, 27 May 2021, on-line interview.
107   CERD, Observations and remarks of the Commissioner for Human Rights on Poland's implementation of recommendations contained in point 10(a), point 12, point 16(b), (c) and (d) and point 18(a) of the Concluding remarks of the Committee on the Elimination of Racial Discrimination presented after examining the joint XXII and XXIV periodic report submitted by Poland (CERD/C/POL/CO/22–24).
108   Commissioner for Human Rights statement, 28 June 2019. The election commercial is still available for viewing on the official Twitter account of the ruling party; see <https://twitter.com/pisorgpl/status/1052530980190334977?s=20> accessed 11 April 2022.
109   Commissioner for Human Rights address to the District Court in Warsaw, XI.518.66.2018.MS, 23 September 2018.

5.1.4 Impact on and through Non-state Actors

In 2019 six civil society organisations submitted information to the CERD Cttee, a significant increase compared with earlier reporting processes (two submissions in 2014 and one in 2009). The only organisation that has participated in all three previous reporting cycles is the Helsinki Foundation for Human Rights.[110] The topics mentioned in the report cover racial discrimination (including against migrants), hate crimes, anti-semitism and the activities of the far-right movement in Poland. The submissions also highlighted the underfunding of the NHRI.

5.1.5 Impact of State Reporting[111]

Poland has so far submitted 15 reports to CERD, the first one in 1970 and the most recent in August 2018. Throughout this time, and in particular after the 1989 democratic transition, legislation has overwhelmingly come into line with CERD. Most of the CERD Cttee's recommendations with regard to amending or adopting laws have been substantially realised, and much of the COs in the recent reporting cycles are devoted to implementation and effective policies. For example, in 2019 the CERD Cttee recommended providing the NHRI with necessary human and financial resources, in particular its Department of Equal Treatment, as well as the Governmental Plenipotentiary for Equal Treatment.[112] The CERD Cttee has also been very vocal with regard to the situation of the Roma. The recommendations relate not only to legislative changes, but to better implementation of existing laws and policies.[113]

A recurring subject remains that of hate speech and hate crimes, as the CERD Cttee disagrees with Poland's approach on two issues, recommending two major changes in the legislation: firstly, to ensure that the definition of hate speech in the Criminal Code is in line with the Convention, in particular including all grounds of discrimination recognised in article 1 of CERD; second, to make a racist motive for a crime an aggravated circumstance.[114] In its response to the 2019 COs, Polish authorities informed the CERD Cttee about the

---

110 Helsińska Fundacja Praw Człowieka <https://www.hfhr.pl/> accessed 11 April 2022.
111 In this section findings from a research project 2012/07/B/HS5/03727 funded by the National Science Centre are included see Gliszczyńska-Grabias (n 89) 305–318.
112 CERD Cttee, COs on the 22nd to 24th periodic review of Poland, paras 10, 12.
113 ibid paras 21–22. See also in older COs, for example, CERD Cttee, COs on the 17th, 18th and 19th periodic review of Poland, paras 4 and 5.
114 CERD Cttee, COs on the 22nd to 24th periodic review of Poland, para 16; CERD Cttee, COs on the 20th and 21st periodic review of Poland, para 8.

realisation of the second recommendation.[115] Through an amendment to the Criminal Code in June 2019, violent offences motivated by hatred because of the victim's national, ethnic, racial, political or religious affiliation or because of the victim's lack of religious denomination were added as circumstances incriminating the perpetrator of the act. While this certainly is in line with the CERD Cttee recommendation, the substantiation of the act does not mention CERD or the CERD Cttee.[116] Additionally, the law did not enter into force, as before signing the President referred it to the Constitutional Tribunal, which declared it unconstitutional.[117]

The adoption of the 2010 Anti-Discrimination Act implementing certain European directives on equal treatment[118] also positively advanced domestic legislation in light of the CERD. While the reason for the Act's adoption arose from EU law, in the aspect which concerned discrimination because of ethnic and national reasons, it also advanced CERD, which has been noted by the CERD Cttee.[119] The justification of the 2010 Anti-Discrimination Act did not mention CERD, but indicated that the principle of equality is also guaranteed by the ECHR, CCPR, CESCR and 'several other conventions of a more detailed character'[120] which, one can assume, also includes CERD.

In 2013 the Prime Minister established a Council for the Prevention of Racial Discrimination, Xenophobia and Related Intolerance,[121] which was dissolved in 2016,[122] shortly after the constitutional breakdown[123] began. This action has been criticised by the CERD Cttee, which recommended that Polish authorities re-establish the body or 'establish an alternative multi-stakeholder institution with a similar mandate'.[124] In response the Polish authorities mentioned the appointment in February 2018 of an inter-ministerial team for 'countering the promotion of fascism or other totalitarian systems or offences of incitement to hatred based on national, ethnic, race or religious differences or for reason

---

115 Information received from Poland on follow-up to the COs on its 22nd to 24th periodic reports, CERD/C/POL/FCO/22–24, para 54.
116 Druk sejmowy No 128 from 12 December 2019.
117 Constitutional Tribunal judgment of 14 July 2020, Kp 1/19.
118 Law of 3 December 2010, Dz.U. of 2010, No 254, item 1700.
119 CERD Cttee, COs on the 29th and 21st periodic review of Poland, para 4(c).
120 Druk sejmowy No 3386 of 16 September 2010.
121 Regulation of the Prime Minister of 13 February 2013, MP 2013 poz 79.
122 Regulation of the Prime Minister of 27 April 2016, MP 2016 poz 413. The NHRI criticised dissolving the Council in a statement of 6 May 2016.
123 Sadurski (n 17).
124 CERD Cttee, COs on the 22nd to 24th periodic review of Poland, paras 11(b); 12(b).

of lack of any religious denomination'.[125] The aim of the team was to identify emerging issues, which were then to be handed over for execution to ministries, public prosecutors, the police, and so forth. While the CERD Cttee has not yet responded to those initiatives, it is very unlikely that they will find this satisfactory. First, this clearly is not a multi-stakeholder institution. Second, it was a one-time initiative and not a long-term commitment to change. Third, both the name of the body and the initiative pursued show that at the heart of it 'counteracting fascism and other totalitarian systems' is more important than reacting to racial discrimination and xenophobia. Finally, the CERD Cttee has repeatedly urged Poland to better disseminate the results of the reporting process. The lack of this significantly hinders the impact of the process.[126]

5.1.6   Impact of Individual Communications

While Poland accepted CERD's individual complaints procedure in 1999, to date no communication has been brought against Poland.

5.1.7   Brief Conclusion

CERD has for over five decades been in force with regard to Poland. The substantial legislative and political changes that took place during this time have significantly advanced the situation in the country to be better in line with CERD. However, this has predominantly resulted from changes brought about by the democratic transition. There are still topics that have not yet been well addressed, in particular hate crimes and hate speech, as well as the banning of far-right groups. With the rising acceptance of such views and activities that accompanied the post-2015 constitutional breakdown, this situation will most likely be further intensified and visible in the next reporting cycle.

5.2   *International Covenant on Civil and Political Rights*

5.2.1   Incorporation and Reliance by Legislature and Executive

CCPR was signed by Poland on 2 March 1967 without reservations. Three months after its ratification in 1977, the document entered into force. Poland accepted the individual complaints procedure under OP1-CCPR in 1991, making a reservation to exclude the procedure set out in article 5(2)(a), in cases where the matter has already been examined under another procedure of

---

125   Information received from Poland on follow-up to the COs on its 22nd to 24th periodic reports, CERD/C/POL/FCO/22–24, paras 3–5.
126   CERD Cttee, COs on the 22nd to 24th periodic review of Poland, para 29; Gliszczyńska-Grabias (n 89) 317–318.

international investigation or settlement. OP2-CCPR, aimed at the abolition of the death penalty, was signed by Poland in 2000 and ratified in 2014.

The current Polish Constitution was adopted 20 years after CCPR became effective with respect to Poland. It has been pointed out that CCPR, similar to ECHR, had an important impact on constitutionalising fundamental rights.[127] During the sessions of the Constitutional Commission of the National Assembly in the 1990s, CCPR was mentioned numerous times.[128] The text of the Constitution contains neither direct references to the Covenant, nor other international human rights law. Nevertheless, the constitutional catalogue of rights and freedoms is similar to the treaty catalogue.

In the period between 30 June 1999 and 30 June 2019, CCPR and the HRCttee were referred to numerous times directly by the legislature in parliamentary debates – mostly speaking about the treaty's rights and freedoms (for instance, the right to freedom of expression, the right to non-discrimination, the right to freedom of association) or paying attention to the HRCttee's observations on Poland (for example, on abortion law, discrimination and the protection of minorities).[129] In one instance a member of parliament brought forward a motion to amend the criminal law proposed by his party, *inter alia*, citing its compliance with CCPR.[130] Another example is the member of parliament who argued in a parliamentary debate that the conscience clause for doctors should be removed due to, *inter alia*, the HRCttee's observations on the availability of reproductive health services for women.[131]

It is worth noting that a part of the parliamentary discussion in 2013 was dedicated to the ratification of OP2-CCPR.[132] CCPR and the HRCttee were also mentioned numerous times in questions, enquiries and statements by members of parliament. In most cases the references were merely a citation of the name of CCPR or the HRCttee, but sometimes the treaty and committee were

---

127 E Łętowska, 'O znaczeniu praw człowieka dla polskiego systemu prawa' in T Jasudowicz and C Mik (eds), *O prawach człowieka. W podwójną rocznicę Paktów. Księga Pamiątkowa w hołdzie Profesor Annie Michalskiej* (Dom Organizatora TNOiK 1996) 119.

128 For a discussion on the rights and freedoms catalogue in the Constitution, see for instance Constitutional Commission of the National Assembly, 22–24th session held on 7–20 March 1995, Bulletin XV 18, 21, 23–25, 42, 46, 49, 55, 106–107; Constitutional Commission of the National Assembly, 25–26th session held on 21–22 March 1995, Bulletin XVI 32, 56; Constitutional Commission of the National Assembly, 29–30th session held on 11–12.04.1995, Bulletin XVIII 12.

129 The information collected by the author on analysing online databases of parliamentary works.

130 Record of the parliamentary meeting, 14 February 2001.

131 Record of the parliamentary meeting, 7 February 2014.

132 Record of the parliamentary meeting, 25 July 2013.

referred to more broadly. For instance, the Undersecretary of State, responding to an enquiry regarding provisions on redemption and refusal to initiate proceedings by courts and prosecutor's offices, pointed out that domestic law exceeded the international standards established in the ECHR and CCPR, granting individuals a wider scope of the right to court.[133] Members of parliament sometimes ask about the implementation of COs, for example, in 2006 one of the members of parliament asked the Prime Minister about actions taken in relation to the report published by the HRCttee on Poland in the seventh reporting cycle.[134]

Direct references to CCPR can be found in domestic law, but they are not extensive and consist solely of the name of the treaty. For instance, the name of CCPR was directly cited in the Preamble to the educational law of 2016[135] and in some bilateral treaties.[136] In several executive documents, references to CCPR were also indicated. A resolution of the Council of Ministers on the National Counter-Terrorism Programme for 2015–2019 indicated that one of the assumptions of the anti-terrorist programme was to ensure full respect for human rights, not only in accordance with the principles of the Constitution, but also the principles adopted in international documents on human rights, including CCPR.[137] In the decision of the Minister of National Defence on the implementation of the 'Strategy of informing and promoting the defence of the Ministry of National Defence' press staff and military personnel were obliged to comply with the acts of international law ratified by Poland, including CCPR.[138]

5.2.2 Reliance by Judiciary

The impact of CCPR on the judiciary in Poland is significant. The treaty has been relied upon by the Constitutional Tribunal and Supreme Court, as well as by common and administrative courts.

In the period from 30 June 1999 to 30 June 2019, the Constitutional Tribunal has on several occasions made use of its competence to adjudicate the conformity of a domestic law with CCPR. The applications for examination of

---

133   Official response to inquiry 10243 to the Minister of Justice, 23 July 2009.
134   Parliamentary inquiry 8010 to the Prime Minister, 22 November 2016.
135   Law of 14 December 2016, Dz.U. of 2020, item 910.
136   CCPR has been invoked on the occasion of ratification of the bilateral treaties between Poland and Ukraine on cooperation in the field of information (2008), Poland and Kazakhstan on the readmission of people (2016).
137   Resolution of the Council of Ministers of 9 December 2014, MP of 2014, item 1218.
138   Decision of Minister of National Defence of 6 June 2006, D.Urz.MON of 2006, no 13, item 170.

conformity and questions of law concerned, in particular, the right of peaceful assembly;[139] the right to freedom of association with others;[140] the minimum guarantees during criminal proceedings;[141] the *ne bis in idem* principle;[142] the right to a fair trial;[143] every citizen's right to have access, on general terms of equality, to public services in a country;[144] the right to freedom of expression;[145] the *lex retro non agit in mitius* principle;[146] the guarantee not to be compelled to testify against or to confess guilt;[147] the principle of the presumption of innocence;[148] the *lex severior retro non agit* principle;[149] the *lex retro non agit* principle;[150] and the right to liberty and security of the person.[151] In some cases the Constitutional Tribunal found provisions of domestic law compatible,[152] or in others incompatible with CCPR.[153] For instance, as a result of a judgment in which the Constitutional Tribunal found domestic law imposing double penalties on a person in the event of not paying the social insurance

---

139 Constitutional Tribunal judgment of 28 June 2000, K 34/99; Constitutional Tribunal judgment of 18 September 2014, K 44/12.
140 Constitutional Tribunal judgment of 10 April 2002, K 26/00.
141 Constitutional Tribunal judgment of 9 July 2002, P 4/01.
142 Constitutional Tribunal judgment of 8 October 2002, K 36/00; Constitutional Tribunal judgment of 18 November 2010, P 29/09; Constitutional Tribunal judgment of 11 October 2016, K 24/15; Constitutional Tribunal judgment of 23 November 2016, K 6/14; Constitutional Tribunal judgment of 1 December 2016, K 45/14.
143 Constitutional Tribunal judgment of 5 March 2003, K 7/01.
144 Constitutional Tribunal judgment of 20 April 2004, K 45/02; Constitutional Tribunal judgment of 9 December 2015, K 35/15.
145 Constitutional Tribunal judgment of 5 May 2004, P 2/03.
146 Constitutional Tribunal judgment of 31 January 2005, P 9/04.
147 Constitutional Tribunal judgment of 27 June 2008, K 52/07.
148 Constitutional Tribunal judgment of 2 September 2008, K 35/06.
149 Constitutional Tribunal judgment of 13 October 2009, P 4/08.
150 Constitutional Tribunal judgment of 27 October 2010, K 10/08; Constitutional Tribunal judgment of 16 March 2011, K 35/08; Constitutional Tribunal judgment of 23 November 2016, K 6/14.
151 Constitutional Tribunal judgment of 23 November 2016, K 6/14.
152 Constitutional Tribunal judgment of 10 April 2002, K 26/00; Constitutional Tribunal judgment of 9 July 2002, P 4/01; Constitutional Tribunal judgment of 8 October 2002, K 36/00; Constitutional Tribunal judgment of 5 March 2003, K 7/01; Constitutional Tribunal judgment of 5 May 2004, P 2/03; Constitutional Tribunal judgment of 27 June 2008, K 52/07; Constitutional Tribunal judgment of 13 October 2009, P 4/08; Constitutional Tribunal judgment of 18 September 2014, K 44/12; Constitutional Tribunal judgment of 11 October 2016, K 24/15; Constitutional Tribunal judgment of 1 December 2016, K 45/14.
153 Constitutional Tribunal judgment of 20 April 2004, K 45/02; Constitutional Tribunal judgment of 31 January 2005, P 9/04; Constitutional Tribunal judgment of 18 November 2010, P 29/09; Constitutional Tribunal judgment of 16 March 2011, K 35/08; Constitutional Tribunal judgment of 9 December 2015, K 35/15.

contributions or paying the underestimated amount was incompatible with the Constitution and international law, including CCPR, the unfavourable provisions were removed from the legal system.[154] In another judgment, at the initial stage of the post-2015 constitutional breakdown, the Constitutional Tribunal questioned the possibility of shortening the term of office of the president and vice-president of the Tribunal, referring to the amendments introduced as incompatible with the Constitution and international law, including CCPR.[155] Moreover, in many judgments the Constitutional Tribunal referred to CCPR even if it did not use the treaty as a standard for judicial review.[156] For instance, the Constitutional Tribunal, considering an application to examine the conformity of activities of a political party with the Constitution, made an analysis of the freedom of action of political parties in international law, incorporating extensive references to CCPR, and even quoting a commentary to the treaty.[157]

CCPR was also referred to by the Supreme Court.[158] For instance, the Supreme Court in one case stated that the prosecution and punishment for the offences specified in the decree on martial law was possible only after the decree was published, referring to articles 15 and 4(1) and (2) of CCPR.[159] Common courts (regional courts, district courts and appellate courts) also take the treaty's provisions into consideration in judgments,[160] as do administrative courts.[161]

5.2.3   Impact on and through Independent State Institutions

The NHRI, while performing its duties, has on numerous occasions referred to the international law standards, including CCPR. For example, the NHRI

---

[154] Constitutional Tribunal judgment of 18 November 2010, P 29/09.
[155] Constitutional Tribunal judgment of 16 March 2011, K 35/08.
[156] See for instance Constitutional Tribunal judgment of 3 June 2008, K 42/07; Constitutional Tribunal decision of 24 November 2010, Pp 1/08; Constitutional Tribunal judgment of 10 December 2014, K 52/13; Constitutional Tribunal judgment of 26 June 2019, K 16/17.
[157] Constitutional Tribunal decision of 24 November 2010, Pp 1/08.
[158] Supreme Court judgment of 18 August 1999 r., II CKN 321/99; Supreme Court judgment of 17 January 2001, V KKN 542/98. Supreme Court judgment of 27 June 2003 r., III KK 218/03.
[159] Supreme Court judgment of 27 June 2003 r., III KK 218/03.
[160] See for instance Appellate Court in Katowice decision of 15 January 2003, II AKz 1251/02; Appellate Court in Cracow judgment of 31 May 2006, II AKa 78/06; Appellate Court in Cracow judgment of 13 May 2015, I ACa 286/15; Appellate Court in Wrocław judgment of 27 April 2016, II AKz 139/16.
[161] See for instance Supreme Administrative Court decision on 28 October 2009, I OSK 509/09; Supreme Administrative Court judgment of 4 November 2009, II OSK 1741/08; Provincial Administrative Court in Warsaw of 7 November 2017, IV SA/Wa 2095/16.

participated in the proceedings before the District Court in Lublin regarding the decision prohibiting the organisation of a pride parade, highlighting that everyone has the freedom of peaceful assembly and participation under the Constitution and CCPR.[162] Another example is the case of the anti-refugee and anti-Muslim election advertisement, where the NHRI asked the prosecutor to resume proceedings, mentioning that CCPR obliges state parties to penalise behaviour consisting of the promotion of national, racial or religious hatred, inciting discrimination, hostility or rape.[163]

An analysis of the NHRI's annual reports shows that the Commissioner has referred to CCPR and COs. For instance, in one of the annual reports the NHRI described its address to the Minister of Justice for consideration of a legislative initiative to introduce legal solutions guaranteeing the accused the commencement of the compensation procedure before the final decision in the trial is issued. The Minister responded that in his opinion the current regulations complied with CCPR requirements.[164] Another example is when the NHRI commented on the problem of racial, national, ethnic or religious attacks on foreigners living in Poland, it pointed out that these events caused concern at the HRCttee, which was reflected in the COs adopted during the seventh reporting cycle, and directed attention to the HRCttee's conclusion on the insufficient response of the authorities to this type of crime.[165] The NHRI pointed to its own initiatives supporting the implementation of the COs, which consisted of: an address to the Ministry of Justice-Prosecutor General on not bringing civil cases to the jurisdiction of military courts, a question to the same institution about the progress of legislative work on changing the law in the field of wiretapping, and a suggestion to analyse the law regarding to the time of arrest.[166]

The NHRI also cooperates with the HRCttee, takes part in meetings and provides information and opinions, for instance, on the implementation of the

---

162   Commissioner for Human Rights address to the District Court in Lublin, XI.613.8.2018.AK/AS/ABB/MK, 10 October 2018.
163   Commissioner for Human Rights address to the District Court in Warsaw, XI.518.66.2018.MS, 23 September 2018. The election commercial is available for viewing on the official Twitter account of the ruling party <https://twitter.com/pisorgpl/status/1052530980190334977?s=20> accessed 11 April 2022.
164   Commissioner for Human Rights, *Informacja o działalności Rzecznika Praw Obywatelskich w roku 2015 oraz o stanie przestrzegania wolności i praw człowieka i obywatela* 66.
165   Commissioner for Human Rights, *Informacja o stanie przestrzegania wolności i praw człowieka i obywatela w 2016 r. oraz o działalności Rzecznika Praw Obywatelskich* 421.
166   Commissioner for Human Rights, *Informacja Rzecznika Praw Obywatelskich prof. Adama Zielińskiego za 1999 rok* 17–19.

provisions of CCPR in the years 2008 to 2015.[167] It is also worth noting that the NHRI addressed the Minister of Justice on the draft sixth periodic report on compliance with the CCPR provisions by Poland for the period from 2003 to 2008, presenting its own observations.[168]

5.2.4 Impact on and through Non-state Actors

One of the non-state actors promoting CCPR is the Polish Bar Council. It has the competence to present opinions and conclusions to Bills during legislative procedures. For example, in an opinion on the restrictive anti-abortion regulation the Council expressed concern about non-compliance of the proposed changes with the international standards of human rights protection, including the infringement of article 7 of CCPR.[169] The treaty is also used by legal professionals before courts, in particular when formulating charges in appeal proceedings.[170]

Several NGOs involved with the protection of human rights in Poland have made submissions to the HRCttee with observations and conclusions on the state's reports. During the sixth and seventh reporting cycles statements were submitted by Amnesty International,[171] Helsinki Foundation for Human

---

[167] Commissioner for Human Rights, Information provided by the Commissioner for Human Rights of the Republic of Poland (Rzecznik Praw Obywatelskich) in accordance with the International Covenant on Civil and Political Rights in connection with the consideration of the seventh periodic report of the Republic of Poland covering the period from 15 October 2008 until 31 October 2015, 6 October 2016. Furthermore, the representatives of the Commissioner's office presented the reports on the observance of human rights in Poland from the perspective of the Commissioner at the forum of the HRCttee (see, for instance, Commissioner for Human Rights, *Informacja o działalności Rzecznika Praw Obywatelskich za rok 2010 oraz o stanie przestrzegania wolności i praw człowieka i obywatela* 405; Commissioner for Human Rights, *Informcja o działalności Rzecznika Praw Obywatelskich oraz o stanie przestrzegania wolności i praw człowieka i obywatela w roku 2016* 688; Commissioner for Human Rights, *Informacja o stanie przestrzegania wolności i praw człowieka i obywatela w 2017 r. oraz o działalności Rzecznika Praw Obywatelskich* 639).

[168] Commissioner for Human Rights address to the Undersecretary of State in the Ministry of Justice, RPO-598265-I/08, 15 September 2008.

[169] Polish Bar Council's opinion on the draft of the Law 2146, NRA.12-SM-1.4.2018, 15 January 2018.

[170] See for instance Provincial Administrative Court in Gorzow Wielkopolski judgment of 29 December 2009, II SA/Go 796/09; Supreme Administrative Court judgment of 22 June 2006, I OSK 1270/05; Appellate Court in Warsaw judgment of 29 December 2014, II AKa 442/14; Supreme Court decision of 26 February 2002, I CKN 413/01; Supreme Court judgment of 4 September 2003, IV CKN 420/01.

[171] Amnesty International, *Poland: Submission to the UN HRCttee. 118th session*, 17 Oct-Nov 2016.

Rights[172] and *Ordo Iuris*, supported by others.[173] Furthermore, joint organisation reports were submitted.[174] For example, Amnesty International Poland expressed concerns about changes in Poland when the conservative Law and Justice Party won the election, highlighting 148 new laws and legislative amendments, reversed developments indicated in Poland's submission to the HRCttee in 2015, the lack of progress in protection from discrimination and hate crimes and violations of sexual and reproductive rights.[175] NGOs also perform an educational role, preparing manuals containing international human rights protection standards arising from CCPR, among other treaties.[176]

CCPR and the HRCttee appear in researchers' and academics' works. Researchers from the Poznań Human Rights Centre, the Institute of Law Studies of the Polish Academy of Sciences in 2012 prepared the first and the only Polish Commentary to CCPR and its Optional Protocols.[177]

5.2.5 Impact of State Reporting[178]

In the period from 30 June 1999 to 30 June 2019 Poland submitted three periodic reports to the HRCttee. Some of the observations issued by the

---

[172] Helsinki Foundation for Human Rights, Comments to the list of issues prior reporting submitted for consideration of the UN Human Rights Committee in reference to the session no 111, 16 June 2014; Helsinki Foundation for Human Rights, Submission to the HRCttee 118th session, October 2016.

[173] *Ordo Iuris* Institute for Legal Culture Alternative, Alternative Follow-up Report to the Human Rights Committee on Poland's Follow-up Report.

[174] Federation for Women and Family Planning, Campaign Against Homophobia, Women's Rights Centre, Report and the update paper to the UN Human Rights Committee in connection with the 6th Periodic Review of Poland; Polish Society of Antidiscrimination Law (coordinator of the report works), Federation for Women and Family Planning, TUS Foundation, Trans-Fuzja Foundation, Open Republic – Association Against Anti-Semitism and Xenophobia, Campaign Against Homophobia, KARAT Coalition, Alternative report to the CCPR submitted by the Polish informal coalition for the CCPR for consideration of the HRCttee in reference to the session no 118, 21 July 2016.

[175] Amnesty International, Poland: Submission to the HRCttee, 118th session, 17 Oct-Nov 2016.

[176] See for instance Amnesty International, *Podręcznik sprawiedliwego procesu. Wydanie drugie* <https://www.amnesty.org.pl/wp-content/uploads/2019/07/Podrecznik-Sprawiedliwego-Procesu-Amnesty-wydanie-PL-WEB.pdf> accessed 11 September 2023.

[177] R Wieruszewski (ed), *Międzynarodowy pakt praw obywatelskich (osobistych) i politycznych. Komentarz* (Wolters Kluwer 2012).

[178] In this section findings from a research project 2012/07/B/HS5/03727 funded by the National Science Centre are included; see R Wieruszewski (ed), 'Funkcjonowanie procedury sprawozdawczej do Komitetu Praw Człowieka w odniesieniu do Polski' in R Wieruszewski (ed), *Mechanizmy ochrony praw człowieka w ramach ONZ. Analiza systemowa* (CH Beck 2017) 297–303.

HRCttee[179] were repeated in subsequent cycles. Indeed, in consecutive COs, the HRCttee specified the same problems as before, including no information on investigations into the detention of people accused of terrorism in a secret prison; no provisions guaranteeing protection against discrimination on all grounds mentioned in CCPR; the significant number of female victims of domestic violence and the lack of proper protection mechanisms; the limited participation of women in public life and in the private sector; wage gaps and gender biases and stereotypes; the significant number of illegal abortions that threaten women's lives and health; no provisions protecting victims of human trafficking; insufficient progress in limiting the excessive use of pre-trial detention; the excessive length of court proceedings; limited access to legal aid for detained persons; and the failure to respect the length of contact with a lawyer.[180] In the opinion of Roman Wieruszewski, former member of the HRCttee, 'such a large number of repeated recommendations indicate that they have not been properly responded to by state authorities'.[181]

Particular attention should be paid to the HRCttee's observations after the post-2015 constitutional breakdown. The HRCttee expressed concerns about the negative impact of legislative reforms, including the amendments to the law on the Constitutional Tribunal and about the Prime Minister's refusal to publish the Tribunal's judgment. Thus, the HRCttee recommend that Poland should ensure respect for and protection of the integrity and independence of the Constitutional Tribunal and its judges and ensure the implementation of all its judgments.[182] In response to this recommendation, Poland informed HRCttee that the changes implemented have in no way undermined the Constitutional Tribunal's independence, and that there are no obstacles that could hinder the institution from performing its duties.[183] A completely different opinion on this matter was expressed by NGOs in their alternative reports, claiming that the serious constitutional crisis in Poland had affected the functioning of domestic human rights protection.[184]

---

179   5–7 Report, CCPR, Poland.
180   Wieruszewski (n 178) 300–301.
181   ibid 301.
182   HRCttee, COs on the 7th periodic report of Poland, CCPR/C/POL/CO/7 para 8.
183   Poland's information on follow-up to the COs, CCPR/C/POL/CO/7/Add.1, para 1.
184   Amnesty International, Submission to the HRCttee, 118th session, 17 Oct-Nov 2016. Poland 6–8; Helsinki Foundation for Human Rights, Submission to the HRCttee 118th session, October 2016; p 3–7.

5.2.6 Impact of Individual Communications[185]

The HRCttee has considered eight individual complaints against Poland. Over the period from 30 June 1999 to 30 June 2019, four complaints were submitted, and seven were finalised;[186] with the HRCttee finding five communications inadmissible;[187] and adopting views under article 5(4) of OP1-CCPR in two communications,[188] finding in one that article 9(1) of CCPR had been violated.[189]

In the case of *Fijalkowska v Poland* the author, suffering from schizophrenic paranoia, claimed that her committal to a psychiatric institution against her will and the treatment she received during her confinement amounted to a violation of article 7 of CCPR. The HRCttee noted that no arguments or further information were provided to consider these allegations admissible, but the HRCttee assumed that the facts before it raised issues under the Covenant that were admissible and should be considered on the merits. The HRCttee found that the author's committal was arbitrary under article 9(1) of CCPR as no special circumstances had been advanced as to the issuance of a committal order without assistance or representation sufficient to safeguard her rights. Furthermore, the HRCttee noted that the author's right to challenge her detention was rendered ineffective by the state party's failure to serve the committal order on her prior to the deadline to lodge an appeal and found a violation of

---

185 For further details, see K Łasak, 'Individual Communications Against Poland Before the Human Rights Committee: A Review and Tentative Conclusions' (2017) 7 Adam Mickiewicz University Law Review 55–78.

186 According to the e-mail information received by the author from the Ministry of Foreign Affairs, as at the date of sending the information (28 April 2021), the Ministry has knowledge about 12 complaints brought against Poland. Two of these complaints were closed – *Jan Piwowarczyk v Poland*, Communication 955/2000, for the reason of lost contact with the author, see Report of the Human Rights Committee. Volume I. 79th session (20 October-7 November 2003); 80th session (15 March-2 April 2004); 81st session (5–30 July 2004), A/59/40, para 87 and *Getke Barbara and Mirosław v Poland*, Communication 1025/2001, for the reason of failure to respond to the Committee by the author or counsel despite repeated reminders; see Report of the Human Rights Committee. Volume I. 88th session (16 October-3 November 2006); 89th session (12–30 March 2007); 90th session (9–27 July 2007), A/62/40, para 98. The other two complaints (*Biltaev Arbi and Dovletmurzaeva Petimat v Poland*, Communication 3017/2017 and *Uzhakhov Bagaudin v Poland*, Communication 3870/2021) have not yet been resolved by the Committee.

187 HRCttee, *Kurowski v Poland* (11 April 2003); HRCttee, *Kolanowski v Poland* (29 August 2003); HRCttee, *Bator v Poland* (4 August 2005); HRCttee, *Wdowiak v Poland* (23 November 2006); HRCttee, *MG v Poland* (27 August 2015).

188 HRCttee, *Fijalkowska v Poland* (4 August 2005); HRCttee, *Rastorgueva v Poland* (28 April 2011). See also HRCtee, *Wieslaw Kall v Poland* (14 July 1997), decided before 30 June 1999.

189 HRCttee, *Fijalkowska v Poland* CCPR/C/84/1061/2002 (26 July 2005).

article 9(4) of CCPR.[190] The Committee considered the state party to be under the obligation to provide the author with an adequate remedy and make such legislative changes as are necessary to avoid similar violations in the future. In order to implement the decision of the HRCttee, Poland paid the author compensation. The amount was determined in the course of negotiations with the author and after consultation with the HRCttee, which considered the remedy a satisfactory measure and completed the follow-up procedure.[191] It seems that no legislative changes have been made. However, the applicable regulations provided a possibility to appoint *ex officio* a defence counsel for the author to safeguard her rights, but in the mentioned case were not used by a court.

One communication was also brought to the HRCttee by Polish citizens against Russia. It concerned the inadequate investigation into the killing of Polish prisoners of war during the Katyń massacres in 1940 and was ruled inadmissible in 2020.[192] The case was brought to the HRCCttee after the ECtHR had decided a similar application inadmissible.[193] While the Katyń massacre remains an important event commemorated in Poland, and the ECtHR judgment was widely commented on both in academia and in the media, the HRCttee's decision did not receive such attention.

5.2.7 Brief Conclusion

CCPR had a visible impact on the institutionalisation of human rights in the Constitution of 1997. In the past 20 years, references to CCPR and the HRCttee have been made by the legislature, executive and judiciary. However, most of these consisted solely of invoking the name of the treaty or those articles stating a particular right or freedom, without an in-depth analysis of them. In parliamentary debates CCPR is often referred to as an argument to change the law. In the field of the judiciary, the treaty has repeatedly served as a pattern of judicial review for the Constitutional Tribunal, and has been a source of argumentation for other courts. The standards established by CCPR have often been referenced in the activities of NHRI and Polish NGOs involved with the protection of human rights. Considering that the recommendations of the

---

190   ibid para 9.
191   Response of the Ministry of Foreign Affairs of 28 April 2021 provided in reply to the author's request; CCPR, A/62/40 vol. II (2007), Annex IX ('The Committee considers that the remedy to be satisfactory and does not intend to consider this matter any further under the follow-up procedure').
192   HRCttee, *KK and Others v Russia* (16 January 2020).
193   ECtHR, Grand Chamber, *Janowiec and others v Russia* (21 October 2013).

HRC ttee in relation to Poland have been repeated in subsequent reporting cycles, it must be assumed that Poland is reluctant to implement them.

5.3 International Covenant on Economic, Social and Cultural Rights
5.3.1 Incorporation and Reliance by Legislature and Executive

The ratification of CESCR took place in Poland at the same time as that of CCPR, in 1977. The democratic transition in 1989 has opened the Polish legal space to international human rights law. CESCR was an important point of reference during the parliamentary debates of the Constitutional Commission of the National Assembly. Nevertheless, acceptance of the standards developed by the CESCR Cttee remains slow and incomplete.[194] The justiciability of numerous economic, social and cultural rights is repeatedly undermined by public authorities in state party reports submitted to the CESCR Cttee,[195] contrary to the interpretation included in the General Comments 3 and 9 as well as in the preparatory works of Poland's Constitution.[196] Only two rights, namely, the right to form unions and the right to education, have been expressly defined as individual rights that can be directly invoked by an individual before national courts.[197]

CESCR is rarely invoked in parliamentary debates. Issues such as labour rights, domestic violence, unequal treatment and discrimination, and sexual and reproductive health, although falling into the scope of the Covenant, are

---

[194] Z Kedzia, 'Funkcjonowanie procedury sprawozdawczej do Komitetu Praw Gospodarczych, Socjalnych i Kulturalnych w odniesieniu do Polski' in R Wieruszewski (ed), *Mechanizmy ochrony praw człowieka w ramach ONZ. Analiza systemowa* (CH Beck 2017) 335.

[195] In the COs from 2002, the Committee recommended clarifying in the next periodic report, whether individuals may invoke the rights enshrined in CESCR before domestic courts. See CESCR Cttee, COs on the 4th periodic report of Poland, para 33. In the following periodic review in 2009, the Committee expressed its concern that Poland perceives the Covenant as 'programmatic, aspirational and not justiciable' and recommended to ensure full justiciability of the rights enshrined therein. See CESCR Cttee, COs on the 5th periodic report of Poland, para 8. In response to the COs, the government commented that the majority of the CESCR provisions are not self-enforceable and, therefore, cannot be directly applied. See Comments by the government of Poland on the COs, 29 March 2010, E/C.12/POL/CO/5/Add.1 paras 1–6. The same position was taken by the Polish government during the 6th periodic review in 2016. See CESCR Cttee, List of issues in relation to the 6th periodic report of Poland (Addendum) para 1.

[196] For a discussion on the right to work, see Constitutional Commission of the National Assembly, 26th session held on 22 March 1995, Bulletin XVI 85–106. For a discussion on the right to health and right to social security, see Constitutional Commission of the National Assembly, 27–28th session held between 4 and 5 April 1995, bulletin XVII 26–32.

[197] CESCR Cttee, Comments by the government of Poland on the COs, 29 March 2010, E/C.12/POL/CO/5/Add.1 para 4.

instead discussed in the context of interpretation developed by other treaty bodies (for instance, the CEDAW and CRC Cttees) or international organisations (for instance, the International Labour Organisation). CESCR is referred to in a rather tokenistic manner with article 2 (the non-discrimination clause) and article 9 (right to social security) being among the most frequently invoked provisions.[198]

Although rarely mentioned in the official documents, CESCR standards were invoked in the internal discussions within the ministries (for instance, the Ministry of Family and Social Policy) and, therefore, could have some impact on the legislative measures adopted in 2010.[199]

5.3.2   Reliance by Judiciary

The provisions of CESCR are rarely invoked by the judiciary. The constitutional principles oblige public authorities to respect binding international law (article 9) while also securing the direct applicability of international treaties (article 91), including their precedence over statutes.[200] The constitutional catalogue of the economic, social and cultural rights is similar to that included in the Covenant. Nevertheless, some constitutional provisions impose certain limits on the enforceability of certain rights. For instance, article 81 stipulates that certain rights may be asserted only within the limits established by law (for instance, the right to just and favourable conditions of work, certain elements of the right to adequate standard of living).

Public authorities, including the judiciary, have consequently framed most of the economic, social and cultural rights as 'programmatic norms' that oblige public authorities to 'take appropriate steps ... with a view to achieving the realisation of the rights'.[201] Courts have indicated that these rights are granted weaker protection than political rights,[202] cannot be directly applied,[203] and do not expressly provide for individual rights.[204] During the last periodic

---

198   Art 9 of CESCR has been consequently invoked on the occasion of ratification of the bilateral treaties on social security between Poland and Austria (2000), Luxembourg (2000), Spain (2002), The Netherlands (2003), Bulgaria (2006), Macedonia (2006), Canada (2008), the United States (2008) and Turkey (2017).
199   Zdzisław Kędzia, former Chair and member of the CESCR Cttee, 25 May 2021, on-line interview.
200   Constitution of the Republic of Poland, 2 April 1997, Dz U No 78, item 483.
201   Supreme Court Decision II UKN 374/99 of 8 February 2000.
202   Supreme Administrative Court Decision I OSK 2163/15 of 1 March 2017.
203   Supreme Court Decision II UKN 374/99 of 8 February 2000.
204   This claim was made in reference to the right to social security. See Supreme Administrative Court Decision I OSK 8/06 of 16 May 2006.

review, one of the Committee's members indicated that these arguments do not reflect the interpretation of article 2 of the Covenant as elaborated in General Comments 3 and 9.[205]

CESCR, along with the General Comments, was referred to in several cases before the Constitutional Tribunal on the right to social security and the right to form and join trade unions, but they did not play a substantial role in the considerations of the Court.[206] There were also six cases in which article 7 of the Covenant (the right to the enjoyment of just and favourable conditions of work) was invoked as a standard for judicial review, but all cases were subsequently redeemed.[207] References to the General Comments in the case law of lower courts are only incidental.[208]

5.3.3 Impact on and through Independent State Institutions and Non-state Actors

In 2016 the Commissioner for Human Rights (NHRI) for the first time participated in the treaty-monitoring process of the CESCR Cttee and disseminated COs through its website (along with the Polish translation).[209] The NHRI provided a detailed submission highlighting, among other things, systematic discrimination against the Roma community.[210] These findings were taken into account by the CESCR Cttee in drafting the list of issues. Nevertheless, the significance of CESCR standards in the operation of the NHRI remains rather limited. There was no substantive reference to the COs adopted by the CESCR Cttee in the annual reports of the NHRI in the CESCR reporting cycles (2002 and 2009) although these documents typically include highly-detailed information. The situation changed with the election of the Commissioner

---

205 See CESCR Cttee, Summary record of the 55th meeting held at the Palais des Nations, Geneva, on 21 September 2016, E/C.12/2016/SR.55.
206 Constitutional Court judgments K 43/12 of 7 May 2014, SK 17/09 of 29 May 2012, and K 63/07 of 15 July 2010, K 5/15 of 17 November 2015.
207 Constitutional Court judgments P 6/09 of 2 April 2009, P 95/08 of 8 June 2009, P 111/08 of 15 July 2009, P 73/08 of 17 December 2009, P 40/09 of 19 April 2010, K 32/11 of 19 December 2012.
208 District Court in Szczecin judgment of 11 July 2018, VI U 1316/18; District Court in Elbląg judgment of 7 February 2013, IV U 1389/12.
209 The increased activity of the Commissioner for Human Rights is attributable to the election of Adam Bodnar for the position of Commissioner for Human Rights (term 2015–2021). See Commissioner for Human Rights, Rekomendacje Komitetu Praw Gospodarczych, Społecznych i Kulturalnych ONZ dotyczące Polski, 11 October 2016 <https://www.rpo.gov.pl/pl/content/rekomendacje-komitetu-praw-gospodarczych-spolecznych-i-kulturaln ych-onz-dotyczace-polski> accessed 11 April 2022.
210 CESCR Cttee, Polish Commissioner for Human Rights Submission, 15 September 2016.

for the term 2015–2021 and since then its reports include information on its involvement in the reporting process and major issues highlighted in the COs.[211] Nevertheless, in subsequent years references to the CESCR Cttee have remained limited when compared to other treaty bodies.

NGO interest in the work of the CESCR Cttee remains equally limited, best demonstrated by the scarcity of alternative reports submitted during periodic reviews (none in 2002, two in 2009 and only one in 2016). This is significantly less than in other countries in the region, for instance, Lithuania (10 alternative reports during the last three periodic reviews); Slovakia (13 reports); Czechia (14 reports); and Ukraine (26 reports). Moreover, all the reports concerning the situation in Poland were submitted by international NGOs, namely, Amnesty International, the Open Society Institute Global Drug Policy Programme (both in 2009), and the European Anti-Poverty Network (2016).

Economic, social and cultural rights have recently received particular attention in academia, in particular through the publication of the first comprehensive commentary to CESCR (2018).[212] The commentary is addressed to practitioners (judges, lawyers), but it is too early to evaluate its impact.

5.3.4 Impact of State Reporting[213]

Poland has submitted six periodic state reports to the CESCR Cttee, three of which between 2002 and 2016. The next state party report is due in October 2021. In the last periodic review, the NHRI submitted a separate report, and was also present during the consideration of the state report in Geneva. Little interest was expressed by civil society – only one organisation submitted information to the Committee (the European Anti-Poverty Network which is an international NGO).

The Committee noted with appreciation legislative measures in the areas of labour law, health care, combating poverty and exclusion, higher education, as well as integration of the Roma community. At the same time, the most pertinent issues elaborated in the COs included limited justiciability of the Covenant (see the section *Incorporation and reliance by legislature and*

---

[211] Commissioner for Human Rights, *Informacja o stanie przestrzegania wolności i praw człowieka i obywatela w 2016 r. oraz o działalności Rzecznika Praw Obywatelskich*, 2017 484.

[212] Z Kedzia and A Hernandez-Połczyńska, *Międzynarodowy Pakt Praw Gospodarczych, Socjalnych i Kulturalnych. Komentarz* (CH Beck 2018).

[213] In this section findings from a research project 2012/07/B/HS5/03727 funded by the National Science Centre are included; see Z Kedzia, 'Funkcjonowanie procedury sprawozdawczej do Komitetu Praw Gospodarczych, Socjalnych i Kulturalnych w odniesieniu do Polski' in R Wieruszewski (ed), *Mechanizmy ochrony praw człowieka w ramach ONZ. Analiza systemowa* (CH Beck 2017).

executive); non-comprehensive protection against discrimination (for instance, persistent discrimination against Roma); and domestic violence (for instance, the lack of explicit criminalisation of marital rape). A significant number of the recommendations concerned health care, in particular inadequate access to geriatric health care, cardiology and diabetology services, low accessibility of safe and legal abortion services as well as a lack of adequate funding for mental health institutions and the treatment of drug users.

The selected issues highlighted in the COs have been indirectly addressed, *inter alia*, through the progressive increase of social expenditures, in particular for families with children and elderly persons. Between 2000 and 2019 social expenditure increased from 20,2 per cent to 21,3 per cent of the gross domestic product (GDP) (while the OECD average was 20 per cent in 2019).[214] In 2016 OECD reported that public authorities had taken steps to improve housing accessibility and quality, particularly for young people and with relation to social housing, but the results of the policies adopted have so far been limited.[215] At the same time, negative developments can be observed in other areas, in particular reproductive and sexual health (for instance, restrictive abortion laws became even more restrictive in 2020) and severely limited access to healthcare services due to the COVID-19 pandemic. The latter resulted in Poland having the highest cumulative excess death rate among the EU countries in 2020.[216]

5.3.5 Impact of individual communications

Since Poland has not ratified OP-CESCR, no individual communications against it have been considered by the CESCR Cttee. During the negotiations of the Protocol, the Polish delegation was among the group of states that resisted the proposal to establish an individual complaints mechanism for economic, social and cultural rights (together with, among other states, the United States and Saudi Arabia).[217] This position has remained constant ever since, regardless

---

214 OECD, Social Expenditure (SOCX) <https://stats.oecd.org/Index.aspx?DataSetCode=SOCX_AGG> accessed 11 April 2022.
215 D Glocker and M Plouin, 'Overview of Housing Policy Interventions in Poland' OECD Regional Development Working Papers 2016/07, OECD 2016.
216 Office for National Statistics, Comparisons of all-cause mortality between European countries and regions: 2020, <https://www.ons.gov.uk/peoplepopulationandcommunity/birthsdeathsandmarriages/deaths/articles/comparisonsofallcausemortalitybetweeneuropeancountriesandregions/2020> accessed 11 April 2022.
217 Zdzisław Kędzia, former Chair and member of the CESCR Cttee, 25 May 2021, on-line interview. For the official position of the Polish government, see Official response 3745 of the Minister of International Affairs, 2 August 2006.

of the political affiliation of the government. The main reasons behind it are threefold: (i) the risk of an overly broad interpretation of CESCR provisions by the treaty body; (ii) the financial burden of potential settlements; and (iii) the reluctance on the part of the government to be subject to external control in the area of social policies.[218] In the last periodic review in 2016, the Polish government highlighted that the Covenant had been analysed and it had been concluded that a large number of its provisions did not establish individual rights that could give rise to a judicial remedy.[219]

5.3.6 Brief Conclusion

The implementation of standards developed by the CESCR Cttee in Poland remains limited, due to the questioning of the subjectivity and justiciability of CESCR by the executive as well as the judiciary. The position of the Polish government, regardless of political affiliation, has remained consistent in this matter, which is regularly met with concerns from the CESCR Cttee. For this reason, it is also unlikely to expect Poland to join OP-CESCR in the foreseeable future.

5.4 *Convention on the Elimination of All Forms of Discrimination against Women*

5.4.1 Incorporation and Reliance by Legislature and Executive

Poland ratified CEDAW in 1980 and OP-CEDAW in 2003. There are no examples of Polish law that were introduced or amended directly in order to implement CEDAW or the CEDAW Cttee's recommendations. When the Constitution of 1997 was enacted, CEDAW was recalled in the drafting process of an article on gender equality[220] but it played a rather peripheral role and, therefore, cannot be recognised as having a direct impact on this provision. An analysis of the parliamentary debates held between 2000 and 2019 indicates that references to CEDAW can only be traced to rare statements (mostly questions addressed to the government) by a few members of parliament. These were interventions related, for instance, to issues such as anti-discrimination education[221] and

---

218   See, for instance, the official response 20538 of the Deputy Minister (Ministry of Labour and Social Policy), 20 September 2013. See also CESCR Cttee, Replies to the List of Issues in relation to the 6th periodic report of Poland, para 9.
219   CESCR Cttee (n 205) para 1.
220   Eg Record of the meeting of the Constitutional Commission of the National Assembly, 25 February 1997; Record of the meeting of the Constitutional Commission of the National Assembly, 28 February 1997.
221   Parliamentary inquiry 2562 to the Minister of Education, 14 April 2016.

domestic economic violence.[222] Nevertheless, it seems that neither CEDAW, reporting to the CEDAW Cttee, nor its recommendations have ever been extensively tackled by the Polish Parliament. No institutional framework has been established to implement CEDAW.

As far as state policies are concerned, no policy or strategy focused on CEDAW has been established. CEDAW was mentioned in the National Action Plan for Equal Treatment 2013–2016,[223] in the Polish National Action Plan on Women, Peace and Security 2018–2021[224] and in the National Programme to Combat Family Violence 2014–2020.[225] Usually it was merely listed or briefly described among other international obligations and it is difficult to assess whether its provisions had any direct impact on these strategies.

5.4.2 Reliance by Judiciary

Research on the database of all published judgments passed by the Constitutional Tribunal and the Supreme Court reveals that CEDAW was referred to only in a few cases.[226] The examples identified allow for drawing some general conclusions. First, CEDAW was only occasionally invoked by the Constitutional Tribunal and the Supreme Court, mostly in order to support reasoning and draw an international perspective.[227] Second, most of the cases concerned the domain of labour law, particularly with reference to the retirement age, which for decades has been lower for women than for men (except for a short period when it was equalised). It may be interesting to note that CEDAW has been referred to by the Constitutional Tribunal both when it found that the lower retirement age for women did not violate the ban on discrimination based on sex, as well as when it ruled that the equalisation of retirement age did not constitute gender discrimination. In 2010 it considered a motion lodged by the Commissioner for Human Rights who claimed that the different retirement age for men and women violated the constitutional rule of equality of sexes. By referring to article 4(1) of CEDAW, the Constitutional Tribunal did not find it unconstitutional and ascertained it as a temporary special measure

---

222 Parliamentary inquiry 1652 to the Minister of Family, Labour and Social Affairs, 9 March 2016.
223 National Action Plan for Equal Treatment (2013–2016) of 10 December 2013.
224 Polish National Action Plan on Women, Peace and Security (2018–2021) 22 October 2018.
225 The National Programme to Combat Family Violence (2014–2020), MP of 2014, item 445.
226 Research based on the *Lex* database <https://sip.lex.pl> accessed 11 April 2022.
227 Eg Constitutional Tribunal judgment of 28 March 2000, K 27/99; Supreme Court judgment of 19 March 2008, I PK 219/07; Supreme Court judgment of 25 January 2017, II PK 341/15; Supreme Court judgment of 10 July 2019, III UK 191/18.

for women who were double burdened due to work and family duties.[228] As a result of the equalisation of the retirement age in 2012, another motion was recognised in 2014. It was lodged by a trade union which claimed that levelling up and equalising the retirement age was discriminatory against women. The Constitutional Tribunal acknowledged that ongoing social changes, including the evolving position of women in society and family, legitimised the equalisation of retirement age. It referred to international standards, including CEDAW, on the equal right of men and women to social security.[229]

Judgment K 15/99 of the Constitutional Tribunal, passed in 2000, requires special attention since it remains the only case in which Polish law was found to be inconsistent with CEDAW, namely, with article 11 on gender discrimination in the field of employment. This case concerned the law regulating the pharmaceutical trade, the provisions of which included a requirement that the position of pharmacy manager can only be held by a person who had not reached retirement age. Due to the differing retirement ages for women and men, a woman who turned 60 could still work in a pharmacy but she could no longer be a manager, whereas a man could be a manager until he was 65. Challenging this regulation before the Constitutional Tribunal, the Commissioner for Human Rights referred to the provisions of the Polish Constitution on gender equality together with article 11(1)(b) of CEDAW which stipulates the right to the same employment opportunities, including the application of the same criteria for selection in matters of employment. The Tribunal considered such a restriction contrary to the Constitution and international legal obligations undertaken by Poland due to its ratification of CEDAW.

5.4.3 Impact on and through Independent State Institutions

With regard to the state's reports examined by the CEDAW Cttee in 2007 and 2014, the NHRI presented no written submissions. However, the NHRI was consulted when the state's report was drafted.[230] It also submitted follow-up information in 2017.[231] It may be observed that in recent years the NHRI has been eager to address CEDAW in its activities. It has referred to CEDAW while

---

228 Constitutional Tribunal judgment of 15 July 2010, K 63/07.
229 Constitutional Tribunal judgment of 7 May 2014, K 43/12.
230 CEDAW Cttee, Reply to the list of issues: Poland, para 1. As mentioned in part 4.4 on state reporting, since then the practice of the NHRI changed and the NHRI is not providing input to the state report but submitting alternative reports. Magdalena Kuruś, Director Department for Equal Treatment in the Office of the Commissioner for Human Rights, 27 May 2021, on-line interview.
231 Follow-up Information from Commissioner for Human Rights Office, 25 October 2017.

inquiring from the government about various aspects of women's human rights and calling for their implementation. For instance, CEDAW and the CEDAW Cttee's recommendations were recalled in submissions related to reproductive rights[232] and women on corporate boards.[233]

5.4.4 Impact on and through Non-state Actors

CEDAW seems to be an important point of reference, particularly for the women's and other human rights NGOs. This may be seen through their involvement in the reporting procedure and submission of individual communications (see below). In both the reporting cycles of 2007 and 2014 alternative reports prepared by coalitions of NGOs were submitted to the CEDAW Cttee. These were very comprehensive documents covering all aspects of CEDAW.[234] Representatives of NGOs participated in the CEDAW Cttee's sessions, prepared submissions for the sessions, organised lunch briefings and submitted follow-up information. The project 'CEDAW – A tool to combat discrimination', implemented in 2014–2016, is a good example of cooperation within civil society in the name of CEDAW. It was based on the informal 'Coalition for CEDAW', established in 2011, which consisted of 17 Polish NGOs.[235] The project's activities were centred around Poland's reporting to the CEDAW Cttee in 2014. It included preparing information for the CEDAW Cttee, raising awareness about recommendations addressed to Poland, and monitoring their implementation. NHRI was also actively engaged in this project.[236] In addition to the reporting process, CEDAW has been also invoked in NGO lobbying activities aimed at improving legal standards[237] in

---

232 Statement of the Commissioner for Human Rights, VII.5001.2.2016.AM B.
233 Statement of the Commissioner for Human Rights of 31 May 2019, XI.801.14.2016.KW Ż.
234 Shadow report: Republic of Poland, 2006 on the implementation of the Convention on the Elimination of all Forms of Discrimination Against Women submitted to the UN CEDAW Committee by the Federation for Women and Family Planning; Alternative report on the implementation of the Convention on the Elimination of All Forms of Discrimination Against Women (CEDAW), POLAND 2014, submitted to the UN Committee on the Elimination of Discrimination Against Women by KARAT Coalition.
235 The project was run by the Karat Coalition. For more, see <https://www.karat.org/programmes/womens-human-rights/cedaw-a-tool-to-combat-discrimination/> accessed 11 April 2022.
236 For example, it hosted and co-organised round table discussions on various aspects of implementation of CEDAW <https://www.karat.org/pl/programmes/womens-human-rights/cedaw-narzedziem-zwalczania-dyskryminacji/raport-z-monitorowania/> accessed 11 April 2022.
237 See in particular activities of Federation for Women and Family Planning <https://federa.org.pl/> accessed 11 April 2022.

Poland, in particular in relation to reproductive rights and violence against women.[238]

5.4.5 Impact of State Reporting[239]

From 1999 to 2019 the CEDAW Cttee examined three periodic reports of Poland: two in 2007[240] and one in 2014.[241] In 2017 Poland submitted follow-up information, after a 10-month delay and repeated reminders from the CEDAW Cttee.[242] The CEDAW Cttee found most of the government's responses unsatisfactory, and considered its recommendations not to have been implemented or implemented only partially.[243] This demonstrates a lack of engagement by the government in recent years. This may be attributable to the dramatic decline of human rights and democracy after the post-2015 constitutional breakdown,[244] and to the anti-gender equality campaign pursued by some leading politicians, organisations and the hierarchs of the Catholic Church.[245]

An analysis of the state's practice, however, reveals that the poor implementation of the CEDAW Cttee's recommendations has been long-lasting, regardless of the political forces that governed Poland during the last two decades. These findings are based on recommendations on the institutional and legal framework related to CEDAW.

To date, Poland has not established any legal act that would provide comprehensive protection against gender discrimination.[246] What protection exists is fragmented, incomplete and spread across various legal acts, including labour

---

238 See in particular activities of Women's Rights Centre <https://cpk.org.pl> accessed 11 April 2022 and Feminoteka <https://feminoteka.pl> accessed 11 April 2022.
239 In this section findings from a research project 2012/07/B/HS5/03727 funded by the National Science Centre are included; see K Sękowska-Kozłowska, 'Funkcjonowanie procedury sprawozdawczej do Komitetu do Spraw Likwidacji Dyskryminacji Kobiet w odniesieniu do Polski' in R Wieruszewski (ed), *Mechanizmy ochrony praw człowieka w ramach ONZ. Analiza systemowa* (CH Beck 2017).
240 4–5 Report, CEDAW, Poland; 6 Report, CEDAW, Poland.
241 7–8 Report, CEDAW, Poland.
242 Information provided by Poland in follow-up to the COs (2017).
243 Follow-up letter sent to the state party (2018).
244 W Sadurski, *Poland's Constitutional Breakdown* (Oxford 2019).
245 E Korolczuk and A Graff, '"Worse Than Communism and Nazism Put Together": War on Gender in Poland' in R Kuhar and D Paternotte (eds), *Anti-Gender Campaigns in Europe: Mobilising Against Equality* London (Rowman & Littlefield International 2017); E Korolczuk, 'The Fight Against "Gender" and "LGBT Ideology": New Developments in Poland' (2019) 3 European Journal of Politics and Gender.
246 CEDAW Cttee, COs on combined and periodic report and the 6th periodic report of Poland para 9; CEDAW Cttee, COs on combined 6th and 7th periodic report of Poland, para 11.

law,[247] the law on domestic violence[248] and the law aiming to implement the EU anti-discrimination directives.[249] There is no national machinery for the advancement of women's rights that would effectively coordinate and monitor the implementation of CEDAW.[250]

With regard to selected legal issues, it is worth addressing reproductive rights, violence against women and public participation. As for reproductive rights, in 2014 the CEDAW Cttee recommended[251] amending the restrictive abortion law which permitted the termination of pregnancy only in selected circumstances: as a result of a criminal act; when the woman's life or health was at risk; or in cases of severe foetal impairment.[252] This law was not liberalised. In fact, in 2020 it was tightened due to a Constitutional Tribunal ruling which found that abortion in cases of severe foetal impairment was unconstitutional.[253] CEDAW was not mentioned in this ruling or during proceedings before the Tribunal.[254]

As for domestic violence, the CEDAW Cttee recommended in 2007 and 2014 the introduction to Polish law of a restraining order issued by the police that would allow for evicting the perpetrator of violence in cases of immediate danger.[255] This instrument was finally introduced in Poland in 2020[256] but CEDAW was not mentioned at all during the legislative process.

In 2007 the CEDAW Cttee recommended increasing the representation of women in the Polish Parliament through the adoption of temporary special measures.[257] This recommendation was to some extent fulfilled in 2011 through

---

247 Law of 26 June 1974 with amendments, Dz. U. of 1974, No. 24, item 141.
248 Law of 29 July 2005 with amendments, Dz.U. of 2005, No. 180, item 1493.
249 Law of 3 December 2010, Dz.U. of 2010, No. 254, item 1700.
250 CEDAW Cttee, COs on combined 4th and 5th periodic report and the 6th periodic report of Poland para 11; CEDAW Cttee, COs on combined 6th and 7th periodic report of Poland para 17.
251 CEDAW Cttee, COs on combined 6th and 7th periodic report of Poland para 37.
252 Law of 7 January 1993 with amendments, Dz.U. of 1993, No. 17, item 78, art 4a.
253 Constitutional Tribunal judgment of 22 October, K 1/20.
254 See documents submitted in proceedings <https://ipo.trybunal.gov.pl/ipo/view/spr awa.xhtml?&pokaz=dokumenty&sygnatura=K%201/20> accessed 11 April 2022.
255 CEDAW Cttee, COs on combined 4th and 5th periodic report and the 6th periodic report of Poland para. 19; CEDAW Cttee, COs on combined 6th and 7th periodic report of Poland paras 24–25.
256 Law of 30 April 2020, Dz.U. of 2020, item 956.
257 CEDAW Cttee, COs on combined 4th and 5th periodic report and the 6th periodic report of Poland para 15.

the introduction of 35 per cent quotas for electoral lists.[258] However, CEDAW did not play any significant role during parliamentary proceedings.[259] In 2014 the CEDAW Cttee recommended amending the quota law with a view to placing male and female candidates in alternating positions on electoral lists (the so-called 'slide' or 'zip' system).[260] Despite the fact that this recommendation was submitted via the follow-up procedure,[261] Poland has made no effort to implement it.

5.4.6 Impact of Individual Communications

So far, the CEDAW Cttee has considered two communications against Poland.[262] Both of these were found inadmissible.

5.4.7 Brief Conclusion

To conclude, it can be observed that CEDAW has had a rather insignificant impact on Polish law and practice. It is attributable foremost to the absence of CEDAW in the state's policies. From 1999 to 2019 the state authorities, regardless of the political party in power, made no significant effort to establish an institutional framework or a comprehensive strategy to implement CEDAW. The state's negligence with regard to reporting obligations was also revealed: from two up to 10 years' delays when submitting periodic reports, and a weak engagement with follow-up procedures.

On the other hand, it is evident that CEDAW plays an important role for civil society. Polish NGOs have been actively engaged in reporting to the CEDAW Cttee, including preparing comprehensive alternative reports. They have also attempted (so far unsuccessfully) to use individual complaints to the CEDAW Cttee as a litigation tool. In 2011 the Coalition for CEDAW was created by numerous Polish NGOs, which realised a project aiming to enhance cooperation between various actors, including public institutions, in order to improve the implementation of CEDAW.

---

258 Law of 5 January 2011, Dz.U. of 2011, No 34, item 172.
259 It was mentioned in one statement only: Record of the parliamentary meeting, 18 February 2010.
260 CEDAW Cttee, COs on combined 6th and 7th periodic report of Poland para 29.
261 ibid para 49.
262 CEDAW Cttee, *Polish Society of Anti-Discrimination Law v Poland*, CEDAW/C/73/D/136/2018 (19 July 2019), CEDAW Cttee, *KS v Poland*, CEDAW/C/76/D/128/2018 (6 July 2020).

5.5 Convention against Torture and Other Cruel, Inhuman or Degrading Treatment or Punishment

5.5.1 Incorporation and Reliance by Legislature and Executive

CAT was ratified by Poland in 1989, during the democratic transition. The country's legislative framework advanced significantly to meet the CAT standards through the adoption of the new Constitution in 1997.[263] While CAT and the CAT Cttee have been raised during parliamentary debates, they were predominantly mentioned by the opposition when criticising policies or laws, and not to justify the adoption of laws.

CAT has been mentioned in Parliament in the context of defining torture, when governmental officials argued – just as in the dialogue with the CAT Cttee – that all the elements specified in the definition of torture in CAT are included in the Criminal Code.[264] This appears to be the opinion of members of parliament and authorities throughout the political spectrum, as changes in government did not result in further discussion on the definition of torture. An exception was the Commissioner of Human Rights (NHRI), who has regularly asked the government to introduce the definition to the Criminal Code between 2015 and 2021.

The CAT Cttee's recommendations have been discussed in parliamentary debates and addressed a number of times. Governmental representatives have been asked about implementing the CAT Cttee's recommendations, mentioning in particular gender-based violence and access to abortion.[265] Another recurring topic is incorporation into the Criminal Code of hate crimes, discrimination and violence targeted at persons on the basis of their sexual orientation.[266] The CAT Cttee's recommendations have been invoked not only

---

[263] G Baranowska, 'Funkcjonowanie procedury sprawozdawczej do Komitetu Przeciwko Torturom w odniesieniu do Polski' in R Wieruszewski (ed), *Mechanizmy ochrony praw człowieka w ramach ONZ. Analiza systemowa* (CH Beck 2017) 349.

[264] Official response to inquiry 33371 to the Ministry of Justice, 27 September 2019; Official response to inquiry 3709 to the Ministry of Justice, 3 August 2006; see also Official response 6322 of the Ministry of Justice, 22 May 2001, in which the governmental representatives used the CAT definition of torture to address the question of overpopulation in prisons.

[265] Parliamentary inquiry 33371 to the Minister of the Interior and Administration, 19 September 2019; see also question on collecting statistics Parliamentary inquiry 14062 to the Minister of Justice, 5 July 2017; Record of the parliamentary meeting, 10 January 2021; Parliamentary inquiry 4423 to the Prime Minister, 12 April 2020.

[266] Parliamentary inquiry 23214 to the Ministry of Justice, 6 December 2013. This 2013 recommendation (CAT Cttee, COs on the 5th and 6th periodic report of Poland para 25) has, however, not been repeated in the same way in the 2019 recommendations (see CAT Cttee, COs on the 7th periodic report of Poland para 36(e)).

during parliamentary debates, but also in the substantiation of a motion to amend the Criminal Code.[267] Interestingly, governmental officials also used the CAT Cttee's recommendations in this context, mentioning disseminating them as one of the means of reaction to hate speech and crimes.[268]

The disregard of human rights accompanying the post-2015 constitutional breakdown is also exemplified by the fate of the Council for the Prevention of Racial Discrimination, Xenophobia and Related Intolerance. The Council was set up in 2013[269] and explicitly welcomed by the CAT Cttee,[270] which has repeatedly recommended that the Polish government deal more effectively with racial discrimination. However, the Council was dissolved in 2016, only three years after it was set up.[271] This led to a discussion in Parliament, during which several members of parliament also referred to CAT. During the discussion one of the parliamentarians even argued that the Council was set up in order to address the CAT Cttee's recommendations.[272] However, we found no evidence to support this.[273]

The NHRI was appointed as the National Preventive Mechanism (NPM) and started to conduct this role in 2008.[274] Initially the legal basis for conducting this role was a resolution of the council of ministers. However, in 2011 the law on the Commissioner of Human Rights was amended so as to include this role.[275] While the clear legal basis for the mandate as an NPM is beneficial, it has been argued that this should be a separate law.[276] In the very first report after taking this role, the NHRI urged the state authorities to provide the office

---

267 Druk sejmowy No 128 of 12 December 2019.
268 Official response 21624 of the Ministry of Justice, 22 April 2011.
269 Regulation of the Prime Minister of 13 February 2013, MP 2013 poz 79.
270 CAT Cttee, COs on the 5th and 6th periodic report of Poland para 6(b).
271 Regulation of the Prime Minister of 27 April 2016, MP 2016 poz 413. The NHRI criticised dissolving the Council in a statement of 6 May 2016.
272 Parliamentary inquiry 3285 to the Prime Minister, 16 May 2016. The response to this inquiry by governmental officials did not invoke CAT; see Official response 3745 of the Minister of International Affairs, 30 June 2016.
273 In the reporting process to the CERD the Polish authorities raised that another initiative was launched in the place of the Council. See part on CERD for details.
274 For an analysis of the NPM in light of the CAT's standards, see J Grygiel, 'Gwarancje niezależności krajowych mechanizmów prewencji powołanych na podstawie OPCAT' (2020) 18 Problemy Współczesnego Praw Międzynarodowego, Europejskiego i Porównawczego.
275 Law of 31 August 2011, Dz. U. of 2011 No 168 item 1004.
276 Z Lasocik and A Mężik, 'Krajowy Mechanizm Prewencji Tortur w oczach funkcjonariuszy Służby Więziennej' (2019) 54 Nowa Kodyfikacja Prawa Karnego. One of the authors of this text was an OP-CAT member (Zbigniew Lasocik).

with the means necessary to carry out this mandate,[277] a request that has been repeated many times since.[278] The SPT conducted a visit to Poland in 2018 which was also raised in Parliament during debates on prison conditions.[279]

5.5.2 Reliance by Judiciary

The majority of cases in which CAT was mentioned in court proceedings concerned compensation cases brought by persons deprived of their liberty. CAT was invoked by the courts alongside other documents, such as ECHR and CCPR, to establish the applicable standards.[280] It has further been invoked in the context of defining 'torture'.[281]

CAT standards have also been applied when dealing with non-citizens. For example, in the case of a woman seeking asylum in Poland, the CAT Cttee's findings with regard to her home state were invoked.[282] In another case in 2019, a court decided that the expulsion to Russia of a person sought by the authorities of the Russian Federation would be a violation of CAT.[283]

CAT has also been raised by the Constitutional Tribunal. When analysing whether the limiting of the NHRI's budget was constitutional, the Tribunal also took into consideration that the office was appointed to the role of the NPM.[284] In the October 2020 ruling, which established a near-total ban on abortion, the majority – arguing in favour of the ban – invoked several human rights treaties in its reasoning. However, as one of the concurring judges pointed out, the reasoning was significantly simplified, as 'various bodies wish to raise [abortion] to the rank of a human right', including the CAT Cttee.[285] While CAT did not impact the judgment, the divergent stance it takes on the issue has thus been recognised by one of the judges.

---

277 Record of the parliamentary meeting, 13 June 2008.
278 See information by both subsequent NHRIS: Irena Lipowicz (Record of parliamentary meeting, 8 October 2010) and Adam Bodnar (Record of parliamentary meeting, 14 January 2016).
279 Record of the parliamentary meeting, 9 December 2020.
280 See for example District Court in Sieradz judgment of 19 July 2013, I C 114/11; District Court in Gliwice judgment of 5 April 2017, II C 448/15.
281 District Court in Wrocław judgment of 19 February 2020, IV Ka 1421/19.
282 Provincial Administrative Court judgment of 16 March 2015, IV SA/Wa 974/14.
283 Appellate Court in Katowice judgment of 25 October 2019, II AKz 968/19.
284 Decision of the Constitutional Tribunal of 27 July 2016, K 18/15.
285 Constitutional Tribunal judgment of 22 October 2020, K 1/20. See A Gliszczyńska-Grabias and W Sadurski, 'The Judgment That Wasn't (But Which Nearly Brought Poland to a Standstill): "Judgment"' of the Polish Constitutional Tribunal of 22 October 2020 K1/20' (2022) 17 European Constitutional Law Review.

Additionally, several proceedings were brought to the Constitutional Tribunal by the NHRI in its role as the NPM, for example, in a request to review the legal basis for introducing a system of rewards and penalties at correctional facilities.[286] The activities and relevance of the NPM are also evident in the proceedings of regular courts. For example, while deliberating on the frequency of access to bathing facilities by prisoners, a court invoked the NPM's findings and recommendations.[287] Courts have also analysed the NPM's reports with regard to specific institutions of detention.[288] However, highlighting that in order for complainants to be able to rely on the NPM's findings, these should concern not only the facility, but also the specific premises and rooms where they were deprived of their liberty.[289]

5.5.3 Impact on and through Independent State Institutions

The NHRI's office has been conducting the role of the NPM since 2008. In this capacity it has relied on and invoked CAT and OP-CAT in various activities, as evidenced in the NHRI's annual reports. Representatives of the NPM met with the SPT during its visit to Poland[290] and submitted comments to the SPT's recommendation and observations.[291] The NHRI has been actively engaged with CAT and promoting its standards not only when acting as the NPM. In June 2019 it submitted an alternative report on the seventh periodic review of Poland to CAT. A representative of the NHRI participated in CAT sessions on Poland's report as well as disseminating information on the process.[292] When speaking out regarding violations of the law by policy officers, the NHRI raised both CAT and the CAT Cttee's recommendations.[293]

---

286 Constitutional Tribunal judgment of 2 October 2012, U 1/12; see also Constitutional Tribunal judgment of 31 March 2015, U 6/14.
287 Appellate Court in Warsaw judgment of 10 July 2019, I ACa 443/18.
288 Appellate Court in Katowice judgment of 21 September 2017, I Aca 324/17.
289 Appellate Court in Łódź judgment of 7 November 2019, Aca 1436/18.
290 OP-CAT, Visit to Poland undertaken from 9 to 18 July 2018: recommendations and observations addressed to the state party, Annex 1.
291 OP-CAT, Comments of the national preventive mechanism on the recommendations and observations addressed to it in connection with the Subcommittee visit to Poland undertaken from 9 to 18 July 2018.
292 <https://www.rpo.gov.pl/pl/content/komitet-onz-przeciwko-torturom-cat-pyta-o-tortury-w-polsce> accessed 11 April 2022.
293 <https://www.rpo.gov.pl/pl/content/o%C5%9Bwiadczenie-rzecznika-praw-obywatelskich-w-zwi%C4%85zku-z-reporta%C5%BCem-tvn-%C5%9Bmier%C4%87-w-komisariacie > accessed 11 April 2022.

5.5.4 Impact on and through Non-state Actors

Five documents by non-state actors were submitted to the CAT Cttee in 2019 within the seventh reporting cycle with regard to Poland. Four of those submissions represent the main areas in which non-state actors are using CAT and the CAT Cttee to advance change in Poland: women's reproductive rights;[294] domestic violence;[295] prison conditions;[296] and the rights of non-citizens.[297] A particularly interesting case is the fifth submission by *Ordo Iuris*, which is a conservative organisation gaining influence in particular after the post-2015 constitutional breakdown, which has recently started to use international human rights mechanisms instrumentally, including at the UN.[298] The submission stated that the 'system of counteracting domestic violence in Poland is one of the most effective in Europe',[299] and called for tougher protection of 'unborn children'.[300] It stands out in strong contrast to the other submissions and exemplifies the use of international human rights mechanisms by conservative organisations.

---

294 Supplemental Information on Poland for the Review by the Committee against Torture. Federation for Women and Family Planning, Women Enabled International, Magdalena Szarota (Lancaster University and Association of Disabled Women. ONE.pl) and independent researchers Agnieszka Król and Agnieszka Wołowicz. 21 June 2019.

295 Compliance with the Convention Against Torture and Other Cruel, Inhuman or Degrading Treatment or Punishment. Submitted by the Advocates for Human Rights, a non-governmental organisation in special consultative status with ECOSOC since 1996 and Women's Rights Centre. 68th Session of the Committee Against Torture. 11 November–6 December 2019. Submitted 22 June 2019.

296 Helsinki Foundation for Human Rights, June 2019. Submission to the review of Poland during the 67th session of the Committee Against Torture, 22 July 2019–9 August 2019. The submission also covered the three other areas, namely, abortion rights, domestic violence and rights of non-citizens.

297 Information from the Association for Legal International regarding the seventh periodic report on Poland by the Committee against Torture. For an analysis of information submitted during the 5th and 6th reporting cycle, see Baranowska (n 263) 344–345.

298 'Cultural and Religious Counterrevolution. Is Polish Law Under the Threat of Christian Fundamentalists' Ideology? Publication – Context and summary' (2020 The Great Coalition for Equality and Choice); L Kurasinska 'This Ultra-Conservative Institute has Infiltrated the Polish State, on a Relentless Quest to Ban Abortion' 30 July 2018 https://www.opendemocracy.net/en/5050/ultra-conservative-institute-has-infiltrated-polish-state-to-ban-abortion/ accessed 11 April 2022.

299 *Ordo Iuris*. Institute for Legal Culture, Warsaw 21 June 2019 6.

300 ibid 15.

5.5.5 Impact of State Reporting[301]

Poland has so far submitted six reports to the CAT Cttee, the first in 1998 and the most recent in 2018. An analysis of the reports and the COs makes it possible to identify a number of recurring issues with regard to Poland, which have been repeatedly raised in the CAT Cttee's COs: the definition of torture, pretrial detention, protection from domestic violence, and hate crimes.

The inclusion of the CAT definition of torture into the Criminal Code has been the subject of an ongoing debate between the CAT Cttee and state authorities.[302] The Polish government has repeatedly stated that all the elements specified in the definition of torture in CAT are encompassed in the Criminal Code. Interestingly, the report of 2018 stated that 'the Ministry of Justice started the analysis of whether torture should be included in the Polish Penal Code'.[303] This is somehow different to the authorities' comments in earlier reports, when the government did not state that this issue would be discussed.[304] However, it does not appear that there is a debate taking place. It must therefore be concluded that while the CAT Cttee has been consistent about mentioning the need to adopt a separate crime of torture, this has not influenced the legal framework.

Another recurring topic in the state reporting process is the use of pre-trial detention, which has been raised by the CAT Cttee since its first COs in 1997.[305] In response to the CAT Cttee's comments, the authorities have raised numerous changes to the Polish Code of Criminal Procedure.[306] However, a close analysis of the adopted acts reveals that, while they indeed are aimed at limiting the use of pre-trial detention and shortening its duration, CAT standards and/or the CAT Cttee's COs were not included in the justification for the laws, and they were adopted for other reasons. For example, in the 2012 report Polish authorities mentioned three Acts, out of which two were adopted to implement a judgment of the Constitutional Tribunal,[307] and in the reasons for adopting the third Act the case law of the Constitutional Tribunal was also mentioned.[308]

---

301 In this part findings from a research project 2012/07/B/HS 5/03727 funded by the National Science Centre are included; see Baranowska (n 263).
302 See CAT Cttee, COs on the 2nd periodic report of Poland, para 103; CAT Cttee, COs on the 4th report of Poland, para 6; CAT Cttee, COs on the 5th and 6th report of Poland, para 7.
303 7th report, CAT, Poland, para 3.
304 3rd report, CAT, Poland, para 23; 4th report, CAT, Poland, para 5; 5th and 6th report, CAT, Poland, paras 6–11.
305 See CAT Cttee, COs on the 1st periodic report of Poland, paras 105 and 108.
306 See 5th and 6th report, CAT, Poland, para 33; 7th report, CAT, Poland, para 119.
307 Law of 5 December 2008, Dz.U. of 2009, No 20, item 104; Law of 16 July 2009, Dz.U. of 2009, No. 127, item 1051.
308 Druk sejmowy No 631 of 4 June 2008.

While the legal framework in Poland was indeed adjusted to meet the majority of the CAT Cttee's standards, this has not been reflected in the debates or reasons substantiating the adoption of those acts. The CAT Cttee recognises the positive legislative changes, but continues to call on Poland regarding the application of the laws, for example, to limit pre-trial detention.[309]

As in the case of other treaty bodies, the CAT Cttee has also issued recommendations to Poland on multiple occasions with regard to access to legal abortion, as well as gender-based and domestic violence. The creation of the National Emergency Service for Victims of Domestic Violence (Blue Line) met with the CAT Cttee's approval, as have legislative changes over the years. However, the recommendations to define and introduce domestic violence and marital rape as separate criminal offences into the Penal Code remain outstanding. The same is true for access to legal abortion: the CAT Cttee consequently criticises the current legislation and practice.[310]

5.5.6   Impact of Individual Communications

While Poland accepted CAT's individual complaints procedure in 1993, to date no communication has been brought against Poland.

5.5.7   Impact of Other Measures

OP-CAT setting up the SPT was ratified by Poland in 2006, which resulted in the NHRI being assigned the role of the NPM in 2008. This mandate was initially carried out on the basis of a resolution, and since 2011 has been based on a law. In 2010 an NPM team was designated within the NHRI office, which currently consists of 11 employees. This number allows for carrying out approximately 80 visits per year.[311] Within their mandate the NHRI also undertakes other actions, such as bringing cases to court, including at the Constitutional Tribunal, and launching campaigns – for example, in 2019 a major campaign 'A state without tortures' was initiated.[312] While submitting proposals and observations concerning draft legislation is one of the powers the NPM should be granted (OP-CAT, article 19(c)), in practice the NPM is currently deprived of the possibility to do so. The last relevant draft legislation was submitted to the NPM in March 2019; since then no drafts have been forwarded for consultation.[313]

---

309 CAT Cttee, COs on the 7th periodic review of Poland, paras 17–18.
310 CAT Cttee, COs on the 5th and 6th periodic report of Poland, para 22. CAT Cttee, COs on the 7th periodic report of Poland, paras 33–34.
311 Przemysław Kazimirski, NPM director, 20 May 2021, on-line interview.
312 <https://www.rpo.gov.pl/pl/content/co-jest-krajowy-mechanizm-prewencji> accessed 11 April 2022.
313 Przemysław Kazimirski, NPM director, 20 May 2021, on-line interview.

In July 2018 the SPT conducted a visit to Poland and reported that the NPM in particular is 'facing challenges regarding its institutional and structural framework'.[314] The recommendations of the SPT are substantially identical to those regularly submitted to Poland by the European Committee for the Prevention of Torture and Inhuman or Degrading Treatment or Punishment, and cover in particular the strengthening of anti-torture guarantees, including the definition of torture into the Penal Code and access to lawyers. While the government has responded in time to the SPT's recommendations, no substantive steps were taken to implement these. At the same time, a number of grass-roots initiatives by advocates were recently initiated, to provide detained persons with access to lawyers, which appears to be one of the main challenges within the torture prevention framework in Poland.[315]

The report of the SPT has been subsequently referred to by representatives of the NPM during a parliamentary discussion on the use of violence by the police on those taking part in mass protests following the judgment of the Constitutional Tribunal in October 2020 limiting access to abortion.[316] The unprecedented police brutality towards the protestors has also been addressed by the NMP itself.[317]

5.5.8 Brief Conclusion

Domestic law in Poland is now clearly more harmonised with CAT than when CAT was ratified. This was influenced not only by the CAT Cttee, but also by the democratic transition and various other bodies that recommended similar adjustments (EU, ECtHR). Some legislative changes requested by the CAT Cttee have consequently been denied, such as adopting the CAT definition of torture. A particularly strong impact has been achieved through the creation of the NPM, which assesses and influences the detention system in Poland through regular visits. The active role taken by the NHRI as NPM is of crucial

---

314 SPT Visit to Poland undertaken from 9 to 18 July 2018: Recommendations and Observations addressed to the national preventive mechanism.
315 See in particular the initiative 'Szpila' set up for protestors after the 2020 Constitution Judgment protests <https://oko.press/zatrzymania-pod-numerem-722-196-13-mozesz-lic zyc-na-pomoc/> accessed 11 April 2022, as well as the initiative by the Polish Bar Council to change the Code of Criminal Procedure accordingly <https://www.prawo.pl/prawn icy-sady/dostep-do-adwokata-w-polsce-badany-przez-etpc,508197.html> accessed 11 April 2022.
316 Record of the parliamentary meeting, 9 December 2020.
317 However, the NMP recommendations were rejected by police authorities, who claimed to have acted within the law; Przemysław Kazimirski, NPM director, 20 May 2021, on-line interview.

relevance for the mechanism created under OP-CAT. It has, however, continued to be underfunded, and the dispute around its mandate between 2020 and 2021 is likely to weaken the NRHI as such.

5.6 Convention on the Rights of the Child[318]
5.6.1 Incorporation and Reliance by Legislature and Executive

The proposal to adopt a treaty on the rights of the child was pioneered and formally tabled by Poland in 1978.[319] Throughout the 1980s, the drafting process of CRC was led by the open-ended Working Group.[320] The Convention was ultimately adopted by the UN General Assembly in 1989. Poland ratified CRC in 1991, however, with several reservations and declarations.[321] Ratification of the Protocols on the sale of children, child prostitution and child pornography (OP-CRC-SC) and the involvement of children in armed conflict (OP-CRC-AC) was completed in 2005. Poland signed the Protocol on a communications procedure (OP-CRC-CP) in 2013 but the government remains reluctant to ratify it due to concerns about the legal and financial implications.[322]

In the period between 30 June 1999 and 30 June 2019 CRC and the CRC Cttee were directly referred to in parliamentary discussions on numerous occasions. The references were mostly related to the situation of children with disabilities,

---

[318] The authors wish to thank PhD Anna Natalia Schulz from Poznań Centre for Family Law and Children's Rights Institute of Law Studies Polish Academy of Sciences for her comments on this part.

[319] The draft convention was submitted to the Commission on Human Rights on 7 February 1978. See UN Doc. E/CN.4/L.1366/Rev.1.

[320] The Working Group was chaired by Prof Adam Łopatka from Poland. For the drafting process, see S Detrick (ed), *The United Nations Convention on the Rights of the Child: A Guide to the Travaux Préparatoires* (Martinus Nijhoff Publishers 1992). For further details on Polish involvement in works on CRC, see AN Schulz, 'Funkcjonowanie procedury sprawozdawczej do Komitetu Praw Dziecka w odniesieniu do Polski' in R Wieruszewski (ed), *Mechanizmy ochrony praw człowieka w ramach ONZ. Analiza systemowa* (CH Beck 2017) 179; G Lanzer, 'Images Towards the Emancipation of Children in Modern Western Culture' in JT Todres and SM King (eds), *The Oxford Handbook of Children's Rights Law* (Oxford 2020) 25-26; Office of the UN High Commissioner for Human Rights *Legislative History of the Convention on the Rights of the Child. Volume I* (New York and Geneva 2007).

[321] Declarations that remain in force relate to arts 12–16 and 24(2)(f) and highlight that a child's rights shall be exercised with respect for parental authority, in accordance with Polish customs and traditions whilst family planning and education services for parents should be in keeping with the principles of morality. See CRC Cttee, Reservations, Declarations and Objections Relating to the Convention of the Rights of the Child, 11 July 1994, CRC/C/2/Rev.3.

[322] Official response to petition on ratification OP-CRC-CP from Ministry of Family, Labour and Social Affairs, DWM.II.6401.6.1.2017.JM, 9 February 2017.

the protection of children from violence, access to health services, social security, and discrimination against children. CRC was also cited in the context of adoption, alimony, the mistreatment of children, and the situation of children in civil and criminal proceedings.[323] The references were made during debates on establishing the institution of the Commissioner for Children's Rights in Poland which took place in 1999.[324] Another noteworthy example was in the reasoning behind a motion for amending the regulations concerning alternative care. The Members of Parliament backed their motion by arguing that the draft enables a better and more complete implementation of the provisions in article 7 and 20 of CRC, as well as the values indicated in the Preamble to the Convention.[325] In 2000 a Member of Parliament asked the Minister of Education about obligatory tuition fees for non-Polish citizens in primary school. It was indicated that under CRC the right to education of a child shall not depend on one's citizenship, nationality or the financial situation of their parents.[326] The Minister responded that exemptions from the obligations for foreigners to bear education costs could be made by the director of the school and an amendment to align the situation of Polish and non-Polish citizens was in process.[327] In fact, under the subsequently amended ministry regulations, these fees are no longer charged to the children of foreigners attending public primary schools.[328] Another inquiry with reference to CRC concerned the improvement of access to medical services in schools.[329]

A significant part of the parliamentary debate also concerned OP-CRC-CP and the government's reluctance to ratify it.[330] In 2017 the Undersecretary in the Ministry of Family, Labour and Social Policy, in response to an inquiry on the ratification of OP-CRC-CP stated: 'Being bound by the protocol could lead to the CRC Cttee questioning the provisions of the Polish Constitution and questioning the shape of the applicable law and the implemented policy,

---

323   The information collected by the author on analysis online databases of parliamentary works.
324   See for instance Record of the parliamentary meeting, 8 September 1999.
325   Record of the parliamentary meeting, 9 November 2000.
326   Parliamentary inquiry 5003 to the Minister of Education, 2 November 2000.
327   Official response to inquiry 5003 to the Minister of Education, 20 November 2000.
328   See, for instance, Regulation of Minister of National Education of 1 April 2010, Dz.U. of 2010, no 57, item 361.
329   Parliamentary inquiry 8115 to the Minister of Health and the Minister of National Education, 10 May 2007.
330   See, for instance, Parliamentary inquiry 20506 to the Prime Minister, 20 August 2013; Parliamentary inquiry 26509 to the Minister of Foreign Affairs, 27 May 2014; Parliamentary inquiry 8573 to the Minister of Family, Labour and Social Policy, 9 December 2016.

reflecting the real needs, as well as Polish culture and tradition', referring, *inter alia*, to the differing views of the CRC Cttee on access to safe abortion and contraception.[331] Although this statement was made by the representative of a conservative government, it should be noted that none of the political groups that have governed Poland during the last two decades has taken any steps towards withdrawing the declarations to CRC that relate to family planning.[332]

The Constitution does not refer directly to the Convention, but it expresses the rights and principles derived from CRC, for instance, the principle of child participation in proceedings and the right to be heard. Direct references to CRC can be found in domestic law. Several references to CRC are evident in the law on the entry into Poland, stay and departure from this territory of citizens of EU member states and their family members,[333] in the law on foreigners,[334] in the Preamble to the law on education[335] and in the Preamble to the law on the education system (until the Preamble was repealed in 2017).[336] Another example of a direct impact of CRC on the legislature is the ministerial regulation on the framework statutes for public art schools and institutions in which it is indicated that the statute shall specify, inter alia, the student's rights, including the rights ensured in CRC, and the procedure for submitting complaints in the event of violation of the student's rights.[337] Similar regulations were also issued in relation to other types of school institutions.

5.6.2 Reliance by Judiciary

The impact of CRC on the judiciary in Poland is considerable, in particular in the judgments of the Constitutional Tribunal and Supreme Court.

The Constitutional Tribunal adjudicated on the conformity of domestic law with CRC on several occasions between 1999 and 2019. The applications to the Constitutional Tribunal referred to the right to express the child's views freely;[338] the right of every child to a standard of living adequate for the child's development;[339] the priority of the best interests of the

---

331 Official response to inquiry 8573 to the Ministry of Family, Labour and Social Policy, 11 January 2017 (own translation).
332 See fn 321.
333 Law of 14 July 2006, Dz.U. of 2019, item 293.
334 Law of 12 December 2013, Dz.U. of 2020, item 35.
335 Law of 14 December 2016, Dz.U. of 2020, item 910.
336 Law of 7 September 1991, Dz.U. of 2017, item 2198.
337 Regulation of the Minister of Culture and National Heritage of 5 November 2014, Dz.U. of 2014, item 1646.
338 Constitutional Tribunal judgment of 11 October 2011, K 16/10.
339 Constitutional Tribunal judgment of 23 June 2008, P 18/06.

child;[340] the guarantees for children deprived of their liberty;[341] the special protection of the child deprived of a family environment with the obligation to ensure a disabled child's enjoyment of a full and decent life;[342] and the rights of the child to freedom of association and to freedom of peaceful assembly.[343] In 2005 the Constitutional Tribunal found provisions of law on family benefits incompatible with the Constitution and CRC. The law contained, *inter alia*, regulations contrary to the principle of subsidiarity, according to which the state should support the family and not replace it in carrying out its functions.[344] In another case the Constitutional Tribunal indicated the incompatibility of domestic law with CRC (the impossibility of challenging an order refusing a visit by a juvenile in detention).[345] It is also worth noting the ruling of the Constitutional Tribunal of 2020, in which the Tribunal found the embryopathological condition of termination of pregnancy incompatible with the Constitution, referring, *inter alia*, to CRC, the Preamble and the provisions of which were interpreted in an instrumental manner.[346]

CRC has been referred to on numerous occasions in the judgments of the Polish Supreme Court.[347] For instance, the Polish Supreme Court supported its arguments on the possibility of consenting to the operation on a child by his or her authorised representative, referring to CRC and its systemic interpretation.[348]

---

[340] Constitutional Tribunal judgment of 15 November 2000, P 12/99; Constitutional Tribunal judgment of 26 February 2003, K 1/01.
[341] Constitutional Tribunal judgment of 2 July 2009, K 1/07.
[342] Constitutional Tribunal judgment of 22 July 2008, P 41/07.
[343] Constitutional Tribunal judgment of 18 September 2014, K 44/12.
[344] Constitutional Tribunal judgment of 18 May 2005, K 16/04.
[345] Constitutional Tribunal judgment of 2 July 2009, K 1/07.
[346] Constitutional Tribunal judgment of 22 October 2020, K 1/20. For an analysis of the judgment, see A Gliszczyńska-Grabias and W Sadurski, 'The Judgment That Wasn't (But Which Nearly Brought Poland to a Standstill). "Judgment" of the Polish Constitutional Tribunal of 22 October 2020 K1/20' (2021) 17 European Constitutional Law Review and the statements by NGOs on the judgment: Federation for Women and Family Planning <https://en.federa.org.pl/constitutional-tribunal-rules-to-ban-abortion/>, Human Rights Watch <https://www.hrw.org/news/2020/10/22/polands-constitutional-tribunal-rolls-back-reproductive-rights> accessed 11 April 2022. It is worth noting that the issue of application of CRC's provisions in relation to unborn children has for many years been the subject of lively debate in Poland and a part of society welcomed the judgment.
[347] See for instance Supreme Court judgment of 18 August 1999, II CKN 321/99; Supreme Court decision of 1 December 1999, I CKN 992/99; Supreme Court decision of 5 July 2006, IV CSK 127/06; Supreme Court resolution of 13 May 2015, III CZP 19/15.
[348] Supreme Court resolution of 13 May 2015, III CZP 19/15.

Common courts also take the treaty's provisions into consideration in judgments,[349] especially in family cases, as well as administrative courts.[350] CRC is often invoked in order to highlight the priority of the principle of the best interests of the child.

5.6.3 Impact on and through Independent State Institutions

According to the Law on the Commissioner for Children's Rights (CChR), the CChR safeguards the rights of the child as defined in the Constitution, CRC and other legal provisions, respecting the responsibility, rights and obligations of parents.[351] A significant number of references to CRC can be found in the subsequent annual reports of the CChR's work.[352] In addition, the CChR participated in meetings in an international fora relating to the application of CRC, including the formal and informal sessions of the work group for preparing OP-CRC-CP.[353] In 2011 the CChR requested the Minister of Foreign Affairs to support the signature of the Protocol.[354] The CChR also takes part in reporting cycles, submitting its own reports to the CRC Cttee.[355] Furthermore, the CChR independently implements some of

---

[349] See for instance Appellate Court in Katowice judgment of 25 January 2001, I ACa 1258/00; Appellate Court in Wrocław judgment of 11 December 2013, II AKa 393/13; District Court in Olsztyn judgment of 21 November 2018, VI RCa 301/18; District Court in Szczecin judgment of 12 December 2017, II Ca 789/17.

[350] See for instance Supreme Administrative Court judgment of 29 August 2018, II OSK 1041/18; Supreme Administrative Court judgment of 18 May 2010, I OSK 183/10.

[351] Art 1 s 2 of the Law of 6 January 2000, Dz.U. of 2020, item 141.

[352] See for instance Commissioner for Children's Rights, *Informacja o działalności Rzecznika Praw Dziecka za rok 2010 oraz uwagi o stanie przestrzegania praw dziecka*; Commissioner for Children's Rights, *Informacja o działalności Rzecznika Praw Dziecka za rok 2011 oraz uwagi o stanie przestrzegania praw dziecka*; Commissioner for Children's Rights, *Informacja o działalności Rzecznika Praw Dziecka za rok 2013 oraz uwagi o stanie przestrzegania praw dziecka*; Commissioner for Children's Rights, *Informacja o działalności Rzecznika Praw Dziecka za rok 2017 oraz uwagi o stanie przestrzegania praw dziecka*.

[353] See for instance Commissioner for Children's Rights, *Informacja o działalności Rzecznika Praw Dziecka za rok 2010 oraz uwagi o stanie przestrzegania praw dziecka* 174; Commissioner for Children's Rights, *Informacja o działalności Rzecznika Praw Dziecka za rok 2011 oraz uwagi o stanie przestrzegania praw dziecka*, 206.

[354] Inquiry of Commissioner for Children's Rights to the Minister of Foreign Affairs, ZSM/500/6/2010/AJ, 3 November 2010.

[355] Commissioner for Children's Rights, Report on the Ombudsman for Children on the enforcement of the UN Committee on the Rights of the Child Recommendations of the 4th October 2002; Commissioner for Children's Rights, Information of the Ombudsman for Children prepared in relation to the list of issues prior to reporting (LOIPR) for Poland being drafted by the Committee on the Rights of the Child on the implementation of the Convention on the Rights of the Child on 29 June 2018.

the Committee's recommendations, for instance, by running a helpline for children. The office of the CChR also prepared a voluminous monograph with comments on CRC provisions.[356] Also, the CChR is one of the few institutions that constantly disseminates knowledge about CRC and its Protocols by publishing information and documents on its website.[357]

CRC standards also remain an important point of reference for the NHRI. For instance, the NHRI noted the problem of the inability of persons who actually care for the child, for instance, grandparents, to receive benefits instead of parents, and requested the Minister of Family, Labour and Social Affairs to amend the law, referring to the provisions of CRC that constitute special protection for a child deprived of his or her family environment.[358] In addition, the NHRI regularly intervenes when public authorities refuse to enter the birth certificate of children from same-sex marriages in the Polish civil status record, pointing out that the obligation to transcribe a foreign civil status record is a part of broad system of protection of the rights of the child, established in CRC.[359] Also, over recent years the NHRI has called on the authorities to ratify OP-CRC-CP.[360] Numerous references to CRC and the CRC Cttee's recommendations are also indicated in the NRHI's annual reports.[361]

5.6.4 Impact on and through Non-state Actors

On two occasions, in 2017 and 2020, civil society organisations submitted a petition to public authorities calling for the ratification of OP-CRC-CP.[362] Among the arguments most frequently used in advocacy is the fact that

---

[356] SL Stadniczenko (ed), *Konwencja o Prawach Dziecka. Wybór zagadnień (artykuły i komentarze)* (Biuro Rzecznika Praw Dziecka 2015).

[357] See the CChR website <https://brpd.gov.pl/konwencja-o-prawach-dziecka/>, <https://brpd.gov.pl/2019/10/22/prawa-dziecka-po-ludzku/>, <https://brpd.gov.pl/prawa-dziecka-dokumenty-organizacji-narodow-zjednoczonych/> accessed 11 April May 2022.

[358] The Commissioner for Human Rights address to the Minister of Family, Labour and Social Affairs, 25 February 2019, III.7064.1.2019.JA.

[359] See for instance the description of the entire strategic procedure on the Commissioner for Human Rights website <https://www.rpo.gov.pl/pl/content/transkrypcja-aktu-urodzenia-dla-dziecka-urodzonego-w-londynie-z-małżeństwa-jednopłciowego> accessed 11 April 2022.

[360] See for instance the Commissioner for Human Rights address to the Minister of Foreign Affairs, 31 October 2016, VII.7021.1.2016.MKS.

[361] See for instance: Commissioner for Human Rights, *Informacja Rzecznika Praw Obywatelskich prof. Andrzeja Zolla za 2000 r* 23–24; Commissioner for Human Rights, *Informacja Rzecznika Praw Obywatelskich za 2004 r* 159, 171; Commissioner for Human Rights, *Informacja o działalności Rzecznika Praw Obywatelskich za rok 2009 oraz o stanie przestrzegania wolności i praw człowieka i obywatela* 449–484.

[362] In 2017 the petition was dismissed by the Ministry of Family, Labour and Social Affairs. See DWM.II.6401.6.1.2017.JM, 9 February 2017. In December 2020 another petition, prepared

Poland was one of the pioneers of CRC.[363] The major actor in the area of children's rights is UNICEF Poland, which coordinated several NGOs to submit a joint report in 2015 and 2020. In 2019 UNICEF launched a country-wide promotional campaign on the thirtieth anniversary of CRC which involved more than 3 000 schools.[364] Another noteworthy example is the activity of the Empowering Children Foundation which refers to CRC standards on numerous occasions (in particular article 19 on protection from violence).[365] Although education on children's rights remains limited in school curricula, the availability of promotional materials (in particular those developed by UNICEF)[366] translates into numerous grassroots initiatives undertaken by the schools and teachers.

In the periodic review in 2015, 15 NGOs grouped into two competing alliances submitted their joint reports to the CRC Cttee. The alliance coordinated by UNICEF consisted of nine NGOs working primarily in the areas of criminal procedure, education, alternative care, health care, and special protection of vulnerable groups (for instance, children with disabilities, unaccompanied minors, abused children, Roma children). Several recommendations adopted in the COs are inspired by the information provided in this joint report (for example, that the maximum length of stay in juvenile shelters should not exceed three months).[367] The competing alliance, coordinated by the ultraconservative organisation *Ordo Iuris*, consisted of five NGOs and provided an alternative report highlighting in particular reproductive issues (such as abortion and sex education). The latter included a solid, albeit biased, legal analysis of international human rights law, including references to CRC General

---

by 20 NGOs and coordinated by the Helsinki Foundation for Human Rights, was submitted to Parliament and is currently awaiting an official response. See Petition P-10-127/20 of 9 December 2020.

[363] For instance, the Commissioner for Children's Rights criticised the government for the reservations to CRC indicating that this 'casts a shadow' over Poland's involvement in the creation of CRC. See: Record of the parliamentary meeting, 18 March 2010.

[364] UNICEF Poland, Miasta i szkoły z całej Polski dołączyły do międzynarodowych obchodów 30. rocznicy Konwencji o prawach dziecka, 18 November 2019 <https://unicef.pl/co-robimy/aktualnosci/dla-mediow/miasta-i-szkoly-z-calej-polski-dolaczyly-do-miedzynarodowych-obchodow-30.-rocznicy-konwencji-o-prawach-dziecka> accessed 11 April 2022.

[365] See for instance M Sajkowska (ed), Dzieci się liczą 2017. Raport o zagrożeniach bezpieczeństwa i rozwoju dzieci w Polsce, 2017; J. Podlewska, R Szredzińska and J Włodarczyk, Analiza polskiego systemu ochrony dzieci przed krzywdzeniem, 2019.

[366] UNICEF Poland, Akcje edukacyjne <https://unicef.pl/wspolpraca/wspolpraca-z-placowkami-edukacyjnymi/akcje-edukacyjne> accessed 11 April 2022.

[367] CRC Cttee, COs on the combined 3rd and 4th periodic reports of Poland, para 53(a). For comparison, see CRC Cttee, Alternative report of Poland, 30 October 2014 39.

Comments. After the publication of the COs, *Ordo Iuris* published a critical analysis of the recommendations adopted.[368] In the joint reports submitted in 2020 (within the procedure of drafting the list of issues prior to reporting) the *Ordo Iuris*-led alliance was enlarged to nine NGOs while the UNICEF-led alliance grew to 13 organisations. It is also worth noting that a number of Polish NGOs in their activities refer to CRC and the CRC Cttee's recommendations, for instance, the Committee for the Protection of Children's Rights (KOPD).

5.6.5 Impact of State Reporting[369]

Poland has submitted four periodic state reports to the CRC Cttee, two of these between 2002 and 2015 (the latter was a combined report III and IV). The latest report (Reply to the List of Issues) was submitted in 2020 and will be considered by the Committee in September 2021. Additionally, a report was submitted under CRC-OP-AC as well as CRC-OP-SC (both in 2007). In 2010 the periodic report prepared for CRC was submitted to Parliament for plenary discussion, and resulted in a heated debate concentrated primarily on the issues of poverty, the right to education as well as the role of the family in the child's development.[370] Nevertheless, the arguments raised by the parliamentarians were built neither on the COs nor on the General Comments.[371]

The impact of the COs remains limited while references to the Convention in legislative procedures are rather superficial.[372] The tokenistic role of CRC is best demonstrated by the practice of invoking article 6 (the right to life) in legislation aimed at restricting abortion law,[373] which remains contrary to the COs.[374] One of the few examples of a direct and substantive reference to

---

[368] *Ordo Iuris, Komitet Praw Dziecka ONZ narusza postanowienia Konwencji*, 20 September 2016 <https://ordoiuris.pl/rodzina-i-malzenstwo/komitet-praw-dziecka-onz-narusza-postanowienia-konwencji> accessed 11 April 2022.

[369] In this part findings from a research project 2012/07/B/HS5/03727 funded by the National Science Centre are included; see AN Schulz, 'Funkcjonowanie procedury sprawozdawczej do Komitetu Praw Dziecka w odniesieniu do Polski' in R Wieruszewski (ed), *Mechanizmy ochrony praw człowieka w ramach ONZ. Analiza systemowa* (CH Beck 2017) 357.

[370] Record of the parliamentary meeting, 18 March 2010.

[371] The only argument that invoked the CRC Cttee was related to the recommendation on the anonymous birth and preservation of identity formulated by the Committee toward Luxembourg. See CRC Ctte, COs on the 2nd periodic report of Luxembourg para 29.

[372] Schulz (n 369).

[373] Proposal for amending the law on abortion submitted to Parliament on 14 September 2016 by the ultra-conservative organisation *Ordo Iuris* <http://orka.sejm.gov.pl/petycje.nsf/nazwa/145-122-16/$file/145-122-16.pdf> accessed 2 April 2022.

[374] CRC Cttee, COs on the combined 3rd and 4th periodic reports of Poland para 39(b).

CRC standards in the normative part of the legislation is the law on foreigners. One of its provisions provides that a foreigner shall not be subject to the return procedure if 'it would violate the rights of a child, as specified in the CRC, adopted by the UN General Assembly on 20 November 1989, to the extent threatening child's mental and psychical development'.[375] This normative construction obliges public authorities to conduct their assessment through the prism of the latest standards adopted by the CRC Cttee, including the General Comments.

In general, Poland has implemented most of the recommendations formulated in the COs, in particular in the areas of criminal procedure, migration, and counteracting sexual abuse. However, the impact of the CRC Cttee itself is difficult to determine.[376] At the same time, several issues are repeatedly and consequently raised by the Committee, in particular the ratification of OP-CRC-CP. Other debatable issues include access to abortion services, education on sexual and reproductive health as well as the existence of baby boxes that allow for the anonymous abandonment of children. Recommendations touching upon these topics have been criticised by the government in a statement submitted to the CRC Cttee in response to the latest COs adopted in 2015.[377]

5.6.6 Brief Conclusion

CRC remains a vivid instrument, in particular due to the activities undertaken by the Commissioner for Children's Rights. Moreover, the fact that Poland was among the authors of CRC is invoked on numerous occasions. Nevertheless, the awareness of the legislature, executive and the judiciary remains limited to the Convention itself and, therefore, rarely entails references to the COs or General Comments. In fact, this tokenistic approach to CRC is widely applied by ultra-conservative organisations and parliamentarians to openly advocate more restrictive abortion laws, or to impose further limitations on sex

---

375   Dz. U. 2013 poz. 1650.
376   Schulz (n 369).
377   The most critical position was taken towards the recommendation on abortion law. The government indicated that the interpretation included in General Comments 3 (HIV/AIDS and the Rights of the Child), 4 (Adolescent Health and Development in the Context of the Convention on the Rights of the Child), and 15 (The Right of the Child to the Enjoyment of the Highest Attainable Standard of Health) goes beyond the scope of the Convention. To support this statement, Poland had also invoked the final document of the Conference on population and development (Cairo, 1994) which specifies *inter alia* that '[i] no case should abortion be promoted as a method of family planning' (s 8.25). See Statement of Poland on the COs of the Committee on the Rights of the Child, 10 March 2016.

education – even though these proposals are contrary both to the COs as well as the General Comments. Taking into account the position of the Polish government, the ratification of OP-CRC-CP should not be expected in the forthcoming years.

5.7 Convention on the Rights of Persons with Disabilities

5.7.1 Incorporation and Reliance by Legislature and Executive

Poland ratified CRPD in 2012. It made reservations to articles 23(1)(a) and (b) and 25(a) of the Convention and interpretative declaration regarding article 12, which affects certain rights of persons with disabilities. The reservations refer to the limitation on the right of persons with mental disabilities to marry,[378] to the permissibility of institutional incapacitation of persons with mental disabilities, and to the state not recognising an individual right to abortion.

Since ratification, Poland has introduced some legislative changes aimed at better protecting the rights of persons with disabilities. These were, for instance, amendments to electoral law[379] and broadcasting law,[380] introducing adjustments for persons with disabilities. CRPD was neither mentioned in these laws nor in their explanatory memoranda. CRPD was directly addressed in amendments to the construction law[381] stipulating that public utility facilities and multi-family housing have to be accessible for persons with disabilities. CRPD also had a direct impact on the shape of the law on accessibility[382] which has explicitly endorsed the definitions of universal design and reasonable accommodation contained in CRPD. Reference to CRPD was also included in an ordinance establishing school curricula.[383]

CRPD has been referenced in parliamentary debates, mostly in questions addressed to the government by members of parliament. These were inquiries related in general to the implementation of CRPD[384] or to its specific aspects,

---

[378] According to the Polish Code on Family and Guardianship a disabled person whose disability results from a mental illness or mental disability and who is of marriageable age, cannot get married without the court's approval based on the statement that the health or mental condition of that person does not jeopardise the marriage, nor the health of prospective children, and on condition that such a person has not been fully incapacitated.

[379] Law of 11 July 2014, Dz.U. of 2014, item 1072.

[380] Law of 25 March 2011, Dz.U. of 2011, No. 85, item 459.

[381] Law of 5 July 2018, Dz.U. of 2018, item 1496.

[382] Law of 19 July 2019, Dz.U. of 2019, item 1696.

[383] Regulation of Ministry of Education of 14 February 2017, Dz.U. of 2017, item 356.

[384] Eg Official response to inquiry 7268 of the Minister of Labour and Social Affairs, 29 September 2014; Official response to inquiry 19104 of the Minister of Family, Labour and Social Affairs, 8 March 2018.

such as education[385] and access to justice.[386] The government was also questioned about the ratification of OP-CRPD by Poland.[387] Poland is not yet a party to this treaty, and has demonstrated no political will to accede, despite the recommendation of the CRPD Cttee[388] and the actions undertaken by the NHRI, which in 2016 addressed to the Prime Minister an appeal to ratify OP-CRPD, supported by 170 NGOs.[389] The reasons for not ratifying OP-CRPD are the same as those relating to OP-CESCR: controversies on justiciability of economic, social and cultural rights and the possible consequences of decisions against Poland.[390]

Pursuant to article 33(1) of CRPD, Poland has designated a focal point within the government, the Ministry of Family and Social Policy. It has also been designated as the mechanism coordinating the implementation of CRPD. In exercising this function, the Minister is supported by the Government Plenipotentiary for Persons with Disabilities. Besides this, a Team for the Implementation of the Provisions of the Convention on the Rights of Persons with Disabilities was appointed. It is composed of representatives of the ministries involved in the implementation of CRPD, and acts as a coordinating mechanism. However, this framework has been assessed by NHRI[391] and several NGOs[392] as insufficient, in particular because in their opinion it is focused mostly on social policy. The role of the independent monitoring mechanism is performed by NHRI, the Commissioner for Human Rights. These duties have been imposed on this body without the inclusion of any relevant provisions in the Act on the Commissioner for Human Rights.[393] This is a serious negligence that has so far not been remedied (see subsection on NHRI).

---

385 Parliamentary inquiry 4406 to the Minister of Education, 24 June 2016.
386 Parliamentary inquiry 25615 to the Minister of Investment and Development, 27 August 2018.
387 Parliamentary inquiry 323 to the Prime Minister, 5 December 2019.
388 CRPD Cttee, COs on the initial report of Poland para 6.
389 Information of the Commissioner for Human Rights on measures taken by the Republic of Poland in 2015–2017 in order to implement the provisions of the Convention on the Rights of Persons with Disabilities 4.
390 Official response to inquiry 323 of the Minister of Family, Labour and Social Affairs, 29 January 2020.
391 Information of the Commissioner for Human Rights 30.
392 Eg Alternative Report on the Implementation of the UN Convention on the Rights of Persons with Disabilities, Foundation KSK (2015) 66–67.
393 For comparison, the relevant provision on the mandate of NPM under OP-CAT, which is also performed by the Commissioner, was included in the Act.

For almost a decade since ratification, Poland has adopted no comprehensive strategy for implementing CRPD,[394] a situation that has seriously affected its implementation and led to criticism by NHRI,[395] NGOs[396] and the CRPD Cttee.[397] CRPD was mentioned in some policies, for instance, those related to older persons,[398] health services for persons with disabilities[399] and accessibility.[400]

5.7.2 Reliance by Judiciary

Taking into account that CRPD is one of the latest human rights treaties incorporated into the Polish legal system, it has had quite a significant impact on the judiciary. The Constitutional Tribunal examined the conformity of Polish law with CRPD in a few cases. These were judgments concerning issues such as the right to organise assembly by persons deprived of legal capacity,[401] accessibility of the local train transport[402] and facilitating access to driving licence tests for persons with disabilities.[403] Some judgments of the Constitutional Tribunal have been criticised for not sufficiently taking CRPD into account, and thus not challenging legal provisions where their conformity with CRPD has been uncertain.[404] In one case this concerned the prohibition contained in the civil code on persons with intellectual or mental disabilities entering into marriage.[405] Another one concerned provisions of the electoral code that a person who was permanently unable to work due to his or her disability could not hold the office of mayor.[406]

---

[394] This type of document was adopted by the government in 2021: Strategy for Persons with Disabilities (2021–2030), MP of 2021, item 218.
[395] Information of the Commissioner for Human Rights para 98.
[396] Helsinki Foundation for Human Rights – Alternative Report on the Implementation of the UN Convention on the Rights of Persons with Disabilities in Poland 4.
[397] CRPD Cttee, COs on the initial report of Poland, para 5.
[398] Long-term Senior Policy (2014–2020), MP of 2014, item 118.
[399] Governmental programme on the public medical services for persons with disabilities (2020), MP of 2020, item 856.
[400] Governmental Programme 'Accessibility Plus' (2018–2025) of 17 July 2018.
[401] Constitutional Tribunal judgment of 18 September 2014, K 44/12.
[402] Constitutional Tribunal judgment of 7 July 2015, K 47/12.
[403] Constitutional Tribunal judgment mentioned of 8 June 2016, K 37/13.
[404] Eg R Stefanicki, 'Glosa do wyroku TK z dnia 22 listopada 2016 r., K 13/15' (2017), Prokuratura i Prawo 11; D Lis-Staranowicz, 'Glosa do wyroku TK z dnia 23 stycznia 2014 r., K 51/12' (2014), Przegląd Sejmowy 2.
[405] Constitutional Tribunal judgment of 22 November 2016, K 13/15.
[406] Constitutional Tribunal judgment of 23 January 2014, K 51/12.

CRPD was invoked by the Supreme Court in a few cases, mostly related to protection of the rights of persons with disabilities during court proceedings.[407] Certainly, CRPD has been most often addressed in proceedings before the administrative courts. It can be observed that CRPD is well known and readily used by claimants in proceedings against public institutions, for example, in cases related to entitlement to social benefits or other forms of public support,[408] or access to education.[409] Although CRPD has been referred to in the process of interpreting law,[410] courts often deny recognition of it as a basis for individual claims,[411] a problem that overshadows the impact of CRPD on the judiciary. Arguments about the reluctance of courts to recognise the justiciability of some of the rights provided for by CRPD have been also raised by the government as an obstacle to the ratification of OP-CRPD.[412]

5.7.3 Impact on and through Independent State Institutions

The NHRI, which is also an independent mechanism under article 33 of CRPD, has been actively engaged in the promotion and monitoring of CRPD. Pursuant to article 33(3) of CRPD, an Expert Committee on Persons with Disabilities operates within the Office of the Commissioner as a consultative body. The NHRI has initiated research and formulated recommendations related to various issues covered by CRPD, such as access to health care,[413] access to election facilities[414] and access to justice.[415] It has advocated the ratification of

---

407 Decision of the Supreme Court of 8 December 2016, III CZ 54/16; Decision of the Supreme Court of 26 February 2015, III CZP 102/14; Decision of the Supreme Court of 21 December 2017, III CZP 66/17.
408 Supreme Administrative Court judgment of 20 December 2017, I OSK 1691/17; Supreme Administrative Court judgment of 15 February 2017, I OSK 2068/15.
409 Supreme Administrative Court judgment of 23 June 2017, I OSK 552/17; Supreme Administrative Court judgment of 24 January 2019, I OSK 1703/18.
410 Supreme Administrative Court judgment of 22 October 2018, V SA/Wa 362/18.
411 Decision of the Supreme Administrative Court of 17 January 2017; I OSK 2894/16; Provincial Administrative Court of Bydgoszcz judgment of 13 February 2019, I SA/Bd 933/18.
412 Official response to inquiry 323 to the Minister of Family, Labour and Social Affairs of 29 January 2020.
413 A Mikołajczyk, 'Dostępność usług opieki zdrowotnej dla osób z niepełnosprawnościami– analiza i zalecenia' (2020), Zasada Równego Traktowania. Prawo i praktyka 2.
414 J Zbieranek, *Dostosowanie lokali obwodowych komisji wyborczych do potrzeb wyborców z niepełnosprawnościami. Raport Rzecznika Praw Obywatelskich z wyborów samorządowych w 2018 roku* (Biuro Rzecznika Praw Obywatelskich 2019).
415 A Błaszczak-Banasiak, K Majdzińska and M Zima-Parjaszewska, 'Dostęp osób z niepełnosprawnościami do wymiaru sprawiedliwości – analiza i zalecenia' (2016), Zasada równego traktowania. Prawo i praktyka, nr 21.

OP-CRPD by Poland, and called on the government to undertake relevant actions.[416] The NHRI has been also a leading actor challenging the conformity of Polish law with CRPD by initiating proceedings before the Constitutional Tribunal.[417] In 2018 the NHRI submitted a report to the CRPD Cttee presenting the main challenges and recommendations related to the implementation of CRPD in Poland.[418] With regard to its mandate as an independent monitoring mechanism under CRPD, it highlighted the lack of a proper legal framework for performing this task, and the lack of a sufficient budget.[419] The NHRI has also been involved in the constructive dialogue, including by participating in the informal meetings with the CRPD Cttee's rapporteur on the Polish report.[420] These issues were addressed by CRPD Cttee in its recommendations,[421] but an improvement in the situation has not yet been achieved.

5.7.4 Impact on and through Non-state Actors

As in many other countries around the world, disability rights organisations in Poland have been active supporters of the ratification and implementation of CRPD. For instance, an extensive report on conformity of Polish law with CRPD was prepared in 2008 by experts related to NGOs and academia.[422] CRPD has had a strong impact on civil society in Poland, and served as an umbrella for various initiatives undertaken in cooperation with numerous organisations of persons with disabilities. Some examples of these initiatives include: monitoring the implementation of CRPD by ministries and public bodies, drafting projects for legal acts, organising annual congresses on the rights of persons with disabilities, and prizes for 'ambassadors of CRPD'. As a result of the cooperation of dozens of NGOs and individual experts, a detailed alternative report

---

416 Statement of the Commissioner for Human Rights of 21 January 2016, XI.516.1.2015.AB.
417 Eg Constitutional Tribunal judgment of 23 January 2014, K 51/12; Constitutional Tribunal judgment of 7 July 2015, K 47/12; Constitutional Tribunal judgment of 8 June 2016, K 37/13; Constitutional Tribunal judgment of 22 November 2016, K 13/15.
418 Information of the Commissioner for Human Rights on measures taken by the Republic of Poland in 2015–2017 in order to implement the provisions of the Convention on the Rights of Persons with Disabilities.
419 For instance, in 2013 the budget allocated to the Commissioner for performing tasks as independent mechanism under CRPD was around 160 000 EUR; Information of the Commissioner for Human Rights 13.
420 Magdalena Kuruś, Director Department for Equal Treatment in the Office of the Commissioner for Human Rights, 27 May 2021, on-line interview.
421 CRPD Cttee, COs on the initial report of Poland, para 56.
422 Polska droga do Konwencji o prawach osób niepełnosprawnych ONZ, AM Waszkielewicz (ed), Fundacja Instytut Rozwoju Regionalnego 2008.

covering all aspects of CRPD was prepared and submitted to the CRPD Cttee.[423] It should be emphasised that the reporting by Poland to the CRPD Cttee in 2018 met with unprecedented interest from civil society in Poland. Apart from the alternative report previously mentioned, at least seven other submissions were delivered to the CRPD Cttee by NGOs. Nevertheless, the need for inclusion of smaller NGOs and a more intersectional approach towards CRPD has been indicated.[424]

5.7.5 Impact of State Reporting

Since the first COs on Poland were only issued by the CRPD Cttee in October 2018, it is too early to thoroughly assess their impact on national law and practice. As mentioned, some positive developments, such as laws on accessibility, have already been introduced. Nevertheless, there are still many challenges and problems to tackle, as emphasised during the reporting process by the CRPD Cttee, the NHRI, NGOs and other actors. The most burning issues and areas that will require systemic changes include the replacement of the institution of incapacitation with a supported decision-making system; the introduction of a unified system of disability assessment based on the level of support required by an individual person, not on health dysfunctions; the transition from institutional care to community-based support; repealing the prohibition on persons with intellectual or mental disabilities entering into marriage and creating a support system for persons with disabilities exercising parental roles; and the introduction of systemic solutions with regard to personal assistance.[425] Poland has so far not declared any intention to withdraw its reservations and declarative interpretation.[426]

5.7.6 Brief Conclusion

Although CRPD is a relatively new human rights treaty within the Polish legal system, it seems to be more visible and influential in comparison to other anti-discrimination treaties such as CEDAW and CERD. It has been present in political debates, and the state authorities have undertaken some activities to establish institutional framework and policies related to CRPD. Provisions of CRPD

---

423 Alternative Report on the Implementation of the UN Convention on the Rights of Persons with Disabilities, Foundation KSK (2015).
424 M Kocejko, 'Nic o nas bez nas? Zaangażowanie ruchu osób z niepełnosprawnościami w monitoring wdrażania Konwencji ONZ o prawach osób niepełnosprawnych w Polsce. Studium przypadku' (2018) 4 Studia z Polityki Publicznej 20.
425 Information of the Commissioner for Human Rights 4.
426 CRPD Cttee, Summary Records (initial report of Poland) paras 41–42.

have been reflected in some legal acts. Significant efforts to promote CRPD and monitor its implementation have been made by civil society and the NHRI. Nevertheless, Poland has still failed to implement many of its obligations under CRPD. This results from various factors, including limited financial resources, but the key issue is the lack of a proper, systemic approach towards the rights of persons with disabilities. Poland still has to internalise the paradigm shift from medical to social model of disability and to adjust its institutions in order to guarantee individual autonomy, inclusion and non-discrimination of persons with disabilities.

6   Conclusion

As a founding member of the UN, Poland has for several decades been engaged with the treaty body system. It has accepted as binding seven of the nine core human rights treaties (CERD, CCPR, CESCR, CEDAW, CRC, CAT and CRPD). The impact of these treaties and their monitoring bodies on Polish law and policies has been related to the political circumstances shaping the state's attitude to human rights in general. Under the Communist regime, although it ratified UN treaties, Poland did so mostly for propaganda reasons, without protecting individual rights (especially civil and political rights) in practice. As a result of the democratic transition initiated in 1989, much effort was undertaken to build democratic institutions and to incorporate human rights within the state's structure. The Constitution, which includes a comprehensive human rights catalogue, was adopted in 1997, and independent courts were established. Most provisions of UN human rights treaties have been reflected in Polish law, but a direct impact is barely visible. Aspirations to join the CoE and the EU and implementation of the regional standards certainly played the major role for advancement of human rights in Poland, whereas the UN system was relegated to a secondary role.

After democratic transition, while securing political and economic stability, Poland had the chance to focus on implementing international human rights obligations. This became a missed opportunity, since no general institutional framework was established, nor any strategy to implement UN human rights treaties and the recommendations of their monitoring bodies. This situation may be attributable, at least to some extent, to the nature of the UN human rights system, based as it is on voluntary cooperation and dialogue with the state parties, without a robust enforcement mechanism. Besides this, subsequent Polish governments, regardless of the political parties in power, evaded responsibility for violations in individual cases by denying the ratification to OP-CRPD, OP-CESCR and OP-CRC.

The impact on law, the judiciary and politics is not related to the amount of time that a given treaty has been in force in relation to Poland or to any reservations that were entered. For instance, CRC and CRPD have been encumbered with reservations, but have had a stronger impact than prior and fully-accepted CERD and CEDAW. In comparison to other treaties, CRC and CRPD are fairly visible in law and practice, but for different reasons. In the case of CRC, Polish 'authorship' of this treaty has been regularly and eagerly invoked in parliamentary debates, albeit without more substantive references to its norms. Besides being addressed in a token manner, CRC has also been misused to restrict access to reproductive rights. As for CRPD, it became part of Polish law thanks to the successful mobilisation of numerous organisations of persons with disabilities. It has frequently been used in litigation before domestic courts. In contrast to other treaties, an institutional mechanism (albeit with many imperfections) has been established for implementation, which could arise from the treaty provision that directly imposes such an obligation on states. Another specific example is CESCR, the implementation of which remains limited due to the 'programmatic' interpretation of the economic, social and cultural rights by the executive and judiciary in Poland. These are but some of the noted peculiarities.

Certainly, UN human rights treaties play an important role for other actors, in particular the NHRI and NGOs. This can be observed through the instances of active engagement in the reporting process, including a growing number of submissions to the Committees. Treaties and recommendations of the treaty bodies are also employed in advocacy activities. It may be expected that in case human rights in Poland continue backsliding, as has been the case since the post-2015 constitutional breakdown, their significance for the human rights movement in Poland will increase.

CHAPTER 15

The Impact of the United Nations Human Rights Treaties on the Domestic Level in the Russian Federation

Aslan Abashidze, Aleksandra Koneva and Alexander Solntsev

1   Introduction to Human Rights in the Russian Federation

Russia as an independent state was established in the ninth century. The Russian Federation was formed as the successor of the Union of Soviet Socialist Republics (USSR) after proclaiming its sovereignty in the Declaration of State Sovereignty of 12 June 1990. As a successor of the USSR Russia has inherited participation in various treaties, including core international human rights treaties – the International Convention on the Elimination of All Forms of Racial Discrimination (CERD); the International Covenant on Economic, Social and Cultural Rights (CESCR); the International Covenant on Civil and Political Rights (CCPR); the Convention on the Elimination of All Forms of Discrimination against Women (CEDAW); and the Convention Against Torture and Other Cruel, Inhuman, or Degrading Treatment or Punishment (CAT).

While the USSR experience was useful for Russia, especially the trend of active ratification of international treaties, the withdrawal of reservations to human rights treaties in 1989 and the focus on the protection of economic, social and cultural rights, Russia has chosen to follow the track of assuming new international human rights obligations on the basis of a different approach and traditions compared to the approach of the USSR, which was mostly grounded on the Communist ideology.

During the new historical period the Russian engagement with the human rights treaties system was now largely guided by the new Constitution, adopted by a popular vote on 12 December 1993. The 1993 Constitution proclaimed the Russian Federation as a democratic, federal, social state with a republican form of government, 'whose policy is aimed at creating conditions for a worthy life and a free development of man'.[1] At its start, the Constitution establishes

---

1   The Constitution of the Russian Federation <http://www.constitution.ru/en/10003000-01.htm> accessed 12 April 2022.

an obligation of the state to recognise and protect human rights as they are regarded as the supreme values of the state. Chapter 2 of the Constitution contains a catalogue of all categories of human rights, which was largely influenced by the International Bill of Human Rights.[2] Chapter 2 of the Constitution may not be revised by the Federal Assembly (the Parliament). There might be a proposal for the revision of the Constitution, but the procedure is very complex and may result in the drafting of a new Constitution (article 135 of the Constitution). According to article 72 of the Constitution 'the protection of the rights and freedoms of man and citizen' is under the joint jurisdiction of the Russian Federation and its federal subjects, currently numbering 85.

A comprehensive machinery responsible for the protection of human rights was developed in the country. Human rights are protected by the legislature, the executive and the judiciary. The President of the Russian Federation is the guarantor of the Constitution and of human and civil rights and freedoms. Article 103 of the Constitution provided the basis for the establishment of the national human rights institution – the Office of the High Commissioner for Human Rights in the Russian Federation (Ombudsman).[3] The process of formalising the legal status of the Ombudsman was intensified due to the accession of Russia to the Council of Europe,[4] and finalised with the adoption of the Federal Constitutional Act 1 of 26 February 1997, pursuant to which the main task of the Ombudsman is to receive and consider complaints from rights holders against decisions, acts or omissions of Russian state bodies, local administrations and officials violating their rights. The Ombudsman is authorised to refer the matter to court, and also to participate in the legally-prescribed manner in the legal proceedings. The Ombudsman may also submit complaints to the Constitutional Court of the Russian Federation concerning the violation of citizens' constitutional rights. It is independent and is not subordinate to any state bodies or officials. In 2015 it received status 'A' accreditation from the Global Alliance of National Human Rights Institutions (GANHRI) and, therefore, is fully compliant with the principles relating to the status of national institutions (Paris Principles).[5] The system of regional

---

2   VA Kartashkin and AP Vihryan, 'Konstituciya Rossii: prava i svobody cheloveka' ('The Constitution of Russia: Human Rights and Freedoms') (2018) 12 Modern Law 20–28.
3   The article states: 'The jurisdiction of the State Duma includes: f. appointment and dismissal of the Commissioner for human rights, who acts according to the federal constitutional law'.
4   Parliamentary Assembly, 'Opinion 193 (1996). Application by Russia for Membership of the Council of Europe' (25 January 1996) Doc 7463.
5   O Goncharenko, 'Preimushhestva statusa "A" dlja Upolnomochennogo po pravam cheloveka v Rossijskoj Federacii (obzor dejatel'nosti)' ('Benefit of "A" Status for the High Commissioner for Human Rights in the Russian Federation (overview of the activities)') Materials of the II

commissioners for human rights has been established in all 85 subjects of the Federation. Under the legislation of three Russian regions special posts have been created for commissioners for the rights of indigenous peoples of the North and the Far East.

With a view to the further development of an institutional human rights structure, commissioners for children's rights and for the rights of entrepreneurs have been set up within the Office of the President of the Russian Federation in 2009 and 2012, respectively, to function alongside the Ombudsman. Commissioners for children's rights have been established in 83 federal subjects.

There currently are many human rights issues that attract the attention of the state federal, regional and local bodies, including civil society, regional and universal human rights mechanisms. Among them one should mention issues such as the state's regulation of the activities of non-governmental organisations (NGOs) that perform functions of 'foreign agents';[6] the right to freedom of association; domestic violence; indigenous peoples' rights; the right to a healthy environment; the rights of detainees; the right to health; the right to housing; and the right to social security. The state policy on regulating the activities of NGOs that perform functions of 'foreign agents' has raised discussions in society and at state level about its effectiveness with regard to the organisations that deal with human rights problems and attempt to cooperate with international human rights bodies. Specifically, the criticism was targeted at the existing law provisions establishing the obligation of such organisations to register as 'foreign agents' and the provision of administrative sanctions for violations of these rules, as well as at the grounds and procedure for declaring the activities of a foreign or international NGOs undesirable in the territory of Russia.

Another problematic aspect relates to developments in the pension system which resulted in the adoption of Federal Law N 350-FZ of 3 October 2018 that provided for the gradual increase of the retirement age with the aim of the subsequent growth in the amount of retirement benefits. This reform is perceived by the authorities as one of the most difficult decisions of the state in recent years. The tensions in society and among state officials[7] persist with a group

---

International conference 'Problems of the Protection of Human Rights in Eurasia: Exchange of Best Practices of Ombudsmen' (2019) 216–223.

6 'Foreign agents' are NGOs that receive foreign funding and engage in political activity, as enshrined in the Federal Law 121-FZ of 20 July 2012.

7 Moskalkova (the Ombudsman) raised new issues occurring in the retirement sphere. Ria novosti (news) (14 June 2019) <https://ria.ru/20190614/1555565709.html> accessed 12 April 2022.

of parliamentarians from the non-ruling political parties having requested the Constitutional Court to consider the compatibility of the provisions of the law with the provisions of the Constitution.[8]

Another noteworthy human rights development is the recent increase in the powers of the Constitutional Court with regard to considering the compatibility of the interpretations of its international obligations in the decisions of the interstate human rights bodies with the Constitution and their possibility to be executed in Russia upon the request of the competent state bodies.[9] The situation has led to more discussions when the Court rendered its first rulings on the impossibility of executing the two judgments of the European Court of Human Rights (ECtHR) – *Anchugov and Gladkov v Russia* and *OAO Neftyanaya Kompaniya Yukos v Russia*. The initiators and supporters of such reforms and rulings of the Court referred to the fact that such an approach offers a possibility to search for a constructive dialogue between the Constitutional Court and international bodies, particularly the European Court.[10] They consider that the situations of discrepancies between the Constitution and the decisions of these bodies may be exceptional due to the compatibility of the Constitution with the international treaties accepted by the Russian Federation. Furthermore, the precedent was invoked by other European states following a similar approach towards implementation of the European Convention on Human Rights (ECHR). Notwithstanding such argumentation, some researchers, civil society representatives and officials[11] characterised this novelty as a 'sharp

---

[8] In April 2019 the Court decided that the determination of the retirement age is the prerogative of the legislator, therefore the Russian Constitution does not exclude the possibility of changing the retirement age. The Constitutional Court found it legal to increase the retirement age. RBC information agency (4 April 2019) <https://www.rbc.ru/society/04/04/2019/5ca526f19a794734c12179bf> accessed 12 April 2022.

[9] Federal Constitutional Law of 14 December 2015 No 7-FKZ 'On Amending the Federal Constitutional Law' 'On the Constitutional Court of the Russian Federation' <http://www.consultant.ru/document/cons_doc_LAW_190427/> accessed 12 April 2022.

[10] AKh Abashidze, MV Ilyashevich and AM Solntsev, '*Anchugov & Gladkov v Russia*' (2017) 111 (2) American Journal of International Law 461.

[11] S Yu Marochkin, 'A Russian Approach to International Law in the Domestic Legal Order: Basics, Development and Perspectives' (2016) 26 Italian Yearbook of International Law 15; see also N Chaeva, 'The Russian Constitutional Court and its Actual Control over the ECtHR Judgment in Anchugov and Gladkov' (2016) EJIL: Talk! <https://www.ejiltalk.org/the-russian-constitutional-court-and-its-actual-control-over-the-ecthr-judgement-in-anchugov-and-gladko/> accessed 12 April 2022.

political and juridical turn away from European cooperation and fulfillment of the ECtHR's judgments'.[12]

Among the positive developments in the country, the progress achieved in the protection of children's rights deserves attention. One of the most important steps is the adoption and implementation of the 2012–2017 National Children's Interests Action Strategy and proclamation of 2018–2027 period as a Decade of Childhood in Russia. The work performed by the Ombudsman and the Office of the Commissioner for Children's Rights has achieved demonstrable positive results.[13] Another positive pattern is the progressive approach developed by the judiciary with regard to the enforcement of the views of the treaty bodies. Although Russia did not adopt legislation regulating the legal status of the views, the Constitutional and the Supreme Courts developed a practice of applying the views as grounds for revising the court decision on new circumstances in criminal and civil proceedings.[14]

2   Relationship of the Russian Federation with the International Human Rights System in General

As one of the world's great powers and creators of the Anti-Hitler Coalition, the USSR played a key role in establishing the United Nations (UN). It was the USSR that proposed the inclusion of the provision on 'promoting and encouraging respect for human rights and fundamental freedoms for all without distinction as to race, sex, language, or religion' in the text of article 1(3) of

---

12   Marochkin (n 11) 15, 40.
13   Common core document; Interview with Olga Goncharenko, Senior Adviser, International Relations Department, Office of the High Commissioner of Human Rights of the Russian Federation (18 July 2019), by email; interview with Alexander Molokhov, advocate, Head of a working group on international legal issues in the Permanent mission of Crimea under the President of Russia, Chairperson of administrative council, non-profit non-governmental public organisation 'Taurida international association' (17 June 2019), telephonically; interview with the 1st representative of the Ministry of Foreign Affairs of the Russian Federation (17 July 2019), by email; interview with Professor Tatiana Zrazhevskaya, Commissioner for Human Rights in Voronezh Region, Doctor of Legal Sciences, Honoured Lawyer of the Russian Federation (22 August 2019), by email; interview with Professor Sergey Baburkin, Commissioner for Human Rights in Yaroslavl Region, Doctor of Political Sciences (29 July 2019), by email. (All notes of interviews on file with authors.)
14   Decision of the Constitutional Court of the Russian Federation N 1248-O (28 June 2012); Decision of the Presidium of the Supreme Court of the Russian Federation N 128-П18ПР (10 October 2018).

the UN Charter.[15] Subsequently, the USSR was also one of the initiators of the establishment of the Economic and Social Council and has always been among the active participants in the drafting of the UN international human rights treaties.

The state has for a long time been at the forefront of the developments taking place in the human rights treaty body (UNTB) system. It was Russia that in 2012 initiated, with the support of a group of states, the launch of the UN intergovernmental process of the General Assembly on strengthening and enhancing the effective functioning of the treaty body system,[16] which resulted in UN GA Resolution 68/268 of 9 April 2014. Russia also cooperates with other universal human rights mechanisms, including the UN Human Rights Council (HRC),[17] the Universal Periodic Review (UPR) and the Special Procedures. Russia was a member of the HRC in 2006–2012 and 2013–2016. As stated by the Permanent Representative of the Russian Federation to the UN Office and other international organisations in Geneva, Mr G Gatilov, although not being a member of the Council, 'we continue to actively work in this organ through promoting our initiatives'.[18] In 2019 Russia applied for membership of the HRC for the period 2021–2023. Russia has undergone three cycles of the UPR (the most recent one in May 2018).

The country is not among those states that issued a standing invitation to Special Procedures. The most recent visits to Russia were conducted by the Special Rapporteur on the negative impact of unilateral coercive measures on the enjoyment of human rights in 2017, the Special Rapporteur on the independence of judges and lawyers in 2013 (second mission) and the Special

---

15 VA Kartashkin, 'Princip vseobshchego uvazheniya i soblyudeniya prav i osnovnyh svobod cheloveka. Mezhdunarodnyĭ bill' o pravah cheloveka. Mezhdunarodnaya zashchita prav cheloveka: uchebnik' ('The Principle of Universal Respect for and Observance of Human Rights and Fundamental Freedoms. The International Bill of Human Rights') in AKh Abashidze (ed), *International Protection of Human Rights* (RUDN University 2017) 89.

16 UN Doc A/66/L.37 (16 February 2012).

17 During the membership in the Council Russia proposed the adoption of various resolutions by the Council, including on the protection of the Roma; on human rights and the arbitrary deprivation of nationality; on promoting human rights through sport and the ideals of the Olympic movement; on the 50th anniversary of the adoption and 40th anniversary of the entry into force of the International Covenants on Human Rights; and on the 70th anniversary of the Universal Declaration of Human Rights and 25th anniversary of the Vienna Declaration and Programme of Action. Russia also initiated a number of conferences within the platform of the HRC, including on the protection of Christians in the world, in particular in the Middle East, in March 2015.

18 Russia will apply again for membership in the UN Human Rights Council. *Interfax* (news) (12 March 2019) <https://www.interfax.ru/russia/653899> accessed 12 April 2022.

Rapporteur in the field of cultural rights in 2012. Among the special mechanisms that have sent Russia their requests for visits and are awaiting the response are the Special Rapporteur on the situation of human rights defenders, the Special Rapporteur on the promotion and protection of human rights and fundamental freedoms while countering terrorism, the Special Rapporteur on the promotion and protection of the right to freedom of opinion and expression, and the Working Group on Enforced or Involuntary Disappearances. The visit of the Special Rapporteur on the human rights of internally displaced persons may well be scheduled later, since Russia has given its acceptance of the visit request to this mandate.

Apart from participation in the core international treaties and cooperation with the UN human rights mechanisms, Russia has also committed itself to obligations under other human rights treaties adopted within the UN[19] and its specialised agencies, including the International Labour Organisation (ILO)[20] and the United Nations Educational, Scientific and Cultural Organization (UNESCO).[21] Russia signed the International Criminal Court (ICC) Statute in 2000, but withdrew its signature in 2016.[22]

A significant component of the national human rights system in Russia is provided by the treaties and activities of the Council of Europe (CoE). In 2018 Russia celebrated 20 years of its membership in the CoE and the ratification of the ECHR. On this occasion a special issue on Russia and the European Convention on Human Rights was prepared with the analysis of 20 cases that influenced the Russian legal system.[23] Significantly, under the Russian legislation the decisions of the ECtHR are regarded as 'new evidence', which discovery provides a ground for reopening of the court proceedings.[24] During these

---

19   United Nations Convention against Transnational Organised Crime and the related Protocol to Prevent, Suppress and Punish Trafficking in Persons, Especially Women and Children.

20   A member to 77 Conventions and 2 Protocols. See <https://www.unesco.org/en/countries/ru/conventions> accessed 15 September 2023.

21   Russian Federation <https://www.unesco.org/en/countries/ru/conventions> accessed 15 September 2023.

22   AY Skuratova, 'Rossiya i Rimskij statut Mezhdunarodnogo ugolovnogo suda' ('Russia and the Rome Statute of the International Criminal Court') (2016) 4 Moscow Journal of International Law 125–137 <https://www.mjil.ru/jour/article/view/205?locale=ru_RU> accessed 12 April 2022.

23   Russia and the European Convention on Human Rights: 20 Years Together. 20 Cases that Changed the Russian Legal System. Case Law of the European Court of Human Rights Special Issue 5'2018 <https://rm.coe.int/20th-anniversary-of-russia-s-accession-to-the-european-convention-on-h/168088f64b> accessed 12 April 2022.

24   Art 413 § 4(2) of the Criminal Procedure Code of the Russian Federation; art 392 of the Code of Civil Procedure; art 311 of the Arbitration Procedure Code.

20 years Russia has gained vast experience in the execution of the decisions of the ECtHR.[25]

The membership of the CoE was marked by various events attracting the attention of the international community with the recent one associated with the suspension of the rights of the delegation of Russia in the Parliamentary Assembly of the CoE. During that period some Russian officials were even expressing ideas on leaving the ECHR and the ECtHR jurisdiction.[26] In July 2019 the Parliamentary Assembly of the Council of Europe (PACE) restored voting rights to Russia.[27] Therefore, the crisis seems to be left at this stage. The Russian Federation has a good record of participation in various CoE treaties and cooperation with its monitoring mechanisms.[28]

The domestic legal system of Russia demonstrates openness to the international law norms. The basis for this approach is provided by the Constitution. Under article 15(4) of the Constitution, the international agreements to which the Russian Federation is a party and the generally-recognised principles and rules of international law are forming part of the Russian national legal system and take precedence in the application over domestic laws. Under article 17, human rights are guaranteed, first, in accordance with the generally-recognised principles and rules of international law, and, second, in conformity with the Constitution. Significantly, the Constitution establishes the direct enforceability of human rights.

Article 46 of the Constitution guarantees the international dimension of the right of judicial protection, as everyone has a right to appeal to international human rights bodies in accordance with the international treaties of the Russian Federation in case of exhaustion of the national remedies.

---

25   In 2013 the Plenum of the Supreme Court of Russia summarised and systematised important questions dealing with the implementation of the ECtHR decisions.
26   Russia considers types of exclusion. Russia is ready to stop cooperation with the Council of Europe <https://www.kommersant.ru/doc/3961860> accessed 12 April 2022.
27   Russia returned to PACE. The powers of the Russian delegation are fully restored <https://www.vedomosti.ru/politics/articles/2019/06/26/805138-rossiya-vernulas-v-pase> accessed 12 April 2022.
28   Russia is a party to the European Social Charter; the Framework Convention for the Protection of National Minorities; the European Convention for the Prevention of Torture and Inhuman or Degrading Treatment or Punishment; the Council of Europe Convention on the Protection of Children Against Sexual Exploitation and Sexual Abuse; the Marrakesh Treaty to Facilitate Access to Published Works for Persons Who Are Blind, Visually Impaired, or Otherwise Print Disabled; the European Convention on Mutual Assistance in Criminal Matters.

The Supreme Court of Russia provided important clarifications on the status of international law in its rulings of 2003 No 5 (with amendments of 5 March 2013),[29] stating that the constitutional provisions of article 15(4) oblige and simultaneously provide the state authorities, including the courts, with an opportunity to directly apply the international treaties of the Russian Federation. Particularly, the Supreme Court stipulated in its Resolution of the Plenum of 31 October 1995 No 8 'On some issues of application of the Constitution of the Russian Federation by courts in the administration of justice' that when administering justice the courts should proceed from the fact that the generally-recognised principles and norms of international law, enshrined in the international covenants, conventions and other documents (in particular, the Universal Declaration of Human Rights, CCPR, CESCR) and international treaties to which the Russian Federation is a party, are the integral part of Russian legal system, in accordance with part 4 of article 15 of the Constitution.

There are many examples where courts invoke treaties as a justification of their decisions and indicate that these are not only compulsory for Russia, but also that they are in effect.[30] Thus, the norms of seven core international human rights treaties are directly enforceable in Russia as part of its national legal system. Many provisions of these treaties were integrated in the Russian Constitution and legislation and are applied by courts. Individuals or groups of individuals have a constitutional right to lodge communications to the treaty bodies on the violations of their rights by Russia after the exhaustion of local remedies. Importantly, in the opinion of the Supreme Court, when considering cases, the Russian courts must take into account the legal positions of the UNTBs, which activities constitute a 'subsequent practice in the application of the treaty which establishes the agreement of the parties regarding its interpretation' within the meaning of article 31(3)(b) of the 1969 Vienna Convention on the Law of Treaties.[31]

---

29   Resolution of the Plenum of the Supreme Court of the Russian Federation N 5 'On the application by courts of general jurisdiction of generally accepted principles and norms of international law and international treaties of the Russian Federation' (10 October 2003).
30   Marochkin (n 11) 15, 23.
31   Review of the jurisprudence of the Supreme Court of the Russian Federation N 1 (28 March 2018).

3 At a Glance: Formal Engagement of the Russian Federation with the UN Human Rights Treaty System

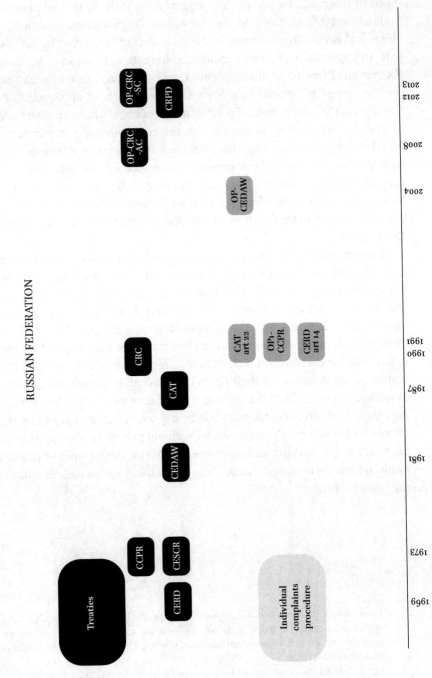

4   Role and Overall Impact of the UN Human Rights Treaties in the Russian Federation

4.1   *Role of UN Human Rights Treaties*

4.1.1   Formal Acceptance

Russia ratified seven core international human rights treaties, namely, CERD, CCPR, CESCR, CEDAW, CAT, CRC, CRPD, and OP-CRC-SC and OP-CRC-AC. Participation in CERD, CCPR, CESCR, CEDAW and CAT was inherited from the USSR by Russia in the context of succession. The ratifications were mostly motivated by the willingness of the USSR to confirm its commitment to international cooperation in the field of human rights together with the initiative to follow the general trend of other countries joining particular treaties.[32]

The first treaty to be ratified, in 1969, was CERD, followed by the ratification of CCPR and CESCR in 1973, as a preparatory measure for the participation of the USSR in the Conference on Security and Cooperation in Europe.[33] In 1981 the Soviet Union ratified CEDAW as a country that was among the initiators of the elaboration of this treaty.[34] Ratification of CAT took place in 1987, at a time of substantial political, economic and social reformation in the USSR (so-called *perestroika*) as an additional step on the path to democracy. In 1990, right after proclaiming its independence, Russia ratified the CRC with the same motivation of following the democracy path.

In 2008 and 2013, respectively, OP-CRC-SC and OP-CRC-AC were ratified based on the willingness of Russia to comply with international norms to protect child rights together with the development of legal cooperation with other states in this field.[35] The additional motivation for OP-CRC-AC was the implementation of the recommendation of the CRC Cttee to ratify this treaty. In 2012 Russia ratified CRPD, after having signed it in the aftermath of the victories of Russian citizens at the Paralympic Games in 2006. The subsequent ratification

---

[32] Y Kolosov and Y Reshetov 'Russia' in C Heyns and F Viljoen (eds), *The Impact of the United Nations Human Rights Treaties on the Domestic Level* (Kluwer Law International 2002) 499–500.

[33] ibid 499.

[34] Initial Report, CEDAW, Union of Soviet Socialist Republics, UN Doc CEDAW/C/5/Add.12 (9 March 1983) 1.

[35] Transcripts of the discussion of Bill No 35523-5 'On the ratification of the Optional Protocol to the Convention on the Rights of the Child on the involvement of children in armed conflict' (6 June 2008) The State Duma of the Russian Federation <http://api.duma.gov.ru/api/transcript/35523-5> accessed 12 April 2022; Explanatory note to the draft federal law 'On the ratification of the Optional Protocol to the Convention on the Rights of the Child on the Sale of Children, Child Prostitution and Child Pornography' <http://www.kremlin.ru/events/president/news/17891> accessed 12 April 2022.

of the treaty is related to the willingness to comply with international norms to protect the rights of persons with disabilities.[36]

Russian authorities periodically consider the prospects for accession to the International Convention on the Rights of All Migrant Workers and Members of their Families (CMW), the International Convention for the Protection of All Persons from Enforced Disappearance (CED) and OP-CAT as part of the policy aimed at gradually increasing its international obligations.[37] Russia considers that it is premature to join CMW. The decision not to join CMW is influenced by the fact that very few countries had ratified the treaty (mainly 'sending' countries), and that its ratification will demand much more of an effort on the part of Russia, as a 'receiving' country. Among the factors preventing the ratification of the treaty are economic reasons (the lack of resources for ensuring the implementation of the Convention's requirements); legal reasons (difficulties in reforming national legislation); and institutional reasons (the absence of necessary institutes for a comprehensive implementation of the Convention's norms).[38] In the same vein Russia considers it premature to accede to CED. However, many provisions of this treaty are said to be incorporated into the national legislation.[39]

With regard to OP-CAT, Russia contends that due to its active engagement with the European Committee for the Prevention of Torture (CPT) the work of the SPT established under OP-CAT largely overlaps with CPT. Meanwhile, the idea of joining the treaty and establishing a National Preventive Mechanism in line with it is quite popular among civil society. The Ombudsman proposed the establishment of such a mechanism in the form of 'the Ombudsman +' model without the accession of Russia to the Protocol.[40]

Unlike the USSR, which for a long time has insisted that the provisions of the treaties on individual complaints are interfering in the internal affairs of

---

[36] Russian President Dmitry Medvedev signed the Decree 'On Signing the Convention on the Rights of Persons with Disabilities' Official website of the Ministry of Labour and Social Affairs of the Russian Federation (2008) <https://rosmintrud.ru/social/invalid-defence/24> accessed 1 November 2019.

[37] Position on the Recommendations Presented to the Russian Federation by Foreign Delegations during the Third Cycle of the Universal Periodic Review <https://www.ohchr.org/EN/HRBodies/UPR/Pages/RUindex.aspx> accessed 12 April 2022.

[38] ZHA Zayonchkovskaya, 'The Protection of the Rights of Migrants Workers in the Countries of Central and Eastern Europe and the CIS and Perspectives of Joining the 1990 UN Convention' UNESCO Series of Country Reports on the Ratification of the UN Convention on Migrants (2004) UN Doc SHS/2004/MC/6/REV.

[39] Position on the Recommendations Presented to the Russian Federation by Foreign Delegations during the Third Cycle of the Universal Periodic Review <https://www.ohchr.org/EN/HRBodies/UPR/Pages/RUindex.aspx> accessed 12 April 2022.

[40] Commissioner for Human Rights in the Russian Federation. Report for 2018 183, 188. <http://ombudsmanrf.org/upload/files/docs/lib/doclad_2018.pdf> accessed 12 April 2022.

states and violate their sovereignty,[41] Russia opened a new page of accepting the competence of the treaty bodies to consider communications and conduct inquiries.[42] Four UNTBS (the HRCttee, the CAT Cttee, the CEDAW Cttee and the CERD Cttee) may consider individual communications against Russia and two UNTBS (the CAT Cttee and the CEDAW Cttee) may initiate inquiry procedure with regard to Russia. Right after its formation, on 1 October 1991, Russia accepted the competence of the HRCttee, the CAT Cttee and the CERD Cttee to consider individual communications and the competence of the CAT Cttee to conduct inquiries. In 2004, the Russian Federation ratified OP-CEDAW[43] as a step to demonstrate commitment to democratic tendencies in the field of gender equality, to raise the interest of Russian women in defending their rights in court and to enhance the awareness of international norms in this area.[44]

In 2017 the head of the Russian delegation informed the CESCR Cttee that accession to OP-CESCR was 'unnecessary, as national legislation was sufficiently well developed to provide for adequate protection measures for economic, social and cultural rights'[45] and that the NHRI was represented in all regions and maintained a website through which complaints could be filed.[46]

It is claimed that Russia's accession to OP-CRPD can be considered once the Russian national legislation, enforcement system and judicial practice have been fully developed to implement each norm of CRPD. This process is still ongoing.[47]

The majority of Russian state authorities do not see legal obstacles to the approval of OP-CRC-CP. However, the Ministry of Foreign Affairs together with the Ministry of Justice cautions against rushing into ratification due to the possible expansive interpretations of the phrase 'exhaustion of all internal mechanisms for the protection of the rights of the child' in the text of the Protocol.[48]

---

41 VA Kartashkin, 'To the 50th Anniversary of the Covenants on Human Rights' (2016) <https://eurasialaw.ru/nashi-rubriki/persona-grata/intervyu-s-kartashkinym-vladimirom-alekseevichem> accessed 12 April 2022.

42 AKh Abashidze and AE Koneva, Dogovornye organy po pravam cheloveka: uchebnoe posobie (Human Rights Treaty Bodies: textbook) (2nd edn, RUDN University 2015) 27.

43 Federal law N 52-FZ 'On ratification of the Optional Protocol to the Convention on the Elimination of All Forms of Discrimination against Women' (19 June 2004).

44 Russian women will now find it easier to defend their rights at the international level. Ministry of Foreign Affairs of the Russian Federation. RIA Novosti (2004) <https://ria.ru/20040603/604906.html> accessed 12 April 2022.

45 CESCR Cttee, 'Summary record of the 60th meeting', UN Doc E/C.12/2017/SR.60 (25 September 2017) para 18.

46 ibid.

47 CRPD Cttee, 'List of issues in relation to the initial report of the Russian Federation. Addendum. Replies of the Russian Federation to the list of issues', UN Doc CRPD/C/RUS/Q/1/Add.1 (23 November 2017).

48 The Federation Council supports the accession of the Russian Federation to the international mechanism for handling children's complaints about violations of their rights by

4.1.2 Reservations

The USSR made similar reservations to CERD, CAT and CEDAW, considering itself not bound by their provisions to refer disputes between parties over the interpretation or application of these treaties to the International Court of Justice (ICJ) for a decision, and that for referral of the dispute to the ICJ the consent of all parties to a particular dispute would be necessary. The motivation was the general reluctance of the USSR to accept the compulsory jurisdiction of the ICJ.[49] These reservations were subsequently withdrawn in 1989 'as a step towards a realisation of the "new thinking" in foreign policy conceptions and international law policies' in the period of *perestroika*.[50] The USSR also made a reservation to article 20 of CAT authorising the Committee to conduct inquiries, which was withdrawn in 1991.

4.1.3 General Attitude of State towards UN Treaty System

The state gives significant attention to cooperation with the UN treaty system as a key element of the universal human rights system. Russia regularly submits its periodic reports, takes part in the dialogues with the treaty bodies and presents follow up information on the recommendations received. It is the understanding of Russia that the treaties do not determine the legal status of the committees' recommendations (COs, views).[51] Russia considers that these are of a non-binding nature and no sanctions are established for their implementation.[52] Russia advocates its sovereign right to choose how the views are to be fulfilled with the recognition that they carry great weight and are taken seriously by its authorities.[53]

---

the state (post of 29 February 2012) The Russian Federation' Federation Council's official site <http://council.gov.ru/events/news/15920/> accessed 12 April 2022.

49 Kolosov and Reshetov (n 32) 501.

50 Th Schweisfurth, 'The Acceptance by the Soviet Union of the Compulsory Jurisdiction of the ICJ for Six Human Rights Conventions' (1991) 2 European Journal of International Law 110, 111.

51 Position of the Ministry of Justice with regard to CCPR and CAT. Information presented by the Ministry of Justice of the Russian Federation in connection with the interview questions related to this project (19 August 2019). Notes of all interviews on file with authors.

52 UN Committee Against Torture published COs on another report of Russia (14 August 2018) <https://www.advgazeta.ru/novosti/komitet-protiv-pytok-oon-opublikoval-zaklyuchitelnye-zamechaniya-na-ocherednoy-doklad-so-storony-rossii/> accessed 12 April 2022.

53 Periodic Report, CCPR, the Russian Federation, UN Doc CCPR/C/RUS/6 (20 December 2007) 7.

4.1.4 Level of Awareness

Given the vast territory of Russia and differences between urban and rural conditions, the level of awareness of the treaties is not even throughout the country. The majority of interviewees mentioned that the awareness of the treaties is generally inadequate in the country.[54] While the state organises various educational programmes and awareness-raising campaigns for state officials,[55] the knowledge of the treaties is demonstrated mostly by the officials of the governmental structures and the judiciary who are directly involved in the process of preparation and presentation of reports to the committees.[56] Some respondents even mentioned the problem of the low awareness about the recommendations of the treaty bodies by the state bodies that are in the position of taking the relevant measures.[57] A wide awareness-raising initiative is being realised in relation to the judiciary through professional training, and the programme includes international law norms, which is obligatory for all

---

54 Interview with Olga Goncharenko, Senior Adviser, International Relations Department, Office of the High Commissioner of Human Rights of the Russian Federation (18 July 2019), by email; interview with Alexander Molokhov, advocate, Head of a working group on international legal issues in the Permanent mission of Crimea under the President of Russia, Chairperson of administrative council, non-profit non-governmental public organisation 'Taurida international association' (17 June 2019), telephonically; Mikhail Todyshev, Chairperson of the Association of Shor People, Head of the Council of Elders of the Shor People, Vice President of the Russian Association of Indigenous Peoples of the North (RAIPON), Director of the Centre for Legal Resources of Indigenous Peoples, adviser to the member of the State Duma A.I. Otke (21 July 2019), Moscow, (notes on file with authors); interview with the 1st representative of the Ministry of Foreign Affairs of the Russian Federation (17 July 2019), by email; interview with Tatiana Zrazhevskaya, Commissioner for Human Rights in Voronezh Region, Doctor of Legal Sciences, Professor, Honoured Lawyer of the Russian Federation (22 August 2019), by email; interview with Sergey Baburkin, Commissioner for Human Rights in Yaroslavl Region, Doctor of Political Sciences, Professor (29 July 2019), by email.

55 'Responses to the list of issues (E/C.12/RUS/Q/5) to be discussed in connection with the consideration of the 5th periodic report of the Russian Federation (E/C.12/RUS/5)' UN Doc E/C.12/RUS/Q/5/Add.1 (25 February 2011), para 41; CEDAW Cttee, COs, the Russian Federation, UN Doc CEDAW/C/RUS/CO/8 (20 November 2015), paras 7, 42(b); SV Polenina, Pravovaya politika Rossijskoj Federacii v sfere gendernyh otnoshenij (Legal Policy of the Russian Federation in the Sphere of Gender Relations) Proceedings of the Institute of State and Law of the Russian Academy of Sciences, 2016 62–80.

56 Interview with the 1st representative of the Ministry of Foreign Affairs of the Russian Federation (17 July 2019), by email.

57 Interview with Tatiana Zrazhevskaya, Commissioner for Human Rights in Voronezh Region, Doctor of Legal Sciences, Professor, Honoured Lawyer of the Russian Federation (22 August 2019), by email.

judges in accordance with the 1992 Law on the Status of Judges in the Russian Federation.[58]

Nevertheless, it is hard to ensure the awareness of numerous judges across the entire country about the UN human rights treaties, taking into account that they annually hear more than 30 million cases.[59] Many legal practitioners are said not to be sufficiently familiar with the treaties and the committees and with the ways in which to use their powers at the national level.[60] There are few, if any, professional training organised for lawyers in this field.[61] Various training opportunities organised for lawyers, including by the Russian Federal Bar Association, mostly focus on developing skills for leading the case in the ECtHR, rather than the treaty bodies.[62]

The international human rights system is forming a part of the university curriculum and is studied within the general course on international law as well as in the context of special educational programmes at Bachelor, Master's and PhD levels. An example of such a programme is the joint Master's programme International Protection of Human Rights, which was established in 2009 as the first Master's programme in human rights in Russia, supported by the Office of the United Nations High Commissioner for Human Rights.[63] The programme is realised by the Consortium of nine Russian universities across Russia with the RUDN University as a leading university.[64] The programme

---

[58] The Supreme Court maintains the database 'Kontur,' which contains decisions and COs of treaty bodies for the use by the judiciary. The Supreme Court starting from 2016 also publishes on its website thematic volumes with summaries of treaty bodies decisions on various human rights issues (right to work, social security, freedom of associations, freedom from torture) as well as quarterly reviews of the practice of intergovernmental human rights bodies (summaries and full texts).

[59] Interview with Bogdan Zimnenko, Deputy Head of the Department for Systematisation of Legislation and Analysis of Judicial Practice – Head of the Department of International Law, Supreme Court of the Russian Federation (29 July 2019), Moscow (notes on file with authors).

[60] J van Uffelen, 'Effective Advocacy at the United Nations. Training Lawyers for Lawyers in the Russian Federation' (2019) <https://lawyersforlawyers.org/en/effective-advocacy-at-the-united-nations/> accessed 12 April 2022.

[61] The exclusion is training 'Effective Advocacy at UN Human Rights Mechanisms' that took place in Moscow on 19–20 April 2019 <https://lawyersforlawyers.org/en/training-course-on-effective-advocacy-at-the-united-nations-human-rights-mechanisms-in-moscow/> accessed 12 April 2022.

[62] Russian Federal Bar Association. Higher professional training courses for advocates (programme) <https://fparf.ru/> accessed 12 July 2019.

[63] UNHCR 'Progress report on the implementation of the World Programme for Human Rights Education' (26 June 2012) UN Doc A/HRC/21/20.

[64] Official website of the programme <https://riuc.ru/> accessed 12 April 2022.

focuses on teaching the basics of the universal and regional human rights systems, while some core international human rights treaties and UNTBs are studied in-depth in specialised courses.[65]

A sound contribution to the promotion of legal education in human rights is made by the Federal High Commissioner, who with the support of the President and Chairperson of the government, since 2017 has been working on the development of a human rights educational programme for schoolchildren and students (bachelor and specialist degree levels), including training for students of the above-mentioned Master's programme and lecture courses in Russian universities; and managing the specialised satellite website on human rights education.[66]

It seems that among the variety of Russian NGOs those that use treaties in their work are mostly those few that have experience in presenting alternative reports to the committees.[67] The level of awareness of the other NGOs is therefore low. Furthermore, there is a view that sometimes Russian NGOs misunderstand the legal significance of treaty bodies' COs (pointing to the obligation of the state to implement these as if they are legally binding) and the objective character of these recommendations, which is not always so.[68]

The local researchers are aware of the treaties and cite them in their work. However, there is more interest in the realisation of the ECHR and the analysis of the practice of the ECtHR, rather than the UN human rights treaties.[69] There is a perception that the academic papers and textbooks sometimes

---

[65] Discrimination and gender issues in current international law; protection of rights of indigenous peoples and minorities; promotion and protection of vulnerable groups human rights in international law; international legal basis for protection of right to health; protection of environmental human rights; international legal standards in the realisation of the right to work.

[66] See Summary Report on the activities of the High Commissioner for Human Rights in the Russian Federation for 2018 <http://ombudsmanrf.org/upload/files/docs/lib/Itog1.pdf> accessed 12 April 2022.

[67] Interview with Mikhail Todyshev, Chairperson of the Association of Shor People, Head of the Council of Elders of the Shor People, Vice President of the Russian Association of Indigenous Peoples of the North (RAIPON), Director of the Centre for Legal Resources of Indigenous Peoples, adviser to the member of the State Duma A.I. Otke (21 July 2019), Moscow; Tatiana Zrazhevskaya, Commissioner for Human Rights in Voronezh Region, Doctor of Legal Sciences, Professor, Honoured Lawyer of the Russian Federation (22 August 2019), by email.

[68] Interview with the 1st representative of the Ministry of Foreign Affairs of the Russian Federation (17 July 2019), by email.

[69] Interview with Sergey Baburkin, Commissioner for Human Rights in Yaroslavl Region, Doctor of Political Sciences, Professor (29 July 2019), by email.

contain incorrect or politically-motivated interpretations of the mandates of the treaty bodies.[70]

The Russian public is the least informed about the treaty system layer of society.[71] No information concerning translation of treaties into local languages has been found with the exception of translation of the main provisions of CRPD into Russian sign language.[72]

4.1.5 General Attitude of Russia towards UN Treaty System

Representatives of the Russian state authorities usually positively perceive the work of the committees and are willing to develop constructive dialogue with them.[73] However, there were a few instances when the state raised concerns on the content of some recommendations adopted by them. Specifically, Russia refused to accept the recommendations of the HRCttee on the situation in South Ossetia and insisted on their exclusion from the COs in question.[74] Another example was the State's reaction to the COs of the CERD Cttee relating to the situation in Crimea following a review of Russia's last periodic report. In particular, the Committee's right to make recommendations on issues that were not raised and considered as part of the consideration of the periodic

---

70 Interview with the 1st representative of the Ministry of Foreign Affairs of the Russian Federation Affairs (17 July 2019), by email.

71 Interview with Alexander Molokhov, advocate, Head of a working group on international legal issues in the Permanent mission of Crimea under the President of Russia, Chairperson of administrative council, non-profit non-governmental public organisation 'Taurida international association' (17 June 2019), telephonically; interview with Tatiana Zrazhevskaya, Commissioner for Human Rights in Voronezh Region, Doctor of Legal Sciences, Professor, Honoured Lawyer of the Russian Federation (22 August 2019), by email; interview with Sergey Baburkin, Commissioner for Human Rights in Yaroslavl Region, Doctor of Political Sciences, Professor (29 July 2019), by email.

72 The All-Russian Society of the Deaf. Convention on the Rights of Persons with Disabilities in Russian Sign Language (June 2016) <https://voginfo.ru/world/2016/06/23/theconventionontherightsofpersonswithdisabilitiesonrsl/> accessed 12 April 2022.

73 Deputy Minister of Justice, Mikhail Galperin, 'On the Investigation of the Torture Incidents in the Yaroslavl colony' (26 July 2018) TASS <https://tass.ru/obschestvo/5407195> accessed 30 August 2019. In this post the Deputy Minister of Justice mentioned that Russia attaches great importance to the development of cooperation with the CAT Cttee and human rights treaty bodies in general.

74 HRCttee, 'Comments from the Russian Federation concerning the COs issued by the Human Rights Committee (CCPR/C/RUS/CO/6) after consideration of the country's sixth periodic report on implementation of the International Covenant on Civil and Political Rights', UN Doc CCPR/C/RUS/CO/6/Add.1 (19 February 2010) para 7.

report was questioned.[75] There is also a view that the treaty bodies have in recent years discredited themselves due to the politicised character of their work, the tendency to impose their own interpretation of the provisions of the international treaties as legal obligations of states, an unwillingness to accept objective information and conceptual differences in the approaches of experts and Russian authorities.[76]

4.1.6 Media Coverage

There was a marked increase in media coverage of activities of the treaty bodies in comparison to the previous research results. Most often the media covers information about the ratification of treaties, the consideration of state reports and recommendations of the committees.[77] As of the beginning of 2018 there were more than 77 500 media registered in Russia,[78] which makes it challenging to provide quantitative research in this field. What may nonetheless be concluded is that media resources of an anti-governmental political leaning tend to reveal the problems in the realisation of the treaties in Russia more frequently[79] than the media belonging to governmental political

---

[75] Comments to COs under consideration of reports submitted by state parties <https://tbinternet.ohchr.org/Treaties/CERD/Shared%20Documents/RUS/INT_CERD_COB_RUS_29435_E.pdf> accessed 12 April 2022.

[76] Interview with the 1st representative of the Ministry of Foreign Affairs of the Russian Federation (17 July 2019), by email.

[77] International Day of Human Rights. RIA Novosti (December 2018) <https://ria.ru/20181210/1547522225.html> accessed 15 January 2019; 'Russia will report in Geneva on the fulfilment of its obligations under the Convention against Torture.' (12 April 2022) TASS <https://tass.ru/politika/5396918> accessed 12 April 2022; The State Duma ratified the Optional Protocol to the Convention on the Elimination of All Forms of Discrimination against Women. RIA Novosti (June 2004) <https://ria.ru/20040602/603342.html> accessed 12 April 2022.

[78] <https://www.mos.ru/upload/documents/files/9928/MonitoringsostoyaniyarinkapechatnihSMIipoligrafii_2020.pdf> accessed 7 December 2019.

[79] Who's Taking Russia to the Rack (2018) *Novaya Gazeta* <https://novayagazeta.ru/articles/2018/10/08/78095-kto-podnimaet-rossiyu-na-dybu> accessed 15 September 2023; 'It was Their Lives or His?' Leading women's rights attorney Mari Davtyan explains the domestic violence case that is bringing Russians out into the streets (27 June 2019) Meduza <https://meduza.io/en/feature/2019/06/27/it-was-their-lives-or-his> accessed 12 April 2022; 'People, Government and Neuropsychiatric Boarding Schools. Why There Is No Reform of Neuropsychiatric Boarding Schools' (7 December 2019) Kommersant <https://www.kommersant.ru/doc/4180226> accessed 15 September 2023.

leaning.[80] Among all the treaties ratified by Russia, CAT is the one that receives less attention on the internet.[81] The most popular treaty on the internet is CRPD.

4.1.7 State Reporting

Russia has submitted in total 55 reports with some reports submitted in a combined format.[82] The delay period for submitting the report is usually ranging from a few months to a year with the longest delays of four years (one report under CCPR, one report under CAT) and seven years (one report under CEDAW). Through time the submission delays have shortened with even some cases of earlier submission of the reports (CEDAW, CRPD, CRC, OP-CRC-AC).

A mechanism has been introduced for distributing responsibility between the executive state bodies for cooperation with the treaty bodies in accordance with the 2003 Decree of the government.[83] Under this Decree the relevant ministries and governmental bodies (minimum two, maximum five) were appointed as responsible for cooperation (preparation of periodic reports and participation in the constructive dialogue) together with the Ministry of Foreign Affairs as a coordinating body for each of the committees.[84] For instance, within the task of preparing a report the Ministry of Justice[85] as the body responsible for cooperating with the HRCttee and the CAT Cttee, sends

---

80 Vice-Speaker of the Federation Council: The Russian Federation Demonstrates Progress in the Protection of Women's Rights (27 October 2015) RIA Novosti <https://ria.ru/20151027/1308992128.html> accessed 12 April 2022; Russia has become better at protecting the rights of persons with disabilities (28 February 2018) Rossiyskaya Gazeta <https://rg.ru/2018/02/28/v-rossii-stali-luchshe-zashchishchat-prava-invalidov.html> accessed 12 April 2022.

81 The search box of Google reveals the following number of results for each treaty: CCPR 162 000; CESCR 137 000; CERD 170 000; CAT 115 000; CEDAW 244 000; CRC 662 000; CRPD 1 320 000.

82 The state describes itself as a world leader in the number of reports submitted to the UNTBs. See National Report, HRC, Russian Federation, UN Doc A/HRC/WG.6/4/RUS/1 (10 November 2008), at 3.

83 Government Decree N 323 'On approval of the interdepartmental distribution of responsibilities for ensuring the participation of the Russian Federation in international organisations of the UN system' (3 June 2003).

84 CESCR Cttee – Ministry of Labour and Social Protection, Ministry of Health, Ministry of Science and Higher Education, Ministry of Education; HRCttee and CAT Cttee – the Ministry of Justice; CERD Cttee – the Federal Agency for Nationalities; CEDAW Cttee and CRPD Cttee – the Ministry of Labour and Social Protection; CRC Cttee – the Ministry of Labour and Social Protection, the Ministry of Education; preparation of report under OP-CRC-AC – the Ministry of Defense of the Russian Federation.

85 Department of International Law and Cooperation.

requests to the relevant state bodies[86] with a view to obtaining information on the main developments, implementation of the COs and comments on the Committee's concerns.[87] On the basis of this information, the Ministry of Justice prepares the report and forwards it to the Ministry of Foreign Affairs, which submits the report to the relevant Committee.

While the procedural aspects of activities of the responsible structures and their concrete powers are not disclosed in detail in their regulatory legal acts, for one treaty (CRPD) special procedure for the preparation of reports has been introduced by the Decree of the government of 11 June 2015.[88] Under this document the Ministry of Labour and Social Protection forms the interdepartmental working group with the participation of representatives of government bodies and constituent entities of Russia, state extra-budgetary funds, scientific organisations, and public organisations of persons with disabilities. Responsible executors of the sections of the report (that correspond to relevant articles of CRPD) are the relevant state bodies indicated in the Annex to the Decree.[89]

The state in its reports usually mentions that within their preparation consultations with various NGOs have been upheld, but the authors could not obtain adequate information on the involvement of particular NGOs, what the content of these consultations and their results were.[90] The interviewees mentioned that NGOs and the NHRI provide concrete information that is subsequently included in the state's reports.[91] Still a view was expressed on the need to ensure a more active participation of civil society and NGOs in the preparation of reports.[92] For one treaty (CRPD) the state provided the legal basis for

---

[86] The Constitutional Court, the Supreme Court, the Ministry of Internal Affairs, the General Prosecutor's Office, the Investigative Committee, the Federal Penal Correction Service.

[87] Information presented by the Ministry of Justice of the Russian Federation in connection with the interview questions related to this project (19 August 2019).

[88] Decree of the Government of the Russian Federation 'On the procedure for preparing a report on measures taken to fulfill the obligations of the Russian Federation under the Convention on the Rights of Persons with Disabilities' of 11 June 2015 No 585 (18 August 2015) Rossiyskaya Gazeta <https://rg.ru/2015/06/16/doklad-site-dok.html> accessed 26 November 2019.

[89] ibid, para 9.

[90] With the exception of CRPD.

[91] Interview with the 1st representative of the Ministry of Foreign Affairs of the Russian Federation (17 July 2019), by email; interview with Olga Goncharenko, Senior Adviser, International Relations Department, Office of the High Commissioner of Human Rights of the Russian Federation (18 July 2019), by email.

[92] Interview with Sergey Baburkin, Commissioner for Human Rights in Yaroslavl Region, Doctor of Political Sciences, Professor (29 July 2019), by email.

more active participation of NGOs in the process of preparation of reports and implementation of the COs together with the state authorities.

The UNTBS have welcomed the improvement of the content and structure of Russia's reports in conformity with their respective guidelines on reporting. As was mentioned in the previous research, Russian reports have gradually become more critical. However, the reports tend to provide information on the developments in the legal regulation and the policy measures with smaller attention given to the difficulties encountered by the state.[93] Nonetheless, the annexes to the reports and written replies to the list of issues are quite frank as they contain current statistics that do not always reflect positive tendencies in the country.

Reports of the Russian Federation to the UNTBS are always presented by the high-level ministerial delegation. Representatives of the relevant state agencies/services and higher courts are also included in the delegation.[94]

There is no common Russian website where COs of all committees are published. COs usually are published in the media, including the websites of the responsible ministries (the Ministry of Foreign Affairs, the Ministry of Justice, the Ministry of Labour and Social Protection) as well as on the websites of

---

[93] See, for example, CESCR Cttee, 'Joint written statement submitted by the Russian non-governmental organisations Patients' Defenders League, Independent Psychiatric Association of Russia, Independent Institute for Social Policy, Civil Society Foundation, Centre for Educational Monitoring and Statistics, Centre for the Development of Democracy and Human Rights and Centre for Social and Labour Rights with the support of non-governmental organisations in special consultative status with the United Nations Economic and Social Council, the International Helsinki Federation and the Network of Russian NGOs to promote and protect social and economic rights in the Russian Federation using international instruments, UN Doc E/C.12/2003/NGO/1 (11 September 2003); Ministry of Labour prepared the first Report for the UN on Russia's compliance with the Convention on the Rights of Persons with Disabilities (19 August 2014) <https://www.asi.org.ru/news/2014/08/19/mintrud-rossii-podgotovil-pervyj-doklad-v-oon-o-vypolnenii-v-rossii-norm-i-polozhenij-konventsii-o-pravah-invalidov/> accessed 17 April 2022.

[94] For example, the Russian delegation during consideration of its 7th periodic report to the HRCttee included the Representative of the Russian Federation at the EctHR, representatives of such ministries as the Ministry of Foreign Affairs, Ministry of Internal Affairs, Ministry of Justice, Ministry of Defence, Ministry of Labour and Social Protection, representatives of such state agencies/services as Federal Penitentiary Service, Federal Migration Service, as well as representatives of the Supreme Court of the Russian Federation. For the full list of the delegation, see List of the Russian Federation delegation/participants to the 113th Session of the Human Rights Committee <https://tbinternet.ohchr.org/Treaties/CCPR/Shared%20Documents/RUS/INT_CCPR_LOP_RUS_19828_E.pdf> accessed 17 April 2022.

some NGOs. As was mentioned earlier, the COs are published in the database Kontur managed by the Supreme Court for use by the judiciary.

4.1.8 Dialogues with Treaty Bodies in the Context of Presenting Its State Reports

Russia had seven dialogues with the HRCttee (in 1978, 1984, 1988, 1995, 2003, 2009 and 2014); six dialogues with the CESCR Cttee (in 1980, 1984, 1997, 2003, 2011, 2017); six dialogues with the CAT Cttee (in 1989, 1996, 2002, 2006, 2012, 2018); seven dialogues with the CERD Cttee (in 1978, 1984, 1989, 1995, 2003, 2009, 2014); seven dialogues with the CEDAW Cttee (in 2015, 2010, 2002, 1998, 1995, 1989, 1983); four dialogues with the CRC Cttee (in 1993, 1999, 2005, 2014); one dialogue with the CRC Cttee under OP-CRC-AC in 2014; one dialogue with the CRC Cttee under OP-CRC-SC in 2018; and one dialogue with the CRPD Cttee in 2018. In total Russia had 40 dialogues with treaty bodies.

4.1.9 Submission of Reports by NGOs and Independent State Institution

While the previous research indicated that NGOs presented their reports to the CAT Cttee, the CERD Cttee and the CRC Cttee, the treaty body database does not contain the texts of these reports. The database demonstrates the texts of the NGOs' reports only starting from 2003 (for the CESCR Cttee). It seems that that was the period when the NGOs started to actively express their interest in the reporting process in Russia and to submit alternative reports to the committees. The database demonstrates that for each treaty from cycle to cycle the number of alternative reports has been growing significantly. Russian NGOs submit joint alternative reports prepared by their coalitions and also reports prepared by single NGOs separately. The reports are both comprehensive and thematic. For some treaties (CESCR and CRPD) NGOs submit their reports both for the session and for the list of issues.

While the issue of reprisals against journalists and human rights defenders is continuously raised by different treaty bodies (the HRCttee, the CESCR Cttee, the CAT Cttee) it is unclear whether these cases were related to the activists directly involved in the reporting process. In May 2013 the CAT Cttee sent two letters to Russia regarding the initiation of administrative case against the NGOs Memorial[95] and Public Verdict[96] due to the fact that these organisations,

---

[95] CAT Reprisals. NGO 'Memorial' Russia (17 May 2013) <https://tbinternet.ohchr.org/Treaties/CAT/Shared%20Documents/RUS/INT_CAT_RLE_RUS_13175_E.pdf> accessed 6 December 2019.

[96] CAT Reprisals. NGO 'Public Verdict' (28 May 2013) <https://tbinternet.ohchr.org/Treaties/CAT/Shared%20Documents/RUS/INT_CAT_RLE_RUS_13176_E.pdf> accessed 6 December 2019.

performing the functions of foreign agents, carried out their activities in violation of the relevant provisions of the Code of Administrative Offences. The Committee was concerned that quotes from the 2012 alternative reports of these organisations were cited among the bases for the charges.[97] In response to these concerns Russia stressed that it is the right to participate in political and public life guaranteed in article 25 of CCPR that is applicable to the case. Therefore, such 'matters do not fall within the mandate of the Committee',[98] and are discussed in the national reports of Russia to the HRC ttee.[99]

The High Commissioner has started to submit reports to the committees since 2017, when her first report to the CESCR Cttee[100] was considered. In 2018 the High Commissioner submitted her first reports to the CAT Cttee,[101] CERD Cttee[102] and CRPD Cttee.[103]

---

[97] <https://tbinternet.ohchr.org/Treaties/CAT/Shared%20Documents/RUS/INT_CAT_RLE_RUS_13175_E.pdf> accessed 17 April 2022.

[98] Periodic Report, CAT, the Russian Federation, UN Doc CAT/C/RUS/6 (27 December 2016) para 265.

[99] ibid.

[100] Parallel report of the High Commissioner for Human Rights in the Russian Federation to the 6th periodic report of the Russian Federation to the Committee on Economic, Social and Cultural Rights <https://tbinternet.ohchr.org/_layouts/15/TreatyBodyExternal/countries.aspx?CountryCode=RUS&Lang=EN> accessed 17 April 2022.

[101] Alternative Report of the Commissioner for Human Rights in the Russian Federation to the Committee Against Torture (CAT), 64th Session July 2018. Information provided by the Accredited National Human Rights Institution of the State under review in full compliance with the Paris Principles (June 2018) <https://tbinternet.ohchr.org/_layouts/15/treatybodyexternal/Download.aspx?symbolno=INT%2fCAT%2fNHS%2fRUS%2f31605&Lang=en> accessed 17 April 2022.

[102] Shadow report of the High Commissioner for Human Rights in the Russian Federation to the 23rd and 24th periodic reports of the Russian Federation to the Committee on the Elimination of Racial Discrimination <https://tbinternet.ohchr.org/_layouts/15/treatybodyexternal/Download.aspx?symbolno=INT%2fCERD%2fIFN%2fRUS%2f28204&Lang=en> accessed 17 April 2022; representative of the High Commissioner informed the UN on the problem of elimination of racial discrimination (3 August 2017) <http://ombudsmanrf.org/news/novosti_upolnomochennogo/view/predstavitel_upolnomochennogo_vystupila_v_oon_po_probleme_likvidacii_rasovoj_diskriminacii> accessed 17 April 2022.

[103] See info from NHRIs (for the session). Submission of the High Commissioner for Human Rights in the Russian Federation (the Russian Ombudswoman) (30 January 2018) <https://tbinternet.ohchr.org/_layouts/15/treatybodyexternal/Download.aspx?symbolno=INT%2fCRPD%2fIFU%2fRUS%2f30078&Lang=en> accessed 6 December 2019.

4.1.10 Domestic Implementation Mechanism

There is no coordinated domestic process or institutional arrangement to implement COs. The implementation process is organised on an *ad hoc* basis for each treaty separately. For instance, the Ministry of Justice as the responsible body for the cooperation with the HRCttee stressed that it tries to implement its international human rights obligations, including in relation to the realisation of the COs, in good faith.[104] For one treaty (CRPD) the government has established a procedure to implement COs through adopting an action plan of activities on the implementation of the COs in 2018, which includes a set of concrete measures to be undertaken by responsible authorities within concrete deadlines.[105] A similar action plan was claimed to be developed for implementing the COs of the CEDAW Cttee after the consideration of Russia's report in 2010,[106] but no information on this plan was found by the authors.

4.1.11 Treaty Body Membership

Russia has traditionally had members in the committees. During the Soviet era Soviet experts were present in the HRCttee,[107] the CERD Cttee[108] and the CEDAW Cttee.[109] Since the formation of Russia to the present time Russia has members in the majority of UNTBs in respect of treaties to which Russia is a party. From 2002 to 2010 Professor YM Kolosov served as a member of the CESCR Cttee. Since 2010 to today (until 2023) the membership in the Committee has been taken by Professor AKh Abashidze. Due to efforts of Prof. Abashidze a joint Master's programme International Protection of Human

---

104 Information presented by the Ministry of Justice of the Russian Federation in connection with the interview questions related to this project (19 August 2019).
105 The Action Plan for the implementation of the recommendations contained in the COs of the Committee on the Rights of Persons with Disabilities on the initial report of the Russian Federation on the implementation of the Convention on the Rights of Persons with Disabilities, approved by the Deputy Chairman of the Government of the Russian Federation (28 December 2018 No 11011p-P12) <https://rosmintrud.ru/uploads/magic/ru-RU/Document-0-8537-src-1547799349.338.pdf> accessed 17 April 2022.
106 Speech by First Deputy Minister of Labor and Social Protection of the Russian Federation AV Vovchenko at the 62nd session of the UN Committee on the Elimination of Discrimination against Women on the defence of the 8th periodic report of the Russian Federation on the implementation of the provisions of the Convention on the elimination of all forms of discrimination against women <https://tbinternet.ohchr.org/Treaties/CEDAW/Shared%20Documents/RUS/INT_CEDAW_STA_RUS_22045_R.pdf> accessed 17 April 2022.
107 Prof AP Movchan (1976–1988); Prof RA Myullerson (1988–1992).
108 Prof YA Reshetov (1988–2003).
109 Ms Aleksandra P Biryukova (1982–1986), Ms Elvira Novikova (1987–1990).

Rights was launched in nine universities across Russia, where significant attention is given to the study of all core human rights treaties and the work of treaty bodies, including the impact of these treaties in Russia. Also, each year the Department of International Law of the RUDN University organises conferences and seminars with the participation of governmental authorities and representatives of NGOs that spread knowledge about the treaties and their committees in Russia. From 2003 up to 2019 Prof AS Avtonomov performed the activities of a member of the CERD Cttee. Currently the position of one of the CAT Cttee's experts is held by Prof Bakhtiyar R Tuzmukhamedov. From 1991 to 1994 Ms Tatiana Nikolaeva was a member of the CEDAW Cttee. From 1991 to 1999 Professor YM Kolosov served as a member of CRC Cttee. From 2012 up to the present time the membership in this Committee has been taken up by Ms Olga Khazova. From 2016 up to 2019 Mr Valery Rukhledev was elected as member of the CRPD Cttee. In 2019 his position was taken by Mr Dmitry Rebrov, since Mr V Rukhledev had to withdraw from his membership for health reasons before the expiry of his mandate on 31 December 2020.

4.2 Overview of Impact of UN Human Rights Treaties

All seven ratified treaties and one Optional Protocol (OP-CRC-SC) were partially incorporated and have been a source of inspiration in the drafting of the Constitution and Russian legislation. Salient examples are: the incorporation of the majority of provisions of CCPR and CESCR into the Constitution; the adoption of the 2001 Labour Code, which was directly inspired by the provisions of CESCR; the adoption of the 1995 Family Code, which was inspired directly by the provisions of CRC; significant legislative reform of amending more than 40 federal and approximately 750 regional laws to bring the legislation in conformity with CRPD.

While Russia usually adopts various policies that are related to the issues covered by the treaties, these documents do not contain direct reference to the relevant treaties. They generally mention that they are adopted in accordance with the international treaties accepted by Russia in the specific area, with more attention given to the treaties adopted within the CoE. For instance, the majority of policies and programmes that are related to the issues covered by CCPR and CAT, especially in the area of improving the penal system, are mostly aimed at fulfilling the obligations taken within the ECHR and the European Prison Rules as well as requirements of the ECPT.

A few more examples of UN human rights treaties influencing the development of policies in the state may be identified. The most influential treaties are CEDAW (due to the adoption of the National Strategy for women for the period 2017–2022 to comply with the COs of the CEDAW Cttee), CRPD (due to the adoption of the Accessible Environment Programme for 2011–2025, developed in line with article 27 of the Convention even before its ratification) and CRC (due to the adoption of National Children's Interests Action Strategy for the period 2012–2017).

Treaties also influenced the institutional landscape in the country. The pertinent institutional reform was the establishment in January 2011 of the Investigative Committee as an independent state body in charge of investigations, separate from the Procuracy, as a measure to give effect to the recommendations of the CAT Cttee.[110] Another relevant example was the creation in 2012 of a new structure (Department on the Persons with Disabilities) within the Ministry of Labour and Social Protection to monitor the activities of executive bodies to implement CRPD and to prepare state reports for the CRPD Cttee.[111] In line with the CRC Cttee's COs steps were taken to set up an office of the Commissioner for children's rights (at federal and regional level).[112]

4.2.1   Reliance by Judiciary

According to the database of the court practice available to the authors,[113] the following statistics of the use of the human rights treaties by Russian higher and lower courts, indicating reference to the treaty at least once in a particular domestic court case (from the most frequently-used to the least used-treaty): CCPR (around 305 700 decisions); CRC (around 23 300 decisions); CESCR (around 20 000 decisions); CRPD (around 4 700 decisions); CAT (around 4 400 decisions); CERD (around 100 decisions); OP-CRC-SC (around 40 decisions); CEDAW (9 decisions). In their practice, Russian higher and lower courts rely on the treaties' provisions as a guide to interpretation (with regard to all treaties). As a source of information and interpretation the judiciary also refers to the following treaty body documents: General Comments of the

---

110   CAT Cttee, COs, the Russian Federation, UN Doc CAT/C/RUS/CO/5 (11 December 2012) para 4(a); see also CAT Cttee, 'Conclusions and Recommendations of the Committee against Torture', UN Doc CAT/C/RUS/CO/4 (6 February 2007) para 12.

111   The Regulation on the Department on the Persons with Disabilities of the Ministry of Labour and Social Protection of the Russian Federation (approved by Decree of the Ministry of Labour and Social Protection of the Russian Federation (4 September 2012)) No 165 <https://rosmintrud.ru/docs/mintrud/handicapped/9> accessed 29 November 2019.

112   Pursuant to Presidential Decree No 986 of 1 September 2009, the post of Presidential Commissioner for Children's Rights was established. CRC Cttee, Consideration of reports submitted by state parties, 4th and 5th periodic reports of Russia, 2011, CRC/C/RUS/4–5 para 42. See also CRC Cttee, COs, the Russian Federation, CRC/C/RUS/CO/3 (23 November 2005) paras 13–14.

113   State Automated System of the Russian Federation 'Justice' <https://bsr.sudrf.ru/bigs/portal.html> accessed 10 September 2019.

CESCR Cttee and HRCttee; treaty bodies' jurisprudence (HRCttee, CAT Cttee, CEDAW Cttee); periodic reports and COs (CERD Cttee, CAT Cttee). Another important trend is the application of the treaty bodies' decisions as a source of a remedy in cases where the Russian courts supported the applicant's reference to the Committee's decision in his or her plea for reviewing a court ruling on the basis of new circumstances (HRCttee, CEDAW Cttee).[114]

4.2.2   Impact on and through Independent State Institutions

A noticeable impact of the treaties is demonstrated through the activities of the Ombudsman. The NHRI refers to the provisions of the human rights treaties when giving legal assessment of various situations dealing with the realisation of human rights, when considering measures taken to implement the treaties (CAT and CRPD), launching legislative initiatives in the area of application of the treaties (endorsing a legal norm in the Code of Civil Procedure for reconsidering the court ruling on the basis of the decisions of the HRCttee, recommending to the government to develop draft comprehensive federal law 'On Combating Domestic Violence'). Additionally, the High Commissioner expresses her position with regard to issues that are also addressed in the COs. For instance, the NHRI shares the critiques of the law on the decriminalisation of beatings by the CESCR Cttee and the CAT Cttee, supported the position of the CAT Cttee on introducing in the Russian Criminal Code a separate article on torture and the CEDAW Cttee's view on the need for the adoption of comprehensive legislation to prevent and address domestic violence against women. There are also examples when the High Commissioner opposes the position of the treaty body. Thus, she disagreed with the position of the CERD Cttee that manifestations of racism remain deeply rooted among football fans in Russia.[115]

4.2.3   Impact on and through Non-state Actors

It is difficult to provide an actual assessment of the use of the treaties by the lawyers due to a lack of information on this issue. However, the UNTBs tend to point to a lack of knowledge of the treaties among the representatives of the

---

114   With regard to the cases *Khoroshenko v Russian Federation* (29 March 2011) Communication No 1304/2004 CCPR/C/101/D/1304/2004; *Igor Kostin v Russian Federation* (21 March 2017) Communication No 2496/2014 CCPR/C/119/D/2496/2014; *S Medvedeva v Russia* (25 February 2016) Communication No 60/2013 CEDAW/C/63/D/60/2013.
115   Summary report on the activities of the High Commissioner for Human Rights in the Russian Federation for 2018 313, para 7.4 <http://ombudsmanrf.org/upload/files/docs/lib/Itog1.pdf> accessed 30 August 2019.

legal profession and recommend that the state should provide and enhance training for them. This view is sometimes supported by scholars and civil society representatives.[116] Sometimes practising lawyers publish articles, where they refer to treaty provisions and the interpretations of the Committee, including on communications where they represented applicants (relevant for the CEDAW Cttee).[117] While there are almost no professional training related to treaty bodies in general or specific committees, one professional training has been planned to be organised in November 2019 for lawyers that focused on the practice of the CEDAW Cttee to address violence against women.[118]

Among NGOs that use the treaties and the Committees' jurisprudence in their activities are mostly those that provide alternative reports to the treaty bodies. There are few examples of the use of the provisions of the treaties and their recommendations in the legal argumentation of the initiatives launched by NGOs. The examples are the initiatives with regard to abolishing the administrative punishment for prostitution and the introduction of substitution therapy programmes for the treatment of drug users, that invoke the legal positions of the CESCR Cttee and the CEDAW Cttee, as well as the #allJobs4all-Women campaign launched by the ADC Memorial, which was supporting the communication of Ms Medvedeva to the CEDAW Cttee, with the aim of lifting discriminatory labour bans for women.[119] Another salient example is the project of the All-Russian Society of the Deaf on translating CRPD into the Russian sign language.[120]

---

116 SV Polenina, 'Pravovaya politika Rossijskoj Federacii v sfere gendernyh otnoshenij' ('Legal Policy of the Russian Federation in the Sphere of Gender Relations') Proceedings of the Institute of State and Law of the Russian Academy of Sciences (2016) 62–80.

117 Analysis of the view of the CEDAW Cttee in the case of *Svetlana Medvedeva v Russia* of 25 February 2016 by Commentary by Dmitry Bartenev (4 May 2016) <https://academia.ilpp.ru/blog/analiz-soobrazhenij-komiteta-oon-po-delu-svetlana-medvedeva-protiv-rossii-ot-25-fevralya-2016-goda/> accessed 24 November 2019; V Frolova, 'Take into Account Domestic Violence: On International Standards for the Resolution of Child Disputes' (2019) Lawyer's newspaper <https://www.advgazeta.ru/mneniya/uchityvat-nasilie-v-seme/> accessed 2 December 2019.

118 Practice of the CEDAW Cttee in domestic violence cases. Webinar of 13 November 2019. Federal Chamber of Lawyers <https://fparf.ru/education/events/praktika-komiteta-oon-po-likvidatsii-diskriminatsii-v-otnoshenii-zhenshchin-po-delam-o-domashnem-nas/> accessed 2 December 2019.

119 'All Jobs for All Women. Forbidden to Women Professions – Gender Discrimination' Human Rights Report of ADC Memorial (March 2018) <https://adcmemorial.org/wp-content/uploads/forbidden_2018RUwww.pdf> accessed 25 November 2019.

120 The All-Russian Society of the Deaf. Convention on the Rights of Persons with Disabilities in Russian Sign Language (24 June 2016) <https://voginfo.ru/world/2016/06/23/theconventionontherightsofpersonswithdisabilitiesonrsl/> accessed 7 December 2019.

The interest of Russian scholars in the treaties is growing from year to year with CRC and CRPD being the most popular treaties used in their publications, followed by CCPR, CESCR, CEDAW, CAT and CERD.[121]

4.2.4 Impact of State Reporting

For the majority of the recommendations of the treaty bodies, it is difficult to establish a direct link between these and the developments taking place in the state. One may note here more the contribution, rather than the concrete influence of the COs. The discernible contribution could be demonstrated mostly through chronological sequence and within the follow-up procedure. Among the examples of such impact are the 2017 amendments to Federal Law 'On the Minimum Wage' establishing the minimum wage in the amount of the worker's minimum subsistence level (CESCR Cttee COs); the steps taken to eliminate the cases of imprisonment as a penalty for defamation (HRCttee COs); and the adoption of an action plan for the socio-economic and ethnocultural development of Roma and subsequent establishment of implementing agencies, timelines, and monitoring processes for this plan (CESCR Cttee and CERD Cttee COs).

However, a few examples of concrete measures where the influence of the treaty or the COs, being the motivators for the changes, could be identified are the following: the ratification of OP-CRC-AC in order to implement the COs of the CRC Cttee; an update by the Ministry of Justice of the instructions for the organisation of the access system to detention centres to ensure prompt access of detained persons to a lawyer (CAT Cttee COs); the adoption of the national strategy for women (2017–2022); and the revision of the list of restricted occupations and sectors for women (CEDAW Cttee COs).

It seems that the COs of the HRCttee and the CESCR Cttee demonstrate a lower impact than the treaty-specific committees. This could be due to the fact that these two committees cover many issues in their COs and, in this sense, it is difficult to see the impact of the lengthy list of the recommendations. Furthermore, their COs touch upon questions that are also covered by treaty-specific committees. Thus, a cumulative effect may take place, while it seems that the state's attention to these questions increases when they are addressed

---

121 In accordance with the data from the scientific electronic library (integrated with Russian science index), which contains publications of Russian scholars in various fields of science, the following number of publications use the treaties in their texts: CRC (670 publications); CRPD (511 publications); CCPR (190 publications); CESCR (74 publications); CEDAW (54 publications); CAT (53 publications); CERD (14 publications) <https://www.elibrary.ru/defaultx.asp> accessed 10 September 2019.

by the treaty-specific committee, rather than the Covenant Committee. It seems that the committees with the strongest impact are the CEDAW Cttee and CRC Cttee,[122] while the CRPD Cttee has the potential to demonstrate a strong impact in the future when more concrete measures will be adopted in accordance with the action plan of activities on the implementation of its COs.

The important reason for the limited impact of the COs is the variance of the state's position with the views of the Committees on a number of issues, some of which are of joint concern to two and more UNTBS. It also often is the case that no consensus on these issues is reached among state officials, civil society and citizens. Among such issues are the regulation of the activities of NGOs acting as 'foreign agents' (CESCR Cttee, HRCttee, CAT Cttee, CERD Cttee); the protection of rights of lesbian, gay, bisexual and transgender (LGBT) persons (CESCR Cttee, HRCttee); the lack of a separate article on 'torture' in Russian legislation (CAT Cttee); the situation of domestic violence (HRCttee, CAT Cttee, CEDAW Cttee); and access to quality medical and rehabilitation services within the existing healthcare system for drug users (CESCR Cttee, CRPD Cttee).

Another noteworthy aspect is the linkage with the ECHR and the decisions of the ECtHR, which is demonstrated with regard to the COs of the HRCttee and CAT Cttee, which could be both limiting or enhancing the impact of the COs.

4.2.5   Impact of Individual Communications

There were 69 communications lodged against Russia under CCPR; two under CERD; ten under CAT; and eight under CEDAW. The total number of communications under all treaties is 89. Russia was found in violation in 46 cases (39 under CCPR, three under CAT and four under CEDAW). The 2003 Decree of the government appointing responsible governmental bodies for cooperation with the treaty bodies provides the basis for the interaction of Russian authorities with the relevant committee during the consideration of the communication. However, no institutionalised or coordinated mechanism for the implementation of the views has been established in the country.

The state's approach towards implementing the views could be demonstrated through its position regarding the views of the HRCttee. While the HRCttee is continuously pointing to the non-implementation of its views,[123]

---

122   Confirmed by the majority of the interviewees.
123   HRCttee, COs, the Russian Federation, UN Doc CCPR/CO/79/RUS (1 December 2003) para 8; HRCttee, COs, the Russian Federation, UN Doc CCPR/C/RUS/CO/6 (24 November 2009) para 5; HRCttee, COs, Russian Federation, UN Doc CCPR/C/RUS/CO/7 (28 April 2015) para 5.

Russia insists on its position that the Committee does not have the functions of a court and its views are of a recommendatory nature.[124] The state advocates its sovereign right to choose how the views are to be fulfilled, with the recognition that they carry great weight and are taken seriously by its authorities.[125] In the state's view, OP1-CCPR contains no provisions on the obligation to inform the Committee on the measures taken to implement its views. That is why in many instances Russia does not present follow-up information to the Committee.[126]

Noting that the treaty body database contains little information on the implementation of the majority of the views and the lack of information available to the authors of this chapter in that regard, it is difficult to provide an assessment of the real state of affairs with regard to the implementation status of the views in the country. The authors of the communications most often point to the state's refusal to carry out a proper investigation or reopen the procedures, or to pay compensation, while the state stresses that the author's allegations and the Committee's conclusions after particular scrutiny may not be proved, and the state's conclusions remain the same.

The impact of the individual communications procedure is demonstrable in two cases considered by the HRCttee (*Khoroshenko v Russia* and *Kostin v Russia*)[127] and one case by the CEDAW Cttee (*Medvedeva v Russia*).[128] These cases reveal a positive tendency in the practice of Russian higher and lower courts of finding legal grounds for revising judicial acts the basis that treaty body views constitute new circumstances or facts. While the Russian legislator is not yet ready to regulate the legal status of the views of the committees, these progressive legal positions of Russian courts have the potential to be confirmed and developed in subsequent judicial practice with regard to the views of any treaty body whose competence to consider communications was recognised by Russia. The case of *Medvedeva v Russia* showed a deeper impact in the country due to the efforts of the Ministry of Labour and Social Protection that

---

124 Periodic Report, CCPR, the Russian Federation, UN Doc CCPR/C/RUS/6 (20 December 2007) 7.
125 Periodic Report, CCPR, Russian Federation, UN Doc CCPR/C/RUS/8 (17 May 2019) para 47.
126 Interview with the 2nd representative of the Ministry of Foreign Affairs of the Russian Federation (5 September 2019), telephonically.
127 Decision of the Constitutional Court of the Russian Federation N 1248-O (28 June 2012); Decision of the Supreme Court N 128-П18ПР (10 October 2018).
128 Decision of the Supreme Court of the Russian Federation, Judicial Chamber on Civil Cases N 46-КГ17–24 (24 July 2017).

were prompted, *inter alia*, by civil society,[129] resulting in the revision in 2019 of the list of restricted occupations and sectors for women.[130]

5 Impact of the Different UN Human Rights Treaties on the Domestic Level in the Russian Federation

5.1 *Convention on the Elimination of All Forms of Racial Discrimination*
5.1.1 Incorporation and Reliance by Organs of State

The state stresses that the prohibition of racial discrimination is one of the staple provisions of the Russian Constitution[131] and that anti-discrimination principles enshrined in the Constitution have been systematically incorporated in different branches of law governing the protection of human rights in education, labour, health care, the courts, social protection and culture. This set of laws together with the Constitution and the Criminal Code constitutes comprehensive anti-discrimination legislation.[132] However, the Committee notes that such legislation covers only limited spheres of life and is not compliant with the requirements of article 1 of CERD.[133] The Committee also points to a lack of comprehensive anti-discrimination legislation containing a definition of all forms of racial discrimination covering all fields of law and public life.[134] Thus, the provisions of the Convention have been partially incorporated into Russian legislation.

---

129 Seafarer's Union of Russia 'The Supreme Court of the Russian Federation Demanded to Reconsider the Case of Svetlana Medvedeva' (25 July 2017) <http://www.sur.ru/ru/news/lent/2017-07-25/verkhovnyj_sud_rf_potreboval_peresmotret_delo_svetlany_medvedevoj/> accessed 19 April 2022; 'All Jobs for All Women. Forbidden to Women Professions – Gender Discrimination' Human Rights Report of ADC Memorial (March 2018) <https://adcmemorial.org/wp-content/uploads/forbidden_2018RUwww.pdf> accessed 19 April 2022.

130 Order of the Ministry of Labour and Social Protection of the Russian Federation of 18 July 2019 No 512H 'On approval of the list of productions, works and positions with harmful and (or) dangerous working conditions, on which the use of women's labour is limited' (15 August 2019) <http://publication.pravo.gov.ru/Document/View/0001201908150010?index=0&rangeSize=1> accessed 19 April 2022.

131 Art 19 establishes the principle of equality of all before the law and the court together with arts 17, 55, 29.

132 Periodic Report, CERD, the Russian Federation, UN Doc CERD/C/RUS/23–24 (27 May 2016) paras 28, 31.

133 CERD Cttee, COs, Russian Federation, UN Doc CERD/C/RUS/CO/23–24 (1 July 2016) paras 9–10.

134 ibid.

The state has adopted various strategies/policies that are related to the issues covered by CERD, but these documents do not contain a direct reference to the Convention.[135] They generally mention that they are adopted in accordance with the international treaties of Russia in the specific area. One example of direct reference to CERD was found, namely, the federal target programme 'Strengthening the unity of the Russian nation and the ethnocultural development of the peoples of Russia (2014–2020)'.[136] The programme mentions that ensuring ethnocultural diversity is in line with international obligations of the Russian Federation, enshrined in particular in CERD and the Council of Europe Framework Convention for the Protection of National Minorities.

In 2015 a new mechanism – the Federal Agency for Ethnic Affairs (FADN) – was established to, among others, analyse the implementation by the Russian Federation of international obligations in accordance with multilateral legal acts relating to the elimination of racial discrimination, and to prepare draft national reports of Russia in this area.[137] Thus, the FADN is the state body mandated to monitor implementation of CERD and to cooperate with the CERD Cttee.

5.1.2   Reliance by Judiciary

In its 23th to 24th periodic reports Russia mentioned that all Russian courts are guided in their work by the Convention and 'routinely hear criminal, civil and administrative cases involving racial discrimination'.[138] However, the Committee in its 2017 COs noted that no concrete examples of court cases in which the Convention's provisions were applied were provided by the state.[139]

---

135   Decree of the President of the Russian Federation N 1666 'On the strategy of the state national policy of the Russian Federation for the period until 2025' (19 December 2012); Decree of the President of the Russian Federation of N 310 'On measures to ensure coordinated actions of state authorities in the fight against manifestations of fascism and other forms of political extremism in the Russian Federation' (23 March 1995) Consultant Plus accessed 27 August 2019.

136   Decree of the Government of the Russian Federation N 718 'On the federal target programme "Strengthening the unity of the Russian nation and the ethnocultural development of the peoples of Russia (2014–2020)"' (20 August 2013) The government of the Russian Federation <http://government.ru/docs/all/88389/> accessed 19 April 2022.

137   Presidential Decree N 168 'On the Federal Agency for Nationalities' (31 March 2015) <http://kremlin.ru/acts/bank/39565> accessed 19 April 2022; Decree of the Government of the Russian Federation of 18 April 2015 N 368 'On the Federal Agency for Nationalities' (31 March 2015) para 5.18. <https://base.garant.ru/70980460/> accessed 19 April 2022.

138   Periodic Report, CERD, the Russian Federation, UN Doc CERD/C/RUS/23–24 (27 May 2016) paras 100–106.

139   This issue was raised by CERD in its COs. CERD Cttee, COs, the Russian Federation, UN Doc CERD/C/RUS/CO/23–24 (20 September 2017) para 6.

Court practice after that reveals examples of direct reference to the Convention and the interpretations of the CERD Cttee. Thus, references to the Convention provisions (article 4) may be found in the practice of lower courts with regard to defining the grounds of race or nationality as the cause of violence, persecution or real risk of persecution.[140] There are also references to the Convention in the cases dealing with the refusal to grant asylum/refugee status in Russia.[141] When considering cases on expulsion of persons to the states where there are possibilities for that person to be subjected to ill-treatment and political persecution, certain courts refer to the periodic reports and COs as a source of information.[142]

5.1.3 Impact on and through Independent State Institutions

The Ombudsman in its activities deals with complaints of racial discrimination and intolerance and monitors information on possible manifestations of racial discrimination. However, it is unclear whether the NHRI uses CERD and the Committee's legal positions in these activities. In the High Commissioner's view, there is a stable situation in the sphere of interethnic relations and a tendency to decrease in cases of xenophobia and racial intolerance is revealed.[143] The High Commissioner became actively involved in the consideration of periodic reports of Russia by the CERD Cttee in 2018, when she presented her first report[144] and her representative met the Committee during its session in

---

140   Appellate Determination of the St Petersburg city court N 33a-12723/2018 (9 July 2018) on the case N 2A-3670/2017; Appellate Determination of the Saint-Petersburg city court N 33a-3366/2017 (27 February 2017) on the case of N 2A-3111/2016; Appellate Determination of the Saint-Petersburg city court N 33a-23748/2016 (5 December 2016) on the case of N 2A-2832/2016.

141   Appellate Determination of the Moscow city court N 33a-9766/2018 (26 November 2018); Appellate Determination of the Moscow city court N 33a-1395/2018 (16 March 2018).

142   Appellate Ruling of the Judicial Collegium for Criminal Cases of the Supreme Court of the Russian Federation of N 82-АПУ17–1 (30 January 2017) Consultant Plus accessed 30 August 2019; Appellate ruling of the Judicial Collegium for Criminal Cases of the Supreme Court of the Russian Federation N 5-АПУ16–40 (9 June 2016) Consultant Plus accessed 30 August 2019. Judgment of the Central district court of Novosibirsk N 5–468/2017 (18 December 2017).

143   Representative of the High Commissioner informed the UN on the problem of elimination of racial discrimination (3 August 2017) <http://ombudsmanrf.org/news/novosti_u polnomochennogo/view/predstavitel_upolnomochennogo_vystupila_v_oon_po_prob leme_likvidacii_rasovoj_diskriminacii> accessed 19 April 2022.

144   Shadow report of the High Commissioner for Human Rights in the Russian Federation to the 23rd and 24th periodic reports of the Russian Federation to the Committee on the Elimination of Racial Discrimination <https://tbinter net.ohchr.org/_layouts/15/treatybodyexternal/Download.aspx?symbolno=INT%2fC ERD%2fIFN%2fRUS%2f28204&Lang=en> accessed 19 April 2022.

Geneva.[145] Subsequently, in her 2018 annual report the Ombudsman opposed the Committee's COs that manifestations of racism remain deeply rooted among football fans in Russia, by noting that during the 2018 World Cup, conflict situations related to racial discrimination were nullified, and the rights and security of both Russian citizens and arrived guests were maximally respected.[146]

5.1.4 Impact on and through Non-state Actors

The examples of direct reference to the Convention and the interpretations of the CERD Cttee in courts may lead to the conclusion that practising lawyers use the treaty in their arguments. However, this does not reveal the actual picture of the awareness and use of CERD by the legal profession.

There are a few NGOs that deal with issues of racial discrimination in Russia and that are actively submitting alternative reports to the Committee.[147] These NGOs may rely on the Convention in their activities, for instance, when conducting research in places of compact gypsy settlements and providing assessment of the practice of segregation in education faced by Roma children[148] or organising workshops/seminars on the educational problems of Roma in Russia.[149] Some NGOs also develop proposals for narrowing the definition of extremist activity in the anti-extremist legislation and to abolish the federal list of extremist materials, which are in line with the Committee's recommendations, although it is unclear whether these NGOs refer to the Convention and the Committee to support these initiatives.[150]

Russian academics do not pay much attention to CERD and its application in Russia. The majority of publications deal with the perspectives and

---

145 Representative of the High Commissioner informed the UN on the problem of elimination of racial discrimination (3 August 2017) <http://ombudsmanrf.org/news/novosti_upoln omochennogo/view/predstavitel_upolnomochennogo_vystupila_v_oon_po_probleme _likvidacii_rasovoj_diskriminacii> accessed 19 April 2022.
146 Summary report on the activities of the High Commissioner for Human Rights in the Russian Federation for 2018 313 para 7.4 <http://ombudsmanrf.org/upload/files/docs/lib/Itog1.pdf> accessed 19 April 2022.
147 Moscow-Helsinki Group, ADC Memorial, SOVA Centre.
148 'Violation of Romani Children's Rights at School' (15 June 2011) <https://adcmemorial.org/novosti/glavnoe/narusheniya-prav-tsyiganskih-detey-v-shkolah/> accessed 19 April 2022.
149 Periodic Report, CERD, Russian Federation, UN Doc CERD/C/RUS/20–22 (6 June 2012) para 511.
150 Proposals for the liberalization of anti-extremist legislation (17 August 2018) Sova-Centre <https://www.sova-center.ru/misuse/publications/2018/08/d39858/> accessed 19 April 2022.

the analysis of the case *Ukraine v Russian Federation*[151] in the International Court of Justice;[152] a few publications refer to the Convention in the context of elimination of extremism[153] and the right of indigenous peoples to marine resources.[154]

5.1.5 State Reporting and Its Impact

The documents related to the follow-up procedure reveal a few examples of the impact of COs. A certain impact is thus demonstrated in the area of fighting intolerance or incitement to hatred fueled by officials. In its follow-up report the state demonstrated legislative developments in the area of establishing mandates and responsibilities of governmental and municipal bodies at all levels and civil servants in the area of inter-ethnic relations and ensuring equal and fair treatment of all physical and legal persons.[155] In its follow-up

---

[151] International Court of Justice. Application of the International Convention for the Suppression of the Financing of Terrorism and of the International Convention on the Elimination of All Forms of Racial Discrimination (*Ukraine v Russian Federation*) <https://www.icj-cij.org/en/case/166> accessed 19 April 2022.

[152] VL Tolstykh, 'Reshenie Mezhdunarodnogo Suda OON ot 8 noyabrya 2019 g. o primenenii Konvencii o bor'be s finansirovaniem terrorizma 1999 g. i Konvencii o likvidacii vsekh form rasovoj diskriminacii 1965 g. (predvaritel'nye vozrazheniya, Ukraina protiv Rossii) i kommentarij k nemu' ('Judgment of the International Court of Justice in the Application of the International Convention for the Suppression of the Financing of Terrorism and of the International Convention on the Elimination of All Forms of Racial Discrimination (8 November 2019, Preliminary Objections, *Ukraine v Russian Federation*) and the comment thereto') (2019) 137 Eurasian Law Journal 30–35; Ekspertnoe obsuzhdenie postanovleniya Mezhdunarodnogo Suda OON o primenenii vremennyh mer po delu Ukraina protiv Rossii (Expert discussion on the Judgment of the International Court of Justice on the Application of Provisional Measures in the Case *Ukraine v Russian Federation*) (2017) 23 International Justice 119–137.

[153] O Alpeeva, O mezhdunarodno-pravovoj reglamentacii protivodejstviya ekstremizmu i ee meste v deyatel'nosti tamozhennyh organov RF ('On International Regulation of Counteraction to Extremism and its Place in RF Customs Bodies Activities') (2009) 9 Eurasian Law Journal 80–87.

[154] IV Ponedelnik, 'The Right of Indigenous Peoples to Marine Resources'(2016) 18 Actual Scientific Research in the Contemporary World 129–132.

[155] Amendments to Federal Act N 79-FZ of 27 July 2004 on the Civil Service; Federal Act N 284 of 2 October 2013 amending certain legislative acts establishing the mandates and responsibilities in the area of inter-ethnic relations of the government bodies of the constituent entities of the Russian Federation, local self-government bodies and their officials. See CERD Cttee, 'Information received from the Russian Federation on follow-up to the COs' (15 May 2014), UN Doc CERD/C/RUS/CO/20–22/Add.1 paras 6–26.

letter sent to the state the CERD Cttee 'applauded the state party for increased legislative protections against interethnic and interreligious discrimination'.[156]

A possible impact could be demonstrated through the elaboration of the draft law on invalidating article 282 of the Criminal Code 'inciting hatred or hostility, and humiliation of human dignity' in 2018 due to the fact that its *corpus delicti* is vague and the article may be applied arbitrarily for political ends.[157] This initiative is in line with the Committee's earlier recommendation to amend the definition of extremism in article 282 of the Criminal Code to ensure that it is clearly and precisely worded.[158] However, the Convention and the CERD Cttee were not mentioned in the documents related to the consideration of the draft law in the state Duma. The law was not approved by the state Duma due to the opposing view on this issue expressed by the authorised State Duma Committee, the government and the Supreme Court.[159]

One of the issues that the Committee is regularly looking at is the realisation of indigenous peoples' rights. Notwithstanding the developments, welcomed by the Committee,[160] a number of issues remain the subject of concern,[161] which are also confirmed by the Russian human rights experts working in this area, including the absence of federally-protected territories and the lack of compliance with the requirement of free, prior and informed consent of

---

156 Follow-up letter sent to the state party (15 May 2015) 2 <https://tbinternet.ohchr.org/Treaties/CERD/Shared%20Documents/RUS/INT_CERD_FUL_RUS_20672_E.pdf> accessed 19 April 2022.

157 Explanatory note to the draft federal law 360083–7 'On Amending the Criminal Code of the Russian Federation and the Criminal Procedure Code of the Russian Federation with regard to invalidating Article 282 of the Criminal Code of the Russian Federation' <https://sozd.duma.gov.ru/bill/360083-7#bh_histras> accessed 29 January 2020. (This website can however only be accessed through a virtual private network (VPN) from outside the Russian Federation.)

158 CERD Cttee, COs, the Russian Federation, UN Doc CERD/C/RUS/20–22 (17 April 2013) paras 107–113; CERD Cttee, COs, the Russian Federation, UN Doc CERD/C/RUS/CO/23–24 (20 September 2017) para 12.

159 See official reviews of the draft Federal Law prepared by the government and the Supreme Court as well as the conclusion of the responsible committee (State Duma Committee on State Building and Legislation). Official web-page of the draft federal law N 360083–7 'On Amending the Criminal Code of the Russian Federation and the Criminal Procedure Code of the Russian Federation with regard to invalidating Article 282 of the Criminal Code of the Russian Federation' <https://sozd.duma.gov.ru/bill/360083-7#bh_histras> accessed 29 January 2020.

160 State ethnic policy for the period to 2025, policy framework for the sustainable development of the small indigenous peoples of the North, Siberia and the Russian Far East, approved by Government Order No 132-r of 4 February 2009.

161 See, for example, CERD Cttee, COs, the Russian Federation, UN Doc CERD/C/RUS/CO/23–24 (20 September 2017) paras 23–26.

indigenous peoples'.[162] Among the various reasons for such concerns, experts mention that the treaty body does not take into account the specifics of the country approach,[163] the absence of the coordinated structure for the implementation of treaty bodies' recommendations and the low level of awareness about them among the relevant state bodies.[164] The other reason is the Russian position of non-endorsement of the 2007 UN Declaration on the Rights of Indigenous Peoples, which prevents certain action in ensuring the rights of indigenous peoples'.[165]

5.1.6 Individual Communications and Their Impact

There were two registered communications against the Russian Federation, which were found inadmissible.[166] However, although the Committee considered that it was not within its competence to examine the first communication, it noted the racist and xenophobic nature of the actions of the identified author of the offensive leaflets that were directed against the native Roma community and reminded the state of its obligations under CERD to 'prosecute *ex officio* all statements and actions which attempt to justify or promote racial hatred and discrimination in any form, regardless of whether or not there was a formal request from the alleged victim(s) to initiate criminal proceedings under

---

162 Interview with Mikhail Todyshev, Chairperson of the Association of Shor People, Head of the Council of Elders of the Shor People, Vice President of the Russian Association of Indigenous Peoples of the North (RAIPON), Director of the Centre for Legal Resources of Indigenous Peoples, adviser to the member of the State Duma AI Otke (21 July 2019); MA Todyshev, Zashchita prav korennyh narodov v deyatel'nosti dogovornyh organov po pravam cheloveka sistemy OON ('Protection of Indigenous Peoples' Rights in the Activities of the UN Human Rights Treaty Bodies') Contemporary Issues of Modern International Law: Proceedings of the XIV International Congress 'Blishchenko Readings': in 2 parts (2016) 121–138.

163 Interview with Olga Goncharenko, Senior Adviser, International Relations Department, Office of the High Commissioner of Human Rights of the Russian Federation (18 July 2019).

164 Todyshev (n 162) 121–138.

165 See CERD Cttee, COs, the Russian Federation, UN Doc CERD/C/RUS/CO/23–24 (20 September 2017) para 24(f); MA Todyshev, 'Activities of the UN Permanent Forum on Indigenous Issues and the Expert Mechanism on the Rights of Indigenous Peoples in the Light of the Provisions of the UN Declaration on the Rights of Indigenous Peoples' (Deyatelnost Postoyannogo foruma OON po voprosam korennyh narodov i Ekspertnogo mehanizma po pravam korennyh narodov v svete polozhenij Deklaracii OON o pravah korennyh narodov) Contemporary issues of modern international law: Proceedings of the XVI International Congress 'Blischenko Readings' in 3 parts (2018) 129–151.

166 *AS v Russian Federation* (19 September 2011) Communication No 45/2009 CERD/C/79/D/45/2009; *MM v Russian Federation* (7 August 2015) Communication No 55/2014 CERD/C/87/D/55/2014.

article 282 of the Criminal Code'.[167] The Committee also encouraged Russia to follow-up on its COs regarding combating racially-motivated violence against the Roma.[168] The state was afterwards continuously building dialogue within the reporting procedure on the measures it is undertaking in this area.

5.1.7 Brief Conclusion

A certain impact could be demonstrated through the judiciary due to the presence of examples of court cases with direct reference to CERD and the CERD Cttee documents as well as the activities of the NHRI and NGOs.[169] The state is constantly developing dialogue with the Committee within the reporting procedure on many issues. However, a direct link between the Committee's COs and the developments in the state is difficult to establish. A few examples of discernible linkage are demonstrated through the follow-up procedure and due to chronological sequence. Among the factors limiting the impact of the treaty is a difference in the approaches of the state and the Committee on some issues, in particular on introducing a more exact definition of extremism in the Russian legislation, reviewing the laws on 'foreign agents', and the adoption of comprehensive anti-discrimination legislation.

5.2 *International Covenant on Civil and Political Rights*

5.2.1 Incorporation and Reliance by Organs of State

Most of the rights and freedoms guaranteed in CCPR are introduced in Part II of the Constitution. Some experts mention that the Constitution lacks such CCPR rights as freedom from slavery and servitude and equality before the law.[170] In its fourth periodic report to the Committee Russia demonstrated how the CCPR provisions (article by article) are reflected in Russian legislation.[171] However, the reliance is rather indirect. CCPR is directly mentioned in

---

167 ibid para 7.4.
168 ibid.
169 Before the consideration of the 20–22 periodic reports of Russia in 2013 the Committee received no alternative reports from NGOs. In 2013 seven alternative reports were submitted by the NGOs. In 2017, in connection with the consideration of the 23–24 periodic reports of Russia, more than 10 alternative reports from NGOs were received.
170 VS Ivanenko, Vseobshchaya deklaraciya prav cheloveka i Konstituciya Rossijskoj Federacii ('Universal Declaration of Human Rights and the Constitution of the Russian Federation') (1998) 4 Jurisprudence 12–22.
171 See Periodic Report, CCPR, Russian Federation (22 February 1995), UN Doc CCPR/C/84/Add.2 <https://tbinternet.ohchr.org/_layouts/treatybodyexternal/Download.aspx?symbolno=CCPR%2FC%2F84%2FAdd.2&Lang=en> accessed 19 April 2022.

two laws: the Federal Constitutional Law 'On the State of Emergency'[172] and the Federal Law 'On ratification of the European Convention on Extradition, the Additional Protocol and the Second Additional Protocol to it'.[173] While Russia develops a large number of policies and programmes that are related to the issues covered by CCPR and the Committee's COs, these policies are not directly based on the treaty.

5.2.2   Reliance by Judiciary

The databases of the court practice available to the authors revealed a large number of court decisions (around 305 647)[174] where references to CCPR were made. The text below contains examples of the application of the treaty provisions and interpretations that are most frequently referred to by the courts. Russian higher and lower courts tend to rely on the provisions of CCPR as a source of interpretation. Most often there are references to article 7 (freedom from torture),[175] article 12 (right to liberty of movement),[176] article 14 (equality before the court),[177] and article 19 of the Covenant (freedom of expression).[178] The higher courts also developed a practice of applying the General Comments of the HRCttee as a guide to interpretation. Specifically, the Constitutional Court relied on the General Comment on the right to freedom of movement[179] and the General Comment on the right to vote.[180] The Supreme Court of Russia

---

172 Federal Constitutional Law N 3-FKZ 'On the State of Emergency' (30 May 2001), art 37 Consultant Plus accessed 15 January 2019.

173 Federal Law N 190-FZ 'On ratification of the European Convention on Extradition, the Additional Protocol and the Second Additional Protocol to it' (25 October 1999), art 1 Consultant Plus accessed 15 January 2019.

174 State Automated System of the Russian Federation 'Justice' <https://bsr.sudrf.ru/bigs/portal.html> accessed 10 September 2019.

175 Supreme Court of the Russian Federation, Judicial Board on Criminal Cases, N 82-АПУ17-1, Appellate Determination (30 January 2017); Supreme Court of the Russian Federation, Judicial Chamber on Criminal Cases, N 18-АПУ18–11, Appellate Determination (18 July 2018).

176 Supreme Court of the Russian Federation, Judicial Board for Administrative Cases, N 77-КГ18–25, Cassation Determination (27 February 2019).

177 Supreme Court of the Russian Federation, Judicial Board on Civil Cases, N 5-КГ18–304, Determination (18 March 2019); Supreme Court of the Russian Federation, Judicial Board on Criminal Cases, N 1-АПУ19–6, Appellate Determination (14 March 2019); Supreme Court of the Russian Federation, Judicial Board on Civil Cases, N 18-КГ18–253, Determination (11 March 2019). Sverdlovsk district court of Perm, N 2–3556/2017, Decision *in absentia* (26 May 2017).

178 Moscow City Court, N 4ra-6932/2017, Appellate decision (13 June 2017).

179 Constitutional Court of the Russian Federation, N 14-П/2012, Ruling (7 June 2012) 8.

180 Constitutional Court of the Russian Federation, N 14-П/2012, Ruling (7 June 2012); Constitutional Court of the Russian Federation, N 1-P, Ruling (19 January 2017);

has appealed to the General Comment on the right to equality before courts and tribunals and to a fair trial.[181]

Referring to the jurisprudence of the HRCttee, the courts do not give specific comments on a particular decision, but simply confirm the existence of such decisions, often in terms of the plaintiff's plea to recognise a particular legal position of the Committee in cases dealing with the extradition of persons to another state or granting temporary asylum,[182] and cases concerning the rights of sexual minorities and their right to peaceful assembly.[183] Finally, the Committee's jurisprudence is also applied as the source of a remedy in cases where the Russian courts supported the applicant's reference to the Committee's decision in his plea for reviewing a court decision on the basis of 'new circumstances'.[184]

5.2.3 Impact on and through Independent State Institutions

The Ombudsman frequently refers to the provisions of CCPR when giving a legal assessment to various situations of violations of rights of Russian citizens inside and outside Russia.[185] The website of the High Commissioner informs the public about the possibility to file a complaint to the HRCttee and shows the difference between the work of the ECtHR and the Committee.[186] In 2010 the Ombudsman suggested to the state Duma to endorse a legal norm in the Code of Civil Procedure for reconsidering the court decision on the basis of the decisions of the ECtHR and the HRCttee.[187] The High Commissioner is also actively involved in raising awareness of CCPR and the Committee through supporting and organising various conferences and seminars, including

---

Constitutional Court of the Russian Federation, N 12-P, Ruling (19 April 2016) Consultant Plus accessed 15 January 2019.

181 Supreme Court of the Russian Federation, Judicial Board on Criminal Cases, N 73-APU15-27, Appellate Determination (23 December 2015) 3.

182 Sverdlovsk regional court, N 33a-16151/2017, Appellate Determination (28 September 2017); Oktyabrsky district court of Murmansk, N 2a-1631/2018, Decision (27 March 2018).

183 Central district court of Kemerovo, N 2a-8133/2016 ~ M-8170/2016, Decision (16 December 2016); Tambov regional court, N 33a-4732/2018, Appellate determination (14 January 2019).

184 Constitutional Court of the Russian Federation, N 1248-O, Determination (28 June 2012); Supreme Court of the Russian Federation, Presidium, N 128-П18ПР, Ruling (10 October 2018).

185 <https://map.ombudsmanrf.org/Karta_Yadro/prav_z_karta/v_mire/v_mire_2019/sotrud_s_megdunar_organ/sotrud_s_megdunar_organweb.pdf> accessed 19 April 2022.

186 'Question-Answer' <http://ombudsmanrf.org/pravo/faq/mezhdunarodnoepravo> accessed 19 April 2022.

187 <http://old.ombudsmanrf.org/news/novosti_upolnomochennogo/1453-2011-03-31-13-06-25> accessed 15 January 2020.

on the occasion of the anniversary of the adoption of the two international Covenants[188] and within the framework of the joint Master's Programme 'International Protection of Human Rights.'[189]

5.2.4 Use by Non-Governmental Actors

It is difficult to provide an actual assessment of the use of the treaty by the lawyers due to a lack of information. No concrete examples of professional training organised for the lawyers and dealing specifically with the implementation of the Covenant and the legal positions of the Committee were found. Since there is an understanding that the courts in their decisions tend to refer to the provisions of the international treaty when the lawyers use these in their argumentation before these courts, it seems that the use of CCPR is quite high due to the fact that the number of the court decisions applying CCPR is the largest compared to other UN human rights treaties (as the statistics showed).

CCPR and its provisions are rarely mentioned and used by NGOs in framing their activities in Russia. However, the NGOs actively participate in sessions of consideration of periodic reports of Russia in the HRCttee. Particularly, they present their own alternative reports and even commentaries to the Committee's follow-up documents.

Russian scholars publish articles, monographs and textbooks, outlining the history of the adoption of the Covenant, the practice and problems of its application in Russia, including implementation of the COs and the decisions of the HRCttee.[190] Russian universities also host scientific conferences devoted

---

[188] Round table entitled 'State institutions for the protection of human rights: experience and development perspectives in the context of the adoption of the International Covenants on Human Rights' was organised by the High Commissioner together with the Federation Council Committee on Constitutional Legislation and State Building in December 2016. 2016 annual report of the High Commissioner <http://ombudsmanrf.org/www/upload/files/docs/appeals/doc_2016_medium.pdf> accessed 15 January 2020.

[189] Opening of the Master's Programme 'International Protection of Human Rights' (23 October 2019) <http://ombudsmanrf.org/pravo/news/partnerskie_proekty/view/otkrytie_magisterskoj_programmy_acirclaquomezhdunarodnaja_zashhita_prav_chelovekaaci rcraquo> accessed 19 April 2022.

[190] AKh Abashidze (ed), Mezhdunarodnaya zashchita prav cheloveka: uchebnik (*International Protection of Human Rights*) (RUDN University 2017); RA Myullerson, Prava cheloveka: idei, normy, real'nost' ('Human Rights: Ideas, Norms, Reality') (1991) Legal literature 160; K Ipatova, Problema implementacii reshenij Komiteta po pravam cheloveka pri OON v Rossijskoj Federacii (Problem of Implementation of Decisions of the UN Human Rights Committee in the Russian Federation) Actual problems of lawmaking and law enforcement in the Russian Federation: Intern. scientific-practical conf., dedicated 120th anniversary of the birth of the first dean of jurid. fac. ISU, Prof VP Domanzho (Irkutsk, 9 April 2011) in 3 volumes. V. 3. Irkutsk: Publishing house of Irkut. State University 18–20; EV

to CCPR together with CESCR which are followed by the publication of conference proceedings.[191] These conferences and their publications are mostly focused on the fiftieth anniversary of the Covenants.[192]

5.2.5   State Reporting and Its Impact

As to the examples of impact, in 2003 the Committee welcomed the establishment of the position of the High Commissioner for Human Rights in accordance with Federal Constitutional Law 1 of 26 January 1997, which was 'in line with the Committee's previous recommendations'.[193]

The Ministry of Justice as a body responsible for the cooperation with the HRCttee stressed that it attempts to implement its international human rights obligations, including in relation to the realisation of the COs, in good faith. Thus, referring to the eight periodic report of Russia submitted in April 2019, the Ministry provided an example of measures taken to improve the legislation on combating extremism in response to the previous COs (paragraph 20).[194] Specifically, a new version of article 282 of the Criminal Code was adopted by Federal Act No 519-FZ of 27 December 2018, 'to rule out criminal responsibility for one-off offences of inciting hatred or enmity or degrading a person or

---

Sychenko, Zamechaniya Komiteta OON po pravam cheloveka k Rossii, prinyatye 31 marta 2015 g.: ih pravovoj status i problema zashchity prav cheloveka na territorii Vostochnoj Ukrainy ('Observations of the UN Human Rights Committee on Russia, adopted on 31 March 2015: Legal status and the problem of protecting human rights in Eastern Ukraine') (2015) 3 International Relations 313–317.

191   IV Logvinova, 'International Covenants on Human Rights of 1966 in the Context of the Development of Universally Recognised Rights and Freedoms of the Individual' (2017) 1 International Law and International Organisations 56, 64.

192   50th anniversary of the International Covenants on Human Rights: Proceedings of international scientific conference. Moscow, RUDN, 17 December 2016 – M.: RUDN, 2017. – 184 p.; RUDN University. Department of International Law <http://intlaw.rudn.ru/files/blischenko/2019BlischenkoCongressProceedingsIVEng.pdf> accessed 25 May 2019; Joint programme of the Russian Federation and the Office of the United Nations High Commissioner for Human Rights (OHCHR), UN in Russia <http://www.unrussia.ru/ru/agencies/sovmestnaya-programma-rf-i-upravleniya-verkhovnogo-komissara-oon-po-pravam-cheloveka-uvkpch> accessed 25 May 2019; TA Soshnikova and NV Kolotova (eds), Mezhdunarodnye pakty o pravah cheloveka: cennostnye harakteristiki / materialy mezhdunarodnoj nauchno-prakticheskoj konferencii (*International Covenants on Human Rights: Value Characteristics: Proceedings of the International Scientific Conference*) (Moscow Humanitarian University 2016) 313 <https://mosgu.ru/nauchnaya/publications/2016/proceedings/International-Covenants-on-Human-Rights-2016.pdf> accessed 25 May 2019.

193   HRCttee, COs, Russian Federation, UN Doc CCPR/CO/79/RUS (1 December 2003) para 6.

194   Position of the Ministry of Justice with regard to CCPR and CAT. Information presented by the Ministry of Justice of the Russian Federation in connection with the interview questions related to this project (19 August 2019).

group of persons that do not seriously endanger the foundations of the constitutional system and state security'.[195] However, in paragraph 20 of the COs, the HRCttee urged the state to clarify the vague definition of 'extremist activity' in the Federal Law on Combating Extremist Activity and to ensure that article 280.1 of the Criminal Code (public calls for action aimed at violating the territorial integrity of the state) is applied in consistency with the state party's obligations under article 19 of CCPR.[196] Although the introduced amendments in article 282 aimed at 'limiting the number of absurd convictions that are strongly criticised by the journalists and human rights organisations',[197] which is in line with the HRCttee's concerns, the direct link between the amendment and the content of the COs is not clearly evident.

A certain impact may be demonstrated through the assessment by the Committee within the follow-up procedure of the steps taken in the state to eliminate the cases of imprisonment as a penalty for defamation (article 128.1 of the Criminal Code).[198] The HRCttee welcomed the absence of any custodial sentences for defamation between 2013 and mid-2015, and evaluated this situation with an assessment 'B (Reply/action partially satisfactory)' but, due to the state's refusal to reconsider decriminalising defamation, additional information was required by the Committee on the number of convictions under article 128.1.[199]

The reason why the majority of recommendations of the HRCttee, selected for follow-up, remained unimplemented in view of the Committee (assessment C Reply/action not satisfactory)[200] is the differing opinion of the state on these issues. Among the examples are the denial by the state of the practice of collective punishment of relatives and suspected supporters of alleged terrorists that took place in the past in the North Caucasus[201] and, thus, the non-provision of the information by the state on the remedies granted to victims

---

195 Now the conviction is possible only if a person has committed an administrative offence of a similar nature in the previous year. See Periodic Report, CCPR, Russian Federation, UN Doc CCPR/C/RUS/8 (17 May 2019) para 175.
196 HRCttee, COs, Russian Federation, UN Doc CCPR/C/RUS/CO/7 (28 April 2015) para 20.
197 Parliamentary record of the meeting of 19 December 2018 regarding the draft law on amending art 282 of the Criminal Code <https://sozd.duma.gov.ru/bill/558345-7> accessed 15 December 2020. (This website can however only be accessed through a virtual private network (VPN) from outside the Russian Federation.)
198 HRCttee, COs, Russian Federation, UN Doc CCPR/C/RUS/CO/7 (28 April 2015) para 19.
199 Follow-up letter sent to the state party (18 April 2017) 4 <https://tbinternet.ohchr.org/Treaties/CCPR/Shared%20Documents/RUS/INT_CCPR_FUL_RUS_27219_E.pdf> accessed 19 April 2022.
200 Follow-up letter sent to the state party (18 April 2017) 3.
201 HRCttee, COs, the Russian Federation, UN Doc CCPR/C/RUS/CO/7/Add.1 (21 April 2016) para 34.

of these actions;[202] the position of the state that the legislation requiring non-commercial organisations receiving foreign funding and engaging in 'political activities' to register as 'foreign agents',[203] is intended to ensure greater transparency and openness in the activities of such organisations and does not preclude them from participating in political activities or discriminate against them;[204] the view of the state that the recognition of the special rights of persons with non-traditional sexual orientation cannot be subject to international legal regulation and should be decided in accordance with the cultural and moral traditions of states[205] and that 'discrimination on the grounds of sexual orientation or gender identity is prohibited, as is any other form of discrimination' in Russia.[206]

5.2.6   Individual Communications

Sixty-nine communications were lodged against Russia since the entry into force of OP1-CCPR in 1992. The HRCttee found that there was a violation of the provisions of the Covenant in 39 cases.[207] The majority of communications deal with the violation of the right to a fair hearing by an impartial tribunal (article 14) and setting aside a court sentence.[208]

Since 2003 the HRCttee has regularly demonstrated concerns over the non-implementation of its views by Russia. Russia is constantly recommended to review its position in relation to the Committee's views and to comply with all of these.[209] As some experts state, Russia may be in the list of states that 'have persistently failed to cooperate with the HRC'[210] within the communications

---

202   Follow-up letter sent to the state party (18 April 2017).
203   HRCttee, COs, Russian Federation, UN Doc CCPR/C/RUS/CO/7 (28 April 2015) para 22.
204   Periodic Report, CCPR, Russian Federation, UN Doc CCPR/C/RUS/8 (17 May 2019) paras 317–332.
205   Periodic Report, CCPR, Russian Federation, UN Doc CCPR/C/RUS/7 (29 November 2013) para 167.
206   Periodic Report, CCPR, Russian Federation, UN Doc CCPR/C/RUS/8 (17 May 2019) para 370.
207   Based on an analysis of the database of the Office of the High Commissioner for Human Rights <https://tbinternet.ohchr.org/_layouts/TreatyBodyExternal/Countries.aspx?CountryCode=RUS&Lang=RU> accessed 15 January 2019.
208   This was also confirmed in the interview with the 1st representative of the Ministry of Foreign Affairs of the Russian Federation (July 2019).
209   HRCttee, COs, the Russian Federation, UN Doc CCPR/CO/79/RUS (1 December 2003) para 8; HRCttee, COs, the Russian Federation, UN Doc CCPR/C/RUS/CO/6 (24 November 2009) para 5; HRCttee, COs, Russian Federation, UN Doc CCPR/C/RUS/CO/7 (28 April 2015) para 5.
210   See KF Principi, 'Implementation of Decisions under Treaty Body Complaints Procedures – Do States Comply? How Do They Do It?' Sabbatical leave report (January 2017) 15 <https://hr.un.org/sites/hr.un.org/files/editors/u4492/Implementation%20

procedure. Russia is following a position that CCPR does not contain provisions on the legal status of views adopted by their treaty bodies and that 'it is the sovereign right of the state to choose how the Committee's views as well as international legal obligations are to be fulfilled'.[211] Russia pointed out that 'the Committee does not have the functions of a court or a body endowed with quasi-judicial powers, and it is for that reason that its decisions are termed "views" and are of a recommendatory nature'.[212] The views 'carry great weight and are taken seriously by the Russian authorities, who are unable to ignore them, even where they are at variance with the Russian approach'.[213]

Each communication is forwarded by the Ministry of Foreign Affairs (MFA) to the Ministry of Justice, which prepares its position on the admissibility and merits on the basis of materials received from competent state authorities (the Supreme Court, the General Prosecutor, the Investigative Committee and the Federal Penitentiary Service) and their conclusions, and forwards this position to the Committee through the MFA.[214] In many cases Russia is not presenting the follow-up information to the Committee due to its position that OP1-CCPR contains no provisions on the obligation of states to inform the Committee on the measures taken to implement its views. This information may be presented by the state during its periodic review upon the request of the Committee.[215]

The treaty body database contains information on the implementation of only six decisions against Russia.[216] Certain information on the follow-up to three other cases was presented by Russia within the reporting procedure.[217] For the majority of these cases it is unclear whether the HRCttee continued or suspended the follow-up dialogue. The Committee's follow-up reports on some communications against Russia contain only information presented by the

---

of%20decisions%20under%20treaty%20body%20complaints%20procedures%20-%20Do%20states%20comply%20-%202015%20Sabbatical%20-%20Kate%20Fox.pdf> accessed 19 April 2022. The paper states that Russia did not cooperate in 27 cases.

[211] Periodic Report, CCPR, Russian Federation, UN Doc CCPR/C/RUS/8 (17 May 2019) para 47.
[212] Periodic Report, CCPR, the Russian Federation, UN Doc CCPR/C/RUS/6 (20 December 2007) 7.
[213] ibid.
[214] Information presented by the Ministry of Justice of the Russian Federation in connection with the interview questions related to this project (19 August 2019).
[215] Interview with the 2nd representative of the Ministry of Foreign Affairs of the Russian Federation (5 September 2019), telephonically.
[216] In accordance with the HRCttee follow-up progress reports on individual communications.
[217] Responses to the list of issues (CCPR/C/RUS/Q/6) to be discussed in connection with the consideration of the second periodic report of the Russian Federation (CCPR/C/RUS/6)' UN Doc CCPR/C/RUS/Q/6/Add.1 (7 August 2009) 3–6.

authors with the state's submission being absent.[218] The authors most often claim that they were not provided with an effective remedy due to the state's refusal to carry out a proper investigation, reopen the procedures, or to pay compensation.[219] The state may have a differing position stating that notwithstanding the detailed consideration of the case in the light of the Committee's view, the author's allegations may not be proved and the state's conclusions remain the same,[220] or the investigative activities with regard to the author's claims are still ongoing and the results will be clear at a later stage.[221] There are cases when Russia found the Committee's conclusions of a violation of the author's rights groundless.[222] In a few cases where no information from the author is accessible within the reporting procedure or within follow-up procedure, the state may inform the Committee that it implemented the decision.

In the case of *Lantsova v Russian Federation*,[223] the HRCttee found that Russia had failed to take appropriate measures to protect Mrs Lantsova's son's life as a result of confinement under conditions unfit for human survival. In

---

218 HRCttee, 'Follow-up progress report on individual communications', Communication No. 2099/2011, Polskikh UN Doc CCPR/C/121/R.1 (16 November 2017); 'Follow-up progress report on individual Communications adopted by the Committee at its 116th session (7–31 March 2016)', Communication No 2041/2011, Dorofeev, UN Doc CCPR/C/116/3 (7 October 2016).

219 For example, in accordance with the information presented by the complainants in such cases, as *Babkin v Russian Federation*, *Amirov v Russian Federation*, *Pustovalov v Russian Federation*. See 'Follow-up progress report on individual Communications adopted by the Committee at its 116th session (7–31 March 2016)', Communication No 1310/2004, Babkin UN Doc CCPR/C/116/3 (7 October 2016); Rapport intérimaire du Comité des droits de l'homme sur la suite donnée aux communications individuelles, UN Doc CCPR/C/97/3 (8 October 2009) 10 <https://tbinternet.ohchr.org/_layouts/treatybodyexternal/Download.aspx?symbolno=CCPR%2FC%2F97%2F3&Lang=ru> accessed 19 April 2022; HRCttee, 'Follow-up Progress Report of the Human Rights Committee on Individual Communications', Communication No 1232/2003, Pustovalov, UN Doc CCPR/C/101/3 (25 May 2011).

220 See HRCttee, 'Follow-up Progress Report of the Human Rights Committee on Individual Communications', Communication No 1232/2003, Pustovalov, UN Doc CCPR/C/101/3 (25 May 2011); Report of the Human Rights Committee (3 October 2005) UN Doc A/60/40, Vol II, Supp No 40 521–2.

221 HRCttee, 'Rapport intérimaire du Comité des droits de l'homme sur la suite donnée aux communications individuelles' (8 October 2009), UN Doc CCPR/C/97/3 10 <https://tbinternet.ohchr.org/_layouts/treatybodyexternal/Download.aspx?symbolno=CCPR%2FC%2F97%2F3&Lang=ru> accessed 19 April 2022.

222 HRCttee, 'Follow-up Progress Report of the Human Rights Committee on Individual Communications' (25 May 2011), UN Doc CCPR/C/101/3 26.

223 *Ms Yekaterina Pavlovna Lantsova v Russian Federation* (15 April 2002) Communication No 763/1997 CCPR/C/74/D/763/1997.

the state's reply to the list of issues it was stressed that in order to increase the effectiveness of medical care for suspected, accused and convicted persons, a joint order of the Ministry of Health and Social Development and the Ministry of Justice 'on the organisation of medical care for persons serving a sentence in places of detention and imprisoned'[224] was issued in 2005. It remains unclear whether the author was granted compensation or an official inquiry into the death of Mr Lantsov was initiated.[225]

Russian authorities refer to the case *Khoroshenko v Russian Federation*[226] as a positive example of implementation of the Committee's views.[227] Mr Khoroshenko appealed to the Prosecutor General's Office and the Russian courts to re-examine his criminal case on the basis of the Committee's finding that his criminal conviction and death penalty were based on an unfair trial, torture and arbitrary detention. His claims were not successful due to the understanding of these authorities that the HRCttee's views do not constitute the grounds for review of judicial decisions. The author then applied to the Constitutional Court, which in 2012 refused to satisfy the claim since the disputed legal provisions do not exclude the possibility to reinstitute the criminal proceedings on the basis of the HRCttee's view. The Court found that such views are considered sufficient grounds for a procurator to issue an order to institute proceedings in view of new circumstances, if the violations of the Covenant identified by the Committee could be corrected by no other means.[228] On the basis of this ruling, Mr Khoroshenko appealed against the previous decisions of the Prosecutor General's office and requested that the prosecutor be

---

[224] 'Responses to the list of issues (CCPR/C/RUS/Q/6) to be discussed in connection with the consideration of the second periodic report of the Russian Federation (CCPR/C/RUS/6)' UN Doc CCPR/C/RUS/Q/6/Add.1 (7 August 2009) 4, para 5 <https://tbinternet.ohchr.org/_layouts/treatybodyexternal/Download.aspx?symbolno=CCPR%2FC%2FRUS%2FQ%2F6%2FADD.1&Lang=en> accessed 19 April 2022.

[225] The research on the implementation of the HRCttee's decisions by Russia authored by Karinna Moskalenko and others revealed that no compensation was paid to Mrs Lantsova. See K Moskalenko, M Goldman and CA Fitzpatrick, 'The High Commissioner for Human Rights in the Russian Federation' in FD Gaer and CL Broecker (eds), *The United Nations High Commissioner for Human Rights. Conscience for the World* (Brill 2014) 331–347.

[226] *Khoroshenko v Russian Federation* (29 March 2011) Communication No 1304/2004 CCPR/C/101/D/1304/2004.

[227] Interview with the 1st representative of the Ministry of Foreign Affairs of the Russian Federation (17 July 2019), by email; Interview with Bogdan Zimnenko, Deputy Head of the Department for Systematisation of Legislation and Analysis of Judicial Practice – Head of the Department of International Law, Supreme Court of the Russian Federation (29 July 2019), Moscow.

[228] Decision of the Constitutional Court of the Russian Federation N 1248-O (28 June 2012).

ordered to issue a ruling on the issue of initiation of proceedings in view of the new circumstances. By a decision of the Tverskoy District Court of Moscow of 19 April 2013, the complaint was denied. However, in 2014 the appellate court reversed the decision and sent the materials of the complaint for new judicial review.[229] This fact was not included in the 2014 follow-up report of the Committee on this case. On the basis of the author's submission of 12 June 2016 that the state party had failed to implement the views, the Committee suspended the follow-up dialogue with a note of unsatisfactory implementation due to no follow-up report received after the reminders (assessment criteria D).[230] In its 2015 COs the HRCttee still demonstrated concern over the state party's 'failure to implement the views adopted by the Committee ... despite decision No 1248-o of 28 June 2012 of the Constitutional Court designed to facilitate their implementation'.[231]

The most recent example of the implementation of the Committee's views is the case of I Kostin,[232] where the Committee found the violation of the author's right to defence during cassation proceedings of his criminal case due to failure to inform him of his right to legal aid. The Supreme Court in its decision of 10 October 2018[233] supported the finding of the Committee and ordered the case to be transferred to a new cassation hearing, as was recommended by the Committee.

5.2.7 Brief Conclusion

A strong impact is demonstrated through the judiciary. Among all UN human rights treaties, CCPR is the treaty with the largest number of references in the court practice. The higher and lower courts directly refer to the provisions of the treaty and the HRCttee's General Comments as a guide to interpretation. In 2012 both the Constitutional and Supreme Courts started to rely on the views as the source of a remedy. A certain impact is also demonstrable through the Ombudsman's activities, NGOs, who are active in preparing and submitting alternative reports to the Committee, as well as through researchers and

---

229   See eg Appellate Decision of the Moscow City Court N 10–7574\14 (9 June 2014).
230   HRCttee, 'Follow-up progress report on individual communications' (16 November 2017), UN Doc CCPR/C/121/R.1.
231   HRCttee, COs, Russian Federation, UN Doc CCPR/C/RUS/CO/7 (28 April 2015) para 5.
232   HRCttee, 'Views concerning Communication No 2496/2014' (21 March 2017), UN Doc CCPR/C/119/D/2496/2014; Interview with Bogdan Zimnenko, Deputy Head of the Department for Systematisation of Legislation and Analysis of Judicial Practice – Head of the Department of International Law, Supreme Court of the Russian Federation (29 July 2019), Moscow (notes on file with authors).
233   Decision of the Supreme Court N 128-П18ПР (10 October 2018).

academic institutions. The state is constantly developing dialogue with the Committee within the reporting procedure on many issues. However, a direct link between the Committee's COs and the developments taking place in the state is difficult to establish. A certain impact may be demonstrated through the positive assessment by the Committee of the steps taken to eliminate the cases of imprisonment as a penalty for defamation.

Among a total number of the 39 views revealing violations of CCPR, the impact of the communications procedure is demonstrable in two cases, namely, *Khoroshenko v Russian Federation* and *Kostin v Russian Federation*. The first case is remarkable due to the recognition by the Constitutional Court that the Committee's views constitute sufficient grounds for a procurator to issue an order to institute criminal proceedings in view of new circumstances. In the second case the Supreme Court followed the position of the Committee and ordered to transfer the criminal case to a new cassation hearing. The key factor limiting the impact of the treaty is that the majority of COs, selected for follow-up (human rights violations in the North Caucasus, the legislation on 'foreign agents', discrimination against LGBT persons) remained unimplemented due to the conceptual differences in the approaches of the state and the Committee on these issues.

Another aspect where the approaches of the HRCttee and the state are at variance is the implementation of views. While the Committee is stressing the non-implementation of its views, Russia advocates its sovereign right to choose how the views are to be fulfilled with the recognition that they carry great weight and are taken seriously by its authorities. In the state's view, OP1-CCPR contains no provisions on the obligation to inform the Committee on the measures taken to implement its views. Another issue is the general lack of information on the implementation of the views by Russia in the treaty body database. For the majority of cases it is unclear whether the HRCttee continued or suspended the follow-up dialogue.

A factor that could be both enhancing and limiting the impact of CCPR is the linkage with the ECHR and the decisions of the ECtHR. The developments taking place in the areas of joint concern of the ECtHR and the Committee are motivated mostly by the ECtHR. The HRCttee itself draws the linkage with the ECtHR when raising questions of the implementation of ECtHR's judgments (for instance, *Ananyev and Others v Russia*) in its list of issues, including in relation to improving conditions of detention. The state also draws this connection when demonstrating the developments in ensuring the right to legal proceedings within a reasonable time through mentioning the steps taken to comply with the relevant decisions of the ECtHR (*Burdov v Russia*).

5.3 International Covenant on Economic, Social and Cultural Rights

5.3.1 Incorporation and Reliance by Organs of State

As some commentators consider, the drafting of the catalogue of economic, social and cultural rights in the Constitution has been influenced by the universal human rights standards, including the Covenant.[234] The Constitution guarantees the majority of the rights set forth in the Covenant, including labour rights, the right to social security, housing, health care, education, as well as the right to take part in cultural life.[235] Certain provisions of the Covenant have not received the status of constitutional norms, such as the right to assistance for the family and the right to an adequate standard of living (except for the right to housing).[236] One of the most visible results of the incorporation of the Covenant is the adoption of the Labour Code, which 'was inspired directly by provisions of the Covenant, as well as other pertinent international instruments, including of the International Labour Organisation (ILO)'.[237]

In its COs adopted since 2003 the CESCR Cttee has been welcoming the adoption of various strategies/policies in the state that are related to the issues covered by CESCR.[238] However, these strategies do not contain direct relevance to the Covenant. They generally mention that these are adopted in accordance with the international treaties of Russia in the specific area. The authors have found one strategy with direct reference to CESCR – the strategy of actions in the interests of the citizens of the older generation in the Russian Federation

---

234 A Müller, 'Influence of the ICESCR in Europe' in D Moeckli and H Keller (eds), *The Covenants at 50: Their Past, Present, and Future* (Oxford University Press 2018) 219; Christof Heyns and Frans Viljoen, 'The Impact of the United Nations Human Rights Treaties on the Domestic Level' (2001) 23 Human Rights Quarterly 483, 503.

235 Heyns and Viljoen (n 234) 483, 503.

236 VS Ivanenko, Vseobshchaya deklaraciya prav cheloveka i Konstituciya Rossijskoj Federacii ('Universal Declaration of Human Rights and the Constitution of the Russian Federation') (1998) 4 Jurisprudence 12–22.

237 CESCR Cttee, COs, Russian Federation, UN Doc E/C.12/1/Add.13 (20 May 1997) para 5.

238 Among them are Policy framework for the sustainable development of the small indigenous peoples in the North, Siberia and the Far East of the Russian Federation and the corresponding action plans for all three periods of its realisation (2009–2011 / 2012–2015 / 2016–2025); the Federal Strategy on Sustainable Development of Rural Areas for the period until 2030; the National Strategy to combat corruption and the National Plan to combat corruption for 2010–2011; the National Strategy for Women 2017–2022; the state strategy for the prevention of the spread of HIV in the Russian Federation for the period up to 2020 and beyond; the government anti-drug policy strategy for the period up to 2020; the National Children's Strategy for 2012–2017; the Strategy for the Development of Healthcare in the Russian Federation until 2025; road map for the promotion of continuing adult education until 2025; the state cultural strategy for the period until 2030.

until 2025, which was developed in line with a number of national strategies and the Universal Declaration and international treaties, including CESCR.[239]

In its COs adopted since 2003 the CESCR Cttee has been welcoming a number of institutional measures undertaken in the state, such as the establishment of the Ministry of Regional Development, the Interdepartmental Commission on Equality between Men and Women, and the Presidential Commissioner for Children's Rights. However, it seems doubtful that these measures were taken primarily to comply with CESCR.

The state continuously undertakes steps to the provision of the financial and human resources within the implementation of a variety of policies and legislation in such fields, such as combating corruption, poverty, women's rights, housing, education and health. As the Committee noted, notwithstanding the unilateral coercive measures, the state party was able 'to maintain the level of public spending to implement its obligations under the Covenant'.[240] What is challenging, though, for the state is the equal distribution of resources across the regions and the imperfection of the flat-rate tax system with regard to fighting social inequalities and its inadequacy in maximising the available resources.[241]

5.3.2 Reliance by Judiciary

The databases of the court practice available to authors revealed a large number of court decisions (around 20 000) where references to CESCR were made. Due to the impossibility to read all these decisions the authors analysed the examples of application of CESCR provisions that are most frequently referred to by the Russian courts. Russian higher and lower courts tend to follow the provisions of CESCR as a guide to interpretation. The most frequently-mentioned provisions of CESCR are those concerning the right to an adequate standard of living (article 11),[242] often referred to together with the right to the enjoyment

---

[239] Interestingly, somehow the state did not mention this development in its last report and the Committee also did not refer to that document in its COs. The High Commissioner in her parallel report mentioned this strategy.

[240] CESCR Cttee, COs, the Russian Federation, UN Doc E/C.12/RUS/CO/6 (16 October 2017) para 16.

[241] ibid para 17.

[242] Supreme Court of the Russian Federation, Plenary Session, N 1 'On application by courts of the civil law regulating the relations on obligations owed for causing harm to life or health of the citizen', Ruling (26 January 2010); Supreme Court of the Russian Federation, Judicial Chamber on Civil Cases, N 32-КГ14-20, Cassation Ruling (23 March 2015); Constitutional Court of the Russian Federation, N 14-P, Ruling (7 June 2012); Constitutional Court of the Russian Federation, N 376-O-П 'On the complaint of the citizen Alekseev Roman

of the highest attainable standard of physical and mental health (article 12);[243] the right to strike (article 8);[244] the right to the enjoyment of just and favourable conditions of work, particularly remuneration for work (article 7(a));[245] the right to education (article 13),[246] and, more frequently, the right to housing.[247]

The General Comments of the Committee have been applied to by the Russian Supreme Court, which recognised the health status, in particular the HIV status, as a ground for discrimination in line with the General Comment 20.[248] General Comment 20 has also been referred to by the lower courts in relation to the definition of 'discrimination' and issues related to the right to health.[249]

5.3.3 Impact on and through Non-state Actors and Independent State Institutions

In its COs in 2017 the Committee, while noting the information provided by the delegation on the application of the Covenant by national courts, was concerned about 'the small number of instances in which the provisions of the

---

Vladimirovich on violation of his constitutional rights by point 1 part 2 of article 57 of the Housing code of the Russian Federation', Determination (5 March 2009).

[243] Nalchik city court of the Kabardino-Balkar Republic, N 2-2154/1818, Decision (18 June 2018); Kalininsky district court of Ufa, N 2-5541/2016, Decision (11 August 2016).

[244] Supreme Court of the Russian Federation, Plenary Session, N 8 'On some questions of application of the Constitution of the Russian Federation by courts in regard of justice implementation', Ruling (31 October 1995) para 12.

[245] Sovetsky district court of Omsk, N 2-2726/2018, Decision (25 July 2018); Sovetsky district court of Omsk, N 2-2396/2018 (21 June 2018); Kotlas city court of the Arkhangelsk region, N 2-368/2017, Decision (6 April 2017); Novy Urengoy city court of the Yamalo-Nenets Autonomous district, N 2-2823/2016 (23 June 2016).

[246] Petrozavodsk city court of the Republic of Karelia, N 2-3079/2016, Decision (23 March 2016); Supreme Court of the Republic of Karelia, N 33-3801/2017, Appellate Determination (7 November 2017).

[247] Supreme Court of the Russian Federation, Plenary Session, N 14 'On some questions which have arisen in judicial practice in regard of application of the Housing code of the Russian Federation', Ruling (2 July 2009); Constitutional Court of the Russian Federation, N 2709-O 'On refusal to consider the complaint of administration of the Volsky municipal district of the Saratov region on violation of the constitutional rights and freedoms by part 2 of article 49 of the Housing code of the Russian Federation', Determination (7 December 2017); Kanavinsky district court of Nizhny Novgorod, N 2-2477/2018, Decision (19 March 2018); Yakut city court, N 2-4204/2018, Decision (26 March 2018).

[248] Supreme Court of the Russian Federation, N АКПИ17-31, Decision (13 March 2017).

[249] Moscow city court, N 33a-4867/2019, Appellate Determination (30 August 2019); Belovsky district court of Kemerovo region, N 2a-797/2016, Decision (16 September 2016); Krasnodar territorial court, N 33-13483/16, Appellate Determination (31 May 2016); Central district court of Tula, N 2a-1690/2017, Decision (2 June 2017).

Covenant were invoked before, or applied by, such courts'.[250] In this respect the state was recommended to 'enhance training for judges, lawyers and public officials on the Covenant and undertake awareness-raising campaigns among them about the obligation to give effect to Covenant rights'.[251] Thus, in the Committee's view the extent of reliance on CESCR in the courts by lawyers was rather low. Nonetheless, there are cases of references to the provisions of the Covenant in the statements by some representatives of bar associations and lawyers.[252] However, this does not reveal the actual picture of the awareness and use of CESCR and the Committee's jurisprudence by the legal profession.

Among NGOs that use the treaty and the Committee's jurisprudence in their activities are mostly those that provide reports to the treaty bodies. In 2017 the Russian movement 'Silver rose', which protects the rights of sex workers in Russia, appealed to the President of Russia, the government and the High Commissioner with a request to abolish the administrative punishment for prostitution, which is the basis for acts of violence committed by police officers against women who are engaged in these activities as well as constituting a factor that prevents these women from receiving adequate medical services, including medical treatment for HIV. The NGO was using the provisions of the Covenant and the recommendations of the CESCR Cttee and CEDAW Cttee in the legal argumentation of this request.[253] Another example is the petition submitted to the President of the Russian Federation by Andrey Rylkov Foundation for Health and Social Justice with a view to implement the

---

[250] CESCR Cttee, COs, the Russian Federation, UN Doc E/C.12/RUS/CO/6 (16 October 2017) para 5.

[251] CESCR Cttee, COs, the Russian Federation, UN Doc E/C.12/RUS/CO/6 (16 October 2017) para 6.

[252] M Barshchevsky, 'There is No Eternal Turmoil' (2014) Rossiyskaya Gazeta <https://rg.ru/2014/03/27/stepashin.html>; Y Gusakov, 'It is Time to be Merciful, Humane and Fair in Resolving Issues Related to Residence on the Territory of the Russian Federation and the Expulsion Outside the Russian Federation of Ordinary People Who Are Not Those Who Hold The Power' (2016) Zakon.ru <https://zakon.ru/blog/2016/01/17/pora_byt_miloserd-nymi_gumannymi_i_spravedlivymi_pri_razresheniya_voprosov_kasayushhiesya_proz hivaniy> accessed 3 October 2019.

[253] 'Russian Prostitutes Asked Putin for Protection' Lenta.RU (December 2017) <https://lenta.ru/news/2017/12/15/moresex/> accessed 19 April 2022; see also Silver Rose, 'Violence Against Sex Workers, HIV Infection and Law Enforcement: A Study in St Petersburg: Monitoring Cases of Violence Against Sex Workers in St Petersburg as Barriers to HIV Services' (2018) Saint Petersburg <http://www.afew.org/wp-content/uploads/2018/10/%D0%BE%D1%82%D1%87%D0%B5%D1%82-4-min.pdf> accessed 19 April 2022.

COs of the CESCR Cttee concerning the introduction of substitution therapy programmes for the treatment of drug users.[254]

Russian law and non-law academics use CESCR in their research on various aspects of universal and regional protection of economic, social and cultural rights. Certain works, including PhD theses, deal with the judicial protection of these rights,[255] specific rights (the right to health, the right to education, cultural rights, and the right to social security).[256] Some works cover issues of functioning of universal and regional human rights mechanisms,[257] international protection of economic, social and cultural human rights in general and the protection of these rights in relation to vulnerable groups.[258]

Russian universities also host scientific conferences devoted to CESCR that are followed by the publication of conference proceedings.[259] These

---

[254] Petition by Anna Sarang N 22/01-08 (19 May 2016) <http://rylkov-fond.org/files/2011/10/Medvedev-CESCR-21.07.11.pdf> accessed 19 April 2022.

[255] SY Kuteynikov, The Problems of Judicial Protection of Social and Economic Human Rights in Modern International Law' PhD Sciences 12.00.10 Moscow, 2001.

[256] AA Belousova, 'The Right to Health in Modern International Law' PhD Sciences: 12.00.10 Moscow, 2015; KN Guseynova, 'Human Right to Higher Education in International Law and Problems of its Provision in the Conditions of Globalization' PhD Sciences 12.00.10 Moscow, 2015; NV Volkova, 'Protection of Cultural Human Rights in International Law' PhD Sciences 12.00.10 Moscow, 2013; NV Putilo, F'undamentals of Legal Regulation of Social Rights' PhD Sciences 12.00.01 Moscow, 1999; MI Akatnova, 'Human Right to Social Security in International Acts, Legislation of Foreign Countries and Russia' PhD Sciences 12.00.05 Moscow, 2009.

[257] AKh Abashidze, AE Koneva and AM Solntsev, Mezhdunarodnaya zashchita ekonomicheskih, social'nyh i kul'turnyh prav cheloveka: programma kursa (*International Protection of Economic, Social and Cultural Human Rights: The Course Programme*) (RUDN University 2015); AE Koneva, Znachenie resheniya Afrikanskoj Komissii prav cheloveka i narodov po delu 'o narushenii prav naroda ogopi' ('The Significance of the Decision of the African Commission on Human and Peoples' Rights in the Case "on Violation of the Rights of the Ogoni People"') Problems of Studying Africa in Russia and Abroad. Materials of XI school of young Africanists of Russia / VG Shubin and NA Zherlitsyna – Kazan: Institute of History of the Academy of Sciences (2012) 38–40.

[258] ES Alisievich, Pooshchrenie i zashchita prav uyazvimyh grupp v mezhdunarodnom prave: uchebnoe posobie (*Promotion and Protection of the Rights of Vulnerable Groups in International Law* (RUDN University 2012)); AKh Abashidze and VS Malichenko, 'International Legal Bases of Protection of the Rights of Elderly People' (2014) 1 Successes of Gerontology 17; Yu V Samovich, Mezhdunarodno-pravovye aspekty zashchity interesov lic s ogranichennymi vozmozhnostyami ('International Legal Aspects of Protection of Interests of Persons With Disabilities') (2018) 3 International Law and International Organisations 46.

[259] IV Logvinova, 'International Covenants on Human Rights of 1966 in the Context of the Development of Universally Recognized Rights and Freedoms of the Individual' (2017) 1 International Law and International Organisations 56, 64.

conferences and their publications are mostly focused on the fiftieth anniversary of the adoption of CCPR and CESCR.[260]

The Ombudsman frequently refers to the provisions of the Covenant in his or her annual reports, specifically with regard to the problem of the level of a minimum wage being below the subsistence level in Russia. In the High Commissioner's view, this situation contradicts the Covenant.[261] The Commissioner referred to the COs of the CESCR Cttee in her 2017 annual report,[262] where she shared the Committee's concern on amendments to the Criminal Code that decriminalise a first offence of domestic violence.[263] Although not explicitly referring to the view of the Committee, the High Commissioner criticises the law on the decriminalisation of beatings, which is in line with the position of the Committee on this matter.[264]

5.3.4   Impact of State Reporting

Since 2003 the CESCR Cttee has been concerned with the low level of the minimum wage which for a long time remained well below the minimum subsistence level[265] and has been recommending to the state to ensure the implementation of article 133 of the Labour Code which, in line with the Covenant, stipulates that the minimum wage must not be lower than the worker's minimum subsistence level.[266] In its 2017 COs the Committee noted the drafting of a Bill to raise the minimum wage rate to subsistence level and urged the state

---

260 TA Soshnikova, 'International Covenants on Human Rights: Value Characteristics. Moscow Humanitarian University' (2016) <https://mosgu.ru/nauchnaya/publications/2016/proceedings/International-Covenants-on-Human-Rights-2016.pdf> accessed 19 April 2022. *International Covenants on Human Rights Are 50 Years: Proceedings of Scientific-Practical Conference* Moscow, RUDN, 17 December 2016 (RUDN 2017) 184.

261 Report on the activities, High Commissioner for Human Rights in the Russian Federation (7 April 2003) 10 <http://iskran.ru/cd_data/disk2/r1/048.pdf> accessed 10 September 2019; Report on the activities, High Commissioner for Human Rights in the Russian Federation (11 June 2019) <https://rg.ru/2019/06/11/a1701940-dok.html> accessed 10 September 2019.

262 Report on the activities, High Commissioner for Human Rights in the Russian Federation (2018) <https://rg.ru/2018/04/16/doklad-site-dok.html> accessed 25 October 2019.

263 CESCR Cttee, COs, the Russian Federation, UN Doc E/C.12/RUS/CO/6 (16 October 2017) para 39.

264 Moskalkova called the law on the decriminalisation of family abuse a mistake (2018) <https://rg.ru/2018/12/03/moskalkova-nazvala-oshibkoj-zakon-o-dekriminalizacii-semejnogo-nasiliia.html> accessed 12 July 2019.

265 CESCR Cttee, COs, Russian Federation, UN Doc E/C.12/RUS/CO/5 (1 June 2011) para 18; CESCR Cttee, COs, Russian Federation, UN Doc E/C.12/1/Add.94 (12 December 2003) para 18.

266 CESCR Cttee, COs, Russian Federation, UN Doc E/C.12/RUS/CO/5 (1 June 2011) para 18.

party to adopt this Bill.[267] The amendments of 28 December 2017 to article 1 of the Federal Law of June 19 2000 N 82-Ф3 'On the Minimum Wage' later stipulated that starting from 1 January 2019 and then annually from 1 January, the minimum wage is established in the amount of the the worker's minimum subsistence level at the level of the II quarter of the previous year.[268] However, it is unclear what the key motivation was for the state authorities to introduce these developments. The *verbatim* records of the parliamentary debates concerning the adoption of these amendments reveal only a reference to the requirements of the ILO.[269]

Since 2001 the Committee has been concerned with the situation of Roma rights and among other measures encouraged the state party to adopt a national programme of action for the promotion of the economic, social and cultural rights of Roma, and to allocate sufficient resources for its effective implementation.[270] In its sixth periodic report Russia mentioned a comprehensive plan for the social, economic, ethnic and cultural development of Roma in the Russian Federation over the period 2013–2014.[271]

It is difficult to identify any concrete legal reform that was prompted directly by the recommendations of the Committee. For example, since 2003 the Committee has regularly encouraged Russia to adopt the draft Federal law 'On State Guarantees of Equal Rights and Freedoms, and Equal Opportunities, for Men and Women in the Russian Federation'. However, this Law was developed more in line with CEDAW, rather than CESCR.

As an example of the issues the Committee is continuously concerned about, one could refer to the problem of health care for drug users, which was selected within the follow-up procedure. The Committee is concerned over the punitive approach of the state to address drug problems and the lack of rehabilitation programmes, in particular the prohibition of opioid substitution

---

267 CESCR Cttee, COs, Russian Federation, UN Doc E/C.12/RUS/CO/6 (16 October 2017) para 30; see also CESCR Cttee, 'List of issues in relation to the sixth periodic report of the Russian Federation' UN Doc E/C.12/RUS/Q/6/Add.1 (12 July 2017) para 90.
268 <http://www.consultant.ru/cons/cgi/online.cgi?req=doc;base=PKV;n=192;dst=100541#08822046409048261> accessed 19 April 2022. (This website can however only be accessed through a virtual private network (VPN) from outside the Russian Federation.)
269 <https://sozd.duma.gov.ru/bill/274625-7> accessed 25 May 2019.
270 CESCR Cttee, COs, the Russian Federation, UN Doc E/C.12/RUS/CO/5 (1 June 2011) para 9.
271 Approved by the government of the Russian Federation on 31 January 2013 N 426 p-P 44; Periodic Report, CESCR, Russian Federation, UN Doc E/C.12/RUS/6 (16 September 2016) paras 439–440. However, the text of the plan could not be found. It was only reported that in 2019 the government adopted the third version of such a comprehensive plan.

therapy (OST).²⁷² In its follow-up report the state responded that OST is 'not intended to eradicate it, ie ending drug use and overcoming drug dependence', and 'is in fact the replacement of one addiction with another.'²⁷³ OST using such psychoactive substances is prohibited under Russian legislation in line with relevant international conventions.²⁷⁴

In its submission concerning the follow-up report of Russia the Russian Public Mechanism for Monitoring of Drug Policy Reform argued that the Russian system of drug treatment 'discourages people who use drugs from seeking medical help, prevents patient access to health information, and ultimately drives the HIV and TB epidemics in Russia'.²⁷⁵ The organisation also informed the Committee that during 2018 in response to its requests concerning their plans to implement paragraph 51 of the COs the relevant Russian authorities demonstrated no plans to implement the recommendations.²⁷⁶

5.3.5   Brief Conclusion

The Covenant has influenced legislation, and the majority of the provisions of the treaty were incorporated into the Constitution. The Labour Code was inspired directly by the provisions of the Covenant, together with ILO Conventions. The strong impact of the treaty is demonstrated through widespread reliance of Russian higher and lower courts on the provisions of CESCR and its General Comments as a guide to interpretation. A certain impact is ensured through non-state actors. The activities of the High Commissioner also demonstrate a discernible impact of the Covenant. There are also concrete examples of the use of the Committee's COs by NGOs in their initiatives.

With regard to factors limiting the impact of CESCR it seems relevant to reflect the position of the Ombudsman on the causes of the violations of socio-economic rights in Russia. She determined the three factors, namely, maladministration, inadequacy of legislation (legal gaps) and a decline in funding

---

272   CESCR Cttee, COs, the Russian Federation, UN Doc E/C.12/RUS/CO/6 (16 October 2017) para 51(d).
273   CESCR Cttee, 'Information received from the Russian Federation on follow-up to the COs' (15 July 2019), UN Doc E/C.12/RUS/CO/6/Add.1 paras 43, 44.
274   ibid paras 45–48.
275   Russian Public Mechanism for Monitoring of Drug Policy Reform. Submission concerning information received from the Russian Federation as part of a follow up to the COBs of the CESCR Cttee (E/C.12/RUS/CO/6/Add.1) at 3 <https://tbinternet.ohchr.org/_layouts/15/TreatyBodyExternal/countries.aspx?CountryCode=RUS&Lang=EN> accessed 19 April 2022.
276   ibid.

in a number of industries due to the Western sanctions imposed on Russia.[277] This is a relevant position and it clarifies some of the possible factors that limit the impact of the treaty.

The state is developing a dialogue with the Committee regarding the large number of recommendations it receives from cycle to cycle and provides relevant information requested by the Committee with regard to its recommendations. However, it is difficult to see the impact of the lengthy list of recommendations. The developments taking place in the state in the area of the application of the treaty are hardly directly caused by the treaty and the CESCR Cttee recommendations. This is partly due to the fact that CESCR, compared to other specific treaties, covers a wide range of issues that are also covered by other human rights treaties, to which Russia is a party. Almost no particular reference to the treaty or the Committee is made in the strategies, laws or parliamentary debates. It is more that the connection to ILO Conventions and the CEDAW Cttee recommendations is visible in these developments. This link may be seen as a factor enhancing the impact of CESCR due to the cumulative effect of the recommendations of various international mechanisms in such areas of common concern as discrimination of women in the spheres of labour, domestic violence, and violence and discrimination against women engaged in prostitution. On the other hand, it is clear that the state pays more attention to the recommendations of the committees monitoring specific treaties than the CESCR Cttee. This situation may be also due to the lack of dissemination of the treaty provisions and the recommendations of the CESCR Cttee among the relevant state representatives and non-state actors and thus the low level of awareness.

5.4 Convention on the Elimination of All Forms of Discrimination against Women

5.4.1 Incorporation and Reliance by Organs of State

In its first periodic report the USSR claimed that 'the ratification of the Convention does not create any need for new legislative measures in the USSR, since all the requirements of the Convention have either already been implemented or are being implemented in the USSR, and the relevant legislation has a long history of application'.[278] The provision of article 2 of

---

277 Parallel report of the High Commissioner for Human Rights in the Russian Federation to the 6th periodic report of the Russian Federation to the Committee on Economic, Social and Cultural Rights <https://tbinternet.ohchr.org/_layouts/15/TreatyBodyExternal/countries.aspx?CountryCode=RUS&Lang=EN> accessed 19 April 2022.

278 Initial Report, CEDAW, Union of Soviet Socialist Republics, UN Doc CEDAW/C/5/Add.12 (9 March 1983) para 1.

CEDAW[279] was subsequently fully incorporated in article 19(3) of the Russian Constitution enshrining the principle of equality of rights and freedoms of man and woman.[280] This principle is also enshrined 'everywhere'[281] in the Russian legislation: labour law;[282] regulation of activities of political parties;[283] education;[284] civil service;[285] and service in bodies of internal affairs.[286] However, this legislation does not cite the Convention directly. The 1993 Decree of the President of the Russian Federation 'On the priorities of the state policy on women' provided for the recognition of the state policy on the protection of women's rights as one of the priority areas of the state's social and economic policy 'in connection with the obligations of Russia under the CEDAW'.[287]

While the National Strategy for Women for the period 2017–2022 does not directly refer to the Convention in its text, its adoption was motivated by the COs of the CEDAW Cttee.[288] The strategy was followed by the plan of activities for 2019–2022, which included the preparation of the periodic report of Russia

---

279   'States Parties undertake: (a) to embody the principle of the equality of men and women in their national constitutions or other appropriate legislation'.
280   LV Lazarev (ed), Kommentarij k Konstitucii Rossijskoj Federacii (*Commentary to the Constitution of the Russian Federation*) 'Novaja pravovaja kul'tura' 2009 <https://constitution.garant.ru/science-work/comment/5366634/chapter/f7ee959fd36b5699076b35abf4f52c5c/> accessed 12 July 2019.
281   Periodic Reports, CEDAW, Russian Federation, UN Doc CEDAW/C/USR/7 (9 March 2009) para 4.
282   Labour Code of the Russian Federation N 197-FZ (30 December 2001), art. 3 Consultant Plus accessed 12 July 2019.
283   Federal Law N 95-FZ 'On Political Parties' (11 July 2001) art. 8 Consultant Plus accessed 12 July 2019.
284   Federal Law N 273-FZ 'On Education in the Russian Federation' (29 December 2012) art. 3 Consultant Plus accessed 12 July 2019.
285   Federal Law N 79-FZ 'On the Civil Service of the Russian Federation' (27 July 2004) art 4 Consultant Plus accessed 12 July 2019.
286   Federal Law N 342-FZ 'On Service in Bodies of Internal Affairs of the Russian Federation and Amendment of Certain Legislative Enactments of the Russian Federation' (30 November 2011) art. 4 Consultant Plus accessed 12 July 2019.
287   Decree of the President of the Russian Federation N 337 'On the priorities of the state policy on women' (4 March 1993) para 1 Consultant Plus <http://www.consultant.ru/cons/cgi/online.cgi?req=doc&base=LAW&n=28449&fld=134&dst=100000001,0&rnd=0.36885412805763473#00229604262719544493> accessed 19 April 2022.
288   Interview with Ms.Olga Goncharenko, Senior Adviser, International Relations Department, Office of the High Commissioner of Human Rights of the Russian Federation (July 2019); CEDAW Cttee, 'Information provided by the Russian Federation in follow-up to the COs' (24 April 2018), UN Doc CEDAW/C/RUS/CO/8/Add.1 2; Senator: Russia will develop a national strategy for action for women (2016) RIA Novosti <https://ria.ru/20160224/1380014285.html> accessed 19 April 2022.

to the CEDAW Cttee by the relevant state bodies, listed in this plan, with the deadline in 2019.[289]

5.4.2 Reliance by Judiciary

Court practice of applying CEDAW is not extensive. Among all core human rights treaties, it is the treaty with the smallest number of decisions with direct references to its text. Nevertheless, in most of such court cases questions concerning CEDAW arise from labour disputes. In such cases the courts most often tend to refer to the definition of discrimination against women provided in the Convention.[290]

The courts sometimes also refer to the jurisprudence of the Committee in cases against Russia as a guide to interpretation.[291] One case of application of the Committee's jurisprudence as the source of a remedy was identified. In 2017 the Supreme Court found[292] that the 2016 CEDAW Cttee's opinion indicating gender discrimination against the applicant (S Medvedeva)[293] should be enforced in the Russian Federation and may be regarded as a new circumstance in relation to the provisions of the Code of Civil Procedure for revising a court decision by analogy to the legal consequences of the views of the HRCttee determined by the Constitutional Court in the case of Mr Khoroshenko.[294] On the basis of this decision, the courts of first and second instance reviewed the case[295] and, recognising the binding nature of the Committee's decisions,

---

[289] Plan of activities for 2019–2022 years for the realisation of the National strategy for women for the period 2017–2022. Approved by the Decree of the Government of the Russian Federation of 7 December 2019 N 2943-p <https://deptrud.admhmao.ru/cotsialno-trudovye-otnosheniya/okhrana-truda/natsionalnaya-strategiya-deystviy-v-interesakh-zhenshchin/3724304/plan-meropriyatiy-po-realizatsii-v-2019-2022-godakh-natsionalnoy-strategii-deystviy-v-interesakh-zhe> accessed 19 April 2022.

[290] Supreme Court of the Russian Federation, Judicial Chamber on Civil Cases, N 5-КГ19-54, Determination (27 May 2019); Zherdevsky district court, N 2–319/2018, Decision (13 June 2018).

[291] Frunze district court of St Petersburg, N 2–2549/2019, Decision (9 April 2019); Krasnokamsky interdistrict court of the Republic of Bashkortostan, N 2–1207/2018, Decision (2 October 2018).

[292] Supreme Court of the Russian Federation, Judicial Chamber on Civil Cases, N 46-КГ17–24, Decision (24 July 2017).

[293] CEDAW Cttee (25 February 2016) Communication No 60/2013 CEDAW/C/63/D/60/2013.

[294] Constitutional Court of the Russian Federation, N 1248-O, Determination (28 June 2012).

[295] Samara district court, N 2–1885/2017, Decision (15 September 2017); Samara regional court, Judicial Chamber on Civil Cases, N 33–15262/2017, Appellate Determination (28 November 2017).

IMPACT OF UNHR TREATIES ON DOMESTIC LEVEL IN RUSSIAN FEDERATION 961

followed its position on the fact of discrimination of the applicant in exercising her right to work.[296]

5.4.3   Impact on and through Independent State Institutions

The Ombudsman actively supports the Committee's recommendations. The Commissioner referred to the Committee's COs in her 2017 annual report with a view to supporting her position concerning assistance to women who wish to abandon prostitution.[297] The Commissioner shares the same view with the Committee on the need for the adoption of comprehensive legislation to prevent and address domestic violence against women[298] in her recommendations in the 2017[299] and 2018 reports[300] addressed to the government on developing a draft of comprehensive federal law 'On Combating Domestic Violence'. However, the Commissioner does not explicitly refer to the Committee in these recommendations. The High Commissioner regularly participates in the conferences and events devoted to the protection of women's rights,[301] where the Ombudsman usually stresses the importance of meeting the requirements of CEDAW by Russia.

5.4.4   Impact on and through Non-state Actors

It is difficult to reveal the actual level of awareness and use of the treaty and the Committee's interpretations by the legal profession. In its 2015 COs the Committee noted with concern that there is insufficient knowledge about the

---

296   Samara district court, N 2–1885/2017, Decision (15 September 2017).
297   High Commissioner for Human Rights in the Russian Federation. Annual 2017 report 169 <http://ombudsmanrf.org/upload/files/docs/lib/lite2-doclad_20.04.18.pdf> accessed 19 April 2022.
298   CEDAW Cttee, COs, the Russian Federation, UN Doc CEDAW/C/RUS/CO/8 (20 November 2015) para 22(a).
299   High Commissioner for Human Rights in the Russian Federation. Annual 2017 report 305.
300   High Commissioner for Human Rights in the Russian Federation. Annual 2018 report 33 <http://ombudsmanrf.org/upload/files/docs/lib/doclad_2018.pdf> accessed 19 April 2022.
301   Round Table 'Prevention and Prevention of Social Disadvantage of Women and Violence Against Women: Causes and Ways to Overcome' (29 January 2019). Ombudsman of the Russian Federation. Official site <http://ombudsmanrf.org/news/novosti_upolnomoc hennogo/view/kruglyj_stol_acirclaquoprofilaktika_i_preduprezhdenie_socialnogo _neblagopoluchija_zhenshhin_i_nasilija_v_otnoshenii_zhenshhin:_prichiny_i_puti_pre odolenijaacircraquo> accessed 19 April 2022; Ombudsmen of the world exchanged best practices to protect the rights of women. Ombudsman of the Russian Federation. Official site <http://ombudsmanrf.org/news/novosti_upolnomochennogo/view/ombudsmeny _mira_obmenjalis_luchshimi_praktikami_po_zashhite_prav_zhenshhin> accessed 19 April 2022.

Convention's rights among the branches of government, and recommended to the state 'to provide training to the police and law enforcement officials, as well as awareness-raising campaigns aimed at the general public'.[302] This view is supported by Russian scholars.[303]

Recently one professional training was organised for lawyers that focused on the practice of the CEDAW Cttee to address violence against women.[304] Lawyers publish articles wherein they provide analyses of the legal positions of the Committee, including on communications where they represented applicants,[305] to help practising lawyers to strengthen their positions in courts.[306]

There are a few NGOs that in their activities deal with women's rights and present alternative reports to the CEDAW Cttee: ANNA – Centre for the Prevention of Violence,[307] Anti-Discrimination Centre 'Memorial',[308] Women's Union of Russia,[309] and Consortium of women's non-governmental associations.[310] One of the examples of the use of the treaty by NGOs is the research project of the non-profit organisation the Russian Justice Initiative (RJI) on the practice of female genital mutilation in the North Caucasus. The authors of the research project refer to the Convention and the legal positions of the CEDAW

---

302 CEDAW Cttee, COs, the Russian Federation, UN Doc CEDAW/C/RUS/CO/8 (20 November 2015) paras 7, 42(b).

303 SV Polenina, Pravovaya politika Rossijskoj Federacii v sfere gendernyh otnoshenij ('Legal Policy of the Russian Federation in the Sphere of Gender Relations') (2016) 1 Proceedings of the Institute of State and Law of the Russian Academy of Sciences 62–80.

304 Practice of the CEDAW Cttee in domestic violence cases. Webinar of 13 November 2019. Federal Chamber of Lawyers <https://fparf.ru/education/events/praktika-komiteta-oon-po-likvidatsii-diskriminatsii-v-otnoshenii-zhenshchin-po-delam-o-domashnem-nas/> accessed 19 April 2022.

305 Analysis of the view of the CEDAW Cttee in the case of *Svetlana Medvedeva v Russia* of 25 February 2016 by Commentary by Dmitry Bartenev (4 May 2016) <https://academia.ilpp.ru/blog/analiz-soobrazhenij-komiteta-oon-po-delu-svetlana-medvedeva-protiv-rossii-ot-25-fevralya-2016-goda/> accessed 21 September 2023.

306 V Frolova, 'Take into Account Domestic Violence: On International Standards for the Resolution of Child Disputes' (2019) Lawyer newspaper <https://www.advgazeta.ru/mneniya/uchityvat-nasilie-v-seme/> accessed 2 December 2019.

307 ANNA – Centre for the Prevention of Violence <https://tbinternet.ohchr.org/_layouts/15/treatybodyexternal/Download.aspx?symbolno=INT%2FCEDAW%2FNGO%2FRUS%2F21870&Lang=en> accessed 21 September 2023.

308 Anti-Discrimination Centre 'Memorial' presents yearly alternative reports to the CEDAW. See eg 'List of Issues Related to the Problem of Discrimination Against Women in Vulnerable Situations to the 62nd Session of the CEDAW' <https://tbinternet.ohchr.org/Treaties/CEDAW/Shared%20Documents/RUS/INT_CEDAW_NGO_RUS_19644_E.pdf> accessed 19 April 2022.

309 Women's Union of Russia <http://wuor.ru/activities/rights> accessed 19 April 2022.

310 Consortium of Women's Non-Governmental Associations <http://wcons.net/category/biblioteka/gendernoe-ravenstvo/> accessed 19 April 2022.

Cttee to reinforce their views and formulate proposals on solving this problem.[311] This initiative was supported by other Russian organisations, including the Moscow Helsinki Group.[312] Furthermore, in March 2017 ADC Memorial, which was supporting the communication of S Medvedeva to the CEDAW Cttee, launched the #allJobs4allWomen campaign with the aim of lifting discriminatory labour bans for women. As part of the campaign, successes were achieved not only in judicial protection of women's rights, but also in making the prohibition of professions for women the subject of public discussion in Russia and in the countries of the post-Soviet region.[313]

Russian scholars conduct research on various aspects of implementation of CEDAW in Russia. There are studies devoted to the general issues of incorporation of Convention in the Russian legislation,[314] the analysis of the implementation of the COs of the Committee in Russia,[315] to the analysis of the situation of domestic violence and the application of the Convention.[316] Some scholars focus on the analysis of the discrimination of Russian women

---

[311] YuA Antonova and SV Siradzhudinova, 'Practices of Female Genital Mutilation in the Republics of the North Caucasus: Strategies For Its Elimination' (2018) <https://www.srji.org/upload/iblock/11e/978_5_4490_9470_4_Praktiki_kalechashih_operacij_v_respublikah_Severnogo_Kavkaza_strategii_preodoleniya.pdf> accessed 19 April 2022; YuA Antonova and SV Siradzhudinova, 'The Practice of Female Genital Mutilation in Dagestan: Strategies for its Elimination' (2018) <https://www.srji.org/upload/iblock/957/The_practice_of_female_genital_mutilation_in_Dagestan_strategies_for_its_elimination_15.06.pdf> accessed 19 April 2022.

[312] 'Human Rights Activists Consider Unacceptable the Approval of the Practice of Female Circumcision' (2016) <https://www.asi.org.ru/news/2016/08/17/136776/> accessed 19 April 2022.

[313] 'All Jobs for All Women. Forbidden to Women Professions – Gender Discrimination' Human Rights Report of ADC Memorial (March 2018) <https://adcmemorial.org/wp-content/uploads/forbidden_2018RUwww.pdf> accessed 19 April 2022.

[314] NN Shapovalova, 'International Legal Standards for the Protection of Women's Rights and Their Implementation in European Countries' PhD Sciences 12.00.10 Moscow, 2003; NA Shvedova, Bill' o pravah zhenshchin: tridcatiletnij yubilej ('Bill on Women's Rights: Thirteenth Anniversary') (2009) 52 A Woman in Russian Society 60–72.

[315] VI Sakevich, Vypolnenie Rossiej Konvencii o likvidacii vsekh form diskriminacii v otnoshenii zhenshchin ('Implementation by Russia of the Convention on the Elimination of All Forms of Discrimination Against Women') (2014) 619 Demoscope Weekly 40–41; SV Polenina, Pravovaya politika Rossijskoj Federacii v sfere gendernyh otnoshenij ('Legal Policy of the Russian Federation in the Sphere of Gender Relations') (2016) 1 Proceedings of the Institute of State and Law of the Russian Academy of Sciences 62–80.

[316] AA Nikiforova, Semejnoe nasilie: yuridicheskie aspekty ('Family Violence: Legal Aspects') A study of contemporary problems of society in the context of social work, a collection of scientific articles by students and teachers, Moscow, 2016 92–95; M Davtyan, Razvitie soderzhaniya pozitivnyh obyazatel'stv gosudarstva po bor'be s domashnim nasiliem v praktike Komiteta po likvidacii vsekh form diskriminacii v otnoshenii zhenshchin ('Development of the Content of the Positive Obligations of the State to Combat

in various spheres of life in light of the provisions of the Convention, especially in labour.[317]

5.4.5 Impact of State Reporting

As was mentioned earlier, the example of the direct impact of the COs was the adoption of the National Strategy for Women for the period 2017–2022[318] in response to the recommendation 'on ensuring effective coordination and developing a gender mainstreaming strategy'.[319] However, the Committee considered that the recommendation has been partially implemented due to its regret on the lack of information on an independent gender-responsive budget on the strategy.[320] The establishment of the coordinating council within the government to oversee the strategy's implementation was, as mentioned in its follow-up report, in response to the Committee's recommendation on proceeding with the establishment of a high-level commission on women's rights and providing it with a clear mandate.[321] The Committee considered that this recommendation had been implemented.[322] Another example of impact is the revision in 2019 of the list of restricted occupations and sectors for women, which is a joint effect of the COs and the individual communications procedure, which will be discussed below.

Some impact may be determined in the context of developing draft legislation, in particular the draft federal law 'On state guarantees of equal rights and

---

Domestic Violence in the Practice of the Committee on the Elimination of All Forms of Discrimination Against Women') (2019) 29 International Justice 67–80.

[317] E Sychenko, 'Zakonnaya' diskriminaciya: zapret primeneniya truda zhenshchin na nekotoryh vidah rabot ('"Legal" Discrimination: Prohibition of Women's Labour in certain work activities') (2017) 4 Labour Law in Russia and Abroad 59–62; D Bartenev, Zapreshchyonnye professii dlya zhenshchin: novyj povod dlya dialoga Konstitucionnogo Suda Rossii I Komiteta OON? ('Prohibited Professions for Women: A New Cause for the Dialogue Between the Russian Constitutional Court and a UN Committee?') (2016) 19 International Justice 37–47.

[318] Interview with Ms Olga Goncharenko, Senior Adviser, International Relations Department, Office of the High Commissioner of Human Rights of the Russian Federation (18 July 2019); CEDAW Cttee, 'Information provided by the Russian Federation in follow-up to the COs' (24 April 2018), UN Doc CEDAW/C/RUS/CO/8/Add.1 2.

[319] CEDAW Cttee, COs, the Russian Federation, UN Doc CEDAW/C/RUS/CO/8 para 14(b).

[320] CEDAW Cttee, Follow-up letter sent to the state party (17 December 2018) 2 <https://tbinternet.ohchr.org/_layouts/15/TreatyBodyExternal/countries.aspx?CountryCode=RUS&Lang=EN> accessed 1 November 2019.

[321] CEDAW Cttee, COs, the Russian Federation, UN Doc CEDAW/C/RUS/CO/8 para 14(a); CEDAW Cttee, 'Information provided by the Russian Federation in follow-up to the COs' (24 April 2018), UN Doc CEDAW/C/RUS/CO/8/Add.1 2–3.

[322] CEDAW Cttee, Follow-up letter sent to the state party (17 December 2018) 1.

freedoms and equal opportunities for men and women',[323] and the draft federal law 'On the prevention of domestic violence',[324] which were both drafted and discussed in the state Duma. The explanatory notes to both draft laws referred to the Convention.[325] Neither of these two laws passed the discussion in the state Duma, since no consensus on the conceptual aspects of these laws had been reached among the state officials, civil society and citizens.[326]

5.4.6 Individual Communications and Their Impact

There have been eight individual communications lodged against Russia. In four communications, the CEDAW Cttee found violations. In one communication (*S Medvedeva v Russia*) the Committee dealt with discrimination against the applicant who was denied employment by the company because of her sex, on the basis of an explicit legal prohibition, and the right to protection of health and to safety in working conditions.[327] The Committee adopted two sets of recommendations: (i) regarding the author, it granted her appropriate reparation and adequate compensation commensurate with the seriousness of the infringement of her rights and facilitate her access to jobs for which she is qualified; (ii) in general, it recommended to the state to review and amend article 253 of the Labour Code and periodically revise and amend the list of restricted occupations and sectors in order to ensure that restrictions applying to women are strictly limited to those aimed at protecting maternity in

---

[323] CEDAW Cttee, COs, the Russian Federation, UN Doc CEDAW/C/USR/CO/7 (16 August 2010) para 13; CEDAW Cttee, COs, the Russian Federation, UN Doc CEDAW/C/RUS/CO/8 (20 November 2015) para 14(c).

[324] CEDAW Cttee, COs, the Russian Federation, UN Doc CEDAW/C/USR/CO/7 (16 August 2010) para 23.

[325] Explanatory Note to the Draft Federal Law 'On state guarantees of equal rights and freedoms and equal opportunities for men and women in the Russian Federation'. State Duma of the Russian Federation <http://sozd.duma.gov.ru/download/D9D628DC-D551-4B8E-B77C-93029175BC6C> accessed 27 November 2019; Explanatory note to the draft federal law of the Russian Federation 'On the Prevention of Domestic Violence'. State Duma of the Russian Federation <http://sozd.duma.gov.ru/download/EB347CA2-426F-44EB-8CAF-FED7C1A46F33> accessed 27 November 2019.

[326] 'State Duma Rejected 15-Year-Old Gender Equality Bill' (11 July 2018) <https://tass.ru/obschestvo/5364113> accessed 19 April 2022; CEDAW Cttee, 'Information provided by the Russian Federation in follow-up to the COs' (24 April 2018), UN Doc CEDAW/C/RUS/CO/8/Add.1 3; 'Warrant Against Beatings: Will Domestic Violence Prevention Law Work' (2018) <https://www.rbc.ru/politics/06/12/2018/5c07d0809a79470cc20b13db> accessed 19 April 2022; <https://tbinternet.ohchr.org/Treaties/CEDAW/Shared%20Documents/RUS/INT_CEDAW_STA_RUS_22045_R.pdf> accessed 19 April 2022.

[327] *S Medvedeva v Russia* (25 February 2016) Communication No 60/2013 CEDAW/C/63/D/60/2013.

the strict sense; and after the reduction of the list of restricted occupations, promote and facilitate the entry of women into previously restricted jobs by improving working conditions and adopting appropriate temporary special measures to encourage such recruitment.

Three other communications dealt with the cases of domestic violence against women. In two communications the Committee recommended to the state to provide adequate financial compensation to the author commensurate with the gravity of the violations of rights.[328] In the other communication the Committee recommended to the state with regard to the authors to ensure the review of the judicial proceedings concerning the cases of domestic violence against both authors, grant the authors appropriate reparation and comprehensive compensation; conduct an exhaustive and impartial investigation to determine the failures in the state's structures and practices that have caused the authors to be deprived of protection.[329] In all three cases the Committee recommended to the state to adopt an extensive measures to fulfil its obligations to protect the rights of women to be free from all forms of gender-based violence, including domestic violence, through, among others, the adoption of comprehensive legislation addressing domestic violence.

The decision in the case of *S Medvedeva* received the widest extent of publicity, as it was published by the Supreme Court and in the media.[330] In 2017 the Supreme Court received the complaint by Ms Medvedeva[331] about the annulment of the rulings of the first and second instance courts which did not satisfy her claim for revising the previous court decisions on the basis of the 2016 view of the CEDAW Cttee in her communication. The Supreme Court found that this view should be enforced and may be regarded as a new circumstance in relation to the provisions of the Code of Civil Procedure for revising a court decision. On the basis of the Supreme Court decision, the court of first and

---

328   *ST v Russia* (25 February 2019) Communication No 65/2014 CEDAW/C/72/D/65/2014; *OG v Russia* (6 November 2017) Communication No 91/2015 CEDAW/C/68/D/91/2015.
329   *X and Y v Russia* (16 July 2019) Communication No 100/2016 CEDAW/C/73/D/100/2016.
330   'A Resident of Samara Seeks the Right to Become a Captain Through the UN' (18 August 2016) NTV Channel <https://www.ntv.ru/novosti/1652516/> accessed 19 April 2022; 'The Court in Samara Recognised the Refusal to Hire a Woman for a Position of a Ship Steerer as Discrimination' (18 September 2017) LENTA.RU <https://lenta.ru/news/2017/09/18/discrimination/>accessed 27 November 2019; '456 Types of Work are Prohibited for Women in Russia. Trucker, Assistant Captain and Captain – How They Overcame This Ban' (13 June 2017) Meduza <https://meduza.io/feature/2017/06/13/dlya-zhenschin-v-rossii-zakryty-456-professiy-dalnoboyschitsa-pomoschnitsa-kapitana-i-kapitan-o-tom-kak-oni-preodoleli-etot-zapret> accessed19 April 2022.
331   Decision of the Judicial Chamber on Civil Cases of the Supreme Court of the Russian Federation N 46-KG17–24 (24 July 2017) Consultant Plus accessed 27 November 2019.

second instance reviewed the case and found the fact of discrimination of the abovementioned citizen. However, it did not oblige the company to conclude an employment contract with the claimant, since the legislation does not provide for such an obligation for the company, and also due to the absence of the relevant vacant position in the company at that time.[332] In December 2016 the Russian Union of Seafarers (RPSM), guided by the CEDAW Cttee's decision in the case of *S Medvedeva*, prepared and sent to the government a petition asking for the exclusion of work performed by the members of crews of ships from the list of the banned professions.[333] As a result of all these initiatives and also taking into account the recommendations of the Committee of Experts on the Implementation of the Conventions of the ILO,[334] in August 2019 the Ministry of Labour and Social Protection revised and adopted the new version of the list of professions, which are limited to be performed by women.[335] Importantly, the term 'prohibited' was replaced by the term 'limited'. The new list contains 100 positions, which is 4,5 times shorter than before.

5.4.7 Brief Conclusion

The treaty has influenced the policies on the protection of women's rights. Thus, the adoption of the National strategy for women for the period 2017–2022 was motivated by the COs of the CEDAW Cttee. A measure of impact is ensured through the activities of the High Commissioner, the work of

---

[332] Samara district court, N 2–1885/2017, Decision (15 September 2017); Samara regional court, Judicial Chamber on Civil Cases, N 33–15262/2017, Appellate Determination (28 November 2017).

[333] Seafarer's Union of Russia. The Supreme Court of the Russian Federation demanded to reconsider the case of Svetlana Medvedeva (25 July 2017) <http://www.sur.ru/ru/news/lent/2017-07-25/verkhovnyj_sud_rf_potreboval_peresmotret_delo_svetlany_medvedevoj/> accessed 19 April 2022.

[334] International Labour Conference. 99th Session, 2010. Report of the Committee of Experts on the Application of Conventions and Recommendations (arts 19, 22 and 35 of the Constitution). Third item on the agenda: Information and reports on the application of Conventions and Recommendations. Report III (Part 1A). General Report and observations concerning particular countries, 450–451<https://www.ilo.org/public/libdoc/ilo/P/09661/09661(2010-99-1A).pdf> accessed 19 April 2022; see also 'Women in danger. Russian women will be entrusted with men's work. They've been waiting for this for 40 years' (22 September 2018)<https://lenta.ru/brief/2018/09/22/less_misognia/>accessed 19 April 2022.

[335] Order of the Ministry of Labour and Social Protection of the Russian Federation N 512н 'On approval of the list of productions, works and positions with harmful and (or) dangerous working conditions, on which the use of women's labour is limited' (18 July 2019) <http://publication.pravo.gov.ru/Document/View/0001201908150010?index=0&rangeSize=1> accessed 19 April 2022.

practising lawyers, the increased use in the scholar research and the activities and campaigns of the NGOs, specifically in relation to addressing the problem of female genital mutilation and lifting the restrictions for women to occupy certain professions.

The strongest impact of the Committee's COs, apart from the national strategy for women, was the establishment of the coordinating council within the government to oversee the strategy's implementation. Another pertinent impact was the revision in 2019 of the list of restricted occupations and sectors for women, that is regarded as a joint effect of the COs and the implementation of the decision of the CEDAW Cttee in the communication *S Medvedeva v Russia*. While among all core human rights treaties, CEDAW is the treaty with the smallest number of court decisions with direct references to its text, the Committee's decision in *S Medvedeva v Russia* was recognised by the Supreme Court as enforceable in Russia and regarded as a new circumstance in relation to the provisions of the Code of Civil Procedure for revising a court decision by analogy to the legal consequences of the views of the HRCttee.

Apart from these positive tendencies, there are certain issues raised by the Committee within both the reporting and communications procedure that remain the subject of continuous discussion with the state, especially with regard to the situation with domestic violence. While a certain impact may be determined in the context of developing draft legislation, in particular the law on equal rights for men and women, and the law on the prevention of domestic violence, no consensus on the conceptual aspects of these laws has been reached among the state officials, civil society and citizens. Such situation may be also explained by the understanding of the role of women and the traditional family values by the Russian society that in some aspects may be at variance with the approach of the Committee,[336] which is concerned 'at the persistence of patriarchal attitudes and stereotypes concerning the roles and responsibilities of women and men in the family and in society'.[337]

---

336 See LA Vasilenko and MA Kashina, Gosudarstvo i grazhdanskoe obshchestvo v bor'be s gendernoj diskriminaciej: antagonizm ili sinergiya? ('Government and Civil Society in Combating Gender Discrimination: Antagonism or Synergy?') (2015) 3 Communicology 13–24.

337 CEDAW Cttee, COs, the Russian Federation, UN Doc CEDAW/C/RUS/CO/8 (20 November 2015) para 19.

5.5 Convention against Torture and Other Cruel, Inhuman, or Degrading Treatment or Punishment

5.5.1 Incorporation and Reliance by Organs of State

While Russian legislation does not directly rely on the Convention, it is clear that CAT was taken into account when adopting the 1993 Constitution. The commentary to article 21(2) of the Russian Constitution containing a general prohibition on torture demonstrates that this provision was inspired by international treaties to which Russia is a party, including CAT, CCPR and ECHR.[338] CAT was also a source of inspiration for the drafters of the Russian Criminal Code together with the ECHR and the European Convention against Torture, in particular with regard to ensuring the principle of humanism in criminal legislation (article 7 of the Criminal Code).[339] Russian legislation does not incorporate the definition of torture under article 4 of CAT. Commentators accept a certain discrepancy in the notions of torture under Russian law and CAT.[340] Nonetheless, the Russian criminal legislation (Criminal Code and Criminal Procedure Code) contains a number of provisions 'on the prohibition of any type of unlawful act involving physical or psychological abuse of human beings'.[341] As Russia mentioned in its periodic report, 'in such a case, the law-enforcement agent bases himself on the definition of the concept of 'torture' contained in the Convention'.[342]

Russia has developed a large number of policies and programmes that are related to the issues covered by CAT and the CAT Cttee's COs. These policies, especially the policies in the area of improving the penal system, generally do not directly refer to the treaty. Their implementation is mostly aimed at fulfilling the obligations taken within Russia's membership in the CoE (the ECHR, the European Prison Rules as well as requirements of the CPT) and international treaties of Russia protecting the rights of detained and accused persons.[343]

---

[338] Commentary to the Constitution of the Russian Federation <http://constitutionrf.ru/rzd-1/gl-2/st-21-krf> accessed 25 November 2019.

[339] AV Brilliantov (ed), Kommentarij k Ugolovnomu Kodeksu Rossijskoj Federacii (*Commentary to the Criminal Code of the Russian Federation*) in 2 Volumes. Volume I. The Russian Academy of Justice (2nd edn, Prospekt 2010) 26.

[340] ibid 333.

[341] Periodic Report, CAT, Russian Federation, UN Doc CAT/C/34/Add.15 (5 December 2000) para 8.

[342] ibid.

[343] Decree of the Government of the Russian Federation N 1772-p 'Strategic Concept for the Development of the Penitentiary System of the Russian Federation up to 2020' (14 October 2010); Decree of the Government of the Russian Federation N 540 'On the Federal Target Programme for the Development of the Penal System (2007–2016)' (5 September 2006)

One of the most pertinent institutional reforms is the establishment in January 2011 of the Investigative Committee as an independent state body in charge of investigations, separate from the Procuracy. Although this is not directly provided by CAT, it is related to the treaty, since the Committee itself regarded this measure as giving effect to its recommendations.[344]

5.5.2 Reliance by Judiciary

The fifth periodic report of Russia submitted in 2011 indicated that 'there have been no cases in practice in which the provisions of the Convention have been directly applied by a court'.[345] The sixth periodic report of Russia submitted in 2016 demonstrated progress in that respect, showing that the Russian courts usually refer to article 3 of CAT together with the provisions of CCPR and the ECHR in extradition cases.[346] For example, the Russian Supreme Court considered decisions of the Russian General Prosecutor's office to extradite a person as illegal on the basis of the risk of torture in the requesting state.[347] Russian higher and lower courts also refer to the jurisprudence[348] and COs[349] of the Committee as a source of information and for strengthening argumentation in the cases involving extradition and expulsion of persons to countries such as Ukraine, Kyrgyzstan, Tajikistan and Uzbekistan. Since 2015 the Supreme Court has prepared a compilation of practice and legal positions of treaty and non-treaty human rights bodies on the issues of the protection of the right not to be

---

<http://base.garant.ru/12149380/> accessed 12 July 2019; Federal Target Programme 'Development of the penal system (2018 – 2026)' <http://static.government.ru/media/files/G4WoeqJEeW89TYrAVtuDvoU6wFH32NQr.pdf> accessed 19 April 2022.

344 CAT Cttee, COs, the Russian Federation, UN Doc CAT/C/RUS/CO/5 (11 December 2012) para 4(a); see also CAT Cttee, 'Conclusions and recommendations of the Committee against Torture', UN Doc CAT/C/RUS/CO/4 (6 February 2007) para 12.
345 Periodic Report, CAT, the Russian Federation, UN Doc CAT/C/RUS/5 (28 February 2011) para 11.
346 Periodic Report, CAT, the Russian Federation, UN Doc CAT/C/RUS/6 (27 December 2016) para 131.
347 ibid paras 125–138; Appellate Decision of the Supreme Court of the Russian Federation N 82-АПУ17–1 (30 January 2017).
348 Appellate Decision of the Supreme Court of the Russian Federation N 5-АПУ16–15 (14 April 2016); The overview of judicial practice of the Supreme Court of the Russian Federation N 2. Approved by the Presidium of the Supreme Court (4 July 2018); Decision of the Basmanny district court of Moscow N 2A-333/19 (10 June 2019); Decision Orekhovo-Zuyevo city court of Moscow region N 5–136/2016 (18 February 2016); Decision of the Amur city court of Khabarovsk region N 2A-149/2018 (19 February 2018).
349 Appellate Decision of the Supreme Court of the Russian Federation N 5-АПУ16–15 (14 April 2016).

tortured or be subjected to inhuman or degrading treatment or punishment,[350] which contains positions of the Committee together with the HRCttee and the ECtHR.

5.5.3 Impact on and through Non-state Actors and Independent State Institutions

There is no concrete data on the extent of use of the treaty by the legal profession. The Committee has been pointing to the lack of practical training for state officials and expressed concern that training on the provisions of the Convention is not mandatory for all law enforcement officers, military personnel and judicial officials.[351]

A number of NGOs specifically deal with issues of torture in Russia.[352] There are also NGOs with a broader scope of activities that deal with civil and political rights, including torture. An example of the initiatives of the representatives of civil society is the idea of the inclusion of a separate article on torture in the Russian Criminal Code in order to bring the Russian legislation in conformity with CAT.[353]

Russian scholars conduct research on various aspects of implementation of CAT in Russia. They usually examine the implementation of the Convention together with other international instruments, especially European, such as the 1987 European Convention for the Prevention of Torture and Inhuman or Degrading Treatment or Punishment.[354] Attention is given to the research on

---

350 The Supreme Court of the Russian Federation. Compilation of practice and legal positions of treaty and non-treaty human rights bodies on the issues of the protection of the right not to be tortured, or subjected to inhuman or degrading treatment or punishment (as of 1 December 2018) <http://www.vsrf.ru/documents/international_practice/27506/> accessed 19 April 2022.

351 CAT Cttee, COs, the Russian Federation, UN Doc CAT/C/RUS/CO/6 (28 August 2018) paras 44–45.

352 Interregional Committee against Torture, Public Verdict Foundation, Memorial Human Rights Centre, Soldiers' Mothers of Saint Petersburg Independent Psychiatric Association, and others.

353 Ode to a soft law document. The Federation Council marked the 70the anniversary of the Universal Declaration of Human Rights (14 December 2018) <https://fparf.ru/news/fpa/oda-dokumentu-myagkogo-prava/?sphrase_id=27137> accessed 17 July 2019; *The Presidential Council for Civil Society and Human Rights recommended the Ministry of Justice and the Ministry of Internal Affairs to introduce criminal punishment for torture* (17 December 2018) <https://novayagazeta.ru/articles/2018/12/17/147697-spch-rekomendoval-minyustu-i-mvd-vvesti-ugolovnoe-nakazanie-za-pytki> accessed 21 September 2023.

354 DA Moryakov, 'International Legal Regulation of the Prohibition and Prevention of Torture and the Legal System of the Russian Federation' PhD Science 12.00.10 Kazan, 2008 168; MN Sadovnikova, Prava cheloveka v penitenciarnyh uchrezhdeniyah: zapret pytok

the complementarity of the notion of torture in the Russian criminal legislation with the Convention. Russian scholars support the idea of the inclusion of a separate article on torture in the Russian Criminal Code in accordance with CAT.[355] A number of researchers discuss the perspectives of the establishment of the national preventive mechanism in line with OP-CAT in their work.[356]

The Russian Ombudsman considers the conformity of the Russian legislation with the Convention. In the annual report for 2009, the Ombudsman noted that the provisions of the Federal Law No 76-FL of 10 June 2008 'On Public Control of Ensuring Human Rights in Places of Detention and on Assistance to Persons Located in Places of Detention' do not meet the recommendation of CAT since it excludes the possibility of checking correctional institutions without prior notification of the Russian Federal Prison Service.[357] The Commissioner supported the view on introducing into the Russian Criminal

---

('Human Rights in Penitentiary Institutions: Prohibition of Torture') (2007) 2 Siberian Law Journal 91–95; OA Adoyevskaya, Konvencionnye normy o resocializacii osuzhdennyh ('Convention Norms About the Resocialisation of Convicts') (2019) 5 Legal Bulletin of Samara University 52–58.

[355] OS Logunova, Voprosy kvalifikacii istyazaniya s primeneniem pytki ('Issues of Qualification of Cruel Treatment With the Use of Torture') (2008) 1 Business in Law. Economic and Legal Journal 138–140; KB Toktosunov, Vliyanie norm mezhdunarodnogo prava na kvalifikaciyu prestuplenij svyazannyh s pytkami: na primere ugolovnyh zakonodatel'stv Kyrgyzskoj Respubliki i Rossijskoj Federacii ('Influence of International Law on the Qualification of the Crime of Torture: The Example of the Criminal Laws of the Kyrgyz Republic and the Russian Federation') (2016) 10 Science, New Technologies and Innovations of Kyrgyzstan 211–214; AYa Asnis, Pytki: problemy tolkovaniya i puti sovershenstvovaniya ugolovnogo zakonodatel'stva ('Torture: Problems of Interpretation and Ways of Improving Criminal Law') (2019) 6 Gaps in Russian Legislation 85–94.

[356] YuV Perron, O perspektivah sozdaniya novogo mekhanizma mezhdunarodnogo kontrolya za soblyudeniem prav osuzhdennyh v Rossijskoj Federacii ('On the Perspectives of Establishing a New International Control Mechanism with Regard to the Rights of Convicts in the Russian Federation') (2016) 34 Institute Bulletin: Crime, Punishment, Correction 48–54; NB Hutorskaya, Problemy sozdaniya nacional'nogo preventivnogo mekhanizma v Rossii ('Problems of Creation of National Preventive Mechanism in Russia') Actual Problems of Organising the Activities of Bodies and Institutions of the Penal System. Materials of the interuniversity scientific-practical conference dedicated to the memory of the honored scientist of the RSFSR, Doctor of Law, Professor AI Zubkov and the Day of Russian Science, 2017 252–255.

[357] Federal Law N 76-FL 'On Public Control of Ensuring Human Rights in Places of Detention and on Assistance to Persons Located in Places of Detention' (10 June 2008) <http://www.consultant.ru/document/cons_ doc_LAW_77567/> accessed 17 December 2019; Commissioner for Human Rights in the Russian Federation. Report for 2009 <https://cyberleninka.ru/article/n/doklad-upolnomochennogo-po-pravam-cheloveka-v-rossiyskoy-federatsii-za-2009-god/viewer> accessed 17 December 2019.

Code a separate article on torture[358] and criticised the decriminalisation of the crimes of domestic violence.[359] These ideas reflect the positions of the CAT Cttee, although the Commissioner does not explicitly refer to the Committee when expressing these views.

5.5.4 Impact of State Reporting

Among the examples of the impact is the establishment in 2011 of the Investigative Committee[360] in charge of investigations, separate from the Procuracy. This measure was considered by the CAT Cttee as 'giving effect to the Committee's previous recommendation'.[361]

The Ministry of Justice prepared a draft law on ensuring prompt access of detained persons to a lawyer with a view to implement paragraph 11 of the CAT Cttee's COs on providing all detained persons with prompt access to a qualified independent lawyer.[362] However, the relevant state authorities did not support this law for various reasons.[363] Finally, instead of adopting the law, the Ministry of Justice updated the instructions for the organisation of the access system to detention centres with the direct indication that a lawyer should be given a pass upon presentation of only a lawyer's identification card.[364]

Russian strategies, policies and legislation, which are regarded in the COs as positive aspects, do not clearly demonstrate a direct link with the recommendations of the CAT Cttee. Instead, these developments often refer to the

---

358 Moskalkova supported the introduction of special article on torture in the Criminal Code (29 January 2019) <https://ria.ru/20190129/1550080889.html> accessed 19 April 2022.

359 'Moskalkova: Decriminalisation of Domestic Violence Is a Mistake' (3 December 2018) Pravo.ru <https://pravo.ru/news/207287/> accessed 19 April 2022.

360 Federal Law N 403-FL 'On the Investigative Committee of the Russian Federation' (28 December 2010) Rossiyskaya Gazeta – Federal Issue 375 (296) <https://rg.ru/2010/12/30/sledstvenny-komitet-dok.html>; UN suggested Russia to work on torture (10.08.2018) <https://www.kommersant.ru/doc/3712041> accessed 19 April 2022.

361 CAT Cttee, COs, the Russian Federation, UN Doc CAT/C/RUS/CO/5 (11 December 2012) para 4 (a); see also CAT Cttee, 'Conclusions and recommendations of the Committee against Torture', UN Doc CAT/C/RUS/CO/4 (6 February 2007) para 12.

362 This was directly outlined by the Deputy Minister of Justice. See 'Law enforcers against amendments on unimpeded access of lawyers to pre-trial detention centres. Deputy Minister of Justice Denis Novak mentioned this, speaking about the draft amendments to the Law on Detention' (21 November 2018) <https://www.advgazeta.ru/novosti/pravookhraniteli-protiv-popravok-o-besprepyatstvennom-dostupe-advokatov-v-sizo/> accessed 19 April 2022.

363 ibid.

364 M Shuvalova, 'The Professional Rights of Lawyers: Basic Violations and Methods of Protection' (21 March 2019) <http://www.garant.ru/news/1264584/#ixzz6BfYztKT2> accessed 19 April 2022.

European human rights instruments and their monitoring bodies. What may still point to the presence of a certain impact is the fact that the Committee enquires from Russia on the progress and welcomes results achieved in the implementation of the findings of the European bodies, especially the decisions of the ECtHR, particularly in the area of upgrading the conditions of detention.[365]

In 2018 the government elaborated and submitted to Parliament a draft law on amending relevant legislation which allows prisoners to file administrative law suits in Russian courts with the request for compensation in relation to the failure to provide adequate conditions of detention and imprisonment.[366] The Russian officials and authors of the law stress that the law addresses problems that are considered not only by the ECtHR, but also the CAT Cttee.[367] The content of the law seems to have a direct relation to the Committee's COs.[368] Thus, the draft law may well have become a joint impact of the Committee and the ECtHR.

Among the COs that Russia has not implemented is the introduction of a separate article on torture in the Russian Criminal Code. There is no consensus on this issue in the country. This idea is supported by civil society and the High Commissioner,[369] but the security agencies are opposing it due to a lack of necessity to amend the Code, since parts of the crime of torture are already introduced in different provisions of the Code.[370]

---

365 For example, CAT Cttee, 'Conclusions and recommendations of the Committee against Torture', UN Doc CAT/C/RUS/CO/4 (6 February 2007) para 4.
366 Draft Law N 711788-7 'On Amending Certain Legislative Acts of the Russian Federation On the Improvement of the Compensatory Judicial Remedy for Violations Associated with Failure to Ensure Proper Conditions of Detention and Imprisonment' <https://sozd.duma.gov.ru/bill/711788-7> accessed 19 April 2022. (This website can however only be accessed through a virtual private network (VPN) from outside the Russian Federation.)
367 The Government of the Russian Federation prepares a Bill on compensations for undertaking conditions in the remand centre. Russian Agency for Legal and Judicial Information (14 December 2018) <https://rapsinews.ru/human_rights_protection_news/20181214/292610683.html> accessed 19 April 2022.
368 CAT Cttee, COs, the Russian Federation, UN Doc CAT/C/RUS/CO/5 (11 December 2012) para 20; CAT Cttee, COs, the Russian Federation, UN Doc CAT/C/RUS/CO/6 (28 August 2018) para 27.
369 'The Head of the Council under the President of the Russia Federation on the Development of Civil Society and Human Rights: on the necessity to strengthen the unit of the Investigative Committee of Russia, which investigates criminal cases of torture by law enforcement officers' (26 June 2019) RIA Novosti <https://ria.ru/20190626/1555916140.html> accessed 19 April 2022.
370 'Federal Security Service and Interior Ministry opposed the introduction of an article on torture in the Criminal Code' (29 January 2019) Pravo.ru <https://pravo.ru/news/208612/> accessed 19 April 2022; Comments on the recommendations of the Council under

5.5.5 Individual Communications and their Impact

A total of ten individual communications lodged against Russia were considered by the Committee, of which seven were found to be inadmissible.[371] In three cases the CAT Cttee found violations, specifically that (i) the conditions of the complainant's detention in the temporary confinement ward amounted to cruel, inhuman or degrading treatment (*Kirsanov v Russian Federation*);[372] (ii) the extradition of the complainant to his homeland (Uzbekistan), where torture was expected, would constitute a violation of article 3 of CAT (*X v Russia*);[373] and (iii) the complainant was tortured by police officers during his detention, his confessions were obtained under duress and used in court, and that the state failed to undertake any prompt and impartial investigation regarding the acts of torture against him (*Gabdulkhakov v Russia*).[374] In the first case the CAT Cttee recommended that Russia 'take steps to provide the complainant with redress, including fair and adequate compensation'.[375] In the second case the Committee 'urged the state party to provide redress for the complainant, including his return to the Russian Federation and adequate compensation'.[376] In the third case the Committee recommended to the State

> to provide the complainant with an effective remedy, including (a) conducting an impartial investigation into the complainant's allegations, with a view to the prosecution, trial and punishment of anyone found to be responsible for acts of torture; (b) providing the complainant with a retrial; (c) providing the complainant with redress and the means of rehabilitation for the acts of torture committed; and (d) preventing the recurrence of any such violations in the future.[377]

---

the President of the Russia Federation on the Development of Civil Society and Human Rights following the special meeting 'Transparency and legality – The main guarantees of respect for human dignity in the institutions of the penitentiary system' (19 September 2018) <http://president-sovet.ru/documents/read/ 629/#doc-4> accessed 19 April 2022.

371　*EE v Russia* (16 July 2013) Communication No 479/2011 CAT/C/50/D/479/2011; *NB v Russia* (9 February 2016) Communication No 577/2013 CAT/C/56/D/577/2013; *Olga Shestakova v Russia* (9 January 2018) Communication No 712/2015 CAT/C/62/D/712/2015.

372　*Sergei Kirsanov v Russian Federation* (19 June 2014) Communication No 478/2011 CAT/C/52/D/478/2011.

373　*X v Russia* (30 June 2015) Communication No 542/2013 CAT/C/54/D/542/2013.

374　*Danil Gabdulkhakov v Russia* (26 June 2018) Communication No 637/2014 CAT/C/63/D/637/2014.

375　ibid para 13.

376　*X v Russia* (30 June 2015) Communication No 542/2013 CAT/C/54/D/542/2013 para 13.

377　*Danil Gabdulkhakov v Russia* (26 June 2018) Communication No 637/2014 CAT/C/63/D/637/2014 para 11.

In the case of *Kirsanov v Russian Federation* the following developments took place at the national level. In 2016 Mr Kirsanov appealed to the Constitutional Court with a claim of disputing the constitutionality of article 392 of the Civil Procedure Code, which establishes the basis for the review of court decisions (due to newly-discovered or new circumstances). The applicant referred to the Constitutional Court after the unsuccessful attempts to apply this article to revise on the basis of the Committee's finding in the 2008 Samara District Court decision awarding him compensation for moral damages caused by his prolonged detention in humiliating conditions in the temporary confinement ward. The Constitutional Court refused to accept Mr Kirsanov's claim since his attempts to revise the aforementioned court decision did not concern the responsibility of individuals who committed the cruel, inhuman or degrading treatment,[378] noting that this fact was already mentioned in the Committee's finding.[379] The Constitutional Court stated that in such circumstances article 392 of the Civil Procedure Code does not prevent Russia from fulfilling its international obligations in accordance with CAT and cannot be regarded as violating the constitutional rights of the applicant in this particular case.[380] Thus, the Court did not find procedural obstacles for the applicant to execute the CAT Cttee's decision in future.

5.5.6 Brief Conclusion

CAT was taken into account when drafting and adopting article 21(2) of the Russian Constitution containing a general prohibition of torture and article 7 of the Criminal Code ensuring the principle of humanism in the criminal legislation. The impact of the treaty is demonstrated through recent tendency (since approximately 2016) of reliance by higher and lower courts on CAT and the CAT Cttee's jurisprudence and COs in the cases involving extradition and expulsion of persons.

While the High Commissioner considered the conformity of the Russian legislation with CAT and submitted its first report to the CAT Cttee in 2018,

---

[378] Determination of the Constitutional Court of the Russian Federation 'On the refusal to accept for consideration the complaint of the citizen Kirsanov Sergey Alexandrovich on violation of his constitutional rights by article 392 of the Civil Procedure Code of the Russian Federation' (2016) <http://doc.ksrf.ru/decision/KSRFDecision240 165.pdf> accessed 19 April 2022.

[379] Para 11.4 of the Committee's decision states: 'The Committee further observes that the findings of the civil court resulted in the complainant being awarded a symbolic amount of monetary compensation and that the civil court had no jurisdiction to impose any measures on the individuals responsible for the cruel, inhuman or degrading treatment'.

[380] ibid.

in the current Commissioner's activities there is little direct reliance on the Convention and the CAT Cttee, compared to other treaties.

The impact among the non-state actors is demonstrated mostly by some NGOs and Russian scholars, who support the idea of the inclusion of a separate article on torture in the Russian Criminal Code in order to bring the Russian legislation in conformity with CAT. A few examples of the impact of COs are the establishment in January 2011 of the Investigative Committee; the development by the Ministry of Justice of the draft law on ensuring prompt access of detained persons to a lawyer; and the 2015 amendments to the Russian Criminal Code establishing the investigators' obligation to respect the right of detained persons to notify a relative.

While in general the Russian delegation always enters into dialogue with CAT within the reporting procedure, there are certain issues that are regularly raised by the CAT Cttee, on which the state holds a position different from that of the Committee and representatives of civil society, including the lack of the separate article on 'torture' in Russian legislation, ineffective and impartial investigation of all incidents and allegations of torture and ill-treatment.

Another aspect that influences the impact of CAT in the country is the relationship between the Committee's recommendations and the findings of the European mechanisms, especially the ECtHR, with regard to the particular developments in the state. The Committee itself recommends to Russia to follow the decisions of the ECtHR as part of the implementation of its obligations under CAT. When undertaking certain measures with regard to the questions of joint Committee and ECtHR concern, including in the sphere of detention conditions improvement, the Russian authorities tend to make more references to the ECHR and the ECtHR decisions, rather than to the Convention and the Committee's recommendations. On the one hand, the connection with the ECtHR may be a factor preventing establishment of a concrete impact of CAT. On the other hand, such a linkage may reinforce the effect of the Committee's recommendations in Russia.

5.6   Convention on the Rights of the Child
5.6.1   Incorporation and Reliance by Organs of State

The state stresses that the protection of children is one of the core provisions of the Russian Constitution[381] and that the principles concerning the protection of children have been systematically incorporated in different branches of law governing the protection of human rights in education, health care, the court

---

381   Arts 7, 38, 43 (right to education), 67^1 (4).

system and social protection. This set of laws together with the Constitution form comprehensive legislation in the sphere of protection of children's rights. However, the CRC Cttee has noted that it is important to take all the necessary measures to amend Russian legislation, in particular in the areas of deinstitutionalisation, adoption and non-discrimination, to better reflect the principles and provisions of the Convention. It has also urged the state party to ensure that those laws that are already in conformity with the Convention are fully and effectively implemented.[382] In this situation one may conclude that the provisions of the Convention have been only partially incorporated in the Russian legislation.

In 2017 several changes to the Russian legislation protecting the rights of minor children were made in accordance with the CRC. These are directly relevant to additional mechanisms to counter the stress that has the potential of inducing suicidal behaviour among children. Monthly payments to low-income families due to the birth or adoption of the first or second child are federally established, and there has been an extension to the timeframe for distribution of financial support from the federal budget, which is intended for the implementation of activities of the Fund for Children in Especially Difficult Circumstances.[383]

The state has adopted various strategies and policies that are related to the issues covered by CRC. These policies generally mention that they are adopted in accordance with the international treaties of Russia in the specific area. Some of these documents contain direct references to the Convention.[384] The National Children's Strategy for 2012–2017, which has a direct reference to CRC in its text, is regarded as the most significant development since the Committee welcomed the adoption of this strategy in its COs.[385]

---

[382] CRC Cttee, COs, Russian Federation, UN Doc CRC/C/RUS/CO/4-5 (25 February 2014) para 9.

[383] The Annual 2017 Report on the activity of the High Commissioner for Human Rights in the Russian Federation 108 <https://ombudsmanrf.org/upload/files/docs/lib/104441_l ite.pdf> accessed 19 April 2022.

[384] Decree of the President of the Russian Federation N 761 'National Children's Strategy for 2012–2017' (1 June 2012) Consultant Plus accessed 27 August 2020; Decree of the Government of the Russian Federation N 520-r 'On the approval of the concept for the development of the system for the prevention of neglect and juvenile delinquency for the period until 2020 and the action plan for 2017–2020 for its implementation' (22 March 2017) Consultant Plus accessed 27 August 2020.

[385] CRC Cttee, COs, Russian Federation, UN Doc CRC/C/RUS/CO/4-5 (25 February 2014) para 5.

In 2009 a new mechanism, the office of the Children's Rights Commissioner of the President of the Russian Federation (Presidential Commissioner for Children's Rights), was established. While the CRC Cttee in 2014 noted the establishment of this position at the federal and regional levels, it expressed deep concern that the position is directly linked to the office of the President and not to Parliament, about the non-transparent procedure for appointing commissioners, and reports that many of the commissioners have little experience in protecting children's rights and do not observe the confidentiality of cases and act rather as law enforcement officials. The Committee recommended that Russia introduce a transparent and competitive process, regulated by law, for nominations and appointments to all posts of commissioners for children's rights in full compliance with the principles relating to the status of national institutions for the promotion and protection of human rights (Paris Principles).[386]

5.6.2   Reliance by Judiciary

Court practice reveals examples of direct reference to CRC with a number of cases with references to the interpretations of the CRC Cttee. Reference to CRC provisions concerning the combat against pornography[387] and the principle of the best interests of the child[388] may be found in the practice of superior and lower courts. There are also references to the Convention in cases dealing with the refusal to grant asylum in Russia.[389]

5.6.3   Impact on and through Non-state Actors and Independent State Institutions

The examples of direct reference to the Convention and the interpretations of the CRC Cttee in courts may lead to the conclusion that practising lawyers use

---

[386]   ibid paras 16–17.
[387]   Decision of the Constitutional Court of the Russian Federation N 795-O 'On the refusal to accept for consideration the complaint of the citizen Andrei Aleksandrovich Almazov about the violation of his constitutional rights by paragraphs 'a', 'd' of the second part of Article 242.1 of the Criminal Code of the Russian Federation' (26 March 2020).
[388]   Decision of the Judicial Collegium for Civil Cases of the Supreme Court of the Russian Federation N 18-KG19–166 'Requirement: On divorce, determination of the child's place of residence' (11 February 2020); Resolution of the Plenum of the Supreme Court of the Russian Federation N 56 'On the application of legislation by the courts when considering cases related to the recovery of alimony' (26 December 2017).
[389]   Appellate Determination of the Moscow city court N 33a-9766/2018 (26 November 2018); Appellate Determination of the Moscow city court in the case of N 33a-1395/2018 (16 March 2018); Appellate Determination of the Moscow city court N 33a-1395/2018 (16 March 2018).

the treaty in their arguments. However, this does not reveal the actual picture of the awareness and use of the CRC by the legal profession.

There are few NGOs that deal with issues of children's rights in Russia and that are actively submitting alternative reports to the Committee.[390] These NGOs may rely on the Convention in their activities, for instance, in the area of the use of psychiatry as a punishment tool in children's institutions of Russia;[391] the violation of children's rights belonging to the indigenous small-numbered peoples of the North, Siberia and the Far East of the Russian Federation;[392] HIV and infant feeding;[393] children with disabilities;[394] and the situation of children belonging to vulnerable groups in Russia.[395]

Russian academics give much attention to CRC and its application in Russia. The majority of publications deal with the right of children of persons sentenced to imprisonment to communicate with them;[396] international adoption;[397] the right of parents to communicate with their children after divorce;[398] the application of the rules on the international jurisdiction of cases arising from the legal relationship between parents and children;[399] the concept of

---

390 Anti-Discrimination Centre Memorial, Global Initiative to End All Corporal Punishment of Children, Human Rights Watch, ICCB and Partners Alternative, International Baby Food Action Network (IBFAN), LGBT Organization Coming Out, Russian Association of Indigenous Peoples of the North, Russian LGBT Network.
391 <https://tbinternet.ohchr.org/Treaties/CRC/Shared%20Documents/RUS/INT_CRC_NGO_RUS_16026_E.pdf> accessed 19 April 2022.
392 <https://tbinternet.ohchr.org/_layouts/15/treatybodyexternal/Download.aspx?symbolno=INT%2fCRC%2fNGO%2fRUS%2f15817&Lang=ru> accessed 19 April 2022.
393 <https://tbinternet.ohchr.org/Treaties/CRC/Shared%20Documents/RUS/INT_CRC_NGO_RUS_15973_E.pdf> accessed 19 April 2022.
394 <https://tbinternet.ohchr.org/Treaties/CRC/Shared%20Documents/RUS/INT_CRC_NGO_RUS_21488_E.pdf> accessed 19 April 2022.
395 <https://tbinternet.ohchr.org/Treaties/CRC/Shared%20Documents/RUS/INT_CRC_NGO_RUS_15814_E.pdf> accessed 19 April 2022.
396 NV Kravchuk, Pravo detej lic, osuzhdyonnyh k lisheniyu svobody, na obshchenie s nimi: mezhdunarodnyj i rossijskij kontekst ('The Right of Children of Persons Sentenced to Imprisonment to Communicate With Them: International and Russian Context') (2019) 4 International Justice 70 86.
397 TA Ivanova, Institut mezhdunarodnogo usynovleniya: obshchaya harakteristika, pravovoe regulirovanie ('Institute of International Adoption: General Characteristics, Legal Regulation') (2019) 4 Family and Housing Law 11–14.
398 I Demidova, S kem rebenok ostaetsya posle razvoda ('With Whom the Child Remains After the Divorce. Analysis of Disputes') (2019) 4 Administrative Law 11–18.
399 ML Shelyutto, O primenenii pravil o mezhdunarodnoj podsudnosti del, voznikshih iz pravootnoshenij roditelej i detej ('On the Application of the Rules on the International Jurisdiction of Cases Arising From the Legal Relationship Between Parents and Children') in KB Yaroshenko (ed), *Commentary of Judicial Practice* (IZiSP, KONTRAKT 2019) 156.

'negative impact' on juvenile participants in criminal proceedings;[400] and improvement of legislation in the field of social services for disabled children who are orphans and are brought up in specialised institutions.[401]

The Ombudsman in its activities deals with complaints of violations of children's rights. However, it is unclear whether the NHRI uses CRC and CRC Cttee's legal positions in its activities. In its 2017 annual report, the Ombudsman mentions that it is guided by the fundamental norms of the CRC, the best interests of the child being a primary consideration.[402]

5.6.4 State Reporting and Its Impact

The CRC Cttee has repeatedly asked Russia to provide information on the following issues: the strengthening of its efforts to establish a comprehensive and permanent mechanism within the national statistical system to collect data, disaggregated by sex, age, rural and urban area, nationality and ethnic origin; and making further efforts to ensure the implementation of the principle of respect for the views of the child. In this connection, particular emphasis should be placed on the right of every child, including children who are members of vulnerable and minority groups, to participate in the family, at school, in other institutions and bodies and in society at large; legislation, in particular in the areas of deinstitutionalisation, adoption and non-discrimination, to better reflect the principles and provisions of the Convention; the establishment of effective mechanisms aimed at facilitating the adoption process by removing unnecessary barriers, but at the same time ensuring proper screening of families where children are involved.

The salient example of the impact of COs is the ratification of OP-CRC-AC in 2008. The proposal to ratify the Protocol was submitted to the Russian President by the Ministry of Foreign Affairs together with the Russian Ministry of Defence and other interested ministries in order to implement the

---

400 AA Fedorova, Ponyatie 'negativnoe vliyanie (vozdejstvie)' na nesovershennoletnih uchastnikov ugolovnogo sudoproizvodstva v mezhdunarodnom prave ('The Concept of "Negative Impact (Impact)" on Juvenile Participants in Criminal Proceedings in International Law') (2019) 5 Russian Judge 54–59.

401 DA Semyannikova, Puti sovershenstvovaniya zakonodatel'stva v oblasti social'nogo obsluzhivaniya detej-invalidov, yavlyayushchihsya sirotami i vospityvayushchihsya v specializirovannyh uchrezhdeniyah ('Ways of Improving Legislation in the Field of Social Services for Disabled Children Who Are Orphans and Brought Up in Specialised Institutions') (2019) 2 Social and Pension Law 31–36.

402 The Annual 2017 Report on the activity of the High Commissioner for Human Rights in the Russian Federation 108 <https://ombudsmanrf.org/upload/files/docs/lib/104441_lite.pdf> accessed 19 April 2022.

recommendation of the CRC Cttee to ratify this international treaty as a priority with a view to becoming its full member, as well as taking into account the foreign policy significance and relevance of this step.[403] Another example is the adoption in 2013 of the comprehensive action plan for the socio-economic and ethnocultural development of Roma in Russia for 2013–2014,[404] which falls under the scope of the CO to adopt a national plan of action that includes special measures for the promotion of access by Roma to economic, social and cultural rights.

It is difficult to reveal any concrete legal reform that was prompted directly by the recommendations of the Committee. However, a certain linkage could be demonstrated in the case of the initiative to adopt a law concerning care for orphaned children and children left without parental care, on 2 July 2013; a law aimed at preventing trafficking in children, their exploitation, child prostitution and activities related to production and dissemination of material and objects with pornographic images of minors, on 5 April 2013; the Education Act, on 29 December 2012, which includes a provision on inclusive education for children with disabilities; an Act on amendments to the Criminal Code and other legislative acts of the Russian Federation, which increase punishment for sexual crimes against minors, on 29 February 2012.

5.6.5 Brief Conclusion

A certain impact could be demonstrated through the judiciary due to the presence of examples of court cases with direct reference to CRC. The state is constantly developing dialogue with the Committee within the reporting procedure on many issues. However, a direct link between the Committee's COs and the developments in the state is not easy to establish. A few examples of a discernible linkage are demonstrated through the follow-up procedure and due to chronological sequence. Among these are the reform of the institution of the Ombudsman for the Rights of the Child; the adoption of the National Children's Strategy for 2012–2017; and the ratification of OP-CRC-AC.

---

403 Federal Law of 26 June 2008 N 101-FZ 'On ratification of the Optional Protocol to the Convention on the Rights of the Child on the involvement of children in armed conflict' Consultant Plus accessed 12 September 2019; Transcripts of the discussion of Bill No 35523-5 'On the ratification of the Optional Protocol to the Convention on the Rights of the Child on the Involvement of Children in Armed Conflict' (6 June 2008). The State Duma of the Russian Federation <http://api.duma.gov.ru/api/transcript/35523-5> accessed 19 April 2022.

404 Approved by the government of the Russian Federation on 31 January 2013 No 426 44. However, the text of the plan could not be found.

5.7 Optional Protocol to the CRC on the Sale of Children, Child Prostitution and Child Pornography

5.7.1 Incorporation and Reliance by Organs of State

Before signing and ratifying the Protocol, a number of laws[405] were adopted as part of the preparatory legislative reform.[406] A clear example is federal law 58-FZ of 5 April 2013,[407] which was adopted in order to provide the basis for the fulfilment by Russia of its obligations under OP-CRC-SC and the 2007 Council of Europe Convention on the Protection of Children against Sexual Exploitation and Sexual Abuse (Lanzarote Convention).[408] The ratification of these treaties was followed by further legislative reforms, including the introduction of definitions of the 'sale of children', the 'exploitation of children' and 'victims of the sale and exploitation of children'[409] and the introduction of new articles in the Code of Administrative Offences.[410]

While in its COs the CRC Cttee appreciated the progress achieved in the adoption of national plans and programmes that facilitate the implementation of OP-CRC-SC, including the adoption of the National Strategy on Action

---

[405] Federal Act amending Individual Legal Acts of the Russian Federation in connection with the Adoption of the Federal Act on the Protection of Children from Information that May Be Harmful to their Health and Development N 252-FZ (21 July 2011) <http://ivo.gar ant.ru/#/document/12188176/paragraph/1:0> accessed 19 April 2022; Federal Act amending the Criminal Code of the Russian Federation and Individual Legal Acts of the Russian Federation to Enhance Liability for Crimes of a Sexual Nature Committed against Minors N 14-FZ (29 February 2012) <http://ivo.garant.ru/#/document/70144008/paragraph/1:0> accessed 19 April 2022.

[406] The State Duma ratified the Convention and the Optional Protocol on Combating the Sale of Children, Child Prostitution and Pornography. Press release (26 April 2013) The State Duma of the Russian Federation <http://duma.gov.ru/news/8011/> accessed 19 April 2022.

[407] Federal Act N 58-FZ 'On amendment of Individual Legal Acts of the Russian Federation to Prevent the Sale and Exploitation of Children, Child Prostitution, and Activities Connected with the Generation and Distribution of Materials or Articles with Pornographic Images of Minors' (5 April 2013).

[408] Explanatory note to the draft federal law 'On Amending Certain Legislative Acts of the Russian Federation to Prevent Trafficking in Children, Their Exploitation, Child Prostitution, as well as Activities Related to the Production and Trafficking of Materials or Objects with Pornographic Images of Minors' (13 October 2012) The State Duma of the Russian Federation <http://sozd.duma.gov.ru/download/317D4039-9FFB-471F-BE2F -BCAF18AB98F9> accessed 19 April 2022.

[409] Federal Act N 124-FZ 'On Fundamental Guarantees of the Rights of the Child in the Russian Federation' (24 July 1998), art 1 Consultant Plus accessed 18 December 2019.

[410] 'Facilitation by a legal person of the sale and (or) exploitation of children', 'generation by a legal person of materials or articles with pornographic images of minors and distribution of such materials or articles'. The Code of Administrative Offences of the Russian Federation, arts 6.19, 6.20. Consultant Plus accessed 18 December 2019.

for Children 2012–2017,[411] these policy documents do not directly rely on the Protocol. They generally mention that they are adopted in accordance with the international norms and treaties of Russia in the specific area.

5.7.2   Reliance by Judiciary

In two of its decisions in 2019 the Constitutional Court applied the definition of 'child pornography' in line with OP-CRC-SC.[412] The Protocol was also invoked by lower courts in the cases concerning child pornography.[413]

5.7.3   Impact on and through Independent State Institutions

In its 2018 COs the Committee noted that OP-CRC-SC is disseminated through a legal education system established at the federal and local levels and also through awareness-raising activities by children's rights commissioners. However, the CRC Cttee noted the limited information available on training on the provisions of the Protocol for professionals working with and for children, except for educational staff.[414] Some official websites of the professional law bureaus mention the Protocol in their publications authored by lawyers.[415] Nonetheless, it is difficult to provide the assessment of the level of knowledge and use of the treaty by the legal profession in the state. Among the Russian NGOs that deal with the issues covered by the Protocol, one should mention the Russian Alliance Combating Commercial Sexual Exploitation of

---

411   CRC Cttee, COs, the Russian Federation, UN Doc CRC/C/OPSC/RUS/CO/1 (3 July 2018) para 4.
412   Decision of the Constitutional Court of the Russian Federation N 1823-O 'On the refusal to admit for consideration of the complaint of a citizen Rodionov Sergey Vitalyevich regarding violation of his constitutional rights by the provisions of Articles 64, 132, 134 and 242.2 of the Criminal Code of the Russian Federation' (25 June 2019); Decision of the Constitutional Court of the Russian Federation N 1174-O 'On the refusal to accept for consideration the complaint of citizen Aleksey Germanovich Makarov on violation of his constitutional rights by article 135, notes to article 242.1 and article 242.2 of the Criminal Code of the Russian Federation' (25 April 2019) Consultant Plus accessed 29 July 2019.
413   Decision of the Meshchansky District Court N 01-0731/2018 (23 October 2018) Consultant Plus accessed 29 July 2019.
414   CRC Cttee, COs, the Russian Federation, UN Doc CRC/C/OPSC/RUS/CO/1 (3 July 2018) para 13.
415   'The Constitutional Court did not see the uncertainty in the concept of 'sexual acts' in the Criminal Code'. Advokatskaya Gazeta (2019) <https://www.advgazeta.ru/novosti/ks-ne-uvidel-neopredelennosti-v-ponyatii-deystviya-seksualnogo-kharaktera-v-uk/> accessed 19 April 2022.

Children.[416] In 2018 this Alliance together with ECPAT provided an alternative report to the Committee in relation to the initial report of Russia.[417] The report reveals that the organisation, jointly with ECPAT International, conducted various studies, undertook a number of awareness-raising activities on the risks of internet use, launched a youth volunteer movement and provided training for the staff of some hotels. It seems that in these activities the NGO is guided by the Protocol together with other treaties to which Russia is a party, namely, the 2000 Protocol to Prevent, Suppress and Punish Trafficking in Persons, Especially Women and Children. Russian scholars do not pay much attention to the Protocol in their research. A few publications deal with certain issues of implementation of the Protocol in Russia,[418] and provide the analysis of the notions of 'sexual exploitation'[419] and 'illegal adoption'.[420]

---

[416] An affiliate of the International Network of ECPAT Organisations ('ECPAT' – 'Stop Child Prostitution, Pornography and Trafficking of Children for Sexual Purposes') established by NGOs in St Petersburg in 2004.

[417] Supplementary report to the initial report submitted by the Russian Federation on the implementation of the Optional Protocol to the Convention on the Rights of the Child on the Sale of Children, Child Prostitution and Child Pornography regarding 'Sexual Exploitation of Children in the Russian Federation' submitted by Russian Alliance against CSEC and ECPAT International. 12 April 2018 // Office of the High Commissioner of Human Rights. Treaty bodies database <https://tbinternet.ohchr.org/Treaties/CRC-OP-SC/Shared%20Documents/RUS/INT_CRC-OP-SC_NGO_RUS_31126_E.docx> accessed 19 April 2022.

[418] AG Volevodz, Rossijskoe zakonodatel'stvo ob ugolovnoj otvetstvennosti za prestupleniya v sfere komp'yuternoj informacii ('Russian Legislation on Criminal Liability for Crimes in the Field of Computer Information') (2002) 9 Russian Judge 34-41; A Koneva and D Gugunskiy, Predotvrashchenie torgovli det'mi, detskoj prostitucii i detskoj pornografii v Rossijskoj Federacii v svete trebovanij Fakul'tativnogo protokola k Konvencii o pravah rebenka, kasayushchegosya torgovli det'mi, detskoj prostitucii i detskoj pornografii 2000 g. ('Prevention of the Sale of Children, Child Prostitution and Child Pornography in the Russian Federation in the Light of the Provisions of the 2000 Optional Protocol to the Convention on the Rights of the Child on the Sale of Children, Child Prostitution and Child Pornography') (2019) 128 Eurasian Law Journal 355-358.

[419] IS Alikhadzhieva, O ponyatii seksual'noj ekspluatacii v mezhdunarodnom prave ('On the Concept of Sexual Exploitation in International Law') (2017) 10 Actual Problems of Russian Law 159-167.

[420] VL Kabanov, Nezakonnoe usynovlenie kak narushenie principa nailuchshego obespecheniya interesov rebenka (mezhdunarodno-pravovye aspekty) ('Illegal Adoption as a Violation of the Principle of the Best Interests of the Child (International Legal Aspects)') (2017) 7 Modern Law 124-127.

5.7.4 Impact of State Reporting

In its first and only COs addressed to Russia in 2018 the CRC Cttee paid particular attention to the following problems: the lack of a comprehensive strategy covering all areas under OP-CRC-SC, including all forms of the sale of children; no single national body coordinating activities to implement the Protocol; a lack of awareness of the Optional Protocol by children and their families and non-incorporation of its provisions into school curricula; insufficient efforts to identify children in need of protection among children in vulnerable and marginalised situations; cases of child marriage, especially in the North Caucasus; sex tourism to the state by foreigners and sex tourism of Russian citizens travelling abroad; a significant increase in the number of websites with child pornography since 2009; a lack of provisions on criminal liability of legal persons under the Russian legislation for offences under the Protocol; treatment by law enforcement agencies of victims of offences under the Protocol, including children involved in prostitution, as offenders rather than victims of crimes; inadequate recovery and reintegration services for child victims of offences.

On 3 July 2018 the state Duma of the Federal Assembly of the Russian Federation adopted in first reading the draft federal law No 388776-7 'On Amending the Criminal Code of the Russian Federation and the Code of Criminal Procedure of the Russian Federation in terms of improving mechanisms to combat crimes against sexual inviolability of minors', aimed at strengthening measures to combat crimes against the sexual integrity of minors.[421] This draft law provides for the possibility of the statute of limitations to start from the moment when the victim reaches 18 years (majority) in cases where the perpetrator of a crime against sexual inviolability of this minor (victim), who at the moment of the crime has not reached the age of twelve, has not been identified or there was no notification of such a crime. This provision seems to follow the recommendation of the Committee to remove the statute of limitations for offences under the Protocol.[422]

In its COs the Committee recommended to the state party to incorporate explicitly into its criminal legislation the liability of legal persons for committing offences under the Protocol. Shortly after the adoption of the COs the draft federal law on the introduction of the institute of criminal liability of legal entities,[423] which had been under consideration of the state Duma since

---

[421] Webpage of the Draft Federal Law <https://sozd.duma.gov.ru/bill/388776-7#bh_histras> accessed 19 April 2022. (This website can however only be accessed through a virtual private network (VPN) from outside the Russian Federation.)

[422] CRC Cttee, COs, the Russian Federation, UN Doc CRC/C/OPSC/RUS/CO/1 (3 July 2018) para 27(c).

[423] Draft Federal Law N 750443-6 (archived) 'On Amending Certain Legislative Acts of the Russian Federation in Connection with the Introduction of the Institute of Criminal

March 2015, was declined by the state Duma due to the official review of the government noting that its adoption implied radical changes in the concept of the criminal law and the criminal law doctrine regarding liability of legal entities and thus pointing to the need for the additional in-depth discussion and theoretical justification of this law.[424]

5.7.5 Brief Conclusion

The relatively short period of time after the entry into force of the Protocol allows one to consider that this treaty does not demonstrate a strong impact on the human rights developments in the country. The few examples of its impact are the legislative amendments introduced before and after the ratification, a number of cases of reliance on the Protocol and the Committee's positions by domestic courts, use by the NGOs and researchers. Since the state had only one dialogue with the CRC Cttee with the COs adopted in 2018, it is difficult to make a concrete assessment on their impact. Another aspect that should be taken into account is the link between OP-CRC-SC and the Lanzarote Convention, which ratification coincided with the Protocol's ratification. The fulfillment by Russia of its obligations under this instrument together with the obligations under the Protocol were mentioned as a motivating factor to introduce the relative legislative changes in the state.

5.8 Optional Protocol to the CRC on the Involvement of Children in Armed Conflict

5.8.1 Incorporation into Domestic Law and Policy

Russia in its initial report mentioned that Russian law contains no provisions that hamper the implementation of the Protocol. There is no need to amend Russian law in order to implement the Protocol.'[425] When ratifying the Protocol in the Parliamentary Debate, it was also concluded that (a) the provisions of the Protocol do not contradict Russian legislation;[426] and (b) amendments to

---

Liability of Legal Entities'. The State Duma of the Russian Federation <https://sozd.duma.gov.ru/bill/750443-6> accessed 19 April 2022. (This website can however only be accessed through a virtual private network (VPN) from outside the Russian Federation.)

424 Official review to the Draft Federal Law 'On Amending Certain Legislative Acts of the Russian Federation in Connection with the Introduction of the Institute of Criminal Liability of Legal Entities', submitted to the State Duma by AA Remezkov. The State Duma of the Russian Federation <http://sozd.duma.gov.ru/download/1BD993E9-A01B-4B99-934B-15058B6B0332> accessed 19 April 2022.

425 Initial Report, CRC, Russian Federation, UN Doc CRC/C/OPAC/RUS/1 para 21.

426 Transcripts of the discussion of Law N 35523-5 'On ratification of the Optional Protocol to the Convention on the Rights of the Child on the Involvement of Children in Armed Conflict' (6 June 2008) The State Duma of the Russian Federation <http://api.duma.gov.ru/api/transcript/35523-5> accessed 19 April 2022.

the Russian legislation are not required in connection with the ratification of the Protocol.[427]

5.8.2 Reliance by Judiciary

The Protocol and the relevant positions of the CRC Cttee have been featured several times in reviews of judicial practice compiled by the Supreme Court,[428] but the treaty and the treaty body interpretations have not been relied upon by domestic courts.

5.8.3 Impact on and through Independent State Institutions

No concrete information on the use of OP-CRC-AC by the High Commissioner is available to the authors, except for the fact that the High Commissioner took part in the preparation of the periodic report of Russia under the Protocol.[429] The state's report revealed that in 2010 a study of the provisions of the Protocol was incorporated into the official military training system for staff of the Ministry of Internal Affairs. Further, more than 40 higher education institutions providing vocational training have introduced 'life safety' as a new specialism as well as the qualification of life safety teacher.[430] The training system for the military personnel of the Ministry of Defence of the Russian Federation also provides for the study of the provisions of the Optional Protocol.[431] No concrete information on the use of OP-CRC-AC by NGOs is available to the authors. Russian scholars do not pay much attention to the Protocol in their research. A few publications mention the treaty in the context of analysing

---

427 ibid.
428 Review of judicial practice of the Supreme Court of the Russian Federation N 5 (2017) (approved by the Presidium of the Supreme Court of the Russian Federation on December 27, 2017) Consultant Plus accessed 12 September 2019; Review of the practice of interstate bodies for the protection of human rights and fundamental freedoms N 1 (2019) (prepared by the Supreme Court of the Russian Federation) Consultant Plus accessed 12 September 2019.
429 Initial Report, CRC, Russian Federation, UN Doc CRC/C/OPAC/RUS/1 para 3.
430 ibid para 7.
431 Theses of the opening speech of the Deputy Minister of Defence of the Russian Federation AI Antonov during the consideration of the initial report of the Russian Federation on the implementation of the Optional Protocol to the Convention on the Rights of the Child on the involvement of children in armed conflict during the 65th session of the Committee on the Rights of the Child (Geneva, January 23 2014). The Ministry of Defence of the Russian Federation <https://function.mil.ru/news_page/country/more.htm?id=11895881@egNews> accessed 19 April 2022.

the current issues of international humanitarian law[432] and in the context of considering issues related to the protection of children in armed conflicts.[433]

5.8.4 Impact of State Reporting

In its first and only COs addressed to Russia in 2014 the CRC Cttee paid particular attention to the following problems: the admission to professional military educational institutions and acquiring the status of members of the military performing compulsory military service for the children who have reached the age of 16; military training involving the use of firearms and combat training for children under the age of 18 in both general and military schools; military discipline and punishment of children under the age of 18 who are admitted to cadet schools and higher military institutes; the lack of explicit prohibition in the Criminal Code on the recruitment of any children under the age of 18 by the armed forces or by non-state armed groups and the use, involvement and participation of children in hostilities; the lack of mechanisms in place to identify at an early stage refugee, asylum-seeking and migrant children who may have been involved in armed conflicts in other countries, and the lack of information on the procedures for their protection, recovery and reintegration. While the Ministry of Defence has stressed that the results of the consideration of Russia's report by the Committee will be taken into account in its future

---

[432] VN Rusinova, Prava cheloveka v vooruzhennyh konfliktah: problemy sootnosheniya norm mezhdunarodnogo gumanitarnogo prava i mezhdunarodnogo prava prav cheloveka: monografiya (*Human Rights in Armed Conflict: Problems of Correlation of International Humanitarian Law and International Human Rights Law*) (Moscow, Statute, 2017); SV Nesterova, Vklyuchennost' instituta obespecheniya zashchity uchastnikov vooruzhennogo konflikta v sovremennuyu mezhdunarodnuyu normativnuyu sistemu ('The Inclusion of the Institution of Ensuring the Protection of Participants in an Armed Conflict in the Modern International Regulatory System') (2016) 2 International Law and International Organisations 180–199; VA Batyr, Mezhdunarodnoe gumanitarnoe pravo: Uchebnik dlya vuzov (*International Humanitarian Law: Textbook for Universities*) (2nd edn, Justicinform 2011).

[433] AM Solntsev, Uchastie detej v vooruzhennyh konfliktah na afrikanskom kontinente: problema vozmeshcheniya ushcherba i vosstanovleniya prav (Participation of Children in Armed Conflicts on the African Continent: The Problem of Compensation for Damages and Restoration of Rights') Actual issues of international law in Africa materials of the round table of the X annual All-Russian scientific-practical conference 'Actual problems of modern international law', dedicated to the memory of Professor IP Blischenko, 2012 199–208; A Yu Yastrebova, Mezhdunarodno-pravovye aspekty obshchej i special'noj zashchity detej v usloviyah vooruzhennyh konfliktov ('International Legal Aspects of General and Special Protection of Children Under Conditions of Armed Conflicts') (2010) 80 Scientific Notes of the Russian State Social University 79–83.

work, no concrete information revealing the impact of the COs was found by the authors.[434]

5.8.5 Brief Conclusion

The relatively short period of time after the entry into force of the Protocol allows one to consider that this treaty hardly demonstrates any impact on the human rights developments in the country, except for the inclusion of the Protocol in the study programmes of the higher education institutions and the official training system for the staff of the Ministry of Internal Affairs and the Ministry of Defence.

5.9 *Convention on the Rights of Persons with Disabilities*

5.9.1 Incorporation and Reliance by Organs of State

In the period 2011–2013, 12 legislative acts were passed in order to give effect to different provisions of the Convention[435] in preparation for the instrument's ratification and as part of subsequent efforts to implement it. However, the application of these standards was not enough 'to address the existing systemic failures in the legal regulation of issues concerning the creation of a barrier-free environment and the elimination of disability-based discrimination by means of individual laws'.[436] Thus, on 1 December 2014 the Federal Law No 419-FL[437] was adopted to introduce interconnected amendments to 25 legislative acts with a view to incorporating the Convention. The law provided the basis for the gradual implementation of CRPD in various laws in the field of the social protection of persons with disabilities, particularly in areas such as transport, communications, the electoral process, employment, housing policy, health care, law enforcement, emergency response and culture.[438] In total,

---

434 The initial report of the Russian Federation on the implementation of the Optional Protocol to the Convention on the Rights of the Child on the Involvement of Children in Armed Conflict was considered in Geneva (25 January 2014). The Ministry of Defence of the Russian Federation <https://function.mil.ru/news_page/country/more.htm?id=11895880@egNews> accessed 19 April 2022.
435 Initial Report, CRPD, Russian Federation, UN Doc CRPD/C/RUS/1 (13 March 2015) para 5; See also Annex 2 to the initial report of the Russian Federation. Information sheet of federal laws adopted in connection with ratification of the CRPD 21–35 <https://rosmintrud.ru/docs/mintrud/handicapped/74> accessed 19 April 2022.
436 Initial Report, CRPD, Russian Federation, UN Doc CRPD/C/RUS/1 (13 March 2015) para 7.
437 Federal Law of the Russian Federation N 419-FL 'On Amending Certain Legislative Acts of the Russian Federation on the Social Protection of Persons with Disabilities in Connection with the Ratification of the Convention on the Rights of Persons with Disabilities' (1 December 2014) <https://rg.ru/2014/12/05/invalidi-dok.html> accessed 19 April 2022.
438 See Annex 4 in the Reply of Russia to List of Issues.

significant changes to bring the Russian legislation in line with the CRPD have been introduced into the 1995 Social Protection for Persons with Disabilities Act, the Civil and Criminal Procedure Codes, as well as 40 other federal and 750 regional laws.[439]

National implementation of the Convention's provisions in establishing a barrier-free environment is being carried out at all levels through the implementation of the Accessible Environment Programme for 2011–2025, which was developed in accordance with article 27 of the Convention even before ratification.[440] The programme together with its three sub-programmes is one of the major initiatives for phased state planning for the long-term perspective to implement the Convention.[441] The programme provides for the adoption of the comprehensive measures with a view to establishing a barrier-free environment, to improving the system of examination and rehabilitation of persons with disabilities, to developing their education, employment, cultural services, as well as to engaging in sports, tourism, social life, to ensuring individual mobility and to improve information and communication conditions. In addition, in line with the Federal Law No 419-FL the government has approved the procedures for elaboration by the state authorities of sectoral, regional and municipal plans ('road maps')[442] in the areas of established activity to gradually increase the values of accessibility indicators for facilities and services for persons with disabilities.[443]

---

[439] Opening Statement of the Head of Delegation of the Russian Federation in connection with the consideration of the initial report of the State on the implementation of the CRPD (27 February 2018).

[440] The Programme was approved by the government in 2011 for the period of 2011–2015 and after its extension until 2020 its duration was finally extended up to 2025 (29 March 2019). Decree of the Government of the Russian Federation N 363 'On Approval of the State Programme of the Russian Federation 'Accessible Environment'' (11 April 2019) <http://www.consultant.ru/document/cons_doc_LAW_322085/> accessed 26 November 2019. See also Ministry of Labour of the Russian Federation. State Programme Portal <https://rosmintrud.ru/ministry/programms/3/0> accessed 26 November 2019.

[441] Programme includes 5 stages (1 January 2011–31 December 2012; 1 January 2013–31 December 2015; 1 January 2016–31 December 2018; 1 January 2019–31 December 2020; 1 January 2021–31 December 2025).

[442] Decree of the Government of the Russian Federation N 599 'On the Procedure and Terms for the Development by Federal Executive Bodies, Executive Bodies of the Constituent Entities of the Russian Federation and Local Governments of Measures to Increase the Values of Accessibility Indicators for Persons with Disabilities of Facilities and Services in Established Areas of Activities' (17 June 2015) <https://rg.ru/2015/06/22/pravila-site-dok.html> accessed 19 April 2022.

[443] An Action Plan (road map) for improving the state system of medical and social expertise for the period until 2020. Approved by the Ministry of Labour and Social Protection

The Ministry of Labour and Social Protection acts as the coordinating body within the government for matters related to the categorisation of disability and social protection for persons with disabilities.[444] The Ministry established the Department on the Persons with Disabilities as a new department specialising in disability issues,[445] which performs tasks related to the implementation of the Convention and cooperation with the CRPD Cttee, specifically monitoring the activities of federal executive bodies and state bodies of the constituent entities of the Russian Federation to implement the Convention, as well as preparing reports to the CRPD Cttee.[446]

The Accessible Environment Programme determines the size of the total budget allocation of the federal funds and of state extra-budgetary funds for its realisation with clarification for the budgeting in each year. The programme also determines separately the volume of funding for each of its three subprogrammes with clarification for the budgeting in each year. Additionally, state support is provided to all-Russian public organisations of persons with disabilities.[447] These organisations have a wide network of territorial and local branches that provide individual assistance through subsidies to persons with disabilities.

5.9.2 Reliance by Judiciary

Despite the relatively recent ratification, Russian courts tend to refer to the CRPD more actively than to other treaties that were acceded to earlier. The higher courts in their practice apply the definition of discrimination on the basis of disability[448] reflected in CRPD. They also refer to CRPD provisions on the rights of children with disabilities.[449] The Supreme Court drew attention to the provision of the Convention in respect of ensuring the right to

---

of the Russian Federation (20 May 2017) <https://rosmintrud.ru/docs/mintrud/handicapped/162> accessed 28 November 2019.

[444] Initial Report, CRPD, Russian Federation, UN Doc CRPD/C/RUS/1 (13 March 2015) para 454.

[445] The Regulation on the Department on the Persons with Disabilities of the Ministry of Labour and Social Protection of the Russian Federation (approved by Decree of the Ministry of Labour and Social Protection of the Russian Federation N 165) (4 September 2012) <https://rosmintrud.ru/docs/mintrud/handicapped/9> accessed 29 November 2019.

[446] ibid paras 6.36, 6.37.

[447] Russian Federation. Government Decree N 2919-p. On the distribution in 2019 of subsidies for State support of all-Russian public organisations of persons with disabilities (24 December 2018) <https://www.consultant.ru/document/cons_doc_LAW_314235/b8759 6476ed67f1a676bb04d6753f38a26b9df39/> accessed 21 September 2023.

[448] Decision of the Supreme Court of the Russian Federation, N АКПИ12–1299, (14 November 2012). <http://vsrf.ru/stor_pdf.php?id=513846> accessed 19 April 2022.

[449] Determination of the Supreme Court of the Russian Federation, Judicial Chamber on Civil Cases, N 51-КГ19–7,(14 October 2019) <http://vsrf.ru/stor_pdf.php?id=1830098> accessed 21 September 2023; Determination of the Supreme Court of the Russian Federation,

work of persons with disabilities,[450] their effective access to justice.[451] The Constitutional Court stressed the obligations of the state to protect the right of persons with disabilities to an adequate standard of living and social protection.[452] The Russian lower courts refer to the provisions of CRPD on the right to social protection,[453] and the right to the highest attainable standard of health.[454] The Supreme Court in its 'Overview of judicial practice' summarises the CRPD Cttee decisions[455] and encourages the Russian courts to use the positions of the Committee in their practice. This fact was welcomed by the Committee in its COs.[456]

5.9.3 Impact on and through Independent State Institutions

Since ratification of the Convention, the NHRI has constantly referred to the provisions of this instrument. The Commissioner in the 2012 annual report welcomed the ratification of the Convention and analysed the measures undertaken to implement it, including the Accessible Environment Programme.[457] In the 2014 and 2015 reports, the Ombudsman emphasised, among other things,

---

Judicial Chamber on Civil Cases, N 14-КГ19–10 (7 October 2019) <https://legalacts.ru/sud/opredelenie-sudebnoi-kollegii-po-grazhdanskim-delam-verkhovnogo-suda-rossiiskoi-federatsii-ot-07102019-n-14-kg19-10/> accessed 21 September 2023; Determination of the Supreme Court of the Russian Federation, Judicial Chamber on Civil Cases, N 29-КГ19–1 (12 August 2019) <http://vsrf.ru/stor_pdf.php?id=1806678> accessed 19 April 2022; Ruling of the Constitutional Court of the Russian Federation, N 17-П/2017, (27 June 2017).

450 Determination of the Supreme Court of the Russian Federation, Judicial Chamber on Civil Cases, N 25-КГ19–7, (12 August 2019) <http://vsrf.ru/stor_pdf.php?id=1804376> accessed 19 April 2022.

451 Determination of the Supreme Court of the Russian Federation, Judicial Chamber on Administrative Cases, N 74-КГ15–4 (20 May 2015) <http://vsrf.ru/stor_pdf.php?id=1341964> accessed 19 April 2022.

452 Ruling of the Constitutional Court of the Russian Federation, N 20-П/2014 (1 July 2014); Ruling of the Constitutional Court of the Russian Federation, N10-П/2018 (26 February 2018); Determination of the Constitutional Court of the Russian Federation, N 593-О/2018 (13 March 2018).

453 Decision of the Tuapse city court of Krasnodar region, N 2–985/2016 (12 July 2016); Decision of the Kropotkin city court of Krasnodar region, N 2a-1768/2016(12 September 2016).

454 Decision of the Samara district court, N 2–1039/2018(20 June 2018); Decision of the Kropotkin city court of Krasnodar region, N 2–219/2017 (1 February 2017).

455 Supreme Court of the Russian Federation, N 1 'Review of Court Practice of the Supreme Court of the Russian Federation' (13 April 2016); Supreme Court of the Russian Federation, N 2 'Review of Court Practice of the Supreme Court of the Russian Federation' (26 April 2017); Supreme Court of the Russian Federation, N 2 'Review of Court Practice of the Supreme Court of the Russian Federation' (4 July 2018).

456 CRPD Cttee, COs, the Russian Federation, UN Doc CRPD/C/RUS/CO/1 (9 April 2018) para 4.

457 High Commissioner for Human Rights in the Russian Federation. Report for 2012 <http://www.consultant.ru/cons/cgi/online.cgi?req=doc&base=EXP&n=553542#hEhOm7T5bjRJNiwe> accessed 19 April 2022.

the need to draw attention to the observance of the rights of persons with disabilities in places of detention in line with the provisions of the Convention.[458] In the 2017 report the Commissioner provided assessment of the wide scope of measures taken to ensure the rights of persons with disabilities in line with the Convention and noted the problems in this area, including the deficiency of the new standards of disability approval procedure that was developed in 2015, resulting in a more difficult procedure for re-assessing the existing disability.[459] In the 2018 report the Ombudsman mentioned her participation in the 19th session of the Committee, where her first shadow report to the report of the Russian Federation was presented.[460]

5.9.4 Impact on and through Non-state Actors

In accordance with Federal Law No 419-FL legal acts of 12 federal ministries define the procedures and programmes for training specialists and staff working with persons with disabilities on providing assistance and services to persons with disabilities in compliance with accessibility requirements in line with the provisions of the Convention.[461] The federal ministries have set up special educational institutions and optional workshops to provide specialised training for those working in sectors involved in the implementation of the Convention.[462] The framework for the implementation of the Accessible Environment Programme provides for the organisation of professional training for managers and specialists responsible for providing relevant services.[463] The professional training and seminars organised for the judges and court staff

---

458 High Commissioner for Human Rights in the Russian Federation. Report for 2014, at 66–67 <http://ombudsmanrf.org/www/upload/files/docs/appeals/doklad2014.pdf> accessed 8 December 2019; High Commissioner for Human Rights in the Russian Federation. Report for 2015, at 72 <https://ombudsmanrf.org/storage/74a0484f-7d5a-4fe4-883d-a1b5ba1dd5f8/documents/67953745-2e1a-4363-8d8a-9d2e25bfc113/fdb011ca-97a8-44fe-ad1a-8a0ff5d6d92d.pdf> accessed 15 September 2023.

459 High Commissioner for Human Rights in the Russian Federation. Report for 2017 <http://ombudsmanrf.org/upload/files/docs/lib/104441_lite.pdf> accessed 19 April 2022.

460 Summary report on the activities of the High Commissioner for Human Rights in the Russian Federation for 2018 <http://ombudsmanrf.org/upload/files/docs/lib/Itog1.pdf> accessed 19 April 2022.

461 CRPD Cttee, 'List of issues in relation to the initial report of the Russian Federation. Addendum. Replies of the Russian Federation to the list of issues', UN Doc CRPD/C/RUS/Q/1/Add.1 (23 November 2017) para 12.

462 ibid paras 16–17.

463 See Detailed schedule of the implementation of the state programme of the Russian Federation 'Accessible Environment', approved by Decree of the Government of the Russian Federation of March 29, 2019 No. 363, for 2019 and for the planned period 2020 and 2021 <https://rosmintrud.ru/docs/mintrud/orders/1350> accessed 19 April 2022.

members include questions related to the Convention and the Committee's practice, including the consideration of individual communications.[464]

However, as some representatives of civil society mention, the country lacks experienced lawyers familiar with the issue of protecting the rights of persons with disabilities and willing to work at the local level. They point to the fact that no court cases have yet been registered under the CRPD's article on non-discrimination on the basis of disability.[465] There are a few NGOs dealing with the protection of the rights of persons with disabilities, that post information on the CRPD and the work of the Committee on their websites,[466] and provide their alternative reports to the Committee. Examples of the initiatives of using the CRPD include the initiatives of the All-Russian Society of the Deaf to provide bank branches with the ability to ensure Russian sign language for hearing-impaired clients[467] and the project of translating the CRPD into Russian sign language.[468] Since the treaty's ratification the Russian scientific community has been conducting research and publishing a wide range of works on issues related to the implementation of the CRPD provisions in Russia,[469] including

---

464   CRPD Cttee, 'List of issues in relation to the initial report of the Russian Federation. Addendum. Replies of the Russian Federation to the list of issues', UN Doc CRPD/C/RUS/Q/1/Add.1 (23 November 2017) para 102.
465   'It became clear, what theUN recommends Russia to undertake in order to protect the rights of persons with disabilities in Russia'(13 March 2018) <https://www.miloserdie.ru/news/stalo-izvestno-chto-rekomenduyut-v-oon-dlya-zashhity-prav-invalidov-v-rossii/> accessed 19 April 2022.
466   All-Russian Society of the Disabled Persons <www.voi.ru/> accessed 19 April 2022; All-Russian Society of the Deaf. Official website <www.voginfo.ru/> accessed 19 April 2022; All-Russian Society of the Blind <www.vos.org.ru/> accessed 19 April 2022; Russian Union of Patients <www.patients.ru/en> accessed 19 April 2022; Regional Public Organisation of Persons with Disabilities 'Perspektiva' <www.perspektiva-inva.ru> accessed 19 April 2022; Anti-discrimination Centre Memorial <www.adcmemorial.org/> accessed 19 April 2022; The Andrey Rylkov Foundation for Social Justice and Health <https://rylkov-fond.org/> accessed 19 April 2022.
467   All-Russian Society of the Deaf. Sign language translation in the offices of Sberbank (16 September 2019) <http://www.voginfo.ru/novosti/newsvog/item/3277-surdoperevod-v-ofisakh-sberbanka.html> accessed 19 April 2022; Sberbank. Full list of cities and addresses of branches with sign language translation service <https://www.sberbank.ru/ru/person/specialbank/surdo/surdo_map> accessed 19 April 2022.
468   The All-Russian Society of the Deaf. Convention on the Rights of Persons with Disabilities in Russian Sign Language (24 June 2016) <https://voginfo.ru/world/2016/06/23/theconventionontherightsofpersonswithdisabilitiesonrsl/> accessed 19 April 2022.
469   Yu V Samovich and NV Kozlova, Zashchita prav lichnosti v Komitete po pravam invalidov ('Protection of Individual Rights in the Committee on the Rights of Persons with Disabilities') International Scientific and Practical Conference 'Implementation of the UN Convention on the rights of persons with disabilities: experience, problems, solutions' Kemerovo 14 December 2016; SA Vasin and others, Organizaciya i provedenie

on the right to education,[470] the right to work[471] and the rights of children with disabilities.[472] For a relatively short period of time the CRPD has received more attention by the Russian researchers than other human rights treaties that had been ratified much earlier.

5.9.5 Impact of State Reporting

The Committee's COs raised many issues that were also pointed out in the alternative reports of NGOs and the Ombudsman.[473] Among these are the necessity

---

kompleksnogo monitoringa zhiznennogo polozheniya invalidov v Rossii v svete Konvencii OON o pravah invalidov ('Organisation and Conduct of Comprehensive Monitoring of the Situation of Persons With Disabilities in Russia in the Light of the UN Convention on the Rights of Persons with Disabilities') RANEPA Moscow, 2014; G Kuleshov, Obespechenie dostupnoj i bezbar'ernoj sredy dlya invalidov v ramkah ratifikacii Konvencii o pravah invalidov ('Providing Accessible and Barrier-Free Environment for Disabled People in the Context of Ratification of the Convention on the Rights of Persons With Disabilities') (2017) 2 Socio-Political Sciences 80–81.

470 R Zhavoronkov, Problemy tolkovaniya Konvencii OON o pravah invalidov: inklyuzivnoe obrazovanie ('Problems of Interpretation of the Convention on the Rights of Persons with Disabilities: Inclusive Education') (2018) 13 Yearbook of Russian Educational Legislation 119–136; N Volkova and E Pulyaeva, Konvenciya OON o pravah invalidov i razvitie inklyuzivnogo obrazovaniya v Rossijskoj Federacii ('United Nations Convention on the Rights of Persons with Disabilities and the Development of Inclusive Education in the Russian Federation') (2017) 249 Journal of Russian Law 55–66.

471 V Shestakov and others, Pravoprimenitel'naya praktika sudov obshchej yurisdikcii po realizacii prav invalidov na trud i zanyatost' v ramkah ispolneniya Konvencii OON o pravah invalidov ('Practice of Courts of General Jurisdiction Regarding Exercise of Disabled Person's Rights to Labour and Employment Within the Framework of Fulfilment of the UN Convention on the Rights of Persons With Disabilities') (2015) 11 Russian Judge 19–23; E Starobina, Sodejstvie trudoustrojstvu invalidov s narusheniem oporno-dvigatel'nogo apparata v svete Konvencii OON o pravah invalidov ('Promoting Employment for Disabled People With Muscle-Skeleton Disorder in the Light of the UN Convention on the Rights of Persons With Disabilities') (2015) 60 Bulletin of the All-Russian Guild of Orthopedic Prosthetists 62–67.

472 V Shestakov and others, Osnovnye napravleniya pravovoj reglamentacii na regional'nom urovne po voprosam realizacii prav detej-invalidov v ramkah ispolneniya polozhenij ('The Main Areas of Regional Legal Regulation of the Issues of Exercising of Rights of Disabled Children within the Framework of Compliance with the Provisions of the UN Convention on the Rights of Persons with Disabilities') (2018) 2 Social and Pension Law 20–24; V Perminov, Ocenka sootvetstviya prav detej-invalidov normam i principam Konvencii OON 'O pravah invalidov' (na primere Tomskoj oblasti) ('Assessment of Conformity of the Rights of Disabled Children with the Norms and Principles of the UN Convention on the Rights of Persons With Disabilities (With the Example of the Tomsk Region)') (2015) 18 Medical and Social Expertise and Rehabilitation 44–49.

473 Interview with Olga Goncharenko, Senior Adviser, International Relations Department, Office of the High Commissioner of Human Rights of the Russian Federation (18 July 2019), by email.

to revise the term 'disabled person' that is officially used in Russia, as it does not reflect the human rights model; the need to amend the relevant articles of the Code of Administrative Offences to increase the amount of fines provided for the violation of the rights of persons with disabilities; the necessity to promote the rights of children and adults with disabilities living in boarding schools and other closed institutions to independent living and involvement in the local community; ensuring access of the deaf to the emergency call system by a single number 112 using text messages and other technologies; the lack of a sufficient number of sign language interpreters and documents in accessible formats during all judicial and administrative proceedings; the unlawful or arbitrary deprivation or restriction of freedom of persons with psychosocial disorders, and their placement in psychiatric hospitals or other institutions; cases of the forced sterilisation of persons with disabilities; the practice of segregated education, and the lack of transparent financial resources allocated and mechanisms established to ensure equal conditions and support for persons with all types of impairment; and the lack of full and effective participation of persons with disabilities in the monitoring process through their representative organisations, including by providing the necessary funding.[474]

After receiving recommendations of the Committee, on 28 December 2018 the government endorsed the Action Plan for the implementation of the COs of the CRPD Cttee,[475] which includes 38 activities aimed at implementing concrete recommendations with each activity having its deadlines, the responsible authorities and public organisations of disabled people, the outcome document to be adopted. On the basis of this Action Plan the state authorities of the constituent entities of Russia started developing regional plans for the realisation of the COs in accordance with the relevant federal government orders.

Since then a number of legislative initiatives have been launched in the state. The higher officials of the Ministry of Labour and Social Protection mention the amendments in the regulations of the work of the employment services, who are now responsible for taking proactive measures with a view to providing accompanied employment assistance for persons with

---

[474] UN experts pointed out the main violations of the rights of persons with disabilities in Russia (2018) <https://dislife.ru/materials/1402> accessed 19 April 2022.

[475] The Action Plan for the implementation of the recommendations contained in the COs of the Committee on the Rights of Persons with Disabilities on the initial report of the Russian Federation on the implementation of the Convention on the Rights of Persons with Disabilities, approved by the Deputy Chairman of the government of the Russian Federation N 11011p-P12 (28 December 2018) <https://rosmintrud.ru/uploads/magic/ru-RU/Document-0-8537-src-1547799349.338.pdf> accessed 19 April 2022.

disabilities and organising the interaction of these persons with the employers.[476] Furthermore, according to the Ministry of Labour and Social Protection a Bill is being prepared on improving the employment of persons with disabilities using the updated quota system for jobs.[477] The Ministry is also considering the possibility of increasing the amount of fines for violating the requirements of accessibility of facilities, services and information for people with disabilities.[478]

In parallel with that the government is amending the rules for recognising a person as disabled with a view to simplifying the procedure through, *inter alia*, approving a list of diseases, which form the basis for establishing disability permanently upon first appeal, and for children under 18 years,[479] extending the criteria for providing status of 'disabled child',[480] and reducing to three days the term for establishing disability for a patient after a limb amputation surgery.[481]

5.9.6 Brief Conclusion

As a recently ratified treaty, in force for only a relatively short period of time, CRPD has made a significant impact on the human right situation in the state. Far-reaching changes have been introduced into more than 40 federal and about 750 regional laws in order to bring Russian legislation in line with the Convention. The Accessible Environment Programme for 2011–2025, developed in line with article 27 of the Convention even before its ratification, together with sectoral, regional and municipal plans ('road maps') in various fields of activities, provide a framework for state planning for the long-term perspective to implement the Convention. The Ministry of Labour and Social Protection as a body responsible for cooperation with the CRPD Cttee established a new structure (Department on the Persons with Disabilities) that monitors the

---

[476] 'Deputy Minister Grigory Lekarev: Russia continues to bring legislation into line with the Convention on the Rights of Persons with Disabilities' (2019) <https://rosmintrud.ru/social/invalid-defence/424> accessed 6 December 2019.

[477] ibid.

[478] ibid.

[479] This measure helps to exclude multiple annual examinations of citizens with a deliberately unfavourable course of the disease <https://rg.ru/2018/04/12/invalid-dok.html> accessed 19 April 2022.

[480] Decree of the Government of the Russian Federation N 823 'On Amending the Rules for Recognising a Person with Disability' (27 June 2019) <https://www.garant.ru/products/ipo/prime/doc/72181066/> accessed 19 April 2022.

[481] Decree of the Government of the Russian Federation N 715 'On Amending the Rules for Recognising a Person with Disability' (4 June 2019) <https://base.garant.ru/72262122/> accessed 15 September 2023.

activities of state executive bodies to implement the CRPD and is responsible for preparing reports for the Committee. Despite the relatively recent ratification, Russian higher and lower courts tend to refer to CRPD more readily than to other treaties that were joined earlier. A discernible impact is also demonstrated through the activities of the High Commissioner and NGOs, as well as increased attention to the Convention in the research of local scholars.

Since the state had only one dialogue with the Committee with the COs adopted in 2018, it is difficult to make a concrete assessment of their impact. However, unlike in the case of other treaties, the government has established a procedure for the preparation of the report to the CRPD Cttee, which was enshrined in the legal act as well as adopted an action plan of activities on the implementation of the COs. At this point the state has taken certain measures in accordance with this plan, which include the introduction of accompanied employment assistance for persons with disabilities, updating the quota system for jobs and simplifying the disability approval procedure. The state provided the legal basis for more active participation of NGOs in the process of preparation of reports and implementation of the COs together with the state authorities, distinguishing the impact of CRPD from other treaties.

Due to the short time of realisation of the treaty it is difficult to make an assessment of factors inhibiting its impact. However, a possible inhibiting factor could be the state of transition in the country from the medical approach to a human rights-based approach to the issue of disability. As was mentioned in the COs, Russia continues to rely on medical care and rehabilitation, while not giving enough attention to mainstream the access of persons with disabilities to services within existing systems and their inclusion in the community across all regions. Some elements of the social/human rights model that were already introduced are not always understood as effective in the society and by the rights holders. The new standards of disability approval procedure, including its technical deficiencies, make it more difficult for some individuals to reconfirm their disability status.[482] This new methodology needs to be tested in practice and assessed by experts. Therefore, time is required to integrate the human rights model in the Russian society in a most effective way.

Another factor is that CRPD in its COs was encouraging Russia to follow the recommendations in the COs of the CESCR Cttee[483] with regard to ensuring

---

[482] As expressed by the High Commissioner in her reports and in the interview with Ms Olga Goncharenko, Senior Adviser, International Relations Department, Office of the High Commissioner of Human Rights of the Russian Federation (18 July 2019).

[483] CRPD Cttee, COs, the Russian Federation, UN Doc CRPD/C/RUS/CO/1 (9 April 2018) paras 51–52.

access to quality medical and rehabilitation services in the context of applying a human rights-based approach to drug users.[484] Such cross-referencing may be a factor enhancing the impact of the recommendations of both Committees in that area. On the other hand, it may be difficult in the future to distinguish between the impact of each of the Committees in this sphere.

Notwithstanding the efforts taken, some experts still mention that another problematic aspect in implementing the Convention deals with the lack of the awareness in society about the Convention and the possibilities it provides.[485]

6 Conclusion

Compared to the 1999 research, the overall impact of the treaties has increased in various directions, which is in general due to the state's policy aimed at increasing its international obligations in the sphere of human rights and steps taken by the state on the path towards democratisation. Since 1999 the country has expanded its participation in the UN treaty system significantly through joining more human rights treaties (a total of seven) and accepting the competence of four committees to consider communications and of two treaty bodies to conduct inquiries.

The general level of awareness of the treaties has increased due to wider media coverage, the promotion of legal education in human rights and the launch of specialised educational programmes in this area, growing academic interest and the organisation of various training, scientific and awareness-raising events in the sphere of application of the treaties.

A more institutionalised process for the preparation of reports was established in 2003 through Governmental Decree on the distribution of the responsibilities of executive state bodies for cooperation with the treaty bodies. In the case of one treaty (CRPD) a special procedure for the preparation of reports was introduced by the 2015 Governmental Decree together with the procedure to implement the Committee's COs through the adoption of an action plan of activities on their implementation.

---

[484] CESCR Cttee, COs, the Russian Federation, UN Doc E/C.12/RUS/CO/6 (16 October 2017) paras 50–51.

[485] 'It became clear, what the UN recommends Russia to undertake in order to protect the rights of persons with disabilities in Russia' (13 March 2018) <https://www.miloserdie.ru/news/stalo-izvestno-chto-rekomenduyut-v-oon-dlya-zashhity-prav-invalidov-v-rossii/> accessed 19 April 2022.

The involvement of NGOs in the reporting process has increased due to the growth in the number of NGOs in Russia and their rising interest in presenting alternative reports to the UNTBs and providing information to the state authorities for subsequent inclusion in the state reports.

A noticeable impact of the treaties is demonstrated through the activities of the NHRI. The High Commissioner uses the treaties when giving legal assessment of various human rights issues, when considering measures taken to implement the treaties, launching legislative initiatives in the area of application of the treaties. Significantly, since 2017 the NHRI started contributing to the reporting process through submitting alternative reports to the committees and meeting the committees during constructive dialogue.

The reliance of the judiciary on treaties and treaty jurisprudence demonstrates a salient positive trend, which is achieved through the organisation of professional training for judges and publishing and dissemination by the Supreme Court of the texts of the recommendations of the treaty bodies among the judiciary. Russian higher and lower courts rely on the treaties' provisions, General Comments, treaty bodies' jurisprudence, periodic reports and COs as a guide to interpretation. An outstanding trend is the application of the treaty bodies' decisions as the source of a remedy in cases where the Russian courts supported the applicant's reference to the Committee's decision (HRC Cttee, CEDAW Cttee) in their plea for reviewing a court decision on the basis of new circumstances.

Some impact is demonstrated through the partial incorporation of all seven treaties and one Optional Protocol (OP-CRC-SC) in the Constitution and Russian legislation, with CRPD being most influential. Three treaties provided the direct basis for the development of a policy, namely, CEDAW, CRC and CRPD. The impact of the reporting procedure is not very strong in the country since it is difficult to establish a direct link between the majority of COs and the measures adopted. It seems that the TBs with the strongest impact in terms of the treaty or the COs being the motivation for the changes are the CEDAW Cttee, the CRC Cttee and the CRPD Cttee. The impact of the individual communications procedure is lower than the impact of the reporting procedure with some examples of the effect of the committees' views, which was ensured mostly through the judiciary.

The impact of the UN treaty system has a linkage with the impact of the treaties and bodies of the CoE, especially the ECHR and the decisions of the ECtHR, which could be both limiting and enhancing the impact of the COs and the views.

It seems that the overarching obstacles to the impact of the core human rights treaties in Russia are the low level of awareness of the treaties and the recommendations among the relevant state authorities, the legal profession and the general public; the lack of a coordinated approach towards preparation of reports and implementation of COs; the variance of the state's approach with the position of the TBS on a number of conceptual issues that are usually the subject of joint concern by the committees.

In order to gradually overcome these obstacles and to ensure the more effective influence of the treaties in Russia, a coordinating state structure should be created that would be responsible for distributing the responsibilities among the relevant state authorities for the preparation of reports, the implementation of the COs and considering the possibility of enforcing the views. Such a structure would be also responsible for distributing the COs and views among the respective executive, legislative and judicial authorities. On the basis of the order by such a coordinating structure the responsible executive bodies would be encouraged to develop the action plans for the implementation of the COs with the example of the action plan already developed by the government with regard to the CRPD Cttee's COs.

The coordinating structure would be mandated to organise, with the support of the academic institutions and practising lawyers, various professional training on the issues of application of the treaties for the staff of the relevant state bodies, NHRIs (federal and regional), NGOs and lawyers. The coordinating structure may also launch and monitor the permanent database containing all recommendations of the treaty bodies accessible to the relevant responsible authorities and all interested actors.

Since a number of issues are addressed by a few committees simultaneously, it would be highly recommendable for the treaty bodies to use cross-referencing to each other's COs, which may enhance their cumulative impact and influence the human rights situation in the country more effectively.

CHAPTER 16

The Impact of the United Nations Human Rights Treaties on the Domestic Level in Senegal

Ibrahima Kane

1   Introduction to Human Rights in Senegal*

A small country of West Africa and former French colony, Senegal has since its independence in 1960 established itself as a country that respects the rule of law, democracy, and human rights. As a result of the country's perseverance in this process, it is one of the rare countries in West Africa that has not experienced a military *coup d'état* and is ranked among the democracies of the continent.

Senegal is a secular republic with a strong presidential regime under which the President of the Republic, the National Assembly, the Economic, Social and Environmental Council (CESE) and the Higher Local Authorities Council of (HCCL) work closely together under the aegis of a Constitutional Council. Two peaceful political power changeovers have already taken place since 2000 and transformed the country into 'a model of stability and democracy, albeit without being a model of development'.[1] The country is made up of administrative districts[2] and local authorities,[3] and implements a very ambitious decentralization policy that bestows considerable powers on local authorities, especially in the areas of health and education.[4] However, the capacity of these local authorities to properly play their role is undercut by limited local resources at their disposal.

Ranked as one of the world's least developed countries,[5] Senegal has since 1960 put in place a strategy of rapid economic and social development based

---

* In memory of Professor Birame Ndiaye, pioneer in human rights education in Senegal.
1   See National Commission for Good Governance, *Rapport national d'auto-évaluation du Sénégal*, March 2016 4.
2   The country has 14 regions, 45 departments and 125 districts.
3   There are 42 Departmental Councils and 557 communes.
4   See Act 2013–10 of 28 December 2013 on the Local Authorities Code.
5   A country is regarded as belonging to the least developed category if its population has a low standard of living (gross domestic product below US $745), is poor in human resources and has an undiversified economy. See the United Nation list at <https://unctad.org/topic/least-developed-countries/list> accessed 30 September 2021.

on forward planning.[6] However, the Senegal was weakened by sluggish economic performance between the 1970s and 1980s, persistent social tensions[7] and numerous crises among the ruling elite, which led to the country falling under the tutelage of the World Bank and the International Monetary Fund (IMF) with the implementation of so-called structural adjustment policies. These policies, however, have systematically led to the dismantling and accelerated privatisation of social sectors such as health and education,[8] wherever they have been implemented. During this period of accelerated privatisation of the economy and 'poverty reduction',[9] the authorities endorsed 'investment programmes and accompanying policy reforms in order to maximise resource efficiency, safeguard essential public financing and mobilise new funding sources whenever possible'.[10] The immediate consequence of this redirection of public policies has been a 'marked slowdown'[11] in government investment in social welfare, especially in terms of building schools, hospitals and health centres and establishing new primary social services for the population; in short, protecting the rights of the most vulnerable segments of Senegalese society.

At the end of the 1990s the realisation of the disastrous consequences of structural adjustment led to Senegal's leaders negotiating the establishment of specific transitional programmes with their development partners. Unfortunately, these programmes had very limited effects on the enjoyment of human rights because of persistent corruption, poor management of public resources, ineffective institutions for the governance of public affairs and, above all, the rapid acquisition of wealth by a large segment of the political class.[12]

From 2014, in the wake of the country's second changeover of power, the Senegalese authorities embarked on the promotion of a new economic and social development model known as the Emerging Senegal Plan (PSE) of which the objective is to fast-track Senegal's progress towards emergence

---

6   See Rolan Colin, 'Sénégal, notre pirogue. Au soleil de la Liberté. Journal de bord 1955–1980' *Présence Africaine* 2007.

7   See Abdoulaye Bathily, 'Mai 1968 à Dakar ou la révolte universitaire et la démocratie, le Sénégal cinquante ans après' *L'Harmattan* 2018.

8   On this issue, see Fred Eloko, 'Repenser l'action publique en Afrique : du SIDA à l'analyse de la globalisation des politiques publiques' Karthala, 2015.

9   Senegal adopted a Poverty Reduction Strategy Paper in 2002.

10 See Pilotage des politiques publiques au Sénégal de 1960 à 2012, led by Seydou Nourou Toure, *L'Harmattan* 2019 368.

11 ibid 399.

12 On this issue, see Momar Coumba Diop, *'Essai sur 'l'art de gouverner ' le Sénégal ' in Gouverner le Sénégal; entre ajustement structurel et développement durable,* Karthala, 2004 9–35.

through three strategic focus areas, with one of the aims being to 'strengthen security, stability and governance, protect rights and freedoms and consolidate the rule of law in order to create the best conditions for social peace and promote the full development of the country's potential'.[13] Poverty remains high in the country,[14] with a large majority of families still reliant on international remittances for survival.[15] This also explains why Senegal has achieved only three of the eight United Nations Millennium Development Goals (MDGs).[16] In the health sector, for example, the country's low level of coverage in health infrastructure[17] and medical personnel[18] is still noticeable, which is largely due to budget constraints imposed by the country's development partners, especially during the structural adjustment period. The education sector has not fared any better, because the introduction of a 10-year period of mandatory education at the primary and secondary levels has proven inadequate to increase access to education due to low school enrolment rates and a serious lack of infrastructure. Classroom facilities remain very scarce[19] and much remains to be done to make the school environment a suitable environment

---

13 See Republic of Senegal, Plan Sénégal Émergent, February 2014 viii.
14 <https://www.ndarinfo.com/Etat-de-la-pauvrete-au-Senegal-467-de-la-population-senegalaise-vivent-dans-la-misere_a18716.html> accessed 20 May 2022.
15 In 2018 Senegal is believed to have received nearly $2,9 billion in international money transfers, which would represent 13% of the country's GDP. See <https://www.riamoneytransfer.com/vi-nz/blog/history-remittances-immigration-in-senegal/> accessed 15 September 2023.
16 With regard to the prevalence rate of HIV, access of populations to drinking water and the conservation of biodiversity and management of environmental resources, see Republic of Senegal, Plan Sénégal Émergent, February 2014 17.
17 In 2016 Senegal had 35 hospitals (one hospital per 422 853 inhabitants, whereas the World Health Organisation (WHO) standards recommend one hospital per 150 000 inhabitants); 100 health centres (one health center per 147 999 inhabitants, whereas the WHO standards recommend one health centre per 50 000 inhabitants); 1 548 health posts (one health post per 10 151 inhabitants, which corresponds to the WHO standards, ie one health post per 10 000 inhabitants). Private health facilities (three hospitals, 359 medical practices, 115 clinics, 443 paramedical facilities, 132 company facilities, 111 health posts, 26 medical analysis laboratories and about ten medical imaging services) complete this health care and services facilities. On all these issues, see Agence nationale de la statistique et de la démographie (ANSD), 'Senegal: Enquête continue sur la prestation des services de soins de santé (ECPSS)' 2017 3.
18 Senegal has 1 813 medical doctors (one doctor per 9100 inhabitants where WHO standards require one doctor per 100.000 inhabitants); 7562 nurses (one nurse per 2181 inhabitants where WHO standards require one nurse per 300 inhabitants); and 3781 midwives (one midwife for 4363 inhabitants where WHO standards require one midwife per 300 inhabitants).
19 In 2017, 9% of classrooms will be used as temporary shelters.

for its users.[20] At the pre-school level, the enrolment rate stood at 17,57 per cent in 2017, with very substantial regional disparities.[21] At the primary level, the enrolment rate averaged 87,3 per cent and was also marked by considerable regional disparities.[22] The adult literacy rate is stable at 52,10%.[23]

The judiciary has also been affected by the weakening capacity of the state of Senegal to uphold the rule of law and guarantee the enforcement of fundamental rights and freedoms. In fact, saying that this sector is understaffed is an understatement. According to the Ministry of Justice, the country needs 1 355 judges and 2 710 court clerks to operate the country's courts, which in 2017, had only 484 judges and 333 court clerks.[24] This situation directly 'compromises the performance of the courts in general, but also impedes the specialisation policy initiated by the authorities'.[25] With regard to paralegals, their low numbers[26] are largely due to the restrictive recruitment policies applied by the state and professional bodies. In addition, these legal workers are highly concentrated in the capital of the country, which prevents the smooth performance of the public service and affects the quality of legal debates and court decisions.[27]

All this contrasts with the provisions of the Senegalese Constitution which stipulates that all citizens, regardless of their status, are equal before the law

---

20   While the percentage of schools with access to drinking water and latrines has improved, the electricity penetration rate in schools is 23% and the computer and internet penetration rate is 3,5%.

21   According to Senegal's *Revue nationale volontaire des Objectifs de Développement Durable* (June 2018, para 156), the highest rate was recorded in the Ziguinchor region (48,5%) and the lowest in the Kaffrine region (4,9%).

22   Here, too, the Ziguinchor region has the highest rate (124,11%), while the Kaffrine region still has the lowest rate (47,2%). See the *Revue nationale volontaire des Objectifs de Développement Durable* June 2018, para 152.

23   See *Revue nationale volontaire des Objectifs de Développement Durable* June 2018, para 170.

24   See Ministry of Justice, Lettre de politique sectorielle de développement de la Justice, December 2017 17, 18. The document also notes that 'the shortage of human resources must be combined with the advanced age of a large part of this staff, which will result in the retirement of 22 judges and 131 registrars over the period 2015–2035. These retirements, which represent 45.77 per cent of the current number of judges and 39.33 per cent of the number of registrars, must be compensated for by urgent recruitment, otherwise the justice system will find it hard to operate'.

25   See Ministry of Justice, Lettre de politique sectorielle de développement de la Justice, December 2017 18.

26   In 2017 Senegal had 363 lawyers, 55 judicial officers, 51 notaries and 28 auctioneers.

27   To take just the example of lawyers, only 32 have chosen to open their offices in the internal regions of the country: Thiès (9); Saint-Louis (6); Ziguinchor (5); Kaolack (3); Mbour (3); Pikine (2); Diourbel (1); Kolda (1); Rufisque (1); and Tambacounda (1).

and establishes the democratic nature of the national political system which, in principle, is marked by the separation, independence and cooperation of the executive, legislative and judicial branches. The country's early constitutions,[28] which were strongly influenced by its former colonial rulers,[29] contained an entire chapter dedicated to 'civil liberties and the human person'.[30] The 2001 Constitution, which was adopted shortly after the first democratic changeover of power, through its numerous innovations, appeared to establish individual freedom as the basis for national construction. It provided a constitutional framework for all the human rights treaties ratified by Senegal, especially those adopted by the United Nations (UN), re-qualified the citizens' rights and freedoms as fundamental rights, recognized new individual and collective rights for citizens and, most importantly, imposed duties on them.

The judiciary, which is the 'custodian of rights and freedoms',[31] has also been entrusted with the responsibility of allowing citizens to freely exercise all the rights guaranteed by the country's Constitution and legislation. It fulfils this responsibility through the country's courts and tribunals, ranging from the Supreme Court to the magistrate's courts, Courts of Appeal, High Courts, Labour Courts and Commercial Courts.[32]

These regulatory and institutional advances, however, are yet to produce the significant changes expected in the country because fundamental freedoms such as freedom of expression and demonstration[33] are yet to become a tangible reality in the country; and the idea that children have rights is not yet

---

28 See Preamble to the Constitution of the Republic of Senegal, Act 59–003 of 24 January 1959. See also the Preambles to the Constitutions of 1960, 1963 and 2001 in Textes Constitutionnels du Sénégal du 24 janvier 1959 au 15 mai 2007 réunis et présentés par Ismaila Madior FALL, CREDILA, 2007 17.
29 By affirming the attachment of the Senegalese people 'to fundamental rights as defined in the Declaration of the Rights of Man and of the Citizen of 1789 and the Universal Declaration of December 10, 1948' and the recognition of 'the existence of inviolable and inalienable human rights as the basis of all human community, peace and justice in the world'.
30 Arts 2 of 16 of the 1959 Constitution.
31 See art 91 of the 2001 Constitution.
32 See Act 2014–26 of 3 November 2014 on the organisation of the judiciary and Act 2017–14 of 19 June 2017 on the establishment, organisation and functioning of commercial courts and commercial chambers of appeal and Decree 2015–1145 of 3 August 2015 on the composition and jurisdiction of courts of appeal, courts of first instance and magistrate's courts.
33 Bans on demonstrations are still being imposed by the authorities and citizens are still being embroiled for not obeying their injunctions. See, for example, Sud Quotidien 7978 of Saturday 21-Sunday 22 December 2019 'Repression of the unauthorised rally of the NOO LANK Collective in downtown Dakar' 1, 2.

widely shared in Senegalese society;[34] women also still continue to experience various forms of violence at a time when equality between men and women is yet to be achieved in a country where 'households are structured around a valued culture based on women's subordination and men's domination';[35] and sexual orientation remains a forbidden subject and is not addressed in legislation.[36]

An increasingly diverse and dynamic civil society is working strenuously locally and nationally to address all these concerns in an often inauspicious legal, economic and social environment. This civil society is made up of associations, non-governmental organizations (NGOs), trade unions and other non-profit organizations with different legal statuses. While associations are subject to a system of preliminary registration,[37] NGOs and other organizations must be formally recognized.[38] Some organizations are granted tax exemptions by the Senegalese authorities,[39] which contribute to the financing of the activities of the trade unions and organisations of the private press.[40] Other associations share funding made available to them by a number of foreign foundations, Western embassies and certain UN agencies established in Senegal[41] to

---

[34] The Archbishop of Dakar, Monsignor Benjamin Ndiaye, recently stated that '[i]t is high time for our country to go beyond symbolic actions, to dare to fully put into practice our good intentions towards children. *For a society that knows how to take care of its children is forging a strong mentality to take better care of the youngest.*' See the newspaper *L'Enquête* 26 December 2019 2 (emphasis added).

[35] See Republic of Senegal: National Strategy for Gender Equity and Equality (SNEEG) 2016–2025 29.

[36] See Ndeye Gning, '*Les motifs de l'illégitimité sociale de l'homosexualité au Sénégal*' *Africultures* 96, 6/2013 22–39.

[37] According to art 812 of Act 68–08 of 26 March 1968 amending Chapter II relating to associations of Book VI of the Code of Civil and Commercial Obligations and repressing the constitution of illegal associations 'the association *is freely formed without any other formality than the prior declaration* and registration of this declaration' (emphasis added).

[38] NGOs are 'regularly declared or authorised private, non-profit-making associations or bodies whose purpose is to contribute to national economic, social and cultural development policy'. See art 1 of Decree 2015–145 establishing the modalities of intervention of non-governmental organisations (NGOs).

[39] According to Decree 2015–145 establishing the modalities of intervention of non-governmental organisations (NGOs), the state 'grants NGOs exemption from duties and taxes on materials, equipment and services' (art 14) and 'grants them temporal admission of vehicles for commercial use ... for the realisation of their investments'(art 16).

[40] Every year the Senegalese state provides in its annual budget a sum of more than CFAF 1 billion (approximately US $2 million) to subsidise the activities of Senegalese trade unions and press organs.

[41] These include the United Nations Children's Fund (UNICEF); the Regional Office of the United Nations High Commissioner for Human Rights (OHCHR); UN-Women; the United

promote and protect human rights in the country. These organisations, however, are constrained by the fact that they can, only in rare circumstances,[42] file complaints in human rights cases because in Senegal 'civil action for compensation for damage caused by any offence can be filed by anyone who has personally suffered damage directly caused by such an offence'.[43]

2   Relationship of Senegal with the International Human Rights System in General

Senegal has attempted to maintain cordial and mutually respectful relations with the human rights protection mechanisms. This has enabled four UN Special Rapporteurs,[44] two working groups[45] and the Sub-Committee on Prevention of Torture and Other Cruel, Inhuman and Degrading Treatment or Punishment (SPT)[46] to visit Senegal between 2000 and 2015. Many Senegalese nationals played a pre-eminent role in the UN system,[47] especially in relation to international human rights law,[48] and the country was elected president of

---

Nations Population Fund (UNFPA); the Regional Office of the United Nations High Commissioner for Refugees (UNHCR); the United Nations Development Programme (UNDP); and the International Organisation for Migration (IOM).

[42] To this day, Senegalese law authorises only environmental protection associations approved by the state (see art L 107, para 2 of Act 2001-01 of 15 January 2001 on the Senegalese Environment Code) and those that provide care for victims of trafficking in persons (articles 16 and 17 of Act 2005-06 of 10 May 2005 on the fight against trafficking in persons and similar practices and the protection of victims) to 'exercise the rights granted to the civil party in respect of acts constituting an offence ... and directly or indirectly prejudicing the collective interests which they are intended to defend'.

[43] See art 2 para 1 of Act 65-61 of 21 July 1965, as amended, on the Code of Criminal Procedure of Senegal.

[44] The UNSR on the Human Rights of Migrants (August 2009), on the Sale of Children, Child Prostitution and Child Pornography (October 2009), on the Right to Education (January 2010) and on the human right to safe drinking water and sanitation (November 2011).

[45] The WG on arbitrary detention and on discrimination against women in law.

[46] In December 2012.

[47] Two Senegalese have served as judges on the International Court of Justice of The Hague. They are Isaac Foster (1964–1982) and Kéba Mbaye (1982–1991).

[48] Prof Ibrahima Fall was Director of the Human Rights Centre before its transformation into the Office of the High Commissioner for Human Rights; Mr. Pierre Sane, Secretary-General of Amnesty International and Mr. Adama Dieng, Secretary-General of the International Commission of Jurists (ICJ) before joining the United nations as the Special adviser of the Secretary general on the prevention of genocide.

the Assembly of State Parties to the Rome Statutes in 2016, and President of the United Nations Human Rights Council[49] in 2017.

Senegal's openness to human rights was also facilitated by the political culture of its leaders, particularly the late President Léopold Sedar Senghor, who observed that 'humanity is one and indivisible and the basic needs of man are the same everywhere [and that] there are no borders or races when it comes to safeguarding the freedoms and rights of the human person'.[50] At the end of the 1970s he initiated the process that led to the adoption in 1981 by the Heads of State and Government of the Organization of African Unity (OAU) of the African Charter on Human and Peoples' Rights (African Charter), which laid down the foundation of the culture of human rights that African countries are now experiencing. His successor, President Abdou Diouf, through a genuine human rights-based diplomacy, contributed to the enforcement of the African Charter, the eradication of the apartheid system in South Africa and, most importantly, the reinforcement of the international human rights protection system.[51]

The architect of the first political changeover of power in Senegal in 2000, Abdoulaye Wade, also contributed to this process by incorporating international human rights standards into the Constitution, based on his conviction that 'any regime, regardless of its nature, must necessarily uphold universally recognised human rights [and] that these rights may not be infringed[52] under any circumstances, and especially not for the sake of development'. As a champion of pan-Africanism, he also expressed the belief that upholding human rights goes hand in hand with economic, social and cultural progress, which is why he 'can hardly see how Africa could make progress if the Africans people's freedom of design and expression, and their sense of creativity and imagination'[53] are stifled.

Senegal is now party to almost all the African human rights treaties[54] and has contributed to the establishment of an effective human rights mechanism

---

49 Senegal is expected to assume the presidency of the 13th cycle in 2019.
50 Speech at the opening ceremony of the meeting for the drafting Committee of the African Charter on Human and Peoples' Rights cited by Keba Mbaye in Les Droits de l'homme en Afrique, 2nd edition, Pedone 2002, p 173.
51 Senegal will thus be the first country in the world to ratify the Rome Statute creating the International Criminal Court (ICC).
52 See Abdoulaye Wade, 'Un destin pour l'Afrique' Michel Lafon 2005 46.
53 ibid 47.
54 Namely, the African Charter on Human and Peoples' Rights and its Protocols; the OAU Convention Governing the Specific Aspects of Refugee Problems in Africa; the Convention for the Protection and Assistance of Internally Displaced Persons in Africa;

in West Africa known as the Court of Justice of the Economic Community of West African States (ECOWAS).

This progress also has been linked with the establishment, under the presidencies of Abdou Diouf and Macky Sall, of inclusive and streamlined reporting procedures that have been highly effective in finalising reports within the deadlines set by the treaty bodies.[55] Paradoxically, it is the liberal government of President Abdoulaye Wade, whose contribution to the national human rights system has been the most noticeable, that has contributed the least in this area because of incompetence and ignorance of the issues at stake. Between 2000 and 2012 only five periodic reports were defended before the UN bodies. Mr. Wade's liberal regime was certainly characterized by a strong determination to deconstruct the institutional legacy bequeathed by the regime of President Abdou Diouf.

Since then, a kind of opportunistic nationalism has created, within the ruling class, an attitude of mistrust towards the UN human rights system. It now reacts very badly, and sometimes aggressively, to the decisions or requests of certain treaty bodies in cases pointing to the government's responsibility for rights violations experienced by prominent leaders of opposition parties in Senegal.

Thus, responding to the findings of the Human Rights Committee (HRCttee) which, hearing a case submitted for its consideration, had found that 'the facts brought to its attention showed violations', by Senegal of article 14(5)[56] of the International Covenant on Civil and Political Rights (CCPR) and requested a review of the 'conviction and sentence' of the complainant,[57] Senegal's Justice Minister was of the view that the HRCttee did not have the power to overturn the judgment of the Court for the Suppression of Unlawful Enrichment (CREI) because 'it is not a judicial body, but a committee of independent experts whose decisions are devoid of any binding authority'. Accordingly, in his view, reforming decisions issued by national courts does not fall under its powers.[58]

---

and the Protocol to the Treaty Establishing the African Economic Community Relating to Free Movement of Persons, Right to Residence and Right to Establishment.

[55] Between 1973 and 2000 and between 2012 and 2019, 26 of the 37 initial and periodic reports due were transmitted to the treaty bodies.

[56] Paragraphe 12.6 des Constatations adoptées par le Comité au titre de l'article 5 du Protocole facultatif concernant la Communication No 2783/2016 CCPR/C/124/D/2783/2016 *Karim Meissa Wade c. Sénégal*.

[57] Para 13 of the Views adopted by the Committee under art 5 of the Optional Protocol in respect of Communication 2783/2016 CCPR/C/124/D/2783/2016 *Karim Meissa Wade v Senegal*.

[58] See Official Communiqué of the Minister of Justice dated 14 November 2018.

A former Minister of Justice went so far as to argue, in relation to the same case, that 'the legal and judicial sovereignty of countries takes precedence over the opinions of 18 experts who act individually'.[59]

Recently, some senior officials had incurred the irritation of the President when confronted with the replies they had given to the members of a treaty body on the implementation of its recommendations. Indeed, the chief of staff of the State Secretary to the Human Rights Promotion and Good Governance Minister and the Human Rights Director at the Ministry of Justice were removed from office because, during the examination of Senegal's periodic report, they maintained that the national authorities had started implementing the recommendations set out in the findings of the HRCttee on Communication 2783/2016, *Karim Meissa Wade v Senegal*.[60]

This decision had been preceded by a statement by the Minister for Foreign Affairs in which he stated that 'information published on this subject is completely baseless and reflects a lack of knowledge of Senegalese legal procedures and Senegal's previous and clearly expressed positions on the issue'.[61] More specifically, the spokesperson for the President of the Republic stressed that 'unless the state of Senegal violates all the rules of law, by trampling on the rules of procedure and the judicial organization of the country, it could not, and in any way whatsoever, commit itself, before anybody whatsoever, on these two points: pay compensation to the victim (Karim Wade) or have his case reviewed'.[62]

Commenting on the condemnation of the criminalization of homosexuality in Senegal at a session of the HRCttee, the new Director of Human Rights at the Ministry of Justice argued that this UN instrument was intended to 'force Senegal to accept unnatural relations, to legalize homosexuality, but that Senegal is not willing to accept it'.[63]

These strong reactions are in contrast to the positions held by previous Senegalese governments on similar issues[64] and the current authorities'

---

[59] See interview of Mrs Aminata Toure in Seneplus <https://www.seneplus.com/politique/le-pds-et-les-avocats-de-karim-wade-pretent-au-comite-des-droits> accessed 14 February 2021.
[60] See 'Dans les coulisses du limogeage de Moustapha KA et de Samba Ndiaye Seck' *L'Observateur* 4817 22 October 2019 4.
[61] See 'Le ministère des Affaires étrangères démentément' *Le Soleil* 14816 18 October 2019.
[62] See 'Surréaliste débat sur la révision d'un procès' *Le Soleil* 14818 21 October 2019 7.
[63] See interview with Mbaye Babacar Diop, Director of Human Rights at the Ministry of Justice in *Le Quotidien* 2 December 2019 7.
[64] See Views adopted by the Committee under article 5 of the Optional Protocol in respect of Communication 386–1989, CCPR/C/52/D/386/1989.

commitment not to intimidate or retaliate against individuals contributing to the work of the human rights treaty bodies.[65] Is this signal the beginning of a shift in the Senegalese authorities' attitude towards the UN treaty bodies? That may well be the case, especially since some treaty bodies are now also 'wading into' national debates with very firm positions that may offend the Senegalese leadership. This is precisely what the Chairperson of the CAT Cttee did when, following information disseminated by Hissène Habré's lawyers on the health status of their client, he wrote to the Senegalese authorities to draw their attention 'to the allegations of possible amnesty for or release of Hissène Habré, reiterating that prematurely releasing the perpetrators of the most serious international crimes is inconsistent with obligations under articles 2, 4, 7 and 14 of the Convention'.[66]

If this trend were to be confirmed, it would put the Senegalese authorities in total contradiction with the Senegalese Constitution, which clearly states that 'treaties or agreements that have been duly ratified or approved shall, as soon as they are published, take precedence over laws, subject, for each agreement or treaty, to its application by the other party'.[67]

3 At a Glance: Formal Engagement of Senegal with the UN Human Rights Treaty System

Refer to the chart on the next page.

4 Role and Overall Impact of United Nations Human Rights Treaties on Senegal

4.1 General
4.1.1 Formal Acceptance

Senegal has accepted all nine core UN human right treaties. It also accepted OP-CRC-AC, OP-CRC-SC and the Optional Protocol to the Convention against Torture and Other Cruel, Inhuman or Degrading Treatment or Punishment

---

65 See para 8 of the replies to General Assembly Resolution 68/268 adopted by the Office of the United Nations High Commissioner for Human Rights on 9 April 2014 by the Human Rights Directorate of the Ministry of Justice of Senegal.
66 See the national daily *Le Soleil* 3 January 2020, 'Éventuelle amnistie et libération de Hissène Habré: le Comite de l'ONU aux droits de l'homme dit Non' 15.
67 Art 98 of the Senegalese Constitution of 2001.

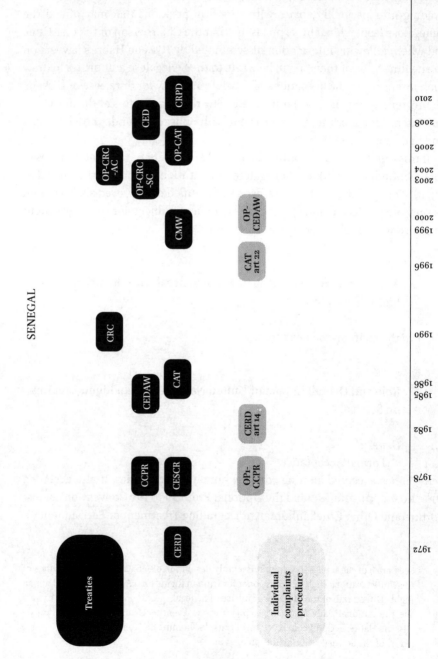

OP-CAT. It did not ratify OP2-CCPR, although it had abolished the death penalty. This omission appears to be connected to the desire of the then President not to offend religious groups who were not happy with the measure he had passed without discussing this with them.

In the early 1970s Senegal ratified the Convention on the Elimination of All Forms of Discrimination against Women (CEDAW) and the two 1966 Covenants. Supported by international organisations such as the International Commission of Jurists, which held a congress in Dakar in 1967,[68] the Senegalese authorities' approach was also based on the humanistic philosophy of the father of the country's independence, President Léopold Senghor, who believed that the purpose of any political action was to 'develop human beings in all fields on the basis of two major principles: rationality and, hence, effectiveness, on the one hand, and social justice, based on human solidarity, on the other hand'.[69] Senegal ratified CEDAW, CAT, CRC and CMW under the presidency of Abdou Diouf, CED, CRPD and the Optional Protocols to CAT and CRC under the presidency of Abdoulaye Wade.

Senegal has accepted four of the complaint's mechanisms, by making the article 14 declaration under CERD, the article 22 declaration under CAT, and by ratifying OP1-CCPR and OP-CEDAW. Three cases have been filed against Senegal – two before the HRCttee, and one to the CAT Cttee. The non-acceptance of the contentious procedures under the other treaties appears not to be deliberate. This seems to be caused by the negligence of officials of the ministries concerned and by the lack of strong advocacy by civil society organisations, which certainly are not impressed by the efficiency of such mechanisms. The impression is that Senegalese are only interested in international procedures when it comes to exposing state behaviour at the international level.

Senegal also accepted the inquiry procedures under article 8 of CEDAW, article 20 of CAT, article 33 of CED, and by ratifying OP-CAT, accepted the visits by the SPT.

4.1.2 Attitude towards the UN Treaty System

The UN mechanisms have always considered Senegal a valued partner on the African continent when it comes to dealing with human rights issues, on account of the fact that democracy is firmly rooted in this country and due to the institutional recognition of the importance of life and human dignity.

---

[68] See on this question Kéba Mbaye, *Les droits de l'homme en Afrique* (2nd edn, A Pedone) 80, 81.

[69] Léopold Sédar Senghor, 'Rapport introductif Pour une société sénégalaise socialiste et démocratique' Conseil National du Parti Socialiste sénégalais, 27 December 1976, quoted by Amadou Diop, *Sénégal: Repères et Grandeur d'une Diplomatie*, Sentinelles 90.

This sound approach has contributed to educating officials in the culture of human rights and has led to a gradual understanding of the spirit and letter of the various treaties. It has also made it possible for human rights concerns to be gradually incorporated into the numerous social policy documents drawn up by the state.

A number of technical partnerships have thus been established between the state of Senegal and UN agencies such as the United Nations Children's Fund (UNICEF), the United Nations Development Programme (UNDP), UN Women, the Regional Office of the High Commissioner for Human Rights (OHCHR) and the IOM, to support it in achieving its ambitions in this area. Based on this cooperation, a number of training schools for state officials have started incorporating human rights modules into their curricula, which is helping introduce a human rights culture into the country's security services.[70] The contribution of the Dakar-based regional office of the OHCHR, through its project to strengthen the capacity of the Senegalese civil service, will ultimately provide quality resource persons who can train future managers on the issue in Senegal.[71] The same is true of the good collaboration between UN Women and the National Statistics and Demography Agency (ANSD) for the production of statistical data on women in Senegal.[72]

Between 1978 and 2019,[73] Senegal had approximately 10 national experts elected to serve as members of treaty bodies in order to contribute to reinforcing the promotion and protection of human rights at the international level.

The Senegalese authorities have made considerable efforts to uphold their commitments and thus implement the recommendations set out in the Concluding Observations (COs) or findings of the treaty mechanisms. The recommendations made by the HRCttee in the *Famara Kone* case, regarding

---

[70] The National School of Administration (ENA); the Judicial Training Centre (CFJ); the National School for Gendarmerie Officers and Non-Commissioned Officers (ENG); the National Police School (ENP); and the National School of Penitentiary Administration (ENAP), to name but a few.

[71] As a result of this training, Senegal now has a pool of human rights trainers consisting of one official from the National Statistics and Demography Agency (ANSD), one official from the Public Policy Planning Directorate of the Ministry of the Economy and Finance and two officials from the Ministry of Foreign Affairs.

[72] See ANSD and UN-Women, 'Gender-based Violence and Women's Empowerment' December 2019.

[73] HRCttee: Mr Abdoulaye Dieye (4 years); Birame Ndiaye (12 years); CESCR Cttee: Mr Samba Cor Konate (8 years); CAT Cttee: Mr Guibril Camara (12 years); CMW Cttee: Mr Ahmadou Tall (2 years); and CDF: Mr Cheikh Tidiane Coulibaly (4 years).

the unlawful arrest and detention of a Senegalese citizen, have been fully implemented by the government.[74] Those of the Convention Against Torture and Other Cruel, Inhuman, or Degrading Treatment or Punishment (CAT) in the *Souleymane Guengueng* case, concerning the trial of a former President of Chad accused of torture and crimes against humanity, were more difficult to implement due to complications resulting from President Wade's refusal to have Hissène Habré put on trial in Senegal.[75]

4.1.3 Level of Awareness of the Public

Generally speaking, the administrative authorities' acceptance of recommendations and citizens' access to these mechanisms have never been easy, especially in view of the limited information available in the media and from civil society organisations. It was only in 2006 that Senegal, with the support of local civil society organisations, set up a local system of which the main function was to inform the population about their rights, to improve access to the public legal service and to help relieve congestion in courts. The system was structured as follows:

- nineteen legal aid offices[76] deployed throughout the country, in local communities. From 2013, some Counselling Offices were set up in 11 of those local authorities with the support of UN Women, in order to provide legal assistance to women and girls who were victims of gender-based violence, by facilitating their access to justice, ensuring their cases were taken care of and providing financial support to victims who were in a precarious situation;
- eighteen Reception and Referral Offices (BAOJs) set up in some of the courts[77] to welcome and inform court users; an

---

[74] Reparation had been negotiated between the victim and the state authorities, the Criminal Code had been revised to reduce lengthy pre-trial detention and a mechanism for compensating victims of lengthy detention had been established.

[75] Act 2012-29 of 28 December 2012 creating the Extraordinary African Chambers in the Senegalese courts to try Hissène Habré was only passed after he left power.

[76] These are the communes of Dangalma, Dahra, Diamaguene-Sicap-Mbao, Fatick, Gossas, Grand-Yoff, Hlm, Kaolack, Kedougou, Keur Massar, Koungheul, Mbacke, Mbour, Parcelles-Assainies, Richard-Toll, Rufisque, Tambacounda, Tivaouane and Ziguinchor.

[77] There currently are 14 of these courts: Act Courts of Lat Dior, Pikine, Kaolack, Diourbel, Louga, Saint-Louis, Courts of Appeal of Kaolack and Saint-Louis, District Courts (TGI) of Mbour, Kaolack, Zigninchor, Tivaouane and Kaffrine and the Regional Courts (TGI) of Kaolack and Ziguinchor.

– four Citizen Advice Bureaus (BIJs) housed in some of the country's universities[78] to promote legal literacy among students and make them important relays for the dissemination of legal information throughout Senegalese society.

Between 2006 and 2018 these legal aid offices received nearly 400 000 people, advised 184,546 people on their rights, handled 142 567 mediation cases with an overall successful conciliation rate of 75 per cent, and assisted 57 493 people in their relations with the authorities.[79] As for the BAOJs, they play an important role in combating crooked brokers swarming around courts and also improving the reputation of the judiciary in society, depending on the city and the jurisdiction. For example, in 2018 the BAOJ of the Palais de Justice in Thiès had 56 831 visitors.[80]

The Senegalese female Lawyers' Association (AJS) is also contributing to this with its seven legal aid offices nationwide,[81] serving as legal and judicial advisory, counselling and psychosocial assistance centres for women and collaborating with the legal aid offices. Health facilities and courts occasionally refer to cases of women seeking legal, judicial or psychosocial assistance. AJS has also a Legal Aid Fund that enables it to provide them with proper legal representation in their cases.[82]

There are also instances of collaboration between civil society organisations and Parliament[83] and the judiciary[84] to help raise awareness and encourage greater respect for human rights.

Human rights education is yet to be formally introduced into the Senegalese school system but has made a minor foray into higher education thanks to the

---

[78] University Cheikh Anta Diop of Dakar; University Gaston Berger of Saint-Louis; University of Thies; and University Assane Seck of Ziguinchor.
[79] See Ministry of Justice, *Les Maisons de justice au Sénégal*, Rapport annuel 2018 9.
[80] ibid 24.
[81] In Dakar, Pikine, Ziguinchor, Kolda, Thies, Kaolack and Sedhiou.
[82] On all issues related to the operation of law shops, see Amy Sakho, 'La prise en charge des victimes de violence dans les boutiques de l'Association des Juristes Sénégalaises (AJS)' <https://femmesjuristes.org/?page_id=426> accessed 15 September 2023.
[83] The laws of 1999 (on violence against women), 2005 (on women's reproductive health), 2008 (on women's access to the military, gendarmerie and police forces) and 2010 (on HIV/AIDS) are the result of close collaboration between women MPs and women's organisations in the country.
[84] See, for example, the Supreme Court study days of 26 and 27 November 2018 on the theme of 'The judge and the protection of liberties' <https://www.coursupreme.gouv.sn/sites/default/files/2021-04/RACS-2018.pdf> accessed 15 September 2023.

Human Rights and Peace Institute (IDHP)[85] of Cheikh Anta Diop University in Dakar. The IDHP also works in collaboration with the Interschool Centre for Children's Rights (CIDE) of the University of Geneva (Switzerland) to train the staff of organisations and institutions working in social affairs and the promotion of children's rights.

In addition to seminars organised by specialised state bodies and the OHCHR, which often target the educated segments of the population, various ministries celebrate human rights days[86] and weeks,[87] while civil society organisations focus on advocacy campaigns and prosecutions.[88] The introduction of human rights modules in training courses for police officers, gendarmes, judges and other medical personnel has also helped make progress in the fight against torture, trafficking in persons and the protection of civil liberties.

The publicity that surrounded Senegal's appearances before the Human Rights Council within the framework of the Universal Periodic Review (UPR), the handling of the Hissène Habré case by CAT and, more importantly, the forceful reactions of the Senegalese authorities regarding the HRCttee's handling of the *Karim Meissa Wade* case, a former minister and son of the former Senegalese President Abdoulaye Wade who accused the government of arbitrary detention, have changed the Senegalese public's perception of these mechanisms, that is, the instruments created by the former colonial powers to 'perpetuate' unequal power dynamics between rich and poor states, and impose Western views on such sensitive issues as the place of women and children in African societies and people's sexual orientation. What remains to be done now is to persuade the public of the universal nature of all the principles and rules conveyed by these legal instruments.

4.1.4 State Reporting

Preparation of initial and periodic reports: Traditionally, the Ministry of Justice has been at the heart of all government human rights initiatives, including the drafting of Senegal's initial and interim reports to regional and international

---

85 Professional and research Master's are offered on human rights, humanitarian action, citizenship and peace.
86 World Days for Literacy, Food, Albinism, Diabetes, Leprosy, AIDS, Water, Freedom of the Press, African Children, Population, Environment, International Days for Human Rights, Migrants, Women, People Living with Disabilities, and so forth.
87 Such as the National Week of Persons with Disabilities, National Basic School Week, National African Child Week and the Women's Fortnight.
88 See the section 'Legal assistance in police misconduct' in the 2017–2018 Activity Report of the Ligue sénégalaise des droits de l'homme (LSDH) 9.

bodies.[89] It was only in 1997 that the new National Human Rights Institution Act[90] granted the CSDH with the responsibility to draft the periodic reports. The constitutional cacophony and chronic instability of the administrative staff that characterised the liberal presidency of Abdoulaye Wade[91] prevented the CSDH from fully accomplishing the mission that had just been entrusted to it. As a matter of fact, the Office of the High Commissioner for Human Rights and Peace, which was established alongside the CSDH in 2004, was responsible not only for monitoring the implementation of international human rights treaties and participating in their transposition into domestic law but also, and more importantly, for coordinating the preparation and presentation of periodic reports, responding to questions that international bodies addressed to Senegal and following up on the authorities' implementation of the opinions and recommendations of those bodies.[92] In 2011 a Human Rights Directorate was established at the Ministry of Justice and assisted by a National Human Rights Advisory Council (CCNDH)[93] directly attached to the office of the Minister of Justice. It was tasked with coordinating the preparation and submission of periodic reports and documents drawn up by the government and intended for regional and international human rights monitoring bodies. This body assisted Senegal to make up for its considerable delay in submitting its reports, thanks in particular to the professionalism and dedication of its administrators.[94] In the interests of efficiency, the government broadened the mandate of the CCNDH by entrusting it, in addition to preparing and submitting reports, with coordinating information collection and collaborating with the bodies responsible for producing such information.[95] In the performance

---

89 The procedure was detailed in paras 2 to 5 of Senegal's most recent periodic report to the Committee on the Elimination of Discrimination against Women (CEDAW/C/SEN/8 of 12 December 2019).
90 See art 3 of Act 97–04 of 10 March 1997.
91 In 12 years of power, President Wade has appointed five Prime Ministers and 122 ministers. See <https://www.seneweb.com/news/Politique/rappelez-vous-quand-wade-nommait-122-ministres-en-10-ans-la-liste-de-tous-les-ministres_n_117413.html> accessed 10 April 2021.
92 See Decree 2004–657 of 2 June 2004.
93 It is composed of the Minister of Justice, the Secretary-General of the Ministry of Justice, the Director of Human Rights and his deputy, a representative of the office of the Prime Minister, a representative of each ministerial department and one representative of each national civil society organisation working in the field of human rights.
94 Particularly noteworthy is the remarkable work of Judge Mouhamadou Seye who headed the Human Rights Directorate for six years.
95 See art 2 of Decree 2018–1969 establishing the tasks, composition and functioning of the National Advisory Council on Human Rights and International Humanitarian Act.

of this mission, the CCNDH could rely on the close collaboration of ministries, the ANSD and other specialised public bodies, Parliament, the judiciary, the CSDH and civil society.

Process of implementation of Concluding Observations: The Ministry of Justice instituted a practice of convening a feedback meeting on Senegal's participation in the state reporting process, once the official delegation returned to the country. This was an opportunity for participants to share their views on the implementation of the recommendations and the role to be played by certain key ministries in information gathering and sharing. Concomitantly, civil society members who had taken part in the discussions or had received reliable information on Senegal's appearance before a treaty body would, as far as possible, shared their impressions with journalists who sometimes made a point of widely disseminating highlights of the COs. The establishment of the CCNDH, whose roles include 'coordinating and monitoring the follow-up of the implementation, on a national scale, of treaty obligations and recommendations issued by international human rights and international humanitarian law mechanisms',[96] somewhat changed administrative practices and led to the establishment of more formal reporting procedures:

- A trip report would be drafted by the head of the delegation and shared with the members of the CCNDH.
- Once the text of the COs has been officially received, the Director of Human Rights would convene a meeting of the CCNDH to discuss the measures to be taken by each ministry concerned and the timeframe for implementing the commitment made by the authorities.
- A note would be prepared for each recommendation of the COs and sent by the Minister of Justice in person to the Minister concerned.
- Line ministries, in turn, would organise sharing workshops with their partners in order to identify pragmatic implementation strategies. In a large majority of cases, especially in the area of children's rights, the financial constraints facing the state are a serious obstacle to the implementation of recommendations.
- Progress and difficulties in implementation are analysed at the monthly meetings of the CCNDH on the basis of reports prepared by the Director of Human Rights and proposals are made for action by the administrative bodies concerned. While this new approach has enabled the Senegalese authorities to provide more regular information on the country's response

---

96 See art 2, para 1 of Decree 2018–1969 establishing the tasks, composition and functioning of the National Advisory Council on Human Rights and International Humanitarian Law.

to COs of the treaty bodies,[97] it has not improved public information on both the content of the periodic reports and on the measures taken to remedy shortcomings reported by the treaty bodies. No official government website, let alone the websites of the independent mechanisms established through the work of the treaty bodies, contained information on those procedures. Civil society organisations are working to fill the void, but their limited communication capacity makes it impossible for them to make a difference.

4.1.5 Role of the Independent State Human Rights Institution

The CSDH was the first national human rights institution to be established in sub-Saharan Africa.[98] In 1997, following the adoption of the Paris Principles by the United Nations General Assembly, a law was passed to turn the national human rights institution into 'an independent institution for consultation, observation, evaluation, dialogue, consultation and the promotion of human rights'.[99] Since then the CSDH may, on its own initiative or at the request of any national authority, work in collaboration with all UN bodies or any regional or national institutions with a role in human rights promotion and protection; and give its opinion on any report or document intended for these bodies and ensure that Senegal complies with its obligations under the international and regional conventions to which it is a party.[100]

The CSDH was granted Status A upon its accreditation with the International Coordinating Committee of National Human Rights Institutions. Under the regime of President Abdou Diouf, it was the country's flagship institution and contributed to Senegal's compliance with its treaty obligations, in particular by implementing the findings of the treaty bodies[101] and raising awareness among the population and the authorities about the content of the treaties.[102] The reforms introduced by Abdoulaye Wade's liberal regime, marked by the creation of the OHCHR, the Human Rights Directorate and the CCNDH,

---

97 See Committee on Enforced Disappearances, Information received from Senegal on follow-up to COs, CED/C/SEN/CO/1/Add.1 of 17 May 2018 and Committee against Torture, Information received from Senegal on follow-up to COs, CAT/C/SEN/CO/4/Add.1 of 7 March 2019.
98 See Decree 70–453 of 22 April 1970.
99 Art 1 of Act 97–04 of 10 March 1997.
100 Art 3 of Act 97–04 of 10 March 1997.
101 Implementation of the *Famara Kone v State of Senegal* decision cited above.
102 Celebration of International Human Rights Day with great pomp and circumstance every 10 December and holding of sectoral meetings with the penitentiary administration now attached to the Ministry of Justice, Courts and Tribunals, and so forth.

contributed to the marginalisation of the CSDH in the state's human rights promotion and protection mechanism, leading to the institution being downgraded to Status B under the presidency of Macky Sall, due mainly to a lack of tangible support, especially financial, from the Senegalese authorities, a lack of diversity in its composition and its lack of independence. By appointing a member of his party and mayor of a city to head the CSDH, President Macky Sall created a feeling of unease within the human rights movement, some of the most influential members of which decided simply to cease all forms of collaboration with the national human rights institution.

4.1.6 Role Played by Civil Society

Since the early 1990s national and foreign civil society organisations have become key players in all matters relating to human rights promotion and protection in Senegal. They very soon recognised the value of working together to influence the Senegalese authorities' policy in a rather sensitive area. Alongside foreign NGOs,[103] which essentially implement individual programmes, local organisations have often chosen to form coalitions[104] in order to interact with the authorities as part of an advocacy strategy or exert pressure on them.

The relations between the Senegalese authorities and civil society are generally good in times of social tranquility, to such an extent that the authorities have sometimes been able to appoint some of its members as advisers[105] or include them in state delegations tasked with interacting with UN bodies. However, they usually deteriorate during pre-election or election periods when civil society organisations are often perceived as opponents.

The passing of a law on electronic communications that should theoretically allow 'specific protection of users' personal data in accordance with the

---

103   These include Amnesty International, Human Rights Watch (HRW), the International Federation for Human Rights (FIDH) and The World Alliance for Citizen Participation (CIVICUS).
104   These include the Senegalese Coalition of Human Rights Defenders (COBSEDDH), which brings together 18 human rights organisations, and the National Coalition of Associations and NGOs for Children (CONAFE), which brings together 217 organisations for the defence and promotion of children's rights, the Siggil Jiggen Network (Women's Rights), the Right Here, Right Now Platform (RHRN) of Senegal (bringing together 13 organisations), the Committee to Combat Violence Against Women and the Coalition of Organisations in Synergy for the Defence of Public Education (COBSYDEP).
105   This was the case of a former President of the AJS and an influential official of RADDHO who were respectively Technical Adviser to the President of the Republic and Technical Adviser No 1 to the Minister of Human Rights.

requirements of security and public order'[106] was also seen as a way to restrict freedom of expression, especially through censorship of content posted online.

More recently, a controversy arose following the publication, by a religious organisation, of a list of associations allegedly defending lesbian, gay, bisexual and transgender (LGBT) rights,[107] forcing the Interior Ministry to launch an investigation into the possible recognition of LGBT organisations in Senegal.[108] This was seen by many Senegalese organisations as the beginning of a 'witch hunt' in a country known for its liberal legislation regarding associations.[109]

Lastly, one should mention the existence of a fairly diversified[110] and dynamic[111] the media sector that is really beginning to play an essential role, not only in informing the public about the activities of the treaty bodies but also, and above all, in educating the population about societal issues such as child begging, safe abortion, homosexuality and violence against women. However, regrettably, these media are under-used by civil society and the public authorities when it comes to promoting human rights or in social debates.

4.1.7 Local Process for Implementing COs and Findings of Treaty Mechanisms

On the surface, the implementation process is very clear, since by law, the CCNDH has a mandate to 'review legislation and regulations and ensure that they are consistent with international and regional human rights and international humanitarian law instruments ratified by Senegal'.[112] In practice, this operation is made more complex by competition between the NCCDH and

---

106   See the Explanatory Memorandum to Act 2018–28 of 12 December 2018 on the Electronic Telecommunications Code.
107   See <https://www.pressafrik.com/Jamra-publie-un-echantillon-de-listes-d-associations-d-homosexuels-et-de-lesbiennes_a208275.html> acceded 10 January 2021.
108   See L'Enquête No 2573 du 4 février 2020 'Récépissé délivrés a des associations LGBT: la Direction des Libertés publiques ouvre une enquête' 3.
109   See L'Observateur No 4903 of 3 February 2020 'La vie cachée des associations pro-gay à Dakar' 6 and 'D Diouf, Président de l'Association AIDES-SENEGAL: Beaucoup se tueraient si les homosexuels de ce pays étaient dévoilé' 7.
110   In Senegal, there are 22 community radio stations, 48 commercial and six international radio stations, 31 television stations and 11 online daily newspapers. See <https://www.teledakar.net/2017/10/10/ya-276-radios-31-televisions-senegal/> (acceded on 10 January 2021) and the site of the Autorité de Régulation des Télécommunications et des Postes (ARTP), <https://artp.sn/> accessed 15 September 2023.
111   Some media outlets have created programmes on human rights or regularly organise debates on societal issues.
112   See art 2, para 2 of Decree 2018–1969 establishing the tasks, composition and functioning of the National Advisory Council on Human Rights and International Humanitarian Law.

other state bodies with the same mandate conferred by law. These include the CSDH which is responsible for 'ensuring that Senegal complies with its obligations under the international or regional conventions to which it is a party',[113] the Legal Instruments Monitoring Commission, which is responsible for 'ensuring that legal instruments are consistent with international and community standards',[114] and the Child Protection Support Unit (CAPE).[115] Experience has shown a difference in approach depending on whether it is about implementing COs or the findings of treaty mechanisms.

4.1.8 Implementation of COs

The implementation of COs may be achieved through the formulation of a national policy that takes account of the state's commitments under the treaty in question[116] or through the revision of an existing law by Parliament to ensure that it complies with the state's new obligations.[117] In many cases, the procedure is initiated by the government itself at the request of some technical partners (UNICEF, the United Nations Population Fund (UNFPA), IOM, UNDP, UN Women, OHCHR, among others) and institutional partners concerned with advancing the fulfillment of certain basic rights. A political authority particularly concerned about the plight of a vulnerable group may also be behind the implementation of the recommendations of the UN mechanisms. This was the case when President Macky Sall, following the death of many street children in March 2013, urged the Minister for Women and Children to take special measures to protect these children.[118] In Senegal, most reforms are politically motivated and therefore tend to serve only the immediate interests of their initiators. The reform of the Nationality Act in 2013, which resulted in Senegalese women being granted the right to pass on citizenship to their children and spouses, is a case in point. In the memorandum submitted to the Minister of Justice, who had initiated the reform, a group of NGOs drew the Minister's attention to a number of discriminatory provisions found in Senegalese law,

---

113 See para 2 of Act 97–04 of 10 March 1997 on the Senegalese Human Rights Committee.
114 See art 2 of the Order of the Minister of Justice 4789 dated 25 March 2016.
115 See art 4 of Presidential Decree 02131 of 12 March 2008, which provides that 'CAPE also facilitates the coordination of actions carried out by the various ministerial departments involved in child protection and the activities carried out by other national and international structures'.
116 One example is the National Child Protection Strategy adopted on 28 December 2013 by the government of Senegal.
117 For example, the reform of the Nationality Code in July 2013 to give women the same rights as men to transmit their nationality to their children and spouses.
118 See 'Diagnosis of Macky Sall's missed shots' *L'Observateur* 4877 3 January 2020 4.

including those related to disability. However, being a good politician, she was concerned only about discrimination affecting women, who made up a large proportion of her party's voters in the forthcoming elections.

4.1.9 Membership of Treaty Bodies

Senegal has always encouraged and supported its citizens with recognised expertise in the field of human rights to apply for positions available within the treaty bodies. Since the end of the 1970s to mid 2021, eleven Senegalese nationals have contributed or are still contributing, based on their expertise, to enhancing the prestige of these human rights protection and promotion mechanisms. Senegalese nationals participated in the activities of UNTB:

UNTB	Person's name	Number of years
CERD Cttee	Mr Jacques Baudin	(unknown dates)
	Mr Ibrahima Guisse	2019–2023 (4 years)
HRCttee	Mr Abdoulaye Dieye	1978–1982 (4 years)
	Prof Birame Ndiaye	1982–1986/1986–1990/1990–1994 (12 years)
CESCR Cttee	Mr Samba Cor Konate	1986–1988/1988–1992 (8 years)
CAT Cttee	Judge Guibril Camara	1995–1999/1999–2003/2003–2007 (12 years)
CMW Cttee	Mr Ahmadou Tall	2017–2021 (4 years)
	Ms Fatima Diallo	2021–2025 (4 years)
CED Cttee	Judge Sheikh Ahmed Tidiane Coulibaly	2019–2021 (2 years)
	Mr Matar Diop	2021–2023 (2 years)

The UNTB membership of judges contributed to the education of the judiciary on a number of issues, including the eradication of torture in the country. As a member of CAT and president of the Cour de Cassation, Justice Guibril Camara contributed to the development of a jurisprudence that made sure that nobody was, even the security forces, above the law when it comes to the application of CAT. Late Professor Birame Ndiaye was, during his mandate as a member of the HRCttee, in charge of the course on human rights at the Faculty of Law of the University of Dakar, which contributed to the training of the first cohort of human rights activists who created the first human rights organisations of the country (ONDH, RADDHO, LSDH, Forum du Justiciable and AJS). (Falling beyond the study's cut-off mark: Maitre Bacre Waly Ndiaye was elected to the HRCttee in 2022 for a mandate of four years (2022-2026).)

4.2 Overview of the Overall Impact of UN Standards

The efforts deployed over the years by state authorities, civil society organisations and the country's technical and financial partners to ensure that citizens benefit as much as possible from the country's commitment to UN human rights treaties, have paid off. The government, without major financial resources but with the critical support of civil society, is trying, with little success, to fulfil its treaty obligations, notwithstanding heavy administrative procedures and religious and societal pressures. The implementation, however timid, of the UN treaties has enabled Senegal to make significant progress in the protection of human life and dignity. The practice of torture by security forces belongs now to the past and the efforts for the effective protection of civil and political rights continue with the promise of a noticeable change in mentalities in a country practically 'hostage' to its social and cultural traditions. While state structures are beginning to get used to the culture of dialogue with UN mechanisms, the strong politicisation of the fight for the respect of the rule of law is slowing down progress and further weakening a civil society with outdated working methods and little experience of intergenerational dialogue.

4.2.1 Domestication of UN Human Rights Treaties into Domestic Law

The inclusion of UN standards[119] in the Constitution and the introduction of the concept of basic rights and new economic and environmental rights in the Constitution seem to have given new impetus to the Senegalese government's determination to honour the commitments it has made to the treaty bodies. Since then, it has prioritised the effective alignment of national legislation with the legal instruments ratified by Senegal in order to 'guarantee legal governance that is more respectful of the rights'[120] they contain.

---

119 Preamble to the Constitution in which it is stated that 'the People of sovereign Senegal ... affirms its adherence ... to the international instruments adopted by the United Nations ... in particular the Universal Declaration of Human Rights of 10 December 1948, the *Convention on the Elimination of All Forms of Discrimination against Women of 18 December 1979, the Convention on the Rights of the Child of 20 November 1989*.' (emphasis added). This, in concrete terms, also means a constitutionalisation of the rights of women and children.

120 According to the expression of President Macky Sall in the preface to the Study on the harmonization of Senegalese national legislation with international legal instruments

- The Senegalese state has innovated by encouraging interested administrations to prepare documents laying down the parameters of their actions in the areas covered by international treaties within a given period of time and creating agencies responsible for implementing the commitments made. This approach was designed to enable 'the state to better report on the progress made in the implementation of legal instruments [and] ... to put all actors into perspective' by giving priority to:
- the implementation of ratified international standards in order to integrate them into programmes and policies;
- the empowerment of players responsible for directly implementing these rights for the benefit of the various segments of the population, especially women and men, based on the fact that these are rights that should be met and not potential needs that may need to be met;
- the support to implementers, especially governments, for the implementation of rights and the definition of legal measures that stakeholders, technical and financial partners, communities of international and national civil society organisations and citizens can take charge of and could call upon in the event of failure to fulfill their commitments; and
- the adoption of human rights indicators and regular monitoring measures to ensure fulfillment of legal commitments.[121]

The following national policy documents are directly connected to the commitments made by the government in ratifying UN human rights instruments:
- In the area of children's rights, the National Child Protection Strategy (SNPE) document adopted on 28 December 2013 'is based on the state's commitments and obligations to protect the rights and well-being of children as stipulated by the CRC, the African Charter on the Rights and Welfare of the Child and the recommendations of the 5th Pan-African Forum on Children'[122] and backed up by a National Action Plan for its implementation.
- In the area of women's rights, the National Strategy for Gender Equity and Equality (SNEEG) document, is 'an operational instrument ... for the elimination of gender discrimination with a view to achieving an emerging Senegal that guarantees equal opportunities between women and men'.[123] It

---

relating to the rights of the child carried out by the Child Protection Support Unit (CAPE) of the Presidency of the Republic of Senegal.

121 See Republic of Senegal: National Strategy for Gender Equity and Equality (SNEEG) 2016–2026 149.
122 See Republic of Senegal: National Child Protection Strategy, December 2013 7.
123 See Republic of Senegal: National Strategy for Gender Equity and Equality (SNEEG) 2016–2026 12.

is interesting to note that the document states that 'the actions to be developed will be based on the human rights approach defined as a conceptual and normative framework for a planning and programming process based on the implementation of international and national standards for the protection and promotion of human rights'. Based on this principle, policy making that will be the basis for translating the principle of gender equality will be based on 'right' and not on needs.[124]

- In the area of economic, social and cultural rights, National Economic and Social Development Strategy (SNDES) documents, National Social Protection Strategy (SNPS) (2015–2035), National Health Development Plan (PNDS) (2009–2018) was followed by a Strategic Plan for Digital Health (PSSD-2018–2023), a Decennial Education and Training Programme (2001–2010) followed by a Programme for Improved Quality, Equity and Transparency in Education (PAQUET).
- Regarding Justice, the Letter for Sectoral Policy for the Development of the Justice system has the objective to set the main orientations and priorities of the Ministry of Justice 'with a view to contributing to the consolidation of the rule of law and guaranteeing the application of the fundamental rights and freedoms recognised by the Constitution of the Republic of Senegal'.[125]

A number of these documents subsequently served as a basis for the adoption of policy legislation to translate the ambitions set out in the strategic documents into legislation. The adoption of the Social Orientation Act 2010-15 of 6 July 2010, on the promotion and protection of the rights of persons with disabilities, for example, followed the adoption in 2006 of the National Community-Based Rehabilitation Programme designed to improve access to the country's rehabilitation services for persons with disabilities. Senegal's ratification of the Convention on the Rights of Persons with Disabilities (CRPD), in a sense, has forced the Senegalese authorities to develop a reference framework for the institutional arrangements to be put in place to ensure that persons with disabilities are cared for and integrated into Senegalese society. It should be noted that the first two implementing decrees[126] already enacted

---

124 ibid 148.
125 See Republic of Senegal: Lettre de politique sectorielle de développement du secteur de la justice (2018–2022) 5.
126 Decree 2010–99 of 27 January 2010 on the Construction Code, arts R18 to R20 which deal with measures for the physical accessibility of buildings by persons with disabilities (art 3 of the Convention) and Decree 2012–1038 of 2 October 2012 establishing two departmental technical commissions responsible for examining applications for equal opportunity cards and promoting special education (art 32 of the Convention).

out of the 15 or so instruments[127] that the government intends to adopt to implement the Convention are those that have the least financial implications for the state.

It is in the area of women's and children's rights that the Senegalese authorities have made commendable efforts to put an end to the discrimination experienced by Senegalese women and to protect children more effectively against certain social practices in Senegalese society. At the request of the UN treaty bodies, significant amendments have been made to certain Senegalese legal provisions:

- Act 91–22 of 16 February 1991, on educational guidance, which provided for compulsory and free elementary education, was revised in 2004 by Act 2004–37 of 15 December 2004, to raise the age of compulsory schooling from six to 16 years as requested by CESCR in its COs dated 24 September 2001 (paragraph 57);
- Act 99–05 of 29 January 1999 amended the Criminal Code in order to address violence against women as recommended by the HRCttee in its COs dated 19 November 1997 (paragraphs 12 and 13);
- Act 2005–15 of 19 July 2005 granted women the right to make decisions regarding their reproductive health at the demand of CESCR in its COs dated 24 September 2001 (paragraph 47);
- Act 2008–02 of 1 January 2008 introduced equal tax treatment for men and women as formulated by CESCR in its COs dated 24 September 2001 (paragraphs 35, 37 and 40);

---

127 These are the draft decrees approving the National Community-Based Rehabilitation Programme (art 5 of the Convention); establishing a High Authority for the Promotion and Protection of the Rights of Persons with Disabilities (art 48 of the Convention); establishing the support fund for persons with disabilities (art 47 of the Convention); establishing an information and disability prevention programme (art 12 of the Convention); laying down the conditions for the recruitment of persons with disabilities in public and private bodies (art 29 of the Convention); and the modalities for supporting persons with disabilities in setting up businesses (art 30 of the Convention); the conditions of access for persons with disabilities to cultural and leisure institutions (art 41 of the Convention); and draft inter-ministerial decrees establishing the modalities of admission of children and adolescents with disabilities to ordinary and specialised institutions and the conditions for taking examinations and competitive examinations (art 18 of the Convention); setting the modalities of technical and material support for special and inclusive education structures (art 18 of the Convention); the modalities for the admission of persons with disabilities to regular and specialised technical and vocational training centres, educational follow-up and the conditions for examinations and competitive examinations (art 26 of the Convention); and the rate of reduction in public transport for persons with disabilities who hold an equal opportunities card (art 34 of the Convention).

- Act 2010–11 of 28 May 2010[128] introduced total parity between men and women in fully and partially elective bodies as demanded by CEDAW in its COs dated 27 January 1994 (paragraph 725);– Act 2013–05 of 8 July 2013[129] granted women the right to pass on citizenship to their children and spouses as recommended by CEDAW in its COs dated 27 January 1994 (paragraph 695);
- Act 2019–20 of 27 December 2019[130] amended Act 65–60 of 21 July 1965 to criminalise rape and pedophilia at the request of the HRCttee in its COs dated 11 December 2019 (paragraph 17);

In some cases, the reforms also produced infra-legislative norms, such as the Circular 004379 of 11 October 2007 of the Ministry of National Education authorising pregnant girls to pursue their studies. This decision followed the formal demand of the CESCR in its COs dated 24 September 2001 (paragraph 47).

4.2.2 Interpretation of Treaties by the Judiciary

The Senegalese judges and lawyers' level of expertise in international human rights law is difficult to assess. This is due in particular to the inaccessibility of judicial decisions. The rare sources of information accessible in Senegal are the website of the Supreme Court of Senegal,[131] Sunulex[132] – which provides information on Senegalese law – and the websites of the Organisation for the Harmonisation of Business Law (OHADA), African Legal Publishers (EDJA) and JURICAF (Jurisprudence of Francophone Supreme Courts).[133]

Cases referring to UN human rights treaties are not numerous on these sites and this situation is due to the parties involved in the proceedings controlling the procedure,[134] to the judges' poor understanding of these treaties and to the fact that the treaties are not very often invoked before the courts by lawyers and litigants. Another factor is the limited interest among the local media in cases relating to the enforcement of these standards, but over the last two years, the media have become more and more interested in the application of international standards of human rights.

---

128 COs of CEDAW, 27 January 1994 para 725.
129 ibid para 695.
130 COs of CCPR, 11 December 2019 para 17.
131 <www.coursupreme.sn> accessed 1 September 2023.
132 <https://www.coursupreme.gouv.sn/> accessed 1 September 2023.
133 <www.juricaf.org> accessed 14 April 2022.
134 Only the administrative courts offer the possibility for groups to act on behalf of their members (see Supreme Court, Judgment of 5 July 1978, *Mamadou Laity Ndiaye and Amicale des fonctionnaires du Cadre des Affaires étrangères*). The Environment Code and

The judges indeed are beginning to refer in their decisions to international treaties ratified by Senegal, particularly the Convention on the Rights of the Child (CRC), and lawyers are invoking provisions of these treaties on issues related to torture and civil and political rights in general. This has contributed to a timid emergence of local jurisprudence on the application of the provisions of UN treaties in Senegal. Clearly, all Senegalese highest courts, whether constitutional,[135] administrative[136] or judicial,[137] are called upon to protect human rights with reference to the UN treaties, and even lower courts also rule on these issues, either directly[138] or when dealing with electoral matters.[139]

More specifically, few cases dealt with by the administrative judge[140] make reference to international treaties on issues related to citizens' equality before the law,[141] the protection of the right to property,[142] religious

---

the Trafficking in Persons Act also allow associations to bring civil action in cases before the courts.

135 See Constitutional Council, Case 1/C/2014 ruling on an appeal for unconstitutionality against the order issued on 17 April 2013 by the Investigation Commission of the Court for the Suppression of Illicit Enrichment in the case between Mr Karim Meissa W and the State of Senegal (see paras 8–11).

136 This is the most extensive case law. These include Ruling 12 of 29 June 2000 of the Court of Cassation, *Association nationale des handicapés moteurs du Sénégal v State of Senegal*; Ruling 35 of 13 October 2011 of the Administrative Chamber of the Supreme Court of Senegal, *Alioune Tine v State of Senegal*; and Ruling 37 of 9 June 2016, *Amnesty International Senegal v State of Senegal*.

137 See Supreme Court of Senegal, Civil and Commercial Chamber, Ruling 64 of 16 June 2010, *Société New Baron and Levesque International, Société George Forrest International v Ciments du Sahel*.

138 See Tribunal de Grande Instance Hors Classe de Dakar, Judgment 044bis/2018 on the treatment of minors before the law.

139 See the numerous judgments handed down by the Senegalese courts on the respect of parity in party lists during local elections: Dakar Court of Appeal, General Assembly Judgment 78 of 21 August 2014, *Ms Woraye Sarr, head of the majority list of the PDS in the Commune of Medina Gounas, Department of Guediawaye*; Kaolack Court of Appeal, General Assembly. Ruling 12 of 25 July 2014, *Mbenda Ndiaye v Baba Ndiaye and Others*.

140 See Communication from Judge Adama Ndiaye, 'La jurisprudence sénégalaise en matière de protection des droits et libertés', presented at the Study Days of the Supreme Court on 26 and 27 November 2018 on Le Juge et la protection des libertés: regards croisés des juges administratifs et des juges judiciaires <https://www.impact.sn/Cour-Supreme-la-jurisprudence-senegalaise-en-matiere-de-protection-des-droits-et-libertes-voir-document-joint_a17487.html> accessed 11 September 2023.

141 Supreme Court, Administrative Chamber, Ruling 1 of 9 January 2014, *Mame Thierno Dieng v Rector of the University Cheikh Anta Diop*, Ruling 5 of 27 January 2017, *Regroupement des diplômés sans emploi du Sénégal v Minister of Justice*; Ruling 63 of 28 December 2017, *Colette Gueye v State of Senegal*.

142 See Supreme Court, Administrative Chamber, Ruling 61 of 24 November 2016, *Collectivité Leboue de Ouakam v Préfecture de Dakar and Agent judiciaire de l'État*; Ruling 21 of 10 April

freedom,[143] freedom of association,[144] freedom of movement,[145] right to trade union[146] and freedom of assembly.[147] With regard to this latter point, the numerous annulments of state decisions banning public demonstrations[148] do not seem to have changed the behaviour of the administration, which continues to disregard freedom of assembly as a fundamental human right that must be respected by all.[149]

By contrast, the increased number of cases of torture and inhuman or degrading treatment brought against the state security services (police and *gendarmerie*)[150] and schools[151] before the courts has rapidly changed state practice. The numerous convictions of police officers, *gendarmes* and teachers, which attracted a great deal of media attention, have contributed to a drastic reduction in allegations of torture and ill-treatment in police stations and gendarmerie brigades throughout the country. It is also true that in most cases these convictions have led to the removal of the perpetrators of these vicious acts from the ranks of the security services.

2014, *Gilbert Khayat v State of Senegal*; Ruling 10 of 22 February 2018, *Commune de Diokoul Diawrigne v Mamadou Lo and Others.*

143 See Supreme Court, Administrative Chamber, Ruling 41 of 28 June 2018, *Église du Christianisme Céleste 'Paroisse Jéhovah Elyon' v State of Senegal.*

144 See Supreme Court, Administrative Chamber, Ruling 48 of 30 August 2018, *Alliances of Democratic Forces v State of Senegal*; Ruling 50 of 24 December 2009, *And Jef/African Party for Democracy and Socialism (AJ-PADS) v State of Senegal.*

145 See Supreme Court, Administrative Chamber, Ruling 5 of 13 January 2015, *Sidia Bayo v State of Senegal*; Ruling of 12 January 2008, *Aboubacar Diakite dit Tomba v State of Senegal.*

146 Supreme Court, Administrative Chamber, Ruling 61 of 12 December 2013, *Ndiaga Soumare v State of Senegal and Director General of Customs.*

147 Supreme Court of Senegal, Administrative Chamber, Ruling 35 of 13 October 2011, *Alioune Tine v State of Senegal*; Ruling 37 of 9 June 2016, *Amnesty International Senegal v State of Senegal*; Ruling 19 of 23 May 2019, *Assane Ba and 2 Others v State of Senegal.*

148 See Supreme Court, Administrative Chamber, Ruling 19 of 23 May 2019, *Assane Ba and 2 Others v State of Senegal*; Ruling 37 of 9 June 2016, *Amnesty International Senegal v State of Senegal*; Ruling 35 of 13 October 2011, *Alioune Tine, President of the African Human Rights Meeting (RADDHO) v State of Senegal.*

149 The diagnosis established by the CNRI in the Report of the Commission for Institutional Reforms to the President of the Republic was that 'concerning rights and freedoms, we cannot fail to note, on the one hand, a lack of effectiveness of some of them and, on the other hand, the persistence in our law of certain liberticidal provisions'. (See section B of the Report).

150 See a list of these cases in Senegal's 4th periodic report to the CTC, CAT/C/SEN/4 30–33.

151 See Cour d'Appel de Thiès, Chambre criminelle, Arrêt No 01 du 23 mai 2017, *Ministère public et Abdou Samb.*

Concerning the independence of the judiciary, the state continues, despite the call of the HRCttee for 'urgent measures to protect the full autonomy, independence and impartiality'[152] of the body, to periodically undermine it[153] by failing to abide by the institutional guarantees enshrined in the Constitution[154] and the country's legislation.[155] The Judges' Union of Senegal (UMS) has been trying for some years, without much success, to reform the status of judges in order to restore guarantees of independence, establish greater transparency in the management of judges' careers, reform the Higher Council of the Judiciary (CSM) in order to reduce the influence of the executive on the functioning of the legal system[156] and grant a minimum of fiscal autonomy to enable the public justice service to direct its actions towards the real priorities of the sector.[157]

4.2.3 Changes within Civil Society

Since the early 2000s the human rights movement,[158] through its expertise and reputation that now extends beyond the boundaries of Senegal, its ability to effectively advocate and influence government actions and the impact it is beginning to have on the population, has strengthened its visibility and legitimacy in society to the point where some of its leaders tend to become politically engaged.[159] This process has encouraged many leaders of civil society[160] to take up positions on critical human rights issues in the central government

---

152   See COs of the HRCttee dated 11 December 2019 (para 37).
153   In its 2013 Report to the President of the Republic, the CNRI deplored the fact that 'the judiciary, which is supposedly independent, finds itself under some degree of dependence *vis-à-vis* the executive branch'. See ch C of the Report of the Institutional Reform Commission to the President of the Republic.
154   Art 88 of the Constitution provides that 'the judiciary is independent of the legislature and the executive'.
155   See in particular Organic Act 2017–10 of 17 January 2017 on the Statutes of Magistrates.
156   On these questions, see *'the synthesis of the study days organised by the UMS in the jurisdictions of the Courts of Appeal'* in L'indépendance de la justice au Sénégal: État des lieux et perspectives de reformes, Actes du Colloque national, UMS, Dakar, September 2018 217–219.
157   See interview with the President of the UMS, Mr Souleymane Teliko in *L'Enquête* 16 December 2019 5.
158   This is the term used by the local media to refer to members of civil society working in the human rights sector.
159   ibid.
160   Mr Alioune Tine, icon of this movement and former Secretary-General of RADDHO, was President of the CSDH for a few years and Mouhamadou Mbodj cumulated, until his death in March 2018, his functions as President of the Civil Forum with that of member of the Autonomous National Electoral Commission (CENA) of Senegal.

that they had previously not been able to move forward. In fact, this situation has revealed a number of weaknesses of Senegalese civil society:
- a serious lack of autonomy on the part of these organisations, which rely on local and international partners to finance their activities;
- low institutional and professional capacity;
- very weak internal democracy and relatively non-transparent governance;[161]
- a decline in activism within these organisations, linked to the disappearance of traditional modes of mobilisation within Senegalese society; and
- a lack of synergy and close collaboration between organisations.

A joint study by Civicus, the Civil Forum and the West African Civil Society Institute (WACSI)[162] had already observed this limited impact of Senegalese civil society on public policies,[163] in general, and human rights issues, in particular, and attributed it to a number of difficulties, including those mentioned above.[164] The solutions they proposed included the following:[165]
- maintaining a proper balance in their relations with political authorities and deepening the ongoing dialogue between the government, the private sector, CSOs and citizens in order to consolidate democracy and the rule of law;
- strengthening technical expertise in the civil society organisations' areas of specialisation; and
- developing a culture of evaluation that allows people to accept constructive criticism and to take responsibility for their mistakes.

4.2.4 Impact of State Reporting

Much of the progress made in the areas of equality between men and women, particularly in the administration, in the delivery of justice, in the production of human rights data, and so forth, can be directly linked to the implementation of the recommendations made by the UN treaty bodies. However, recommendation relates to societal or religious issues. Recommendations in relation to religion and societal issues are the most difficult to implement due to the caution of the political authorities to engage in such reforms, but also, and

---

161 Few human rights organisations hold renewal meetings of their bodies when their term expires.
162 CIVICUS, Forum Civil and WACSI, Civil Society Index –Rapid Assessment Study of civil society in Senegal: A strong identity for civil society, but a need to complete awakening of civic consciousness, 2014.
163 ibid 20.
164 ibid 22, 23.
165 ibid 20.

above all, because Senegal is perceived by the majority of its citizens 'as a land where people's souls are yearning and thirsting for the absolute and for the highest spiritual values'.[166]

The erratic nature of the presentation of the periodic reports[167] also adds to the difficulty of making an objective assessment of the impact that this procedure has had on the perception that the authorities and citizens have of these rights which nevertheless continue to be at the heart of their often-tumultuous relations. The government of President Abdou Diouf in 1997 began[168] to formally implement the recommendations of the treaty bodies. This practice was maintained by President Abdoulaye Wade, who made efforts to address them in the numerous public policies that his government developed and applied under his leadership. This approach made it possible to transpose the relevant provisions of these legal instruments into Senegalese law in a more or less opportunistic, realistic and sometimes partial manner.

It should be noted, however, that Senegal has more easily implemented its procedural obligations, such as the prohibition of lengthy pre-trial or arbitrary detention or those relating to compensation for victims of rights violations. It has been nuanced and vague whenever its commitments relate to social or culturally-relevant issues, such as discrimination or equality, child protection or sexual orientation.

The attitude of the Senegalese state towards child abuses through begging in *daaras*[169] is a good example of the ambiguity of its approach to UN human rights treaties. Child begging,[170] a widespread phenomenon in the country and in the sub-region, has been clearly identified by all human rights advocates in Senegal as 'a serious and manifest violation of the fundamental rights of the child in that it undermines children's physical integrity and the harmonious development of their personality and deprives them of the right to grow

---

166 Quotations credited to Prof Sékéné Mody Sissoko by Ambassador Amadou Diop in his book titled *Sénégal: Repères et grandeurs d'une diplomatie*, Edition Sentinelles, May 2006 29.

167 Twenty-one years and four months separated the submission of Senegal's 3rd and 4th periodic reports to the HRCttee; 14 years and 11 months between Senegal's 2nd and 3rd periodic reports to CESCR, and six and a half years between Senegal's 18th and 19th periodic reports to CERD.

168 See the recommendations in paras 11 and 13 of the COs on the 5th periodic report of Senegal (CCPR/C/79/Add.82 of 19 November 1997).

169 The term refers to a traditional school in which children, called *talibés*, study and sometimes live under the responsibility of a Koranic master.

170 This is a practice which, under the pretext of Islamic education of children, consists of sending a child to beg in order to exploit him or her financially.

up in a family environment, in a climate of love, happiness and understanding'.[171] This explains why there is unanimous opposition to child begging and why it has been condemned by all the treaty mechanisms[172] and many special procedures[173] that have taken up the issue. Although the state of Senegal has expressed its will 'to build a state governed by the rule of law that places children at the heart of its mechanism for the promotion and protection of the fundamental rights of citizens'[174] and has developed national policies for children and established a legal framework and institutions to combat the phenomenon, the *talibés* are still on the streets where they continue to suffer all kinds of abuse.[175] More recently, the CESCR Cttee, echoing the requests made by almost all the human rights bodies,[176] has asked the Senegalese authorities 'to send a strong signal of the political will to end the practice of forced child begging'.[177]

In retrospect, the ineffectiveness of the efforts by the state of Senegal can be attributed to the following causes:

Religious: Even though it is now considered a violation of children's rights, begging by young people living in *daaras* has for a very long time been perceived in the predominantly Muslim Senegalese society as an essential educational practice that is intended to 'prepare children for adult life by instilling in them the values of humility, asceticism and endurance' and help 'form well-rounded men, freed from any obstructive ego, capable of surviving and

---

[171] See evaluation and analysis of the international, regional and national legal framework on the rights of the child and the status of implementation of the recommendations of human rights protection mechanisms relating to the rights of the child, Study of the West Africa Regional Office of the Office of the High Commissioner for Human Rights, 2018 11.

[172] Recommendations from the 31st session of the UPR (A/HRC/40/5), General Comments of CRC (/C/SEN/CO/3–5), CAT (CAT/C/SEN/CO/4), CERD (CERD/C/SEN/CO/16–18), MTC (CMW/C/SEN/CO/2–3), CESCR (E/C.12/SEN/CO/3) and HRCttee (CCPR/C/SEN/CO/5).

[173] See the Report on the Mission to Senegal of Ms Najat Maalla M'Jid, Special Rapporteur on the sale of children, child prostitution and child pornography (A/HRC/16/57/Add.3), the Report on the Mission to Senegal of Mr Kishore Singh, Special Rapporteur on the right to education (A/HRC/17/29/Add.2) and the Report on the Mission to Senegal of Mr Jorge Bustamante, Special Rapporteur on the human rights of migrants (A/HRC/17/33/Add.2).

[174] In the words of His Excellency Macky Sall, President of the Republic of Senegal in the preface to the Study on the Harmonisation of Senegalese National Legislation with International Legal Instruments on the Rights of the Child carried out by the Child Protection Support Unit (CAPE) of the Presidency of the Republic of Senegal.

[175] Corporal punishment, psychological and sexual violence, among others.

[176] See CCPR/C/SEN/CO/5 (para 41(a)), CAT/C/SEN/CO/4 (para 32(a)), CRC/C/SEN/CO/3–5 (paras 68 and 70) and CMW/C/SEN/CO/2–3 (para 57).

[177] See COs of CESCR dated 13 November 2019 (para 27(a)).

evolving in all environments'.[178] The economic crisis of the 1980s and the PAS imposed by the Bretton Woods institutions (World Bank and International Monetary Fund) soon turned the *daaras* into an instrument for acquiring resources,[179] and gradually created a real child 'alms market' controlled by the Quranic teachers, with the accelerated impoverishment of the population and resulting rural depopulation. The Senegalese people's propensity, 'for reasons related to their cultural beliefs and practices, to internalise almsgiving in their daily lives'[180] and the almost total control exercised by religious leaders over religious education explain, in part, the timid attitude of the Senegalese public authorities in managing this sector, which gives the impression that child protection is not really a priority in the structuring of the Senegalese social order. A review of administrative practice on the subject provides some insights.

Administrative aspects: Despite the involvement of the Office of the President of the Republic[181] and six ministries[182] in child protection activities, and the concerns raised by CESCR on 'the inadequate availability of inclusive and quality education in public schools, to the benefit of potentially expensive private schools and Franco-Arab and Qur'anic schools, which are generally free but whose current curricula do not ensure the same level of education as in public institutions',[183] inconsistencies remain in the administrative response to child begging. Private religious education, which is still strongly rooted in the country's sociological fabric, is marginalised in the education system: It still lacks a pedagogical content determined by the public authorities, is unregulated[184] and receives, on average, only 3 per cent of the annual national education budget.[185] There is even a perception of 'total

---

178   See Les nouveaux talibés-mendiants: genesis and persistence of a social pathology, Université Gaston Berger 2014–2015 19, 20.
179   According to the United Nations Office on Drugs and Crime (UNODC), the 'work' of Dakar's 30 000 beggars would have brought in more than US$10 million in 2016.
180   See Les nouveaux talibés-mendiants: genesis and persistence of a social pathology, Université Gaston Berger 2014–2015 48.
181   Through a Special Advisor on Children.
182   The Ministries of National Education, Women, the Family, Gender and Child Protection, Justice, the Interior, the Civil Service and Public Service Renewal, and Health and Social Action.
183   See COs of CESCR dated 13 November 2019 (para 41).
184   There is no legal framework organising the establishment and operation of Koranic schools and specifying the conditions for the recruitment and training of Koranic masters.
185   For example, a *marabout* that had 300 Koranic schools, employed 500 teachers and 125 service staff received only US $1 400 in state subsidies compared to US $1 100 000 for the 100 non-Islamic religious schools in the country. See Les nouveaux talibés-mendiants: genèse et persistance d'une pathologie sociale, Université Gaston Berger 2014–2015 42 fn 70. For the fiscal year 2020, it represents only 0,03% of the budget of the Ministry of National

discrimination'[186] on the part of the government towards this non-formal branch of the education system because of the striking difference between how Senegalese children enrolled in formal schools and those enrolled in *daaras* are cared for. Anti-begging services lack almost everything: quality human resources,[187] working tools and, most importantly, funding, greatly reducing their capacity to deal effectively with situations experienced in the field. There is a lack of coordination and synergy both within the administration[188] and between the programmes of the government, technical partners[189] and civil society.[190] This is so obvious at the local level[191] where the state has set up several response bodies that many actors now accept that 'there are different experiences, but not a unifying platform for all the initiatives to make them more coherent and replicate them if necessary'.[192]

Political aspects: In Senegal, political leaders have always shown a certain degree of caution on the issue of child begging, which some have equated with weakness towards the powerful religious brotherhoods that have always supported religious education through the *daaras*. President Macky Sall may well have urged his government, during cabinet meetings, 'to pursue the considerable efforts undertaken to fight against child begging, in particular through the effective implementation of the National Child Protection Strategy, the modernisation of and support for the *daaras*'[193] or even ordered the 'emergency

---

Education (see <http://www.finances.gouv.sn/wp-content/uploads/2019/11/LFI-2020.pdf> accessed 15 April 2022).

186 See Les nouveaux talibés-mendiants: genesis and persistence of a social pathology, Université Gaston Berger 2014–2015 43.

187 According to the HRW report cited above (37), in 2017, the famous WSB of the Dakar-based police had only about ten agents to manage the situation of the country's 100 000 *talibés*.

188 On this issue, see Human Right Watch report, La place de ces enfants n'est pas dans la rue: une feuille de route pour mettre fin à la maltraitance des talibés au Sénégal, December 2019. On page 77 it states that 'the widespread exploitation and abuse of *talibé* children cannot be resolved without coherent and coordinated efforts by law enforcement, justice and social services, as well as among child protection actors, both governmental and non-governmental'.

189 The main ones are the International Labour Organisation (ILO), the International Organisation for Migration (IOM), the United Nations Population Fund and UNICEF.

190 In 2015 there were 15 international and 28 national non-governmental organisations working on the issue of child begging.

191 In addition to the village level CVPEs, there are CQPEs and CCPEs at the city level and CDPEs at the administrative department level.

192 See Les nouveaux talibés-mendiants: genesis and persistence of a social pathology, Université Gaston Berger 2014–2015 72.

193 See Communiqué of the Council of Ministers of Senegal of 22 June 2016.

removal of street children' and the closure of all Quranic institutions that encourage begging, in the wake of the atrocious death of nine *talibés*, who were burned alive in the fire of their insalubrious room in Dakar in March 2013, but children remain present on the streets of many cities in the country. Recently, Quranic teachers who ransacked the courthouse of the city of Louga[194] to oppose the conviction of one of their colleagues who was found guilty of physically abusing the *talibé*, were not at all worried, let alone prosecuted, as the President of the Republic preferred to settle the case directly with the head of the powerful Mouride Brotherhood to which the offending Quranic teacher belonged. What was more ironic was the cancellation, by President Abdoulaye Wade, in the middle of a meeting of the Council of Ministers, of a measure prohibiting begging on the public highway taken by the Prime Minister of Senegal, in application of Act 2005–06 relating to trafficking in persons, on the grounds that 'almsgiving is a practice recommended by religion'.[195] These facts demonstrate religious leaders' hold on politics and explain the government's reluctance to present the draft Children's Code[196] to the Council of Ministers and the deputies to review legislation on the modernisation of *daaras*, which has been sitting in the office of Parliament since 6 June 2018.[197]

Judiciary: Despite the existence of legislation enabling parents, state prosecutors and civil society organisations to take legal action against child begging, and the formal request by CRC 'to ensure the effective enforcement of article 298 of the Penal Code which criminalises physical abuse and wilful neglect of children',[198] the Senegalese judiciary is struggling to play an important role in eradicating the phenomenon. Although the courts have started to indict and prosecute Koranic teachers, the number of cases brought before the courts seems to be very small compared to the magnitude of the problem. Between 2014 and 2015, only a dozen Koranic school teachers were prosecuted for acts of violence perpetrated against *talibés*; however, the figure, according to Human Rights Watch, rose to 25 cases between 2017 and 2018 'resulting in at

---

[194] See 'Louga: Violence during the trial of Cheikhouna Gueye et Cie les maitres coraniques se déchaent' *Le Quotidien* 5029 of 28 November 2019 3. See also *L'Enquête* 2517 of 28 November 2019, 'Mendicité, sévices corporels sur enfants: Shameful!'.
[195] 11th para of the Communiqué of the Council of Ministers of Senegal of 7 October 2010.
[196] However, on 19 June 2019 President Macky Sall had still 'instructed the government to evaluate the implementation of the national child protection strategy, to ensure the urgent adoption of the bill on the child code'.
[197] See Communiqué of the Council of Ministers of Senegal of 6 June 2018.
[198] See COs of CRC dated 7 March 2016 38(a).

least 21 prosecutions and 18 convictions during this period'.[199] There are many reasons behind this situation: (i) a tendency on the part of Senegalese authorities, both national and local, to give preference to 'mediation' rather than legal proceedings against the perpetrators of abuses against *talibés*. This reduces the capacity of the prosecuting authorities, mainly the prosecutor-general, to take a proactive stance in cases involving *talibés*; (ii) the fact that parents, if they are not accomplices of the perpetrators, refuse to lodge complaints, especially for financial and cultural reasons related to the social influence of Quranic teachers; (iii) the pressure exerted by religious leaders and Quranic teachers on the judiciary;[200] (iv) the lack of legal aid services and legal aid funds[201] dedicated specifically to children and the few existing legal aid services are based in the major cities.[202] All in all, the treatment of child begging in Senegal, in addition to exposing poor governance, sheds light on the violations of children's rights of which the state itself is guilty by discriminating against non-formal education and, worst of all, by failing to take its obligations under all the UN treaties it has ratified seriously. This is all the more so since, on the specific issue of begging, the financial resources of the state's technical partners have not been lacking.[203]

In light of all the above, one may wonder whether considering national realities is not crucial in the fight for human rights. As Professor Mireille Delmas Marty affirmed, 'acknowledging differences implies acknowledging that the perception of human rights can be shaped by history and by various political, cultural, religious, economic and social factors, and that every person achieves humanness only through the mediation of a specific culture'[204] – which seems to be the case of the Senegalese.

---

199 See HRW, 'These Children's Place is Not on the Street: A Roadmap to End Talibé Abuse in Senegal' December 2019 54.

200 See the recent ransacking of the premises of the Louga Tribunal in December 2019 to force the judges not to convict a master *coranique* accused of mistreating a *talibé*.

201 The current Legal Aid Fund, housed at the level of the National Bar Association, covers the costs of lawyers mainly in criminal cases where their presence is mandatory to assist the persons being prosecuted.

202 The main one is the AJS, which provides free legal assistance to child victims of violence.

203 UNICEF, the International Labour Office (ILO), UNODC and USAID are major contributors to state programmes to combat begging.

204 Mireille Delmas Marty, Trois défis pour un droit mondial, Éditions du Seuil 1998 26.

4.2.5 Impact of Individual Communications

Compared to the 15 or so cases heard by the Court of Justice of ECOWAS concerning Senegal,[205] only three cases were decided by the UNTBS against Senegal. The figures seem to indicate a clear preference among the Senegalese population for sub-regional jurisdiction, owing largely to its accessibility and the possibility for the Court to travel to the country concerned to hold its hearings. The views of the UN human rights bodies have had mixed fortunes in their implementation by the Senegalese authorities, as some of them helped to bring about changes in the Senegalese judicial system, especially with regard to lengthy litigation[206] and the hearing of the most serious cases of crimes[207] while others, politically sensitive, were simply ignored.

4.2.6 Impact of SPT Visit

The SPT's 2012 visit to Senegal played a distinct role in making the National Detention Centre Observatory (ONLPL) more compliant with OP-CAT requirements.

---

205 EWC/CCJ/APP/06/06, *Mrs Alice R Chukwudolue and 7 Others v Senegal*, EWC/CCJ/APP/07/08; *Mr M Hissène Habré v Senegal*, EWC/CCJ/APP/05/08; *Ocean King Ltd v Senegal*, EWC/CCJ/APP/05/08; Senegal, EWC/CCJ/APP/28/11 *El-Hadj Abdou Gaye v Senegal*, EWC/CCJ/APP/28/11; *Mr Hissène Habré v Senegal*, EWC/CCJ/APP/05/08; *Ocean King Ltd Barthelemy Toye Dias v Senegal*, EWC/CCJ/APP/22/12; *Mr Abdoulaye Balde v Senegal*, EWC/CCJ/APP/11/13; *Mr Hissène Habré v Senegal*, EWC/CCJ/APP/11/13; *Mr Hissène Habré v Senegal*, EWC/CCJ/APP/11/13; *Mr Hissène Habré v Senegal*, EWC/CCJ/APP/22/13 Mr. Hissène Habré v Senegal, EWC/CCJ/APP/22/13 *Mr Hissène Habré v Senegal*, EWC/CCJ/APP/22/14; *Mr Hissène Habré v Senegal*, EWC/CCJ/APP/22/15 Senegal, EWC/CCJ/APP/09/13; *Mr Karim Meissa Wade v Senegal*, EWC/CCJ/APP/03/12; *RADDHO v Senegal*, EWC/CCJ/APP/55/18; *Mr Karim Meissa Wade v Senegal*, EWC/CCJ/APP/32/16; *Mr Ndiaga Soumare v Senegal*, EWC/CCJ/APP/54/18; *Mr Ndiaga Soumare v Senegal*, EWC/CCJ/APP/54/18; *Mr Ndiaga Soumare v Senegal*, EWC/CCJ/APP/32/16; *Mr Ndiaga Soumare v Senegal*, EWC/CCJ/APP/54/18; *Assane Diouf and Others v Senegal*, EWC/CCJ/APP/01/18; *Mr Khalifa Ababacar Sall and Others v Senegal*, EWC/CCJ/APP/04/19; *Mr Khalifa Ababacar Sall v Senegal* and EWC/CCJ/APP/17/17 *Mr Charles Sunday v Senegal*.
206 See *Famara Koné v Senegal* CCPR/C/52/D/386/1989.
207 See *Souleymane Guengueng v State of Senegal* CAT/C/36/D/181/2001.

5 Detailed Impact of the Various United Nations Human Rights Treaties in Senegal

5.1 *Convention on the Elimination of Racial Discrimination*

CERD has been covered by some 20 periodic reports.[208] The Senegalese legislature has experimented with a model for transposing this international human rights treaty into domestic law, which was again quickly abandoned. In addition to adopting CERD's definition of racial discrimination and extending it to religious discrimination,[209] Act 81–77 of 10 December 1981 revised several other Senegalese instruments to make them compatible with the Convention, following its introduction into the Senegalese domestic legal system. These included:

- The Senegalese Criminal Code was amended to include provisions criminalising certain acts.[210]
- The Associations Act[211] was revised to allow for the dissolution of associations that in practice incite or encourage racial discrimination.[212]
- The Political Parties Act was amended to force political parties to abide by the Constitution, respect national sovereignty and democracy.[213]

Since then, the Senegalese legislature and other actors had entered into a kind of hibernation for at least 15 years before being 'awakened' by the Committee's repeated requests for the effective implementation of the Convention.[214]

The UN mechanism's insistence in the early 2000s,[215] which has been

---

208 See the latest periodic report of Senegal CERD/C/SEN/19–23 received on 21 August 2019.
209 See art 3 of Act 81–77 of 10 December 1981.
210 Acts of racial, ethnic and religious discrimination, any dissemination of ideas based on racial superiority or hatred, incitement to ethnic or religious discrimination, acts of violence directed against any person because of his or her origin or membership of an ethnic group, race or religion, with the same severity as premeditation or ambush.
211 Act 65–40 of 22 May 1965 and Act 79–02 of 4 January 1979 repealing and replacing paras 2 and 3 of art 814 of the Code of Civil and Commercial Obligations (COCC).
212 Provoking armed demonstrations in the streets, presenting the character of combat groups or private militias, undermining territorial integrity or attacking the republican form of government and disrupting the functioning of the constitutional regime by illegal means.
213 See art 2 of Act 89–36 of 12 October 1989 amending Act 81–17 of 15 May 1981 on political parties.
214 The Rencontre Africaine pour la Défense des Droits de l'Homme (RADDHO), to our knowledge, is the only Senegalese organisation to have submitted to CERD an alternative report on the application of the Convention in Senegal.
215 In its Concluding Observation dated 21 August 2002, CERD mentioned the absence in the Senegalese of 'statistics relating to the ethnic breakdown of the population and the representation of the various ethnic groups in Senegal political institutions, as well as their

reiterated since,[216] on the availability of statistical data on the exercise of human rights, especially those relating to the ethnic composition and representation of the various ethnic groups, explains the redefinition by Senegal of the legislative[217] and institutional[218] frameworks for the production of statistics with a view to adapting 'legislative instruments to the new economic realities, [and] conducting a coherent and efficient economic and social policy in accordance with its commitments to international institutions'.[219] The creation of ANSD, of which the central mission is to 'provide public administrations, regional and international institutions, businesses and non-governmental organisations, the media, researchers and the public with up-to-date statistical information relating to all areas of national life, particularly economic, social, demographic, cultural and environmental',[220] seems to be the government response to the need of data formulated by all the UN human rights mechanisms. The ANSD, which is governed by a policy council, has sectoral sub-committees[221] organised into thematic groups[222] to carry out its mission and provide public administrations with valuable information on human rights-related topics. Although the ANSD has not yet produced detailed data on the implementation of all UN treaties, it has already carried out numerous studies and surveys on the economic and social situation in the country.[223] With the support of some

---

participation in public bodies entrusted with ensuring respect for human rights'. See COs dated 21 August 2002 para 441 A/57/18/(SUPP) paras 435–450.

[216] See the COs of CERD dated 24 October 2012 para 10, where it recommended to Senegal to 'collect and publish reliable and comprehensive statistical data on the ethnic composition of its population, including immigrants, as well as socio-economic indicators disaggregated by ethnic origin'.

[217] Act 2004–21 of 21 July 2004 on the organisation of statistical services.

[218] Decree 2005–2249 of 17 March 2005 on the National Statistics and Demography Agency (ANSD) of Senegal.

[219] See para 1 of the report on the presentation of Decree 2005–2249 of 17 March 2005.

[220] ibid.

[221] These include the Sub-Committees on Gender Equity, Culture, Education and Training, Labour and Professional Organisations, Health, Environment and Natural Resources, Family and National Solidarity, Justice (see art 2 of Ministerial Order 07245/MEF/ANSD of 28 July 2009 creating and establishing the rules for the organisation and functioning of the Sub-Committees).

[222] All thematic groups have a link with human rights as defined by UN treaties (see art 3 of Ministerial Order 07245/MEF/ANSD of 28 July 2009 creating and setting the rules for the organisation and functioning of the sub-committees).

[223] See the list of studies and surveys on the ANSD website http://www.ansd.sn/ Examples include surveys on child labour, civil registration in Senegal, gender-based violence, poverty and family structures, 'à l'écoute du Sénégal', and so forth.

international organisations,[224] it has set up open data platforms to monitor, in a harmonised manner, the indicators for the achievement of the UN Sustainable Development Goals in Senegal.[225] In addition, two national policy documents were produced between 2008 and 2019, namely, the Statistics Master Plan (SDS) and the National Statistics Development Strategy (SNDS). The ANSD is also working to integrate an ethnic dimension into its field surveys.[226]

Issues relating to the government's failure to bring racial discrimination cases before Senegalese courts[227] and the lack of awareness-raising activities on the Convention in Senegal[228] undoubtedly have a bearing on the establishment, by the state, of a local justice system of which the main mission is to improve access to justice, in particular by providing legal information and encouraging civil society to do the same. However, the sensitivity of discrimination issues, the financial situation of victims and their families, the lack of a legal aid fund specifically reserved for victims of racial discrimination and the preference of state authorities for 'mediation' rather than prosecution of potential perpetrators limit the impact of the judicial approach. Cases with a motive on issues of racial discrimination, including caste issues, still exist[229] but they are very often not classified as such because they end up in court for other reasons. For example, the court in *Tambacounda* tried several caste-related cases but under the heading of assault and battery on others.[230]

The same attitude was adopted by Senegal to the Committee's proposals for solutions to the Casamance crisis. In its COs dated October 2012, CERD recommended, as a way of ending the violence in the southern part of the

---

224 Notably the United Nations family of agencies (UN-Women, UNICEF, UNFPA, UNDP, UNESCO and the Office of the OHCHR), USAID and GIZ.
225 See the report of the International Conference on Sustainable Development Goals: What Agenda for Senegal? *Le Soleil* 28 October 2016 15–18.
226 This was the case in the 4th General Population Census (see Census Objectives on 24 of the Final Report of the EARPGN 2013), the Socio-demographic Characteristics of Persons with Disabilities study and the Report on Gender Analysis of Existing Databases.
227 See the COs of CERD dated 21 August 2002 para 442.
228 See the COs of CERD dated 24 October 2012 para 11.
229 See Tribunal de Grande Instance (TGI) de Tambacounda, Jugement No 66/2020 du 12 février 2020, *Ministère public et Association GAMBANÉ contre Bakary CAMARA* on insults to persons by electronic means on the grounds of their affiliation to groups distinguished by their descent, national and ethnic origin.
230 See TGI de Tambacounda, Jugement No 51/2020 du 13 novembre 2020, *Ministère public et Bakary BATHILY contre Abdou Karim DIAKITE et Oumar DOUCARA* for assault and injury causing temporary incapacity to work (TIW) and TGI de Tambacounda, Jugement No 02/2021 du 8 janvier 2021, *Ministère public contre Mamadou FOFANA, Moussa FOFANA, Mamadou KANOUTE dit Dora, Mamadou Mohamed WASSA et Arona GAKOU* concerning violence and physical assault with TIW.

country, a dialogue between the government and the *Mouvement des Forces Democratiques de Casamance* (MFDC) accompanied by a programme of reparation and compensation for victims of the conflict in Casamance, 'so as to create a climate of trust that will make possible a peaceful and lasting solution to the conflict'. More importantly, CERD invited the Senegalese government to also 'implement the planned measures for boosting economic development and opening up Casamance as soon as possible and to ensure the active participation of the people who will benefit from this by consulting them and involving them in decisions that affect their rights and interests'.[231] This explains why, in addition to the Peace Agreement signed on 30 December 2004 between the government and the Secretary-General of the MFDC, the adoption of a special law granting special tax status to tourist businesses established in the region[232] and numerous socio-economic projects,[233] the government included new actions to prevent racial discrimination in the public sphere. These include the reception and commissioning, in December 2014, by the National Assembly, of a simultaneous translation system enabling members of parliament to express themselves in national languages, and the creation of a National Broadcasting Regulatory Council (CNRA) of which the mandate is to 'ensure preservation of cultural identities'[234] and 'respect for national unity, territorial integrity and the secular nature of the Republic in the content of audiovisual messages'.[235]

Despite the insistence of CERD for a follow-up to the Durban Declaration and Programme of Action by the Senegalese government, it also seems that the elaboration and implementation of a National Action Plan in accordance with such Declaration is not on the agenda in a country that nevertheless organised the African regional preparatory meeting for the 2001 Durban Conference against Racism, Racial Discrimination, Xenophobia and Related Intolerance. The local NGOs' lack of interest in the subject and the deep silence observed by society as a whole on major discrimination issues such as the caste issue account for such a situation.

---

[231] See the COs of CERD dated 24 October 2012 para 12.

[232] The government justifies the adoption of this law by 'a strong awareness ... that uniform treatment, in the name of a principle of absolute egalitarianism, of parts of the territory that are objectively in differentiated situations could lead to economic and social deadlock or even generate inequities'. See the text of the agreement in <http://theirwords.org/media/transfer/doc/sn_mfdc_2004_01-d339554f0f2d97c081cf738cf842d1a4.pdf> accessed 1 September 2023.

[233] Such as the Casamance Development Support Programme, the Casamance Development Pole Project, the Lower Casamance Livestock Development Project and the Support Project for the Promotion of Youth Employment in Casamance.

[234] See s 7(2) of the Act.

[235] See s 9(2) of the Act.

5.2   *International Covenant on Civil and Political Rights*

Senegal's inconsistent submission of its periodic reports,[236] especially between 1997 and 2019, makes it difficult to properly measure the impact of the HRCttee's recommendations. Nevertheless, it can be said that in recent years the Senegalese authorities have shown an increasingly resolute zero tolerance attitude towards the security forces on the issue of torture and inhuman and degrading treatment, and a more effective handling of the issue of violence against women and the treatment of prisoners. However, on the issue of equality between men and women, non-discrimination or the primacy of the Covenant over national laws, the authorities still allow 'a cultural, social or legal system that more or less tolerates violations'[237] of the rights protected by CCPR.

5.2.1   Torture

Faced with the numerous accusations brought against its security forces, especially during military operations against the Casamance rebellion, the Senegalese authorities multiplied their initiatives to show national and international public opinion that torture was no longer tolerated[238] in the country. Some of the important measures taken include the following:

The concerns expressed by the HRCttee in its COs dated 19 November 1997 at recurring problems of overcrowding and poor health and sanitary conditions in many prisons[239] led to the ratification of OP-CAT, on 18 October 2006, which main objective is to establish a system of regular visits undertaken by independent international and national bodies to places where people are deprived of their liberty, in order to prevent torture and other cruel, inhuman or degrading treatment or punishment. The establishment of the ONLPL (Act 2009-13 of 2 March 2009) contributed to the improvement of the prisons conditions and the prevention of acts of torture, especially in police custody. Since its establishment in December 2012, the ONLPL has increased the number

---

236 Between 1997 and 2019 there were only two reports submitted compared to three in the period 1987 and 1997. See <https://onlpl.sn/formation-des-agents-dexecution-des-lois/> accessed 11 September 2023.
237 See Ministry of Women, Family and Children, National Action Plan to Combat Gender-based Violence and Promote Human Rights in Senegal, October 2015 22.
238 In 2004 an amnesty law was passed, justified by the fact that the policy applied by President Abdoulaye Wade 'must be reinforced by forgiving and forgetting acts that deserve to be put on the shelf of sad memories' (Explanatory memorandum to Act 2004-20 of 6 July 2004).
239 See COs of HRCttee, 19 November 1997 para 15.

of initiatives that have contributed to the effective implementation of the HRCttee's recommendations on the prevention of torture:
- the training of law enforcement officers and students (police officers, gendarmes, prison officers, customs officers and water and forest officers) as suggested by the COs of the HRCttee dated 19 November 1997 (paragraph 11) to instill in them a culture of non-violence;[240]
- visits to detention facilities[241] to monitor law enforcement officers' compliance with their obligations *vis-à-vis* persons under arrest;
- awareness-raising activities for administrative authorities and civil society organisations in seven regions and six departments; and
- the organisation of awareness-raising programmes on torture with 13 community radio stations.

The concerns expressed by the HRCttee in its COs dated 19 November 1997 about the lack of access to counsel by detainees in police stations[242] led to the revision of the Code of Criminal Procedures (article 55 of Act 2016–30 of 8 November 2016 on the presence of a lawyer during custody and article 669 of Act 2007–05 of 12 February 2007 on the implementation of the Treaty of Rome establishing the International Criminal Court). A Circular 00179/MJ/DACG/MN of 11 January 2018 specifying arrangements for the implementation of article 5 of Regulation 05/CM/UEMOA on legal assistance upon arrest[243] was released by the Ministry of Justice.

The number of decisions taken by the justice system shows that it now stands as guarantor of the strict enforcement of the relevant provisions of the Covenant and other treaties relating to torture against members of the security services found guilty of acts of torture or inhuman or degrading treatment.[244] The severity of the judges is sometimes thwarted by the state, especially when, during the settlement of the Casamance crisis, the state decided to grant amnesty to the perpetrators of acts of torture committed in that part of the country on the grounds that the search for peace 'must be strengthened by forgiving and forgetting acts that should be relegated to the chapter of sad memories'.[245] However, the severity of judicial decisions has greatly changed

---

240 In 2017–2018, 883 student officers and 422 enforcement officers were trained.
241 ibid.
242 See COs of HRCttee, 19 November 1997 para 14.
243 ibid.
244 See Court of Appeal of Thiès, Criminal Division, Ruling 1 of 23 May 2017 Public Prosecutor's Office and *Abdou Samb v Almamy Lawaly Toure, Thiendella Ndiaye, Mame Cor Ndong and Ousmane Ndao*.
245 See the Explanatory Memorandum to Act 2004–20 of 6 July 2004 on the Amnesty Act.

the behaviour of security service officers *vis-à-vis* citizens in police stations or gendarmerie brigades.

Moreover, the concerns about the 'passiveness of the government in conducting timely investigation of reported cases of ill-treatment of detainees, of torture and of extra-judicial executions'[246] forced the state to make available to citizens new procedures for the protection of their fundamental rights.[247] With regard to administrative matters, an expedited procedure, known as summary administrative proceedings, has been introduced to allow the judge to issue rulings within a short period of time whenever warranted by the nature of the case referred to them. For example, when an administrative decision is subject to annulment proceedings, the court may order that its execution be suspended, or that some of its effects be interrupted, 'where warranted by the urgency of the situation and where there is evidence that, during the investigation, there is a serious doubt as to the lawfulness of the decision'.[248] In such cases the term 'temporary suspension order' is used.

It may also 'order any measures necessary to safeguard a fundamental freedom which a legal person governed by public law or a private law body entrusted with the management of a public service has, in the exercise of one of its functions, seriously and manifestly unlawfully[249] interfered with'. The judge in chambers should then review a freedom summary procedure and rule on the matter within 48 hours. Another example is the administrative referral case, which is initiated by the chief justice of the Supreme Court when a local authority's act referred to them is likely to jeopardise the exercise of a public or individual freedom. In such cases, the chief justice of the Supreme Court may order the suspension of the referral within 48 hours of the Supreme Court being seized of the matter.

There are also cases of administrative proceedings[250] initiated by the chief justice of the Supreme Court when the act of a local authority referred to them is likely to jeopardise the exercise of a public or individual freedom.[251] In such cases, the chief justice may suspend the administrative proceedings within 48 hours of referral to the Supreme Court. Exemption from the requirement of a deposit in the Supreme Court for persons filing family rights lawsuits can also be mentioned.[252] Lastly, the procedure known as the exception

---

246   See the COs of HRCttee dated 18 December 1992 para 5.
247   See Organic Act 2017–09 of 17 January 2017 on the Supreme Court.
248   Art 84 of Organic Act 2017–09 of 17 January 2017 on the Supreme Court.
249   ibid art 85.
250   ibid.
251   ibid art 80.
252   ibid para 2 of art 34.

of unconstitutionality, which may be initiated by a court of appeal or the Supreme Court 'when the solution of a dispute is subject to an assessment of the consistency of the provisions of a law or the stipulations of an international agreement with the Constitution'.[253] In such cases the petitioning court shall defer ruling on the dispute until the Constitutional Council has ruled on the matter.

5.2.2 Prisons

The state of Senegal has addressed, with very mixed results, the issue of lengthy pre-trial detention, alternatives to imprisonment and the renovation of Senegalese prisons.[254]

- The Criminal Code[255] and the Code of Criminal Procedures[256] have been revised respectively to introduce new sanctions and alternatives to imprisonment[257] and to introduce, in the Senegalese judiciary, a judge responsible for enforcing sentences and two new bodies specifically responsible for dealing with issues relating to the adjustment of sentences.[258]
- The concept of 'community service'[259] has been introduced into the Criminal Code as a substitute for a prison sentence of up to six months to enable a convicted person to perform 30 to 300 hours of work for a public law legal person or a public utility organisation.[260]
- The prison computer system has been upgraded to facilitate the decongestion and renovation of prisons.
- To address prison overcrowding, a new 1 500-place detention centre was built in Sebikotane to relieve congestion in Dakar, and some measures were taken to build six new departmental remand prisons with 500 places each, and the remand prisons in Thiès, Foundiougne, Fatick and Koutal were renovated to either create units for minors and women or to increase the prison's capacity.

---

253 Art 22 of Organic Act 2016–23 of 14 July 2016 on the Constitutional Council.
254 See COs of HRCttee, 19 November 1997 para 15.
255 Act 2000–38 of 29 December 2000 on methods of mitigating punishment (paras 1 to 8 of art 44).
256 Act 2000–39 of 29 December 2000.
257 According to the explanatory memorandum to Act 200–38 of 29 December 2000, the reform 'is in line with the International Covenant on Civil and Political Rights'.
258 These include day parole (ss 693(2) and (3)), parole (ss 699–703), work release (s 693(1)) and temporary absences (s 693(8)).
259 Para 3 of art 44 amended.
260 Act 2016–29 of 8 November 2016 amending the Criminal Code.

- Numerous measures have also been taken to improve the living conditions of detainees: Libraries, telephone booths, televisions and fans have been installed in several prisons, a medical-social centre and a dental surgery have been built to relieve congestion in the special wing of the Aristide Le Dantec Hospital and to provide care to detainees in the Dakar region.

As a result of these improvements, between 2013 and 2018 the amount of the allowance per prisoner and per day has increased from CFAF 600 to CFAF 1 023 and the juvenile penal population has decreased from 4,1 per cent to 1,8 per cent. The only major problem continues to be the occupancy rate in Senegalese prisons, which averaged 230 per cent during the period covered by this report.[261] With the increased number of prisons, the government is considering the adoption of an order setting out the standards for accommodation in prisons and the ratio of supervisors per prisoner.

5.2.3 Women

In dealing with the HRCttee's concern about the 'continued existence' of laws and customs, in particular those affecting equality between men and women, which impede the full observance of CCPR,[262] Senegal undertook to reduce inequalities in the participation of women in political life and institutional governance. In addition to the clear provisions of the Constitution on equality between men and women, the country adopted a law establishing absolute parity between men and women[263] in elected and semi-elected positions[264] and an observatory[265] responsible for 'the implementation, follow-up, monitoring and evaluation of protection and security measures to prevent and combat inequalities between men and women at all levels of life in society'.[266] Bodies hitherto inaccessible to females are beginning to open up to them,[267]

---

261 See Department of Justice 2018 Annual Review 51.
262 See COs of HRCttee, 19 November 1997 para 4.
263 See arts 7, 18, 19 and 22.
264 See Act 2010–11 of 28 May 2010, which in its Explanatory Memorandum makes a clear reference to CEDAW and Decree 2011–819 of 16 June 2011 implementing the Act establishing the absolute male-female component at the level of all fully or partially elective institutions. Subsequently, Act 2012–01 of 5 January 2012 repealing and replacing the Act on the Electoral Code (amended legislative part) was adopted to harmonise it with that of 2010.
265 See Decree 2011–309 of 7 March 2011 revised by Decree 2013–279 of 14 February 2013 establishing, organising and operating the National Gender Observatory (ONP).
266 See para 2 of art 3 of Decree 20122–309 of 7 March 2011.
267 These are the territorial administration, the police, the *gendarmerie*, the army, customs and water and forestry.

and administrative measures have been taken to remedy the gender gap in the civil service. Women's representation in elected institutions and the republican security forces has improved significantly (42 per cent in Parliament; 47 per cent in local authorities (municipalities and departmental councils); 22 per cent in the police;[268] 11 per cent in the armed forces and the gendarmerie) but remains relatively low in the rest of government (23,4 per cent in the civil service; 23 per cent in the diplomatic service; 17 per cent in the judiciary; and only 1,58 per cent in territorial government).[269]

The implementation of the Gender Parity Law was severely tested during the 2014 local elections. First, there was the refusal of the ruling coalition, Benno Bokk Yakaar, to apply total parity on the electoral lists in the commune of Touba-Mosquée – a holy city built on the values of Islam. Second, there was a different interpretation of the law by Senegalese courts, which required the supreme judge to step in and set the record straight. In the first case, the Independent National Electoral Commission (CENA), to save face following this religious insubordination, had to step in and grant a special status to the holy city to organise the ballot in that part of the country,[270] before recommending to the public authorities, once the ballot was over, to revise the law in order to take into consideration the 'sociological dimension'[271] of the realities of Senegal.

In the other case, resistance to parity, observed in the Ministry of the Interior[272] and the judiciary, especially at the Kaolack Court of Appeal, was resolved by the Supreme Court's clarification of the spirit and letter of the 2010 Act. While the General Local Government Code was clear on gender parity in the offices of these elected bodies,[273] the Kaolack Court of Appeal, hearing a legal action for an annulment of the election of members of the City Council Bureau, rejected the request on the grounds that the free and individual nature of a mayoral candidacy did not allow for the application of the

---

268 These figures are contained in the WISAT report, National Evaluation of Gender Equality and the Knowledge Society in Senegal, May 2017 40–42.
269 See in this connection the 8th periodic report submitted by Senegal under art 18 of the Convention, CEDAW/C/SEN/8 8, 20.
270 See on this issue <www.pambazuka.org/fr/gouvernance/senegal-liste-non-paritaire-de-touba-mosquee-pour-les-elections-locales-indignez-vous> accessed 14 April 2021.
271 See ANEC, The Report on the Departmental and Municipal Elections of June 29, 2014, 23.
272 In instructions addressed to the territorial administration officials responsible for supervising the installation of the newly-elected teams, the Minister of the Interior had clearly implied that 'the law does not impose respect for gender parity in the composition of the offices' (see Circular 004547/MINT.SP./DGAT/SP of 10 July 2014, para 4.1).
273 See arts 31 and 92 of the General Code for Local Authorities.

Parity Act, which 'did not provide for the practicalities of respecting parity in elections with individual candidates, such as mayor or deputy mayor elections'.[274] On the other hand, the Dakar Court of Appeal, dealing with the same subject, noted that 'Article 1 of Act No. 2010-11 of May 28, 2010 establishing absolute gender parity in all fully or partially elective institutions and Article 2 of Decree No. 2011-819 of June 16, 2011 implementing the said Act, require the election, within the Municipal Council, of a board composed of persons of both sexes alternately'.[275]

It took two 'historic'[276] Supreme Court[277] decisions, one overturning the decision of the Kaolack Court of Appeal and the other upholding that of the Dakar Court of Appeal, to make it clear that

- the 2010 Act was designed to 'correct women's under-representation in politics';
- the Municipal Council, its board and commissions are part of fully or partially elective institutions;
- the spirit of the Act, which entails promoting the equal access of men and women to electoral mandates and elective functions in order to correct women's under-representation in political bodies, must always be the guiding light for judges, whenever they are called upon to interpret their relevant provisions.

Following these two decisions, the election of the members of the board of the Keur Massar Municipal Council was re-run, while in Kaolack the complainants were disqualified from the municipal team, which had close ties with the ruling party and was tacitly complicit with the authorities who took no action to implement the Supreme Court's decision. This confirms, once again, that the state of Senegal is not yet prepared to implement its obligations under the Convention by confronting the powerful Muslim brotherhoods head-on, even if it means alienating the support of human rights organisations.

---

[274] See Kaolack Court of Appeal, Judgment 14/14 of 25 July 2014 *Case Mbenda Ndiaye and Others v Kaolack City Council Office*.

[275] See Dakar Court of Appeal, Ruling 77 of 21 August 2014, *Case Amadou Barry, Municipal Councillor of the Municipality of Keur Massar v the Office of the Municipal Council of Keur Massar*.

[276] See Observatoire national de la Parité (ONP), 'La parité à l'épreuve des élections départementales et municipales du 29 juin 2014: enseignements tirés des recours devant les juridictions compétentes' July 2015 15.

[277] See Supreme Court of Senegal, Administrative Chamber Judgment 2 of 8 January 2015, *Case Ms Mbenda Ndiaye and Others v Office of the Municipal Council of Kaolack* and Judgment 17 of 26 February 2015, *Case Amadou Barry, Municipal Councillor of the Municipality of Keur Massar v Office of the Municipal Council of Keur Massar*.

5.2.4 Impact of Views on Communications

The HCttee found Senegal in violation of CCPR in three cases: *Famara Koné v Senegal* (CCPR/C/52/D/386/1989); and *Karim Meissa Wade v Senegal* (CCPR/C/124/D/2783/2016). The views of the UN human rights bodies have had mixed fortunes in their implementation by the Senegalese authorities, as some of them helped to bring about changes in the Senegalese judicial system, especially with regard to lengthy litigation[278] and the hearing of the most serious cases of crimes[279] while others, politically sensitive, were simply ignored.

When the CSDH met, at a formal request of the President of the Republic in 1997, to discuss the implementation of the views of the HRCttee on the *Famara Kone* case, a number of solutions were proposed not only to give a fair compensation to the victim but also to deal with the delays in trials and to give the possibility, under Senegalese law, to victims of such human rights violations, the right to seek a remedy. It took a few years to implement the proposals of the CSDH, partly because Famara Kone was not satisfied with the compensation proposed. After a few additional negotiations, the victim accepted a piece of land, a sum of 4 million CFA to build his house, and permanent medical support, as he was suffering from mental health problems.

Regarding legal reforms requested by the HRCttee, the CSDH recommended that the President have the Code of Criminal Procedure revised to make it impossible for people to be held in prolonged pre-trial detention and establish a compensation mechanism for victims of long and arbitrary detention. The new laws were passed and enforced in 2008 and 2016 to align Senegalese legislation with CCPR. Today a Compensation Commission for victims of lengthy pre-trial detention[280] exists at the Supreme Court and individuals are granted fair compensation by the state for mistakes made by Senegalese courts in relation to their detention. So far it has made a few interesting decisions regarding long and unlawful detention in Senegalese prisons.[281] The Code of Criminal Procedure was reviewed in 2016 to, among other issues, 'combat prison overcrowding and prolonged detention'[282] as denounced in the case. The OP-CAT

---

278   See *Famara Koné v Senegal* CCPR/C/52/D/386/1989.

279   See *Souleymane Guengueng v Senegal* CAT/C/36/D/181/2001.

280   See art 4 of Organic Act 2008–35 of 8 August 2008 on the Supreme Court and arts 107 to 110 of Organic Act 2017–09 of 17 January 2017 on the Supreme Court.

281   See Compensation Commission: Cases 002/CS/CI/2018 *Mamadou Ndiaye dit Tyson*, 003/CS/CI/2018 *Serigne Cheikh Mbaye*, 005/CS/CI/2018 *Fatou Keita* and 006/CS/CI/2018 *Assane Danso*.

282   See the explanatory memorandum to Act 2016–30 of 8 November 2016 amending Act 65–61 of 21 July 1965 on the Code of Criminal Procedure in the Official Gazette (JO) of Senegal 6976 of 26 November 2016.

was ratified to allow the creation of a national mechanism to monitor the conditions in which people are detained or transferred in order to ensure compliance with their human rights and prevent torture,[283] and its principal officer submits an annual report on the situation in Senegalese prisons.[284]

In a more politicised case, that of *Karim Meissa Wade*, the request of the HRCttee to Senegal to review the conviction and sentencing of a former Senegalese minister who was accused of corruption and mismanagement of public resources[285] was rejected by the Senegalese authorities on the basis that it was in contradiction with a ruling of the ECOWAS Court of Justice[286] on the same subject and that 'the Head of State cannot review a trial and ... cannot make a citizen pay compensation either'.[287]

The implementation of the views of the HRCttee in the *Karim Wade* case was raised during the review of Senegal's periodic report by the HRCttee in October 2019. Answering a question from a member of the Committee regarding the implementation of its views, the Human Rights Director replied: 'Senegal is not refusing to pay compensation, but requests the person concerned to come forward so that the judges in charge could determine the extent of the prejudice. We are ready. If the person concerned refers the matter to the competent courts to seek redress, there is no obstacle to the State of Senegal granting such redress.'[288]

The official's statements, which were perceived as an acknowledgment of the Senegalese government's responsibility in that politically-charged affair,[289] were quickly refuted by the country's senior authorities who, a few days later, dismissed the Human Rights Director from his position. President Macky

---

283   See Act 2009–13 of 2 March 2009 establishing the National Observatory of Places of Deprivation of Liberty.

284   In 2013, for example, he had proposed reforms of the CP and the CPP to put an end to the practice of returning prosecutors, limiting the warrant of committal in criminal cases to a maximum of three years, returning to the correction of drug-related offences and amending art 44(2) of the CP so as not to absolutely restrict judges' freedom of appreciation by means of textual limits.

285   Case of *Karim Meissa Wade v Senegal* CCPR/C/124/D/2783/2016, para 14.

286   See the interview with Mr Mbaye Babacar Diop, Director of Human Rights at the Ministry of Justice in *Le Quotidien* appreciation by means of textual limits. Case of *Karim Meissa Wade v Senegal* CCPR/C/124/D/2783/2016, para 14. See the interview with Mr Mbaye Babacar Diop, Director of Human Rights at the Ministry of Justice in *Le Quotidien* 5032 dated 2 December 2019 7.

287   See Abdou Latif Coulibaly, 'Surrealist debate on the revision of a trial' *Dakar News* 20 October 2019.

288   CCPR/C/SR.3649, para 19.

289   On file with author.

Sall's spokesperson, who justified the ministerial decision[290] to remove him from office, nevertheless recognised that there was an urgent need 'to initiate (national) procedures, especially in matters of criminal law and criminal procedure, in order to align them with the international standards on the basis of which Karim Wade's trial was appraised on the international scene. It was no longer enough to abide by our domestic law; it was necessary to adapt and align it with these standards.'[291]

5.2.5 Other Impact

The concern related to the fact that foreign workers were barred from holding official position in local trade unions was directly addressed by article L 9 of the Labour Code, which was adopted a few weeks after Senegal's appearance before the Committee,[292] and by article 12 of the 2001 Constitution. Similarly, recommendations on ethnic minorities were effectively addressed by the 2001 Constitution[293] and the numerous agreements on the crisis in Casamance. Keeping the public informed of the Committee's meetings and findings is still the Achilles heel of the Senegalese authorities. This task which, in principle, is the responsibility of the Human Rights Directorate and the National Advisory Council on Human Rights, has not been properly carried out by the state's bodies. Professor Ismaïla Madior Fall, a former Minister of Justice, had made it a habit, after each round of talks with UN mechanisms, to organise a meeting with the media[294] to brief them on the positions defended by Senegal before these bodies. His successor did not deem it useful to maintain these meetings, which forced citizens to rely on the Senegalese media, especially newspapers, which were now beginning to cover committee sessions on a regular basis, especially when covering current events, as was the case in 2019 with the *Karim Wade* case.[295]

---

290 ibid.
291 ibid.
292 Act 97–77 of 1 December 1997, arts 7 and 29.
293 In particular by the second paragraph of art 1, art 5, art 8 and art 24.
294 See 'Senegal refuses 35 UN directives' *Sud Quotidien* 27 November 2018.
295 See *Le Quotidien* 4995 18 October 2019 '*Affaire Karim Wade au Comité des droits de l'homme:* Cacophonie au Sommet de l'Etat'; *Sud Quotidien* 7926 19–20 October 2019 "Engagement de "rehabilitation"" *de Karim Wade devant les ... Nations Unies: Ba on the tightrope!* ' 1; *L'Observateur* 4814 18 Octobre 2019 '*Passage du Sénégal devant le Comité des droits humains de l'ONU: K de mini crise au sommet de l'État* ' 1; and *Le Soleil* 14816 18 October 2019 '*Supposée réhabilitation de Karim Wade et réparation d'un préjudice qu'il aurait subi: L'État dément*', 1.

5.3 International Covenant on Economic, Social and Cultural Rights

Despite its limited interaction with the state of Senegal over the past 20 years,[296] the CESCR Cttee has been able to identify key areas where the authorities need to make considerable efforts in order to fulfill their treaty obligations.

5.3.1 Non-discrimination

This component has been of great interest of CESCR to the Senegalese authorities over the past 20 years because of the scale of discrimination against women in the country. Unfortunately, legal, political, economic and institutional efforts have yet to achieve the critical mass needed to reverse the trend in favour of women:

- at the legal level, efforts focused on women's fiscal autonomy,[297] the suppression of discriminatory provisions to enable women civil servants,[298] administrative contract[299] workers or employees[300] to take care of their husbands and children, especially in medical care, the reduction of gender inequalities in agricultural activities[301] and the opening-up of certain professional trades to women,[302] the guarantee of the right to education for pregnant girls[303] and the equal participation of women and men in politics;[304]

---

[296] Only three reports were submitted by the Senegalese government in 1978 and 2019.

[297] See Act 2008–01 of 8 January 2008 amending arts 379 and 380 of the General Tax Code.

[298] See Decree 2006–1309 of 23 November 2006 repealing and replacing art 1 of Decree 72–215 of 7 March 1972 on social security for civil servants.

[299] See Decree 2006–1310 of 23 November 2006 repealing and replacing arts 32 and 33 of Decree 74–347 of 12 April 1974 on the special regime applicable to non-state employees.

[300] See Decree 2006–1310 of 23 November 2006 repealing and replacing arts 1 and 8 of Decree 75–895 of 14 August 1975 on the organisation of company or inter-company health insurance institutions and making the establishment of such institutions compulsory.

[301] See Ministerial Circular 0989 of 5 June 2018.

[302] See Decrees 2003–696 of 23 September 2003 on discipline in the National Army, 2006–515 of 9 June 2006 on the exceptional and transitional recruitment of female personnel in the *gendarmerie* and 2007–1244 of 19 October 2007 on the recruitment of female personnel in the armed forces, 2008–1012 of 18 August 2008 on the special status of *gendarmerie* personnel, 2009–490 of 28 May 2009 setting the terms of application of Act 2009–18 of 9 March 2009 on the status of national police personnel, 2013–1367 of 21 October 2013 on the Regulations of General Discipline in the Armed Forces.

[303] See Circular 004379 of 11 October 2007 from the Minister of National Education authorising pregnant girls to continue their studies.

[304] See Decree 2011–819 of 6 June 2011 implementing the Act establishing absolute parity between men and women in elective assemblies.

- at the political level, strategies have been developed to include gender equality and the autonomy of women and girls in national development plans;[305]
- at the economic level, programmes,[306] projects[307] and funds have been set up[308] to address the concerns of women living in poverty and to promote positive discrimination in favor of women, especially rural women;
- at the institutional level, the establishment, at the Ministry of Justice, of a committee to review laws and regulations discriminating against women[309] and of a Delegation-General for the Rapid Entrepreneurship of Young People and Women.

More specifically, with regard to women's access to land and security of tenure, discrimination persists despite the enshrinement of the principle of equal access to land, due to social, political and cultural constraints, including difficulties in accessing financing mechanisms, production factors, agricultural extension services and, more importantly, the effects of climate change, which is drastically reducing the amount of arable land. Observing that between 2014 and 2017, women's access to land only increased from 13,8 to 28,8 per cent,[310] the government in 2018 decided to expedite this process by applying a quota policy.[311]

---

305 These are mainly the National Strategy for Economic and Social Development (SNDES), the SNEEG, the National Strategy for the Economic Empowerment of Women (SNAEF) and the Digital Senegal Strategy (2016–2025).
306 See the programmes for social protection, support for the development of entrepreneurship among women and young people (PADEFJ), strengthening of economic and social dynamics (PRODES).
307 See Projet d'appui à la promotion de l'emploi des jeunes et des femmes (PAPEFJ).
308 See the National Fund for the Promotion of Women's Entrepreneurship (FNPEF), the National Credit Fund for Women (FNCF), the Economic and Social Development Support Programme (PADES) and the Programme for Literacy and Apprenticeship for Poverty Alleviation (PALAM).
309 See Order 00936 of 27 January 2016. It clearly states that the mission of this committee is to study and propose the revision and harmonisation of national laws and regulations with the international conventions ratified by Senegal.
310 See Senegal's National Report on the Implementation of the Beijing+25 Declaration and Platform for Action, June 2019, 25.
311 See Ministerial Circular 0989 of 5 June 2018 of the Minister of Agriculture and Rural Equipment on the reduction of gender inequalities in agricultural activities. These include allocating at least 15% of the developments to be carried out, 20% of subsidised fertilisers, 20% of certified rice and groundnut seeds, at least 10% of subsidised tractors, 40% of agricultural financing, 20% of agricultural research projects and 20% of representation in agricultural decision-making bodies to women.

5.3.2 Protection of Families

This is an area where the Senegalese administration has progressed 'at a snail's pace' due to social and religious constraints. Calls for amendments to the Family Code[312] relating to paternal authority (article 152), the minimum marriage age for girls (article 111), the selection of the household's residence (article 153), the prohibition of paternity testing (article 196), as well as the issue of medical abortion and the nagging issue of child begging, have not yet been met, and there are indications that they will not be in the immediate future, unless the Instruments Review Committee decides to take up these requests.

5.3.3 Right to Health Care

Fulfilling economic and social rights in a poor country such as Senegal can be extremely difficult, especially when the resources essential for the enjoyment of such rights are lacking. This is the case, in particular, for the right to health care, with respect to which the Senegalese authorities were asked, in 2001, to remedy the lack of hospitals and health facilities by distributing these equitably throughout the national territory and encouraging medical personnel to work elsewhere than in the major cities in the western part of the country. Guided by the Constitution, which imposed 'the duty to take responsibility for the physical and moral health of the family' and the obligation to 'guarantee to those living in rural areas,[313] in particular, access to healthcare services and well-being', the government established a national health policy.[314] Under this policy, in principle, 'all individuals, all households and all communities have universal access to quality promotional, preventive and curative health services without any form of exclusion'.[315]

An increase in the annual health budget,[316] the introduction of a self-financing system for health facilities, the implementation of an emergency

---

312 See COs of CESCR, 24 September 2001 para 15.
313 See art 17 of the Constitution of Senegal.
314 Taken from the Integrated Health Development Programme (PDIS (1998–2002)) and the National Health Development Plan (PNDS (2009–2018)).
315 See ANSD, Situation économique et sociale du Sénégal en 2016, Chapter V Santé, February 2019, 106. This health policy was articulated around the following points: access to quality health care guaranteed to the entire population; deepening decentralisation and local health governance; promotion of health insurance coverage; protection of vulnerable groups; strengthening the public-private partnership; alignment of external assistance with national health priorities; and the culture of results-based management.
316 Between 2012 and 2017 the health budget increased from $220 million to nearly $340 million, an increase of nearly 49%. It still constitutes only 8% of the national budget, far from the 15% recommended by the World Health Organisation (WHO).

plan for the modernisation[317] of border road networks[318] and the state's efforts to ensure that certain social categories[319] have equal access to health services have, unfortunately, failed to significantly reduce the gap between rural and urban areas.

Although between 2011 and 2015 new medical infrastructures were built up inside the country,[320] major heavy equipment was acquired by the government[321] and mobile health services were set up, especially in hard-to-reach areas. However, due to the lack of an effective mechanism for forward-looking management of jobs and skills in the sector, the low contribution of local and regional authorities to health financing because of limited resources, a decrease in the state's financial partners' contribution to health financing,[322] the high level of household contributions to health expenditure[323] and the huge disparities in the availability of certain basic commodities required for the installation of health facilities,[324] the government is finding it difficult to honour its obligations under the Convention.

For the time being, the Senegalese authorities seem to be setting their sights on a Universal Health Coverage Programme (CMU), launched in 2015, which aims to extend basic health coverage to at least 80 per cent of the country's population by 2021 through community-based mutual health insurance, and a national family security scholarship programme started in 2013, of which the ambition is to help break the intergenerational transmission of poverty, increase household resilience and foster the development of human capital in rural areas.

---

317 See ANSD, Situation économique et sociale du Sénégal en 2016, Chapter V Santé, February 2019, 110.
318 This aims, among other things, to provide border populations with basic social infrastructure and equipment of sufficient quality and quantity.
319 In this regard, the creation of an equal opportunity card for persons living with a disability, the promotion of access for vulnerable groups such as sex workers, MSM and persons living with HIV, free care for women (Caesarean section), full coverage of health care costs for children up to five years of age and persons aged 60 and over, reduction of treatment costs for certain conditions (cancer, diabetes, kidney failure), are worth mentioning.
320 Four hospitals in Rufisque, Ziguinchor, Matam and Pikine and hundreds of health centres throughout the country.
321 Twelve oxygen generators installed in the health facilities, 13 scanners, one angiography machine, 169 ambulances, and so forth.
322 Between 2008 and 2013, it went from 21% to 13%.
323 It was 58% in 2013. This is both a source of exclusion from health services and a risk of household impoverishment.
324 For example, while almost all health facilities (98%) have an improved water source, only 65% have an emergency transport system, 57% have regular electricity, 50% have computers and 52% have internet access.

5.4 Convention on the Elimination of All Forms of Discrimination against Women

The issue of effectiveness in combating violence against women was frequently raised during the review of Senegal's first seven CEDAW reports. In addition to calling on the Senegalese authorities to take steps to correct or eliminate the stereotypes and harmful practices that contribute to persistent violence against women, the Committee also stressed the need for legislative reform to reclassify offences, make statistics on the judicial aspects of violence against women available and, more importantly, ensure that the national community takes better care of victims while educating the various actors on women's rights with a view to eliminating social prejudices relating to violence against women.[325] An analysis of the local context of violence and an evaluation of the measures taken by the authorities shows that it is difficult to deal with a phenomenon of which the implications have not always been properly understood by the mechanism.

The Senegalese socio-cultural context is characterised by the following:
- the multifaceted[326] nature of violence in society, which is intimately linked to the breakdown of family values, the economic living conditions of the population, prevailing poverty, illiteracy and religious obscurantism;
- the legitimation, in certain cultural circles, of violence through the socio-cultural roles assigned to men and women;
- the degree of violence depending on regions, cultures, ethnic groups and beliefs[327] and, above all, the 'tolerance' by the state of these social and cultural systems that violate women's rights.

The Committee's recommendations have forced Senegal to integrate CEDAW into the national legal system, to implement new policies and create institutions designed to better protect women from such societal violence.

From a legal standpoint, in addition to the adoption of two laws on violence against women, one on female genital mutilation,[328] and another on violations of privacy and the representation of the individual through image or sound

---

[325] See COs of CEDAW, 28 July 2015 paras 19 and 21.
[326] To take only those of a sexual nature, we can cite rape (individual, gang or marital), sexual harassment, indecent assault, paedophilia, misappropriation of minors, touching, and so forth.
[327] Particularly domestic violence, forced marriages, child marriages, female genital mutilation, violence in polygamous families, child fostering, and so forth.
[328] Act 99–05 of 29 January 1999 on excision and Act 2020–05 of 10 January 2020 amending the Criminal Code.

recordings,[329] only a few symbolic measures have been taken at the administrative level to strengthen the framework for combating violence:
- at the administrative level, institutionalisation of gender units in the ministries[330] to take into account the different needs and interests of women and men in the Senegalese public administration;
- at the national education level, authorisation for young mothers, who were systematically expelled from school when pregnant, to return to school after giving birth, and creation of a body of school life inspectors to deal with cases of violence in schools.

At the political level, the state has taken numerous initiatives, including the adoption of –
- a National Action Plan for the Abandonment of Female Genital Mutilation (2000–2005),[331] one of the components of which was 'better management of excision and violation of the law prohibiting it across Senegal';
- a National Action Plan for the eradication of gender-based violence, one of the aims of which is 'the strengthening and harmonisation of the international, regional and national legal, political and institutional framework, for better protection, compliance and effective implementation of the human rights of victims of violence, including girls, boys, persons living with a disability, the elderly, and so forth';[332]
- a National Gender Equity and Equality Strategy (NEGES)[333] of which the purpose is to 'promote attitudes and practices that are conducive to equity and equal recognition, treatment, opportunities and outcomes for women and men';
- a National Children's Rights Promotion and Protection Policy, which aims to promote, protect and implement all human rights of children, including girls' rights;[334]
- a programme to support girls' education.[335]

---

[329] Act 2016–29 of 8 November 2016 amending Act 65–60 of 21 July 1965 on the Penal Code.
[330] Decree 2017–313 of 15 February 2017. Since 25 ministries have gender units housed in the General Secretariat of the Ministry.
[331] See COs of CEDAW, 28 July 2015 paras 19(a) and (b).
[332] See Ministry of Women, Family and Children, National Action Plan to Combat Gender-based Violence and Promote Human Rights in Senegal, October 2015 12.
[333] See COs of CEDAW, 28 July 2015 para 25.
[334] ibid para 27(b).
[335] ibid para 27(a).

It is at the institutional level that the impact of the Committee's recommendations has been most significant, since some 10 ministries[336] have established mechanisms for the prevention of or care for victims of gender-based violence. These include the establishment, in the Ministry of Health and Social Welfare, of a Bureau for Violence and Trauma Prevention, reception and psychological care facilities in a number of the country's hospitals, and the implementation of the Universal Medical Coverage (CMU), the main objective of which is to reduce inequalities in access to health care.

As for the Ministry of Justice, in addition to its Human Rights Directorate, it has a Supervised Education and Social Protection Directorate which, as the gateway to judicial services and psychosocial care, plays a key role in caring for victims of violence nationwide, the CNLTP and the Community Justice Coordination Unit, which is responsible for coordinating the activities of the 19 legal aid offices providing shelter and assistance to women victims of violence.

The ANSD has also made an extraordinary effort to supply political decision makers[337] with detailed statistics on violence against women. It is now known that the practice of excision is highly influenced by ethnicity[338] and varies from region to region.[339] The surveys have also painted a picture of domestic violence and its geographical distribution throughout the country,[340] thereby providing valuable information to policy makers and civil society organisations for them to take action to help eradicate it.

With regard to public awareness and education, a citizen platform to combat excision and a youth network to promote the abandonment of excision and harmful practices had been established, and the Ministry of Women's Affairs had developed a wide-ranging training programme for judges, criminal investigation police officers and gendarmes on the content of the law. Legal aid

---

336 These include the Ministries of Justice, Health and Social Action, Youth, Women, Family and Children, Armed Forces, Interior, Civil Service, Tourism, Livestock, Sport, Transport, Agriculture and Industry and Mines.

337 ANSD's first report, DHS 2015 and Gender-based Violence, May 2017, welcomes the work as part of the recommendations of the UN mechanisms (8).

338 74,7% among the Mandingues, 63,3% among the Soninké, 58,6% among the Diolas and 49,3% among the Halpullars. See ANSD, Gender-Based Violence and Women's Empowerment, December 2019 19.

339 91% in Kedougou, 75,6% in Sedhiou, 73,3% in Matam, 71,8% in Tambacounda, 68,2% in Ziguinchor and 63,6% in Kolda. See ANSD, Gender-based Violence and Women's Empowerment, December 2019 19.

340 According to ANDS (see ANSD, Gender-based Violence and Women's Empowerment, December 2019, 42), Sedhiou has the highest rate of domestic violence in Senegal with 42%, followed by Kolda 37%, Tambacounda 32%, Fatick 30% and Kédougou 30%. The lowest rates are in Louga (16%) and Diourbel (17%).

offices have started operating in peripheral regions[341] to provide legal, judicial and psycho-social assistance to victims.

However, the implementation of these various measures has highlighted serious shortcomings, such as
- gaps in victim protection laws passed so far;
- a lack of specialised bodies to deal with violence within government health services;
- the very limited number of law firms in the regions, especially those where violence is endemic;[342]
- the non-existence of state reception and refuge centres in the internal areas of the country;[343]
- illiteracy and women's ignorance of their rights;
- practices linked to interpretations, sometimes misinterpretations, of religion;
- poor governance in a state that itself fails to address issues of violence against women;
- cultural and social norms that are out of step with women's daily lives.

Faced with the religious and cultural burden of some of the issues raised, the state of Senegal seems to prefer keeping a low profile in order not to upset religious leaders who are important supporters of politicians, especially during election periods or acute political crises.

5.5 Convention against Torture and Other Cruel, Inhuman or Degrading Treatment or Punishment

The fight against torture is the only human rights area where, over the past two decades, the state of Senegal has preferred a case-by-case approach to a coherent policy aimed at fully transposing the relevant provisions of the Convention into local legislation. Every time it was challenged in its convictions about how individuals were treated in police stations or gendarmerie brigades, the government opted to back off in order to avoid being accused of complicity in the perpetration of these crimes rather than methodically tackling this abominable crime. However, when accusations gained momentum, as in the case of the Senegalese courts' treatment of the Hissène Habré case, the government finally agreed, when the law implementing the Rome Treaty establishing the International Criminal Court was adopted,[344] to introduce the rule of

---

341   The regions of Sedhiou, Kolda and Kédougou.
342   See COs of CEDAW 28 July 2015 paras 13(a) and (b).
343   This issue was highlighted by CEDAW in its COs 28 July 2015 para 21(c).
344   Act 2007–05 of 12 February 2007 amending the CPP.

'universal jurisdiction'[345] into Senegalese legislation and to revise the definition of torture in the Senegalese Criminal Code,[346] which differed somewhat from that of the Convention.[347]

With the adoption of the Terrorism Act, the authorities also enshrined in Senegalese criminal law a rule requiring the presence of a lawyer as soon as a person is arrested.[348] This slow approach to the transposition of CAT into Senegalese criminal law poses enormous problems for law enforcement officials in Senegal.[349]

Regarding the National Observer of Detention Centres, it was established by an Act of 2009, supplemented by a Decree of 2011. According to the law, the observer enjoys independence from the state authorities and budgetary autonomy, but these elements were reviewed by the SPT during a visit to Senegal.[350] The visit of the SPT (10–14 December 2012) helped the government to better understand the characteristics and role of the mechanism proposed by the OP-CAT. Created in 2009, the National Detention Centre Observatory (ONLPL) was only operationalised in 2011. Following the advisory visit to the ONLPL,[351] the SPT noted a number of constraints preventing the mechanism from playing an effective role in preventing torture within the country. These included, with regard to the independence of the mechanism, its attachment to the Ministry of Justice; the procedure for appointing the observer; the impossibility of choosing the collaborators; and the exclusion of certain detention centres (those under the jurisdiction of the army) from its jurisdiction. With regard to its working methods, concerns raised include the absence of a work plan and strategy for action; the instability of the resources allocated to the facility; and the lack of visibility.

---

345   See the provisional report of the Coordinating Committee for the Reform of the Criminal Code and the Code of Criminal Procedure, which states, at 21, that the introduction of the rule is intended 'to enable Senegal to comply with its commitments under … the Convention against Torture and Other Cruel, Inhuman or Degrading Treatment or Punishment'.
346   The first para of article 295.
347   See the Senegalese government's explanations in Senegal's 4th Periodic Report, 2.
348   See art 55 of Act 2016–30 of 8 November 2016 amending Act 65–61 of 21 July 1965 on the Code of Criminal Procedure.
349   Act 2009–13 of 12 March 2013.
350   See Report on the visit made by the Sub-Committee on Prevention of Torture and Other Cruel, Inhuman or Degrading Treatment or Punishment for the purpose of providing advisory assistance to the national preventive mechanism of Senegal CAT/OP/SEN/2.
351   See CAT/PO/SEN/R.2.

Based on these factors, a number of recommendations were made.[352] Since the visit, the places of detention of the security services were included in the list of places of detention covered by the institution, a five-year action plan was adopted, information concerning the observer of places of detention within the administration was popularized, the guide for visits to places of detention was revised. However, problems that have not yet been formally resolved are the independence of the institution from the supervisory ministry and the size of the annual budget allocated to carry out monitoring activities in places of detention. The formal commitment made by the Minister of Justice in 2014 to settle the issue of the autonomy of the mechanism has not yet materialised and the annual budget allocated does not yet match the SPT's proposals.[353]

When it establishes a grave violation of the fundamental rights of a person deprived of liberty, the Observer communicates its findings and gives the authority concerned a period of time within which to determine whether or not the reported violation has been put to an end. If he considers it necessary, he shall make public the content of his observations and the replies received.

With the installation of focal points in five pilot regions of Senegal, the ongoing training of security service personnel and the access of lawyers to their clients from the moment of arrest, the prevention of acts of torture is more effective than before and explains, in part, the decrease in cases of torture on the territory.

The CAT Cttee found Senegal in violation in one case: *Souleymane Guengueng v Senegal* (CAT/C/36/D/181/2001). The implementation of the CAT findings was laborious because of the sensitivity of the issue being dealt with, that is, the trial of former President Hissène Habré accused of having ordered the torture of his opponents in prison when he was the President of the Republic of Chad. Following the rejection of the complaint by the Senegalese courts, the victims seized CAT which found that Senegal was obliged to adopt the necessary measures, including legislative measures, to establish its jurisdiction over the acts referred to and to submit the present case to its competent authorities for the purpose of prosecution or, failing that, since Belgium has made and extradition request, to comply with that request, or, should the

---

352 See CAT/OP/SEN/2/Add.1.
353 See Replies of the national preventive mechanism of Senegal to the recommendations and questions put forward by the Sub-Committee on Prevention of Torture and Other Cruel, Inhuman or Degrading Treatment or Punishment in its report on its advisory visit, CAT/OP/SEN/2/Add.1, para 3.

case arise, with any other extradition request made by another state, in accordance with the Convention.[354]

The Senegalese authorities refused to extradite former President Hissène Habré to Belgium and turned to the African Union for a solution to the legal crisis it had created. Finally, a decision of the African Union[355] authorised the government of Senegal to put the former Chadian President on trial in Senegal. As a result of this decision, a law was passed to create the Extraordinary African Chambers attached to the Senegalese courts to put Hissène Habré on trial and convict him.[356]

5.6 Convention on the Rights of the Child

CRC is the treaty that drew the largest number of recommendations from both the CRC Cttee[357] and other UN mechanisms.[358] These have focused on better coordination and ownership of actions for children and more effective harmonisation of national legislation with the Convention.

According to the National Child Protection Strategy (SNPE), the idea of coordinating and supporting actions to protect children is based on article 19 of the Convention, which states that effective, efficient and sustainable protection of children is based on pooling resources, experiences and shared visions at all levels.[359] A National Intersectoral Child Protection Committee (CINPE) has thus been established to provide a forum for exchange and sharing among all actors involved in child protection issues in Senegal,[360] with a general secretariat, technical commissions and departmental child protection committees. The CINPE was, in principle, responsible for developing action plans, mobilising budgetary resources for child protection, monitoring and evaluating

---

354 See *Souleymane Guengueng and Others v Senegal* CAT/C/36/D/181/2001 para 10.
355 Assembly/AU/Dec.127 (VII) (2007).
356 Statute of the Extraordinary African Chambers within the courts of Senegal created to prosecute international crimes committed in Chad between 7 June 1982 and 1 December 1990.
357 For example, the COs on the 3rd to 5th periodic reports of Senegal (CRC/C/SEN/CO/3-5) contained some 40 recommendations.
358 The report Evaluation and analysis of Senegal's international, regional and national legal framework on the rights of the child and the state of implementation of the recommendations of human rights protection mechanisms relating to the rights of the child, 2017, mentions the recommendations of the UPR, CESCR, CCT, CED, CTM and those of special procedures such as the SRs on the sale of children, the right to education and the rights of migrants.
359 See Republic of Senegal, National Child Protection Strategy, December 2013 13.
360 See Primatorial Order 01333 of 24 January 2014, replaced by Primatorial Order 06788 of 29 April 2016.

programmes and, more importantly, preparing and submitting reports to the authorities on the implementation of the SNPE. Due to its rather cumbersome structure[361] and the 'competition' of several administrative bodies performing similar functions, it soon fell into lethargy.

Another institution of which the creation had been strongly recommended by the Committee is the ombudsman for children.[362] An instrument for the establishment of this independent authority has been prepared by the government. It consists of a person appointed for a non-renewable term of six years whose independence is guaranteed by law. This person has complete freedom of investigation and may refer cases to the public prosecutor under certain conditions. The legislation has not yet been reviewed by the government, let alone sent to Parliament for discussion.

Recognising that 'the diversity of the instruments and the scattered nature of the provisions relating to child protection are not conducive to their ownership by the various stakeholders, let alone their effective enforcement', the Senegalese authorities have undertaken to adopt a Children's Code, the main aim of which is to 'harmonise national legislation with the international conventions signed and ratified by Senegal ... reaffirm the responsibilities of the various stakeholders in this area and ... establish mechanisms for monitoring the effective implementation of the provisions protecting children'.[363] The purpose of the instrument is to transpose the rules and principles contained in the Convention, but is struggling to do so unambiguously.[364] Even worse, crucial issues relating to begging, forced or early marriages, protection and assistance to children who are victims of violations of their rights have not been dealt with consistently in the document. The hostility of Senegalese religious groups to the provisions defining the child, the rules of non-discrimination against children and the arrangements for the child's religious education, among others, forced the national authorities to postpone consideration of the Bill by Parliament.

---

361   More than 59 members, including 33 representatives of ministries, according to the report entitled Evaluation and analysis of Senegal's international, regional and national legal framework on the rights of the child and the status of implementation of the recommendations of human rights protection mechanisms relating to the rights of the child, 2017 71.
362   See the COs of CRC dated 7 March 2016, para 18(a).
363   See Republic of Senegal, Bill on the Children's Code, Preamble, 3.
364   See the criticisms of the Bill contained in the Report on the Evaluation and analysis of Senegal's international, regional and national legal framework on the rights of the child and the status of implementation of the recommendations of human rights protection mechanisms relating to the rights of the child, 2017, 81–88.

5.7 Convention on the Rights of Persons with Disabilities

A year after ratifying the CRPD in 2009, and even before submitting its initial report in 2015, Senegal adopted its Social Orientation Act on the Promotion and Protection of the Rights of Persons with Disabilities, which may be regarded as a law implementing CRPD, as the definition of the disability is extracted from the treaty.[365] Such legislative activism seems to be also linked to the choice of Senegal by the African Union as an ambassador country for the Second Decade of Persons with Disabilities in Africa (2009–2019). Although the Act is very holistic in its handling of the rights of persons living with disabilities, it omits essential aspects of these rights such as the right to life (article 11); women's rights (article 6); equal recognition of legal personality (article 12); access to justice (article 13); freedom from torture (article 15); and participation in political and public life (article 29).

The aforementioned text reproduces the definition of a person with disabilities contained in the UN Convention almost word-for-word,[366] and sets out the institutional framework for the treatment and integration of persons with disabilities in Senegalese society. Out of the 14 draft decrees that accompanied the Law's elaboration, at least three address important aspects of the Convention:

- Decree 2012–1038 of 2 October 2012 sets up two departmental technical commissions responsible for examining applications for the Equal Opportunity Card and the promotion of special education. This card enables its holder to enjoy rights and benefits in terms of access to health care, rehabilitation, technical and financial assistance, education, training, employment, transport, as well as any other benefit likely to contribute to the promotion and protection of the rights of persons with disabilities. Order 4867/MSAS/DPPPH of 30 March 2015 set the conditions for the creation and issuance of the card. The issuing of the card does not seem to have been accelerated because, as of 30 December 2017, only 50 000 out of the 800 000 persons with disabilities identified in Senegal have received their equal opportunity cards. Nearly 20 000 card holders have been enrolled in mutual health insurance and 30 000 of these have also benefited from family security grants.
- Decree 2018–1236 of 5 July 2018 approving the national community-based rehabilitation programme provided for by the Convention in its article 26. Rehabilitation is defined by the government as an inclusive development strategy, which makes it possible to meet the needs of people with

---

365 See art 1 of the Act.
366 See art 1 of the Loi d'orientation sociale 2010–15 of 6 July 2010.

disabilities on a larger scale, with the aim of ensuring their participation and inclusion in society and improving their quality of life.
- Decree 2010–99 of 27 January 2010 on the Construction Code in articles R18 to R20 deals with measures for the physical accessibility to buildings by persons with disabilities.[367]

Two other drafts have been prepared but have not yet been adopted. These are:
- the draft Decree instituting a High Authority for the promotion and protection of the rights of the disabled.[368] The text has been drafted since May 2014 but has not yet been signed. However, a Directorate for the Promotion and Protection of People with Disabilities was created in 2012 at the Ministry of Health and Social Action and persons with disabilities were appointed as advisors to the Presidency of the Republic, the Economic, Social and Environmental Council (CESE) and the High Council of Local Authorities;
- a draft inter-ministerial Decree laying down the conditions for admission and passage of pupils with special educational needs to the examination for entry to the sixth form and the final examinations for the elementary school certificate and the intermediate school certificate has been drawn up and is awaiting signature by the Minister of National Education.[369]

A National Disability Measurement Instrument was adopted in November 2016 by the National Demography and Statistics Agency,[370] which has already conducted two surveys on disability in Senegal.[371] Finally, a National Action Plan on Disability (2017–2021) has been adopted and is being implemented by the Ministry of Health and Social Action.

5.8 Convention on the Protection of the Rights of All Migrant Workers and Members of Their Families

Senegal has reported twice under CMW and is up to date with its reporting obligations. Its reports were considered, and led to the adoption of COs issued in 2010 and 2016. Among the numerous issues raised by the CMW Cttee, the following can be highlighted:

---

367 See art 9(b) of the Convention. See also COs of CRPD, 13 May 2019 para 16(b).
368 See art 4(a) of the Convention.
369 See art 24(2)(a) of the Convention.
370 See COs of CRPD of 13 May 2019 para 54.
371 See Recensement général de la population 2013, Chapitre V Personnes en situation de handicap, September 2014 and Atlas démographique du Sénégal, Rapport final, August 2016.

Statistics: In its interactions with the Senegalese authorities, the CMW Cttee strongly recommended the establishment of a 'solid'[372] and 'centralised'[373] database enabling the generation of quantitative and qualitative information on all aspects of the Convention. The UN Special Rapporteur on the Human Rights of Migrants also highlighted this after his visit to Senegal in 2009.[374] Within a few years, the ANDS has made progress in supplying data on migration in the country. Since 2009, chapter 2 of the annual analysis of the Economic and Social Situation of Senegal has covered migration. In the 2017–2018 report,[375] the ANSD provided useful information on migration flows in the country, such as internal migration, international migration, including refugees and asylum seekers, irregular migration, return migration and remittances. A national survey on migration in Senegal, conducted jointly by ANSD and IOM in 2018, looked further into migration trends and characteristics of migrants, effects and governance of migration. As a result, they identified numerous gaps in migration data collection, including the absence of judicial statistics on human trafficking, the fact that the labour statistics file does not take into account the nationality of the owner of the declared enterprise registered in Senegal, making it difficult to establish the number of foreign nationals involved in business creation in Senegal. The study even proposed that migration be considered a development priority in the country and that all other aspects of migration be integrated into national development plans. It also recommended that the country's migration profile be updated every two years. Furthermore, the state of Senegal has decided to carry out a census of all Senegalese abroad, with the support of the ANSD. The results are expected in July 2021.

Voting rights and the right to be elected for Senegalese living abroad:[376] The participation of Senegalese migrants in the presidential and legislative elections of their country has made progress after the referendum organised in 2016 for the adoption of a new constitution, which recognised the entrance of the representatives of Senegalese abroad into Parliament. Currently Senegalese

---

372   See para 12 of the COs of CMW of 10 December 2010.
373   See para 19 of the COs of CMW of 20 May 2016.
374   See para 93 of the Report of the Special Rapporteur on the human rights of migrants, Jorge Bustamante, mission to Senegal, A/HRC/17/33/Add.2.
375   See ANSD, Situation économique et sociale du Sénégal 2017–2018L Chapitre II Migration, juillet 2020.
376   See CMW/C/SEN/CO/2–3 para 45 (COs of 20 May 2016): Senegal is urged to provide information 'on the opportunities available to Senegalese nationals living abroad to take part in their country's public affairs and on their participation in presidential and legislative elections' in its next report.

living abroad can vote and be elected to the Senegalese National Assembly. Law 2017–12 of 18 January 2017 amending the Electoral Code increased the number of Members of Parliament to 165, 15 of whom must represent Senegalese living abroad. The first Members of Parliament from the diaspora were consequently elected during the legislative elections of 30 July 2017.

Transfer of earnings and savings of Senegalese workers and efforts to reduce the cost of these operations for migrant workers:[377] The Senegalese authorities have accepted the introduction of mobile phone or prepaid bank card money transfer systems and retail money platforms in the country to facilitate the transfer of migrants' funds and to reduce the exorbitant fees charged by foreign money transfer companies such as Western Union and MoneyGram. The three telecom operators[378] in the country offers money transfer possibilities from Burkina Faso, Côte d'Ivoire, Guinea Bissau, Mali and Niger to Senegal using their networks of retail agents. The Senegalese Post Office also has a mobile phone transfer service called Post One. More recently, an electronic money institution (EME), named FERLO, was authorised to offer money transfer solutions by card and mobile phone at national and regional level. All these initiatives are designed to improve the conditions for money transfers in Senegal.

5.9 Convention on the Protection of All Persons from Enforced Disappearance

This certainly is the treaty that has influenced local legislation the least despite the increase in enforced disappearances in recent years in Casamance due to the criminal activities of armed groups.[379] One reason for the limited impact is that CED has only examined one report from Senegal since the country's ratification of the Convention. The issues addressed in the CED Cttee's first COs[380] and in the document produced by the Senegalese government on the follow-up to these Observations[381] relate essentially to the amendments that need to be made to Senegalese legislation, in particular the Criminal Code and the Code of Criminal Procedure, in order to bring it into compliance with state's obligations under CED.

---

377 ibid para 49(b): Senegal must 'step up its efforts to reduce the cost of sending and receiving funds, including through the application of preferential rates, in accordance with target 10.c of the Sustainable Development Goals'.
378 Orange, Free and Expresso.
379 See <https://www.seneplus.com/article/douze-d%C3%A9mineurs-enlev%C3%A9s-par-des-pr%C3%A9sum%C3%A9s-rebelles-en-casamance> accessed 15 April 2022.
380 See para 6 of the COs of CED of 18 April 2017.
381 See information received from Senegal on follow-up to the COs, 17 May 2018 CED/C/SEN/CO.1/Add.1.

Given that the Penal Code and the Code of Criminal Procedure have not been formally amended, Senegalese law cannot be said to have been brought into compliance. However, two draft Bills demonstrate a clear intention of the Senegalese authorities to fulfill their treaty obligations. This is the case with regard to the definition of 'enforced disappearance' in article 153–1 of the draft Penal Code, which not only reproduces the exact definition of the Convention but makes 'enforced disappearance' an autonomous offence. On a number of legal issues, it seems clear that the Senegalese authorities will have to review the legislation since it does not take into consideration the relevant nuances introduced by the Convention concerning

- the inclusion of enforced disappearance as an element of a crime against humanity;
- the conditions that must govern investigations into cases of enforced disappearance;
- the content of registers of persons deprived of their liberty;-
- the definition of the victim and his or her right to obtain reparation; and
- the legal situation of disappeared persons and their relatives.

The Senegalese authorities promised to address all these issues when revising the Penal Code and the Code of Criminal Procedure. However, the reform is still slow in taking shape.

6   Conclusion

Concluding his study on the impact of UN human rights treaties in Senegal, late professor Birame Ndiaye estimated, twenty years ago, that it was 'significant'[382] as CCPR, CEDAW and CAT have really impressed the minds of Senegalese citizens. The current study shows that the country has not really made progress in paving the way for a new dawn of respect for life and human dignity in Senegal.

Nobody can deny that the ratification of UN treaties has brought changes in the domestic legal order. These reforms vary from one legal instrument to another, depending on the areas covered, the links they have with the religions and traditions of the communities of Senegal, the influence of civil society organizations, the level of involvement of the technical and financial partners of the country and, more importantly, the degree to which local actors are ready to defend their rights and interests.

---

382 See Frans Viljoen and Birame Ndiaye, 'Senegal' in Christof Heyns and Frans Viljoen (eds), *The Impact of the UN Human Rights Treaties on the Domestic Level* (Kluwer Law International 2002) 518, 537.

Over the last two decades of constructive dialogue with UN mechanisms, dozens of laws were adopted, and new norms were incorporated in public policies, with a view to bringing national legislation up to the level of the UN treaties. Often, legislation was passed due to pressure from local and external actors without sufficient political will on the part of the state. In retrospect, it appears that the task proved more difficult when legal issues touched on morality or religion, and that it was easier where the issues were related to judicial procedures or to protecting the authority of the judiciary. Even in respect of these issues, the results were not always commensurate with the expectations raised by the recommendations of the treaty bodies.

Now that economic and social development is on the horizon, the government must explore a new approach to the incorporation and use of such legal instruments. In the current Senegalese social and cultural context, the realistic approach would be to seek 'harmonization', that is, a 'rapprochement' between national standards and those of the UN system.[383] This would be the first step towards a possible unification of the two systems, in the sense that 'harmonization is politically more acceptable when the divergences are wide, because it merely brings the systems closer to each other without eliminating the differences'.[384]

This would facilitate an emergence of 'minimal common rules which, precisely because they are minimal, will not lead to the adoption of a unique law that would encounter strong resistance'.[385] In short, the aim will be to 'build fragile compromises whereby the decision is not so much between good and evil, between black and white, as between grey and grey, or, in a most tragic scenario, between the bad and the worse'.[386] This would help in a progressive and consensual implementation of these standards as 'universality is not to be taken for granted. It is to be experienced through multiple struggles and in the way – still difficult to understand – in which these struggles converge and are waged together in solidarity, with a view to pursuing a common horizon towards emancipation'.[387]

---

383 See Mireille Delmas-Marty, Trois défis pour un droit mondial, Éditions du Seuil, 1998, page 106.
384 ibid 121.
385 ibid 122.
386 See Paul Ricoeur, Le Juste 1, Revue Esprit, 1995, 220.
387 Souleymane Bachir Diagne, 'De l'universel et de l'universalisme' in Souleymane Bachir Diagne and Jean-Loup Amselle (eds), En quête d'Afrique(s), Universalisme et Pensée décoloniale (Albin Michel 2018) 85.

The harmonization strategy could capitalize on the gains made since the establishment of relations between Senegal and the UN system, notably in the areas of statistical data collection and analysis, and in the management of specific social issues including disability, gender and violence through public policies. The aim would be to convince Senegalese people of the importance of human rights in the transformation of the Senegalese society to ensure better respect for human life and dignity. The task is extremely delicate as, to persuade, it is necessary to obtain 'support ... after having gone through the rigour, intransigence and impartiality of abstract morality, and having confronted the drama of actions'.[388]

All these seem to be preconditions for an effective rapprochement between Senegal and the human rights treaty bodies. In addition, the Senegalese government needs to increase awareness, in national languages, on the content of international human rights instruments and promote education on human rights in all Senegalese as one can only defend and promote the rights that he or she knows. This could be easily done with the support of its technical and financial partners.

It should also be ready to take up its responsibilities regarding the implementation of human rights treaties in the country. The establishment, within the Senegalese central administration, of a National Law Reform Commission, as a permanent structure responsible for the preparation for accession and, above all, assisting the State of Senegal in the transposition of the relevant provisions of the treaties it ratifies into the national legal order, seems fundamental. Its primary role would be, immediately after the negotiation and before the signing of a treaty, to inform the public authorities of the implications of accession and to identify all the laws that need to be changed in the event of accession to the said instrument, and once this has taken place, to suggest to the national authorities the appropriate amendments that would enable the government to honour its treaty obligations.

Human rights modules should be introduced in the initial and continuing professional development of all law enforcement officials, in particular police officers, gendarmes and the judiciary. For the latter, this will mean an in-depth understanding of international human rights law so that they are able to appreciate all the nuances of such law and implement them appropriately in the complex political and social context of Senegal.

The civil society should increase its interventions to be more effective and efficient in the promotion and protection of human rights and identify

---

[388] See Paul Ricoeur, 221.

strategies through which social practices that are inconsistent with the core provisions of UN legal instruments can be challenged by consensus. It should also submit, every year, to the authorities a comprehensive report on the state of implementation of the recommendations of treaty bodies.

CHAPTER 17

The Impact of the United Nations Human Rights Treaties on the Domestic Level in South Africa

Foluso Adegalu and Tess Mitchell

1   Introduction to Human Rights in South Africa

South Africa has an ancient, rich and diverse history marred by flagrant human rights abuses, particularly during the colonisation and apartheid eras. Since democracy, milestones have been achieved in the progressive realisation of human rights for all South Africans, but much progress is still required.

South Africa was home to some of the oldest known ancestors of modern human beings, and later became inhabited by diverse indigenous communities.[1] South Africa's colonial history began with the establishment of a Dutch settlement in the seventeenth century. British colonisation followed in the nineteenth century. Dutch and British colonial powers governed South Africa in whole or in part from 1652 to 1910. The Anglo-Boer War (1899–1902) led to the creation in 1910 of the Union of South Africa as a dominion state within the British empire, when the boundaries of present-day South Africa came into being. However, the majority black population was neither consulted about the formation of the Union nor did the colonial authorities heed the protests against increasing racial exclusion and other violations of human rights.[2] In 1948 the National Party came to power, and the government elevated *de facto* racial segregation into a formal framework of social engineering that came to be known as 'apartheid'. South Africa became a Republic in 1961 and left the British Commonwealth. Under apartheid South Africans were segregated on the basis of race. Black, Indian and 'Coloured' persons were systematically discriminated against, oppressed and denied basic human rights. Internal resistance to apartheid, including the Sharpeville massacre in 1960 and the Soweto riots in 1976, was met by violent and repressive measures enforced by the state security. South Africa was increasingly condemned and isolated by the

---

1   Committee on the Elimination of Racial Discrimination, 2005, CERD/C/461/Add.3; South African History Online, 'Mapungubwe' (2019) <https://www.sahistory.org.za/article/mapungubwe> accessed 11 February 2021.
2   Committee on the Elimination of Racial Discrimination (n 1).

international community, including through United Nations (UN)-authorised economic sanctions.

The unbanning of various political movements and the release from imprisonment of political leaders in 1990 symbolically marked the start of negotiations which resulted in the dismantling of apartheid and the adoption of the interim Constitution in 1993. Justiciable human rights and a new court, the Constitutional Court, were first introduced into the Constitution under the interim Constitution in 1993.[3] The parliament chosen as a result of the first democratic elections in 1994 sat as a constitutional assembly and drafted a final Constitution for a constitutionally-democratic South Africa. The Constitution of the Republic of South Africa, 1996, became effective on 4 February 1997 and remains in force. The Constitution provides for a Bill of Rights, which protects both civil and political rights as well as economic, social and cultural rights. These developments led to South Africa being welcomed back into the international community of states and becoming a state party to various international human rights instruments.

There are numerous domestic institutions responsible for the promotion and protection of human rights in South Africa. As part of the process of democratisation, the Truth and Reconciliation Commission played an instrumental role in addressing violations committed during apartheid. The Commission for the Restitution of Land Rights has also sought to equitably redistribute land. Other key institutions include the South African Human Rights Commission (SAHRC), mandated by the Constitution to protect, promote and develop human rights; the Commission for Gender Equality (CGE); the Commission for the Promotion and Protection of the Rights of Cultural, Religious and Linguistic Communities (CRL Rights Commission); and the Electoral Commission. Further, the Public Protector functions to uphold human rights and support and defend democracy and protect the South African population in its engagement with the public administration.

Following the democratisation of South Africa, the Judicial Service Commission (JSC) was introduced and functions to make recommendations for the appointments of judges and deals with complaints brought about judges.[4] The JSC functions to ensure an inclusive representative process of judicial appointment and replaces exclusive executive discretion.

---

3   For the first time political equality was guaranteed for all South Africans in the interim Constitution.
4   The Judicial Service Commission was established by s 178 and its powers are set out in s 178(5) of the Constitution of South Africa.

There are many human rights issues in South Africa. The main concerns are poverty, vast inequality and structural injustice; racism and xenophobia; harmful cultural traditions and practices, such as *ukuthwala*; corporal punishment; institutional attacks on human rights defenders; hate crimes and speech; violence against women; gender-based violence; the criminalisation of sex work; sexual orientation-based violence; discrimination based on HIV status; conditions in places of detention; violations of indigenous peoples' rights; and barriers in access education for persons with disabilities.

However, there have also been significant human rights milestones in South Africa: basic social and economic rights such as the right to education, to housing and to food, and to social security have, since the demise of apartheid, been extended to many more South Africans. The judiciary in South Africa is very active in the realisation of human rights. The Constitutional Court has played a vital role in the realisation of human rights and holding the government accountable for violations of human rights. For example, the Constitutional Court declared the death penalty unconstitutional as a violation of the right to life and the right to dignity.[5] In other ground-breaking cases the Constitutional Court held the government accountable for the realisation of socio-economic rights. The courts adopted a 'reasonableness' test to determine whether the measures employed to achieve progress are adequate. This approach has been instrumental regarding the right to access to clean water[6] and access to housing in relation to eviction.[7] Constitutional jurisprudence illustrates the important role the judiciary plays in social justice in South Africa.

2 Relationship of South Africa with the International Human Rights System in General

South Africa is part of the international human rights system at both the global and regional level and since 1994 has played an active role in the international human rights community.

---

5 *S v Makwanyane* 1995 (6) BCLR 665 (CC). Justice Mahomed held that '[i]n its obvious and awesome finality, [the death penalty] makes every other right, so vigorously and eloquently guaranteed by ... the Constitution, permanently impossible to enjoy' (para 269).
6 See eg *S v Mazibuko* 1988 (87) ZASCA 25.
7 *Port Elizabeth Municipality v Various Occupiers* 2005 (1) SA 217 (CC); *S v BlueMoonlight* 2012 (2) BCLR 150 (CC).

At the UN level, it has been a member of the Human Rights Council (HRC) twice for three-year terms since 2006.[8] In addition to participating in the UN treaty body (UNTB) system, South Africa has been reviewed by the Universal Periodic Review (UPR) in 2008, 2012, and 2017. The Working Group's recommendations include the need for South Africa to implement international human rights obligations, including civil and political rights; economic, social and cultural rights; women's rights; children's rights; and rights of other specific groups and persons.[9] Special procedures of the HRC also conducted visits to South Africa to determine the extent to which South Africa is complying with international human rights standards. There have been 14 completed and reported Special Procedure visits to and reports on South Africa related to thematic matters such as violence against women; racism; independence of judges; and on indigenous people.[10]

Regarding international criminal law, South Africa has ratified the International Criminal Court (ICC) Statute. Noticeably, while the ICC has not opened an investigation in respect of events in South Africa, there has been a turbulent relationship between the ICC and South Africa. In 2017 the ICC held that South Africa was in breach of its obligations when it failed to arrest Oman Al-Bashir, the President of Sudan.[11] This issue also highlights South Africa's contradictory obligations as African Union (AU) member and under the ICC Statute. The AU's call on its members to respect the immunity of heads of state,[12] stood in stark contrast to the ICC Statute which requires South Africa to arrest Al-Bashir and cooperate under article 86 of the ICC Statute. South Africa took steps to withdraw from the ICC Statute after the ICC had

---

8   United Nations Human Rights Council, 2020, Membership of the Human Rights Council <https://www.ohchr.org/EN/HRBodies/HRC/Pages/Membership.aspx> accessed 11 February 2021.

9   Rights addressed in the Universal Periodic Reviews include equality and non-discrimination; right to life, liberty and security of the person; administration of justice, impunity, and the rule of law; freedom of religion or belief, expression, association and peaceful assembly, and right to participate in public and political life; right to work and to just and favourable conditions of work; right to social security and to an adequate standard of living; right to health; right to education; rights of persons with disabilities; and rights of migrants, refugees and asylum-seekers; A/HRC/WG.6/13/ZAF/3; A/HRC/WG.6/27/ZAF/3.

10   United Nations Human Rights of the High Commissioner, 'View Country Visits of Special Procedures of the Human Rights Council since 1998' <https://spinternet.ohchr.org/ViewCountryVisits.aspx?visitType=all&country=ZAF&Lang=en> accessed 12 February 2021.

11   ICC, Decision Under Article 87(7) of the Rome Statute on the Non-Compliance by South Africa with the Request by the Court for the Arrest and Surrender of Omar Al-Bashir, ICC-02/05–01/09, para 17.

12   ICC (n 12) para 133.

found that it was in breach of its obligations under the ICC Statute. The government tabled the International Crimes Bill before Parliament in December 2017, which would have repealed the Rome Statute Implementation Act and commence the process of South Africa's withdrawal from the ICC Statute. However, this was reversed by the High Court, deeming the decision to withdraw unconstitutional.[13]

On the regional plane, South Africa is a member of the AU, has ratified the African Charter on Human and Peoples' Rights (African Charter), the Organisation of African Unity (OAU) Convention on Refugee Rights,[14] and the African Charter on the Rights and Welfare of the Child (African Children's Charter), which to a large extent corresponds with the UN Convention of the Rights of the Child (CRC).[15] However, the regional system has not been instrumental in the realisation of human rights in South Africa. South Africa has accepted the jurisdiction of the African Court on Human and Peoples' Rights (African Court), but has not accepted individual direct access to the Court,[16] therefore complainants have to submit their complaints first to the African Commission on Human and Peoples' Rights (African Commission).[17]

Although South Africa has a dualist system of law, the South African Constitution is very 'international human rights law friendly'.[18] The President is empowered to negotiate and sign international agreements.[19] As a general rule these treaties must be ratified by Parliament in order to bind the country. An international agreement becomes part of domestic law only once it has been

---

13   *Democratic Alliance v Minister of International Relations and Cooperation and Others (Council for the Advancement of the South African Constitution Intervening)* 2017 (1) SACR 623 (GP).
14   OAU Convention on the Specific Aspects of Refugee Problems in Africa, ratified 15 December 1995.
15   African Charter on the Rights and Welfare of the Child, 1990; ratified 7 January 2000.
16   South Africa has not deposited the art 34(6) declaration in cases involving individuals and non-governmental organisations.
17   African Court on Human and Peoples' Rights 'Jurisdiction' (2021) <https://www.african-court.org/wpafc/jurisdiction/> accessed 12 February 2021; African Court on Human and Peoples' Rights 'Declarations' (2021) <https://www.african-court.org/wpafc/declarations/> accessed 12 February 2021.
18   D Tladi, 'Interpretation and international law in South African courts: The Supreme Court of Appeal and the Al Bashir saga' (2016) 16 African Human Rights Law Journal 310–338, <http://www.scielo.org.za/scielo.php?script=sci_abstract&pid=S1996-20962016000200002> accessed 15 September 2023.
19   International treaties must be signed and ratified by the President of the Republic of South Africa.

incorporated into legislation.[20] In cases where the provisions of the treaty are self-executing, they may be implemented directly and are immediately binding on South Africa – unless they are 'inconsistent with the Constitution or an Act of Parliament'.[21] The last phrase suggests that international (human rights) law has a status inferior to domestic legislation.

International law further influences South Africa through the judiciary. International human rights law *must* be considered when a court interprets the Bill of Rights;[22] and every court must favour an interpretation of legislation that is consistent with international law over one that is inconsistent with it.[23] Additionally, during such interpretation, courts must 'promote the spirit, purport and objects of the Bill of Rights'.[24] The Bill of Rights is largely based on the main international human rights instruments.

The conduct of officials offers insight into the nature of the relationship between international human rights systems and South Africa. For example, reported human rights violations at centres for refugees and asylum seekers, such as the Lindela Repatriation Centre, have given rise to findings by the UN that have been disregarded by officials. Despite being party to various refugee treaties, South Africa has not implemented these obligations into domestic legislation. Organisations, including Human Rights Watch and Lawyers for Human Rights, have reported a 'worrying extent of human rights violations'.[25] Such reports have been prevalent since at least 1998.[26] In 2017 the UN Human Rights Council urged the South African government to provide adequate health care and redress human rights abuses.[27] However, little has been done to rectify the conduct towards refugees and asylum seekers.[28]

---

20   S 231 1996 Constitution. Only one international treaty with an impact on human rights, the Hague Convention on the Civil Aspects of International Child Abduction, has in fact been incorporated into national law.
21   S 231(4) Constitution of the Republic of South Africa, 1996.
22   S 39(1)(b) Constitution of the Republic of South Africa, 1996.
23   S 233 Constitution of the Republic of South Africa, 1996.
24   S 39(2) Constitution of the Republic of South Africa, 1996.
25   J van Dyk, 'Rough Welcome: Could South Africa's New Border Detention Centres Turn Deadly?' (2017) <https://bhekisisa.org/article/2017-05-24-00-rough-welcome-could-south-africas-new-border-detention-centres-turn-deadly/> accessed 20 July 2019.
26   Human Rights Watch, '"*Prohibited Persons*" : Abuse of Undocumented Migrants, Asylum Seekers, and Refugees in South Africa' 1 March 1998, 1-56432-181-9 <https://www.refworld.org/docid/3ae6a8430.html> accessed 20 August 2019.
27   A/HRC/17/33/Add.4 'Report of the Special Rapporteur on the Human Rights of Migrants, Jorge Bustamante, Addendum, Mission to South Africa'.
28   Médecins sans Frontières and others and The Department of Home Affairs and others (SAHRC) Baseline Investigations Report (GP/2012/0134).

3 At a Glance: Formal Engagement of South Africa with the UN Human Rights Treaty System

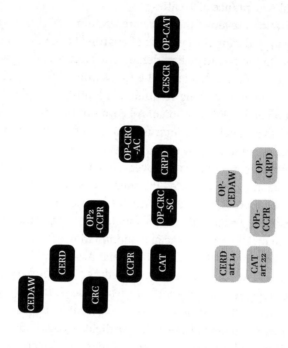

SOUTH AFRICA

4 Role and Overall Impact of the UN Human Rights Treaties in South Africa

4.1 Role of the UN Human Rights Treaties

4.1.1 Formal Acceptance of Treaties

South Africa has ratified seven of the nine core UN human rights treaties.

On 29 January 1993, during the last days of apartheid and at the start of the transitional phase to the country's first democratic elections, the government of then President FW de Klerk signed the Convention Against Torture and Other Cruel, Inhuman or Degrading Treatment or Punishment (CAT), the CRC and the Convention on the Elimination of All Forms of Discrimination against Women (CEDAW) as a signal to the international community that the flagrant human rights abuses committed during apartheid and South Africa's isolation from the international community were over. Upon transition to a democratic government in 1994, the newly-elected President, Nelson Mandela, signed the International Covenant on Civil and Political Rights (CCPR), the International Covenant on Economic, Social and Cultural Rights (CESCR) and the Convention on the Elimination of All Forms of Racial Discrimination (CERD) on 3 October 1994 to coincide with his visit to the UN General Assembly.[29] One year into democracy, the South African Parliament ratified CRC and CEDAW on 16 June and 15 December 1995, respectively, without reservations. Before the ratification of CRC, there were efforts to address issues of children, repression and the law in South Africa.[30] Leaders of the anti-apartheid struggle, such as Nelson Mandela and Oliver Tambo, placed enormous importance on children's rights. On 16 June 1994, when the National Children's Rights Committee (NCRC) task team delivered the National Programme of Action for Children (NPAC) to then President Nelson Mandela, he emphasised the need for a new democratic South Africa to place children's rights at the highest level. The promise of Nelson Mandela to place children's rights at the highest level was reflected in the establishment of the Office on Child Rights within the presidency to coordinate children's rights. In 2009 children's rights were moved to the Department for Women, Children and Persons with Disabilities (DWCPD), and in 2014 children's rights were moved to the Department of Social Development. The historical importance of children's rights in a new democratic South Africa has contributed massively to the huge impact that CRC has had in South Africa, compared to other treaties.

The democratic government took another monumental step in fulfilling South Africa's international commitments when it ratified CERD, CCPR and

---

[29] CH Heyns and F Viljoen, *The Impact of the UN Human Rights Treaties on the Domestic Level* (2002) 544.

[30] *Mail & Guardian*, 'Twenty-Five Years of Children's Rights'<https://mg.co.za/article/2014-11-21-00-twenty-five-years-of-childrens-rights/> accessed 12 February 2021.

CAT on 10 December 1998. The motivation behind the ratification of the three treaties was that it was considered a fitting gesture because South Africa chaired the UN Commission on Human Rights in 1998, and was eager to ratify some of the treaties it has already signed to coincide with the fiftieth celebration of the Universal Declaration of Human Rights (UDHR).[31]

On 30 March 2007 South Africa signed the Convention on the Rights of Persons with Disabilities (CRPD). Six months later, on 30 September 2007, the country's Parliament ratified CRPD. The prompt signing and ratification of CRPD by South Africa is connected to the participation of South Africa in the CRPD drafting process and the role of the country as one of the leading forces in the campaign for, and eventual adoption of, CRPD.[32]

The ratification of CESCR did not take place until 12 January 2015, over 20 years after the country had signed the treaty. The long delay in ratification has been ascribed to bureaucratic issues with respect to the lead department that was expected to take the lead process in the ratification of the treaty.[33]

South Africa is yet to ratify the Convention on the Protection of the Rights of All Migrant Workers and Members of Their Families (CMW) and the Convention for the Protection of All Persons from Enforced Disappearance (CED). While the political atmosphere and general hostility towards foreigners may be a crucial factor in the non-ratification of CMW, the non-ratification of CED may be as a result of bureaucratic hurdles.

The four substantive Optional Protocols to the UN treaties have been acceded to or ratified by South Africa. The Second Optional Protocol to CCPR (OP2-CCPR) was acceded to on 28 August 2002. South Africa acceded to the Optional Protocol to the CRC on the Sale of Children, Child Prostitution and Child Pornography (OP-CRC-SC) and ratified the Optional Protocol to the Convention on the Rights of the Child on the Involvement of Children in Armed Conflict (OP-CRC-AC) on 30 June 2003 and 24 September 2009, respectively. Even though the Optional Protocol to CAT (OP-CAT) was signed on 20 September 2006, South Africa only ratified OP-CAT on 20 June 2019.[34] The ratification of OP-CAT was delayed because of the delay of South Africa to pass legislation criminalising torture.[35] This obstacle was removed with the

---

31　Heyns and Viljoen (n 29) 546.
32　White Paper on the Rights of Persons with Disabilities, 33 <https://www.gov.za/sites/default/files/gcis_document/201603/39792gon230.pdf> accessed 12 February 2021.
33　Heyns and Viljoen (n 29) 546.
34　<https://www.ohchr.org/EN/HRBodies/CAT/Pages/CATIntro.asp> accessed 14 March 2020.
35　Report of the Portfolio Committee on Justice and Correctional Services on OP-CAT. In his response to a parliamentary question, the Deputy Minister of Justice explained that the ratification had taken long because government had to wait for the Preventive and Combating of Torture of Persons Act 13 of 2013 to be passed <https://static.pmg.org.za/190313pcjusticereport.htm.pdf> accessed 10 July 2019.

enactment of the Prevention and Combating of Torture of Persons Act, 2013. A further delay in the ratification was due to discussions and consultations on the appropriate National Preventive Mechanism (NPM) model to be implemented in compliance with the requirements of OP-CAT.[36]

With respect to the individual complaint mechanisms, South Africa accepted the individual complaint mechanisms of CERD and CAT by making the article 14 declaration and article 22 declaration under the respective treaties on 10 December 1998. The individual complaint mechanisms of the Human Rights Committee (HRCttee), the CEDAW Cttee and the CRPD Cttee were accepted through the ratification of the First Optional Protocol to CCPR (OP1-CCPR), the Optional Protocol to CEDAW (OP-CEDAW) and the Optional Protocol to CRPD (OP-CRPD) on 28 August 2002, 18 March 2005 and 30 November 2007 respectively.

South Africa is yet to ratify the Optional Protocol to CESCR (OP-CESCR), but is in the process of considering the Optional Protocol's consistency with domestic and international law to which South Africa is obligated, with a view to ratifying OP-CESCR.[37] South Africa also has not ratified the Optional Protocol to CRC on a Complaints Procedure (OP-CRC-CP). The argument given by the government for non-ratification is that the country's domestic legal framework offers sufficient protection for children's rights.[38]

4.1.2 Level of Awareness

The level of awareness of the treaties among government officials is fairly high. Government departments such as the Department of Justice and Constitutional Development, the Department of Basic Education, the Department of Arts and Culture, and independent state institutions such as the SAHRC and the CGE implement programmes that are designed to increase awareness of the rights in international human rights treaties and the Constitution of South Africa.[39] Various government agencies and departments speak to the steps

---

[36] Parliamentary Monitoring Group 'Convention Against Torture and Other Cruel, Inhuman or Degrading Treatment or Punishment: Briefing, with Deputy Minister' <https://pmg.org.za/committee-meeting/28159/> accessed 14 March 2020.

[37] Written reply to National Assembly Parliamentary Question 3042, submitted on 9 November 2018 <https://www.google.com/url?sa=t&rct=j&q=&esrc=s&source=web&cd=&cad=rja&uact=8&ved=2ahUKEwiN6MKbx9jpAhUBu3EKHUg-CEEQFjABegQIAxAB&url=https%3A%2F%2Fpmg.org.za%2Ffiles%2FRNW3042-181115.docx&usg=AOvVaw3Kjnia Ll9t3jgw_Bk36Xr> accessed 12 February 2021.

[38] Report of the 32nd session of the African Committee of Experts on the Rights and Welfare of the Child, 12–20 November 2018 22.

[39] Initial report, CCPR, South Africa 2.

they have taken in the implementation of UN treaties in their departments when appearing before Parliamentary Portfolio Committees. The requirement of mainstreaming of human rights across various government departments has led to a general increase in the awareness of the treaties among government officials. The presidency has on certain occasions expressly referred to the UN treaties.[40] Beyond high-ranking government officials, the level of awareness of the treaties is not really high. The prospectus of the Justice College, a state institution responsible for the development of a professional and legally-capable public sector, reveals that human rights and international human rights are completely absent from the curriculum of the College.[41] The South African Government News Agency, a news service published by the department of communication, occasionally make reference to the treaties.[42] The Agency also occasionally refers to the discussions of cabinet on state reports, but it does not cover submission of reports to treaty bodies and issuance of Concluding Observations (COs).[43]

The treaties have also been frequently discussed in parliamentary debates. The National Assembly has raised the issue of the implementation of the treaties, COs as well as the submission of state reports during parliamentary debates. Generally, Parliament becomes aware of the treaties and its reporting mechanisms through the engagement of its oversight committees with lead departments that are in charge of the different UN treaties.[44]

---

40 State of the Nation Address by President Jacob Zuma 17 June 2014 <https://pmg.org.za/briefing/19063/> accessed 12 February 2021. The Minister for Women, Youths and Persons with Disabilities made reference to CRPD in her speech on the discussion of the rights of persons with disabilities during COVID-19. See <https://www.gov.za/speeches/minister-maite-nkoana-mashabane-webinar-upholding-rights-persons-disabilities-22-may-2020> accessed 12 February 2021.

41 <https://www.justice.gov.za/juscol/jcp/JusticeCollegeProspectus-2019-2020.pdf> 15 September 2023.

42 South African Government News Agency, 'SA Advocating for Economic, Social, Cultural Rights' <https://www.sanews.gov.za/south-africa/sa-advocating-economic-social-cultural-rights> accessed 1 June 2020; South African News Agency, 'Defence Amendment Bill on its Way to Parliament' 30 March 2017 <https://www.sanews.gov.za/south-africa/defence-amendment-bill-its-way-parliament> accessed 12 November 2020. The coverage of the treaties on the website are mostly related to events that are political in nature. For example, the SA news agency reported on the address of the Deputy Minister of Social Development at the 8th session of the Conference of States Parties to the Convention on the Rights of Persons with Disabilities (CRPD) held in New York.

43 <https://www.sanews.gov.za/search?keyword='convention%20on%20the%20rights%20of%20persons%20with%20disabilities'&sort_by=search_api_time_adjusted_relevance&sort_order=DESC> accessed 12 February 2021.

44 Parliamentary Monitoring Group 'Country Reports (2nd, 3rd and 4th for 1998–2012) on UN Convention & African Charter on Rights of the child'

The level of awareness in the media and among the public is generally low. The treaty bodies have constantly required South Africa to take steps to ensure greater dissemination of the treaties and the COs issued by the treaty bodies.[45] The low level of public awareness has also been raised in non-governmental organisation (NGO) reports.[46] In one of its reports, the government acknowledged that weaknesses in coordination, implementation and monitoring and evaluation have largely detracted from the awareness of the UN treaties.[47] However, there has been occasional media coverage of the treaties and events around the treaties.[48]

The level of awareness of the treaties in the judiciary is generally high. As will be discussed througout this chapter, the treaties have featured prominently in the decisions of South African courts. However, because of the status of international law in the South African legal system, the treaties have mostly played interpretive roles in court decisions. Additionally, the treaties have generally featured in decisions where NGOs are parties in strategic litigations or have made *amicus curiae* submissions before the court. It is highly doubtful

---

<https://pmg.org.za/committee-meeting/15551/> accessed 2 June 2020; <https://pmg.org.za/search/?q=%22convention+on+the+rights+of+persons+with+disabilities%22&filter%5Btype%5D=hansard; https://pmg.org.za/hansard/25646/; https://pmg.org.za/hansard/18293/> accessed 1 June 2020.

45 See eg CEDAW Cttee, COs on the Combined Second, Third and Fourth Periodic Report of South Africa para 13.

46 Centre for the Study of Violence and Reconciliation People Opposing Women Abuse Western Cape Network on Violence Against Women, (2011) NGO Shadow Report 19.

47 Initial Report, CRPD, South Africa, para 57.

48 See eg South African Human Rights Commission, 'SAHRC Welcomes Ratification of UN Torture Agreement' <https://www.sahrc.org.za/index.php/sahrc-media/news/item/1819-sahrc-welcomes-ratification-of-un-torture-agreement> accessed 15 September 2023; *Times Live*, 'Fees Must Fall: Joint Statement from Amnesty International University Groups iLIVE' <https://www.timeslive.co.za/ideas/2015-10-22-fees-must-fall-joint-statement-from-amnesty-international-university-groups-ilive/> accessed 1 June 2020; South African Government News Agency, 'Defence Amendment Bill on its Way to Parliament' <https://www.sanews.gov.za/south-africa/defence-amendment-bill-its-way-parliament> accessed 1 June 2020; Staff Report, 'Mom at Work' *Mail & Guardian* (2008) <https://mg.co.za/article/2008-09-18-mom-at-work/> accessed 1 June 2020; K Farise, 'Ban Harmful Virginity 'Testing'' *Mail & Guardian* (2019) <https://mg.co.za/article/2019-12-12-00-ban-harmful-virginity-testing/> accessed 1 June 2020; C Rickard, 'Sorry, You Can Only Be a Girl for this Election' *Sunday Times* (2005) <https://www.timeslive.co.za/sunday-times/lifestyle/2005-07-17-sorry-you-can-only-be-a-girl-for-this-election> accessed 1 June 2020; TMG Digital, 'Scholarships for Virgins Holds Girls to a Different Sexual Standard than Boys: LHR' *Times Live* (2016) <https://www.timeslive.co.za/news/south-africa/2016-01-26-scholarships-for-virgins-holds-girls-to-a-different-sexual-standard-than-boys-lhr/> accessed 1 June 2020.

if the level of awareness of the treaties is of a major significance in the legal profession generally.

There is a relatively high level of awareness of the treaties among NGOs, but greater reliance on and more reference is made to the Constitution and national policies. This may be because of the dualist system of South Africa, in which case international treaties are not directly enforceable before the courts except where they have been domesticated as part of South African laws. There is no specific preference for regional treaties over UN treaties among the NGOs. The practice is usually to rely on the instrument that offers the highest form of protection on specific issues.

Generally, the UN treaties form part of the Bachelor of Laws curricula and are taught as part of an optional subject of international human rights law in South African universities.[49] In addition to the Bachelor of Laws curricula, there are different university departments that offer specialised programmes on specific treaties. The Centre for Human Rights (CHR) at the University of Pretoria offers advanced short courses on different thematic rights that place extensive reliance on the UN human rights treaties.[50] The CHR also offers five different Masters' programmes which, among other things, educate students on the different UN human rights treaties.[51] The University of Cape Town also offers a Higher Certificate in Disability Studies which is anchored in the Department of Health and Rehabilitation Sciences.[52] The Faculty of Law, Stellenbosch University, through its Socio-Economic Rights and Administrative Justice Research Project, promotes the role of law in improving access to administrative justice and socio-economic rights.[53] Further, at the Dullah Omar Institute,

---

[49] For example, at Rhodes University, International Human Rights Law optional course for final year Bachelor of Laws students and is taught in conjunction with International Humanitarian Law. Students are taught about 'Implementation of human rights law: Charter-based and treaty-based mechanisms and implementation: The African human rights system' (Rhodes University, Faculty of Law Course Outline for International Human Rights/Humanitarian Law (2020)).

[50] Centre for Human Rights: 'Advanced Human Rights Courses (AHRC)' <https://www.chr.up.ac.za/ahrc> accessed 12 February 2021.

[51] Centre for Human Rights: 'Academic Programme' <https://www.chr.up.ac.za/academic> accessed 12 February 2021: <https://dullahomarinstitute.org.za/socio-economic-rights/international-covenant-on-economic-social-and-cultural-rights-icescr> accessed 10 October 2022.

[52] <http://www.dhrs.uct.ac.za/dhrs/divisions/disability/undergraduate/requirements> accessed 1 June 2020.

[53] The research project is co-directed by Professor Sandra Liebenberg, a member of the Committee on Economic and Socio-Cultural Rights, and Professor Geo Quinot.

University of the Western Cape (UWC), the Socio-Economic Rights Project advocated for the ratification of CESCR.[54]

The CRC, CEDAW, CRPD and CESCR are the four treaties that have generally received the highest level of attention from stakeholders. Considering South Africa's history of racial discrimination, CERD has surprisingly received the lowest level of attention from stakeholders and the level of awareness of CERD seems to be the lowest among the treaties.

4.1.3 Human Rights Defenders

Civil society organisations (CSOs) in South Africa are diverse and very active. The high level of CSO engagement in South Africa has its roots in the struggle against numerous injustices perpetrated by the apartheid regime. However, CSOs that is advocacy oriented, as opposed to service oriented CSOs, have received less financial support and protection from the government.[55] Generally, there are hostility between the state and human rights defenders who advocate on sensitive national issues such as land and housing, labour rights, gender-based violence, sexual orientation and gender identity rights, corporate and government accountability and transparency, and the impact of extractive industries on local people, and the environment.[56] The Minister of State Security stated that some human rights defenders were collaborating with foreign countries to disrupt the country.[57] The UN Rapporteur on Human Rights Defenders has also reported on the lack of response from South Africa on the situation of human rights defenders.[58] Human rights defenders have also been attacked and killed by unknown third parties, and in most of these instances there has been poor investigation by the state.[59]

---

54 <https://dullahomarinstitute.org.za/socio-economic-rights/Advocacy/Campaigns> accessed 5 November 2022.

55 M Forst, 'World Report on the Situation of Human Rights Defenders' (2018) *United National Special Rapporteur on the Situation of Human Rights Defenders* 146.

56 See, generally, Forst (n 55). The CESCR Cttee in its COs to South Africa expressed its concerns over the harassment of human rights defenders in the mining and environmental sectors. The CESCR Cttee recommended that South Africa should review the Regulation of Gatherings Act of 1993 and ensure a safe and favourable environment for human rights defenders. CESCR Cttee COs E/C.12/ZAF/CO/1, para 13. The HRCttee also expressed concerns about the safety of human rights defenders working on 'corporate accountability, land rights and transparency issues, as well as lesbian, gay, bisexual, transgender and intersex persons and HIV activists'. See CCPR/C/ZAF/CO/1, para 40.

57 Forst (n 55) 148.

58 ibid 149.

59 In November 2017, Sibonelo Patrick Mpeku, a member of Abahlali baseMjondolo, a grassroots organisation that advocates the rights of shack dwellers, was stabbed to death; his fellow member Soyiso Nkqayini was also killed a month later. In April 2011 Noxolo

4.1.4 Domestic Implementation Mechanism/Process

In 2012, the Department of Justice and Constitutional Development, together with the SAHRC, established the Interdepartmental Committee on International Treaty Obligations (IDC), to facilitate the data gathering, drafting and consultation processes required for the finalisation of state reports. The IDC has its membership in all government departments. However, the IDC has generally been ineffective and the country has usually resorted to *ad hoc* processes through lead government departments to prepare state reports to the different treaty bodies.[60] The Department of Justice and Constitutional Development has embarked upon a process to develop a National Mechanism for Reporting and Follow-Up (NMRF) on South Africa's human rights treaty obligations. Recommendations received from the various treaty bodies are taken for noting by cabinet. Government departments are notified of recommendations through the IDC and through workshops held to publicise the recommendations and the implementation and planning needed in light of received recommendations.[61]

4.1.5 Treaty Body Membership

Generally, in order to select nominees domestically, the Department of International Relations and Cooperation requests nominations from different government departments. After these names have been submitted, the department makes a final selection. However, research revealed that this approach has not been consistent in practice.[62] One of the treaty members whose appointment has increased the visibility of a UN treaty is Sandra Liebenberg, a member and Vice-Chairperson of the CESCR Cttee.[63] Although her appointment as a member of the CESCR Cttee was not covered in the local

---

Nogwaza, a woman human rights defender, was subject to sexual orientation-based violence and was raped and murdered; in 2016 Mr Sikhosiphi Rhadebe, the chairperson of Amadiba Crisis Committee (ACC) who was at the forefront of a campaign opposing opencast mining of titanium in the Xolobeni area, was shot dead.

60 Common Core Document Forming Part of State Report, South Africa para 147.
61 ibid para 149.
62 One of the treaty body members interviewed was directly approached by the DIRCO because of expertise and significant contributions in the field of human rights. Another treaty body member was referred to the Department of Justice for nomination by a UN agency. According to the interviewees, the DIRCO took active steps to ensure the success of their nomination.
63 <https://www.ohchr.org/Documents/HRBodies/CESCR/FormerMembers.docx> accessed 1 June 2020.

newspapers,[64] she has engaged in several activities to promote the impact of CESCR in South Africa.[65] Ann Skelton, a member of the CRC Cttee, has also played several roles in promoting CRC among government officials and stakeholders in South Africa.[66] Another treaty body member whose appointment has had significant influence on the impact of the UN treaty system is the late Christof Heyns, who was a member of the HRCttee between 2017 and 2020. He has been involved in numerous activities to promote the influence of the treaty system within and beyond South Africa.[67] Two South African nationals have been nominated and elected to the CEDAW Cttee. South Africa nominated Mavivi Myakayaka-Manzini as a member of the CEDAW Cttee. She was elected, and served from 1999 to 2002. Hazel Gumede Shelton was elected and served as a member in 2007.[68] Their elections were not covered in the media, and did not lead to greater treaty awareness. Another South African who served as members of the treaty bodies is Zonke Zanele Majodina (HRCttee, 31 December 2010 to 31 December 2014). The most recent South African to be appointed to the treaty body is Faith Dikeledi Pansy Tlakula (CERD Cttee, 2020–2024).

---

[64] Her election, however, was reported by the NGO Studies in Poverty and Inequality Institute. See <http://spii.org.za/wp-content/uploads/2016/04/WEB-13-04-2016-Sandra-Liebenberg.pdf> accessed 1 June 2020.

[65] Interview with Prof. Sandra Liebenberg, Member, CESCR Cttee. Skype interview conducted in Pretoria on 6 September 2019. Among other things, she has been involved in several workshops and consultations with the Department of International Relations and Cooperation (DIRCO), the Department of Justice and Constitutional Development and other South African government officials about the procedures of the CESCR Cttee. She has also been involved in guiding NGOs in the submission of shadow reports before the CESCR Cttee. All interview notes on file with the author.

[66] Interview with Prof. Ann Skelton, Member, CRC Cttee. Physical interview conducted at the University of Pretoria, South Africa on 8 January 2020. On 10 December 2019, Prof. Skelton, alongside Prof. Heyns, a member of the HRCttee, was invited by the South African government to deliver a seminar on the treaty system to government officials. In contrast, Ms Esther Margeret Queen Mokhuane, who served on the CRC Cttee from 27 February 1997 to 28 February 2001, was criticised by NGOs as inactive. See Heyns and Viljoen (n 29) 564.

[67] Most notably, in 1999 Christof Heyns and Frans Viljoen coordinated a study on the domestic impact of the UN treaty system on 20 countries, including South Africa. The study to date is the most comprehensive study of the UN treaty system (see Heyns and Viljoen (n 29)).

[68] OHCHR, 'Committee on the Elimination of Discrimination Against Women' *Membership* (2020) <https://www.ohchr.org/EN/HRBodies/CEDAW/Pages/Membership.aspx> accessed 1 June 2020.

4.2 Overall Impact of the UN Human Rights Treaties

4.2.1 Incorporation and Reliance by Legislature and Executive

The seven treaties ratified by South Africa have had a significant impact on laws and policies in South Africa. In most instances the laws and policies made express references to the relevant treaties; on a few occasions, to the COs of the treaty bodies, and in other instances the impact was realised through the utilisation of the treaties by stakeholders during the drafting of the laws and policies.[69] The ratification of OP-CAT has also influenced institutional reforms.[70]

4.2.2 Reliance by Judiciary

By virtue of section 231(4) of the Constitution, South Africa is a dualist state. As such, international law only becomes law in South Africa when it has been enacted into law by national legislation. The only exception to the rule is when the provision of the treaty is self-executing, but the jurisprudence is not yet clear on the meaning of self-executing treaties. Section 39(1)(b) of the Constitution obliges South African courts to consider international law as a tool to interpret the Bill of Rights. To this extent, the treaties have generally been applied as interpretive guides on different occasions by the judiciary. However, there are also instances in which the state reporting process was used as a basis of factual scenarios and set of circumstances to influence the opinions of courts.[71] The South African judiciary has also influenced the jurisprudence of the UN treaty bodies.[72]

The impact of the treaties on the South African judiciary can be enhanced or impeded by the approach of different judges. In the case of *Gauteng Provincial Legislature In Re: Dispute Concerning the Constitutionality of Certain Provisions of the School Education Bill of 1995*,[73] the lead judgment by Mahomed DP for example made no reference to CERD. However, Sachs J in a separate judgment, which applied internationally accepted principles of minority rights protection, made reference to CERD in espousing the principle of affirmative action.[74]

---

69   This form of impact was mostly found in constitutional debates.
70   See pt 5 for a detailed discussion on specific treaties.
71   See pt 5 for a detailed discussion on reliance by the judiciary.
72   CESCR Cttee General Comment 24: State obligations under the International Covenant on Economic, Social and Cultural Rights in the context of business activities, para 4. The CESCR Cttee also referred to the decision of the Constitutional Court in the case of *Daniels v Scribante and Others* Case CCT 50/16, judgment of 11 May 2017, paras 37–39.
73   1996 (4) BCLR 537 (CC).
74   Para 82.

4.2.3 Impact on and through Independent State Institutions

The treaties have had the most impact on the work of the South African Law Reform Commission (SALRC), the SAHRC[75] and the CGE. The Truth and Reconciliation Commission on some occasions made reference to CAT in its final report. Apart from the above stated state institutions, the treaties have not had a discernible influence on the work of other independent state institutions such as the CRL Rights Commission, the Office of the Military Ombud, and the Judicial Inspectorate for Correctional Services (JICS). However, with the establishment of the NPM, OP-CAT could likely become more influential in the works of the JICS.[76]

4.2.4 Impact on and through Non-state Actors

CSOs have played crucial roles in promoting the influence of the UN treaty system in South Africa. CSOs have advocated the compliance with South Africa's obligations under the different treaties and have even ingeniously deployed the state reporting process through strategic litigation. There has been a robust engagement by CSOs with the treaty body state reporting process. However, there have not been significant engagement with the complaint mechanisms of the UN treaty system. The lack of engagement with the individual complaint mechanisms of the UN is connected with the existence of a reliable and independent judicial system in South Africa.

4.2.5 Impact of State Reporting

The state reporting process has gained more traction over the years. There are signs of improvement in the quality of the state reports and conformity with reporting guidelines and increased participation of CSOs in the state reporting process. There is also increasing awareness of the importance of

---

75 The SAHRC generally interprets its mandate to include how South Africa gives effect to its obligations in terms of international treaties. See SAHRC Annual Report 2006/2007 1. The SAHRC has a Committee on Policy and International Coordination that deals with international treaty reports. The Policy and International Co-ordination Committee of the SAHRC attended a four-day training course on UN Treaty Report Writing in Pretoria, 20–23 September 1999. See SAHRC 4th Annual Report 1998/1999 73. The SAHRC has a sub-programme called International Treaty Body Monitoring. The sub-programme monitors the government's follow-up of recommendations from treaty bodies and contributes towards general awareness raising of South Africa's international and regional human rights obligations. See SAHRC Annual Report 2010 48.

76 The inspecting judge of the JICS reported that he represented JICS on the National Preventive Mechanism (NPM) as required by OP-CAT. See Judicial Inspectorate for Correctional Services Annual Reports 2018/2019 10.

the reporting process among government officials.[77] As discussed above, the reporting process contributed to the eventual ratification of OP-CAT. Although the influence of COs of the treaty bodies is relatively low, it is anticipated that the planned establishment of the NMRF will most likely improve the impact of the COs in South Africa. However, there is a need to improve the visibility and publicity of the treaties and the reporting process in the media.

4.2.6 Impact of Individual Communications

The influence of the individual communications procedure has been minimal, with only three communications submitted over the study period.[78] Only one treaty body, the HRCttee, has found a single violation against South Africa.[79] The low level of utilisation of the individual complaint procedure in South Africa is connected to the general belief by stakeholders that the country's domestic legal framework offers sufficient protection for human rights.[80]

The government's response suggests that it does not accept the legitimacy of UN individual complaint mechanisms. South Africa did not cooperate with the HRCttee during the case of Bradley McCallum, the only case in which it was found to be in violation. It also took no significant steps to implement the decision of the HRCttee.[81] In defending the approach of the country to the HRCttee's decision, the Minister of Justice and Correctional Services in his briefing before the National Assembly's Committee on Justice and Correctional Services, stated:[82]

---

[77] South African Government News Agency, 'SA Advocating for Economic, Social, Cultural Rights' 21 September 2015 <https://www.sanews.gov.za/south-africa/sa-advocating-economic-social-cultural-rights> accessed 12 November 2020.

[78] HRCttee, *McCallum v South Africa* (2 November 2010); HRCttee, *Gareth Anver Prince v South Africa* (14 November 2007; no violation found) and CPRD Cttee, *ANP v South Africa*, CRPD/C/23/D/73/2019 (submitted 19 September 2017; declared inadmissible 28 August 2020).

[79] HRCttee, *McCallum v South Africa* CCPR/C/100/D/1818/2008 (25 October 2010).

[80] The use of individual complaints in South Africa is also the same at the regional level. South Africa has had four individual cases and was not found to be in violation. South Africa is also yet to accept the direct individual access competence of the African Court. A government official stated that the treaty body members do not understand the peculiarities of South African society and cannot do better than the Constitutional Court justices. (Interview with anonymous government official. Physical interview conducted at the University of Pretoria on 29 July 2019).

[81] The decision was used by the SAHRC to advocate the criminalisation of torture and ratification of OP-CAT.

[82] Parliamentary Monitoring Group, 'Minister on National Council for Correctional Services Appointments; Correctional Services Contingent Liability and Legal Services Capacity; POPI Act appointments' <https://pmg.org.za/committee-meeting/21819/> accessed 1 June 2020.

We are compliant with international conventions on offender policy. For example, the St Albans matter in which a gang member killed a correctional facility official, required significant clean-up to the extent of almost war. However, these offenders ran to the UN and claimed maltreatment and torture that resulted in a finding against SA by the UN that the Department intends to challenge. Previous cases have found on the side of SA that officials did not act too heavily. Only two individual complaints have been filed against South Africa and the country was found in violation in one of the cases. These officials work in extremely difficult conditions.

5 Detailed Impact of the Different UN Human Rights Treaties in South Africa

5.1 *International Convention on the Elimination of All Forms of Racial Discrimination*

5.1.1 Incorporation and Reliance by Legislature and Executive

Even though South Africa had not ratified CERD as at the time of drafting the Constitution, traces of the Convention are evident in the 1996 Constitution. The prohibition of hate speech in section 16(2) of the South African Constitution was influenced by article 4 of CERD.[83] The influence of CERD is also evident in the express reference to CERD in the Promotion of Equality and Prevention of Unfair Discrimination Act (PEPUDA),[84] the Prevention and Combating of Hate Crimes and Hate Speech Bill,[85] and the Employment Equity Act.[86] In terms of government policies, CERD was influential in the definition of racial discrimination and the role of government in combating and eliminating racism, racial discrimination, xenophobia and related intolerance.[87]

---

83 Heyns and Viljoen (n 29) 553.
84 Promotion of Equality and Prevention of Unfair Discrimination Act, Preamble. Section 2(h) of the PEPUDA also states that the objects of the Act include to 'facilitate further compliance with international law obligations including treaty obligations in terms of, amongst others, the Convention on the Elimination of All Forms of Racial Discrimination and the Convention on the Elimination of All Forms of Discrimination against Women'.
85 Prevention and Combating of Hate Crimes and Hate Speech Bill B9 – 2018, Preamble para 3. The influence of CERD on the Bill was also acknowledged by the DOJ & CD in its Annual Report 2009/2010 145, 146.
86 Explanatory Memorandum to the Employment Equity Act 9.
87 National Action Plan to Combat Racism, Racial Discrimination, Xenophobia and Related Intolerance 7, 37.

5.1.2 Reliance by Judiciary

CERD was influential in the Gauteng High Court's decision in the case of *Duduzile Baleni and Others v Minister of Mineral Resources and Others*.[88] In that case, the fifth respondent, Transworld Energy and Mineral Resources (SA) Property Limited (TEM), an Australian company, had applied for a mining right for titanium ores and other heavy minerals in the Xolobeni area of the Eastern Cape. The Court placed great reliance on General Recommendation 23 of the CERD Cttee on indigenous people in deciding that the consent of (as opposed to mere consultation with) the community members who will be negatively affected by the mining operation is the appropriate requirement for TEM to mine on the ancestral lands of the applicants' community.[89] Similarly, the Equality Court used CERD as an interpretive guide in the case of *Nelson Mandela Foundation Trust and Another v Afriforum NPC*.[90] In that case the defendant contended that section 10(1) of the Equality Act applies only to hate speech communicated by words. The Equality Court stated that article 20(2) of the ICCPR and article 4 of the CERD prohibit hate speech in the widest sense to include any expression of ideas and neither instrument draws a distinction between verbal or non-verbal advocacy or communication of racial hatred.[91] The Court ruled that hate speech goes beyond mere words and that the display of the previous ('apartheid era') South African flag constitutes hate speech against black people.[92] CERD has also been quite influential in the jurisprudence of the Labour Court. In the case of *Francis Kanku and Others v Grindrod Fuelogic*,[93] the Labour Court referred to CERD in conjunction with section 9(3) of the Constitution in reaching its conclusion that nationality as a reason for dismissal is discriminatory. In addition to the above, CERD has generally been applied as interpretive guide by the Constitutional Court,[94] the High

---

88 [2019] 1 All SA 358 (GP).
89 See para 79. The Court also made extensive reference to the decision of the HRCttee in the case of *Angela Poma poma v Peru* and the CESCR Cttee General Comment 21.
90 2019 (10) BCLR 1245 (EqC).
91 *Nelson Mandela Foundation Trust and Another v Afriforum NPC*, 2019 (10) BCLR 1245 (EqC) paras 150 & 151.
92 *Nelson Mandela Foundation Trust and Another v Afriforum NPC*, 2019 (10) BCLR 1245 (EqC) para 177.
93 [2017] ZALCCT 26. See also *Solidarity v Minister of Labour and Others* [2020] 1 BLLR 79 (LC) and *Director General, Department of Labour v Win-Cool Industrial Enterprise (Pty) Ltd* [2007] 9 BLLR 845 (LC).
94 *Gauteng Provincial Legislature in re: Dispute Concerning the Constitutionality of Certain Provisions of the School Education Bill of 1995* 1996 (4) BCLR 537 (CC); *Certification of the Amended Text of the Constitution of the Republic of South Africa*, 1996 1997 (1) BCLR 1 (CC);

Court,[95] the Equality Court,[96] and the Land Claims Court.[97]

5.1.3 Impact of State Reporting

South Africa has submitted two reports to the CERD Cttee. The two reports were each submitted after a delay of approximately four years.

There is no indication as to whether the reports were prepared in consultation with CSOs.[98] The SAHRC submitted shadow reports to CERD both these reports and made oral presentations before the CERD Cttee. The active participation of the SAHRC in the CERD reporting process resulted in recommendations by the CERD Cttee urging the state to implement the recommendations of the SAHRC and increase the budget of the SAHRC. There is no record of NGO submission of shadow reports to the initial report, but two NGOs submitted shadow reports to the combined fourth to eighth periodic report.[99] The two reports were comprehensive and addressed thematic issues contained in CERD.[100] The presentation of the initial report was made by the Minister of Justice while the combined fourth to eighth periodic report was presented by the Deputy Minister of Justice.

Law Society of South Africa and Others v Minister for Transport and Another 2011 (2) BCLR 150 (CC); *Jacques Charl Hoffmann v South African Airways* 2000 (11) BCLR 1211 (CC); *Annette Brink v Andre Kitshoff NO* 1996 (6) BCLR 752 (CC) para 38.

[95] *Isimangaliso Wetland Park and Another v Sodwana Bay Guest Lodge and Another* (01/2017) [2018] ZAKZDHC 60.

[96] See *Afri-Forum and Another v Julius Sello Malema and Others* 2011 (12) BCLR 1289 (EqC); *South African Human Rights Commission on behalf of South African Jewish Board of Deputies v Masuku and Another* [2017] 3 All SA 1029 (EqC, J).

[97] *Richtersveld and Others v Alexkor Limited and Another* [2001] ZALCC 10.

[98] In its COs to South Africa's initial report, the CERD Cttee requested that South Africa should consult with CSOs and the SAHRC in connection with the preparation of its next periodic report.

[99] Solidarity Trade Union's Centre for Fair Labour Practices argued that South Africa through laws and policies such as the Employment Equity Act and the Broad-Based Black Economic Empowerment Act seeks to promote a demographic representative society which in reality promotes neo-racism. The application of affirmative action under the constitutional ideology of unfair discrimination is contrary to the provisions of art 1(4) of CERD. On the other hand, Police and Prisons Civil Rights Union contended that transformation in the form of affirmative action such as the Employment Equity Act and the Broad-Based Black Economic Empowerment Act is required to achieve equality and redress apartheid disparities in South Africa. The organisation argued that the special measures taken by South Africa comply with the Convention.

[100] An illustration of the quality of the CERD report is exemplified in the request by two members of the CERD Cttee that the South African report should be sent to their home countries of Brazil and Guatemala. Summary Record of CERD Initial Report, South Africa, CERD/C/SR.1766, pages 8, 9.

The initial COs of the CERD Cttee required South Africa to provide additional information on the country's population and promotion of native languages, among other issues. The first periodic report addressed the concerns of the CERD Cttee about inadequate information on the composition of the country's population;[101] the promotion of languages of native and minority communities;[102] information on the CRL Commission;[103] the role of traditional leadership and on the status of customary law in South Africa;[104] and on measures adopted to address the situation of *de facto* segregation.[105] Apart from the request for information, there is no discernible impact of the CERD Cttee's COs to South Africa's initial report. South Africa did not submit an interim report to the CERD Cttee as requested in the COs to the initial report. In its dialogue with the CERD Cttee during the presentation of its second periodic report, the Deputy Minister of Justice stated that because the vision of the government is that of a people united in their diversity, and not divided along ethnic and tribal lines, the government does not as a rule disaggregate statistical data according to ethnicity.[106]

The key issues in the COs to the combined fourth to eighth periodic report are statistical data; institutional strengthening of the SAHRC; hate crime and hate speech; special measures for disadvantaged communities; the situation of black and marginalised ethnic women and girls; situation of indigenous peoples; and the situation of non-citizens. In line with the requirements of the CERD Cttee, South Africa submitted a follow-up report on measures taken to strengthen and comply with the recommendations of the SAHRC, and Prevention and Combating of Hate Crimes and Hate Speech Bill.

Although some positive progress was reported on these issues, the impact of the COs on the reported measures is not discernible. In an interview, a government official stated that the dialogue with the CERD Cttee was not particularly useful because the CERD Cttee does not understand the South African context.[107] There also is some perception that since CERD was largely drafted as a response to the apartheid regime in South Africa, it has lost its relevance with the end of apartheid.

---

101   CERD First Periodic Report, South Africa, CERD/C/ZAF/4–8, paras 11–17.
102   ibid para 19.
103   ibid para 20.
104   ibid para 56.
105   ibid para 86.
106   Summary Records of CERD First Periodic Report, South Africa, CERD/C/SR.2460, para 8.
107   Interview with an anonymous government official. Physical interview conducted at the University of Pretoria on 29 July 2019.

5.1.4 Impact on and through Independent State Institutions

CERD has impacted the work of the SAHRC. For the purposes of article 14(2) of CERD, the SAHRC is the competent body to receive and consider petitions from individuals or groups of individuals who claim to be victims of any of the rights in CERD. The SAHRC relied extensively on the provisions of CERD and the COs of the CERD Cttee to South Africa in determining South Africa's compliance with international law obligations with respect to the implementation of special measures.[108] In advocating comprehensive and disaggregated socio-economic data for purposes of special measures, the SAHRC referred to the CERD Cttee's 2006 and 2016 COs that requested government to provide more exhaustive statistical demographic data that includes social and economic indicators and, furthermore, accounts for indigenous groups and non-citizens.[109]

There is no discernible impact of CERD on the work of other independent national institutions.

5.1.5 Impact on and through Non-state Actors

CERD has influenced the activities of trade union organisations in South Africa. The state reporting process of CERD was used by Solidarity Trade Union's Centre for Fair Labour Practices, and the Police and Prisons Civil Rights Union (POPCRU) to voice opinions on the Broad-Based Black Economic Empowerment Act.[110]

5.1.6 Other Measures

Following the devastating incidents of xenophobic attacks in South Africa in 2008, the CERD Cttee on 11 March 2011, under its early warning measures procedures, sent a letter to South Africa,[111] expressing its concerns about xenophobic attacks and racist violence on refugees and asylum seekers in South Africa. The CERD Cttee requested South Africa to provide information on measures taken or envisaged to combat xenophobic attitudes and to stop racist violence

---

108 SAHRC Equality Report 2017/2018.
109 SAHRC Equality Report, 2017/2018 34.
110 See shadow reports submitted to the CERD Cttee in the consideration of CERD First Periodic Report, South Africa, CERD/C/ZAF/4–8by Solidarity Trade Union's Centre for Fair Labour Practices and Police and Prisons Civil Rights Union. See also 'Solidariteit: Our Visit to the UN: Questions and Answers' <https://regsfonds.solidariteit.co.za/en/our-visit-to-the-un-quick-questions-and-answers/> accessed 1 June 2020.
111 <https://www.ohchr.org/Documents/HRBodies/CERD/EarlyWarning/SouthAfrica_11March2011.pdf> accessed 1 June 2020.

against non-South African citizens living in South Africa. However, South Africa did not respond to the letter from the CERD Cttee.

5.1.7   Brief Conclusion

Even though the CERD has had some impact in South Africa, its influence has mostly been in the form of indirect impact on laws, policies, judicial decisions and on the work of non-state actors in South Africa.

One of the reasons for the high level of indirect influence of CERD in South Africa is the enactment of national laws that are specifically targeted at addressing South Africa's particular history of racial injustice as a result of apartheid. One of the major focuses of a new South African democracy was the need to address residual and systemic racism that arose from a legacy of previously institutionalised injustices. The need to deal with the social legacy of legalised racism has resulted in the promulgation of several policy frameworks on the elimination of racial discrimination and affirmative actions for previously disadvantaged groups.[112] The availability of national laws and policies that are more specific to the South African reality has resulted in more reliance on national laws than on CERD.[113] The constructive dialogue between the CERD Cttee and the South African delegates reveals that the CERD Cttee and the delegates were not able to reach a standpoint on issues of statistical information and the South African concept of 'unfair discrimination'.[114]

---

[112] Some of the laws enacted to combat the residue of apartheid in South Africa include the Film and Publication Act of 1996; the South African Schools Act of 1996; the Culture Promotion Amendment Act of 1998; the National Empowerment Fund Act of 1998; the Refugees Act of 1998; the Employment Equity Act of 1999; and the Promotion of Equality and Prevention of Unfair Discrimination Act of 2000.

[113] In its initial report to the CERD Cttee, South Africa elaborated on the 'South African concept of unfair discrimination'. The country stated that the distinction between fair and unfair discrimination as permitted under national laws is 'slightly different from that which underpins' CERD. See CERD Initial Report, South Africa 10. In its discussion with the CERD Cttee, the Cttee consistently asked the South African delegates to clarify the concept of 'unfair discrimination'. See Summary Record of CERD Initial Report, South Africa,, CERD/C/SR.1766, pages 4, 6. In his response to the CERD Cttee members, the Deputy Minister of Justice maintained that contrary to the position of the CERD Cttee members on unfair discrimination, 'article 1(4) of the Convention amounted to an acknowledgment that, in certain circumstances, special measures could be taken to promote the advancement of human rights and freedoms and that those measures should not be deemed to be discriminatory'.

[114] Summary Records of CERD First Periodic Report, South Africa, CERD/C/SR.2460 paras 33 and 38.

5.2 *International Covenant on Civil and Political Rights*

5.2.1 Incorporation and Reliance by Legislature and Executive

The influence of CCPR on the South African Constitution can be derived from the strong overlap between some of the rights in CCPR and the Bill of Rights in the Constitution. The Bill of Rights provides for equality,[115] the right to life,[116] the abolition of slavery,[117] and liberty and security of the person,[118] which includes a prohibition against arbitrary arrest. Propaganda for war and advocacy of racial hatred is prohibited in both.[119] Section 31 of the Bill of Rights is a replica of article 27 of CCPR.[120] CCPR was also used by stakeholders in their submissions to the committee responsible for the Bill of Rights in the final Constitution.[121]

Apart from the similarities between the rights provided for in CCPR and the rights guaranteed in some national laws, such as the Electoral Act, the Municipal Electoral Act,[122] the National Water Act, the Employment Equity Act, the Social Assistance Act, the Labour Relations Act, the Recognition of Customary Marriages Act, the Municipal Structures Act, and the Choice on Termination of Pregnancy Act,[123] the influence of CCPR is difficult to ascertain.

Some influence of CCPR can be found in the provisions of the National Action Plan to Combat Racism, Racial Discrimination, Xenophobia and Related Intolerance, launched on 25 March 2019. The National Action Plan referred to article 2 of CCPR and General Comment 31 of the HRCttee in asserting that states assume obligations and duties under international law to respect, protect and fulfill human rights for all persons within their territory or jurisdiction, without discrimination of any kind.[124]

---

115 Arts 2, 3 CCPR; Constitution of the Republic of South Africa, 1996, s 9.
116 Art 6 CCPR; Constitution of the Republic of South Africa, 1996, s 11.
117 Art 8 CCPR; Constitution of the Republic of South Africa, 1996, s 13.
118 Art 9 CCPR; Constitution of the Republic of South Africa, 1996, s 12.
119 Art 20 CCPR; Constitution of the Republic of South Africa, 1996, s 16(2).
120 Constitution of the Republic of South Africa, 1996, s 31(1)(a) provides that '[p]ersons belonging to a cultural, religious or linguistic community may not be denied the right, with other members of the community, to enjoy their culture, practice their religion and use their language'. Its inclusion is the result of a compromise, and is an attempt to appease fears that especially the Afrikaner identity will not be accorded sufficient protection under the Constitution.
121 Theme Committee 4 Fundamental Rights Report and Explanatory Memorandum on Children's Rights to the Constitutional Assembly 11.
122 Initial Report, CCPR, South Africa, para 9.
123 Initial Report, CCPR, South Africa, para 57.
124 National Action Plan to Combat Racism, Racial Discrimination, Xenophobia and Related Intolerance 54.

5.2.2 Reliance by Judiciary

The provisions of CCPR have, to a significant extent, been referred to or invoked by the judiciary.

Among the notable instances where CCPR played a significant role in the Court's reasoning is the case of *Amabhungane Centre For Investigative Journalism NPC and Another v Minister of Justice and Correctional Services and Others*.[125] The North Gauteng High Court referred to the COs[126] of the HRCttee to South Africa's initial report in its consideration of the legality of sections 30, 35 and 37 of the Regulation of Interception of Communications and Provision of Communication-Related Information Act (RICA) 2002. The HRCttee in its COs had required South Africa to ensure that the interception of communications by law enforcement and security services is carried out only on the basis of the law and under judicial supervision.[127] The Court ruled that the absence of judicial oversight within the RICA's regime for the management, usage and accessibility controls of data that are intercepted not only amounts to an ineffective safeguard, but is no safeguard at all.

Similarly, in the case of *Mlungwana and Others v State and Another*,[128] the Constitutional Court referred to the decision of the HRCttee in the case of *Kivenmaa v Finland* as an interpretive guide in ruling that '[t]he possibility of a criminal sanction prevents, discourages, and inhibits freedom of assembly, even if only temporarily'.[129]

The Constitutional Court has also used the CCPR as interpretive guide in the cases of *Kaunda and Others v The President of the RSA and Others*;[130] *Alex Ruta v Minister of Home Affairs*;[131] *DE v RH*;[132] *The State v Makwanyane and Mchunu*;[133] *MEC for Education: KwaZulu-Natal and Others v Pillay*;[134] *Richard Gordon Volks NO v Ethel Robinson and Others*;[135] *Centre for Child Law and Others v Media 24 Limited and Others*; *Kruger v National Director of Public*

---

125 2020 (1) SA 90 (GP).
126 *Amabhungane Centre For Investigative Journalism NPC & Another v Minister of Justice and Correctional Services and Others* para 99.
127 ibid, para 91.
128 2019 (1) BCLR 88 (CC).
129 Para 47.
130 2005 (4) SA 235 (CC) paras 34, 98, 119, 216, 223 & 263.
131 2019 (2) SA 329 (CC).
132 2015 (5) SA 83 (CC).
133 1995 (3) SA 391 (CC).
134 Case 2008 (1) SA 474 (CC).
135 2005 (5) BCLR 446 (CC) paras 53 & 83.

Prosecutions;[136] *Freedom of Religion South Africa v Minister of Justice and Constitutional Development and Others;*[137] *AB and Another v Minister of Social Development;*[138] *Xolile David Kham and Others v Electoral Commission and Another;*[139] *Doctors for Life International v The Speaker of the National Assembly and Others;*[140] and *Jonathan Zealand v Minister for Justice and Constitutional Development of Correctional Services.*[141] CCPR has also been referred to in cases on the right to a fair hearing,[142] and the protection of family under article 23(1).[143]

5.2.3 Impact on and through Independent State Institutions

Evidence of the impact of CCPR is visible in the work of the SALRC on Sexual Offences and Adult Prostitution;[144] and on Privacy and Data Protection.[145] The SAHRC submitted its own report to the HRCttee.

5.2.4 Impact on and through Non-state Actors

The findings of the HRCttee against South Africa in the case of *Bradley McCallum v South Africa* was published on the website of the African Policing Civilian Oversight.[146] A review of the shadow reports submitted to the HRCttee illustrates the influence of CCPR on the work of CSOs such as Gender DynamiX (GDX), Iranti-Org, and Legal Resources Centre.

5.2.5 Impact of State Reporting

South Africa has submitted only one report to the HRCttee. The report was submitted after a prolonged delay of 14 years. South Africa submitted the report after the HRCttee had announced its intention to review South Africa in the

---

136 2019 (6) BCLR 703 (CC); here the Court also makes reference to HRCttee General Comment 32, art 14: Right to Equality Before Courts and Tribunals and to Fair Trial.
137 2020 (1) SA 1 (CC).
138 CCT 2017 (3) SA 570 (CC).
139 2016 (2) SA 338 (CC).
140 2006 (6) SA 416 (CC).
141 2008 (4) SA 458 (CC) para 30.
142 *Pather v Financial Services Board* 2018 (1) SA 161 (SCA) para 15; *City of Cape Town v South African National Roads Authority Limited and Others* 2015 (3) SA 386 (SCA) para 13.
143 *Hattingh v Juta* 2013 (3) SA 275 (CC) para 14.
144 SALRC Discussion Paper on Sexual Offences and Adult Prostitution 2009 93, 94.
145 SALRC Discussion Paper on Privacy and Data Protection 2006, ch 2, 2. See also SALRC Issue Paper 29, The Review of the Witchcraft Suppression Act 3 of 1957, 2014.
146 African Civilian Policing Oversight '*McCallum v South Africa*, UN Doc CCPR/C/100/D/1818/2008 (2 November 2010)' <https://acjr.org.za/resource-centre/southafrica_iccpr_t5_1818_2008.pdf/view> accessed 1 June 2020.

absence of a report.[147] The delay in the submission of the report was because South Africa had to prepare several reports under the UN and AU human rights system.[148]

The report was prepared without consultations with civil society.[149] The effect of the lack of consultation in the preparation of the state report was the submission of 13 thematic and four joint shadow reports to the initial report. The SAHRC also submitted a shadow report.[150]

The delegation that presented the report in Geneva was high level and experienced. The Minister in the Presidency responsible for women, the Deputy Minister of the Department of International Relations, the Deputy Minister of Justice and Constitutional Development and the Deputy Permanent Representative of South Africa in Geneva were among the delegates who attended the session of the HRCttee in which the report was considered.[151] The report was presented by the Deputy Minister of Justice and Constitutional Development.[152]

The pertinent issues in the COs are racism and xenophobia; harmful cultural traditions and practices; the protection of the rights of persons living with HIV; violence based on gender, sex, sexual orientation and gender identity; corporal punishment; excessive and disproportionate use of force by the police; and violence, torture, ill-treatment, deaths, and conditions of places of detention. The COs also highlighted human rights violations in the areas of juvenile justice; migration; the protection of human rights defenders; the right to privacy and interception of private communications; and indigenous peoples' rights.[153]

The key recommendations selected for follow-up by the HRCttee are the implementation of recommendations of the TRC and conditions of places of detention. Even though South Africa has fully engaged with the follow-up

---

147   <https://thoughtleader.co.za/lukasmuntingh/2014/10/27/sas-failures-in-the-international-human-rights-system/> accessed 1 June 2020.
148   CCPR Initial Report, South Africa, CCPR/C/ZAF/1, page 4.
149   This information is contained in at least two shadow reports submitted to the Human Rights Committee. See 'Thematic Report on Criminal Justice and Human Rights in South Africa'; 'Civil Society Report on the Implementation of the ICCPR'. See also Summary Records of CCPR First Periodic Report, South Africa, CCPR/C/SR.3235 page 4.
150   See generally South African Human Rights Commission, List of Issues Report to the Human Rights Committee on South Africa's Implementation of the International Covenant on Civil and Political Rights.
151   South Africa List of Delegate, Ref: 32/2016.
152   Summary Records of CCPR First Periodic Report, South Africa, CCPR/C/SR.3234, page 2.
153   See, generally, COs on the CCPR Initial Report of South Africa, CCPR/C/ZAF/CO/1.

procedure of the HRCttee COs and submitted a follow-up report on 12 May 2017,[154] much of the information in the follow-up report is based on existing policies, laws and processes that predate the recommendations of the HRCttee. To this effect, it is doubtful if the COs have had any significant impact on laws and policies in South Africa.

5.2.6 Individual Communications

Two individual communications (*Gareth Anver Prince v South Africa* and *Bradley McCallum v South Africa*)[155] have been lodged and finalised against South Africa. In the case of *Bradley McCallum v South Africa*, the HRCttee found South Africa to be in violation of article 7 of CCPR read in conjunction with article 2(3) and article 10(1) of CCPR.[156] The HRCttee required South Africa to investigate the claims of Bradley McCallum, prosecute those responsible for the violation of his rights, provide reparation and adequate compensation to him, submit information on measures taken on the HRCttee's views within 180 days and publish the HRCttee's views.[157] The government did not cooperate with the HRCttee during the process of consideration by the Committee. Despite several requests from the HRCttee, the state did not submit any information on the admissibility or the substance of McCallum's claim.[158] However, the South African government published the findings of the HRCttee in national newspapers in 2011 and outlined the findings of the HRCttee and actions taken by the government.[159] The Department of Correctional Services reopened the investigation into the actions of its officials with respect to the claims of McCallum.[160] However, the National Prosecuting Authority decided not to prosecute anybody as there was not enough evidence for prosecution.[161] The state is yet to pay reparation or compensate the victim in accordance with the views of the HRCttee. Disciplinary proceedings were not pursued against officers involved in the incident because of a legal opinion on the matter.[162]

---

154 <https://tbinternet.ohchr.org/_layouts/15/TreatyBodyExternal/FollowUp.aspx?Treaty=CCPR&Lang=en> accessed 1 June 2020.
155 <https://tbinternet.ohchr.org/_layouts/15/TreatyBodyExternal/countries.aspx?CountryCode=ZAF&Lang=EN> accessed 1 June 2020.
156 HRCttee, *McCallum v South Africa* (2 November 2010) para 7.
157 ibid para 9.
158 ibid para 4.
159 CCPR Initial Report, South Africa, CCPR/C/ZAF/1 para 88.
160 ibid para 89.
161 ibid.
162 Summary Records of CCPR First Periodic Report, South Africa, CCPR/C/SR.3234, CCPR Initial Report, South Africa, CCPR/C/ZAF/1, para 29.

South Africa has not engaged with the follow-up procedures of the HRCttee. The HRCttee indicated in its follow-up progress report that it has not received any follow-up response from South Africa and there is no ongoing follow-up dialogue with South Africa.[163]

In the case of *Gareth Anver Prince v South Africa*, the HRCttee found that South Africa had not breached any article of CCPR.[164]

5.2.7 Brief Conclusion in Respect of CCPR

CCPR has had some influence on policies and legislation in South Africa. The treaty has also in some way impacted on the work of the SAHRC and the SALRC. Beyond the normative provisions of the treaties, the COs of the HRCttee has also impacted the courts. However, it appears that the general influence of CCPR is restricted because of the general nature of the categories of rights covered in the treaty. There is a general preference among stakeholders to substantially use other specialised treaties that provide for the rights of specific categories of persons as opposed to the general provisions of CCPR. There is a need for more awareness in government departments about CCPR. This need transpires from the 2017/2018 annual report the Department of Justice and Constitutional Development: While reporting on the submission of South Africa's CCPR initial report, it erred by referring to the 'Human Rights Committee' as the 'Human Rights Council'.[165]

5.3 *International Covenant on Economic, Social and Cultural Rights*

5.3.1 Incorporation and Reliance by Legislature and Executive

CESCR played an important role in the enactment of socio-economic rights in the South African Constitution. It was relied on by stakeholders during the drafting of the final Constitution.[166] The Constitution provides for socio-economic rights, such as the right to basic and further education,[167] the right

---

163   HRCttee, Follow-up progress report on individual communications received and processed between June 2014 and January 2015, CCPR/C/113/3, 48.
164   HRCttee, *Gareth Anver Prince v South Africa* (14 November 2007) para 8.
165   The report stated that 'South Africa's initial report to the United Nations Human Rights Council was submitted in 2014 and deliberated on in 2016 by the body of independent experts that monitors the implementation of the ICCPR by the State parties to this covenant'. See Department of Justice and Constitutional Development Annual Report 2017–2018 67.
166   Heyns and Viljoen (n 29) 553.
167   Constitution of the Republic of South Africa, 1996, s 29.

of children to basic nutrition, shelter and health care,[168] the right to health,[169] the right to housing,[170] and the right to a clean and sustainable environment.[171]

In terms of policies, the influence of CESCR is discernible from direct reference to CESCR in the following policies: the National Health Insurance Bill;[172] the 2003 White Paper on National Health Insurance Policy;[173] the White Paper on Corrections in South Africa;[174] and the National Strategic Plan on HIV, TB and STIs 2017–2022. In addition to referencing CESCR, the National Action Plan to Combat Racism, Racial Discrimination, Xenophobia and Related Intolerance and the White Paper on the Rights of Persons with Disabilities also referred to General Comment 21[175] and General Comment 3[176] of the CESCR Cttee.

5.3.2 Reliance by Judiciary

CESCR has on several occasions been influential in the pronouncements of South African courts on socio-economic rights.

Notable among the cases is the case of *Equal Education and Others v Minister of Basic Education and Others*.[177] The crux of the matter was the constitutionality of the suspension of the National Schools Nutrition Programme (NSNP) as a result of the closure of schools in South Africa in response to the COVID-19 pandemic. The Department of Education had argued that the NSNP by its very nature was merely a supportive programme to achieve substantive equality and to protect and advance children disadvantaged by unfair discrimination in terms of section 9(2) of the Constitution.[178] The North Gauteng High Court relied on the submissions of South Africa in its initial report to the CESCR Cttee to interpret the nature and obligation of state departments with respect to the realisation of the right to basic nutrition. In reaching its decision that the state has a constitutional duty in terms of section 29(1)(a) of the Constitution to provide basic nutrition, the Court looked at the goals and the description of

---

168 Constitution of the Republic of South Africa, 1996, s 28.
169 Constitution of the Republic of South Africa, 1996, s 27.
170 Constitution of the Republic of South Africa, 1996, s 26.
171 Constitution of the Republic of South Africa, 1996, s 24.
172 National Health Insurance Bill (2019) 2.
173 CESCR was merely listed alongside the Universal Declaration of Human Rights as one of the many international treaties and instruments to which South Africa is a signatory that protect individual rights to health and well-being.
174 White Paper on Corrections in South Africa 80 para 11.7.5.
175 National Action Plan to Combat Racism, Racial Discrimination, Xenophobia and Related Intolerance 46.
176 White Paper on the Rights of Persons with Disabilities 11.
177 [2020] 4 All SA 102 (GP).
178 Para 35.

the NSNP in various documents including South Africa's initial report to the CESCR Cttee. The Court ruled that on the respondents' 'own documents the stance that the nutritional aspects of the NSNP is just a by-product of their duty to educate is simply wrong'.[179]

In the case of *Geneva Claasen and Others v The MEC for Transport and Public Works Western Cape Province and Another*,[180] the Western Cape High Court applied CESCR Cttee General Comment 7 and the report of the Special Rapporteur on adequate housing in giving an order compelling the MEC for Transport and Public Works, Western Cape Provincial Department and the City of Cape Town, to provide suitable alternative accommodation for the applicants before effecting an eviction order. The Court specifically quoted the relevant paragraph of the Special Rapporteur's report which emphasised the duty of the state to provide alternative housing for citizens who must be evicted from their residence due to unavoidable circumstances.

In the case of *Lindiwe Mazibuko and Others v City of Johannesburg and Others*,[181] the Constitutional Court placed strong emphasis on the principle of progressive realisation under article 2(1) of CESCR. In this case the issue in question was whether the City of Johannesburg had taken reasonable steps to provide the residence with enough water. In addressing this question, the Court relied on General Comment 3 of the CESCR Cttee on progressive realisation and the concept of minimum core obligations under paragraphs 9 and 10.[182] The Court found that the City of Johannesburg, by constantly reviewing its policies, had taken reasonable measures to realise the right to access water.[183]

The Court has also made reference to in respect of the right to adequate housing,[184] the right to social security,[185] the right to education,[186] and the

---

179   Para 40.
180   [2016] ZAWCHC 167.
181   2010 (4) SA 1 (CC) paras 41 & 52.
182   ibid, paras 40 & 62.
183   ibid, para 40.
184   *Government of the Republic of South Africa and Others v Irene Grootboom and Others* 2000 (11) BCLR 1169; *Minister of Health and Others v Treatment Action Campaign* 2002 (5) SA 721; *City of Johannesburg v Rand Properties (Pty) Ltd* 2007 (6) BCLR 643 (SCA); *Pontsho Doreen Motswagae and Others v Rustenburg Local Municipality and Another* 2013 (2) SA 613 (CC).
185   *The Minister of Social Development of the Republic of South Africa and Others v Neti Applied Technologies South Africa (Pty) Ltd and Others*; *The Black Sash Trust and Others v The CEO: The South African Social Security Agency and Others* [2018] ZASCA 129.
186   *Governing Body of the Juma Musjid Primary School and Others v Ahmed Asruff Essay NO and Others* 2011 (8) BCLR 761 (CC) paras 40 & 41; *Equal Education and Others v Minister of Basic Education and Others* 2018 (9) BCLR 1130 (ECB).

right to non-discrimination in economic, social and cultural rights on the basis of sexual orientation.[187]

At the international level, the South African judiciary has also influenced the General Comment[188] and individual communication of the CESCR Cttee.[189]

5.3.3   Impact on and through Independent State Institutions

The impact of CESCR on and through independent state institutions has not gained much traction in South Africa. This may be due to the fact that CESCR was not ratified by South Africa until 2015. However, the SALRC referred to the principle of progressive realisation encapsulated in CESCR in its Discussion Paper on Sexual Offences and Adult Prostitution.[190]

5.3.4   Impact on and through Non-state Actors

As is evident from the shadow reports submitted during the consideration of South Africa's CESCR initial report, CESCR had a significant impact on the work of CSOs in South Africa.[191]

5.3.5   Impact of State Reporting

South Africa has submitted only one state report to the CESCR Cttee. The report was submitted by the deadline. The prompt reporting on CESCR may be ascribed to the momentum created by the coalitions between NGOs and government departments during the activities that led to the ratification of CESCR by South Africa.[192] The report was prepared with inputs from a consultative workshop between the government, the SAHRC and civil society organisations.[193] In addition to the state report, South Africa provided supplementary information to the list of issues raised by the CESCR Cttee. The South African delegate, led by the Deputy Minister of Justice, had a constructive dialogue with the CESCR Cttee.[194]

---

[187]   *Jade September v Mr Subramoney* [2019] 4 All SA 927 (WCC) para 91.
[188]   CESCR Cttee General Comment 24: State Obligations under the International Covenant on Economic, Social and Cultural Rights in the context of business activities, para 4.
[189]   Case CCT 50/16, judgment of 11 May 2017, paras 37–39.
[190]   SALRC Discussion Paper on Sexual Offences and Adult Prostitution 2009, 93 & 94.
[191]   Some of the organisations include the Centre for Applied Legal Services, Sex Workers Education and Advocacy Task Force and Dullar Omar Institute.
[192]   Interview with Prof Ebenezer Durojaye, Project Head, Socio-Economic Rights Project, Dullah Omar Institute, University of Western Cape, in-person interview conducted at the University of Western Cape on 22 August 2019.
[193]   CESCR Initial Report, South Africa, E/C.12/ZAF/1 page 4.
[194]   COs on the CESCR Initial Report of South Africa, E/C.12/ZAF/CO/1, page 1.

The initial report to the CESCR Cttee attracted alternate reports from approximately 20 CSOs, including the SAHRC. Two factors are responsible for the high number of alternate reports: the long delay in the ratification of CESCR, which had resulted in the existence of different coalitions for the ratification of CESCR, and the historical importance attached to socio-economic rights as a pathway to erase the economic inequalities created by apartheid and the status of socio-economic rights in the South African Constitution.[195]

Concerns expressed by the CESCR Cttee in its COs to South Africa include the absence of the right to work and the right to an adequate standard of living from the South African Constitution; the introduction of austerity measures to relieve debt levels without defining the time frame within which such austerity measures should be re-examined or lifted; the poverty ratio in South Africa; and the need to expedite the adoption of the Social Assistance Amendment Bill of 2018 to address some of the economic inequalities in the country.

In terms of impact, the recommendation of the CESCR Cttee on the adoption of the Social Assistance Amendment Bill and provision of access to social assistance for people between the ages of 18 and 59 was used as an advocacy tool during the public hearing on the Social Assistance Amendment Bill.[196] Hoodah Fayker-Abrahams, Black Sash National Advocacy Manager, while addressing the Portfolio Committee, stated that '[o]ne of the four priority recommendations that the UN has requested a report on by October 2020, include the need to address the lack of social assistance for poor people between the ages of 18 and 59'.[197] While acknowledging her support for the proposals to the amended Bill, she reiterated that the Portfolio Committee would have to work towards compliance with the CESCR recommendations by the October 2020 deadline. On 22 October 2020 the Social Assistance Amendment Bill was passed by the National Council of Provinces and was sent to the President for assent.[198] The amended Bill addressed some of the concerns of the CESCR Cttee about the poverty ratio in South Africa and the need for improvement of social assistance by South Africa. The amended Bill provides for additional

---

[195] CESCR Initial Report, South Africa, E/C.12/ZAF/1 page 4.
[196] Parliamentary Monitoring Group 'Social Assistance Amendment Bill [B8– 2018]: public hearings' <https://pmg.org.za/committee-meeting/29901/> accessed 14 November 2020.
[197] ibid.
[198] Parliamentary Monitoring Group 'Social Assistance Amendment Bill (B8–2018)' <https://pmg.org.za/bill/781/> accessed 14 November 2020. In the explanatory memorandum to the Bill, it was stated that subject to approval of funding, the National Treasury has made a provisional allocation of R524m and R1,487bn for implementation of the additional payments for the Child Support Grant (CSG top-up) during the 2019/20 and 2020/21 financial years, respectively.

payments linked to social grants; payment of benefits to a child-headed household; and provide for social relief of distress in the event of a disaster.

5.3.6 Brief Conclusion

Even though there was a delayed ratification of CESCR in South Africa, this treaty has played a significant role in South Africa, and in particular, through the judiciary. Two factors may be responsible for this. One factor is the status of socio-economic rights in the South African legal system. Based on the extensive protection of socio-economic rights in the Bill of Rights, judicial enforcement of socio-economic rights has resulted in the litigation of numerous domestic socio-economic rights cases. The second factor is derived from the first. The abundance of national litigation on socio-economic rights brings to the fore section 39(1)(b) of the South African Constitution, which requires courts to consider international law (including CESCR) in interpreting the Bill of Rights.

5.4 *Convention on the Elimination of All Forms of Discrimination against Women*

5.4.1 Incorporation and Reliance by Organs of State

As CEDAW was formally accepted during the democratisation process in South Africa, it has played and continues to play a vital role in the development of legislation and policies, and has contributed to significant institutional and domestic legal reform.

CEDAW contributed to the women's rights and equality rights contained in the South African Constitution. It functioned to resolve tensions between certain traditional leaders and customary laws, women's rights organisations and civil society during the drafting process of the South African Constitution.[199] The norms of CEDAW such as equality,[200] and women's rights, including reproductive rights,[201] are enshrined in the South African Bill of Rights.

CEDAW has played an important role in domestic legal reform notably with regard to equality,[202] the recognition of customary marriage,[203] reproductive rights,[204] trafficking[205] and domestic violence.[206]

---

[199] Heyns and Viljoen (n 29) 554.
[200] Constitution of the Republic of South Africa s 9.
[201] Constitution of the Republic of South Africa s 27(1)(a).
[202] Promotion of Equality and Prevention of Unfair Discrimination Act 4 of 2000; CEDAW Cttee, COs on the combined second, third and fourth periodic report of South Africa, paras 26–28. Women Empowerment and Gender Equality Bill [B50–2013].
[203] Recognition of Customary Marriages Act 120 of 1998.
[204] Choice of Termination of Pregnancy Act 96 of 1992.
[205] Prevention and Combating of Trafficking in Persons Act 7 of 2013.
[206] CEDAW is invoked explicitly in the Preamble to the Domestic Violence Act 116 of 1998 and Criminal Law (Sexual Offences and Related Matters) Amendment Act 32 of 2007.

In terms of policies, South Africa's National Policy Framework for Women Empowerment and Gender Equality refers to South Africa's obligations in terms of CEDAW and notes that 'the vision outlined (in the policy) is based on the Reconstruction and Development Programme (RDP), the Women's Charter for Effective Equality, the National Policy for Women's Empowerment, the Convention on the Elimination of All Forms of Discrimination Against Women, and the Platform of Action of the Fourth World Conference on Women in Beijing, 1995'.[207] The South African Integrated Programme of Action Addressing Violence Against Women and Children (2013–2018) also made reference to CEDAW.

Under-resourcing, however, continues to be a challenge to the effective implementation of state obligations under CEDAW.[208]

5.4.2   Reliance by Judiciary

The judiciary has played a prominent role by incorporating CEDAW into South African jurisprudence. CEDAW's requirements have contributed to transformative landmark decisions including cases on inheritance and customary law,[209] the recognition of Muslim marriages,[210] and violence against women.[211]

---

[207] South Africa's National Policy for Women's Empowerment and Gender Equality, Executive Summary 20.

[208] CGE Shadow Report notes that there 'has been operating without adequate human resource capacity for extended periods of time. Coupled with a high turnover of staff, this ultimately contributed to a lack of performance in meeting its mandate effectively.' CGE, Report to the CEDAW Cttee on South Africa's implementation of CEDAW: 1998–2008 15. In the NGO Shadow Report on Beijing +15, it noted: 'Despite the State's reliance on civil society organizations to provide services to survivors of violence, it fails to adequately resource these organizations.' (People Opposing Women Abuse (POWA) with the AIDS Legal Network (ALN); One in Nine Campaign and the Coalition for African Lesbians (CAL), Criminal Injustice: Violence Against Women In South Africa (2010)).

[209] *Bhe and Others v Magistrate, Khayelitsha and Others* 2005 (1) BCLR 1 (CC); *Shibi v Sithole and Others* CCT 69/03; *South African Human Rights Commission and Another v President of the Republic of South Africa and Another* 2005 (1) SA 850 (CC); 2005 (1) BCLR 1 (CC); *Gumede v President of the Republic of South Africa and Others (Women's Legal Centre Trust as Amicus Curiae)* [2008] ZACC 23; *Shilubana v Nwamitwa* 2009 (2) SA 66 (CC).

[210] *Daniels v Campbell NO and Others* 2004 (7) BCLR 735 (CC).

[211] *Carmichele v Minister of Safety and Security and Another (Centre for Applied Legal Studies Intervening)* 2001 (4) SA 938 (CC); *S v Baloyi and Others* 2000 (2) SA 425 (CC); *Masiya v Director of Public Prosecutions Pretoria and Another (Centre for Applied Legal Studies, Tshwaranang Legal Advocacy Centre as Amici Curiae)* 2007 (8) BCLR 827 (CC).

5.4.3 Impact on and through Independent State Institutions

CEDAW has to a significant extent impacted on the work of the CGE. The CGE has facilitated workshops on CEDAW,[212] and has referred to CEDAW in its annual reports.

CEDAW has also influenced the research of the SALRC.[213] In the reports of the SALRC on the harmonisation of common law and customary law,[214] domestic violence,[215] maintenance,[216] HIV[217] and sex work,[218] it explicitly refers to CEDAW and its conclusions and findings illustrate the impact of CEDAW. The SALRC did not refer to the CEDAW Cttee COs to South Africa on the practice of *ukuthwala* in its Discussion Paper 132, 'The Practice of *Ukuthwala*', 2014. The SALRC, however, referred to general recommendations of the CEDAW Cttee and CRC Cttee.[219]

5.4.4 Impact on and through Non-state Actors

CEDAW is used by NGOs that referred to the CEDAW requirements in their reports and blogs.[220] Increasingly, research, reports, blogs and workshop

---

212   CGE, Annual Report 2009–2010 32.
213   On 30 March 2009 Ms. Clark, a staff member of the SALRC, attended a seminar on Harmful Traditional Practices for a Joint Research Undertaking on CEDAW.
214   (SALRC, Project 90 The Harmonisation of the Common Law and the Indigenous Law Report on Customary Marriages (1998)). However, in its 2003 report on Islamic marriages the SALRC did not refer to CEDAW. See SALRC, Project 59 Islamic Marriages and Related Matters Report (2003). See also SALRC Issue Paper 3 on the Harmonisation of the Common Law and the Indigenous Law, 1996 viii and SALRC Twenty Fifth Annual Report, 1997, 74.
215   SALRC's Research Paper on Domestic Violence relies on the provisions in CEDAW dealing with domestic violence, as well as on General Comment 19 adopted by the CEDAW Cttee in 1992 (SALRC, 'Research Paper on Domestic Violence,' April 1999, para 4.8.6).
216   SALRC Issue Paper 28 Review of the Maintenance Act 1998, 2014 10.
217   SALRC Discussion Paper on Aspects of the Law Relating to AIDS – Compulsory HIV Testing of Persons Arrested in Sexual Offence Cases, 1999 122, 123, 132 & 138.
218   SALRC Discussion Paper 85, Sexual Offences: The Substantive Law, 1999, 30–40. The SALRC also referred to the initial report of South Africa to the CEDAW Cttee in which the country admitted that some of its laws on prostitution may violate constitutional rights. See SALRC Issue Paper 19 Sexual Offences: Adult Prostitution 2002 37. See also SALRC Discussion Paper on Sexual Offences and Adult Prostitution 2009 53–54 and 94–96 and SALRC, Report Project 107, Sexual Offences and Adult Prostitution (2015) 20.
219   See Discussion Paper 132, 'The Practice of Ukuthwala' 2014 32.
220   Sonke Gender Justice, 'Sonke Participates in a Number of Landmark Global Conferences' (2009) <https://genderjustice.org.za/news-item/sonke-participates-in-a-number-of-landmark-global-conferences/> accessed 1 June 2020; Sonke Gender Justice, 'Sonke's ED presents on VIDC Panel in Vienna, Austria on Sexual Violence in Conflict' (2012) <https://genderjustice.org.za/news-item/sonkes-ed-presents-on-vidc-panel-in-vienna-austria-on-sexual-violence-in-conflict/>; Sonke Gender Justice, 'Sex Work and Human Rights'

resources make use of regional treaties and domestic documents.²²¹ NGO shadow reports highlight that South Africa 'has a duty to promote human rights by awareness campaigns of treaties like CEDAW'.²²² Further, they criticise the government's lack of sufficient evidence in the country periodic reports of whether it has fulfilled this duty and information of how many women 'know about CEDAW or the rights it protects'.²²³ Finally, an NGO report held that '[d]uring the consultations held in preparation for this report, almost all participating NGOs indicated that knowledge levels [regarding CEDAW] among women ... are very low'.²²⁴

CEDAW is frequently discussed, applied to pertinent issues and referred to in law journals,²²⁵ academic research and

(2015) <https://genderjustice.org.za/publication/sex-work-and-human-rights?> accessed 15 September 2023; Masimanyane Women's Rights International, 'About Us' <https://www.masimanyane.org> accessed 15 September 2023; Women's Legal Centre, 2012 Annual Report (2012) <https://wlce.co.za/wp/wp-content/uploads/2017/10/WLC-Annual-Report-2012.pdf>; Women's Legal Centre, 'Opinion: Sex Work in South Africa Must Be Decriminalised – In a Democratic Society, This Cannot be Put on the Back Burner Any Longer' <https://wlce.co.za/sex-work-in-south-africa-must-be-decriminalised/>.

221 L Foster, Country Papers, South Africa, The First CEDAW impact Study (2010), 115. <http://iwrp.org/wp-content/uploads/2010/06/South-Africa.pdf> accessed 15 October 2022; The Herald, Demystifying the convention on the elimination of violence against women (2017) <https://www.herald.co.zw/demystifying-convention-on-elimination-of-discrimination-against-women/> accessed 15 October 2022; Mail & Guardian, Gender-sensitive budgets can help end inequality (2017) <https://mg.co.za/article/2018-09-07-00-gender-sensitive-budgets-can-help-end-inequality/> accessed 15 October 2022; N Farisè, Mail & Guardian, Ban harmful virginity 'testing', <https://mg.co.za/article/2019-12-12-00-ban-harmful-virginity-testing/> accessed 15 October 2022; N Farisè, T Jeewa, Mail & Guardian, Yet another treaty aims to protect African women. But how will it be enforced? (2020) <https://mg.co.za/africa/2020-12-09-yet-another-treaty-aims-to-protect-african-women-but-how-will-it-be-enforced/> accessed 15 October 2022; S Barkley, 'A Crisis of Violence against Women: Has South Africa Fulfilled its Obligations in terms of the Convention on the Elimination of All Forms of Discrimination against Women?' (2020) Acta Juridica, 165 – 196; L Isaacs S Mzantsi, UN experts slam SA's 'alarming' scale of GBVF (2021) <https://www.iol.co.za/capetimes/news/un-experts-slam-sas-alarming-scale-of-gbvf-e1405536-7593-4978-842e-45a0d93ae438> accessed 15 October 2022.

222 South African Shadow Report of the CEDAW, submitted to the CEDAW Cttee's 48th session (17 January-4 February 2011) by Centre for the Study of Violence and Reconciliation, People Opposing Women Abuse, Western Cape Network on Violence Against Women 7.

223 South African Shadow Report of the CEDAW, submitted to the CEDAW Cttee's 48th Session (17 January-4 February 2011) by Centre for the Study of Violence and Reconciliation, People Opposing Women Abuse, Western Cape Network on Violence Against Women 7.

224 ibid. 16 <https://tbinternet.ohchr.org/Treaties/CEDAW/Shared%20Documents/ZAF/INT_CEDAW_NGO_ZAF_48_10362_E.pdf> accessed 1 June 2020.

225 F Kathree, 'Convention on All Forms of Discrimination Against Women' (1995) 11 *SAJHR* 421; NM Ngema, 'Considering the Abolition of *Ilobolo*: Quo Vadis South Africa?' (2002) 2

textbooks.[226] In non-law-related research CEDAW has been discussed, but to a lesser extent. In other domains such as sociology and philosophy CEDAW has also been referred to.[227]

5.4.5 Impact of State Reporting

The initial report to the CEDAW Cttee was submitted in 1998, almost a year late.[228] The consolidated second, third and fourth reports were also submitted late: the second due in 2001, the third in 2005 and the fourth report was due on 14 January 2009. The consolidated report was submitted on 2 July 2009. The fifth periodic report was due on 1 February 2015 and submitted on 9 May 2019.

The content of the reports, particularly the initial report, has been of a high quality and the reports have largely followed the guidelines.[229] However, the consolidated second, third and fourth report did not keep to the guideline length.[230]

The lead government department has differed between reports: The Department of Welfare led the initial report process; the Ministry for Women,

---

Speculum Juris 30–46.; A Rudman, 'Women's Access to Regional Justice as a Fundamental Element of the Rule of Law: The Effect of the Absence of Women's Rights Committee on the Enforcement of the African Women's Protocol' (2018) 18 African Human Rights Law Journal 319; R Kovacs, S Ndashe and J Williams, 'Twelve Years Later: How the Recognition of Customary Marriages Act of 1998 is Failing Women in South Africa' (2013) Acta Juridica 273.

226 J Linnegar and K McGillivray, *Women and the Law in South Africa* (Juta & Company (1998); D Brand and C Heyns *Socio-Economic Rights in South Africa* (PULP 2005); H Britton, J Fish and S Meintjes *Women's Activism in South Africa: Working Across Divides* (University of Kwa-Zulu Natal Press 2009); M Payandeh and others, *The Implementation of International Law in Germany and South Africa* (PULP 2015); S Hassim, *The ANC Women's League: Sex, Gender Politics* (Ohio University Press 2015).

227 L Kapp, 'Employment Equity in SANDF: Practical Implications and Challenges' (2002) Industrial Sociology in the School of Behavioural Sciences at the Faculty Vaal Triangle of the Potchefstroom University for Christian Higher Education.; K de Villiers Graaf, 'Masculinities and Gender-Based Violence in South Africa: A Study of a Masculinities-Focused Intervention Programme' PhD thesis, University of Stellenbosch, 2017.

228 The Initial report was due on 14 January 1997, but was only submitted on 5 February 1998. This delay of almost a year may be ascribed to the fact that this was South Africa's first country report, and that a system had not yet been put in place to oversee the reporting obligation.

229 The CEDAW Cttee has commended the country reports as being clear and frank Summary Records of CEDAW Initial Report, South Africa, CEDAW/C/SR.387 page 7.

230 The CEDAW Cttee invited South Africa to follow the Harmonised Guidelines (HRI/MC/2006/3 and Corr.1) which require 'the treaty specific document to be limited to 40 pages, while the updated common core document should not exceed 80 pages'. COs on the CEDAW First Periodic Report of South Africa, CEDAW/C/ZAF/CO/4, para 51.

Children and People with Disabilities headed the preparation of the consolidated second, third and fourth report. The drafting committee, consisting of representatives of various departments and civil society was largely inclusive.[231] However, in response to the consolidated second, third and fourth report the CEDAW Cttee recommended broader participation of all ministries and the consultations of a variety of women's rights and human rights organisations.[232] South Africa has been lauded for the high level and experienced delegation presenting the report in Geneva, in particular regarding the initial report.[233]

There are numerous shadow reports by civil society and NGOs. These enrich the report and offer an alternative, in some cases contrary, view to the state report. NGO and civil society shadow reports are comprehensive,[234] and deal with issues such as disabilities, domestic violence, gender equality and sexual orientation. Some reports are thematic, focusing on a particular issue, for example, disabilities.[235] The CGE also presented a report to South Africa's consolidated second, third and fourth country report, commenting on South Africa's implementation of CEDAW during the period 1998 to 2008.[236]

The CEDAW Cttee's COs have focused on issues such as stereotypes and harmful practices (including *ukuthwala*);[237] participation in political and public life;[238] employment;[239] health services;[240] violence against women;[241]

---

[231] Mr Jackie Selebi, Director-General of Foreign Affairs, Opening Address to NAP Workshop, 20 June 1998.
[232] COs on the CEDAW First Periodic Report of South Africa, CEDAW/C/ZAF/CO/4 para 49.
[233] CEDAW Initial Report, South Africa, CEDAW/C/ZAF/1, para 110; COs on the CEDAW First Periodic Report of South Africa, CEDAW/C/ZAF/CO/4, para 3.
[234] South African Shadow Report of the CEDAW, submitted to the CEDAW Cttee 48th session (17 January-4 February 2011) Submitted by Centre for the Study of Violence and Reconciliation, People Opposing Women Abuse, Western Cape Network on Violence Against Women.
[235] In 2010 the International Disability Alliance provided both recommendations for disability-relevant questions to be included in the list of issues 46th Pre-Sessional Working Group (2–6 August 2010) <https://tbinternet.ohchr.org/Treaties/CEDAW/Shared%20Documents/ZAF/INT_CEDAW_NGO_ZAF_48_10359_E.pdf>. In 2011 it provided disability-relevant recommendations to be included in the COs for CEDAW for the 48th Session (17 January-4 February 2011).
[236] Commission of Gender Equality, Report to the CEDAW Cttee on South Africa's Implementation of CEDAW: 1998–2008 (2010).
[237] COs on the CEDAW First Periodic Report of South Africa, CEDAW/C/ZAF/CO/4, para 21.
[238] ibid para 30.
[239] CEDAW Initial Report, South Africa, CEDAW/C/ZAF/1, para 131; COs on the CEDAW First Periodic Report of South Africa, CEDAW/C/ZAF/CO/4, para 34.
[240] CEDAW Initial Report, South Africa, CEDAW/C/ZAF/1, para 134.
[241] COs on the CEDAW First Periodic Report of South Africa, CEDAW/C/ZAF/CO/4, para 25.

education;[242] the position of rural women;[243] trafficking and exploitation of prostitution;[244] sexual orientation;[245] marriages and family relations;[246] discrimination against women;[247] and the need for wider dissemination of CEDAW, in particular at local community level.[248]

In terms of impact, South Africa has not implemented most of the CEDAW's Cttee's recommendations, in particular, regarding the implementation of the Women Empowerment and Gender Equality Bill (WEGE)[249] and the establishment of a unified family code. Significantly, these recommendations were highlighted by the Committee as important and it requested South Africa to provide, by 2013, written information on the steps undertaken to implement these recommendations.[250] South Africa not only responded late but it had not implemented the recommendations. South Africa held that the WEGE Bill had not been implemented as it would be redundant, due to other existing mechanisms and legislation that 'are in place to protect women against discrimination, violence, including sexual violence and promote women empowerment and rights of women'.[251] The lack of a unified marriage code, according to the fifth periodic report, is not desirable in South Africa as 'a unified family code might result in achieving formal equality which, in many instances, discriminates against others indirectly. The aim of recognising diversity is to ensure substantive equality for all.'[252] This reasoning indicates, to some extent, South Africa's relationship with the CEDAW Cttee, suggesting discord between some of the recommendations and the nuanced realities for women in South Africa.

However, to some extent the state reporting process has influenced resource allocation to prevent and address discrimination against women.[253] Also,

---

242   ibid para 32.
243   ibid para 38.
244   ibid para 28.
245   ibid para 40.
246   ibid para 42.
247   ibid paras 15 & 42.
248   CEDAW Initial Report, South Africa, CEDAW/C/ZAF/1, para 137; COs on the CEDAW First Periodic Report of South Africa, CEDAW/C/ZAF/CO/4, para 46.
249   COs on the CEDAW First Periodic Report of South Africa, CEDAW/C/ZAF/CO/4, para 15.
250   ibid para 48.
251   Follow-up Report to CEDAW First Periodic Report, South Africa, CEDAW/C/ZAF/CO/4/Add.1, paras 24 and 33.
252   CEDAW Second Periodic Report, South Africa, CEDAW/C/ZAF/5 paras 266–281.
253   In the CEDAW Cttee, COs on the CEDAW First Periodic Report of South Africa, the CEDAW Cttee expressed its concerns at the 'weak institutional capacity of this Ministry (for Women, Youth and People with Disabilities), including inadequate human, financial and technical resources' and the impact this may have on effectively discharging its duties (CEDAW Cttee, COs on the combined second, third and fourth periodic report of South

some influence of the CEDAW Cttee COs is evident in the National Action Plan to Combat Racism, Racial Discrimination, Xenophobia and Related Intolerance.[254]

5.4.6 Brief Conclusion

To some extent CEDAW has had an impact on the rights of women in South Africa and *de jure* gender equality. It has played a substantial role since the transition to democracy, influencing not only the Constitution but also being relied on and incorporated by the legislature and the judiciary. Despite notable strides, legislation specifically addressing women's empowerment has not been implemented, as recommended by the CEDAW Cttee. Of concern is the lack of implementation of the recommendations of the CEDAW Cttee. The strong presence of NGOs and civil society in South Africa and their significant involvement in the reporting process are significant and ensure greater accountability.

5.5 Convention against Torture and Other Cruel, Inhuman or Degrading Treatment or Punishment

5.5.1 Incorporation and Reliance by Legislature and Executive

The influence of CAT on the South African Constitution is discernible from the reliance of stakeholders on CAT.[255]

CAT has also been impactful on national legislation. The Prevention and Combating of Torture of Persons Act 2013 (PCTPA) in its Preamble conspicuously reaffirmed the commitment of South Africa to preventing and combating the torture of persons and seeks to ensure that no person is subjected to torture as required by CAT.[256] CAT has also influenced the Draft Refugees Amendment Bill, 2015 (Act 130 of 1998). The draft Bill amended section 4 of the

---

Africa, para 18). In response, the Ministry of Women, according to its CEDAW Second Periodic Report, reviewed 'the Department's institutional capacity and is putting in place human, financial and technical resources in order to strengthen its capacity to monitor and evaluate the impact of programmes on women's empowerment, to report and make recommendations, to coordinate stakeholders and its outreach capacity' (CEDAW Second Periodic Report, South Africa, CEDAW/C/ZAF/5, South Africa, para 35).

254 National Action Plan to Combat Racism, Racial Discrimination, Xenophobia and Related Intolerance 23.
255 ANC Preliminary Submission, Theme Committee 4: Our Broad Vision of a Bill of Rights for South Africa <https://www.justice.gov.za/legislation/constitution/history/SUBMISS/ANC.pdf> accessed 1 June 2020.
256 The Prevention and Combating of Torture of Persons Act 13 of 2013, Preamble.

principal Act (Refugees Act of 1998) to include the commission of torture as defined in article 1 of CAT.[257]

In terms of government policies, the influence of CAT is evident in the White Paper on the Rights of Persons with Disabilities. The White Paper strongly relied on CAT in advocating that by recognising and reframing violence and abuse perpetrated against persons with disabilities as torture or other cruel, inhuman or degrading treatment or punishment, victims and advocates can be afforded stronger legal protection and redress for violations of human rights.[258] The White Paper on Remand Detention Management in South Africa, which provides for the policies on orderly, safe and secure remand detention in South Africa, listed CAT and OP-CAT among the several prescripts that form the basis for ensuring the good order, safety and security of remand detainees.[259]

The South African Police Services Policy on the Prevention of Torture and the Treatment of Persons in Custody states that the ratification and requirement of CAT 'necessitated a re-evaluation of the treatment of persons in custody of the South African Police Service, and the approach of the South African Police Service towards interrogation methods, detention, etc'.[260]

OP-CAT has influenced institutional reforms. Upon the ratification of OP-CAT, the government has designated a multiple-body national preventive mechanism (NPM), to be coordinated by the SAHRC. The South African NPM will include institutions such as the JICS, the Independent Police Investigative Directorate, the Military Ombud and the Health Ombud.[261]

5.5.2 Reliance by Judiciary

The case of *Sonke Gender Justice NPC v President of the Republic of South Africa and Others*[262] demonstrates the significant influence of OP-CAT on the South

---

[257] <https://www.gov.za/sites/default/files/gcis_document/201508/39067gen806.pdf> accessed 1 June 2020.
[258] White Paper on the Rights of Persons with Disabilities 69.
[259] White Paper on Remand Detention Management in South Africa 12 <https://www.gov.za/sites/default/files/gcis_document/201607/white-paper-remand-detention-management-south-africaa.pdf> accessed 1 June 2020.
[260] Policy on the Prevention of Torture and the Treatment of Persons in Custody of the South African Police Service 1.
[261] *Mail & Guardian*, 'Introducing South Africa's Mechanism for the Prevention of Torture' <https://mg.co.za/article/2020-05-04-introducing-south-africas-mechanism-for-the-prevention-of-torture-and-degrading-treatment-or-punishment/> accessed 1 June 2020. See also Parliamentary Monitoring Group, Convention against Torture and Other Cruel, Inhuman or Degrading Treatment or Punishment: Briefing, with Deputy Minister <https://pmg.org.za/committee-meeting/28159/> accessed 1 June 2020.
[262] 2019 (2) SACR 537 (WCC).

African judiciary. In this case the accession of South Africa to OP-CAT strongly influenced the reasoning of the Court in determining the adequacy of the operational and financial independence of the JICS. The Court, relying on section 7(2) of the Constitution and article 18 of OP-CAT, ruled that the JICS lacks sufficient independence that would conform with South Africa's international obligations as provided for in OP-CAT, read with the Paris Principles and other relevant international instruments. In considering whether to give orders to Parliament to correct the defects in the JICS Act, the Court considered the possible restructuring of JICS, and a revamping of the oversight role(s) played by different institutions in correctional services by virtue of South Africa's accession to OP-CAT.

In the case of *Khosa, Mphephu & Others v Minister of Defence and Military Veterans and Others*,[263] the Gauteng North High Court placed extensive reliance on South Africa's CAT second periodic report and the CAT Cttee COs to South Africa's second report in reaching its conclusion that the country does not have sufficient torture complaint mechanisms to ensure a prompt and impartial investigation of complaints of torture against the South African Police Service and the South African National Defence Force. The Court ruled that the lack of proper investigation into the death of Khosa and the assaults on the applicants show that 'the existing investigative bodies are either not competent or not committed to comply with article 12 of the Torture Convention'.[264] The Court ordered the respondents in the case (Minister of Defence and Military Veterans, the Minister for Defence, the Chief of the South African National Defence Force, the Minister of Police, the National Commissioner of the South African Police Service and the Acting Chief of the Johannesburg Metropolitan Police Department) to 'establish a freely accessible mechanism for civilians to report allegations of torture or cruel, inhuman or degrading treatment or punishment committed by members of the SANDF, the SAPS or any MPD for the duration of state of disaster'.[265]

The courts have also utilised CAT as interpretive guides in cases of non-refoulement,[266] and prohibition of

---

263 2020 (5) SA 490 (GP).
264 ibid para 137.
265 ibid para 146(5).
266 *Khalfan Khamis Mohamed and Another v President of South Africa and 6 Others* 2001 (3) SA 893 (CC). See also *Tantoush v Refugee Appeal Board* 2008 (1) SA 232 (T); *Alex Ruta v Minister of Home Affairs* 2019 (3) BCLR 383 (CC); *Dobrosav Gavrić v Refugee Status Determination Officer and Others* 2019 (1) BCLR 1 (CC); *Emmanuel Tsebe and Society for the Abolition of the Death Penalty in South Africa v The Minister of Home Affairs and Others* 2012 (1) BCLR 77 (GSJ). The South Gauteng High Court, after quoting art 3 of CAT, stated that '[t]he

torture.[267]

5.5.3 Impact on and through Independent State Institutions

CAT has impacted significantly on the work of the SAHRC. The SAHRC Section 5 Committee on Torture works on the compliance of South Africa with CAT. Through its education, training and public awareness programme, the SAHRC was involved in the ratification of OP-CAT, has co-hosted a roundtable discussion on OP-CAT and also made presentations to Parliament on OP-CAT.[268] The SAHRC also launched a media briefing in Cape Town on 17 July 2019 on the launch of the NPM.[269] The influence of CAT on the work of the Truth and Reconciliation Commission is discernible from its final report.[270] Surprisingly, CAT has not had any significant impact in the work of the SALRC.[271]

5.5.4 Impact on and through Non-state Actors

CAT has featured prominently in the works of Article5 Initiative (A5I), a partnership between the University of Cape Town (Gender, Health and Justice Research Unit), the University of the Western Cape (Civil Society Prison Reform Initiative at the Dullah Omar Institute), the University of Bristol (Human Rights Implementation Centre) and the African Policing Civilian Oversight Forum. A5I is supported by the European Union (EU) through the European Instrument for the Development of Human Rights (EIDHR).[272] A5I hosted

---

evidence referred to above in paragraphs [61] to [67] constitute in our view proof of 'a consistent pattern of gross, flagrant ... violations of human rights' as contemplated in the above Convention'.

267 *National Commissioner of the South African Police Service v Southern African Human Rights Litigation Centre and Another* 2015 (1) SA 315 (CC); *Bongani Mthembu v The State* 2008 3 All SA 159 (SCA).
268 SAHRC, Annual Report 2007/2008 13, 18, 29; SAHRC, Annual Report 2006/2007 32; SAHRC, Annual Report 2008/2009 13.
269 SAHRC, Annual Report Human Rights Advocacy and Communications Unit 31.
270 Truth and Reconciliation Commission of South Africa, Report, vol 1 78. The Commission in its report referred to the HRCttee cases of *Bleier v Uruguay* (Case No 30/1978); *Camargo v Columbia* (Case No 45/1979); *Dermit v Uruguay* (Case No 84/1981); *Quinteros v Uruguay* (Case No 107/1981); *Baboerem v Suriname* (Cases No 146/1983 & 148–154/1983); *Muiyo v Zaire* (Case No 194/1985). The Commission also referred to the communication by the CAT Cttee to the government of Argentina that it should ensure that victims of torture receive adequate compensation. See Truth and Reconciliation Commission of South Africa Report, vol 5 173.
271 However, the SALRC listed CAT alongside CEDAW, CRC and OP-CRC-SC as one of the international conventions that regulates trafficking in persons. See SALRC, Issue Paper 25 Trafficking in Persons 2004 5–8.
272 <http://apcof.org/wp-content/uploads/2016/06/A5I-Practical-Monitoring-Tools-to-Promote-Freedom-from-Torture.pdf> accessed 1 June 2020.

a workshop on the prevention and eradication of torture in South Africa.[273] The workshop was aimed at identifying the main challenge and developing opportunities for reform in domesticating CAT and, more specifically, in implementing the Prevention and Combating of Torture of Persons Act 13 of 2013 and amending the Act where it is not compliant with CAT.[274] The Practical Monitoring Tools to Promote Freedom From Torture that was developed by the project was heavily influenced by CAT.[275]

The Centre for the Study of Violence and Reconciliation (CSVR) has used CAT in its advocacy works.[276] The CSVR relied on CAT in advocating a civil case against the police ministry following the death of a taxi driver after he had been dragged by a police van. It stated that 'the ill-treatment of Macia [the taxi driver] and the alleged subsequent beating in the police holding cells amounts to torture, cruel, inhuman and degrading treatment, under the definition of torture in article 1 of the UN Convention against Torture'.[277] The CSVR also highlighted the CAT as one of the key international instruments for the protection of torture, in its analysis of the act and facts of torture in South Africa.[278] As part of its advocacy campaign on addressing torture in South Africa, the CSVR has also developed a booklet on torture that deals with the obligations of South Africa under CAT and the role of civil society in the work of the CAT Cttee.[279]

The Detention Justice Forum (DJF), composed of civil society organisations concerned with the rights of detainees, has also expresse concerns about OP-CAT.[280]

---

273 Dullah Omar Institute: A5I hosted a workshop on the prevention and eradication of torture in South Africa <https://dullahomarinstitute.org.za/news/a5i-hosted-a-workshop-on-the-prevention-and-eradication-of-torture-in-south-africa> accessed 1 June 2020.
274 ibid.
275 <http://apcof.org/wp-content/uploads/2016/06/A5I-Practical-Monitoring-Tools-to-Promote-Freedom-from-Torture.pdf> accessed 1 June 2020.
276 <https://www.csvr.org.za/docs/torture/torturebooklet.pdf> accessed 27 May 2020.
277 Centre for the Study of Violence and Reconciliation, 'From Horror to Healing: Remembering Torture Victims and Their Families on June 26, 2016: The International Day in Support of Torture Victims and Their Families' <https://www.csvr.org.za/media-articles/all-csvr-in-the-media/2644-statement-to-be-read-on-world-torture-day-in-three-communities-to-commemorate-world-torture-day> accessed 1 June 2020.
278 CSVR 'Torture in South Africa: The Acts and the Fact' <https://www.csvr.org.za/pdf/Torture%20in%20South%20Africa.pdf> accessed 15 September 2023.
279 See Lukas Muntingh 'Preventing and Combating Torture in South Africa: A Framework for Action under CAT and OPCAT' CSVR, 2008 <https://www.csvr.org.za/docs/torture/torturebooklet.pdf> accessed 15 September 2023.
280 Sonke Gender Justice, 'Detention Justice Forum Annual General Meeting 2015: Forging Synergies for Human Rights and Dignity' <https://genderjustice.org.za/news-item/detention-justice-forum-annual-general-meeting-2015-forging-synergies-for-human-rights-and-dignity/> accessed 1 June 2020.

5.5.5 State Reporting and Its Impact

South Africa has submitted two CAT state reports. The two reports were submitted after lengthy delays. The delay of the second CAT report was occasioned by the democratic transitioning of South Africa and burgeoning international treaty and reporting obligations of the country.[281] The second report was shared by the government with national human rights institutions and civil society organisations.[282]

The initial report of South Africa to the CAT Cttee did not conform with the CAT Cttee's guidelines on preparation of initial reports. While the second report was an improvement on the initial report, it contains much general information and did not specifically address the issue of implementation of COs. South Africa's second periodic report was presented by a high-level delegation led by the Deputy Minister of Justice. The SAHRC submitted a report for the consideration of the second to third periodic report. Three and five shadow reports, respectively, were submitted to the initial and second periodic report of South Africa.[283]

In terms of impact of the COs, apart from the general measures that at best can be linked with CAT, the COs of the CAT Cttee have not had any significant impact in South Africa. These recommendations have had an insignificant impact, as seen by South Africa's response to the list of issues raised by the CAT Cttee. South Africa responded to each of the issues, except for the requested information on the implementation of COs from its initial report. South Africa has not engaged with the follow-up procedure of the CAT Cttee. On 25 April 2008 the Rapporteur for follow-up on COs of the CAT Cttee wrote a reminder letter to the Permanent Mission of South Africa in Geneva, requesting follow-up information on select recommendations in South Africa's initial report.[284]

The key recommendations that were selected by the CAT Cttee in South Africa's initial report for follow-up include information on the extradition of Rashid and Mohamed (*non-refoulement*), torture of non-citizens detained in

---

281 CAT First Periodic Report, South Africa, CAT/C/ZAF/2 page 3.
282 CAT First Periodic Report, South Africa, CAT/C/ZAF/2 page 28.
283 The three CSOs are Amnesty International, Global Initiative to End All Corporal Punishment of Children and World Organisation Against Torture.
284 <https://tbinternet.ohchr.org/Treaties/CAT/Shared%20Documents/ZAF/INT_CAT_FUR_ZAF_12358_E.pdf> accessed 5 November 2022.

repatriation centres and lack of oversight mechanism for repatriation centres, access to justice and compensation for victims of torture and rape and sexual violence. Even though the CAT Cttee had requested information on the extradition of Khalid Mehmood Rashid and Mohammed Hendi, from South Africa, the issue was not addressed in South Africa's periodic report.[285] In response to the recommendations of the Committee that South Africa should combat ill-treatment of non-citizens detained in repatriation centres, particularly Lindela Repatriation Centre, the state responded that Lindela Repatriation Centre cannot be considered a detention centre, that the centre is equipped with a fully-serviced medical centre, and complies with minimum standard rules for the treatment of persons deprived of their liberty.[286] In response to the recommendations of CAT, the government stated that it had designated violent crimes against women and children as high priority crimes and embarked on specialised investigations and prosecution of violence against women and children within the criminal justice system.[287] Although the report referred to certain measures on sexual violence, such as the creation of Thutuzela care centres for victims of sexual violence, the re-establishment of the sexual offences court, increase in prosecution rates for sexual violence, and the enactment of the Criminal Law (Sexual Offences and Related Matters) Amendment Act, 2007, it is difficult to establish a link between these measures and the CAT Cttee's recommendations on sexual violence.[288]

5.5.6 Brief Conclusion

The ratification of OP-CAT has signalled the country's commitment to the prohibition of torture and other forms of degrading treatment in South Africa. It also kick-started a process of institutional reform. It is anticipated that the institutional reforms occasioned by the ratification of OP-CAT will improve the influence of CAT and OP-CAT in South Africa.

---

285 South Africa's First Periodic Report to the CAT Cttee was focused on general descriptions of national policies and measures as opposed to responding to the CAT Cttee's previous concerns on non-refoulement. The long delay in the submission of the report and absence of institutional memory with respect to state reporting may be a crucial factor in the vagueness of the responses in the first periodic report.
286 CAT First Periodic Report, South Africa, CAT/C/ZAF/2 paras 67–69.
287 CAT First Periodic Report, South Africa, CAT/C/ZAF/2 para 74. This response did not directly address the previous recommendation that required South Africa to undertake research into the high rate of rape and sexual violence and establish awareness-raising campaigns.
288 The difficulty is also exacerbated by the fact that the CERD Cttee has issued similar recommendations on sexual violence to South Africa.

5.6 Convention on the Rights of the Child

5.6.1 Incorporation and Reliance by Organs of State

CRC was influential in the elaborate provisions on children's rights in section 28 of the South African Constitution.[289] CRC was extensively relied on in the proposals and suggestions made by stakeholders to the Technical Committee during the drafting of the interim Constitution.[290] In the drafting of the Constitution of the Republic of South Africa, 1996, various submissions made by children's rights stakeholders to Theme Committee 4 (the theme committee responsible for the Bill of Rights in the final Constitution) were influenced by CRC.[291]

CRC has had a significant impact on children-related laws in South Africa. The 1996 Amendment to the Child Care Act shifted the focus of the Act from 'unable' or 'unfit' parents to 'the child in need of care', in accordance with the provisions of CRC.[292] The Children's Act 38 of 2005 (as amended) aligns the age of a child with that stipulated in CRC. The Act provides a comprehensive framework for the protection of children from all forms of abuse, neglect and exploitation, in response to South Africa's obligations under OP-CRC-SC.[293] The Child Justice Act introduced changes that harmonise the law more closely with article 40 of CRC. The Act increased the minimum age of criminal capacity from 7 to 10 years, and established a rebuttable presumption of criminal incapacity in the case of children between 10 and 14 years of age.[294] The Defence Act (2002) aligned the law with the provisions of OP-CRC-AC. The Act changed the minimum age for recruitment into the national defence force from 17 to 18 years.[295] The Maintenance Act, the Domestic Violence Act, the Children's Act (2005), the Criminal Law (Sexual Offences and Related Matters) Amendment Act 32 of 2007 all made express references to the need for South Africa to fulfill its obligations under CRC.

CRC has had a significant influence on government policies, particularly as it relates to children and women. The influence of CRC is quite noticeable, mostly on the National Plan of Action for Children (NPAC) (2012–2017). The policy, in its introduction, stated that '[i]n view of South Africa having ratified

---

289 Heyns and Viljoen (n 29) 555.
290 ibid.
291 Theme Committee 4, Fundamental Rights Report and Explanatory Memorandum on Children's Rights to the Constitutional Assembly 8, 10, 12.
292 CRC Initial Report, South Africa, CRC/C/51/Add.2, para 310.
293 CRC First Periodic Report, South Africa, CRC/C/ZAF/2, para 38(a).
294 ibid para 38(h).
295 ibid para 38(i). Unlike the previous Acts, the Defence Act did not make express reference to OP-CRC-AC.

the CRC, it is obligated to develop a Plan of Action for children'.[296] The policy stated that CRC is a major guide to the policy and it reproduced the provisions of CRC, OP-CRC-AC and OP-CRC-SC in its annexure,[297] and specified the different obligations that the different articles of CRC impose on the state. The NPAC was designed to monitor the progress of the implementation of CRC.[298] The NPAC referenced CRC in outlining the roles that local municipalities have to play in the realisation of children's rights,[299] and also referred to article 42 of CRC as the provision underpinning the requirement of the policy that the public is involved in the development of the NPAC and it is published and accessible to the public.

The influence of CRC is evident in the following policies through the specific reference to South Africa's legal obligations under the CRC in the following documents: the training manual on enforcing the law on child labour in South Africa;[300] the 1996 National Programme of Action;[301] the National Drug Master Plan 1999;[302] the national integrated early childhood development policy;[303] the National Policy Framework for Orphans and Other Children Made Vulnerable by HIV and AIDS;[304] the National School Health Policy and Implementation Guidelines;[305] the Infant and Young Child Feeding Policy;[306] the amended

---

296 Department of Women, Children and People with Disabilities, National Plan of Action for Children (2012–2017) 9.
297 CRC was reproduced in annexure B1; OP-CRC-SC was reproduced in annexure B1.1; OP-CRC-AC was reproduced in annexure B1.2.
298 National Programme of Action for Children (2012–2017) 13.
299 ibid 98.
300 Heyns and Viljoen (n 29) 549.
301 The National Programme of Action comprehensively listed the different articles of CRC that are relevant to each of the policy areas that it covered. National Programme of Action for Children, 'Framework' <https://www.gov.za/documents/national-programme-action-children-framework> accessed 10 January 2020. See also Initial Report, CRC, South Africa para 4.
302 Drug Advisory Board, National Drug Master Plan 1999 (unpaged document) <https://www.gov.za/sites/default/files/gcis_document/201409/drugplano.pdf> accessed 1 June 2020. It is worth noting that the National Drug Master Plan of 2006 merely referred to the ratification of CRC by South Africa and the 2013 National Drug Master Plan did not refer to CRC.
303 Department of Social Development, National Integrated Early Childhood Development Policy 2015 (2015) 50.
304 The National Policy Framework for Orphans and Other Children Made Vulnerable by HIV and AIDS made reference to arts 2, 3, 5, 6, 8, 9, 11, 12, 13, 15, 16, 17, 18, 19, 20, 21, 24, 25, 27, 28–29, 31, 32, 33 and 34 of CRC. See Department of Social Development, National Policy Framework for Orphans and Other Children Made Vulnerable by HIV and AIDS 50.
305 National School Health Policy and Implementation Guidelines 6, 12.
306 Department of Health, Infant and Young Child Feeding Policy iii, 2, 4.

National Policy Framework on Child Justice; the Integrated School Health Policy;[307] the Integrated Programme of Action Addressing Violence Against Women and Children (2013–2018);[308] the National Strategy for the Prevention and Management of Alcohol and Drug Use amongst Learners in Schools;[309] the National Adolescent Sexual and Reproductive Health and Rights Framework Strategy;[310] the Practice Guidelines on Inter-Country Adoption;[311] the National Consolidated Guidelines for the Prevention of Mother-to-Child Transmission of HIV (PMTCT);[312] the Disclosure Guidelines for Children and Adolescents in the Context of HIV, TB and Non-Communicable Diseases;[313] and the National Policy Guidelines on Victim Empowerment.[314]

Despite its significant contributions to government policies, CRC has not led to visible institutional reforms. In its response to the CRC Cttee's requirement for the establishment of a separate budget for children, South Africa responded that there is no mechanism within the setup of the cabinet to assess government spending on children because government departments do not generally regard children as a separate homogenous group.[315] However, there have been efforts to train the police on the provisions of CRC as it relates to the right to privacy of children, and the UN juvenile justice documents have been simplified and contextualised in South Africa.[316]

---

[307] Department of Health and Department of Basic Education, Integrated School Health Policy (2012) 3, 5.

[308] South African Integrated Programme of Action Addressing Violence Against Women and Children (2013–2018) 2, 8. The policy further listed OP-CRC-AC and OP-CRC-SC together with other treaties ratified by South Africa in its annexure.

[309] Department of Basic Education, National Strategy for the Prevention and Management of Alcohol and Drug Use Amongst Learners in Schools 2013 iv, 13.

[310] Ministry of Social Development, National Adolescent Sexual and Reproductive Health and Rights Framework Strategy 2014–2019 21.

[311] Practice Guidelines on Inter-Country Adoption 3.

[312] Department of Health, National Consolidated Guidelines for the Prevention of Mother-to-Child Transmission of HIV (PMTCT) and the Management of HIV in Children, Adolescents and Adults 18.

[313] Department of Health, Disclosure Guidelines for Children and Adolescents in the Context of HIV, TB and Non-Communicable Diseases 2016 13.

[314] National Policy Guidelines on Victim Empowerment 7. See also Second Periodic Report, CAT, South Africa, para 102.

[315] CRC Initial Report, South Africa, CRC/C/51/Add.2, para 20.

[316] ibid para 185.

5.6.2 Reliance by Judiciary

Generally, the provisions of CRC, the CRC Cttee's General Comments and the CRC Cttee's COs have played crucial roles in the arguments of counsel and decisions of the judiciary in South Africa.

In the case of *YG v The State*,[317] the appellant was convicted of assault on his son. The appellant contested the conviction on the ground that the actions deemed assault were nothing more than an exercise of his right as a parent to chastise his son by meting out reasonable corporal punishment for his son's indiscipline. The South Gauteng High Court in its judgment stated that '[a]s recently as October 2016, the Committee [CRC Cttee] had cause to comment on South Africa's second report on the implementation of its obligations under the CRC. The Committee made the following pertinent remarks: It was "concerned that corporal punishment in the home has not been prohibited and is widely practiced". With reference to the Committee's General Comment 8, it recommended that South Africa 'expedite the adoption of legislation to prohibit all forms of corporal punishment in the home, including "reasonable chastisement"'.[318] The Court ruled as follows:[319]

> For all of these reasons, I find that the limitations imposed by the reasonable chastisement defence are not constitutionally justifiable under section 36. It is time for our country to march in step with its international obligations under the CRC by recognising that the reasonable chastisement defense is no longer legally acceptable under our constitutional dispensation.

---

[317] 2018 (1) SACR 64 (GJ).

[318] Para 56. The court also referred to a similar recommendation of the African Committee of Experts on the Rights and Welfare of the Child that called upon South Africa to ban corporal punishment in the home. See para 57. The Court noted that the ratification of CRC by South Africa has spawned specific legislation establishing a detailed framework for the protection of children (para 48). The Court stated that even though CRC does not expressly deal with physical chastisement, the CRC Cttee in General Comment 8 had stated that corporal punishment is incompatible with CRC. The Court also replicated 5 paras from the CRC Cttee General Comment 13 in its judgment.

[319] Para 85. Even though the Constitutional Court upheld the High Court's decision on appeal, it made no reference to CRC or the COs in its judgment. The Court based its decision on the provisions of section 12 of the Constitution. See *Freedom of Religion South Africa v Minister of Justice and Constitutional Development and Others* 2019 (11) BCLR 1321 (CC) para 73.

In the case of *C & Others v Department of Health and Social Development*,[320] the Constitutional Court was required to confirm the declaration of constitutional invalidity of sections 151 and 152 of the Children's Act. The High Court had previously declared the aforementioned sections unconstitutional to the extent that they allow the removal of a child from the care of the family without the option for automatic review of the removal before the children's court. The Constitutional Court in its majority judgment held that the provisions of sections 151 and 152 of the Children's Act constituted a limitation of the child's right to 'family care or parental care'. In elaborating on the right to family care or parental care, the Court relied on the provisions of articles 7(1) and 8(1) of CRC, which guarantee children's rights 'to know and be cared for by his or her parents' and to 'preserve his or her identity, including ... family relations as recognised by law and without unlawful interference'.[321]

Other cases in which CRC has been influential are *Minister for Welfare and Population Development v Fitzpatrick and Others*;[322] *AD and Another v DW and Others*;[323] *J v NDPP and Another*;[324] *Centre for Child Law v Minister for Justice and Constitutional Development and Others*;[325] *TMC v TC*;[326] *Ester Nel v Valerie Deodot Byliefeldt and Another*;[327] *KM v JW*;[328] and *Helen Margaret Ford v Michael George William Ford*.[329]

5.6.3 Impact on and through Independent State Institutions

CRC has been highly influential on the work of the SALRC. CRC, OP-CRC-SC and the COs of the CRC Cttee under the OP-CRC-SC were highly influential in the work of the SALRC on sexual offences, pornography and children. The discussion paper on SALRC's Project 107C (Sexual Offences (Pornography and Children)) that was considered by the SALRC on 16 March 2019 includes recommendations aimed at ensuring compliance with South Africa's obligations in terms of international instruments such as the OP-CRC-SC.[330] Seven

---

320 2012 (4) BCLR 329 (CC).
321 ibid para 25.
322 2000 (7) BCLR 713 (CC).
323 2008 (4) BCLR 359 (CC) para 38.
324 2014 (2) SACR 1 (CC) para 40.
325 2009 (11) BCLR 1105 (CC).
326 NCHC 268/2013 para 14.
327 NHGC 27748/2015 para 26.
328 NHGC 95071/2016 para 16.
329 SCA 52/05 para 8.
330 South African Law Reform Commission Report 2018/ 2019 27. SALRC Discussion Paper 85, Sexual Offences – The Substantive Law, 1999 18–30. See also SALRC Discussion Paper on Aspects of the Law Relating to AIDS – Compulsory HIV Testing of Persons Arrested in

observations of the CRC Cttee to South Africa's OP-CRC-SC report were applied by the SALRC in the discussion paper to review the legislative framework of South Africa that applies to children in respect of pornography.[331]

CRC also played a crucial role in the work of the SALRC on the Child Care Act.[332] The SALRC relied on South Africa's obligations under CRC to broadly interpret its mandate to investigate and review the Child Care Act, 1983 and to make recommendations to the Minister for Social Development for reform to include the reform of all statutory, common, customary and religious law affecting children.[333] The SALRC used CRC in its work on the review of juvenile justice in South Africa.[334] The SALRC also relied on CRC in its work on harmonisation of the common law and the indigenous law;[335] customary marriages;[336] maternity and paternity benefits for self-employed workers;[337] the

---

Sexual Offence Cases, 1999 139. Also, see generally SALRC, Issue Paper 10 on Sexual Offences Against Children, 1997; SALRC, Discussion Paper 149 Sexual Offences Pornography and Children 2019 XXII, 2–7. SALRC, Issue Paper 30 Sexual Offences: Pornography and Children 2015, 48, 49, 52, 60, 95.

[331] See generally SALRC, Discussion Paper 149 Sexual Offences Pornography and Children 2019 2–7.

[332] SALRC, Discussion Paper 103 Review of the Child Care Act, 2002; SALRC, Executive Summary Review of the Child Care Act. See also SALC Bulletin Vol 3 No 1, May 1998 1, 2. See also SALRC, Review of the Child Care Act Report, 2002 3.

[333] SALRC Review of the Child Care Act Report, 2002 3.

[334] See SALRC, Issue Paper on Juvenile Justice, 1997. In the opening paragraph of the Issue Paper the Commission stated that '[b]y ratifying the Convention, South Africa is now obliged, in terms of article 40(3) thereof, to establish laws, procedures, authorities and institutions specifically applicable to children in conflict with the law'. See also SALC Bulletin Vol 2 No 2, June 1997, and SALC Bulletin Vol 2 No 3, October 1997 5.

[335] SALRC, Discussion Paper on the Harmonisation of the Common Law and the Indigenous Law, 1997 5, 8, 74, 80. In one of its recommendations in the discussion paper, the SALRC stated that '[i]t is recommended that, under the Constitution and the United Nations Convention on the Rights of the Child, a parent's power to consent to marriage must be exercised only in the child's best interests. Accordingly, a guardian may not unreasonably prevent a ward's marriage' (82).

[336] During August 1997 the SALRC published a discussion paper on customary marriages for general information and comment. One of the recommendations in the discussion paper is that in accordance with s 28(3) of the Constitution and the United Nations Convention on the Rights of the Child, the child's best interests should govern all aspects of custody, guardianship and access to children. Because the best interests principle has no specific content, cultural expectations may be accommodated by the courts. To avoid unfair discrimination against women, mothers should have equal rights to children. See SALRC, Twenty Fifth Annual Report, 1997 75.

[337] SALRC, Research Proposal Paper on Maternity and Paternity Benefits for Self-Employed Workers, 2017 14–15.

best interests of the child;[338] maintenance;[339] the right of the child to be heard in divorce cases;[340] and the relationship between children's rights and social, political, religious and cultural contexts.[341]

OP-CRC-AC has had an impact in South Africa through the work of the SAHRC. The SAHRC has engaged in follow-up to ensure the compliance of South Africa with the requirements of OP-CRC-AC. The engagement of the SAHRC with the Department of Foreign Affairs and the South African national defence force (SANDF) led to an agreement to raise the age of recruits to the army to 18 years. The efforts of the SAHRC resulted in the compliance of South Africa with the OP-CRC-AC, thereby removing the barrier to South Africa's ratification of OP-CRC-AC.[342]

The SAHRC also published an article on the 25th anniversary of CRC. The article detailed the historical significance of children's rights issues in South Africa and the regression in the protection of children's rights in South Africa due to bureaucratic issues in government departments.[343]

5.6.4 Impact on and through Non-state Actors

CRC has gained traction in South Africa's judiciary through the work of the Centre for Child Law (CCL), an impact litigation organisation situated in the Faculty of Law, University of Pretoria. The CCL has deployed CRC and the COs of the CRC Cttee to South Africa in its litigation on numerous children rights cases before South African courts.[344] The influence of CRC can also be seen in the work of organisations such as the Children's Institute, University of Cape

---

[338] The SALRC received a request to establish whether the prohibition in the Children's Act 38 of 2005 on revealing the identity of a surrogate mother and a sperm donor violates the 'best interest of the child' principle, as provided for in the Constitution and the UN Convention on the Rights of the Child. Report on Activities of the SALRC 2013/2014 68.

[339] SALRC, Issue Paper 28 Review of the Maintenance Act 1998, 2014 10.

[340] SALRC, Issue Paper 31 Family Dispute Resolution: Care of and Contact with Children 2015 32, 65.

[341] ibid 7.

[342] South African Human Rights Commission 4th Annual Report 1998/1999 70.

[343] In 1987 a conference was held on Children, Repression and the Law in Apartheid South Africa in Zimbabwe. In 1990 the National Committee on the Rights of the Child (NCRC) comprising of more than 200 children's rights organisations was formed. In 1992 an international conference on the rights of children in South Africa was hosted by the Community Law Centre, University of the Western Cape. See *Mail & Guardian*, 'Twenty-Five Years of Children's Rights' <https://mg.co.za/article/2014-11-21-00-twenty-five-years-of-childrens-rights/> accessed 1 June 2020.

[344] See eg *Equal Education and Others v Minister of Basic Education and Others* (n 173); *C and Others v Department of Health and Social Development* 2012 (2) SA 208 (CC).

Town,[345] the Equal Education Law Centre, Lawyers for Human Rights, Legal Resources Centre and Scalabrini Centre of Cape Town.

5.6.5 Impact of State Reporting

The initial report of South Africa under CRC was submitted within four months of the due date for submission. However, the second periodic report was submitted after a delay of 12 years. The delay in submission may be connected with the shuffling of the lead department on children's rights. When the Department of Women, Children and Persons with Disabilities was established in 2009 it was discovered that the 2002 and 2007 UN reports, although prepared, had never been submitted to the UN, and South Africa had also never submitted any reports to the AU.[346] The country submitted a combined second to fourth periodic report and the report also served as the initial report for the optional protocol on the involvement of children in armed conflict. The consolidated second to fourth periodic report was prepared with technical support from UNICEF and there was input from the provinces and civil society.[347]

In terms of structure and content, the initial report to the CRC Cttee was quite comprehensive on general information but did not provide much specific information on the implementation of the provisions of CRC. The dialogue of the Committee with the representatives of South Africa also reflected the enthusiasm of the representatives in discussing children's rights in general, as opposed to focusing on the implementation of the rights contained in the Convention. The initial report was presented by a high-ranking delegation and the CRC Cttee acknowledged in its COs that the presence of a high-ranking delegation allowed for a fuller assessment of the situation of children in South Africa. The structure of the combined second to fourth periodic report followed the general guidelines of the CRC Cttee. The delegation that presented the combined second to fourth periodic report was led by the Deputy Minister of the Department of Social Development (DSD).

CSOs did not submit shadow reports during the consideration of the initial reports of South Africa but they participated in the preparation of the state report.[348] The SAHRC submitted a report for the consideration of the second

---

[345] Children's Institute, University of Cape Town, Project 28: Promoting Children's Socio-Economic Rights.
[346] Parliamentary Monitoring Group, 'Country Reports (2nd, 3rd and 4th for 1998–2012) on UN Convention and African Charter on Rights of the Child' <https://pmg.org.za/committee-meeting/15551/> accessed 2 June 2020.
[347] CRC First Periodic Report, South Africa, CRC/C/ZAF/2 page 13.
[348] Summary Records of CRC Initial Report, South Africa, CRC/C/SR.609 page 2.

to fourth periodic report. During the consideration of South Africa's combined second to fourth periodic report, nine shadow reports were submitted for the consideration of the CRC Cttee. Two coalition reports (South African Alternate Report Coalition[349] and Alternate Report Coalition – Children's Rights South Africa ARC-CRSA) were submitted by 23 and 13 NGOs, respectively.

In terms of publicity, the DWCPD published copies of the initial state report and COs and, with the support of civil society, has distributed it among governmental departments and NGOs. It has further conducted consultations on, and raised awareness of, CRC with national, provincial and local-level stakeholders in rural as well as urban areas.[350] South Africa's second periodic report to CRC was also reported on the website of the Department of Basic Education.[351]

In terms of impact of the COs, there are some instances of influence of the CRC Cttee's COs. During the drafting of the Child Justice Act 75 of 2008, the CRC Cttee had recommended that South Africa should reassess the draft legislation on criminal responsibility with a view to increasing the proposed legal minimum age of ten years.[352] However, section 7 of the Child Justice Act set the minimum age of criminal capacity at 10 years. Section 8 of the Act, however, provided for the review of the minimum age of criminal capacity by the responsible cabinet minister within five years of the commencement of the Act. In the presentation of its review before the Portfolio Committee on Justice and Correctional Services, the DOJ & CD referred to articles 3(1) and 40(3) of CRC and CRC Cttee General Comment 10: Children's Rights in Juvenile Justice.[353] The Child Justice Amendment Bill[354] now sets the minimum age of criminal capacity at 12 years.[355] The amendment has been described as an alignment of South Africa's criminal justice law with 'recommendations from

---

[349] This report was a revision of the 2014 Complementary Report submitted during the consideration of South Africa's state report by the African Committee of Experts on the Rights and Welfare of the Child.

[350] CRC First Periodic Report, South Africa, CRC/C/ZAF/2, para 54.

[351] <https://www.education.gov.za/Portals/0/Documents/Reports/Convention%20on%20 the%20Rights%20of%20a%20Child%202013.pdf?ver=2015-04-08-101801-837> accessed 20 June 2020.

[352] COs on the CRC Initial Report of South Africa, CRC/C/15/Add.122, para 17.

[353] Department of Justice and Constitutional Development, Briefing by the Department of Justice and Constitutional Development on the Review of the Age of Criminal Capacity (Section 8 Read with Section 96(4) and (5) of the Child Justice Act, 2008) (Act 75 of 2008) <https://static.pmg.org.za/160907age_of_criminal_capacity_presentation-DojCD .pdf> accessed 27 June 2020.

[354] [B32B-2018].

[355] <https://justice.gov.za/legislation/bills/201809-ChildJustice-AmendmentBill-OCSLA .pdf> accessed 1 June 2020.

the United Nations Committee on the rights of the child to increase the minimum age to at least 12 years'.[356]

South Africa also reported that the provisions in the Children's Act include outlawing and/or regulating harmful customary practices, such as virginity testing and male circumcision, among children younger than 16 years were a response to the CRC Cttee's concerns about harmful practices for children.[357] In the second periodic report of South Africa it was reported that the increase in the legal minimum age for sexual consent in the Criminal Law (Sexual Offences and Related Matters) Amendment Act 32 of 2007 was a response to the recommendation of CRC.[358]

5.6.6   Brief Conclusion

CRC is highly influential in the work of state and non-state actors in South Africa. The high level of impact of CRC is connected to the importance attached to children's rights in the early post-apartheid South Africa and the crucial role of CRC in the drafting of the Constitution.[359] The high impact of CRC in South Africa has also been aided by technical and financial support received from UN specialised agencies such as UNICEF, UNAIDS, UNFPA and UNDP.[360] The

---

356   <https://www.iol.co.za/pretoria-news/child-criminal-capacity-age-raised-to-12-49149209> accessed 1 June 2020. Skelton posited that Parliament likely set the minimum age of criminal responsibility for children at 12 years in order to align the Act with other domestic legislation passed around the same time as the Child Justice Act. See Ann Skelton, 'Proposals for the Review of the Minimum Age of Criminal Responsibility' 2013 *South African Computer Journal* 257, 272–273 <https://repository.up.ac.za/bitstream/handle/2263/40378/Skelton_Proposals_2013.pdf?sequence=1&isAllowed=y> accessed 15 September 2023.

357   CRC First Periodic Report, South Africa, CRC/C/ZAF/2 page15. S 12(4) of the Children's Act prohibits virginity testing for children under 16 years of age. S 12(5) of the Act permits the testing of children older than 16 only (a) if the child has given consent to the testing in the prescribed manner; (b) after proper counselling of the child; and (c) in the manner prescribed. Furthermore, s 12(8) of the Act prohibits circumcision of male children under the age of 16, except when (a) circumcision is performed for religious purposes in accordance with the practices of the religion concerned and in the manner prescribed; or (b) circumcision is performed for medical reasons on the recommendation of a medical practitioner.

358   Ss 15 & 16 of Criminal Law (Sexual Offences and Related Matters) Amendment Act 32 of 2007. See CRC First Periodic Report, South Africa, CRC/C/ZAF/2 page 19.

359   Interview with Prof. Ann Skelton, Member, CRC Cttee. Physical interview conducted at the University of Pretoria, South Africa on 8 January 2020.

360   South Africa also receives international aid from development agencies such as IDC, USAID and Save the Children towards the promotion of children's rights. See CRC 2nd-4th Periodic Report 17; CRC First Periodic Report, South Africa, para 52. UNICEF South Africa, 'UNICEF South Africa and SA Human Rights Commission Partner to Advance Children's

presence of highly active children's rights CSOs has also enhanced the impact of CRC in South Africa.

The impact of CRC in South Africa has been impeded by cultural and religious beliefs. Some of the normative standards in the treaties appear to be in conflict with long-established cultural and religious beliefs such as virginity testing and abortion. In one of the dialogues with the CRC Cttee, a member of the South African delegation, Pahad, explained to the Committee that the termination of pregnancies has been met with stiff opposition by religious groups.[361] Male circumcision was also described as a cultural practice guaranteed by the Constitution by South African representatives during the consideration of South Africa's CRC initial report. Also, with respect to corporal punishment, the efforts of the Department of Basic Education to reduce corporal punishment in schools have been hampered by parents who considered corporal punishment an appropriate way of training children.[362] There is also evidence of tension between government policies and international law. When the CRC Cttee asked the state officials about the possibility of a specific budget for children, the official answered that he doubted if the Minister of Finance would subscribe to the idea of a separate or specific budget for children.[363]

5.7   Convention on the Rights of Persons with Disabilities

5.7.1   Incorporation and Reliance by Organs of State

CRPD has had some influence on laws and policies in South Africa. During the review of the Electronic Communications Amendment Bill, a definition was inserted for 'persons with disabilities', to align it with the White Paper definition that is based on CRPD.[364] Also, the Women Empowerment and Gender Equality Bill identifies its objective to include facilitating South Africa's compliance with its commitments to international agreements, including CRPD.[365] The biggest influence of CRPD on government policies may be gleaned from

---

Rights' <https://www.unicef.org/southafrica/press-releases/unicef-south-africa-and-sa-human-rights-commission-partner-advance-childrens-rights> accessed 1 June 2020. Department of Social Development, 'The Children's Act Explained' <https://www.justice.gov.za/vg/children/dsd-Childrens_Act_Explained_Booklet3_June2009.pdf> accessed 1 June 2020. Parliamentary Monitoring Group, 'Country Reports (2nd, 3rd and 4th for 1998–2012) on UN Convention and African Charter on Rights of the Child' <https://pmg.org.za/committee-meeting/15551/> accessed 2 June 2020.

361   Summary Records of CRC Initial Report, South Africa, CRC/C/SR.610 page 7.
362   CRC First Periodic Report, South Africa, CRC/C/ZAF/2 page 31.
363   Summary Records of CRC Initial Report, South Africa, CRC/C/SR.610 page 5.
364   Electronic Communications Amendment Bill B31–2018 35 para 3.1.
365   Women Empowerment and Gender Equality Bill B 50D-2013 5.

the White Paper on the Rights of Persons with Disabilities. The White Paper relies heavily on the provisions of CRPD as well as OP-CRPD. For example, the White Paper further relied on and adopted the definition of legal and mental capacity as espoused in the General Comment of the CRPD Cttee on article 12 of CRPD, which interprets the 'legal capacity of persons with disabilities'.[366]

The influence of CRPD is discernible through express reference in the South African Policy on Disability, developed by the Department for Social Development;[367] the White Paper on Sport and Recreation;[368] the National Development Plan: Vision 2030;[369] the Strategic Policy Framework on Disability for the Post School Education and Training System;[370] the National Strategic Plan for HIV and AIDS, STIs and TB, 2012–2016;[371] the South African Integrated Programme of Action Addressing Violence Against Women and Children (2013–2018).

Currently there is no specific legislation that has comprehensively domesticated CRPD. However, it is envisaged that the 2015 White Paper on the Rights of Persons with Disabilities will be developed into legislation to complete the domestication of CRPD.[372] There is no express mention of budgetary allocation for disability mainstreaming. This may be due to the state department responsible for disability mainstreaming being situated within the Department of Women, Children and Persons with Disabilities (DWCPD). During the press briefings by the minister in charge of the department, the issue of limited budgets within the department has always come up. The department has cited challenges, including with respect to enhancing disability mainstreaming pursuant to CRPD in the country due to a limited budget.[373]

---

366 White Paper on the Rights of Persons With Disabilities 2016 19 <https://www.gov.za/sites/default/files/gcis_document/201603/39792gon230.pdf> accessed 1 June 2020.
367 DSD Policy on Disability 11 <https://www.westerncape.gov.za/assets/departments/social-development/national_disability_policy.pdf> accessed 1 June 2020. See also Department of Social Development Annual Report 2012/2013 63.
368 Department of Social Development Annual Report 2012/2013 15.
369 CRPD Initial Report, South Africa, CRPD/C/ZAF/1 para 1.
370 The Strategic Policy Framework on Disability for the Post School Education and Training System <http://www.dhet.gov.za/SiteAssets/Gazettes/Approved%20Strategic%20Disability%20Policy%20Framework%20Layout220518.pdf> accessed 1 June 2020.
371 CRPD Initial Report, South Africa, CRPD/C/ZAF/1 para 275.
372 White Paper on the Rights of Persons with Disabilities 2015 15.
373 Press briefings by the Minister of the Department of Women, Children and Persons with Disabilities <https://pmg.org.za/search/?q=%22convention+on+the+rights+of+persons+with+disabilities%22&filter%5Btype%5D=briefing> accessed 1 June 2020.

5.7.2 Reliance by Judiciary

CRPD has not featured prominently in the jurisprudence of South African courts. The Convention has only been used as an interpretive guide in five instances by South African courts.

The Constitutional Court in the case of *Anna-Marie de Vos NO and Others v Minister of Justice and Constitutional Development and Others*[374] relied on the provisions of CRPD in holding that the provisions of section 77(6)(a)(i) of the Criminal Procedure Act 51 of 1977 were unconstitutional to the extent that it provided for the compulsory detention of persons found guilty of criminal offences, regardless of their various status, including mental disabilities. Similarly, the Court in *Director of Public Prosecutions, Transvaal v Minister for Justice and Constitutional Development*[375] referred to CRPD as one of the instruments that provide for the rights of children, particularly on the principle of the best interests of the child.

The Western Cape High Court in the case of *Murray John Martyn Bridgman NO v Witzenberg Municipality*[376] referred to CRPD in determining whether the parents of the plaintiff in the case were partly liable for the rape of their daughter on the respondent's premises. In particular, the Court referred to the rights against discrimination on the basis of disability, equality before the law, as well as the right to live independently, pursuant to articles 1, 8, 12 and 19 respectively.[377] The Western Cape High Court also referred to CRPD in the case of *Western Cape Forum for Intellectual Disability v Government of the Republic of South Africa and Government of the Province of the Western Cape.*[378]

5.7.3 Impact on and through Independent State Institutions

The SAHRC has conducted several trainings and workshops on the principles furthered by CRPD. The training and workshops have been focused on particular articles of CRPD, among them articles 19, 24 and 27. The SAHRC has also developed a framework, guidelines and toolkits to guide state and non-state entities on implementing the provisions of CRPD. These include the 2017 SAHRC Disability Monitoring Framework and guidelines (2017); 'Promoting the Right

---

[374] 2015 (2) SACR 217 (CC).
[375] 2009 (4) SA 222 (CC).
[376] 2017 (3) SA 435 (WCC).
[377] *Murray John Martyn Bridgman NO v Witzenberg Municipality* para 11.
[378] 2011 (5) SA 87 (WCC). The Equality Court also applied the principles of CRPD in *Parvathi Singh v The Minister of Justice and Constitutional Development, The Director General for the Department of Justice and Constitutional Development and Magistrates Commission* paras 34 and 35.

to Work of Persons with Disabilities: A Toolkit for South African Employers'; and the right to education for special needs learners (2017/2018). It is, however, acknowledged that capacity challenges within the Commission cause significant delays in the effective investigation and finalisation of complaints.[379] The inaugural Equality Report of the SAHRC released in 2012 includes two chapters on disability. The report asserted that CRPD can be a useful tool in the realisation of equity for persons with disabilities.[380]

CRPD significantly impacted on the work of the SALRC on an assisted decision-making Bill. In its annual report the SALRC stated that the finalisation of the SALRC's draft report and draft Bill on Assisted Decision Making was interrupted by a request from the SAHRC in September 2009 that the report and draft Bill should take CRPD into account.[381] On the advice of the Department of International Relations and Cooperation (DIRCO), the SALRC in January 2010 embarked on further research to establish a draft interpretation of the articles of CRPD that are relevant to the SALRC's draft proposals on assisted decision making. The SALRC completed the review and amendment of the proposed draft Bill on Assisted Decision Making for compatibility with CRPD in draft form in December 2010. An information and consultation session aimed at government stakeholders, the disability sector and public interest lawyers on the compatibility of the draft Bill with CRPD was held on 16 February 2012.[382] In line with the terminology of CRPD, the SALRC's final recommendations and proposed draft Bill were changed to 'supported decision making' as opposed to 'assisted decision making'.[383] Because of the significant impact of CRPD on the Commission's recommendations, the Commission in its final report dedicated a chapter on the relevance of CRPD to its research on assisted decision making for persons with disabilities.[384]

Additionally, in May 2018 the SALRC received a request from DOJ & CD for investigation into the necessity for legislation for the domestication of CRPD. The object of this investigation was to ascertain the necessity of a single or

---

379   CRPD Initial Report, South Africa, CRPD/C/ZAF/1, para 53.
380   SAHRC, Equality Report: Commentaries on Equality: Race, Gender, Disability and LGTBI Issues 2012 33.
381   SALRC 38th Annual Report, 2010/2011 39–40.
382   SALRC 39th Report, 2011/2012 59.
383   SALRC Project 122 Assisted Decision-Making Report 2015 1. See also SALRC Issue Paper 31 Family Dispute Resolution: Care of and Contact with Children 2015 88, 89.
384   The SALRC premised its recommendations on the interpretation that favours art 12(2) of CRPD as it relates to legal capacity. Several sections of the final draft Bill by the Commission reflected the provisions of art 12 of CRPD. See SALRC Project 122 Assisted Decision-Making Report 2015 111–114.

cross-cutting legislation on disability rights in South Africa in response to CRPD. On 16 March 2019 a pre-investigation proposal paper into the domestication of CRPD was considered and approved. The meeting recommended that the investigation be placed on the research programme of the SALRC.[385]

Traces of CRPD are also evident in the work of the Commission for Employment Equity (CEE). The Commission for Employment Equity, in setting out their key strategic objectives from 2010, highlighted that it would be advising the Minister of Labour on policy matters which include, but not limited to the review of the Code of Good Practice on People with Disabilities and Employment and its Technical Assistance Guidelines to bring it in line with any new developments, including CRPD.[386]

5.7.4 Impact on and through Non-state Actors

CRPD has reflected in the work of the Centre for Human Rights, which has issued a publication on its website explaining the state reporting process of CRPD, the key summary of the recommendations of the CRPD Cttee to South Africa and urged the government of South Africa to implement the COs.[387] The influence of CRPD is also reflected in the works of Cape Mental Health and Epilepsy South Africa. These organisations also participated in the shadow reports that were submitted to the CRPD Cttee in 2018.

CRPD has also been influential in academic publications. The annual *African Disability Rights Yearbook*, which is published by the Pretoria University Law Press, contains articles touching on the impact of CRPD in South Africa. The publications identified discuss topics such as the rights of South African women with disabilities;[388] criminal capacity and psychosocial disability in South African law;[389] access to justice;[390] and a country report for South Africa

---

385 South African Law Reform Commission Report, 2018/2019 55.
386 11th Commission for Employment Equity Annual Report 2010–2011 2.
387 Centre for Human Rights, 'Taking Stock of the Committee on the Rights of Persons with Disabilities COs to South Africa' <https://www.chr.up.ac.za/latest-news/83-news-chr/1912-taking-stock-of-the-committee-on-the-rights-of-persons-with-disabilities-concluding-observations-to-south-africa> accessed 1 June 2020.
388 A Holoboff and S Phillips, 'Leveraging the International Human Rights System to Advance Local Change for South African Women with Disabilities' (2019) 7 African Disability Right Yearbook 247.
389 H Combrinck, 'Rather Bad Than Mad? A Reconsideration of Criminal Incapacity and Psychosocial Disability in South African Law in Light of the Convention on the Rights of Persons with Disabilities' (2018) 6 African Disability Rights Yearbook 3–26 <http://doi.org/10.29053/2413-7138/2018/v6a1> accessed 1 June 2020.
390 R White and D Msipa, 'Implementing Article 13 of the Convention on the Rights of Persons with Disabilities in South Africa: Reasonable Accommodations for Persons with

in 2013.[391] The *African Human Rights Law Journal* has also featured an article on 'violent attacks against persons with albinism in South Africa'.[392]

5.7.5 Impact of State Reporting

South Africa presented its initial report to CRPD on 26 November 2014, seven years after ratifying the treaty. The country report covered the period between May 2008 and March 2012. Pursuant to the initial report, the delay in submitting the report was occasioned by changes in departmental arrangements resulting from the transition from the Office on the Status of Disabled Persons in the Presidency to the Department of Women, Children and Persons with Disabilities, which impacted negatively on government's capacity in the short term to finalise and deposit the first country report.

The preparation of the report involved various government departments and persons with disabilities organisations.[393] The first draft of the report was also published on the government website for public comments in November 2012, and released to multiple stakeholders by electronic means.[394]

The SAHRC submitted a shadow report and eight other shadow reports were submitted, including a joint submission from nine NGOs. The South African delegation was led by the Minister of Social Development.

In terms of impact, the state reporting process of CRPD has been used as a medium for dialogue on the development of policies. The comments and submissions received on the 2013 draft baseline country report to CRPD were some of the mediums of consultations with relevant stakeholders to develop the White Paper on the Rights of Persons with Disabilities.[395] In response to the CRPD Cttee's recommendation that South Africa should expedite the designation of an independent monitoring mechanism (IMM) under article 33 of

---

Communication Disabilities' (2018) 6 African Disability Rights Yearbook 99 <http://doi.org/10.29053/2413-7138/2018/v6a5> accessed 1 June 2020.

391   I Grobbelaar-Du Plessis and C Grobler, 'South African Country Report on Disability' (2013) 1 African Disability Rights Yearbook 307.
392   M Nswela, 'Violent Attacks Against Persons with Albinism in South Africa: A Human Rights Perspective' (2017) 17 African Human Rights Law Journal 114 <http://www.ahrlj.up.ac.za/mswela-m> accessed 1 June 2020.
393   CRPD Initial Report, South Africa, CRPD/C/ZAF/1, para 16.
394   See <https://www.gov.za/sites/default/files/gcis_document/201409/draft-country-report-crpd-public-comment-26-nov-2012.pdf> accessed 1 June 2020.
395   White Paper on the Rights of Persons with Disabilities 10.

CRPD, the SAHRC has embarked on a SAHRC/EU project on the establishment of an independent monitoring mechanism in South Africa under CRPD.[396]

5.7.6 Impact of Individual Communications

Although South Africa was one of the first states to ratify OP-CRPD in 2007, only one complaint has thus far been submitted, and was declared inadmissible.[397]

5.7.7 Brief Conclusion

South Africa has acknowledged that the impact of CRPD has been impeded partly due to the lack of an effective monitoring and evaluation system to track implementation of CRPD in the country.[398] It is anticipated that the influence of CRPD will improve once the process of establishing the IMM under article 33 of CRPD has been completed.

The impact of CRPD has also been impeded by the absence of a special government agency or department working to mainstream disability rights and enhance the implementation of CRPD. Currently, the responsible department is that of Women, Children and Persons with Disabilities. This department has often raised the issue and challenges of a limited budget. It is also evident, from the press briefings at Parliament, that the department has placed more focus on the rights of children and women. The Department of Social Development Policy on Disability inexplicably listed CRC as one of the 'national and international disability instruments' but omitted CRPD.

The impact of the treaty also is only feasible at national level. The South African Local Government Association and the former Department of Provincial and Local Government released the Disability Framework for Local Government 2009–2014, aimed at enabling local government and other role players to mainstream disability considerations in the development programmes of municipalities. The framework, despite being released after the ratification of CRPD, does not expressly refer to CRPD. The implementation of the framework has also regrettably lagged behind.

The level of awareness of CRPD among government officials seems to be relatively low. There are a number of important disability rights documents

---

396 Interview with Innocentia Mgijima, Manager Disability Rights Unit, Centre for Human Rights, University of Pretoria. Physical interview conducted at the University of Pretoria on 12 August 2019.

397 It was submitted in 2017, and declared inadmissible after the cut-off mark for this study (CPRD Cttee, *ANP v South Africa*, CRPD/C/23/D/73/2019 (submitted 19 September 2017; declared inadmissible 28 August 2020).

398 CRPD Initial Report, South Africa, CRPD/C/ZAF/1 page 37.

that should have incorporated the CRPD but did not in any way make reference to it. The South African National Policy Guidelines for Victim Empowerment prioritise persons with disabilities as a target group for intervention. Despite listing 'abused people living with disabilities' as one of its priority target groups for victim empowerment, the guidelines did not refer to CRPD as part of the legislative base for the policy. The National Development Plan of 2012 promotes an accelerated roll-out of inclusive education that will enable everyone to participate effectively in a free society and acknowledges that education provides knowledge and skills that persons with disabilities can use to exercise a range of human rights, such as the right to political participation, the right to work, the right to live independently and contribute to the community, the right to participate in cultural life, and the right to raise a family. Despite being released in 2012, and relying on the principles provided for in article 24 of CRPD, it does not expressly refer to CRPD.

6   Conclusion

Trends: In comparison to the 1999 study, there is a general increase in the level of impact of the treaties on legislation, policies and judicial decisions. However, in terms of the level of influence among the treaties, the findings of the current study are similar to the 1999 study. As stated above, CRC and CEDAW remain the treaties with the highest level of influence among the seven treaties ratified by South Africa. As compared to the pre-2000 consideration of state reports, the post-2000 reports witnessed an increase in submission of shadow reports to the treaty bodies, especially by national NGOs. The national NGOs have also shown more awareness of the treaties and have played crucial roles both directly and indirectly in improving the impact of the treaties in South Africa. The SAHRC has also been more involved in the state reporting process and has submitted several shadow reports to the treaty bodies. The CSOs that were involved in the early stages of the state reporting process did not understand the cyclical nature of the reporting process and, thus, they did not actively follow up on the COs. However, the trends have improved and the current set of CSOs involved in the reporting process are mobilising around the COs and use the COs at the national level. This is exemplified in the ingenious deployment of the COs in strategic litigation by the Centre for Child Law and the reference to the COs by the CESCR Cttee by Black Sash. The current set of treaty body members has also significantly contributed to the increase in the visibility of their respective treaties as opposed to the findings in the previous studies where the appointment of treaty members has not had much impact on the visibility of their respective treaties. There is a significant increase in the involvement of treaty body members in enlightening government officials and helping CSOs understand the usefulness and use of the treaty system. This is in sharp contrast to the findings in the 1999 study where the CRC Cttee member was criticised by NGOs as inactive and non-interactive. The current members such as Ann Skelton, Sandra Liebenberg and Pansy Tlakula are human rights advocates and scholars as opposed to, for example, the previous CRC member who was a clinical psychologist.

General findings of the study: The research found that the UN human rights treaties have had a considerable influence on laws, policies and decisions in South Africa. The influence on laws, policies and decisions varies among the treaties, with CRC, CEDAW, CRPD and CAT having the highest level and most discernible form of influence. The high level of influence of CRC may be attributed to the presence of strong CSO coalitions and the inputs of UN specialised agencies such as UNICEF and UNESCO, and the historical relevance of CRC in South Africa.

Generally, the treaties and COs have generally had their most significant impact through the deployment of the treaties by CSOs and independent state human rights institutions. The desire of the country to maintain a good human rights reputation within the international community has also in some instances motivated the state to comply with its obligations under the UN human rights treaties.

Several factors have impeded the impact of the UN human rights treaties in South Africa. One of these factors is the disparity between national principles and international law. This factor may be deduced from the conversations of the state delegates with the treaty bodies. For instance, in its response to the CERD Cttee's request for disaggregated data based on ethnic origin, South Africa responded as follows: 'South Africa's vision is that of a united people, united in our diversity, and not divided along ethnic and tribal groups. We are thus not in a position to provide disaggregated statistical data regarding ethnic groups.' This factor was also observed in the Equality Report of the SAHRC. In the initial report of South Africa to the CRC Cttee, the government explained that there is no mechanism within the setup of the cabinet to assess government spending on children because government departments do not generally regard children as a separate homogenous group.[399] When the CRC Cttee asked the state officials about the possibility of a specific budget for children, the official answered that he doubted if the Minister of Finance would

---

399   CRC Initial Report, South Africa, CRC/C/51/Add.2, para 20.

subscribe to the idea of a separate or specific budget for children.[400] Closely aligned to the disparity between national principles and international law is the perception of state officials that the treaty bodies do not fully understand the South African context in issuing its COs.[401] This factor was demonstrated in the case of *Amabhungane Centre for Investigative Journalism NPC and Another v Minister of Justice and Correctional Services and Others*.[402] Even though the HRCttee had recommended that South Africa should consider revoking or limiting the requirement for mandatory retention of data by third parties, the Court was of the opinion that the authorisation prescribed by the Regulation of Interception of Communications and Provision of Communication Related Information Act (RICA) for the retention of data by telecommunication companies for up to a maximum period of five years is consistent with the prescripts of section 36 of the South African Constitution. The Court aligned itself with the argument of the respondents that the investigation of crime in South Africa takes a longer time than in other jurisdictions with shorter duration, hence the period of five years is reasonable in the South African context.

Another factor that has impeded the impact of the UN treaties in South Africa are bureaucratic and capacity issues. For example, the long delay in the ratification of CESCR was a result of bureaucratic issues with respect to the lead department that is expected to take the lead process in the ratification of the treaty. Bureaucratic and capacity issues are also reflected in the lack of coordination and cooperation among government departments.[403] The lack of cooperation by other departments is the reason why the OP-CRC-AC report was, as at 30 June 2019, yet to be submitted because the DWCPD was unable to receive information from the Department of Defence despite several requests. According to some of the interviewees, some departments are generally more receptive to the human rights system, while some are extremely resistant. The lack of coordination has also been exacerbated by the problem of inadequate data collection systems.[404] The lack of coordination and cooperation among different departments has also made it difficult to adequately assess the impact of the COs in South Africa. Apart from the CRC second report, there is insufficient qualitative and quantitative data on measures undertaken by

---

400 Summary Records of CRC Initial Report, South Africa, CRC/C/SR 610 page 5.
401 The lack of contextual understanding was also stated by a government official. (Interview with anonymous government official. Physical interview conducted at the University of Pretoria on 29 July 2019).
402 2020 (1) SA 90 (GP).
403 CRC First Periodic Report, South Africa, CRC/C/ZAF/2, paras 106 & 108.
404 ibid.

South Africa to address the COs.[405] While the lack of adequate qualitative data can readily be ascribed to a low level of implementation of the COs, the problem is further exacerbated by the lack of coordination among the different government departments in the preparation of state reports and the low level of involvement of CSOs in the state reporting process in South Africa.[406] The lack of coordination between the different levels of government has also hampered the implementation of the COs of the UN treaty bodies.[407] The Parliamentary Committee on the DWCPD during its deliberation on the draft CRC report agreed that reporting by the state needed to improve, and intersectoral coordination strengthened. The Committee agreed that monitoring and evaluation also needed to be strengthened.[408] During the presentation to the Portfolio Committee, Dr September stated that the main issue was the country's attitude and subsequent commitment with regard to the report. To date, the submission of the report was seen as merely a technical exercise.[409] At the time of presenting the draft report before the portfolio committee, ten departments (the Departments of Sport and Recreation, Arts and Culture, Cooperative Governance and Traditional Affairs, Communication, Agriculture, Forestry and Fisheries, Energy, Economic Development, Trade and Industry, Public Works and Mineral Resources) were yet to submit their inputs to the DWCPD.[410] In order to improve collaboration among departments, there is the need for the lead department to be upfront, to guide each department on the relevant articles on what it needs to report, and to internalise the system and understand the cyclical nature of reporting.

---

405 The lack of qualitative and quantitative information was raised in the COs of the treaty bodies to South Africa.
406 The CERD Cttee in its COs on the CERD First Periodic Report of South Africa, CERD/C/ZAF/CO/4–8 required South Africa to involve the SAHRC and CSOs in the preparation of its next periodic report.
407 CRC First Periodic Report, South Africa, CRC/C/ZAF/2, para 107.
408 Parliamentary Monitoring Group 'Country Reports (2nd, 3rd and 4th for 1998–2012) on UN Convention and African Charter on Rights of the Child' <https://pmg.org.za/committee-meeting/15551/> accessed 2 June 2020.
409 ibid.
410 ibid.

CHAPTER 18

The Impact of the United Nations Human Rights Treaties on the Domestic Level in Spain

Carlos Villán Durán

1 **Introduction to Human Rights in Spain**

The 1931 democratic Constitution of the Second Republic was disrupted in 1936 by a military *coup d'état* conducted by General Franco, followed by a bloody civil war (1936–1939) and a long military dictatorship led by General Franco until his death (1939–1975). Gross and systematic violations of human rights and humanitarian law during this extended period continue unpunished due to the 1977 Amnesty Act, including crimes against humanity, such as 150 000 disappeared persons, among them 30 000 children. Substantive measures of transitional justice recommended by the United Nations (UN) to address the truth, justice, reparation of victims and adoption of guarantees of non-recurrence are still pending.

Franco's appointed successor, King Juan Carlos I, led a political transition to democracy that in 1978 culminated in the adoption of the current Constitution,[1] by which a monarchy with a democratic government elected by Parliament was established. However, the transition was not peaceful, since a military *coup d'état* attempt was registered on 23 February 1981, in reaction to ETA (Basque Country and Freedom) military and terrorist activities. Furthermore, on 11 March 2004 Madrid suffered a massive terrorist attack attributed to Islamic fundamentalist groups belonging to Al Qaeda, with a toll of 193 deaths and some 2 000 persons injured.

The 1978 Constitution recognised fundamental human rights and public liberties, mainly civil and political rights and the right to education, including the appeal on *amparo* before the Constitutional Court (article 53(2)). However, economic, social and cultural rights, such as the rights to food and housing, are considered principles inspiring the economic and social policy that would require further legislative development to enable them to be

---

1   BOE 311, 29 December 1978; see <https://www.boe.es/eli/es/c/1978/12/27/(1)/con> accessed 22 March 2022.

© CARLOS VILLÁN DURÁN, 2024 | DOI:10.1163/9789004377653_020
This is an open access chapter distributed under the terms of the CC BY-NC-ND 4.0 license.

adjudicated by the judiciary (article 53(3)).[2] The Constitution also recognised that Spain is composed of nationalities and regions (article 2), paving the way to the establishment of 17 autonomous communities (regions) with limited self-government. Nevertheless, the Constitution failed to recognise the right of peoples to self-determination, a right still claimed by strong pro-independence groups, in particular in the Basque country and Catalonia.

In the Basque country the National Liberation Movement was supported by the armed group ETA, responsible for the killing of 829 persons between 1968 to 2010. In reaction, the state adopted counter-terrorism legislation and restrictive administrative practices that are still in force, although ETA declared a ceasefire in 2011. In addition, Spain supported the organisation of paramilitary groups responsible for some summary executions and enforced disappearances. Counter-terrorism legislation also facilitated arbitrary detention, torture and other human rights violations that remain unpunished. Only victims of ETA were recognised as victims of human rights violations.

In Catalonia, political parties supporting the independence as well as the regional parliament and government (*Generalitat*) forced a referendum of self-determination on 1 October 2017, which was declared unconstitutional by the Constitutional Court. Subsequently, the police violently opposed those attempting to vote. Twelve top officials of the regional government and civil society leaders were charged with rebellion, sedition and other grievances. Nine of them were jailed on pre-trial detention – so-called 'political prisoners' – and others were forced to go into exile, including the then President of the *Generalitat*. In 2018 his extradition to Germany and Belgium was requested, but the respective domestic courts refused the charge of rebellion. In April 2019, the UN Working Group on Arbitrary Detention declared the detention of seven top Catalan leaders to be arbitrary.[3]

---

2   Consolidated jurisprudence which was confirmed by the Constitutional Court's judgment 32/2019 of 28 February FJ 6. BOE 73 of 26 March 2019. See <https://www.boe.es/boe/dias/2019/03/26/pdfs/BOE-A-2019-4447.pdf> accessed 26 March 2022.
3   WGAD, opinion 6/ 2019 (*Cuixart, Sánchez and Junqueras v Spain*), adopted on 25 April 2019. WGAD, opinion 12/ 2019 (*Forn, Rull, Romeva and Bassa v Spain*), adopted on 26 April 2019. These opinions are accessible from the WGAD search engine: https://wgad-opinions.ohchr.org/Search/Search.

2   Relationship of Spain with the International Human Rights System in General

With the support of the United States of America (USA) and the Vatican, the Spain of dictator Franco joined the UN in 1955. In 2019 Spain became a member of the Human Rights Council (HRC). It has extended a standing invitation to visits by thematic special procedures, albeit under the understanding that the terms of reference of each visit should be agreed upon by the government.

Eleven thematic special procedures visited Spain between 2003 and 2019,[4] submitting country reports to the consideration of the HRC.[5] Under the Universal Periodic Review (UPR) Spain was examined in 2010 and 2015.[6] The outcome and the added value of this rather promotional mechanism was rather poor, since relevant recommendations made by individual states were not accepted by the government, such as the ratification of the International Convention on the Protection of the Rights of All Migrant Workers and Members of Their Families (CMW).

As far as the adoption of the 1978 Constitution was in progress, Spain ratified nine UN core human rights treaties. It also accepted the individual complaints procedure before eight UN committees and the inquiry procedure before five UN committees.[7]

Within the International Labour Organisation, Spain is party to 87 conventions in force, including the eight fundamental conventions dealing with human rights.[8] It has also ratified four United Nations Educational, Scientific and Cultural Organisation (UNESCO) conventions in the field of human rights, as follows: the Convention against Discrimination in Education (1960); the Protocol Instituting a Conciliation and Good Offices Commission to be Responsible for Seeking the Settlement of any Disputes which may Arise between States Parties to the Convention against Discrimination in Education

---

[4] <https://spinternet.ohchr.org/ViewCountryVisits.aspx?visitType=all&country=ESP&Lang=en> accessed 26 March 2022.
[5] The reports on visits to Spain by relevant thematic special procedures are available at <http://ap.ohchr.org/documents/dpage_e.aspx?c=172&su=171> accessed 26 March 2022.
[6] See <https://www.ohchr.org/en/hr-bodies/upr/es-index> accessed 26 March 2022.
[7] An official table showing the ratification of UN human rights treaties, as well as UN individual complaints procedures and UN inquiry procedures relevant to Spain is available at <https://tbinternet.ohchr.org/_layouts/TreatyBodyExternal/Treaty.aspx?CountryID=163&Lang=EN> accessed 26 March 2022.
[8] See <https://www.ilo.org/dyn/normlex/en/f?p=1000:11200:0::NO:11200:P11200_COUNTRY_ID:102847> accessed 26 March 2022.

(1962); the Convention concerning the Protection of the World Cultural and Natural Heritage (1972); and the Convention on the Protection and Promotion of the Diversity of Cultural Expressions (2005).

Spain also joined the Council of Europe (in 1977) and the European Convention on Human Rights (ECHR). The European Convention entered into force in 1979. Since then the European Court of Human Rights (ECtHR) found violations of the ECHR in 100 cases against Spain dealing with, among others, unlawful detention, torture, the right to a fair trial, the right to privacy and freedom of expression.[9]

In addition, Spain ratified the 1961 European Social Charter (in 1980), the 1998 Additional Protocol (in 2000) and the 1991 Amending Protocol (in 2000). However, Spain is neither party to the Protocol of 1995 providing for a system of collective complaints nor to the Revised European Social Charter of 1996.[10] In December 2017 the European Committee of Social Rights reached its twenty-first supervising cycle of national reports on implementation of the European Social Charter, including reports submitted by Spain.[11]

Moreover, Spain ratified the European Convention for the Prevention of Torture and Inhuman or Degrading Treatment or Punishment (in 1987) and received 17 visits (seven periodic and 10 *ad hoc*) by the European Committee for the Prevention of Torture and Inhuman or Degrading Treatment or Punishment (CPT).[12]

Spain also became a party to the Framework Convention for the Protection of National Minorities (in 1995) and the European Charter for Regional or Minority Languages (in 2001). In addition, Spain is participating at the European Commission against Racism and Intolerance (ECRI) (since 2002), which has

---

9   See the ECHR 100 judgments on Spain at <https://hudoc.echr.coe.int/eng#{%22respondent%22:[%22ESP%22],%22documentcollectionid2%22:[%22JUDGMENTS%22]}> accessed 26 March 2022.

10 See European Committee of Social Rights, Activity report 2019 <https://rm.coe.int/activity-report-2019-of-the-european-committee-of-sosial-rights/16809fcf8b> accessed 26 March 2022.

11 The conclusions on Spain adopted by the European Committee of Social Rights are available at <https://hudoc.esc.coe.int/eng/#{%22ESCPublicationDate%22:[%222009-02-21T00:00:00.0Z%22,%222019-02-21T00:00:00.0Z%22],%22ESCStateParty%22:[%22ESP%22]}> accessed 26 March 2022.

12 CPT 16 published reports on Spain are available at <https://hudoc.cpt.coe.int/eng#{%22sort%22:[%22CPTDocumentDate%20Descending,CPTDocumentID%20Ascending,CPTSectionNumber%20Ascending%22],%22CPTState%22:[%22ESP%22]}> accessed 26 March 2022.

produced five reports on Spain, the last one published on 27 February 2018.[13] Moreover, since 1 May 1999 Spain has been participating in the Group of States against Corruption (GRECO).[14]

In addition, Spain has been a member of the European Union (EU) since 1986 and its Charter of Fundamental Rights; it also cooperates with the European Agency for Fundamental Rights. Moreover, Spain in 1994 joined the Organisation for Security and Cooperation in Europe (OSCE).

In 1982 Spain joined the North Atlantic Treaty Organisation (NATO) while its full integration into the military command structure was achieved in 1996. Spain also ratified the Rome Statute of the International Criminal Court (ICC).

In accordance with article 96(1) of the Constitution, 'validly concluded international treaties, once officially published in Spain, shall be part of the internal legal system'. Therefore, the integration system of international treaties into the Spanish domestic law is monist, since it does not require their transformation into national law. However, all treaties shall be published in the official gazette (*Boletín Oficial del Estado* (*BOE*)) in order to be compulsory to all public powers, including the judiciary. In case of conflict between international standards and domestic law, the provisions of treaties published in Spain shall prevail over domestic law. As stated in article 96(1) of the Constitution, treaty provisions 'may only be repealed, amended or suspended in the manner provided for in the treaties themselves or in accordance with the general rules of international law'. Consequently, once published the international treaties have a supra-legal but infra-constitutional status under Spanish law. Finally, article 10(2) of the Constitution states that '[p]rovisions relating to the fundamental rights and liberties recognised by the Constitution shall be interpreted in conformity with the Universal Declaration of Human Rights and the international treaties and agreements thereon ratified by Spain'. The constitutional provisions were complemented by Law 25/2014, of 27 November, on Treaties and Other international Agreements.[15] In accordance with article 29: 'All public authorities, organs and agencies of the State must respect the obligations of the international treaties in force in which Spain is a party and ensure the proper compliance with those treaties'. And article 30(1) states that they will be self-executing, unless they require additional domestic regulations to be implemented.

---

13   See the five ECRI reports on Spain at <https://www.coe.int/en/web/european-commission-against-racism-and-intolerance/spain> accessed 26 March 2022.
14   See the five GRECO reports on Spain at <https://www.coe.int/en/web/greco/evaluations/spain> accessed 26 March 2022.
15   See <https://www.boe.es/eli/es/l/2014/11/27/25> accessed 26 March 2022.

3 At a Glance: Formal Engagement of Spain with the UN Human Rights Treaty System

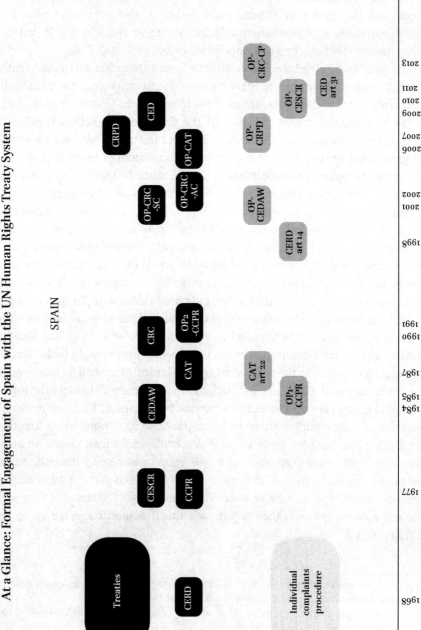

4 Role and Overall Impact of the UN Human Rights Treaties in Spain

4.1 *Role of UN Human Rights Treaties*

4.1.1 Formal Acceptance

In the period of the adoption of the 1978 Constitution and the restoration of democracy (1968–1990), Spain ratified most of the UN core human rights treaties, with the exception of the Convention on the Protection of the Rights of All Migrant Workers and Members of their Families (CMW). In parallel, Spain joined the most relevant Council of Europe (CoE) and European Union (EU) human rights treaties (1979–2007). Spain has also accepted the individual complaints procedure before eight UN treaty bodies (UNTBS), with the exception of CMW Cttee, in the period 1985 to 2014, and the inquiry procedure before five UNTBS, with the exception of the CESCR Cttee, in the period 1987 to 2014.

Neither early warning measures by the CERD Cttee nor urgent actions by the CED Cttee were adopted regarding Spain. The SPT paid a visit to Spain in 2017. The CRPD Cttee conducted an inquiry visit to Spain in 2017.

Spain entered an interpretative declaration to the Optional Protocol to CCPR (OP1-CCPR) to preserve the competence of the ECtHR; a reservation to the Convention on the Elimination of All Forms of Discrimination against Women (CEDAW) to preserve the constitutional provisions concerning succession to the Spanish crown (preference to male heirs); and minor reservations to articles 21(d) and 38 of the Convention on the Rights of the Child (CRC).

4.1.2 Non-Acceptance of CMW[16]

CMW currently has 57 state parties, but none of them is a member of the European Union (EU),[17] largely because the EU takes the view that its position was not considered when the Convention was drafted and adopted by the UN General Assembly. In 2010 and 2015 Spain reported to the Universal Periodic Review (UPR) that, as in the case of all other developed countries that are destinations for international migratory flows, it is not a signatory to CMW. It further noted that 'Part III of the Convention confers rights on all workers and their families without distinction, ie regardless of whether or not they are in a regular situation (articles 8 to 35)'.[18] However, the Spanish Aliens Act[19] sets

---

16　Sub-sec co-drafted by Carmelo Faleh Pérez, Ph Dr Professor of Public International Law and Human Rights at University of Las Palmas de Gran Canaria; member and legal adviser of the Spanish Society for IHRL.
17　See <https://treaties.un.org/Pages/ViewDetails.aspx?src=TREATY&mtdsg_no=IV-13&chapter=4&clang=_en> accessed 11 September 2023.
18　A/HRC/WG.6/8/ESP/1, 19 February 2010, para 20; A/HRC/29/8, 13 April 2015 para 131.
19　Organic Act No. 4/2000, of 11 January, on the rights and freedoms of foreigners in Spain and their social integration, as amended. See <https://www.boe.es/eli/es/lo/2000/01/11/4> accessed 11 September 2023.

forth two categories of rights and freedoms for foreigners in Spain: (a) rights to which all foreigners are entitled, namely, fundamental rights; and (b) social rights that only foreigners lawfully residing in Spain may exercise.

As discussed by some academics, the Spanish accession to CMW would allow the rights of all migrant workers and their families to be extended along with the principle of non-discrimination established by the CCPR and the International Convention on the Elimination of All Forms of Racial Discrimination (CERD), irrespectively of their administrative status. However, it will require the amendment of discriminatory provisions in the 2000 Aliens Act, which are allowed by article 13 of the Constitution.[20]

Finally, many treaty bodies recommended that Spain join CMW. This is the case of the most recent Concluding Observations (COs) adopted by the CESCR Cttee,[21] the CRC Cttee,[22] the CEDAW Cttee,[23] the CAT Cttee[24] and the CERD Cttee.[25]

4.1.3 General Attitude of Spain towards UN Treaty System

Spain considers that recommendations contained in COs, as well as interim measures and views adopted by UN committees, are merely recommendations and, therefore, not legally binding.[26] Since the recovery of democracy, the judiciary has for a long time followed this pattern. The Supreme Court judgment

---

20 See eg J de Lucas, C Ramón and A Solanes, *Informe sobre la necesidad y oportunidad de la ratificación por España de la Convención Internacional de la Organización de las Naciones Unidas de 1990 sobre la protección de los derechos de todos los trabajadores migratorios* (2008) Institut Català de Drets Humans; Universitat de Valencia; C Faleh Pérez, 'La Convención sobre los Derechos de los Trabajadores Migratorios y sus Familias' in APDHE, *Derecho Internacional de los Derechos Humanos: su vigencia para los Estados y los ciudadanos* (Madrid 2009) 103–112; Mª Ángeles Cano, 'Protección internacional de los Derechos Humanos de los trabajadores migratorios' (2010) 63 *Persona y Derecho* 137–162; and C Villán Durán 'La protección internacional de los trabajadores migrantes y de sus familiares' in Fundación Paulino Torras Domenech (ed), *Derecho, inmigración y empresa* (Publicaciones Itinera, Barcelona 2010) 449–512.
21 E/C.12/ESP/CO/6, 25 April 2018, para 51.
22 CRC/C/ESP/CO/5–6, 5 March 2018, para 50.
23 CEDAW/C/ESP/CO/7–8, 29 July 2015, para 43.
24 CAT/C/ESP/CO/6, 29 May 2015, para 25.
25 CERD/C/ESP/CO/18–20, 8 April 2011, para 18.
26 See María Gemma López Martín, 'La doctrina del Consejo de Estado sobre los efectos jurídicos de los dictámenes de los comités de derechos humanos de Naciones Unidas' in Carlos Fernández de Casadevante Romaní (ed), *Los efectos jurídicos en España de las decisiones de los órganos internacionales de control en materia de derechos humanos de naturaleza no jurisdiccional* (Dykinson, Madrid 2019) 171–200; Valentín Bou Franch, 'Las comunicaciones individuales contra España presentadas en el Comité de Derechos Humanos y su incidencia en el Derecho español' in Romaní (above) 17–64; Carlos Villán Durán, 'El valor jurídico de las decisiones de los órganos establecidos en tratados de las Naciones Unidas en materia de derechos humanos', in Romaní (above) 99–123.

of 17 July 2018 unexpectedly found that the state has an obligation to comply with the views emanating from CEDAW and its Optional Protocol.[27] Therefore, it paved the way towards a more significant impact of the treaties and the committees' decisions in the future.[28]

4.1.4 Level of Awareness

As a general trend there is not a high level of awareness of the treaties among the executive, the legislative, the judiciary and legal practitioners.[29] UNTBs are not part of the school and university curricula, including the judiciary school. Treaties are not officially translated into local languages. Only a few law schools offer courses related to UNTBs at master's degree level. Therefore, awareness of UNTBs is confined to some university researchers and a few human rights non-governmental organisations (NGOs) specialising in particular treaties.[30] When the media sporadically covers treaty body activities relevant to Spain, the information provided often is inaccurate or manipulated.[31]

4.1.5 State Reporting

Spain generally meets its reporting obligations, while occasionally accumulating some delays and some overdue reports.[32] Reports on CERD were submitted 20 months late; the fifth periodic report on the Convention Against Torture and Other Cruel, Inhuman, or Degrading Treatment or Punishment (CAT) was received more than three years late.

---

27 See below *Impact of individual communications*.
28 See Eduardo Jiménez Pineda, 'A commentary on the Supreme Court's judgment of 17 July 2018 (STS 1268/2018) and its supposed impact for a legally binding value of the decisions adopted by the Committee on the Elimination of Discrimination against Women (CEDAW)' (2019) 23 *SYbIL* 129–145 <http://www.sybil.es/documents/ARCHIVE/Vol23/6_JimenezPineda.pdf> accessed 26 March 2022. See also Carolina Jiménez Sánchez, 'Human Rights Committees: Their nature and legal relevance in Spain' (2019) 23 *SYbIL* 104–128 <http://www.sybil.es/documents/ARCHIVE/Vol23/5_JimenezSanchez.pdf> accessed 26 March 2022; Jorge Cardona LLoréns, '*The* legal value of views and interim measures adopted by the United Nations treaty bodies' (2019) 23 *SYbIL* 146–165 <http://www.sybil.es/documents/ARCHIVE/Vol23/7_Cardona.pdf> accessed 26 March 2022.
29 See newspaper *Público*, 25 November 2019, <https://www.publico.es/sociedad/espana-incumple-mandatos-internacionales-juzgar.html> accessed 26 March 2022.
30 See e.g. Open Society Foundations and Rights International Spain (2019), *Bajo sospecha. Impacto de las prácticas policiales discriminatorias en España*, 20 p. <https://rightsinternationalspain.org/wp-content/uploads/2022/03/BAJO-SOSPECHA-.pdf> (September 2019) accessed 11 September 2023 and <http://rightsinternationalspain.org/uploads/publicacion/of2da70d30d454c678b63afc6571c5641b313e86.pdf> (December 2019) accessed 27 March 2022.
31 See eg 'La ONU reprende a España por torturar al etarra Lupiáñez' *Deia* (21 May 2019).
32 On 6 March 2020 Spain had three overdue reports. See <https://tbinternet.ohchr.org/_layouts/15/treatybodyexternal/Download.aspx?symbolno=INT/CHAIRPERSONS/CHR/32/31688&Lang=en> p. 6 accessed 26 March 2022.

The Human Rights Office within the Directorate-General for the United Nations and Human Rights at the Ministry of Foreign Affairs, European Union and Cooperation is the lead agency for coordinating reporting on human rights obligations. This unit prepares the draft reports incorporating inputs from relevant departments and ministries. Reports are formally shared with NGOs only once they have been finalised and sent to Geneva.

The reports are rather formal since they refer extensively to legal texts, but they lack sufficient data to evaluate real treaty implementation by the executive and the judiciary. Shortcomings are not recognized.

In 2002 the CAT Cttee commended Spain for sending 'a large and highly-qualified delegation'.[33] Since then none of the delegations sent to treaty bodies included high-ranking officials, with the exception of the delegation sent in 2004 to the CEDAW Cttee, headed by the Minister of Equality;[34] in 2018 the CRC Cttee received a 'high-level and multisectoral delegation'.[35]

The National Ombudsman (*Defensor del Pueblo*) only submitted one alternative report to the CERD Cttee (2011).[36] In its capacity as national mechanism for the prevention of torture, it submitted alternative reports to the CAT Cttee in 2009 and 2015.[37] The National Ombudsman as well as the Basque and Catalan Ombudsmen also submitted their own reports to the CRC Cttee.

The CERD Cttee received six alternative reports from NGOs in relation to Spain's twenty-first to twenty-third periodic reports[38] and four with respect to the eighteenth to twentieth periodic reports.[39] Coalitions of NGOs submitted alternative reports to the HRCtte and the CRC, CED, CESCR and CEDAW Cttees.

Both the Spanish Committee of Representatives of Persons with Disabilities (CERMI) and *Defensor del Pueblo* (national human rights institution with UN

---

33 CAT/C/CR/29/3, para 3.
34 CEDAW/C/ESP/CO/6, para 3.
35 CRC/C/ESP/CO/5–6, para 2.
36 CERD/C/ESP/CO/18–20, para 3.
37 See 'Observaciones del Defensor del Pueblo sobre el sexto informe periódico de España ante el Comité contra la Tortura de la Organización de las Naciones Unidas' Defensor del Pueblo, 2015; and 'Observaciones del Defensor del Pueblo sobre el quinto informe periódico de España ante el Comité contra la Tortura de la Organización de las Naciones Unidas' Defensor del Pueblo, 2009.
38 The following NGOs submitted alternative reports: the Apache-Ndé-Nneé Working Group; Institut de Drets Humans de Catalunya; International Human Rights Advocacy Group; Rights International Spain; and, Sociedad Civil Africana y Afrodescendiente <https://tbinternet.ohchr.org/_layouts/treatybodyexternal/SessionDetails1.aspx?SessionID=1072&Lang=en> accessed 27 March 2022.
39 The following NGOs submitted alternative reports: Amnesty International; Asociación Española para el Derecho Internacional de los Derechos Humanos; Consejo Indio Exterior; and a joint submission by SOS Racismo España, Secretariado Gitano and Comisión Española de Ayuda al Refugiado <https://tbinternet.ohchr.org/_layouts/treatybodyexternal/SessionDetails1.aspx?SessionID=399&Lang=en> accessed 27 March 2022.

status A) have been formally appointed in 2011 as national independent monitoring mechanisms in accordance with article 33 of the Convention on the Rights of Persons with Disabilities (CRPD).[40]

4.1.6 Domestic Implementation Mechanisms

Concluding Observations are posted on the official website of the Ministry of Justice. They are summarised by some media and are not translated into local languages. A few NGO websites offer COs and, more rarely, general comments or recommendations adopted by committees.[41] The Human Rights Office of the Ministry of Foreign Affairs is also responsible for following up and monitoring the implementation of the committees' recommendations. However, outputs are not shared with NGOs. In 2012 the National Plan on Human Rights dealing with the implementation of COs was discontinued.

No reprisals against human rights defenders engaging in the reporting process have been reported. However, in individual cases victims and their lawyers were slandered in the media.[42]

4.1.7 Treaty Body Membership

There is no national process for nomination of treaty body members. The following seven committees had or have Spanish members: the CRC Cttee;[43] the CESCR Cttee;[44] the CEDAW Cttee;[45] the CAT Cttee;[46] the CED Cttee;[47] the CERD Cttee;[48] and the SPT.[49] Most of these members are officials from different ministries or university professors. Their activities are rarely reported in domestic media.

---

40 See Royal Decree 1276/2011 <http://ennhri.org/Ombudsman-of-Spain-Defensor-del-Pueblo> accessed 27 March 2022.

41 See eg <https://doc.es.amnesty.org/ms-opac/search?search?norm=siai&q=mssearch_fl d41:DESC> accessed 27 March 2022.

42 Following the WGAD opinion 17/2009 of 4 September 2009 (*Karmelo Landa v Spain*); both the victim and his lawyers from SSIRHL were considered 'terrorists' in the media.

43 Mr Jorge Cardona Lloréns (2011–2019).

44 Ms María de los Ángeles Jiménez Buitragueño (1986–2000) and Mr Mikel Mancisidor (2012–2020).

45 Ms Carlota Bustelo García del Real (1989–2000) and Ms Ana Peláez Narváez (2019–2022).

46 Mr Fernando M Mariño Menéndez (2002–2013). From 2003 to 2005 he served as Chairperson.

47 Mr Juan José López Ortega (2011–2023).

48 Mr Nicolás Marugán Zalba (2015–2019); on 3 February 2019 he resigned. On 8 April 2019 Spain appointed Ms María Teresa Verdugo Moreno to serve the remainder of Mr Marugán's term of office, expiring on 19 January 2020 (see A/74/18, para 8).

49 Ms Carmen Comas-Mata Mira (2019–2022).

4.2 Overall Impact of the UN Human Rights Treaties

4.2.1 Incorporation and Reliance by Legislature and Executive

In accordance with article 96(1) of the 1978 Constitution and article 23 of Act 25 of 2014, on treaties and other international agreements, treaties ratified by Spain, once published in the official gazette, form part of the Spanish legal system and are directly applicable by the executive and the judiciary. In addition, article 10(2) of the Constitution provides that fundamental rights and freedoms recognised by the Constitution will be interpreted in accordance with the Universal Declaration of Human Rights and international treaties and agreements on the same matters ratified by Spain. Nevertheless, comprehensive definitions of criminal offences (for instance, torture[50] and enforced disappearances) included in international treaties have to be adopted first through amendments to the domestic Criminal Code to be directly applicable by Spanish courts.

In addition, article 53(3) of the Constitution states that economic, social and cultural rights, with the exception of the right to education, are considered principles inspiring the economic and social policy. Therefore, they would require further legislative development to enable them to be protected by the judiciary.

Based on recommendations by treaty bodies, Spain revised some domestic legislation to comply with international treaties. Upon adoption of the HRCttee's views of 20 July 2000, Organic Act 19 of 2003 introduced the principle that would allow the establishment of appeal proceedings in high courts ensuring that all convictions and judgments can be reviewed in a second instance to comply with article 14(5) of CCPR. Similarly, in 2015 the Spanish Criminal Code was revised with a view to better tackling hate crimes,[51] and legislation was enacted to strengthen support for victims of crime, including racially-motivated acts.[52]

Following the recommendations made by the CRC Cttee in 2002, Spain modified article 154 of the Civil Code to delete the provision stipulating that parents could reasonably and moderately discipline their children.[53] However, in 2002 CRC Cttee reiterated its previous recommendation that Spain appropriately integrate the general principles of CRC, namely, articles 2, 3, 6 and 12, in all relevant legislation concerning children. It further

---

50 CAT Cttee considers that art 174 of the Criminal Code does not fully reflect the definition contained in art 1 CAT. See CAT/C/ESP/CO/6, para 8.
51 CERD/C/SR.2424, para 2.
52 Act No 4/2015 of 27 April, on the status of victims of offences. *Ibidem*, para 3.
53 Act No 54/2007 of 28 December.

recommended the approval of an integral law on violence against children.[54] In 2018 the CRC Cttee welcomed new legislative amendments introduced by Act 26 of 2015 on the modification of the system for the protection of children and adolescents.[55] However, it recommended the adoption of additional extensions to the statute of limitations in child sexual abuse cases, and to ensure the alignment of regional legislation with national legal frameworks related to children's rights. In 2010 it also recommended the development of systematic educational programmes on the principles and provisions of CRC for the general public, children, families and professionals working with children, including judges, lawyers, law enforcement officials, teachers, health personnel and social workers.

Spain enacted Act 26 of 2011, on normative adaptation to CRPD to ensure appropriate harmonisation of domestic legislation with the treaty. By Legislative Royal Decree 1 of 2013, the Consolidated Text of the General Act on the Rights of Persons with Disabilities was approved. However, in March 2019 the CRPD Cttee found the text not in compliance with the human rights model of disability.[56] The CRPD Cttee commended Spain for taking steps to guarantee the right to vote of all persons with disabilities on an equal basis with others. Spain adopted many laws and regulations, as well as policies and practical measures in implementing CRPD. However, major challenges persist in key areas of CRPD such as the full recognition of legal capacity of persons with disabilities; the right to inclusive education; accessibility; and the right of persons with disabilities to live independently and being included in the community. Official budgets were either insufficient or not allocated in line with CRPD. Women with disabilities continue to experience intersectional discrimination based on disability, gender and other statuses limiting their advancement, development and empowerment as actors of change. More needs to be done in the key area of raising awareness of CRPD and the human rights model of disability, as the medical model of disability continues to be largely entrenched in society, and contributes to perpetuate negative stereotyping, prejudices and stigma against persons with intellectual, psychosocial and multiple disabilities.[57] In 2019 the CRPD Cttee lamented the lack of training for professionals in fields such as education and health and the judiciary to raise awareness about the rights of persons with disabilities. It also regretted the

---

54   CRC/C/ESP/CO/3-4, para 38.
55   BOE 180, 29 July 2015. See <https://www.boe.es/eli/es/l/2015/07/28/26> accessed 27 March 2022.
56   CRPD/C/ESP/CO/2-3, para 6.
57   ibid, para 10.

overall lack of awareness about the provisions of CRPD among lawyers, court staff, judges, prosecutors and law enforcement officials.[58]

The Constitution recognises the principle of equality as one of the highest values of the legal system (article 1(1)) and elevates it to a fundamental right (article 14). Pursuant to article 53, the principle of equality is also binding on all public authorities and enjoys the protection of the courts. However, article 13(1) of the Constitution provides that 'foreigners in Spain shall enjoy the public freedoms guaranteed in this title under the terms established by treaties and the law'. Unfortunately, the 2000 Aliens Act sets forth two categories of rights and freedoms for foreigners in Spain.[59]

4.2.2   Reliance by Judiciary

In many of the judicial proceedings quoting CERD the participation of NGOs, through private prosecutions or the public right of action, has been fundamental.

References to CCPR were found in 238 judgments and 68 court orders by the Constitutional Court. In 2006 it reiterated the important hermeneutical function that the international human rights treaties ratified by Spain have to determine the content of fundamental rights, having expressly stated that the content of human rights recognised in CCPR is also part of fundamental rights, 'forming the minimum and basic standard of fundamental rights of every person in the Spanish legal system'.

In 2012 the Plenary of the Constitutional Court warned about the need to build the legal culture of rights, not only from the systematic and literal interpretation of legal texts, but also taking into account the international treaties, the jurisprudence of the international bodies that interpret them, and the opinions and views elaborated by the competent organs of the UN system.[60] However, in 2018 the Constitutional Court regarded as constitutional the Organic Act 1 of 2014, which had drastically reduced the application of the universal jurisdiction principle in Spain.[61]

---

58   ibid, paras 24 and 25.
59   See n 19.
60   CC judgment 198/2012 of 6 November. *BOE* 286, 28 November 2012. See <https://hj.tribunalconstitucional.es/es-ES/Resolucion/Show/23106> accessed 27 March 2022.
61   CC judgment 140/2018 of 20 December 2018 (*BOE* 22, 25 January 2019). See <https://hj.tribunalconstitucional.es/es/Resolucion/Show/25823> accessed 27 March 2022. See Irene Vázquez Serrano, *El principio de jurisdicción universal y su encrucijada (¿Utopía o el mundo real?)* (Madrid, Thomson Reuters Aranzadi 2019) 642.

References to the International Convention on Economic, Social and Cultural Rights (CESCR) were only found in 12 judgments of the Constitutional Court.[62] In 2012 the CESCR Cttee recommended to Spain to ensure that the provisions of CESCR are fully justiciable and applicable by domestic courts; to carry out awareness-raising campaigns for rights holders on the justiciability of economic, social and cultural rights; and to provide training to the actors responsible for the implementation of CESCR (especially judges, lawyers, law enforcement officials, members of Parliament and others).[63] CAT, CEDAW and CRC are regularly invoked in judgments by domestic courts, strictly for interpretative purposes. The reception of CRPD by domestic tribunals is diverse, from both a qualitative and a quantitative point of view. It is not always referenced in domestic judgments and the interpretation of CRPD by domestic courts is not always in line with the human rights model of disability enshrined in both CRPD and general comments of the CRPD Cttee.[64]

4.2.3 Impact on and through Non-state Actors and Independent State Institutions

Publications of human rights NGOs and basic textbooks on law generally cite human rights treaties. There is a remarkable research production by university academics about CCPR, CESCR, CAT, CEDAW, CRC and OPs.[65]

The participation of NGOs in the examination of periodic reports has increased significantly between 2015 and 2018, reaching 13 before the HRCttee, 15 before the CESCR Cttee and seven before the CAT Cttee.

For the last two reports on CESCR, the National Ombudsman (*Defensor del Pueblo*) also contributed his own reports as the national human rights institution recognised by the UN.

CERMI has since 2008 published annual reports on disability and human rights. In 2011 the Ombudsman (*Defensor del Pueblo*) published a national report on human rights and disability.[66] The annual reports of the Ombudsman also include chapters on the implementation of the rights of persons with disabilities. CERMI acknowledges that different awareness-raising measures have been adopted, but they lack systematic and structural dimensions.[67] Priority

---

62 E/C.12/ESP/Q/5/Add.1, para 2.
63 E/C.12/ESP/CO/6, paras 6(b) and (c).
64 CRPD/C/20/3, paras 70–74.
65 See below the respective sub-sections.
66 <https://www.defensordelpueblo.es/informe-monografico/las-personas-discapacidad-informe-anual-del-defensor-del-pueblo-2018/> accessed 27 March 2022.
67 <https://www.cermi.es/es/colecciones/derechos-humanos-y-discapacidad-informe-espa%C3%B1a-2013> accessed 27 March 2022.

actors, which require systematic attention, are the national and regional parliaments, public administrations and judges. CERMI's 2013 annual report reproduces the recommendations of the CRPD Cttee and describes the measures adopted by Spain in implementing these.[68]

4.2.4 Impact of State Reporting

Most of the recommendations contained in the COs adopted by treaty bodies remain unimplemented. As they are considered by Spain to be not binding, there is no effective national follow-up mechanism to ensure their appropriate implementation. International mechanisms to follow up are also weak. The sporadic replies by Spain are insufficient since they do not meet the required criteria established by the treaty bodies. This situation generates frustration among victims of human rights violations and other stakeholders that discontinue their cooperation with treaty bodies. Only a limited number of NGOs are aware of the relevance of the recommendations and continue their advocacy in an attempt to persuade both the executive and the legislative to take urgent action on unattended recommendations. As an example, in 2015 the HRCttee selected three issues to follow up, requesting Spain to report within one year on the implementation of recommendations dealing with ill-treatment and excessive use of force by the police, past human rights violations and unaccompanied minors. Spain replied on 21 July 2016.[69] One NGO submitted its follow-up report on 22 May 2017.[70] On 18 April 2018 the Special Rapporteur on follow-up, having assessed a lack of substantive progress, transmitted the HRCttee's decision to discontinue the procedure.[71]

4.2.5 Impact of Individual Communications[72]

Up to 30 June 2019, six treaty bodies out of eight adopted a total of 37 views on Spain finding violations of conventional norms, as follows: HRCttee (26); CESCR Cttee (2); CEDAW Cttee (1); CAT Cttee (3); CRC Cttee (4); and CRPD Cttee (1).

---

68 ibid.
69 CCPR/C/ESP/CO/6/Add.1, 27 September 2016 19.
70 See <http://aedidh.org/wp-content/uploads/2017/05/Seguimiento-a-OF-2015.pdf> accessed 27 March 2022.
71 See <https://tbinternet.ohchr.org/_layouts/15/treatybodyexternal/Download.aspx?symbolno=INT%2fCCPR%2fFUD%2fESP%2f30919> accessed 27 March 2022.
72 Sub-sec co-drafted by Carmen Rosa Rueda Castañón, former Secretary of the HRCttee's Working Group on Communications and member of the Spanish Society for IHRL.

The prevailing position of Spain has been that the recommendations emanating from views where committees found violations of the respective treaties are not binding, since the committees are not courts and their decisions are mere opinions and not judgments.[73] Furthermore, there has for a long time been no mechanism in the Spanish legal order by which the victims of violations declared by international bodies can seek reparation. Spain also maintained that the respective treaties do not include the obligation of state parties to establish such mechanisms. As this rigid and very conservative position has over the years become problematic, particularly with respect to the judgments of the ECHR, an amendment to the Organic Act of the Judiciary was adopted in 2015.[74] According to its article 5*bis*, victims of violations found in judgments of the ECHR can file a review appeal before the Supreme Court in order to seek reparation. Unfortunately, views of the UNTBs were left out of the scope of this new provision, with the result that victims continue to be confronted with the refusal by the government and domestic courts to take measures of reparation. Consequently, the vast majority of views remain unimplemented.

This situation may evolve in the right direction following the unexpected Supreme Court judgment of 17 July 2018[75] in connection with the reparations ordered by the CEDAW Cttee in the case of *Ángela González Carreño*.[76] While acknowledging that article 5*bis* of the Act of the Judiciary does not apply to decisions by the UN treaty bodies, the Court declared that the state had the obligation to comply with the views emanating from CEDAW and its OP, since it voluntarily acknowledged the competence of the CEDAW Cttee to examine individual complaints. Furthermore, CEDAW was part of the Spanish legal system, as set up in articles 96 and 10(2) of the Constitution. The Court also indicated that the views are the result of a legal procedure conducted by the CEDAW Cttee with full participation of Spain and voluntarily entered into by Spain.[77] Accordingly, such views are part of the Spanish legal system

---

73   See for all Santiago Ripol Carulla, 'Las decisiones de los órganos de tratados de derechos humanos de las Naciones Unidas en el Derecho español', in Romani (n 26) 201–233.

74   Organic Act 7/2015 of 21 July, amending Organic Act of the Judiciary 6/1985 of 1 July. *BOE* of 22 July 2015. See <https://www.boe.es/diario_boe/txt.php?id=BOE-A-2015-8167> accessed 27 March 2022.

75   Judgment 1263/2018 of 17 July of the Supreme Court, Administrative Chamber, Section Four. See <https://supremo.vlex.es/vid/735629461> accessed 27 March 2022.

76   CEDAW, views adopted on 16 July 2014. See CEDAW/C/58/D/47/2012 of 18 July 2014 <https://juris.ohchr.org/Search/Details/1878> accessed 27 March 2022.

77   See Concepción Escobar Hernández, 'Sobre la problemática determinación de los efectos jurídicos internos de los "dictámenes" adoptados por comités de derechos humanos. Algunas reflexiones a la luz de la STS 1263/2018, de 17 de julio' (2019) 71 *REDI* 241–250.

and have the supra-legal value provided to them by articles 95 and 96 of the Constitution. This strong judgment by the Supreme Court sets a precedent that will be difficult to ignore. It paves the way for a more significant impact of the treaties and the UNTBs' decisions not only in the lives of human rights victims, but also in the Spanish legal system as a whole. As proposed by some academics, the legislative should again revise article 5*bis* of the Organic Act of the Judiciary to include decisions by both the UN committees and the UN Working Group on Arbitrary Detention along with judgments of the ECtHR.[78]

4.2.6 Impact of Other Measures: Inquiry by CRPD Cttee and Visit by SPT

The CRPD Cttee carried out an inquiry in Spain in 2017 regarding systematic violations of article 24 CRPD (right to education).[79] It found violations of the right to an inclusive and quality education related primarily to certain features of the education system that have been maintained despite reforms and that continue to exclude persons with disabilities – particularly those with intellectual or psychosocial disabilities or multiple disabilities – from mainstream education on the basis of assessments conducted according to the medical model of disability. In 2018 Spain rejected the CRDP Cttee's findings arguing that the report did not reflect the real situation in the country.[80] In 2019 the CRPD Cttee remained concerned about the limited progress made by Spain with regard to inclusive education, including the lack of a clear policy and

---

[78] Carlos Villán Durán and Carmelo Faleh Pérez, *El sistema universal de protección de los derechos humanos. Su aplicación en España* (Tecnos, Madrid 2017) 58–65. Similarly, Valentín Bou Franch, 'El cumplimiento en España de las sentencias y dictámenes de los órganos de control del cumplimiento de los derechos humanos establecidos en tratados internacionales. Comentario a la STS núm 2747/2018, de 17 de julio (ROJ: 2747/2018)' (2019), *Rev Boliv de Derecho*, nº 27, 434–457; Cesáreo Gutiérrez Espada, 'La aplicación en España de los dictámenes de comités internacionales: la STS 1263/2018, un importante punto de inflexión' (2018) 10 *Cuadernos de Derecho Transnacional* 836–851; Carlos Fernández de Casadevante Romaní, 'La obligación del Estado de reconocer y aceptar los efectos jurídicos de las decisiones de los órganos internacionales de control en materia de derechos humanos' in Carlos Fernández de Casadevante Romaní (ed), *Los efectos jurídicos en España de las decisiones de los órganos internacionales de control en materia de derechos humanos de naturaleza no jurisdiccional* (Dykinson, Madrid 2019) 237–277; and Cesáreo Gutiérrez Espada, 'Reflexiones sobre la ejecución en España de los dictámenes de los comités de control creados por los tratados sobre derechos humanos' in Romaní (above) 279–297.
[79] CRPD/C/20/3.
[80] CRPD/C/20/5.

action plan for the promotion of inclusive education, and called upon Spain to implement all the recommendations contained in its inquiry report.[81]

The SPT visited Spain from 15 to 26 October 2017. It addressed one report to the state and one to the national preventive mechanism. Spain also replied in 2018.[82] Against NGO opinion,[83] the national preventive mechanism was established in 2009 as part of the National Ombudsman's mandate. It is composed of a unit within the organisational structure of the Office of the Ombudsman created to that effect and an advisory board of independent experts. The SPT reported that the budget allocated to the national preventive mechanism is included, without differentiation, in the overall budget of the Office of the Ombudsman, which makes it difficult for the national preventive mechanism to effectively fulfil its mandate. The mechanism does not have a sufficiently large team of professionals to perform its mandate on a national scale. Furthermore, it does not adequately engage in constructive dialogue with senior authorities with a view to effectively monitoring the implementation of its recommendations. Finally, it should increase its interaction with civil society and the offices of the ombudsman of the autonomous communities (regions).[84]

4.2.7 Additional

The treaty body system is complemented by Charter-based HRC special procedures. Among them, 11 thematic special procedures paid relevant visits to Spain between 2003 and 2019,[85] producing many recommendations – still unimplemented – that reinforce recommendations adopted by treaty bodies addressing inter alia incommunicado detention, the 1977 Amnesty Act and the human rights of migrants.

---

81 CRPD/C/ESP/CO/2–3, para 46.
82 The SPT Sub-Cttee reports to Spain and NPM, as well as the reply of Spain, are discussed in detail below.
83 See Carlos Villán Durán and Carmelo Faleh Pérez, 'Contribución de la AEDIDH a la aplicación en España del Protocolo Facultativo de la Convención contra la Tortura y Otros Tratos o Penas Crueles, Inhumanos o Degradantes' in Fernando M Mariño Menéndez and Alicia Cebada Romero (eds), *La creación del mecanismo español de prevención de la tortura* (Iustel, Madrid 2009) 267–298.
84 CAT/OP/ESP/2, para 19.
85 See *supra*, sec 2.

5 The Impact of the Different UN Human Rights Treaties on the Domestic Level in Spain

5.1 *International Convention on the Elimination of All Forms of Racial Discrimination*[86]

Spain acceded to CERD on 13 September 1968.[87] On 13 January 1998, it made the optional declaration under article 14 recognising the competence of the CERD Cttee to receive and consider individual complaints.[88]

5.1.1 Incorporation and Reliance by Legislature and Executive

Article 1(1) of the 1978 Constitution recognised the principle of equality as one of the highest values of the legal system and elevated it to a fundamental right (article 14).[89] Pursuant to article 53(2), this principle is also binding on all public authorities and enjoys the protection of the courts.[90] In addition, the Constitution requests public authorities to remove any obstacles that prevent or hinder the full enjoyment of freedom and equality of individuals and the groups to which they belong and reminds them of their obligation to facilitate participation of all citizens in political, economic, cultural and social life (article 9). Article 13(1) of the Constitution provides that 'foreigners in Spain shall enjoy the public freedoms guaranteed in this title under the terms established by treaties and the law'. Accordingly, pursuant to article 3(1) of the Aliens Act,[91] foreigners in Spain enjoy the rights and freedoms recognised in Title I of the Constitution under the terms established in international treaties, in this Act and in laws regulating the exercise of such rights and freedoms.[92]

---

86 Sub-sec 5.1 was drafted by Dr Javier Leoz Invernón, staff member of OHCHR.
87 BOE 118, 17 May 1969.
88 BOE 139, 11 June 1998. On 22 October 1999 the government informed the Secretary-General that it had decided to withdraw its reservation in respect of art 14 made upon accession. See United Nations Treaty Collection, Chapter IV.2 Declarations and reservations.
89 'Spaniards are equal before the law and may not in any way be discriminated against on account of birth, race, sex, religion, opinion or any other personal or social condition or circumstance'; art 14 of the Constitution.
90 By means of a preferential and summary procedure before ordinary courts and, where appropriate, an application to the Constitutional Court for *amparo*, art 53(2) Constitution.
91 Organic Act 4/2000 of 11 January, on the rights and freedoms of foreigners in Spain and their social integration, as amended. See n 19.
92 According to the information provided by Spain in its 21st to 23rd periodic reports, 'Act No 4/2000 explicitly sets forth a series of rights for foreigners and establishes the general interpretative rule that foreigners may exercise the statutory rights on equal terms with Spaniards. The Constitution states that foreigners and Spaniards have equal rights, under the conditions provided for in international instruments to which Spain is a party and in national legislation. However, foreigners and Spaniards are not entirely equal in the

In 2015 the Spanish Criminal Code was revised with a view to better tackling hate crimes,[93] and legislation was enacted to strengthen support for victims of crime, including racially-motivated acts.[94] The Comprehensive Strategy against Racism, Racial Discrimination, Xenophobia and Related Forms of Intolerance, adopted in 2011, is currently the main instrument for action in this sphere and implementing Spain's obligations under various international human rights treaties. The Strategy also provides a framework for institutional cooperation and coordination and for collaboration with civil society.[95] The Council for the Elimination of Racial and Ethnic Discrimination,[96] which was created in 2003, includes among its functions to provide independent assistance to victims of direct or indirect discrimination on racial or ethnic origin when it processes their claims.[97] Another measure worth mentioning is the appointment of special prosecutors on hate crime.[98]

5.1.2 Reliance by Judiciary

A detailed listing of recent judicial decisions relating to the provisions of articles 1 to 7 of CERD can be found in the twenty-first to twenty-third periodic reports of Spain.[99] In many of these judicial proceedings the participation of

---

exercise, enjoyment and protection of the rights listed in Title I, inasmuch as the underlying legal basis is either an international treaty or a national law. The Aliens Act sets forth two categories of rights and freedoms for foreigners in Spain: rights to which all foreigners are entitled, namely, fundamental rights ... and social rights that only foreigners lawfully residing in Spain may exercise ... Art 23 of the Act establishes that discrimination in any act that, directly or indirectly, involves any distinction, exclusion, restriction or preference directed against a foreigner on the basis of race, colour, descent, national or ethnic origin or religious beliefs and practices, and whose purpose or effect is to vitiate or curtail the recognition or equal exercise of human rights and fundamental freedoms in the political, economic, social and cultural spheres. Art 24 states that judicial protection against any discriminatory practice that violates fundamental rights and freedoms can be sought through the procedure provided for in art 53(2) of the Constitution, as provided by law. Art 54 of the Act, regarding very serious violations, stipulates that discriminatory behaviour on racial, ethnic, national or religious grounds, as set out in art 23, is a very serious violation, where it does not constitute an offence.' CERD/C/ESP/CO/21–23, paras 50–54 ff; CERD/C/ESP/CO/18–20, para 6; and, CERD/C/64/CO/6, paras 4–8.

93 See CERD/C/SR.2424, para 2.
94 Act 4/2015 of 27 April, on the status of victims of offences. See CERD/C/SR.2424, para 3.
95 CERD/C/ESP/21–23, paras 14–15 and 50; CERD/C/SR.2424, paras 4–5.
96 Pursuant to art 33 of Act No 62/2003 of 30 December, and regulated by Royal Decree No 1262/2007 of 21 December, on the composition, authority and functioning of the Council. See also CERD/C/ESP/CO/18–20, paras 125–128.
97 CERD/C/ESP/18–20, para 127.
98 CERD/C/ESP/21–23, para 112.
99 CERD/C/ESP/21–23 para 73.

NGOs, through private prosecutions or the public right of action, has been fundamental.[100]

5.1.3 Impact on and through Non-state Actors

Human rights NGOs generally cite CERD in their publications and other outputs and follow the work of the CERD Cttee. They submit shadow reports, follow the examination of periodic reports, contest inaccurate and/or misleading statements by the government, and send information to the media and social media.[101]

5.1.4 Impact of State Reporting

The CERD Cttee considered the sixteenth and seventeenth,[102] eighteenth to twentieth[103] and twenty-first to twenty-third[104] periodic reports of Spain at its sixty-fourth (February-March 2004), seventy-eighth (February-March 2011) and eighty-ninth (April-May 2016) sessions, respectively.[105] On average, the state party's reports under article 9 of CERD were submitted 20 months late.[106] The preparation of the twenty-first to twenty-third periodic reports was coordinated by the Human Rights Office of the Ministry of Foreign Affairs and Cooperation, with the support of the Racism and Xenophobia Monitoring Centre,[107] which is also responsible for following up and monitoring the

---

100 ibid para 74.
101 See eg 'El Comité para la Eliminación de la Discriminación Racial examina a España', Rights International Spain, 29 April 2016.
102 CERD/C/431/Add.7.
103 CERD/C/ESP/18–20.
104 CERD/C/ESP/21–23.
105 The information submitted by Spain on follow-up to COs can be found in CERD/C/ESP/CO/21–23/Add.1 and CERD/C/ESP/CO/18–20/Add.1. See also CERD/C/ESP/21–23, paras 10–4. Spain's combined 24th to 26th periodic reports are due on 4 January 2020 (see CERD/C/ESP/CO/21–23, para 43).
106 Spain submitted its combined 16th and 17th periodic reports on 6 June 2003. These reports should have been submitted on 4 January 2000 (CERD/C/304/Add.95, para 16). Again, the combined 18th to 20th periodic reports, which were due on 4 January 2008 (CERD/C/64/CO/6, para 20) were only submitted on 5 May 2009. The combined 21st to 23rd periodic reports, which were due on 4 January 2014 (CERD/C/ESP/CO/18–20, para 25) were submitted on 5 August 2014.
107 The Racism and Xenophobia Monitoring Centre is attached to the General Secretariat for Immigration and Emigration of the Ministry of Employment and Social Security. The following bodies took part in the preparation of the report: the Ministries of Education, Culture and Sport, Employment and Social Security, Industry and Tourism, Internal Affairs, Justice and Health, and Social Services and Equality, along with the Attorney-General's Office and the General Council of the Judiciary.

implementation of the CERD Cttee's recommendations.[108] Consultations were also held with NGOs specialising in this field.[109]

In its 2011 COs the CERD Cttee welcomed the contribution made by the Ombudsman Institution (*Defensor del Pueblo*).[110] However, the national human rights institution did not submit a public alternative report in relation to Spain's twenty-first to twenty-third periodic reports in 2016. In its 2004 COs, the CERD Cttee acknowledged that the sixteenth and seventeenth periodic reports of Spain had addressed many of the concerns and recommendations included in its previous COs.[111] Nevertheless, in 2014 the CERD Cttee again noted that the periodic reports of Spain did not contain recent, reliable data on economic and social indicators that could be used, in particular, to compare the status of minorities and immigrants with that of the general population.[112]

Six alternative reports were submitted to the CERD Cttee in relation to Spain's twenty-first to twenty-third periodic reports[113] and four with respect to the eighteenth to twentieth periodic reports.[114] In its 2011 COs the CERD Cttee welcomed the active engagement and contributions from NGOs.[115] In 2004 the CERD Cttee welcomed the attendance of a large delegation,[116] while in 2011 it appreciated that Spain had sent a high-level delegation.[117]

There have been no communications sent to the government by the Committee's Focal Point for Reprisals.[118]

---

[108] See OHCHR, *National Mechanisms for Reporting and Follow-up. A Study of State Engagement with International Human Rights Mechanisms*, UN, New York and Geneva, 2016, 37–38.
[109] CERD/C/ESP/21–23, paras 6–7.
[110] CERD/C/ESP/CO/18–20, para 3.
[111] CERD/C/SR.1616, paras 19 and 22.
[112] CERD/C/ESP/CO/21–23, para 5.
[113] The following NGOs submitted alternative reports: the Apache-Ndé-Nneé Working Group; Institut de Drets Humans de Catalunya; International Human Rights Advocacy Group; Rights International Spain; and Sociedad Civil Africana y Afrodescendiente. All submissions are available at <https://tbinternet.ohchr.org/_layouts/treatybodyexternal/SessionDetails1.aspx?SessionID=1072&Lang=en> accessed 28 March 2022.
[114] The following NGOs submitted alternative reports: Amnesty International; Asociación Española para el Derecho Internacional de los Derechos Humanos; Consejo Indio Exterior; and a joint submission by SOS Racismo España, Secretariado Gitano and Comisión Española de Ayuda al Refugiado. All submissions are available at <https://tbinternet.ohchr.org/_layouts/treatybodyexternal/SessionDetails1.aspx?SessionID=399&Lang=en> accessed 28 March 2022.
[115] CERD/C/ESP/CO/18–20, para 3.
[116] CERD/C/64/CO/6, para 3.
[117] CERD/C/ESP/CO/18–20, para 2.
[118] See <https://tbinternet.ohchr.org/_layouts/TreatyBodyExternal/TBSearch.aspx?Lang=en&TreatyID=6&DocTypeID=130> accessed 28 March 2022.

During the period under review, identity checks and police raids carried out on the basis of ethnic and racial profiling were a recurrent cause for concern.[119] The CERD Cttee expressed grave concern over the practice of the Spanish security forces of summarily returning irregular migrants and potential asylum seekers to Morocco from the cities of Ceuta and Melilla, thereby depriving them of access to the asylum procedure.[120] In this connection, the CERD Cttee was concerned about reports of ill-treatment perpetrated during deportation operations by both Spanish and Moroccan officials operating on Spanish soil.[121] The CERD Cttee expressed concern over the persistent difficulties in finding employment, housing and access to education faced by the Gypsy/Roma population in the country;[122] the healthcare restrictions imposed on irregular migrants;[123] the poor conditions of detention and services in migrant detention centres;[124] and the lack of independence and adequate resources of the Council for the Elimination of Racial and Ethnic Discrimination.[125]

In 2016 the CERD Cttee requested Spain to provide, within one year, information on the implementation of the recommendations in paragraphs 12 (reinstatement of universal public health care) and 28 (measures against identity checks based on racial and ethnic profiling) of the COs.[126] On 7 November 2017 Spain submitted its follow-up replies.[127] Subsequently, in a letter dated 17 May 2018, the CERD Cttee's Chairperson expressed appreciation for the information provided concerning Decree Law 16/2012 and the extent to which it and other laws allow undocumented individuals to access public health services, although it requested Spain to provide further information on the practical application of these laws.[128]

In 2016 the CERD Cttee commended Spain for the publication of a training handbook to assist members of the security forces in recognising and documenting racist and xenophobic incidents.[129] Recently, various

---

119 CERD/C/ESP/CO/21–23, para 27; CERD/C/ESP/CO/18–20, para 10.
120 CERD/C/ESP/CO/21–23, para 17.
121 CERD/C/ESP/CO/21–23, para 19.
122 CERD/C/ESP/CO/21–23, paras 23 and 31; CERD/C/ESP/CO/18–20, paras 15 and 16.
123 CERD/C/ESP/CO/21–23, para 11.
124 CERD/C/ESP/CO/21–23, paras 13 and 21.
125 CERD/C/ESP/CO/21–23, para 7(c); CERD/C/ESP/CO/18–20, para 9.
126 CERD/C/ESP/CO/21–23, para 41.
127 CERD/C/ESP/CO/21–23/Add.1, 4.
128 The state party was also requested to include in its next periodic report statistical information on incidents of racial or ethnic profiling. See <https://tbinternet.ohchr.org/Treaties/CERD/Shared%20Documents/ESP/INT_CERD_FUL_ESP_31256_E.pdf> accessed 28 March 2022.
129 CERD/C/ESP/CO/21–23, para 4(a).

public information and awareness-raising actions have been launched aimed at increasing knowledge in this area and promoting the training of key actors.[130]

During the period under review, the CERD Cttee's consideration of periodic reports generated significant media coverage.[131] Spanish media has also reported about the submission of complaints to the CERD Cttee under article 14 of CERD.[132]

5.1.5 Impact of Individual Communications

There have been no views adopted by the CERD Cttee on alleged violations of CERD.

5.2 *International Covenant on Civil and Political Rights*[133]

Spain ratified CCPR on 13 April 1977 without making any reservation to its provisions; it entered into force on 27 July 1977. On 17 January 1985 Spain acceded to OP1-CCPR.[134] Under article 41 CCPR,[135] Spain recognised the competence of

---

130 See eg 'Guía práctica: cómo actuar ante actos de discriminación y delitos de odio' and 'Manual para la prevención y detección del racismo, la xenofobia y otras formas de intolerancia en las aulas'.

131 See eg 'España no lucha contra el racismo de forma efectiva, según la ONU', *infoLibre*, 17 May 2016; 'Naciones Unidas examinará a España sobre lucha contra la discriminación racial', *Europa Press*, 19 April 2016; 'Naciones Unidas examinará a España este martes y miércoles sobre su lucha contra la discriminación racial', *La Vanguardia*, 26 April 2016; 'La ONU pide a España que acabe con las detenciones "indiscriminadas" de inmigrantes', *ABC*, 15 March 2011.

132 See eg 'España, denunciada ante la ONU por discriminación racial en la frontera con Marruecos', *eldiario.es*, 26 June 2016.

133 Sub-secs 5.2.1 to 5.2.5 were prepared by Carmelo Faleh Pérez, Ph Dr Professor of Public International Law and Human Rights at the University of Las Palmas de Gran Canaria; member and legal adviser of the Spanish Society for IHRL.

134 OP1 entered into force on 25 April 1985. Spain stated that art 5(2) OP1 means that the HRCttee shall not consider any communication from an individual unless it has ascertained that the same matter has not been or is not being examined under another procedure of international investigation or settlement.

135 A *note verbal*, dated 28 January 1998, transmitting the text of the statement made by Spain recognizing the competence of the HRCttee under art 41 CCPR, was deposited on 30 January 1998. Subsequently, the Secretary-General received a *note verbal* of Spain dated 9 March 1998, transmitting a corrected text of the statement which was deposited on 11 March 1998. See BOE No 290 of 4 December 2001. Previous statements were received on 25 January 1985 and 21 December 1988, and expired on 25 January 1988 and 21 December 1993, respectively.

the HRCttee to receive inter-state complaints. On 22 March 1991 Spain ratified OP2-CCPR.[136]

5.2.1 Incorporation and Reliance by Legislature and Executive

In accordance with articles 96(1) of the Constitution and 23 of the Law 25/2014, as of 27 November, on Treaties and other International Agreements, CCPR and its two OPs, once published, are part of the Spanish legal system and are directly applicable.[137]

Based on the HRCttee's views of 20 July 2000,[138] legislative amendments were made to recognise the right to double criminal instances required by article 14(5) of CCPR. Thus, in 2003 the Organic Act of the Judiciary (1985) was modified in order to create an Appeals Chamber in the National Court, to hear the appeals against decisions issued by the Criminal Chamber of this Court (article 64*bis*). In addition, Civil and Criminal Chambers of the Superior Courts of Justice (regional) were given knowledge of the appeals against the decisions issued in the first instance by the Public Administrations. These reforms generalised the second criminal instance, promoting the reviewing powers of the Superior Courts of Justice and creating an Appeal Chamber in the National Court. It should also be noted that the Supreme Court has converted the appeal into a true appeal, allowing a review of the facts.[139] This extensive 'jurisprudential' reconstruction of the cassation allows the appellant to discuss not only the application of the law, but also the assessment of the evidence on which the court based the appellant's conviction.

However, in 2015 the HRCttee noted that despite article 10(2) of the Constitution, CCPR is not directly applicable in the domestic legal order. It also regretted the absence of a specific procedure to implement the HRCttee's views under OP1-CCPR. Therefore, Spain should ensure that the domestic legal

---

[136] On 13 January 1998 Spain withdrew its reservation made upon ratification of OP2 by which it had reserved the right to apply the death penalty in the exceptional and extremely serious cases provided for in Fundamental Act No 13/1985 of 9 December 1985 regulating the Military Criminal Code, in wartime as defined in art 25 of that Act. *BOE* No 81 of 4 April 1998.

[137] CCPR was officially published in *BOE* of 30 April 1977; OP1 in *BOE* 79 of 2 April 1985; and OP2 in *BOE* 164, of 10 July 1991.

[138] Case of *Gómez Vázquez v Spain*. See CCPR/C/69/D/701/1996.

[139] Judgment 8048/2004 of the Criminal Chamber of the Supreme Court of 13 December 2004, where it stated that in judicial practice the review carried out by the Court of Cassation is progressively approaching that carried out by the Courts of Appeal, not only through the assessment of the legality or illegality of the evidence, but the content of the evidence and verification of whether it can be considered incriminating or of charge, or if on the contrary it lacks consistency to raise the presumption of innocence (FJ 1).

system fully complies with its obligations under CCPR and, to this end, it must take appropriate measures, including legislative measures, to ensure the full implementation of CCPR.[140]

5.2.2 Reliance by Judiciary

In several judgments of Provincial Courts and Superior Courts of Justice (regional), the application of different provisions of CCPR was considered. However, the reference to CCPR has greater relevance in the decisions of the Constitutional Court. The search for decisions in which the Court mentions CCPR reached 238 judgments and 68 court orders.[141] Among others, a judgment of 2006 is particularly relevant, since the Court reiterated the important hermeneutical function that the international human rights treaties ratified by Spain have to determine the content of fundamental rights, having expressly stated that the content of human rights recognised in the Covenant is also part of fundamental rights, 'forming the minimum and basic standard of fundamental rights of every person in the Spanish legal system'. To this end, the Court emphasised that this interpretation of the constitutional norms on human rights 'cannot do without what, in turn, guarantee bodies established by those same international treaties and agreements'.[142]

In 2012 the Plenary of the Constitutional Court warned about the need to build the legal culture of rights taking into account the international activity of states manifested in the international treaties, the jurisprudence of the international bodies that interpret them, and the views by the competent organs of the UN system.[143]

5.2.3 Impact on and through Non-state Actors and Independent State Institutions

In its fifth periodic report, Spain informed that CCPR is widely disseminated, as evidenced by the constant references made to it by the courts. Since it has

---

140 See CCPR/C/ESP/CO/6, para 5.
141 See <https://hj.tribunalconstitucional.es/> (as of 27 July 2019).
142 Constitutional Court (1st Chamber), Judgment 116/2006 of 24 April 24 (FJ 5). *BOE* 125 of 26 May 2006. In another judgment, the Court resorts to the jurisprudence of the HRCttee in order to affirm that, in relation to art 26 CCPR, the HRCttee 'has stressed that the prohibition against discrimination based on sex includes discrimination based on sexual orientation' (notably, views of 4 April 1994, Communication 488/1992, *Toonen v Australia*, para 8.7; and views of 18 September 2003, Communication 941/2000, *Young v Australia*, para 10.4). Constitutional Court (2nd Chamber), judgment 41/2006, of 13 February (FJ 3). *BOE* 64 of 16 March 2006.
143 Constitutional Court (Plenary), judgment 198/2012 of 6 November (FJ 9). *BOE* 286 of 28 November 2012.

been incorporated into national legislation, CCPR is included in all basic textbooks on law, together with other treaties on fundamental rights and freedoms ratified by Spain.[144] However, judicial references to CCPR should be accompanied by the interpretation provided by the HRCttee, which is exceptional. In 2015 the HRCttee included in the list of issues related to the sixth periodic report of Spain a question on the dissemination of information on CCPR and its OP, as well as detailed information on the participation of civil society, NGOs and the national human rights institution in the preparation of the report.[145] Spain replied that CCPR and its OPs, along with the HRCttee's activities, are covered in training and outreach activities undertaken by the Human Rights Office of the Ministry of Foreign Affairs and Cooperation. In addition, the periodic report was shared with the Ombudsperson and with a wide spectrum of a highly-representative sample of civil society organisations. It was also presented for information to the Foreign Affairs Committee of the Congress of Deputies.[146] There is an increasing number of studies by university scholars on CCPR and the OPs, and the practice of the HRCttee, demonstrating a greater understanding of CCPR than in the past.[147] Some NGOs are

---

144 CCPR/C/ESP/5, para 16.
145 See CCPR/C/ESP/Q/6, para 24.
146 ibid. See also CCPR/C/ESP/Q/6/Add.1, para 63.
147 See eg Valentín Bou Franch, 'Las comunicaciones individuales contra España presentadas en el Comité de Derechos Humanos y su incidencia en el Derecho español', in Romaní (n 26) 17–64; Carlos Villán Durán, 'El valor jurídico de las decisiones de los órganos establecidos en tratados de las Naciones Unidas en materia de derechos humanos' in Romaní (n 26) 99–123; Jorge Cardona LLoréns, 'Hacia la configuración de un 'sistema' de protección de los derechos humanos de las Naciones Unidas'(2016) *Cursos de Derecho Internacional y Relaciones Internacionales de Vitoria-Gasteiz* 2015; Navarra, Aranzadi; Carlos Fernández de Casadevante Romaní (eds), *España y los órganos internacionales de control en materia de derechos humanos* (Madrid, Dilex 2010); Julia Ruiloba Alvariño, 'El Comité de Derechos Humanos. Examen de los informes y las quejas individuales presentadas contra España' in Romaní (above) 51–107; JL Monereo Pérez (ed), *El sistema universal de los derechos humanos* (Comares, Granada 2014); Natalia Ochoa Ruíz, *Los mecanismos convencionales de protección de los derechos humanos en las Naciones Unidas* (Civitas, Madrid 2004); Ana Gemma López Martín, 'La reclamación individual como técnica de control del respeto a los derechos humanos, Comité de Derechos Humanos de Naciones Unidas o Tribunal Europeo de Derechos Humanos?' (2004) 5 *Cursos de derechos humanos de Donostia-San Sebastián* 225–260; Fernando Mariño Menéndez (ed), Carmen Pérez González & Alicia Cebada Romero (eds), *Instrumentos y regímenes de cooperación internacional* (Trotta, Madrid 2017); C Villán Durán and C Faleh Pérez, *Prácticas de Derecho internacional de los derechos humanos* (Dilex, Madrid 2006); C Villán Durán and C Faleh Pérez, *El sistema universal de protección de los derechos humanos. Su aplicación en España* (Tecnos, Madrid 2017). In addition, frequent references to the HRCttee's views are published in

especially active in the promotion and defence of the rights recognised in CCPR.[148]

5.2.4 Impact of State Reporting

The HRCttee considered the fifth[149] and sixth[150] periodic reports of Spain during its 94th (13-31 October 2008) and 114th sessions (29 June-24 July 2015), respectively. Since 2008, the participation of NGOs in the examination of periodic reports has increased significantly: Thirteen and 11 NGOs contributed to the respective reports.

The Spanish delegation attending the review of the fifth periodic report (2008) was composed of representatives of the Permanent Mission in Geneva and representatives of the Ministries of Foreign Affairs and Cooperation, Interior and Justice.[151] The Spanish representation was much broader and more representative when the sixth periodic report (2015) was examined, since four representatives of the Permanent Mission were part of the Spanish delegation, as well as representatives of the Office of the Attorney-General of the state (2); Ministries of Foreign Affairs and Cooperation (1); Justice (29); Interior (4); Education, Culture and Sports (2); Employment and Social Security (2); and Health, Social Services and Equality (4).[152]

5.2.5 Issues of Concern and Recommendations

In 2015 the HRCttee recommended to Spain to adopt the second human rights plan; to provide the Council for the Elimination of Racial and Ethnic Discrimination with resources and independence; to eliminate the use of

---

the jurisprudence section of the Spanish Journal of International Law (*Revista Española de Derecho Internacional*) and the Electronic Journal of International Studies (*Revista Electrónica de Estudios Internacionales*).

148 This is the case, among others, of the following Spanish NGO that have participated in the process of examining the periodic reports of Spain before the HRCttee: the Spanish Society for International Human Rights Law (SSIHRL); Association for Human Rights of Andalusia (APDHA); Amnesty International-Spain; Basque Observatory for Human Rights (BEHATOKIA); Coordinator of Historical Memory Associations of Andalusia; Coordinator for the Prevention of Torture; Association for Human Rights of Spain (APDHE); Foundation for Human Rights Action; Observatory of the Criminal System and Human Rights (OSPDH); and Rights International Spain (RIS).

149 CCPR/C/ESP/5.

150 CCPR/C/ESP/6.

151 See <https://tbinternet.ohchr.org/_layouts/15/treatybodyexternal/Download.aspx?symbolno=INT%2fCCPR%2fLOP%2fESP%2f94%2f10986&Lang=en> accessed 28 March 2022.

152 ibid.

ethnic profiling by the police; to ensure equal treatment for everyone in its territory or under its jurisdiction; to ensure that immigrants, foreigners and ethnic minorities do not suffer discrimination in access to housing, employment, education, equal pay and health care; to obtain the free and informed consent of persons with disabilities whenever sterilisation is practised; to increase participation by women in the public and private sectors and to reduce the wage gap; to combat violence against women and young girls; to prevent and eliminate torture and ill-treatment providing more human rights training for law enforcement officials; to establish independent complaint bodies to address claims of ill-treatment by the police; to ensure that all complaints of torture and ill-treatment are investigated promptly, thoroughly and independently and that victims receive appropriate reparation and rehabilitation; to prohibit the granting of pardons to persons found guilty of torture; and to ensure the recording of interrogations of all persons deprived of liberty in places of detention.

In addition, the HRCttee recommended to Spain to avoid the detention of asylum seekers; to ensure that the detention of foreigners is resorted to for the shortest period possible, only where existing alternatives have been considered inappropriate; to put an end to incommunicado detention and to guarantee the rights of all detainees to medical services and to freely choose and consult (in complete confidentiality) a lawyer, who can be present at interrogations; to repeal or amend the 1977 Amnesty Act; to encourage investigations into all past human rights violations; to investigate allegations of trafficking in persons; to determine the age of unaccompanied children; to ensure that in accordance with the principle of the best interests of the child, this is given due consideration in all decisions concerning unaccompanied children; to ensure that the Code of Criminal Procedure meets full compliance with article 14 of CCPR; and to ensure that all individuals fully enjoy their rights to freedom of expression, association and peaceful assembly in accordance with General Comment 34.[153]

The follow-up mechanism was discontinued by the HRCttee in 2018 having assessed a lack of substantive progress.[154]

5.2.6 Impact of Individual Communications[155]

The HRCttee adopted 26 views in which it found violations of various provisions of CCPR. Spain generally cooperated with the procedure by providing

---

153 CCPR/C/ESP/CO/6, paras 6–25. Concluding Observations adopted on 20 July 2015.
154 See above, *Impact of state reporting*. See also n 71.
155 Sub-sec co-drafted by Carmen Rosa Rueda Castañón, former Secretary of the HRCttee's Working Group on Communications and member of the Spanish Society for IHRL.

the Committee with comments to the allegations formulated by the complainant.[156] The vast majority of complaints were submitted by individual lawyers not linked to a specific NGO.

Fourteen out of the 26 views in which the HRCttee found violations of CCPR concern the right of everyone convicted of a crime to have the conviction and sentence being reviewed by a higher tribunal (article 14(5) CCPR). Communication 701/1996 (*Gómez Vázquez v Spain*)[157] was the first case in which the HRCttee found that the review in second instance of the complainant's conviction and judgment, carried out by the Supreme Court through a cassation appeal, did not comply with the requirements of CCPR, as such review had been limited to the formal or legal aspects of the conviction and, according to the domestic law, the evidence had to be evaluated exclusively by the first instance court. Accordingly, the HRCttee stated that the complainant's conviction had to be reviewed in accordance with article 14(5) of CCPR.

In its response Spain on several occasions has maintained that, following the HRCttee's position on the matter, the jurisprudence of the Supreme Court had enlarged the scope of the cassation appeal to comply with the provisions of CCPR. Spain also argued that the right to an appeal may also be interpreted as the right to a review of the lawfulness of a lower court's ruling, but not necessarily a review of the whole trial, in accordance with CCPR and the jurisprudence of ECHR.

As the HRCttee continued to reiterate its position in subsequent views, Organic Act 19 of 2003 introduced the principle that would allow the establishment of appeal proceedings in high courts ensuring that all convictions and judgments can be reviewed in a second instance.[158]

While this system does not seem to be operational, the HRCttee observed an evolution in the practice and jurisprudence of the Supreme Court when deciding cassation appeals in criminal cases in the sense that the Court would not only consider formal aspects regarding the application of the law by the lower court, but would also carry out some examination of the facts and evidence on the basis of which the conviction was established. In many

---

156 See Javier Chinchón Álvarez and Jorge Rodríguez Rodríguez, 'La actividad cuasi-judicial del Comité de Derechos Humanos, Comité contra la Tortura y Comité contra las Desapariciones Forzadas' in Héctor Olasolo *et al* (eds), *Alcance y limitaciones de la justicia internacional* (Tirant lo blanch, Valencia 2018) 153–182.
157 CCPR/C/69/701/1996 (20 July 2000).
158 A/69/40 (Vol 1) 213–214.

of the cases decided by the HRCttee this was considered to be sufficient in order to satisfy the requirements of article 14(5) of CCPR.[159] While the new approach has contributed to a better protection of the right enshrined in this provision, the HRCttee's requests in 14 complaints that the conviction and judgment should be reviewed remain unimplemented, and those victims who initiated domestic proceedings seeking such review did not find satisfaction.[160]

No measures of reparation were taken in other types of communications. For instance, in Communication 1473/2006 (*Morales Tornel*) of 20 March 2009, where the HRCttee found a violation of article 17(1) of CCPR in connection with the refusal of prison authorities to facilitate contacts between a sick prisoner and his family and requested to grant compensation, after several exchanges the HRCttee decided to suspend the follow-up dialogue, with a finding of unsatisfactory implementation of the recommendation.[161]

Communication 1493/2006 (*Williams Lecraft*),[162] where the HRCttee found a violation of article 26 of CCPR for discrimination on the basis of racial profiling, up to now is the only case where the HRCttee considered that the response provided by Spain was satisfactory and decided to close the follow-up procedure. Spain informed the HRCttee that the text of the views had been included in the information bulletin of the Ministry of Justice and had been sent to all main judicial bodies and organs related to them, including the General Council of the Judiciary, the Constitutional Court, the Supreme Court, the General Attorney's Office and the Ministry of Interior. Furthermore, the Minister of Foreign Affairs and other high officials at his Ministry had met with Ms Williams Lecraft and offered to her apologies for the acts of which she was a victim. She had also received oral and written apologies from the Deputy Interior Minister for Security Affairs.[163]

---

[159] See, for instance, the inadmissibility decision in CCPR/C/107/D/1943/2010 (*HPN v Spain*) of 25 March 2013, para 7.7.

[160] See, for instance, the HRCttee's statement regarding non-implementation of its recommendations in Case 1363/2005 (*Gayoso v Spain*) A/68/40 (Vol 1) 198–200.

[161] Follow-up progress report on individual communications adopted by the HRCttee at its 116th session, CCPR/C/116/3, 69.

[162] Views adopted on 27 July 2009.

[163] A/66/40 (Vol 1), 170–171.

5.3 International Covenant on Economic, Social and Cultural Rights[164]

Spain ratified CESCR on 13 April 1977 without making any reservation to its provisions. Spain also on 23 September 2010 ratified OP-CESCR.[165] This entered into force on 5 May 2013.

5.3.1 Incorporation and Reliance by Legislature and Executive

In accordance with articles 96(1) of the Constitution and 23 of the Law 25/2014, on Treaties and other International Agreements, CESCR is part of the Spanish legal order, and is directly applicable.[166] However, the CESCR Cttee is concerned that rights recognised in CESCR continue to be viewed as nothing more than guiding principles for social and economic policy (with the exception of the right to education, which is one of the fundamental rights enshrined in the Constitution) and that, as a result, they can be invoked before the courts only after having been developed by domestic law or in connection with other rights that enjoy full protection, such as the right to life.[167]

5.3.2 Reliance by Judiciary

Spain has reported that CESCR has been invoked before domestic courts, both by the parties and by the judges themselves, as legal grounds for the defence and protection of the rights enshrined therein.[168] The impact of CESCR in the jurisprudence of the Constitutional Court has been limited, since only 12 judgments refer to it.[169]

In 2012 the CESCR Cttee recommended that Spain take appropriate measures to ensure that the provisions of CESCR are fully justiciable and applicable by domestic courts.[170] It also recommended to carry out awareness-raising campaigns for rights holders on the justiciability of economic, social and cultural rights and to provide training to the actors responsible for the implementation of CESCR (especially judges, lawyers, law enforcement officials, members of Parliament and others) on the content of the rights recognised,

---

[164] Sub-secs 5.3.1. to 5.3.5. were prepared by Carmelo Faleh-Pérez, Ph Dr Professor of Public International Law and Human Rights at the University of Las Palmas de Gran Canaria; member and legal adviser of the Spanish Society for IHRL.
[165] BOE 48 of 25 February 2013.
[166] CESCR was officially published in BOE of 30 April 1977.
[167] See E/C.12/ESP/CO/6, para 5 and E/C.12/ESP/CO/5, para 6.
[168] See some examples in E/C.12/ESP/6, para 125.
[169] See E/C.12/ESP/Q/5/Add.1, para 2.
[170] See E/C.12/ESP/CO/5, para 6.

including the Committee's general comments concerning what those rights cover, and on the possibility of invoking CESCR before the courts.[171]

Unfortunately, the Constitutional Court consolidated jurisprudence against the justiciability of economic, social and cultural rights was confirmed in 2019 in relation to the right to housing, maintaining that when article 11(1) CESCR states the right of persons to a sufficient standard of living to ensure adequate housing, it is not recognising a subjective right; it is rather a mandate for state parties to adopt appropriate measures to promote public policies aimed at facilitating the access of all citizens to decent housing.[172]

5.3.3 Impact on and through Non-state Actors

University researchers have studied and researched about CESCR and its OP and followed the practice of the CESCR Cttee.[173] Some NGOs are especially

---

171 E/C.12/ESP/CO/6, paras 6(b) and (c).
172 Constitutional Court (Plenary), judgment 32/2019 of February 28. See above, *Introduction to human rights in Spain*.
173 See eg Carlos Villán Durán, 'El Protocolo Facultativo del Pacto Internacional de Derechos Económicos, Sociales y Culturales' in Concepción Escobar Hernández (ed), *Los derechos humanos en la sociedad internacional del siglo XXI* Vol I (Escuela Diplomática/AEPDIRI, Madrid 2008) 311–330; Felipe Gómez Isa, 'Obligaciones transnacionales en el campo de los derechos económicos, sociales y culturales' (2009) 18 *Revista Electrónica de Estudios Internacionales*; Carlos Fernández de Casadevante Romani, 'La práctica española relativa a los órganos internacionales de control de los derechos humanos: un estudio introductorio' in Romani, *España y los órganos internacionales de control en materia de derechos humanos* (Dilex, Madrid 2010) 17–48; Antonio Pastor Palomar, 'El Comité de Derechos Económicos, Sociales y Culturales' in *España y los órganos internacionales de control en materia de derechos humanos* (above) 109–124; Ana G López Martín, 'La protección internacional de los Derechos Sociales. A propósito de la ratificación española del Protocolo Facultativo del Pacto de Derechos Económicos, sociales y culturales de 2008' (2011) 13 *Foro: Revista de Ciencias Jurídicas y Sociales* 13–59; Julia Ruiloba Alvariño, 'El pacto internacional de derechos económicos, sociales y culturales de 16 de diciembre de 1966' in Romani, *Derecho internacional de los derechos humanos* (2011) 169–185; Rosa Riquelme Cortado, 'El Protocolo Facultativo del Pacto Internacional de Derechos Económicos, Sociales y Culturales. Comunicaciones de personas o grupos como piedra angular' (2012) 24 *Revista Electrónica de Estudios Internacionales*; Laura Salamero Teixidó, *La protección de los derechos sociales en el ámbito de las Naciones Unidas. El nuevo Protocolo Facultativo del Pacto Internacional de Derechos Económicos, Sociales y Culturales* (Civitas, Pamplona 2012) 183; F Javier Quel López, 'Un paso esencial hacia la eficacia internacional de los derechos económicos sociales y culturales. Luces y sombras del Protocolo Facultativo del Pacto de Derechos Económicos, Sociales y Culturales' in *El derecho internacional en el mundo multipolar del siglo XXI. Obra homenaje al profesor Luis Ignacio Sánchez Rodríguez* (2013) 837–859; Soledad Torrecuadrada García-Lozano, 'España y el Pacto de Derechos Económicos, Sociales y Culturales' (2013) 180 *El Cotidiano* 53–66; Carmelo Faleh Pérez, 'La seguridad humana en la práctica del Comité de Derechos Económicos,

active in the promotion and defence of the rights recognised by CESCR.[174] The coverage of the CESCR Cttee's work in the media is relatively important in recent times, as the media only addresses some economic, social and cultural rights, such as the right to food, housing and health.[175]

5.3.4 Impact of State Reporting

The CESCR Cttee considered the fourth,[176] fifth[177] and sixth[178] periodic reports of Spain during its thirty-second (26 April-14 May 2004); forty-eighth (30 April-18 May 2012) and sixty-third sessions (12–19 March 2018), respectively. The participation of NGOs in the examination of periodic reports has increased notably in the fifth and sixth reports, receiving 15 non-governmental reports. The National Ombudsman (*Defensor del Pueblo*) also contributed to the review process with his own reports as the national human rights institution with UN status A.[179]

Sociales y Culturales' in Carmelo Faleh Pérez & Carlos Villán Durán (eds), *El derecho humano a la paz y la (in)seguridad humana. Contribuciones atlánticas* (Velasco Ediciones, Oviedo 2017) 77–98; and Carmelo Faleh Pérez, 'Los dictámenes del Comité de Derechos Económicos, Sociales y Culturales y sus efectos jurídicos en España' in Carlos Fernández de Casadevante Romaní (ed), *Los efectos jurídicos en España de las decisiones de los órganos internacionales de control en materia de derechos humanos de naturaleza no jurisdiccional* (Dykinson, Madrid 2019) 65–97.

174 See Observatori DESC (ESCR Observatory) <http://observatoridesc.org/es> accessed 28 March 2022; Coalition of national NGOs preparing shadow reports to CESCR Cttee. See also Amnesty International, *La receta equivocada. El impacto de las medidas de austeridad en el derecho a la salud en España* (2018) <https://www.amnesty.org/es/documents/eur41/8136/2018/es/> accessed 11 September 2023.

175 See eg 'Proteger el derecho a la vivienda no admite dilaciones' *El Diario* (21 January 2019); 'La ONU llamó la atención a España en 2012 por excluir de la Sanidad a las personas en situación irregular' *El Diario* (4 May 2016); '20 ONG denuncian a España ante la ONU por el recorte de derechos' *El País* (7 May 2012); 'Españoles sin derechos frente al hambre' *El País* (4 April 2017); 'La ONU critica la escasa protección del derecho a la vivienda y a la salud en España' *Público* (3 April 2018); 'Entidades y ONG piden en el Congreso un grupo de seguimiento tras el 'suspenso' de la ONU a España en derechos sociales' *Infolibre* (7 April 2018).

176 E/C.12/4/Add.11.
177 E/C.12/ESP/5.
178 E/C.12/ESP/6.
179 See <https://tbinternet.ohchr.org/_layouts/15/treatybodyexternal/SessionDetails1.aspx?SessionID=443&Lang=es> (fifth report) accessed 28 March 2022; and <https://tbinternet.ohchr.org/_layouts/15/treatybodyexternal/Download.aspx?symbolno=INT%2fCESCR%2fIFR%2fESP%2f22946&Lang=en> (sixth report) accessed 28 March 2022.

5.3.5 Issues of Concern and Recommendations

In 2004 CESCR Cttee referred to (i) the precarious situation of undocumented immigrants, which only enjoyed a limited protection of their economic, social and cultural rights and were victims of xenophobic incidents; (ii) the vulnerable situation of the Roma population especially with regard to employment, housing, health and education; (iii) the promotion of gender equality; (iv) the high level of unemployment and the precarious situation of the large number of persons employed under short-term temporary contracts and the high number of occupational accidents; (v) the vulnerable situation of domestic workers, unaccompanied migrant children arriving in Spain and the growing problem of homelessness; (vi) the rising number of fatal cases of domestic violence; (vii) the deteriorating conditions of housing; (viii) the high abortion rate among adolescent women; and (ix) the high rate of drug and alcohol abuse and tobacco smoking, particularly among young people.

In 2012 the CESCR Cttee urged Spain to ensure the effective protection of economic, social and cultural rights of all persons residing within its territory, and to promote the regularisation of undocumented immigrants.[180]

In 2018 the CESCR Cttee recommended to Spain to (i) ensure that companies comply with their obligation to perform human rights with due diligence; (ii) address the disparities between the different autonomous communities (regions); (iii) address the impact of austerity measures on the effective enjoyment of economic, social and cultural rights; (iv) assess the fiscal policy to address the adverse effects of the growing social inequality; (v) ensure non-discrimination, including multiple discriminations and persistent *de facto* discrimination; (vi) address the gender stereotypes in society; (vii) address the wage gap between men and women; (viii) address the criminal prosecution of workers who have participated in strikes; (ix) address the deficit shown by the pension system; (x) address the high percentage of the population at risk of poverty and social exclusion; (xi) address the social housing deficit and evictions; and (xii) address the difficulties experienced by migrants, asylum seekers and refugees with regard to the enjoyment of their economic, social and cultural rights.[181]

As a follow-up, the CESCR Cttee requested Spain to provide information within 18 months on the action taken to give effect to the recommendations referred to austerity measures, evictions and right to health.[182]

---

[180] E/C.12/ESP/CO/5, para 6 and following.
[181] E/C.12/ESP/CO/6, para 8 and following.
[182] E/C.12/ESP/CO/6, paras 8–55. On 25 October 2019 Spain informed on (a) the adoption of a National Strategy for the Prevention and Fight against Poverty and Social Exclusion

5.3.6 Impact of Individual Communications[183]

By 2019, the CESCR Cttee had received around 75 complaints against Spain, out of which only two had by 30 June 2019 been concluded with findings of violations. Most of the cases did not pass the test of admissibility or a friendly settlement was reached. Compared to other state parties to the OP-CESCR, the number of cases submitted against Spain has been particularly high,[184] revealing a real interest of Spanish civil society in this rather new procedure. Spain generally cooperates with the formal procedure by formulating observations to the complainants' allegations.[185]

In Communication 5/2015 (*Djazia and Bellili v Spain*) the CESCR Cttee found violations of the complainants' rights under article 11(1) of CESCR.[186] The issue raised was whether the complainants' eviction from their rental accommodation by court order on grounds that their contract had ended, and the authorities' failure to grant alternative housing constituted a violation of the right to adequate housing, taking into account the fact that the complainants were

---

2019–2023 and the approval of the National Strategy against Energy Poverty 2019–2024; (b) modifications of the laws regulating evictions to comply with the CESCR Cttee recommendations; and (c) the approval of Royal Decree-Law 7/2018, of July 27, on universal access to the National Health System (E/C.12/ESP/FCO/6, 4). See <https://tbinternet.ohchr.org/_layouts/15/treatybodyexternal/Download.aspx?symbolno=E%2fC.12%2fESP%2fFCO%2f6&Lang=es> accessed 28 March 2022. On 15 June 2020 the CESCR Cttee assessed the legal reforms insufficient. See <https://tbinternet.ohchr.org/Treaties/CESCR/Shared%20Documents/ESP/INT_CESCR_FUL_ESP_42482_S.pdf> accessed 28 March 2022.

183 Sub-sec co-drafted by Carmen Rosa Rueda Castañón, former Secretary of the HRCttee's Working Group on Communications and member of the Spanish Society for IHRL.

184 On 16 March 2020 the CESCR Cttee had 135 pending cases from Spain related to art 11 CESCR (eviction of families that occupied flats without legal title or were unable to pay mortgages or the rent). See <https://www.ohchr.org/EN/HRBodies/CESCR/Pages/PendingCases.aspx>.

185 See Ricardo Izquierdo and Ana Lucía Ugalde, 'La actividad cuasi-judicial del sistema de protección universal del Comité de Derechos Económicos, Sociales y Culturales, Comité para la Protección de los Trabajadores Migrantes y Comité para la Protección de las Personas Discapacitadas: alcance y limitaciones' in Héctor Olasolo *et al* (eds), *Alcance y limitaciones de la justicia internacional* (Tirant lo Blanch, Valencia 2018) 221–252; and Carmelo Faleh Pérez, 'Los dictámenes del Comité de Derechos Económicos, Sociales y Culturales y sus efectos jurídicos en España' in Carlos Fernández de Casadevante Romaní (ed), *Los efectos jurídicos en España de las decisiones de los órganos internacionales de control en materia de derechos humanos de naturaleza no jurisdiccional* (Dykinson, Madrid 2019) 65–97.

186 E/C.12/61/D/5/2015 (20 June 2017). See <https://tbinternet.ohchr.org/_layouts/15/treatybodyexternal/Download.aspx?symbolno=E%2fC.12%2f61%2fD%2f5%2f2015&Lang=en> accessed 27 March 2022.

left homeless. The CESCR Cttee considered the arguments provided by Spain insufficient to demonstrate that it had made all possible effort, using all available resources, to realise, as a matter of urgency, the right to housing of persons who, like the complainants, were in a situation of dire need. As reparation the CESCR Cttee requested that the complainants be provided, among others, with an effective remedy and compensation.

In Communication 2/2014 (*IDG v Spain*)[187] the complainant claimed shortcomings in the manner in which she had been notified of mortgage enforcement proceedings, which had resulted in lack of protection by courts of her right to housing. The CESCR Cttee examined the system of notification used by the court and concluded that Spain had not shown that the court had exhausted all available means to serve notice in person and that the irregularities in the notice procedure revealed a violation of article 11(1) of CESCR. As for remedies, the CESCR Cttee held that Spain had an obligation to ensure that the auction of the author's property did not proceed unless she had due procedural protection and due process.

At the time of writing, these cases were still under the follow-up procedure. Accordingly, the CESCR Cttee had not yet taken a position on whether Spain had implemented the measures of reparation requested.

5.4 Convention on the Elimination of All Forms of Discrimination against Women

Spain ratified CEDAW on 5 January 1984.[188] OP-CEDAW entered into force on 6 October 2001.[189]

5.4.1 Incorporation and Reliance by Legislature and Executive

CEDAW and its OP are part of the Spanish legal order pursuant to articles 96(1) of the Constitution, 1(5) of the Civil Code and 23 of Act 25 of 2014, on Treaties and other International Agreements. Therefore, they are directly applicable. Upon ratification, Spain entered a reservation, indicating that it shall not affect constitutional provisions concerning succession to the Spanish crown (preference being given to male heirs).

In its COs of the fifth periodic report of Spain, the CEDAW Cttee expressed concern that no specific definition of discrimination against women in line with

---

187 E/C.12/55/D/2/2014 (17 June 2015). See <https://tbinternet.ohchr.org/_layouts/15/treatybodyexternal/Download.aspx?symbolno=E/C.12/55/D/2/2014&Lang=en> accessed 27 March 2022.
188 BOE 69, 21 March 1984.
189 BOE 190, 9 August 2001.

article 1 of CEDAW had been included in domestic legislation.[190] Subsequently, on the occasion of the sixth periodic report of Spain, the CEDAW Cttee noted that Organic Act 3 of 2007 on effective equality for men and women included a definition of discrimination against women in line with CEDAW. In addition, Organic Act 1 of 2004 on integral protection measures against gender violence, and Act 33 of 2006 on the equality of men and women in the order of succession to titles of nobility, were based on CEDAW.[191]

Spain also adopted Act 4 of 2015 on the legal status of the victims of crime; Organic Act 1 of 2015 amending the Criminal Code with regard to violence against women; Act 12 of 2009 on asylum and subsidiary protection, which implemented EU directives on asylum and explicitly recognised gender-based persecution of women as grounds for refugee recognition. Moreover, Spain adopted a National Strategy for the Eradication of Violence against Women (2013–2016); the Strategic Plan on Equal Opportunities (2014–2016); and the Action Plan for Equality between Women and Men in the Information Society (2014–2017).

In 2015, however, the CEDAW Cttee requested Spain to revise its legislation on violence against women to include other forms of gender-based violence, such as violence by care providers, police violence and violence in public spaces, workplaces and schools.[192]

In its fifth periodic report, Spain pointed out that it adopted policies in compliance with its obligations under CEDAW such as the fourth Plan of Action for Equal Opportunities, the Second Comprehensive Plan against Domestic Violence, the Optima Program for Women in Business and annual Plans of Action for Employment, the Social Inclusion Plan and the Comprehensive Family Support Plan, all of which include a gender dimension.[193]

Yet, in 2015 the CEDAW Cttee noted with concern that restructuring of the Spanish national machinery for the advancement of women had affected the ability of Spain to ensure the development and effective implementation of gender policies. It further noted the absence of a consistent strategy on gender equality at the national level and insufficient institutionalised and systematic coordination between the autonomous communities (regions) and the central administration.[194] While noting the adoption of a framework protocol for the

---

190   A/59/38 (Part II), para 330.
191   CEDAW/C/ESP/CO/6, para 4.
192   CEDAW/C/ESP/CO/7-8, para 21.
193   A/59/38 (Part II), paras 318 and 327.
194   CEDAW/C/ESP/CO/7-8, para 14.

protection of victims of trafficking in human beings, the CEDAW Cttee was concerned about the prevalence of the trafficking of women and girls to Spain and the absence of comprehensive anti-trafficking legislation, as well as the failure of Spain to criminalise all forms of trafficking. It further expressed concern about the limited definition of pimping, which could impede the adequate prosecution of the exploitation of prostitution.[195]

5.4.2 Reliance by Judiciary

In 2015 concerns were raised noting that women themselves, especially women in rural areas and migrant women, were unaware of their rights under CEDAW and thus lacked the information necessary to claim such rights.[196] The CEDAW Cttee requested Spain to provide mandatory training for judges, prosecutors, police officers and other law enforcement officials on CEDAW and its OP,[197] and to increase women's awareness of and access to education, health and social services, training and employment, as well as to familiarise them with their rights to gender equality and non-discrimination.[198] In a landmark judgment of 17 July 2018[199] the Supreme Court acknowledged that CEDAW and its OP are part of domestic law. Therefore, the CEDAW Cttee's views are obligatory for Spain.

5.4.3 Impact on and through Non-state Actors

Human rights NGOs, as well as other civil society organisations, generally refer to CEDAW in their legal and advocacy activities.[200] The CEDAW Cttee's consideration of periodic and follow-up reports, as well as its views under OP-CEDAW, generated significant media coverage.[201]

---

195   ibid para 22.
196   ibid para 10.
197   ibid para 21.
198   CEDAW/C/ESP/CO/6, para 32.
199   Judgment 1263/2018. See below *Impact of individual communications*.
200   See eg <https://www.la-politica.com/wp-content/uploads/2018/11/AMNISTIA-INTERNACIoNAL-Ya-es-hora-que-me-creas.pdf> accessed 27 March 2022.
201   See eg <https://www.eldiario.es/sociedad/ONU-Espana-parcialmente-recomendaciones-violencia_0_714978696.html>; <https://www.europapress.es/epsocial/derechos-humanos/noticia-cedaw-suspende-espana-violencia-genero-tratamiento-reciben-mujeres-ninas-refugiadas-20170714115313.html; https://elpais.com/sociedad/2014/08/04/actualidad/1407137771_603454.html> accessed 27 March 2022.

5.4.4 Impact of State Reporting

The CEDAW Cttee considered the fifth,[202] sixth[203] and combined seventh and eighth[204] periodic reports of Spain at its thirty-first session (July 2004), forty-fourth session (July-August 2009) and sixty-first session (July 2015), respectively. The sixth periodic report was prepared under the leadership of the Women's Institute, an autonomous agency operating under the Ministry of Labour and Social Affairs. It included information provided by other ministries and the autonomous communities. There was no specific information available on the process of preparation of the fifth and combined seventh and eighth periodic reports by Spain. In the examination of its combined seventh and eighth period report, the Spanish delegation was composed of the Permanent Representative in Geneva and representatives of the Office of the Public Prosecutor and six ministries. In the examination of its sixth report, the CEDAW Cttee commended Spain for its large and high-level delegation, headed by the Minister of Equality, which included representatives of various ministries.[205]

5.4.5 Issues of Concern and Recommendations

Although the CEDAW Cttee took note of the measures implemented and efforts made by Spain to comply with its obligations under CEDAW, it raised some similar issues of concern that were recurrent in its three COs in relation to persistence of entrenched traditional attitudes and stereotypes concerning the roles and responsibilities of women and men in the family and in society, which were a root cause of violence against women and contributed to women's disadvantaged position in a number of areas, including in the labour market and in decision-making positions.[206]

While welcoming Spain's measures to combat and eliminate violence against women such as the adoption of Organic Act 1 of 2004 on integral protection measures against gender violence, the CEDAW Cttee was concerned about the prevalence of violence against women, including sexual violence, and by the high percentage of women who had died as a result of a gender-based violence,

---

[202] A/59/38 (Part II), paras 316–355.
[203] CEDAW/C/ESP/CO/6.
[204] CEDAW/C/ESP/CO/7–8.
[205] CEDAW/C/ESP/CO/6, para 3.
[206] A/59/38 (Part II), para 332, CEDAW/C/ESP/CO/6, para 17, and CEDAW/C/ESP/CO/7–8, para 18.

particularly the alarming number of reported murders of women by current and former spouses or partners.[207]

In its COs with respect to the fifth period report, while commending Spain for its legal and other measures against trafficking, the CEDAW Cttee remained concerned about increasing incidents of trafficking in women and girls,[208] as well as the under-representation of women in senior positions in some areas of professional and public life, such as the judiciary and the foreign service.[209] It was also concerned that Roma women remained in a vulnerable and marginalised situation, especially with regard to education, employment, housing and health.[210] It further noted the continuing high level of unemployment among women, the high number of women in part-time and temporary jobs as well as the wage discrimination faced by women.[211]

With regard to the sixth periodic report, the CEDAW Cttee expressed concern by the continuing prevalence of trafficking in women and girls; exploitative prostitution;[212] the participation of women in the labour market;[213] the high rates of unwanted pregnancies and voluntary interruptions of pregnancy; the increasing rates of HIV among women;[214] the relegation of women in rural areas to secondary roles and their difficulties to benefit fully and equally from legislative and policy framework for the promotion of gender equality;[215] and the situation of Roma women, women of ethnic and minority communities, migrant women and women with disabilities, who might be more vulnerable to poverty and violence and were at risk of multiple forms of discrimination with respect to education, health, employment and social and political participation.[216]

On the occasion of the combined seventh and eight periodic report, the CEDAW Cttee also expressed concerns about the prevalence of the trafficking of women and girls to Spain;[217] the low participation of women in political and public life;[218] the persistent gender wage gap and low representation of women

---

207   A/59/38 (Part II), para 334, CEDAW/C/ESP/CO/6, para 19, and CEDAW/C/ESP/CO/7–8 para 20.
208   A/59/38 (Part II), para 336.
209   ibid para 342.
210   ibid para 344.
211   ibid para 350.
212   CEDAW/C/ESP/CO/6, para 21.
213   ibid para 23.
214   ibid para 25.
215   ibid para 27.
216   ibid paras 29 and 31.
217   CEDAW/C/ESP/CO/7–8, para 22.
218   ibid para 24.

in managerial and decision-making positions and on boards of directors;[219] the situation of migrant women, Roma women, older women and women with disabilities; and the disproportionate impact on women, particularly women with disabilities, older women and women domestic workers, by the austerity measures introduced in response to the economic and financial crisis.[220]

At its sixty-eighth session (November 2017) the CEDAW Cttee examined the follow-up report of Spain[221] concerning its previous COs. It noted *inter alia* the measures and steps taken by Spain to amend its legislation on violence against women, for instance, to include other forms of gender-based violence against women, including in its Criminal Code. Yet it considered that such measures were insufficient to fully implement its recommendations, since some forms of gender-based violence, such as violence perpetrated by care providers, police violence and other violence in public spaces and workplaces, had not been addressed by Spain.[222]

5.4.6   Impact of Individual Communications[223]

Over the period under review, the CEDAW Cttee has examined three complaints against Spain,[224] out of which only one, Communication 47/2012 (*Ángela González Carreño v Spain*), ended with a finding of violation.[225] The complainant claimed violations of CEDAW in connection with the events leading to the killing of her minor daughter by the latter's father, and the question before the CEDAW Cttee concerned the responsibility of the state for not having fulfilled its duty of diligence in connection with the father's visiting rights in a context of domestic violence. The CEDAW Cttee noted that Spain

> had adopted a broad model for dealing with domestic violence which included legislation, awareness-raising, education and capacity-building. However, in order for a woman victim of domestic violence to see the practical realisation of the principle of non-discrimination and

---

219   ibid para 28.
220   ibid para 8.
221   CEDAW/C/ESP/CO/7–8/Add.1, 23 August 2017 8.
222   <https://tbinternet.ohchr.org/Treaties/CEDAW/Shared%20Documents/ESP/INT_CE DAW_FUL_ESP_29559_E.pdf> accessed 27 March 2022.
223   Sub-sec co-drafted by Carmen Rosa Rueda Castañón, former Secretary of the HRCttee's Working Group on Communications and member of the Spanish Society for IHRL.
224   See Ruth Abril Stoffels, 'El Comité de la CEDAW ante las comunicaciones individuales: requisitos de admisión y medidas provisionales' (2015) 30 *Revista Electrónica de Estudios Internacionales* 23 <http://www.reei.org> accessed 15 September 2023.
225   CEDAW/C/58/D/47/2012 (16 July 2014).

substantive equality and enjoy her human rights and fundamental freedoms, the political will expressed by that model must have the support of public officials who respect the obligations of due diligence by the state party. These include the obligation to investigate the existence of failures, negligence or omissions on the part of public authorities which may have caused victims to be deprived of protection.[226]

In this case, that obligation had not been discharged and, as a result, Spain had infringed the rights of the complainant and her deceased daughter under articles 2(a)-(f), 5(a) and 16(1)(d) of CEDAW. As a remedy, the CEDAW Cttee requested Spain to grant the complainant appropriate reparation and comprehensive compensation commensurate with the seriousness of the infringement of her rights; and to conduct an exhaustive and impartial investigation to determine whether there had been failures in the state's structures and practices that had caused the complainant and her daughter to be deprived of protection.[227]

Following the CEDAW Cttee's views, the complainant initiated administrative and judicial proceedings for the implementation of the recommendations. She failed to obtain satisfaction in first and second instance courts, until she finally reached the Supreme Court in cassation. In a landmark judgment of 17 July 2018,[228] the Court acknowledged the infringement of the complainant's rights and ordered the state to grant her €600 000 as reparation for moral damages.

5.5 Convention against Torture and Other Cruel, Inhuman or Degrading Treatment or Punishment[229]

Spain ratified CAT on 21 October 1987.[230] At the time of ratification it did not enter any reservation, and it recognised the competence of the CAT Cttee to receive individual and inter-state complaints under articles 21 and 22 of CAT. Spain did not opt out of the inquiry procedure under article 20 of CAT.[231]

5.5.1 Incorporation and Reliance by Legislature and Executive

CAT forms part of the Spanish legal order, in accordance with article 96(1) of the Constitution,[232] and is directly applicable. Nevertheless, it should be noted

---

226 ibid para 9.9.
227 ibid paras 10 and 11(a).
228 Supreme Court judgment 1263/2018. See above 4.2.5 and 5.4.2.
229 Sub-secs 5.5.1 to 5.5.4 drafted by Dr Javier Leoz Invernón, staff member of OHCHR.
230 BOE 268 of 9 November 1987.
231 See ch IV.9 of the United Nations Treaty Collection.
232 See CAT/C/17/Add.10.

that comprehensive definitions of criminal offences included in international instruments have to be adopted first through amendments to the domestic Criminal Code to be directly applicable by Spanish courts.[233]

5.5.2 Reliance by the Judiciary

CAT is regularly invoked in judgments by domestic courts, strictly for interpretative purposes.[234]

5.5.3 Impact on and through Non-state Actors

Researchers and NGOs generally cite CAT in their publications and other outputs and follow the work of the CAT Cttee at the examination of periodic reports, contesting inaccurate and/or misleading statements by government representatives, and sending information to the media and social media.[235] Awareness by lawyers of the provisions of CAT is focused among those whose areas of expertise include criminal law and international human rights law.[236]

5.5.4 Impact of State Reporting

The fourth,[237] fifth[238] and sixth[239] periodic reports of Spain were considered during the CAT Cttee's twenty-eighth (11–22 November 2002), forty-third (2–20 November 2009) and fifty-fourth (20 April-15 May 2015) sessions, respectively. Spain submitted its fourth and sixth periodic reports with minor delays of less than two months, but its fifth periodic report was received more than three years after the due date.[240] On 4 June 2019 Spain submitted its seventh periodic report[241] in response to the list of issues prior to reporting prepared under the simplified reporting procedure.[242]

---

233 CAT/C/ESP/6, para 12.
234 For a list of Supreme Court and National High Court judgments that mention CAT in the grounds for the decision, see CAT/C/ESP/6, para 13.
235 See eg 'El Comité contra la Tortura de la ONU suspende a España', Rights International Spain, 18 May 2015; *eldiario.es*, 6 April 2019 <https://www.eldiario.es/catalunya/suicidios-carcelas-catalanas-regimen-aislamiento_0_885061901.html> accessed 28 March 2022.
236 See eg *'Comentarios de la Asociación Libre de Abogados de Zaragoza 'ALAZ' con motivo del 6º informe periódico del Comité contra la Tortura de la ONU de España'*, ALAZ, abril 2015.
237 CAT/C/55/Add.5.
238 CAT/C/ESP/5.
239 CAT/C/ESP/6.
240 See <https://tbinternet.ohchr.org/_layouts/TreatyBodyExternal/Countries.aspx?CountryCode=ESP&Lang=EN> accessed 28 March 2022.
241 CAT/C/ESP/7.
242 CAT/C/ESP/QPR/7.

The Human Rights Office within the Directorate-General for the United Nations and Human Rights at the Ministry of Foreign Affairs, European Union and Cooperation is the lead agency for coordinating reporting on human rights obligations. This unit prepares the draft reports incorporating inputs from relevant departments and ministries, and finalises them in consultation with some stakeholders. It is also responsible for following up and monitoring the implementation of treaty body recommendations.[243]

The Ombudsman Institution (*Defensor del Pueblo*), in its capacity as national mechanism for the prevention of torture, submitted alternatives reports to the CAT Cttee for its consideration during the reviews of Spain's fifth and sixth periodic reports in 2009 and 2015, respectively.[244]

In 2002 the CAT Cttee observed that although Spain's fourth periodic report contained abundant information on legislative developments, it provided little information on the implementation in practice of CAT.[245] In response to the subsequent COs, a database was established within the State Secretariat for Security to collect information on claims of torture or ill-treatment and deprivation of rights during police custody.[246] This database was used to supply the detailed statistics contained in Spain's sixth periodic report.[247] Nevertheless, the CAT Cttee has continued to lament the scarcity of available data.[248]

During the last CAT Cttee review of Spain's report in 2015, seven alternative reports were submitted by human rights NGOs and other civil society actors.[249]

---

243   See OHCHR, *National Mechanisms for Reporting and Follow-up. A Study of State Engagement with International Human Rights Mechanisms* (UN, New York and Geneva 2016) 37–38.
244   See '*Observaciones del Defensor del Pueblo sobre el sexto informe periódico de España ante el Comité contra la Tortura de la Organización de las Naciones Unidas*', Defensor del Pueblo 2015; and '*Observaciones del Defensor del Pueblo sobre el quinto informe periódico de España ante el Comité contra la Tortura de la Organización de las Naciones Unidas*', Defensor del Pueblo 2009.
245   CAT/C/CR/29/3, para 2.
246   CAT/C/SR.1302, para 5.
247   ibid.
248   CAT/C/ESP/CO/6, paras 19(e) and 20.
249   The following NGOs submitted alternative reports during the review of the 6th periodic report of Spain: Amnesty International; Argituz and others; Asociación Libre de Abogados de Zaragoza (ALAZ); Basque Observatory of Human Rights; Coordinadora para la Prevención y la Denuncia de la Tortura; Fundación Acción Pro Derechos Humanos; and, Rights International Spain. All reports available at <https://tbinternet.ohchr.org/_layouts/treatybodyexternal/SessionDetails1.aspx?SessionID=961&Lang=en> accessed 28 March 2022.

There had been nine NGO/CSO submissions in relation to the previous periodic report.[250]

Despite the fact that in 2002 the CAT Cttee appreciated Spain's sending 'a large and highly-qualified delegation',[251] none of the delegations sent by Spain to the CAT Cttee's reviews since then included high-ranking officials.

There have been no communications sent to Spain by the CAT Cttee's Rapporteur on reprisals under article 19 of CAT.[252]

The CAT Cttee expressed serious concern at Spain's failure to effectively investigate allegations of torture and ill-treatment committed during incommunicado detention, as well as instances of excessive use of force by the police, with particular reference to social protests and abuses carried out against immigrants by border officials.[253] It recommended that Spain ensure the prosecution and punishment of perpetrators, noting with concern the fact that officials accused of these crimes seem to be given light sentences or are granted pardons.[254] Concerns have also been raised about the insufficient emphasis placed on the prohibition of torture and the legitimate use of force in law-enforcement human rights training programmes.[255] The difficulties faced by victims in obtaining reparation owing to the absence of proper investigation was an additional matter of concern.[256]

The CAT Cttee repeatedly recommended that Spain review the incommunicado detention regime with a view to its abolition, and to ensure that all persons deprived of their liberty enjoy fundamental legal safeguards from the

---

[250] Shadow reports submitted by Amnesty International; Asociación Española de Neuropsiquiatría; Asociación Pro Derechos Humanos de España; Basque Observatory of Human Rights; Coordinadora para la Prevención de la Tortura; International Commission for Jurists; International Federation of Action by Christians for the Abolition of Torture; Spanish Society for International Human Rights Law; and Womens' Link Worldwide. In addition, the Directorate for Human Rights within the Basque Government's Justice, Labour and Social Security Department submitted an alternative report. All reports available at <https://tbinternet.ohchr.org/_layouts/treatybodyexternal/SessionDetails1.aspx?SessionID=334&Lang=en> accessed 28 March 2022.

[251] CAT/C/CR/29/3, para 3.

[252] <See https://www.ohchr.org/EN/HRBodies/CAT/Pages/ReprisalLetters.aspx> accessed 28 March 2022.

[253] CAT/C/ESP/CO/6, paras 18–19; CAT/C/ESP/QPR/7, paras 3 and 26; CAT/C/CR/29/3, para 15.

[254] CAT/C/ESP/CO/6, para 19.

[255] CAT/C/ESP/CO/6, para 23. See also CAT/C/ESP/6 paras 86–96 and annex 'Training in the National Police Force and the Civil Guard'.

[256] CAT/C/ESP/CO/6, para 20.

moment of their arrest.[257] Spain was also urged to impose a total ban on prolonged solitary confinement.[258]

While the Spanish Criminal Code was amended in 2003 with the aim of explicitly including discrimination among the purposes for inflicting torture, in compliance with a former recommendation by the CAT Cttee,[259] CAT members still considered that article 174 of the Criminal Code does not fully reflect the definition contained in article 1 CAT.[260] The CAT Cttee also recommended that Spain ensure appropriate penalties for acts of torture[261] and that torture is never subjected to a statute of limitations.[262]

The 1977 Amnesty Act remains an issue of grave concern for CAT experts.[263] They urged Spain to take all necessary measures to ensure, in law and in practice, that crimes of torture, including enforced disappearances, are not subject to amnesty or a statute of limitations. They also noted with concern that extradition requests in respect of persons suspected of crimes of torture under the Franco regime had been denied by Spain on grounds that the acts of which they were accused did not constitute crimes against humanity and, therefore, were subject to a statute of limitations.[264]

Other issues of serious concern included the continuing high level of overcrowding in temporary migrant holding centres and the appalling material conditions in these facilities;[265] the practice of summary forced return of irregular migrants and asylum seekers with no prior risk assessment of their personal circumstances;[266] as well as other alleged breaches of the principle of *non-refoulement*.[267]

As follow-up the CAT Cttee requested Spain to inform on the steps taken to carry out recommendations on incommunicado detention and fundamental legal safeguards; temporary migrant holding centres; solitary confinement;

---

257 CAT/C/ESP/CO/6, para 10; CAT/C/ESP/CO/5, para 12; CAT/C/CR/29/3, para 10.
258 CAT/C/ESP/CO/6, para 17; CAT/C/ESP/QPR/7, para 22.
259 CAT/C/CR/29/3, paras 9 and 12.
260 CAT/C/ESP/CO/6, para 8. In its previous COs, the CAT Cttee pointed out that two important elements should be explicitly added to the offence of torture contained in art 174 of the Criminal Code: that the act of torture can also be committed by 'other person acting in an official capacity'; and that the purpose of torture may include 'intimidating or coercing him or a third person' (CAT/C/ESP/CO/5, para 7).
261 CAT/C/ESP/CO/5, para 8; CAT/C/ESP/CO/6, para 8.
262 CAT/C/ESP/CO/5, para 22.
263 CAT/C/ESP/CO/5, para 21; CAT/C/ESP/CO/6, para 15.
264 CAT/C/ESP/CO/6, para 14.
265 CAT/C/ESP/CO/6, para 16; CAT/C/ESP/QPR/7, para 20.
266 CAT/C/ESP/CO/6, para 13. See also CAT/C/ESP/CO/5, para 15.
267 CAT/C/ESP/CO/6, para 12.

and the excessive use of force by law enforcement officials. In the light of the information provided by Spain,[268] the CAT Cttee considered that the recommendations had still not been fully implemented and requested updated information on the steps taken to achieve their implementation.[269]

In 2015 there was some media coverage of the consideration of the sixth periodic report of Spain[270] and the subsequent adoption of the COs by the CAT Cttee.[271] The focus was placed on incommunicado detention, solitary confinement, the lack of effective investigation of torture allegations and *non-refoulement*.

5.5.5   Impact of Individual Communications[272]

Between July 1999 and 30 June 2019, the CAT Cttee found violations of CAT in three communications concerning Spain:[273]

In Communication 212/2002 (*Urra Guridi v Spain*),[274] decided on 17 May 2005, the complainant alleged violations of CAT in view of the light sentence and subsequent pardon granted to the three civil guards who had been found guilty of torture in his regard. The CAT Cttee was of the view that, in the circumstances of the case, the measures taken by Spain were contrary to the obligation in article 2 of CAT, according to which states must take effective measures to prevent acts of torture. It also considered that the imposition of light penalties and the granting of pardons were incompatible with the duty under article 4(2) of CAT to impose appropriate punishment. Violations of article 14 of CAT were also found in that the compensation received did not cover all damages suffered by the complainant. Therefore, it urged Spain to ensure that the complainant receive full redress.

---

268   CAT/C/ESP/CO/6/Add.1.
269   CAT/C/ESP/QPR/7, para 1.
270   See eg 'El Comité contra la Tortura critica incomunicación de detenidos en España' *La Vanguardia* (28 April 2015); 'El Comité contra la Tortura de la ONU reprocha a España la falta de datos concretos' *20 Minutos* (29 April 2015).
271   See eg 'España 'apenas avanza' en la prevención y castigo de la tortura según la ONU' (18 May 2015); 'La ONU insta a España a revisar la legislación de inmigración y asilo' *Europa Press* (15 May 2015); 'La ONU suspende a España por no actuar contra la tortura' *Diagonal* (18 May 2015).
272   Sub-sec co-drafted by Carmen Rosa Rueda Castañón, former Secretary of the HRCttee's Working Group on Communications and member of the Spanish Society for IHRL.
273   In addition, falling outside the timeframe of this study, the CAT Cttee adopted its decision of 26 November 2019 in communication 818/2017 (ELG v Spain), disclosing a violation of art 2(1) read in conjunction with art 16; art 11, read alone and in conjunction with art 2; and art 16 CAT. See <https://juris.ohchr.org/Search/Details/2696> accessed 27 March 2022.
274   CAT/C/34/D/212/2002 (24 May 2015).

Regarding Communication 368/2008 (*Sonko v Spain*),[275] the CAT Cttee on 25 November 2011 decided that the information before it disclosed a violation of articles 12 and 16 of CAT in connection with the circumstances in which the complainant's brother died after having been rescued by a civil guard vessel, when he was swimming to enter the Spanish city of Ceuta. It urged Spain to carry out a suitable investigation into the events and to provide an effective remedy to the family. As follow-up, Spain on 28 July 2015 informed that the competent court had revoked the decision by which it declared the preliminary inquiry closed and reopened the investigation. Mr Sonko's relatives were informed of the new legal avenues opened to them in that regard. However, since none of the relatives submitted an application to that effect, the inquiry concerning the death of Mr Sonko was again closed. Furthermore, the relatives did not initiate domestic proceedings in order to seek compensation. The follow-up procedure remains open.[276]

Finally, in Communication 453/2011 (*Gallastegi v Spain*),[277] the complainant claimed that the allegations made to the courts of having been subjected to torture and ill-treatment while being held incommunicado did not lead to a prompt, independent and impartial investigation. The CAT Cttee could find nothing to justify the failure of the courts to take evidence that was relevant. It therefore considered that Spain was under an obligation to provide the complainant with an effective remedy, including a full and thorough investigation of his claim. As follow-up, Spain informed that, while disagreeing with the CAT Cttee's findings, it had adopted the following measures: (a) in September 2012, the decision was published in the Official Bulletin of the Ministry of Justice; and (b) the decision was notified to all judicial and other concerned authorities.[278]

In a case decided in the period predating the time frame of this study,[279] some measures relevant to implementation may be noted. In this communication, the CAT Cttee found that the lack of investigation of the complainant's allegations, which had been made to the forensic physician and repeated before the judge of the National High Court, and the length of time that passed between the reporting of the facts and the initiation of judicial proceedings, were incompatible with the obligation to proceed to a prompt investigation enshrined in article 12 of CAT. The CAT Cttee also found violations of article 13 CAT in connection with the refusal of the judge to interview witnesses

---

275 CAT/C/47/D/368/2008 (25 November 2011).
276 CAT/C/56/2, p. 2.
277 *Orkatz Gallastegi Sodupe v Spain* CAT/C/48/D/453/2011 (23 May 2012).
278 A/68/44 204.
279 Communication 59/1996 (*Blanco Abad v Spain*) CAT/C/20/D/59/1996, (14 May 1998).

proposed by the complainant. Despite these findings, the CAT Cttee did not request any particular measure of reparation, limiting itself to request that Spain provide information on any relevant measures taken in accordance with its views. Following the decision, Spain on 25 May 2009 informed the CAT Cttee that it had been sent to all judges for information, as well as the office of the prosecutor which drafted guidelines for all prosecutors to the effect that all claims of torture should merit a reply by the judiciary. The follow-up procedure remains open.[280]

5.5.6 Impact of SPT Visit[281]

Spain ratified OP-CAT on 4 April 2006.[282] The SPT visited the country from 15 to 26 October 2017. As a result, it addressed one report to the state,[283] and one to the national preventive mechanism (NPM).[284] Spain replied in 2018.[285]

The SPT recommended to Spain to harmonise article 174 of the Criminal Code with the definition of torture in article 1 of CAT; to remove the distinction between severe and non-severe torture; to establish appropriate penalties for perpetrators of torture which take into account the seriousness of the offence in accordance with article 4(2) of CAT; and to establish the non-applicability of statutory limitations to all acts of torture.[286]

While incommunicado detention was reduced in 2015 from 13 to 10 days, the SPT recommended its abolishment and, in the interim, to prohibit it to juveniles between the ages of 16 and 18 years.[287] It noted that coercive measures in prison should be used only on an exceptional basis, and not used as a punishment for persons deprived of their liberty who are at risk of committing suicide.[288] Solitary confinement should not exceed 15 days and should be used

---

280 A/66/44 185.
281 Sub-sec co-drafted by Carmen Rosa Rueda Castañón, former Secretary of the HRCttee's Working Group on Communications and member of the Spanish Society for IHRL.
282 *BOE* 148, 22 June 2006.
283 CAT/OP/ESP/1. Spain authorised its publication on 2 October 2019. See <https://tbinternet.ohchr.org/_layouts/15/treatybodyexternal/Download.aspx?symbolno=CAT%2fOP%2fESP%2f1&Lang=en> accessed 27 March 2022.
284 CAT/OP/ESP/2, of 4 September 2018. See <https://tbinternet.ohchr.org/_layouts/15/treatybodyexternal/Download.aspx?symbolno=CAT%2fOP%2fESP%2f2&Lang=en> accessed 27 March 2022.
285 CAT/OP/ESP/2/add1 of 27 July 2018. See <https://tbinternet.ohchr.org/_layouts/15/treatybodyexternal/Download.aspx?symbolno=CAT%2fOP%2fESP%2f2%2fadd1&Lang=en> accessed 25 March 2022.
286 CAT/OP/ESP/1 (n 305) para 17.
287 ibid para 19.
288 ibid para 22.

only as a last resort in exceptional cases and under proper medical examination.[289] The closed regime should not be extended indefinitely; persons subjected to it should receive appropriate medical attention and have access to group activities and common areas, including the library.[290]

In addition, Spain should ensure that complaints of torture or ill-treatment are investigated in an efficient, thorough and transparent manner; that those responsible for such acts are prosecuted and punished; and that impunity is combated by having an independent mechanism to carry out transparent investigations into all allegations of torture or ill-treatment by law enforcement officials.[291] Persons who have reported cases of torture or ill-treatment should be protected against reprisals.[292] Persons accused or convicted of acts of terrorism should not be systematically transferred to detention centres far from their families, in violation of rule 59 of the Nelson Mandela Rules.[293] The SPT also recommended further development of current training programmes for judges, prosecutors, public defenders, doctors[294] and psychiatrist,[295] including instruction concerning the Manual on the Effective Investigation and Documentation of Torture and Other Cruel, Inhuman or Degrading Treatment or Punishment (Istanbul Protocol).[296] Places of confinement should be established for patients with psychiatric disorders.[297] Finally, it addressed recommendations dealing with persons belonging to groups deprived of their liberty in vulnerability, such as women, migrant, children and adolescents.[298]

Against civil society's preferred view,[299] the NPM was established in 2009 as part of the National Ombudsman's mandate.[300] It is composed of a unit and an advisory board of independent experts. The NPM is responsible for conducting periodic visits to places of deprivation of liberty that are overseen by various public authorities, in order to make recommendations with a view to

---

289   ibid para 27.
290   ibid para 29.
291   ibid para 35.
292   ibid para 37.
293   ibid paras 40–41.
294   ibid paras 63–64.
295   ibid para 70.
296   ibid para 46.
297   ibid para 71.
298   ibid paras 72–106.
299   See *Manifiesto de Madrid para la erradicación de la tortura y los malos tratos* of 26 June 2008, signed by many CSOs including the SSIHRL and the Coordination to Prevent Torture. Cf Fernando M Mariño Menéndez and Alicia Cebada Romero (eds), *La creación del mecanismo español de prevención de la tortura* (Iustel, Madrid 2009) 339–344.
300   Organic Act 1/2009 of 3 November.

preventing torture and other cruel, inhuman or degrading treatment or punishment. In its first eight years of its existence the NPM carried out 754 visits.[301] Out of these 107 were conducted in 2017, 52 of which were follow-up visits.[302]

In accordance with the 2018 report of the SPT to the NPM, the budget allocated to it is included, without differentiation, in the overall budget of the Office of the Ombudsman, which makes it difficult for the NPM to effectively fulfil its mandate. In this connection, the NPM does not have a sufficiently large team of professionals to perform its mandate on a national scale, with the result that it needs to recruit specialists, such as doctors and psychologists, in order to build its capacities in an interdisciplinary manner.[303] Therefore, the SPT recommended that the NPM submit a proposal to the legislature in order to obtain a budget of its own and to build an interdisciplinary team of specialists and professionals that will enable it to perform its mandate.[304] These observations were welcomed by the NPM. While indicating that, over the years, its budget had increased gradually, allowing the hiring of additional staff and external experts, it replied that it would address a request to Parliament in order to adjust the budget to its mandate and functions.[305]

The SPT also noted that the NPM does not adequately engage in constructive dialogue with senior authorities with a view to effectively monitor the implementation of its recommendations. It thus recommended that, after each visit, the NPM should submit rapidly recommendations to the relevant authorities and conduct follow-up visits promptly. The NPM should also establish, together with the relevant authorities if possible, an effective mechanism for monitoring the implementation of its recommendations.[306] The NPM replied that it considered it feasible to strengthen the mechanism.

The SPT further recommended that the NPM take steps to effectively increase its interaction with civil society and the offices of the ombudsmen of the autonomous communities.[307] The NPM showed its readiness to take initiatives in this respect. Concerning cooperation with the offices of the ombudsmen of the autonomous communities, a decision had been taken in 2013 by which staff from the latter participates in some of the visits carried out by the NPM. This cooperation could be strengthened in the future.[308]

---

301 National Preventive Mechanism, Annual Report 2017 328.
302 ibid 25.
303 CAT/OP/ESP/2 para 18.
304 ibid para 19.
305 CAT/OP/ESP/2/Add.1, of 27 July 2018.
306 CAT/OP/ESP/2 paras 26–27.
307 ibid para 28.
308 CAT/OP/ESP/2/Add.1 of 27 July 2018.

Following its visits to places of deprivation of liberty, the NPM addresses suggestions or recommendations to the public authorities, an account of which is contained in its annual reports. As an example, the NPM refers in 2017 to the follow-up to its recommendation concerning the premises of the local police in the town of Barbastro (Huesca). It found that the cells were not appropriate to hold detainees and recommended their closure while awaiting full renovation; the mayor of Barbastro ordered such closure.[309] A similar recommendation was made regarding the cells in the Civil Guard premises of Armunia (León), as a result of which the cells were closed.[310] Still, the NPM indicates that a large number of its recommendations are not implemented and that its follow-up mechanisms need to be strengthened.[311]

5.6 Convention on the Rights of the Child[312]

Spain ratified CRC on 3 November 1990,[313] making reservations regarding articles 21(d) and 38(2) and (3) of CAT of CRC.[314] Spain also ratified OP-CRC-SC;[315] OP-CRC-AC;[316] and OP-CRC-CP.[317]

5.6.1 Incorporation and Reliance by Legislature and Executive

In accordance with articles 96(1) of the Constitution and 23 of the Act 25 of 2014, on Treaties and other International Agreements, CRC is part of the Spanish legal order and is directly applicable. However, in 2002 the CRC Cttee was concerned because the principles of non-discrimination, the best interests of the child, the right to life, survival and development of the child and respect for the views of the child were not fully reflected in the Spanish legislation and administrative and judicial decisions, as well as in policies and programmes relevant to children at both national and local levels. Consequently, it reiterated previous recommendation that Spain appropriately integrate the general principles of CRC, namely, articles 2, 3, 6 and 12, in all relevant legislation concerning children.[318]

---

309   NPM, Annual Report 2017 57.
310   ibid 58.
311   ibid 34–35.
312   Sub-secs 5.6.1 to 5.6.4 drafted by Dr Carmelo Faleh Pérez, Professor on Public International Law and Human Rights, University of Las Palmas de Gran Canaria and Legal Adviser to the Spanish Society for IHRL.
313   BOE 313 of 31 December 1990.
314   See above, *Table of formal engagement of Spain with the UN human rights system*.
315   BOE 27 of 31 January 2002.
316   BOE 92 of 17 April 2002.
317   BOE 27 of 31 January 2014.
318   CRC/C/15/Add.185, paras 25–26.

In 2010 the CRC Cttee recommended to Spain to ensure that legislation and administrative regulations in all the autonomous communities fully comply with the principles and provisions of CRC. It also requested to improve an effective and adequate coordination system within the central administration and between the autonomous communities to implement policies for the promotion and protection of children. Besides, it welcomed the recognition in the domestic legislation of the child's right to be heard and other children's participation rights. Nevertheless, it was concerned that, in certain circumstances, recourse to higher courts was still necessary in order to obtain recognition for the right of a child to appear independently of his or her legal guardians before a court, in particular in judicial and administrative procedures affecting the child.[319] In 2018 it asked Spain to ensure the alignment of regional legislation with national legal frameworks related to children's rights, ensuring its homogeneous implementation and adequate and sufficient human, technical and financial resources.[320] The CRC Cttee further recommended that all the provisions of CRC be widely known and understood by adults and children, and called on Spain to develop systematic educational programmes on the principles and provisions of CRC for the general public, children, families and professionals working with children, including judges, lawyers, law enforcement officials, teachers, health personnel. and social workers.[321]

5.6.2   Reliance by the Judiciary

CRC is regularly invoked in judgments by domestic courts, strictly for interpretative purposes.[322] It is legally encouraging to verify the incorporation of the CRC Cttee jurisprudence in judicial decisions. For example, the Supreme Court judgment 41/2018 of 15 January 2018 in a matter relating to the regime of visits between grandparents and grandchildren noted that a flexibility criterion must be applied that allows the judge to issue a prudent and weighted trial, taking into account the particularities of the case and always having as a fundamental guide the principle of the best interests of the child (article 3 CRC),

---

[319]   CRC/C/ESP/CO/3–4, paras 10–12 and 29.
[320]   CRC/C/ESP/CO/5–6, para 5.
[321]   CRC/C/ESP/CO/3–4, para 20.
[322]   According to the search made in the electronic database *Tirant on Line*, for the period 1997–2018, CRC appears in 40 judgments, as follows: criminal courts (3 judgments), social courts (1); provincial courts (27); Superior Courts of Justice (2); Supreme Court (6); and Constitutional Court (1). For the same period, the electronic database *Thomson Reuters Aranzadi* offers the following results: First Instance Courts (1 judgment); Contentious-Administrative Courts (1); provincial courts (82); Superior Courts of Justice (5); National Court (1); Supreme Court (24); and Constitutional Court (25).

which derives from article 8(1) of CRC. Precisely, for the establishment of this regime of visits and communications, the will of the child must be considered in accordance with article 12 of CRC as well as General Comment 14 (2013) of the CRC Cttee on the right of the child to have his or her best interests taken as a primary consideration.[323]

5.6.3 Impact on and through Non-state Actors

CRC has been widely studied by university researchers[324] and is widely invoked by non-governmental actors. Some NGOs are especially active in the promotion and defence of CRC. This is the case of the UNICEF-Spanish National Committee, *Fundación Raíces, Noves Vies, Defence of Children International, Sociology Group of Childhood and Adolescence*, the Federation of Associations for the Prevention of Child Mistreatment (FAPMI)[325] and *Spanish Multidisciplinary Association for Research on Parental Interferences* (ASEMIP).

---

323   Supreme Court judgment 18/2018 of 15 January 2018. See <http://www.poderjudicial.es/search/documento/TS/8269360/Proteccion%20de%20menores/20180126> accessed 28 March 2022.

324   See eg Cástor Miguel Díaz Barrado, 'La convención sobre los derechos del niño' (1991) 1 *Estudios jurídicos: en conmemoración del X aniversario de la Facultad de Derecho* 181–222; Pilar Rodríguez Mateos, 'La protección jurídica del menor en la Convención sobre los derechos del niño de 20 de noviembre de 1989' (1992) 44 *REDI* 465–498; Juan Soroeta Liceras, 'La protección Internacional del niño I. La convención de Naciones Unidas sobre los Derechos del Niño' *Lecciones de derechos humanos: aspectos de Derecho internacional y de Derecho español* (1995) 271–286; José A Paja Burgoa, *La convención de los derechos del niño* (Madrid 1998) 188; Manuel Calvo García and Natividad Fernández Sola (eds), *Los derechos de la infancia y de la adolescencia* (2000); María Linacero de la Fuente, *Protección jurídica del menor* (Madrid 2001) 717; Ministerio de Trabajo e Inmigración, *Los derechos del niño: estudios con motivo del X aniversario de la Convención de los derechos del niño* (2002); Isaac Ravetllat Ballesté and Carlos Villagrasa Alcaide (eds), *El desarrollo de la Convención sobre los derechos del niño en España* (2006); Jorge Cardona Llorens, 'La Convención sobre los derechos del niño: significado, alcance y nuevos retos' (2012) 30 *Educatio siglo XXI: Revista de la Facultad de Educación* 47–68; María del Rosario Carmona Luque, 'Incidencia de la Convención sobre los Derechos del Niño en la precisión del *ius cogens* internacional' (2012) 27 *American University International Law Review* 511–542; Jorge Cardona Lloréns, 'El interés superior del niño: balance y perspectivas del concepto en el 25º aniversario de la Convención sobre los Derechos del Niño' (2014) 34 *Revista Española de Desarrollo y Cooperación* 21–40.

325   FAPMI reported on the commercial sexual exploitation of children and adolescents in Spain, referring to the implementation of OP1 to CRC. See FAPMI *Needs and Proposals to Combat Commercial Sexual Exploitation of Boys, Girls and Adolescents in Spain* (2017) 33 <https://tbinternet.ohchr.org/_layouts/15/treatybodyexternal/Download.aspx?symbolno=INT%2fCRC%2fNGO%2fESP%2f27129> accessed 28 March 2022.

The UNICEF Spanish Committee, for instance, covers all autonomous communities, focusing on political advocacy for the rights of children, the situation of children and education on rights, promoting a rights-based approach in classrooms and educational centres. In 2017 it reported to the CRC Cttee on general measures for the implementation of CRC and its general principles, the rights and civic freedoms of children, violence against children, the family environment, disability in childhood, educational, cultural and leisure measures or special protection measures in the event of trafficking in minors and migrant and refugee children.[326]

In April 2017 *Fundación Raíces* and *Noves Vies* reported to the CRC Cttee on the situation of MENA (unaccompanied migrant children), addressing issues such as location and immediate care; identification and documentation; the age assessment procedure; immigration detention centres (*CIE*); residence and work authorisations; the right of children to be informed about their rights; the right to education; institutional violence; deportations without guarantees; and a lack of resources in the child protection system.[327]

In 2017 DCI Spain (*Defence of Children International*) and GSIA (*Sociology Group of Childhood and Adolescence*) also reported to the CRC Cttee on civil and political rights and migratory itineraries of children and adolescents in Spain.[328] Finally, ASEMIP reported on the consequences for children and adolescents of delays in Spanish civil jurisdiction procedures.[329]

Regarding coverage of the CRC Cttee's work in the media, it has since 2015 become relatively important, but remains incomplete. The media fails to provide references to COs or general comments, while it should contribute to

---

[326] See <www.unicef.es> accessed 28 March 2022. UNICEF Spanish National Committee, *Complementary Report to the V and VI Report on Implementation of the Convention on the Rights of the Child in Spain* (2017) 48 <https://tbinternet.ohchr.org/_layouts/15/treatybodye xternal/Download.aspx?symbolno=INT%2fCRC%2fNGO%2fESP%2f27128> accessed 28 March 2022.

[327] Fundación Raíces & Noves Vies, *Unaccompanied Migrant Children in Spain* (2017) 41 <https://tbinternet.ohchr.org/_layouts/15/treatybodyexternal/Download.aspx?symbo lno=INT%2fCRC%2fNGO%2fESP%2f27130> accessed 28 March 2022.

[328] DCI Spain and GSIA, *Thematic Reports to the Committee on the Rights of the Child 2017* (2017) 31 <https://tbinternet.ohchr.org/_layouts/15/treatybodyexternal/Download.aspx- ?symbolno=INT%2fCRC%2fNGO%2fESP%2f27132> accessed 28 March 2022.

[329] ASEMIP, 'Statistical analysis in Spain, which enables us to learn the variables and harmful effects that occur in children and adolescents involved in the process of their parents breaking up, when there is a procedural delay in setting up the provisional measures and drafting the psychosocial reports from the psychological and legal point of view' (2017) 36 <https://tbinternet.ohchr.org/_layouts/15/treatybodyexternal/Download.aspx?symbo lno=INT%2fCRC%2fNGO%2fESP%2f27345> accessed 28 March 2022.

disseminating and raising awareness of the importance of CRC by making a broader reference to relevant COs, rather than selecting specific issues within the broad framework of rights covered by CRC.[330]

5.6.4 Impact of State Reporting

The CRC Cttee considered the second,[331] third/fourth (combined)[332] and fifth/sixth (combined)[333] periodic reports of Spain on the implementation of CRC during its thirtieth (21 May-7 June 2002), fifty-fifth (13 September-1 October 2010) and seventy-seventh (15 January-2 February 2018) sessions, respectively. It also considered the initial reports of Spain regarding OP-CRC-SC on sale of children, child prostitution and the use of children in pornography[334] and OP-CRC-AC on the participation of children in armed conflicts.[335]

More than ten NGOs submitted alternative reports in the framework of the examination procedure of the fifth and sixth reports. The National Ombudsman as well as the Basque and Catalan Ombudsmen also submitted their own reports.

In the examination of the third/fourth (combined) reports (2010), the delegation of Spain was composed of members of the Permanent Mission and 13 representatives of seven ministries. In the examination of the fifth/sixth (combined) reports (2018), the Spanish delegation consisted of the Secretary of State for Social Services and Equality, five members of the Permanent Mission, 17 representatives from seven different ministries, two representatives of the State Attorney-General's Office, one of the General Council of the Judiciary, and three representatives of the Autonomous Community of Galicia.

In 2002 the CRC Cttee welcomed the legislative amendments to ensure better compliance with CRC along the lines indicated by previous recommendations made in 1994.[336] This is the case of the amendment of the Civil Code and the Civil Proceedings Act (the Protection of Minors Act, 1996), the

---

330 See eg 'La lucha por los sentidos del derecho a la educación' *El País* (29 August 2017); 'Hay que blindar la protección de los niños migrantes' *El País* (18 December 2017); 'La ONU pide a España que prohíba la participación de niños en corridas de toros' *Diario Público* (8 February 2018); 'Los niños españoles, aún 'huérfanos' de una ley integral contra la violencia' *El Confidencial* (21 February 2015); 'La Plataforma de Infancia ve "positiva" pero "insuficiente" la subida de la prestación por hijo' *Europa Press* (15 January 2019).
331 CRC/C/70/Add.9.
332 CRC/C/ESP/3-4.
333 CRC/C/ESP/5-6. Concluding Observations adopted on 2 February 2018.
334 CRC/C/OPSC/ESP/1, of 17 October 2006.
335 CRC/C/OPAC/ESP/1, of 16 October 2006.
336 CRC/C/15/Add.28 and CRC/C/15/Add.185, para 3.

improvement of safeguards in the cases of intercountry adoption (Act 1/1996) and the amendments to the Criminal Code with reference to offences against sexual integrity (1999). In 1999 the Observatory for Children was established and some autonomous communities created institutions or services specifically responsible for children. However, the CRC Cttee regretted that Spain had insufficiently addressed its previous recommendations relating, *inter alia*, to coordination mechanisms existing in its constitutional and legislative framework: data collection; resources for children; to prevent discriminatory attitudes or prejudices towards vulnerable groups of children (including migrant children and gypsies); and the situation of asylum-seeking and unaccompanied children. In addition, the CRC Cttee asked Spain to guarantee children's equal access to the same standard of services, irrespective of where they are living, in the areas of health, education and other social welfare services. It further recommended to Spain to (i) increase the minimum age of marriage; (ii) appropriately integrate the general principles of CRC (articles 2, 3, 6 and 12 CRC) in domestic legislation and practice; (iii) amend article 154 of the Civil Code in order to delete the reference to reasonable chastisement and prohibit all forms of violence; (iv) ensure that protection procedures for children have a minimum common standard and are compatible with the best interests of the child; (v) adopt measures and policies to address domestic violence and abuses, teenage pregnancies or female genital mutilation; (vi) ensure regular attendance at schools and the reduction of truancy and drop-out rates, to prevent bullying and violence in schools and to promote the culture of peace and tolerance; and (vii) address other concerns related to labour and sexual exploitation of minors, unaccompanied minors and vulnerable groups or the administration of juvenile justice.[337] Some of the concerns raised were reiterated in the 2010 COs.[338]

Regarding the general principles, the CRC Cttee welcomed the efforts to combat the discrimination suffered by children belonging to vulnerable groups and to include the principle of the best interests of the child in the legislation and in the judicial decisions affecting the children. Moreover, it

---

[337] CRC/C/15/Add.185, paras 4, 5, 8, 11, 18, 26, 30–31, 37–41, 44, 48, 50, 52 and 54.
[338] This is the case of disparities in the laws and regulations applied by the autonomous communities; the need to intensify the effective and adequate coordination between the central administration and the autonomous communities; the difficulties in allocating specific and priority budgetary resources in favour of children; the fragmentary data collected (insufficient to cover the entire CRC); the minimum age for marriage; and the discrimination experienced by children of foreigners in an irregular situation in educational and health services. See CRC/C/ESP/CO/3–4, paras 10–24.

recommended the adoption of a strategy against *de facto* discrimination and a uniform process to determine what constitutes the best interests of the child at national and regional level, as well as to continue and strengthen efforts to fully implement and promote due respect for the views of the child at any age in administrative and judicial proceedings.[339]

Following the recommendations made by the CRC Cttee in 2002, Spain modified article 154 of the Civil Code to delete the provision stipulating that parents could reasonably and moderately discipline their children, stating that parental authority shall always be exercised for the benefit of children, according to their personality 'and with respect for their physical and psychological integrity'.[340]

The CRC Cttee further recommended the approval of an integral law on violence against children, which would guarantee the reparation of their rights and minimum attention standards in the different autonomous communities. Other concerns were linked to the family environment and alternative care; basic health and health care; education, leisure and cultural activities; and special protection measures in favour of asylum-seeking children, refugees and unaccompanied foreign children, victims of sexual exploitation and abuse, and in the field of administration of juvenile justice.[341]

In 2018 the CRC Cttee welcomed new legislative amendments introduced by Act 26 of 2015, on the modification of the system for the protection of children and adolescents.[342] However, it recommended to Spain to adopt additional extensions to the statute of limitations in child sexual abuse cases.[343] In addition, it required Spain to adopt urgent measures in the following areas: the allocation of resources; non-discrimination; children deprived of a family environment; the standard of living; education; asylum-seeking and refugee children; and unaccompanied foreign children.[344] In addition, Spain should,

---

339   ibid paras 27–30.
340   This modification was the result of Act 54/2007 of 28 December, to meet the requirements of the CRC Cttee regarding the faculty of moderate correction that up to now was granted to parents and guardians in contravention of art 19 CRC. The same Act strengthened guarantees for inter-country adoption processes by providing clear regulatory instruments to ensure that the rights and interests of the child are observed.
341   CRC/C/ESP/CO/3-4, paras 34, 38, 44 and 57–64.
342   CRC/C/ESP/CO/5-6, para 3. In fact, Act 26/2015 referred to important social changes that affect the situation of minors and demand an improvement of legal protection instruments. Among them, the Act mentions specifically CRC Cttee's general comment 13 (2011) on the right of the child not to be the object of any form of violence and the COs made to Spain in 2010. The CRC Cttee also welcomed the fact that the obligation to evaluate the impact on children and adolescents of all draft legislation has been included in the Act.
343   ibid para 23(a).
344   CRC/C/ESP/CO/5-6 paras 9,15, 28, 38, 40 and 43–45.

inter alia, (i) ensure that the business sector complies with the rights of the child; (ii) remove exceptions to the minimum age for marriage under 18 years; (iii) ensure that children born through international subrogation have access to information about their origins; (iv) monitor and enforce the prohibition of corporal punishment; (v) guarantee the integral protection of children against violence; (vi) strengthen the fight against the sexual exploitation of children; and (vii) end the use of incommunicado detention of all children, increase the number of specialised judges for children, ensure the availability of specialised juvenile court facilities and child-friendly procedures and strengthen capacity building and awareness raising of judges on CRC and its OPs.[345]

Regarding OP-CRC-SC, the CRC Cttee recommended the establishment of a central database for registering violations of the OP disaggregated by age, sex, minority group and origin;[346] to make the OP widely known, particularly to children, their families and communities,[347] raising the age of sexual consent (13 years);[348] bringing its Criminal Code in full compliance with articles 2 and 3 of OP-CRC-SC, including the provisions on remuneration and improperly induced consent,[349] criminalising trafficking in persons in accordance with the Protocol to Prevent, Suppress and Punish Trafficking in Persons, Especially Women and Children; ratifying or acceding to the CoE Convention on Action against Trafficking in Human Beings (2005) and the Convention on Cybercrime (2001);[350] prosecuting child pornography and allocate more resources to investigating crimes of child prostitution and the sale of children;[351] and earmarking resources to strengthen social reintegration and physical and psychosocial recovery measures, in accordance with article 9(3) of OP-CRC-SC.[352] Finally, regarding OP-CRC-SC, the CRC Cttee made a number of recommendations in 2007, including the reform of the Criminal Code.[353] In 2018 it reiterated that Spain should increase the number of professionals providing assistance for the physical and psychological recovery and social reintegration of asylum-seeking and refugee children who may have been involved in hostilities abroad.[354] No reply has been received.

---

345   ibid paras 4, 12, 13, 19, 21–23 and 47.
346   CRC/C/OPSC/ESP/CO/1, para 9. COs adopted on 5 October 2007.
347   ibid para 16(a).
348   ibid para 24.
349   ibid para 26.
350   ibid.
351   ibid para 28.
352   ibid para 34(e).
353   CRC/C/OPAC/ESP/CO/1. COs adopted on 5 October 2007.
354   CRC/C/ESP/CO/5–6, para 49.

5.6.5 Impact of Individual Communications[355]

The CRC Cttee found Spain in violations of the CRC in four instances:[356]

First, in *NBF v Spain*,[357] a case concerning the age assessment procedures as applied to unaccompanied migrant children, the CRC Cttee concluded that the absence of a multidisciplinary age assessment procedure and the lack of safeguards led to a finding that the best interests of the child were not a primary consideration in the age determination procedure to which the complainant, who alleged to be a minor, was subjected, in breach of articles 3 and 12 of CRC. The Committee also concluded that by not taking the interim measure of providing the complainant with accommodation in a centre for unaccompanied minors, as requested, Spain breached its obligations under article 6 of OP-CRC-CP. The CRC Cttee indicated no specific measure of redress in connection with the complainant, but limited itself to remind Spain of its obligation to prevent similar violations in the future. At the time of writing Spain had not yet submitted information on measures taken in accordance with the views.

Second, in *DD v Spain*,[358] the CRC Cttee found violation of articles 3, 20 and 37 of CRC when the police in 2014 deported a Malian minor from Melilla to Morocco. The victim was allowed no protection as a minor. Spain should provide him with adequate reparation, including financial compensation and rehabilitation for the harm suffered; prevent similar violations from occurring in the future, in particular by revising Organic Act 4 of 2015 on safeguarding the security of citizens, which was adopted on 1 April 2015; and revise the tenth additional provision of that law, on the special regime applicable in Ceuta and Melilla, which would authorise the practice of indiscriminate automatic deportations at the border.

---

355 Sub-sec co-drafted by Carmen Rosa Rueda Castañón, former Secretary of the HRCttee's Working Group on Communications and member of the Spanish Society for IHRL.

356 The CRC Cttee adopted a significant number of decisions finding Spain in violation of the CRC in the period immediately following the cut-off mark of this study, see eg Communications 21/2017 (*AD v Spain*) (4 February 2020), 26/2017 (*MBS v Spain*) (28 September 2020), 28/2017 (*MB v Spain*) (28 September 2020), 38/2017 (*BG v Spain*) (28 September 2020), 40/2018 (*SMA v Spain*) (28 September 2020), 24/2017 (*MAB v Spain*) (7 February 2020), 17/2017 (*MT v Spain*), (18 September 2019), and 27/2017 (*RK v Spain*) (18 September 2019). See also Pablo Espiniella, 'Unaccompanied Children out of Their Country of Origin. Trapped in the Administrative Net' in Fannie Lafontaine and François Larocque (eds), *Doing Peace the Rights Way. Essays in International Law and Relations in Honour of Louise Arbour* (Intersentia, Cambridge/Antwerp/Chicago 2019) 121–143.

357 CRC/C/79/D/11/2017 (27 September 2018) (Communication 11/2017).

358 CRC/C/80/D/4/2016 (1 February 2019) (Communication 4/2016).

Third, in *AL v Spain*,[359] the CRC Cttee found violation of articles 3, 8 (Spain failed to respect the identity of the author by denying that the birth certificate had any probative value) and 12 CRC (the best interests of the child were not a primary consideration in the age determination process); and article 6 of OP-CRC-CP (failure to implement the requested interim measure of transferring the author to a child protection centre).

The fourth finding, in *JAB v Spain*, similar to *NBF* and *AL*, concerns violations in the context of age determination of an unaccompanied minor.[360]

Consequently, the CRC Cttee recommended that Spain provide the authors with adequate reparation, and prevent similar violations in the future by ensuring that all procedures for determining the age of possible unaccompanied children are carried out in a manner consistent with CRC and, in particular, that in the course of such procedures they are granted prompt access to a qualified representative free of charge. As follow-up, Spain should within 180 days provide information about the measures it has taken to give effect to the CRC Cttee's views, to publish them and to widely disseminate them. However, no reply has been received.

5.7 International Convention for the Protection of All Persons from Enforced Disappearance

Spain ratified CED on 24 September 2009 without reservations; and it has been in force since 23 December 2010.[361] It also recognised the competence of the CED Cttee, under articles 31 and 32 of CED, in respect of individual and interstate complaints.

5.7.1 Incorporation and Reliance by Legislature and Executive

Once published, CED is part of the domestic legislation,[362] and the latter should be interpreted in line with CED.[363] CED can be invoked directly before domestic tribunals.[364]

The CED Cttee noted as a positive development the adoption of Instruction 12/2009 by the State Secretariat for Security regulating the Register of Detainees; and Instruction 12/2007 on the behaviour required of members of

---

359 CRC/C/81/D/16/2017 (31 May 2019) (Communication 16/2017).
360 *JAB v Spain* CRC/C/81/D/22/2017 (31 May 2019) (Communication 22/2017).
361 BOE 42, 18 February 2011.
362 Constitution, art 96(1); Act 25/2014 of 27 November, <https://www.boe.es/boe/dias/2014/11/28/pdfs/BOE-A-2014-12326.pdf> accessed 27 March 2022.
363 Constitution, art 10(2).
364 Act 25/2014, art 30.

the security forces and units to guarantee the rights of detainees and persons in police custody.[365] However, the Cttee recommended that Spain ensure that security forces of which the members are suspected of having committed an enforced disappearance do not participate in the investigation.[366] In addition, the search for persons who have been the victims of enforced disappearance and efforts to clarify their fate are obligations of the state even if no formal complaint has been laid; relatives are entitled to know the truth about the fate of their disappeared loved ones. Therefore, Spain should set up 'an *ad hoc* body responsible for searching for persons who were the victims of enforced disappearance'.[367]

In accordance with article 24(2) of CED, all victims of enforced disappearance have the right to know the truth. The CED Cttee recommended that Spain set up 'a commission of independent experts charged with establishing the truth about past human rights violations, in particular enforced disappearances'.[368] Unlike the national government, some regional governments made investigations of disappearances during the Franco dictatorship. This is the case of Catalonia, Andalusia and the Basque country governments.[369]

5.7.2 Reliance by Judiciary

In 2012 the Supreme Court confirmed that the Amnesty Act of 1977 does not allow the judiciary to investigate the fate of disappeared persons in the period 1936 to 1952. It then dismissed a suit brought by a group of associations for the recovery of historical memory that had been initially accepted by Magistrate B Garzón.[370] Judgments 75/2014 and 478/2013 of the Provincial Court of Madrid both confirmed that criminal proceedings are not the proper avenue for seeking satisfaction for the claims of complainants on the exhumation of the remains of family members in the Valle de los Caídos. However, the CED Cttee recommended that Spain ensure that the courts' exercise of jurisdiction over offences of enforced disappearance is guaranteed, in accordance with the obligations arising from article 9 of CED and, in particular, the principle of *aut dedere aut judicare*.[371] Moreover, all cases of enforced disappearances should

---

365 CED/C/ESP/CO/1, of 12 December 2013, para 5.
366 ibid para 18.
367 ibid para 32.
368 ibid para 33.
369 See Basque Country government, *Informe de vulneraciones de derechos fundamentales entre 1936–1978. Público.es*, 3 July 2019.
370 Supreme Court judgment 101/2012, of 27 February 2012. See <https://vlex.es/vid/prevaricacion-crimenes-franquismo-injusticia-356948146> accessed 27 March 2022.
371 CED/C/ESP/CO/1 para 14.

'remain expressly outside military jurisdiction and can only be investigated by ordinary courts'.[372] Finally, Spain should provide the necessary judicial assistance, including providing all evidence at its disposal, to the authorities of other states that may request it in connection with investigations into possible cases of enforced disappearance.[373]

5.7.3 Impact on and through Independent State Institutions

The Ombudsman (*Defensor del Pueblo*) has not submitted reports to the CED Cttee. The annual reports of the Ombudsman do not deal with the issue of disappearances.[374] The CED Cttee recommended to Spain to 'ensure that the Office of the Ombudsman has sufficient financial, human and technical resources effectively to perform its role as the mechanism for the prevention of torture'.[375]

5.7.4 Impact on and through Non-state Actors

One NGO on 30 April 2008 submitted a report on the rights of victims of disappearances in Spain;[376] a statement of 27 November 2008 before the Working Group on Enforced or Involuntary Disappearances;[377] and a report of 16 February 2010 on the incompatibility of the 1977 Amnesty Act with international law,[378] which was supported by numerous NGOs and academics.[379] Two NGOs in November 2014 reported that all recommendations of the CED Cttee remained unimplemented.[380] On 30 August 2018 four NGOs addressed persistent shortcomings to the Spanish authorities both from the executive and the judiciary.[381] The reply of 26 September 2018 from the Attorney-General stated

---

372 ibid para 16.
373 ibid para 20.
374 See eg DEFENSOR DEL PUEBLO, *Informe anual 2018*, 11 June 2019, <https://www.defensordelpueblo.es/informe-anual/informe-anual-2018/> accessed 27 March 2022.
375 CED/C/ESP/CO/1 para 28.
376 See <http://www.aedidh.org/sites/default/files/dictamen%20mayo%2008-1_0.pdf> accessed 27 March 2022.
377 See <http://www.aedidh.org/sites/default/files/ComparecenciaCDH_AEDIDH.pdf http://www.aedidh.org/sites/default/files/ComparecenciaCDH_AEDIDH.pdf> accessed 27 March 2022.
378 See <http://aedidh.org/sites/default/files/informe-final-auto-varela-garaon-aedidh.pdf> accessed 27 March 2022.
379 See <http://aedidh.org/sites/default/files/listado-de-adhesiones-al-informe-en-derecho-15032010.pdf> accessed 27 March 2022.
380 See <https://tbinternet.ohchr.org/_layouts/15/treatybodyexternal/Download.aspx?symbolno=CED%2fC%2f9%2f2&Lang=en> accessed 28 March 2022.
381 See <http://aedidh.org/wp-content/uploads/2018/09/Carta-Gobierno-Desapaiciones-Forzadas.pdf> accessed 27 March 2022.

that the Supreme Court's judgment of 2012 was a consolidated jurisprudence preventing any investigation of past disappearances.[382]

5.7.5 Impact of State Reporting

The CED Cttee considered the report of Spain[383] at its 62nd and 63rd meetings, held on 5 and 6 November 2013. At its 74th meeting, held on 13 November 2013, it adopted the COs.[384]

Spain was asked to take legislative measures 'to make enforced disappearance a separate offence in line with article 2 CED'; the offence 'should be punishable by appropriate penalties';[385] to ensure that 'the term of limitation actually commences at the moment when the enforced disappearance ends'; 'all disappearances are investigated thoroughly and impartially'; 'remove any legal impediments to such investigations in domestic law, notably the interpretation given to the 1977 Amnesty Act'; 'perpetrators are prosecuted and, if found guilty, punished in accordance with the seriousness of their actions'; and 'victims receive adequate reparation that includes the means for their rehabilitation and takes account of gender issues'.[386]

Spain was further requested 'to prohibit carrying out an expulsion, *refoulement*, rendition or extradition when there are substantial grounds for believing that the person would be in danger of being subjected to enforced disappearance';[387] to ensure that all persons, regardless of the offence with which they are charged, enjoy all the safeguards provided for in article 17 of CED;[388] that 'the right to apply for *habeas corpus* may be neither suspended nor restricted under any circumstances, even when a state of emergency or siege has been declared';[389] to establish a definition of victim that conforms to that contained in article 24(1) of CED.[390]

---

382 See <http://aedidh.org/wp-content/uploads/2018/10/doc02380820180928131834.pdf> accessed 27 March 2022.
383 CED/C/ESP/1.
384 CED/C/ESP/CO/1, of 12 December 2013. See <https://tbinternet.ohchr.org/_layouts/15/treatybodyexternal/Download.aspx?symbolno=CED%2fC%2fESP%2fCO%2fi&Lang=en> accessed 28 March 2022.
385 ibid para 10.
386 ibid para 12.
387 ibid para 22.
388 ibid para 24.
389 ibid para 26.
390 ibid para 30.

Finally, the CED Cttee recommended to Spain to incorporate as specific offences the acts described in article 25(1) of CED on removal of children and to provide appropriate penalties that take into account the extreme seriousness of the offences; 'to search for and identify any children who may have been the victims of removal, enforced disappearance and/or identity substitution', in conformity with article 25(2) of CED; and to ensure that 'national DNA bank holds genetic samples for all cases that have been reported whether through administrative or judicial channels',[391] given that children who are victims of enforced disappearance are especially vulnerable to numerous human rights violations, including identity substitution.[392]

As follow-up, by 15 November 2014 Spain was required to provide information on its implementation of selected recommendations;[393] and no later than 15 November 2019 on the implementation of all its recommendations; and to facilitate the participation of civil society, in particular organisations of relatives of victims, in the preparation of this information.[394]

The information provided by Spain in its 2015 response revealed no progress on the implementation of recommendations selected for follow-up.[395] Spain indicated that it did not share the interpretation provided by the CED Cttee of article 35 of CED dealing with its own competence *ratione temporis* regarding individual complaints, since it sets forth a broad interpretation extending its competence to encompass an unspecified length of time in the past; it will also entail a duplication of efforts and a clear overlap with other human rights treaty bodies and, in particular, with the Working Group on Enforced or Involuntary Disappearances.[396]

No urgent actions under article 30 of CED or reports of reprisals have been received by CED Cttee regarding Spain.

5.7.6 Impact of Individual Communications

No individual complaints from Spain were received by the CED Cttee.

---

[391] ibid para 35.
[392] ibid para 37.
[393] ibid para 39.
[394] ibid para 40.
[395] ibid paras 14–42.
[396] CED/C/ESP/CO/1/Add.1, 23 February 2015, paras 3 and 9. See <https://tbinternet.ohchr.org/_layouts/15/treatybodyexternal/Download.aspx?symbolno=CED%2fC%2fESP%2fCO%2f1%2fAdd.1&Lang=en> accessed 28 March 2022.

5.8 Convention on the Rights of Persons with Disabilities

CRPD was ratified on 3 December 2007, and it entered into force on 3 May 2008.[397] No reservations to the treaty were made. Spain also ratified OP-CRPD on the same date, accepting the individual complaints and the inquiry procedure.

5.8.1 Incorporation and Reliance by Legislature and Executive

CRPD is part of the domestic legislation,[398] and the latter should be interpreted in line with the Convention.[399] CRPD can be invoked directly before domestic tribunals.[400] Spain enacted Act 26 of 2011, on normative adaptation to CRPD to ensure appropriate harmonisation of domestic legislation with the treaty. According to this Act, all proposed laws and regulations should include, when relevant, analytical studies on their impact on the equality of opportunities, non-discrimination and accessibility of persons with disabilities.[401]

In the period 2006 to 2016, 42 laws, 75 Royal Decrees and 14 Ministerial Orders were adopted in relation to persons with disabilities.[402] Act 26 of 2011 was regulated by the Royal Decree 1276/2011, which in turn amended 11 Royal Decrees.[403] By Legislative Royal Decree 1/2013, the Consolidated Text of the General Act on the Rights of Persons with Disabilities was approved.[404] However, the text was found not in compliance with the human rights model of disability when the CRPD Cttee considered the second and third periodic reports of Spain in March 2019.[405] The Committee commended Spain for taking steps to guarantee the right to vote of all persons with disabilities on an equal basis with others.[406]

---

[397] United Nations, Office of Legal Affairs Website, Status of Treaties, Chapter IV at <https://treaties.un.org> accessed 28 March 2022.

[398] Constitution, art 96(1); Act 25/2014 of 27 November <https://www.boe.es/boe/dias/2014/11/28/pdfs/BOE-A-2014-12326.pdf> accessed 28 March 2022.

[399] Constitution, art 10(2).

[400] Act 25/2014, of 27 November, art 30(1) ('International treaties shall be directly applicable, unless it is clear from their text that such application is subject to the approval of the relevant laws or regulations.').

[401] Act 26/2011 of 1 August, additional provision fifth <https://www.boe.es/buscar/act.php?id=BOE-A-2011-13241> accessed 28 March 2022.

[402] Spanish Committee of Representatives of Persons with Disabilities (CERMI), *2006–2016 Ten years of the Convention on the Rights of Persons with Disabilities, Assessment of its implementation in Spain* 29.

[403] ibid 35. The Royal Decree 1276/2011 is available at <http://noticias.juridicas.com/base_datos/Admin/rd1276-2011.html> accessed 28 March 2022.

[404] ibid 37.

[405] CRPD/C/ESP/CO/2-3, 13 May 2019, para 6.

[406] ibid para 4(a).

In 2009 Spain adopted the Third Plan of Action for persons with disabilities 2009–2012. It was followed by the long-term strategy for persons with disabilities (2012–2020), which included objectives for the short and medium term.[407]

Both the Spanish Committee of Representatives of Persons with Disabilities (CERMI) and *Defensor del Pueblo* (UN status A) have been formally appointed as the National Independent Monitoring Mechanisms following article 33 of CRPD.[408]

With regard to budget allocations, in key areas of CRPD such as accessibility, inclusive education and living independently and being included in the community, the CRPD Cttee observed that public budgets were either insufficient or not allocated in line with CRPD.[409]

With regard to accessibility, in 2019 the CRPD Cttee expressed concern over the ineffectiveness of policies regarding accessibility in public administration, the lack of sufficient budget allocations and the lack of mandatory admissibility criteria in public procurement at all levels.[410]

With regard to the implementation of the right to live independently and being included in the community, the CRPD Cttee regretted 'the continuing investment of public funds in the construction of new residential institutions for persons with disabilities'.[411]

On 22 February 2019 the government established 3 May as the national day of CRPD.

5.8.2 Reliance by Judiciary

The reception of CRPD by domestic tribunals is diverse, from both a qualitative and a quantitative point of view. It is not always referenced in domestic judgments and the interpretation of CRPD by domestic courts is not always in line with the human rights model of disability enshrined in CRPD and general comments of the CRPD Cttee. As an example, a judgment of the Civil Chamber of the Supreme Court considered that the restrictions to the right to vote of a person with a disability was compatible with CRPD.[412] On the right to education, the Constitutional Court, in its judgment 10/2014 of 27 January, found

---

407 CRPD/C/ESP/CO/1, 19 October 2011, paras 7 and 8; CERMI 142.
408 See Royal Decree 1276/2011 and <http://ennhri.org/Ombudsman-of-Spain-Defensor-del-Pueblo> accessed 28 March 2022.
409 CRPD/C/ESP/CO/2-3, paras 16–17 and 37–38. See also CRPD/C/20/3, para 82.
410 CRPD/C/ESP/CO/2-3 para 16.
411 ibid para 37(b).
412 Supreme Court judgment 181/2016, 17 March 2016 <https://supremo.vlex.es/vid/631962033> accessed 28 March 2022.

segregation from the mainstream educational system based on impairment assessment compliant with CRPD.[413] However, in 2015 the Superior Court of Justice of Catalonia considered that such segregation infringed upon the right to equal treatment and the prohibition of non-discrimination.[414] Also, in judgment 3/2018 of 22 January, the Constitutional Court highlighted the importance of reasonable accommodation and the prohibition of discrimination on the basis of disability.[415]

5.8.3 Impact on and through Independent State Institutions

In 2011 the Ombudsman (*Defensor del Pueblo*) published a national report on human rights and disability.[416] The annual reports of the Ombudsman regularly include chapters on the implementation of the rights of persons with disabilities.[417]

CERMI has since 2008 published annual reports on disability and human rights.[418] These are based on a variety of sources such as information collected by grassroots organisations of persons with disabilities, decisions of public administrations, decisions and judgments of tribunals, and information from the media. CERMI acknowledges that different awareness-raising measures have been adopted by Spain, but indicates that they lack systematic and structural dimensions.[419] CERMI identifies as priority actors, which require systematic attention, national and regional parliaments, public administrations and judges.

CERMI submitted an alternative report to the initial report of Spain, and the *Defensor del Pueblo* submitted an alternative report prior to the adoption by the CRPD Cttee of the list of issues under the simplified reporting procedure.[420] Other civil society organisations also submitted alternative reports.[421]

---

413 Constitutional Court judgment 10/2014, 27 January <http://hj.tribunalconstitucional.es/es-ES/Resolucion/Show/23770> accessed 28 March 2022.
414 Supreme Court of Justice of Catalonia judgment 794/2015, 9 November <https://www.magisnet.com/2015/12/el-tsjc-obliga-a-escolarizar-en-un-instituto-a-un-joven-con-discapacidad/> accessed 28 March 2022.
415 Constitutional Court judgment 3/2018, 22 January <http://hj.tribunalconstitucional.es/es-ES/Resolucion/Show/25560> accessed 28 March 2022.
416 CERMI 127.
417 ibid 214.
418 See eg <http://www.convenciondiscapacidad.es/publicaciones/> accessed 28 March 2022.
419 CERMI 241.
420 Available on the *Defensor del Pueblo*'s website <https://www.defensordelpueblo.es/grupo-social/personas-con-discapacidad > accessed 28 March 2022.
421 See, eg, <https://tbinternet.ohchr.org/_layouts/treatybodyexternal/SessionDetails1.aspx?SessionID=1304&Lang=en> accessed 28 March 2022.

CERMI's 2013 annual report, which is available on CERMI's website, reproduces the recommendations of the CRPD Cttee and describes the measures adopted by Spain in implementing those recommendations. Both CERMI and the *Defensor del Pueblo* submitted alternative reports in relation to the consideration of the second and third periodic reports of Spain.[422]

In 2018 CERMI pointed out the lack of awareness about CRPD and the human rights model of disability among professionals, public officers and service providers in key areas of CRPD such as the right to equal recognition before the law, inclusive education, and the prohibition of forced sterilisation or involuntary institutionalisation. CERMI explains this lack of understanding of CRPD by the fact that diverse and multiple training activities lack a comprehensive strategy on the subject.[423]

In 2019 the CRPD Cttee noted with regret the lack of training for professionals in fields such as education, health and the judiciary to raise awareness about the rights of persons with disabilities. It also lamented the overall lack of awareness about the provisions of CRPD among lawyers, court staff, judges, prosecutors and law enforcement officials.[424]

5.8.4 Impact of State Reporting

Spain submitted its initial report on 3 May 2010, exactly two years after the entry into force of CRPD in Spain.[425] The report was considered by the CRPD Cttee on 20 September 2011. It did not identify recommendations for follow-up as this procedure was only subsequently adopted.[426]

The CRPD Cttee adopted a list of issues under its simplified reporting procedure regarding Spain in April 2017,[427] and requested it to submit its combined second and third reports in May 2018. Spain complied with this requirement by submitting these on 3 May 2018.[428] This report does not specify whether organisations of persons with disabilities and civil society organisations were consulted. Both the initial report and the combined second and third reports described in detail the laws, policies and measures adopted in the

---

422 ibid.
423 CERMI's alternative report to the CRPD Cttee <https://tbinternet.ohchr.org/_layouts/15/treatybodyexternal/Download.aspx?symbolno=INT%2fCRPD%2fNHS%2fESP%2f33561&Lang=en> accessed 28 March 2022.
424 CRPD/C/ESP/CO/2–3, para 24(c). See also *Accesibilidad y educación: España suspende en la protección de las personas con discapacidad*. CERMI, 22 June 2019.
425 CRPD/C/ESP/1, 3 May 2010.
426 In April 2012. See for example initial report on Peru, CRPD/C/PER/CO/1, 12 August 2012.
427 List of Issues Prior to Reporting, CRPD/C/ESP/QPR/2–3, 28 April 2017.
428 CRPD/C/ESP/2–3, 3 May 2018. COs were adopted on 29 March 2019.

implementation of CRPD. During the first constructive dialogue held with the CRPD Cttee in September 2011, the delegation of Spain responded openly to the questions raised by members of the CRPD Cttee.[429]

In 2019 the CRPD Cttee expressed concern on several areas where there was not significant progress since 2011. These areas include abolishing legal provisions that reinforce a negative perception of disability by allowing the late termination of pregnancy based on foetal impairments; abolishing legislative initiatives aimed at allowing euthanasia in case of disability;[430] 'the predominance of a paternalistic approach and the lack of human rights-based provisions within mental health systems';[431] and 'the lack of training for professionals in fields such as education, health and the judiciary to raise awareness about the rights of persons with disabilities'.[432]

Spain was asked to 'prohibit multiple and intersectional discrimination on the grounds of disability, sex, age, ethnicity, gender identity, sexual orientation and any other status, in all areas of life'; and 'recognise the denial of reasonable accommodation as a form of discrimination'.[433] Spain was also asked to 'provide protection from multiple discrimination against women and girls with disabilities, in particular women and girls with intellectual or psychosocial disabilities';[434] to 'end the institutionalisation of children with disabilities';[435] to 'ensure accessibility in all areas, including buildings and facilities open or provided to the public';[436] to 'address gender-based violence against women with psychosocial disabilities';[437] to 'repeal all discriminatory legal provisions with a view to fully abolishing substituted decision-making regimes';[438] to 'remove barriers for persons with disabilities in their access to justice';[439] to 'prohibit forced institutionalisation and treatment on the grounds of disability';[440] to 'ensure the free and informed consent of the person concerned in all procedures and stages of the mental health system';[441] and to 'establish an

---

429 CRPD/C/6/SR.3 and CRPD/C/SR.4.
430 CRPD/C/ESP/2–3, para 6(b).
431 ibid para 6(a).
432 ibid para 6(d).
433 ibid para 9.
434 ibid para 11(a).
435 ibid para 13(a).
436 ibid para 17.
437 ibid para 19.
438 ibid para 23.
439 ibid para 25(a).
440 ibid para 27(a).
441 ibid para 30(b).

independent human rights-based mechanism for monitoring mental health facilities and services in all autonomous communities'.[442]

In addition, Spain was requested to 'repeal article 156 of Organic Act No 10/1995 to fully abolish the administration of sterilisation, medical treatment and research on all persons with disabilities without the full and informed consent of the person concerned';[443] to 'recognise the right to personal assistance in law, ensuring that all persons with disabilities are entitled to personal assistance';[444] to 'discontinue the use of public funds to build residential institutions for persons with disabilities';[445] and to expedite legislative reform in line with CRPD, in order to 'clearly define inclusion and its specific objectives at each educational level' and 'to view inclusive education as a right'.[446]

As follow-up, the CRPD Cttee in 2019 requested Spain to pay urgent attention 'to the recommendations contained in paragraphs 34, on protecting the integrity of the person, and 46–47, on inclusive education'.[447] No reply has been received.

No reports of reprisals have been received by the CRPD Cttee regarding Spain.[448]

5.8.5   Impact of Individual Communications

By 30 June 2019 the CRPD Cttee has found Spain in violation of the CRPD in one communication, *VFC v Spain*.[449] In the complaint, dealing with a municipal employee who, due to an accident leading to motor disability was compelled to go on mandatory retirement and was refused the possibility of modified-duty assignment, the Cttee concluded that Spain failed to fulfil its obligations under articles 27(a), (b), (e), (g), (i) and (k), read alone and in conjunction with articles 3(a), (b), (c), (d) and (e); articles 4(1)(a), (b) and (d) and (5); and articles 5(1), (2) and (3) of CRPD.[450] As for individual-focused remedies, the CRPD Cttee

---

442 ibid para 30(d).
443 ibid para 34.
444 ibid para 38(a).
445 ibid para 38(b).
446 ibid para 46.
447 ibid para 64.
448 Interview with the Secretariat of the CRPD Cttee, 15 January 2019 (notes on file with author).
449 *VFC v Spain* CRPD/C/21/D/34/2015 (2 April 2019) Communication 34/2015. In 2020, the Cttee also found violations in Communications 37/2016, 41/2016.
450 CRPD/C/21/D/34/2015, para. 9. Views adopted on 2 April 2019. See <https://tbinternet.ohchr.org/_layouts/15/treatybodyexternal/Download.aspx?symbolno=CRPD%2fC%2f21%2fD%2f34%2f2015&Lang=es> accessed 28 March 2022.

stated that the victim has the right to compensation and to undergo an assessment of fitness for alternative duties for the purpose of evaluating his potential to undertake modified duties or other complementary activities, including any reasonable accommodation that may be required. As for general measures, the CRPD Cttee recommended that Spain take measures to prevent similar violations in the future; to align the modified-duty regulations of the Barcelona municipal police and their application with the principles enshrined in CRPD to ensure that assignment to modified duty is not restricted to persons with a partial disability; and similarly harmonising the variety of local and regional regulations governing the assignment of public servants to modified duty.[451] As follow up, Spain should within six months report on any action taken in light of the present views; to publish them, to have them translated into the official languages of the state and to circulate them widely, in accessible formats, in order to reach all sectors of the population.[452]

5.8.6 Impact of Inquiry

The CRPD Cttee carried out an inquiry on Spain regarding grave or systematic violations of article 24 of CRPD (right to education), on the basis of information received from NGOs alleging structural exclusion and segregation of persons from the mainstream education system on the basis of disability. The period examined spanned from 2011 to June 2017 and the inquiry included a visit to the country conducted from 30 January to 10 February 2017.[453] The CRPD Cttee found violations of the right to an inclusive and quality education related primarily

> to certain features of the education system that have been maintained despite reforms and that continue to exclude persons with disabilities – particularly those with intellectual or psychosocial disabilities or multiple disabilities – from mainstream education on the basis of assessments conducted according to the medical model of disability. This, in turn, results in educational segregation and denial of the reasonable

---

451 ibid paras 9(a) and (b).
452 ibid para 10. On 16 November 2020, judgment 173/2020 by Administrative Court 4 of Barcelona recognised that the CRPD Cttee's views were legally binding and ordered the Municipality of Barcelona to comply with them.
453 CRPD/C/20/3, 4 June 2018, para 11. See <https://tbinternet.ohchr.org/_layouts/15/treatybodyexternal/Download.aspx?symbolno=CRPD/C/20/3&Lang=en> accessed 28 March 2022.

accommodation needed to ensure the non-discriminatory inclusion of those with disabilities in the mainstream education system. This segregation ... [affected] around 20 per cent of persons with disabilities, with negative repercussions on their social inclusion.[454]

On 25 May 2018 Spain rejected the CRPD Cttee's findings arguing that the report did not reflect the real situation in the country. Inclusive education was a principle that had prevailed in the legislation and policies of successive governments, both at the central and regional levels, but it was a permanent process in the course of which adjustments were required in accordance with the principle of the best interests of the child.[455]

In 2019 the CRPD Cttee remained concerned about the limited progress made by Spain with regard to inclusive education, including the lack of a clear policy and action plan for the promotion of inclusive education. It was particularly concerned that Spain has maintained regulatory provisions on special education and a medical impairment-based approach. It regretted that a high number of children with disabilities, including autism, intellectual or psychosocial and multiple disabilities, are still receiving segregated education. The CRPD Cttee called upon Spain to implement all the recommendations contained in its inquiry report.[456]

5.8.7 Brief Conclusion

Spain has adopted many laws, regulations, policy and practical measures to implement CRPD. While progress has been made in several areas, resulting in broader social inclusion of persons with disabilities, major challenges persist in key areas of CRPD such as the full recognition of legal capacity of persons with disabilities;[457] the right to inclusive education;[458] accessibility;[459] and the rights of persons with disabilities to live independently and being included in the community.[460] Women with disabilities continue to experience intersectional discrimination based on disability, gender, and other statuses limiting their advancement, development and empowerment as actors of change.[461]

---

[454] ibid para 23.
[455] CRPD/C/20/5.
[456] CRPD/C/ESP/CO/2–3, paras 45 and 46.
[457] ibid paras 22 and 23.
[458] ibid paras 45, 46 and 47.
[459] ibid paras 16 and 17.
[460] ibid paras 37 and 38.
[461] ibid paras 10 and 11.

More needs to be done at all levels – national, regional and local levels – in the key area of raising awareness of CRPD and the human rights model of disability, as the medical model of disability continues to be largely entrenched in society, and contributes to perpetuate negative stereotyping, prejudices and stigma against persons with disabilities and, particularly, against persons with intellectual, psychosocial and multiple disabilities.[462]

6   Conclusion

As in the case of other EU members, Spain is party to all the UN core human rights treaties, with the exception of CMW. It has also accepted the individual complaints procedure before eight committees and the inquiry procedure before five committees, with the exception of the CESCR Cttee. Formally speaking, Spain regularly cooperates with UN treaty bodies, meeting the reporting requirements with minor delays. It also formally cooperates with the individual complaints, inquiry and SPT procedures. However, most of the recommendations contained in the COs adopted by treaty bodies remain unimplemented.[463] As they are considered not binding, there is no effective national mechanism to follow up that could ensure their appropriate implementation.

International mechanisms to follow up are also weak. The formal replies received from Spain are insufficient, since they do not meet the required criteria established by the treaty bodies.

Six treaty bodies adopted a total of 37 views on Spain, finding violations of conventional norms. Therefore, the individual complaints procedure was under-utilised during the period under review due to a lack of both knowledge and effectiveness.[464] Since recommendations emanating from views were considered not binding, there is no mechanism in the domestic legal order by which victims of violations declared by international bodies can seek reparation.

This situation generated frustration among victims and other stakeholders that discontinued their cooperation with treaty bodies. Only a limited number of local NGOs are aware of the relevance of recommendations/views unimplemented and continue their advocacy trying to persuade both the executive and the legislative to comply with them.

---

462   ibid paras 6, 7, 14, and 5.
463   A similar assessment was made in the first edition of this book (2002) 605–609.
464   This trend was already observed in the first edition of this book (2002) 610.

Thanks to the excellent litigation – both domestic and international – carried out by an international NGO,[465] it was achieved the Supreme Court's judgment of 17 July 2018[466] in connection with the reparations recommended by the CEDAW Cttee in its first case concerning Spain, namely, the case of *Ángela González Carreño*.[467] The Court stated that Spain has the obligation to comply with the views emanating from CEDAW and its OP, since it voluntarily acknowledged the competence of the CEDAW Cttee to examine individual complaints. Furthermore, CEDAW and views under OP are part of the Spanish legal system, as set up in articles 96 and 10(2) of the Constitution, and have the supra-legal value provided to them by articles 95 and 96 of the Constitution.

This unexpected judgment of the Supreme Court sets a precedent[468] which paves the way for a more significant impact of the treaties and the committees' decisions, not only in the lives of human rights victims, but also in the Spanish legal system as a whole.

Therefore, Spain should fully comply with UN human rights mechanisms. First, it should adhere to CMW and accept the inquiry procedure of the CESCR Cttee. Second, it should fully comply with recommendations from COs and general comments, accepting their legal effect and establishing an effective and transparent national mechanism to follow up. Third, it should amend article 5*bis* of the 2015 Organic Act of the Judiciary, to include decisions by both the UN Committees and the HRC Working Group on Arbitrary Detention along with judgments of ECHR, to ensure that all victims may seek domestic redress following international decisions.

Treaty bodies could also do more: first, updating their internal rules to expedite and harmonise common procedures; second, improving procedures of follow up to recommendations of both COs and views or interim measures, generalising visits in the field; third, asserting the legal effect of their own decisions; fourth, increasing cooperation with HRC special procedures.

The UN should increase the regular budget allocated to OHCHR and the High Commissioner for Human Rights should revise the budget priorities given to

---

465 Women's Link Worldwide.
466 Judgment 1263/2018, of 17 July of the Supreme Court, Administrative Chamber, Section Four. See <https://supremo.vlex.es/vid/735629461> accessed 28 March 2022.
467 Views adopted on 16 July 2014, CEDAW/C/58/D/47/2012. See <https://juris.ohchr.org/Search/Details/1878> accessed 28 March 2022.
468 This precedent was followed by judgment 173/2020 of 16 November 2020, Administrative Court 4 of Barcelona. See n 480. However, judgment 401/2020 of 12 February of the Supreme Court regarding views adopted by the HRCttee was a set back to the traditional position. See <http://www.poderjudicial.es/search/AN/openDocument/fa633d2d95d772a1/20200221> accessed 28 March 2022.

UPR and other promotional activities, in detriment of protection mechanisms, namely, treaty bodies and HRC special procedures.

Finally, Spain should seek technical support from OHCHR to raise awareness of UNTBS, among judicial,[469] legislative and administrative authorities, civil society and local NGOs, as well as the general public.

Acknowledgements

The author wishes to acknowledge valuable contributions received, inter alia, from Dr Javier Leoz Invernón, staff member of OHCHR (CERD and CAT); Dr Carmelo Faleh Pérez, Professor of Public International Law and Human Rights, University of Las Palmas de Gran Canaria and Legal Adviser to the Spanish Society for IHRL (CCPR, CESCR, CRC and CMW) (carmelo.faleh@ulpgc.es); and Carmen Rosa Rueda Castañón, former Secretary of the HRCttee's Working Group on Communications and member of the Spanish Society for IHRL (individual complaints and SPT SubCttee). The views expressed herein are those of the author and do not necessarily reflect the views of the United Nations.

---

[469] As already stated in the first edition of this book (2002): 'Most government officials, lawyers and judges are not familiar with international law. Judicial training is of the utmost importance' (610).

CHAPTER 19

The Impact of the United Nations Human Rights Treaties on the Domestic Level in Turkey*

Başak Çalı, Betül Durmuş and İlayda Eskitaşçıoğlu

1 Introduction to Human Rights in Turkey

The history of fundamental rights protections in Turkey traces back to developments in the early nineteenth century Ottoman Empire: The 1876 Basic Law was the first document to recognise the rights of citizens.[1] In the Republican era starting in 1923, the 1961 Constitution provided a comprehensive list of fundamental rights. The constitutional protection of rights has continued with the 1982 Constitution. According to the Turkish Constitution, the Turkish Republic is a democratic, secular, welfare, rule of law state based on respect for human rights.[2]

Until 2012, constitutional rights were justiciable before the Turkish Constitutional Court only by way of 'norm review', subject to referral by the President of Turkey, members of parliament or lower domestic courts. Since 2012 there exists a right to individual petition before the Turkish Constitutional Court.[3] This, however, applies only to rights that are protected by both the Constitution and the European Convention on Human Rights and Fundamental Freedoms.[4] Turkey established the office of an Ombudsman capable of receiving, among others, human rights complaints also in 2012, while the Human Rights and Equality Institution (the country's NHRI) was established in 2016.

Military *coups*, states of emergency, and the Kurdish question play important roles in Turkey's contemporary human rights history.[5] Turkey's multi-party

---

* This chapter uses Turkey as the country name as it covers documents and events before 2022.
1 Ottoman Constitution of 1876.
2 Constitution of the Republic of Turkey 1982, art 2.
3 Constitution of the Republic of Turkey 1982, arts 148, 149 (with the amendment of 12 September 2010 (Law 5982)); Law on the Establishment and Rules of Procedures of the Constitutional Court (No 6216) 2011, arts 45–51.
4 Law on the Establishment and Rules of Procedures of the Constitutional Court (No 6216) 2011, art 45.
5 Zehra F Kabasakal (ed) and Richard Falk, *Human Rights in Turkey* (University of Pennsylvania 2007).

democratic regime, established in 1946, has been interrupted by a military *coup* in 1960, a military memorandum in 1971, and another military *coup* in 1980. Turkey also experienced an attempted military *coup* in 2016. The effects of military rule, in particular that of the 1980 military regime, have left a long-lasting legacy with approximately 650 000 people detained and 49 people executed, alongside enforced disappearances and deaths from torture in custody.[6] The state of emergency regime in the east and south-east provinces of Turkey aimed at combating the Kurdistan Workers' Party (PKK) lasted from 1987–2002. In this period, an estimated 950 000 to 1 200 000 people were displaced from their homes and 1 352 people were subjected to enforced disappearances.[7] After the attempted *coup* of July 2016, Turkey was under a fully-fledged state of emergency until July 2018. According to data gathered by the Turkey Human Rights Joint Platform, at least 228 137 people were detained during the state of emergency and over 100 000 civil servants were purged, including one quarter of the judiciary.[8]

Turkey is a country with longstanding institutional ties to Europe. It is a member of the Council of Europe, the Organisation for Security and Co-operation in Europe (OSCE) and the North Atlantic Treaty Organisation (NATO). Since Turkey's acceptance of the right to individual petition before the European Court of Human Rights (ECtHR) in 1990, the ECtHR has played a central role in Turkey. Turkey's candidacy to the EU in 1999 also led to significant legal human rights reforms, in particular between 1999 and 2004.[9] In 2004, Turkey abolished the death penalty in all circumstances.[10]

Women and girls face discrimination and domestic violence in Turkey. Turkey ranks as the 130th state in the global gender gap index of UN Women.[11] Poverty and socio-economic deprivation have become highly prevalent in recent years. Although the poverty rate in Turkey declined from 27,3 to 9,9

---

6 Turkish Human Rights Association, 'No to 12 September Darkness' (12 September 2019) <https://www.ihd.org.tr/12-eylul-karanligina-hayir/> accessed 24 March 2022.

7 Özgür Sevgi Göral, Ayhan Işık and Özlem Kaya, *Unspoken Truth: Enforced Disappearances* (Truth Justice Memory Centre 2013).

8 İnsan Hakları Ortak Platformu, 27 Temmuz 2016–20 March 2018 Olağanüstü Hal Uygulamaları: Güncellenmiş Durum Raporu, 17 April 2018 <https://www.ihd.org.tr/wp-content/uploads/2018/04/Olağanüstü-Hal_17042018.pdf> accessed 24 March 2022.

9 Meltem Müftüler-Bac, 'Turkey's Political Reforms: The Impact of the European Union' (2009) 10(1) South European Society and Politics 16–30.

10 Law on the Amendment of the Constitution of the Republic of Turkey (No 5170) 2004, art 5.

11 UN Women, Global Database on Violence against Women: Turkey <https://evaw-global-database.unwomen.org/en/countries/asia/turkiye> accessed 24 March 2022.

per cent between 2004 and 2016, economic growth significantly slowed down in the second half of 2018.[12] Unemployment climbed between May 2018 and May 2019, from 10,6 to 14 per cent, leaving 4,5 million people unemployed.[13] Likewise, the youth unemployment rate increased sharply to 25,5 per cent from 19,4 per cent in 2019.[14] Inequality has increased over the last decade in Turkey: Although the Gini index, measuring the degree of inequality in the distribution of family income, decreased from 42,2 per cent in 2003 to 39 per cent before the economic crisis in 2008, it rose back to 41,9 per cent in 2016.[15] As of 2017, 13,5 per cent of the population lives below the national poverty line.[16] In addition, over three million Syrians who have arrived in Turkey since 2011 face challenges in accessing human rights protections.[17]

2   Relationship of Turkey with the International Human Rights System in General

International human rights law enjoys the status of domestic law under article 90 of the Turkish Constitution. No appeal to the Constitutional Court can be made with regard to these treaties on the grounds that they are unconstitutional.[18] Significantly, article 90 of the Constitution holds that in the case of a conflict between human rights treaties and domestic law the provisions of international treaties shall prevail. In the case of *Sevim Akat Eşki* (2013), the Constitutional Court also formulated a direct effect doctrine of international human rights treaties under the Constitution.[19]

Turkey has a long history of engagement with United Nations (UN) human rights mechanisms. Turkey was considered under the former '1503' procedure focusing on gross and systematic human rights violations, between 1983 and 1986. Since 2001, UN Special Rapporteurs have enjoyed a standing invitation from Turkey. The most recent visits by the UN Special Rapporteurs to

---

12   Facundo Cuevas, World Bank Group Poverty and Equity Brief: Turkey (2019) <https://databank.worldbank.org/data/download/poverty/33EF03BB-9722-4AE2-ABC7-AA297 2D68AFE/Global_POVEQ_TUR.pdf> accessed 24 March 2022.
13   ibid.
14   ibid.
15   ibid.
16   ibid.
17   Burcu Toğral Korca, 'Syrian Refugees in Turkey: From "Guests" to "Enemies"?' (2016) 54 New Perspectives on Turkey 55.
18   Constitution of the Republic of Turkey, art 90.
19   Turkish Constitutional Court, App No 2013/2187 (19 December 2013) para 42.

Turkey were carried out by the Special Rapporteur on Torture and the Special Rapporteur on Freedom of Expression after the attempted *coup* of Summer 2016. The Working Group on Enforced or Involuntary Disappearances also undertook a visit to Turkey in 2016, Turkey also accepted the inquiry into the killing of Jamal Khashoggi, the Saudi Arabian journalist who was murdered in the Saudi Arabian consulate in Istanbul. This inquiry was conducted by the Special Rapporteur on Extrajudicial, Summary or Arbitrary Killings in 2019.

The Ministry of Foreign Affairs is the governmental contact point for all issues regarding the UN human rights mechanisms. This includes nominations for membership of the UN treaty bodies, preparing state reports and defending the government when there is an individual complaint before UN treaty bodies.

Turkey has a policy of having as wide a representation as possible of Turkish citizens in UN human rights mechanisms.[20] It has also been successful in securing the election of Turkish citizens in UN treaty bodies (UNTBS) and Special Procedures. Yet, the procedures for nominations for UNTB positions are highly opaque at the domestic level, where there is no transparent call for candidates or clear standards for selection.[21] The Ministry of Foreign Affairs enjoys full discretion in these nominations. So far, successful candidates have included academics, former diplomats and bureaucrats.

Turkey generally exhibits a co-operative attitude towards UN human rights mechanisms that visit Turkey. In recent years, however, there has also been strong criticism of the UN human rights machinery. For example, the two reports of the United Nations High Commissioner for Human Rights, one analysing the clashes between the state security forces and the PKK or affiliated groups between July 2015 and 2016 and one on the impact that the declaration of the state of emergency had on human rights between January and December 2017, received strong criticism.[22] In 2018, the Ministry of Foreign Affairs accused the High Commissioner for exhibiting prejudice against

---

20   Interview with the Ministry of Foreign Affairs, 15 January 2020, Ankara, Turkey. Notes of all interviews (including this one) are on file with the authors.

21   ibid.

22   See Office of the United Nations High Commissioner for Human Rights, Report on the Human Rights Situation in South-East Turkey: July 2015 to December 2016 (2017) <https://www.ohchr.org/Documents/Countries/TR/OHCHR_South-East_TurkeyReport_10March2017.pdf> accessed 24 March 2022; Office of the United Nations High Commissioner for Human Rights, Report on the Impact of the State of Emergency on Human Rights in Turkey, Including an Update on the South-East January-December 2017 (2018) <https://www.ohchr.org/Documents/Countries/TR/2018-03-19_Second_OHCHR_Turkey_Report.pdf> accessed 24 March 2022.

Turkey.[23] This concern regarding Western double standards against Turkey was also raised in interviews conducted with government representatives.[24]

On certain occasions, criticisms by the international human rights system of Turkey's commitment to international human rights law go beyond reactions to specific reports. Gender equality has been one such area. President Erdoğan, for example, has said that men and women are not equal, and he has also criticised feminists for not understanding the importance of motherhood.[25] These views have also been echoed in the activities of the Human Rights and Equality Institution of Turkey. One outcome declaration of a symposium organised by this institution included statements against gender equality and respect for the rights of the lesbian, gay, bisexual and transgender (LGBT) individuals. This declaration called for changing or revoking domestic law and international treaties that are deemed to have a detrimental effect on families. These include the Istanbul Convention and Law No 6284 to Protect Family and Prevent Violence against Women.[26] Turkey withdrew from the Istanbul Convention in March 2021.

3 At a Glance: Formal Engagement of Turkey with the UN Human Rights Treaty System

Refer to the chart on the next page.

4 Role and Overall Impact of the UN Human Rights Treaties in Turkey

4.1 *Role of UN Human Rights Treaties*
4.1.1 Formal Acceptance

Turkey is a state party to eight of the nine core UN human rights treaties, as well as OP2-CCPR, OP-CRC-AC, OP-CRC-SC and OP-CAT. The first treaty that

---

23 Ministry of Foreign Affairs, No 79, Press Release Regarding the OHCHR Turkey Report published on 20 March 2018 (20 March 2018) <https://www.mfa.gov.tr/no_-79-bm-insan-haklari-yuksek-komiserli%C4%9Finin-ulkemize-iliskin-olarak-20-mart-2018-tarihinde-yayimladigi-belge-hk_en.en.mfa> accessed 24 March 2022.
24 Interview with MP Hakan Çavuşoğlu, Human Rights Commission of the Grand Assembly, 23 October 2019, Ankara, Turkey.
25 Agence France-Presse in Istanbul, 'Recep Tayyip Erdoğan: "Women not Equal to Men"' *The Guardian* (24 November 2014) <https://www.theguardian.com/world/2014/nov/24/turkeys-president-recep-tayyip-erdogan-women-not-equal-men> accessed 24 March 2022.
26 Human Rights and Equality Institution of Turkey, Final Declaration of the Human Rights Symposium on the Right to Protection of the Family (2019) <https://www.tihek.gov.tr/ailenin-korunmasi-hakki-sonuc-bildirisi/> (in Turkish) accessed 24 March 2022.

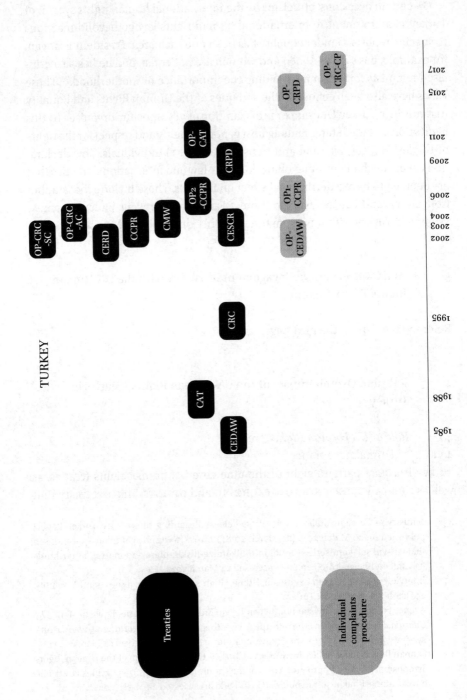

Turkey ratified was CEDAW in 1985, followed by the Convention Against Torture and Other Cruel, Inhuman or Degrading Treatment or Punishment (CAT) in 1988 and the Convention on the Rights of the Child (CRC) in 1995. Turkey ratified the older UN human rights treaties, namely, the International Covenant on Civil and Political Rights (CCPR), the International Covenant on Economic, Social and Cultural Rights (CESCR) in 2003 and the International Convention on the Elimination of All Forms of Racial Discrimination (CERD) in 2002. Turkey ratified the International Convention on the Protection of the Rights of All Migrant Workers and Members of Their Families (CMW) in 2003 and the Convention on the Rights of Persons with Disabilities (CRPD) in 2009. The surge in ratifications in the 2000s and the late ratification of the twin Covenants in 2003 correspond with Turkey's Europeanisation process. In this period Turkey undertook major human rights reforms to make its legal framework more compatible with the European Union (EU) *Acquis communautaire* in the context of its EU accession negotiations.[27] In this context Turkey's increased commitment to UN treaties was driven by its membership negotiations with the EU.

Turkey is not a state party to the International Convention for the Protection of All Persons from Enforced Disappearance (CED), and the ICC Statute. Turkey exited from a human rights treaty for the first time in its history in 2021, the Council of Europe Convention on Preventing and Combating Violence Against Women and Domestic Violence, better known as the Istanbul Convention.[28] Although Turkey has not ratified CED, the campaign for its ratification by domestic NGOs is ongoing: The Human Rights Foundation of Turkey, the Human Rights Association, the Saturday Mothers and the Truth Justice Memory Centre have on several occasions called for the ratification of CED, including through the stakeholder reports they have submitted to the Universal Periodic Review (UPR).[29] Our interlocutors pointed out two possible reasons for the lack of ratification of CED. The first concerns the enforced disappearances in Cyprus which may be attributable to Turkey, and the second concerns the widespread

---

27   Council of Ministers Decision No 2001/2129 (24 March 2001); Council of Ministers Decision No 2003/5930 (24 July 2003); interview with Prof Dr Bertil Emrah Oder, Koç University, 26 March 2019, Istanbul, Turkey.
28   İlayda Eskitaşçıoğlu, 'Turkey's Withdrawal from the Istanbul Convention: A Sudden Presidential Decision in the Dead of the Night and an Alarming Setback' *Völkerrechtsblog* (27 March 2021) <https://voelkerrechtsblog.org/turkeys-withdrawal-from-the-istanbul-convention/> accessed 24 March 2022.
29   Interview with Adem Arkadaş Thibert, Child Rights International Network, 5 August 2019, Istanbul, Turkey.

enforced disappearances in Turkey in the 1990s.[30] It is argued that the state does not have the political will to be under international scrutiny with respect to their military operations abroad or with respect to accountability for high-level state officials for enforced disappearances that took place in the context of the security operations against the PKK.[31] There furthermore are new dimensions to this problem with current concerns regarding possible enforced disappearances in the post-*coup* period after 15 July 2016. Taken together, the question of enforced disappearances has always been an overly political and sensitive topic for Turkish authorities acting as a barrier against the ratification of CED as well as against fighting impunity through domestic courts.[32]

Turkey's ratifications of the UN human rights treaties came with substantive and procedural reservations. The substantive reservations primarily aim to limit the legal effects of provisions that seek to protect people belonging to minorities. For Turkey, the definition of minorities is limited to non-Muslim minorities with reference to the Lausanne Peace Treaty of 1923, thereby only covering Jewish, Greek and Armenian minorities. Turkey's procedural reservations focus on its non-recognition of Cyprus and limiting access to the International Court of Justice (ICJ) in cases of bilateral disputes arising from UN human rights treaties. In the case of the Convention on the Elimination of All Forms of Discrimination Against Women (CEDAW) and in parallel with the amendments to the Turkish Civil Code in 2001 and 2004, reservations concerning article 15(2) and (4), and article 16(1)(c), (d), (f) and (g) were withdrawn on 20 September 1999.[33]

The motivations for ratifying UN human rights treaties and their subsequent impact on political discourse, courts, academia, and civil society are closely interlinked in Turkey. The ratification processes of all treaties emerge as top-down processes. While there has been a campaign for the ratification of CEDAW by the Turkish women's rights movement in the 1980s, the ratification of CEDAW is best explained by the post-1980 *coup* civilian government's decision to signal better integration to the international community.[34] Yet, the

---

[30] Interview with Emel Ataktürk Sevimli, Truth Justice Memory Centre, 25 July 2019, Istanbul, Turkey.

[31] ibid; interview with Asst Prof Dr Murat Önok, Koç University, 24 December 2019, Istanbul, Turkey.

[32] Interview with Dr Kerem Altıparmak, Ankara Bar Association Human Rights Centre, 6 August 2019, Istanbul, Turkey.

[33] Communication by the Secretary-General of the United Nations regarding Turkey's partial withdrawal of reservations to CEDAW, Communication No CN 895.1999.TREATIES-7 (5 October 1999).

[34] Interview with Prof Dr Ayşe Feride Acar, Middle East Technical University, 22 October 2019, Ankara, Turkey.

early mobilisation of the women's movement around CEDAW has certainly increased its impact and led to the process of the lifting of reservations. The ratification of CAT in 1988 corresponds to a time where practices of torture in custody in Turkey were systemic. The government of the time saw this ratification as a useful tool to deflect criticism about its torture practices and to criticise the torture practices of other states.[35]

Turkey is a selective ratifier of optional protocols and clauses that enable the right to individual petition before the UN treaty bodies. It accepted the right to launch petitions before CAT in 1988, and ratified OP-CEDAW in 2004, OP1-CCPR in 2006, OP-CRPD in 2016 and OP-CRC-CP in 2017 (with reservations). The lack of acceptance of right to individual petition with respect to CERD and CMW may be explained by widespread views holding that racial discrimination is alien to the Turkish context,[36] and that Turkey is a migrant sender country rather than a migrant receiving one.[37] The lack of ratification of OP-CESCR coheres with views concerning the non-justiciability of economic, social and cultural rights under the Turkish Constitution.[38]

4.1.2   Domestic Processes

The top-down dynamics and concerns for its international reputation that drove Turkey's increased commitment to the UN human rights treaties also help to explain the lack of long-standing legislative engagement with UN treaties as a basis for domestic legal reform in the country. Turkey has not carried out broad consultative processes to make its legal frameworks compatible with the UN human rights treaties prior to the ratification of these treaties. In legislative changes following ratification, explicit references to UN treaties are scarce. Yet, in the preceding decades there have also been many legal reforms that indeed have brought domestic legal frameworks more in line with the UN treaties and their interpretations by their committees. However, these legal reforms correspond to the dynamics of Turkey's EU membership negotiations. In addition, there are no clear, public and transparent domestic institutional mechanisms to follow up on COs and views by UNTBS. COs are neither systematically translated nor disseminated by state authorities. There therefore is a very important information gap about the COs of UNTBS.

---

35   Interview with Asst Prof Dr Murat Önok.
36   See Section 5.1. on CERD.
37   See Section 5.7 on CMW.
38   See Section 5.3 on CESCR.

4.1.3 State Reporting

Overall, Turkey is slow in reporting. Significantly, following the ratification of the twin Covenants in 2003, it has reported only once, its next reports being more than seven years late. The trend repeats itself with respect to CAT: Turkey is overdue to report by eight years. Turkey fares better concerning its reports to CRC, CEDAW and CERD. The Ministry of Foreign Affairs explains that these delays are not due to an unwillingness to report, but due to bureaucratic delays and the length of time that is required to compile the required information from all state agencies.[39]

There are cross-cutting issues in the reports which Turkey has submitted to the UNTBs which have been asked by the various treaty bodies to make further progress and undertake legal reforms. The first common area of concern is Turkey's reservations. All UNTBs have issued calls for Turkey to withdraw these. Closely related to this is the concern over the protection of rights of those belonging to minorities, in particular the rights of Kurdish citizens. Women's rights, and the need to take comprehensive steps to end violence against women, are also a cross-cutting issue. Finally, all UNTBs have called on Turkey to establish a national human rights institution (NHRI) in line with the Paris Principles.

4.2 Overall Impact of UN Human Rights Treaties

In respect of all these common areas of concern there has been no significant progress, with one exception: the creation of a NHRI. Turkey first established a NHRI in 2014 entitled the Human Rights Institution and subsequently reconstituted it as the Human Rights and Equality Institution in 2016. Yet, the top-down creation of this institution has attracted strong domestic civil society criticism, noting that this institution does not fulfill the criteria of independence under the UN Paris Principles,[40] and that it falls significantly short in terms of the UN's definition of equality and investigative powers. This institution has not received accreditation in line with the Paris Principles.

The impact of the UN treaties on judicial decision making varies from treaty to treaty and also between the Constitutional Court, other apex courts and first instance courts. A key difficulty in this regard is the lack of public reporting of

---

39   Interview with the Ministry of Foreign Affairs.
40   In 2016 nearly 30 Turkish civil society organisations signed a petition entitled Bu Kanunla Olmaz ('Repeal This Law') to underline problems with the law establishing the Human Rights and Equality Institution <https://bukanunlaolmaz.wordpress.com> accessed 24 March 2022.

court decisions in Turkey and the absence of comprehensive databases of all case law, as well as the dearth of academic studies on citations of UN treaties and their COs and General Comments.

Based on our research of the publicly available judgments of the Constitutional Court, the High Court of Appeals and the Council of State, we find that CRC attracts the most frequent references, in particular its 'best interests of the child' maxim and the right to participation (article 12 of CRC) followed by references to CEDAW. In contrast, references to CRPD, CERD, CMW, CAT, CCPR and CESCR are scarce. The references at the level of the Constitutional Court, however, after the introduction of the right to individual petition in 2012, demonstrate that the Constitutional Court is open to making use of all UN treaties that Turkey has ratified as persuasive authority alongside the case law of the European Court of Human Rights. There has been one case in which the Constitutional Court has relied on CCPR to offer a more permissive interpretation of religious freedom than the one offered by the European Court.[41]

Data collected through interviews with members of civil society and academia shows that the reach of the UN human rights treaties in domestic advocacy, teaching and research, is thin. Overall, interlocutors point to the fact that UN human rights treaties are not well known.[42] Some also point to the fact that knowing the names of treaties such as CRC and CEDAW does not mean that actors are fully versed in their content and transformative potential.[43] In the case of CEDAW, some also point out that despite a general level of awareness, the treaty is only partially invoked. For example, no systematic attention is paid to the protection of the economic and social rights of women by CEDAW.[44]

Several factors are put forward to explain the meagre reach of UN treaties in Turkey. First and foremost, there is an important language barrier to accessing the UN treaty body mechanisms and their outputs. While most decisions against Turkey from the European Court of Human Rights are translated by the Ministry of Justice and are comparatively accessible, this is not the case with UN treaty body documents. The translation of these documents does not fall squarely within the mandate of a specific agency or ministry. This means that while some of these documents are translated by specialised

---

41 Turkish Constitutional Court, App No 2014/256 (25 June 2016).
42 Interview with Emel Ataktürk Sevimli; interview with Hakan Özgül and Süleyman Akbulut, Social Rights and Research Society (TOHAD), 24 September 2019, Istanbul, Turkey; interview with Murat Köylü, Kaos GL, 26 November 2019, Istanbul, Turkey.
43 Interview with Adem Arkadaş Thibert.
44 Interview with Prof Dr Bertil Emrah Oder.

ministries, or by civil society initiatives, most of them are not. Second, there are no institutionalised domestic channels of input to the treaty reporting process by civil society. The lack of domestic channels of engagement only leaves the opportunity to engage with the system through shadow reports. Yet, members of civil society in Turkey face resource and capacity problems to engage with UNTBs. The EU is the key funder of civil society organisations in Turkey. Domestic philanthropic sources are scarce and often do not support rights-based advocacy efforts, but rather development projects in the fields of women's empowerment, public health and education. These barriers are also confirmed by the number of domestic shadow reports submitted to the UN treaty bodies. To this day, most of the shadow reports submitted to the UN are prepared by international non-governmental organisations (NGOs) or NGOs that work outside Turkey rather than domestic organisations. The fact that the state authorities write their reports only in English further inhibits the participation of NGOs in shadow reporting. There are, however, exceptions to this pattern as seen by the shadow reports submitted to CEDAW, CAT and CRPD.

International human rights law is not part of the compulsory curriculum of law schools in Turkey. While some universities have made this compulsory, in many others it is either an elective course or not offered at all. Courses in the fields of constitutional, criminal and public law may include references to human rights law, but the case law of the European Court takes the centre stage in these courses.[45] In public international law courses, too, international human rights law may be covered as a single module at best. This means that most lawyers have a very limited knowledge of UN human rights treaties at the time of their graduation from law school. Legal professional education, too, is primarily geared towards learning to bring complaints before the European Court. Having said this, there has been recent interest in learning more about UN petition mechanisms in Turkey[46] due to the dissatisfaction with the slow progression of cases before the European Court and the large number of cases from Turkey that are declared inadmissible.

---

45 Interview with Prof Dr Bertil Emrah Oder; interview with Asst Prof Dr Murat Önok.
46 Interview with Tuğçe Duygu Köksal, Istanbul Bar Association Human Rights Centre, 29 July 2019, Istanbul, Turkey; interview with Dr Kerem Altıparmak.

5 Detailed Impact of the Different UN Human Rights Treaties on the Domestic Level in Turkey

5.1 *International Convention on the Elimination of All Forms of Racial Discrimination*

5.1.1 Incorporation and Reliance by the Legislature and Executive

Since its ratification of CERD in 2002, Turkey has had a number of reforms in its domestic frameworks that relate to CERD. In 2002. the changes to the Law on Foreign Language Education and Teaching enabled the opening of private courses to teach local languages other than Turkish.[47] In 2004, the new Penal Code criminalised incitement to hatred (article 216). In 2011, the law prohibited defamation and discrimination on the basis of race or colour in media services.[48] In 2013, the Criminal Procedural Code was amended to allow defendants to express themselves in languages other than Turkish.[49] In 2014, the election law was changed to allow the use of languages other than Turkish in election campaigns.[50]

In addition to these legal changes, the most notable public policy giving effect to the provisions of CERD was the 'democratic opening' or 'Kurdish opening' which was initiated in 2009. This was aimed at increasing democratic standards and preventing terrorism, and paved the way for peace negotiations called 'the reconciliation process'. This initiative officially started in 2013, but collapsed in 2016. Subsequently, this democratic initiative was also extended to the Roma. Yet, in none of these changes was CERD cited as a reason. Thus, while the congruence of the domestic framework and CERD has increased over time, it is not possible to attribute such changes to the ratification of the treaty as such.

5.1.2 Reliance by the Judiciary

CERD is not a treaty that receives a significant number of citations by the domestic courts. It has been cited only once by the High Court of Appeals,[51] and twice by the Turkish Constitutional Court. In the latter cases, the Turkish

---

47   Law No 4771, art 11.
48   The Law on the Establishment of Radio and Television Enterprises and Their Media Services, arts 8 and 9.
49   Law No 6411, art 1.
50   Law No 6529, art 1.
51   The High Court of Appeals, File No 2017/4–1734 Decision No 2018/668 (4 April 2018).

Constitutional Court referred to the definition of racial discrimination in article 1(1) and to articles 2 and 4 of CERD.[52]

5.1.3 Impact on and through Independent State Institutions

The Human Rights and Equality Institution of Turkey has the competence to receive individual applications alleging violations of non-discrimination and issue administrative sanctions. However, the Institution has not cited or applied CERD in individual applications. This is also the case for the office of the Ombudsman.

5.1.4 Impact on and through Non-state Actors

CERD has had a very slight impact on non-state actors. None of the interlocutors reviewed for this report viewed CERD as a well-known treaty in Turkey. The monitoring process before the CERD Cttee, however, attracted the attention of ten different international and domestic organisations. Although international reporting organisations outnumber domestic organisations, it is important to note that all domestic NGOs submitted their shadow reports in 2015 without collaborating with an international organisation.

5.1.5 Impact of State Reporting

Turkey submitted two reports to the CERD Cttee: the first in 2007 and the second in 2014. The 2007 report contains strong statements such as 'racial segregation or apartheid are concepts alien to the Turkish society'[53] and 'anti-Semitism has traditionally been alien to Turkish society'.[54] This approach is also followed in the 2014 report which states that 'in the fight against terrorism, Turkey does not discriminate in purpose or effect on the grounds of race, color or any other grounds, and individuals are not subjected to racial or other profiling or stereotyping',[55] and that the 'concept of racial discrimination by those who rent or sell houses or apartments is alien to Turkish society'.[56]

In the COs, the CERD Cttee asked Turkey to make specific legal adjustments by adopting a clear and comprehensive definition of racial discrimination

---

52 Turkish Constitutional Court, File No 2009/47, Decision No 2011/51 (17 March 2011); Turkish Constitutional Court – GK, B. 2014/12225 T. 14.7.2015.
53 Third periodic reports of state parties due in 2007 – Addendum – Turkey, 13 February 2008, CERD/C/TUR/3, para 88.
54 ibid para 137.
55 Combined fourth to sixth periodic reports of state parties due in 2013 – Turkey, 17 April 2014, CERD/C/TUR/4–6, para 85.
56 ibid para 114.

including all elements in article 1 of CERD;[57] ensuring that the interpretation and application of article 216 of the Turkish Penal Code are in compliance with article 4 of CERD;[58] ensuring that the new article 301 of the Turkish Penal Code is interpreted and applied in conformity with CERD;[59] enacting comprehensive anti-discrimination legislation covering all rights in article 5 of CERD,[60] including the motive of ethnic, racial or religious hatred as an aggravating circumstance in the Penal Code;[61] and considering further amendments to the legislation to allow the teaching of languages traditionally used in Turkey in the general public education system.[62]

Only a limited number of these recommendations have been implemented to date. With the entry into force of the Law establishing the Human Rights and Equality Institution of Turkey, the Committee's recommendations to enact comprehensive anti-discrimination legislation and to include ethnic origin as a protected ground have been implemented.[63] The Committee's recommendation to grant work permits to refugees has also been implemented by the coming into force of the Regulation on Work Permit of Refugees under Temporary Protection entered into force on 15 January 2016.[64]

Despite these positive developments towards implementation, some of the comments made by Turkey in the state reports or in the follow-up reports to the COs may be interpreted as showing its reluctance to implement the recommendations. The government, for example, does not intend to withdraw its reservations.[65] Furthermore, Turkey refuses to collect, maintain or use either qualitative or quantitative data on ethnicity since it 'is a sensitive issue, especially for those nations living in diverse multicultural societies for a long period of time'.[66]

---

57   ibid para 11.
58   ibid para 14.
59   ibid para 16.
60   ibid para 17.
61   ibid para 23.
62   ibid para 20.
63   The Law on Human Rights and Equality Institution of Turkey (Law No 6701) 2016, arts 2 and 3. This is included in the follow-up letter sent to the state party, 17 May 2017, CERD/92nd/FU/GH/HH/ks; see also information received from Turkey on follow-up to the COs, 9 February 2017, CERD/C/TUR/CO/4–6/Add.1, para 7–10.
64   CERD/C/TUR/CO/4–6/Add.1, para 93.
65   CERD/C/TUR/4–6, para 4.
66   CERD/C/TUR/4–6, para 7; Comments by the Government of Turkey on the COs of the Committee on the Elimination of Racial Discrimination, 30 March 2009, CERD/C/TUR/CO/3/ADD.1, para 5.

Regarding article 216 of the Penal Code, Turkey holds that the provision aims to strike a balance between freedom of expression and the obligation to combat incitement to hatred.[67] According to the follow-up report of 2009, the number of languages traditionally used in Turkey may reach into the hundreds and it therefore is beyond the capacity of the state to offer teaching in all of these languages in the public education system. Furthermore, Turkey argues that 'any act in favour of one or two languages traditionally used in Turkey can be interpreted as discrimination against other languages and their respective speakers'.[68]

Regarding the COs on the impact of anti-terror measures on the Kurdish community, Turkey has raised strong objections in the follow-up report of 2017. Turkey rejects the fact that its criminal procedure is discriminatory,[69] and calls for distinguishing between PKK terrorism and 'the possible legitimate expectations of the citizens of Kurdish origin in Turkey'.[70] Turkey's objections also extend to the recommendation on the elimination of economic disparities between Kurdish provinces and the rest of the country. Turkey stated that it is misleading to make a differentiation between provinces based on ethnicity and claimed that the fact that certain regions face economic hardship stems from geographical or economic characteristics of those regions and not from ethnicity, religion or language of the residents.[71]

The Committee, in its follow-up letter sent to Turkey on 17 May 2017, raised concerns about the implementation of recommendations with Syrian and Iraqi refugees. It noted the lack of information regarding the efforts to protect these refugees from racial discrimination and hatred, and the fact that mother tongue education is not provided to refugee children.[72]

5.1.6   Brief Conclusion

The impact of CERD since its ratification in 2002 in Turkey has been limited. This is partly due to the fact that Turkey maintains that racial discrimination is alien to Turkey and partly because the CERD Cttee's approach to the interpretation of the treaty incorporates the treatment of minorities. CERD also is not

---

[67]   CERD/C/TUR/3, para. 68–69; CERD/C/TUR/CO/3/ADD.1, para 4; CERD/C/TUR/CO/4–6/Add.1, paras 45–46.
[68]   CERD/C/TUR/CO/3/ADD.1, para 6.
[69]   CERD/C/TUR/CO/4–6/Add.1, para 52.
[70]   CERD/C/TUR/CO/4–6/Add.1, para 72.
[71]   CERD/C/TUR/CO/4–6/Add.1, para 74.
[72]   CERD/92nd/FU/GH/HH/ks.

a treaty to which the judiciary, the legal profession, civil society and academia have paid systematic attention since its ratification.

5.2 International Covenant on Civil and Political Rights

5.2.1 Incorporation and Reliance by Legislature and Executive

While no compatibility analysis of the domestic legal framework with CCPR was carried out prior to the ratification of CCPR in 2003, legal reforms undertaken in the 2000s have nevertheless increased the level of compatibility between the two. The abolition of the death penalty in peacetime in 2002[73] and the abolition of the death penalty in all circumstances, that is, inclusive of times of war or imminent threat of war, in 2004;[74] the new Labour Law No 4857;[75] and the new Penal Code No 5237[76] are notable examples. CCPR has been mentioned in the explanatory notes of some draft Bills.[77]

In addition to CCPR, Turkey ratified both OP1-CCPR and OP2-CCPR in 2006. In the explanatory notes for both ratifications, it was indicated that all EU members and EU candidates have already ratified the Protocol, that the ratification of the Protocol has been among the criteria Turkey has to fulfill according to the 2003 EU Accession Partnership document and that the ratification is necessary to become a party to international human rights law documents and to 'accelerate the completion of a comprehensive human rights framework'.[78]

---

[73] Law on the Amending Various Laws (No 4771) 2002, art 1.

[74] Law on the Abolishment of Death Penalty and on Amending Various Laws (No 5218) 2004.

[75] The most remarkable changes may be listed as change of the 'workplace' definition and introduction of 'flexible work' (art 2); introduction of the 'non-discrimination principle' for the workplace (art 5); introduction of 'job security' protection for the workers (arts 18–20); increase in the annual paid leave and maternal leave (arts 53, 74); integration of ILO standards for child labour (art 71); improvements regarding occupational health and safety (arts 80–83). For further information, see Celal Emiroğlu and Sultan Özer, 'Eski ve Yeni İş Yasası: Ne getirdi? Ne götürdü?' (2003) 4(15) Sağlık ve Güvenlik Dergisi (2003) 4–8.

[76] The new Penal Code has brought some positive changes in line with international human rights law standards, such as the introduction of genocide and crimes against humanity in the Penal Code for the very first time (arts 76–77) and the aggravation of sentences regarding gender-based violence (arts 102–105). However, it also includes restrictive and retrogressive articles considering freedom of the press and freedom of expression (art 218), and comprehensive regulations on crimes against the state (arts 247–339) and the crime of insulting the President (art 299).

[77] For example, the Explanatory Notes of the Draft Law on the Human Rights and Equality Institution of Turkey (28 January 2016) <https://www.tbmm.gov.tr/sirasayi/donem26/yil01/ss149.pdf> accessed 24 March 2022; Explanatory Notes of the Draft Law on the Execution of Punishments and Measures (30 November 2004) <https://www2.tbmm.gov.tr/d22/1/1-0933.pdf> accessed 24 March 2022.

[78] The explanatory notes are available at <https://www5.tbmm.gov.tr/tutanaklar/TUTANAK/TBMM/d22/c016/tbmm22016089ss0150.pdf> accessed 24 March 2022.

In the explanatory notes for the ratification of OP2-CCPR, particular emphasis is placed on the abolishment of the death penalty in 2004 through the constitutional amendment and Turkey's ratification of Protocols No 6 and 13 to the European Convention on Human Rights (ECHR).[79]

Turkey has officially informed the UN Secretary-General about the state of emergency in 2016 and derogated from CCPR. Following the end of the state of emergency on 19 July 2018, Turkey withdrew the derogation in accordance with article 4.[80]

5.2.2   Reliance by the Judiciary

Interviews with the representatives of human rights commissions of bar associations and NGOs indicate that CCPR in recent years has become one of the better-known UN human rights treaties among the judiciary.[81] Indeed, CCPR has been cited by the High Court of Appeals, the Constitutional Court and the Council of State. However, courts in general do not provide detailed discussions of the scope of the provisions, general comments or case law, but instead refer only to the relevant articles in the cases that we reviewed.[82] We have found CCPR citations in at least 26 decisions of the General Assembly of Civil Chambers and Penal Chambers of the High Court of Appeals. The Constitutional Court has referred to CCPR in 39 individual application decisions, with 18 of these including references to the General Comments or the COs of the HRCttee. Among them, references to General Comment 22, which further explains article 18 stand out.[83] The Council of State has referred to CCPR in four decisions. Compared to the references to the jurisprudence of the European Court, references to CCPR are rare.

---

79   The explanatory notes are available at <https://www5.tbmm.gov.tr/tutanaklar/TUTANAK/TBMM/d22/c094/tbmm22094004ss0793.pdf> accessed 24 March 2022.
80   Answer by Minister of Foreign Affairs to the Written Question No 7/633 submitted by MP Kamil Okyay Sındır (11 January 2019) <https://www2.tbmm.gov.tr/d27/7/7-0633sgc.pdf> accessed 24 March 2022.
81   Interview with Dr Kerem Altıparmak; interview with Tuğçe Duygu Köksal.
82   There are 71 decisions that include at least one reference to ICCPR. This information was reached via LexPera through searching for 'Medeni ve Siyasi Haklara İlişkin Uluslararası Sözleşme' on 29 January 2020.
83   Some of these cases include Turkish Constitutional Court Decision No 2015/51 (27 May 2015); Turkish Constitutional Court Decision No 2014/17354 (22 May 2019); Turkish Constitutional Court Decision No 2009/4 (11 December 2009); Turkish Constitutional Court Decision No 2016/22169 (20 June 2017).

5.2.3 Impact on and through Independent State Institutions

The Ombudsman cited CCPR in 22 decisions. These citations are mostly made to articles 5, 6, 17, 18, 19, and 25(c). One reference has been made to the HRCttee's General Comment 25 on the right to participate in public affairs, voting rights and the right of equal access to public service.[84] There are seven decisions[85] by the Equality and Human Rights Institution of Turkey in which CCPR has been briefly mentioned, with a specific emphasis on article 7 and one reference to the HRCttee's General Comment 22 on the right to freedom of thought, conscience and religion.

5.2.4 Impact on and through Non-state Actors

Given the significant level of overlap between the ECHR and CCPR in terms of their coverage of civil and political rights, CCPR competes with the ECHR for the attention of civil society. Yet, there is evidence that the increased difficulty of accessing the ECtHR has enhanced interest in the individual petition mechanisms of CCPR among the Turkish legal profession. There is increasing demand and interest towards training on the individual petition mechanisms, according to the representative of the bar associations.[86] There also is an increase in the knowledge and visibility of CCPR, specifically after the *coup* attempt in 2016 and the cases following thousands of expulsions. During our interviews, many NGOs stated that CCPR is one of the well-known UN human rights treaties among human rights activists, particularly in terms of the right to life, citizenship, non-discrimination and self-determination. The low level of ownership of UN human rights treaties within the judiciary, the political discourse and the curricula of law schools are criticised by academics and NGOs.[87] However, they have also noted that CCPR and the HRC jurisprudence was referred to by the Constitutional Court concerning freedom of religion cases and, particularly, in cases concerning the wearing of headscarves.[88]

---

[84] The Ombudsman Institution of Turkey, File No 2015/2608 (27 October 2015) para 17.4.

[85] Equality and Human Rights Institution of Turkey, File No 2018/99 (30 October 2018); Equality and Human Rights Institution of Turkey, File No 2018/99 (30 October 2018); Equality and Human Rights Institution of Turkey, File No 2018/83 (18 July 2018); Equality and Human Rights Institution of Turkey, File No 2019/04 (8 January 2019); Equality and Human Rights Institution of Turkey, File No 2019/07 (12 February 2019); Equality and Human Rights Institution of Turkey, File No 2019/24 (9 April 2019); Equality and Human Rights Institution of Turkey, File No 2019/26 (16 April 2019).

[86] Interview with Tuğçe Duygu Köksal; interview with Asst Prof Dr Kerem Altıparmak.

[87] Interview with Prof Dr Bertil Emrah Oder; interview with Asst Prof Dr Murat Önok.

[88] Turkish Constitutional Court, App No 2014/256 (25 June 2014); Turkish Constitutional Court, App No 2013/7443 (20 May 2015); interview with Prof Dr Bertil Emrah Oder.

5.2.5 State Reporting and Its Impact

Turkey has submitted only one initial report to the HRCttee, in 2011. Turkey's second report, which has not yet been submitted, was due on 31 October 2016. The initial report states that consultations with civil society were held as part of the reporting process, and that civil society has provided decisive input in establishing priority issues in the report. However, detailed information is not available.[89]

Only a few COs and key recommendations have so far seen implementation. The Turkish NHRI was established in 2016, and its founding law includes provisions regarding anti-discrimination and equality and, thus, indirectly the law functions as anti-discrimination legislation. The recommendations regarding adopting a strict timeline to protect women and family members from violence, zero tolerance of so-called honour killings and awareness-raising programmes have been partially fulfilled through the ratification of the İstanbul Convention in 2011, the adoption of the Law on the Protection of Family and Prevention of Violence against Women No 6284 and the establishment of ŞÖNIMs (Centres for Prevention of Violence and Monitoring) in 2012, as well as the consecutive adoption of the National Action Plans for Combating Domestic Violence against Women (2007–2010), (2012–2015), and (2016–2020). Despite these policies and action plans, however, gender-based violence has in recent years increased.[90]

5.2.6 Impact of Individual Communications

The HRCttee found violations in three individual communications with respect to Turkey.

The first was delivered in the case of *Atasoy and Sarkut v Turkey* in 2012.[91] This case concerns the conscientious objection of two Jehovah's Witness citizens to military service, in which the Committee found a violation to the right to freedom of thought, conscience and religion under article 18, and that Turkey is under an obligation to provide the authors with an effective remedy, including expunging their criminal records and providing them with adequate compensation. No information has been found on whether Atasoy and Sarkut received individual remedies. To this day conscientious objection to military service is not permitted in Turkey.

---

89 CCPR/C/TUR/1, para 4.
90 See GREVIO, Baseline Evaluation Report: Turkey (2018) <https://rm.coe.int/eng-grevio-report-turquie/16808e5283> accessed 24 March 2022.
91 CCPR/C/104/D/1853–1854/2008 (19 March 2012).

The second individual communication is *Türkan v Turkey*, which was decided in 2018.[92] It concerns the refusal of university admission to the author, who was wearing a wig substituting for a head scarf, in which the Committee found a violation of article 18 (the right to freedom of thought, conscience and religion) and article 26 (anti-discrimination), and of article 3 (equal rights of men and women) read in conjunction with article 18, and stated that Turkey was obligated to provide the author with adequate compensation, including as a result of her lost employment opportunities, and to ensure that she is afforded the full opportunity to pursue her higher education studies, should she seek it. Turkey explained that due to recent amendments of the Law No 2547 in 2008 on higher education, the author now is entitled to be enrolled and to continue her education. No information has been found whether Türkan has received compensation. By the time this case was decided, Turkey had already liberalised the legal regime on limiting the wearing of headscarves in all public institutions.

The third communication is *Özçelik, Karaman and IA v Turkey*, delivered in 2019.[93] This case concerns two individuals who are considered to be connected to the Gülen movement by the Turkish authorities and who were detained and forcibly removed from Malaysia without an extradition hearing or a judicial decision. The Committee, recalling that a derogation (following the *coup* attempt on 15 July 2016) cannot justify a deprivation of liberty that is unreasonable or unnecessary, found a violation of article 9 (the right to liberty and security) of the Covenant, and asked Turkey to release Özçelik and Karaman within 180 days and to provide them with adequate compensation for the violations. Turkey contested the admissibility of both communications on grounds of non-exhaustion of domestic remedies, and argued that the authors' claims under articles 9, 10 and 14 are inadmissible as Turkey had derogated from the Covenant in accordance with article 4. Özçelik and Karaman have not been released although the 180-day period has passed. This is the first opinion adopted by the HRCttee considering arbitrary detention and derogations in the aftermath of the *coup* attempt in Turkey, and the opinion was covered in the media.[94] No information has been found on any kind of follow-up

---

92 CCPR/C/123/D/2274/2013 (17 July 2018).
93 CCPR/C/125/D/2980/2017 (26 March 2019).
94 Büşra Taşkıran, 'BM'nin uygulanması için Türkiye'ye 180 gün verdiği karar hakkında hukukçular ne diyor?' Euronews (1 July 2019) <https://tr.euronews.com/2019/07/01/bm-nin-uygulanmasi-icin-turkiyeye-180-gun-verdigi-karari-hakkinda-hukukcular-ne-diyor> accessed 24 March 2022.

concerning implementations, either concerning individual redress for Özçelik and Karaman, or broader legal reform.

5.2.7 Brief Conclusion

While the Turkish legal framework has over time become more compatible with CCPR, this is largely a consequence of EU pressures to make Turkish institutions more compatible with European human rights law. In some other fields, such as freedom of religion, Turkey has aligned more closely with the HRCttee case law.

5.3 *International Covenant on Economic, Social and Cultural Rights*

5.3.1 Incorporation and Reliance by Legislature and Executive

As is the case with CCPR, Turkey did not carry out a compatibility analysis prior to the ratification of CESCR in 2003. However, legal reforms undertaken in the 2000s also improved the compatibility of domestic legal frameworks with CESCR. Some major domestic legislative changes of this kind include the new Labour Law No 4857, which has partially improved workers' rights, and the Social Security and Universal Health Insurance Law No 5510, which introduced the private pension system and a new system for universal health care.

Turkey has still not signed or ratified OP-CESCR. During the 46th session of the CESCR Cttee in 2011, in which Turkey's initial report was considered, the Turkish delegation could not give any date for ratification, but assured the Committee that Turkey was examining the matter.

5.3.2 Reliance by the Judiciary

The provisions of CESCR have been relied upon by the High Court of Appeals, the Council of State and the Constitutional Court in a number of decisions. However, the courts have not discussed these clauses in detail, but instead have only referred to the relevant articles in general terms, either by only mentioning the relevant article or by citing the Turkish texts of the articles without additional comments. We found CESCR citations in at least six decisions of the General Assembly of Civil Chambers and Penal Chambers of the High Court of Appeals.[95] The Constitutional Court has referred to CESCR in 14 decisions; in nine of them there are references to the General Comments of the

---

[95] There are 40 decisions including at least one reference to CESCR. This information is reached via LexPera through searching for 'Ekonomik, Sosyal ve Kültürel Haklara İlişkin Uluslararası Sözleşme' on 29 January 2020.

Committee.[96] Concerning labour-related rights, references to ILO Conventions rather than CESCR are dominant in the jurisprudence.

5.3.3 Impact on and through Independent State Institutions

The involvement of the Ombudsman Institution and the Equality and Human Rights Institution of Turkey with the Convention or the Committee is very limited. There are only two Ombudsman decisions[97] among those published on their official website that have cited CESCR, which is limited to the text of the relevant clauses only.

5.3.4 Impact on and through Non-state Actors

NGOs have undertaken some activities with a focus on CESCR. In particular, the Human Rights Agenda Association has authored, published and distributed a booklet that explains social, economic and cultural rights in accessible language. Although several NGOs have acknowledged CESCR as an important UN human rights treaty, it is not well-known or widely used by civil society.[98] Academics and NGOs agree that although economic and social rights could have been a rather easier area to campaign for (from a developmental point of view and considering rights on non-political areas) labour unions are not at all active considering the Covenant.[99] Indeed, labour unions have not been actively involved with CESCR and no labour unions have submitted a shadow report.

5.3.5 Impact of State Reporting

Turkey submitted its initial report to the CESCR Cttee in 2008 after a four-year delay. Turkey's second report was due in 2016. In the initial report, there are no references to any consultation with civil society. Only a few key recommendations made in the COs have to date been implemented. Apart from the regular operations and projects of the Ministry of Family, Labour and Social Services

---

96 Some of these cases are Turkish Constitutional Court Decision No 2011/6 (26 January 2012); Turkish Constitutional Court Decision No 2015/68 (29 November 2017); Turkish Constitutional Court Decision No 2012/174 (8 November 2012; The High Court of Appeals 17th Penal Chamber, File No 2015/15665 Decision No 2015/10872 (10 December 2015); The High Court of Appeals 17th Penal Chamber, File No 2016/5390 Decision No 2017/15604 (11 December 2017); The High Court of Appeals 13th Penal Chamber, File No 2014/36407 Decision No 2016/659 (18 January 2016).

97 The Ombudsman Institution of Turkey, File No 03.2013/687 (6 March 2014) para 10; The Ombudsman Institution of Turkey, File No 04.2003/1707 (26 February 2014) para 85.

98 Interview with Adem Arkadaş Thibert.

99 ibid.

regarding assistance to older persons, the rights of disabled people, rural development and youth employment, which might be considered as partially fulfilling the relevant recommendations of the Committee to take measures in these areas, no specific action has been taken to implement the recommendations. No parliamentary questions were raised and no draft legislations were proposed as a result of the COs.[100]

5.3.6 Brief Conclusion

The impact of CESCR in Turkey has been limited, except in the case of crosscutting recommendations such as that of establishing the national human rights institution. There have also been times when the object of CESCR and Turkish domestic policy have aligned, such as was the case with social security reform. A central explanation for the lack of deeper impact of CESCR in Turkey concerns the limitations to the justiciability of economic social and cultural rights directly under the Turkish Constitution. Whilst the Turkish Constitution recognises state duties with respect to social and economic rights,[101] these parts of the Constitution are not justiciable as a matter of individual rights.

5.4 Convention on the Elimination of All Forms of Discrimination against Women

5.4.1 Incorporation and Reliance by Legislature and Executive

CEDAW is the longest-standing human rights treaty adhered to by Turkey. Following its ratification in 1985, a significant number of legislative reforms brought the legal and constitutional framework in line with the Convention. The rise of women's rights activism, particularly second-wave feminism in Turkey, and the ratification of CEDAW has coincided with an era of post-*coup* democratisation in the mid-1980s.[102] This started with the reform of the Civil Code in 2001 to define a family as an entity that is 'based on equality between the spouses', removing the previous recognition of the man as the head of family; the reform of rights over the family domicile and representational power; and the equalisation of minimum marriage ages for both sexes. In 2004, equality between men and women was added into article 10 of the Constitution. In 2010, the inclusion of the provision 'any measures to be taken to this aim shall not be contrary to the principle of equality' provided the constitutional recognition of temporary special measures. The Turkish Penal Code also saw significant improvements in 2005 with the amendment of the 'hatred and

---

100 E/C.12/TUR/CO/1/Add.1, para 3.
101 Constitution of the Republic of Turkey, art 65.
102 Interview with Prof Dr Bertil Emrah Oder.

discrimination' provisions, specific amendments to combat violence against women, the criminalisation of marital rape and harassment at the workplace. Turkey also introduced the Law on Protection of Family and Prevention of Violence against Women No 6284 in 2012. In addition, between 2011 and 2014, 31 laws were reviewed with a gender perspective in consultation with local governments and NGOs.[103]

CEDAW has received several mentions during the parliamentary discussions concerning women's rights: A total of eight written questions from parliamentary members to the government have been submitted solely on the implementation of CEDAW provisions.[104] The Minister Responsible for Women's Affairs (which ministry was later put under the command of the Minister of Family, Labour and Social Services) often responded to these questions in a timely manner. There are also several mentions of CEDAW among the minutes of the general meetings of Parliament, particularly in the course of discussions regarding violence against women.[105]

Turkey has adopted general national action plans in the field of women's rights and in a majority of these national action plans, there are explicit references to CEDAW articles, state reports, COs and shadow reports.[106]

Alongside these, a range of institutions have been established that relate directly to the implementation of CEDAW. In 2002, the National Task Force to Combat Trafficking was founded.[107] In 2004, the General Directorate on the Status and Problems of Women was restructured and the Directorate on the Status of Women was established.[108] In 2007, the Monitoring Committee on Violence Against Women was founded.[109] In 2009, the Parliamentary

---

103   CEDAW/C/TUR/7, para 23. For the report (in Turkish) see Kevin Devaux, Toplumsal Cinsiyet Eşitliği Mevzuatının Uygulanmasının İzlenmesi Raporu (2014) < http://ceidizleme.org/ekutuphaneresim/dosya/367_1.pdf > accessed 24 March 2022.
104   For example, Answer by Minister Responsible for Women's Affairs to the Written Question No 7/10647 submitted by MP Nevin Gaye Erbatur (27 October 2009); Answer by Minister Responsible for Women's Affairs to the Written Question No 7/21722 submitted by MP Ayşe Gülsün Bilgehan (23 March 2007) <https://cdn.tbmm.gov.tr/KKBSPublicFile/D22/Y5/T7/WebOnergeMetni/986f8d03-f384-4185-b7dd-4fe05393ccec .pdf> accessed 24 March 2022.
105   For example, Speech by MP Mehmet Şandır (22 November 2011) <https://www5.tbmm .gov.tr//develop/owa/Tutanak_B_SD.birlesim_baslangic?P4=21045&P5=B&PAGE1 =81&PAGE2=86> accessed 24 March 2022.
106   CEDAW/C/TUR/6 at 63; CEDAW/C/TUR/7, para 197.
107   ibid 21.
108   ibid 5.
109   CEDAW/C/TUR/6, 12.

Commission on Equal Opportunities for Women and Men (KEFEK) was established.[110] The Commission monitors and informs Parliament of national and international developments with respect to gender equality, and provides opinions upon request on draft laws and decree laws submitted to Parliament. Following the adoption of Law No 6284 to Protect Family and Prevent Violence Against Women (2012), Centres for Preventing and Monitoring Violence (ŞÖNİM) have also been established nationwide.[111]

5.4.2   Reliance by the Judiciary

Interviews with the representatives of human rights commissions of bar associations and NGOs indicate that CEDAW is among the better-known UN human rights treaties among the judiciary.[112] We found CEDAW citations[113] in over 100 decisions of the General Assembly of Civil Chambers and Penal Chambers of the High Court of Appeals. The Turkish Constitutional Court has referred to CEDAW in 15 individual application decisions and the Council of State has referred to CCPR in four decisions. On the one hand, in the majority of these judgments the clauses were not discussed in detail and the relevant articles were merely cited. On the other hand, the Constitutional Court has used CEDAW as a basis for progressive legal interpretation in a few precedent-setting cases. In 1990, the Constitutional Court annulled article 159 of the former Civil Code which required the permission of the husband for married women to work outside the home.[114] In 1998, it annulled articles 440 and 441 of the former Penal Code which demarcated a husband's and wife's adultery on separate grounds.[115] In 2013, in the case of *Sevim Akat Eşki*,[116] the Constitutional Court found the automatic change of a woman's name after marriage unconstitutional. The judiciary overall, however, refers to CEDAW less than the jurisprudence of the ECtHR and the Istanbul Convention. Despite this, CEDAW clauses, jurisprudence and General Comments are well-known among lawyers

---

110   CEDAW/C/TUR/6, 5.
111   CEDAW/C/TUR/CO/6/Add.1, para 32.
112   Interview with Prof Dr Bertil Emrah Oder; interview with Tuğçe Duygu Köksal.
113   There are 127 decisions including at least one reference to CEDAW. This information is reached via LexPera through searching for 'Kadınlara Karşı Her Türlü Ayrımcılığın Önlenmesi Sözleşmesi' on 29 January 2020.
114   Turkish Constitutional Court, App No 1990/30 (29 November 1990).
115   Turkish Constitutional Court, App No 1998/3 (23 June 1998).
116   Turkish Constitutional Court, App No 2013/2187 (19 December 2013) para 43.

who specialise in gender-based violence cases and are often used by women's rights NGOs in their petitions concerning cases of gender-based violence.[117]

5.4.3 Impact on and through Independent State Institutions

CEDAW has been named as one of the most well-known and most widely used UNTBs by Ombudsperson Tunçak.[118] We found two Ombudsman decisions[119] among those published on their official website that have cited provisions of CEDAW. The Human Rights and Equality Institution of Turkey, on the other hand, hosted several conferences in which women's rights were discussed exclusively as a part of the family unit and several panelists have heavily criticised CEDAW and the Istanbul Convention for not being in line with traditional Islamic family values.[120]

5.4.4 Impact on and through Non-state Actors

Women's rights NGOs and activists have been very actively involved with the Committee and the procedures since the ratification of the Convention. CEDAW's impact on civil society has been far greater than its impact on the judiciary or the political discourse in Turkey.[121] It is not possible to state that the ratification process has been the outcome of the civil society efforts only; rather, the progressive political atmosphere has contributed significantly.[122] However, after the ratification, several petitions have been launched by women's rights NGOs, activists and prominent feminist academics for the implementation of CEDAW clauses and for the withdrawal of reservations.[123] One of the most prominent of these campaigns led to the amendment of the Civil Code. Women's rights NGOs not only succeeded in collecting hundreds of thousands of signatures for this campaign,[124] but also used CEDAW effectively to enable the legal redefinition 'family' as an entity that is based on equality

---

117 Interview with Yeşim Erkan Yetişer, Women for Women's Human Rights – New Ways, 9 October 2019, Istanbul, Turkey; interview with Tuğçe Duygu Köksal; interview with Adem Arkadaş Thibert.
118 Interview with Celile Özlem Tunçak, Ombudsperson, 16 October 2019 Ankara, Turkey.
119 The Ombudsman Institution of Turkey, File No 2013/2 (20 September 2013) para 68; The Ombudsman Institution of Turkey, File No 04.2003.1707 (26 February 2014) para 83.
120 Human Rights and Equality Institution of Turkey, Final Declaration of the II. Human Rights Symposium on the Right to Protection of the Family (2019) <https://www.tihek.gov.tr/ailenin-korunmasi-hakki-sonuc-bildirisi/> accessed 24 March 2022.
121 Interview with Prof Dr Bertil Emrah Oder.
122 Interview with Prof Dr Ayşe Feride Acar.
123 ibid.
124 ibid.

between the spouses and to eliminate discriminatory clauses in the Civil Code. A collective for NGOS named the Executive Committee for NGO Forum on CEDAW has been established for the specific purpose of preparing shadow reports to be submitted to CEDAW. This NGO collective has presented detailed, high-quality shadow reports through consecutive reporting cycles.

NGOS, academics and representatives of bar associations view CEDAW as among the most well-known and used UN human rights treaties within civil society.[125] The state has been in a closer dialogue with the NGOs considering CEDAW compared to other UNTBS: For example, consultation meetings have been organised by the General Directorate on the Status of Women and several NGOS have been invited. CEDAW has been described as the constitution of women's human rights by the women's rights movement.[126] Academics and NGOS acknowledge the lack of clauses considering gender-based violence and employment in CEDAW.[127] However, they emphasise article 5 on stereotyping and cultural prejudices and article 4 on affirmative action as major achievements. Article 4 has been the basis for arguments in favour of affirmative action in Turkey, particularly considering quota systems for women's participation in politics and regarding the introduction of the affirmative action concept to the Turkish Constitution.[128]

5.4.5 Impact of State Reporting

Turkey has submitted a series of reports to CEDAW, in all cases accompanied by delay. In its reports Turkey stated that all state reports have been prepared in a participatory process, integrating the contributions of relevant government agencies, academicians and NGOS.[129] This has also been confirmed by NGO representatives.[130] In addition, the NGO Forum on CEDAW, a civil society collective consisting of 20 independent women's rights organisations, was established with a view to submit regular shadow reports to CEDAW.

Regarding the implementation of the key recommendations of COs, it has been stated by the Committee in the 2005 COs that Turkey has implemented some of the recommended legal reforms aimed at the promotion of gender

---

125 Interview with Yeşim Erkan Yetişer; interview with Tuğçe Duygu Köksal; interview with Adem Arkadaş Thibert.
126 Interview with Prof Dr Bertil Emrah Oder.
127 Interview with Prof Dr Ayşe Feride Acar; interview with Prof Dr Bertil Emrah Oder.
128 Interview with Prof Dr Bertil Emrah Oder.
129 CEDAW/C/TUR/6, 3.
130 Interview with Yeşim Erkan Yetişer; interview with Beydağ Tıraş Öneri and Özlem Yılmaz, Human Rights Agenda Association, 4 July 2019, Istanbul, Turkey.

equality and the elimination of discrimination against women, and combating domestic violence, such as the amendments of articles 10 and 90 of the Constitution, the adoption of the Civil Code of 2001, the Penal Code of 2004 and the criminalisation of marital rape.[131] The Committee also noted that Turkey has increased the duration of compulsory education from five to eight years with a focus on increasing the enrolment of girls, and ratified the Optional Protocol to the Convention, in accordance with the previous recommendations.[132] Turkey has also withdrawn its declaration to article 9, paragraph 1, of the Convention in 2008.[133]

In addition, a wide range of legislative measures, policies and programmes have been adopted, in accordance with the recommendations of the Committee such as the adoption of the Gender Equality National Action Plan, the amendments to the Penal Code to combat violence against women, the creation of the Parliamentary Commission on Equal Opportunities for Women and Men,[134] the adoption of the Law No 6284 on the Prevention of Violence against Women and the Protection of the Family in 2012,[135] and the National Action Plan on the empowerment of rural women (2012–2016).[136]

Turkey has actively engaged in the follow-up procedures and provided follow-up reports and additional information in reply to the follow-up letters.

5.4.6   Impact of Individual Communications

The CEDAW Cttee has examined three individual complaints. While *Rahime Kayhan v Turkey*[137] and *NM v Turkey*[138] were found inadmissible, the Committee found a violation in one instance, *RKB v Turkey*.[139]

RKB v Turkey is a unique case about a female hairdresser dismissed from her position based on a claim of having an affair with a male colleague, while the male colleague was not dismissed. RKB claimed that her employer had unfairly

---

131   A/60/38(SUPP) paras 350–387.
132   ibid para 346.
133   CEDAW/C/TUR/CO/6, para 4.
134   ibid paras 5–7.
135   CEDAW/C/TUR/CO/7, paras 4–6.
136   ibid para 6.
137   *Rahime Kayhan v Turkey*, CEDAW/C/34/D/8/2005 (27 January 2006). The case concerns the expulsion of a civil servant woman from her teaching position for wearing a headscarf at the workplace. This was found inadmissible by the Committee due to a failure to exhaust domestic remedies.
138   *NM v Turkey* CEDAW/C/70/D/92/2015 (9 July 2018). The case was submitted by a Singaporean woman who was married to a Turkish man and had two children by him. It was found inadmissible due to a failure to exhaust domestic remedies.
139   *RKB v Turkey* CEDAW/C/51/D/28/2010 (24 February 2012).

terminated her contract of employment based on gender stereotypes. The first degree labour court ruled that dismissing her but not her male colleague was not discriminatory but only that the termination was unjustified, and the Court of Cassation dismissed the appeal without reference to gender discrimination. Turkey claimed that the violation claims of the author were manifestly ill-founded and not sufficiently substantiated, and that she had been dismissed on the grounds that she failed to have regular work attendance and did not act in line with business ethics, without properly mentioning the gender stereotypes aspect of the case. The CEDAW Cttee concluded that the Turkish courts based their decisions on gender stereotypes, tolerating allegations of extramarital relationships by male employees but not by female employees and that articles 5(a), 11(1a) and 11(1d) of CEDAW had been violated.[140] The Committee also emphasised that despite the appropriate legislative measures, the state has an obligation to improve women's position in society and to eliminate wrongful stereotypes.[141] The Committee decided that adequate compensation should be paid; that the state should take measures to implement laws on gender equality in the work environment; and that the state should provide training to judges, lawyers and law enforcement personnel on women's rights and gender-based stereotypes.[142]

Regarding the implementation of this decision, the Working Group on Communications under OP-CEDAW reported in 2015 the finding of a partly satisfactory implementation of the Committee's recommendations concerning the *RKB* case.[143] In an addendum to the 2014 state report, Turkey reported that although the first degree labour court refused the demand for a retrial – with the justification that the decisions of the CEDAW Cttee, which are advisory in nature, do not provide the conditions for a retrial and that a retrial requires a final decision by the Turkish Constitutional Court – yet it also decided on a compensation payment of 4 446 Turkish Liras to RKB.[144]

---

140 *RKB v Turkey*, para 8.10.
141 ibid.
142 ibid.
143 CEDAW/C/2015/II/CRP.Add para 11(d).
144 INT/CEDAW/ADR/TUR/19028/E (Annex to the State Report Submitted by Turkey for the 7th Reporting Cycle, dated 2014). <https://tbinternet.ohchr.org/Treaties/CEDAW/Shared%20Documents/TUR/INT_CEDAW_ADR_TUR_19028_E.pdf > accessed 24 March 2022.

5.4.7 Brief Conclusion

CEDAW enjoys the widest implementation constituency in government, Parliament and civil society. Compared to all other treaties there also is a more robust institutional infrastructure that is able to connect CEDAW case law with national actors. This infrastructure not only carries out key functions such as the translation of the CEDAW COs into Turkish, but also inactions between civil society and state actors. Compared to other treaties, the jurisprudence of CEDAW is more widely translated and better disseminated. Yet, the decline in the quality of the state reports over time, and anti-women's rights discourse adopted by some members of the government, also raise concerns about the sustainability of the impact of CEDAW over time. As a retrogressive institutional change, for example, the Ministry for Women and Family in 2011 was replaced by the Ministry of Family and Social Policies, thereby reducing the emphasis on women's rights and strengthening the focus on traditional, patriarchal family life and women as caretakers of their families.

5.5 Convention against Torture and Other Cruel, Inhuman or Degrading Treatment or Punishment

5.5.1 Incorporation and Reliance by Legislature and Executive

CAT was ratified in 1988 when systemic torture in Turkish prisons and detention centres remained a key concern. As the explanatory notes indicate, the motivation of the government was to align with the 'Western powers moving in the same direction' and to obtain a tool to 'speak up against any kind of human rights violations'.[145] The latter is also confirmed by one member of Parliament stating that the ratification of CAT would increase Turkey's negotiation capacities.[146]

CAT has been incorporated into domestic law 11 years after the entry into force in 1999 by way of amendments made to the Penal Code. These amendments broadened the definition of torture with direct reference to CAT and increased the maximum sentence of imprisonment from five to eight years for the crime of torture.[147] The legislative history of the amendments points to the direct impact of CAT. The explanatory notes of the amendment explicitly

---

[145] The Reports of the Justice Commission and the Commission on Foreign Affairs on the Draft Law on the Approval of CAT (8 February 1988) <https://www5.tbmm.gov.tr/tutanaklar/TUTANAK/TBMM/d18/c010/tbmm18010061ss0041.pdf> accessed 24 March 2022.
[146] The 61st Session of the Parliament (21 April 1988) <https://www5.tbmm.gov.tr/tutanaklar/TUTANAK/TBMM/d18/c010/tbmm18010061.pdf> accessed 24 March 2022.
[147] The Law on the Amendment of Certain Provisions of the Penal Code (No 4449) 1999, arts 1 and 2.

refer to the definition of torture in CAT.[148] Furthermore, during the relevant parliamentary debates three separate MPs referred to its provisions.[149] The direct influence of CAT can also be seen in the adoption of the new Penal Code in 2004. Article 94 broadens the definition of torture and also increases the maximum sentence to 12 years. The legislative history shows the CAT figures as part of the explanatory notes, where direct references to articles 1, 4 and 16 are made.[150]

In addition to these legal developments, the most remarkable executive policy regarding torture and other forms of ill-treatment has been the Zero Tolerance for Torture which was initiated in 2003. This was later emphasised in the programmes of the 60th government in 2007 and the 61st government in 2011.[151]

5.5.2 Reliance by the Judiciary

The reliance of the domestic courts on CAT has been limited to the definition of torture. The High Court of Appeals cited CAT in 16 different cases and in all these cases quoted the definition of torture.[152] This is also the case for the Turkish Constitutional Court which cited article 1 of CAT in 27 different cases. In these cases, the TCC cited CAT to emphasise that torture carries a particular intent different from other forms of ill-treatment.[153] While the definition of

---

[148] The explanatory notes are available at <https://www5.tbmm.gov.tr/tutanaklar/TUTANAK/TBMM/d21/c012/tbmm21012058ss0141.pdf> accessed 24 March 2022.

[149] In the words of one MP, '[t]he Convention against Torture and Other Cruel, Inhuman or Degrading Treatment or Punishment has entered into force by our country's signature and has become a domestic legal document. With the signature and ratification of this Convention, the obligation to implement its content has arisen.' See the records of the 58nd Session of the Parliament (26 August 1999) <https://www5.tbmm.gov.tr/tutanak/donem21/yil1/bas/b058m.htm> accessed 24 March 2022.

[150] Niyazi Güney, Kenan Özdemir and Yusuf S Balo, *Gerekçe ve Tutanaklarla Karşılaştırmalı Yeni Türk Ceza Kanunu* (Adil Yayınevi 2004) 304.

[151] The programme for the 60th government, <https://www.resmigazete.gov.tr/eskiler/2007/09/20070907M1-1.htm> accessed 24 March 2022; the programme of the 61st government, <https://www.resmigazete.gov.tr/eskiler/2011/07/20110717-1.htm> accessed 24 March 2022.

[152] Some of these cases are The High Court of Appeals the 8th Penal Chamber, File No2017/468 Decision No 2017/4455 (20 April 2017); The High Court of Appeals the 8th Penal Chamber, File No 2010/12567 Decision No 2011/10230 (28 September 2011); The High Court of Appeals Penal General Council, File No 2002/191 Decision No 2002/362 T. 15.10.2002; The High Court of Appeals the 8th Penal Chamber, File No 1998/10667 Decision No 1998/12819 (12 October 1998).

[153] TCC used CAT to emphasise that torture carries a particular intent different from other forms of ill-treatment in 2014 in the case referenced as App No 2013/293 (17 July 2014).

torture in the Convention attracts the occasional interest of the judiciary, the work of the Committee against Torture, however, goes largely unnoticed. Only in one case before the TCC has a judge referred to the COs of the Committee concerning Canada in his dissenting opinion.[154]

5.5.3 Impact on and through Independent State Institutions

Since 28 January 2014, the Human Rights and Equality Institution of Turkey has functioned as the national prevention mechanism pursuant to OP-CAT. Due to this specific mandate, the Law on the Human Rights and Equality Institution of Turkey and its relevant regulation explicitly mention OP-CAT.[155] As of January 2020, the Institution has issued 13 reports on the visits conducted pursuant to OP-CAT. In each report there is a reference to OP-CAT as the main reason behind the visit.[156] In the work of the Institution, particularly in its decisions on the complaints regarding detention conditions, there are references to article 2 of CAT.[157] However, these references are only made in passing. The Ombudsman, meanwhile, has referred to CAT in only one of its decisions.[158]

5.5.4 Impact on and through Non-state Actors

CAT has had a substantial impact through non-state actors. The Human Rights Association and Human Rights Foundation of Turkey, which were founded in 1986 and 1990 respectively, are considered the leading organisations in campaigning against torture and providing medical and legal aid to the victims of torture.[159] These two organisations contributed significantly to the monitoring process of the CAT Cttee by submitting five shadow reports in three different

---

This reasoning was followed in other cases such as App No 2014/2871 (27 October 2016); App No 2015/13100 (31 October 2018); App No 2014/7296 (29 September 2016); App No 2014/19954 (12 June 2018).

154 Turkish Constitutional Court, App No 2015/14363 (3 April 2019).
155 The Law on the Human Rights and Equality Institution of Turkey (No 6701) 2016, art 2/1(k) and art 9/1(1); The Regulation on the Law and Procedure of the Implementation of the Law on the Human Rights and Equality Institution of Turkey, art 4/1(bb) and art 24/1(1).
156 See the Report No 2018/19 (December 2018) <https://www.tihek.gov.tr/upload/file_editor/2019/06/1560845325.pdf> accessed 24 March 2022.
157 See the Decision No 2018/104 (27 November 2018); Decision No 2018/99 (30 October 2018); Decision No 2018/98 (30 October 2018); Decision No 2018/83 (18 July 2018); Decision No 2019/04 (8 January 2019); Decision No 2019/24 (9 April 2019); Decision No 2019/26 (16 April 2019).
158 See the Decision No 2013/90 (3 December 2013).
159 Interview with Gulan Kaleli and Barış Yavuz, Human Rights Foundation of Turkey, 15 November 2019, Istanbul, Turkey, interview with Emel Ataktürk Sevimli.

cycles. Despite the work of these strong organisations, the 'politicised' nature of torture[160] and overall denial by the government that torture takes place[161] prevent CAT from having a wider reach. The impact of CAT on non-state actors was more evident before the adoption of the new Penal Code. When the definition of torture was limited, non-state actors referred to the definition of CAT to widen the existing scope of domestic provisions.[162]

5.5.5 Impact of State Reporting

Turkey has reported to CAT, albeit with significant delays. In its 2010 report, Turkey pointed to its reporting burden to other UN human rights treaty bodies and the European Committee for the Prevention of Torture (CPT) as the reason for late reporting.[163]

In the COs, the Committee asked Turkey to make specific legal reforms including amending article 161/5 of the Criminal Procedure Code which requires special permission to prosecute high-level officials;[164] reviewing the Law on the Right to Access to Information so that information regarding detention facilities is not subject to restrictions;[165] aligning the definition of torture in article 94 of the Penal Code with article 1 of CAT;[166] repealing article 47 of the Penal Code;[167] raising the age of criminal responsibility;[168] prohibiting corporal punishment of children in the home, school and penal institutions;[169] and amending the Penal Code to ensure that the crime of torture is not subject to any statute of limitations.[170]

As recommended by the Committee, Turkey removed the statute of limitations for the crime of torture[171] and this was endorsed by the

---

160 Interview with Dr Kerem Altıparmak.
161 Interview with Gulan Kaleli and Barış Yavuz.
162 ibid.
163 Third periodic report of state parties due in 1997; the present report is submitted in response to the list of issues (CAT/C/TUR/Q/3) transmitted to the state party pursuant to the optional reporting procedure (A/62/44, paras 23 and 24) – Turkey, 26 January 2010, CAT/C/TUR/3, para 326.
164 COs of the Committee against Torture: Turkey, 20 January 2011, CAT/C/TUR/CO/3, para 8.
165 CAT/C/TUR/CO/3, para 17.
166 COs on the fourth periodic reports of Turkey, 2 June 2016, CAT/C/TUR/CO/4, paras 17–18.
167 CAT/C/TUR/CO/4, para 36.
168 CAT/C/TUR/CO/3, para 21.
169 ibid para 22.
170 ibid para 24.
171 Art 94 of the Penal Code has been amended by art 9 of the Law No 6459. See CAT/C/TUR/4, para 231. It is noteworthy that in the third periodic report, Turkey rejected this recommendation by arguing that it would be against the principle of equality to remove the statute of limitation for one crime. See CAT/C/TUR/3, para 149.

Committee.[172] However, no reference has been made to the CAT Cttee in the drafting history nor in the parliamentary debates of this removal.[173] Some recommendations of CAT, however, were openly rejected by Turkey. For instance, the recommendation to amend the Law on the Right to Access to Information has not been implemented. Turkey stated that the Law includes no restrictions on access to information about detention facilities.[174] Similarly, the recommendation to provide data on complaints related to torture disaggregated by ethnic origin, age and gender has not been implemented.[175] The issue of impunity may be regarded as an area with a low level of implementation as the Committee selected that issue for follow-up both in the third and fourth cycles.

5.5.6   Impact of Individual Communications

Only one communication has been decided by the CAT Cttee against Turkey; it was found inadmissible.[176]

5.5.7   Impact of Other Measures

The SPT conducted its first visit to Turkey in October 2015, and its report was published in December 2019. The report noted that the Law on the Human Rights Institution of Turkey (No 6332) dated 2012 did not provide a sufficient legal basis for this institution to act as the national preventive mechanism.[177] It further asked for clarification with respect to the functions of the institution as a national preventive mechanism.[178] The first concern was partly remedied by the adoption of the new Law on Human Rights and Equality Institution of Turkey (No 6701) in 2016, which clearly endowed the institution with the mandate to act as the national preventive mechanism pursuant to the OP-CAT.[179]

---

172   CAT/C/TUR/CO/4, para 5(a).
173   The Draft Law on the Amendment of Some Laws in the Context of Human Rights and Freedom of Expression (No 6459) (7 March 2013) <https://www5.tbmm.gov.tr/tutanaklar/TUTANAK/TBMM/d24/c048/tbmm24048090ss0445.pdf> accessed 24 March 2022.
174   CAT/C/TUR/4, para 272.
175   ibid para 273.
176   The applicant, REG, who was granted refugee status in France alleged that he had been tortured and ill-treated in Turkey. The Committee found this application inadmissible on the basis of non-exhaustion of domestic remedies. See CAT, *REG v Turkey*, Communication 4/1990 (29 April 1991).
177   Report on the visit made by the Subcommittee on Prevention of Torture and Other Cruel, Inhuman or Degrading Treatment or Punishment for the purpose of providing advisory assistance to the national preventive mechanism of Turkey, 12 December 2019, CAT/OP/TUR/1, para 19.
178   ibid, para 20.
179   See arts 1 and 9.

However, the functions of the mechanism remain indistinguishable from the general functions of the national human rights institution. Turkey explained that combining all these functions under one institution pursued the 'goal of avoiding possible duplication among different institutions'.[180]

Similar to the concerns raised by other treaty bodies, the SPT also commented on the independence of the national human rights institution, and noted that its members are selected at the discretion of the executive branch.[181] Turkey commented that with the changes brought by Law No 6701 in 2016 a wide range of stakeholders including lawyers, NGOs, media representatives and academics were able to propose membership.[182] However, members were still appointed by the President of Turkey and the Council of Ministers. After the amendments in July 2018, the President directly appoints the members without being notified by any proposals for membership.[183]

5.5.8 Brief Conclusion

CAT has had a direct impact on legislative changes, judicial decisions and the work of non-state actors with regard to the definition of torture. However, this substantial impact does not extend to procedural obligations arising from CAT as impunity is one of the most raised and repeated issues by the CAT Cttee. It is also worth noting that some of the legislative and executive changes in this field can readily be attributed to the European Court case law.

5.6 *Convention on the Rights of the Child*

5.6.1 Incorporation and Reliance by the Legislature and Executive

Turkey ratified the CRC in 1995. Although Turkey did not engage in a comprehensive review of its domestic law before or after ratification, there have been many changes increasing the impact of CRC. First, the Law on the Competence and Functioning of the Juvenile Courts was amended in 2003 to include children above the age of 15. The explanatory notes cite the definition of the child in CRC to justify this amendment.[184] Second, the new Penal Code that was

---

180 Comments of Turkey on the recommendations and observations addressed to it in connection with the Subcommittee visit undertaken from 6 to 9 October 2015, 16 December 2019, CAT/OP/TUR/CSPRO/1, para 33.
181 CAT/OP/TUR/1, para 24.
182 CAT/OP/TUR/CSPRO/1, para 20. This referred to art 10(2) of the Law no 6701 before the amendment of 2 July 2018.
183 Statutory Decree (No 703) 2018, art 149.
184 The Draft Law on the Amendment of Certain Laws (23 July 2003) <https://www5.tbmm.gov.tr/tutanaklar/TUTANAK/TBMM/d22/c025/tbmm22025113ss0262.pdf>; <https://www2.tbmm.gov.tr/d22/1/1-0282.pdf> accessed 24 March 2022.

adopted in 2004 defines 'child' as any person below the age of 18 years and sets the age for criminal responsibility as 12 years. CRC is not cited explicitly in the text of the Code. However, the explanatory notes cite CRC as the source for the definition of the child as such.[185]

Third, the most comprehensive domestic framework – the Law on Child Protection – was adopted ten years after ratification. There is no direct reference to CRC in the formal text of the Law or in the explanatory notes presented by the government.[186] However, during the parliamentary proceedings on 3 July 2005, Cemil Çiçek, who at the time was the Minister of Justice, stated the Draft Law was aimed at incorporating the obligations arising from CRC into the domestic law.[187]

Fourth, in 2010 legal changes were made to the Anti-Terror Law regarding children charged with terror-related offences who are publicly known as 'stone-throwing children'.[188] It was accepted under the new provisions that the crime of resistance and the crime of terrorist propaganda during assemblies are not applicable to children. Furthermore, the clause under the Anti-Terror Law increasing the penalties for terror-related crimes has been changed to exclude children from its scope. Although there is no direct reference to CRC in the wording of the legal amendment, the explanatory note quotes article 40 of CRC to show the obligation to take preventive instead of punitive measures and not to apply penalties for children unless they are of last resort.[189]

Finally, CRC had an impact on the 2010 constitutional amendments. First, 'the rights of the child' was added to the title of article 41, which now reads 'Protection of the family and the rights of the child'. Second, the 2010 amendments added the third and fourth paragraphs to article 41 which ascribe children

---

[185] Erdener Yurtcan, *Yargıtay Kararları Işığı Altında Türk Ceza Kanunu (Genel Hükümler) Cilt-1* (Türkiye Barolar Birliği 2015) 106.

[186] The Draft Law on Child Protection (10 March 2005) <https://www5.tbmm.gov.tr/sirasayi/donem22/yil01/ss963m.htm> accessed 24 March 2022.

[187] 'This draft under concern is about the protection of children. The Turkish Grand National Assembly has adopted the United Nations Convention on the Rights of the Child a while ago. Therefore, Turkey implements an international obligation with this draft about which we are debating today and which we will evaluate soon. It is about adapting the obligations arising from the Convention on the Rights of the Child into our domestic law.' The 125th Session of the Parliament (3 July 2005) <https://www5.tbmm.gov.tr/tutanaklar/TUTANAK/TBMM/d22/c091/tbmm22091125.pdf> accessed 24 March 2022.

[188] 'Stone-Throwing Youths Face up to 58 Years in Prison in Turkey' *Hurriyet Daily News* (1 December 2008) <http://www.hurriyet.com.tr/gundem/stone-throwing-youths-face-up-to-58-years-in-prison-in-turkey-10480767> accessed 24 March 2022.

[189] The Draft Law on the Amendment of the Anti-Terror Law and Other Laws (10 November 2009) <https://www5.tbmm.gov.tr/tutanaklar/TUTANAK/TBMM/d23/c076/tbmm23076137ss0526.pdf> accessed 24 March 2022.

'the right to protection and care and the right to have and maintain a personal and direct relation with his/her mother and father unless it is contrary to his/her best interests', and assign a duty to the state to protect children from all kinds of abuse and violence. Third, the rule which sets out that the measures taken for children are not deemed to be against the principle of equality was added to article 10 of the Constitution.[190] The explanatory notes provided by the government in 2010 state that the amendment to article 41 aims to incorporate the universal principles on the rights of the child as established by CRC and the European Convention on the Exercise of Children's Rights.[191]

5.6.2   Reliance by the Judiciary

CRC has been widely cited in the decisions of the domestic courts. The vast majority of these decisions emanate from the High Court of Appeals.[192] In criminal cases, the High Court of Appeals consistently cites CRC as authority that the child cannot be charged for the cost of the proceedings.[193] In civil cases, the High Court of Appeals refers to article 12 of CRC to emphasise the requirement to take the child's opinions into account in custody cases.[194] It also refers to article 3 of CRC in many cases to show that the best interests of the child are the main principle guiding custody cases.[195] The Turkish Constitutional Court also refers to CRC, particularly in recent years in its decisions on individual applications. The impact of CRC on these decisions range

---

[190] The Law on the Amendment of the Constitution of the Turkish Republic (No 5982) 2010, art 1.

[191] The Draft Law on the Amendment of the Constitution of the Turkish Republic <https://www5.tbmm.gov.tr/tutanaklar/TUTANAK/TBMM/d23/c066/tbmm23066088ss0497.pdf> accessed 24 March 2022, art 4.

[192] There are 1655 decisions including at least one reference to CRC. This information is reached via LexPera through searching for 'Çocuk Haklarına Dair Sözleşme' on 7 November 2019.

[193] Some of these cases are The High Court of Appeals 17th Penal Chamber, File No 2015/15665 Decision No 2015/10872 (10 December 2015); The High Court of Appeals 17th Penal Chamber, File No 2016/5390 Decision No 2017/15604 (11 December 2017); The High Court of Appeals 13th Penal Chamber, File No 2014/36407 Decision No 2016/659 (18 January 2016).

[194] Some of these cases are The High Court of Appeals 2nd Civil Chamber, File No 2008/3840 Decision No 2009/6670 (8 April 2009); The High Court of Appeals 2nd Civil Chamber, File No 2010/12050 Decision No 2011/12818 (20 July 2011); The High Court of Appeals 2nd Civil Chamber, File No 2012/25767 Decision No 2013/17834 (24 June 2013).

[195] Some of these cases are The High Court of Appeals 2nd Civil Chamber, File No 2014/26364 Decision No 2015/11749 (4 June 2015); The High Court of Appeals 2nd Civil Chamber, File No 2013/5542 Decision No 2013/25510 (7 November 2013); The High Court of Appeals 2nd Civil Chamber, File No 2017/2281 Decision No 2017/14852 (19 December 2017); The High Court of Appeals 2nd Civil Chamber, File No 2016/23674 Decision No 2016/16251 (20 December 2016).

from the best interests of the child and the right to participation,[196] the right to health,[197] to the right not to be separated from parents.[198]

When it comes to the work of the CRC Cttee, the number of references decreases dramatically. The High Court of Appeals twice cited General Comment 14.[199] The TCC also referred to the General Comments[200] and the COs on Turkey in a few decisions.[201] These references were made in passing and do not seem to have directly affected the outcome of the cases.

5.6.3   Impact on and through Independent State Institutions

The establishment of the Ombudsman in 2012 and the establishment of the Human Rights and Equality Institution of Turkey in 2016 were major developments enhancing the impact of CRC. The Office of Ombudsman allocates one ombudsman to the rights of the child and women's rights.[202] Similarly, the Human Rights and Equality Institution of Turkey accepts individual applications from children. These applications can be made anonymously.[203] While the Institution has not relied on CRC in any complaints, the Ombudsman cited CRC in six decisions,[204] and General Comment 9 in one decision.[205]

---

196 Turkish Constitutional Court, App No 2015/13760 (18 July 2018); Turkish Constitutional Court, App No 2015/10826 (17 July 2018); Turkish Constitutional Court, App No 2014/13936 (8 March 2018).
197 Turkish Constitutional Court, App No 2015/4664 (11 October 2018); Turkish Constitutional Court, App No 2015/4662 (10 October 2018); Turkish Constitutional Court, App No 2015/13136 (30 October 2018); Turkish Constitutional Court, App No 2015/1863 (30 January 2015); Turkish Constitutional Court, App No 2015/326 (11 October 2018).
198 Turkish Constitutional Court, App No 2013/6382 (9 March 2016); Turkish Constitutional Court, App No 2013/8846 (9 March 2016); Turkish Constitutional Court, App No 2013/3181 (3 February 2016).
199 See The High Court of Appeals 4th Civil Chamber, File No 2016/9024 Decision No 2018/6595 (25 October 2018); and The High Court of Appeals 4th Civil Chamber., File No 2016/12541 Decision No 2018/7636 (5 December 2018).
200 Turkish Constitutional Court, App No 2014/5974 (26 December 2017); Turkish Constitutional Court App No 2014/18179 (25 October 2017); Turkish Constitutional Court App No 2013/2928 (18 October 2017); Turkish Constitutional Court, File No 2015/68, Decision No 2017/166 (29 November 2017).
201 Turkish Constitutional Court App No 2014/18179 (25 October 2017); Turkish Constitutional Court App No 2013/3262 (11 May 2016).
202 Law on the Institution of Ombudsman (No 6328), art 7(1)(f).
203 Law on Human Rights and Equality Institution of Turkey (Law No 6701), art 17(7).
204 Complaint No 02.2013/378 (27 January 2014); Complaint No 2014/3164 (2 October 2014); Complaint No 2017/1293 (11 January 2018); Complaint No 2015/5175 (31 March 2016); Complaint No 2015/5629 (23 August 2016); Complaint No 2015/4978 (15 April 2016).
205 Complaint No 02.2013/1064 (6 June 2014).

5.6.4 Impact on and through Non-state Actors

Many interlocutors with whom we engaged referred to CRC as one of the well-known human rights treaties.[206] They consider that CRC is well-known because it is deemed 'non-political',[207] 'harmless'[208] and 'sympathetic',[209] to some extent it overlaps with women's rights[210] and it has institutional support under the Ministry of Family.[211] The work of the United Nations Children's Fund (UNICEF) has also increased awareness of CRC.[212] According to the interlocutors, the impact of CRC has been seen in the following areas: the right to participation of children;[213] changing perceptions of childhood;[214] the definition of the child;[215] and the best interests of the child principle.[216]

5.6.5 State Reporting and Its Impact

In the COs, the CRC Cttee asked for specific legal reforms such as increasing the marriage age of girls to equal that of boys (from 15 to 17 years) and instituting the same age for the end of compulsory education and the beginning of employment;[217] amending the Civil Code of 1926 which excludes children from forming, joining and leaving associations;[218] raising the minimum legal age for criminal responsibility;[219] establishing juvenile courts in every province;[220] and prohibiting corporal punishment in the home and in alternative care settings.[221]

---

206 Interview with Prof Dr Bertil Emrah Oder; interview with Gulan Kaleli and Barış Yavuz; interview with Hakan Özgül and Süleyman Akbulut; interview with Beydağ Tıraş Öneri and Özlem Yılmaz; interview with Dr Taylan Barın, Turkish Constitutional Court Rapporteur, 22 October 2019, Ankara, Turkey; interview with MP Hakan Çavuşoğlu.
207 Interview with Dr Kerem Altıparmak.
208 Interview with Adem Arkadaş Thibert.
209 Interview with Celile Özlem Tunçak.
210 Interview with Prof Dr Ayşe Feride Acar.
211 Interview with Zehra Güleç Kayış and Mehmet Aktaş, Human Rights and Equality Institution of Turkey, 23 October 2019, Ankara, Turkey.
212 Interview with Prof Dr Ayşe Feride Acar.
213 Interview with Bayram İnce, Child Services Unit at the Ministry of Family, Labour and Social Services, 23 October 2019, Ankara, Turkey; interview with Emrah Kırımsoy, 1 August 2019, Istanbul, Turkey.
214 Interview with Emrah Kırımsoy.
215 Interview with Gulan Kaleli and Barış Yavuz.
216 Interview with Beydağ Tıraş Öneri and Özlem Yılmaz.
217 COs of the Committee on the Rights of the Child: Turkey (9 July 2001) CRC/C/15/Add.152, para 26.
218 CRC/C/15/Add.152, para 38.
219 CRC/C/15/Add.152, para 66.
220 CRC/C/15/Add.152, para 66.
221 COs: Turkey (20 July 2012) CRC/C/TUR/CO/2-3, para 45(a).

During the 60th session in 2012, the Committee endorsed the steps taken in the following areas that were among the COs taken in 2001:[222] amendments to the counter-terrorism law that softens the penalties for children (2010); the adoption of the Law on Child Protection (2005); legal amendments regarding persons with disabilities (2005); increasing the minimum age of criminal responsibility (2004); the entry into force of the Turkish Civil Code (2005); and the ratification of the Optional Protocols to CRC. Nonetheless, the Committee stressed that Turkey had not fully or sufficiently implemented the previous recommendations of the Committee in the following areas:[223] reservations to the Convention on the Rights of the Child; coordination between public agencies; an independent and effective monitoring mechanism; data collection; honour killings; the prohibition of discrimination against children belonging to minorities not recognised under the Treaty of Lausanne of 1923; disparities affecting children living in the eastern and south-eastern regions and in rural areas especially with regard to their access to adequate health and education; corporal punishment; and the administration of juvenile justice, including long detention periods and poor conditions in some prisons.

5.6.6 Brief Conclusion

CRC has had a direct impact on legislative changes, executive policies, judicial decisions and non-state actors. The definition of the child, the right to participation and the best interests of the child principle are the thematic areas in which CRC is well-known and has had the most significant impact. Some interlocutors pointed out that this impact could be attributed to the comparatively less politicised nature of CRC. Yet, there is also resistance to CRC, in particular where it conflicts with the political stance of the government, as is the case with children belonging to minorities and the marriage age for children.

5.7 International Convention on the Protection of the Rights of All Migrant Workers and Members of Their Families

5.7.1 Incorporation and Reliance by the Legislature and Executive

Turkey ratified CMW in 2004. A number of domestic laws indirectly speak to Turkey's obligations under the Convention on Migrant Workers, although none of them make explicit reference to it. Of these, the Law on Work Permits of Foreigners No 4817 of 2003, the Law on Foreigners and International Protection No 6458 of 2013, followed by the establishment of the Directorate General of

---

222 CRC/C/TUR/CO/2-3, paras 3-4.
223 CRC/C/TUR/CO/2-3, para 7.

Migration Management, and the Law on International Workforce No 6735 of 2016, are of most relevance. Turkey additionally listed the Law on Passports No 5682, the Law on Child Protection No 5395, and the Attorneyship Law No 1136 as laws that realise the aims of the Convention in its state report.[224]

Although migration, with a specific focus on the influx of Syrian refugees (as of 25 November 2020 Turkey hosts 3 635 288 registered Syrian refugees)[225] has been intensively discussed in the Turkish Grand National Assembly, CMW has received limited attention in such debates. The discussions on migration and asylum mainly concern the domestic legislations, social services and budgetary allocations for Syrian refugees and the EU-Turkey deal of 2016.

There are no direct references to the Convention in the process of the formulation of policies. The Presidency for Turks Abroad and Related Communities established in 2010,[226] the General Directorate of Migration Management and the Department of Protection of Human Trafficking Victims established in 2013 under the Law on Foreigners and International Protection No 6458, however,[227] are prominent institutions in the field of migration. Turkey works closely with other UN institutions and other stakeholders, namely, the UNHCR, IOM and the EU, in the field of migrants and refugees.[228]

5.7.2 Reliance by the Judiciary

CMW is one of the least known UN human rights treaties among lawyers, prosecutors and judges. The treaty has been briefly mentioned in one decision of the High Court of Appeals' General Assembly of Civil Chambers.[229]

5.7.3 Impact on and through Non-state Actors

CMW is largely unknown within civil society and academia. There are many NGOs working with a focus on refugee rights in Turkey, particularly after the arrival of Syrian refugees. However, these NGOs do not seem to be actively using CMW. Instead they focus on international documents and mechanisms that focus directly on the protection of refugees. No domestic NGOs have submitted shadow reports to the Committee. CMW was not mentioned throughout

---

224 CMW/C/TUR/1, para 12.
225 UNHCR, Syrian Regional Refugee Response (2020) <https://data2.unhcr.org/en/situations/syria/location/113> accessed 24 March 2022.
226 CMW/C/TUR/1, para 160.
227 CMW/C/TUR/1, para 27.
228 IOM, IOM Refugee Response Operations in Turkey (2019) <https://turkiye.iom.int/sites/g/files/tmzbdl1061/files/documents/Refugee_Response_One_Pager_FEB-APR19_EN_Web.pdf> accessed 24 March 2022.
229 High Court of Appeals, File No 2005/618 (16 November 2005).

our interviews with NGOs, academics, representatives of bar associations and other interlocutors.

5.7.4   Impact of State Reporting

Turkey has only submitted an initial report concerning CMW in 2016 with a 10-year delay. Turkey stated in its report that it was not possible to cooperate with the NGOs during the preparation process.[230]

COs have not been translated into Turkish and are not accessible on public websites. For the implementation of the key recommendations within the COs, Turkey continues to invest in policies and projects aiming to improve the living and working conditions of migrant workers and their families in a few areas in accordance with the key recommendations, such as education, the right to be informed and medical care. However, it is not possible to state to what extent these measures have been taken as a result of the COs. The key recommendations have not been implemented in some critical areas, such as expulsions, remuneration, conditions of work, and the right to join trade unions.

In the months following the COs, the International Labour Force Law No 6735 was enacted regulating, among others, work permit applications for foreign nationals. However, there are no references to CMW in the new law. No parliamentary questions were raised, no draft legislations were made as a result of the COs and there have been no follow-ups.

5.7.5   Impact of Individual Communications

While Turkey made a declaration that the competence of the Committee would be recognised at a later time, the individual complaint mechanism has not yet entered into force for CMW.

5.7.6   Brief Conclusion

The ratification of the Convention on Migrant Workers by Turkey is best understood as support from a migrant-sending country. As is well known, there is very limited support for CMW from migrant-receiving countries around the world. Yet, alongside the significant presence of migrants from Turkey, in particular, in Europe, the Syrian conflict of the past decade has significantly transformed Turkey's position as a migrant-sending country. Turkey now is home to a large number of refugees, as well as migrant workers in the domestic care and other sectors.[231] Despite this fundamental change, Turkey has not yet systematically

---

230   CMW/C/TUR/1, para 36.
231   According to the 2018 statistics published by the Ministry of Family, Labour and Social Security, the highest percentage of work permits given to foreigners is for

engaged with this Convention with a focus on migrant workers within Turkey, but rather with a focus on migrant workers from Turkey elsewhere. This can be seen both in the emphasis placed on the protection of Turkish migrant workers in the activities of the NHRI, and in the Parliamentary Human Rights Commission and state reporting.

5.8 Convention on the Rights of Persons with Disabilities

5.8.1 Incorporation and Reliance by the Legislature and Executive

Turkey ratified CRPD in 2009. It is worth noting that at the time of ratification, Turkey already had a comprehensive law – the Turkish Disability Act – which was enacted on 1 July 2005. The legal amendments after ratification show limited impact of CRPD.

In 2010, the constitutional amendments to article 10 of the Constitution enshrined that the special measures taken for the persons with disabilities are not against the principle of equality. Yet, the explanatory notes of the 2010 constitutional amendments which added this sentence to article 10 contain no reference to CRPD. In 2013, the term *özürlü* ('with defect'), which has a defamatory meaning in Turkish, was replaced by *engelli* ('with disability') in all the relevant laws including the Turkish Disability Act. During the parliamentary proceedings on this amendment, many members of Parliament discussed the rights of persons with disabilities and referred to CRPD.[232] In 2014, several provisions of the Turkish Disability Act were amended. These amendments expanded the purposes of disability services, added an anti-discrimination provision, including indirect discrimination and reasonable accommodation, and stipulated the general principles in the fields of labour and education.[233] Despite these important changes, there is only one explicit reference to CRPD in the parliamentary debates in 2014.[234]

On the question of how well CRPD is known by the government, the interlocutors point out that disability rights are known only with respect to the fields such as education and health. There is a lack of awareness regarding the

---

domestic/household employees. See Ministry of Family, Labour and Social Security, 2018 Statistics: Work Permits of Foreigners (2019) <https://www.csgb.gov.tr/media/63117/yabanciizin2019.pdf.> accessed 24 March 2022.

[232] The 97th Session of the Parliament, 25 April 2013 <https://www5.tbmm.gov.tr/tutanaklar/TUTANAK/TBMM/d24/c049/tbmm24049097.pdf> accessed 24 March 2022.

[233] Law No 6518, 2014, arts 62–75.

[234] The 54th Session of the Parliament (29 January 2014) <https://www5.tbmm.gov.tr/tutanaklar/TUTANAK/TBMM/d24/c070/tbmm24070054.pdf> accessed 24 March 2022.

right to autonomy. Therefore, the authorities are reluctant to change laws that are capable of creating more autonomy in civil rights and employment such as the Civil Code, the Law on Notary, and the Law on Judges and Prosecutors.[235]

5.8.2 Reliance by the Judiciary

CRPD has attracted almost no attention from the domestic courts. The Turkish Constitutional Court has cited CRPD in three decisions,[236] while the High Court of Appeals, the Council of State and the Court of Accounts have once referred to CRPD in their decisions.[237] The domestic courts have not referred to any of the general recommendations or COs of the CRPD Cttee.

5.8.3 Impact on and through Independent State Institutions

The Human Rights and Equality Institution applied reasonable accommodation by reference to CRPD in one individual application complaining about the failure to adjust working conditions to the individual's disability.[238] The Ombudsman has also cited CRPD in nine different cases.[239]

5.8.4 Impact on and through Non-state Actors

The monitoring process of the CRPD Cttee has attracted the attention of many domestic NGOs working in the field of disability rights. Most of the reports submitted to the Committee are collaborative work of many organisations. For instance, the report led by the Network for the Rights of Children with Disabilities (EÇHA) received contributions from 73 domestic organisations. Despite this high interest in the CRPD mechanisms, the representatives of the Social Rights and Research Society (TOHAD) have indicated that for most of the disability organisations in Turkey, CRPD is known only by its name. Many organisations have no detailed information of the obligations of CRPD, or its

---

235 Interview with Hakan Özgül and Süleyman Akbulut.
236 Turkish Constitutional Court, App No 2014/19352 (24 May 2018); Turkish Constitutional Court App No 2015/17844 (7 March 2019); Turkish Constitutional Court, File No 2012/102, Decision No 2012/207 (27 December 2012).
237 The Court of Accounts, No 1304 (28 January 2010); The High Court of Appeals 12th Civil Chamber, File No 2011/7964 Decision No 2011/7497 (25 April 2011); The Council of State, File No 2008/2220 Decision No 2012/2239 (21 November 2012).
238 Decision No 2019/06 (15 January 2019).
239 Complaint No 02.2013/1064 (6 April 2014); Complaint No 2016/2600 (24 April 2017); Complaint No 2016/4990 (31 July 2017); Complaint No 2017/384 (24 August 2017); Complaint No 2016/1863 (28 October 2016); Complaint No 2016/102 (26 September 2016); Complaint No 2015/5862 (19 May 2016); Complaint No 2015/5496 (27 July 2016); Complaint No 2016/719 (10 October 2016).

mechanisms.[240] Due to this low level of awareness, they do not have the capacity to create pressure on the government to make necessary changes.[241]

5.8.5   Impact of State Reporting

The COs for Turkey were delivered in April 2019. The Committee asked Turkey to make a number of changes in civil law including replacing the guardianship regime with support decision-making mechanisms; abolishing the requirement of the presence of two witnesses under the Notary Law; and revising the Civil Code which subjects the right to marry and the right to vote of persons with intellectual disabilities to medical authorisation.[242] Turkey should also repeal the provisions of the Civil Code that deny the right of persons with disabilities to marry and support them to raise their children at home.[243] In the field of access to justice, Turkey is asked to amend the Law on Judges and Prosecutors to allow persons with disabilities to participate in the justice system.[244] The Committee also requested Turkey to repeal the criterion of 'dangerousness' as a basis for depriving persons with disabilities of their liberty[245] and to abolish the requirements of medical reports and third-party authorisation to travel.[246] Lastly, Turkey is asked to strengthen the capacity of the General Directorate of Social Services for Persons with Disabilities and the Elderly.[247]

5.8.6   Brief Conclusion

It is difficult to assess the impact of CRPD as the Committee delivered its first COs on Turkey in April 2019. It is interesting to note that the rights of persons with disabilities were legalised before the adoption of CRPD. The parliamentary debates on the legal amendments show clearly that there is an overall knowledge of CRPD at the legislative level. This is not the case for the judiciary, probably because it is a new instrument. The strongest impact of CRPD clearly is on the NGOs and the monitoring process before the CRPD Cttee attracted more attention from many domestic organisations than any UNTB ever has.

---

[240]   Interview with Hakan Özgül and Süleyman Akbulut.
[241]   ibid.
[242]   COs on the Initial Report of Turkey (9 April 2019), CRPD/C/TUR/CO/1, para 26.
[243]   CRPD/C/TUR/CO/1, para 47.
[244]   CRPD/C/TUR/CO/1, para 28.
[245]   CRPD/C/TUR/CO/1, para 30.
[246]   CRPD/C/TUR/CO/1, para 41.
[247]   CRPD/C/TUR/CO/1, para 67.

6 Conclusion

The impact of UNTB in Turkey significantly varies based on the treaty. Despite Turkey's monist stance towards international law as reflected in its Constitution, the treaties that have had the most direct impact on the practices of the judiciary are those treaties that have been embedded in domestic law, even if only partially. We observe this particularly in the cases of CEDAW, CAT and CRC. It is when certain standards, such as the definition of torture, the definition of a child or the definition of the head of family in line with UN human rights treaties, are incorporated in domestic laws that their impact becomes routine and normalised. In contrast, in cases that lack such domestic incorporation such as CERD, the impact of UN human rights treaties has only been superficial. The impact of the Covenants that encompass a wide range of rights, on the other hand, is inhibited due to their general formulations of rights. In the field of civil and political rights, the state authorities and the judiciary are strongly socialised into relying on the European Convention on Human Rights. All the individual petition case law of the Turkish Constitutional Court, too, focuses on the intersection of the Convention and the Constitution. CCPR is unable to compete with this highly-institutionalised embedded quality of the ECHR in the Turkish system. With respect to CESCR, the non-justiciability of economic, social and cultural rights *qua* human rights in Turkey and in the Constitution, in particular, constitutes a barrier to impact.

There are important ideological barriers to impact across the full spectrum of treaties. In the case of the enforced disappearance treaty, this takes the form of non-ratification; in the case of the protection of rights of persons belonging to minorities, it results in reservations. In the case of racial discrimination and the rights of migrant workers, while Turkey is a state party to both, there is a general perception that violations of these rights only occur in other places in the world, for example, in Europe. In the case of CESCR, these rights are viewed as programmatic and not justiciable. While CRC and CRPD are subject to comparatively fewer ideological barriers, the domestic perception of these rights continues to be through the lens of assistance and vulnerability. CEDAW is also subject to ideological barriers based on a patriarchal understanding of families and women's sexuality.

Institutionally, UN human rights treaties are not well entrenched at the domestic level. While there is specialised institutional ownership of CEDAW, CRC and CRPD at dedicated ministries, the rest of the treaties are within the general purview of the Ministry of Foreign Affairs. In addition, there is no intra-governmental coordination concerning the follow-up to treaty body recommendations or structured dialogues between the executive and the legislative branches on such recommendations.

Our study reveals that the impact of UN human rights treaties on civil society is strongly hampered by capacity constraints, most notably language barriers. This is exacerbated by the fact that even the UN state reports are not prepared in Turkish, but in English. The translation of reports, COs and General Comments are piecemeal and incomplete. Despite these difficulties, UN treaties have enabled important mobilisation for domestic civil society organisations when it comes to CEDAW, CAT, CRC and, more recently, CRPD. We found that between 1999 and 2020 the treaties with the weakest impact in Turkey have been CESCR, CERD and CMW.

CHAPTER 20

The Impact of the United Nations Human Rights Treaties on the Domestic Level in Zambia

O'Brien Kaaba

1   Introduction to Human Rights in Zambia

The Republic of Zambia gained its independence from Britain in 1964. At independence in 1964 it inherited a Constitution with an enforceable Bill of Rights modelled on the 1963 Nigerian Constitution.[1] The Nigerian Bill of Rights in turn was modelled on the European Convention on Human Rights 1950, which in turn was modelled on the Universal Declaration of Human Rights 1948 (UDHR). The Zambian Bill of Rights, therefore, can be said to mirror the civil and political rights contained in the UDHR. Although the Bill of Rights was entrenched,[2] the entrenchment provision was removed by an amendment in 1969 achieved by the 'referendum to end all referenda'.[3] This made it easy for the government to hold a further amendment in 1973 that abolished multipartyism in favour of one-party rule. However, in 1991 the Constitution was revised to reinstate multiparty politics. The 1991 Constitution brought back the entrenchment clause to 'lock in' the Bill of Rights, that is, no amendment to it could be achieved unless the proposed amendment was subjected to a referendum and the people approved the proposed amendment.

The rights protected in the Bill of Rights are the right to life; personal liberty; protection from slavery and forced labour; protection from inhuman treatment; protection from deprivation of property; privacy; the right to a fair trial; religious freedom; freedom of expression; freedom of movement; protection from discrimination; and protection of young persons from exploitation. The Bill of Rights does not include economic, social and cultural rights. In January 2016 the Zambian Constitution, except for the Bill of Rights, was amended. This amendment brought into existence the Constitutional Court. The draft

---

1   Alfred Chanda, *Human Rights Law in Zambia: Cases and Materials* (University of Zambia Press 2007) 4.
2   Art 72(3) Constitution of Zambia 1964.
3   Muna Ndulo and Robert Kent, 'Constitutionalism in Zambia: Past, Present and Future' (1996) 40 African Law Journal 264.

Bill of Rights, which incorporated social, economic and cultural rights, was subjected to a referendum in August 2016 but was rejected by the people.

Although the country has a Constitutional Court, the constitutional mandate for enforcing human rights vests in the High Court.[4] The anomalous position is due to the fact that the draft Bill of Rights which assigned that role to the Constitutional Court failed to pass in the 2016 referendum. The courts have churned out a mixed jurisprudence on human rights. In some cases, the courts were courageous in enforcing human rights, especially relating to freedom of expression, fair trial, assembly and association.[5] However, in more politically-sensitive cases, courts tend to defer excessively to the executive. An example of this approach was taken in the case of *M'Membe and Mwape v The People* (1995–1997) ZR 118, in which the Supreme Court declined to declare as unconstitutional a provision in the Penal Code criminalising the defamation of the President for offending the clause on freedom of expression in the Constitution. Rather, the Court appeared to have a misconceived role of the President, placing him or her above everyone else and not a public servant, stating:

> It was also an attempt to reduce to the common ranks the central executive authority and first citizen of the country. The election of any person to the office of President, I would have thought to be self-evident, has legal and constitutional consequences, quite apart from any other result. The constitution itself ordains that the become Head of State and of Government; that the executive power of the state vest in him and that he can be endowed with the various matters, powers and functions described in the constitution. I do not see how it can be argued that the President should stand before the law equally with the rest of us.

Apart from the courts, Zambia has a Human Rights Commission (HRC), established under the Constitution.[6] The mandate of the Commission includes investigating and reporting human rights violations, helping redress human rights violations through negotiation and conciliation, carrying out research on human rights and raising awareness about human rights.[7] The Commission

---

4 Art 28 Constitution of Zambia.
5 See, for example, the cases of *Christine Mulundika & Others v The People* (1995) ZR 105; *Thomas Mumba v Attorney-General* (1984) ZR 38; *Resident Doctors Association & Others v The Attorney-General* SCZ No 12 2003.
6 Art 230 Constitution of Zambia.
7 ibid art 230(2).

has no authority to enforce its decisions, but can only make recommendations. Although the HRC in its earlier years (approximately the first ten years) generally was perceived as acting courageously in condemning human rights abuses, its vibrancy has died down and plays an insignificant role in the human rights and governance discourse of the country.[8]

In 2015 Parliament enacted the Gender Equity and Equality Act 22 of 2015. The Act established a Gender Equity and Equality Commission.[9] The Commission has a broad mandate to help realise women's rights and, specifically, it is empowered to help mainstream gender equality, to monitor, lobby or investigate violations of women' rights, and to recommend appropriate measures to other authorities in order to ensure gender equality.[10] However, the government has not appointed commissioners and, therefore, the Commission is not yet functional.

Examples of major human rights violations in Zambia include arbitrary killings by state agents; the excessive use of force by police; harsh and life-threatening prison conditions; arbitrary arrests; interference with privacy; restrictions on freedom of the press, speech, and assembly; state-sanctioned looting or high-level official corruption; trafficking in persons; and the criminalisation and arrest of persons engaged in consensual same-sex sexual relations.[11] Prior to that, perhaps the most well-known examples of police arbitrary killings are the shooting to death of two female youths, Mapenzi Chibulo and Vespers Shimuzhila,[12] for which no officer has been prosecuted. The civil liberties of assembly and expression appear to be overwhelmingly restricted. The government often deploys repressive laws to curtail freedom of expression, and also through the use of threats, actual violence against and arrest and detention of journalists, opposition leaders, critical civil society leaders.[13] For example, a group of civil society activists who met at a church to critique

---

[8] Felicity Kayumba Kalunga and O'Brien Kaaba, 'The State of Administrative Justice in Zambia' in Hugh Corder and Justice Mavedzenge (eds), *Pursuing Good Governance: Administrative Justice in Common-Law Africa* (Siber Ink 2019) 35.

[9] S 6 Gender Equity and Equality Act 22 of 2015.

[10] ibid s 9(1).

[11] Department of State, Zambia 2017 Human Rights Report (March 2018) 1.

[12] 'Murdered UPND Supporter Mapenzi Chibulo to be Buried Today' <https://www.lusakatimes.com/2016/07/11/murdered-upnd-supporter-mapenzi-chibulo-buried-today/> accessed 19 April 2019; Zondiwe Mbewe, 'Vesper's Mother Weeps as UNZA Clinical Officer Testifies' <https://diggers.news/local/2019/04/05/vespers-mother-weeps-as-unza-clinical-officer-testifies/> accessed 19 April 2019.

[13] Amnesty International, 'Human Rights in Africa: Review of 2019 – Zambia' <https://www.amnesty.org/en/countries/africa/zambia/report-zambia/> accessed 19 April 2019.

the national budget in October 2018 were arbitrarily arrested and detained by police.[14]

A leader of an activist NGO summarised the reasons why the current regime was adverse towards civil society and closed political space:[15]

> This government is much more resentful of civil society, previous regimes saw us as a necessary evil, but they also respected us and the space that we occupied. That has changed a lot, since PF came into office. Not only for civil society, but also for opposition parties. I think what PF did was to recognise how it came to power and then closed those avenues for anyone else. PF came into power being close to civil society and having space as an opposition party. It then comes into power and deliberately closes off these spaces.

In March 2019 the government suspended the operating licence of Prime TV, a critical private television station. Freedom of assembly and association equally is adversely affected.[16]

The heavy-handedness towards civil society in general has also been applied by the state towards the opposition. In April 2017, for example, Hakainde Hichilema, leader of the main opposition party, the United Party for National Development (UPND), was arrested and detained for more than 120 days on trumped-up charges of treason. He was only released following interventions by the Commonwealth.[17] In July 2017 President Lungu declared a threatened state of emergency, effectively allowing him to suspend the enjoyment of human rights by decree.[18]

Although previous regimes tended to generally take human rights violations seriously, especially if reported in the media, the Patriotic Front (PF) regime shows a lack of interest and often applies the law selectively to prosecute or punish individuals who committed abuses and mostly targeted those who

---

14 Interview with A (Executive Director of a governance NGO) on 19 March 2019, Lusaka. All notes of interviews on file with the author.
15 Interview with B (Executive Director of a good governance NGO) on 26 February 2020, Lusaka.
16 ibid.
17 O'Brien Kaaba and Babatunde Fagbayibo, 'Promoting the Rule of Law Through the Principle of Subsidiarity in the African Union: A Critical Perspective' (2019) 8 Global Journal of Comparative Law 27–51.
18 See Statutory Instrument 53 of 2017.

were critical of the ruling party or were perceived supporters of the opposition.[19] Since the election of the PF in 2011, Zambia has gradually become more autocratic. Further, impunity remained a major problem, as ruling party supporters and officials were either not prosecuted for serious crimes or, if prosecuted, released after serving small fractions of prison sentences.[20] In fact, political violence is on the rise in Zambia.[21] Wahman has established that the fear of political violence has been escalating and as of 2017, at least 50 per cent of the Zambians were fearful of being victims of political violence. This is not surprising considering that Zambia, which was considered a beacon of regional stability in Southern Africa, in recent years has been backsliding and is now considered among the top 10 autocratising countries in the world.[22]

Corruption, especially by senior government officials, is rife and often goes unpunished. This, together with incompetence of the government, has led to a public debt and economic crisis.[23] *Africa Confidential* in January 2018 reported: 'A key reason behind the lack of certainty about the exact debt figures is that many of the loans that were contracted in 2016 and 2017 ended up in the pockets of individuals and cannot be accounted for.'[24] The Financial Intelligence Centre (FIC), an autonomous public institution created to investigate suspicious financial transactions, has documented cases of official corruption. In its 2016 report FIC stated that over K3 billion (approximately US $300 million) had been received by public officials or their associates through

---

19 Alastair Fraser, 'Post-Populism in Zambia: Michael Sata's Rise, Demise and Legacy' (2018) 34 International Political Science Review 456–472.

20 <https://www.state.gov/j/drl/rls/hrrpt/humanrightsreport/index.htm#wrapper> accessed 19 April 2019; see also Department of State, Zambia 2018 Human Rights Report (March 2019) 1.

21 Michael Wahman, 'Violence and Money: A Constituency-Level Survey of Pre-Election Manipulation' in Tinenenji Banda, O'Brien Kaaba, Marja Hinfelaar and Muna Ndulo (eds), *Democracy and Electoral Politics in Zambia* (Brill 2020) 288. In 2019 a commission of inquiry set up to investigate political violence and voting patterns concluded its work and submitted its report in January. It discusses the dynamics of political violence in more detail. See Republic of Zambia, Report of the Commission of Inquiry into Voting Patterns and Electoral Violence (January 2019).

22 Seraphine F Maerz and others, 'State of the World 2019: Autocratisation Surges – Resistance Grows' (2020) 27 Democratisation 909–927. See also Marja Hinfelaar and O'Brien Kaaba, 'Adjust, Resist, or Disband: How Does Civil Society Respond to Repression in Zambia?' PRIO Working Paper 2019.

23 The World Bank Group, 'Zambia Economic Brief: How Zambia Can Borrow Without Sorrow' 10th Zambia brief (December 2017).

24 'Lungu's Costly Power Play' *Africa Confidential* (January 2018) Vol 59, No 2 <https://www.africa-confidential.com/article-preview/id/12226/Lungu%27s_costly_power_play> accessed 20 April 2019.

kickbacks from public contracts.[25] In 2017 the FIC figures more than doubled. FIC reported that politically-exposed persons received more than K6.3 billion (US $630 million) in kickbacks mainly from the infrastructure contracts.[26] Considering that these are only figures for one year, and only capturing suspicious transactions through the formal banking system, one can safely conclude that what was reported is only the tip of the iceberg.

Government's contempt for accountability is manifest in its response to the revelations and calls for accountability. When FIC reported the substantial amount of kickbacks received by government officials, the government responded by withholding funding to the entity.[27] When the Auditor-General exposed the abuse of resources in the construction sector, the government resorted to victimising the Auditor-General by launching an investigation into alleged 'irregularities' and 'lack of transparency' in the office of the Auditor-General.[28] Perhaps more telling was President Lungu's encouragement of senior government and ruling party officials to steal, but not to finish everything.[29]

2 Relationship of Zambia with the International Human Rights System in General

Zambia joined the United Nations (UN) on 1 December 1964. It is a state party to all the core UN human rights treaties, except the International Convention on the Protection of the Rights of All Migrant Workers and Members of Their Families (CMW). In ratifying the treaties, Zambia has entered only one reservation. This is in relation to article 13(2)(a) of the International Covenant on Economic, Social and Cultural Rights (CESCR) regarding the provision of free and compulsory primary education.[30]

---

25 Financial Intelligence Centre, 'Money Laundering and Terrorist Financing Trends Report 2017'.
26 ibid 10.
27 Joseph Mwenda, 'Govt Withholds Salaries for FIC Employees' *News Diggers* (17 January 2018) <https://diggers.news/local/2018/01/17/govt-withholds-salaries-for-fic-employees/> accessed 13 May 2018.
28 'Auditor-General to be Probed' *Daily Nation* (16 May 2018).
29 Marilyn Rose, 'You can steal … but tabatila kulya nembuto kumo – Lungu' *The Mast* (12 February 2018) <http://www.themastomline.com/2018/02/12/you-can-stealbut-tabatila-kulya-nembuto-kumo-lungu> accessed 5 May 2018.
30 <https://www.lusakavoice.com/2018/02/23/ubomba-mwibala-alya-mwibala-stays-chungu/> accessed 20 July 2020.

Since Zambia is a common law jurisdiction, treaties, once ratified, do not become directly applicable; the legal effect of such instruments is dependent on their realisation in domestic law. Article 63(2)(e) of the Constitution vests in the National Assembly the power to approve international agreements before these are ratified or acceded to. Consequently, the key Zambian Act of Parliament that regulates and provides for the domestication of international obligations is the 2016 Ratification of International Agreements Act. The Act's purpose is to 'provide for the ratification of international agreements and the domestication process; and provide for matters connected with, or incidental to, the foregoing'.[31] Prior to 2016, the ratification process was provided for in the Constitution as amended in 1996, article 44(2)(d) of which stated that the President had the powers to 'negotiate and sign international agreements and to delegate the power to do so'.[32] Therefore, prior to the 2016 constitutional amendment, the signing, ratification or accession to international treaties was a purely executive function. The 2016 Act defines what is meant by 'domestication', indicating that it means to give 'legal effect to an international agreement or a part of an international agreement, through legislation or any other enforceable means'.

The legal status of ratified international treaties in Zambia is not clear as article 7 of the Constitution, which lists sources of law applicable in Zambia, omits international law. However, it has long been assumed that the ratification of a number of treaties and conventions indicates a willingness on the part of the Zambian Parliament to act consistently with such provisions and that Zambia feels somewhat 'morally bound' to interpret grey areas of domestic law in line with such international agreements.[33] This assumption is affirmed in the case of *Amnesty International v Zambia,* in which the lawyer for the government of Zambia 'affirmed Zambia's commitment to abide by the treaties it is party to'.[34]

The Zambian judiciary has often stated that international law can be relied upon as a persuasive aid to interpretation or to fill gaps where domestic law is

---

[31] The Ratification of International Agreements Act (2016) 34 of 2016 s 2 <http://www.parliament.gov.zm/sites/default/files/documents/acts/The%20Ratification%20of%20International%20Agreements%20Act%20No.%2034%20of%202016.pdf> accessed 15 November 2018.

[32] Constitution of Zambia (Amendment) Act 18 of 1996 <https://www.ilo.org/dyn/natlex/docs/ELECTRONIC/26620/90492/F735047973/ZMB26620.pdf> accessed 15 November 2018.

[33] R Mbambi, 'Domestication and Implementation of the CRC in Zambia: The Rights of the Child Victim of Defilement' (2014) 45 Zam LJ 111.

[34] *Amnesty International v Zambia* Communication 212/98 42 <http://www.refworld.org/cases,ACHPR,52ea5ca34.html> accessed 15 November 2018.

inadequate or has *lacunae*. In *Longwe v Intercontinental Hotel*, for example, the Court declared:[35]

> Before I end, I have to say something about the effect of International Treaties and Conventions which the Republic of Zambia enters into and ratifies ... It is my considered view that ratification of such documents by a nation State without reservations is a clear testimony of the willingness by that State to be bound by the provisions of such a document. Since there is that willingness, if an issue comes before this court which would not be covered by local legislation but would be covered by such international document, I would take judicial notice of the Treaty or Convention in my resolution of the dispute.

Similarly, in the case of *Attorney-General v Clarke* the respondent claimed a violation of his rights to freedom of expression and non-discrimination. The Supreme Court held that '[w]e agree that in applying and construing our statutes we can take into consideration international instruments to which Zambia is a signatory. However, these international instruments are only of persuasive value unless they are domesticated in our laws'.[36] This approach was again followed in 2011 by the Supreme Court. In *Kingaipe & Another v Attorney-General* Muyovwe JS found that the courts indeed have the authority to 'consider and take into account provisions of international instruments and decided cases in other courts. Zambian courts are not operating in isolation and any decision made by other courts on any aspect of the law is worth considering.'[37]

At the regional level, Zambia has been a member of the African Union (AU) and its predecessor, the Organisation for African Unity (OAU), since 1964 when it attained its independence. In July 2018 Zambia signed an agreement with the AU to host the Economic, Social and Cultural Council (ECOSOCC) of the AU in Zambia.[38] It ratified the African Charter on Human and Peoples' Rights (African Charter) in 1984;[39] the African Charter on the Rights and Welfare

---

35 1992/HP/765 (HC) 19.
36 *Attorney-General v Clarke* (96A/2004) [2008] ZMSC 4 (23 January 2008) 26 <https://zambialii.org/akn/zm/judgment/zmsc/2008/4/eng@2008-01-23> accessed 15 September 2023.
37 *Kingaipe & Another v Attorney-General* 2009/HL/86.
38 <https://www.lusakatimes.com/2018/07/01/zambia-signs-agreement-with-au-to-host-ecosocc-secretariat-in-lusaka/> accessed 19 April 2019.
39 <https://au.int/sites/default/files/treaties/7770-sl-african_charter_on_human_and_peoples_rights_2.pdf> accessed 19 April 2019.

of the Child (African Children's Charter) in 2008;[40] and the Protocol to the African Charter on Human and Peoples' Rights on the Rights of Women in Africa (African Women's Protocol) in 2006.[41] In the case of *Legal Resources Foundation v Zambia* the African Commission on Human and Peoples' Rights (African Commission), in its interpretation of the African Charter, considered the approach that Zambia was taking to its responsibilities under international law.[42] The case challenged article 34(3)(b) in the 1996 Constitution which barred presidential candidates who could not prove that both their parents were Zambian citizens by birth or descent. It was argued that the provision violated article 2 (non-discrimination) and articles 13 and 19 (political participation). Despite the African Commission's recognition that international agreements are not self-executing in Zambia and despite finding that Zambia was not avoiding its treaty responsibilities, it asserted its position that 'international treaties which are not part of domestic law and which may not be directly enforceable in the national courts nonetheless impose obligations on states parties'.[43]

Zambia's past commitment to respect for international human rights systems could be measured by its cooperation with international human rights entities created to bring to justice those who are accused of grave human rights violations. Zambia has in the past cooperated with the international community and institutions to bring to justice fugitives who had committed grave human rights violations. For example, as the first conviction by the International Criminal Tribunal for Rwanda (ICTR) for sexual violence and rape as a crime of genocide, Jean-Paul Akayesu was captured in Zambia in 1995. The Zambian authorities cooperated with the Tribunal to have him extradited to stand trial there.[44] Zambia became a state party to the Rome Statute establishing the International Criminal Court (ICC) in November 2002.[45]

---

40 <https://au.int/sites/default/files/treaties/7773-sl-african_charter_on_the_rights_and_welfare_of_the_child_1.pdf> accessed 19 April 2019.

41 <https://au.int/sites/default/files/treaties/7783-sl-protocol_to_the_african_charter_on_human_and_peoples_rights_on_the_rights_of_women_in_africa_7.pdf> accessed 19 April 2019.

42 *Legal Resources v Zambia* Communication 211/98 African Commission on Human and Peoples' Rights (2001) <http://hrlibrary.umn.edu/africa/comcases/Comm211-98.pdf> accessed 15 September 2023.

43 ibid.

44 <https://blogs.lse.ac.uk/vaw/landmark-cases/a-z-of-cases/jean-paul-akayesu-case/> accessed 19 April 2019.

45 <https://asp.icc-cpi.int/en_menus/asp/states%20parties/african%20states/Pages/zambia.aspx> accessed 19 April 2019.

Although no cases involving Zambians have been dealt with by the ICC, the ICC seems to enjoy popular support among ordinary Zambians. In 2017, the Patriotic Front (PF) government considered withdrawing from the ICC, and authorised the Minister of Justice to undertake public consultations. However, this initiative was shelved when the majority of those consulted disapproved of withdrawal.[46] In relation to the ICC arrest warrant against then Sudanese President, Omar al-Bashir, the Zambian government in 2012 asserted that it would arrest and hand him over to the ICC if he ever visited Zambia.[47]

3 At a Glance: Formal Engagement of Zambia with the UN Human Rights Treaty System

Refer to the chart on the next page.

4 Role and Overall Impact of Human Rights Treaties in Zambia

4.1 *Role of Human Rights Treaties*
4.1.1 Formal Acceptance
Zambia is a state party to eight out of the nine core UN human rights treaties. It has not yet ratified the International Convention on the Protection of the Rights of All Migrant Workers and Members of their Families 1990 (CMW). Although there is no formal explanation given by the government for

---

46 <https://www.lusakatimes.com/2017/02/13/cabinet-table-icc-withdrawal-motion/>; <https://www.lusakatimes.com/2017/05/23/zambians-overwhelmingly-vote-remain-icc/>; <https://zambia24.com/citizens-reject-move-for-zambia-to-leave-icc/> accessed 19 April 2019.
47 'Zambia Ready to Arrest Sudan's Al Bashir' <https://www.faceofmalawi.com/2012/05/21/zambia-ready-to-arrest-sudans-al-bashir/> accessed 20 July 2020.

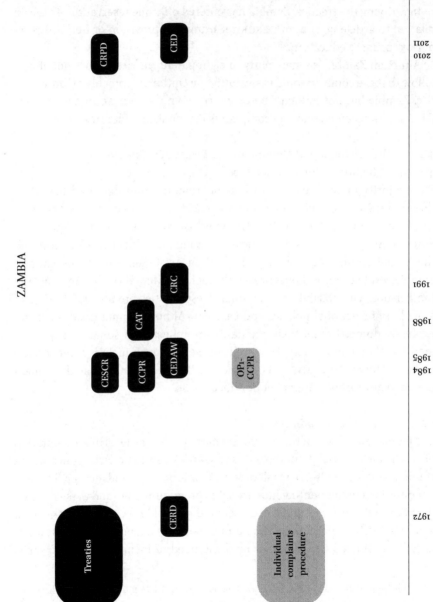

not ratifying this treaty, it seems that unlike other treaties around which many international and local organisations implement programmes, there is no organisation in Zambia specifically advocating for the rights of immigrants. Generally, apart from the influence of lobbying civil society organisations, there is no dominant discernible pattern that influences Zambia's decision to ratify international human rights treaties.

In ratifying the treaties, Zambia has entered only one reservation. This is in relation to article 13(2)(a) of CESCR regarding the provision of free and compulsory primary education.[48]

Although Zambia is a state party to eight parent treaties, it does not always follow that the country would easily ratify the Optional Protocols to those treaties. Zambia has not ratified OP2-CCPR, OP-CAT, OP-CRC-AC or OP-CRC-SC. Zambia has accepted only the complaints mechanism under OP-1-CCPR.

4.2 Overall Impact of Human Rights Treaties in Zambia

4.2.1 Incorporation and Reliance by Organs of State

The majority of the treaties are not incorporated into domestic law. Only three (CEDAW, CRC and CRPD) are domesticated, in whole or in part by local legislation. CEDAW, for example, is domesticated by the Gender Equity and Equality Act 2015; CRC is domesticated through the Education Act 2011 and the Affiliation and Maintenance of Children Act Chapter 64 of the Laws of Zambia, while CRPD is domesticated through the Mental Health Act 2019 and the Persons with Disabilities Act 2012. These treaties are also referred to in a plethora of national policies and case law. Although some treaties are not expressly domesticated, their standards are reflected in some laws and are mentioned in national policies as well as case law. These include CCPR, CESCR and CAT. Only CERD, CMW and CED seem to be neither incorporated nor mentioned in any formal national policy documents.

4.2.2 Level of Awareness

The level of awareness of the treaties seems to mirror the level of incorporation of treaties in Zambia. CRC, CEDAW and CRPD seem to be well known in the country. This is mainly as a result of several international and local civil society organisations implementing human rights programmes around these treaties. Apart from these, CCPR and CESCR seem to be well known. CCPR is the most commonly-cited international human rights treaty in court cases. CESCR has usually dominated the debate around the need to include economic, social

---

48 <https://treaties.un.org/pages/ViewDetails.aspx?src=IND&mtdsg_no=IV-3&chapter=4&clang=_en#EndDec> accessed 20 July 2020.

and cultural rights in the national Constitution. Although CAT is not very well known, its influence seems to be growing as a result of the interventions of the Human Rights Commission and other stakeholders, leading to a cabinet decision to approve proposals to enact specific legislation proscribing torture. CERD, CMW and CED do not seem to be known beyond academic circles.

4.2.3 Use by Non-Governmental Actors

CEDAW, CRC and CRPD seem to be the most referred to by non-state entities. Several UN agencies, international organisations and local civil society organisations actively promote the standards of these treaties in their programming. These treaties are also actively studied and commented upon by scholars. As a result, they are the most covered in the media. Apart from these, CCPR and CESCR also seem to be well known and often cited in the context of major national political debates. CCPR has influenced political debate around civil and political rights, while CESCR has had an influence on the national debate about incorporating economic, social and cultural rights into the national Constitution. Only CERD, CMW and CED are hardly made use of in the country.

4.2.4 State Reporting

Zambia has never been consistent and efficient in submitting its reports. Its reports usually are delayed for many years and often, as a result, the country has to combine two or three reports in order to catch up. Albeit always late, Zambia has reported to seven of the eight treaty bodies to which it is a member, but it is yet to submit its initial state party report to the CED Cttee. The report was due on 4 May 2013. The reports are prepared under the Ministry of Justice, which has a designated department dealing with international treaty obligations. Earlier reports tended to be drafted entirely in-house with little or no consultation. However, the practice has evolved where the Ministry consults widely and engages all major stakeholders, including civil society organisations, in the preparation of reports. The reports are usually presented to treaty bodies by high-ranking state officers such as the Minister of Justice, permanent secretaries, the attorney-general or the solicitor-general. The government, however, does not publish its reports locally.

In the context of presenting its reports, Zambia has had a total of 14 dialogues with treaty-monitoring bodies (two under CERD; three under CCPR; two under CESCR; three under CEDAW; two under CAT; and two under CRC). There have been no dialogues in relation to CRPD and CED as the country is yet to submit its initial reports. In terms of quality, the earlier or older reports seem to have been of poor quality and contained very little relevant information and were not prepared in line with guidelines. This seems to have changed over time as later reports have often been praised by treaty bodies as having been prepared in line with guidelines and containing essential information. Although the reports have improved markedly, they generally tend to be less self-critical. It should also be noted that international organisations and bilateral partners have usually provided financial and material support to help draft state party reports. These have often been in relation to CRC and CEDAW treaties around which many implement programmes. As a result, these seem to be better researched and drafted reports. In general, concluding observations, although not often popularized by the state, are implemented. The choice and vigour of the implementation are often informed by the nature or popularity of the treaty, local political dynamics and priorities as well as technical support and interest from civil society organisations and other international actors.

4.2.5 Individual Communications

There have only been individual communications to the Human Rights Committee (HRCttee) under CCPR as Zambia has not allowed individual communications under other treaty bodies. The HRCttee found ten violations against Zambia. The implementation of the findings largely depends on the remedy proposed. Where the remedy has been compensation, this seems to have been relatively easy for the state to implement. At least three of the complainants are known to have been compensated. However, where the proposed remedy is at variance with the domestic legal order, this has been impossible to implement. For example, a number of cases challenged the death penalty and findings were made against Zambia. Considering that these sentences were brought by domestic courts and exhausted all appeal options, it means in those specific cases that the decisions of the courts cannot be reversed, despite the finding of the HRCttee. In such cases, the only option is through a moratorium or pardon by the President. Although this frequently occurs, it is difficult to attribute it to any specific treaty as the President relies on domestic law in making the decisions. This, however, does not absolve the state from the duty to amend its laws to align them with its international human rights law responsibilities under the treaty.

4.2.6 Treaty Body Membership

There is no formalised process for the nomination of committee members from the country. Zambia currently has membership in the CRC Cttee, represented by Professor Cephas Lumina. His mandate ends in 2021. No other Zambian national holds membership in other treaty bodies or has in the past been a member.

4.2.7 Additional

There seems to be no reference to the UN Charter in national laws and policies. However, the UDHR is often cited in national policies and case law (see, for example, the cases of *MacDonald Chipenzi & Others v The People*;[49] *Stanley Kingaipe and Charles Chookole v Attorney-General*;[50] *Gift Nkanza v The People*;[51] *Lipepo Others v The People*;[52] and *George Mwanza and Melvin Beene v Attorney General*).[53] The Zambian Bill of Rights in the Constitution is also modelled on the UDHR.[54]

5 The Impact of the Different UN Human Rights Treaties on the Domestic Level in Zambia

5.1 *International Convention of the Elimination of All Forms of Racial Discrimination*

Zambia ratified CERD on 4 February 1972, without any reservations.[55] It has not accepted individual complaints procedures under the treaty.

5.1.1 Incorporation and Reliance by Organs of State

The treaty has not been expressly incorporated in any domestic law. There is no known public policy document incorporating or referring to the treaty. However, articles 11 and 23 of the Zambian Constitution outlaw discrimination based, *inter alia*, on race, although 'race' is not defined.

5.1.2 Level of Awareness

The treaty seems not to be well known in Zambia, possibly because of its political history in which race and racial segregation were not a major problem, relative to other colonial states. Apart from the academia, the Human Rights Commission and lawyers and officials at the Ministry of Justice, there seems to be little or no awareness of the treaty. At the academic level, the Law School at the University of Zambia incorporates the treaty in its course on human

---

49 *MacDonald Chipenzi & Others v The People* HPR/03/2014 (4 December 2014).
50 *Stanley Kingaipe and Charles Chookole v Attorney-General* 2009/HL/86 (27 May 2010).
51 *Gift Nkanza v The People* Selected Judgment No 31 of 2015.
52 *Lipepo & Others v The People* (Appeal No 389, 390, 391, 392/2013[2014]).
53 *George Mwanza and Melvin Beene v Attorney-General* Selected Judgment No 33 of 2019.
54 Alfred Chanda, *Constitutional Law in Zambia* (University of Zambia Press 2012) 23.
55 <https://treaties.un.org/Pages/ViewDetails.aspx?src=TREATY&mtdsg_no=IV-2&chapter=4&clang=_en> accessed 19 April 2019.

rights.[56] The Human Rights Commission mentions the treaty in its 2014–2016 Strategic Plan as among the international human rights treaties it has a mandate to promote.[57] There are no publicly-available official references to the treaty from senior government officials and there seems to be no press references to the same treaty. No civil society organisation is known to have made reference to the treaty in its work in Zambia.

5.1.3 Use by Non-Governmental Actors

There is no evidence of the legal profession, NGOs and media making reference to the treaty. The treaty, however, is covered in the main locally-published human rights law textbook used in the School of Law at the University of Zambia.[58]

5.1.4 State Reporting and Its Impact

Zambia's reporting to the CERD Cttee has been erratic and characterised by long delays. It has reported five times to the Committee. It submitted its first report on 1 March 1975 after a delay of a year and 11 months; its second report was submitted on 22 December 1982 after seven years and eight months; it submitted its third report on 22 February 1993 after a delay of seven years and 11 months; it submitted its fourth report on 13 July 2004 after nine years and three months; and it submitted its fifth and most recent report on 14 February 2018 after eight years and 11 months.[59] The government has given no explanations for the delayed reporting.

The reports have traditionally been prepared privately under the Ministry of Justice, without external consultation. To this effect, the 1993 country report categorically stated that '[i]nformation for the preparation of human rights reports is obtained from within Zambia and the contents are not subject to public debate'.[60] The reports have usually lacked depth and substance and were not prepared in line with the guidelines. In its 1993 COs, for example, the Committee noted that the country report had 'gaps' and further noted that

---

56 See The University of Zambia, LPU 3975 Human Rights Law Course Outline; and The University of Zambia Institute of Distance Education, LPU 3975 Human Rights Module (2018).
57 <file:///C:/Users/elvin/Downloads/HRC%20Strategic%20Plan%202014%20-%202016.pdf> accessed 19 April 2019.
58 Carlson Anyangwe, *Introduction to Human Rights and Humanitarian Law* (University of Zambia Press 2004).
59 <https://tbinternet.ohchr.org/_layouts/TreatyBodyExternal/Countries.aspx?CountryCode=ZMB&Lang=EN> accessed 19 April 2019.
60 Zambia Country Report 22 February 1993 CERD/C/239/Add.2, para 17.

the report had 'not been prepared in accordance with the Committee's general guidelines for the preparation of reports, made the Committee's task more difficult'. The 2005 report was praised by the Committee as having been prepared in accordance with the guidelines and containing relevant information.[61] Equally, the 2018 report appears to have been a remarkable improvement. Not only was it consultative (involving NGOs, the Human Rights Commission and government agencies) but it had more substance than previous reports and responded to almost every recommendation made in the last COs in 2007.[62] The report, however, was lacking in critical reflection. For example, it said very little about the possibility that xenophobic attacks against foreigners, which rocked the country in 2016, might have been fuelled by anti-foreigner rhetoric by politicians and government officials.[63]

There have been no alternative or complementary reports by civil society or NGOs to the Committee. The state has had two dialogues in the context of presenting its reports, that is, in 1993 and in 2005. The Zambian delegation has usually been led by the Minister of Justice, the attorney-general, the solicitor-general or the permanent secretary in the Ministry of Justice.[64]

The most recent COs are those of 2007. The Committee was concerned about the need to amend article 23(4) of the Constitution, which allows discrimination in the area of personal law.[65] In response to this the state party report for 2018 stated that an attempt had been made to reform the provision but the draft Bill of Rights was defeated in a 2016 referendum.[66] The Committee requested the state party to include in its report statistical information on complaints of racial discrimination. The state included this in the 2018 report, indicating that it had six reported cases of racial discrimination.[67] The Committee also recommended that the state party should enhance the effectiveness of the Human Rights Commission in redressing human rights violations, in particular to improve its funding. However, in the 2018 report

---

61 COs of the Committee on the Elimination of All Forms of Racial Discrimination Zambia 27 March 2007 CERD/C/ZM/CO/16, para 2.
62 Zambia Country Report 14 February 2018 CERD/C/ZM/17–19, p 17–19.
63 <https://www.lusakatimes.com/2016/04/18/xenophobic-attacks-lusaka-spread/>; <https://www.chronicle.co.zw/xenophobic-attacks-erupt-in-zambia/> accessed 20 April 2019.
64 Zambia Country Report 22 February 1993 CERD/C/239/Add.2, and COs of the Committee on the Elimination of All Forms of Racial Discrimination Zambia 27 March 2007 CERD/C/ZM/CO/16.
65 COs of the Committee on the Elimination of All Forms of Racial Discrimination Zambia 27 March 2007 CERD/C/ZM/CO/16, para 9.
66 Zambia Country Report 14 February 2018 CERD/C/ZM/17–19, para 5.
67 ibid para 33.

Zambia does not indicate how it effected this. Instead, it simply states that the Human Rights Commission is empowered to receive funds from international institutions or any other source deemed appropriate.[68] The COs have not been translated into local languages and are not widely publicised. In fact, they are not hosted by any government institution website. Therefore, they are inaccessible to many Zambians.

5.1.5 Brief Conclusion

The treaty seems insignificant in the political discourse of Zambia. It is hardly used by NGOs as a tool for advocacy or lobbying. This could be because of the colonial history of the country which, unlike other colonies, did not experience instances of extreme racial segregation.

5.2 *International Covenant on Civil and Political Rights*

Zambia acceded to the treaty on 10 April 1984, without any reservations.[69] It also at the same time acceded to the OP1-CCPR allowing for individual complaints. Zambia, however, is not a party to OP2-CCPR.

5.2.1 Incorporation and Reliance by Organs of State

Although provisions of the treaty have not been expressly incorporated into domestic law, many of the rights provided for in the treaty are also reflected in the Zambian Constitution. These include the right to life; freedom from torture, inhuman or cruel punishment; freedom from slavery; the right to liberty; freedom of movement; the right to a fair trial; the right to privacy; religious freedom; freedom of expression; freedom of assembly; and freedom of association. No compatibility study or programme of domestic reform has been embarked upon to expressly give effect to the provisions of the treaty. However, the treaty is recognised in several public documents. For example, the Human Rights Commission's strategic plan mentions it as one of the human rights treaties to which Zambia subscribes, which the Commission incorporates in its programmes.[70]

---

68 ibid para 46.
69 <https://treaties.un.org/Pages/ViewDetails.aspx?src=TREATY&mtdsg_no=IV-4&chapter=4&clang=_en> accessed 19 April 2019.
70 Human Rights Commission, Strategic Plan 2014–2016: Building a Sustainable Human Rights Culture Together (2014) 7.

5.2.2   Reliance by Judiciary

The treaty also is often cited in judgments by courts. The cases that cite treaties or General Comments relating to the treaty include the cases of *Attorney-General v Roy Clarke*[71] (dealing with the issue of freedom of expression); *MacDonald Chipenzi & Others v The People*[72] (in which the High Court declared a provision in the Penal Code criminalising the sharing of false information as unconstitutional); *Stanley Kingaipe and Charles Chookole v Attorney-General*[73] (dealing with inhuman treatment and discrimination against soldiers who were dismissed from employment after being subjected to mandatory HIV testing without their consent); *Gordon Maddox Mwewa & Others v Attorney-General*[74] (in which the applicants were challenging the constitutionality of the Mental Disorders legislation); *Gift Nkanza v The People*[75] (dealing with the right to fair trial of criminal defendants); *Sata v Post Newspapers & Another*[76] (in which the Supreme Court had to deal with the interplay between the law of defamation and freedom of expression); and *Major Isaac Masonga v The People*[77] (seized with the issue of fair trial). In the case of *George Mwanza and Melvin Beene* the Supreme Court partly relied on the treaty to hold that prisoners had the right to food of adequate nutritional value, arising from their right to life.[78]

5.2.3   Level of Awareness

The treaty is among the most well-known human rights treaties in Zambia.

It has directly or indirectly shaped political discourse. For example, in 1997 the then main opposition leader and former President, Dr Kenneth Kaunda, and his ally, Dr Rodger Chongwe, were shot at by police. Chongwe brought a case (discussed further below) against the state at the Human Rights Committee, the treaty body responsible for enforcing the treaty body. The enforcement of the decision by the Committee and the need to compensate him have often shaped political debate and featured prominently in the media.[79] The case

---

71   *Attorney-General v Roy Clarke* (2008) 1ZR 38.
72   *MacDonald Chipenzi & Others v The People* HPR/03/2014 (4 December 2014).
73   *Stanley Kingaipe and Charles Chookole v Attorney-General* 2009/HL/86 (27 May 2010).
74   *Gordon Maddox Mwewa & Others v Attorney-General* 2017/HP/204 (9 October 2017).
75   *Gift Nkanza v The People* Selected Judgment No 31 of 2015.
76   *Sata v Post Newspapers Limited & Another* 1995.
77   *Major Isaac Masonga v The People* SCZ Judgment No 24 of 2009.
78   *George Mwanza and Melvin Beene v Attorney-General* Selected Judgment No 33 of 2019.
79   <https://www.lusakatimes.com/2009/12/08/chongwe-family-speaks-on-perceived-compensation/>; <https://www.lusakatimes.com/2009/12/09/rodger-chongwe-v-zambia-communication-no-8211998-submitted-by-blogger-nick-edwards/>; <https://www.zambiawatchdog.com/grant-the-barotseland-agreement-and-stop-fooling-around/amp/>; <https://maravi.blogspot.com/2009/12/rupiah-and-chongwes-59m-compensation.html>;

dominated the political landscape between 2008 and 2011 when the government showed a willingness to compensate Chongwe. The general reaction against the government decision centred on the fact that the amount ordered to compensate Chongwe was excessive.

The treaty has also been used by Barotseland activists to either assert their right to internal self-determination or secession from mainland Zambia. For example, in a paper presented at the Barotse National Council in 2012, Muyuwa Liuwa argued that article 1 of CCPR recognises the rights of people to self-determination and that, therefore, Barotseland was entitled to determine its own future as a sovereign nation.[80] Barotseland, officially the western province of Zambia, enjoyed a semi-autonomous state under colonial rule and proceeded to be part of Zambia at independence on the assurance of its semi-autonomy. However, subsequent Zambian governments never honoured the undertaking and forced Barotseland into the unitary Zambian state. This has been a source of tension and political mobilisation in Barotseland, culminating in the resolutions of the Barotse National Council in 2012 that voted to secede from the rest of Zambia.[81]

The treaty, including all major international human rights law treaties to which Zambia is a party, is taught in secondary schools as part of civic education.[82] The treaty is regularly cited by legal scholars. For example, in arguing against political violence, Professor Muna Ndulo relied in part on provisions of CCPR in a 2013 article.[83] The treaty is also widely cited by Zambian postgraduate law students in their research. Linda Kasonde, for example, cited the treaty in arguing for an expanded national Bill of Rights that contains enforceable economic, social and cultural rights.[84] Similarly, in arguing for the inclusion of

---

<https://www.lusakatimes.com/2009/12/18/govt-is-liable-to-compensate-dr-chongwe-%E2%80%93-george-kunda/>; <https://www.lusakatimes.com/2009/12/16/roger-chongwe-claim-must-be-registered-%E2%80%94-laz/>; <https://www.lusakatimes.com/2009/12/17/chongwe-tells-off-laz/> accessed 19 April 2019.

80 Muyuwa Liuwa, 'The Impasse on Barotseland Agreement 1964: Available Options' Paper Presented at the Barotse National Council, Limulunga, 26–27 March 2012 7.
81 Resolutions of the 2012 Barotse National Council held at Limulunga on 26–27 March 2012.
82 Republic of Zambia, Civic Education High School Syllabus Grade 10–12 (Lusaka: Curriculum Development Centre, 2004).
83 Muna Ndulo, 'Political Violence in Zambia and State Responsibility' <http://saipar.org/wp-content/uploads/2013/09/Ndulo_Political-Violence-in-Zambia-and-State-Responsibility.pdf> accessed 19 April 2019.
84 Linda Kasonde, 'The Need for Justiciable Socio-Economic Rights in the Bill of Rights in the Zambian Constitution' LLM dissertation, University of Cape Town, 2014 16.

economic, social and cultural rights in the Constitution, Sam Mwapela relies in part on CCPR.[85]

5.2.4   Use by Non-state Actors

The treaty is widely used by NGOs in their human rights programmes and human rights campaigns. In 2015 the Jesuit Centre for Theological Reflection (JCTR), under funding from the United Nations Development Programme (UNDP), for example, conducted human rights training for members of parliament to equip them with appropriate human rights skills in their legislative work. The module for the training incorporates CCPR human rights standards.[86] The Media Institute of Southern Africa Zambia Chapter (MISA Zambia) often uses the treaty's provisions in the training of journalists in human rights reporting. For example, in 2017, with support from GIZ, MISA Zambia organised training for journalists from community radio stations. The training focused on human rights reporting and included provisions of CCPR.[87] Similarly, the NGO Southern African Centre for Constructive Resolution of Disputes (SACCORD), in collaboration with the Human Rights Commission, under funding from the Germany Development Cooperation (GIZ) in 2014, developed guidelines for use by police in managing public order.[88] The guidelines specifically refer to article 21 of CCPR which entitles people to peaceful assembly.[89]

5.2.5   State Reporting

Zambia's reports to the Human Rights Committee have been intermittent and characterised by long periods of delay. The country so far has submitted only three reports. The first report was submitted on 24 June 1987, after a delay of one year and 11 months. The second report was submitted on 27 January 1995 following a delay of four years and five months. The third and last report was

---

[85]   Sam Mwapela, 'Economic, Social and Cultural Rights: Prospects and Challenges for their Inclusion in the Next Constitution of Zambia' LLM dissertation, University of Zambia, 2015.

[86]   JCTR, 'Tools for Promoting Respect, Protection and Promotion of Human Rights for Members of Parliament' (2015).

[87]   O'Brien Kaaba and Mubanga Chikuta, 'Human Rights Issues to be Considered in Journalism' Paper presented at the MISA workshop for community radio Journalists in Lusaka, 2–3 October 2017.

[88]   Guidelines on Freedom of Peaceful Assembly and Application of the Public Order Act in Zambia, 2014.

[89]   ibid 18.

submitted on 12 December 2005, after a delay of seven years and five months.[90] The state currently is approximately seven years behind its reporting schedule.

The responsibility for compiling state party reports is under the Ministry of Justice in Zambia. Although traditionally reports were generated within the Ministry without public engagement, the state has moved towards a more consultative approach whereby it seeks the input of NGOs and quasi-governmental entities such as the Human Rights Commission.[91] Zambia's reports have tended to be very short, lacking in depth and critical reflection. This was noted by the Committee in its 1996 COs:[92]

> However, the Committee regrets that although the report provides information on general legislative norms in Zambia, it largely fails to deal with the actual state of implementation of the Covenant in practice and the difficulties encountered in the course of implementation.

The 2006 report, however, seems very detailed and a marked improvement from previous reports.[93]

Civil society has generally been active in submitting alternative reports. Alternative CSO reports in relation to Zambian are largely a post-2000 phenomenon. In 2006 the Global Initiative to End All Corporal Punishment of Children submitted a briefing memorandum to the Human Rights Committee's pre-session Working Group on the status of corporal punishment against children under Zambian law.[94] In 2007 a coalition of Zambian NGOs, with support from the World Organisation Against Torture (OMCT), submitted two shadow reports, one focusing on women's rights with the other focusing on children's rights in Zambia.[95] Similarly, the Global Initiative in 2007 submitted an alternative report to the Human Rights Committee focusing on the violation of the rights of the LGBT community in Zambia.[96] In 2009 three Zambian NGOs, with

---

90 <https://tbinternet.ohchr.org/_layouts/TreatyBodyExternal/Countries.aspx?CountryCode=ZMB&Lang=EN> accessed 19 April 2019.
91 Interview with C (lawyer at Ministry of Justice) 20 February 2019.
92 COs of the Human Rights Committee on Zambia (3 April 1996) CCPR/C/79/Add.62 para 2.
93 Zambia State Party Report (2006) CCPR/C/ZMB/3.
94 Briefing from the Global Initiative to End All Corporal Punishment of Children (October/November 2006).
95 OMCT, Human Rights Violations in Zambia: Child Rights Situation (Shadow Report to the UN Human Rights Committee July 2007); OMCT, Human Rights Violations in Zambia: Women's Rights (Shadow Report to the UN Human Rights June 2007).
96 Global Initiative, The Violations of the Rights of Lesbian, Gay, Bisexual and Transgender Persons in Zambia (2007).

support from the Centre for Civil and Political Rights, submitted a joint report to the Human Rights Committee focusing on the progress on the follow-up to the COs.[97] Reports by NGOs generally tend to focus on narrow thematic areas of interest of concerned NGOS.

Zambia normally sends a high-level delegation to the Human Rights Committee, usually led by a permanent secretary, the attorney-general or the solicitor-general.[98] Zambia has had only three dialogues with the Committee, that is, in 1988, 1996 and 2007. The main human rights concerns that emerged from those dialogues, as captured in COs, include the lack of clarity on the legal provisions governing the introduction and administration of a state of emergency; high maternal mortality rates; sexual and domestic violence against women; the criminalisation of same-sex activities between consenting adults; corporal punishment; compliance of customary law with rights provided for in the Covenant; the abolition of imprisonment for civil debt; discrimination against women; torture and ill-treatment of prisoners; and the harmonisation of domestic law with the Covenant.

The government does not disseminate COs widely and, therefore, they are largely inaccessible to the public. Although the state has acted to change the situation in relation to some of the concerns, in other areas the government position has tended to be counter-COs proposals. For example, corporal punishment has been abolished[99] and laws against gender violence strengthened. However, the position of the government against same-sex relations has been hardened, as the government in 2016 attempted to pass a constitutional clause expressly banning marriage between people of the same sex.[100]

Zambia has been the subject of follow-up mechanisms. The state has, however, not been fully responsive to the requests for further information requested. For example, following the 2007 COs and the request for further information therein, the Special Rapporteur in 2009 reminded the country to submit the information requested in the COs. Zambia duly submitted the information but the information was found to be inadequate. Several reminders were sent to the state party to submit more detailed information, but these have not been heeded.[101]

---

97   AWOMI, WILDAF and ZCEA, NGO Progress Report on the Follow-up to the COs CCPR/C/ZMB/CO/3 (2009).
98   Interview with C (lawyer at the Ministry of Justice) 20 February 2019.
99   *John Banda v The People* HPA/6/1998; *The People v Ian Kainda* (HLR/01/2000) (unreported).
100 See the Draft Bill of Rights 2016.
101 Human Rights Committee, Consideration of Reports Submitted by States Parties Under Article 40 of the Covenant: Zambia (CCPR/C/ZMB/CO/3/Add.1) (18 December 2009); Human Rights Committee, Report of the Special Rapporteur for Follow-Up on COs

5.2.6 Individual Communications and Their Impact

There have been 12 individual complaints against Zambia. Ten of these communications led to adverse findings against Zambia.[102] The state is only known to have provided compensation in three cases (*Peter Chiiko Bwalya v Zambia*; *Alex Soteli Chambala v Zambia*; and *Kalenga v Zambia*). It has been reported that Mwamba received a presidential pardon and was released; and that Chisanga's sentence was commuted to life imprisonment.[103] No remedies were provided by the state in the other cases. There have been no general measures to avoid recurrence of these violations, such as law reform.

5.2.7 Brief Conclusion

CCPR is among the most popular and well-known treaties in Zambia. It is referred to in government documents, taught in secondary schools and as part of human rights law at university. A plethora of judgments make express reliance on the treaty. While in some cases the state has made efforts to implement treaty standards, in some areas, such as same-sex relations, the state seems to be adopting counter-treaty standards.

(95th session, March 2009) (CCPR/C/95/2) (20 February 2009) 27; Letter of the Special Rapporteur for Follow-Up on COs to the Republic of Zambia dated 26 April 2010; Letter of the Special Rapporteur for Follow-up on COs to the Republic of Zambia dated 28 September 2010; Letter of the Special Rapporteur for Follow-up on COs to the Republic of Zambia dated 20 April 2011; Letter of the Special Rapporteur for Follow-up on COs to the Republic of Zambia dated 25 November 2011.

102 *Kalenga v Zambia* Communication 326/1988 (27 July 1993) (CCPR/C/48/D/326/1988); *Mukunto v Zambia* Communication 768/1997 (23 July 1999) (CCPR/C/66/D/768/1997); *Peter Chiiko Bwalya v Zambia* Communication 314/1988 (30 March 1988)(CCPR/C/WG/33/D/314/1988); *Mwamba v Zambia* Communication 1520/2006 (10 March 2010) (CCPR/C/98/D/1520/2006); *Lubuto v Zambia* Communication 390/1990 (31 October 1991) (CCPR/C/55/D/390/1990); *Chongwe v Zambia* Communication 821/1998 (25 October 2000) (CCPR/C/70/D/821/1988); *Chisanga v Zambia* Communication 1132/2002 (18 October 2005) (CCPR/C/85/D/1132/2002); *Chambala v Zambia* Communication 856/1999 (15 July 2003) (CCPR/C/78/D/856/1999); *Chiti v Zambia* Communication 1303/2004 (26 July 2012) (CCPR/C/105/D/1303/2004); *Kamoyo v Zambia* Communication 1859/2009 (23 March 2012) (CCPR/C/104/D/1859/2009). Two communications were found to be inadmissible: *Silva & Others v Zambia* (CCPR/C/75/D/825-828/1998), and *EMM v Zambia* (CCPR/C/116/D/1145/2002).

103 See Human Rights Implementation Law Project (HRLIP) Case template for decisions adopted by the UN and Regional Human Rights Bodies involving Burkina Faso, Cameroon and Zambia <http://www.bristol.ac.uk/media-library/sites/law/hric/Confidential%20c onsolidated%20case%20templates%20Africa%20English.pdf> accessed 21 March 2022.

5.3 *International Covenant on Economic, Social and Cultural Rights*

Zambia ratified CESCR on 10 April 1984.[104] The state party entered a reservation to article 13(2)(a) of the Covenant regarding provision of free and compulsory primary education.[105] Zambia has accepted neither the individual complaints procedure nor the inquiry procedure.[106]

5.3.1 Incorporation and Reliance by Organs of State

CESCR is used as a standard for economic, social and cultural rights by the national human rights commission and is expressly mentioned in its strategic plan.[107] Although the National Vision document does not expressly mention the treaty, it incorporates social, economic and cultural rights as its development targets to be achieved in turning the country into a middle-income country by 2030.[108] The draft National Land Policy refers to the Covenant as among other international human rights treaties it seeks to domesticate.[109]

The treaty has not been incorporated into domestic law and, therefore, is not directly enforceable by domestic courts. There was an effort in 2016 to amend the Constitution in order to incorporate economic, social and cultural rights.[110] The expanded draft Bill of Rights, however, was defeated in the referendum. As noted above, CESCR is incorporated into the national human rights commission's strategic plan. There has never been a treaty compatibility survey. In the case of *George Mwanza and Melvin Beene* the Supreme Court partly relied on the treaty to hold that prisoners had the right to food of adequate nutritional value, arising from their right to life.[111] The case is significant as it was filed by two HIV-positive inmates on anti-retroviral treatment. They argued that the food with which they were provided in prison was inadequate both in quantity and nutritional value, hence it was in violation of their right to life considering their medical condition. At first instance, the High Court dismissed

---

[104] <https://tbinternet.ohchr.org/_layouts/TreatyBodyExternal/Treaty.aspx?CountryID=194&Lang=EN> accessed 20 April 2019.

[105] Zambia State Party Report to the Committee on Economic Social and Cultural Rights E/1990/5/ADD.60 (1 September 2003) 10; see also Committee on Economic, Social and Cultural Rights, 'List of Issues to be Taken Up in Connection with the Consideration of the Initial Report of Zambia' E/C.12/Q/ZMB/1 (1–5 December 2003) para 35.

[106] ibid.

[107] Human Rights Commission, Strategic Plan 2012–2016: Building a Sustainable Human Rights Culture Together (2014) 7.

[108] Republic of Zambia, Vision 2030: A Prosperous Middle-Income Country by 2030 (December 2006).

[109] Republic of Zambia, Draft National Land Policy (December 2017) 47.

[110] Draft Bill of Rights 2016.

[111] *George Mwanza and Melvin Beene v Attorney-General* Selected Judgment No 33 of 2019.

the case, holding that the Zambian Constitution did not provide for social and economic rights. On appeal, the Supreme Court, however, held that the right to life included all the social goods such as health and food that enhanced the quality of life. Its decision was informed mainly by the treaty and comparative jurisprudence from India.[112]

There seem to be no court decisions expressly referring to the treaty.

5.3.2 Level of Awareness

CESCR is among the most well-known UN treaties in Zambia. It has informed the proposals in various constitution-making initiatives to expand the Bill of Rights to include economic, social and cultural rights since 1996. Although the treaty has not been officially translated into local languages, some NGOs have translated excerpts of the treaty in the course of raising awareness about human rights. For example, the Women in Law and Development in Africa (WiLDAF), with support from Plan International, in 2007 to 2009 translated some economic, social and cultural rights into local languages and printed these on posters for purposes of community engagement and human rights awareness.[113]

The treaty seems to be well known by the media. It is often cited by name or indirectly by referring to its norms in several reports by the leading press. This includes the leading daily newspapers such as the *Zambia Daily Mail*[114] and *The Mast*.[115] The Media Institute of Southern Africa (MISA) Zambia, the umbrella association for media in Zambia, included the treaty in its training of community radio journalists in 2017.[116]

The treaty also forms part of the curriculum both at secondary and tertiary level, particularly in law schools. At the University of Zambia, the treaty is part of the human rights law curriculum.[117] The University of Zambia also offers a postgraduate diploma in human rights law which incorporates the treaty.[118]

---

112 ibid.
113 Kwaba Project Posters 2007–2009.
114 <https://www.daily-mail.co.zm/towards-16-days-of-activism-against-gbv/> accessed 15 September 2023.
115 <https://www.themastonline.com/2017/08/23/pf-govt-reversing-human-rights-culture-says-zcea/>; <https://web.facebook.com/themastzambia/posts/1817773171814065:0?_rdc=1&_rdr> accessed 19 April 2019.
116 O'Brien Kaaba and Mubanga Chikuta, 'Human Rights Issues to be Considered in Journalism' Paper presented at the MISA workshop for community radio journalists in Lusaka, 2–3 October 2017.
117 University of Zambia School of Law, LPU 3975 Human Rights Law Course Outline.
118 University of Zambia School of Law, Postgraduate Diploma in Human Rights Law.

The University of Lusaka also offers human rights courses at both undergraduate and postgraduate level.[119] Similarly, Cavendish University Zambia provides human rights training at both undergraduate and postgraduate levels.[120]

The treaty is also widely cited by academics and Zambian postgraduate law students in their research. In 2013 O'Brien Kaaba and Franziska Bertz authored an article urging inclusion of economic, social and cultural rights in the Constitution.[121] Linda Kasonde cited the treaty in arguing for an expanded national Bill of Rights that contains enforceable economic, social and cultural rights.[122] Similarly, in arguing for the inclusion of economic, social and cultural rights in the Constitution, Sam Mwapela relies in part on CCPR.[123] Equally, Simson Mwale cites the treaty in arguing for expanding the Bill of Rights in the Zambian Constitution in order to incorporate economic, social and cultural rights.[124] The treaty is also referred to in local human rights textbooks.

5.3.3 Use by Non-state Actors

The treaty has mostly been widely used by local NGOs in the context of constitution making in order to urge the government to include economic, social and cultural rights. The Jesuit Centre for Theological Reflection (JCTR), for example, in 2009 relied on the treaty to urge the Constitution Review Commission to incorporate economic, social and cultural rights in the Constitution.[125]

5.3.4 State Reporting and Its Impact

Zambia has reported only twice under CESCR, in 1985 and in 2003.[126] The reporting has been characterised by delays. The second report was presented

---

119 <https://www.educartis.co.zm/courses/master-of-laws-llm-mphil-human-rights-law; https://eduloaded.com/zambia/unilus-programmes/> accessed 19 April 2019.
120 <http://cavendishza.org/enrolment/index.php/programmes-2> accessed 19 April 2019.
121 O'Brien Kaaba and Franziska Bertz, 'Implications of Enshrining Economic, Social and Cultural Rights in the Bill of Rights of the Zambian Constitution' (2013) JCTR Bulletin.
122 Linda Kasonde, 'The Need for Justiciable Socio-Economic Rights in the Bill of Rights in the Zambian Constitution' LLM dissertation, University of Cape Town, 2014 16.
123 Sam Mwapela, 'Economic, Social and Cultural Rights: Prospects and Challenges for their Inclusion in the Next Constitution of Zambia' LLM dissertation, University of Zambia, 2015.
124 Simson Mwale, 'Zambia's Economic, Social and Cultural Rights: Why Should They Be in the New Constitution?' JCTR Report December 2004.
125 JCTR, 'Inclusion of Economic, Social and Cultural Rights in the New Bill of Rights in the New Constitution of Zambia,' Submissions by JCTR to the Human Rights Committee of the National Constitutional Conference 2009.
126 <https://tbinternet.ohchr.org/_layouts/TreatyBodyExternal/Countries.aspx?CountryCode=ZMB&Lang=EN> accessed 19 April 2020.

four years after its due date. Since 2003 Zambia has not submitted its report, which is approximately nine years overdue.

The Ministry of Justice is responsible for coordinating the drafting and submission of the reports. The initial report submitted in 1985 seems to have been drafted in-house without collaboration with other stakeholders such as civil society organisations. The subsequent report of 2003 was drafted with technical and financial support from the Swedish government. The process was consultative and included civil society organisations.[127] The initial report was lacking in substance and critical self-reflection and was not done in line with the guidelines. This was attributed to the lack of experience by the country in drafting such reports, for which technical assistance was recommended.[128] The 2003 report was more detailed and provided more relevant information, although it was not self-critical. The Committee acknowledged that the 2003 report conformed with the guidelines but indicated that the information provided was insufficient for purposes of the Committee being able to assess the status of the implementation of the treaty.[129]

There have so far been no alternative or supplementary reports by civil society organisations.

Zambia's delegations to the Committee have been high level. The delegation that presented the 2003 report was led by the permanent secretary for the Ministry of Justice. Zambia has had two dialogues with the Committee, in 1986 and 2005.

The Committee published its COs in 1986 and 2005. The main concerns arising out of the COs include the lack of incorporation of the Covenant into the domestic legal order; inadequate funding of the national human rights commission; the lack of desegregated data on measures taken by the state to implement the treaty; customary law that discriminates against women and girls; inadequate representation of women at high-level decision-making bodies of the state; the high levels of unemployment; restrictions on the right to form trade unions; the social impact of HIV/AIDS; widespread child labour; and low funding for health care.[130] The COs are neither published nor widely disseminated by Zambia.

---

127 Zambia State Party Report to the Committee on Economic, Social and Cultural Rights E/1990/5/Add.60 (September 2003) 6.
128 Zambia State Report to the Committee on Economic, Social and Cultural Rights E/1986/WG.1/SR4 (1985) paras 2,18 and 22.
129 COs of the Committee on Economic, Social and Cultural Rights, Zambia, E/C.12/1/Add.106 (25 April-13 May 2005) para 2.
130 ibid paras 11–32.

Although Zambia has not acted on many of these concerns, the state has made efforts to increase the numbers of women in decision-making bodies. The 2016 constitutional amendment, for example, includes a provision that requires the electoral system to ensure 'gender equity in the National Assembly and Council'.[131] The Constitution further requires that any person with the power to nominate persons for public office should ensure that 50 per cent of each gender is represented.[132] Further, Parliament in 2015 enacted the Gender Equity and Equality Act 22 of 2015 which applies not only to the public sector but also to the private sector and prescribes quotas for women in decision making and provides for sanctions for a failure to implement its standards. Although the law has been significantly tilted in favour of enhancing the numbers of women in decision-making positions, the letter of the law is rarely observed and not implemented. For example, women remain underrepresented in the National Assembly and only account for 18,4 per cent while men account for 81,6 per cent.[133] Of the 28 ministers in the cabinet, only nine are women.[134]

The state has had no engagement over follow-up mechanisms relating to the treaty.

5.3.5 Brief Conclusion

The treaty is fairly well known in Zambia. It is referred to in government documents and informs civil society programmes. Zambia has taken some measures to implement some of the treaty standards. These have tended to be those mostly relating to women's rights. However, much remains to be done.

5.4 *Convention on the Elimination of All Forms of Discrimination against Women*

Zambia ratified CEDAW on 21 June 1985 without any reservation. The state has not accepted optional mechanisms such as the individual complaints and inquiries procedures.[135]

---

131 Art 45(1)(d) Constitution of Zambia (Amendment) Act 2 of 2016.
132 ibid art 259(1)(b).
133 <http://www.parliament.gov.zm/members/gender> accessed 19 April 2019.
134 <http://www.parliament.gov.zm/ministers/cabinet> accessed 19 April 2019.
135 <https://treaties.un.org/Pages/ViewDetails.aspx?src=TREATY&mtdsg_no=IV-8&chapter=4&clang=_en>;<https://treaties.un.org/Pages/ViewDetails.aspx?src=TREATY&mtdsg_no=IV-8-b&chapter=4&clang=_en> accessed 19 April 2019.

5.4.1 Incorporation and Reliance by Organs of State

There are several laws and national policies domesticating certain provisions of the treaty or simply referring to the treaty articles as guiding norms domestically. These include the Gender Equity and Equality Act 22 of 2015 which promotes the representation of women in key decision-making positions; the Human Rights Commission Strategic Plan 2014–2016, which refers to the treaty among other human rights treaties it promotes domestically; the draft National Land Policy 2017 which attempts to implement some of the treaty provisions in ensuring that women have equal access to land; and the National Gender Policy 2014 which is the main national policy document governing the national aspirations for gender equality and empowerment of women. CEDAW is also referred to in the police guidelines for managing cases of gender-based violence, developed with support from the United Nations Children's Fund (UNICEF).[136] When Zambia self-reviewed its governance performance in order to relate good governance and economic development, CEDAW was one of the benchmarks against which the country evaluated itself.[137]

In 2004 the Zambian government in collaboration with the World Bank carried out a detailed strategic country gender assessment.[138] Although the assessment primarily focused on gender in development and poverty reduction, it highlighted human rights concerns affecting women. Civil society organisations have also done their own assessments, usually focusing on specific areas of interest. For example, WiLDAF in 2015 carried out a national assessment of the participation of women in electoral and democratic processes in Zambia.[139]

Although the Anti-Gender Based Violence Act 1 of 2011 provides the Anti-Gender-Based Violence Fund for purposes of promoting activities aimed at fighting the physical and psychological abuse of women, the actual funds have never been provided by the government.

5.4.2 Level of Awareness

CEDAW is one of the most well-known treaties as it is widely promoted by international and national NGOs, such as Women in Law and Development

---

136 Zambia Police Service, Gender-Based Violence: Victim Support Unit Experience (2014).
137 Republic of Zambia, 2009 State of Governance Report-Zambia (Lusaka: Governance Secretariat, 2010).
138 The World Bank, Zambia Strategic Country Gender Assessment: A Report of the World Bank (June 2004).
139 WiLDAF, Assessment of Women's Participation in Electoral and Democratic Processes in Zambia (May 2015).

(WiLDAF) and the Non-Governmental Gender Coordinating Council (NGOCC). As noted above, it is referred to in national laws and policies. Several civil society organisations working in this area have translated simplified versions of the treaty for purposes of awareness raising about women's rights. For example, in 2007 WiLDAF carried out extensive awareness raising around the country and developed simplified versions of the treaty which were translated into seven major local languages.[140] The treaty forms part of the human rights curriculum taught in all major law schools in Zambia at both undergraduate and graduate levels. It is also referred to in several standard human rights textbooks. Perhaps the most well-known detailed treatment of CEDAW is by Professor Munalula.[141] This is the leading local textbook on gender and law.

5.4.3 Use by Non-state Actors

CEDAW is well known in the NGO sector and widely promoted by NGOs with an interest in women's rights. It has shaped discourse about women's rights as it has been used by NGOs to mobilise for the domestication of its standards locally, and this arguably led to three major legal reforms. The first was in 2005 when the Penal Code was amended to enhance sentences in crimes of sexual violence.[142] The second was the drafting of a Sexual Offences and Gender Violence Bill by a coalition of women NGOs led by WiLDAF with support from UNICEF in 2006.[143] This Bill was used as a basis by the NGOs to lobby the government to pass a law addressing gender and domestic violence. These efforts resulted in the enactment of the Anti-Gender-Based Violence Act in 2011.[144] Third, lobbying efforts by women NGOs to promote the participation of women in high-level decision-making bodies led to the enactment of the Gender Equity and Equality Act.[145]

The treaty continues to inform the work of many NGOs promoting women's rights. For example, WiLDAF, a local NGO promoting women's rights, incorporated CEDAW in its paralegal training manual.[146] Several NGOs with specific focus on promoting women's rights in line with CEDAW dominate the local

---

140 WiLDAF, CEDAW booklets in Tonga, Nyanja, Bemba, Kaonde, Lunda, Lozi, and Luvale (2007).
141 Mulela Margaret Munalula, *Women, Gender Discrimination and the Law: Cases and Materials* (University of Zambia Press 2005).
142 See Penal Code (Amendment) Act 15 of 2005.
143 Proposed Sexual Offences and Gender Violence Bill 2006.
144 Anti-Gender-Based Violence Act 1 of 2011.
145 Gender Equity and Equality Act 22 of 2015.
146 Women in Law and Development in Africa (WiLDAF) Zambia, Paralegal/Community Legal Rights Promoters Training Manual (2010).

NGO landscape. These include NGOCC; WiLDAF; Women and Law in Southern Africa (WLSA); Women for Change (WFC); Women in Action; and the Young Women's Christian Association.

5.4.4 State Reporting

Zambia has reported three times to the CEDAW Cttee. Its first report was submitted in 1991 after a delay of four years and seven months; the second report was submitted in 1999 after a delay of one year; and the third report was submitted in 2010 following a delay of two years and five months. The subsequent report was due on 1 July 2015 but has not yet been submitted.[147] The lead agency coordinating the state report is the Ministry of Justice. While the initial report was prepared in-house, without much consultation, subsequent reports have been consultative, bringing together both government and civil society.

The quality of reports has shown progressive improvement.[148] The CEDAW Cttee, for example, found the 2010 report better than the previous ones as it was more detailed and was prepared in line with the guidelines. However, the Committee noted that the 2010 report lacked adequate sex-disaggregated data on the situation of women in relation to rights covered by CEDAW.[149] The reports have usually been presented by high-level technocrats, usually led by the permanent secretary at the Ministry of Justice or the attorney-general. This, however, does not entail that the head of the delegation is conversant with the CEDAW provisions or national reports. For example, in the 1994 COs the Committee observed that the presentation of the Zambian report had to be delayed as the delegation leader had not read the report and was not conversant with its contents and, therefore, had to be given time to appraise himself.[150]

International NGOs have been very active in submitting complementary reports to the CEDAW Cttee. For example, at least four international organisations submitted reports to the 2011 pre-session review of Zambia. These

---

[147] <https://tbinternet.ohchr.org/_layouts/15/TreatyBodyExternal/Countries.aspx?CountryCode=ZMB&Lang=EN> accessed 19 April 2019.

[148] See Zambia State Party Report to the CEDAW Committee CEDAW/C/ZAM/1-2 (November 1991); Zambia State Party Report to the CEDAW Committee CEDAW/C/ZAM/3-4 (12 August 1999) 5; and Zambia State Party Report to the CEDAW Committee CEDAW/C/ZMB/5-6 (18 May 2010) 5.

[149] Concluding Observations of the Committee on the Elimination of all Forms of Discrimination Against Women Zambia CEDAW/C/ZMB/CO/5-6 (19 September 2011) para 2.

[150] COs of the Committee on the Elimination of all Forms of Discrimination Against Women Zambia (12 April 1994) paras 328 and 358.

are the International Disability Alliance which submitted a report focusing on the rights of women with disabilities;[151] the Human Rights Watch, which submitted a report that raised concerns about the health and sexual abuse of women in detention in Zambia;[152] the African Rights Monitor, which submitted a detailed report on the state of the implementation of CEDAW;[153] and the Centre for Reproductive Rights, which evaluated the performance of the country in implementing CEDAW.[154]

Zambia has had three dialogues with the CEDAW Cttee, that is, in 1994, 2002 and 2011. The most pertinent issues raised by the Committee in the COs include the lack of incorporation of the treaty into domestic law; the persistence of traditional sex roles; sex, gender and domestic violence against women; constitutional and statutory provisions permitting gender discrimination; the limited participation of women in political and public life; the high level of maternal and infant mortality rates; the increased rate of HIV and the lack of adequate care for infected women; the high rate of unemployment among women; low levels of literacy among women; insufficient efforts by the state to promote visibility of CEDAW; cultural practices adverse to women's rights; and trafficking and commercial exploitation of women. Although the Zambian government has made efforts to domesticate the treaty by incorporating parts of CEDAW in specific statutes mentioned above, and has significantly improved the enrolment of girls in schools, many other concerns remain largely unattended to and continue to affect the realisation of CEDAW domestically.

There have been two follow-up letters from the Rapporteur for Follow-up on COs of the Committee on the Elimination of Discrimination Against Women, that is, in 2013 and 2014.[155] The follow-up letters sought further information from the state in relation to the concerns raised in the 2011 COs. As of 2019 Zambia had not responded to the follow-up letters.

---

151 International Disability Alliance, Suggestions for Disability Relevant Recommendations to be Included in the COs CEDAW Committee 49th Session (11–22 July 2011).
152 Human Rights Watch, Pre-Session Review of Zambia (15 September 2010).
153 African Human Rights Monitor, Submissions Related to the Discussion of the Country Situation in Zambia and its Performance in Upholding the Convention on the Elimination of All Forms of Discrimination Against Women (July 2011).
154 Centre for Reproductive Rights, Supplementary Information on Zambia Scheduled for Review During the 49th Session of the CEDAW Committee (31 May 2011).
155 See Letter by Barbra Bailey, Special Rapporteur on Follow-up CEDAW Committee to the Republic of Zambia AA/follow-up/Zambia/56 (15 November 2013); letter by Barbra Bailey, Special Rapporteur on Follow-up CEDAW Committee to the Republic of Zambia AA/follow-up/Zambia/58 (10 September 2014).

5.4.5 Brief Conclusion

CEDAW is among the most well-known treaties in the country. This is largely as a result of very active women's organisations promoting women's rights. As a result of their lobbying, the country has enacted statutes that attempt to domesticate CEDAW. However, even where these laws have been passed, the country is far from effectively implementing its own laws.

5.5 Convention against Torture and Other Cruel, Inhuman or Degrading Treatment or Punishment

Zambia ratified the treaty on 7 October 1998 without any reservations.[156] However, Zambia is not a state party to OP-CAT.

5.5.1 Incorporation and Reliance by Organs of State

There has been no treaty compatibility study by the state. The treaty has not yet been incorporated into domestic law. However, the Zambian Constitution prohibits torture in absolute terms.[157] Although the treaty has not been incorporated into domestic law, the Human Rights Commission (HRC), in collaboration with the Zambia Law Development Commission (ZLDC),[158] has led a strong campaign lobbying government to pass specific legislation domesticating CAT and specifically criminalising torture. This was part of the HRC's Anti-Torture Campaign Strategy 2015–2019.[159] The campaign led to government drafting the Anti-Torture Bill, which was approved by cabinet on 4 December 2017 and was intended to be submitted to parliament for enactment in 2018.[160] The Bill is yet to be enacted into law. If enacted, the Bill intends to domesticate CAT by criminalising acts of torture and other inhuman or degrading treatment or punishment; to provide for the protection of victims of torture; to provide mechanisms for the compensation and rehabilitation or restitution of victims; and to establish a national anti-torture fund.[161]

---

156 <https://tbinternet.ohchr.org/_layouts/15/TreatyBodyExternal/Countries.aspx?CountryCode=ZMB&Lang=EN> accessed 19 April 2019.
157 Art 15 Constitution of Zambia 1991.
158 <http://www.zldc.org.zm/index.php/k2-blog/with-sidebar-2/item/50-torture-in-zambia> accessed 19 April 2019.
159 <https://tbinternet.ohchr.org/_layouts/15/TreatyBodyExternal/Countries.aspx?CountryCode=ZMB&Lang=EN> accessed 19 April 2019.
160 ibid.
161 ibid.

5.5.2 Reliance by Judiciary

Although there are no known cases in domestic courts directly referring to the treaty, there have been cases by domestic courts finding violations of torture, inhuman or degrading treatment on the basis of the Constitution. In the case of *John Banda v The People*,[162] the High Court declared the use of corporal punishment as a judicial sentence unconstitutional. Similarly, in the case of *The People v Ian Kainda*,[163] the High Court held that corporal punishment cannot be used as a form of punishment for offending juveniles. In the case of *Benjamin Banda and Cephas Kufa Miti v The Attorney-General*,[164] however, the Supreme Court declined to rule that the death penalty was inhuman or degrading on account that it is allowed under the Constitution.

5.5.3 Level of Awareness

The treaty does not seem to be well known among many civil society organisations and the public. The HRC, however, in 2015 (to 2019) launched an anti-torture campaign, popularising CAT and lobbying government to domesticate the treaty. As part of the campaign, the HRC held conferences in almost all major towns in the country to sensitise key stakeholders.1[165] It further opened a FaceBook page dedicated to sharing messages about this campaign, with a hashtag #JoinTheAntiTortureCampaign and provided a toll free number (8181) for reporting torture.[166] The page has approximately 8 300 followers.

Government officials make occasional reference to CAT. For example, while giving a key note address in March 2015 at a conference convened by the HRC, Vice-President Inonge Wina expressed her support for the criminalisation of torture on the ground that Zambia is a state party to CAT.[167] The Minister of

---

162 HP/A6/1998.
163 HLR 1 of 2000.
164 SCZ 2007 unreported.
165 Shikanda Kawanga, 'Let's Criminalise Torture-Inonge' *Zambia Daily Mail* <http://www.daily-mail.co.zm/lets-criminalise-torture-inonge/> accessed 19 April 2019.
166 <https://www.facebook.com/hashtag/jointheantitorturecampaign?source=feed_text&epa=HASHTAG&__xts__[0]=68.arbrsP7ifsCPI-NjNRKenSaHUww8feznSGH623l3Djt8Q9W9QEKvK-p6r108zHwEutHyldy1FuFrtb4ZEoIkkpiscTTWU_3rC45AkMQITjhTdB6e25jLofaQSodbFdYkwP79_xm0ex0qE5IO9mHPzi_YJ1Gh3jzqSjDZO1ntlHsr17ZnZx-wPLNUShv_5obvcI94pSdiJIFFZxL5uoZEih1S_Qo9OIi1KmfdMJAK1pGaGvjVovpD2DopdWzS4Dn81qSQlAo3b-OUSJmNey4mQ2hujtTcc6tlc6-PboY_SM70MdBaTosZkEVvh4mE3zfPP48IZ983FJtEi56RLOfFrQ&__tn__=*NK-R> accessed 19 April 2019.
167 Kawanga (n 165).

Justice, Given Lubinda, in June 2017 indicated that government would enact the Anti-Torture Act in furtherance of its international obligations.[168]

CAT forms part of the human rights curriculum taught in all major law schools in the country. It is also often referred to by academicians in their publications and public interest commentaries. For example, when the Zambian government deported Zimbabwean opposition leader, Tendai Biti, who was seeking asylum in Zambia in August 2018, renowned Zambian legal scholar, Michelo Hansungule, wrote an article condemning the act. He argued, in part, that the deportation of Biti violated Zambia's obligations under CAT as article 3 forbids member states to return an asylum seeker to a country where they are likely to face torture.[169] Similarly, in condemning torture by the police, Prof Muna Ndulo in an article in May 2017 in part relied on the provisions of CAT.[170]

5.5.4 Use by Non-state Actors

The treaty seems to be known by NGOs working around good governance and human rights issues. For example, in 2013 a coalition of 24 local NGOs led by SACCORD, working in this sector, submitted an alternative report to the Human Rights Council on the occasion of the 14 session of the Universal Periodic Review at which occasion Zambia was being reviewed. The alternative report documented instances of the violations of CAT by state agencies, especially the police, and made recommendations on how the state should redress such violations.[171]

Although the treaty does not seem to be frequently cited by practitioners in court proceedings, the Law Association of Zambia included it in its training programmes for human rights defenders in 2018.

The treaty is well known in academia and features in the curriculum on human rights in all major universities in the country. It is often cited in

---

168 'Government to Criminalise Torture in Zambia – Lubinda,' *Lusaka Times* <https://www.lusakatimes.com/2017/06/27/government-criminalize-torture-zambia-lubinda/> accessed 19 April 2019.
169 Michelo Hansungule, 'Deportation of Tendai Biti Low, Low Point for Zambian Regime' *Zambian Watchdog* <https://www.zambiawatchdog.com/deportation-of-tendai-biti-low-low-point-for-zambian-regime/> accessed 19 April 2019.
170 Muna Ndulo, 'Torture and Police Brutality in Zambia: The Need to End Impunity' *Lusaka Times* <https://www.lusakatimes.com/2017/05/26/torture-police-brutality-zambia-need-end-impunity/> accessed 19 April 2019.
171 SACCORD Submission to the Universal Periodic Review 2012 5. See also 'NGOs Worried About Situation Ahead of Zambia's Human Rights Review by the UN' <https://www.zambiawatchdog.com/ngos-worried-about-situation-ahead-of-zambias-human-rights-review-by-un/> accessed 12 July 2019.

commentaries by academics, especially in the context of police brutality against opposition political party supporters. The leading commentaries in this regard are by Zambian legal scholar, Professor Muna Ndulo.[172]

The media only cites the treaty in the context of commentaries made by the Human Rights Commission, NGOs and academics. There seems to be no independent media appreciation of the treaty. The media, however, frequently reports cases of torture by police and other state agencies.[173]

5.5.5   State Reporting

Zambia has only submitted two reports to the CAT Cttee. The first was submitted on 1 December 2000, a year after its due date, and the second was submitted on 15 December 2005, two years after the due date. The subsequent report was due on 30 June 2016 but has not yet been submitted by the state.

The Ministry of Justice is responsible for coordinating the reporting processes to treaty bodies. In preparation of the initial report, the Ministry of Justice constituted an Inter-Ministerial Committee to draft the report. The Committee had representation from NGOs and academia. The process was supported by the Swedish Embassy in Zambia and the Raoul Wallenberg Institute for Human Rights and Humanitarian Law of the University of Lund in Sweden provided technical support to the drafting process.[174] The 2005 report was similarly produced under the tutelage of the Ministry of Justice, with consultation from NGOs, the judiciary and academia.[175] The CAT Cttee considered the initial report to have been frank and thorough.[176]

There seems to have been no alternative reports by NGOs to the CAT Cttee.

Zambia has had two dialogues with the CAT Cttee, namely, in 2002 and 2008. In both instances Zambia sent a high-level delegation. The Zambian delegation in 2002 was led by the attorney-general while in 2008 it was led by the permanent secretary at the Ministry of Justice.

The main concerns raised in the COs of both 2002 and 2008 include the lack of domestication of the treaty; the lack of definition of torture in domestic

---

172   Ndulo (n 170); 'Zambia Degenerating Into a Police State – Prof Ndulo' <https://www.lusakatimes.com/2017/04/14/zambia-degenerating-police-state-prof-ndulo/> accessed 19 April 2019.
173   See for example 'The Death of Detainee Whilst in Police Custody Sparks a Riot in Nakonde' <https://www.lusakatimes.com/2013/10/04/the-death-of-detainee-whist-in-police-custody-sparks-a-riot-in-nakonde/> accessed 12 July 2019.
174   Zambia's State Party Report to the CAT Committee CAT/C/47/Add.2 (26 March 2001).
175   Zambia's State Party Report to the CAT Committee CAT/C/ZMB/2 (9 February 2006).
176   Report of the CAT Committee Twenty-Seventh Session (12–23 November 2001) and Twenty-Eighth Session (29 April-17 May 2002) No 44/A/57/44 para 60.

law; the lack of criminalisation of torture, poor prison conditions; and violence against women in society. Apart from case law noted above declaring corporal punishment unconstitutional, very little seems to have been done in terms of law reform to implement the treaty domestically. Although the state has indicated that it has drafted a Bill domesticating CAT, this has not been enacted. In fact, the CAT Cttee in the 2008 COs indicated its displeasure at the fact that the state had not implemented all of its recommendations made in the 2002 COs.[177]

In terms of follow-up mechanisms, the CAT Cttee in its 2008 COs listed more pressing issues upon which it requested the state to furnish the Committee with further information within a year. The state did not supply the requisite information, prompting the Rapporteur for Follow-up on the COs of the CAT Cttee to send a follow-up letter in November 2009 following up on the same issue.[178] As of 2019 there was no response from the state.

5.5.6 Brief Conclusion

The treaty is among the least-known human rights treaties in the country. However, the Human Rights Commission has had extensive sensitisation across the country raising awareness about the treaty standards. Further, the Human Rights Commission, in collaboration with the Zambia Law Development Commission, have helped the government develop a Bill aimed at criminalising torture. The Bill has been approved by Cabinet but is yet to be presented in Parliament to be enacted into law. The treaty, however, seems to be well known among legal scholars, who have written several commentaries on it.

5.6 *Convention on the Rights of the Child*

Zambia ratified CRC on 6 December 1991 without any reservations. However, Zambia has not yet ratified OP-CRC-AC and OP-CRC-SC. The treaty itself was ratified two months after Zambia had ended 27 years of one-party rule and elected a new government in multiparty elections.

5.6.1 Incorporation and Reliance by Organs of State

The state has not undertaken a compatibility assessment of the legal framework with CRC. However, two statutes or national laws expressly indicate that they are domesticating CRC. These are the Education Act[179] and the Affiliation

---

177 COs of the CAT Committee on Zambia CAT/C/ZMB/CO/2 (26 May 2008) para 2.
178 Letter of the Rapporteur of the CAT Committee for Follow-up on COs to the Republic of Zambia, 12 November 2009.
179 23 of 2011; see specifically the long title or Preamble to the Act.

and Maintenance of Children Act.[180] Besides these, a plethora of national policies expressly indicate that they are incorporating CRC standards. These policies include the National Child Labour Policy;[181] the National Action Plan for the Elimination of the Worst Forms of Child Labour;[182] the National Plan of Action for the 2015 Youth Policy;[183] the National Gender Policy;[184] and the National Strategy on Ending Child Marriage in Zambia.[185]

5.6.2 Level of Awareness

CRC probably is the most well-known international human rights treaty in Zambia. This is largely due to a number of international and national organisations working in this sector supporting the realisation of children's rights. Such organisations include UNICEF;[186] Save the Children International;[187] Plan International;[188] Caritas Zambia;[189] Children in Need Network (CHIN);[190] and the Undikumbukire Project.[191]

CRC is well covered in the local media and often referenced in relation to stories relating to children's rights.[192] Government officials refer with approval to CRC as setting standards towards which the country strives to achieve. For example, in November 2018 the Minister of Youth, Sport and Child

---

180 Ch 64 of the Laws of Zambia.
181 Republic of Zambia, National Child Labour Policy: Securing a Better Future for Our Children (2011) 1.
182 Republic of Zambia, National Action Plan for the Elimination of the Worst Forms of Child Labour in Zambia 2010–2015 (2011) 6.
183 Republic of Zambia, National Plan of Action for the 2015 Youth Policy (2015) 5.
184 Republic of Zambia, National Gender Policy (2014) 9.
185 Republic of Zambia, National Strategy on Ending Child Marriage in Zambia 2016–2021 (2016) 12.
186 <https://www.unicef.org/zambia/> accessed 19 April 2019.
187 <https://zambia.savethechildren.net/about-us> accessed 19 April 2019.
188 <https://plan-international.org/zambia> accessed 19 April 2019.
189 <https://www.caritas.org/where-caritas-work/africa/zambia/> accessed 19 April 2019.
190 <https://chinzambia.org/> accessed 19 April 2019.
191 <http://www.upzambia.org/contact> accessed 19 April 2019.
192 See, for example, 'Zambia Making Strides in Children's Rights' <http://www.daily-mail.co.zm/zambia-making-strides-childrens-rights/> accessed 19 April 2020; 'Stealing From the Disabled is Beyond Cruelty, Evil' <https://diggers.news/opinion/2018/12/06/stealing-from-the-disabled-is-beyond-cruelty-its-evil/> accessed 19 April 2019; 'Legal Framework, Policies to Enhance Child Protection in Zambia' <http://www.daily-mail.co.zm/legal-framework-policies-to-enhance-child-protection-in-zambia/> accessed 19 April 2019; 'Barriers Affecting Children's Rights' <http://www.daily-mail.co.zm/barriers-affecting-childrens-rights/> accessed 19 April 2019; 'UNHCR Praises Zambia Over Children's Rights' <http://www.daily-mail.co.zm/unhcr-praises-zambia-childrens-rights/> accessed 19 April 2019.

Development, Moses Mawere, stated that as a result of ratifying CRC, the government had adopted policies aimed at protecting children's rights.[193]

A simplified version of CRC has been translated into seven major local languages with support from UNICEF.[194] The treaty is also widely cited in academic research and publications.

5.6.3 Use by Non-state Actors

CRC is widely used by non-governmental entities and the legal profession. The Law Association of Zambia (the regulatory body for lawyers) held a series of workshops from August 2018 to April 2019 in which it trained a number of lawyers as human rights defenders, with technical and financial support from the National Endowment for Democracy (NED). The training included CRC.[195]

UN agencies and NGOs are the leading promoters of CRC locally. These often have programmes based on promoting aspects of CRC. The leading agencies on this aspect seem to be UNICEF; Save the Children International; Plan International; Caritas Zambia; Children in Need Network (CHIN); WiLDAF; and Undikumbukire Project (UP).

Caritas Zambia, for example, has developed a Child Protection Manual, which revolves around realising children's rights as articulated in CRC.[196] WiLDAF also has a child protection manual which includes several chapters discussing CRC.[197] CRC is also the subject of academic research and writing, especially by graduate students.[198] As alluded to above, CRC is also often referred to by the media in stories relating to children's rights.

5.6.4 State Reporting

Zambia has only reported twice to the CRC Cttee. It submitted its first report in 2001, six years and nine months after the due date, and submitted a combined

---

[193] 'Zambia Making Strides in Children's Rights' <https://www.lusakatimes.com/2018/11/20/zambia-boast-of-protecting-childrens-rights/>; see also 'Zambia Committed to Children's Welfare – Bota' <http://www.daily-mail.co.zm/zambia-committed-childrens-welfare-bota/> accessed 20 April 2019.

[194] 'UNICEF Annual Report 2015 – Zambia' <https://www.unicef.org/about/annualreport/files/Zambia_2015_COAR.pdf> accessed 20 April 2019.

[195] The President's Report, Law Association of Zambia (April 2019) 26.

[196] Caritas Zambia, *Child Protection Manual 2019*.

[197] WiLDAF, Child Protection Training Manual: Protecting Children Through the Law (2012).

[198] See, for example, Davies Chali Mumba, 'The Juvenile Criminal Justice System in Zambia vis-à-vis the International Protection of Children's Rights' LLM dissertation, University of Zambia, 2011; EM Simaluwani, 'The Juvenile Justice System in Zambia,' PhD thesis, University of London, 1994; Ruth L Mbambi, 'Crisis of the Girl Child's Rights: Victims of Defilement in Zambia' LLM dissertation, University of Zambia, 2017.

second, third and fourth periodic report in 2013, some three years and six months after the fourth periodic report was due.[199] The process of reporting is coordinated by the Ministry of Justice but is consultative and includes NGOs. The 2013 report, for example, not only included consultation with NGOs, but included consulting children themselves through provincial forums.[200] The reports have been developed with both technical and financial support from UNICEF and appear to be consistent with the guidelines. The CRC Cttee, for example, praised the 2001 Zambian report for being 'self-critical and constructive'.[201]

There were no alternative reports accompanying Zambia's reporting cycle. However, the second report was accompanied by several alternative reports from NGOs. For example, the Global Initiative submitted a brief focusing on corporal punishment,[202] IPAS Zambia submitted a report focusing on children's health,[203] and *Terres des Hommes* submitted a detailed report focusing on the impact of pollution emanating from lead mining on children.[204]

Zambia has sent high-level delegations usually led by either the Minister of Justice or the attorney-general. It has had two dialogues with the CRC Cttee, namely, in 2003 and 2016.[205] Some of the main concerns that emerged in the 2003 and 2016 COs include the lack of a consistent definition of a child in the national legal framework; the low age of criminal responsibility for children (eight years); discrimination against vulnerable children; principles of CRC such as the best interests of the child that are not fully incorporated into domestic laws; the low civil registration of children with fewer than 10 per cent registered at birth; the fact that corporal punishment was still being widely practised despite being outlawed; torture and ill-treatment of children in conflict with the law; and the impact of HIV/AIDS on children.[206]

---

199 <https://tbinternet.ohchr.org/_layouts/15/TreatyBodyExternal/Countries.aspx?CountryCode=ZMB&Lang=EN> accessed 19 April 2019.
200 Zambia State Party Report to the CRC CRC/C/ZM/2-4 (27 January 2015) para 1.
201 CRC Committee COs on Zambia CRC/C/15/Add.206 (2 July 2015) para 2.
202 Global Initiative, Briefing on Zambia for the Committee on the Rights of the Child – Professional Working Group (June 2015).
203 IPAS Zambia, Supplementary Information on Zambia (March 2015).
204 Terres des Hommes, Alternative Report to the UN Committee on the Rights of the Child on the Occasion of Zambia's Combined Second, Third and Fourth State Party Report: The Child Rights Impact of Pollution Caused by Lead Mining (January 2016).
205 <https://tbinternet.ohchr.org/_layouts/15/TreatyBodyExternal/Countries.aspx?CountryCode=ZMB&Lang=EN> accessed 19 April 2019.
206 CRC Committee COs on Zambia CRC/C/15/Add.206 (2 July 2003); CRC Committee COs on Zambia CRC/C/15/Add.206 (2 July 2015).

There are many changes to the domestic legal framework that can be attributed to CRC. These include the Education Act 23 of 2011 which enshrines the education rights of children, outlaws corporal punishment in schools and prohibits child marriages, and the Affiliation and Maintenance of Children Act Chapter 64 of the Laws of Zambia which purports to end discrimination between marital and non-marital children with regard to custody, maintenance and affiliation. In addition to these statutes, policies aimed at ending child labour and child marriages have been adopted.[207]

There have so far been no follow-up measures with Zambia under CRC.

5.6.5   Treaty Body Membership

Professor Cephas Lumina, a Zambian, was a member of the CRC Cttee.[208] His term ended in 2021.

5.6.6   Brief Conclusion

CRC probably is the most well-known treaty in Zambia. This is due to the multiplicity of UN agencies, international organisations and local NGOs with a specific focus on children's rights that actively promote the treaty in their programmes. The treaty features prominently in several national policies and is domesticated, to some extent, in at least two pieces of legislation.

5.7   *International Convention for the Protection of All Persons from Enforced Disappearance*

Zambia ratified CED on 4 May 2011 without any reservations. The treaty was ratified at a time when the then ruling party, the Movement for Multiparty Democracy (MMD), enjoyed a very low public rating and was often criticised for corruption and abuse of human rights by the international cooperating partners. Ratification of the treaty at that time may have been intended as a show of goodwill and to show a commitment to human rights.[209]

---

[207] Republic of Zambia, National Child Labour Policy: Securing a Better Future for Our Children (2011); Republic of Zambia, National Action Plan for the Elimination of the Worst Forms of Child Labour in Zambia 2010–2015 (2011); Republic of Zambia, National Plan of Action for the 2015 Youth Policy (2015); Republic of Zambia, National Gender Policy (2014); Republic of Zambia, National Strategy on Ending Child Marriage in Zambia 2016–2021 (2016) 12.

[208] <https://ohchr.org/EN/HRBodies/CRC/Pages/Membership.aspx> accessed 19 April 2019.

[209] Human Rights Commission, Strategic Plan 2014–2016.

5.7.1 Incorporation and Reliance by Organs of State

The treaty has not been domesticated into national law. There are no laws, policies or official statements referring to the treaty. Equally, there have been no court cases making reference to the treaty.

5.7.2 Level of Awareness

The treaty is hardly known domestically. There are no records of it being mentioned in official public statements. It is not even specifically mentioned in the National Human Rights Commission strategic plan as being among the international human rights treaties it was implementing for that period.[210] It has not been translated into any of the local languages. A search through the main media publications reveals no mention of the treaty. However, it is known among academics and is taught in human rights courses.[211]

5.7.3 Use by Non-state Actors

There is no evidence of use of the treaty by NGOs and there seems to be no academic research on the treaty.

5.7.4 State Reporting

Zambia's initial report was due on 4 May 2013, but has not been submitted.[212]

5.7.5 Brief Conclusion

Except in academic circles, the treaty is hardly known in Zambia. There are no NGOs that have activities around the treaty. Zambia is yet to submit its initial state report relating to the treaty.

5.8 *Convention on the Rights of Persons with Disabilities*

Zambia ratified CRPD on 1 February 2010 without any reservations.[213] As in the case of CED, this treaty was ratified at a time when the country seemed to be attempting to assert its good governance credentials.[214]

---

210 Human Rights Commission, Strategic Plan 2014–2016 7.
211 See, for example, University of Zambia School of Law, Human Rights Law Course Outline 2017.
212 <https://tbinternet.ohchr.org/_layouts/15/TreatyBodyExternal/countries.aspx?CountryCode=ZMB&Lang=EN> accessed 19 April 2019.
213 <https://tbinternet.ohchr.org/_layouts/15/TreatyBodyExternal/Treaty.aspx?CountryID=194&Lang=EN> accessed 19 April 2019.
214 Human Rights Commission, Strategic Plan 2014–2016.

5.8.1 Incorporation and Reliance by Organs of State

There are two statutes that expressly indicate that they are domesticating or giving effect to CRPD: the Mental Health Act 6 of 2019[215] and the Persons with Disabilities Act 6 of 2012. The latter statute establishes a government agency, the Zambia Agency for Persons with Disabilities (ZAPD) to coordinate the government's initiatives of realising the rights of persons with disabilities.[216] The statutes are also complemented by the National Policy on Disability in 2013. In 2015 the government, through the Central Statistical Office and the Ministry of Community Development, carried out a national disability survey. The survey, however, did not focus on the compatibility of national laws with CRPD, but largely focused on the prevalence of disability and the economic challenges accompanying disability.[217] The survey was carried out with financial support from the Department for International Development (DFID), Irish Aid, the Swedish Embassy, the embassy of Finland and UNICEF.

5.8.2 Reliance by Judiciary

The treaty has also been specifically mentioned in court judgments. It was recently cited in the case of *Gordon Maddox Mwewa & Others v Attorney-General & Others*,[218] which challenged the constitutionality of the now repealed Mental Disorders Act, and the case of *Brotherton v Electoral Commission of Zambia*,[219] in which the High Court found that by not providing persons with disabilities with facilities for easy access to polling stations, persons with disabilities were discriminated against.

5.8.3 Level of Awareness

Awareness about the treaty is growing as the treaty seems to have become the standard framework of reference in the disability discourse in Zambia. Public officers, courts and civil society organisations often refer to it. The media often reports on the disability theme, making reference to the treaty.[220] The treaty is also taught as part of human rights law in the major law schools in the country.

---

215 The Mental Health Act 2019 replaces the Mental Disorders Act 1949, which was passed in colonial times and was manifestly overdue for reform. There is no doubt that the reform was propelled by the ratification of the CRPD.
216 <http://www.zapd.org.zm/?page_id=96> accessed 19 April 2019.
217 Republic of Zambia, National Disability Survey 2015.
218 2017/HP/204.
219 HP/818/2011.
220 See, for example, 'Promotion of Rights of Persons with Mental Disabilities on Course' <http://www.daily-mail.co.zm/promotion-of-rights-of-persons-with-mental-disabilities-on-course/> accessed 20 April 2019.

In the case of the School of Law at the University of Zambia, the treaty is also taught as part of a specialised elective undergraduate course in disability law.[221]

5.8.4 Use by Non-state Actors

The treaty is also widely used by NGOs in their programmes. With funding from UNDP, the Jesuit Centre for Theological Reflection (JCTR), for example, in 2017 carried out an extensive national survey of the accessibility of public places of persons with disabilities.[222] Several local NGOs are active in the disability sector. Both cases noted above were actually brought to court as part of public interest litigation by civil society organisations working in the disability sector. The treaty is widely cited in research and publications of Zambian scholars and institutions. For example, it was cited in two relatively recent publications focusing on disability in Zambia.[223] The media equally makes extensive reference to the treaty in the context of reporting on stories touching on disabilities.[224]

5.8.5 State Reporting

Zambia is yet to submit a report to the treaty body. Its initial report was due on 1 March 2012.[225]

5.8.6 Other Measures

The Special Rapporteur on the Rights of Persons with Disabilities visited Zambia in April 2016. Her visit was not widely covered in the media. Although she noted that major aspects of the treaty were not comprehensively domesticated in local legislation, she lauded the enactment of the Persons with Disabilities Act and other government efforts to protect the rights of persons living with disabilities.[226] Although the enactment of the Mental Disabilities

---

221   University of Zambia School of Law, Disability Law Course Outline 2017.
222   JCTR, Accessibility of Public Places to Persons with Disabilities in Zambia (May 2017).
223   FK Kalunga and Chipo Mushota, 'Protection of the Rights of Persons with Mental Disabilities to Liberty and Informed Consent to Treatment: A Critique of *Gordon Maddox Mwewa and Others v Attorney General and Another*' (2018) African Disability Yearbook; Linda Asare and Erica Tennant, 'Removing Barriers Towards Inclusion: Sensitisation and Mainstreaming Intellectual Disabilities at Community and National Levels in Zambia' SAIPAR Occasional Papers September 2017.
224   See, for example, 'Without Good Laws Disability Means Inability' <http://www.daily-mail.co.zm/without-good-laws-disability-means-inability/> accessed 19 April 2019.
225   The CRPD Cttee received this report (CRPD/C/ZM/1) on 19 September 217; it was scheduled to be considered after the cut-off mark for this study.
226   Report of the Special Rapporteur on the Rights of Persons with Disabilities on her Visit to Zambia A/HRC/34/58/Add.2(19 December 2016), para 21: 'The Special Rapporteur was particularly concerned about the discriminatory provisions against persons with

Act in 2019 cannot be attributed solely to her visit, it is possible that her visit contributed momentum to its enactment as it was one of the issues raised during her visit.[227]

5.8.7 Brief Conclusion

The treaty is growing in popularity and is already referred to in national policies and legislation, as well as in case law of the courts. Several NGOs exist that champion the implementation of its standards. However, Zambia is yet to submit its initial report to the treaty-monitoring body.

6 Conclusion

Zambia is a state party to eight of the nine core human rights treaties. Many of these treaties are well known and inform national laws, policies and public discourse. However, the treaties are not uniformly implemented in Zambia. While some treaties have been expressly incorporated into domestic law, such as CEDAW, CRC and CRPD, others such as CED and CERD are conspicuously absent from national discourse, national policies and laws.

There are several lessons to be drawn from this. First, the popularity of treaties domestically seems to be driven by two factors: political context and mobilization by civil society organisations. Treaties such as CCPR and CESCR are contextually relevant as they speak to certain developments in the country. In relation to civil society, treaties such as CRC, CEDAW and CRPD have been popularised by civil society organisations that promote them and use them as a standard of reference in their programming. Therefore, it is hardly surprising that these three are the ones specifically incorporated into Zambian law.

Second, although the treaties are implemented to varying degrees, they still matter and are important. Their relevance and popularity may depend on political developments in the country at particular times. For example, as a result of seemingly declining professionalism in the Zambian Police Service, the implementation of CAT seems cardinal and its importance is on the upswing.

Third, the implementation of treaties and decisions of treaty bodies involves a relatively complex interplay of international obligations and the structure of the national legal system. Where remedies such as compensation were

---

psychosocial disabilities contained in the outdated Mental Disorders Act of 1951, which is not compliant with the Convention but which continues to be in effect and applied by national authorities'.

227 ibid.

ordered, the state seems to have relatively easily complied. But where remedies had implication likely to alter the domestic legal system, such as abolishing death penalty, or relaxing anti-gay rules, the state has been hesitant to yield to the views of treaty bodies. Overall, the human rights treaties provide a common framework of reference for national and international stakeholders operating in Zambia. In the Zambian context, this is also helped by the fact that the Bill of Rights in the constitution is modelled on the UDHR, which entails that many civil and political rights recognized internationally are already enforced under the constitution.

Finally, it should be noted that often, adherence to international human rights standards is driven by political will to respect the rule of law. Examples cited above suggest declining respect for human rights during the rule of the Patriotic Front (PF), especially under the leadership of President Edgar Lungu (2015–2021). In August 2021, however, a new government, led by Hakainde Hichilema was elected on a platform of law reform, respect for human rights and fighting corruption. It is yet to be seen which direction the new government will take once it settles down.

Conclusion

Contours of a Conclusion, into the Sixth UN Treaty System Decade

Frans Viljoen and Rachel Murray

1   Introduction

This conclusion cannot possibly do justice to the rich and nuanced material contained in the comprehensive chapters covering the 'impact' of nine core United Nations (UN) human rights treaties, ten UN treaty bodies (UNTBS), and three substantive protocols in divergent contexts over a period of 20 years. We therefore are deliberately modest in our ambitions for this chapter. While we aim to highlight some illustrative examples, and suggest some trends, we take caution not to arrive at expansive overarching and cross-cutting conclusions. Our thoughts and tentative insights are aimed at opening the door to others, to encourage future researchers to delve deeper into and more closely analyse the rich body of evidence contained in the pages of the 20 country study chapters. We draw some comparison between this study's conclusions and those of the first (1999) study (and the 2002 book).[1] Having covered the three decades between the entry into force of the first treaty body in 1969 and 1999 in the first study, this book contains further reflection on the fourth and fifth UNTB decades (2000 to 2019). What is incontrovertible, though, is that the country reports amplify the finding in the previous study that the treaties have had 'an enormous influence'.[2]

2   Reflections on Methodology

As noted in the introduction, there are a number of complexities in measuring impact. These are further highlighted by the chapters in this book.

First, there are different forms of impact, manifesting at different levels. We saw numerous examples where state authorities engage at the UN level (for instance, in Japan, in development of standards) or cooperate with the UNTBS procedurally but then fail to implement the obligations in practice. Even states

---

[1] C Heyns and F Viljoen *The Impact of the United Nations Human Rights Treaties on the Domestic Level* Kluwer Law International 2002 (*Impact* 2002).

[2] *Impact* 2002, 5.

such as Canada, Colombia (in particular in respect of CAT), Finland and Spain, that mostly present reports on time, routinely fail to take measures to implement the UNTB recommendations. Impact may be felt domestically if, for example, the UNTB recommendations align with political priorities (Australia), but this may be 'sporadic and uncoordinated' (Canada). Furthermore, while some states show legislative and institutional changes, violations still occur in practice (Mexico). 'Influence' is an open-ended concept, and its specific meaning under a particular set of circumstances lies on a continuum (such as, in respect of the development of legislation on the minimum wage in Russian Federation, where the UNTBs influence was characterised as a 'contribution', rather than 'concrete influence').

Second, in many instances it is difficult to show the causal link between the UN system and measures taken by the state. At the most basic level, in many countries there is *no effective follow-up process at the national level* or a lack of coordination across government, thereby making it difficult to assess implementation and impact of UNTB recommendations. In other countries, such as Jamaica, changes to domestic law or policy were considered by some to be 'coincidental'. A *range of domestic factors* may enhance or curb the influence of the UN system. In Egypt, for example, it is difficult to dissect mobilisation by civil society and pressure from donors from the effect of the UNTB Concluding Observations. Even if the sequence of events may be compelling, the route of influence may not be conclusive. For example, Canada in 2018 established a Canadian Ombudsperson for Responsible Enterprise, following – in temporal terms but without any explicit reference to the CCPR or HRCttee – the HRCttee's 2015 recommendation to Canada to establish an independent mechanism to investigate allegations of human rights abuses committed by Canada-based resource companies operating abroad.

Domestic action may not always be attributed to a *particular treaty*. Treaties exert influence in tandem with one another, for example, when a domestic court relies on more than one treaty in arriving at a decision.

The UNTBs also may effect change together with other parts of the UN system, including the Universal Periodic Review (UPR) and special procedures. UN special procedures undertook numerous visits to all 20 study countries. All but five of these countries (Egypt, Jamaica, Nepal, the Russian Federation and Senegal) have issued standing invitations, indicating that they are open to visits by all special procedures. Since 2000, between eight and 24 special procedures have visited each of the study countries. This contrasts with the average of around two visits per country by special procedures in the preceding period of 30 years. Indications are that these visits and the work of UNTBs are mutually reinforcing. However, when the contributions of different UNTBs and special procedures overlap, accurate attribution of influence becomes almost impossible. The influence of the various bodies should rather be viewed as intersecting and cumulative, as exemplified by the visit of the Special Rapporteur on the Rights of Persons with Disabilities to Zambia in 2016 as reinforcing the CRPD Cttee's role in the enactment of the Mental Disabilities Act in 2019.

The relative contribution of the regional human rights systems further complicates the assessment of the role of the UN treaties, as is shown in Senegal with respect to the Convention against Torture and Other Cruel, Inhuman or Degrading Treatment or Punishment (CAT) recommendations and the building of a new prison. Because of this interplay between the regional and UN systems, it often is difficult to disentangle the impact of the two systems. As the chapter on Estonia highlights, it is not always feasible to differentiate between the impact on policy of the Covenant on Economic, Social and Cultural Rights (CESCR) and the Convention on the Elimination of All Forms of Discrimination against Women (CEDAW), on the one hand, and subject-related European treaties, on the other.

Using Mexico as but one example, the interrelatedness of various human rights regimes is striking. As the issue of violence against women in Ciudad Juarez illustrates, particular and largely similar implementing measures may be required by multiple procedures within the same treaty body,[3] by different treaty bodies,[4] by a UN special procedure,[5] in numerous UPR recommendations,[6] at the regional level in recommendations contained in an

---

3 In respect of violence against women, through state reporting (CEDAW Cttee, Concluding Comments of the Committee on the Elimination of Discrimination against Women: Mexico, 23 August 2002 (CEDAW/C/MEX/5); Committee on the Elimination of Discrimination against Women, Concluding Comments of the Committee on the Elimination of Discrimination against Women: Mexico, 25 August 2006 (CEDAW/C/MEX/CO/ 6)); and art 8 visit (Committee on the Elimination of Discrimination against Women, Report on Mexico Produced by the Committee on the Elimination of Discrimination against Women under Article 8 of the Optional Protocol to the Convention, and Reply from the Government of Mexico, 27 January 2005 (CEDAW/C/2005/OP.8/ MEXICO)).
4 Committee against Torture, Consideration of Reports Submitted by States Parties under Article 19 of the Convention. Conclusions and Recommendations of the Committee against Torture. Mexico, 6 February 2006 (CAT/C/MEX/CO/4)).
5 Special Rapporteur on Violence against Women, its Causes and Consequences, Report of the Special Rapporteur on Violence against Women, its Causes and Consequences, Yakin Ertürk. Addendum. Mission to Mexico, 13 January 2006 (E/CN.4/2006/61/Add. 4).
6 Human Rights Council, Report of the Working Group on the Universal Periodic Review. Mexico, 3 March 2009 (A/HRC/11/27).

Inter-American Commission of Human Rights (IACHR) report,[7] and even in other regional systems, such as a resolution of the Committee of Ministers of the Council of Europe (CoE).[8] While the extent of overlap and levels of reinforcement may detract from methodological clarity, it highlights the potential cumulative effect of the overlapping systems.

Third, the chapters also indicate that impact is not linear, and the engagement with and influence of the system can 'wax and wane' (Australia), from a 'golden age' to a period of domestic challenges to human rights (Finland). The extent of treaty system influence may depend on the government at the time (Brazil, India, Mexico), as well as interest shown in the system by civil society organisations, as illustrated by the relationship between the government in South Africa and CEDAW. Impact can also vary over the life stages of a treaty. Ratification appears to be an important moment for some countries in which 'compatibility studies' are undertaken prior to or immediately following ratification. For example, such a process resulted in changes to national legislation and policies (Finland and Japan) upon ratification, after which attention waned. For others, however, insufficient ground work was done prior to ratification, which impacted on its ultimate implementation (for instance, Nepal and the Convention on the Rights of Persons with Disabilities (CRPD)). Indeed, it is useful to consider the 'function' that the UN system serves for a particular government, as explored in the chapter on Egypt: At various times, it can be used to display the government's ambition to play a leading role in the international system, or to legitimise its actions in the eyes of the international community. One of the primary reasons why treaty impact differs is the difference in the length of time allowing for potential treaty influence. Some of the countries have only recently ratified certain treaties, or final views were adopted only close to 30 June 2019, the cut-off mark for our study.

3   Impact on Legislation and Policies

The material impact of the UN treaty system can most often be traced to legislative reform and policy measures. As the chapter on India illustrates, treaties that have been ratified by the state, with the exception of the Convention on

---

7   Inter-American Commission on Human Rights, The Situation of the Rights of Women in Ciudad Juarez, Mexico: The Right to Be Free From Violence and Discrimination, 7 March 2003 (OEA/ Ser.L/V/II.117).
8   Council of Europe-Committee of Ministers, 'Disappearance and Murder of a Great Number of Women and Girls in Mexico'. Parliamentary Assembly Recommendation 1709 (2005).

the Elimination of Racial Discrimination (CERD), as well as those that have been signed, have been used by the legislature in the country. This is seen especially in the case of CAT. CEDAW helped to change attitudes towards women in Egypt, resulting in the criminalisation of sexual harassment in the Penal Code, and the introduction of electoral quotas, thereby increasing the number of women in the House of Representatives. Mexico has implemented the Concluding Observations of the Committee on the Rights of the Child (CRC Cttee) through legal and policy reforms, although these have often not yet been translated into practice, and CRPD has been enforced through federal and state level legislation in Canada.

Other examples of legislative measures influenced by UNTBS are the following:

- criminalisation of torture (Australia, in 2010, as part of reforms required in the CAT Cttee's Concluding Observations issued in 2008);
- prohibition of *refoulement* (Australia, in 2011, as part of reforms required in the CAT Cttee's Concluding Observations issued in 2008);
- domestic and other forms of violence against women (Mexico adopted the 2007 Law of Access of Women to a Life Free from Violence, relying on CEDAW Cttee recommendations).

The impact of some treaties on policies and policy-related initiatives has been 'substantial', for example, eliminating discrimination towards lesbian, gay, bisexual and transgender (LGBT) persons in Brazil in the areas of education, food and health. Similarly, in Mexico, CERD has had a significant impact on official recognition, through the census and Constitution, of people of African descent. For Canada, in response to the CEDAW Cttee's Concluding Observations, the authorities committed to a national action plan for murdered indigenous women and girls, and there is evidence of impact in developing a strategy around housing and targets to reduce homelessness. CRC influenced and was referred to in Egypt's 2018 Strategic Framework and the National Plan for Childhood and Motherhood in Egypt 2018–2030 (prepared with the support of the United Nations Children's Fund (UNICEF), citing CRC as a basic reference). The adoption by the Russian Federation of the National Strategy for Women 2017–2022 (in response to the Concluding Observation recommendation to ensure 'effective coordination and developing a gender mainstreaming strategy'), and the adoption in 2013 of an action plan for the socio-economic and ethnocultural development of Roma in the Russian Federation for 2013–2014 (in response to the Concluding Observation to adopt a national plan of action that includes special measures for the promotion of access by Roma to economic, social and cultural rights), are examples of the direct impact of the COs.

CONCLUSION

In many instances, the COs of UNTBs do not display domestic salience. In Jamaica, for example, the CEDAW Cttee's pertinent COs were not raised as part of the legal reform process related to marital rape and abortion; and in Canada, CERD was not referenced in Canada's or Nova Scotia's current anti-racism strategies or Ontario's Anti-Racism Act.

The country studies stress the importance of symbolic impact. In many countries, especially those in transition to becoming 'full democracies' (such as Nepal and Zambia), the treaties provide a 'common framework of reference' and a 'guiding force', respectively, for stakeholders working on the issues, building upon rights that are in the constitution. In these countries, in particular, but in study countries more generally, the reframing role of UN human rights treaties is often emphasised. The CRC and CRPD have most prominently contributed to transforming legal and cultural understandings, approaches and practices. In the wake of these treaties being accorded national prominence, children and persons with disabilities are increasingly being accepted as autonomous subjects and holders (rather than objects) of rights; and are included in public spaces (for example, Egypt).

4 Reliance by National Judiciaries

One measure of treaty impact is the extent and frequency of judicial reference to or reliance placed on treaty provisions and UNTB decisions or soft law standards by national judiciaries. The significance and domestic effect of 'reliance' on treaties or UNTB findings differ greatly depending on whether the domestic court invokes the treaty as a source of remedy within the national system (direct reliance) or relies on the treaty or UNTB output for interpretive guidance (indirect reliance). Since direct reliance has been recorded only in exceptional cases, the focus here falls on indirect reliance.

Some of the chapters provide quantitative data on judicial reliance, mostly by the country's highest court(s). The number of cases in which a treaty is cited becomes only meaningful as an indicator if the number is expressed as a total of the likely or possible cases in which reliance was likely or possible. It is to be expected that the extent of judicial reliance on a group-specific treaty with a narrow thematic focus (CERD, CAT, the Convention on the Protection of the Rights of All Migrant Workers and Members of Their Families (CMW), the Convention for the Protection of All Persons from Enforced Disappearance (CED) and CRPD) would not be comparable to group-specific treaties with a more general thematic scope (CEDAW, CRC) or to general treaties (the Covenant on Civil and Political Rights (CCPR) and CESCR). The data provided below largely confirms this expectation as far as CCPR and CRC are concerned, but less so in respect of CESCR and CEDAW. Country dynamics are clearly also at play.

Overall, reference to UN treaties by higher courts in the 20 countries has significantly increased in the last two decades, compared to the previous study period. In Finland, for example, the number of references to UN treaties in higher court decisions grew from 17 to 142. We further observe that the instances of reliance on treaties differ markedly from country to country. The assumption that treaty reliance would be greater in respect of more general treaties is to a large extent supported, with particular 'group-specific' treaties receiving more judicial attention than others. Most frequently, CCPR is the most referred to treaty (for instance, Finland, Poland, Spain). However, particular treaties resonate differently with the judiciaries of different countries. CESCR has had judicial salience in a number of countries (Czech Republic, referred to in 91 decisions of Constitutional and Supreme Courts). Overall, CRC is the group-specific treaty most frequently referred to. CEDAW is invoked by female asylum seekers (for instance, in Australia); CAT in cases involving *refoulement* and extradition (in most countries); and CRC for the best interests of the child principle in various contexts (in most countries). CERD seems less used (rarely, Czech Republic, Turkey). The country chapters also confirm that reliance by courts is largely determined by the issues that litigants introduce and legal bases they invoke.

On the one end of the scale are countries in which courts have seldomly or only on rare occasions referred to or relied on treaties (for instance, Australia, Estonia, Jamaica and Japan). Jamaican courts have only placed minimal reliance on UN human rights treaties, with only CCPR recording more than one instance of reliance. The Supreme Court of Estonia made references in a total of 14 cases, with CCPR (6) the highest, followed by CRC (3), CESCR (2), CAT, CERD and CRPD (one each) and CEDAW (0).

Occupying the middle ground, a total of 142 references to UN treaties by Finnish higher courts were recorded over the study period: CCPR (95); CRC (16); CERD (12); CRPD (8); CESCR (7); CAT (3); and CEDAW (1).

At the other end of the scale are Colombia, Canada, Mexico and India, where the numbers are much higher.[9] Over the life of the treaties (covering both the initial and current study periods), the Colombian Constitutional Court made reference to the core treaties in 6 771 cases: CCPR (2 282), CESCR (2 137), CRC

---

9 Table 2 in the Mexico chapter (ch 11). The number of courts surveyed is a relevant factor in the difference in number of reliance. The Mexican courts canvassed clearly are many more than the single Estonian court canvassed.

CONCLUSION 1327

(1 025), CEDAW (538), CRPD (321), CERD (216), CAT (168), CMW (51), CED (33). Over the same period, Canadian courts made some 2 870 references to the treaties ratified by Canada: CAT (1 997); CRC (710); CCPR (67); CEDAW (56); CESCR (22); CRPD (16); and CERD (2). The Mexican federal judiciary (National Supreme Court, Collegiate Circuit Courts and Circuit plenums) made a total of 648 mentions to the core treaties over the study period, with CRC the highest (250), followed by CCPR (184), CESCR (92), CRPD (52), CEDAW (47), CED (11), CAT (6), CMW (5) and CERD (1). Indian courts made reference in a total of 995 cases, with CCPR (390), CRC (206), CESCR (188), CEDAW (138), CRPD (50), CERD (13) and CAT (10).

Going beyond mere numbers, many of the chapters show that treaties (such as CRPD) have steered domestic courts towards particular interpretations and solutions.[10] The Japanese judiciary, in the context of discrimination for those born out of wedlock, have made clear reference to CCPR and CRC. Similarly, CERD's definition of discrimination was crucial in the development of affirmative action programmes by Brazil's Federal Supreme Court (STF), and the Convention is visible in the decisions of higher courts in the country. The extent and depth of interpretive reliance has markedly increased since the International Law Association in its 2004 report concluded that the 'number of cases in which a treaty body finding is a significant factor in influencing the outcome of a decision is a small minority of the cases'.[11] The Colombian Constitutional Court, in Ruling C-376/10 in 2010 for example accepted that CESCR should prevail over the letter of the Constitution as it provided a more generous protection to the right of education, and held that primary education in public schools has to be free of charge, despite the contrary position set out in article 67 of the Constitution.

It is not only the meaningful reliance, but also the eventual enforcement of any relevant decision that matter. For example, it is one thing that the Polish Constitutional Tribunal found domestic law imposing double penalties in relation to social insurance payments to be incompatible with CCPR; it is another that these provisions were subsequently removed from the statute books. In Poland, CEDAW was relied upon to ensure greater equality between men and women of retirement age. CAT has been influential in the outcome

---

10 See eg the *Habeas Corpus* case, in which the Brazilian STF had to decide on alternatives to preventive custody of imprisoned women who are guardians of persons with disabilities, and the South African Constitutional Court's reliance on CRPD in *De Vos NO* to declare provisions of the Criminal Procedure Act unconstitutional.
11 Final Report on the Impact of Findings of the United Nations Human Rights Treaty Bodies para 179 <https://docs.escr-net.org/usr_doc/ILABerlinConference2004Report.pdf> accessed 30 November 2022.

of expulsion cases (for instance, in Poland, Czech Republic). The influence of UN treaties on domestic courts may vary from issue to issue. While the Czech Constitutional Court rejected the HRCttee's case law in respect of restitution of property, in 32 cases it relied on CCPR to annul lower court decisions, most frequently based on fair trial rights.

The reference to and reliance on treaty body jurisprudence and soft law standards are much less frequent than reliance on the treaties themselves. Although the Colombian Constitutional Court has made considerable reference to UNTBs, with 2 130 mentions in its case law over the life of the treaty system, this figure is much smaller than the number of corresponding mentions of the treaties themselves (6 771). In Mexico, the same cohort of courts, mentioned above, which made 2 870 references to treaties, made only 51 'mentions' to the treaty bodies. Some of the reasons are that treaty body decisions are given less visibility, even in official state resources (Estonia). Another reason for the greater reliance being placed on UN treaties than treaty bodies is that domestic courts mostly invoke or 'mention' treaties rather than use them as the basis for close interpretation based on extensive argumentation (Estonia, Mexico). Domestic courts in Europe and Latin America place greater reliance on the decisions of regional courts, compared to treaty body decisions, as they are considered more accessible and effective (based on their binding nature) (Estonia, Mexico). Generally, the most extensive reliance is on the HRCttee. However, the CESCR Cttee is by far the most cited UNTB by the Colombian Constitutional Court, most likely because it provides guidance, especially in its General Comments and increasingly in findings based on OP-CESCR, which the European and Inter-American Courts of Human Rights (ECHR and IACtHR), on which the Court usually most frequently relies, do not.

The role of individual judges can be crucial, if they have a good knowledge of the international system, as the role of individual judges such as Kirby J and Bell J (in the Australian High Court and Victoria Court of Appeal, respectively) and the *Mwansa* case in Zambia illustrate.

It should be kept in mind that this 'impact' relates to the highest or higher courts. There has been little recorded impact beyond these courts, with little change to the practices of lower court judges (for instance, Mexico).

Only in the rarest of cases do national courts directly 'apply' UN treaties, in the sense of finding violations of the treaty provisions in respect of disputes before them. Mostly, in dualist states, courts have held that they lack the competence to adjudicate disputes alleging violations of UN treaties because these treaties did not form part of (or 'were not incorporated into') domestic law (Australia). In monist states, where this possibility exists in principle, courts have chosen a similar path because they considered the relevant treaty

5 Domestic Effect Given to Findings in Communications

While there has over the last two decades been a significant increase in the number of submitted and finalised communications, they remain small in number, relative to the universe of potential cases at the national level that could benefit from international recourse, and compared to the sheer volume of cases before at least one regional body, the European Court of Human Rights (ECtHR). Only a modest number is being finalised yearly, due in part to the modest number of submitted complaints, and to inadequate secretarial resources at treaty body level to expeditiously deal with incoming cases. The extent of justice provided to individual complainants should therefore not be the most prominent measure of treaty body impact.

Implementation by states of the remedial recommendations in findings has been erratic and inadequate. Writing in 1994, McGoldrick concluded that compliance by states with the HRCttee's views has been 'disappointing'.[12] In the previous study, the impact of this mechanism has also been part of 'very limited demonstrable impact' of the UN treaty bodies. In 2009, the HRCttee reported that only around 30 per cent of follow-up replies display a willingness to implement on the part of states.[13]

Best practice examples of impact derived from communications among the study countries are limited, and mostly relate to individual measures. In the period under study, some very specific instances of implementation in individual cases have been recorded.

The more far reaching impact of the treaty bodies' individual complaints mandate lies in the general measures identified to ensure non-repetition.[14] An example of individual measures being adopted, but general measures neglected, is the case *Pimentel v Brazil*.[15] Alyne da Silva Pimentel, the author's

---

[12] D McGoldrick, *The Human Rights Committee: Its Role in the Development of the International Covenant on Civil and Political Rights* (Oxford Clarendon Press 1994) 202.

[13] Human Rights Committee Report of the HRC, 1 January 2009, UN Doc.A/64/40 Vol Suppl No 40 paras 230–236.

[14] In response to the HRCttee's finding in *Gómez Vázquez v Spain*, adopted in 2000, Spain in 2005 reconstructed its system of criminal appeals/cassation.

[15] CEDAW, *Pimentel v Brazil*, Communication 17/2008, UN doc, CEDAW/C/49/D/17/2008, 10 August 2011 (emphasis added).

daughter, was killed by her father during an unsupervised visit, despite prior warning signs that he posed a threat to her and her mother. The CEDAW Cttee found a violation of the right to life and health under articles 2 and 12 of CEDAW. Brazil implemented its obligation to provide 'appropriate reparation' through an amicable settlement of some US $55 000, as well as symbolic reparation in the form of a certificate recognising governmental responsibility handed to the mother during a solemn public ceremony. However, there is much less clarity about the implementation of the recommendations aimed at non-repetition. The only indications of a broader effect are that some federal states in Brazil adopted laws (at state and municipal levels) to protect the maternity and reproductive rights subsequent to the CEDAW finding, but these measures are not explicitly linked to the decision.

Non-implementation by states found in violation is the order of the day, often on the basis of disagreement about the finding on the merits. States not infrequently take issue or reject the UNTB's views on the merits also during the follow-up stage. In respect of the numerous findings that its legislation dealing with restitution of property confiscated from the Communist government was discriminatory, the Czech Republic, for example, indicated that it did not share the HRCttee's legal opinion regarding the discriminatory nature of the restitution condition of citizenship. It therefore opted to rely on the case law of the Constitutional Court – which contradicts the HRCttee's views – to resolve such matters. The following response during the follow-up procedure by Australia is a further telling example:

> As Australia does not agree with the Committee's view that a violation of article 9(1) of the Covenant has occurred, *it does not accept the Committee's view* that Australia is obliged to take steps to prevent similar violations in the future.[16]

Also illustrative is Canada's response to a follow-up request, ending with this rather abrupt statement: 'the State party concludes that it *will not take any further measures to give effect* to the Committee's views'.[17]

A more pervasive and promising change over the last two decades has been the adoption, at the domestic level, of various mechanisms or procedures to facilitate implementation of remedial recommendations. These include

---

16   HRCttee, Follow-Up Progress Report on Individual Communications, CCPR/C/119/3 (30 May 2017) in respect of Communication 2005/2010, *Hicks v Australia* (emphasis added).
17   CCPR/C/127/3; Follow-Up Progress Report on Individual Communications (8 July 2021) in respect of Communication 2348/2014, *Toussaint* (19 July 2018) (emphasis added).

administrative, legislative and constitutional processes. A striking example of legislation enacted to deal with this issue is the Czech Republic's 2011 Act on the Cooperation in the Proceedings before International Courts and Other International Supervisory Bodies, which requires the competent bodies to immediately take all necessary individual and general measures intended to halt and prevent any violation of CCPR or any other international treaty. Some legislation, such as the Polish 1997 Code of Criminal Procedure, allows the decisions of UNTBS to be a ground for automatic reopening of criminal proceedings. Colombia's Law 288 of 5 July 1996, which enables awards of compensation made by UNTBS to be enforced in domestic law, has not had much practical application.

Domestic courts may also play an important role in giving domestic effect to UNTB findings, especially when national legislation is ambiguous or restrictive. In Spain, the relevant legislation (article 5*bis* of Organic Act of the Judiciary) provides that the Spanish Supreme Court may review and set aside a domestic judicial decision on the basis that it contradicts the ECHR.[18] In *Ángela González Carreño v Ministry of Justice*,[19] a judgment of 2018, the Spanish Supreme Court found that the state had an obligation to comply with the views emanating from CEDAW and its Optional Protocol (OP-CEDAW). The Court accepted that, in a literal interpretation, article 5*bis* does not apply to decisions by UN treaty bodies. However, adopting a purposive approach, the Court declared that the state had the obligation to comply with the views emanating from CEDAW and its OP, since it voluntarily acknowledged the competence of the CEDAW Cttee to examine individual complaints, and fully participated in a legal procedure conducted by this Committee.[20] This judicial revolution can be explained with reference to the broader constitutional context, and particularly articles 10(2) and 96 of the Constitution. However, these provisions – which are contained

---

18   Organic Law on the Judiciary 6/1985, amended in 2015 (by Law 7/2015), to include art 5*bis*: 'An appeal for review can be lodged before the Supreme Court against a final judicial ruling, in accordance with the procedural regulations of each judicial sphere, where the European Court of Human Rights has affirmed that the ruling in question violates any of the rights enshrined in the European Convention for the Protection of Human Rights and Fundamental Freedoms and its Protocols, providing that the violation, in view of its nature and gravity, gives rise to effects that persist and cannot be eradicated by any other means, apart from such review'.

19   <http://www.poderjudicial.es/search/openDocument/14eef2e1ad3680ea/20180723> accessed 1 September 2023; see also CEDAW/C/58/D/47/2012 of 16 July 2014.

20   The Court also noted that CEDAW was part of the Spanish legal system, as set up in art 96 ('validly concluded international treaties, once officially published in Spain, shall be part of the internal legal system') and art 10(2) of the Constitution (constitutional rights must be interpreted in conformity with international treaties).

in many 'monist' constitutions – may be necessary but are not sufficient to explain this remarkable judicial outcome. It remains to be seen how far reaching this decision will be in practice, and if judiciaries in states with similar legislation (such as Estonia), would follow suit.

6 Impact by Country

Against the background of expanding norms, the unsurprising conclusion is that the impact of the UNTB system has increased significantly over the last 20 years. Its impact has increased in all the study countries. However, impact remains variable, differing according to country, and along the relevant time frame. Still, two countries stand out as having seen a pronounced difference in the level of impact over the last two decades. One of these, Nepal, was not part of the initial study. The other, Mexico, is a Group of Latin America and Caribbean Countries (GRULAC) country in which ground-breaking political changes have occurred.

The initial study concluded that the UNTB system has had a 'very limited impact' in Mexico.[21] 'Lack of political will' and 'reluctance by the government to allow international supervision of its human rights record' were identified as the primary reasons. The radically different conclusion of the follow-up study (namely, that the UNTB system plays a key role in political and juridical dynamics pertaining to human rights in the country) underscores the pertinent role of the political context as a predictor of UNTB impact. In the early 2000s Mexico experienced an important political transition from a one-party regime to a more competitive multi-party political system. Importantly, the political transition was anchored constitutionally, in the form of an amendment to article 1 of the 1917 Constitution, which was introduced in 2011. It provides that everyone enjoys the human rights recognised in international treaties to which the Mexican state is a party, and that human rights norms will be interpreted in conformity to the Mexican Constitution and relevant international treaties.

The government of President Vicente Fox (2000 to 2006) brought about a paradigmatic shift in Mexico's human rights foreign policy. This shift is evidenced by the establishment of a permanent representative of the Office of the United Nations High Commissioner for Human Rights (OHCHR) in Mexico City; an 'open and standing' invitation being issued to UN special procedures; the acceptance in 2002 of the individual communications procedures under

---

21 *Impact*, 2002 444.

four of the UN treaty bodies; and the fact that Mexico is also the only country among the 20 to have become a party to all nine core treaties. Not only the executive and legislature, but also the judiciary have been very open to UN treaties, as reflected in the graph in the country chapter (chapter 11) depicting the sharp increase, between 2000 and 2019, in the number of decisions by Mexico's federal judiciary that mention UN human rights treaties. However, it should also be noted that under the presidency of Enrique Peña Nieto (2012–2018), the Mexican government has become less tolerant of international criticism.

7 Impact by Treaty

Across countries and even within one country, the impact of the different treaties often differs markedly. The length of time that a treaty has been in force does not necessarily guarantee greater impact. Although the influence of CCPR has in most countries expanded and been enhanced over time, the same is not observed for CERD, the oldest of the nine core treaties. There are many examples indicating that the various treaties may each be approached differently by the state. As is shown in Canada, the authorities may 'cherry-pick' to which recommendations they will respond. Different parts of the treaty system may experience different levels of impact in the same state, as shown particularly in the chapters on India (where only CRC has significantly influenced policy), Japan and South Africa. The particular impact of two treaties adopted in the last two decades – OP-CAT, adopted in 2002 and CRPD, adopted in 2006 – is highlighted below. While the influence of CRPD has been mostly normative, that of OP-CAT has predominantly been at the level of processes and procedures. The fact that both these treaties are at the vanguard of rooting international supervision in national institutional processes underscores the important role of empowered domestic constituencies in serving as a bridge between UN treaties and rights holders in state parties to these treaties.

7.1   CRPD

Despite these variables, one treaty, CRPD, in our view also stands out in terms of its consistent impact across the 20 study countries. CRPD, the first of the treaties adopted in the new century, is foregrounded as a treaty that has achieved great salience across all the study countries. Its consistently significant influence on legislation is shown in the Table below.

The adoption of these laws is an example of direct material impact. In most instances, there is a discernible domestic influence of the CRPD derived from the chronological sequence, explicit recognition in documentary form, and

TABLE 21.1 Legislation implementing CRPD in 20 study countries

Country	Year CRPD ratified	National law adopted	Further evidence
Australia	2008	– 2009 amendments to the Disability Discrimination Act 1992 (Cth)	National Disability Insurance Scheme established (2013)
Brazil	2008	– Law No 13,146 of 6 July 2015, on the Inclusion of Persons with Disabilities	first treaty with supra-constitutional status (Legislative Decree No 186 of 9 July 2008)
Canada	2010	– 2019 Accessible Canada Act	The Preamble to the Act explicitly references the treaty as adding 'to the existing rights and protections for people with disabilities'.
Colombia	2011	– Law 1618, adopted in 2013, to implement CRPD – Law 1996, adopted in 2019, protecting the autonomy and legal capacity of persons with disabilities	new social paradigm on disability, such as 'reasonable accommodation', 'universal design' introduced Law 1996 (art 2) must be construed and applied in conformity with CRPD.
Czech Republic	2009	– Anti-Discrimination Act – amendment of Building Act – National Plan for the Promotion of Equal Opportunities for Persons with Disabilities (2015–2020)	Each ministry has to assess priorities in line with the National Plan.
Egypt	2008	– Law 10 on Persons with Disability of 2 February 2018 – Law 11 of 5 March 2019 establishing the National Council for Persons with Disabilities – Law 2733 of 2018 which set out the ground for the implementation of Law 10 (executive bylaw)	

CONCLUSION 1335

TABLE 21.1 Legislation implementing CRPD in 20 study countries (*cont.*)

Country	Year CRPD ratified	National law adopted	Further evidence
Estonia	2012	– enshrined in several articles of the 2014 Constitution – Law 10 on Persons with Disability of 2 February 2018 – Law 11 of 5 March 2019 establishing the National Council for Persons with Disabilities – Law 2733 of 2018 facilitating the implementation of Law 10	The Law on Persons with Disability, divided into eight parts, closely echoes CRPD structure; and its objective makes specific reference to CRPD.
Finland	2016	– amendments to the Act of Special Care for Persons with Intellectual Disabilities, the Non-Discrimination Act, and the Municipality of Residence Act and the Social Welfare Act were especially considered necessary prior to ratifying the treaty	referred to at least in 51 government Bills considered by Parliament. In that period, the references to CRPD or the CRPD Cttee may be found at least in 25 documents of the parliamentary committees.
India	2007	– Rights of Persons with Disabilities Act, 2016	Preamble states that it is enacted to give effect to CRPD. Mental Healthcare Act, 2016 states that it is enacted to 'align and harmonise the existing laws with CRPD'.
Jamaica	2007	– 2014 Disabilities Act	Parliamentary debates indicate CRPD influence.

TABLE 21.1 Legislation implementing CRPD in 20 study countries (cont.)

Country	Year CRPD ratified	National law adopted	Further evidence
Japan	2014	– revision of Basic Act for Persons with Disabilities (2011), Services and Supports for Persons with Disabilities Act (2012) – enactment of 2013 Act for Eliminating Discrimination against Persons with Disabilities	definition of 'persons with disabilities' changed to include social model; reasonable accommodation introduced
Mexico	2007	– 2011 General Law on the Inclusion of Persons with Disabilities	CRPD mentioned several times in General Law; repeatedly cited in draft Bills preceding its adoption
Nepal	2010	– 2017 Disability Rights Act, repealing the previous Disabled Persons Welfare Act 1982	2017 Act serves as adherence to its general obligation under CRPD, not recognised in 1982
Poland	2012	– amendments to electoral law and broadcasting law, introducing adjustments for persons with disabilities	without referencing CRPD in either the law or the explanatory reports
Russian Federation	2012	– Federal law No. 419-FL – amendments to 25 legislative Acts with a view to incorporate the Convention	aligned with CRPD
Senegal	2010	– Social Orientation Act on the Promotion and Protection of the Rights of Persons with Disabilities (Social Framework Act)	definition of 'disability' in Social Framework Act is extracted from CRPD

TABLE 21.1 Legislation implementing CRPD in 20 study countries (cont.)

Country	Year CRPD ratified	National law adopted	Further evidence
South Africa	2007	– Decree No 2012 implementing the Social Framework Act (No 2010-15) of 6 July 2010 on the promotion and protection of the rights of persons with disabilities – Decree No 2010-99 of 27 January 2010 on the Construction Code, of which articles R 18 to R 20 deal with measures for the physical accessibility to buildings by people with disabilities – White Paper on the Rights of Persons with Disabilities – South African Law Reform Commission (SALRC) project on domestication of CRPD (2018 –)	explicit mention of CRPD
Spain	2007	– Act 26 of 2011, on normative adaptation to CRPD to ensure appropriate harmonisation with Legislative Royal Decree 1/2013 – General Act on the Rights of Persons with Disabilities	42 laws, 75 Royal Decrees and 14 Ministerial Orders consolidated into General Act
Turkey	2009	– 2010 constitutional amendment (allowing 'special measures') – Pre-existing 2005 Turkish Disability Act underwent comprehensive amendment in 2014.	no mention in Act; no mention in debate
Zambia	2010	– Persons with Disabilities Act 2012 – Mental Health Act 2019	explicit mention of aim to domesticate CRPD in Preamble of both statutes

explicit recognition acknowledged and recorded during interviews. The role of the CRPD in steering the increasing replacement of the welfare and medical approaches to disability with a human rights model exemplifies its symbolic impact. In most countries, CRPD is closely associated with a paradigm shift from medical to social models of disability and the adjustment of institutions in order to guarantee individual autonomy, inclusion and non-discrimination of persons with disabilities. In a number of countries, CPRD has influenced terminology (for instance, the replacement of 'mentally-handicapped person' with 'person with disability' in Nepal). In Estonia there has been a dramatic change in the way in which disability was regarded in Soviet times compared to how it is now viewed. CRPD is also often more frequently cited than expected by the judiciary (as exemplified in Mexico, and in Brazil, where the STF referred more frequently only to CCPR).

The following factors appear to us to be relevant to the relative pronounced influence and impact of CRPD in the study countries:

Political context and the willingness of political elites based on popular support: The extent of willingness among political elites is reflected in the near-universal ratification of this treaty (184 state parties). The subject matter of disability does not provoke deep-seated political sensitivities. Different to the two other treaties that entered into force in the twenty-first century (CMW, dealing with migrant workers, and CED, dealing with enforced disappearances), the thematic of disability is more commonplace and generalised. It touches many people personally either directly or through their family members, and is cross-cutting in that it affects society as a whole: Disability intersects with all genders, races, ages and persons of all social or economic status.

Active civil society involvement: The drafting of CRPD was characterised by the most meaningful involvement by civil society of all treaties. Civil society organisations work to advance the rights of persons with disabilities in all 20 countries. In terms of the number and intensity of their activities, disabled persons' organisations (DPOs) and civil society organisations have been a very active segment of civil society. They have advocated the ratification of CRPD and have subsequently continued to push for the treaty's full implementation. As is the case with CRC and CEDAW, coalitions of civil society organisations to initiate various activities have been formed in particular around state reporting. Some pertinent examples are unprecedented civil society interest in reporting (Poland, Turkey); the Council of Canadians with Disabilities, which produced very thorough yet accessible articles, guidebooks and other materials on various aspects of CRPD to assist with shadow reports and informing the general public (Canada); and 170 civil society organisations supported a campaign by the national human rights institution for ratification of OP-CRPD (Poland).

National (as opposed to international) monitoring: This is a treaty-specific factor. CPRD sets out an elaborate system of national monitoring.[22] It operates at three levels: a focal point serving as a coordination mechanism within the executive; a monitoring mechanism from one or more state entities that are compliant with the Paris Principles; and monitoring by non-governmental organisations (NGOs) and, particularly, organisations of persons with disabilities.[23] Establishing an intra-governmental focal point has the potential to smoothen out inter-governmental blockages. The visibility, domestic stature and legitimacy of CRPD has been enhanced by the designation of national human rights institutions as national independent monitoring mechanisms, and by the active and constructive role many of these have played.

CRPD as a transformative instrument: Another treaty-specific factor is the transformative nature of the treaty itself. It does not merely catalogue a series of rights, but it postulates the possibility of a paradigm shift, a movement from 'darkness into light',[24] based on a human rights – as opposed to a welfare and medical – approach to disability, with persons with disabilities viewed as subjects or rights and not as objects of social protection (Australia (Supreme Court of Victoria)). Its transformative potential is most acute where cultural dispositions are mitigated against the self-determination of persons with disabilities (for instance, Nepal, India).

CRPD is a detailed and content-specific treaty: In respect of the Russian Federation, it was reported that treaties that are subject-specific treaties may have a greater impact because of the specificity and detail with which they deal with a particular thematic area, compared to the generalised and often unhelpful way in which general treaties such as CCPR and CESCR deal with issues due to the breadth of the scope of their mandates. This insight is applicable particularly to CRPD.

---

22 CRPD, art 33.
23 See also LFA Gatjens, 'Analysis of Article 33 of the UN Convention: The Critical Importance of National Implementation and Monitoring' (2011) 8 Sur: Revista Internacional de Direitos Humanos 1; Sébastien Lorion, 'A Model for National Human Rights Systems? New Governance and the Convention on the Rights of Persons with Disabilities' (2019) 37 Nordic Journal of Human Rights 234.
24 Rosemary Kayess and Phillip French, 'Out of Darkness into Light? Introducing the Convention on the Rights of Persons with Disabilities' (2008) 8 Human Rights Law Review 1–34.

Country-specific factors: Some factors relevant to impact are specific to a particular country: its constitutional status (CRPD is the first treaty to acquire supra-constitutional status in Brazil, in line with the 2005 Constitutional Amendment 45, which gives international human rights treaties that have been approved in two rounds by three-fifths of the members of each House of Congress the status of constitutional amendments); and connection to participation in the CRPD drafting process and the role as one of the leading forces in the campaign for, and eventual development of CRPD (South Africa). European Union (EU) member states are bolstered by the fact that the EU has also, as an intergovernmental organisation, formally adhered to CRPD. In the case of the Russian Federation, a uniquely special procedure for the preparation of reports and for the adoption of action plans to implement Concluding Observations was introduced. Hosting the Paralympic Games in 2006 is reported to be an impetus for the ratification of CRPD and the adoption of measures for its implementation by the Russian Federation.

CRPD as a complement to regional human rights law: It has been pointed out that there are significant gaps between the 'lived realities' of a majority of person with disabilities in many countries of the Global South (such as Egypt, India, Nepal, Senegal and Zambia) especially in underserved rural communities, on the one hand, and the rhetorical promises of CRPD, on the other.[25] A recognition of this disjuncture at least in part motivated the drafting and adoption of an African counterweight to CRPD, the 2018 Protocol to the African Charter on the Rights of Persons with Disabilities in Africa (African Disability Rights Protocol). It requires 15 state parties to secure its entry into force. While 50 African UN member states have become party to CRPD, only five African states have as yet ratified the African treaty.[26] A further region-specific treaty, the Inter-American Convention on the Elimination of all Forms of Discrimination against Persons with Disabilities (Inter-American Disability Convention), was adopted by the Organization of American States in 2001, but it too seems to have little salience (with the exception of, perhaps, Mexico). Although it is in force, very few states have subsequent to the adoption of CRPD in 2008 become party to the Inter-American Disability Convention. This discrepancy in adherence to UN and autochthonous treaties should be further interrogated: Does it reflect a crude cost-benefit analysis by political elites,

---

25   Helen Meekosha and Karen Soldatic, 'Human Rights and the Global South: The Case of Disability' (2011) 32 Third World Quarterly 1383–1397.
26   <https://au.int/en/treaties/protocol-african-charter-human-and-peoples-rights-rights-persons-disabilities-africa> accessed 31 March 2023; ratified by Angola, Burundi, Kenya, Mali, Rwanda.

CONCLUSION 1341

or skewed agenda setting by civil society? In other regions, such as Europe, the absence of a parallel regional treaty contributed to enhancing the impact of CRPD.

7.2 OP-CAT

OP-CAT spearheaded the idea that implementation of international standards needs to be grounded in national mechanisms. In addition to the standard approach of UN treaties, to create a treaty body to monitor implementation (in this case, the Subcommittee on Prevention of Torture (SPT)) the innovation provided by OP-CAT was the requirement that states also establish, designate or maintain a 'national preventive mechanism (NPM)', a single entity or a combination of independent bodies that have the mandate to prevent torture and ill-treatment through visits and other means.

For European states, such as Estonia, which already were party to the European Convention for Prevention of Torture, the ratification of OP-CAT may have had significant impact because of the work of its national preventive mechanism, but may have made little difference in terms of the international monitoring. Indeed, this has enabled states such as the Russian Federation to argue that engagement with the European committee is sufficient, given the overlap with the mandate of the SPT.

Beyond this, however, one can see the impact of OP-CAT in a number of ways.

Strengthening existing bodies: The extent to which OP-CAT has contributed to the strengthening of existing bodies is variable. For some state parties to OP-CAT it may be business as usual for those existing bodies that visit and monitor places of detention, providing no additional resources or legislative framework in light of OP-CAT requirements (Australia), or not ring-fencing a budget or staff to enable an ombudsperson institution to develop its national preventive mechanism role (as in Spain). Although existing bodies may have been adapted after OP-CAT ratification, they may still lack full compliance with OP-CAT criteria (Brazil). However, in other countries OP-CAT has led to an extension of the body's mandate (for instance, Czech Republic's Ombudsman) and resulted in the body itself, having taken on the national preventive mechanism mantle, to then adapt its own methodologies and approach, for example broadening the type of place of detention to be visited in line with the breadth of article 4 of OP-CAT (for instance, the Chancellor of Justice in Estonia now visits care homes). The ability of the SPT to address recommendations not only to the states but also the national preventive mechanism itself, can be a powerful tool to engage with the mechanism. Visits to countries prior to the official designation of a national preventive mechanism have also been very influential, as in Senegal, in developing a national preventive mechanism that complies with OP-CAT criteria.

Cross-pollination of other treaty body recommendations: Being creatures of both domestic and international law, national preventive mechanisms have drawn upon recommendations from other treaty bodies, not only the SPT, to corroborate their own findings or raise awareness of their existence. Therefore, as the National Detention Centre Observatory (ONLPL) in Senegal did with respect to recommendations of the HRCttee, such approaches can contribute to the implementation of those findings. Moreover, after visits to Mexico, the SPT reiterated Concluding Observations of CAT, albeit with questionable success in terms of their ultimate implementation. Furthermore, there is evidence in some countries of increased visibility of CAT after the ratification of OP-CAT and designation of a national preventive mechanism. For instance, in Finland, the Parliamentary Ombudsman's reference to OP-CAT, an increase in frequency of its visits, and drawing attention to violations led to an increase in prominence of CAT at some, if not all, levels. A similar impact can be found in Poland. In contrast, some national preventive mechanisms, such as the Human Rights and Equality Institution in Turkey, do not appear to have made full use of the opportunity to cite CAT in their own decisions. The SPT itself is able to identify, on its visits to states, incidents of torture and ill-treatment, which have led to changes in policy (as in Brazil after a visit by the SPT in 2015) and legislation (for instance, to Spain's Criminal Code after its visit in 2017).

Judicial activism: One influence of OP-CAT has been on the judiciary in some jurisdictions where they have used OP-CAT to bolster and strengthen the mandate and funding of existing bodies (for example, with respect to remuneration of the national preventive mechanism in Brazil; and the independence of the Judicial Inspectorate for Correctional Services (JICS) in South Africa). Furthermore, the judiciary has embedded the status of the national preventive mechanism in the domestic legal framework by, as in Estonia, holding that the findings of not only the SPT but also the national preventive mechanism can be relied upon by the national courts.

8   Domestic Factors that Explain Impact

8.1   *Domestic Politics, Context and History*

Depending on the historical context and current political contestations or priorities, some treaties are taken more seriously than others. One factor that plays a prominent role is whether the UNTB recommendations and standards align with national politics: As is seen in Zambia and Jamaica, the government

CONCLUSION 1343

may be more willing to contradict the UN treaty bodies on issues that have particular sensitivity, such as the death penalty or the rights of LGBT persons. Conversely, those treaties that deal with topics that are considered less controversial, such as monitoring detention and children's rights in Estonia and Turkey, generally have greater salience. UN treaty impact is also influenced by the presence or lack of national political or social consensus. National consensus or a 'general consensus in society' often is more likely around the rights of women, children and persons with disabilities, allowing CEDAW, CRC and CRPD generally to have more impact than other treaties. In the Russian Federation, on the other hand, treaty body impact has been minimised by the lack of societal consensus among state officials, civil society and citizens on issues such as the regulation of the activities of NGOs acting as 'foreign agents'; the protection of rights of LGBT persons; and domestic violence.

Historical context, such as colonial history, can influence the extent to which the treaty is seen as significant in the political discourse of the country (for instance, CERD in Zambia). In South Africa, a lingering and widespread perception is that, since CERD was adopted as a response to apartheid, its relevance has subsequently diminished. The influence of a treaty may be affected if it is 'weaponised' for political purposes, exemplified by the use of CCPR by the Barotse National Council in its efforts to secede from the Zambian state.

Different governments, as is seen in Brazil, Colombia and Mexico, will display varying degrees of willingness to be open to international scrutiny and engagement.

Finally, in some jurisdictions, religion and customs will also play a part, the chapter on Senegal providing a fascinating insight into the role of religious groups towards the state.

8.2   Domestic Actors

Numerous chapters indicate that domestic actors play a key role in ensuring the impact of UN treaty bodies. A lack of coordination among government bodies is raised as one issue that explains in part the failure of Canada to fully implement UNTB recommendations. Where there is greater clarity on who is leading on submissions or cooperating with particular UN treaty bodies, for example, as there now is in South Africa, this appears to have had some influence on state reporting and implementation of Concluding Observations and views. Indeed, putting some structure or mechanism in place to facilitate coordination, as in the Czech Republic, can be a sign of government commitment to the UNTB system. However, even when such structures or processes do exist, they may deal only with decisions from, say, the ECtHR (as Spain's Organic Act of the Judiciary enables victims of violations before the European Court to file a review before the Supreme Court for reparation) and not with the UN treaty bodies at all, or only with some (as in Finland).

In addition, the experiences of Jamaica and Zambia suggest that the existence of UN agencies in the country may also play a role. Civil society's choice to prioritise certain treaties over others (for example, CRPD and CRC in Zambia) and with which ministry responsibility lies, are also relevant factors in some jurisdictions. For example, it is pointed out that apart from women, children and CPRD, all other treaties fall within the Ministry of Foreign Affairs, which tends not to have ownership over the reporting process in the same way as a specific ministry. Relatedly, the existence of state agencies with a mandate in respect of a particular treaty may also result in greater impact, as can be seen in Jamaica with CEDAW, CRC and CRPD.

National courts, particularly Supreme or Constitutional Courts, have shown particular influence in some of the studies, prompting debate on how to ensure constructive dialogue between the state authorities and UNTBS, as the courts consider the compatibility of constitutions with international obligations (for instance, Russian Federation). The chapters also provide examples of domestic courts using the treaty provisions and other international human rights principles on a regular basis (for instance, India) and going further to uphold rights of individuals (Zambia) including through references in *amicus* submissions (for example, South Africa and the use of CRC Concluding Observations with respect to parents' chastisement of children). Developing practices that enable them to enforce the views of UN treaty bodies is another approach (for instance, in Spain, where the Supreme Court held that Spain had an obligation to comply with views of the CEDAW Cttee) such that remedies can be provided to victims of violations found by the UN treaty bodies. Conversely, however, a judiciary that is unaware of the international system can slow the rate of change and degree of impact.

This study also provides evidence for the role that civil society organisations play in keeping a treaty alive at the national level (Japan, or CERD in Brazil) or for advocacy (such as in India and South Africa) influencing different actors in a state to take action. Conversely, where civil society is weaker, as in Senegal, there may be fewer submissions to the UNTBS.

The chapters also show that statutory or constitutional bodies such as ombudspersons or national human rights institutions can also influence impact. The use of CRC in influencing domestic legislation change by the Chancellor of Justice in Estonia is one such example.

8.3 Nature and Extent of Protection Available under Domestic Legal System

Monist systems do not guarantee impact. The direct applicability of treaties in some jurisdictions does not always, it would seem from examples in this book, guarantee impact. As the chapters on the Czech Republic, the Russian Federation, Senegal and Turkey illustrate, the practical application of this approach indicate that even though, in theory, an individual victim can base their case at the domestic level on international treaty provisions, in practice they will tend to employ national legislation, this being that with which the state authorities are most familiar. The perceived strength offered by the national Constitutions of Egypt, Japan and South Africa, for example, can be a disincentive to look to international standards, including UN treaties. The existence of more detailed or promises of more responsive provisions under national law also explains reliance on national law. In South Africa, for example, the availability of national laws and policies on the elimination of racial discrimination and affirmative actions (in the form of the Promotion of Equality and Prevention of Unfair Discrimination Act (PEPUDA)), which speaks more specifically to the South African reality, has resulted in more reliance on national laws than on CERD.

9 International-Level Factors Play a Part in Explaining Impact

9.1 Geopolitics

Geopolitical factors often frame the horizon of possibilities of domestic impact. A decline in funding in a number of industries due to the Western sanctions, for example, constrained the Russian Federation's ability to give effect to CESCR.

9.2 Membership of Treaty Bodies

The commitment and presence of nationals as members of UN treaty bodies can influence the level of awareness among domestic actors, for example in Poland, and among the judiciary in Senegal, and assist in the development of national jurisprudence. In other countries, such as Egypt, however, a relatively high number of members on UN treaty bodies has not resulted in the submission of more or up-to-date reports, a deeper engagement with UN treaty obligations, or acceptance of any optional complaints mechanisms.

9.3 Criticism of Treaty Bodies

There are a number of criticisms levelled at the UN treaty bodies' credibility as an explanation for why the UN instruments or treaty body findings have not had an impact. Some chapters, including those on Finland and the Russian Federation, highlight examples of government officials arguing that the UN treaty bodies display a 'lack of nuance' in appreciating the domestic context. Several chapters, such as those on Estonia and Jamaica, indicate concerns that Concluding Observations and other findings of the UN treaty bodies are not accurate or are not thought through. With respect to CAT in the Czech Republic, it has been argued that particular UN treaty bodies have overstepped their mandate. In a similar vein, as one Australian official put it, 'mission creep', going beyond the scope of the treaty, weakens their credibility. These criticisms have also arisen through questioning, as the judiciary have done in Jamaica, whether a UNTB, as quasi-judicial and not judicial body, has the authority to interpret the relevant treaty.

9.4 Legally Binding Nature of the Treaty Bodies' Findings

There are numerous examples of state authorities foregrounding the argument that treaty body views and Concluding Observations are not legally binding (for instance, Australia, Canada, Jamaica, Russian Federation, Senegal and Spain). This can have a number of consequences. First, it is perceived as an option for the state to choose to implement, but only if the issue is considered to be in line with national policies (Australia) and the right to choose how such recommendations are to be dealt with (Russian Federation). In addition, it can prompt reluctance from civil society, for example in Spain, to submit cases to the UNTBs. Conversely, the chapter on Egypt notes that the government finds it 'relatively easy' to comply with soft law commitments pertaining to economic, social and cultural rights as they align with the 'Arab social contract', under which the government undertakes to provide social services to the people 'in return for their political acquiescence'.

9.5 Regional Human Rights Systems Deepen and Detract from Impact of UN Treaties

Several chapters raise the inter-relationship between the UN and regional systems, and the influence this has on the impact of the UN treaties. These are chapters dealing with countries that are members of the African Union (AU) (Egypt, Senegal, South Africa, Zambia), the CoE (Czech Republic, Estonia, Finland, Poland, Russian Federation,[27] Spain, Turkey) and the Organization of

---

27 The Russian Federation's membership of the CoE ended after the cut-off date for this study (30 June 2019). The CoE expelled the Russian Federation on 16 March 2022, causing

American States (OAS) (Brazil, Canada, Colombia, Jamaica, Mexico). This issue is evidently of less relevance in regions where no developed regional human rights system exists (Australia, India, Japan, Nepal).

In the first two decades of the new millennium, the three regional human rights systems have more firmly established themselves. On the one hand, the impact of UN treaties is often deepened by regional systems but, on the other, it could be that UN treaties are largely eclipsed by them. Attention to the regional system can result in limited reference to UN treaties, by the judiciary (in Estonia), government (Russian Federation), civil society or the legislature (Brazil, Finland and Mexico), and a preference among CSOs to submit complaints to regional bodies such as IACHR (Colombia). National judiciaries in Latin America and Europe routinely place more reliance on regional than UN precedents. The Brazilian judiciary, for example, is more likely to place reliance on specific Inter-American treaties, such as the Inter-American Convention on Forced Disappearance of Persons, than on CED. The regional system can be perceived, as the European system is in Turkey, as offering more financial opportunities, training and knowledge of particular issues. In Senegal, there is a preference for the geographical accessibility of the sub-regional Economic Community of West African States (ECOWAS) Court of Justice over the UN – and the regional – system.

The UN system is then considered supplementary to the regional. If the recommendations from the UNTBs dovetail with those from the regional system, this may result in effective implementation and impact of the former, as an example with respect to racial discrimination in the Czech Republic illustrates. A clear example of a mutually-supportive relationship between the UNTB system and the CoE system is the recommendation in the CEDAW Cttee's view in Communication 100/2916 that the Russian Federation should sign and ratify the CoE Convention on Preventing and Combating Violence against Women and Domestic Violence.

In other instances, the possibility of forum shopping may give rise to a sense of competition. In the Czech Republic, the study reports, victims of torture are more likely to file a complaint with the ECtHR than to submit an individual communication under CAT. Also, deciding on differentiation between non-citizens and Czech citizens in the legislation dealing with restitution of property, the Czech Constitutional Court relied on analogous cases decided

---

it to cease being a party to the ECHR on 16 September 2022. However, the ECtHR still deals with applications submitted against Russia alleging ECHR violations occurring until 16 September 2022, and the Committee of Ministers continues to supervise the execution of judgments and friendly settlements.

by the European Commission on Human Rights to substantiate a conclusion contradicting the HRCttee's finding.[28]

Of the three regional systems, the African features less as a factor that either enhances or limits the impact of the UNTB system. Although an African-specific children's rights treaty, the African Charter on the Rights and Welfare of the Child (African Children's Charter), is in place, African states appear to pay more heed to their obligations under CRC than under the African treaty. It has been suggested that the actively supportive role of UNICEF in advancing CRC (in Africa as elsewhere) provides an explanation for the prioritisation of CRC (eg South Africa). As the African system grows into maturity, the weight of reliance and influence may shift to the regional system.

10 Decentralisation

The shift from standard setting to norm implementation has been mirrored by a turn away from a dominant focus on the national level (by states, academics and UNTBs)[29] to much greater appreciation for the important role in treaty implementation of more decentralised units within states, especially those with a federalist constitutional structure. Particularly the fifth treaty body decade (2010–2019) has seen a marked increase in awareness and understanding of the crucial role of decentralised units (sub-national units such as provinces and states in federal states, and local government structures within unitary states).[30] There is much greater acknowledgment that, while the state party's federal government remains the primary duty bearer throughout the territory, implementation depends on legislative and other administrative practices at the state, provincial, regional or municipal level. Emerging also is the need for data that is disaggregated by decentralised units to avoid masking

---

[28] *Šimůnek v Czech Republic* and *Adam v Czech Republic*.

[29] See eg CRPD Cttee expressing concern about the harmonisation of national legislation with CRPD at the sub-national level in Mexico.

[30] See eg Roberta Ruggiero, 'Ombudspersons for Children in Selected Decentralised European States: Implementing the CRC in Belgium, Spain and the United Kingdom' (2013) 18 Interdisciplinary Journal of Family Studies 65; Conrad Mugoya Bosire, 'Local Government and Human Rights: Building Institutional Links for the Effective Protection and Realisation of Human Rights in Africa' (2011) 11 African Human Rights Law Journal 147–170; Judith Wyttenbach, 'Systemic and Structural Factors Relating to Quality and Equality of Human Rights Implementation in Federal States: A Critical Assessment of the Practice of Human Rights Treaty Bodies' (2018) 7 International Human Rights Law Review 43–81.

the disproportionate vulnerability of particular groups in regionals that lack autonomy.

The study countries include a number of federal states. Australia, Brazil, Canada, India, the Russian Federation and Mexico have strong federalist features, while other states (such as Colombia, South Africa and Spain) have less developed 'spheres' of decentralised government in place. A shared feature among these states is an increase in measures to establish decentralised bodies with a mandate to oversee human rights. In India, for example, state-level human rights commissions have been established in 25 out of 26 states. In Brazil, decentralised bodies created for monitoring and guiding the gender questions have a significant impact, with a fledgling system of Municipal Councils for the Rights of the Child (CMDCAs) being put in place at the municipality level, and State Councils for the Rights of the Child (CEDCAs) created in all states. The South African National Plan of Action for Children (NPAC) (2012–2017) underlined the role that local municipalities have to play in the realisation of children's rights. However, despite these examples, the influence of international law remains limited at the sub-national level, leaving important harmonisation challenges to be overcome in the future.[31] Judiciaries at the local level, being further away from the harmonising and centralising pull of the centre, tend to be less aligned to international jurisprudential trends.

11   Conclusion

We acknowledge that the study is part of a process. Given our cut-off mark of 30 June 2019, it is already outdated. It is part of a broader community of work-in-progress,[32] and of an ongoing conversation between scholars.[33] Taking the long view, spanning five decades, the study confirms that the UNTB system is 'one of the greatest achievements' of the international community's efforts to promote and protect human rights.[34] With the UPR gaining much interest and domestic resonance, the results of this study should be correlated and

---

[31]   For example, across the 32 federal states in Mexico.
[32]   For example, on the UPR, see eg UPR Info, 'Beyond Promises: The Impact of the UPR on the Ground' (2014) <https://www.graduateinstitute.ch/sites/internet/files/2020-11/2014_beyond_promises.pdf> accessed 21 September 2023 and Rhona Smith, '"To See Themselves as Others see Them": The Five Permanent Members of the Security Council and the Human Rights Council's Universal Periodic Review' (2013) 35 Human Rights Quarterly 1-32.
[33]   See eg Audrey L Comstock, *Committed to Rights: UN Human Rights Treaties and Legal Paths for Commitment and Compliance* (Cambridge University Press 2021).
[34]   Navanethem Pillay, 'Strengthening the United Nations human rights treaty body system: A report by the United Nations High Commissioner for Human Rights', June 2012.

compared with information and findings on national implementation of UPR recommendations.[35] The same applies to the influence of regional human rights systems.[36] A more holistic view of 'impact' of the various layers of human rights systems departs from the insight that what matters in the end is the effect of international human rights law on the lives of individuals within each of the UN member states, irrespective of the source of the applicable law.

Independent and state actors with a mandate to monitor and implement UN treaties have come a long way since our initial study. With its requirement not only that there be internationals supervision under the SPT, but also that states establish national mechanisms, OP-CAT planted the seed for other UN instruments, such as the CRPD, to consider that implementation of treaty obligations may necessitate not just a supranational but also a national system of monitoring and supervision. The proliferation of independent bodies such as NPMS under OP-CAT and article 33(2) mechanisms under the CRPD, in addition to recommendations by UNTBs that states create similar independent entities to monitor the implementation of other treaties, is a significant contribution of the UN system in the last two decades. In parallel, the recommendations made by Navi Pillay in her 2012 report that states should establish 'standing national reporting and coordination mechanisms' were based on the need to strengthen national capacity to implement treaties and also that they would 'considerably strengthen the building of expertise and institutional memory on human rights within the State machinery'.[37] With their increasing number, development of expertise, and expansions of their respective roles, the relationship between these national-level actors has become increasingly complex.[38]

---

[35] See eg Nadia Bernaz, 'Reforming the UN Human Rights Protection Procedures: A Legal Perspective on the Establishment of the Universal Periodic Review Mechanism' in Kevin Boyle (ed), *New Institutions for Human Rights Protection* (Oxford University Press 2009) 75–92.

[36] See eg Brice Dickson, *International Human Rights Monitoring Mechanisms: A Study of Their Impact in the UK* (Edward Elgar 2022), who considers the joint impact of monitoring under UN and European mechanisms on human rights protection in the UK.

[37] Strengthening the United Nations human rights treaty body system. A report by the United Nations High Commissioner for Human Rights, Navanethem Pillay, June 2012, para 4.5.4.

[38] OHCHR, 'Regional consultations on experiences and good practices relating to the establishment and development of national mechanisms for implementation, reporting and follow-up. Report of the Office of the United Nations High Commissioner for Human Rights', UN Doc A/HRC/50/64, 2022, para 52.

While the various chapters reveal many shortcomings in domestic implementation and in the workings of the UNTB system, the overriding impression is positive. Insight from the country studies may also be helpful in the ongoing treaty 'strengthening' process. The study confirms the utility of some of the changes that have been introduced, in particular the simplified reporting procedure, but also highlights the need for greater alignment in the practices and procedures of the various UNTBs; for concise, focused, concrete, prioritised, contextualised and implementable COs; for a fixed, comprehensive and transparent state reporting calendar; and for more reviews in member States or regions.[39]

In many ways, the first three decades in the life of the UN human rights system constituted a period of optimism: from the belief in a fledgling system in the 1970s and 1980s, to the golden era of possibilities in the 1990s following the fall of the Berlin Wall. Notwithstanding the erosive influence of the 'war on terror' and the global financial crisis of the 2000s and the rise in right-wing populism in the 2010s, the studies unequivocally conclude that the last 20 years have witnessed a significant increase in the relevance and impact of the UN treaty system in the world. The details of each of the country studies have much to offer towards the improvement in domestic impact of the UN human rights system, the growth of the human rights movement, and the discourse on the future effectiveness of international human rights law.

---

39 See also A/75/601, Report on the process of the consideration of the state of the United Nations human rights treaty body system, 17 November 2020.

Index

Academics/academia   47, 184, 189–190, 198, 210, 367–368, 376, 498, 577–578, 707, 840, 1000
Adequate standard of living, right to   108, 195, 263, 322, 323, 511, 556, 615*n*35, 722, 863, 950, 951, 993, 1080*n*9, 1111
Affirmative action (*See* special measures)
African Charter on Human and Peoples' Rights   28, 358, 1010, 1081, 1280–1281
African Charter on the Rights and Welfare of the Child   28, 1028, 1081, 1348
African Commission on Human and Peoples' Rights   28, 954*n*257, 1081, 1281
African Court on Human and Peoples' Rights   28, 360, 1081
African Union   28, 1067, 1069, 1080, 1280, 1346
Alternative reports (*See* Shadow reports)
American Convention on Human Rights   108, 162, 231, 254, 572, 701
Amnesty International   203, 232, 316*n*83, 360, 378, 391, 488*m*12, 629*n*83, 727*n*112, 742*m*187, 750*n*7, 857, 865, 1023*n*103, 1193*n*250, 1275*n*13
Arab Human Rights Charter   358–359
Arbitrary detention   42*n*47, 65, 186, 571, 720, 947, 1019, 1036, 1054, 1148, 1245
Assembly, freedom of   506, 625*n*71, 664, 842, 847–848, 1033, 1103, 1276, 1290
Association, freedom of   197, 365, 374, 378*n*49, 384, 413, 452, 510, 534, 806, 810, 852, 854, 885, 901, 1033, 1276, 1290
Association of Southeast Asian Nations (ASEAN)   612
Australia
    Asylum seekers   34–36, 51, 71, 78, 332, 619, 659–660, 665, 667, 780, 1071, 1082, 1100, 1170, 1176, 1182, 1194, 1326
    Australian Human Rights Commission   34, 46, 61, 82, 83*n*283, 85*n*293, 86–87
    Bill of Rights   33, 156, 157*n*5, 273, 636, 1078, 1082, 1093, 1102, 1112, 1126, 1273–1274, 1287, 1289, 1292, 1297–1299, 1319
    Constitution   33
    DFAT   40, 42, 45, 47–84, 64, 74
    Ombudsman offices   35
    Parliamentary Joint Committee on Human Rights (PJCHR)   41
Brazil
    Commission on Human Rights and Minorities   136
    Constitution   98*n*11
    National Council of Human Rights   13, 98, 357, 375*n*43, 381*n*55
    National Mechanism for Prevention and Combat of Torture   103, 136, 139, 1156, 1192
    National Truth Commission   135
Canada
    Canadian Human Rights Commission (CHRC)   159, 175, 185, 188, 199*nn*244–245, 201, 204, 210, 216, 217, 220
    Charter of Rights and Freedoms   156, 176, 178, 195, 197, 201, 207, 217
    Constitution   191*n*199, 222*n*384
    Continuing Committee of Officials on Human Rights (CCOHR)   157
    Truth and Reconciliation Commission   14*n*27, 191, 758, 1122
Convention against Torture and Other Cruel, Inhuman and Degrading Treatment or Punishment (CAT)
    Art 22   38, 80, 135, 270, 340, 465
CAT Committee (CAT Cttee)   15, 16, 75–80, 92, 140–142, 176–177, 209–212, 225–226, 249*n*50, 270–272, 335, 337, 342, 369, 377–378, 399, 403–405, 419, 434, 469, 474, 469, 499, 515–521, 658, 674, 683, 690, 710, 730–733, 800–803, 819–820, 833, 839*n*75, 844–847, 874–881, 911, 916–929, 970*n*344, 971*n*351, 973–974, 1013–1015, 1066, 1121–1125, 1156–1161, 1190–1197, 1259–1260, 1309–1310
CCPR (*See* International Covenant on Civil and Political Rights)

CED (*See* International Convention for the Protection of all Persons from Enforced Disappearance)
CED Committee (CED Cttee) 16–23, 178, 282–285, 348, 689–691, 710, 740–746, 847, 1153, 1157, 1209–1213, 1285
CEDAW Committee (CEDAW Cttee) 16, 73–75, 131–133, 134*n*146, 107, 175, 177, 205–207, 221, 225, 240–241, 266–269, 331–334, 363–372, 393, 395*n*101, 397*n*117, 398, 412, 433, 436, 462–465, 495–499, 512–518, 560, 578–580, 597–598, 629*n*85, 666, 673–684, 725–728, 764, 791, 839, 844, 868–873, 913, 921–929, 953, 962, 965, 1001, 1119, 1154–1163, 1184–1190, 1223, 1254, 1304*n*148, 1305, 1324, 1330, 1331, 1344
CERD (*See* International Convention on the Elimination of All Forms of Racial Discrimination)
CERD Committee 38, 58, 251, 657
CESCR (*See* International Covenant on Economic, Social and Cultural Rights)
CESCR Committee (ESCR Cttee) 593
Charter of Fundamental Rights of the EU 27–28, 428, 471
Child/children
Best interest of the child 1132*n*338
Corporal punishment 84, 189, 214, 216, 316*n*83, 473–474, 577, 600, 601*n*153, 610, 613*n*27, 684, 686, 806–807, 810, 1079, 1105, 1129, 1136, 1207, 1258, 1264–1265, 1294–1295, 1307, 1310, 1313–1314
Child labour 273, 536, 788, 804, 809–810, 1127, 1300, 1311, 1313–1314
Child marriage 514, 556, 766, 774, 787, 794, 795, 797, 804, 986, 1311
Citizenship 128, 145, 273, 301–302, 307, 315–320, 324, 444, 447, 451, 492, 767, 781, 791, 883, 1025, 1031, 1243, 1330
CMW (*See* International Convention on the Rights of All Migrant Workers and Members of their Families)
CMW Committee (CMW Cttee) 412–414, 603, 738–739, 1070–1071, 1153
Colombia
Colombian Ombudsman (La Defensoría del Pueblo) 260

Constitution 234*n*21, 246, 250, 255, 287
Commonwealth 33, 48, 55, 59–61, 72*n*225, 75–77, 86, 88, 423, 569, 1276
Complaints 18–29, 109, 125, 163, 166, 186, 190, 239–240, 259, 263, 270, 272, 295, 296, 309, 311, 318, 320, 340, 345, 363, 411, 449, 478, 490, 508–509, 517, 527, 584, 589, 605, 625*n*70, 634, 697, 760, 781, 783, 789, 820, 831–832, 851, 860, 866, 873, 880, 910, 1095*n*80, 1096, 1149, 1153, 1163, 1166, 1253, 1287, 1290, 1296–1297, 1301, 1329, 1331
Compliance 4, 5, 16, 30, 38*n*34, 43, 92, 105, 126, 142, 151, 170, 176, 218, 225, 289, 292, 296, 298, 302, 306, 308, 324, 328, 352, 393, 395, 413, 435, 440, 529, 581, 586, 606, 648, 651, 657, 745–751, 764, 767, 771, 786, 810, 815, 825, 852, 936, 979, 994, 1022, 1048, 1055, 1062, 1072, 1086, 1100, 1122, 1132, 1136, 1151, 1159, 1176, 1185, 1194, 1204, 1207, 1214, 1239, 1295, 1329, 1341
Concluding Observations (COs) 3, 15, 49, 58, 238–239, 251, 256, 257, 262, 266–267, 276, 280, 432, 493, 629*n*85, 645, 666, 1016, 1021, 1087, 1154, 1157, 1286, 1321, 1340–1346
Convention on the Elimination of All Forms of Discrimination Against Women (CEDAW) 5, 41, 72–75, 95, 97, 128–143, 166, 200–212, 231, 239, 242, 264–272, 295, 327–334, 362, 386, 388, 393–399, 462–470, 556–560, 595–599, 671–681, 724–729, 789–797, 867–873, 958–968, 1061–1064, 1112–1119, 1184–1190, 1248–1255, 1301–1306
Convention on the Rights of Persons with Disabilities (CRPD) 11, 41, 85–92, 217–220, 277–281, 475–479, 525–528, 565–566, 604–605, 891–897, 1069–1070, 1136–1143
Art 33 30, 1167*n*96, 87, 217, 476–477, 526–527, 636, 659, 692, 843, 892, 894, 1167*n*96, 1215, 1350
Corruption 263–264, 291, 400, 700, 951, 1004, 1055, 1151, 1275, 1277, 1314, 1319
Council of Europe 12, 291, 297, 299, 423, 463, 480*n*334, 484, 829, 900–906, 932, 983, 1150, 1153, 1226, 1231, 1323

INDEX

Court of Justice of the European Union   835
Courts (*See* Judiciary)
Convention on the Rights of the Child
   (CRC)   5, 40, 80–85, 143–146, 166,
      212–220, 273–277, 342–346, 405–411,
      470–475, 521–525, 562–566, 683–688,
      733–740, 804–810, 882–891, 977–982,
      1067–1070, 1126–1136, 1200–1209, 1260–
      1265, 1310–1314
   CRC Committee (CRC Cttee)   25, 84–85, 146,
      176, 178, 212–215, 274–276, 344–345,
      369, 372, 377, 409, 472, 495, 521–524,
      562, 579, 580, 600, 601, 662, 684–687,
      734–736, 759–760, 808, 832–835, 844,
      882–909, 921–923, 979–989, 1001, 1114,
      1129–1136, 1144, 1156–1158, 1162, 1200–
      1209, 1264, 1312–1314, 1324
CRPD (*See* Convention on the Rights of
   Persons with Disabilities)
CRPD Committee (CRPD Cttee)   16, 52, 89,
   91, 152, 178, 278–281, 352–353, 370, 476–
   478, 525–528, 580, 605, 694, 744–746,
   813, 816–817, 832–836, 839, 893–896,
   911n47, 921–929, 992–1001, 1086, 1137,
   1140, 1153, 1159, 1161–1164, 1214–1221,
   1269, 1270
CSOs/NGOs   4, 16, 36, 137, 387, 602, 660,
   671, 676
Czech Republic
   Constitution   289, 303, 346
   Government Commissioner for Human
      Rights   291, 298, 299, 310n59, 316, 331
   Government Council for Human
      Rights   291, 299, 301, 317, 326, 345
   Office of the Public Defender of Human
      Rights   290, 297n22, 330n130, 570
   Roma   251, 291, 304–326, 331, 338, 345,
      447–448, 501, 506, 515, 835, 847–849,
      864–866, 888, 923, 934–938, 956, 982,
      1170, 1182, 1188–1189, 1237, 1324
   Supreme Court   314

Death penalty   14, 19, 61, 108, 189, 236, 254,
   386–389, 409, 418, 432, 466, 505, 554,
   571, 576, 585, 590m105, 606, 613, 616n38,
   624, 664, 666, 667n243, 681, 696, 702,
   729, 852, 947, 1015, 1079, 1172n136, 1226,
   1241, 1242, 1286, 1307, 1319, 1343

Deportation   51, 66, 67, 79, 175, 189, 194, 202,
   210, 471, 499, 517–520, 561, 602, 619, 626,
   660, 665, 682, 689n352, 1170, 1308
Detention conditions (*See* Prison)
Dialogue   49–50, 98, 179, 194, 238, 253, 268,
   276, 280, 284, 309–310, 326, 404, 494,
   520, 630, 634, 653, 671, 730, 769, 795,
   799, 834, 843, 848, 874, 895, 897, 902,
   916, 918, 921, 938, 948–949, 977, 982,
   987, 999, 1001, 1022, 1027, 1035, 1046,
   1074, 1099, 1107, 1110, 1133, 1141, 1165, 1178,
   1199, 1218, 1252, 1344
Disability/persons with disability   88, 90,
   415, 1334–1335
Discrimination   66, 72, 89, 91, 102, 111, 159,
   201, 205, 251, 266, 290, 323, 327–328,
   338, 342, 381, 383, 448, 459, 478, 504,
   581, 587, 596, 604, 648n161, 657, 663,
   664, 743, 745, 770–772, 788, 849,
   944, 1184–1185, 1188, 1216, 1218, 1253,
   1265, 1327
District authority   30, 58, 95, 138, 303, 648,
   650, 770, 847, 1049, 1142, 1249, 1348–1349
Domestic violence   71, 95, 131, 190, 195, 203,
   205, 266, 316, 321, 326, 331, 460, 515, 518,
   530, 596, 610, 669, 682 727, 794, 795,
   829, 841, 844, 859, 862, 866, 872, 878–
   880, 901, 926, 929, 955, 958, 961, 963,
   965, 966, 968, 973, 1063, 1112, 1114, 1117,
   1182, 1189, 1205, 1226, 1253, 1295, 1303,
   1305, 1343
Dualist/dualism   37, 163, 178, 232, 573, 1081,
   1089, 1093, 1328

Early warning   58–59, 114–115, 180, 186, 655–
   656, 727, 775, 1100, 1153
Egypt
   Constitution   386, 416
   Egyptian Human Rights
      Organisation   368, 370, 388, 400,
      401, 404
   Law of Associations   357, 383, 387, 388
   Mubarak, President   13, 360, 363
   National Council for Human
      Rights   381n54
   National Council for Childhood and
      Motherhood   375, 398, 406
   National Council of Women   394n97

Egypt (*cont.*)
  Permanent Supreme Committee for Human Rights   369–370
  Sisi, President   359, 392, 397–398, 419
  Supreme Court   357, 374, 384, 388, 416
Enforced disappearance   11, 40, 147–152, 281–287, 346–354, 688–691, 740–743, 1072–1073, 1209–1213, 1314–1315
Environment   83, 93–96, 278, 299, 352, 405, 414, 538, 592, 693, 722, 778, 785, 788, 798, 817, 885, 887, 901, 1005, 1008, 1037, 1090, 1108, 1203, 1206, 1254
Estonia
  Chancellor of Justice   425, 438–445, 452–453, 461, 466–483, 508, 516, 521, 524, 528, 1341, 1344
  Child protection   471
  Constitution   422, 424, 426, 451, 458, 468
  Estonian Institute of Human Rights   437, 438
  European human rights treaties   354, 442, 480
  Gender Equality and Equal Treatment Commissioner   425, 438, 440, 441, 459
  Right-wing movement   228, 486, 680
  Soviet Union   423, 461, 469, 479, 481, 909
  Supreme Court   425, 434, 479, 1326
European Commission against Racism and Intolerance (ECRI)   445, 1150
European Committee for the Prevention of Torture (ECPT)   15, 27, 292, 336, 342, 881, 910, 1150, 1258
European Convention on Human Rights   291, 423, 484, 589, 902, 905, 1150, 1225, 1242, 1271, 1273
European Court of Human Rights (ECtHR)   27, 164, 289, 434, 486, 490, 829, 902, 1150, 1226, 1235, 1329, 1331*n*18
European Union (EU)   291, 412, 428, 484, 829, 1122, 1151, 1153, 1231, 1340
Executive   109–110, 116–117, 121–123, 128–129, 135–137, 143–144, 147, 149–150, 178, 303–305, 311–313, 320–322, 327–329, 334–336, 342–343, 346–347, 348–352, 388–389, 393–394, 411–412, 442–444, 450–452, 457, 462, 465–466, 470–471, 475–477, 495–497, 500–501, 504–506, 509–510, 512–513, 517, 521–522, 525–526, 549, 551, 554, 556–557, 562, 565, 581–583, 586, 587–588, 592, 595–596, 599–600, 602–603, 604, 715–716, 718, 721, 840–841, 846–847, 851–853, 862–863, 867–868, 874–876, 883–884, 891–893, 1093–1094, 1102, 1107–1108, 1119–1120, 1158–1160, 1166–1167, 1172–1173, 1179, 1184–1186, 1190–1191, 1200–1201, 1209–1210, 1214–1215, 1237, 1241–1242, 1246, 1248–1249, 1255–1256, 1261–1262, 1265–1266, 1268–1269

Fair trial, right to   254, 854, 1150, 1273, 1290
Federal/provincial   30, 158, 159, 176–182, 191, 200, 807, 1348
Finland
  Constitution   484
  Ombudsman for Children   216, 472, 483–484, 496, 499, 508, 516, 521, 523, 524, 529, 886*n*355, 1068
  Parliamentary Ombudsman   483, 493, 496, 498, 504, 508, 512–529
  Supreme Administrative Court   323, 497, 502–527
  Supreme Court   523
Food   108, 332, 389, 538, 556, 721, 733, 754, 785–786, 828, 1079, 1147, 1181, 1291, 1297, 1298, 1324
Foreign workers   411, 413, 657, 669, 1056
Freedom of expression   162, 183, 358, 502, 508, 575, 587, 618, 664, 750, 777, 828, 852, 854, 1024, 1150, 1176, 1228, 1240, 1275, 1280, 1290–1291

Gender based violence   202, 204, 328, 596, 673, 874, 966, 1017, 1062, 1079, 1090, 1185–1189, 1218, 1244, 1251–1252, 1302
Geneva Conventions   157*n*11, 231
General Comment   70, 89, 190, 249, 256–261, 274–275, 278, 280–281, 314, 322*n*103, 338, 352, 451, 457, 459, 465, 552–555, 593, 594, 686, 716, 719, 725, 816, 939, 940, 952, 102, 1108, 1137, 1176, 1202, 1242, 1243, 1263
General Recommendation   70, 185, 266, 267, 556, 557, 648, 713, 716, 719, 725, 735, 738, 1097
Girls   89, 95, 160, 168, 170, 172, 175, 181, 190, 201–206, 221, 225, 332, 352, 367, 396, 408, 513, 520, 673, 687, 726, 745, 787, 794–796, 805, 808, 817, 828, 1017, 1031, 1058, 1059, 1062, 1176, 1188, 1218, 1226, 1253, 1264, 1300, 1305, 1324
Global Alliance of National Human Rights Institutions   290, 825, 900

INDEX

Housing   35, 47, 69, 108, 175, 196, 200, 205, 222, 259, 306, 309, 321, 323, 326, 327, 332, 359, 392, 535, 549, 555, 571, 615*n*35, 665, 786, 866, 891, 901, 950, 952*n*247, 990, 1079, 1090, 1108, 1147, 1170, 1176, 1180–1188, 1324
Human Rights Committee (HRCttee)   369, 719, 720, 734, 742, 839
Human Rights Council
   UPR   10, 37, 105, 161, 239, 291, 359, 427, 486, 539, 572, 613, 753, 829, 904, 1019, 1080, 1149, 1153, 1231, 1308, 1321
Human Rights Watch   119, 148, 151, 232, 758*n*40, 1040, 1082, 1305

Ill-treatment   76, 120, 140, 141, 211, 339, 340, 403, 659, 665, 667, 682, 771, 798, 933, 977, 1033, 1049, 1105, 1123, 1162, 1170, 1176, 1192–1198, 1256, 1295, 1313, 1341–1342
Independent state institutions (*See also* National Human Rights Institutions)   111–113, 118, 124–125, 130–131, 138–139, 144, 203–204, 209–210, 219–220, 302, 323–324, 329, 375, 381, 385, 395, 398, 401, 412, 417, 445, 452–453, 459, 463, 467–468, 472, 477–478, 498, 502–503, 507, 510–511, 514, 518–519, 523, 527, 738, 842–843, 848, 855–856, 864–865, 869–870, 877, 886–887, 894–895, 926, 933–934, 940–941, 952–953, 961, 971–972, 979–980, 984–985, 988–989, 993–994, 1086, 1094, 1100, 1104, 1110, 1114, 1122, 1130–1131, 1138–1139, 1161–1162, 1173–1174, 1211, 1216–1217, 1238, 1243, 1247, 1251, 1257, 1263, 1269
India
   Constitution   532, 544, 553
   National Human Rights Commission   533, 546, 751, 754, 767, 772–779, 786, 789, 799, 807, 813, 820, 821
   Supreme Court   551–566
Indigenous peoples   55, 58, 64, 95, 97, 113–115, 127, 128, 160, 175, 180, 181, 185, 187, 195, 199, 219, 236, 250, 253, 264, 508, 647, 715–717, 723, 724, 901, 935–937, 950*n*238, 1079, 1099, 1105
Inquiry   25–26, 387, 418, 432, 705, 833, 1015, 1164, 1220–1221
Inter-American Commission on Human Rights   97, 102, 119, 163*n*45, 232, 572, 583, 289, 702, 1323

Inter-American Court of Human Rights   30, 162, 239, 259, 572
International Criminal Court   98, 157*n*11, 163, 231, 241, 243, 275, 359, 428, 486, 540, 612, 701, 828, 905, 1048, 1064, 1080, 1151, 1281
International Criminal Tribunal for Rwanda   1281
Immigration   34, 36, 44, 49, 57, 63, 64, 78, 101, 168, 175, 186, 193, 202, 207, 210, 433, 602, 604, 626, 666, 681, 682, 688, 1203
Individual communication   65–67, 107, 340, 432, 449
Interim measures   51, 67–68, 79–80, 221, 1154, 1209
International Convention for the Protection of all Persons from Enforced Disappearance (CED)   11, 40, 147–152, 281–287, 346–354, 688–691, 740–743, 1072–1073, 1209–1213, 1314–1315
   Art   31 16
International Convention on the Elimination of All Forms of Racial Discrimination (CERD)   1, 38, 55–60, 109–116, 181–187, 249–254, 303–311, 379–383, 442–450, 500–504, 549–551, 586–587, 644–657, 715–717, 769–777, 846–851, 931–938, 1043–1046, 1096–1110, 1166–1171, 1237–1241, 1287–1290
   Art   14 17
International Convention on the Rights of All Migrant Workers and Members of their Families (CMW)   11, 40, 100, 166, 167, 296, 363, 432, 490, 542, 575, 611, 706, 758, 831, 910, 1085, 1149, 1153, 1278, 1282, 1325
International Covenant on Civil and Political Rights (CCPR)   60–68, 116–121, 188–195, 254–259, 311–320, 383–388, 450–456, 504–509, 551–554, 587–591, 657–667, 718–721, 777–783, 851–862, 938–949, 1047–1056, 1102–1107, 1171–1178, 1241–1246, 1290
International Covenant on Economic, Social and Cultural Rights (CESCR)   68–72, 121–128, 195–200, 259–264, 320–327, 388–393, 457–462, 509–512, 554–556, 592–595, 667–671, 721–724, 783–789, 862–867, 950–958, 1057–1060, 1107–1112, 1179–1184, 1246–1248, 1297–1301
International Labour Organisation (ILO)   231, 273, 292, 465, 759, 863, 905, 950, 1149

International Monetary Fund (IMF)   338, 392, 1004, 1038
International Organisation for Migration (IOM)   1009n41, 1016, 1025, 1071, 1266
Iran   6, 12, 208, 613, 682, 684, 689
Istanbul Convention   27, 332, 334, 464, 465, 498, 514, 827, 829, 1229, 1231, 1244, 1250, 1251

Jamaica
  Charter of Fundamental Rights and Freedoms   572–573
  Constitution   570
  Office of the Public Defender (OPD)   570, 588, 589, 593, 597, 601, 603
  Office of the Children's Advocate (OCA)   570, 583, 599, 600, 602, 606
Japan
  Buraku people   610n9, 647–657
  Diet   608, 620, 628n51, 637, 643, 645, 647, 652, 661, 674, 679, 696
  Korean schools   613n27, 670, 671
  Okinawa people   619, 655, 656
Judiciary   102, 710, 712, 716, 718, 722, 725, 730, 734, 738, 741, 743, 1327, 1333
Justiciability of economic, social and cultural rights   19, 69, 72, 198, 287, 457, 461, 484, 485, 638, 785, 832, 833, 845, 862, 865, 867, 892, 1161, 1179, 1180, 1233, 1248, 1271

Lanzarote Convention   12, 27, 983, 987
Legal aid   59, 140, 332, 339, 404, 485, 571, 752, 777, 859, 948, 1017, 1018, 1041, 1045, 1063, 1257
LGBTQ\+ (*See* sexual orientation and gender identity)
Life, right to   162, 197, 200, 242, 312, 337, 538, 552, 765, 778, 834, 844, 889, 1102, 1200, 1243, 1273, 1290, 1291, 1296, 1297, 1298, 1330
Local authority (*See* district)

Maputo Protocol (*See* Protocol to the African Charter on Human and Peoples' Rights on the Rights of Women in Africa)
Media   3, 43, 93, 172–174, 184, 192, 211–212, 248, 252, 257, 262, 265, 275, 279, 283, 326, 365–374, 404, 437, 472, 477, 491–492, 560, 632, 677, 763, 764, 810, 835, 917–918, 1088, 1171, 1186, 1195
Mexico
  Constitution   721, 733, 737, 740
  National Council for the Prevention of Discrimination   715, 744
  National Human Rights Commission   701, 708, 713, 716, 719, 725, 730, 735, 738, 745n202
Migrant workers   40, 71, 168, 355, 364, 411–413, 419, 653, 759, 760, 832, 1154, 1267, 1278, 1338
Minorities   46, 108, 159, 175, 181, 195, 199, 289, 293, 303, 307, 316, 382, 424, 447, 460, 484, 493, 513, 538, 553, 594, 651, 670, 696, 761, 808, 819, 829, 852, 940, 1169, 1232, 1234, 1240, 1265, 1271
Monist/monism   232, 1151, 1271, 1328, 1332, 1345

National Human Rights Institution (NHRI) (*See also* Independent state institutions)   29–30, 98, 185, 199, 204, 210, 220, 229, 290, 296, 323, 354, 371, 401, 425, 442, 483, 491, 493, 594, 607, 610, 635, 709, 760, 825, 900, 1022, 1124, 1161, 1169, 1174, 1181, 1234, 1248, 1260, 1339, 1344
National preventive mechanism (NPM)   30, 76, 290, 336, 340, 466, 467, 469, 493, 517, 843, 875, 910, 1072, 1086, 1120, 1165, 1197, 1259, 1341, 1342
National mechanism for implementation, reporting and follow-up   29, 672, 709, 1169n108, 1350
NEPAD   360
Nepal
  Constitution   783
  Commission of Enforced Disappeared Person   782
  National Human Rights Commission   784
  Truth and Reconciliation Commission   755, 758, 782, 819, 822
Non-refoulement   61, 64, 68, 76, 207, 517, 520, 536, 561, 659, 681, 682, 781, 1121, 1124, 1194, 1195

OAS   28, 106, 153, 162, 1347

INDEX 1359

OHCHR   13, 205*n*282, 232, 242, 359, 371, 580*n*52, 615*n*35, 619*n*52, 754, 786, 1092*n*68, 1223, 1332, 1350*n*388
Older persons   26, 123, 483, 484, 518, 526, 893, 1248
OP1-CCPR   19, 20, 39, 99, 165, 237, 294, 431, 489, 544, 585, 704, 757, 830, 908, 1014, 1083, 1152, 1230, 1283
OP2-CCPR   13, 14, 154, 431, 489, 757, 830, 1152
OP-CAT   13, 15, 29, 39, 40, 137, 138, 294, 431, 489, 830, 1014, 1083, 1012
OP-CEDAW   18, 19, 25, 240, 433
OP-CESCR   19, 20, 25*n*35, 69, 705, 866–867, 911, 1086, 1183–1184, 1233
OP-CRC-CP   19, 20, 25, 887–888
OP-CRPD   18, 25, 90–91, 296, 579, 894, 911, 1142, 1219–1220
OSCE   292, 315, 428, 465, 829, 1151, 1226

Parliament/legislature   109–110, 116–117, 121–123, 128–129, 135–137, 143–144, 147, 149–150, 178, 303–305, 311–313, 320–322, 327–329, 334–336, 342–343, 346–347, 348–352, 388–389, 393–394, 411–412, 442–444, 450–452, 457, 462, 465–466, 470–471, 475–477, 495–497, 500–501, 504–506, 509–510, 512–513, 517, 521–522, 525–526, 549, 551, 554, 556–557, 562, 565, 581–583, 586, 587–588, 592, 595–596, 599–600, 602–603, 604, 715–716, 718, 721, 840–841, 846–847, 851–853, 862–863, 867–868, 874–876, 883–884, 891–893, 1093–1094, 1102, 1107–1108, 1119–1120, 1158–1160, 1166–1167, 1172–1173, 1179, 1184–1186, 1190–1191, 1200–1201, 1209–1210, 1214–1215, 1237, 1241–1242, 1246, 1248–1249, 1255–1256, 1261–1262, 1265–1266, 1268–1269
Philippines   6, 168*n*77
Places of detention   14, 27, 30, 77, 140, 186, 339, 843, 947, 972, 1066, 1079, 1105, 1176, 1341
Poland
    Commissioner for Children's Rights   835, 839, 843, 883, 890
    Commissioner for Human Rights   886–887
    Constitution   823–897

Constitutional Tribunal   823–897
Supreme Court   834, 841, 853, 884, 885, 894
Police   41, 58, 60, 62, 66, 94, 114, 117, 121, 136*n*150, 140, 175, 186, 205, 307, 316, 339, 341, 347, 362, 383, 403, 456, 520, 538, 570, 578, 619, 630, 687, 729, 732, 763, 778, 794, 799, 802, 803, 804, 827, 845, 872, 881, 953, 975, 1033, 1047, 1052, 1064, 1120, 1148, 1170, 1176, 1186, 1189, 1193, 1200, 1210, 1275, 1293, 1308, 1318
Populism   2, 94, 429, 481, 1351
Prison   60, 64, 78, 80, 95, 102, 108, 120, 136, 140, 155, 194, 210, 335, 339, 467, 518, 521, 552, 610, 630, 658, 662, 777, 859, 878, 969, 1048, 1054, 1066, 1122, 1178, 1197, 1275, 1277, 1297, 1310, 1322
Protocol to the African Charter on Human and Peoples' Rights on the Rights of Women in Africa   28

Race   49, 55, 60, 102, 107, 109, 110, 125, 127, 139, 175, 205, 251, 335, 380, 441, 443, 445, 549, 586, 669, 774, 823, 850, 903, 933, 1077, 1237, 1287
Ratification   55, 60–62, 68–69, 72–73, 75–77, 80–82, 168*n*71, 882, 909, 1279, 1314, 1323
Refugee   5, 36, 78, 103, 202, 207, 210, 519, 561, 682, 688, 780, 933, 989, 1081, 1082, 1185, 1206, 1240, 1266
Religion   33, 42, 108, 256, 307, 335, 380, 441, 443, 460, 505, 522, 532, 769, 774, 788, 823, 903
Reservations   60, 69, 75, 101, 128, 154, 162, 169, 358, 363, 364, 377, 393, 401, 405, 409, 411, 414, 420, 425, 429, 432, 488, 504, 543, 575, 625, 832, 851, 891, 896, 912, 1232, 1233, 1239, 1271, 1287, 1306, 1314, 1315
Roma (Romani)   251, 291, 303–345, 474, 484, 502, 506, 835, 847, 849, 865, 888, 928, 934, 956, 982, 1170, 1188, 1324
Romania   6
Rome Statute (*See* International Criminal Court)
Russian Federation
    Constitutional Court   900, 902, 939, 947, 948, 949, 976
    Constitution   900–1003

Russian Federation (*cont.*)
  Duma   936, 940, 965, 987
  Office of Commissioner for
    Human Rights in the Russian
    Federation   900, 914
  Office of the Commissioner for Children's
    Rights   903, 925, 979
  Ombudsman   900, 910, 926, 933, 940,
    948, 955, 957, 961, 972, 981, 992, 996

Schools   182, 191, 222, 262, 279, 297, 306, 324,
  353, 367, 383, 388, 436, 470, 472, 474,
  475, 492, 530, 670, 692, 763, 808, 824,
  883, 888, 989, 997, 1016, 1038, 1062, 1108,
  1128, 1136, 1185, 1205, 1243, 1296, 1303,
  1308, 1316, 1327
Self-execution/self-executing treaty
  provisions   3, 4, 10, 224, 373, 457, 548,
  577, 697, 822, 927, 939, 958, 1151, 1302,
  1325, 1328, 1344, 1345
Senegal
  Constitution   1003–1076
  National Human Rights Advisory Council
    (CCNDH)   1020–1022
  National Intersectoral Committee for the
    Protection of Children   1067
  National Advisory Council on Human
    Rights and International Humanitarian
    Law (CCNDHIH)   1056
Sexual abuse   27, 78, 82, 273, 474, 687, 781,
  790, 804, 890, 983, 1159, 1206, 1305
Sexual orientation and gender identity   26,
  585, 590, 610, 616, 1090, 1105
Sexual and reproductive rights   279, 858
Shadow reports (alternative reports)   48,
  104, 272, 330, 395, 709, 713, 735, 744, 808,
  1098, 1105, 1110, 1117, 1124, 1133, 1140, 1168,
  1236, 1249, 1252, 1266, 1294, 1338
SIMORE   106
Slavery, freedom from   127, 938, 1102, 1290
Social security   33, 69, 70, 108, 259, 273, 302,
  324, 349, 350, 458, 571, 671, 750, 785, 795,
  842, 863, 869, 901, 950, 1079, 1109, 1175,
  1246, 1248
Solitary confinement   60, 175, 210, 560, 666,
  1194–1197
South Africa
  Centre for Child Law   1103, 1130, 1132
  Centre for Human Rights   1089, 1140
  Commission for Gender
    Equality   1078, 1094
  Constitution   1077–1147
  Constitutional Court   1078, 1103, 1109,
    1130, 1138, 1147
  South African Human Rights
    Commission   1078, 1086, 1093, 1098,
    1099, 1100, 1107, 1110, 1120, 1122, 1132,
    1138–1139, 1144
  South African Law Reform
    Commission   1094, 1104, 1107, 1110,
    1114, 1122, 1130–1131, 1139–1140
  Lawyers for Human Rights   1082, 1133
Spain
  Constitution   1147–1151, 1158–1160,
    1163, 1223
  National Ombudsman (*Defensor del
    Pueblo*)   1156, 1161, 1169, 1181, 1192, 1211,
    1215, 1216
  Spanish Committee of Representatives
    of Persons with Disabilities
    (CERMI)   1156, 1215
Special measures   56, 108, 110–111, 113, 264,
  266, 277, 872, 966, 982, 1025, 1093,
  1098n99, 1099, 1100, 1101, 1248, 1252,
  1268, 1324, 1337, 1345
Special Rapporteur on Extrajudicial,
  Summary or Arbitrary
  Killings   540n63, 572, 1228
Special Rapporteur on Torture   38, 572, 706,
  801, 803, 1228
State reporting
  Delays   15, 18, 47
  Simplified procedure   15
Sterilisation   89, 90, 209, 212, 280, 281, 300,
  301, 307, 308, 316, 317, 324, 331, 333, 464,
  679, 997, 1176, 1217, 1219
Sub-Committee on Prevention of Torture
  (SPT)   14–15, 26, 30, 107–108, 141, 732–
  733, 845, 877, 880–881, 1009, 1065–1066,
  1165, 1197–1199, 1259–1260, 1341–1342
Sustainable Development Goals (SDGs)   197,
  607, 790, 795, 1045

Terrorism   64, 76, 78, 119, 359–360, 386, 853,
  859, 935n151, 935n152, 1065, 1148, 1198,
  1237, 1238, 1240, 1265
Trade union   124, 349, 390–392, 1056,
  1267, 1300

INDEX

Trafficking in persons   74, 78, 80, 81, 133, 201, 213, 273, 291, 316, 331, 373, 377, 379, 411–414, 420, 513, 514, 518, 599, 603, 673–674, 688, 727, 766–767, 780, 859, 983, 985, 1019, 1040, 1071, 1112, 1176, 1186, 1188, 1207, 1249, 1266, 1305

Torture   75–80, 135–143, 207–212, 270–273, 334–340, 399–405, 465–470, 517–521, 560–561, 599–602, 681–683, 729–733, 797–804, 874–882, 969–977, 1064–1067, 1119–1125, 1190–1200, 1255–1260, 1306–1310

Treaty Body Membership   53, 59, 68, 71, 75, 80, 85, 91, 106, 176–178, 300, 372, 495, 547, 580, 636, 764, 839–840, 923, 1091, 1157–1158, 1286, 1314

Turkey
  Constitution   1225–1270
  Human Rights and Equality Institution   1225, 1229, 1238, 1239, 1251, 1257, 1259, 1263, 1269
  Office of the Ombudsman   1238

Türkiye (*See* Turkey)

UN Declaration on the Rights of Indigenous Peoples (UNDRIP)   56*n*142, 187, 191, 222

UNICEF   145, 406, 437, 523, 545, 599, 784, 1016, 1264, 1302, 1324

United Nations (UN)   1, 38, 94, 231, 357, 423, 483, 539, 572, 611, 701, 750, 1147, 1227, 1278, 1320

Universal Declaration of Human Rights (UDHR)   436, 443, 470, 539, 548, 551, 1085, 1273, 1287, 1319

Universal Periodic Review (UPR) (*See* Human Rights Council)

Universities   9, 46, 110, 111, 112, 306, 337, 357, 367, 379, 390, 435, 492, 494, 708, 834, 924, 1236, 1308

UN Security Council   6, 162, 429, 437, 480

UN Working Group on Arbitrary Detention   619, 1148, 1164, 1223

Urgent measures   272, 1034, 1206

Water   78, 122, 209, 225, 261, 360, 533, 538, 784, 1048, 1102, 1109

Women   72–75, 128–135, 200–207, 264–270, 327–334, 393–399, 462–465, 512–517, 556–560, 595–599, 671–681, 724–729, 789–797, 867–873, 958–968, 1061–1064, 1112–1119, 1184–1190, 1248–1255, 1301–1306

Work, right to   70, 195, 307, 323, 961, 1111, 1143

World Trade Organisation (WTO)   428

Zambia
  Constitution   1273–1319
  Gender Equity and Equality Commission   1275
  Human Rights Commission   1285, 1287, 1288, 1289, 1290, 1294, 1297, 1300, 1302, 1306, 1309, 1310, 1315